1998

HISTORIC
DOCUMENTS
OF
1998

1998

HISTORIC
DOCUMENTS
OF
1998

Cumulative Index, 1994–1998

Congressional Quarterly Inc.

Historic Documents of 1998

Editors: Martha Gottron, John Felton, Bruce Maxwell
Production and Associate Editor: Kerry V. Kern
Indexer: Victoria Agee

Copyright © 1999 Congressional Quarterly Inc.
1414 22nd Street, N.W.
Washington, D.C. 20037

Printed in the United States of America

The Library of Congress cataloged the first issue of this title as follows:

Historic documents. 1972-
      Washington. Congressional Quarterly Inc.

      1. United States—Politics and government—1945- —Yearbooks.
2. World politics—1945- —Yearbooks. I. Congressional Quarterly Inc.

E839.5H57   917.3'03'9205   72-97888

ISBN 1-56802-442-8
ISSN 0892-080X

PREFACE

For almost all of 1998, Americans were inundated with news about a sex-and-lies scandal that led to the impeachment of President Bill Clinton. The rest of the world was more concerned about a flood of economic news—most of it bad—stemming from the financial crisis that had gripped much of Asia beginning the year before. These two matters had little direct influence on one another, except to the extent that Washington's focus on scandal distracted the attention of politicians and policymakers from a worldwide economic downturn that had the potential to reach the United States.

The worst American political scandal in a generation began in January with allegations that President Clinton had lied under oath to cover up his extramarital affair with Monica S. Lewinsky, a former White House intern who was only a few years older than Clinton's daughter. In December the House of Representatives impeached Clinton in nearly straight party-line votes, charging him with four counts of perjury and obstruction of justice. In the intervening months, the American public watched in a mixture of fascination and revulsion as intimate and graphic details of the president's personal life were made public. They were also subjected to the wrenching experience of hearing the leader of the world's most powerful nation admit that he had deliberately misled his family, his aides, and the American people. Throughout his ordeal, however, Clinton maintained that he had not committed perjury or obstructed justice.

The Senate was not expected to convict Clinton when it took up the impeachment early in 1999. Clinton's job ratings remained high throughout the year, and the Republicans were unlikely to muster the two-thirds majority vote needed for conviction. But the events leading up to the impeachment had already taken a toll. Clinton's place in history would forever be marred by his becoming only the second American president to be impeached. The impeachment debate itself had heightened the mistrust between the two political parties to its highest point in decades, and the American people grew even more cynical about their elected representatives in Washington.

Ironically, the Republicans who pursued impeachment sustained more immediate political damage than did Clinton. Despite clear signals that the majority of Americans did not want Clinton impeached, House leaders could not resist the opportunity to go after the man many considered their political

---

How to Use This Book

The documents are arranged in chronological order. If you know the approximate date of the report, speech, statement, court decision, or other document you are looking for, glance through the titles for that month in the table of contents.

If the table of contents does not lead you directly to the document you want, turn to the index at the end of the book. There you may find references not only to the particular document you seek but also to other entries on the same or a related subject. The index in this volume is a five-year cumulative index of *Historic Documents* covering the years 1994–1998. There is a separate volume, *Historic Documents Index, 1972–1995*, which may also be useful.

The introduction to each document is printed in italic type. The document itself, printed in roman type, follows the spelling, capitalization, and punctuation of the original or official copy. Where the full text is not given, omissions of material are indicated by the customary ellipsis points.

---

nemesis. The price was high: a loss of five House seats in the November elections and the resignation of two top House leaders, Speaker Newt Gingrich of Georgia and his designated successor, Rep. Robert S. Livingston, R-La.

Aside from further souring the American public on Washington politics and creating endless opportunities for racy coverage in the news media, the partisan bickering over the Lewinsky scandal seemed to have little impact on the nation as a whole. The American economy continued to produce its best performance in a generation with high rates of job creation, low rates of unemployment, and no sign of inflation on the horizon.

The nation's growth enabled the federal government to claim in October that the budget for the 1998 fiscal year had shown a surplus for the first time in nearly thirty years. That claim was somewhat exaggerated—a deficit in government's actual operating budget was masked by a large surplus in the Social Security program. Even so, the news was encouraging because the trend was away from deficit spending, and it dramatically altered the shape of the debate in Washington on budget issues. For nearly a generation, Republicans and Democrats had argued over what to do about recurring deficits; starting in 1998 leaders of the two parties began disputing what to do with multibillion-dollar surpluses that were expected in the succeeding years. Clinton was the first to seize the high ground. In his State of the Union speech he offered a simple phrase—"save Social Security first"—that undercut plans by Republicans to use most of the budget surplus to pay for tax cuts. From that moment forward, politicians in Washington competed for ways to claim credit for ensuring that the Social Security system would remain solvent in the second and third decades of the twenty-first century, when the tens of millions of Americans in the post–World War II "baby boom" generation would reach retirement age.

A variety of reports issued during the year by government and private agencies painted a picture of a nation in transition at the close of the twentieth century. The 1996 welfare reform law—coupled with continued economic growth—appeared to be sharply reducing the nation's welfare rolls. At the same time, the Department of Housing and Urban Development reported that economic prosperity was still eluding many of the nation's cities. Nearly all the growth in employment during the 1990s was taking place in suburban areas ringing the cities, leaving inner-city residents with the choice of taking low-pay service jobs or trying to commute to the suburbs.

Americans did not have much company when it came to celebrating good economic news during 1998. Most other countries were either still struggling to escape the worldwide recession that had peaked at the beginning of the 1990s, or they were suffering the "contagion" effect from the Asian financial crisis. The Asian crisis was to have a much broader impact than anyone envisioned in the months after July 1997, when the collapse of the currency in Thailand set off financial turbulence throughout Asia. By the beginning of 1998, the Japanese economy—the world's second largest, after the United States—had fallen into a deep recession. Most other east Asian nations already had fallen into recession during late 1997 or were experiencing sharply reduced growth.

Countries where democracy had taken root, including the Philippines, South Korea, and Thailand, managed to weather the economic turbulence with little social unrest. But the economic crisis demonstrated the fragility of one of the world's longest-reigning dictatorships. President Suharto, who had ruled Indonesia with an iron hand since 1967, was toppled from power with amazing ease in May following a series of mass demonstrations by university students. The Indonesian economy was the hardest hit in Asia; according to one estimate by the World Bank, nearly 75 percent of the nation's businesses went bankrupt during the year, throwing millions of people out of work. The impact of the overall Asian financial crisis was worsened by a severe drought. The International Monetary Fund (IMF) offered Indonesia a $40 billion rescue package but imposed tough conditions, including the dismantling of monopolies controlled by Suharto and his family members.

Japan, with a much stronger economy and a more open political system than Indonesia, nevertheless suffered an economic downturn that severely undermined national confidence. The Japanese economy had been sluggish ever since the worldwide recession at the beginning of the decade, and by early 1998 that sluggishness had turned into a full-scale recession. As happened elsewhere in Asia, the plunge exposed inherent weaknesses in the Japanese economic system, most importantly the government's failure to monitor lending by Japanese banks. By late 1998 most experts estimated that

Japanese banks were holding upwards of $1 trillion worth of bad loans. The government of Prime Minister Ryutaro Hashimoto offered several economic rescue plans in 1997 and early 1998, none of which had any dramatic impact. Voters in parliamentary elections in July rebuffed Hashimoto's Liberal Democratic Party, forcing the prime minister from office. Party leaders selected Foreign Minister Keizo Obuchi as Hashimoto's successor, despite Obuchi's lack of experience in economic matters. Obuchi put forward a modest economic stimulus plan in August and then a more substantial plan in November, including proposals to help banks deal with their bad loans. By year's end the IMF was estimating that the Japanese economy would come close to reaching positive growth in 1999.

Another major victim of the Asian financial crisis was Russia, which in 1998 was still trying to overcome economic and political instability resulting from its transition from communism. After a few heady years of Wild West-style capitalism in the mid-1990s, Russia by 1998 was faced with the reality of dealing with its communist legacy, including antiquated factories, unskilled workers, and a lack of political consensus about the nation's direction. American and European investors, who had poured billions of dollars into speculative schemes in Russia, began pulling back in 1998, partly in response to the Asian economic crisis and partly in response to continuing uncertainty in Russia. President Boris Yeltsin in March dramatically fired his longtime prime minister, Viktor S. Chernomyrdin, and replaced him with a team pledged to radical economic reform. But the nation's economic slide continued despite a pledge of $17 billion in aid from the IMF. In mid-August the Russian government took steps that had the effect of devaluing the ruble and defaulting on short-term loans. That action set off panic alarms all over the world and caused a sudden drop in financial markets, including Wall Street. Yeltsin tried to bring Chernomyrdin back as prime minister, but was blocked by parliament. In September he finally succeeded in getting parliament to approve foreign minister Yevgeny M. Primakov as prime minister. Primakov cobbled together a budget and won approval for it in parliament but was unable to develop a coherent long-term plan for the nation's economic future. By the end of the year Russia was forced into the humiliating position of appealing to the United States and European governments for food aid.

China, which was also making a transition from a purely communist system to a melding of communism and capitalism, escaped the worst of the year's economic turmoil. The country's economic growth rate, which had been averaging nearly 10 percent a year for more than a decade, fell to about 7 percent for 1998—still a remarkable performance given the economic free fall in the rest of Asia. But the Chinese communist leaders faced the most intense international scrutiny of their leadership in years. Visiting China in June, President Clinton offered some words of praise for the leaders in Beijing but lectured them on the virtues of democracy. Weeks after Clinton's visit, the government launched a sustained crackdown, imprisoning several dissidents who were trying to form an opposition party.

Another abrupt reminder of the limits of American influence came August 7, when nearly simultaneous bomb explosions destroyed the U.S. embassy buildings in Nairobi, Kenya, and Dar es Salaam, Tanzania. The bombings killed more than 250 people, including twelve Americans, and wounded several thousand others, most of them civilians in Nairobi. The Clinton administration quickly identified a terrorist group headed by exiled Saudi millionaire Usama bin Laden as responsible for the bombings. On August 20 U.S. warplanes and cruise missiles attacked remote camps in Afghanistan, where bin Laden was said to have his headquarters, and a chemical factory in the Sudan, which U.S. officials said had manufactured chemical weapons for the use of terrorists. Bin Laden survived the attack in Afghanistan, but U.S. officials hoped the massive response to the bombings would convince Afghanistan to expel him.

In December U.S. military power was called into play once again in the Middle East—this time in a place familiar to Pentagon planners: Iraq. After it lost the Persian Gulf War in 1991, Iraq was ordered by the United Nations Security Council to hand over to a UN commission all of its ballistic missiles and chemical, biological, and nuclear weapons. During its eight years of work, the UN commission managed to locate and destroy many of Iraq's weapons of mass destruction—but the Iraqi government never provided a full accounting of the vast arsenal of chemical and biological weapons it had accumulated before the Gulf War. After a series of moves by Iraq to frustrate its work, the commission suspended its operations on December 15 and reported to the Security Council that Iraq had failed to cooperate. The next day, the United States and Great Britain launched air attacks on military targets in Iraq. In a televised speech from the White House, Clinton said he had ordered the attacks because Iraqi leader Saddam Hussein was continuing to pose a military threat to other Middle East nations. The military action came just one day before the House of Representatives was scheduled to begin debating articles of impeachment against Clinton—causing some Republican leaders to charge that Clinton was using U.S. military power to stall the impeachment. Most of the Republicans later backed down on that charge, but their willingness to make it demonstrated the climate of mistrust in Washington.

A scourge that military power could not hope to overcome was the seemingly relentless advance of the AIDS epidemic throughout much of the world. According to UN estimates, the number of people with HIV, the virus that caused the incurable disease, rose 10 percent in 1998, to 33.4 million. In parts of sub-Saharan Africa, one of every four adults had either HIV or AIDS; in nine African countries, life expectancy, which had been rising, was now expected to fall over the next ten to fifteen years. Although the disease was worst in Africa and Southeast Asia, health workers were finding evidence of it spreading through previously little touched countries, including China, India, and several Eastern European countries. In the United States, deaths from AIDS continued to decline significantly, but the rate of new HIV infections held steady, at about 40,000 a year.

Not all news was doom and gloom during the year. Millions of Americans watched for weeks on end as two baseball players—Mark McGwire of the St. Louis Cardinals and Sammy Sosa of the Chicago Cubs—battled each other for the honor of breaking one of the most important records in American sports: Roger Maris's total of sixty-one home runs in a single season (1961). In the end, both McGwire and Sosa broke the record, but McGwire won the overall title with seventy home runs, a figure that had seemed inconceivable before the 1998 season.

Americans enjoyed a bit of nostalgia in October when John Glenn returned to space. In 1962 Glenn had been the first American astronaut to circle the globe; his journey in space had helped restore the confidence of Americans who were worried at that time about the cold war and the Soviet Union's lead in the space race. Glenn later served three terms as a senator from Ohio, but he always wanted another trip in space. His chance came when he persuaded the National Aeronautics and Space Administration (NASA) to take him as a crew member on the shuttle *Discovery* for experiments on how weightlessness in space affected the aging process. Glenn and six other astronauts spent nine days in space in late October and early November. The results of the experiments on the seventy-seven-year-old Glenn had not been made public by the end of the year, but the mission reignited public interest in manned space ventures and was an enormous public relations success for NASA.

These are only some of the topics of national and international interest chosen by the editors for *Historic Documents of 1998*. This edition marks the twenty-seventh volume of a Congressional Quarterly project that began with *Historic Documents of 1972*. The purpose of the series is to give students, librarians, journalists, scholars, and others convenient access to documents on a wide range of topics that set forth some of the most important issues of the year. In our judgment, the official statements, news conferences, speeches, special studies, and court decisions presented here will be of lasting interest.

Each document is preceded by an introduction that provides context and background material and, when relevant, an account of continuing developments during the year. We believe these introductions will become increasingly useful as memories of current times fade.

John Felton and Martha Gottron

CONTENTS

January

February

the Health, Education, and Human Services Division of the General
Accounting Office, in which she set forth the options for restoring long-
term solvency to the Social Security system.

March

April

May

June

ruled that employers could be held vicariously liable for sexual harassment of their employees by company supervisors and laid out steps the
employers could take to defend against such liable claims.

September

October

November

January

CONGRESSIONAL COMMISSION REPORT ON COLLEGE COSTS
January 21, 1998

A congressionally mandated commission on January 21 urged American colleges and universities to do a better job of controlling costs and explaining those costs to the public. The commission noted that students, parents, and public policymakers were becoming increasingly concerned about the escalating costs of college and warned that these concerns could undermine public support for America's system of higher education.

Congress created the National Commission on the Cost of Higher Education in 1997 and asked for a review of why college costs had increased faster than the rate of inflation and for recommendations on how those costs could be controlled. Numerous members of Congress had insisted that college tuition levels had increased so fast that higher education faced a crisis. The commission released an interim report in December 1997 concluding that such fears were overblown. That interim report caused a storm of protest on Capitol Hill.

Acknowledging Public Concerns

The eleven-member commission included college administrators, faculty members, and representatives of nonprofit philanthropic and research organizations. The chairman was William E. Troutt, president of Belmont University in Nashville.

In its final report released in January, the commission appeared to respond to the controversy generated by its interim assessment playing down public concerns about tuition increases. The report, entitled "Straight Talk About College Costs and Prices," acknowledged that the issue could create a "gulf of ill will" between the public and institutions of higher education. "Public anxiety about college prices has risen along with increases in tuition," the commission said. "It is now on the order of anxiety about how to pay for health care or housing, or cover the expenses of taking care of an elderly relative. Financing a college education is a serious and troublesome matter to the American people."

The commission urged students, their families, and the public to draw a comparison between paying for college and buying a car. The former was a long-term investment that would pay dividends throughout life, the commission said, while the latter was a short-term purchase of an item that immediately declined in value. To dramatize the comparison, the commission used the term sticker price *as a substitute for* tuition.

Throughout its report, the commission attempted to explain the complexities of higher education finance, including terminology. It noted, for example, that members of the public often confused college "costs" (how much it costs to run an institution of higher education) with "prices" (the amounts that students and their families actually pay for tuition, books, room and board, and other fees). Although costs and prices were related, they should not be confused with each other, the commission said, because students never pay the full cost of their education; "subsidies," such as financial aid, endowments, state funding, and grants from governments and foundations, make up the difference.

In general, the commission found that the prices paid by students increased more than the costs of running institutions of higher education between 1987 and 1996—but costs still exceeded prices. For example, the commission noted that per-student instructional costs at public four-year colleges and universities rose by 57 percent during that period (to $12,416 on average); tuition rose by 132 percent (to $3,918 on average). Similar trends were found at private institutions and at public two-year colleges.

Basing its findings on numerous studies, some of which it had sponsored, the commission said several factors led to the sharp increases in both costs and prices. Costs had risen, the commission said, because nearly every aspect of higher education was becoming more complex. Colleges needed more administrators than in the past, in part to deal with government regulations and mandates. The commission cited an estimate by Stanford University that complying with government regulations consumed 7.5 percent of every tuition dollar. Enrollment increases and the need to accommodate "special needs" cases had forced colleges to build or repair classrooms, dormitories, and laboratories. Adding capacity for computer-based instruction had been costly—especially in the case of older campus buildings. Students also were expecting more of colleges than in the past, such as gymnasiums equipped with state-of-the-art exercise equipment and dormitories wired for computers. Paying for all these rising costs and meeting rising expectations took money, and so the prices that students paid went up, the commission said.

The commission called for further study on one issue raised by some members of Congress: whether the widespread availability of federal loans to students had contributed to the increase in college costs. The commission cited two studies that appeared to lend credence to the arguments that student loans made it easier for colleges to spend more and therefore to charge more. The commission said it found "no conclusive evidence" on the question, however, and suggested a more detailed analysis of it. The commis-

sion noted its concern about "sharp increases" in student borrowing to finance education.

Commission Recommendations

While noting the variety of factors that led to rising college costs, the commission said members of the public were less interested in complex explanations than in learning how they could afford college for themselves or their children. Parents considered a college degree "as essential to their children's future," the commission said, and they were becoming worried that "access and opportunity are slipping away."

To address such concerns, the commission recommended more than forty actions for colleges, parents, federal and state governments, and philanthropic agencies. One set of ten recommendations dealt with controlling costs on campus. For example, the commission called for cooperative efforts by colleges in such areas as joint use of facilities and purchasing goods and services, and it suggested detailed national studies of how to devise innovative ways for colleges to save money. Colleges should not shrink from examining such potentially controversial issues as faculty tenure and alternatives to traditional classroom instruction.

In another set of recommendations, the commission said colleges needed to be more open in explaining financial issues to their various publics, including students and parents. Colleges should issue annual financial reports that are clear and understandable, the commission said, and agencies such as the federal Department of Education should improve the collection of nationwide higher education data. Noting the impact of government regulations on colleges, the commission called for new approaches "to ensure public accountability in ways that are less costly and more easily manageable." As an example, the commission called on Congress to repeal a section of a 1997 tax law (PL 105–34) that required colleges to report to the Internal Revenue Service personal financial information provided by parents and students. That requirement had the potential to add "major administration costs" for colleges, the commission said.

The commission also advocated more efficient ways for accrediting institutions of higher education and specific academic programs. In addition to regional agencies that reviewed entire institutions, some sixty specialized agencies had jurisdiction over more than one hundred academic programs. The accreditation process was complex, costly, and time-consuming and needed to be simplified, the commission said. In a final set of recommendations, the commission proposed a streamlined system of student financial aid, especially those programs funded by the federal government. Administering the complex series of scholarships, grants, loans, and other aid programs was very costly for colleges, the commission noted.

Congressional Action

When it formed the commission in 1997, Congress had said it wanted more information for its work during 1998 in extending the Higher Edu-

cation Authorization Act, which covered federal programs on student aid and other issues. During its work on the act, Congress took two important actions to ensure continued availability of financial aid for needy students. For low-income college students, Congress boosted the maximum amount of the "Pell grant" to $5,800 in academic year 2003–2004, up from the existing maximum of $3,000. Congress also approved a new formula for setting interest rates on student loans; the new formula was intended to give commercial banks enough of a profit to ensure that they would continue making the loans. Congress cleared its five-year extension of the higher education act (PL 105–244) in late September.

> *Following are excerpts from the report, "Straight Talk About College Costs and Prices," issued January 21, 1998, by the National Commission on the Cost of Higher Education:*

The phenomenon of rising college tuition evokes a public reaction that is sometimes compared to the "sticker shock" of buying a new car. Although this reference to automobile prices may irritate some within the higher education community, it serves to remind all of us that higher education is a product, a service and a life-long investment bought and paid for, like others.

Rising college tuitions are real. In the 20 years between 1976 and 1996, the average tuition at public universities increased from $642 to $3,151 and the average tuition at private universities increased from $2,881 to $15,581. Tuitions at public two-year colleges, the least expensive of all types of institutions, increased from an average of $245 to $1,245 during this period.

Public anxiety about college prices has risen along with increases in tuition. It is now on the order of anxiety about how to pay for health care or housing, or cover the expenses of taking care of an elderly relative. Financing a college education is a serious and troublesome matter to the American people.

Each member of this Commission understands this anxiety. We treat it seriously. We do not take lightly the public concern generated by increases in tuition. Worry about college prices, the difficulty of planning for them, and the amount of debt they entail dominated a discussion group of parents convened by the Commission in Nashville in November 1997. Members of the Commission are equally convinced that if this public concern continues, and if colleges and universities do not take steps to reduce their costs, policymakers at the Federal and state levels will intervene and take up the task for them.

What concerns this Commission is the possibility that continued inattention to issues of cost and price threatens to create a gulf of ill will between institutions of higher education and the public they serve. We believe that such a development would be dangerous for higher education and the larger society.

In the end, academic institutions must be affordable and more accountable. The Commission is worried that many academic institutions have not seriously confronted the basic issues involved with reducing their costs—and that most of them have also permitted a veil of obscurity to settle over their basic financial operations. . . .

Facts about Higher Education, Its Cost, and Its Price

The diversity of American higher education is unequaled in the world and is, without question, one of this nation's great strengths. Approximately 3,700 not-for-profit colleges and universities which vary in terms of size, geography, sector, selectivity, and mission comprise the academic spectrum: flagship state universities expanding the boundaries of human knowledge; four-year public institutions providing access at very low prices; private universities, many of them among the most prestigious in the world; liberal arts colleges proud of their tradition of encouraging intellectual development in small, intimate settings; and two-year community colleges offering everything from high school and transfer programs to retirement planning and technical training.

Although there are more private colleges and universities than public ones, more than three quarters (78 percent) of all students—and 81 percent of all undergraduates—are enrolled in public two- and four-year institutions. In recent years, the number of part-time students has increased substantially. Indeed, the student profile has changed radically in recent decades profoundly affecting the way colleges look at and do their jobs. In addition to the traditional 18-to-22 year-old full-time students, higher education enrollments now include large numbers of older, married individuals, many of them parents, with limited means, demanding personal schedules, and a tendency to move in and out of the student population on a part-time basis. Current students are the most racially and ethnically diverse group ever served by any nation's system of higher education. A high percentage of these students, including many undergraduates, are financially independent of their parents. In fact, the percentage of undergraduates enrolled part-time increased from 28 percent of all enrollments (two- and four-year) in 1980 to 42 percent in 1994, with the greatest concentration of part-time students in two-year institutions.

The diversity within American higher education is also reflected in the prices institutions charge students to attend. The average undergraduate tuition ranged from $1,245 in public two-year colleges in the Fall of 1996 to $15,581 in private universities. Tuition, however, generally does not cover the full cost of the students' education. This means that all students—both those in public and private institutions—receive a subsidy.

Posted tuition does not include other education-related costs borne by students such as books, special laboratory fees, and living expenses (room and board if living on campus, or rent or related housing costs if the student lives off campus). Furthermore, for a large percentage of students and families, the price actually paid to attend college bears little resemblance to the tuition charged and other education-related expenses. This occurs because many students receive some form of financial aid. In 1995-96, for example, 80 percent of full-time undergraduates at private four-year institutions (and 70 percent of part-time students) received aid. For public four-year institutions, 66 and 48 percent respectively received aid, and for two-year institutions, 63 and 36 percent.

Finally, since financial aid awards are often based on financial need, students from lower income families tend to pay less to attend the same institution as students from higher income families. In 1995-96, full-time undergraduates who were financially dependent on their parents and whose family incomes were less than $40,000 paid, on average, $5,412 to attend a public university (this estimate subtracts all financial aid awards from tuition and other education-related expenses). Undergraduates whose family incomes exceeded $80,000 paid almost twice as much, $10,376. Indeed, while much of the public attention focuses on increases in tuition, tuition is but one element of the price of attending college. . . .

Trends in Costs, Prices, and Subsidies

Although most public discussion of the affordability of higher education focuses on tuition charges and increases, tuition (i.e., "sticker price") is but one component of the college cost/price picture. As noted, the total price (tuition plus other educational expenses), net price, and instructional cost per student—and the complex interrelationships among these concepts—should all be included in discussions of why the price of attending college may be increasing. Below we present what we have learned about costs, prices, and generalized subsidy for our three types of institutions and how they have changed over time.

Public four-year colleges and universities

Between 1987 and 1996, the instructional cost per student increased from $7,922, on average, to $12,416, an increase of 57 percent. During this same period, the sticker price increased considerably faster, 132 percent, from an average of $1,688 to $3,918. The general subsidy, which averaged $6,234 in 1987, increased 36 percent, to approximately $8,500 in 1996. Thus, the sticker price, or tuition, increased much faster than either instructional costs or the subsidy. During part of this period—between fiscal years 1990–91 and 1992-93—state appropriations in 16 states declined and tuitions in many of these states increased much higher than in previous years. In most of these states, appropriations began to increase again in 1994. Thus, declines in state appropriations to higher education during a small portion of this period cannot totally account for the rate at which public four-year tuitions rose between 1987 and 1996. In public four-year colleges and universities, the percentage of total student costs covered by the general subsidy declined from 79 percent to 68 percent.

Private four-year colleges and universities

In these institutions, the cost per student increased between 1987 and 1996 from an average of $10,011 to $18,387. This represents a 69 percent increase. Tuition, or sticker price, increased by 99 percent—lower in percentage terms than for the public four-year colleges, but higher in real-money terms because of the higher base, from $6,665 to $13,250. Even in the private sector, the percentage of per-student costs covered by the general subsidy declined by 11 percentage points, from 39 percent in 1987 to 28 percent in 1996. The Commission does not understand the sources of subsidies in private institutions as well as it does subsidies in public institutions; endowment income cannot be a complete explanation since it only represents a significant contribution to a relatively small number of colleges and universities.

Public two-year colleges

For these institutions, total costs per student increased by 52 percent between 1987 and 1996, from an average of $5,197 to $7,916. Sticker prices increased 85 percent, from $710 to $1,316. Similar to the situation for public four-year colleges and universities, subsidies to public two-year colleges declined for part of this period. Among all three institutional types, the decrease in the general subsidy was lowest for public two-year colleges; here the percentage of total costs covered by the general subsidy declined only from 86 to 83 percent.

In all three institutional categories, tuition (or sticker price) increased faster than cost per student between 1987 and 1996. It may be tempting to conclude that institutions acted irresponsibly, by charging students and their families higher tuition but not spending the additional revenue to improve or maintain the quality of the education provided. However, tuition is not the sole source of institutional revenue, and if other revenues declined, institutions may have been forced to increase their tuition revenue. We know that state appropriations to public higher education declined during part of this period and tuitions in many state institutions escalated even faster at that time. At best we can conclude that tuition appears to have increased faster than institutional costs in all types of colleges and universities. We believe that institutions themselves should explain to the public why this occurs. . . .

Convictions and Recommendations

Based on its review of college affordability, this Commission has arrived at five key convictions about the college cost and price crisis:

Conviction 1: The concern about rising college prices is real. The Commission has observed the anxiety in parents' faces as they talk about the price of sending their children to college. People consider a college degree as essential to their children's future, as something of great value because it promises their children a better life. And, they also worry that access and opportunity are slipping away. These are genuine public fears to which academic institutions must respond.

Although concerns and perceptions about price are not entirely wrong, they are not always based on sound factual information. Moreover, as we have noted, institutions of higher education are not always fiscally transparent. Academic leaders must address these issues.

Here, however, academic institutions face a genuine challenge. It is quite clear from parents this Commission talked with, that many members of the general public have little interest in complicated explanations of higher education finance. As important as these matters are for institutional leaders, parents are interested simply in what they will have to pay when their children go to college—indeed if they can afford to send them at all. In responding to public concerns about prices, academic leaders must provide information that is comprehensive, comprehensible, accessible, and persuasive.

Conviction 2: The public and its leaders are concerned about where higher education places its priorities. We have relearned something most academic leaders always knew: higher education costs are driven by people and by how these people spend their time.

But, because academic institutions do not account differently for time spent directly in the classroom and time spent on other teaching and research activities, it is almost impossible to explain to the public how individuals employed in higher education use their time. Consequently, the public and public officials find it hard to be confident that academic leaders allocate resources effectively and well. Questions about costs and their allocation to research, service, and teaching are hard to discuss in simple, straightforward ways—and the connection between these activities and student learning is difficult to draw. In responding to this growing concern, academic leaders have been hampered by poor information and sometimes inclined to take issue with those who asked for better data. Academic institutions need much better definitions and measures of how faculty members, administrators, and students use their time.

The skepticism underlying this concern about where higher education places its priorities is a major consequence of higher education's inability to explain its cost and price structure convincingly to the public. Some cost data are unavailable; much of the information that is provided is hard to understand. College finances are far too opaque. Higher education has a major responsibility to make its cost and price structures much more "transparent," i.e., easily understandable to the public and its representatives.

Conviction 3: Confusion about cost and price abounds and the distinction between the two must be recognized and respected. Issues of cost, price, subsidy, and net price have been difficult for the members of this Commission to master. They are equally, if not more confusing to members of the public. These are complex topics, and higher education must strive continuously to clarify and communicate them clearly and candidly.

Beyond that, American families are confused and poorly informed—not only about costs and prices, but also about the entire matter of how to access higher education and its complicated system of financial aid.

The Commission believes that the message about prices (what students and families actually pay) is more encouraging than much of the public dialogue acknowledges, even if it is not entirely comforting. Moreover, the increase in the price students are asked to pay has begun to moderate in recent years. Academic institutions must continue their efforts to control costs—and hence prices—or risk the unpalatable alternative of government intervention.

Conviction 4: Rising costs are just as troubling a policy issue as rising prices. This Commission is concerned because institutional costs (not just prices) are also rising. Unless cost increases are reduced, prices in the long run cannot be contained without undermining quality or limiting access.

Some of the factors behind these cost increases can be understood and explained. As noted previously, tuition tends to go up as public subsidies go down. Administrative costs have increased as a share of total expenditures. The expense of building or renovating facilities and of acquiring and implementing modern technologies has the potential of becoming a significant cost driver. The cost of providing institutional aid (or discounting tuition sticker prices) for needy students increased by nearly 180 percent in the ten years between 1987-88 and 1996-97. Federal, state, and local laws, regulations, and mandates have undoubtedly added to academic costs.

Some policymakers worry that Federal financial aid might have encouraged tuition increases. This Commission is confident that Federal grants have not had such an effect, at either public or private institutions. The Commission believes no conclusive evidence exists with respect to Federal loans and believes this issue deserves serious and in-depth additional study.

Aside from such general observations, the Commission does not have solid information to help identify specific factors driving cost and price increases. The simple truth is that no single factor can be identified to explain how and why college costs rise. The Commission suspects that part of the underlying dynamic is the search for academic prestige and the academic reward systems governing higher education. This institutional emphasis on academic status is reinforced by a system of regional and specialized accreditation that often encourages increased expenditures by practically every institution.

The complexity of the interrelationships among these and other factors convinces the Commission that policymakers should avoid simple, one-size-fits-all solutions to the challenge of controlling or reducing college costs. Costs are increasing for a variety of reasons. The response to these mixed and subtle causes, must be similarly mixed and sophisticated.

Conviction 5: The United States has a world-class system of higher education. The United States has a diverse system, one that provides more opportunities to acquire a high-quality education, for citizens of all ages and backgrounds, than any other society. American higher education is a public and a private good. American academic institutions represent an investment in the nation's future, one that yields dividends every day, for both individuals and society. It is little wonder that the world has beaten a path to the door of the American university.

Nonetheless, Academic leaders cannot take the continued pre-eminence of their institutions for granted. Although it requires a long time to build an outstanding nationwide system of higher education, such a system can deteriorate very rapidly. In the Commission's judgment, one of the few things capable of precipitating such a decline in the United States would be an erosion of public trust so serious that it undermined ongoing financial support for the nation's academic enterprise. Continued inattention to the imperative to make academic institutions more financially transparent threatens just such an erosion.

Recommendations: An Action Agenda

The Commission believes its analysis of some of the national data about higher education finance has broken new ground, especially in clarifying the connections between and among cost, price, subsidy, and affordability. Nevertheless, the best national data are insufficient to provide the kind of clear information on these trends that policymakers and the general public need. For example, the terms of analysis used by different parties are not always consistently defined: institutional costs and student costs are two different things; prices and costs are not the same; and prices charged and prices paid often bear little relationship to each other.

The persistent blurring of terms (both within and beyond higher education) contributes to system-wide difficulties in clarifying the relationship between cost and quality; defining the difference between price and cost; distinguishing between what institutions charge and what students pay; and ultimately to systemic difficulties in controlling costs and prices.

If we are to clarify these relationships and control expenses, several things must happen. Academic institutions should start to use these terms systematically and regularly; policymakers must realize that costs and subsidies need to be better managed if prices are to be controlled; and academic leaders must acknowledge that, before they can manage costs and explain prices to the public, they themselves have to do a better job of measuring and understanding both.

The Commission organizes its recommendations around a five-part action agenda grounded in the concept of shared responsibility. Many different participants have contributed to the academic cost dilemma; all of them must be involved in resolving it. In the Commission's view, these actors have a shared responsibility for achieving five policy goals:

- strengthening institutional cost control;
- improving market information and public accountability;
- deregulating higher education;
- rethinking accreditation; and
- enhancing and simplifying Federal student aid.

Sharing Responsibility. The Commission is convinced that many different stakeholders have contributed to the college cost and price crisis; consequently, all of them will have to contribute to the solutions. We believe institutions of higher education, government at all levels—Federal, state and local—the philanthropic community, and families and students have essential and complementary roles to play in maintaining affordable, high-quality education well into the future. Each of these stakeholders in some fashion influences or subsidizes the cost and price of American higher education. They have a common obligation to respond to the issues outlined in this report: Government needs to invest in higher education as a public good; foundations should continue to support policy research and the search for innovation; parents should be prepared to pay their fair share of college expenses; and students should arrive at college prepared for college-level work.

But without doubt, the greatest benefits depend on academic institutions shouldering their responsibility to contain costs, and ultimately prices. Although the responsibility for controlling costs and prices is widely shared, the major onus rests with the higher education community itself.

I. Strengthen Institutional Cost Control

The Commission Recommends *that academic institutions intensify their efforts to control costs and increase institutional productivity.*

The Commission is convinced that academic institutions have done a lot to control costs but they must achieve more in the way of cost containment and productivity improvement. The drive for greater efficiency, productivity, and fiscal transparency requires an expanded definition of academic citizenship, one that is broadly participatory, involving faculty, administrators, students, staff, and trustees.

The effort the Commission is calling for should challenge the basic assumptions governing how institutions think about quality and costs. This will require a greater willingness to focus institutional resources on a few priority areas where excellence can be sustained. It should include new cost saving partnerships among institutions.

The Commission believes it is impossible to formulate an effective single set of directives on cost control applicable to the diverse institutional settings and missions of American colleges and universities. The responsibility for cost control, like the responsibility for quality improvement, must be shouldered by each institution. In recent years, American colleges and universities have made major efforts to reduce expenditures and control costs. The Commission applauds this progress; however, it also believes that much more must be accomplished. To do so, the academic community must focus sustained attention on its own internal financial structures, the better to understand and ultimately control costs and prices. To that end, the Commission makes ten implementing recommendations to strengthen cost control and improve institutional productivity.

Implementing Recommendations:
1. Individual institutions, acting with technical support from appropriate higher education associations, should conduct efficiency self-reviews to identify effective cost-saving steps that are relevant to institutional mission and quality improvement.
2. Academic leaders should communicate the results of these self-reviews widely, providing the campus community and institutional constituents with information on issues such as administrative costs, faculty teaching loads, average class size, faculty and student ratios, facilities management, and expenditures on technology.
3. The Commission recommends the creation of a national effort led by institutions of higher education, the philanthropic community, and oth-

ers to study and consider alternative approaches to collegiate instruction which might improve productivity and efficiency. The Commission believes significant gains in productivity and efficiency can be made through the basic way institutions deliver most instruction, i.e., faculty members meeting with groups of students at regularly scheduled times and places. It also believes that alternative approaches to collegiate instruction deserve further study. Such a study should consider ways to focus on the results of student learning regardless of time spent in the traditional classroom setting.

4. The Commission recommends similar national attention be devoted to developing new alternative approaches to thinking about faculty careers, beginning with graduate school education and extending to tenure and post-tenure review. These should explicitly consider the many ways in which tenure policies vary across institutions.

5. The Commission recommends greater institutional and regional cooperation in using existing facilities at institutions of higher education. Implementation of this recommendation will vary within and across states. Whenever expansion of higher education is contemplated, the existing capacity of all institutions should be considered, including the promotion of greater access through financial aid.

6. The Commission recommends maximizing the opportunity for cost savings through joint campus purchase of goods and services and joint use of facilities, pursuing these opportunities through many different kinds of partnerships. Where necessary, states should consider statutory changes to make such partnerships possible.

7. The Commission recommends greater use of consortia and joint planning to maximize access to expensive academic programs. While acknowledging that some inefficiencies and redundancies are inevitable in America's diverse and decentralized system of higher education, the Commission believes that greater emphasis on consortia and joint planning offers significant opportunities for cost control. In states and regions with large numbers of institutions, creative ways need to be found to make the programmatic variety of each campus available to as many students as possible.

8. The Commission recommends that the philanthropic community, research institutes, and agencies of state and local government adopt the topic of academic cost control as a research area worthy of major financial support. In addition to grants to support efforts to undertake such changes, best-practice and recognition-award programs should be established and supported.

9. As part of the recognition-award effort, the National Association of College and University Business Officers should, in consultation with major higher education associations, develop programs that publicize innovative institutional practices that help control costs. As part of this effort, higher education associations should jointly seek foundation support for annual awards to public and independent colleges and universities that have pioneered cost-management strategies.

10. Finally, we urge Congress to support academic efforts to control costs and improve productivity by:
    - amending Public Law 100-107 (which created the Malcolm Baldrige Award to recognize continuous quality improvement in the corporate sector) to include education; and
    - authorizing in the next reauthorizing cycle the U.S. Department of Education's Fund for the Improvement of Post Secondary Education (FIPSE) to continue to offer financial support for projects addressing issues of productivity, efficiency, quality improvement, and cost control.

II. Improve Market Information and Public Accountability

The Commission Recommends *that the academic community provide the leadership required to develop better consumer information about costs and prices and to improve accountability to the general public.*

The Commission is convinced that both policymakers and the general public need more useful, accurate, timely, and understandable information on college costs, prices, and the different subsidies that benefit all students. Leadership for this effort should come from the academy, from both institutions and higher education associations; but to be really effective of the entire thrust requires a partnership engaging appropriate Federal agencies, states, leaders of the press and electronic media, and the private sector.

For policymakers and the general public to act in a well-informed manner, more timely and reliable data are essential. The Commission was troubled by the sheer amount of incomplete and outdated information available from academic and government sources. Terms of analysis like cost, price, and subsidy are not clearly defined or generally understood. Financial standards, expenditure reports, and cost-recovery principles all rely on different methodologies. There is no common national reporting standard to measure costs or prices.

What is required, first, are comprehensive, easy-to-understand analyses of cost and price issues for different types of institutions by sector (e.g., public and private institutions, two- and four-year, with distinctions between four-year colleges and universities). These analyses should then be transformed into handbooks, available to the public, that provide the following cost and price information:

- the cost of educating students (i.e., the total institutional expenditure—capital costs included—to provide the education);
- actual tuition charges (i.e., sticker prices);
- the general subsidy (i.e., the cost minus the tuition charge);
- instructional costs by level of instruction;
- the total price of attendance (i.e., tuition, fees and other expenses);
- a net price "affordability" measure (i.e., total price minus grants); and
- a net price "accessibility" measure (i.e., total price minus all financial aid).

15

Although the Commission was not always able to obtain complete data on all these issues, the approach outlined above is consistent with the one used in this report. The Commission is convinced that these materials should also include information on financial-aid availability and options along with information on different types of institutions and their different price structures. To the extent possible, information should also include total and net prices for full- and part-time, dependent and independent students. Above all, to be useful, these data should be issued annually. The aim is to provide up-to-date information and illustrate how all potential students—but especially those of limited financial means—can gain access to high-quality postsecondary education. The Commission understands that new accounting standards have been developed for private institutions and are currently being developed for public institutions. Further, the Commission is aware of efforts underway to redesign the Department of Education's Integrated Postsecondary Education Data Survey (IPEDS) to make it compatible with such standards. The recommendations below are offered to emphasize the Commission's belief in the importance of these efforts to the Commission's call for institutions of higher education to become more fiscally transparent, that is, more straightforward in describing to the public where they get their money and how they spend it. . . .

III. Deregulate Higher Education

The Commission Recommends *that governments develop new approaches to academic regulation, approaches that emphasize performance instead of compliance, and differentiation in place of standardization.*

Members of the Commission believe that institutions of higher education have a responsibility to be good public citizens, not just in their teaching, research, and service missions, but also as employers, vendors, and good neighbors in their communities. The Commission is also aware that a variety of regulations, some accompanying public funding and some independent of it, are intended to ensure public health and safety or accountability in the use of tax dollars. The Commission clearly supports these goals.

But the Commission is equally convinced that a fresh approach to academic regulation is required—on the part of government at all levels. This Commission received a lot of testimony about the impact of the regulatory environment on college costs. Academic institutions handling small amounts of toxic substances, for example, are subject to the same regulations as manufacturing enterprises handling the same materials by the ton. Prohibitions against mandatory retirement ages were imposed on academic institutions in recent years (after several decades in which colleges and universities had been legislatively exempt from them) without considering the implications of the change on tenure or maintaining faculty vitality. And regulations regarding such issues as student privacy, the right of students to examine their records, and the incidence of crime on campus are redundant and repetitive.

New approaches need to be developed to ensure public accountability in ways that are less costly and more easily manageable. The Commission believes it is time to replace the current command-and-control approach to academic regulation with an approach that emphasizes performance and accommodates the type and volume of regulation to institutional history, size, and need. . . .

IV. Rethink Accreditation

The Commission Recommends *that the academic community develop well-coordinated, efficient accrediting processes that relate institutional productivity to effectiveness in improving student learning.*

Accreditation is an honored and essential part of higher education. It assures the education community and the public, as well as funding agencies, that the institutions they are attending or supporting merit their confidence. In addition, it provides a useful tool for institutional self-study and account-ability that would be inappropriate to government.

Accreditation strives to assure educational quality and institutional integrity. Basic to the accreditation process are periodic self-studies that evaluate an institution or program in light of publicly-stated objectives—and peer evaluation of those self-studies by a visiting team of academic col-leagues. Accreditation seeks not only to judge and assure quality and integrity, but to promote improvement through continuous self-study and evaluation. Regional associations accredit an institution as a whole, while specialized accrediting groups accredit specific educational programs within an institution.

The Commission recognizes and encourages the movement underway at all six regional accrediting associations to focus more on assessing student achievement. Accreditation bodies—both regional and specialized—have been inclined to emphasize traditional resource measures as proxies for qual-ity. Such traditional measures are often difficult to link to demonstrated stu-dent achievement. Specialized or professional accreditation has, for the most part, continued to focus on resource measures in making judgments about quality. In fact, to many campus observers, they appear often to be acting more in the economic interest of the professions they represent than in the interest of assuring student achievement.

Moreover, specialized accreditation has, in the eyes of many, taken on a life of its own. It has become too complicated, occurs too often, and makes the case for additional resources to support programs of interest to them without regard to the impact on the welfare of the entire institution.

Today, some 60 specialized accrediting agencies oversee more than 100 dif-ferent academic programs—ranging from architecture, business, and engi-neering to journalism, law, medicine, and far beyond. The time-consuming self-study procedures involved with specialized accreditation, the focus on additional resources without regard to their connection to student learning or the welfare of the larger institution, and the expensive duplication involved with different entities, increase red tape and drive up costs.

17

The Commission believes a great deal of improvement is possible in developing both accrediting standards and evaluation review processes that focus directly on student learning. It believes accreditation should encourage a greater focus at both the program and institutional level on productivity and efficiency. . . .

V. Enhance and Simplify Federal Student Aid

The Commission Recommends *that Congress continue the existing student aid programs and simplify and improve the financial aid delivery system.*

Despite the complexity of the current Federal student-aid system of grants, loans, campus-based aid, and tax benefits, it provides crucial support to students from widely varying personal and financial circumstances. There is value in preserving the current mix of programs that enhance student choice among a variety of institutions. Nevertheless, the manner in which that aid is delivered confuses students and families, and, despite its variety, the aid system struggles to serve the diverse needs of the many different types of students now attending postsecondary institutions. Meanwhile, student aid regulations from the U.S. Department of Education are so extensive, internally inconsistent, and excessive that it is almost impossible for any college, university or other financial aid provider in the country to be sure it is ever in full compliance. . . .

U.S. ADVISORY COMMITTEE
ON RELIGIOUS FREEDOM
January 23, 1998

A State Department advisory committee called on the United States to place greater emphasis on the issue of religious freedom overseas. The committee, in an interim report issued January 23, said human rights—including religious freedom—should be just as important a factor in U.S. foreign policy as economic and political considerations.

Although it did not endorse the full scope of the committee's many recommendations, the Clinton administration during 1998 paid an increasing amount of attention to religious freedom issues. Secretary of State Madeleine K. Albright appointed a senior State Department official to coordinate U.S. efforts on religious freedom overseas. The administration reached a compromise agreement with members of Congress who had wanted to impose U.S. economic sanctions against countries that refused to allow religious freedoms.

Starting with the Carter administration in the late 1970s, the United States had made human rights a cornerstone of its foreign policy. During the 1990s American religious groups stepped up pressure on the government to pay more attention to religious freedom overseas. In particular, conservative Christian groups wanted to focus on the persecution of those who tried to practice Christianity in communist and Islamic countries. Responding to such concerns, the Clinton administration in 1997 stressed freedom of religion in its annual report on human rights practices around the world. The administration in July 1997 also sent Congress a special report on what the United States was doing to promote the rights of Christians and other religious groups. (State Department report, Historic Documents of 1997, p. 562)

Advisory Committee Report

The State Department in late 1996 appointed a twenty-member Advisory Committee on Religious Freedom Abroad to address all issues involving freedom of religion and U.S. foreign policy. The panel included academic and foreign policy specialists and leaders representing a wide range of religions. The committee was chaired by John Shattuck, assistant secretary of state for democracy, human rights, and labor.

In its interim report, released January 23, the committee reviewed the role of religious freedom in the founding of the United States and discussed the importance for democracy of all human rights issues. The report briefly described how many countries restrict the practice of religion, although it did not offer a comprehensive country-by-country review of such restrictions.

The heart of the report was a detailed series of recommendations for putting the issue of religious freedom at the forefront of U.S. foreign policy. From the president on down, the panel said, the government needed to pay more attention to human rights issues—especially religious freedom. The committee said that too often in the past the United States had allowed foreign policy and economic considerations to override concerns about human rights abuses in other countries. Bureaucratic restraints also prevented the U.S. government from adequately addressing human rights issues, the committee noted. In particular, the panel said it found "lingering institutional uncertainty in the State Department about the role of human rights in U.S. foreign policy and about the relative importance of religious freedom when weighed against other foreign policy priorities."

For example, the committee pointed out that many U.S. embassies assigned the task of monitoring human rights issues to junior officers who had neither the training nor the resources to carry out their responsibilities. Similarly, the committee said the Immigration and Naturalization Service did not give its agents the proper training or guidance to enable them to determine whether refugees seeking admission to the United States had a well-founded fear of persecution in their home countries because of their religious beliefs.

The panel listed dozens of steps the government could take to make religious freedom a more important element of U.S. foreign policy. Some recommendations were symbolic in nature, such as a call for the president to make a major speech on the issue and to meet more often with religious leaders during his foreign travels. Many of the directives were intended to force U.S. diplomats and other government officials to pay more attention to religious freedom issues during the normal course of business. Still other recommendations would require unspecified funding increases for U.S. programs, such as aid for nongovernmental organizations that promoted human rights and religious freedom.

The committee said it had not studied in detail whether the United States should impose economic or other forms of sanctions against countries that restricted religious freedom. Existing U.S. law allowed the president to place sanctions against countries that violated human rights, but some members of Congress had been lobbying for legislation requiring sanctions against countries that repressed religious minorities. The committee said it would continue to review the matter.

In releasing the report on January 23, Secretary of State Albright said she was carrying out one of the committee's chief recommendations: creation of a high-level position within the State Department to oversee U.S. activities on religious freedom. Albright in June named Robert Seiple as the department's first special representative for religious freedom; he had the rank of a deputy assistant secretary of state.

The Sanctions Issue

Even as the State Department advisory panel was mulling the sanctions issue, the Clinton administration and members of Congress were dealing with sanctions legislation during 1998. Conservatives in both chambers had proposed legislation requiring U.S. economic sanctions against nations that systematically persecuted their citizens for their religious beliefs. As the legislation was moving through House committees in 1998, the Clinton administration expressed opposition to any requirement for automatic sanctions. Administration officials said the president needed flexibility to take all foreign policy issues into consideration when determining whether to impose sanctions against another country.

The administration and key senators developed a compromise measure that gave the president authority to impose a range of diplomatic and economic sanctions against nations that consistently permitted or endorsed religious persecution. The bill also required annual State Department reports to Congress on religious freedom overseas. The Senate passed the bill on October 9, and the House cleared it the next day; Clinton signed it into law (PL 105–292) on October 27. Administration officials said the law gave the president adequate flexibility to promote religious freedom overseas without forcing him to impose sanctions regardless of other considerations.

> *Following are excerpts from the "Interim Report to the Secretary of State and to the President of the United States," by the Advisory Committee on Religious Freedom Abroad, released January 23, 1998:*

IV. Preliminary Recommendations

In making its preliminary recommendations, the Advisory Committee has focused on reviewing current U.S. Government efforts and finding ways to make them more effective; and identifying new approaches through which the U.S. Government can advance religious freedom and oppose religious persecution.

The Committee has received detailed information from the U.S. Government on its current activities to address issues of religious freedom. We have included this information in the discussion below to set the context for Committee recommendation.

The U.S. Government has demonstrated a commitment to advocate more vigorously for religious freedom and integrate the issue into mainstream policy considerations. We have included recommendations in some areas in which the U.S. Government's current actions or policies are consistent with our proposals. The purpose of their inclusion is to indicate that more needs to be done or that existing policies need to be integrated and strengthened, as well as to provide a comprehensive package of the various areas where action is necessary to ensure an overall, cohesive and effective policy. It is clear that there are many areas where current policies and practices can be strengthened and improved to achieve the goals of ending religious persecution and promoting respect for religious freedom and other universal human rights principles.

The following recommendations reflect the Advisory Committee's preliminary findings and represent some of the areas on which the Committee will continue to focus in greater detail over the coming year. The Committee intends to build and expand on the recommendations offered in this Interim Report for a more comprehensive assessment and set of recommendations in its final report next year.

Presidential Initiatives

Current U.S. Policies: The Clinton Administration has undertaken several initiatives to highlight issues of religious freedom and the role of religion in resolving conflict and promoting human rights. The establishment of the Advisory Committee on Religious Freedom Abroad is one indication of U.S. Government recognition that more can and should be done to address the issue.

The President has publicly affirmed his commitment to advancing religious freedom as a U.S. foreign policy priority and as an issue of concern to the Administration and the American people. The President has raised the issue directly with leaders of other governments. For example, President Clinton has expressed to Russian President Boris Yeltsin the U.S. concern about legislation to curtail religious liberty in Russia.

The President has hosted a wide variety of meetings attended by representatives of diverse religions, including leaders from Christian, Jewish, Islamic, Baha'i, Buddhist, Hindu, and other faiths. The President has met with the Dalai Lama, Pope John Paul II, Ecumenical Patriarch Bartholomew, and other eminent religious leaders from around the world to discuss critical issues affecting religious communities and U.S. diplomatic efforts to advance religious freedom. During his travels abroad, the President has also visited leading religious figures.

Under the President's leadership, the U.S. Government has undertaken diplomatic initiatives in conflicts with a religious dimension, working to promote peace processes in the former Yugoslavia, Northern Ireland, and the Middle East. The First Lady inaugurated an inter-faith humanitarian initiative in Bosnia in 1996 and has raised issues of religious freedom and conflict resolution during her travels.

The President has annually issued proclamations designating January 16 as Religious Freedom Day, as a means of celebrating the diversity of spiritual beliefs that flourish in the United States and underscoring America's commitment to religious freedom.

Recommendations

The President should deliver a major address explaining the importance of religious freedom at home and abroad.

The President should give greater weight and enhanced importance to religious freedom among the issues for consideration in foreign policy decision-making.

The President should take every opportunity to raise specific concerns about religious freedom in meetings with foreign leaders.

The President should stress and highlight, in our bilateral and multilateral international relations, the increased importance which U.S. foreign policy accords issues of religious freedom.

The President should instruct the heads of U.S. Government agencies to support and reinforce U.S. policies to promote religious freedom and agencies of the U.S. Government should give appropriate priority to this concern.

The President should encourage greater dialogue on issues of religious freedom among a broad spectrum of Americans to encourage understanding, tolerance, and activities to end violations of religious freedom.

The President should direct additional U.S. funds towards U.S. Government programs, offices, and bureaus with oversight on human rights issues, including religious freedom, in order to enhance work on and consideration of these issues.

The Department of State

Current U.S. Policies: In recent years, the State Department has instituted several initiatives which can be further developed to promote religious freedom and combat religious persecution. Secretary [Madeleine] Albright, in one of her first statements after taking office, announced clearly and publicly that religious freedom must be treated as a foreign policy priority. Through a series of world-wide cables, Secretaries Christopher and Albright instructed all U.S. diplomatic posts to give greater attention to religious freedom both in their reporting and in their advocacy, emphasizing the need for State Department employees and foreign governments alike to treat religious liberty as a priority in U.S. foreign policy.

The creation of the Secretary of State's Advisory Committee on Religious Freedom Abroad introduces an important new opportunity for partnership towards dialogue, information gathering, and parallel action by government and religious institutions in addressing persecution, and promoting conflict resolution and respect for human rights.

The State Department currently provides extensive, comprehensive reports on religious freedom and persecution. The Spokesmen for both the State Department and White House have begun to issue more frequent public statements condemning specific acts and policies of persecution in various parts of the world. Religious persecution has also been the topic of reports and editorials on the Voice of America and other U.S. Government broadcasting organs, which have focused on China, Tibet, Burma, Sudan, Iran, and Vietnam, among other places where persecution has occurred.

Despite a positive trend and several constructive new initiatives, however, the State Department and U.S. Embassies often approach religious freedom issues in an ad hoc and reactive manner. Responses to particular problems have often been shaped by factors such as congressional or media interest, U.S. Ambassadors' attitudes on intervention in human rights cases, and Embassy staffing levels. The result is an approach that varies somewhat from case to case and country to country. This pattern is attributable, in part, to lingering institutional uncertainty in the State Department about the role of human rights in U.S. foreign policy and about the relative importance of religious freedom when weighed against other foreign policy priorities.

Recommendations

The Secretary of State should build on her current initiatives to reflect the importance of this issue by dedicating more resources to focus on integrating policies that promote religious freedom, coordinating actions among bureaus and agencies, and implementing the policies that advance religious freedom, including the recommendations of the Advisory Committee that are accepted by the Secretary of State. For example, the Secretary of State should dedicate for this purpose a high-level position, support staff, and an office at the State Department, in an appropriate bureau, such as the Bureau of Democracy, Human Rights and Labor or another relevant bureau.

The Advisory Committee should meet on a semi-annual basis with the Under Secretaries of State for Political Affairs, Global Affairs, Economic Affairs, and others, and with appropriate Assistant Secretaries, including those from regional bureaus, to review religious freedom issues and take stock of U.S. diplomatic efforts.

The State Department should incorporate religious freedom concerns into all appropriate high-level meetings and visits.

The State Department should instruct embassies to raise routinely through diplomatic channels cases of imprisoned religious believers and other individual cases where religious freedom is violated.

The State Department's Spokesperson and other officials should speak out forcefully and frequently on instances of religious persecution and when religious freedom is violated.

The State Department and other relevant U.S. Government agencies should pay special attention to the status of religious freedom as a human rights concern when considering arms sales, military assistance, or economic aid. To the greatest extent possible, the U.S. Government should also be in consultation with U.S. and foreign religious communities before deciding on policies that will effect religious communities abroad.

The Secretary of State should instruct all Under Secretaries and Assistant Secretaries to ensure that foreign affairs officers receive human rights training by attending courses, including enhanced training on religious freedom offered at the National Foreign Affairs Training Center (NFATC).

The annual evaluation of State Department officers should include an evaluation of their understanding of the status of human rights in their region, especially on religious freedom, their advocacy on religious freedom and other human rights with foreign governments, and their engagement with local religious and belief communities, as well as with local human rights groups.

Embassies

Current U.S. Policies: U.S. Embassies include the promotion of human rights in their missions. In almost every country of the world, the U.S. Embassy is comparatively the most active member of the local diplomatic community on issues of human rights and religious freedom. U.S. Embassy officials at all levels are instructed to and regularly raise concerns about limitations on or violations of religious freedom in meetings with foreign leaders and their representatives. In addition, the State Department and U.S. Embassies in many parts of the world have begun to engage in dialogue with religious leaders and advocates of religious freedom.

Nevertheless, human rights and religious freedom issues compete for attention among other important foreign policy priorities determined at Embassies. It is essential that the Foreign Service attach as great importance to global issues such as human rights, as it does to commercial promotion and political and military affairs. Especially in countries with poor human rights records, the human rights issues are a consistent part of the dialogue between Ambassadors, and other top level Embassy personnel, and officials of the host government. However, human rights advocacy is also viewed by some U.S. officials as an impediment to good relations with foreign governments, rather than as the promotion of a core U.S. interest.

Primary responsibility for maintaining contact with human rights organizations and for drafting the annual human rights report is generally assigned to junior political officers. It is important that senior Embassy officers devote as much time and energy to establishing contacts in the human rights and religious communities as they do to building relationships with local officials and business leaders. In addition, reduced staffing, in part determined by congressional appropriations, has sometimes impeded the capacity of Embassies to advocate on behalf of human rights and religious freedom.

The Committee understands that the U.S. has multiple foreign policy goals, and that these goals must be carefully balanced and pursued. Human rights advocacy calls for the highest standards of diplomatic professionalism. Human rights advocacy should not be hesitant and cautious, although such advocacy, to be effective, must sometimes be conducted in a low-key manner and behind the scenes. The Committee believes that routine diplomatic practice must incorporate and act with the understanding that human rights, including religious freedom, are core American values and universal principles that require treatment as priority U.S. interests.

Recommendations

U.S. Embassies should assign priority importance to investigating, monitoring, and reporting on issues of religious freedom. They should seek information from local and international religious groups and other non-governmental organizations that monitor religious freedom and other human rights conditions.

Adequate staffing should be assigned to Embassies in the countries where religious persecution is an issue.

The promotion and protection of religious freedom should be integrated into all Embassy annual mission program plans, wherever religious freedom is an issue.

Issues of religious freedom should be included in ongoing diplomatic communications with host governments.

U.S. Embassy staff should seek meetings with imprisoned religious leaders and dissidents, as well as access to prisons.

U.S. Embassy staff should regularly intervene on behalf of victims of religious persecution and raise their cases directly and firmly with the host government.

U.S. Embassy personnel should maintain dialogue and outreach with religious leaders, religious groups, and experts on local religious life. They should contact members of majority and minority religious communities, including both government-sponsored and unregistered groups.

U.S. Embassy personnel should be alert to and distinguish the different treatment accorded to groups within the same religion, and should reflect these distinctions in their reporting and policy.

U.S. Embassies should coordinate with local, international, and American non-governmental organizations, particularly those that focus on promoting religious freedom, to facilitate their human rights and humanitarian activities and support their access to difficult regions.

When determining the allocation of program funds, U.S. Embassies should allocate funds for non-governmental projects that promote religious freedom, such as programs that protect human rights, facilitate reconciliation, and strengthen the rule of law and civil society. Embassies should also support initiatives to integrate fully religious freedom as a central element of existing programs.

U.S. Embassies should press host governments to accord independent human rights monitoring groups full and unimpeded access to regions throughout the country.

U.S. Ambassadors should be personally involved in and review their Embassy's human rights reports. . . .

Asylum & Refugee Assistance

Current U.S. Policies: The Administration has indicated that the State Department and the Immigration and Naturalization Service (INS) should give more attention to religious persecution and the growing numbers of claims resulting from it, and is committed to improving and strengthening measures and provisions necessary to achieving this goal. Inadequate training and/or insensitivity to the nature of the claim can result in the disregard or the dismissal of claims based on religious persecution and on other human rights violations.

In this context, the State Department and the INS are working to insure that the issue of religious persecution is taken into account in the various asylum adjudication processes. Efforts are underway to update and strengthen the information used by asylum adjudicators to determine the human rights conditions in foreign countries and to provide them with current information on religious persecution. Most of the country condition reports prepared by the State Department's Office of Asylum Affairs have been brought up to date and strengthened, although this has been a problem in the past.

A new "summary exclusion" provision prevents individuals who arrive in the U.S. without proper documents from applying for asylum without first establishing a credible fear of persecution. It is crucial that INS and the State Department be well-informed, attentive, and sensitive to situations of religious persecution and other human rights violations. Otherwise, there is a strong possibility that individuals who are unable to demonstrate immediately that they have a "credible fear" of persecution, when in fact they do, could be wrongly deported and returned to the hands of their persecutors. Generally, there are insufficient safeguards in the current asylum procedures to prevent the mistaken return of persons who are too fearful, confused, or unfamiliar with procedures to make a clear and accurate claim.

Recommendations

Training of INS and State Department personnel should include courses that promote sensitivity to religious persecution and other human rights issues and provide up-to-date information on these subjects.

The NFATC [National Foreign Affairs Training Center] and its counterpart in INS should introduce training on religious persecution, including country-specific conditions, and the handling of such cases and claimants, including guidance on interview techniques to readily identify individuals suffering the trauma of religious persecution. Successful completion of a mandatory training course in this subject for all State Department and INS personnel associated with asylum or refugee processes could significantly increase the level of sensitivity to religious persecution.

Refugee and human rights non-governmental organizations should be incorporated into the training programs.

Asylum and refugee personnel should periodically be provided with updated information and on-site refresher courses. Statistical analysis and data should be uniformly gathered, reported and available for evaluation. Detailed information should be gathered about the assessments and results of the "credible fear" interview, the determinations reached by primary and secondary inspectors, the overseas refugee adjudication, asylum officer referrals, and immigration removal proceeding determinations.

The summary exclusion law of the immigration act should be repealed. At a minimum, procedural safeguards in the summary exclusion screening process for "credible fear" should be strengthened and improved in order to ensure against the return of victims of religious persecution.

Those arriving to the United States without proper documents and seeking to apply here for asylum should be referred immediately to asylum officers for a "credible fear" interview. Those officials responsible for referring individuals for "credible fear" screening should be provided with a list of countries, nationalities and ethnic populations known to be at "high risk" of religious persecution.

Inspectors empowered to detain individuals during the primary or secondary inspection process should follow strict guidelines that prevent the detention of individuals with legitimate asylum claims, while retaining important security procedures that permit the detention of suspected terrorists, criminals, and other significant security risks.

To the extent possible, claimants should have access to non-governmental, independent, and competent, on-site translators, eliminating the need for INS officials to serve as translators.

The Office of the U.N. High Commissioner for Refugees (UNHCR) and relevant non-governmental organizations should be given access to claimants and be made available at all stages of the process to provide claimants with information, guidance and assistance in preparing their claims and to monitor the process.

The INS, in coordination with the UNHCR and non-governmental organizations, should make every effort to provide claimants with information, including explanations and findings, in their native language, either written or oral, to facilitate the claimant's understanding of the decisions and available procedures.

The overseas refugee processing should be strengthened. Expanding the size of the professionally trained asylum corps and better integrating it into the refugee adjudication corps would strengthen overseas refugee processing and could improve assistance to legitimate victims of religious persecution. In addition, individuals seeking refugee protection who claim serious human rights violations, including religious persecution, should be identified as "groups of special humanitarian concern" to the U.S. Government.

UNHCR should be pressed to identify cases of religious persecution not easily accessible to our current refugee processing apparatus. However, UNHCR referrals must not be the only path to adjudication in such cases. Greater use of refugee, human rights and faith-based non-governmental organizations should be made by U.S. missions abroad to identify groups or individuals victimized by religious persecution.

The size of the State Department's Office of Asylum Affairs and the INS Resource Center should be increased to ensure they are capable of providing assistance and up-to-date information, especially on religious persecution, to U.S. consulates and other USG personnel involved in summary exclusion or "credible fear" screening, asylum adjudication or removal proceedings. . . .

Multilateral Diplomacy

Current U.S. Policies: The United States has championed efforts to raise the profile of religious freedom in multilateral institutions, including the U.N. General Assembly, the U.N. Human Rights Commission, and the Organization for Security and Cooperation in Europe. The United States played a leading role in creating the position of the U.N. Special Rapporteur on Religious Intolerance and has continued to support renewal of his mandate. Promotion of religious freedom was a priority for the U.S. delegation at the 1997 United Nations Human Rights Commission, as well as an important issue for the U.S. Delegation at the U.N. General Assembly in September. The U.S. has also taken a lead on specific country resolutions that cite serious violations of religious freedom.

Although the U.S. has taken several steps to promote and integrate the issue of religious freedom at international fora, the issue remains a peripheral one which is not yet fully integrated into the mainstream of deliberations, nor is it mentioned consistently in relevant country resolutions. It is still unclear whether this is a priority issue for the Office of the U.N. High Commissioner for Human Rights. The U.N. Special Rapporteurs are under-funded and has weak international support. Although some Special Rapporteurs for countries with violations of religious freedom are tasked specifically to consider religious freedom, others are not. . . .

PAPAL ADDRESS ON OPENNESS AND RELIGIOUS FREEDOM IN CUBA
January 25, 1998

The image was powerful: Two aging men, symbols of opposing twenti-eth-century forces, greeting each other warmly in the tropical sun. Pope John Paul II, the frail seventy-seven-year-old leader of the Roman Catholic Church and longtime anticommunist crusader, was welcomed to Cuba on January 21 by President Fidel Castro, at seventy-one a rare survivor from the losing communist side of the cold war. As an apostle of understanding, John Paul urged Castro to open his totalitarian society to the ideals of the outside world, including "freedom, mutual trust, social justice, and lasting peace." John Paul also called on the rest of the world—the United States in particular—to be more willing to help Cuba change its society, including dropping the decades-old U.S. economic embargo.

The pope's first visit to Cuba had been under consideration for nearly ten years, and it took a year to work out the logistical and diplomatic details. All the planning appeared to be worth the trouble, as the pontiff delivered a series of messages that stirred the Cuban people and gave the outside world its closest look at Cuba since Castro's revolution in 1959.

Any hopes that the pope's visit would lead Castro to relax his grip were soon dashed, however. In response to a papal appeal, Castro released sev-eral dozen prisoners, including some held for their political beliefs. But human rights groups and other observers reported no significant reduction of communist control in Cuba. Months after the visit, Vatican officials expressed frustration at the lack of progress in Cuba.

There was one tangible result for the Vatican: The pope's visit appeared to spur renewed interest in the church on the part of the Cuban people. The Miami Herald *reported on June 26 that more Cubans were attending mass regularly than in decades. Castro's government announced in December that Cubans would be allowed to celebrate Christmas legally for the first time since the revolution.*

The Pope's Appeals

Pope John Paul II spent five days in Cuba, conducting religious services for large crowds at several points around the island. Castro accompanied the pope on some of the stops—even attending mass despite his declared atheism—and the two men met privately for fifty minutes at the Palace of the Revolution. Out of respect for the pope, Castro shed his customary military uniform and wore a blue business suit. The Cuban leader also was solicitous of his guest's frail health and at one point gave the pontiff an affectionate pat on the back.

Each leader had an obvious agenda for the visit, and each managed to accomplish at least parts of that agenda. Before the visit, the pope said he wanted the Cuban people to be able to express their religious faith and to hear a call for human rights and religious freedom. His visit offered Cubans more opportunities in that regard than at any point since the 1959 revolution.

In a country where religious expression had been discouraged and often suppressed, Castro allowed the pope to perform open-air masses that were attended by tens of thousands and broadcast over state radio and television to the entire nation. For his part, Castro wanted international attention for himself and his revolution and a papal denunciation of the U.S. economic embargo against Cuba. Castro got both. Brushing aside the pontiff's criticisms, Castro attempted to portray the visit as a sign of international backing for the revolution that the United States had tried for so long to crush.

Although disagreeing on most major issues between them, the two men did share views on the dangers of capitalism. Throughout his papacy, John Paul had warned against the dehumanizing effects of an unbridled free market that places profits above all social considerations. He expressed this view in his final address on January 25, declaring his opposition to "capitalist neoliberalism which subordinates the human being to blind market forces." Castro construed such statements to be an endorsement of his anticapitalist position.

Many of the pope's statements were appeals to Castro and his government on human rights and religious freedom, but the pontiff also spoke directly to the Cuban people about moral values and their own roles in society. On the second day of his visit, for example, the pope spoke to an audience in the southeastern city of Santa Clara about the importance of family life. He denounced the country's high rates of divorce and abortion and called on Cuban parents to be more serious about their responsibilities to their children. But even in this speech the Pope challenged the government for its policy of forcing many students to attend high school far away from home—a practice he said weakened family bonds.

The culmination of the pope's visit was his celebration of an open-air mass in the Plaza of the Revolution in central Havana. Reporters estimated the crowd at about a quarter-million people, while the Vatican put the turnout at "over a million." The Plaza frequently had been the site of most of Castro's famed hours-long speeches to his subjects.

During the mass a giant portrait of Cuban revolutionary hero Che Guevara faced the crowd on one side, while a freshly painted mural of Jesus dominated the stage from which the Pope spoke. Castro and other government leaders sat in the front row and heard a blistering papal attack on the fundamentals of their revolutionary state: communism, materialism, atheism, isolation from the outside world, and restrictions on virtually all forms of individual human endeavor.

Later on January 26, as he was preparing to leave Cuba, the pope uttered the words Castro had been waiting for throughout the visit: a denunciation of the U.S. embargo that had been in effect against Cuba since 1962. In a prepared statement, John Paul said that "imposed isolation strikes the population indiscriminately, making it ever more difficult for the weakest to enjoy the bare essentials of decent living, things such as food, health, and education." The suffering of the Cuban people had many causes, he said, including "oppressive economic measures, unjust and ethically unacceptable, imposed from outside the country."

Release of Prisoners

At the outset of the pope's visit, Vatican officials gave the Castro government a list of about three hundred prisoners for whom the pontiff was asking clemency. During a visit to a hospital near Havana on January 24, the pope directly appealed for release of "prisoners of conscience" in Cuba. "What they want is to participate actively in life with the opportunity to speak their mind with respect and tolerance," he said. "I encourage efforts to reinsert prisoners into society."

The pope's words had limited effect. On February 13 the Cuban government announced that it was releasing about one hundred prisoners. Many of those released were common criminals near the end of their sentences; a few had been imprisoned because of political dissent. Nevertheless, international human rights groups and the U.S. government denounced Castro's regime for continuing to hold several hundred political dissidents in prison. During the summer of 1998, Vatican officials expressed frustration with the lack of progress toward political openness in Cuba.

U.S. Eases Restrictions

The Clinton administration swiftly rejected the pope's call for lifting the U.S. economic embargo against Cuba, saying that the suffering of the Cuban people resulted from the policies of the Castro regime rather than U.S. sanctions. Even so, Secretary of State Madeleine K. Albright on March 20 announced that the United States would ease some restrictions on Cuba, such as making it easier for relief agencies to provide food, medicine, and other humanitarian supplies to the Cuban people. The administration also agreed to allow Cuban Americans to send up to $300 per quarter to family members back in Cuba. Several of the administration's steps softened *restrictions that had been imposed in 1994 and again in 1996 in response to Cuba's downing of civilian airplanes flown by Cuban exiles.* (Historic Documents of 1996, p. 93)

Albright said the U.S. steps were inspired by the pope's visit and were an effort "to reach out to the people of Cuba to make their lives more tolerable." She said Cubans "are beginning to think beyond Castro. We need to do the same." Albright said the United States would maintain its economic embargo against Cuba—despite the pope's criticism—because Castro "appears as autocratic as ever."

Late in the year, the U.S. embargo came under fire from two quarters, one expected and the other unexpected. The former was the latest version of an annual resolution in the United Nations General Assembly denouncing the embargo. For the seventh year in a row, an overwhelming majority of nations supported the resolution; the vote on October 14 was 157–2 (the United States and Israel), with 12 nations abstaining. The vote against the U.S. position was the highest ever; 143 nations supported a similar resolution in 1997.

A more unusual call for a review of U.S. policy came on November 7 from a bipartisan group of senators and former diplomats. Organized by Sen. John Warner, R-Va., former secretary of state Lawrence Eagleburger, and former State Department official William D. Rogers, the group called for a presidential commission to review all aspects of U.S. policy toward Cuba, including the embargo. The group did not take a specific position on the embargo, but its call for a policy review was generally viewed as sign of diminished domestic support for the long-standing policy. The group included several conservative Republican senators (such as Rick Santorum of Pennsylvania and Rod Grams of Minnesota) and former secretaries of state Henry M. Kissinger and George P. Shultz.

> *Following are excerpts from a sermon delivered by Pope John Paul II on January 25, 1998, to an open-air mass in Havana, Cuba. The pope spoke in Spanish; this translation was provided by the Vatican:*

1. "This day is holy to the Lord your God; do not mourn or weep" (Neh 8: 9). With great joy I celebrate Holy Mass in this José Martí Plaza on Sunday, the Lord's Day, which should be dedicated to rest, prayer and family life. The word of God calls us together to grow in faith and to celebrate the presence of the risen Lord in our midst, for "by one Spirit we were all baptized into one body" (1 Cor 12: 13), the Mystical Body of Christ which is the Church. Jesus Christ unites all the baptized. From him flows the fraternal love among Cuban Catholics and Catholics everywhere, since all are "the body of Christ and individually members of it" (1 Cor 12: 27). The Church in Cuba is not alone or isolated; rather, it is part of the Universal Church which extends throughout the whole world.

2. With affection I greet Cardinal Jaime Ortega, the Pastor of this Arch-diocese, and I thank him for his kind words at the beginning of this celebration, telling me of the joys and the hopes which mark the life of this ecclesial community. I likewise greet the Cardinals present from different countries, my Brother Bishops in Cuba, and the Bishops from other places who have wished to take part in this solemn celebration. I cordially greet the priests, the men and women religious and all the faithful assembled here in such numbers. I assure each one of you of my affection and closeness in the Lord. I respectfully greet President Fidel Castro Ruz, who has wished to take part in this Mass.

I also thank the civil authorities who have wished to be present today and I am grateful for the co-operation which they have provided.

State must allow every person to live his faith freely

3. "The Spirit of the Lord is upon me, because he has anointed me to preach good news to the poor" (Lk 4: 18). Every minister of God has to make his own these words spoken by Jesus in Nazareth. And so, as I come among you, I wish to bring you the Good News of hope in God. As a servant of the Gospel I bring you this message of love and solidarity which Jesus Christ, by his coming, offers to men and women in every age. In absolutely no way is this an ideology or a new economic or political system; rather, it is a *path of authentic peace, justice and freedom.*

4. The ideological and economic systems succeeding one another in the last two centuries have often encouraged conflict as a method, since their programmes contained the seeds of opposition and disunity. This fact profoundly affected their understanding of man and of his relations with others. Some of these systems also presumed to relegate religion to the merely private sphere, stripping it of any social influence or importance. In this regard, it is helpful to recall that *a modern State cannot make atheism or religion one of its political ordinances.* The State, while distancing itself from all extremes of fanaticism or secularism, should encourage a harmonious social climate and a suitable legislation which enables every person and every religious confession to live their faith freely, to express that faith in the context of public life and to count on adequate resources and opportunities to bring its spiritual, moral and civic benefits to bear on the life of the nation.

On the other hand, various places are witnessing the resurgence of a certain *capitalist neoliberalism* which subordinates the human person to *blind market forces* and conditions the development of peoples on those forces. From its centres of power, such neoliberalism often places unbearable burdens upon less favored countries. Hence, at times, *unsustainable economic programmes* are imposed on nations as a condition for further assistance. In the international community, we thus see *a small number of countries growing exceedingly rich at the cost of the increasing impoverishment of a great number of other countries;* as a result the wealthy grow ever wealthier, while the poor grow ever poorer.

The teachings of Jesus maintain their full force

5. Dear brothers and sisters: *the Church is a teacher in humanity*. Faced with these systems, she presents *a culture of love and of life*, restoring hope to humanity, hope in the transforming power of love lived in the unity willed by Christ. For this to happen, it is necessary to follow *a path of reconciliation, dialogue and fraternal acceptance* of one's neighbour, of every human person. This can be called the social Gospel of the Church. The Church, in carrying out her mission, *sets before the world a new justice*, the justice of the kingdom of God (cf. Mt 6: 33). On various occasions I have spoken on social themes. It is necessary to keep speaking on these themes, as long as any injustice, however small, is present in the world; otherwise the Church would not be faithful to the mission entrusted to her by Christ. *At stake here is man*, the concrete human person. While times and situations may change, there are always people who need the voice of the Church so that their difficulties, their suffering and their distress may be known. Those who find themselves in these situations can be certain that they will not be betrayed, for the Church is with them and the Pope, in his heart and with his words of encouragement, embraces all who suffer injustice.

After a long burst of applause, the Holy Father said:

I am not against applause because when you applaud the Pope can take a little rest!

On the threshold of the Year 2000, the teachings of Jesus maintain their full force. They are valid for all of you, dear brothers and sisters. In seeking the justice of the kingdom we cannot hesitate in the face of difficulties and misunderstandings. If the Master's call to justice, to service and to love is accepted as good news, then the heart is expanded, criteria are transformed and a culture of love and life is born. This is the great change which society needs and expects; and it can only come about if there is first a conversion of each individual heart, as a condition for the necessary changes in the structures of society.

6. *"The Spirit of the Lord has sent me to proclaim release to the captives . . . to set at liberty those who are oppressed"* (Lk 4: 18). The Good News of Jesus must be accompanied by a proclamation of freedom based on the solid foundation of truth: *"If you continue in my word, you are truly my disciples, and you will know the truth and the truth will make you free"* (Jn 8: 31–32). The truth of which Jesus speaks is not only the intellectual grasp of reality, but also *the truth about man* and his transcendent condition, *his rights and duties, his greatness and his limitations*. It is the same truth which Jesus proclaimed with his life, reaffirmed before Pilate and, by his silence, before Herod; it is the same truth that led him to his saving Cross and his glorious Resurrection.

A freedom which is not based on truth conditions man in such a way that he sometimes becomes the object and not the subject of his social, cultural, economic and political surroundings; this leaves him almost no initiative for his personal development. At other times that freedom takes on an individualistic cast and, with no regard for the freedom of others, imprisons man in his own egoism. *The attainment of freedom in responsibility is a duty which no one can shirk.* For Christians, *the freedom of the children of God* is not only a gift and a task, but its attainment also involves an invaluable witness and a genuine contribution to the journey towards the liberation of the whole human race. *This liberation cannot be reduced to its social and political aspects*, but rather reaches its fullness in the exercise of *freedom of conscience, the basis and foundation of all other human rights.*

To the crowds who were shouting: "The Pope is free and wants us all to be free", the Holy Father replied:

Yes, he lives with that freedom for which Christ has set you free.

For many of the political and economic systems operative today the greatest challenge is still that of *combining freedom and social justice, freedom and solidarity*, so that no one is relegated to a position of inferiority. *The Church's social doctrine* is meant to be a reflection and a contribution which can shed light on and reconcile the relationship between the inalienable rights of each individual and the needs of society, so that people can attain their profound aspirations and integral fulfilment in accordance with their condition as sons and daughters of God and citizens in society. Hence *the Catholic laity* should contribute to this fulfilment by the *application of the Church's social teachings in every sector* open to people of goodwill.

7. In the Gospel proclaimed today, justice is seen as intimately linked to truth. This is also evident in the *enlightened thinking of the Fathers of your country.* The Servant of God *Fr Félix Varela*, inspired by his Christian faith and his fidelity to the priestly ministry, sowed in the heart of the Cuban people the seeds of justice and freedom which he dreamed of seeing blossom in an independent Cuba.

The teaching of José Martí on love between all people had profoundly evangelical roots, and thus overcame the false conflict between faith in God and love and service to one's country. This great leader wrote: "Pure, selfless, persecuted, tormented, poetic and simple, the religion of the Nazarene enthralled all honourable men. . . . *Every people needs to be religious.* Not only as part of its essence, but for its own practical benefit it needs to be religious. . . . An irreligious people will die, because nothing in it encourages virtue. Human injustices offend virtue; it is necessary that heavenly justice guarantee it".

As everyone knows, *Cuba has a Christian soul* and this has brought her a *universal vocation.* Called to overcome isolation, she needs to open herself to the world and the world needs to draw close to Cuba, her people, her sons and daughters who are surely her greatest wealth. *This is the time to start out on the new paths* called for by the times of renewal which we are experiencing at the approach of the third millennium of the Christian era!

8. Dear brothers and sisters: *God has blessed this people with true educators of the national conscience*, clear and firm models of the Christian faith as the most effective support of virtue and love. Today the Bishops, with the priests, men and women religious and lay faithful, are striving to build

bridges in order to bring minds and hearts closer together; they are fostering and strengthening peace, and *preparing the civilization of love and justice.* I am present among you *as a messenger of truth and hope.* For this reason I wish to repeat my appeal: *let Jesus Christ enlighten you; accept without reservation the splendour of his truth,* so that all can *set out on the path of unity through love and solidarity,* while avoiding exclusion, isolation and conflict, which are contrary to the will of God who is Love.

May the Holy Spirit enlighten by his gifts those who, in different ways, are responsible for the future of this people so close to my heart. And may Our Lady of Charity of El Cobre, Queen of Cuba, obtain for her children the gifts of peace, progress and happiness.

At the end of his homily the Holy Father spoke extemporaneously:

This wind today is very significant because wind symbolizes the Holy Spirit. "Spiritus spirat ubi vult; Spiritus vult spirare in Cuba". My last words are in Latin, because Cuba also has a Latin tradition: Latin America, Latin Cuba, Latin language! "Spiritus spirat ubi vult et vult Cubam"! Goodbye.

STATE OF THE UNION ADDRESS AND REPUBLICAN RESPONSE
January 27, 1998

President Bill Clinton on January 27 pulled off what many people did not think was possible. Under siege for a week by reports that he had had an affair with a former White House intern and had urged her to lie about it, Clinton strode into the Capitol and delivered a rousing State of the Union address that repeatedly brought cheers and applause from members of both parties. Facing the greatest peril of his presidency—including talk that he might be impeached or forced to resign—Clinton forged ahead with proud boasts about the country's economic health and proposals for a series of new spending programs.

In many ways, Clinton's sixth State of the Union speech turned out to be a preview of how he would get through the rest of a very troubled year. Standing before both houses of Congress, he never mentioned the subject on everyone's mind: his alleged affair with former White House intern Monica Lewinsky. With rare exceptions, Clinton stuck to that pattern the rest of the year, allowing his aides and lawyers to deal with the constant barrage of media reports and political developments surrounding the scandal. In his speech, and in most of his follow-up actions throughout 1998, Clinton tried to keep the public's focus on specific policy issues. Clinton was especially eager to concentrate on those issues that had helped him win reelection in 1996: protecting social security and the environment and widening educational opportunities.

Clinton's bravura performance left Republicans shaking their heads in wonder at his amazing political skills. Most Republicans found themselves agreeing with many of the president's proposals, although complaining about the high cost of some of them and expressing skepticism about his sincerity on others. (Clinton/Lewinsky scandal, pp. 564, 632, 695, 958)

The Lewinsky Scandal

The Lewinsky scandal broke on January 21, with news reports that Kenneth W. Starr, the independent counsel investigating Clinton's involvement in a failed Arkansas land deal called "Whitewater," was widening his inquiry into the president's alleged sexual misconduct. The reports said Clinton had conducted an affair with Lewinsky when she had been an intern at the White House and had asked her to lie about it. The reports also said both Clinton and Lewinsky had denied the affair in sworn testimony for a civil lawsuit brought against Clinton by Paula Jones. Jones had accused Clinton of sexually harassing her while he was governor of Arkansas and she was a state employee.

The core elements of the Lewinsky scandal—sex, perjury, and political power—raised immediate questions not only about the president's legal difficulties but about how much political damage he had suffered. Most political commentators and politicians of both parties appeared to assume there was some element of truth to the allegations, and they openly asked whether Clinton would face an impeachment inquiry or might be forced to resign.

Clinton tried to quiet the scandal during a news conference on January 26. "I did not have sexual relations with that woman, Miss Lewinsky. I never told anyone to lie about it," he said. The president's denial did little to calm the uproar, however, and for months afterward there was a daily barrage of leaks from legal sources (including from Starr's office) and of speculation with little apparent basis in fact.

It was in this context that Clinton entered the House chamber on the evening of January 27 to deliver his State of the Union address. Having developed into a routine exercise, the State of the Union ceremony years before had lost most of its political significance. Clinton's 1998 speech held a special interest only because most observers were looking for evidence of how he had been affected by the Lewinsky scandal. But even the most careful observer could find no such evidence in the president's words or behavior.

Clinton made no mention of the alleged affair, directly or indirectly, and he appeared as poised and confident as at any time in his remarkable political career. After a brief eulogy for two House members who had died, Clinton trumpeted the nation's economic state of health and gave a detailed series of policy proposals. He spoke for seventy-two minutes—not at all a lengthy speech for this loquacious president—and never faltered.

Democrats leapt to their feet more than three dozen times to cheer the president's remarks, and even the Republicans in the chamber responded warmly to many of his points. In their remarks to reporters immediately after the speech, most Republican members of Congress refused to criticize or even comment on the president directly; instead, they talked about the president's policy proposals they wished to support or oppose.

Domestic Policy Proposals

As with most Clinton speeches, the 1998 State of the Union address was full of specific proposals on various issues of the day. From the global economy to teenage smoking, Clinton offered concrete ideas for government action—all leading to an overarching goal of "an America which leads the world to new heights of peace and prosperity."

Many of the president's proposals centered around budgetary matters, and so he proudly announced that he was about to send Congress a pro-

posed balanced budget for fiscal year 1999, the first in thirty years. Clinton said it was possible that the budget might end up in surplus even earlier, in fiscal 1998. A booming economy made that happen; fiscal year 1998 ended on September 30 with a $70 billion surplus. (Budget, p. 500)

If there was a centerpiece proposal in Clinton's speech, it was his prescription for using any surpluses once the budget came into balance. Many Republicans had talked about using surpluses to cut taxes or pare back the national debt. Clinton offered his own plan in just four words: "Save Social Security first." Every penny of any surplus should be saved, he said, "until we have taken all the necessary measures to strengthen the Social Security system for the twenty-first century." Clinton said he would hold a White House conference on Social Security in December and would work with congressional leaders in 1999 on legislation to keep the Social Security system solvent when the gigantic generation of postwar "baby boomers" reached retirement in the second and third decades of the twenty-first century.

Clinton kept his promise of a conference on Social Security; held at the White House on December 8 and 9, the meeting reviewed various options for financing the system. Clinton participated in the second day of the session. It was his first detailed discussion of Social Security options with congressional leaders of both parties. (Social security issues, p. 98)

For the most part, Clinton also achieved his goal of protecting the budget surplus during the year; Congress did not touch the fiscal 1998 surplus and spent only about $20 billion worth of anticipated surpluses starting in fiscal 1999. Congressional restraint resulted more from discord than from support for Clinton's surplus-saving plan. Republicans were unable to reach agreement on a tax cut that would have taken the biggest single bite out the budget surplus during fiscal 1999.

Most of the other specifics advocated by Clinton during his State of the Union message fell by the wayside during 1998. Congress took no action on his proposal to raise the minimum wage. Several other important Clinton proposals, such as campaign finance reform, a "consumer bill of rights" for people under managed-care health insurance plans, and tax breaks for child care all made some headway in Congress but ultimately fell short of approval.

Republican Response

Trent Lott of Mississippi, the Senate majority leader, offered the official Republican response to the president's State of the Union address. Speaking from his Senate office, Lott offered a low-key rebuttal to many of Clinton's proposals. Lott also joined the president in making no direct mention of the Lewinsky scandal. Several of Lott's remarks, however, were widely seen as indirect references to the president's troubles, including his closing comment about building "the kind of government you can trust."

Lott emphasized Republican themes that had become traditional in recent years: cutting taxes, reducing government regulations, and offering parents more choice in where their children attend school. On each issue, Lott insisted that Clinton and the Democrats represented "big government" solutions whereas the Republicans wanted to put individual citizens at the forefront.

Following are texts of President Bill Clinton's State of the Union address, delivered to a joint session of Congress on January 27, 1998, and the Republican response by Senate Majority Leader Trent Lott of Mississippi:

STATE OF THE UNION ADDRESS

Mr. Speaker [Newt Gingrich], Mr. Vice President [Al Gore], members of the 105th Congress, distinguished guests, my fellow Americans:

Since the last time we met in this chamber, America has lost two patriots and fine public servants. Though they sat on opposite sides of the aisle, Representatives Walter Capps [D-Calif.] and Sonny Bono [R-Calif.] shared a deep love for this House and an unshakable commitment to improving the lives of all our people. In the past few weeks they've both been eulogized. Tonight, I think we should begin by sending a message to their families and their friends that we celebrate their lives and give thanks for their service to our nation.

For 209 years it has been the President's duty to report to you on the state of the Union. Because of the hard work and high purpose of the American people, these are good times for America. We have more than 14 million new jobs; the lowest unemployment in 24 years; the lowest core inflation in 30 years; incomes are rising; and we have the highest homeownership in history. Crime has dropped for a record five years in a row. And the welfare rolls are at their lowest levels in 27 years. Our leadership in the world is unrivaled. Ladies and gentlemen, the state of our Union is strong.

With barely 700 days left in the 20th century, this is not a time to rest. It is a time to build, to build the America within reach: an America where everybody has a chance to get ahead with hard work; where every citizen can live in a safe community; where families are strong, schools are good and all young people can go to college; an America where scientists find cures for diseases from diabetes to Alzheimer's to AIDS; an America where every child can stretch a hand across a keyboard and reach every book ever written, every painting ever painted, every symphony ever composed; where government provides opportunity and citizens honor the responsibility to give something back to their communities; an America which leads the world to new heights of peace and prosperity.

This is the America we have begun to build; this is the America we can leave to our children—if we join together to finish the work at hand. Let us strengthen our nation for the 21st century.

Rarely have Americans lived through so much change, in so many ways, in so short a time. Quietly, but with gathering force, the ground has shifted beneath our feet as we have moved into an Information Age, a global economy, a truly new world.

For five years now we have met the challenge of these changes as Americans have at every turning point—by renewing the very idea of America: widening the circle of opportunity, deepening the meaning of our freedom, forging a more perfect union.

We shaped a new kind of government for the Information Age. I thank the Vice President for his leadership and the Congress for its support in building a government that is leaner, more flexible, a catalyst for new ideas—and most of all, a government that gives the American people the tools they need to make the most of their own lives.

We have moved past the sterile debate between those who say government is the enemy and those who say government is the answer. My fellow Americans, we have found a third way. We have the smallest government in 35 years, but a more progressive one. We have a smaller government, but a stronger nation. We are moving steadily toward an even stronger America in the 21st century: an economy that offers opportunity, a society rooted in responsibility and a nation that lives as a community.

First, Americans in this chamber and across our nation have pursued a new strategy for prosperity: fiscal discipline to cut interest rates and spur growth; investments in education and skills, in science and technology and transportation, to prepare our people for the new economy; new markets for American products and American workers.

When I took office, the deficit for 1998 was projected to be $357 billion, and heading higher. This year, our deficit is projected to be $10 billion, and heading lower. For three decades, six Presidents have come before you to warn of the damage deficits pose to our nation. Tonight, I come before you to announce that the federal deficit—once so incomprehensibly large that it had 11 zeroes—will be, simply, zero. I will submit to Congress for 1999 the first balanced budget in 30 years. And if we hold fast to fiscal discipline, we may balance the budget this year—four years ahead of schedule.

You can all be proud of that, because turning a sea of red ink into black is no miracle. It is the product of hard work by the American people, and of two visionary actions in Congress—the courageous vote in 1993 that led to a cut in the deficit of 90 percent—and the truly historic bipartisan balanced budget agreement passed by this Congress. Here's the really good news: If we maintain our resolve, we will produce balanced budgets as far as the eye can see.

We must not go back to unwise spending or untargeted tax cuts that risk reopening the deficit. Last year, together we enacted targeted tax cuts so that the typical middle class family will now have the lowest tax rates in 20 years. My plan to balance the budget next year includes both new investments and new tax cuts targeted to the needs of working families: for education, for child care, for the environment.

But whether the issue is tax cuts or spending, I ask all of you to meet this test: Approve only those priorities that can actually be accomplished without adding a dime to the deficit.

Now, if we balance the budget for next year, it is projected that we'll then have a sizable surplus in the years that immediately follow. What should we do with this projected surplus? I have a simple four-word answer: Save Social Security first. Thank you.

Tonight, I propose that we reserve 100 percent of the surplus—that's every penny of any surplus—until we have taken all the necessary measures to strengthen the Social Security system for the 21st century. Let us say to all Americans watching tonight—whether you're 70 or 50, or whether you just started paying into the system—Social Security will be there when you need it. Let us make this commitment: Social Security first. Let's do that together.

I also want to say that all the American people who are watching us tonight should be invited to join in this discussion, in facing these issues squarely, and forming a true consensus on how we should proceed. We'll start by conducting nonpartisan forums in every region of the country—and I hope that lawmakers of both parties will participate. We'll hold a White House Conference on Social Security in December. And one year from now I will convene the leaders of Congress to craft historic, bipartisan legislation to achieve a landmark for our generation—a Social Security system that is strong in the 21st century. Thank you.

In an economy that honors opportunity, all Americans must be able to reap the rewards of prosperity. Because these times are good, we can afford to take one simple, sensible step to help millions of workers struggling to provide for their families: We should raise the minimum wage.

The Information Age is, first and foremost, an education age, in which education must start at birth and continue throughout a lifetime. Last year, from this podium, I said that education has to be our highest priority. I laid out a 10-point plan to move us forward and urged all of us to let politics stop at the schoolhouse door. Since then, this Congress, across party lines, and the American people have responded, in the most important year for education in a generation—expanding public school choice, opening the way to 3,000 new charter schools, working to connect every classroom in the country to the Information Superhighway, committing to expand Head Start to a million children, launching America Reads, sending literally thousands of college students into our elementary schools to make sure all our 8-year-olds can read.

Last year I proposed, and you passed, 220,000 new Pell Grant scholarships for deserving students. Student loans, already less expensive and easier to repay, now you get to deduct the interest. Families all over America now can put their savings into new tax-free education IRAs. And this year, for the first two years of college, families will get a $1,500 tax credit—a HOPE Scholarship that will cover the cost of most community college tuition. And for junior and senior year, graduate school, and job training, there is a lifetime learning credit. You did that and you should be very proud of it.

And because of these actions, I have something to say to every family listening to us tonight: Your children can go on to college. If you know a child from a poor family, tell her not to give up—she can go on to college. If you know a young couple struggling with bills, worried they won't be able to send their children to college, tell them not to give up—their children can go on to college. If you know somebody who's caught in a dead-end job and afraid he can't afford the classes necessary to get better jobs for the rest of his life, tell him not to give up—he can go on to college. Because of the things that have been done, we can make college as universal in the 21st century as high school is today. And, my friends, that will change the face and future of America.

We have opened wide the doors of the world's best system of higher education. Now we must make our public elementary and secondary schools the world's best as well—by raising standards, raising expectations, and raising accountability.

Thanks to the actions of this Congress last year, we will soon have, for the very first time, a voluntary national test based on national standards in 4th grade reading and 8th grade math. Parents have a right to know whether their children are mastering the basics. And every parent already knows the key: good teachers and small classes.

Tonight, I propose the first ever national effort to reduce class size in the early grades. Thank you.

My balanced budget will help to hire 100,000 new teachers who have passed a state competency test. Now, with these teachers—listen—with these teachers, we will actually be able to reduce class size in the 1st, 2nd, and 3rd grades to an average of 18 students a class, all across America.

If I've got the math right, more teachers teaching smaller classes requires more classrooms. So I also propose a school construction tax cut to help communities modernize or build 5,000 schools.

We must also demand greater accountability. When we promote a child from grade to grade who hasn't mastered the work, we don't do that child any favors. It is time to end social promotion in America's schools.

Last year, in Chicago, they made that decision—not to hold our children back, but to lift them up. Chicago stopped social promotion, and started mandatory summer school, to help students who are behind to catch up. I propose—I propose to help other communities follow Chicago's lead. Let's say to them: Stop promoting children who don't learn, and we will give you the tools to make sure they do.

I also ask this Congress to support our efforts to enlist colleges and universities to reach out to disadvantaged children, starting in the 6th grade, so that they can get the guidance and hope they need so they can know that they, too, will be able to go on to college.

As we enter the 21st century, the global economy requires us to seek opportunity not just at home, but in all the markets of the world. We must shape this global economy, not shrink from it. In the last five years, we have led the way in opening new markets, with 240 trade agreements that remove foreign barriers to products bearing the proud stamp "Made in the USA." Today, record high exports account for fully one-third of our economic growth. I want to keep them going, because that's the way to keep America growing and to advance a safer, more stable world.

All of you know whatever your views are that I think this a great opportunity for America. I know there is opposition to more comprehensive trade agreements. I have listened carefully and I believe that the opposition is rooted in two fears: first, that our trading partners will have lower environmental and labor standards which will give them an unfair advantage in our market and do their own people no favors, even if there's more business; and, second, that if we have more trade, more of our workers will lose their jobs and have to start over. I think we should seek to advance worker and environmental standards around the world. I have made it abundantly clear that it should be a part of our trade agenda. But we cannot influence other countries' decisions if we send them a message that we're backing away from trade with them.

This year, I will send legislation to Congress, and ask other nations to join us, to fight the most intolerable labor practice of all—abusive child labor. We should also offer help and hope to those Americans temporarily left behind by the global marketplace or by the march of technology, which may have nothing to do with trade. That's why we have more than doubled funding for training dislocated workers since 1993—and if my new budget is adopted, we will triple funding. That's why we must do more, and more quickly, to help workers who lose their jobs for whatever reason.

You know, we help communities in a special way when their military base closes. We ought to help them in the same way if their factory closes. Again, I ask the Congress to continue its bipartisan work to consolidate the tangle of training programs we have today into one single G.I. Bill for Workers, a simple skills grant so people can, on their own, move quickly to new jobs, to higher incomes and brighter futures.

We all know in every way in life change is not always easy, but we have to decide whether we're going to try to hold it back and hide from it or reap its benefits. And remember the big picture here: While we've been entering into hundreds of new trade agreements, we've been creating millions of new jobs.

So this year we will forge new partnerships with Latin America, Asia, and Europe. And we should pass the new African Trade Act—it has bipartisan support. I will also renew my request for the fast track negotiating authority necessary to open more new markets, create more new jobs, which every President has had for two decades.

You know, whether we like it or not, in ways that are mostly positive, the world's economies are more and more interconnected and interdependent. Today, an economic crisis anywhere can affect economies everywhere. Recent months have brought serious financial problems to Thailand, Indonesia, South Korea, and beyond.

Now, why should Americans be concerned about this? First, these countries are our customers. If they sink into recession, they won't be able to buy the goods we'd like to sell them. Second, they're also our competitors. So if their currencies lose their value and go down, then the price of their goods will drop, flooding our market and others with much cheaper goods, which makes it a lot tougher for our people to compete. And, finally, they are our strategic partners. Their stability bolsters our security.

The American economy remains sound and strong, and I want to keep it that way. But because the turmoil in Asia will have an impact on all the world's economies, including ours, making that negative impact as small as possible is the right thing to do for America—and the right thing to do for a safer world.

Our policy is clear: No nation can recover if it does not reform itself. But when nations are willing to undertake serious economic reform, we should help them do it. So I call on Congress to renew America's commitment to the International Monetary Fund. And I think we should say to all the people we're trying to represent here that preparing for a far-off storm that may reach our shores is far wiser than ignoring the thunder until the clouds are just overhead.

A strong nation rests on the rock of responsibility. A society rooted in responsibility must first promote the value of work, not welfare. We can be proud that after decades of finger-pointing and failure, together we ended the old welfare system. And we're now we replacing welfare checks with pay-checks.

Last year, after a record four-year decline in welfare rolls, I challenged our nation to move 2 million more Americans off welfare by the year 2000. I'm pleased to report we have also met that goal, two full years ahead of schedule.

This is a grand achievement, the sum of many acts of individual courage, persistence and hope. For 13 years, Elaine Kinslow of Indianapolis, Indiana, was on and off welfare. Today, she's a dispatcher with the a van company. She's saved enough money to move her family into a good neighborhood, and she's helping other welfare recipients go to work. Elaine Kinslow and all those like her are the real heroes of the welfare revolution. There are millions like her all across America. And I'm happy she could join the First Lady tonight. Elaine, we're very proud of you. Please stand up.

We still have a lot more to do, all of us, to make welfare reform a success—providing child care, helping families move closer to available jobs, challeng-ing more companies to join our welfare-to-work partnership, increasing child support collections from deadbeat parents who have a duty to support their own children. I also want to thank Congress for restoring some of the bene-fits to immigrants who are here legally and working hard—and I hope you will finish that job this year.

We have to make it possible for all hard-working families to meet their most important responsibilities. Two years ago, we helped guarantee that Americans can keep their health insurance when they change jobs. Last year, we extended health care to up to 5 million children. This year, I challenge Congress to take the next historic steps.

One hundred sixty million of our fellow citizens are in managed care plans. These plans save money and they can improve care. But medical decisions ought to be made by medical doctors, not insurance company accountants. I urge this Congress to reach across the aisle and write into law a Consumer Bill of Rights that says this: You have the right to know all your medical options, not just the cheapest. You have the right to choose the doctor you want for the care you need. You have the right to emergency room care, wherever and whenever you need it. You have the right to keep your medical records confidential. Traditional care or managed care, every American deserves quality care.

Millions of Americans between the ages of 55 and 65 have lost their health insurance. Some are retired; some are laid off; some lose their coverage when their spouses retire. After a lifetime of work, they are left with nowhere to turn. So I ask the Congress: Let these hard-working Americans buy into the Medicare system. It won't add a dime to the deficit—but the peace of mind it will provide will be priceless.

Next, we must help parents protect their children from the gravest health threat that they face: an epidemic of teen smoking, spread by multimillion-dollar marketing campaigns. I challenge Congress: Let's pass bipartisan, comprehensive legislation that improve public health, protect our tobacco farmers, and change the way tobacco companies do business forever. Let's do what it takes to bring teen smoking down. Let's raise the price of cigarettes by up to $1.50 a pack over the next 10 years, with penalties on the tobacco industry if it keeps marketing to our children.

Tomorrow, like every day, 3,000 children will start smoking, and 1,000 will die early as a result. Let this Congress be remembered as the Congress that saved their lives.

In the new economy, most parents work harder than ever. They face a constant struggle to balance their obligations to be good workers—and their even more important obligations to be good parents. The Family and Medical Leave Act was the very first bill I was privileged to sign into law as President in 1993. Since then, about 15 million people have taken advantage of it, and I've met a lot of them all across this country. I ask you to extend that law to cover 10 million more workers, and to give parents time off when they have to go see their children's teachers or take them to the doctor.

Child care is the next frontier we must face to enable people to succeed at home and at work. Last year, I co-hosted the very first White House Conference on Child Care with one of our foremost experts, America's First Lady. From all corners of America, we heard the same message, without regard to region or income or political affiliation: We've got to raise the quality of child care. We've got to make it safer. We've got to make it more affordable.

So here's my plan: Help families to pay for child care for a million more children. Scholarships and background checks for child care workers, and a new emphasis on early learning. Tax credits for businesses that provide child care for their employees. And a larger child care tax credit for working families. Now, if you pass my plan, what this means is that a family of four with an income of $35,000 and high child care costs will no longer pay a single penny of federal income tax.

I think this is such a big issue with me because of my own personal experience. I have often wondered how my mother, when she was a young widow, would have been able to go away to school and get an education and come back and support me if my grandparents hadn't been able to take care of me.

She and I were really very lucky. How many other families have never had that same opportunity? The truth is, we don't know the answer to that question. But we do know what the answer should be: Not a single American family should ever have to choose between the job they need and the child they love.

A society rooted in responsibility must provide safe streets, safe schools, and safe neighborhoods. We pursued a strategy of more police, tougher punishment, smarter prevention, with crime-fighting partnerships with local law enforcement and citizen groups, where the rubber hits the road. I can report to you tonight that it's working. Violent crime is down, robbery is down, assault is down, burglary is down—for five years in a row, all across America. We need to finish the job of putting 100,000 more police on our streets.

Again, I ask Congress to pass a juvenile crime bill that provides more prosecutors and probation officers, to crack down on gangs and guns and drugs, and bar violent juveniles from buying guns for life. And I ask you to dramatically expand our support for after-school programs. I think every American should know that most juvenile crime is committed between the hours of 3:00 in the afternoon and 8:00 at night. We can keep so many of our children out of trouble in the first place if we give them someplace to go other than the streets, and we ought to do it.

Drug use is on the decline. I thank General McCaffrey for his leadership. And I thank this Congress for passing the largest antidrug budget in history. I ask you to join me in a ground-breaking effort to hire 1,000 new border patrol agents and to deploy the most sophisticated available new technologies to help close the door on drugs at our borders.

Police, prosecutors, and prevention programs, as good as they are, they can't work if our court system doesn't work. Today there are large number of vacancies in the federal courts. Here is what the Chief Justice of the United States wrote: Judicial vacancies cannot remain at such high levels indefinitely without eroding the quality of justice. I simply ask the United States Senate to heed this plea, and vote on the highly qualified judicial nominees before you, up or down.

We must exercise responsibility not just at home, but around the world. On the eve of a new century, we have the power and the duty to build a new era of peace and security. But, make no mistake about it, today's possibilities are not tomorrow's guarantees. America must stand against the poisoned appeals of extreme nationalism. We must combat an unholy axis of new threats from terrorists, international criminals and drug traffickers. These 21st century predators feed on technology and the free flow of information and ideas and people. And they will be all the more lethal if weapons of mass destruction fall into their hands.

To meet these challenges, we are helping to write international rules of the road for the 21st century, protecting those who join the family of nations and isolating those who do not. Within days, I will ask the Senate for its advice and consent to make Hungary, Poland, and the Czech Republic the newest members of NATO. For 50 years, NATO contained communism and kept

America and Europe secure. Now these three formerly communist countries have said yes to democracy. I ask the Senate to say yes to them—our new allies.

By taking in new members and working closely with new partners, including Russia and Ukraine, NATO can help to assure that Europe is a stronghold for peace in the 21st century.

Next, I will ask Congress to continue its support for our troops and their mission in Bosnia. This Christmas, Hillary and I traveled to Sarajevo with Senator and Mrs. [Bob] Dole and a bipartisan congressional delegation. We saw children playing in the streets, where two years ago they were hiding from snipers and shells. The shops are filled with food; the cafes were alive with conversation. The progress there is unmistakable—but it is not yet irreversible.

To take firm root, Bosnia's fragile peace still needs the support of American and allied troops when the current NATO mission ends in June. I think Senator Dole actually said it best. He said, "This is like being ahead in the 4th quarter of a football game. Now is not the time to walk off the field and forfeit the victory."

I wish all of you could have seen our troops in Tuzla. They're very proud of what they're doing in Bosnia. And we're all very proud of them. One of those brave soldiers is sitting with the First Lady tonight—Army Sergeant Michael Tolbert. His father was a decorated Vietnam vet. After college in Colorado, he joined the Army. Last year, he led an infantry unit that stopped mob of extremists from taking over a radio station that is a voice of democracy and tolerance in Bosnia. Thank you very much, Sergeant, for what you represent.

In Bosnia and around the world, our men and women in uniform always do their mission well. Our mission must be to keep them well-trained and ready, to improve their quality of life, and to provide the 21st century weapons they need to defeat any enemy.

I ask Congress to join me in pursuing an ambitious agenda to reduce the serious threat of weapons of mass destruction. This year, four decades after it was first proposed by President Eisenhower, a comprehensive nuclear test ban is within reach. By ending nuclear testing we can help to prevent the development of new and more dangerous weapons and make it more difficult for non-nuclear states to build them.

I'm pleased to announce four former Chairmen of the Joint Chiefs of Staff—Generals John Shalikashvili, Colin Powell, and David Jones, and Admiral William Crowe—have endorsed this treaty. And I ask the Senate to approve it this year.

Together, we also must also confront the new hazards of chemical and biological weapons, and the outlaw states, terrorists and organized criminals seeking to acquire them. Saddam Hussein has spent the better part of this decade, and much of his nation's wealth, not on providing for the Iraqi people, but on developing nuclear, chemical, and biological weapons—and the missiles to deliver them. The United Nations weapons inspectors have done a truly remarkable job, finding and destroying more of Iraq's arsenal than was destroyed during the entire Gulf War. Now Saddam Hussein wants to stop them from completing their mission.

I know I speak for everyone in this chamber, Republicans and Democrats, when I say to Saddam Hussein: You cannot defy the will of the world. And when I say to him: You have used weapons of mass destruction before; we are determined to deny you the capacity to use them again.

Last year, the Senate ratified the Chemical Weapons Convention to protect our soldiers and citizens from poison gas. Now we must act to prevent the use of disease as a weapon of war and terror, The Biological Weapons Convention has been in effect for 23 years now. The rules are good, but the enforcement is weak. We must strengthen it with a new international inspection system to detect and deter cheating.

In the months ahead, I will pursue our security strategy with old allies in Asia and Europe, and new partners from Africa to India and Pakistan, from South America to China. And from Belfast, to Korea to the Middle East, America will continue to stand with those who stand for peace.

Finally, it's long past time to make good on our debt to the United Nations. More and more, we are working with other nations to achieve common goals. If we want America to lead, we've got to set a good example. As we see so clearly in Bosnia, allies who share our goals can also share our burdens. In this new era, our freedom and independence are actually enriched, not weakened, by our increasing interdependence with other nations. But we have to do our part.

Our founders set America on a permanent course toward "a more perfect union." To all of you I say it is a journey we can only make together—living as one community. First, we have to continue to reform our government—the instrument of our national community. Everyone knows elections have become too expensive, fueling a fundraising arms race. This year, by March 6th, at long last the Senate will actually vote on bipartisan campaign finance reform proposed by Senators [John] McCain [R-Ariz.] and [Russell] Feingold [D-Wis.]. Let's be clear: A vote against McCain and Feingold is a vote for soft money and for the status quo. I ask you to strengthen our democracy and pass campaign finance reform this year.

At least equally important, we have to address the real reason for the explosion in campaign costs—the high cost of media advertising. To the folks watching at home, those were the groans of pain in the audience. (Laughter.) I will formally request that the Federal Communications Commission act to provide free or reduced-cost television time for candidates who observe spending limits voluntarily. The airwaves are a public trust, and broadcasters also have to help us in this effort to strengthen our democracy.

Under the leadership of Vice President Gore, we've reduced the federal payroll by 300,000 workers, cut 16,000 pages of regulation, eliminated hundreds of programs and improved the operations of virtually every government agency. But we can do more. Like every taxpayer, I'm outraged by the reports of abuses by the IRS. We need some changes there—new citizen advocacy panels, a stronger taxpayer advocate, phone lines open 24 hours a day, relief for innocent taxpayers. Last year, by an overwhelming bipartisan margin, the House of Representatives passed sweeping IRS reforms. This bill must not now languish in the Senate. Tonight I ask the Senate: follow the House, pass the bipartisan package as your first order of business.

I hope to goodness before I finish I can think of something to say, "follow the Senate" on, so I'll be out of trouble. (Laughter.)

A nation that lives as a community must value all its communities. For the past five years, we have worked to bring the spark of private enterprise to inner city and poor rural areas—with community development banks, more commercial loans in the poor neighborhoods, cleanup of polluted sites for development. Under the continued leadership of the Vice President, we propose to triple the number of empowerment zones, to give business incentives to invest in those areas.

We should also should give poor families more help to move into homes of their own, and we should use tax cuts to spur the construction of more low-income housing.

Last year, this Congress took strong action to help the District of Columbia. Let us renew our resolve to make our capital city a great city for all who live and visit here. Our cities are the vibrant hubs of great metropolitan areas. They are still the gateways for new immigrants, from every continent, who come here to work for their own American Dreams. Let's keep our cities going strong into the 21st century. They're a very important part of our future.

Our communities are only as healthy as the air our children breathe, the water they drink, the Earth they will inherit. Last year, we put in place the toughest-ever controls on smog and soot. We moved to protect Yellowstone, the Everglades, Lake Tahoe. We expanded every community's right to know about the toxins that threaten their children. Just yesterday, our food safety plan took effect, using new science to protect consumers from dangers like E. coli and salmonella.

Tonight, I ask you to join me in launching a new Clean Water Initiative, a far-reaching effort to clean our rivers, our lakes, our coastal waters for our children. Our overriding environmental challenge tonight is the worldwide problem of climate change, global warming, the gathering crisis that requires worldwide action. The vast majority of scientists have concluded unequivocally that if we don't reduce the emission of greenhouse gases, at some point in the next century we'll disrupt our climate and put our children and grandchildren at risk. This past December, America led the world to reach a historic agreement committing our nation to reduce greenhouse gas emissions through market forces, new technologies, energy efficiency. We have it in our power to act right here, right now. I propose $6 billion in tax cuts and research and development to encourage innovation, renewable energy, fuel-efficient cars, energy-efficient homes.

Every time we have acted to heal our environment, pessimists have told us it would hurt the economy. Well, today our economy is the strongest in a generation, and our environment is the cleanest in a generation. We have always found a way to clean the environment and grow the economy at the same time. And when it comes to global warming, we'll do it again.

Finally, community means living by the defining American value—the ideal heard round the world that we are all created equal. Throughout our history, we haven't always honored that ideal and we've never fully lived up to it. Often it's easier to believe that our differences matter more than what we have in common. It may be easier, but it's wrong.

What we have to do in our day and generation to make sure that America becomes truly one nation—what do we have to do? We're becoming more and more and more diverse. Do you believe we can become one nation? The answer cannot be to dwell on our differences, but to build on our shared values. We all cherish family and faith, freedom and responsibility. We all want our children to grow up in a world where their talents are matched by their opportunities.

I've launched this national initiative on race to help us recognize our common interests and to bridge the opportunity gaps that are keeping us from becoming one America. Let us begin by recognizing what we still must overcome. Discrimination against any American is un-American. We must vigorously enforce the laws that make it illegal. I ask your help to end the backlog at the Equal Employment Opportunity Commission. Sixty thousand of our fellow citizens are waiting in line for justice, and we should act now to end their wait.

We also should recognize that the greatest progress we can make toward building one America lies in the progress we make for all Americans, without regard to race. When we open the doors of college to all Americans, when we rid all our streets of crime, when there are jobs available to people from all our neighborhoods, when we make sure all parents have the child care they need, we're helping to build one nation.

We, in this chamber and in this government, must do all we can to address the continuing American challenge to build one America. But we'll only move forward if all our fellow citizens—including every one of you at home watching tonight—is also committed to this cause.

We must work together, learn together, live together, serve together. On the forge of common enterprise Americans of all backgrounds can hammer out a common identity. We see it today in the United States military, in the Peace Corps, in AmeriCorps. Wherever people of all races and backgrounds come together in a shared endeavor and get a fair chance, we do just fine. With shared values and meaningful opportunities and honest communication and citizen service, we can unite a diverse people in freedom and mutual respect. We are many; we must be one.

In that spirit, let us lift our eyes to the new millennium. How will we mark that passage? It just happens once every thousand years. This year, Hillary and I launched the White House Millennium Program to promote America's creativity and innovation, and to preserve our heritage and culture into the 21st century. Our culture lives in every community, and every community has places of historic value that tell our stories as Americans. We should protect them. I am proposing a public-private partnership to advance our arts and humanities, and to celebrate the millennium by saving American's treasures, great and small.

And while we honor the past, let us imagine the future. Think about this—the entire store of human knowledge now doubles every five years. In the 1980s, scientists identified the gene causing cystic fibrosis—it took nine years. Last year, scientists located the gene that causes Parkinson's Disease—in only nine days. Within a decade, "gene chips" will offer a road map for prevention of illnesses throughout a lifetime. Soon we'll be able to carry all the phone calls on Mother's Day on a single strand of fiber the width of a human hair. A child born in 1998 may well live to see the 22nd century.

Tonight, as part of our gift to the millennium, I propose a 21st Century Research Fund for path-breaking scientific inquiry—the largest funding increase in history for the National Institutes of Health, the National Science Foundation, the National Cancer Institute.

We have already discovered genes for breast cancer and diabetes. I ask you to support this initiative so ours will be the generation that finally wins the war against cancer, and begins a revolution in our fight against all deadly diseases.

As important as all this scientific progress is, we must continue to see that science serves humanity, not the other way around. We must prevent the misuse of genetic tests to discriminate against any American. And we must ratify the ethical consensus of the scientific and religious communities, and ban the cloning of human beings.

We should enable all the world's people to explore the far reaches of cyberspace. Think of this—the first time I made a State of the Union speech to you, only a handful of physicists used the World Wide Web. Literally, just a handful of people. Now, in schools, in libraries, homes and businesses, millions and millions of Americans surf the Net every day. We must give parents the tools they need to help protect their children from inappropriate material on the Internet. But we also must make sure that we protect the exploding global commercial potential of the Internet. We can do the kinds of things that we need to do and still protect our kids.

For one thing, I ask Congress to step up support for building the next generation Internet. It's getting kind of clogged, you know. And the next generation Internet will operate at speeds up to a thousand times faster than today.

Even as we explore this inner space in a new millennium we're going to open new frontiers in outer space. Throughout all history, humankind has had only one place to call home—our planet Earth. Beginning this year, 1998, men and women from 16 countries will build a foothold in the heavens—the international space station. With its vast expanses, scientists and engineers will actually set sail on an unchartered sea of limitless mystery and unlimited potential.

And this October, a true American hero, a veteran pilot of 149 combat missions and one, five-hour space flight that changed the world, will return to the heavens. Godspeed, John Glenn. John, you will carry with you America's hopes. And on your uniform, once again, you will carry America's flag, marking the unbroken connection between the deeds of America's past and the daring of America's future.

Nearly 200 years ago, a tattered flag, its broad stripes and bright stars still gleaming through the smoke of a fierce battle, moved Francis Scott Key to scribble a few words on the back of an envelope—the words that became our national anthem. Today, that Start Spangled Banner, along with the Declaration of Independence, the Constitution and the Bill of Rights, are on display just a short walk from here. They are America's treasures and we must also save them for the ages.

I ask all Americans to support our project to restore all our treasures so that the generations of the 21st century can see for themselves the images and the words that are the old and continuing glory of America; an America that has continued to rise through every age, against every challenge, of people of great works and greater possibilities, who have always, always found the wisdom and strength to come together as one nation—to widen the circle of opportunity, to deepen the meaning of our freedom, to form that "more perfect union." Let that be our gift to the 21st century.

God bless you, and God bless the United States.

LOTT'S REPUBLICAN RESPONSE

Tonight I'd like to share with you our plans, here in the Congress, for a safer, stronger, and more prosperous America.

Those plans are shaped by our commitment to family, to faith, and to freedom. And they highlight some real differences, between the Republican Party and the President, concerning what government should do—and how much of your money government should take.

Big Government or families? More taxes or more freedom?

We believe the choice is clear: The first priority of your representatives in Washington must be to fight for the interests of the American family.

That's why one of the first things we'll tackle is REAL reform of the IRS. I'll have more to say about that later, but the bottom line is this: We are going to stop the abuses the IRS is inflicting on American taxpayers.

You've got our word on it!

Also, we'll be building on the progress of the last few years, when our Republican Congress, working with the nation's governors, took some historic first steps.

We took the first step in transforming welfare into workfare.

We started reducing taxes, especially for families with children. And with considerable difficulty, we finally worked out a long-term agreement with the President for a balanced budget.

We protected Medicare. And in that same way, we're going to protect Medicare, this year, against any changes that would imperil its financial stability.

We strengthened education opportunities for disabled youngsters, launched a long-overdue reform of the nation's troubled foster care system, made adoption easier, and encouraged alternatives to abortion.

We proved that people of good will and strong faith can work together to deal with the problems that face our nation and our neighborhoods.

But we have only just BEGUN the difficult job of stopping Big Government, making it more responsive, and—perhaps hardest of all—rebuilding the trust you used to have in your elected officials.

That's especially important when it comes to education, to taxes, and to the twin plagues of drugs and crime. Those are the three areas where the American people are most dissatisfied ... and where our freedom is most threatened.

Parents—and good teachers, as well—are dissatisfied with schools where kids don't learn, and in many cases, where they aren't even safe. When one-quarter—one out of four—of our high school students can barely read, isn't it obvious the current system isn't working?

I know we are all fed up with the criminal justice system that has tragically failed to halt the poisonous epidemic of drugs that is undermining family life in our country. Violent crime is turning the Land of the Free into the Land of the Fearful.

Today's workers and today's savers are angry and disillusioned with a tax code that benefits only tax lawyers and Big Government.

Let's take a look at the typical family budget. The typical family pays more than 38 percent of its income in taxes. That's nearly forty cents of every dollar. That's not just bad policy. It's immoral. Our tax system should not penalize marriage, hard work, or savings, not to mention your efforts to keep up with the cost of living. We believe these high taxes mean less freedom overall.

And yet, President Clinton now wants the government to spend billions of dollars more. But I don't have to tell you, if the government spends more, you'll wind up getting taxed more. You know that. He knows that.

Instead, Republicans want you—the people who work hard for the money—to keep more of what you earn. The President seems to think that Big Government can solve all your children's problems if you will just give government more of your money—and more control over your lives. Nonsense!

We think the best things for safe, healthy children are healthy, stable families—not more government programs that require parents to work longer, take home less, and spend less time with the kids. That's why we fought for a $500 per child tax credit last year.

Once again, the choice is clear:

Big Government? Or families?

More taxes? Or more freedom?

The American people elected us in the Congress to listen to you and then to lead. So while we listen respectfully to the President's ideas, we can not wait on them.

One example is the drug crisis. With all due respect, for the past five years, we've had all kinds of wrong signals.

It took the President four years to admit the need to reduce the tax burden on the American people, as we finally did in the Balanced Budget Act last year. That was a welcome reversal of the pile-on-the-taxes approach of his first four years in office. But you know that Americans are still over-taxed, over-regulated, and over-governed.

This chart shows how the income of the federal government, over the last 30 years, has gone up almost 1,000 percent. But during the same period, family incomes rose only half as much. Government has gotten fat, while families are working overtime just to stay where they were.

We believe hard-working Americans deserve a break. So our focus in 1998 will be to increase family income by CUTTING taxes and making government more accountable for the way it spends your money.

But tax relief is only the first step.

As I said earlier . . . the only way to limit government and expand individual freedom is to eliminate the IRS as we know it today. It is morally wrong for a free people to live in fear of any government agency. It is morally wrong for citizens in a democracy to be presumed guilty until proven innocent.

But IRS reform alone isn't enough. The real problem lies with the tax code itself. It is too long. It is too complicated. It is simply unfair. It punishes achievement. It discourages work, savings, and innovation.

As Republicans, we pledge to replace the tax code with a new system that is fair, consistent, easy to understand, and less frightening to the American taxpayer—a tax code that will end the fear and encourage savings and investment.

Finally, because the Republican balanced budget plan is now working, we should commit, here and now, not to spend any budget surplus on unnecessary government programs. If there is a surplus, we should use part of it to pay down the national debt, and return the rest to you, the taxpayer. After all, it is your money.

Like those tax proposals, the Republican education plan proposes the same fundamental change from what we have now. As a father, and a prospective grandfather, I realize that nothing is more important than the education of our young people. Washington today has more than 750 education programs, in 39 different bureaucracies. That just doesn't make sense.

And it doesn't make sense for Washington to tax the people in your community and, then, give the money back with strings attached. We want to cut those strings and to remove the out-of-date rules and restrictions that hold back our schools from the future. For example, if your community needs to build new schools or rehabilitate old ones, YOU should be able to do that. If you want to offer merit pay for great teachers, YOU should be able to do that too.

We've heard a lot from the President about testing. But he thinks Washington should administer the tests. Wrong again. We think that you—the parents, the teachers and local officials— should do the job.

Republicans in Congress strongly support that kind of state testing, just as we support an even more important kind: Periodic testing for teachers. You won't hear much about that from the President. On this subject, the President disagrees with us. And, we disagree with him. But good teachers—like my Mother, who taught public elementary school for 19 years—don't object to testing. They want it. They say, teacher testing will be a key step in implementing the kind of merit pay program that attracts star teachers. They also say, even the best teachers can't get good results when their school is a dangerous, violent place.

We hope the President, this year, will finally see the wisdom in our proposal to give freedom of choice to low-income families whose children are stuck in dead-end, drug-ridden schools. Because we care so deeply about those families, we want them to have the same option exercised by both President Clinton and Vice President Gore, who chose the schools their children attended.

Parental choice and involvement are absolutely essential, but choice in education does not mean abandoning our public schools. It simply means moving decision-making away from Washington, and back to you at your family's kitchen table. That's the first and most important step to launching an era of education renewal that will equip our schools and our students to lead America and the world into the new century.

But don't forget, today's young people confront a danger even worse than poor education. Teen drug abuse has become epidemic, and there are no safe havens from this insidious modern plague. Overall, teenage drug use has nearly doubled since 1992 and, perhaps most frightening of all, nearly half of all 17-year-olds say they could buy marijuana in just an hour's time.

Like the president, I want to stop youth smoking, but the narcotics problem is a far greater threat to teenagers.

First, to solve the drug crisis, we have to start with the family, the school, and with our churches and synagogues. Studies show that teens in families that eat together, play together, and pray together are the ones least likely to try drugs. When the battle against drug abuse is first waged at home, the war is half won.

Second, schools must be drug-free. We must demand absolute accountability and zero tolerance for any drug abuse on school grounds.

Third, there is the critical role of the federal government. We've simply got to be more aggressive in guarding our national borders. Along with that, we must be more vigilant in arresting and prosecuting anyone—yes, anyone—who sells this poison.

And fourth, it's time to get tough on society's predators. We must end parole for violent criminals, crack down on juvenile criminals, increase prison capacity, make the death penalty a real threat, and impose mandatory penalties for crimes committed with a gun.

If we are honestly committed to protecting the innocent, we must do more to punish the guilty. By combining national leadership with community activism, we can—and we will—save America, one child and one neighborhood at a time. We don't pretend to have all the answers here in Washington, but I guarantee you we will ask the right questions. For example, there's the issue of child-care. We say, give families more flexibility in the way they work and care for their children. But how do we do it?

First and foremost, cut the tax burdens on the American family. Don't force both parents to work, and work longer hours, when they could have more time at home with their kids.

Give stay-at-home parents the same tax breaks and benefits available to parents who use day care. After all, all moms work—whether at home or in an outside job.

Let employees negotiate flex-time and comp-time arrangements. Help small businesses provide on-site day care. And make it easier—and more profitable—for older Americans to provide child care for growing families. We're taking this common-sense approach because, as parents and grandparents ourselves, we've learned it takes parents, and parental choice, to raise a child in today's world.

Of course, there are dangers in today's world that demand strong national leadership. Just last week, Pope John Paul's visit to Cuba reminded us that, despite the collapse of communism, tonight the future remains very uncertain over much of the globe.

Let me make one thing clear to Saddam Hussein—or anyone else who needs to be told: Despite any current controversy, this Congress will vigorously support the President in full defense of America's interests throughout the world.

By the same token, we will ask the President to work with us in considering ways to stop the threats of terrorism, international narcotics, and the spread of weapons of mass destruction. As hard as it is to believe, right now, our country has no national defense against missiles carrying nuclear, chemical, or biological warheads. Those who hate America most—in Iraq, Iran, and elsewhere—they know that. President Clinton, I urge you to reconsider your opposition to defending America from missile attack. Join us in taking the steps that will actually deploy a missile defense system for the United States.

There are at least a dozen other important subjects the Congress will deal with in the months ahead. For example, ending the dreadful practice of partial-birth abortions. I urge our Democratic colleagues in the Senate to help us override the President's veto of that legislation.

In addition, we're committed to more positive reforms in health care, protection of worker's rights and paychecks, reform of bankruptcy laws, and legislation to combat teen smoking. All the while, we're going to concentrate on what we call oversight. Which means finding out why you aren't getting your money's worth from government. And why so much of your hard-earned money goes for programs filled with fraud and abuse. Last year, for example, the Administration admitted it paid out $23 billion dollars in ineligible Medicare claims—that's in one year alone—and spent another $5 billion dollars in improper payments in just one welfare program. That's just intolerable!

We intend to make government accountable. From the classrooms to the courts. From the clerks to the President's Cabinet. From the post office to the Presidency.

This isn't a matter of Republicans versus Democrats. It's a question of whether we will learn from past mistakes, in order to restore the great institutions and the cherished values—family, faith, and freedom—that for so long have held us together as a nation.

The President is right to point out our heroes tonight . . . but there are some others who should not be forgotten. Twenty-five years ago next month a small band of Americans returned home after long captivity in Southeast Asia. Some broken in body, but never broken in spirit. Those returning Prisoners of War reminded us, through our cheers and our tears, just how PRECIOUS we hold our freedom.

Now the world has changed greatly—and greatly for the better—in those twenty-five years. But we must remember WHY it changed—WHY we can now look to the century ahead with high hopes—and just WHY we are the envy of the world.

The reason is that Americans, we the people, have been willing to sacrifice everything to protect our families, to practice our faith, and to defend our freedom.

What those heroes fought to preserve, we must now work to recover and strengthen: By renewing American education, restoring the security of the American family, and rebuilding the kind of government that works with you . . . and for you. The kind of government you can trust.

Thank you for listening. Good night and God bless you all.

February

FEDERAL COURT ON GENETIC TESTING IN THE WORKPLACE
February 3, 1998

Advances in genetics in 1998 raised hopes that scientists were on the verge of major breakthroughs in discovering new treatments for repairing human organs and treating genetic diseases. In early November two teams working independently announced that they had isolated and cultivated human embryonic stem cells—the cells that eventually differentiate to form various human tissues, such as blood, bone marrow, and heart muscle. Among other things, scientists hoped that they would be able to use these cells to repair or replace damaged or ailing organs and tissues in humans. In another breakthrough, a laboratory announced that it had developed a technique that would aid parents in selecting the sex of their baby.

While these discoveries held much promise, they also embodied difficult ethical, moral, and legal questions. Under what circumstances should parents be able to choose the sex of their child? Is the use of fetal tissue to extract human stem cells tantamount to abortion? If scientists have the potential to grow all kinds of human tissue, what is to prevent them from eventually cloning human beings? Because it would be years before these discoveries were advanced enough to move out of the laboratory and into the marketplace, ethicists, scientists, academics, government officials, and the general public had time to ponder these and similar questions.

A foreshadowing of the likely debate came in February 1998 when a federal appeals court ruled that a laboratory had violated the constitutional right to privacy of its workers when it tested them for medical and genetic conditions without their consent or knowledge. It was the first time that a federal appeals court had addressed the issue of genetic privacy or outlined limits on the permissible use of genetic testing. Two weeks earlier, the Clinton administration had called on Congress to pass legislation that would bar discrimination in the workplace based on a worker's genetic makeup.

Genetic Privacy

The three-judge panel of the Ninth Circuit Court of Appeals, in California, was unanimous in its February 3 ruling that genetic testing was per-

missible only with the consent of the person being tested or if the testing were done as part of a medical physical for employment and the results were likely to be relevant to the person's ability to perform the job.

The case was brought by seven employees at the Department of Energy's Lawrence Berkeley National Laboratory in California. Years after they were hired, the employees learned that blood and urine samples taken during pre-employment physicals had been tested for syphilis and, in the case of the women, for pregnancy; in addition, the samples from black employees had been genetically tested for sickle cell trait.

The Energy Department began testing prospective employees in the 1960s, and the laboratory's defense attorneys said signs were posted notifying prospective employees of the specific tests they would be given. The seven plaintiffs said they never saw the signs and were stunned when they accidentally learned that the tests had been done. The plaintiffs did not claim that the tests had been used to discriminate against them or that the test results had been disclosed to third parties; they claimed that the tests violated their civil rights as well their right to privacy. Defense attorneys said the tests, which were discontinued in 1995, were intended to uncover any unknown health problems so that employees could be treated. They also argued that even if prospective employees did not see the signs, the tests were justifiable as part of a general physical examination. "When one submits to a medical exam, one expects some invasion of privacy," one of the attorneys argued. A federal district court agreed in 1996, ruling that the testing was a de minimus offense and "a reasonable part of an employment physical."

In overturning the lower court, the appeals court wrote that "few subject areas" were "more personal and more likely to implicate privacy interests than that of one's health or genetic makeup." Although the appeals court ruling applied only to one of twelve circuits in the country, it was widely hailed by those who had long argued not only that genetic testing was a potential tool for discrimination, but also that it was a particularly pernicious invasion of privacy. Supporters of the appeals court decision believed that such tests could reveal intimate physical and behavioral details about a person that might otherwise not be visible and that such information was easily misinterpreted. "Giving your blood for cholesterol testing is one thing but for genetic testing is really something else," Lori Andrews, a professor of law and bioethics at the Chicago-Kent College of Law told the Washington Post. *She added that she was "shocked" by the district court's original decision, which, she said, implied that "an employer can roam around in your genes with impunity."*

The appeals court ruling came just two weeks after Vice President Al Gore urged Congress to pass legislation barring discrimination against workers on the basis of their genetic makeup. "We want legislation that will prevent employers from requesting or requiring genetic information for hiring or for setting salaries, that will stop employers from using this genetic information to discriminate or segregate the workplace, and that will ensure that genetic information is not disclosed without the explicit permission of the individual," Gore said January 20. He also released an administration report detailing specific instances of discrimination against employees or potential employees.

That report, entitled "Genetic Testing and the Workplace," acknowledged that genetic screening and monitoring were appropriate tools to help employers ensure that their workers were not being exposed to occupational hazards that could cause illness. But, the report added, some employers should not be allowed to use genetic testing to avoid hiring workers that the employers thought might take costly sick leave; leave the company early, thus creating costs for hiring and training a replacement; file for worker's compensation; or use health care benefits "excessively." Furthermore, the report said, "the economic incentive to discriminate based on genetic information is likely to increase as genetic research advances and the costs of genetic testing decrease." The report was prepared by the Departments of Labor, Health and Human Services, and Justice, and the Equal Employment Opportunity Commission.

Selecting a Baby's Sex

Doctors at the Genetics and IVF Institute, a private, for-profit medical center in Fairfax, Virginia, announced in September that they had developed a technique for increasing the odds that a couple would have a baby of the sex they preferred. A more sophisticated version of a process used for breeding animals, the technique involved sorting sperm into those that carried the X chromosome, which produced females, and those that carried the Y chromosome, which produced males. Doctors then used artificial insemination to fertilize an egg with a sperm sample that was composed predominantly of cells with X or Y chromosomes, depending on the parents' choice. Because the samples also included chromosomes of the unwanted sex, the technique did not guarantee the sex of the baby. However, according to the researchers, it did improve the odds of having a baby of the sex the parents preferred.

In the September 9 issue of the journal Human Reproduction, *a team of doctors reported their findings concerning parents who wanted girls. Of fourteen pregnancies that had progressed enough for doctors to determine the sex of the fetus, thirteen were girls. Ten of the eleven babies that had been born were girls. The doctors said they expected similar results for boys, where sperm sorting was expected to work about 65 percent of the time, compared with 85 percent for girls.*

A spokesperson for the institute said that the medical center would offer the technique to couples who were at risk of passing on a genetic disease that afflicted virtually only one sex or to couples who already had several children of one sex and wanted one of the other. But, one fertility expert told the New York Times, *"most people feel this is tampering with nature." Other fertility experts and medical ethicists expressed concern that the technique might reinforce cultural or social biases in favor of one sex, leading at best to skewed family patterns and at worst to increased numbers of abortions.*

In cultures such as China, where boys were more highly valued than girls, parents had aborted fetuses shown to be girls by ultrasound testing.

Human Embryonic Stem Cells Isolated

In early November two teams of researchers announced within days of each other that they had isolated "stem cells" from human embryo tissue. These cells quickly differentiate in the growing human embryo into all the various tissues that make up the human body—blood, bone, muscle, brain, and so forth. Scientists hoped eventually to use these cells to grow replacement tissue that could be used to treat a variety of diseases, including certain cancers, heart disease, diabetes, Parkinson's disease, and Alzheimer's disease.

The research was expected to be highly controversial because of its use of fertilized cells that theoretically had the potential to become a human being. The team of researchers led by James A. Thomson at the University of Wisconsin used leftover embryos that otherwise would have been discarded following infertility treatments; the team led by John Gearhart at Johns Hopkins University in Baltimore used gonads from aborted fetuses. Abortion groups and several religious groups, including the Roman Catholic Church and the Southern Baptists, objected to embryonic research, making no distinction between it and abortion. "A human being has an identity at fertilization," said Judie Brown of the American Life League. "It doesn't matter if it's done in the womb or a petri dish, it's still killing." Others who supported a woman's right to abortion also objected to embryonic research. "There is a difference ethically between a single woman's difficult, individual choice and a corporation's doing mass experimentation," said a genetic specialist for the United Methodist Church.

Congress in 1995 prohibited federal funding of embryonic research, and both laboratories were extremely careful to use only private funds to conduct their research. The chief sponsor of that legislation in the House, Rep. Jay Dickey, R-Ark., said he saw no reason to lift the funding ban. But scientists both in and out of government disagreed, arguing that embryonic research should not be left solely in the hands of private companies that were not subject to the ethical and accountability rules that would pertain under federal funding. Both teams of researchers had licensed commercial rights to Geron Corp., a biotechnology firm in Menlo Park, California. One of those who regretted the funding ban was Harold Varmus, director of the National Institutes of Health. The research "has potential health benefits which I think are extremely promising and I am sorry that the law prevented us from supporting it," he said. Use of human embryonic stem cells could also face legal challenges in the nine states that prohibited research on human fetal tissue.

Following are excerpts from the opinion in the case of Marya S. Norman-Bloodsaw et al. v. Lawrence Berkeley Laboratory et al., *in which a three-judge panel of the United States Court of Appeals for the Ninth Circuit unanimously ruled February 3, 1998, that an employer who tested potential employees for genetic diseases without their knowledge violated those employees' guarantee of privacy under the Constitution:*

Opinion

REINHARDT, Circuit Judge:

This appeal involves the question whether a clerical or administrative worker who undergoes a general employee health examination may, without his knowledge, be tested for highly private and sensitive medical and genetic information such as syphilis, sickle cell trait, and pregnancy.

Lawrence Berkeley Laboratory is a research institution jointly operated by state and federal agencies. Plaintiffs-appellants, present and former employees of Lawrence, allege that in the course of their mandatory employment entrance examinations and on subsequent occasions, Lawrence, without their knowledge or consent, tested their blood and urine for intimate medical conditions—namely, syphilis, sickle cell trait, and pregnancy. Their complaint asserts that this testing violated Title VII of the Civil Rights Act of 1964, the Americans with Disabilities Act (ADA), and their right to privacy as guaranteed by both the United States and State of California Constitutions. The district court granted the defendants-appellees' motions for dismissal, judgment on the pleadings, and summary judgment on all of plaintiffs-appellants' claims. We affirm as to the ADA claims, but reverse as to the Title VII and state and federal privacy claims.

Background

Plaintiffs Marya S. Norman-Bloodsaw, Eulalio R. Fuentes, Vertis B. Ellis, Mark E. Covington, John D. Randolph, Adrienne L. Garcia, and Brendolyn B. Smith are current and former administrative and clerical employees of defendant Lawrence Berkeley Laboratory ("Lawrence"), a research facility operated by the appellee Regents of the University of California pursuant to a contract with the United States Department of Energy (the Department). Defendant Charles V. Shank is the director of Lawrence, and defendants Henry H. Stauffer, Lisa Snow, T. F. Budinger, and William G. Donald, Jr., are all current or former physicians in its medical department. The named defendants are sued in both their official and individual capacities.

The Department requires federal contractors such as Lawrence to establish an occupational medical program. Since 1981, it has required its contractors to perform "preplacement examinations" of employees as part of this program, and until 1995, it also required its contractors to offer their employees the option of subsequent "periodic health examinations." The mandatory preplacement examination occurs after the offer of employment but prior to the assumption of job duties. The Department actively oversees Lawrence's occupational health program, and, prior to 1992, specifically required syphilis testing as part of the preplacement examination.

With the exception of Ellis, who was hired in 1968 and underwent an examination after beginning employment, each of the plaintiffs received written offers of employment expressly conditioned upon a "medical examination," "medical approval," or "health evaluation." All accepted these offers and underwent preplacement examinations, and Randolph and Smith underwent subsequent examinations as well. In the course of these examinations, plaintiffs completed medical history questionnaires and provided blood and urine samples. The questionnaires asked, inter alia, whether the patient had ever had any of sixty-one medical conditions, including "[s]ickle cell anemia," "[v]enereal disease," and, in the case of women, "[m]enstrual disorders."

The blood and urine samples given by all employees during their preplacement examinations were tested for syphilis; in addition, certain samples were tested for sickle cell trait; and certain samples were tested for pregnancy. Lawrence discontinued syphilis testing in April 1993, pregnancy testing in December 1994, and sickle cell trait testing in June 1995. Defendants assert that they discontinued syphilis testing because of its limited usefulness in screening healthy populations, and that they discontinued sickle cell trait testing because, by that time, most African-American adults had already been tested at birth. Lawrence continues to perform pregnancy testing, but only on an optional basis. Defendants further contend that "for many years" signs posted in the health examination rooms and "more recently" in the reception area stated that the tests at issue would be administered.

Following receipt of a right-to-sue letter from the EEOC [Equal Employment Opportunity Commission], plaintiffs filed suit in September 1995 on behalf of all past and present Lawrence employees who have ever been subjected to the medical tests at issue. Plaintiffs allege that the testing of their blood and urine samples for syphilis, sickle cell trait, and pregnancy occurred without their knowledge or consent, and without any subsequent notification that the tests had been conducted. They also allege that only black employees were tested for sickle cell trait and assert the obvious fact that only female employees were tested for pregnancy. Finally, they allege that Lawrence failed to provide safe guards to prevent the dissemination of the test results. They contend that they did not discover that the disputed tests had been conducted until approximately January 1995, and specifically deny that they observed any signs indicating that such tests would be performed. Plaintiffs do not allege that the defendants took any subsequent employment-related action on the basis of their test results, or that their test results have been disclosed to third parties.

On the basis of these factual allegations, plaintiffs contend that the defendants violated the ADA by requiring, encouraging, or assisting in medical testing that was neither job-related nor consistent with business necessity. Second, they contend that the defendants violated the federal constitutional right to privacy by conducting the testing at issue, collecting and maintaining the results of the testing, and failing to provide adequate safeguards against disclosure of the results. Third, they contend that the testing violated their right to privacy under Article I, S 1 of the California Constitution. Finally, plaintiffs contend that Lawrence and the Regents violated Title VII by singling out black employees for sickle cell trait testing and by performing pregnancy testing on female employees generally. . . .

Discussion

I. Statute of Limitations

[1] The district court dismissed all of the claims on statute of limitations grounds because it found that the limitations period began to run at the time the tests were taken, in which case each cause of action would be time-barred. Federal law determines when the limitations period begins to run, and the general federal rule is that "a limitations period begins to run when the plaintiff knows or has reason to know of the injury which is the basis of the action." . . .

[2] We find that whether plaintiffs knew or had reason to know of the specific testing turns on material issues of fact that can only be resolved at trial. Plaintiffs' declarations clearly state that at the time of the examination they did not know that the testing in question would be performed, and they neither saw signs nor received any other indications to that effect. The district court had three possible reasons for concluding that plaintiffs knew or should have expected the tests at issue: (1) they submitted to an occupational preplacement examination; (2) they answered written questions as to whether they had had "venereal disease," "menstrual problems," or "sickle cell anemia"; and (3) they voluntarily gave blood and urine samples. Given the present state of the record, these facts are hardly sufficient to establish that plaintiffs either knew or should have known that the particular testing would take place.

The question of what tests plaintiffs should have expected or foreseen depends in large part upon what preplacement medical examinations usually entail, and what, if anything, plaintiffs were told to expect. The record strongly suggests that plaintiffs' submission to the exam did not serve to afford them notice of the particular testing involved. The letters that plaintiffs received informed them merely that a "medical examination," "medical approval," or "health evaluation" was an express condition of employment. These letters did not inform plaintiffs that they would be subjected to comprehensive diagnostic medical examinations that would inquire into intimate health matters bearing no relation to their responsibilities as administrative or clerical employees. . . .

The district court also appears to have reasoned that plaintiffs knew or had reason to know of the tests because they were asked questions on a medical form concerning "venereal disease," "sickle cell anemia," and "menstrual disorders," and because they gave blood and urine samples. The fact that plaintiffs acquiesced in the minor intrusion of checking or not checking three boxes on a questionnaire does not mean that they had reason to expect further intrusions in the form of having their blood and urine tested for specific conditions that corresponded tangentially if at all to the written questions. First, the entries on the questionnaire were neither identical to nor, in some cases, even suggestive of the characteristics for which plaintiffs were tested. For example, sickle cell trait is a genetic condition distinct from actually having sickle cell anemia, and pregnancy is not considered a "menstrual disorder" or a "venereal disease." Second, and more important, it is not reasonable to infer that a person who answers a questionnaire upon personal knowledge is put on notice that his employer will take intrusive means to verify the accuracy of his answers. There is a significant difference between answering on the basis of what you know about your health and consenting to let someone else investigate the most intimate aspects of your life. Indeed, a reasonable person could conclude that by completing a written questionnaire, he has reduced or eliminated the need for seemingly redundant and even more intrusive laboratory testing in search of highly sensitive and non–job-related information.

Furthermore, if plaintiffs' evidence concerning reasonable medical practice is to be credited, they had no reason to think that tests would be performed without their consent simply because they had answered some questions on a form and had then, in addition, provided bodily fluid samples. Plaintiffs could reasonably have expected Lawrence to seek their consent before running any tests not usually performed in an occupational health exam—particularly tests for intimate medical conditions bearing no relationship to their responsibilities or working conditions as clerical employees. The mere fact that an employee has given a blood or urine sample does not provide notice that an employer will perform any and all tests on that specimen that it desires,—no matter how invasive—particularly where, as here, the employer has yet to offer a valid reason for the testing.

[3] In sum, the district court erred in holding as a matter of law that the plaintiffs knew or had reason to know of the nature of the tests as a result of their submission to the preemployment medical examinations. Because the question of what testing, if any, plaintiffs had reason to expect turns on material factual issues that can only be resolved at trial, summary judgment on statute of limitations grounds was inappropriate with respect to the causes of action based on an invasion of privacy in violation of the Federal and California Constitutions, and also on the Title VII claims.

II. Federal Constitutional Due Process Right of Privacy

The district court also ruled, in the alternative, on the merits of all of plaintiffs' claims except the ADA claims. We first examine its ruling with respect to the claim for violation of the federal constitutional right to privacy. While acknowledging that the government had failed to identify any "undisputed legitimate governmental purpose" for the three tests, the district court concluded that no violation of plaintiffs' right to privacy could have occurred because any intrusions arising from the testing were de minimis in light of (1) the "large overlap" between the subjects covered by the medical questionnaire and the three tests and (2) the "overall intrusiveness" of "a full-scale physical examination." We hold that the district court erred. . . .

[4] The constitutionally protected privacy interest in avoiding disclosure of personal matters clearly encompasses medical information and its confidentiality. [Citations omitted.] Although cases defining the privacy interest in medical information have typically involved its disclosure to "third" parties, rather than the collection of information by illicit means, it goes without saying that the most basic violation possible involves the performance of unauthorized tests—that is, the non-consensual retrieval of previously unrevealed medical information that may be unknown even to plaintiffs. These tests may also be viewed as searches in violation of Fourth Amendment rights that require Fourth Amendment scrutiny. The tests at issue in this case thus implicate rights protected under both the Fourth Amendment and the Due Process Clause of the Fifth or Fourteenth Amendments. . . .

[6] The district court erred in dismissing the claims on the ground that any violation was de minimis, incremental, or overlapping. The latter two grounds are actually just the court's explanations for its adoption of its "de minimis" conclusion. They are not in themselves reasons for dismissal. Nor if the violation is otherwise significant does it become insignificant simply because it is overlapping or incremental. We cannot, therefore, escape a scrupulous examination of the nature of the violation, although we can, of course, consider whether the plaintiffs have in fact consented to any part of the alleged intrusion.

[7] One can think of few subject areas more personal and more likely to implicate privacy interests than that of one's health or genetic make-up. . . . Furthermore, the facts revealed by the tests are highly sensitive, even relative to other medical information. With respect to the testing of plaintiffs for syphilis and pregnancy, it is well established in this circuit "that the Constitution prohibits unregulated, unrestrained employer inquiries into personal sexual matters that have no bearing on job performance.". . . The fact that one has syphilis is an intimate matter that pertains to one's sexual history and may invite tremendous amounts of social stigma. Pregnancy is likewise, for many, an intensely private matter, which also may pertain to one's sexual history and often carries far-reaching societal implications. . . . Finally, the carrying of sickle cell trait can pertain to sensitive information about family history and reproductive decisionmaking. Thus, the conditions tested for were aspects of one's health in which one enjoys the highest expectations of privacy.

[8] As discussed above, with respect to the question of the statute of limitations, there was little, if any, "overlap" between what plaintiffs consented to and the testing at issue here. Nor was the additional invasion only incremental. In some instances, the tests related to entirely different conditions. In all, the information obtained as the result of the testing was qualitatively different from the information that plaintiffs provided in their answers to the questions, and was highly invasive. That one has consented to a general medical examination does not abolish one's privacy right not to be tested for intimate, personal matters involving one's health—nor does consenting to giving blood or urine samples, or filling out a questionnaire. As we have made clear, revealing one's personal knowledge as to whether one has a particular medical con-

dition has nothing to do with one's expectations about actually being tested for that condition. Thus, the intrusion was by no means de minimis. Rather, if unauthorized, the testing constituted a significant invasion of a right that is of great importance, and labelling it minimal cannot and does not make it so.

[9] Lawrence further contends that the tests in question, even if their intrusiveness is not de minimis, would be justified by an employer's interest in performing a general physical examination. This argument fails because issues of fact exist with respect to whether the testing at issue is normally part of a general physical examination. There would of course be no violation if the testing were authorized, or if the plaintiffs reasonably should have known that the blood and urine samples they provided would be used for the disputed testing and failed to object. However, as we concluded in Section I, material issues of fact exist as to those questions. Summary judgment in the alternative on the merits of the federal constitutional privacy claim was therefore incorrect.

[Parts III, IV, V, VI, and VII omitted]

Conclusion

Because material and disputed issues of fact exist with respect to whether reasonable persons in plaintiffs' position would have had reason to know that the tests were being performed, and because the tests were a separate and more invasive intrusion into their privacy than the aspects of the examination to which they did consent, the district court erred in granting summary judgment on statute of limitations grounds with respect to the Title VII claims and the federal and state constitutional privacy claims. The district court also erred in dismissing the federal and state constitutional privacy claims and the Title VII claims on the merits. The district court's dismissal of the ADA claims was proper. None of the Secretary's arguments with respect to the claims brought against him in his official capacity has merit.

Affirmed in part, reversed in part, and remanded.

PRESIDENT'S ECONOMIC REPORT, ECONOMIC ADVISERS' REPORT
February 10, 1998

President Bill Clinton and his economic advisers were able to report another stellar year for the American economy in their annual reports to Congress, released February 10, 1998. "Economic growth in 1997 was the strongest in almost a decade," the president said in his report, "and the benefits of that growth are being shared by all Americans." According to administration figures, 14 million new jobs had been created since Clinton became president in 1993, unemployment had fallen below 5 percent for the first time in twenty-four years, and core inflation (the consumer price index excluding food and energy components) was at its lowest level in thirty years. At the same time, the economy grew 3.9 percent in 1997 (as measured by real gross domestic product, GDP). And, for the first time in thirty years, a president was predicting a budget surplus.

Clinton's projection of a surplus in fiscal 1999 was off by a few months. As it turned out, the federal budget produced a total surplus of $70 billion in fiscal 1998, consisting of a $29 billion deficit in government programs, offset by a $99 billion surplus for Social Security and the Postal Service. Overall the economy in 1998 outstripped the administration's projections—and many analysts' expectations. Despite concerns that economic crises in Asia, Russia, and Brazil would eventually slow the U.S. economy, growth continued to be strong, while unemployment remained stable and inflation continued to decline. At year's end, the longest uninterrupted expansion in the nation's history showed few signs of distress.

"Best Performance in a Generation"

Calling the economic record in 1997 "truly remarkable," the Council of Economic Advisers said that the economy had followed the path that the council had forecast at the beginning of the year. What the council had not fully anticipated, the advisers said, was how rapidly the economy would grow. With real GDP growth at 3.9 percent, the economy created 3.2 million jobs in 1997—more than in either of the two previous years. Unemploy-

ment for the year was 4.9 percent, the lowest level since 1973 and well below the 5.3 percent level the administration had predicted. Hourly wages rose 3.9 percent.

In the past, fast growth combined with low unemployment and rising wages usually pushed inflation up. In 1997 inflation declined, as it had in 1996. Core inflation, as measured by the consumer price index for all items except food and energy, rose just 2.4 percent in 1997, its lowest level since 1966.

In short, the council said, it was the "best performance in a generation." The president and his economic advisers noted that Americans of all races were sharing in this economic growth. Unemployment among black Americans was 10 percent for the year, which was its lowest level since 1973. The poverty rate fell to 13.7 percent in 1996 (the last year for which data were available), from 15.1 percent in 1993. Although high at 28.4 percent, the poverty rate for African Americans reached a historic low. Real household income for the 20 percent of the population with lowest incomes rose 2.2 percent between 1993 and 1996, compared with 1.7 percent for the highest-income quintile. Although the country had made progress in narrowing the income disparities among the races, the economic advisers said, that progress had been "very uneven" and "substantial disparities" persisted. The president's race initiative was designed to focus attention on this problem, the advisers said, and several of the administration's empowerment and community developments programs were intended to narrow the income gaps. (Race initiative, p. 665)

Clinton attributed much of the success of the economy to his economic strategy, particularly his deficit reduction plan, which he said "set the nation on a course of fiscal responsibility." When Clinton took office in 1993, the federal budget deficit stood at $290 billion and was projected to go to $400 billion or higher. The new Democratic president managed to push an omnibus package of spending cuts and tax increases through the Democratic-controlled Congress in 1993, and the budget deficits began to decline. The president said he expected the deficit to fall to $10 billion in fiscal 1998 and projected a small surplus for fiscal 1999, to be followed by significantly larger surpluses for the next several years (Budget surplus, p. 500; deficit reduction action, Historic Documents of 1993, p. 181)

Clinton also had the good fortune of coming into office just as a recession was ending and the economy was beginning to grow. This generated higher than anticipated tax revenues, which gave a boost to his deficit reduction measures. "The lion's share of the credit for the economy's performance goes to American workers and firms, who have risen to the challenges of a competitive global economy and rapidly changing technology," the Council of Economic Advisers said. "Using government to complement, not replace, the market and the private sector has been a fundamental guiding principle of this administration's economic strategy from the very beginning. And it is this strategy that has borne fruit over the last five years."

As he had in his State of the Union message, Clinton urged that any budget surplus be "reserved" until the Social Security system had been fixed. The nation's largest pension system was projected to go bankrupt in 2032 unless steps were taken to shore up its long-term financing. Clinton also asked Congress to restore the president's authority to negotiate "fast-track" trade agreements. Fast-tracking permitted a president to negotiate trade agreements and then submit them to Congress for approval on an up-or-down vote, without amendment. Without fast track procedures in place, other countries were generally unwilling to negotiate trade pacts for fear that legislators would reopen the deals to seek concessions on those parts of the agreement with which they disagreed.

That request was denied in September when the House voted down the authorization, 180–243. The administration's request for renewed fast-track authority had also failed in November 1997, when Clinton was unable to muster enough support to overcome opposition from a coalition of Democrats and conservative Republicans. Led by House Minority Leader Richard A. Gephardt of Missouri, Democrats complained that Clinton had not followed through on promises he had made to secure their support for the North American Free Trade Agreement in 1993. (Social Security, p. 98; North American Free Trade Agreement, Historic Documents of 1993, p. 953)

1998: Economic Expectations on a Roller Coaster Ride

The Council of Economic Advisers predicted slower growth of 2 percent in 1998, with unemployment and inflation remaining relatively stable, at 4.9 percent and 2.2 percent, respectively. The advisers said this projection did not mean that was the best the economy could do, but was rather a conservative estimate upon which it based its revenue and spending projections. There was no reason why the current economic growth could not continue, the advisers said. "Expansions do not die of old age," the advisers continued, quoting their own 1996 report. "Instead, recent postwar expansions have ended because of rising inflation, financial imbalances, or inventory overhangs. None of these conditions exists at present. The most likely prognosis is therefore for sustained job creation and continued non-inflationary growth." And that is more or less what happened, despite fears that foreign financial crises might plunge the economy into recession.

Throughout 1998 government and private analysts expressed concern that the continuing economic recession in much of Southeast Asia might spill over into the U.S. economy. Both the Council of Economic Advisers and Federal Reserve Board Chairman Alan Greenspan said the crisis-induced slowdown of American exports to the region probably helped the economy by moderating any underlying inflationary pressures. But they and others also worried that the moderation could quickly turn into a recession.

Those fears were heightened in mid-year after Russia devalued its currency and effectively defaulted on its loans from foreign banks and investors. At the same time several economies in Latin America (notably that of Brazil, the world's ninth largest economy) seemed on the brink of collapse. In response, investors began to move funds out of the American stock markets, which had reached record heights earlier in the summer, and invest their profits in safer instruments, such as U.S. Treasury bonds. On August 4 the Dow Jones industrial average fell 299 points; on two successive trading days at the end of August it lost nearly 900 points. The market rebounded with a 380-point gain on September 8—the single biggest rise in Dow Jones history—only to lose much of that gain on September 10. (Russian financial crisis, p. 601; Asian financial crisis, p. 722)

With strained financial markets a greater threat to the economy's stability than inflation, the Federal Reserve Board reduced its discount rate—the interest rate its charges depository institutions—from 5 percent to 4.75 percent on October 15 and to 4.5 percent on November 17. On October 7 Federal Reserve chairman Alan Greenspan told a group of economists that the outlook for the economy had "weakened measurably" since mid-summer. Even though growth was good and inflation remained low, Greenspan said, "We are clearly facing a set of forces that should be dampening demand going forward to an unknown extent. We do not know how far it will go or how much it will affect consumer and business spending here at home."

The interest rate cuts at home combined with renewed efforts to bolster the sagging economies in Asia and Latin America appeared to restore some measure of confidence in investors. By year's end, the stock markets had regained most of what they had lost in the fall. Despite predictions of slower growth and tighter labor markets, the economy continued its pattern of fast growth coupled with high employment and low inflation. Preliminary figures estimated real growth for 1998 at 3.9 percent—the same level as in 1997, stable unemployment, and even further declines in the rate of inflation.

Following are the text of the Economic Report of the President and excerpts from chapter 1 of the Annual Report of the Council of Economic Advisers, both released February 10, 1998:

ECONOMIC REPORT OF THE PRESIDENT

To the Congress of the United States:

For the last 5 years this Administration has worked to strengthen our Nation for the 21st century, expanding opportunity for all Americans, demanding responsibility from all Americans, and bringing us together as a community of all Americans. Building a strong economy is the cornerstone of our efforts to meet these challenges.

When I first took office in 1993, the Federal budget deficit was out of control, unemployment was unacceptably high, and wages were stagnant. To reverse this course, we took a new approach, putting in place a bold economic strategy designed to bring down the deficit and give America's workers the tools and training they need to help them thrive in our changing economy.

Our strategy has succeeded: the economy has created more than 14 million new jobs, unemployment is at its lowest level in 24 years, and core inflation is at its lowest level in 30 years. Economic growth in 1997 was the strongest in almost a decade, and the benefits of that growth are being shared by all Americans: poverty is dropping and median family income has gone up nearly $2,200 since 1993. We also saw the biggest drop in welfare rolls in history. Many challenges remain, but Americans are enjoying the fruits of an economy that is steady and strong.

The Administration's Economic Strategy

From the beginning, this Administration's economic strategy has had three crucial elements: reducing the deficit, investing in people, and opening markets abroad.

Deficit reduction. In 1993 this Administration's deficit reduction plan set the Nation on a course of fiscal responsibility, while making critical investments in the skills and well-being of our people. When I took office, the deficit was $290 billion and projected to go much higher. This year the deficit will fall to just $10 billion and possibly lower still. That is a reduction of more than 95 percent, leaving the deficit today smaller in relation to the size of the economy than it has been since 1969. And this year I have proposed a budget that will eliminate the deficit entirely, achieving the first balanced budget in 30 years.

Beyond that, it is projected that the budget will show a sizable surplus in the years to come. I propose that we reserve 100 percent of the surplus until we have taken the necessary measures to strengthen the Social Security system for the 21st century. I am committed to addressing Social Security first, to ensure that all Americans are confident that it will be there when they need it.

Investing in our people. In the new economy, the most precious resource this Nation has is the skills and ingenuity of working Americans. Investing in the education and health of our people will help all Americans reap the rewards of a growing, changing economy. Those who are better educated, with the flexibility and the skills they need to move from one job to another and seize new opportunities, will succeed in the new economy; those who do not will fall behind.

That is why the historic balanced budget agreement I signed into law in 1997 included the largest increase in aid to education in 30 years, and the biggest increase to help people go to college since the G.I. Bill was passed 50 years ago. The agreement provided funds to ensure that we stay on track to help 1 million disadvantaged children prepare for success in school. It provided funding for the America Reads Challenge, with the goal of mobilizing a million volunteers to promote literacy, and it made new investments in our schools themselves, to help connect every classroom and library in this country to the Internet by the year 2000.

The balanced budget agreement created the HOPE scholarship program, to make completion of the 13th and 14th years of formal education as widespread as a high school diploma is today. It offered other tuition tax credits for college and skills training. It created a new Individual Retirement Account that allows tax-free withdrawals to pay for education. It provided the biggest increase in Pell grants in two decades. Finally, it provided more funds so that aid to dislocated workers is more than double what it was in 1993, to help these workers get the skills they need to remain productive in a changing economy.

But we must do more to guarantee all Americans the quality education they need to succeed. That is why I have proposed a new initiative to improve the quality of education in our public schools—through high national standards and national tests, more charter schools to stimulate competition, greater accountability, higher quality teaching, smaller class sizes, and more classrooms.

To strengthen our Nation we must also strengthen our families. The Family and Medical Leave Act, which I signed into law in 1993, ensures that millions of people no longer have to choose between being good parents and being good workers. The Health [Insurance] Portability and Accountability Act, enacted in 1996, ensures that workers can keep their health insurance if they change jobs or suffer a family emergency. We have also increased the minimum wage, expanded the earned income tax credit, and provided for a new $500-per-child tax credit for working families. To continue making progress toward strengthening families, the balanced budget agreement allocated $24 billion to provide health insurance to up to 5 million uninsured children—the largest Federal investment in children's health care since Medicaid was created in 1965.

Opening markets and expanding exports. To create more good jobs and increase wages, we must open markets abroad and expand U.S. exports. Trade has been key to the strength of this economic expansion—about a third of our economic growth in recent years has come from selling American goods and services overseas. The Information Technology Agreement signed in 1997 lowers tariff and other barriers to 90 percent of world trade in information technology services.

To continue opening new markets, creating new jobs, and increasing our prosperity, it is critically important to renew fast-track negotiating authority. This authority, which every President of either party has had for the last 20 years, enables the President to negotiate trade agreements and submit them to the Congress for an up-or-down vote, without modification. Renewing this traditional trade authority is essential to America's ability to shape the global economy of the 21st century.

Seizing the Benefits of a Growing, Changing Economy

As we approach the 21st century the American economy is sound and strong, but challenges remain. We know that information and technology and global commerce are rapidly transforming the economy, offering new opportunities but also posing new challenges. Our goal must be to ensure that all Americans are equipped with the skills to succeed in this growing, changing economy.

Our economic strategy—balancing the budget, investing in our people, opening markets—has set this Nation on the right course to meet this goal. This strategy will support and contribute to America's strength in the new economic era, removing barriers to our economy's potential and providing our people with the skills, the flexibility, and the security to succeed. We must continue to maintain the fiscal discipline that is balancing the budget, to invest in our people and their skills, and to lead the world to greater prosperity in the 21st century.

William J. Clinton
The White House
February 10, 1998

THE ANNUAL REPORT OF THE COUNCIL OF ECONOMIC ADVISERS

Promoting Prosperity in a High-Employment Economy

The past year saw the Nation's economy turn in its best performance in a generation. Over the course of 1997, output growth and job creation remained vigorous while inflation declined. Real (inflation-adjusted) gross domestic product (GDP) grew 3.9 percent, and employment rose by 3.2 million, for an average rate of 267,000 jobs per month. The unemployment rate dropped below 5 percent for the first time in 24 years, yet core inflation (as measured by the consumer price index, excluding its volatile food and energy components) averaged only 2.2 percent, its lowest rate in over 30 years. This exceptional economic performance occurred during a period of historic deficit reduction: the Federal budget deficit, which reached $290 billion in the 1992 fiscal year, declined to only $22 billion in fiscal 1997. And the Administration has submitted a budget for fiscal 1999 that projects a balanced budget for the first time since 1969.

As 1998 begins, the prospects for continued growth with high employment and low inflation remain excellent. The economy is remarkably free of the symptoms that often presage an economic downturn—such as an increase in inflation, an accumulation of inventories, or evidence of financial imbalance. Inflation fell in 1997, and developments in East Asia, by reducing U.S. import prices, are likely to exert additional downward pressure on U.S. inflation in 1998. Economic turmoil in East Asia could affect the global economy, but if international efforts to restore stability there succeed, the main effect on the U.S. economy could simply be to allow continued growth and job creation with a more moderate outlook for interest rates. Another sign that an expansion is nearing its end would be a sudden accumulation of inventories, as businesses find their sales falling short of production. Yet sales were strong in 1997, and inventory-sales ratios are near historical lows. Financial imbalances can also threaten to disrupt an expansion. But today banks and other financial institutions do not appear overextended, as they did in the late 1980s and early 1990s, and the stock market shrugged off a one-day plunge in October (although its continuing high valuation relative to earnings is a source of concern to some). Although the business cycle may not have been vanquished, the economy is in fundamentally sound shape and well-equipped to handle any unexpected bouts of rougher weather.

A principal force behind the current expansion has been private fixed investment. Almost none of the growth in GDP over this expansion has come from increased government spending, whereas close to one-third has come from greater private fixed investment.... Because of the Administration's deficit reduction efforts, the contribution of government spending to overall growth has been much lower than in most previous postwar expansions (real Federal Government spending has actually declined), while that of private fixed investment has been substantially higher. One benefit of this burst of investment has been a rapid expansion of industrial capacity: over the past 3 years average annual capacity growth has exceeded every previous growth rate since 1968.

Policies such as deficit reduction have contributed to an investment-led recovery and a climate conducive to sustained economic growth. But the lion's share of the credit for the economy's performance goes to American workers and firms, who have risen to the challenges of a competitive global economy and rapidly changing technology. The role of government in such an economy is not to prop up economic growth with government spending but, more subtly, to provide individuals and businesses with the tools they need to flourish through their own efforts. The range of appropriate government policies in such an economy includes promoting private investment through sound macroeconomic policies, encouraging the formation of skills through training and education, securing opportunity for the marginalized members of our society, and—where necessary—providing assistance to the most vulnerable. Using government to complement, not replace, the market and the private sector has been a fundamental, guiding principle of this Administration's economic strategy from the very beginning. And it is this strategy that has borne fruit over the last 5 years.

Despite the economy's recent exemplary performance, a number of challenges remain. The first is to preserve and nurture the successes achieved so far. And although progress has been made in addressing the longer term problems that have affected the economy since the productivity slowdown of the early 1970s—problems like slow growth in wages and incomes and widening income inequality—more needs to be done. This chapter describes the principles and policies of this Administration for achieving its two basic, overarching goals: securing high and rising living standards now and in the future, and ensuring that the benefits of a higher standard of living are extended to all Americans.

The Administration's Economic Strategy

The Employment Act of 1946 (which created the Council of Economic Advisers), together with its later amendments, gave the Federal Government responsibility for stabilizing short-run economic fluctuations, promoting balanced and noninflationary economic growth, and fostering low unemployment. This Administration's strategy in pursuing this mandate has focused on getting the fundamentals right: reducing the budget deficit, investing in technology and the American people, and opening markets at home and abroad. These were the right policies for encouraging the job creation needed to move the economy to full employment, and they are the right policies for attacking the longer term problems of sluggish productivity growth and widening income inequality that began to afflict the economy in the early 1970s.

But there is more to the Administration's policy agenda than can be measured by aggregate economic statistics alone. Getting the fundamentals right means removing the barriers that block people from realizing their potential; it means promoting their sense of individual responsibility and giving them the tools to succeed. Getting the fundamentals right also means fostering a personal commitment by all Americans to help others, a sense of shared responsibility for our Nation's children, and a sense of community in an increasingly multiethnic society.

A Credible Plan for Deficit Reduction

The policy course set in 1993 has contributed to the Nation's recent economic health and strength. In 1993 the economy was still recovering from the 1990-91 recession, and it labored under the burden of a Federal budget deficit that had ballooned to $290 billion, an all-time record. The linchpin of the Administration's economic strategy was a credible budget plan that could achieve substantial deficit reduction over the longer term, yet be balanced and gradual enough to allow the economy to gather strength and move toward full employment in the short term. The success of this program rested on achieving an interest rate environment conducive to investment, which would allow the economy to grow in the face of a contractionary fiscal policy. This in turn required that financial markets correctly anticipate an appropriately accommodative monetary policy. In large measure, that is exactly what happened. Long-term interest rates fell to 25-year lows in 1993, spurring a pickup in economic growth.

A key feature of the Administration's deficit reduction plan was its credibility. A credible and realistic program for deficit reduction—one that observers and financial markets judged likely to be fully implemented—was a precondition for the reduction in interest rates that spurred investment-led growth. Fundamental to the plan's credibility was the adoption of a set of economic projections that represented conservative, mainstream forecasts of future growth and inflation. These projections eschewed the "rosy scenarios" of previous budgets, which invariably fell short of reality; they weren't meant to indicate the best that the economy could do, but rather how the economy was most likely to perform given past experience. In fact, the economy's performance has been stronger than the Administration projected.

In the 1980s expansive fiscal policy required relatively tight monetary policy in the form of high interest rates to prevent the economy from overheating. This policy mix is particularly unfavorable from the standpoint of fostering longer term growth: high interest rates impede capital formation, while burgeoning government deficits depress national saving and contribute to more borrowing from abroad. The net result of deficit reduction in the 1990s has been to promote a more balanced mix of fiscal and monetary policy. Deficit reduction has also had an important collateral benefit, namely, a restoration of Americans' confidence in the ability of their government to manage its own affairs.

Investing in People and Technology

The primary purpose of deficit reduction, however, is to encourage investment. Hence, this Administration recognized from the outset that a plan that balanced the budget at the expense of the government's own productive investments would ultimately be self-defeating. Far from curtailing public investment, the Administration has given investment in people and technology a major place in its economic agenda.

Government invests in people by promoting public health and safety, encouraging opportunity and individual responsibility, and assisting in the formation of human capital through education and training. This last function is especially vital in today's high-technology economy, where a skilled work force is an essential condition for future growth. Education is critical if Americans are to capitalize on the opportunities created by new technologies and more open global markets. And education and training programs are of particular importance in the present economic environment as a means of preventing poverty and ensuring opportunity for all. The return to education has risen dramatically since the late 1970s; today, highly skilled workers command a large premium in the labor market over their less skilled counterparts. This rising skill premium is an important reason why earnings inequality is greater today than it was in the late 1970s. Governments have an important role to play in ensuring that all Americans have the opportunity to accumulate the skills necessary for economic success. This requires initiatives to improve public education at the primary and secondary levels, as well as programs to make higher education more accessible. It also requires recognizing that learning must be a lifelong activity in an economy where technological change is ongoing.

Investing in basic research and the development of new technologies is another important function of government. The private sector spends billions of dollars every year on research and development. But economists have long recognized that private sector spending alone in these areas will be less than the optimum. Since the fruits of a new scientific discovery, for example, are enjoyed not merely by the discoverer but by society as a whole, the private incentive for pursuing scientific research falls short of the total social benefit. Moreover, new theories of economic growth place a special emphasis on advances in knowledge through research and development as the motive force behind long-run increases in living standards. This analysis implies that the return to government investment in basic research and technology is likely to be especially high.

Opening Markets at Home and Abroad

A third major component of the Administration's economic agenda is the promotion of freer and more competitive markets at home and abroad. Domestically, this has involved the pursuit of initiatives directed at enhancing competition—particularly in such industries as telecommunications, electric power, financial services, and health care—and a vigorous approach to antitrust enforcement. It has also meant addressing market failures in such areas as health care and environmental protection. In some cases the effect of these initiatives is a one-time boost to the level of output, through greater efficiency and lower costs. But these policies can also sometimes lead to a faster rate of economic growth. For example, past experience provides evidence that sensible deregulation can not only help raise efficiency, but also spur continued innovation through greater competition. Moreover, some benefits of these policies are not captured in the GDP statistics at all, but rather take the form of improvements in our quality of life.

The Administration is also committed to reducing the burden of government regulation and ensuring that the benefits of new regulations justify their costs. Many government regulations apply to industries in which technological change is rapidly altering the nature of market competition. A key precept of this Administration's approach to regulation, therefore, is that the regulatory process must be dynamic, with regulatory policies under constant review so as to minimize their burden on consumers and businesses. Another important precept is to refrain from policies that regulate through government fiat in favor of policies that use market-based incentives to attain the desired outcome. Experience with such policies as permit trading for sulfur dioxide emissions suggests that this approach can help ensure that compliance with socially beneficial goals is achieved efficiently and cost-effectively.

This Administration has also worked hard to open markets abroad by encouraging fairer and freer international trade. From his earliest days in office, the President has advocated an outward-looking, internationalist trade policy. During the Administration's first 4 years the United States concluded over 200 trade agreements with other countries. Some of these agreements, such as the North American Free Trade Agreement (NAFTA) and the Uruguay Round agreement of the General Agreement on Tariffs and Trade, were comprehensive in scope, whereas others had much more limited aims—but all are vital to our Nation's competitive future.

Economists generally recognize that an open economy offers both static and dynamic advantages. First, trade benefits an economy by allowing it to specialize in what it does best—a point that economists have made since the early 1800s. Even if a country is more efficient than its neighbors at producing every good it consumes, it can still benefit from trade by specializing in the production of goods in which it is relatively more efficient, and then trading its surplus production for whatever else it wants to consume. In addition, a new view of international trade argues that increased trade actually raises an economy's rate of growth, because increased competition and larger markets spur the acquisition of new skills and the development of new technologies. If so, the case for trade liberalization becomes even more compelling, since raising the economy's growth rate—even by a few tenths of a percentage point per year—has vastly more significance for long-run living standards than even a relatively large one-time increase in the level of output.

A Record of Accomplishment

Focusing on the fundamentals in shaping economic policy has paid off by helping to produce an economy that is stronger than it has been in decades. This past year alone saw a drop in the unemployment rate to its lowest level in a generation and the forging of a budget agreement that promises to bring the Federal deficit under control for the first time in decades. Last year also saw significant advances in this Administration's economic agenda along other fronts.

Benefits of a High-Employment Economy

Driven largely by strong growth in business fixed investment, growth in real GDP and employment picked up in the second half of 1993 and persisted in 1994. This robust growth led to a series of monetary policy tightenings over the course of 1994, which resulted in more moderate growth in 1995. In retrospect, 1995 may have been the pause that refreshes. Economic growth exceeded expectations in 1996, and strong growth continued through 1997. The result has been a high-employment economy with the potential to overcome some of the longer term problems of productivity growth and income distribution that built up in the 1970s and 1980s.

A high-employment economy brings enormous economic and social benefits. Essential to personal economic security is the knowledge that work is available to those who seek it, at wages sufficient to keep them and their families out of poverty. A tight labor market increases the confidence of job losers that they will be able to return to work, lures discouraged workers back into the labor force, enhances the prospects of those already at work to get ahead, enables those who want or need to switch jobs to do so without a long period of joblessness, and lowers the duration of a typical unemployment spell. Returning the economy to full employment yields a direct benefit by ensuring that the economy's resources—human and material—are not squandered by needless cyclical unemployment. On average, reducing the unemployment rate by a percentage point raises output by approximately 2 percent; in 1997, 2 percent of GDP was $160 billion, or roughly $600 for every American man, woman, and child. Wasted resources from not producing at potential, together with the human cost of unemployment, are intolerable; the elimination of this waste is the principal benefit of a sustained return to full employment.

But a high-employment economy in which jobs are plentiful and labor markets tight yields other benefits as well. Short-term economic conditions can affect long-term structural unemployment. A tight labor market encourages participation by those who might otherwise be forced to sit on the sidelines, and makes it easier to absorb less skilled or younger and more inexperienced workers into the labor force. These new labor market entrants gain much-needed job experience, building the skills they will need to hold down a job in the future. The importance of this can be seen from the experience of some European countries: prolonged stagnation or recession may have led to a permanent increase in unemployment there, as the unemployed and the never-employed have seen their skills atrophy or become obsolete. Running a high-employment economy, then, may be one of the surest ways to ensure that an unacceptably large fraction of our citizens are not consigned to long-term joblessness and economic marginalization.

From the 1980s until the early 1990s, the economy's ability to reduce poverty through growth alone was hampered by a strong headwind: sustained declines in wages at the low end of the earnings distribution that offset the benefits of an expanding economy for the poorest Americans. As a result, holding a job no longer ensured that a less skilled worker would be able to lift his or her family out of poverty. This adverse secular trend raises even further the stakes of maintaining a high-employment economy.

Keeping the unemployment rate low and job growth high is also necessary if we are to move current welfare recipients into the work force. Early, indirect evidence here is encouraging: employment and labor force participation rates among single women who maintain families—about two-thirds of whom have children under 18—have increased in the past few years. This is probably in part the result of recent welfare reform: the greatest acceleration in employment rates has occurred among those single women most likely to be affected by welfare reform, namely, those with young children. Nevertheless, it is obvious that fostering an economy in which job opportunities are plentiful plays a crucial part in aiding the transition from welfare to work.

We have begun to see heartening signs that the current expansion is yielding gains in living standards for all Americans, especially those at the bottom of the income distribution. The poverty rate fell to 13.7 percent in 1996, from 15.1 percent in 1993; the poverty rate for black Americans is at a historical low, and in 1997 unemployment among blacks fell to its lowest rate since 1973. Since 1993, household income has grown in each quintile of the income distribution, with the largest percentage increase going to the poorest members of our society. . . . Maintaining a full-employment economy is essential if this progress is to continue.

Deficit Reduction: Completing the Task

The most significant economic policy event of 1997 was the passage of a deficit reduction package that will finish the task of balancing the Federal budget by 1999. This will be the first balanced budget since 1969, and only the ninth since World War II. . . .

Some have claimed that the expanding economy, not government policy, deserves all the credit for vanquishing the deficit. It is certainly true that ups and downs in the business cycle have an important effect on both revenues and outlays, leading to fluctuations in the deficit. But even when cyclical factors are thus accounted for, it is evident that policy has played a major role in bringing the deficit under control. It is also worth noting that in January 1993, before the 1993 deficit reduction package was adopted, the Federal deficit was projected to reach $350 billion in fiscal 1998 and to rise to $650 billion in fiscal 2003, even when the economy was projected to be at full employment. Finally, it is difficult to imagine that the economy's performance would have been anywhere near as strong as it has been without a credible and successful attempt to put the government's fiscal house in order. Improvements in economic conditions have played a part in reducing the deficit, but a balanced budget would not now be in sight had the Nation remained on the fiscal course in place in 1992.

Although a balanced budget is often taken as the goal of fiscal policy, from an economic standpoint the motivation for deficit reduction is to raise national saving, thereby augmenting society's future consumption possibilities. When the government's budget is in surplus, in the sense that revenues exceed outlays, the government makes a positive contribution to national saving. . . . [A] case for higher national saving can be based on the high return on saving in the United States and the fact that private saving remains low. A higher rate of national saving now would lead to a larger economy when the baby-boom generation retires, thus making it easier to provide for their retirement without imposing undue burdens on younger generations. Although a balanced budget does not add to the government's outstanding debt to the public, which past deficits have ballooned, it does not subtract from it either. Leaving a large public debt in place implies that a sizable portion of existing government resources will continue to be absorbed by interest payments, leaving less for all other spending. Indeed, one legacy of the runup in the national debt that accompanied the deficits of the 1980s and early 1990s has been a sharp increase in the share of total outlays that must be used to make interest payments on the debt. . . .

Policies to Raise Growth, Reduce Inequality, and Increase Opportunity

A significant part of the Administration's economic agenda also involves investment in people: in a broad sense, this encompasses education and training, measures to promote health, and policies that extend opportunity to all Americans. A number of policies have been put in place to ensure that these investments are made.

Education

The 1997 balanced budget agreement included the largest Federal investment in education in a generation, in the form of initiatives to improve the quality and accessibility of primary, secondary, and higher education.

Higher education is a particular priority. The earnings of college graduates have risen sharply relative to those of workers with only a high school education; in today's economy, a college degree has become as vital for success as a high school diploma was a generation ago. Even post-high school education that does not lead to a bachelor's degree (such as an associate's degree program or vocational or technical training) boosts earnings substantially over just completing high school . . . .

Moreover, learning must be a lifelong process. A fundamental characteristic of our economy is constant technological change. Such progress holds the promise of higher living standards for all, but it also requires workers to adapt to employers' demands for a well-trained, highly skilled work force. It is therefore critical to provide all individuals—including those not traditionally thought of as "school age"—with access to additional education or training.

The President's higher education initiatives reflect these principles. Specific measures include:

- *The largest Pell grant increase in 20 years.* The balanced budget agreement raises the maximum Pell grant by over 10 percent, to $3,000. Approximately 3.7 million students receive Pell grants, and close to a quarter of a million families will become eligible for the grant for the first time.
- *HOPE scholarships for post-high school education.* In his 1997 State of the Union address, the President called for making the 13th and 14th years of education as universal as a high school education is today. The HOPE scholarship program accomplishes this by providing a tax credit for higher education expenses of as much as $1,500, enough to cover tuition at a typical community college.
- *A tuition tax credit for Americans of all ages.* A 20-percent tax credit for post-high school tuition expenses will be available for the first $5,000 (and after 2002, $10,000) of qualified education expenses. This tax credit is offered not just to school-age Americans but to those already working as well, to permit workers to upgrade their skills at any time during their life.
- *Tax exemptions for employer-provided education benefits.* The budget agreement extends Section 127 of the tax code for 3 years, allowing workers to exclude up to $5,250 of employer-provided education benefits from their taxable income.
- *A tax deduction for interest on student loans.* Up to $1,000 of interest payments on loans for higher education expenses will be tax-deductible in any given tax year, starting in 1998. This deduction will rise by $500 each year until 2001.

Because public education in the United States is largely administered by local authorities, the Federal Government's ability to influence primary and secondary education is somewhat less direct. Nevertheless, this Administration recognizes that there is much that the Federal Government can do to improve our public schools, and has worked to enact programs that will ensure that our children have access to the best possible primary and secondary education. These initiatives include:

- *Establishing national standards.* Research shows that students in countries that have standardized, mandatory examinations do better than students in countries that do not. The Administration's voluntary national testing program has received full funding; this will allow for the development of national fourth-grade reading and eighth-grade mathematics examinations.
- *Expanding Head Start.* The balanced budget agreement raised funding for Head Start by $374 million, to $4.4 billion, to reach the Administration's goal of having 1 million children in the Head Start program by 2002. Since 1993, funding for this program, which has shown great success in preparing low-income preschoolers to enter school, has increased by 57 percent. The program will serve over 830,000 children and their families in 1998, including 40,000 infants and toddlers in the Early Head Start program.
- *Establishing a comprehensive literacy strategy.* Every child should be able to read by the third grade. To meet this basic goal, the President's comprehensive literacy strategy will receive nearly $46 million in new funding in 1998 for State teacher training, family literacy, and tutoring efforts; $210 million was provided in an advance appropriation to be available in 1999, contingent on authorization of a literacy initiative such as the America Reads Challenge.
- *Increasing funding for charter schools.* The President set a goal of having 3,000 locally designed public charter schools in operation by early in the next century. Funding for charter schools is increased by over 50 percent in the balanced budget agreement, to allow the Department of Education to support nearly 1,000 charter schools by the end of 1998.

Health

This Administration has made promoting health, increasing access to health insurance, and improving the functioning of health insurance markets a major priority. The Balanced Budget Act of 1997 allocates $24 billion over 5 years to assist States in providing health insurance for up to 5 million children through Medicaid or State programs. This represents the single largest investment in children's health since Medicaid was begun in 1965. The Administration's 1999 budget proposes to expand access to health insurance further by allowing uninsured Americans between 62 and 65 years old, as well as 55- to 61-year-olds who have been laid off or displaced from their jobs, to buy into the Medicare program. These measures are fully offset so as not to increase the cost of Medicare to the government.

The Balanced Budget Act also takes important steps toward ensuring that Medicare itself remains viable. Structural reforms—such as expanded choice among health care plans and the restructuring of payment systems—will help save $115 billion over 5 years. Recently passed legislation also provides additional funding for preventive care, such as mammograms, which can help keep health care expenses down by catching and treating health problems before they become serious. These and other measures will keep the Medicare trust fund solvent for at least the next decade. The Balanced Budget Act also created a commission to examine long-term solutions to the problems that will face Medicare as a result of the demographic changes coming in the 21st century.

The Administration has also promoted policies to improve the functioning of health insurance markets, increase consumer protection, and improve access to new pharmaceuticals. The Health Insurance Portability and Accountability Act of 1996 helps workers who change jobs by making it easier to carry their health insurance with them to the new job. In 1997 the President's Commission on Consumer Protection and Quality in the Health Care Industry, established to advise the President on changes in the health care system, responded to the President's request to develop and recommend a "Consumer Bill of Rights and Responsibilities." The President urged the Congress to pass appropriate and necessary legislation to ensure that a range of protections are extended to all Americans. And the Food and Drug Administration Modernization Act of 1997, which codifies a number of initiatives taken by this Administration as part of the reinventing government initiative, will help ensure the timely availability of safe and effective new drugs. . . .

Finally, teenage tobacco use is one of the most important public health concerns that the Nation faces, and it has been rising in recent years. The increase in the tobacco tax passed last year not only will help fund the expansions in children's health insurance coverage described above, but also will help reduce teen smoking. The rise in the tax complements recent Food and Drug Administration rules to limit advertising targeted at youth. Finally, the Administration has indicated its support for national legislation designed to achieve large reductions in teen smoking, with strict financial penalties on the tobacco industry if specific targets in this effort are not met.

Welfare Reform and Poverty Alleviation

Welfare reform presents an ongoing challenge: to ensure that our neediest citizens can maintain a decent standard of living without creating incentives that encourage a life of dependency. This Administration has committed itself to a policy that combines work incentives and community efforts to move people off of welfare and into employment. This has contributed to the largest reduction in welfare rolls in history.

The same long-term changes in the wage structure that give greater rewards to education and skill also imply that some workers will find it difficult to raise themselves and their families out of poverty, even with a full-time job. To make work pay, all those who work must be guaranteed a minimum level of earnings. The Administration has made an expansion of the earned income tax credit (EITC), which raises the take-home pay of eligible low-income workers, a cornerstone of its strategy to promote work and reduce poverty. . . . This expansion has occurred alongside two increases in the minimum wage (the second of which, in September 1997, raised the minimum wage from $4.75 to $5.15 an hour).

In August 1996 the President signed into law a comprehensive, bipartisan welfare reform bill, which established the Temporary Assistance for Needy Families program. This created a new system of block grants to States and dramatically altered the nature and provision of Federal welfare benefits in America. This legislation has changed the Nation's welfare system into one that requires work in exchange for time-limited assistance and provides support for families moving from welfare to work.

Although these policies have helped shrink the welfare rolls significantly since 1993, much remains to be done. To that end, two additional initiatives have been put in place to advance this Administration's strategy for moving welfare recipients into employment. The first is a tax credit for employers who hire long-term welfare recipients; the credit rebates to employers up to $3,500 in wages paid in the first year and up to $5,000 in the second. The second initiative is the Welfare to Work Job Challenge Fund, which will assist States and communities in moving long-term welfare recipients into lasting, unsubsidized employment. A hallmark of this fund, for which $3 billion has been earmarked, is that it is targeted to those areas of the country most in need of poverty alleviation.

The Child Tax Credit

The Administration proposed a tax cut to help working families with the expense of raising their children. The Taxpayer Relief Act of 1997 will reduce taxes for 26 million families by providing a tax credit of $500 per child. This credit will benefit over 40 million children under age 17, including over 10 million children from working families with incomes below $30,000. Because the credit is partly refundable, large families who have paid significant out-of-pocket payroll taxes can benefit even if they have little or no income tax liability.

Strengthening Cities and Communities

This Administration has worked to make Federal resources available for investment in our Nation's cities and communities. First, the Administration has sought to expand the number of Empowerment Zones and Enterprise Communities. The initial round of competition, in 1994, led to the establishment of 95 Enterprise Communities and 9 Empowerment Zones; both urban and rural areas were represented. The Taxpayer Relief Act of 1997 established 22 additional Empowerment Zones. To compete for these designations, communities submitted strategic plans for revitalization; this requirement is intended to mobilize local communities and encourage them to harness their talents and resources in framing a plan for local economic development. Designated zones and communities receive tax benefits and flexible grants and are entitled to apply for waivers of certain Federal regulations; the underlying principle of the program is that communities know best how to solve their own problems but may lack the necessary resources.

The Administration has also worked to promote fair access to loans and investment capital for residents of low- and moderate-income areas. Reform of the Community Reinvestment Act regulations required banks to focus on performance—actual lending, investments, and services—rather than paperwork. Since 1993, conventional home mortgage lending to black Americans has increased by 67 percent, lending to Hispanic borrowers is up nearly 50 percent, and lending activity in low- and moderate-income communities has risen by 37 percent. The Administration also obtained $80 million in funding for Community Development Financial Institutions, which make investment capital and other financial products available to low- and moderate-income communities. The President's 1999 budget requests an additional $45 million for this program.

In addition, the President signed into law the "brownfields" program, which will provide tax incentives for the restoration of urban land contaminated by pollution. These incentives will leverage more than $6 billion for nationwide private sector cleanups and the redevelopment of 14,000 contaminated and abandoned sites in economically distressed urban areas.

Several basic principles inform these policies. First, they seek to equip communities with the tools they need in order to flourish—they are helping hands, not handouts. Second, they place the principal responsibility for community development with the communities themselves, because they are closest to their problems. Third, they emphasize private sector engagement rather than government mandates. And finally, they stress results over process: the Enterprise Communities/Empowerment Zones program, for example, gives communities broad scope to determine for themselves the best path for development; similarly, the reformed regulations implementing the Community Reinvestment Act use criteria based on actual outcomes to judge compliance with its provisions.

Strengthening the Performance of Domestic Markets

As part of this Administration's commitment to free and open markets, the Antitrust Division of the Department of Justice has worked together with the Federal Trade Commission to vigorously enforce the Nation's antitrust laws. Recent cases and investigations reveal that the Department of Justice and the Federal Trade Commission have both pursued an aggressive but balanced approach in enforcing antitrust law; in particular, both agencies have sought to ensure the continued growth and competitiveness of high-technology industries. . . .

Opening Foreign Markets

Progress was also made in 1997 toward opening foreign markets to U.S. goods, as a number of important international trade initiatives were made final. Trade agreements affecting three important sectors were reached, concluding some unfinished business from the Uruguay Round of multilateral negotiations. The first of these agreements, the Information Technology Agreement (ITA), will eliminate tariffs on a large array of information technology products, in which U.S. firms tend to be highly competitive. Also successfully concluded were an agreement covering financial services, which will foster broad liberalization of banking, securities, and insurance markets, and a key agreement to liberalize basic telecommunications services (including telephone services). . . .

These negotiations illustrate an important point about trade liberalization. Even though all three agreements involved sectors in which the United States is generally thought to have a competitive advantage, other countries were willing nevertheless to agree to their liberalization. They did so because they recognized that the entry of efficiently produced foreign products in these markets would improve the competitiveness of their own economies: securing goods of the highest quality at the lowest possible price is good for any economy.

Promoting an Economically Sound Environmental Agenda

The Administration took several important steps in 1997 to protect the environment. These included efforts to address global climate change and to improve air quality. In December representatives of the United States and some 160 other countries, meeting in Kyoto, Japan, agreed to establish binding limits on industrial countries' greenhouse gas emissions. These limits are intended to stem the disruptive effects of climate change by stabilizing atmospheric concentrations of greenhouse gases. (Because developing countries will emit an increasing share of global greenhouse gases, the President has indicated that the Kyoto agreement will not be submitted for ratification without meaningful developing-country participation.)

The Administration has proposed several market-based approaches to meeting the Kyoto limits. Domestically, tax incentives for energy-efficient technologies and research and development will spur early efforts to reduce emissions. A national system of tradable permits for greenhouse gas emissions, patterned after the successful permit trading program for sulfur dioxide emissions, will be implemented later under the President's proposal. In addition, the Kyoto agreement allows for trading in greenhouse gas emissions permits on an international scale, as well as opportunities for firms in the industrial countries to receive emissions credits for investing in climate-friendly technologies in developing countries. All of these efforts will help the United States attain its greenhouse gas emissions target in a cost-effective way.

In July 1997 the Environmental Protection Agency (EPA) issued a significantly more stringent standard for ground-level ozone and a new standard for fine particulate matter in the atmosphere. Although the Clean Air Act does not allow for the consideration of costs in setting these standards, under the President's policy the EPA must implement these health-based standards in a cost-effective manner. The Administration's plan for achieving the new air quality standards departs from traditional command-and-control approaches by designing regional strategies that will complement local efforts, and encouraging the development of trading programs for emissions of nitrogen oxides, which are ozone precursors. The nitrogen oxide trading program, like the acid rain program and the trading program envisioned for greenhouse gas emissions, enlists market incentives in controlling pollution and should reduce pollution more cheaply than do traditional regulatory approaches. . . .

Facing the Challenges Ahead

In many ways the U.S. economy today is very different from that in which our parents and grandparents lived and worked. Today, 24 percent of families are headed by a single parent, compared with 14 percent 25 years ago. And three in five married mothers with children under 6 are in the work force—twice as large a share as in 1970. This makes affordable, quality child care a pressing concern for most families. Meanwhile the nature of the labor market has changed significantly: few American workers expect to be working for the same employer—or even to be in the same career—when they retire. Industry has also changed radically: in the 1950s the information technology industry barely existed; today it employs a larger share of the labor force than the automobile industry did in the 1950s and 1960s. And the U.S. population is aging, implying that in the next century there will be fewer workers for every retiree.

This Administration's economic agenda is designed to deal with these changes and the challenges they pose. If the American economy is to maintain its preeminence as the strongest and most dynamic in the world, both policymakers and citizens will have to meet and overcome a number of challenges in the 21st century.

Several such challenges already loom large for this Administration and Congress. Perhaps the most important is preparing for the aging of the population, which requires reforming Medicare and Social Security and promoting retirement security more generally. As reported above, some progress was made in addressing Medicare's immediate problems, but comprehensive reforms are still needed to ensure the program's long-term viability. Likewise, steps will have to be taken to strengthen the finances of the Social Security system.

For almost 60 years Social Security has provided Americans with income security in retirement and protection against loss of family income due to disability or death. A large share of elderly Americans, particularly those with low incomes, rely on Social Security as their primary source of pension income in retirement. The system has enjoyed dramatic success in reducing poverty rates among older Americans. However, many Americans now fear that Social Security will not be there for them when they are ready to retire. This concern reflects the widespread recognition that, under current ``intermediate" projections of the Social Security trustees, the system faces a long-term funding gap: beginning in 2012, unless the system is reformed by then, the government will be unable to pay current Social Security benefits in full out of current payroll taxes; it will then have to draw down the system's trust fund, and by 2029 those funds will be exhausted. If still nothing has been done, the government would then face several options which it could adopt singly or in combination: it could reduce benefits until they are in line with collections, raise payroll taxes to cover an unchanged level of benefits, or finance the shortfall from other parts of the budget, by raising other taxes, cutting expenditures on other programs, or borrowing and allowing the budget deficit to increase. One or more of these measures will have to be taken so long as no changes are made to the present system.

Although the seriousness of the financial imbalance facing Social Security should not be downplayed, its magnitude is not so large as to be insurmountable, particularly if early action is taken. For example, even if nothing is done and the trust fund is exhausted, payroll taxes will still be sufficient to permanently finance roughly 75 percent of benefits. Put another way, the difference between the anticipated income and the anticipated expenditures of the Old Age, Survivors', and Disability Insurance program over the next 75 years amounts to around 2G percentage points of taxable payroll, or approximately 1 percent of GDP. (The imbalance is somewhat larger when viewed over a longer horizon.) These facts suggest that the problem of placing Social Security on a sound financial footing can admit of eventual resolution, and the President has proposed a process to devise an appropriate solution over the next 2 years. The President has also proposed that any budget surpluses should be reserved until Social Security reform is achieved.

Medicare reform presents a somewhat thornier problem, in terms of both its complexity and its scale. Unlike Social Security, Medicare promises not just the payment of a sum of money but the delivery of a service: health insurance. The government has little influence over the rate of increase in the cost of providing this service, which has been rising faster than general inflation for decades, largely driven by technological advances in medical care. Higher costs for medical care are projected to account for the bulk of the increase in Medicare expenditures for the next 25 years or so, after which the aging of the baby-boom generation will act to raise expenditures still further through increases in program enrollment. Hence, any long-term reform will have to involve slowing both the rise in health care prices and the growth in volume and intensity of use of covered services. Neither will be accomplished easily.

Before last year's budget legislation was enacted, the trust fund for the component of Medicare that covers hospital costs was projected to fall to zero in 2001. The 1997 reforms will delay the trust fund's depletion until 2010. The legislation also calls for the establishment of a bipartisan commission to assess and recommend the structural changes that will be needed to ensure Medicare's long-term viability. A second major policy challenge involves continuing the drive for more open international markets. Preferential trade agreements are being negotiated among countries around the world at a rapid pace, and the United States could easily be left behind through inaction. Since 1992, countries in Latin America and Asia have negotiated 20 preferential trade arrangements that exclude the United States. One of these is

MERCOSUR, a customs union among four South American countries. The European Union has begun a process intended to culminate in a free trade agreement with Brazil, Argentina, and the other MERCOSUR nations; the President of one European nation has even gone so far as to declare that the economic interests of Latin America lie with Europe, not the United States. Meanwhile the MERCOSUR nations are attempting to extend their preferential trade arrangement to the entire continent. It is clear that now, more than ever, continued engagement with the world trading system will require an active effort on the part of the United States.

In 1997 the Senate voted to move forward on extending the President's so-called fast-track negotiating authority. This authority allows the President to negotiate trade agreements and submit them to the Congress for a yes-or-no vote, without amendments. However, in the House of Representatives the vote to renew fast-track was postponed. Some have voiced concern that free trade hurts American workers and contributes to the U.S. trade deficit. . . . [M]arket-opening initiatives do not cause net job losses to the U.S. economy as a whole, although they do result in a reallocation of jobs into expanding, export-oriented industries. . . . [T]he jobs created by increased trade are good jobs, offering high pay. But some workers are indeed hurt by more open markets, just as some workers are harmed by technological innovation, even though market-opening initiatives unambiguously benefit the economy as a whole.

This Administration has realized from the beginning that the government can minimize the impact of dislocations affecting workers who lose their jobs, by speeding the adjustment process. For example, one of the key provisions of NAFTA involved monitoring those industries that were in danger of being adversely affected by the agreement, and the Administration committed itself early on to providing for dislocated workers through retraining programs. The President's 1999 budget includes proposals to expand the scope of trade adjustment assistance and to increase funding for these programs. More generally, the Administration's commitment to investing in people through education and training serves as a strong complement to its policy of trade liberalization.

A widespread misconception is that one of the benefits of increased trade comes in the form of an improved balance of trade. Economic policies do indeed affect the current account (the broad measure of U.S. international transactions that includes investment income and transfers as well as trade in goods and services), but it is budget, saving, and investment policies, not trade liberalization policies, that do so. The Nation's current account deficit equals its borrowing abroad to finance any excess of investment over domestic saving. The current account is therefore a macroeconomic phenomenon that mirrors the gap between what we as a Nation invest and what we save. The large Federal budget deficits of the 1980s and early 1990s were a form of negative saving, or dissaving, which reduced the total amount of national saving available to cover the Nation's investment in plant and equipment. In an important sense, the Nation was overconsuming in the 1980s, financing its consumption binge by borrowing from foreigners. The result was a large and persistent current account deficit.

We still have a current account deficit today, but for a very different reason. The near elimination of the budget deficit has left more saving available for investment in plant and equipment by the private sector. National saving has risen. But because of the investment boom during this expansion, the gap between investment and saving has persisted. Once again, this shortfall is made up by borrowing from abroad, and the result is a current account deficit. But there is a big difference between borrowing to invest—as the Nation is doing now—and borrowing to consume, as it did in the 1980s. In fact, running a trade deficit in order to expand the Nation's productive capacity is not new to American history—we did much the same thing in the last century, to build up the Nation's infrastructure, most notably during the railroad construction boom. Ironically, therefore, today's trade deficit reflects the economy's current success in growing more rapidly than our trading partners and investing so much—and not our free trade policies.

It is always difficult to explain this macroeconomic perspective on the trade deficit to those who are primarily concerned with the microeconomics of their daily lives. But making the case in favor of trade is particularly important now, because real danger threatens should countries turn their backs on a progressive and integrated world economic order. Besides postponing the renewal of the President's traditional trade-negotiating authority, the Congress chose not to support the sort of financial participation in international institutions that is vital for the sound functioning of the international system. Meanwhile financial crises in East Asia have made U.S. international engagement more important, rather than less. Other emerging-market countries are themselves in danger of reacting to the East Asian crises by turning inward. It is important for their economic well-being, as well as our own, that they continue along the path toward an outward-oriented market system, on which they had until recently been making such astonishing progress. This will require difficult macroeconomic and structural adjustments on their part, including reducing their dependence on foreign borrowing. As a result, these countries will have to reduce their trade deficits, and in some cases even turn them into trade surpluses. This will inevitably lead to an increase in U.S. bilateral trade deficits with some East Asian countries. Again, however, such deficits are not the proper gauge of the success or failure of U.S. trade policy.

The Nation faces other, broader challenges in shaping economic policies for the 21st century. First, we must act to help families address the problems they face in today's economy. More American workers today are faced with the need to juggle the demands of the workplace with the demands of family and home. Government must act to ease this burden by ensuring that families have access to quality child care and health care. For this reason the President's 1999 budget includes a $21 billion increase in funding for child care, to make it accessible to more families and raise its quality. An important part of this proposal is increased tax credits for 3 million working families to help them pay for child care, as well as an increase in block grants to

States that will directly subsidize child care for low-income families. In addition, the proposal calls for a new Early Learning Fund, along with support for the enforcement of State child care health and safety standards, scholarships for up to 50,000 child care providers per year, and funding for research and consumer education.

We must also continue to invest in our Nation's children. . . . [T]he last 3 years have witnessed notable improvements in children's well-being along several fronts, including decreases in child poverty, increases in consumption of basic health care services, and improvements in health status and in some measures of educational achievement. However, many children remain economically vulnerable. One in five children in the United States lives in a family whose income is below the poverty line, one in seven does not have access to health insurance, and a large proportion of children fail to achieve basic levels of proficiency in science, mathematics, and reading. . . .

Finally, this country's longstanding goal of achieving equality of opportunity among racial and ethnic groups has not yet been attained. . . . Although there has been progress in narrowing these gaps in the postwar period, it has been very uneven, with rapid progress in the 1960s and early 1970s followed by 20 years of stagnation from the early to mid-1970s to the early 1990s. For example, since the mid-1970s the wages of young black college graduates have fallen relative to those of their white counterparts. Although the current expansion has brought signs of renewed progress, substantial disparities in economic status persist. For example, the median wealth of white families is by some estimates 10 times that of black and Hispanic families. More needs to be done to promote equality of opportunity for all Americans. Many of the Administration's current and proposed policies, such as those that encourage community empowerment and education, are intended to address these disparities. And this Administration has pledged itself to furthering a dialogue on race in America.

Conclusion

The United States today enjoys some of the most favorable economic conditions in a generation: high growth and low unemployment combined with low and stable inflation. And the success of Americans in adapting to the new economy in which they find themselves has been truly remarkable. But that success—and the economy's present strength—cannot be taken for granted. Recent developments do not herald the end of inflation, the conquest of the business cycle, or the permanent reversal of such secular trends as weak productivity growth and rising income inequality. Rather, there are still long-term changes at work that demand action by individuals, businesses, and governments alike. This Administration has put in place a set of policies that has allowed the economy to grow and to flourish—in particular by putting the Nation's fiscal house in order. But we must continue to pursue sound policies aimed at opening markets at home and abroad, promoting private and public investment, and ensuring that all Americans, regardless of age or origin, have the skills they need to prosper in a world of change and opportunity.

GAO ON SOLVENCY OF
SOCIAL SECURITY SYSTEM
February 10, 1998

The complicated issue of financing Social Security came under renewed scrutiny in 1998 as President Bill Clinton used the prospect of budget surpluses to open discussions on ensuring the long-term solvency of the nation's public pension system. The system was in little danger of going broke in the near term, but for years experts had warned policymakers that unless something was done Social Security revenues would fall short of the program's benefit obligations when the baby-boom generation began to retire in large numbers in the twenty-first century. Apart from promising that Social Security would "be there" for retirees in the next century, policymakers had done little to heed the warnings, in large part because their choices either so polarized the political parties that no compromise seemed possible or were politically unacceptable to both parties.

Clinton seized the opportunity presented by the first projected federal budget surplus since 1969 to ask Congress to "save Social Security first" before enacting tax cuts or new spending programs. His request during the State of the Union address in January won sustained applause from both sides of the congressional aisle. To build momentum and a political base for action, the administration helped organize forums across the country to educate the public about the need to take action to secure the long-run future of Social Security. Commissioner of Social Security Kenneth S. Apfel said officials from the Social Security Administration had participated in more than 5,000 events and "media opportunities" by December 1998. (State of the Union, p. 38)

These efforts culminated in a White House Conference on Social Security held December 8–9 in Washington, D.C. President Clinton met behind closed doors with forty-eight legislators from both parties to begin to try to forge a consensus on the outlines of a plan for saving Social Security. Members of both parties reported that the meeting was "constructive" and largely without the partisan harshness that had infected so much of the legislative debate during the year. Despite the good will evident at the conference, the

98

administration and legislators were aware that long-standing differences between the parties and the impending impeachment proceedings against the president could jeopardize further efforts to stabilize Social Security financing.

A Complicated Problem

The most popular domestic program on the books, Social Security benefits went to about 44 million Americans, two-thirds of them retirees; the other one-third were survivors and dependents of deceased and disabled workers. Social Security was the sole source of income for 18 percent of all elderly Americans and the primary source for about two-thirds of them. The system was enacted in 1935 after millions of the elderly found themselves in poverty when their pensions and savings were wiped out during the Great Depression. Since its inception, Social Security had reduced the poverty rate among the elderly from more than one in three to a little more than one in ten.

The system was financed by a payroll tax, currently set at 12.4 percent of the first $68,400 of annual earned income (employees and their employers each paid 6.2 percent, while the self-employed paid the full 12.4 percent; employers and their workers each paid another 1.45 percent in payroll taxes to finance Medicare benefits). Social Security benefits were paid based on a lifetime earnings formula. Although the system taxed everyone at the same rate, the system was progressive in that low-income workers received higher benefits in proportion to their contributions than did high-income workers.

The long-term financing problem was largely a result of demographic trends. Social Security was a "pay-as-you-go" pension system, meaning that the taxes collected from current workers were used to pay benefits to current retirees. In 1998 the ratio of workers to beneficiaries was roughly three to one. The Social Security trust funds thus ran a surplus, which was invested in government securities and helped the government meet its operating expenses. But as life expectancy increased and the birth rate declined, that ratio began to shrink. By about 2020 when most of the baby boomers were likely to be retired, the ratio of workers to retirees was expected to be two to one. According to current projections, Social Security revenues were expected to exceed benefits until about 2013, when the system would then begin to use the trust funds to pay benefits. The trust funds were expected to be depleted by 2032, and revenues would be enough to pay only 70 to 75 percent of currently promised benefits.

Finding a Politically Acceptable Solution

In testimony February 10 before the Senate Special Committee on Aging, Jane L. Ross, director of Income Security Issues for the Health, Education, and Human Services Division of the General Accounting Office, outlined the options for dealing with the projected shortfall. These included increasing revenues and reducing expenditures by raising taxes, raising the retirement age, and reducing inflation adjustments—all options that Congress had exercised in 1983, just months before Social Security was projected to run short of funds. That agreement, which came only after years of partisan wrangling, followed the recommendations of a blue-ribbon bipartisan commission and raised payroll taxes, delayed a cost-of-living increase, and gradually raised retirement age from sixty-five to sixty-seven by the year 2027. (Social Security report, Historic Documents of 1983, p. 57)

The options exercised in 1983 seemed politically foreclosed in 1998. Clinton had virtually promised not to raise taxes, while Republicans were still painfully aware of the substantial losses they sustained at the polls in 1982 and 1986 when they tried to cut benefits. Explaining why the issue was so difficult politically, one senator noted that members still get asked about their votes from the 1980s.

Several of the proposals under consideration would change the structure of the program altogether. The most far-reaching and controversial of these were proposals to privatize a portion of the system, allowing or requiring individuals to invest a portion of their payroll taxes in the private market. It was thought that people might realize greater benefits under this option than they would with the current system. Variations of these personal investment accounts were supported by many Republicans and some Democrats, including Sen. Daniel Patrick Moynihan of New York and Sen. Bob Kerrey of Nebraska. "There is no more Democratic idea than building a generation of wealthy Americans who participate in our economy rather than feeling isolated from it," Kerrey said. Many businesses and their representatives, such as the U.S. Chamber of Commerce, the Business Roundtable, and the National Association of Manufacturers, supported private retirement accounts.

Opponents pointed out that a system of 150 million or so private accounts would be an administrative nightmare for business owners, investment advisers, and millions of Americans who might not understand their choices or want the burden of making investment decisions. Some also raised concerns that the lowest-income workers would have the least to invest and so might not have enough retirement income to meet their essential needs. Many Democrats both in and out of Congress were opposed to individual retirement accounts. The Rev. Jesse Jackson, for example, vowed to fight anyone—Democrat or Republican—who advocated individual accounts, saying that the only winners would be on Wall Street. The AFL-CIO, the National Association for the Advancement of Colored People, and the National Urban League announced on December 3 that they had formed a new coalition to oppose private accounts.

Another option was for the government to invest all or part of the Social Security trust funds in the stock market, with the hope of realizing higher returns than the funds now received from their investments in low-yielding government bonds. Skeptics contended that the risk of financial loss was too great and could jeopardize the national pension system. Others said that such investment could give the government too much control over private business. Former Social Security commissioner Robert M. Ball, who favored investing 40 percent of Social Security reserves in common stock by 2015, said that an independent, appointed board could take steps to minimize government interference. He also observed that the government would have little influence over any one stock if it were required to invest only in index funds—financial instruments that matched the holdings of a broad-based stock index, such as the Standard and Poor's 500. Even so, he acknowledged that if Congress started "fussing with the index, dropping firms that didn't have union contracts or something, that of course would defeat the whole plan."

Meeting with legislators from both parties on December 9, Clinton repeated his view that stock market investing should be part of the long-term financing solution, but he neither supported nor opposed individual accounts. Many legislators voiced optimism about the tone of the meeting. "It was a productive discussion that creates some momentum for us to move ahead," said Rep. Jim Kolbe, R-Ariz., a leading proponent of personal accounts.

> *Following is the text of testimony before the Senate Special Committee on Aging on February 10, 1998, by Jane L. Ross, director of income security issues for the Health, Education, and Human Services Division of the General Accounting Office, in which she set forth the options for restoring long-term solvency to the Social Security system:*

Social Security: Restoring Long-Term Solvency Will Require Difficult Choices

Mr. Chairman and Members of the Committee:

Thank you for inviting me to speak about the goals of the Social Security program and the difficult choices that restoring its long-term solvency will require. Social Security is the foundation of the nation's retirement income system. It provides 42 percent of all the income of the elderly, which is twice as much as any other single source. However, because of dramatic demographic changes, Social Security now faces a serious long-term financing shortfall.

Today, I would like to discuss five fundamental choices that Social Security reforms will reflect: (1) balancing income adequacy and individual equity, (2) determining who bears risks and responsibilities, (3) choosing among various benefit reductions and revenue increases, (4) using pay-as-you-go or advance funding, and (5) deciding how much to save and invest in the nation's productive capacity. My testimony is based on work we have done over the past few years.

Background

When Social Security was enacted in 1935, the nation was in the midst of the Great Depression. About half of the elderly depended on others for their livelihood, and roughly one-sixth received public charity. Many had lost their savings. Social Security was created to help ensure that the elderly would have adequate retirement incomes and would not have to depend on welfare. It would provide benefits that workers had earned because of their contributions and those of their employers.

When Social Security started paying benefits, it responded to an immediate need to bolster the income of the elderly. The Social Security benefits that early beneficiaries received significantly exceeded their contributions, but even the very first beneficiaries had made some contributions. Initially, funding Social Security benefits required relatively low payroll taxes because very few of the elderly had earned benefits under the new system. Increases in payroll taxes were always anticipated to keep up with the benefit payments as the system matured and more retirees received benefits. Virtually from the beginning, Social Security was financed on this type of pay-as-you-go basis, with any single year's revenues collected primarily to fund that year's benefits. The Congress had rejected the idea of advance funding for the program, or collecting enough revenues to cover future benefit rights as workers accrued them. Many expressed concern that if the federal government amassed huge reserve funds, it would find a way to spend them.

Over the years, both the size and scope of the program have changed, and periodic adjustments have been necessary. In 1939, coverage was extended to dependents and survivors. In the 1950s, state and local governments were given the option of covering their employees. The Disability Insurance program was added in 1956. Beginning in 1975, benefits were automatically tied to the Consumer Price Index to ensure that the purchasing power of benefits was not eroded by inflation. These benefit expansions led to higher payroll tax rates in addition to the increases stemming from the maturing of the system. Moreover, the long-term solvency of the program has been reassessed annually. Changes in demographic and economic projections have required benefit and revenue adjustments to maintain solvency, such as the amendments enacted in 1977 and 1983.

Profound demographic trends are now contributing to Social Security's long-term financing shortfall. As a share of the total U.S. population, the elderly population grew from 7 percent in 1940 to 13 percent in 1996; this share is expected to increase further to 20 percent by 2050. As it ages, the baby-boom generation will increase the size of the elderly population. However, other demographic trends are at least as important. Life expectancy has increased continually since the 1930s, and further improvements are expected. Moreover, the fertility rate has declined from 3.6 children per woman in 1960 to around 2 children per woman today and is expected to level off at about 1.9 by 2020. Combined, increasing life expectancy and falling fertility rates mean that fewer workers will be contributing to Social

Security for each aged, disabled, dependent, or surviving beneficiary. While 3.3 workers support each Social Security beneficiary today, only 2 workers are expected to be supporting each beneficiary by 2030.

As a result of these demographic trends, Social Security revenues are expected to be about 14 percent less than expenditures over the next 75-year period, and demographic trends suggest that this imbalance will grow over time. By 2030, the Social Security trust funds are projected to be depleted. From then on, Social Security revenues are expected to be sufficient to pay only about 70 to 75 percent of currently promised benefits, given currently scheduled tax rates and the Social Security Administration's (SSA) intermediate assumptions about demographic and economic trends. In 2031, the last members of the baby-boom generation will reach age 67, when they will be eligible for full retirement benefits under current law.

Restoring Social Security's long-term solvency will require some combination of increased revenues and reduced expenditures. A variety of options are available within the current structure of the program, such as raising the retirement age, reducing inflation adjustments, increasing payroll tax rates, and investing trust fund reserves in higher-yielding securities.

However, some proposals would go beyond restoring long-term solvency and would fundamentally alter the program structure by setting up individual retirement savings accounts and requiring workers to contribute to them. Retirement income from these accounts would usually replace a portion of Social Security benefits. Some proposals would attempt to produce a net gain in retirement income. The combination of mandated savings deposits and revised Social Security taxes would be greater than current Social Security taxes, in most cases.

Relative Emphasis Between Income Adequacy and Individual Equity

Helping ensure adequate retirement income has been a fundamental goal of Social Security. While Social Security was never intended to guarantee an adequate income, it provides an income base upon which to build. Virtually all reform proposals also pay some attention to "income adequacy," but some place a different emphasis on it relative to the goal of "individual equity," which seeks to ensure that benefits bear some relationship to contributions. Some proponents of reform believe that increasing the role of individual retirement savings could improve individual equity without diminishing income adequacy.

The current Social Security program seeks to ensure adequate retirement income in various ways. First, it makes participation mandatory, which guards against the possibility that some people would not otherwise save enough to have even a minimal retirement income. Reform proposals also generally make participation mandatory.

Second, the current Social Security benefit formula redistributes income from high earners to low earners to help keep low earners out of poverty. It accomplishes this by replacing a larger share of lifetime earnings for low earners and a smaller share for high earners. In addition, Social Security helps ensure adequate income by providing benefits for dependent and surviving spouses and children who may not have the work history required to earn adequate benefits. Also, it automatically ensures that the purchasing power of benefits keeps pace with inflation, unlike most employer pension plans or individually purchased annuities.

While the Social Security benefit formula seeks to ensure adequacy by redistributing income, it also promotes some degree of individual equity by ensuring that benefits are at least somewhat higher for workers with higher lifetime earnings.

In helping ensure adequate retirement income, Social Security has contributed to reducing poverty among the elderly. Since 1959, poverty rates for the elderly have dropped by two-thirds, from 35 percent to less than 11 percent in 1996. While they were higher than rates for children and for working-age adults (aged 18 to 64), they are now lower than for either group. For more than half the elderly, income other than Social Security was less than the poverty threshold in 1994.

While Social Security provides a strong foundation for retirement income, it is only a foundation. In 1994, it provided an average of roughly $9,200 to all elderly households. Median Social Security benefits have historically been very close to the poverty threshold. Elderly households with below-average income rely heavily on Social Security, which provided 80 percent of income for 40 percent of elderly households in 1994. One in seven elderly Americans has no income other than Social Security. Pockets of poverty remain. Women, minorities, and persons aged 75 and older are much more likely to be poor than other elderly persons. For example, compared with 11 percent for all elderly persons (aged 65 and older) in 1996, poverty rates were 23 percent for all elderly women living alone, roughly 25 percent for elderly blacks and Hispanics, and 31 percent for black women older than 75. Unmarried women make up more than 70 percent of poor elderly households, although they account for only 45 percent of all elderly households.

Proposals that would increase the extent to which workers save for their own retirement would reduce income redistribution because any contributions to individual accounts that would otherwise go to Social Security would not be available for redistribution. Still, proponents of individual accounts assert that virtually all retirees would be at least as well off as they are now and that such reforms would improve individual equity. Citing historical investment returns, they argue that the rates of return that workers could earn on their individual retirement savings would be much higher than the returns they implicitly earn under the current system and that their retirement incomes could be higher as a result. Nevertheless, earning such higher returns would require investing in riskier assets such as stocks. Income adequacy under such reforms would depend on how workers invest their savings and whether they actually earn higher returns. It would also depend on what degree of Social Security coverage and its income redistribution would remain after reform.

In addition to examining the effects of reform proposals on all retirees generally, attention should be paid to how they affect specific subpopulations, especially those that are most vulnerable to poverty, including women, widows, minorities, and the very old. Reform proposals vary considerably in their effects on such subpopulations. For example, since men and women typically have different earnings histories, life expectancies, and investment behaviors, reforms could exacerbate differences in benefits that already exist. An individual savings approach that permits little redistribution would on average generate smaller savings balances at retirement for women, who tend to have lower earnings from both employment and investments, and these smaller balances would need to last longer because women have longer life expectancies.

Who Bears Risk And Responsibility?

The balance between income adequacy and individual equity also influences how much risk and responsibility are borne by individuals and the government. Workers face a variety of risks regarding their retirement income security. These include individually based risks, such as how long they will be able to work, how long they will live, whether they will be survived by a spouse or other dependents, how much they will earn and save over their lifetimes, and how much they will earn on retirement savings. Workers also face some collective risks, such as the performance of the economy and the extent of inflation. Different types of retirement income embody different ways of assigning responsibility for these risks.

Social Security was based on a social insurance model in which the society as a whole through the government largely takes responsibility for all these risks to help ensure adequate income. This tends to minimize risks to the individuals and in the process lowers the rate of return they implicitly earn on their retirement contributions. Social Security provides a benefit that provides income to workers who become disabled and to workers who reach retirement, for as long as they live, and for their spouse and dependents. The government takes responsibility for collecting and managing the revenues needed to pay benefits. By redistributing income, Social Security helps protect workers against low retirement income that stems from low lifetime earnings.

Social Security pays a pension benefit that is determined by a formula that takes lifetime earnings into account. This type of pension is called a defined benefit pension. Many employer pensions are also defined benefit pensions. These pensions help smooth out variations in benefit amounts that can arise from year to year because of economic fluctuations. Defined benefit pension providers assume investment risks and some of the economic risks and take responsibility for investing and managing pension funds and ensuring that contributions are adequate to fund promised benefits. In contrast, defined contribution pensions, such as 401(k) accounts, base retirement income solely on the amount of contributions made and interest earned. Such pensions resemble individual savings.

Retirement savings by individuals place virtually all the risk and responsibility on individuals but give them greater freedom and control over their income. Under reform proposals that increase the role of individual savings, the government role would primarily be to make sure that workers contribute to their retirement accounts and to regulate the management of those accounts. Workers would be responsible for choosing how to invest their savings and would assume the investment and economic risks. Some proposals would allow workers to invest only in a limited number of "indexed" investment funds, which like some mutual funds are managed so they mirror the performance of market indexes like the Standard and Poor 500. Some proposals would require workers to buy an annuity at retirement, while others would place few restrictions on how workers use their funds in retirement.

Social Security places relatively greater emphasis on adequacy and less on individual equity by providing a way for all members of society to share all the risks. An individual retirement savings approach places relatively less emphasis on adequacy and more on individual equity by making retirement income depend more directly on each person's contributions and management of the funds. Reform proposals that would increase the role of individual savings would change the overall mix of different types of retirement income and with it the relative emphasis on adequacy and individual equity embodied by that mix.

In addition to changing the relative roles of Social Security and individual savings, such Social Security reform could indirectly affect other sources of retirement income and related public policies. For example, raising Social Security's retirement age or cutting its benefit amounts could affect employer pensions. Some employers pay supplements to their pensions until retirees start to receive Social Security income, or they set their pension benefits relative to Social Security's. Employers might terminate their pension plans rather than pay increased costs. Reforms would also interact with other income support programs such as Social Security's Disability Insurance or the Supplemental Security Income public assistance program. For example, raising the retirement age could lead more older workers to apply for Social Security's disability benefits because those benefits would be greater than retirement benefits, if they qualify.

Reducing Benefits or Increasing Revenues?

No matter what shape Social Security reform takes, restoring long-term solvency will require some combination of benefit reductions and revenue increases. Within the current program structure, examples of possible benefit reductions include modifying the benefit formula, raising the retirement age, and reducing cost-of-living adjustments. Revenue increases might take the form of increases in the payroll tax rate, expanding coverage to include the relatively few workers who are still not covered under Social Security, or allowing the trust funds to be invested in potentially higher-yielding securities such as stocks. Reforms that increase the role of individual retirement savings would also involve Social Security benefit reductions or revenue increases, which might take slightly different forms. For example, such reforms might include Social Security benefit reductions to offset any contributions that are diverted from the current program or permitting workers to invest their retirement savings in stocks.

The choice among various benefit reductions and revenue increases will affect the balance between income adequacy and individual equity. Benefit reductions could pose the risk of diminishing adequacy, especially for specific subpopulations. Both benefit reductions and tax increases that have been proposed could diminish individual equity by reducing the implicit rates of return the workers earn on their contributions to the system. In contrast, increasing revenues by investing retirement funds in the stock market could improve rates of return. The choice among various benefit reductions and revenue increases—for example, raising the retirement age—will ultimately determine not just how much income retirees will have but also how long they will be expected to continue working and how long their retirements will be. Reforms will determine how much consumption workers will give up during their working years to provide for more consumption during retirement.

Pay-as-You-Go or Advance Funding?

Reform proposals have also raised the issue of increasing the degree to which the nation sets aside funds to pay for future Social Security benefits. Advance funding could reduce payroll tax rates in the long term and improve intergenerational equity but would involve significant transition costs. As noted earlier, Social Security is largely financed on a pay-as-you-go basis. In a pure pay-as-you-go arrangement, virtually all revenues come from payroll taxes since trust funds are kept to a relatively small contingency reserve that earns relatively little interest compared with the interest that a fully funded system would earn.

In contrast, defined benefit employer pensions are generally fully advance funded. As workers accrue future pension benefit rights, employers make pension fund contributions that are projected to cover them. The pension funds accumulate substantial assets that contribute a large share of national saving. The investment earnings on these funds contribute considerable revenues and reduce the size of pension fund contributions that would otherwise be required to pay pension benefits.

Defined contribution pensions and individual retirement savings are fully funded by definition, and investment earnings on these retirement accounts also help provide retirement income. Similarly, Social Security reform proposals that increase the role of individual retirement savings would generally increase advance funding.

Advance funding is possible in the public sector simply by collecting more revenue than is necessary to pay current benefits. However, advance funding in the public sector raises issues that prompted the Congress to reject advance funding in designing Social Security. A fully funded Social Security program would have trust funds worth trillions of dollars. If the trust funds were invested in private securities, some people would be concerned about the influence that government could have on the private sector. If these funds were invested only in federal government securities, as is required under current law, taxpayers would eventually pay both interest and principal to the trust funds and ultimately cover the full cost of Social Security benefits. Moreover, the effect of advance funding in the public sector fundamentally depends on whether the government as a whole is increasing national saving, as discussed further below.

If Social Security reforms increase the balances in privately held retirement funds, interest on those funds could eventually help finance retirement income and reduce the system's reliance on Social Security payroll contributions, which in turn would improve individual equity. At the same time, the relatively larger generation of current workers could finance some of their future benefits now rather than leaving a relatively smaller future generation of workers with the entire financing responsibility. In effect, advance funding shifts responsibility for retirement income from the children of one generation of retirees to that retiree generation itself.

However, larger payroll contributions would be required in the short term to build up those fund balances. Social Security would still need revenues to pay benefits that retirees and current workers have already been promised. The contributions needed to fund both current and future retirement liabilities would clearly be higher than those currently collected.

Thus, increasing advance funding in any form involves substantial transition costs as workers are expected to cover some portion of both the existing unfunded liability and the liability for their own future benefits. Reform proposals handle this transition in a variety of ways, and the transition costs can be spread out across one or several generations. The nature of specific reform proposals will determine the pace at which advance funding is increased. For example, one proposal would increase payroll taxes by 1.52 percent for 72 years to fund the transition and would involve borrowing $2 trillion from the public during the first 40 years of the transition to help cover the unfunded liability.

Saving and Investing for Productivity Growth

Ideally, Social Security reforms would help address the fundamental economic implications of the demographic trends that underlie Social Security's financing problems. Although people are living longer and healthier lives, they have also been retiring earlier and have been having smaller families. Unless these patterns change, relatively fewer workers will be producing goods and services for a society with relatively more retirees. Economic growth, and more specifically growth in labor productivity, could help ease the strains of providing for a larger elderly population. Increased investment in physical and human capital should generally increase productivity and economic growth, but investment depends on national saving, which has been at historically low levels.

Recognizing these economic fundamentals, proponents of increasing the role of individual retirement savings generally observe that a pay-as-you-go financing structure does little to help national saving, and they argue that the advance funding through individual accounts would increase saving. However, reforms would not produce notable increases in national saving to the extent that workers reduce their other saving in the belief that their new accounts can take its place.

Social Security reforms might also increase national saving within the current program structure. Advance funding would increase saving, and it could be applied to government-controlled trust funds as well as to individual accounts. Any additional Social Security savings in the federal budget could add to national saving but only if not offset by deficits in the rest of the federal budget. More broadly, overall federal budget surpluses or deficits affect national saving since they represent saving or dissaving by the government.

To the extent that reforms attempt to increase national saving, they will vary by how much emphasis they place on doing so through individual or government saving. That emphasis will reflect not only judgments about which is likely to be more effective but also values regarding the responsibilities of individuals and governments and attitudes toward the national debt. While these points will be much debated, few dispute the need to be aware of the effect of increasing national saving, although it may be hard to achieve.

Observations

In some form and to varying degrees, every generation of children has supported its parents' generation in old age. In economic terms, those who do work ultimately produce the goods and services consumed by those who do not. The Social Security system and, more broadly, the nation's retirement income policies, whatever shape they take, ultimately determine how and to what extent the nation supports the well-being of the elderly.

Restoring Social Security's long-term solvency presents complex and important choices. These choices include how reforms will balance income adequacy and individual equity; how risks are shared as a community or assumed by individuals; how reforms assign roles and responsibilities among government, employers, and individuals; whether retirements will start earlier or later and how large retirement incomes will be; and how much the nation saves and invests in its capacity to produce goods and services. Whatever reforms are adopted will reflect these fundamental choices implicitly, if not explicitly. . . .

March

NASA FINDINGS ON MOON ICE
March 5, 1998

A U.S. spacecraft provided the first solid evidence during 1998 that water—in the form of ice—exists on the Moon. A satellite orbiting close to the Moon sent information back to Earth enabling scientists to determine that billions of tons of water was frozen at the Moon's north and south poles.

A Pentagon satellite in 1996 had found evidence that led scientists to speculate about the presence of ice on the Moon. Largely in response to those findings, the National Aeronautics and Space Administration (NASA) in January 1998 launched a satellite called the Lunar Prospector *to take a closer look.* Prospector *began sending back information almost immediately and was expected to continue orbiting the Moon for about one year before running out of fuel and crash-landing on the lunar surface.*

Previous Lunar Theories and Explorations

School children may have believed the Moon was made of green cheese, but for many years scientists thought they knew better: the Moon was rocky, cratered, airless, and totally arid. All lunar temperatures were extremes, ranging from nearly 300 degrees below zero Fahrenheit in dark areas to about 250 degrees above zero Fahrenheit at the lunar equator facing the sun.

U.S. and Soviet lunar explorations starting in the mid-1960s—including the American manned lunar landings starting in 1969—tended to confirm the view that the Moon had absolutely no resources to support life of any kind. Those explorations left many questions unanswered, among them: How was the Moon formed and how has it evolved over time? Exactly what material is the Moon made of? Why is the Moon's surface crust much thicker in some places than others?

A Pentagon satellite, named Clementine, *raised interesting questions in 1996, when it sent back data suggesting that the Moon was not totally dry, as most scientists had thought. Using radar,* Clementine *found indications that craters near the Moon's south pole contained ice. (*Clementine findings, Historic Documents of 1996, p. 472)

To check out Clementine's *findings in more detail, NASA developed* Lunar Prospector, *a relatively low-cost project (totaling $63 million) launched on January 6, 1998. Prospector was equipped with five instruments to study the composition of the Moon's surface. The satellite orbited sixty-three miles above the lunar surface until December 19, when mission controllers lowered the orbit to about twenty miles above the surface. Plans called for the satellite to descend to about six miles above the surface early in 1999 for closer studies before crashing onto the Moon. In a tribute to a man revered by many people in the NASA program, the satellite carried a small sample of the ashes of famed astronomer Eugene Shoemaker, who had helped train the Apollo astronauts and had died in an automobile accident in 1997.*

NASA on March 5 announced the first results from Prospector's *findings. Using its neutron spectrometer, the craft had measured evidence of hydrogen, leading scientists to believe that a sizable amount of water was frozen in the areas of the two lunar poles. NASA gave preliminary estimates that the lunar soil could contain between eleven million tons and 330 million tons of water ice spread over a total area about 25,000 square miles at the two poles. Most of the ice likely was contained within the rocky lunar soil (called* regolith*), in very thin concentrations. Alan B. Binder, of the Lunar Research Institute in California and the chief scientists for the mission, said the* Prospector *data had provided the "first unquestionable results" demonstrating that water was present on the Moon. Scientists said it was likely that water reached the moon through the impact of comets, which are essentially giant balls of ice and rock.*

Six months later, on September 3, NASA issued a second statement reporting that scientists had revised upwards their estimates of the amount of water ice present on the lunar surface. Based on additional data from the Prospector *satellite, scientists estimated that the lunar soil might contain up to six billion tons of water ice.*

"Growing evidence now suggests that water ice deposits of relatively high concentrations are trapped beneath the soil in the permanently shadowed craters of both lunar polar regions," the September 3 NASA statement said. Binder said additional data and analysis led NASA scientists to believe that there were layers of "near-pure water ice" lying beneath as much as eighteen inches of lunar soil near the poles.

What the Findings Meant

In the March 3 NASA report, Wesley Huntress, the agency's associate administrator for space science, was quoted as saying that Prospector's *finding of ice was "primarily of scientific interest at this time" because it provided new information on such questions as the history and evolution of the solar system. Such statements, however, did not prevent widespread speculation about whether astronauts might one day be able to make use of the lunar ice.*

Scientists working for NASA and other institutions said the moon's ice might eventually be useful in two ways. The ice could be used in any attempt to colonize the moon—even if for brief scientific observations. In addition, future astronauts could extract the hydrogen from the ice to make rocket fuel for their exploration of the solar system. Either way, tapping the moon's water supplies would eliminate the enormous costs of shipping water or rocket fuel from Earth. The major obstacle to making use of the Moon's ice was the extraordinarily low temperatures at the lunar poles; as of the end of the twentieth century, there was no technology capable of extracting water from ice when the surrounding temperature was nearly 300 degrees below zero Fahrenheit.

Locating Distant Planets

Also during 1998, astronomers reported findings of potential significance for understanding the role of planets in the universe. On April 21, two independent teams of astronomers—working at telescopes in Chile and Hawaii—reported evidence of planets forming around a star in the constellation Centaurus. The astronomers observed a disk of gas and dust surrounding the star HR 4796, approximately 1,300 trillion miles from Earth. The astronomers said this disk appeared to be the initial phase of the formation of planets, similar to what the Earth's solar system went through billions of years of ago.

On May 28, astronomers working with NASA's Hubble Space Telescope published an image that they said showed a planet near two stars in the constellation Taurus. The astronomers said they believed the image was the first ever of a planet outside the solar system. Most scientists had long assumed that planets had developed around stars other than the Sun, and several possible planetary systems had been detected in previous years, but no one had ever captured an image of an existing planet beyond the solar system. Susan Tereby, of the Extrasolar Research Corp. in Pasadena, California, said the object assumed to be a planet (named TMR-1C) may have been formed about the same time as the two stars around which it orbited. The planet was speeding away from the stars at a rate of about twelve miles per second, leading scientists to conclude it had been forced away by the gravitational effect of the stars.

> *Following is the text of a statement, "Lunar Prospector Finds Evidence of Ice at Moon's Poles," released on March 5, 1998, by the National Aeronautic and Space Administration (NASA), followed by the text of a statement, "Latest Lunar Prospector Findings Indicate Larger Amounts of Polar Water Ice," released by NASA on September 3, 1998:*

NASA STATEMENT OF MARCH 5

There is a high probability that water ice exists at both the north and south poles of the Moon, according to initial scientific data returned by NASA's *Lunar Prospector.*

The Discovery Program mission also has produced the first operational gravity map of the entire lunar surface, which should serve as a fundamental reference for all future lunar exploration missions, project scientists announced today at NASA's Ames Research Center, Moffett Field, CA.

Just two months after the launch of the cylindrical spacecraft, mission scientists have solid evidence of the existence of lunar water ice, including estimates of its volume, location and distribution. "We are elated at the performance of the spacecraft and its scientific payload, as well as the resulting quality and magnitude of information about the Moon that we already have been able to extract," said Dr. Alan Binder, Lunar Prospector Principal Investigator from the Lunar Research Institute, Gilroy, CA.

The presence of water ice at both lunar poles is strongly indicated by data from the spacecraft's neutron spectrometer instrument, according to mission scientists. Graphs of data ratios from the neutron spectrometer "reveal distinctive 3.4 percent and 2.2 percent dips in the relevant curves over the northern and southern polar regions, respectively," Binder said. "This is the kind of data 'signature' one would expect to find if water ice is present."

However, the Moon's water ice is not concentrated in polar ice sheets, mission scientists cautioned. "While the evidence of water ice is quite strong, the water 'signal' itself is relatively weak," said Dr. William Feldman, co-investigator and spectrometer specialist at the Department of Energy's Los Alamos National Laboratory, NM. "Our data are consistent with the presence of water ice in very low concentrations across a significant number of craters." Using models based on other *Lunar Prospector* data, Binder and Feldman predict that water ice is confined to the polar regions and exists at only a 0.3 percent to 1 percent mixing ratio in combination with the Moon's rocky soil, or regolith.

How much lunar water ice has been detected? Assuming a water ice depth of about a foot and a half (.5 meters)—the depth to which the neutron spectrometer's signal can penetrate—Binder and Feldman estimate that the data are equivalent to an overall range of 11 million to 330 million tons (10–300 million metric tons) of lunar water ice, depending upon the assumptions of the model used. This quantity is dispersed over 3,600 to 18,000 square miles (10,000–50,000 square kilometers) of water ice-bearing deposits across the northern pole, and an additional 1,800 to 7,200 square miles (5,000–20,000 square kilometers) across the southern polar region. Furthermore, twice as much of the water ice mixture was detected by *Lunar Prospector* at the Moon's north pole as at the south.

Dr. Jim Arnold of the University of California at San Diego previously has estimated that the most water ice that could conceivably be present on the Moon as a result of meteoritic and cometary impacts and other processes is 11 billion to 110 billion tons. The amount of lunar regolith that could have been "gardened" by all impacts in the past 2 billion years extends to a depth of about 6.5 feet (2 meters), he found. On that basis, *Lunar Prospector's* estimate of water ice would have to be increased by a factor of up to four, to the range of 44 million to 1.3 billion tons (40 million to 1.2 billion metric tons). In actuality,

Binder and Feldman caution that, due to the inadequacy of existing lunar models, their current estimates "could be off by a factor of ten in either direction."

The earlier joint Defense Department-NASA Clementine mission to the Moon used a radar-based technique that detected ice deposits in permanently shadowed regions of the lunar south pole. It is not possible to directly compare the results from *Lunar Prospector* to *Clementine* because of their fundamentally different sensors, measurement "footprints," and analysis techniques. However, members of the Clementine science team concluded that its radar signal detected from 110 million to 1.1 billion tons (100 million to 1 billion metric tons) of water ice, over an upper area limit of 5,500 square miles (15,500 square kilometers) of south pole terrain.

There are various ways to estimate the economic potential of the detected lunar water ice as a supporting resource for future human exploration of the Moon. One way is to estimate the cost of transporting that same volume of water ice from Earth to orbit. Currently, it costs about $10,000 to put one pound of material into orbit. NASA is conducting technology research with the goal of reducing that figure by a factor of 10, to only $1,000 per pound. Using an estimate of 33 million tons from the lower range detected by *Lunar Prospector*, it would cost $60 trillion to transport this volume of water to space at that rate, with unknown additional cost of transport to the Moon's surface.

From another perspective, a typical person consumes an estimated 100 gallons of water per day for drinking, food preparation, bathing and washing. At that rate, the same estimate of 33 million tons of water (7.2 billion gallons) could support a community of 1,000 two-person households for well over a century on the lunar surface, without recycling.

"This finding by *Lunar Prospector* is primarily of scientific interest at this time, with implications for the rate and importance of cometary impacts in the history and evolution of the Solar System," said Dr. Wesley Huntress, NASA Associate Administrator for Space Science. "A cost-effective method to mine the water crystals from within this large volume of soil would have to be developed if it were to become a real resource for drinking water or as the basic components of rocket fuel to support any future human explorers."

Before the Lunar Prospector mission, historical tracking data from various NASA Lunar Orbiter and Apollo missions had provided evidence that the lunar gravity field is not uniform. Mass concentrations caused by lava which filled the Moon's huge craters are known to be the cause of the anomalies. However, precise maps of lunar mass concentrations covering the moon's equatorial nearside region were the only ones available.

Lunar Prospector has dramatically improved this situation, according to co-investigator Dr. Alex Konopliv of NASA's Jet Propulsion Laboratory, Pasadena, CA. Telemetry data from *Lunar Prospector* has been analyzed to produce a full gravity map of both the near and far side of the moon. Konopliv also has identified two new mass concentrations on the Moon's nearside that will be used to enhance geophysical modeling of the lunar interior. This work has produced the first-ever complete engineering-quality gravity map of the moon, a key to the operational safety and fuel-efficiency of future lunar missions.

"This spacecraft has performed beyond all reasonable expectations," said NASA's Lunar Prospector mission manager Scott Hubbard of Ames. "The findings announced today are just the tip of the iceberg compared to the wealth of information forthcoming in the months and years ahead."

Lunar Prospector is scheduled to continue its current primary data gathering mission at an altitude of 62 miles (100 kilometers) for a period of ten more months. At that time, the spacecraft will be put into an orbit as low as six miles (10 kilometers) so that its suite of science instruments can collect data at much finer resolution in support of more detailed scientific studies. In addition, surface composition and structure information developed from data returned by the spacecraft's Gamma Ray Spectrometer instrument will be a crucial aspect of additional analysis of the polar water ice finding over the coming months.

The third launch in NASA's Discovery Program of lower cost, highly focused planetary science missions, *Lunar Prospector* is being implemented for NASA by Lockheed Martin, Sunnyvale, CA, with mission management by NASA Ames. The total cost to NASA of the mission is $63 million.

NASA STATEMENT OF SEPTEMBER 3

The north and south poles of the Moon may contain up to six billion metric tons of water ice, a more than ten-fold increase over previous estimates, according to scientists working with data from NASA's Lunar Prospector mission.

Growing evidence now suggests that water ice deposits of relatively high concentration are trapped beneath the soil in the permanently shadowed craters of both lunar polar regions. The researchers believe that alternative explanations, such as concentrations of hydrogen from the solar wind, are unlikely.

Mission scientists also report the detection of strong, localized magnetic fields; delineation of new mass concentrations on the surface; and the mapping of the global distribution of major rock types, key resources and trace elements. In addition, there are strong suggestions that the Moon has a small, iron-rich core. The new findings are published in the Sept. 4 issue of *Science* magazine.

"The Apollo program gave us an excellent picture of the Moon's basic structure and its regional composition, along with some hints about its origin and evolution," said Dr. Carl Pilcher, science director for Solar System exploration in NASA's Office of Space Science, Washington, DC. "*Lunar Prospector* is now expanding that knowledge into a global perspective. The indications of water ice at the poles are tantalizing and likely to spark spirited debate among lunar scientists."

In March, mission scientists reported a water signal with a minimum abundance of one percent by weight of water ice in rocky lunar soil (regolith) corresponding to an estimated total of 300 million metric tons of ice at the Moon's poles. "We based those earlier, conscientiously conservative estimates on graphs of neutron spectrometer data, which showed distinctive dips over the lunar polar regions," said Dr. Alan Binder of the Lunar Research Institute, Gilroy, CA, the Lunar Prospector principal investigator. "This indicated significant hydrogen enrichment, a telltale signature of the presence of water ice.

"Subsequent analysis, combined with improved lunar models, shows conclusively that there is hydrogen at the Moon's poles," Binder said. "Though other explanations are possible, we interpret the data to mean that significant quantities of water ice are located in permanently shadowed craters in both lunar polar regions."

"The data do not tell us definitively the form of the water ice," Binder added. "However, if the main source is cometary impacts, as most scientists believe, our expectation is that we have areas at both poles with layers of near-pure water ice." In fact, the new analysis "indicates the presence of discrete, confined, near-pure water ice deposits buried beneath as much as 18 inches (40 centimeters) of dry regolith, with the water signature being 15 percent stronger at the Moon's north pole than at the south."

How much water do scientists believe they have found? "It is difficult to develop a numerical estimate," said Dr. William Feldman, co-investigator and spectrometer specialist at the Department of Energy's Los Alamos National Laboratory, NM. "However, we calculate that each polar region may contain as much as three billion metric tons of water ice."

Feldman noted he had cautioned that earlier estimates "could be off by a factor of ten," due to the inadequacy of existing lunar models. The new estimate is well within reason, he added, since it is still "one to two orders of magnitude less than the amount of water predicted as possibly delivered to, and retained on, the Moon by comets," according to earlier projections by Dr. Jim Arnold of the University of California at San Diego.

In other results, data from *Lunar Prospector's* gamma ray spectrometer have been used to develop the first global maps of the Moon's elemental composition. The maps delineate large compositional variations of thorium, potassium and iron over the lunar surface, providing insights into the Moon's crust as it was formed. The distribution of thorium and potassium on the Moon's near side supports the idea that some portion of materials rich in these trace elements was scattered over a large area as a result of ejection by asteroid and comet impacts.

While its magnetic field is relatively weak and not global in nature like those of most planets, the Moon does contain magnetized rocks on its upper surface, according to data from *Lunar Prospector's* magnetometer and electron reflectometer. The resultant strong, local magnetic fields create the two smallest known magnetospheres in the Solar System.

"The Moon was previously interpreted as just an unmagnetized body without a major effect on what is going on in the solar wind," explained Dr. Mario

Acuna, a member of the team located at NASA's Goddard Space Flight Center, Greenbelt, MD. "We are discovering that there is nothing simple about the Moon as an obstacle to this continuous flow of electrically charged gas from the Sun."

These mini-magnetospheres are located diametrically opposite to large impact basins on the lunar surface, leading scientists to conclude that the magnetic regions formed as the result of these titanic impacts. One theory is that these impacts produced a cloud of electrically charged gas that expanded around the Moon in about five minutes, compressing and amplifying the pre-existing, primitive ambient magnetic field on the opposite side. This field was then "frozen" into the surface crust and retained as the Moon's then-molten core solidified and the global field vanished.

Using data from *Prospector's* doppler gravity experiment, scientists have developed the first precise gravity map of the entire lunar surface. In the process, they have discovered seven previously unknown mass concentrations, lava-filled craters on the lunar surface known to cause gravitational anomalies. Three are located on the Moon's near side and four on its far side. This new, high-quality information will help engineers determine the long-term, altitude-related behavior of lunar-orbiting spacecraft, and more accurately assess fuel needs for possible future Moon missions.

Finally, *Lunar Prospector* data suggests that the Moon has a small, iron-rich core approximately 186 miles (300 kilometers) in radius, which is toward the smaller end of the range predicted by most current theories. "This theory seems to best fit the available data and models, but it is not a unique fit," cautioned Binder. "We will be able to say much more about this when we get magnetic data related to core size later in the mission." Ultimately, a precise figure for the core size will help constrain models of how the Moon originally formed. . . .

ROMAN CATHOLIC CHURCH ON THE HOLOCAUST
March 16, 1998

Attempting to close wounds that were still festering a half-century after World War II, the Roman Catholic Church on March 16 issued a "repentance" for the roles played by Christians during the Holocaust, or "Shoah." The church acknowledged that some of its "sons and daughters" had participated in the slaughter of six million Jews by Nazi Germany and its allies. The church added that many Christians did not act or speak forcefully enough to try to halt the Nazi drive to exterminate the Jews.

The church's statement on the Holocaust came in a report, "We Remember: A Reflection on the Shoah," produced by the Pontifical Commission for Religious Relations with the Jews. The commission, headed by Australian cardinal Edward Idris Cassidy, had worked on the report for nearly eleven years.

Jewish leaders generally welcomed the church's acknowledgment of Christian complicity in the Holocaust. However, many leaders of Jewish religious and civic organizations expressed disappointment that the commission rejected claims that Catholic teachings may have helped foster the atmosphere in which the Nazi reign of terror developed.

The Vatican report was the latest in a series of apologies stemming from the events of World War II and its aftermath. In 1995, the fiftieth anniversary of the end of the war, the Japanese government apologized for the suffering caused by its aggression, French president Jacques Chirac apologized for French complicity in the forced deportation of thousands of Jews during the war, and President Clinton apologized to the survivors of radiation experiments conducted by the U.S. government from 1944 to 1974. (Japanese apology, Historic Documents of 1995, p. 302; Chirac apology, Historic Documents of 1995, p. 478; Clinton apology, Historic Documents of 1995, p. 633)

The Commission and Its Report

Pope John Paul II appointed the commission and gave it several assignments, including writing a report on the history of relations between

Catholics and Jews during the Holocaust. John Paul, who as a young man experienced the Nazi occupation of his Polish homeland, had taken numerous steps to reconcile his church with the Jewish people. He became the first pope to visit a Jewish synagogue, and he established diplomatic relations between the Vatican and Israel. John Paul's creation of the commission was widely seen as one effort to clear away a dark spot in church history before celebrating the official "Jubilee" marking the dawn of the third millennium after the birth of Christ.

While the commission was working on its report, church officials at lower levels issued statements repenting for Christian complicity in the Holocaust. Among the strongest in this regard were statements in 1995 from the conference of Roman Catholic bishops in Germany and in 1997 from their colleagues in France. The French bishops specifically asked Jews to forgive Catholics.

Cardinal Cassidy and fellow members of the commission released their report March 16 at a news conference at the Vatican. Preceding the report was a brief letter from John Paul expressing hope that it "will indeed help to heal the wounds of past misunderstandings and injustices."

The report was divided into five sections. The first four recalled the "tormented" history of relations between Christians and Jews and the terrors of the Holocaust. The fifth section appealed for a "new relationship" between Christians and Jews in the future.

In its historical review, the commission acknowledged that the overall balance of relations between Christians and Jews during the previous two millennia "has been quite negative." Until the end of the eighteenth century, the commission said, many Christian-led countries actively discriminated against Jews and often treated them brutally. During the nineteenth century, Jews won political and civic rights in some Christian-led countries—but at the same time nationalist forces in those countries developed "anti-Judaism" theories that eventually led to the Nazi attempt to destroy the Jews.

At this point in its report, the commission drew a distinction between the actions of the Roman Catholic Church and of individual Christians. Church teachings emphasized the "unity of the human race" and church leaders condemned Nazi racism, the commission said, citing a series of statements throughout the 1930s. At the same time, the commission said, individual Christians (as well as those repudiating Christian teachings) were among those who adopted the Nazi's anti-Semitic views and carried out the Holocaust.

Many Christians acted to help save the Jews, the commission said. It cited in particular Pope Pius XII, who after becoming pope in 1939 took steps "to save hundreds of thousands of Jewish lives." The commission noted statements of praise for Pope Pius XII made by Jewish leaders after the war, including a eulogy at the time of his death in 1958 by Golda Meir, later a prime minister of Israel.

In the closing section of its report, the commission expressed the hope that an "act of repentance" by the church would help heal the past breach between Christians and Jews. The memory of the Holocaust should serve as a warning that "the spoiled seeds of anti-Judaism and anti-Semitism must never again be allowed to take root in any human heart."

Jewish Reaction

Jewish leaders generally praised the Catholic Church for attempting to confront the role of Christians in allowing the Holocaust to occur. Several Jewish leaders said the commission statement could serve as an important element of church teaching. Robert S. Rifkind, president of the American Jewish Committee, said the report was "a step in the right direction for the future of Catholic-Jewish relations."

However, Rifkind and other Jewish leaders—along with numerous independent commentators in the media and other organizations—criticized the report as falling short on two issues. First, the American Jewish Committee said the church statement "did not go far enough in exploring the role of historic anti-Semitic church teachings in setting the stage for the Holocaust." Second, several Jewish groups said the church statement did not provide a full accounting for the church's failure to act more aggressively against Nazi tyranny. Many of these critics focused particularly on Pope Pius XII who, they said, failed to speak out forcefully against the Holocaust. Criticism of that pope's role had been sparked by the 1963 premiere of a controversial play about the Holocaust, "The Deputy," written by Rolf Hochhuth.

Several church officials said one purpose of the commission report was to counter the widespread view of Pope Pius XII generated by the Hochhuth play. The pope worked behind the scenes to oppose the Holocaust, they said, adding that a more assertive public role might have been counterproductive. Numerous Jewish groups called on the Vatican to open its archives so independent scholars could examine material dealing with the Holocaust in general and Pope Pius's response to it.

A coalition of Jewish groups drafted a unified response to the church report, but the response was not released in 1998. A draft response was prepared by the International Committee on Inter-religious Consultations, which served as a liaison to the Vatican on behalf of major international Jewish groups. According to press reports, the draft said the church report was disappointing because it played down the importance of anti-Semitic teachings by Christians.

Following is the text of "We Remember: A Reflection on the Shoah," a document prepared by the Pontifical Commission for Religious Relations with the Jews and released by the Vatican on March 16, 1998; the report is preceded by a letter to the commission chairman from Pope John Paul II:

PAPAL LETTER

To my venerable brother, Cardinal Edward Idris Cassidy,

On numerous occasions during my pontificate I have recalled with a sense of deep sorrow the sufferings of the Jewish people during the Second World War. The crime which has become known as the Shoah remains an indelible stain on the history of the century that is coming to a close.

As we prepare for the beginning of the third millennium of Christianity, the church is aware that the joy of a jubilee is above all the joy that is based on the forgiveness of sins and reconciliation with God and neighbor. Therefore she encourages her sons and daughters to purify their hearts, through repentance of past errors and infidelities. She calls them to place themselves humbly before the Lord and examine themselves on the responsibility which they, too, have for the evils of our time.

It is my fervent hope that the document, "We Remember: A Reflection on the Shoah," which the Commission for Religious Relations with the Jews has prepared under your direction, will indeed help to heal the wounds of past misunderstandings and injustices. May it enable memory to play its necessary part in the process of shaping a future in which the unspeakable iniquity of the Shoah will never again be possible. May the Lord of history guide the efforts of Catholics and Jews and all men and women of good will as they work together for a world of true respect for the life and dignity of every human being, for all have been created in the image and likeness of God.

From the Vatican, March 12, 1998

Pope John Paul II

STATEMENT ON THE HOLOCAUST

I. The tragedy of the Shoah and the duty of remembrance

The 20th century is fast coming to a close and a new millennium of the Christian era is about to dawn. The 2,000th anniversary of the birth of Jesus Christ calls all Christians, and indeed invites all men and women, to seek to discern in the passage of history the signs of divine providence at work, as well as the ways in which the image of the Creator in man has been offended and disfigured.

This reflection concerns one of the main areas in which Catholics can seriously take to heart the summons which Pope John Paul II has addressed to them in his apostolic letter "Tertio Millennio Adveniente": "It is appropriate that, as the second millennium of Christianity draws to a close, the church should become more fully conscious of the sinfulness of her children, recalling all those times in history when they departed from the spirit of Christ and his Gospel and, instead of offering to the world the witness of a life inspired by the values of faith, indulged in ways of thinking and acting which were truly forms of counterwitness and scandal."

This century has witnessed an unspeakable tragedy, which can never be forgotten: the attempt by the Nazi regime to exterminate the Jewish people, with the consequent killing of millions of Jews. Women and men, old and young, children and infants, for the sole reason of their Jewish origin, were persecuted and deported. Some were killed immediately, while others were degraded, ill-treated, tortured and utterly robbed of their human dignity, and then murdered. Very few of those who entered the camps survived, and those who did remained scarred for life. This was the Shoah. It is a major fact of the history of this century, a fact which still concerns us today.

Before this horrible genocide, which the leaders of nations and Jewish communities themselves found hard to believe at the very moment when it was being mercilessly put into effect, no one can remain indifferent, least of all the church, by reason of her very close bonds of spiritual kinship with the Jewish people and her remembrance of the injustices of the past. The church's relationship to the Jewish people is unlike the one she shares with any other religion. However, it is not only a question of recalling the past. The common future of Jews and Christians demands that we remember, for "there is no future without memory." History itself is "memoria futuri."

In addressing this reflection to our brothers and sisters of the Catholic Church throughout the world, we ask all Christians to join us in meditating on the catastrophe which befell the Jewish people, and on the moral imperative to ensure that never again will selfishness and hatred grow to the point of sowing such suffering and death. Most especially, we ask our Jewish friends, "whose terrible fate has become a symbol of the aberrations of which man is capable when he turns against God," to hear us with open hearts.

II. What we must remember

While bearing their unique witness to the Holy One of Israel and to the Torah, the Jewish people have suffered much at different times and in many places. But the Shoah was certainly the worst suffering of all. The inhumanity with which the Jews were persecuted and massacred during this century is beyond the capacity of words to convey. All this was done to them for the sole reason that they were Jews.

The very magnitude of the crime raises many questions. Historians, sociologists, political philosophers, psychologists and theologians are all trying to learn more about the reality of the Shoah and its causes. Much scholarly study still remains to be done. But such an event cannot be fully measured by the ordinary criteria of historical research alone. It calls for a "moral and religious memory" and, particularly among Christians, a very serious reflection on what gave rise to it.

The fact that the Shoah took place in Europe, that is, in countries of long-standing Christian civilization, raises the question of the relation between the Nazi persecution and the attitudes down the centuries of Christians toward the Jews.

III. Relations between Jews and Christians

The history of relations between Jews and Christians is a tormented one. His Holiness Pope John Paul II has recognized this fact in his repeated appeals to Catholics to see where we stand with regard to our relations with the Jewish people. In effect, the balance of these relations over 2,000 years has been quite negative.

At the dawn of Christianity, after the crucifixion of Jesus, there arose disputes between the early church and the Jewish leaders and people who, in their devotion to the law, on occasion violently opposed the preachers of the Gospel and the first Christians. In the pagan Roman Empire, Jews were legally protected by the privileges granted by the emperor, and the authorities at first made no distinction between Jewish and Christian communities. Soon however, Christians incurred the persecution of the state. Later, when the emperors themselves converted to Christianity, they at first continued to guarantee Jewish privileges. But Christian mobs who attacked pagan temples sometimes did the same to synagogues, not without being influenced by certain interpretations of the New Testament regarding the Jewish people as a whole. "In the Christian world—I do not say on the part of the church as such—erroneous and unjust interpretations of the New Testament regarding the Jewish people and their alleged culpability have circulated for too long, engendering feelings of hostility towards this people." Such interpretations of the New Testament have been totally and definitively rejected by the Second Vatican Council.

Despite the Christian preaching of love for all, even for one's enemies, the prevailing mentality down the centuries penalized minorities and those who were in any way "different." Sentiments of anti-Judaism in some Christian quarters, and the gap which existed between the church and the Jewish people, led to a generalized discrimination, which ended at times in expulsions or attempts at forced conversions. In a large part of the "Christian" world, until the end of the 18th century, those who were not Christian did not always enjoy a fully guaranteed juridical status. Despite that fact, Jews throughout Christendom held on to their religious traditions and communal customs. They were therefore looked upon with a certain suspicion and mistrust. In times of crisis such as famine, war, pestilence or social tensions, the Jewish minority was sometimes taken as a scapegoat and became the victim of violence, looting, even massacres.

By the end of the 18th century and the beginning of the 19th century, Jews generally had achieved an equal standing with other citizens in most states and a certain number of them held influential positions in society. But in that same historical context, notably in the 19th century, a false and exacerbated nationalism took hold. In a climate of eventful social change, Jews were often accused of exercising an influence disproportionate to their numbers. Thus there began to spread in varying degrees throughout most of Europe an anti-Judaism that was essentially more sociological and political than religious.

At the same time, theories began to appear which denied the unity of the human race, affirming an original diversity of races. In the 20th century, National Socialism in Germany used these ideas as a pseudo-scientific basis for a distinction between so called Nordic-Aryan races and supposedly inferior races. Furthermore, an extremist form of nationalism was heightened in Germany by the defeat of 1918 and the demanding conditions imposed by the victors, with the consequence that many saw in National Socialism a solution to their country's problems and cooperated politically with this movement.

The church in Germany replied by condemning racism. The condemnation first appeared in the preaching of some of the clergy, in the public teaching of the Catholic bishops, and in the writings of lay Catholic journalists. Already in February and March 1931, Cardinal Bertram of Breslau, Cardinal Faulhaber and the bishops of Bavaria, the bishops of the province of Cologne and those of the province of Freiburg published pastoral letters condemning National Socialism, with its idolatry of race and of the state. The well-known Advent sermons of Cardinal Faulhaber in 1933, the very year in which National Socialism came to power, at which not just Catholics but also Protestants and Jews were present, clearly expressed rejection of the Nazi anti-Semitic propaganda. In the wake of the "Kristallnacht," Bernhard Lichtenberg, provost of Berlin cathedral, offered public prayers for the Jews. He was later to die at Dachau and has been declared Blessed.

Pope Pius XI, too, condemned Nazi racism in a solemn way in his encyclical letter, "Mit brennender Sorge," which was read in German churches on Passion Sunday 1937, a step which resulted in attacks and sanctions against members of the clergy. Addressing a group of Belgian pilgrims on Sept. 6, 1938, Pius XI asserted: "Anti-Semitism is unacceptable. Spiritually, we are all Semites." Pius XII, in his very first encyclical, "Summi Pontificatus," of Oct. 20, 1939, warned against theories which denied the unity of the human race and against the deification of the state, all of which he saw as leading to a real "hour of darkness."

IV. Nazi anti-Semitism and the Shoah

Thus we cannot ignore the difference which exists between anti-Semitism, based on theories contrary to the constant teaching of the church on the unity of the human race and on the equal dignity of all races and peoples, and the long-standing sentiments of mistrust and hostility that we call anti-Judaism, of which, unfortunately, Christians also have been guilty.

The National Socialist ideology went even further, in the sense that it refused to acknowledge any transcendent reality as the source of life and the criterion of moral good. Consequently, a human group, and the state with which it was identified, arrogated to itself an absolute status and determined to remove the very existence of the Jewish people, a people called to witness to the one God and the Law of the Covenant. At the level of theological reflection we cannot ignore the fact that not a few in the Nazi Party not only showed aversion to the idea of divine providence at work in human affairs, but gave proof of a definite hatred directed at God himself. Logically, such an attitude also led to a rejection of Christianity, and a desire to see the church destroyed or at least subjected to the interests of the Nazi state.

It was this extreme ideology which became the basis of the measures taken, first to drive the Jews from their homes and then to exterminate them. The Shoah was the work of a thoroughly modern neo-pagan regime. Its anti-Semitism had its roots outside of Christianity and, in pursuing its aims, it did not hesitate to oppose the church and persecute her members also.

But it may be asked whether the Nazi persecution of the Jews was not made easier by the anti-Jewish prejudices imbedded in some Christian minds and hearts. Did anti-Jewish sentiment among Christians make them less sensitive, or even indifferent, to the persecutions launched against the Jews by National Socialism when it reached power?

Any response to this question must take into account that we are dealing with the history of people's attitudes and ways of thinking, subject to multiple influences. Moreover, many people were altogether unaware of the "final solution" that was being put into effect against a whole people; others were afraid for themselves and those near to them; some took advantage of the situation; and still others were moved by envy. A response would need to be given case by case. To do this, however, it is necessary to know what precisely motivated people in a particular situation.

At first the leaders of the Third Reich sought to expel the Jews. Unfortunately, the governments of some Western countries of Christian tradition, including some in North and South America, were more than hesitant to open their borders to the persecuted Jews. Although they could not foresee how far the Nazi hierarchs would go in their criminal intentions, the leaders of those nations were aware of the hardships and dangers to which Jews living in the territories of the Third Reich were exposed. The closing of borders to Jewish emigration in those circumstances, whether due to anti-Jewish hostility or suspicion, political cowardice or shortsightedness, or national selfishness, lays a heavy burden of conscience on the authorities in question.

In the lands where the Nazis undertook mass deportations, the brutality which surrounded these forced movements of helpless people should have led to suspect the worst. Did Christians give every possible assistance to those being persecuted, and in particular to the persecuted Jews?

Many did, but others did not. Those who did help to save Jewish lives as much as was in their power, even to the point of placing their own lives in danger, must not be forgotten. During and after the war, Jewish communities and Jewish leaders expressed their thanks for all that had been done for them, including what Pope Pius XII did personally or through his representatives to save hundreds of thousands of Jewish lives. Many Catholic bishops, priests, religious and laity have been honored for this reason by the State of Israel.

Nevertheless, as Pope John Paul II has recognized, alongside such courageous men and women, the spiritual resistance and concrete action of other Christians was not that which might have been expected from Christ's followers. We cannot know how many Christians in countries occupied or ruled by the Nazi powers or their allies were horrified at the disappearance of their Jewish neighbors and yet were not strong enough to raise their voices in protest. For Christians, this heavy burden of conscience of their brothers and sisters during the Second World War must be a call to penitence.

We deeply regret the errors and failures of those sons and daughters of the church. We make our own what is said in the Second Vatican Council's declaration "Nostra Aetate," which unequivocally affirms: "The church . . . mindful of her common patrimony with the Jews, and motivated by the Gospel's spiritual love and by no political considerations, deplores the hatred, persecutions and displays of anti-Semitism directed against the Jews at any time and from any source."

We recall and abide by what Pope John Paul II, addressing the leaders of the Jewish community in Strasbourg in 1988, stated: "I repeat again with you the strongest condemnation of anti-Semitism and racism, which are opposed to the principles of Christianity." The Catholic Church therefore repudiates every persecution against a people or human group anywhere, at any time. She absolutely condemns all forms of genocide, as well as the racist ideologies which give rise to them. Looking back over this century, we are deeply saddened by the violence that has enveloped whole groups of peoples and nations. We recall in particular the massacre of the Armenians, the countless victims in Ukraine in the 1930s, the genocide of the Gypsies, which was also the result of racist ideas, and similar tragedies which have occurred in America, Africa and the Balkans. Nor do we forget the millions of victims of totalitarian ideology in the Soviet Union, in China, Cambodia and elsewhere. Nor can we forget the drama of the Middle East, the elements of which are well known. Even as we make this reflection, "many human beings are still their brothers' victims."

V. Looking together to a common future

Looking to the future of relations between Jews and Christians, in the first place we appeal to our Catholic brothers and sisters to renew the awareness of the Hebrew roots of their faith. We ask them to keep in mind that Jesus was a descendant of David; that the Virgin Mary and the Apostles belonged to the Jewish people; that the church draws sustenance from the root of that good olive tree on to which have been grafted the wild olive branches of the Gentiles (cf. Rom 11:17–24); that the Jews are our dearly beloved brothers, indeed in a certain sense they are "our elder brothers."

At the end of this millennium the Catholic Church desires to express her deep sorrow for the failures of her sons and daughters in every age. This is an act of repentance (teshuva), since, as members of the church, we are linked to the sins as well as the merits of all her children. The church approaches with deep respect and great compassion the experience of extermination, the Shoah, suffered by the Jewish people during World War II. It is not a matter of mere words, but indeed of binding commitment. "We would risk causing the victims of the most atrocious deaths to die again if we do not have an ardent desire for justice, if we do not commit ourselves to ensure that evil does not prevail over good as it did for millions of the children of the Jewish people. . . . Humanity cannot permit all that to happen again."

We pray that our sorrow for the tragedy which the Jewish people has suffered in our century will lead to a new relationship with the Jewish people. We wish to turn awareness of past sins into a firm resolve to build a new future in which there will be no more anti-Judaism among Christians or anti-Christian sentiment among Jews, but rather a shared mutual respect, as befits those who adore the one Creator and Lord and have a common father in faith, Abraham.

Finally, we invite all men and women of good will to reflect deeply on the significance of the Shoah. The victims from their graves, and the survivors through the vivid testimony of what they have suffered, have become a loud voice calling the attention of all of humanity. To remember this terrible experience is to become fully conscious of the salutary warning it entails: the spoiled seeds of anti-Judaism and anti-Semitism must never again be allowed to take root in any human heart.

March 16, 1998.

Cardinal Edward Idris Cassidy
  President

Bishop Pierre Duprey
  Vice-President

Dominican Father Remi Hoeckman, O.P.
  Secretary

INTERNAL REVENUE SERVICE
ON REFORMING ITSELF
March 18, 1998

Members of Congress gave themselves—and American taxpayers—an election-year present by enacting legislation intended to curb alleged abuses by the Internal Revenue Service (IRS). Leading Republicans hoped the legislation would be the first step in a long-term campaign to scrap the complex federal tax code and replace it with a simpler flat tax or national sales tax.

During the 1980s, when it was desperately searching for revenue to counter a burgeoning deficit, Congress tried to bolster IRS tax collection efforts, in part by increasing penalties for noncompliance. By the late 1990s, with the deficit at least temporarily under control, Congress began paying attention to taxpayer complaints about a heavy-handed IRS. The Senate in 1997 held a series of hearings offering aggrieved taxpayers an opportunity to air horror stories about how they had been harassed by the tax collection agency. During those hearings, Michael P. Dolan, the acting IRS commissioner, apologized to those taxpayers and promised that the agency was mending its ways. (IRS mistakes and abuses, Historic Documents of 1997, p. 661)

Dolan's apology represented an unusual admission of institutional wrongdoing by a major federal agency, but it did not stem the political tide that was rising against the IRS. In accordance, the Clinton administration agreed to support legislation reforming the IRS. After a series of negotiations from late 1997 through mid-1998, Congress sent President Clinton an IRS overhaul bill in July, and he promptly signed it into law (PL 105–206).

IRS on "Customer Service"

Even as Congress was working on legislation mandating a more tax-payer-friendly approach at the IRS, the agency was taking steps to reform its own operations. In May 1997 the Clinton administration formed a Customer Service Task Force within the agency to develop ways of making the agency function more like a private business. Sponsored by Vice President

Al Gore and Treasury Secretary Robert E. Rubin, the task force included thirty IRS managers and workers; its recommendations were presented to President Clinton on March 18.

The task force report offered more than two hundred recommendations for specific steps the IRS should take to improve its dealings with taxpayers. The agency had already implemented some of the recommendations, including holding a national "Problem Solving Day." IRS offices opened on a Saturday in November 1997 so taxpayers could try to resolve their problems with the agency. The agency also expanded its hours of telephone service so that, starting in January 1998, taxpayers could call with questions six days a week, sixteen hours a day. The agency was promising to answer its phones seven days a week, twenty-four hours a day, by the start of 1999.

Some of the task force recommendations were general in nature and were intended to refocus the basic way the IRS and its employees dealt with taxpayers. In their summary of the report, Gore and Rubin said the underlying thesis was simple: "The taxpayers don't work for us, we work for them." As an example, the report said the agency should put its notices to taxpayers in "plain language." The report acknowledged that some IRS notices were so detailed and full of jargon that they could be fully comprehended only by taxpayers with accounting or tax law backgrounds. Making notices and tax forms easier to understand would benefit both taxpayers and the government, the task force said, noting that similar efforts at other agencies had improved compliance and efficiency.

Perhaps the heart of the report was its section calling on the IRS to "treat taxpayers as customers." The report took a first step in that direction, referring throughout the document to "customers" rather than "taxpayers."

Citing techniques from the private sector, the report argued that the IRS could improve its service simply by listening to the specific problems and needs of is customers, whether they were individuals, small businesses, or giant corporations. For example, the task force said the agency needed to be more responsive to the complaints and suggestions of taxpayers, in part by training its employees to understand that taxpayers often were right. The task force recommendations also were aimed at ensuring that taxpayers received prompt, accurate answers to their questions when they contacted the IRS.

Many of the recommendations would reform specific procedures within the IRS to reduce some of the most common problems cited by taxpayers. For example, an IRS employee who had been trained to answer a taxpayer's inquiry would be allowed to answer that inquiry whether or not the employee was assigned to that specific issue. This step was intended to reduce the frequency of taxpayers being shuttled from one IRS employee to another. The task force said employees and individual IRS offices should be graded on how well they dealt with taxpayers, rather than just on the amount of tax dollars they collected.

IRS Reform Legislation

The IRS reform legislation enacted by Congress in 1998 dealt with many of the same broad issues that the administration was addressing through internal procedures. The law mandated changes that proponents—including President Clinton—said would force a new way of doing business at the IRS.

The law included what sponsors called a "taxpayer bill of rights" intended to give taxpayers more leverage in dealing with the tax agency. Perhaps the most significant of these rights involved shifting the burden of proof in tax court disputes between the IRS and taxpayers. Under previous law, it was presumed that the IRS was correct in its determination of how much a taxpayer owed, and so it was up to the taxpayer to prove that the IRS was wrong. The new law shifted the presumption in the opposite direction: If the taxpayer could produce credible evidence supporting his position during a tax court dispute, it would be up to the IRS to prove the taxpayer wrong.

In an attempt to ensure that the IRS actually followed through on reforms, the law mandated the creation of a nine-member oversight board to review the administration and overall direction of the agency. Six of the nine members were to represent the private sector—a requirement that sponsors hoped would bring fresh perspectives to the agency. In the past, the IRS commissioner reported only to the secretary of the Treasury.

Republican leaders, especially in the House, said they hoped to use the IRS reform issue to spur interest in a fundamental change in federal tax law. Several Republicans had advocated replacing the complex federal income tax with a simple flat tax (in which all taxpayers paid the same percentage) or a national sales tax. The Republicans acknowledged, however, that passing legislation to reform the IRS was easier to accomplish than totally revamping decades of tax law, much of it written by Congress to satisfy specific interest groups.

>*Following is the text of the summary section of the report, "Reinventing Service at the IRS," released March 18, 1998, by Vice President Al Gore and Treasury Secretary Robert E. Rubin; the report was prepared by an IRS Customer Service Task Force composed of IRS employees and other government officials:*

Far too many Americans feel the Internal Revenue Service is not doing right by them, or that it doesn't treat them with the respect and trust they deserve. Taxpayers can't understand complex IRS forms, notices and procedures. IRS phones and toll-free numbers are often busy. Taxpayers who get through frequently get put on hold or transferred to a person who cannot answer specific questions. Taxpayers who do not speak English are unlikely to reach an employee who speaks their language. And even the simplest problems can take far too long to resolve.

On May 20, 1997, Vice President Al Gore and Treasury Secretary Robert Rubin launched a National Performance Review Study to find ways to improve customer service at the IRS. The IRS Customer Service Task Force consisted of over 60 front-line IRS employees and managers, Department of Treasury officials, and members of the National Performance Review. The Task Force interviewed hundreds of people: it listened to complaints, read letters from taxpayers and met with tax preparers. The Task Force gathered ideas from others in government and the private sector, including businesses that excel in customer service and consultants who help those companies improve customer service.

The Task Force also looked at IRS pilot programs that have improved customer service and compliance and collected ideas from front-line employees. For example, the IRS has run programs with small businesses that were on the verge of bankruptcy because of tax troubles. Special IRS teams moved in to work with these businesses and designed plans that allowed them to pay off tax debts and keep afloat, saving jobs and contributing to the local economy. In the process the IRS doubled the tax revenues collected in one area. As a preventive measure, the teams also set up an intensive taxpayer education program to teach businesses what the IRS expects them to do and how to do it.

The Task Force studied other government reinvention efforts and found ample evidence that enforcement is not the only good method of ensuring compliance with the law. It examined programs that prove that agencies that treat people like customers and partners can be more successful in encouraging people to obey the law, and can then focus enforcement efforts on those who deliberately violate it. For example, until the U.S. Customs Service began working with airlines, importers and the rest of the trade community, Customs at the Miami Airport had a history of long lines for passengers and endless waits for cargo. Customs designed and implemented a plan that enabled them to identify high risk passengers or freight before a plane landed. This resulted in an increase in drug seizures, faster passage through customs for law-abiding passengers and less waiting time for importers. Similar results were found at the Environmental Protection Agency and the Occupational Safety and Health Administration when these agencies joined with the people and companies they regulate to solve problems—results such as cleaner air, fewer injuries and fewer violations and fines.

The report of the Task Force contains more than 200 actions which share a clear goal: to ensure that every taxpayer is treated with fairness and respect and that IRS customer service begins to meet the same standards that characterize private sector firms. Together these actions will make the IRS easier to deal with in everything from finding forms to filing taxes, from getting information to resolving a problem.

Highlights of the Actions

1. Ban Measures That Undermine Fair Treatment of Taxpayers

- The IRS will immediately ban measures such as using enforcement activities to rank districts and assigning dollar goals for districts and service centers.
- The IRS will work with the National Treasury Employees Union to design and test a balanced scorecard to evaluate the IRS and its employees in 1998. The scorecard will rate performance on: (1) customer service, based on customer satisfaction surveys; (2) employee satisfaction; and (3) business results.
- Over the longer term, the IRS will change how it selects, trains, evaluates, rewards and supports its employees so they can better serve customers.

2. Provide Better Telephone Service

- Increase Hours
  To make service more convenient, the IRS will by January 1, 1998 expand telephone service to 6 days a week, 16 hours a day. By January 1, 1999 the IRS will expand telephone service to 7 days a week, 24 hours a day. Currently, callers can get their questions answered by an IRS customer service representative only 5 days a week, 12 hours a day. Expanded phone service will be achieved by putting more of the current workforce on the phones during peak calling periods, using a new national call-routing system to route calls to the next available customer service representative, and forwarding calls to employees in other time zones during late night hours.

- Expand Customized Services
  In 1999 the IRS will begin using new call-routing technology to provide information that is geared to specific customers' needs—such as the tax implications of the sale of a house, retirement or job change and multilingual service. The IRS will also provide nationwide telephone services for tax preparers.

3. Make It Easier To Get Answers

- Institute New "Problem Solving Days"
  Beginning on November 15, 1997 the IRS instituted monthly "Problem Solving Days" in every district, during which employees listen to and resolve taxpayer problems.

- Expand Office Hours
  Beginning in 1998 the IRS will open district offices on Saturdays during the busiest weekends of the filing season.

- Open More Convenient Locations
  Beginning in 1999 the IRS will open additional temporary community-based locations such as banks, libraries or shopping malls during peak tax season to distribute publications and forms. It will also expand the telephone information system so that people can find out when and where they can get help.

- Improve Tracking of Complaints
  Using the Taxpayer Advocate's Problem Resolution Information System (PROMIS), the IRS will track complaints and, if unresolved in a reasonable period of time, to assign the case to the next higher level of management . These changes will go hand in hand with the strengthened Taxpayer Advocate and Citizen Advocacy Panels. . . .

- Review Unnecessary Penalties
  The Administration will undertake a comprehensive review of the fairness and effectiveness of all penalties, report to Congress in 1998 and make recommendations for legislative changes.

4. Reduce and Simplify Forms and Notices

- Rewrite Notices
  By 1999 the IRS will completely rewrite in plain language its most frequently used notices, like those for late payment or mathematical errors. These notices will be released only after they are tested for clarity and acceptance by taxpayers who do not have accounting or tax law backgrounds.

- Eliminate 30% of All Notices
  By the end of 1998 the IRS will eliminate additional unnecessary notices. This will eliminate more than 45 million pieces of mail—almost one-third of the notices the IRS has been sending to taxpayers.

- Simplify Forms and Brochures
  During 1999 the IRS will create easy-to-read brochures to provide important information on tax benefits and obligations when and where taxpayers need it, such as at banks or realty companies after the purchase of a home. By 2000 the IRS will rewrite the basic 1040 instruction package and test it for clarity on ordinary taxpayers.

5. Strengthen Customized Support For Small Businesses

- Help Start-Up Businesses
  Beginning in 1998 the IRS will team up with other federal agencies, financial institutions, tax preparers, state and local authorities and others to provide tax information, training and consultative services to small start-up businesses. These services are designed to make record keeping, filing and payment requirements as simple and easy as possible.

- Provide Specialized Phone Services
  In 1998 the IRS will offer small businesses the opportunity to use Tele-File, expanding a successful pilot program nationwide. The IRS will provide small businesses with 24 hour a day phone assistance geared to their needs by the 1999 tax season.

- Work With Troubled Small Businesses
  The IRS will work with troubled small businesses to help them comply, stay in business and avoid future tax problems, expanding on successful pilot programs in California, Maine and elsewhere.

6. Expand Electronic Filing

- TeleFile
  By 1998 the IRS will increase by 3 million, or about 10 percent, the number of taxpayers who are eligible to use TeleFile—the telephone filing system. Also, the IRS will extend the use of TeleFile for business

- Electronic Filing
  The IRS will increase the number of forms that can be filed electronically and educate customers about the benefits of electronic filing—fewer hassles, fewer contacts with the IRS and faster refunds

- Paperless Taxes
  In 1999 the IRS will work to enable taxpayers to file paperless returns by eliminating the need for mailing in W-2s and other forms and for paper signatures.

7. Introduce New Payment Options

- For the first time, beginning in 1999 taxpayers who file electronically will be able to pay their taxes with a direct withdrawal from their bank accounts. In addition, the IRS is seeking credit industry partners to test credit cards for taxpayers who file electronically in 1999. These new options will build upon the successful experience with about 15 million taxpayers whose refunds are deposited electronically.

8. Eliminate Unnecessary Filing 8640

- In 1998 the IRS will step up its public efforts to inform nearly two million older and lower-income taxpayers who are currently filing federal tax forms that they don't need to file, saving them and the IRS time and money.

9. Upgrade Technology to Improve Customer Service

- In the long term, the IRS Modernization Blueprint will improve assistance to customers by making accurate, electronically accessible and up-to-date information available on taxpayer returns and accounts while providing stringent protection of taxpayer privacy. In 1998, for example, the IRS will pilot a national call-routing system and provide simpler menus to let taxpayers get information more easily, including a much more reliable TeleTax system to check on the status of their refunds.

10. Improve Customer Service Training

- Before the 1998 filing season the IRS will have an intensive agency-wide special training program. This program will initiate the new approach to customer service and make specific plans for the 1999 filing season. In addition, IRS managers, including the Commissioner, will spend time each year serving customers.

* * * * * *

Taken together, these actions promise to introduce a new culture of customer service at the IRS. Accountability at all levels for customer satisfaction, greater access to telephone and walk-in service, easier-to-understand forms and notices, expanded electronic filing, improved technology, an effective complaint system—all this will make it simpler to get questions answered, fill out forms and pay taxes. This program will provide new support for small business, the lifeblood of the American economy and the taxpayers who face the greatest hurdles in achieving compliance.

These actions will help ensure that the IRS meets Vice President Gore's statement that taxpayers have the right to fair treatment. "The goal is this: to treat them with trust, with respect, with accuracy and with fairness. It's that simple."

Top management's recent apology for poor treatment of taxpayers was both courageous and necessary. This action, taken with this report, signals the change within the IRS and in the relationship between the IRS and the American taxpayer. These changes signal a new era in which the IRS employees can earn the trust of the taxpayers and take greater pride in the changes they're making on their behalf.

The more than 100,000 employees of the IRS were represented on the Task Force by people like Nancy Eik, a customer service representative in a walk-in center in Missoula, Montana. Ms. Eik spends every Saturday during the tax season at the public library helping people fill out their tax forms. This is the type of IRS employee service that will help rebuild the pride, energy and professionalism of the IRS.

Task Force members believe that by taking the steps in this report, IRS employees will be able to provide better customer service and work to restore the morale of the workforce. For government reinvention to be successful—legitimate and lasting—it must come from both the front-line workers and the customers. This report is based on that honest feedback from the front lines and the customers of the IRS.

The IRS is the agency of the federal government that most Americans must deal with every year. Nothing else in government reaches out and touches so many Americans so directly. And no agency has a greater responsibility to protect its customers and serve our nation's citizens with fairness, courtesy and respect.

GAO ON HEALTH INSURANCE COVERAGE UNDER 1996 ACT
March 19, 1998

Access to and affordability of health care continued to plague consumers, the health care industry, and policymakers in 1998. The major controversy arose from consumer complaints that their managed care providers cared more about preserving their bottom lines than providing adequate treatment to patients. Congress and the White House spent much of the year bogged down—politically and philosophically—in a debate over setting minimum federal standards of coverage for health maintenance organizations (HMOs) and other managed care providers. President Bill Clinton and the Democrats pushed for minimum federal standards that would guarantee consumers access to appropriate health care, including emergency and specialist services; access to information about treatment options; and procedures to appeal denials of coverage, including the right to sue a provider for damages. Republicans were split on the issue, with some supporting more federal protections for consumers, including the right to sue; other Republicans argued that solutions should be left to the marketplace and that the Democrats' approach would result in higher premiums and thus throw even more people into the ranks of the uninsured.

A series of gloomy reports released throughout the year indicated that health insurance was out of the price reach of a growing number of Americans. In March the General Accounting Office (GAO) reported that a new federal law guaranteeing access to insurance to people who lost their group coverage was not working as well as intended, in some cases because insurers were jacking up the price of the premiums. In September economists in the U.S. Department of Health and Human Services predicted that spending on health care costs would double over the next decade, primarily because the nation had already benefited from most of the savings that came in the late 1980s when the vast majority of Americans switched from traditional fee-for-service insurance to managed care. Later in the month the Census Bureau reported that 16 percent of the population was without health insurance coverage in 1997—the highest level in a decade.

Deadlock on Patients' Bill of Rights

HMOs and other managed care plans surged in popularity in the late 1980s and early 1990s as the health care industry sought ways to hold down soaring costs. By the late 1990s nearly 150,000 million Americans were enrolled in managed care plans, often sponsored by their employers. But dissatisfaction with managed care also surged as consumers realized that HMOs saved money by reducing the length and frequency of hospital stays, restricting access to medical specialists, and requiring preauthorization for many diagnostic procedures and treatments, including emergency room visits. Consumers complained that their managed care providers seemed more concerned about profits than health care.

In response the states, which traditionally regulated insurance, began to adopt laws requiring insurers to provide minimum levels of care if they wanted to do business in that state. But the consumer protections varied from state to state, making it difficult for insurers that operated in more than one state. Moreover, health care plans offered by self-insured employers (generally large corporations) were exempt from state regulation; thus the 48 million people covered under those plans could not sue their insurer for damages under state law (they could sue under federal law, but were not allowed to seek punitive damages). Congress tried to fill some of the gaps left by these state laws, but the piecemeal approach was unsatisfactory to many legislators, who began to explore the possibility of setting federal standards.

President Clinton seized the initiative on the issue in March 1997 when he appointed a Presidential Advisory Commission on Consumer Protection and Quality in the Health Care Industry, which in November issued a health care "bill of rights" to build "a stronger relationship of trust" among patients and their insurers. Clinton immediately challenged Congress to enact this so-called patients' bill of rights. (Health Care Bill of Rights, Historic Documents of 1997, p. 787)

The Republican leadership, much of the managed care industry, and many employer groups opposed federal intervention, saying that such standards would only increase the costs of health care, driving up premiums, forcing more employers to stop providing health care benefits for their employers, and adding more people to the roles of the uninsured. Concerned that they would suffer losses at the polls if they did not take some action to bolster health care protections for their constituents, Republicans in the House passed a version of the patients' bill of rights that offered far fewer protections than the Democrats wanted. Democratic efforts to bring their version of the legislation to the floor of the Senate were unsuccessful and the two parties went into the general elections accusing each other of using the issue to their own political ends and promising to revisit the issue in 1999.

Unintended Consequences of the Portability Law

Policymakers who argued that federal intervention in health insurance could have unwanted consequences were handed a concrete example in

1998. In 1996 Congress enacted the Health Insurance Portability and Accountability Act (PL 104–191), which, among other things, sought to ensure that eligible individuals who lost their group coverage could maintain access to individual health coverage regardless of their health status. Eligible people included those who changed jobs, started their own businesses, or became ill and could no longer work. The law "seals the cracks that swallow as many as 25 million Americans who can't get insurance or who fear they'll lose it," President Clinton said when he signed the bill.

But the law put no limit on the amounts insurers could charge. As a result, a GAO official told a Senate committee hearing on March 19 that some insurers in some states were charging individuals with health problems 140 percent to 600 percent above standard premium rates. This situation was "likely to persist," unless measures were taken to stop it, William J. Scanlon, director of GAO's Health Financing and Systems Issues office told the committee. Scanlon also reported that some insurers were also unwilling to tell consumers that they qualified for the policies, and that some reduced or even refused to pay commissions to agents who sold these policies. In addition, the GAO found that consumers and insurers did not fully understand the new law, which complicated compliance. Moreover, the new law had created new bureaucratic problems for the federal agencies that administered it. The Health and Human Services Department, for example, had to act as insurance commissioner in the five states that had not passed legislation to implement the law.

Members of the Senate Labor and Human Resources Committee were clearly struck by the higher than expected premiums. "With rates of that magnitude, I'm not sure you can still call it insurance," said Sen. James M. Jeffords, R-Vt., the panel's chairman. Other witnesses before the committee agreed. "Consumers' hopes for 'portability' of health insurance when they leave their job are not being met," said one. "Insurance remains unaffordable to many who lose their group coverage." Sen. Edward M. Kennedy of Massachusetts, the ranking Democrat on the panel and a coauthor of the portability law, said he would immediately introduce legislation to stop the "price-gouging." The Kennedy legislation would cap the premiums that insurers could charge eligible individuals at 150 percent of the standard rate for coverage..

Bill Gradison, president of the Health Insurance Association of America and a former Republican House member from Ohio, argued that the GAO report was misleading because it was based on data from only a few states and did not look at the majority of states that had used risk-pooling mechanisms to keep premium costs down. Gradison also said that Congress had been warned that the portability law was likely to increase some premiums and so should not react with surprise when that happened. "As other witnesses have said, [the law] dealt with access, not affordability," Gradison said.

Gradison's organization subsequently released estimates that Kennedy's proposed cap would raise overall premiums for individual health insur-

ance by an average of nearly 11 percent and cause nearly 160,000 people to lose their insurance. Kennedy said that other estimates put the increases at a maximum of 1.6 percent over three years. No action was taken on Kennedy's bill in 1998.

Spending on Health Care Expected to Double

Any debate on health care issues in 1999 was likely to be in the context of rising health care spending. After several years of remaining relatively stable, health care spending began to rise in 1998 and, according to projections by federal economists, was expected to double, from slightly more than $1 trillion in 1997 to $2.1 trillion in 2007. Premiums for private insurance were expected to be increasing by 8.2 percent a year in 2007, compared with a 3.6 percent rate of increase in 1996. The forecast was prepared by economists in the Health Care Financing Administration of the Department of Health and Human Services and was published in the journal Health Affairs.

One important reason for the projected increase was, in effect, the success of managed care in helping to bring medical inflation under control in the late 1980s and early 1990s. With 85 percent of all privately insured Americans now enrolled in HMOs or others forms of managed care, the report said, the nation had already realized most of the "one-time savings" to be had from switching from the more expensive fee-for-service insurance system to a less costly one. Other factors contributing to the spending increase were consumers' increasing consumption of more expensive prescription drugs and their demands to be treated with the most sophisticated medical technology available. Patients who had become frustrated with managed care limitations on their right to choose their doctors and seek treatment from specialists increasingly were enrolling in more expensive plans with more flexible arrangements—and higher premiums.

Growing Numbers of Uninsured

While federal policymakers debated the minimum standards that insured Americans were entitled to, the number and proportion of Americans without any health insurance continued to climb. The Census Bureau reported in September that an estimated 43.4 million Americans were without health insurance for all of 1997—1.7 million more than in 1996 and the highest number of uninsured since 1992. The Census Bureau acknowledged that the sharp increase might seem surprising in a time when the economy was booming and unemployment was at its lowest point in a generation. Rising insurance costs were an important factor. Individuals and employers had long cited high costs as a primary reason for not carrying health insurance.

But the Census Bureau also noted two other factors that it said were contributing to the increase. First, it said, small businesses were creating most of the new jobs, and these businesses were much less likely than big corpo-

rations to give their employees health benefits. Only 28 percent of workers in businesses that employed fewer than twenty-five people had employer-based health insurance in 1997, compared with two-thirds of workers in businesses that employed five hundred people or more.

Second, as a result of welfare reform and the good economy, millions of people had moved from welfare to work in recent years, many of them into low-paying jobs that did not offer health benefits. Welfare recipients were automatically entitled to Medicaid, and while low-wage workers or their children might be eligible for Medicaid, many of them did not realize it. According to the Census Bureau, nearly half of all poor full-time workers were uninsured in 1997. "We are in a time of transition and turmoil in welfare," Diane Rowland, executive director of the Kaiser Commission on Medicare and the Uninsured, told the New York Times. *"While many states are trying to simplify Medicaid enrollment procedures, there are still many barriers. Caseworkers seem to be under greater pressure to find people jobs than to assure they have health insurance coverage."*

The Census Bureau reported that the number of uninsured children remained substantially unchanged from 1996, at 10.7 million. Among ethnic and racial groups, people of Hispanic origin had the highest uninsured rate; nearly one-third had no health insurance in 1997.

In other findings:

- *Thirty percent of adults aged eighteen to twenty-four had no health insurance in 1997, compared with 14 percent of adults aged forty-five to sixty-four. Because they were eligible for Medicare, only 1 percent of elderly adults did not have health insurance.*
- *People with lower incomes were less likely to have health insurance than people with higher incomes. One-fourth of those households with incomes under $25,000 had no insurance in 1997, compared with 8 percent of those with incomes above $75,000.*

Following are excerpts from testimony before the Senate Committee on Labor and Human Resources delivered March 19, 1998, by William J. Scanlon, director of Health Financing and Systems Issue in the General Accounting Office, on unintended consequences of the Health Insurance Portability and Accountability Act of 1996:

Mr. Chairman and Members of the Committee:

We are pleased to be here today to discuss the implementation of the private insurance market provisions of the Health Insurance Portability and Accountability Act of 1996 (HIPAA). Most Americans—some 160 million—rely on the private health insurance market, whether for employer-sponsored group coverage or an individual market policy. HIPAA provides, for the first time, nationwide standards for access, portability, and renewability protection for consumers in this market. To implement these standards, HIPAA requires coordinated action by many stakeholder groups, including federal agencies, state insurance regulators, private insurers, and employers. The Departments of Health and Human Services (HHS), Labor, and the Treasury issued regulations by the April 1, 1997, statutory deadline and were widely commended for the open and inclusive nature of the process. Nonetheless, implementing this new law has been a complex undertaking and, not surprisingly, during HIPAA's first year some challenges have emerged.

Today, I will discuss these challenges as they relate to

- consumers;
- issuers of health coverage, including employers and insurance carriers;
- state insurance regulators; and
- federal regulators.

This statement relies primarily on our two recent reports: Health Insurance Portability and Accountability Act of 1996: Early Implementation Concerns and Health Insurance Standards: New Federal Law Creates Challenges for Consumers, Insurers, Regulators.

In summary, although HIPAA gives people losing group coverage a guarantee of access to coverage in the individual market, consumers attempting to exercise this right have been hindered in some states by carrier practices and pricing and by their own misunderstanding of this complex law. In the 13 states using the "federal fallback" approach to guaranteed access—so called because it is specified by federal law—some carriers initially discouraged people from applying for the coverage or charge them as much as 140 to 600 percent of the standard rate because they believe that people seeking HIPAA's individual market access guarantee will typically be less healthy than others in the individual market. Many consumers also do not fully understand the eligibility criteria that apply and as a result may risk losing their right to coverage.

Issuers of health coverage believe certain HIPAA provisions are burdensome to administer, may create unintended consequences, or may be abused by consumers. For example, although issuers generally appear to be complying with the requirement to provide certificates of creditable coverage to enrollees who terminate health coverage, many continue to suggest that issuing these certificates to all enrollees is unnecessary and costly. Issuers also fear that HIPAA's guaranteed renewal provision could cause those eligible for Medicare to pay for redundant coverage and could also hinder carriers' ability to sell products to children and other targeted populations. And certain protections for group plan enrollees may create an opportunity for consumer abuse, such as the guarantees of credit for prior coverage, which could give certain enrollees an incentive, when they need medical care, to switch from low-cost, high-deductible coverage to more expensive, low-deductible coverage.

State insurance regulators have encountered difficulties implementing and enforcing HIPAA provisions where federal guidance lacks sufficient clarity or detail, such as that pertaining to nondiscrimination and late enrollee requirements in the group market, and to risk-spreading for products available to HIPAA eligibles in the individual market. While acknowledging that in some areas more guidance is needed, federal officials noted that the Congress allowed the regulations to be issued before a notice and comment period, given the need to draft many complex regulations within tight statutory deadlines.

Federal regulators face an unexpectedly large role under HIPAA, which could strain HHS' resources and weaken its oversight. In states that do not pass legislation implementing HIPAA provisions, HHS is required to take on the regulatory role. For at least five states that reported they did not pass implementing legislation by the end of 1997, HHS must perform that role. Since it may have similar responsibility for several other states that have not enacted such legislation or reported on it, the full extent of HHS' regulatory role under this law is not yet known.

Some implementation challenges may soon recede; others are hypothetical and may not materialize. As federal agencies issue more guidance and states and issuers gain more experience with HIPAA, concerns about the clarity of its regulations may diminish. Whether unintended consequences will occur is as yet unknown, in part because sufficient evidence has not accumulated. However, two substantive concerns are likely to persist. First, in federal fall-back states, premiums for group-to-individual guaranteed access coverage are likely to remain high unless regulations with more explicit risk-spreading requirements are issued at the federal or state level or states adopt other mechanisms to moderate these rates. Second, HHS' ability to meet its growing oversight role may prove inadequate given the current level of resources, particularly if more states cede regulatory authority to the federal government.

In any case, as early challenges are resolved during 1998, other challenges to implementing HIPAA may emerge. That fact, coupled with the incompleteness of the evidence, makes a comprehensive assessment of HIPAA's implementation and effects premature and suggests the need for continued oversight.

Background

Among other protections, HIPAA's standards for health coverage, access, portability, and renewability guarantee access to coverage for certain employees and individuals, prohibit carriers from refusing to renew coverage on the basis of a person's health status, and place limits on the use of preexisting condition exclusion periods. However, not all standards apply to all markets or individuals. For example, guarantees of access to coverage for employers apply only in the small-group market, and the individual market guarantee applies only to certain eligible individuals who lose group coverage. . . .

The Departments of Labor and the Treasury and HHS are required to jointly develop and issue regulations implementing HIPAA, and each agency is charged with various oversight responsibilities. Labor is responsible for ensuring that group health plans comply with HIPAA standards, which is an extension of its current regulatory role under the Employee Retirement Income Security Act of 1974 (ERISA). Treasury also enforces HIPAA requirements on group health plans but does so by imposing an excise tax under the Internal Revenue Code on employers or plans that do not comply with HIPAA. HHS is responsible for enforcing HIPAA with respect to insurance carriers in the group and individual markets, but only in states that do not already have similar protections in place or do not enact and enforce laws to implement HIPAA standards.

This represents an essentially new role for that agency.

The implementation of HIPAA is ongoing, in part, because the regulations were issued on an "interim final" basis. Further guidance needed to finalize the regulations has not yet been issued. In addition, various provisions of HIPAA have different effective dates. Most of the provisions became effective on July 1, 1997, but group-to-individual guaranteed access in 36 states and the District of Columbia had until January 1, 1998, to become effective. And although all provisions are now in effect, individual group plans do not become subject to the law until the start of their plan year on or after July 1, 1997. For some collectively bargained plans, this may not be until 1999 or later, as collective bargaining agreements may extend beyond 12 months.

During the first year of implementation, federal agencies, the states, and issuers have taken various actions in response to HIPAA. In addition to publishing interim final regulations by the April 1, 1997, statutory deadline, Labor and HHS have conducted educational outreach activities. State legislatures have enacted laws to implement HIPAA provisions, and state insurance regulators have written regulations and prepared to enforce them. Issuers of health coverage have modified their products and practices to comply with HIPAA.

HIPAA Guarantees Access to Coverage for Individuals Leaving Group Plans, But Some Consumers' Ability to Obtain this Coverage Is Compromised

To ensure that individuals losing group coverage have guaranteed access—regardless of health status—to individual market coverage, HIPAA offers states two different approaches. The first, which HIPAA specifies, is commonly referred to as the "federal fallback" approach and requires all carriers who operate in the individual market to offer eligible individuals at least two health plans. (This approach became effective on July 1, 1997.) The second approach, the so-called "alternative mechanism," grants states considerable latitude to use high-risk pools and other means to ensure guaranteed access. (HIPAA requires states adopting this approach to implement it no later than Jan. 1, 1998.)

Among the 13 states using the federal fallback approach, we found that some initial carrier marketing practices may have discouraged HIPAA eligibles from enrolling in products with guaranteed access rights. After the federal fallback provisions took effect, many consumers told state insurance regulators that carriers did not disclose the existence of a product to which the consumers had HIPAA-guaranteed access rights or, when the consumers specifically requested one, the carrier said it did not have such a product available. Also, some carriers initially refused to pay commissions to insurance agents who referred HIPAA eligibles. Insurance regulators in two of the three federal fallback states we visited told us that some carriers advised agents against referring HIPAA-eligible applicants or paid reduced or no commissions. Recently, though, this practice appears to have abated.

We also found that premiums for products with guaranteed access rights may be substantially higher than standard rates. In the three federal fallback states we visited, we found rates ranging from 140 to 400 percent of the standard rate, as indicated in table 1. Anecdotal reports from insurance regulators and agents in federal fallback states suggest rates of 600 percent or more of the standard rate are also being charged. We also found that carriers typically evaluate the health status of applicants and offer healthy individuals access to their lower-priced standard products. This practice could cause HIPAA products to be purchased disproportionately by unhealthy, more costly individuals, which, in turn, could precipitate further premium increases.

Carriers charge higher rates because they believe HIPAA-eligible individuals will, on average, be in poorer health, and they seek to prevent non-HIPAA-eligible individuals from subsidizing eligibles' expected higher costs. Carriers permit or even encourage healthy HIPAA-eligible individuals to enroll in standard plans. According to one carrier official, denying HIPAA eligibles the opportunity to enroll in a less expensive product for which they qualify would be contrary to the consumers' best interests. In any case, carriers that do not charge higher premiums to HIPAA eligibles could be subject to adverse selection. That is, once a carrier's low rate for eligible individuals became known, agents would likely refer less healthy HIPAA eligibles to that carrier, which would put it at a competitive disadvantage. Finally, HIPAA does not specifically regulate premium rates and, with one exception, the regulations do not require a mechanism to narrow the disparity of rates for products with guaranteed access rights. The regulations offer three options for carriers to provide coverage to HIPAA-eligible individuals in federal fallback states, only one of which includes an explicit requirement to use some method of risk spreading or financial subsidy to moderate rates for HIPAA products. This limited attention to rates in the regulations, some state regulators contend, permits issuers to charge substantially higher rates for products with guaranteed access rights.

A third potential obstacle facing consumers seeking HIPAA products is, we found, widespread consumer confusion about consumers' guaranteed access rights in the individual market. Soon after HIPAA was enacted, insurance regulators in several states received numerous calls from individuals, including the uninsured, who misunderstood their rights and expected to have guaranteed access to insurance coverage. One state reported receiving consumer calls at a rate of 120 to 150 a month, about 90 percent of which related to the group-to-individual guaranteed access provision. Similarly, an official from one large national insurer told us that many consumers believe the law covers them when it actually does not.

Issuers of Health Coverage Are Concerned About HIPAA's Administrative Burden and Possible Unintended Consequences

Issuers of health coverage are concerned about the administrative burden and the unintended consequences of certain HIPAA requirements. One persistent concern has been the administrative burden and cost of complying with the requirement to issue certificates of creditable coverage to all enrollees who terminate coverage. Some issuers are concerned that certain information, such as the status of dependents on a policy, is difficult or time consuming to obtain. Some state officials are concerned that Medicaid agencies, which are also subject to the requirement, may face an especially difficult burden because Medicaid recipients tend to enroll in and disenroll from the Medicaid program frequently. This could require Medicaid agencies to issue a higher volume of certificates. Finally, issuers suggest that many of the certificates will not be needed to prove creditable coverage. Several issuers and state insurance regulators point out that portability reforms passed by most states have worked well without a certificate issuance requirement. Also, many group health plans do not contain preexisting condition exclusion clauses, and therefore the plans do not need certificates from incoming enrollees. While issuers generally appear to have complied with this requirement, some suggest that a more limited requirement, such as issuing the certificates only to consumers who request them, would serve the same purpose for less cost.

Issuers are also concerned that HIPAA's guaranteed renewal requirement may adversely affect certain populations. For example, in the individual market, issuers typically terminate the coverage of enrollees who reach Medicare eligibility age, sometimes offering Medicare supplemental coverage instead. But because HIPAA requires that coverage be renewed, issuers may no longer terminate the coverage, and certain drawbacks may result. Those who elect to retain individual market coverage may miss the 6-month open enrollment window during which they may enroll in a Medicare supplemental policy without preexisting condition exclusions. Furthermore, these consumers could be worse off financially, since individual market coverage generally costs more than Medicare supplemental coverage. In addition, because some states do not permit issuers to coordinate their coverage with Medicare, some consumers may pay for coverage that duplicates their Medicare benefits. Furthermore, the National Association of Insurance Commissioners (NAIC) is concerned that if large numbers of older and less healthy individuals remain in the individual market, premiums for all individuals there could rise as a result. HIPAA's guaranteed renewal requirements may also preclude issuers from canceling enrollees' coverage, once they exceed eligibility limits, in insurance programs that are targeted for low-income populations. Therefore, these programs' limited slots could be filled by otherwise ineligible individuals. Similarly, issuers could be required to renew coverage for children-only insurance products, for children who have reached adulthood—contrary to the design and intent of these products.

Finally, issuers cite some HIPAA provisions that have the potential to be abused by consumers. For example, HIPAA requires group health plans to give new enrollees or enrollees switching between plans during an open enrollment period full credit for a broad range of prior health coverage. Since the law does not recognize differences in deductible levels, issuers and regulators are concerned that individuals may enroll in inexpensive, high-deductible plans while healthy and then switch to plans with comprehensive, low-deductible coverage when they become ill. Federal agencies have sought comments from industry on this matter. In a related example, because HIPAA does not permit pregnancy to be excluded from coverage as a preexisting condition, an individual could avoid the expense of health coverage and then enroll in the employer's group plan as a late enrollee to immediately obtain full maternity benefits. Issuers contend that such abuses, if widespread, could increase the cost of insurance. . . .

Unexpectedly Large Role for Federal Regulators May Strain Resources, Hamper Oversight

States have the option of enforcing HIPAA's access, portability, and renewability standards as they apply to fully insured group and individual health coverage. In states that do not pass laws to enforce these federal standards, HHS must perform the enforcement function. According to HHS officials, the agency as well as the Congress and others assumed HHS would generally not have to perform this role, believing instead that states would not relinquish regulatory authority to the federal government. However, five states—California, Massachusetts, Michigan, Missouri, and Rhode Island—reported they did not pass legislation to implement HIPAA's group-to-individual guaranteed access provision, among other provisions, thus requiring HHS to regulate insurance plans in these states. Preliminary information suggests that up to 17 additional states have not enacted laws to enforce one or more HIPAA provisions, potentially requiring HHS to play a regulatory role in some of these states as well. HHS resources are currently strained by its new regulatory role in the five states where enforcement is under way, according to officials, and concern exists about the implications of the possible expansion of this role to additional states. . . .

Concluding Observations

HIPAA reflects the complexity of the U.S. private health insurance marketplace. The law's standards for health coverage access, portability, and renewability apply nationwide but must take account of the distinctive features of the small-group, large-group, and individual insurance markets, and of employees' movements between these markets. From the drafting of regulations to the responses of issuers, implementation of this complex law has itself been complicated but has nonetheless moved forward. Notwithstanding this progress, though, participants and observers have raised concerns and noted challenges to those charged with implementing this law.

Some challenges are likely to recede or be addressed in the near term. What could be characterized as "early implementation hurdles," especially those related to the clarity of federal regulations, may be largely resolved during 1998, as federal agencies issue further regulatory guidance to states and issuers. Moreover, as states and issuers gain experience in implementing HIPAA standards, the intensity of their dissatisfaction may diminish. In any case, while criticizing the cost and administrative burden of issuing certificates of creditable coverage, issuers still seem able to comply.

According to issuers and other participants in HIPAA's implementation, HIPAA may have several unintended consequences, but predicting whether these possibilities will be realized is difficult. At this early point in the law's history, these concerns are necessarily speculative because HIPAA's insurance standards have not been in place long enough for evidence to accumulate. In addition, possible changes in the regulations or amendments to the statute itself could determine whether a concern about a provision's effects becomes reality.

However, two implementation difficulties are substantive and likely to persist, unless measures are taken to address them. First, in the 13 federal fallback states, some consumers are finding that high premiums make it difficult to purchase the group-to-individual guaranteed access coverage that HIPAA requires carriers to offer. This situation is likely to continue unless HHS interprets the statute to require (in federal fallback states) more explicit and comprehensive risk-spreading requirements or that states adopt other mechanisms to moderate rates of guaranteed access coverage for HIPAA eligibles. In addition, if the range of consumer education efforts on HIPAA provisions remains limited, many consumers may continue to be surprised by the limited nature of HIPAA protections or to risk losing the opportunity to take advantage of them. Second, HHS' current enforcement capabilities could prove inadequate to handle the additional burden as the outcome of state efforts to adopt and implement HIPAA provisions becomes clearer in 1998.

The situation regarding the implementation of HIPAA's insurance standards is dynamic. As additional health plans become subject to the law, and as further guidance is issued, new problems may emerge and new corrective actions may be necessary. Consequently, because a comprehensive determination of HIPAA's implementation and effects remains years away, continued oversight is required. . . .

FORMER SENATOR MANSFIELD
ON CIVILITY IN THE SENATE
March 24, 1998

Mike Mansfield, who during the 1960s and 1970s set a record for length of service as Senate majority leader, returned to the Capitol on March 24 with words of advice for making the Senate a more civilized place of debate and legislating. Mansfield's words had a timeless quality: He had written the speech in November 1963, in response to criticism of his leadership by fellow Democrats, but had never delivered it on the Senate floor because of the assassination that month of President John F. Kennedy.

A Democrat from Montana, Mansfield had served along with some of the most famous and influential senators of the twentieth century, among them Everett M. Dirksen, Barry Goldwater, Hubert H. Humphrey, Jacob K. Javits, Lyndon B. Johnson, Robert and Edward Kennedy, and Edmund S. Muskie. Mansfield was elected majority leader to succeed Johnson when he became vice president. Mansfield retired from the Senate after the 1976 session and by that time was widely considered one of the most successful and most respected congressional leaders ever.

Mansfield had planned to return to private life, but President Jimmy Carter asked him to become ambassador to Japan. He held that post for twelve years, under Carter and also for President Ronald Reagan—once again earning nearly universal praise. At age ninety-five, Mansfield was still working in 1998 as a senior advisor on East Asian affairs at the Washington office of Goldman, Sachs & Company.

The Changed Senate

The current Senate majority leader, Republican Trent Lott of Mississippi, invited Mansfield to inaugurate the "Leaders Lecture Series," intended as a regular event for the Senate. The lecture took place at the Old Senate Chamber in the Capitol—a room that for many years served as chambers for the Supreme Court and then as a storage area and multipurpose room for the Senate until it was restored in 1976 to its early nineteenth-century appearance.

Addressing an audience of senators and invited guests, Mansfield on March 24 recalled the atmosphere surrounding his decision in 1963 to speak to the Senate about the need for more cooperation and genuine debate. The Democrats enjoyed a nearly two-to-one majority over Republicans in the Senate (sixty-five to thirty-five), but many key items of President Kennedy's legislative agenda had been stalled for months. The most controversial of the stalled items was civil rights legislation that southern Democrats vociferously opposed. Some of the Senate's more liberal members—along with several influential political commentators—complained about the slow pace of action in the Senate. A few of the critics blamed Mansfield, saying he was too timid a leader, especially compared with Johnson, who had run the Senate with a disciplined hand bordering on regimentation.

Mansfield said his critics, whether they expressed their views openly or in private, "were equally determined that I, as majority leader, should begin to knock some heads together." Instead, Mansfield put together his speech on "The Senate and Its Leadership" and prepared to deliver it on November 22, 1963. When news of President Kennedy's assassination came that day, Mansfield put his speech aside and later inserted it in the Congressional Record.

Addressing the senators of 1998, Mansfield said he believed the views he had expressed in the speech "are as relevant today as they were more than a third of a century ago." Ever the diplomat, Mansfield did not mention that the 1998 Senate operated in an even more divisive atmosphere than during his leadership days. Numerous observers, and even some senators themselves, had been saying for several years that Capitol Hill had become too partisan and too torn by ideological disputes and personal rancor. Many of the Senate's most respected moderates had voluntarily retired during the mid-1990s; some expressed disgust and frustration at what they said was a poisonous atmosphere on Capitol Hill.

Mansfield's Call for Reason

In his 1963 speech, finally delivered to senators in 1998, Mansfield said the effectiveness of the Senate, or even Congress as a whole, could not be measured by the number of hours spent in session or even the number of bills enacted into law. Instead, he said, the true measure of the worth of Congress was its ability to act over the long term in the national interest.

Mansfield accepted much of the criticism that had been leveled at him and his accommodating leadership style. It was not in his nature to run rough-shod over other senators, he said. "I am what I am, and no title, political face-lifter, or image-maker can alter it."

Mansfield then turned to the core of the disputes surrounding the allegedly unproductive Senate of 1963 and the contentious Senate of 1998. The Senate can function, he said, "only if there is a high degree of accommodation, mutual restraint and a measure of courage—in spite of our weaknesses—in all of us." Expanding on his 1963 remarks, Mansfield reminded the senators that each member "can play only a brief and limited role," while "the Senate's responsibilities go on."

> *Following are excerpts from an address given March 24, 1998, by former senator Mike Mansfield at the Old Senate Chamber in the Capitol; Mansfield incorporated in his address elements from a speech entitled "The Senate and Its Leadership," which he had planned to deliver in the Senate on November 22, 1963:*

. . . There are very few advantages to outliving one's generation. One of them is the opportunity to see how historians describe and evaluate that generation. Some historians do it better than others.

One such historian is Senator Robert C. Byrd [D-W.Va.]. As all of you know, Robert Byrd has combined a participant's insights with a scholar's detachment to produce an encyclopedic four-volume history of the Senate. Near the end of his first volume appear two chapters devoted to the 1960's and '70's. Robert has entitled them "Mike Mansfield's Senate."

Now, I have no doubt that he would be the first to acknowledge the accuracy of what I am about to say. If, during my time as Senate leader, a pollster had asked each Senator the question, "Whose Senate is this?" that pollster would surely have received 99 separate answers—and they would all have been right. Only for purposes of literary convenience or historic generalization could we ever acknowledge that one person—at least during my time—could shape such a body in his own image.

Senator Byrd has been doubly generous in assigning me a seat in the Senate's Pantheon. Volume Three of his history series contains forty-six so-called "classic speeches" delivered in the Senate over the past century and a half. Among them is an address that was prepared for delivery in the final weeks of the 1963 session. My topic was "The Senate and Its Leadership."

By mid-1963, various Democratic senators had begun to express publicly their frustration with the lack of apparent progress in advancing the Kennedy administration's legislative initiatives. Other Senators were less open in their criticism—but they were equally determined that I, as majority leader, should begin to knock some heads together. After all, they reasoned, Democrats in the Senate enjoyed a nearly two-to-one party ratio. With those numbers, anything should be possible under the lash of disciplined leadership. Sixty-five Democrats, thirty-five Republicans! (Think of it, Senator Daschle.) Of course, I use the word "enjoy" loosely. Ideological differences within our party seriously undercut that apparent numerical advantage.

I decided the time had come to put down my views in a candid address. There would then be no doubt as to where I stood. If some of my party colleagues believed that mine was not the style of leadership that suited them, they would be welcome to seek a change.

I had selected a Friday afternoon, when little else would be going on, to discuss "The Senate and Its Leadership.'" The date was Friday, November 22, 1963.

That day's tragic events put an end to any such speechmaking. On the following week, as the nation grieved for President Kennedy, I simply inserted my prepared remarks into the *Congressional Record* (November 27, 1963).

I have waited thirty-five years to give that speech. I wish to quote from that address to present views that I believe are as relevant today as they were more than a third of a century ago. But first, before I do so, I would like to quote Lao Tsu, a Chinese philosopher of ancient times, who said, "A leader is best when the people hardly know he exists. And of that leader the people will say when his work is done, 'We did this ourselves.'"

[The Speech]

"Mr. President, some days ago, blunt words were said on the floor of the Senate. They dealt in critical fashion with the state of this institution. They dealt in critical fashion with the quality of the majority leadership and the minority opposition. A far more important matter than criticism or praise of the leadership was involved. It is a matter which goes to the fundamental nature of the Senate.

"In this light, we have reason to be grateful because if what was stated was being said in the cloakrooms, then it should have been said on the floor. If, as was indicated, the functioning of the Senate itself is in question, the place to air that matter is on the floor of the Senate. We need no cloakroom commandos, operating behind the swinging doors of the two rooms at the rear, to spread the tidings. We need no whispered word passed from one to another and on to the press.

"We are here to do the public's business. On the floor of the Senate, the public's business is conducted in full sight and hearing of the public. And it is here, not in the cloakrooms, that the Senator from Montana, the majority leader, if you wish, will address himself to the question of the present state of the Senate and its leadership. . . . It will be said to all senators and to all the members of the press who sit above us in more ways than one.

"How, Mr. President, do you measure the performance of this Congress—any Congress? How do you measure the performance of a Senate of one hundred independent men and women—any Senate? The question rarely arises, at least until an election approaches. And, then, our concern may well be with our own individual performance and not necessarily with that of the Senate as a whole.

"Yet that performance—the performance of the Senate as a whole—has been judged on the floor. Several senators, at least, judged it and found it seriously wanting. And with the hue and cry thus raised, they found echoes outside the Senate. I do not criticize senators for making the judgment, for raising the alarm. Even less do I criticize the press for spreading it. Senators were within their rights. And the press was not only within its rights but was performing a segment of its public duty, which is to report what transpires here.

"I, too, am within my rights, Mr. President, and I believe I am performing a duty of the leadership when I ask again: How do you judge the performance of this Congress—any Congress? Of this Senate—any Senate? Do you mix a concoction and drink it? And if you feel a sense of well-being thereafter, decide it is not so bad a Congress after all? But if you feel somewhat ill or depressed, then that, indeed, is proof unequivocal that the Congress is a bad Congress and the Senate is a bad Senate? Or do you shake your head back and forth negatively before a favored columnist when discussing the performance of this Senate? And if he, in turn, nods up and down, then that is proof that the performance is bad? . . .

"There is reference (by members and the media), to be sure, to time-wasting, to laziness, to absenteeism, to standing still, and so forth. But who are the time wasters in the Senate, Mr. President? Who is lazy? Who is an absentee? Each member can make his own judgment of his individual performance. I make no apologies for mine. Nor will I sit in judgment of any other member. On that score, each of us will answer to his own conscience, if not to his constituents.

"But, Mr. President, insofar as the performance of the Senate as a whole is concerned, with all due respect, these comments in time wasting have little relevance. Indeed, the Congress can, as it has—as it did in declaring World War II in less than a day—pass legislation which has the profoundest meaning for the entire nation. And by contrast, the Senate floor can look very busy day in and day out, month in and month out, while the Senate is indeed dawdling. At one time in the recollection of many of us, we debated a civil rights measure twenty-four hours a day for many days on end. We debated it shaven and unshaven. We debated it without ties, with hair awry, and even in bedroom slippers. In the end, we wound up with compromise legislation. And it was not the fresh and well-rested opponents of the civil rights measure who were compelled to the compromise. It was, rather, the exhausted, sleep-starved, quorum-confounded proponents who were only too happy to take it.

"No, Mr. President, if we would estimate the performance of this Congress or any other, this Senate or any other, we will have to find a more reliable yardstick than whether, on the floor, we act as time wasters or moonlighters. As every member of the Senate and press knows, even if the public generally does not, the Senate is neither more nor less effective because the Senate is in session from 9 a.m. to 9 p.m., or to 9 a.m. the next day.

"Nor does the length of the session indicate a greater or lesser effectiveness. We live in a twelve-month nation. It may well be that the times are pushing us in the direction of a twelve-months Congress. In short, we cannot measure a Congress or a Senate by the standards of the stretch-out or of the speedup. It will be of no avail to install a time clock at the entrance to the chamber for Senators to punch when they enter or leave the floor.

"There has been a great deal said on this floor about featherbedding in certain industries. But if we want to see a featherbedding to end all featherbedding, we will have the Senate sit here day in and day out, from dawn until dawn, whether or not the calendar calls for it, in order to impress the boss—the American people—with our industriousness. We may not shuffle papers as bureaucrats are assumed to do when engaged in this art. What we are likely to shuffle is words—words to the President on how to execute the foreign policy or administer the domestic affairs of the nation. And when these words pall, we will undoubtedly turn to the Court to give that institution the benefit of our advice on its responsibilities. And if we run out of judicial wisdom, we can always turn to advising the governors of the states, or the mayors of the cities, or the heads of other nations, on how to manage their concerns.

"Let me make it clear that Senators individually have every right to comment on whatever they wish, and to do so on the floor of the Senate. Highly significant initiatives on all manner of public affairs have had their genesis in the remarks of individual Senators on the floor. But there is one clear-cut, day-in-and-day-out responsibility of the Senate as a whole. Beyond all others, it is the constitutional responsibility to be here and to consider and to act in concert with the House on the legislative needs of the nation. And the effectiveness with which that responsibility is discharged cannot be measured by any reference to the clocks on the walls of the chamber.

"Nor can it be measured, really, by the output of legislation. For those who are computer-minded, however, the record shows that 12,656 bills and resolutions were introduced in the 79th Congress of 1945 and 1946. And in the 87th Congress of 1961 and 1962, [that number had increased by] 60 percent. And the records show further that in the 79th Congress, 2,117 bills and resolutions were passed, and in the 87th, 2,217 were passed.

"But what do these figures tell us, Mr. President? Do they tell us that the Congress has been doing poorly because in the face of an 8,000 increase in the biannual input of bills and resolutions, the output of laws fifteen years later had increased by only a hundred? They tell us nothing of the kind.

"If these figures tell us anything, they tell us that the pressures on Congress have intensified greatly. They suggest, further, that Congress may be resistant to these pressures. But whether Congress resists rightly or wrongly, to the benefit or detriment of the nation, these figures tell us nothing at all.

"There is a [more meaningful way to measure] the effectiveness of a Democratic administration. I refer to the approach which is commonly used these days of totaling the Presidential or executive branch requests for significant legislation and weighing against that total the number of congressional responses in the form of law.

"On this basis, if the Congress enacts a small percentage of the executive branch requests, it is presumed, somewhat glibly and impertinently, to be an ineffective Congress. But if the percentage is high, it follows that it is classifiable as an effective Congress. I am not so sure that I would agree, and I am certain that the distinguished minority leader [Senator Everett Dirksen, R-Ill.] and his party would not agree that that is a valid test. The opposition might measure in precisely the opposite fashion. The opposition might, indeed, find a Democratic Congress which enacted little, if any, of a Democratic administration's legislation, a paragon among congresses. And yet I know that the distinguished minority leader does not reason in that fashion, for he has acted time and time again not to kill administration measures, but to help to pass them when he was persuaded that the interests of the nation so required. . . . I see no basis for apology on statistical grounds either for this Congress to date or for the last. But at the same time, I do not take umbrage in statistics. I do not think that statistics, however refined, tell much of the story of whether or not a particular Congress or Senate is effective or ineffective.

"I turn, finally, to the recent criticism which has been raised as to the quality of the leadership. Of late, Mr. President, the descriptions of the majority leader, of the Senator from Montana, have ranged from a benign Mr. Chips, to glamourless, to tragic mistake.

"It is true, Mr. President, that I have taught school, although I cannot claim either the tenderness, the understanding, or the perception of Mr. Chips for his charges. I confess freely to a lack of glamour. As for being a tragic mistake, if that means, Mr. President, that I am neither a circus ringmaster, the master of ceremonies of a Senate night club, a tamer of Senate lions, or a wheeler and dealer, then I must accept, too, that title. Indeed, I must accept it if I am expected as majority leader to be anything other than myself—a Senator from Montana who has had the good fortune to be trusted by his people for over two decades and done the best he knows how to represent them, and to do what he believes to be right for the nation.

"Insofar as I am personally concerned, these or any other labels can be borne. I achieved the height of my political ambitions when I was elected Senator from Montana. When the Senate saw fit to designate me as majority leader, it was the Senate's choice, not mine, and what the Senate has bestowed, it is always at liberty to revoke.

"But so long as I have this responsibility, it will be discharged to the best of my ability by me as I am. I would not, even if I could, presume to a tough-mindedness which, with all due respect to those who use this cliché, I have always had difficulty in distinguishing from soft-headedness or simple-mindedness. I shall not don any Mandarin's robes or any skin other than that to which I am accustomed in order that I may look like a majority leader or sound like a majority leader—however a majority leader is supposed to look or sound. I am what I am, and no title, political face-lifter, or image-maker can alter it.

"I believe that I am, as are most Senators, an ordinary American with a normal complement of vices and, I hope, virtues, of weaknesses and, I hope, strengths. As such, I do my best to be courteous, decent, and understanding of others, and sometimes fail at it.

"I have always felt that the President of the United States—whoever he may be . . . is worthy of the respect of the Senate. I have always felt that he bears a greater burden of responsibility than any individual Senator for the welfare and security of the nation, for he alone can speak for the nation abroad; and he alone, at home, stands with the Congress as a whole, as constituted representatives of the entire American people. In the exercise of his grave responsibilities, I believe we have a profound responsibility to give him whatever understanding and support we can, in good conscience and in conformity with our independent duties. I believe we owe it to the nation of which all our States are a part—particularly in matters of foreign relations—to give to him not only responsible opposition, but responsible cooperation.

"And, finally, within this body, I believe that every member ought to be equal in fact, no less than in theory, that they have a primary responsibility to the people whom they represent to face the legislative issues of the nation. And to the extent that the Senate may be inadequate in this connection, the remedy lies not in the seeking of shortcuts, not in the cracking of nonexistent whips, not in wheeling and dealing, but in an honest facing of the situation and a resolution of it by the Senate itself, by accommodation, by respect for one another, by mutual restraint and, as necessary, adjustments in the procedures of this body.

"The constitutional authority and responsibility does not lie with the leadership. It lies with all of us individually, collectively, and equally. And in the last analysis, deviations from that principle must in the end act to the detriment of the institution. And, in the end, that principle cannot be made to prevail by rules. It can prevail only if there is a high degree of accommodation, mutual restraint, and a measure of courage—in spite of our weaknesses—in all of us. It can prevail only if we recognize that, in the end, it is not the Senators as individuals who are of fundamental importance. In the end, it is the institution of the Senate. It is the Senate itself as one of the foundations of the Constitution. It is the Senate as one of the rocks of the Republic."

Thus ended my abridged observations of November 1963.

In my remarks during the 1976 dedication ceremonies in this chamber, I returned to the themes of 1963. I stated my belief that, in its fundamentals, the Senate of modern times may not have changed essentially from the Senate of Clay, Webster, and Calhoun.

What moved Senators yesterday still moves Senators today. We have the individual and collective strength of our predecessors and, I might add, their weaknesses. We are not all ten feet tall, nor were they. Senators act within the circumstances of their fears no less than their courage, their foibles as well as their strengths. Our concerns and our efforts in the Senate, like our predecessors and successors, arise from our goals of advancing the welfare of the people whom we represent, safeguarding the well-being of our respective States and protecting the present and future of this nation, a nation which belongs—as does this room—not to one of us, or to one generation, but to all of us and to all generations.

The significance of that 1976 gathering—and perhaps of our being here tonight—is to remind us that in a Senate of immense and still unfolding significance to the nation, each individual member can play only a brief and limited role. It is to remind us that the Senate's responsibilities go on, even though the faces and, yes, even the rooms in which they gather, fade into history. With the nation, the Senate has come a long way. And still, there is a long way to go.

CLINTON AND MANDELA ON
U.S. AND SOUTH AFRICAN ISSUES
March 27, 1998

President Bill Clinton traveled around sub-Saharan Africa for twelve days in late March and early April—the longest overseas trip of his presidency and nearly triple the total amount of time all his forty-one predecessors had spent on the continent. Clinton offered messages of regret for the world's indifference to and mistreatment of Africa, but he also expressed hope for a new era in which some African countries were moving toward democracy, human rights, free markets, and economic development.

Clinton encountered joyous and friendly crowds at nearly every stop on his trip, a welcome change of pace from the emphasis on scandal that for months had dogged his every move at home. The president visited six African countries between March 23 and April 2, in this order: Ghana, Uganda, Rwanda, South Africa, Botswana, and Senegal. Jimmy Carter had been the most recent previous president to visit Africa, in 1978.

Expressing Regrets

Although administration planners had intended to use the president's trip to spread an upbeat message about Africa, much of the world's attention during the trip inevitably focused on the bitter past. In his own statements during the first days of his journey, Clinton did much to revive unpleasant memories.

On March 23, the first day of his trip, Clinton told a crowd estimated at nearly 500,000 in Accra, Ghana, that he was trying to overcome American "stereotypes that have warped our view and weakened our understanding of Africa." The next day, Clinton expressed regret for slavery, telling an audience in Uganda: "Going back to the time before we were even a nation, European Americans received the fruits of the slave trade and we were wrong in that." Aides said Clinton's remark was an impromptu one; before the trip the administration had decided against a formal apology for slavery. Clinton also acknowledged that, during the cold war, the United States had tended to view Africa primarily as a battleground against commu-

nism. Washington, he said, for decades was more interested in where African and other Third World nations stood in terms of the U.S.-Soviet conflict "than how they stood in the struggle for their own people's aspirations to live up to the fullest of their God-given abilities."

On the third day of his trip, March 24, Clinton confronted the most recent and painful memory of the world's failures toward Africa. At the airport in Kigali, Rwanda, Clinton met with two groups of survivors of the 1994 Rwandan genocide, in which an estimated one million people died. The killings were carried out by the Rwandan military and vigilante groups, most of them members of the then-dominant Hutu tribe. Most of the victims were members of the rival Tutsi tribe, although tens of thousands of moderate Hutus also were killed. The United States was among the Western countries that rejected calls for a large United Nations peacekeeping force to contain the violence. (East African genocide, p. 614; Historic Documents of 1996, p. 809; Historic Documents of 1994, p. 541)

Speaking informally to a small group of people who lost relatives during the genocide, Clinton said: "We in the United States and the world community did not do as much as we could have and should have done to try to limit what occurred in Rwanda in 1994." Later, in a formal speech to a larger group of genocide survivors, the president expanded on that theme, saying the rest of the world "did not act quickly enough after the killings began." He noted, for example, that outside countries, such as the United States, failed to prevent Hutu killers from turning international refugee camps into "safe havens" from which they could launch their attacks on civilians. Clinton also acknowledged that he was among those who did not pay enough attention at the time to events in the Rwandan killing fields. "It may seem strange to you here, especially the many of you who lost members of your family, but all over the world there were people like me sitting in offices, day after day, who did not fully appreciate the depth and the speed with which you were being engulfed by this unimaginable terror," he said.

Even as Clinton spoke, violence was continuing in Rwanda. Hutu paramilitary forces, driven from the country after a Tutsi uprising in the wake of the 1994 genocide, were conducting raids in the northwestern part of the country, and the Rwandan military was launching counterattacks. Observers said that violence was killing dozens of people every week during the early part of 1998. Indeed, fear of Rwandan violence had led the U.S. Secret Service to oppose Clinton's trip to the country. Although the president was determined to visit Rwanda, security concerns limited his stay to a brief stopover at the airport; a planned ceremony at a nearby genocide memorial was canceled for the same reason.

Praising New Leaders

The president's expressions of regret for past failings caught most of the attention during the trip and undermined his administration's plans to showcase positive developments in Africa. In the weeks before the trip,

State Department officials had emphasized that U.S. policy toward Africa had shifted from the cold war focus of fighting communism to a new focus on trade, economic development, and building civil societies on the continent. A State Department "fact sheet" issued March 3 declared that there was "now more reason for optimism about Africa's future than at any time" since African nations gained their independence from colonial powers in the 1950s and 1960s.

A key element of the Clinton policy was supporting a new generation of African leaders who appeared to be genuinely interested in improving the lives of their people—as opposed to many leaders in the previous generation who were determined to enrich themselves and hold onto power. Although the Clinton administration promoted democracy as an essential element of nation building in Africa, in practice it was willing to support leaders who had gained power through nondemocratic means, so long as they advocated an open economy and the rule of law. Ghana, the first stop on Clinton's trip, illustrated the administration's approach. Jerry Rawlings, the Ghanaian leader who appeared with Clinton before the massive crowd in Accra, had seized power in a military coup d'etat but had implemented free-market economic reforms and had promised to leave office in 2000.

The Clinton administration also had high praise for Ugandan leader Yoweri K. Museveni, who had put his country on the road to economic recovery following years of misrule and corruption. A former guerrilla leader, Museveni appeared to have little interest in democracy and, in fact, had banned opposition parties. Clinton overlooked these shortcomings, however, saying he wanted "to listen and to learn" on his visit to Uganda.

Clinton took a somewhat different approach toward another African leader who, just a few months before, had been praised by Secretary of State Madeleine K. Albright. That leader was Laurent Kabila, another former guerrilla leader, who in 1997 had led the successful drive to oust the corrupt dictator of Zaire, President Mobutu Sese Seko. Now the president of the renamed Democratic Republic of Congo, Kabila appeared to be following in Mobutu's footsteps: repressing political opposition, ignoring calls for elections, and allowing supporters to raid the nation's abundant natural resources for their own gain. Clinton invited Kabila to a meeting in Uganda, along with other regional leaders, but refused to be seen with him in public. Clinton met privately with Kabila for about an hour and, according to aides, pressed him to move toward elections and clean up corruption. During the last half of 1998 Kabila faced an armed insurrection, led by some of his former supporters and backed by several regional governments. The rebellion resulted in many deaths and destabilized Kabila's regime but failed to force him from power. (Mobutu ouster, Historic Documents of 1997, p. 877)

Basking in Mandela's Glow

At the midpoint of his trip, Clinton spent nearly three days in South Africa, meeting with political and business leaders and the public in a *nation that just a few years before had been ruled by a white minority. On March 26, Clinton addressed the multiracial South African parliament, praising the country's budding democracy and promising American political and economic support for it.*

The next day, on March 27, Clinton met privately with South African president Nelson Mandela and then traveled to Robben Island, an apartheid-era prison in the Atlantic Ocean eight miles northwest of Cape Town. Mandela had been a prisoner on Robben Island for eighteen years, forced to break rocks by day and live in a tiny cell at night—all for the crime of opposing white minority rule. Mandela gave Clinton a tour of the prison, which had been turned into a memorial for those who had fought apartheid. "When I come here, I call back into memory that great saga in which the authorities, who were pitiless, insensitive and cruel, nevertheless failed in their evil intentions," Mandela told Clinton. Ushering Clinton into the six foot by six foot cell where he had slept on the floor for fourteen years, Mandela said: "This was my home." The prison visit clearly was an emotional experience for both men. Later in the day, Clinton noted that Mandela had emerged from prison in 1990 "not in anger, but in hope, passion, and determination to put things right." (Mandela prison release, Historic Documents of 1990, p. 65)

Just before the prison visit, Clinton and Mandela held a joint news conference, during which they expressed similar views on the need for political and economic reforms in Africa. But Clinton sat silently as Mandela publicly lectured him on issues of disagreement between South Africa and the United States. Mandela noted that he had maintained cordial relations with Cuba, Iran, and Libya—each of which was subject to U.S. economic and political sanctions. Mandela said those countries had supported the antiapartheid movement. "Those South Africans who have berated me for being loyal to our friends, literally, they can go and throw themselves in a pool," he said. "I'm not going to betray the trust of those who helped us."

Mandela also criticized as "unacceptable" legislation promoted by the Clinton administration, and pending in Congress, that would have given trade preferences to African nations that implemented free market policies and that observed the U.S. sanctions against Cuba, Iran, and Libya. That trade legislation failed in Congress later in 1998.

Following are excerpts from a joint news conference by U.S. president Bill Clinton and South African president Nelson Mandela, held March 27, 1998, in Cape Town, South Africa:

President Mandela: ... President Clinton, a visit by a foreign head of state to a country is, broadly speaking, one of the most significant developments in entrenched strong political and economic relations between the countries concerned. During this last four years, we have received a record number of heads of states and heads of government. They have come from all continents and practically from every country. They have come from the industrial nations; they have come from the developing world. Some have advanced democratic institutions; in others, such institutions are just developing; in others, there are none at all.

We have received all of them, and we have welcomed those visitors because that they have taught us things which we have not known before. We have democratic countries, but where poverty of the masses of the people is rife. We have had countries where there are no popular institutions at all, but they are able to look after their people better than the so-called democratic countries. I have visited one which is a creditor nation, which has got one of the highest standards of living in the world, which is tax-free, which has got one of the best schemes of subsidy and housing, for medical services, and where education is free and compulsory. And yet, the people in that country have no votes, they have no parliament. And yet they are looked after better than in so-called democratic countries. We insist that even in those countries that people must have votes. Even though they may enjoy all the things which the masses of the people in other countries don't enjoy, democratic institutions are still critical.

So we have received heads of states and heads of government from all those countries. But the visit to our country by President Clinton is the high-water mark. And I hope that the response of our parliamentarians yesterday has indicated that very clear.

Our people have welcomed President Clinton with open arms. And it is correct that that should be so, because President Clinton, as well as the First Lady, Hillary, they have the correct instincts on the major international questions facing the world today. Whatever mistakes that they may have made—and we have made many—but there is one thing that you cannot be accused of—of not having the right instincts. And for that reason, I hold him, and almost every South African, in high respect.

The fact that we have high respect for him does not mean that we have no differences. But I would like to declare that when we have differed on an issue, at the end of that, my respect for him is enhanced because I fully accept his integrity and his bona fides, but such differences are unavoidable.

One of the first heads of state I invited to this country was Fidel Castro. I have received in this country ex-President Rafsanjani of Iraq. I have also invited the leader [Libyan president Muammar] Qaddafi to this country. And I do that because our moral authority dictates that we should not abandon those who helped us in the darkest hour in the history of this country. Not only did they support us in rhetoric, they gave us the resources for us to conduct the struggle and the will. And those South Africans who have berated me for being loyal to our friends, literally, they can go and throw themselves into a pool. I am not going to betray the trust of those who helped us.

The United States is acknowledged far and wide as the world leader, and it is correct, that should be so. And we have, today, a leader, as I have said, whose instincts are always correct. I would like to draw attention to a very important provision in the United Nation's Charter, that provision which enjoins, which calls upon all member states to try and settle their differences by peaceful methods. That is the correct position which has influenced our own approach towards problems.

We had a government which had slaughtered our people, massacred them like flies, and we had a black organization which we used for that purpose. It was very repugnant to think that we could sit down and talk with these people, but we had to subject our blood to our brains, and had to say without these enemies of ours, we can never bring about a peaceful transformation in this country. And that is what we did.

The reason why the world has opened its arms to South Africans is because we are able to sit down with our enemies and to say let us stop slaughtering one another—let's talk peace. We were complying with the provisions of the United Nations Charter. And the United States as the leader of the world should set an example to all of us to help eliminate tensions throughout the world. And one of the best ways of doing so is to call upon its enemies to say let's sit down and talk peace. I have no doubt that the role of the United States as the world leader will be tremendously enhanced.

I must also point out that we are far advanced in our relations with the United States as a result of the efforts of Deputy President Thabo Mbeki and Vice President Al Gore. That [Binational] Commission has achieved, has had a high rate of performance far beyond our dreams. And today America has become the largest investor in our country. Trade between us has increased by 11 percent.

And we have the president of the ANC [African National Congress], who carefully pushed me out of this position—and took it over—the president of the ANC and the Deputy President of this country is one of those who, more than anybody else in this country, is committed to the improvement of relations between South Africa and the United States. I hope that when he succeeds in pushing me to step down from the presidency, and the country will put him in that position so that he can be in a position further to improve relations between us. And I have no doubt that we have no better person than him to complete this job.

President Clinton, you are welcome. This is one of our proudest moments, to be able to welcome you. You helped us long before you became President and you have continued with that help now as the President of the greatest country in the world. Again, welcome.

President Clinton: Thank you very much, Mr. President. Thank you and all the people of South Africa for the wonderful welcome you have given to Hillary and me, and to our entire delegation. We have felt very much at home here.

As I have said yesterday in my address to the Parliament, I was very honored to be the first American President to visit South Africa on a mission to Africa to establish a new partnership between the United States and the nations of Africa, and to show the people of America the new Africa that is emerging—an Africa where the number of democratic governments has quadrupled since 1990; where economies are beginning to grow; where deep-seated problems, to be sure, continue to exist, but where hope for the future is stronger than it has been in a generation.

It is in our profound interest to support the positive changes in Africa's life. Nowhere is this more evident than in the miracle you have wrought here in South Africa.

The partnership between our nations is only four years old, but already we are laying the foundation for a greater future. And I think everyone knows that the most important reason for our success is President Mandela.

His emergence from his many years on Robben Island is one of the true heroic stories of the 20th century. And more importantly, he emerged not in anger, but in hope, passion, determination to put things right in a spirit of rec-onciliation and harmony. Not only here, but all over the world, people, espe-cially young people, have been moved by the power of his example.

Yesterday Mr. Mandela said that the only thing that disappointed him about our trip was that Hillary and I did not bring our daughter. Last night our daugh-ter called us and said the only reason she was really sorry not to have made her second trip to Africa was that she didn't get to see President Mandela.

I think that the impact he has had on the children of the world who see that fundamental goodness and courage and largeness of spirit can prevail over power lust, division, and obsessive small news in politics, is a lesson that everybody can learn every day from. And we thank you, Mr. President, for that.

Today we talked about how the United States and South Africa can move into the future together. We have reaffirmed our commitment to increasing our mutual trade and investment, to bringing the advantages of the global economy to all our people. South Africa is already our largest trading partner in Africa, and, as the President said, America is the largest foreign investor in South Africa. And we want to do more.

The presence here of our Commerce Secretary and leaders from our busi-ness community underscores, Mr. President, how important these ties are to us, and our determination to do better. Our Overseas Private Investment Cor-poration is creating there new investment funds for Africa which will total more than three-quarters of a billion dollars. The first of these, the Africa Opportunity Fund, is already supporting transportation and telecommunica-tion projects here in South Africa. The largest of the funds, worth $500 mil-lion, will help to build the road, the bridges, the communication networks Africa needs to fulfill its economic potential.

Increasing trade does not mean ending aid. I am proud that we have pro-vided almost $1 billion in assistance to South Africa since 1991. I am com-mitted to working with Congress to return our aid for all of Africa to its his-toric high levels. We will target our assistance to investing in the future of the African people. If people lack the fundamentals of a decent life, like educa-tion or shelter, they won't be able to seize opportunity.

I announced in Uganda a new $120-million initiative to train teachers, increase exchanges, bring technology into classrooms throughout Africa.

We're also working to help provide better housing for those who have never had it. Yesterday Hillary, with me in tow, went back a year later to visit the Victoria Mxenge housing project in Guguletu, where women are building their own homes for the first time. I'm proud that through our aid projects and our Binational Commission with Mr. Mbeki and Vice President Gore we are providing seed money and technical assistance for this effort. And I want to do more of that throughout this country and throughout the continent.

President Mandela was also kind enough to speak with me at some great length about other nations in Africa and our common goals for Africa in the future. We are determined to help countries as they work to strengthen their democracies. We agree human rights are the universal birthright of all people. I also had a great chance to talk to President Mandela about the progress we made at the regional summit in Entebbe. And he had read the communiqué we put out, and I think that we both agree it was a remarkable document. And if we can make it real, it will change things in a profound way in all the countries that signed off on the statement.

We're also working on security issues, and let me just mention a couple. We are committed to preventing the spread of weapons of mass destruction, to strengthening the Biological Weapons Convention, because we both believe disease must never be used as a weapon of war. We are both at the forefront of the effort to eliminate the scourge of land mines. And now we are joining together to speed this work.

As I said yesterday, and I'd like to emphasize again, I am very pleased that our Department of Defense has decided to purchase new South African de-mining vehicles, called the Cubbies. The vehicles will help us to remove mines more quickly, more safely, and more effectively. And I might say, that's been a terrible problem the world over. Even in Bosnia where there are so many people, we're not taking enough mines out of the land every week. And the new South Africa technology will help us immensely.

Mr. President, for centuries the winds that blow around the Cape of Good Hope have been known for strength and danger. Today the winds blowing through Cape Town and South Africa, and indeed much of this continent, are winds of change and good fortune. I thank you for being so much the cause of the good that is occurring not only in your own country, but throughout this continent.

I am deeply pleased that we're committed to harnessing the winds of change together. And as we meet in your nation, which has seen such remarkable hope arise from the ashes of terrible tragedy, let me again thank you. . . .

Q: Mr. President, you expressed regret the other day that the United States supported authoritarian regimes in Africa during the Cold War. Today, we buy about 50 percent of the oil from Nigeria, propping up a regime the United States says is one of the most oppressive in Africa.—what will the United States do—

President Clinton: Well, first of all, let me restate what I said because I think it's worth saying again. I said that I did not believe the United States had ever been as good a partner to the African nations and the African people as we could have been, and that during the Cold War, when we and the Soviets were worried about the standoff that we had between us, we tended to evaluate governments in Africa and to pick and chose among them and to give aid to them based far more on how they stood in the fight of the Cold War than how they stood toward the welfare of their people. I stand by that. And I think now we're free to take a different course.

President Mandela and I actually talked at some length about this today, and I, frankly, asked for his advice. And Nigeria is the largest country in Africa in terms of population. It does have vast oil resources. It has a large army. It is capable of making a significant contribution to Regional security, as we have seen in the last several months. My policy is to do all that we can to persuade General Abacha to move toward general democracy and respect for human rights—release of the political prisoners; the holding of elections. If he stands for election, we hope he will stand as a civilian.

There are many military leaders who have taken over chaotic situations in African countries, but have moved toward democracy. And that can happen in Nigeria; that is, purely and simply, what we want to happen. Sooner, rather than later, I hope. . . .

Q: On regret again, sir, why are you revisiting those who seek a formal apology from the United States for America's own shameful behavior?

President Clinton: Well, let me say, first of all, there are two different issues here on the slavery issue. Most of the members of the African community with whom I talk at home advise me to keep our race initiative focused on the future.

I don't think anybody believes that there is a living American—I don't think that anyone believes that any living American today would defend, feel proud of, or in any way stand up for the years where we had slavery or the awful legacy which it left in its wake. But we have moved through now in the last 130, almost last 140 years, the 13th, 14th and 15th amendments, a spate of civil rights legislation. We're now focused on what still needs to be done, and it's considerable. So at home we're looking to the future—to closing the opportunity gap, to dealing with the discrimination that still exists, trying to lift up those communities that have done better than others, as we become not primarily just a divided society between blacks and whites, but increasingly multicultural, not only with our large Hispanic and Native American populations, but with people from all over the world.

Now, in addition to that, what I tried to do the other day in Uganda is to recognize that the role of Americans in buying slaves, which were taken out of Africa by European slave traders, had a destructive impact in Africa, as well as for the people who were enslaved and brought to America. And I think that was an appropriate thing to do. I don't think anybody would defend what we did in terms of its destructive impact in Africa. No American President has ever been here before, had a chance to say that.

And I think we want more and more African leaders to do what President [Yoweri Kaguta] Museveni [of Uganda] did the other day when we were in

Entebbee, and he said, I am not one of those leaders who blames everybody else for our problems. I think we've got—you know, you've got to quit going back to the colonial era, we've got to look to the future.

If you want to see more Africa leaders do that, which I do, than it seems to me that we have to come to terms with our past. And stating the facts, it seems to me, is helpful. I think we are going to be a good partner with people who are talking responsibility for their own future, we can't be blind to the truths of the past.

That's what—I think Mr. Mandela has done a remarkable job of balancing those two things here in South Africa. That's why I made the statement I did in Uganda, and I'm glad I did it. . . .

GAO ON GOVERNMENT AIRLINE SAFETY ENFORCEMENT
March 30, 1998

The nation's air traffic safety system—a frequent target of criticism and controversy—came in for more of the same during 1998. As in the past, the chief target of complaints was the Federal Aviation Agency (FAA), the bureau responsible for overseeing safety and security procedures for all U.S. airports, airlines, and airplane repair facilities.

The General Accounting Office (GAO), the investigative arm of Congress, issued several reports during the year that were critical of the FAA. The GAO's most comprehensive report came in a study, released March 30, entitled "Weaknesses in Inspection and Enforcement Limit FAA in Identifying and Responding to Risks." In the report, the GAO reviewed many of the FAA's procedures for inspecting airports and airlines for safety and security problems, along with the FAA's methods of mandating corrections for the problems it found.

The report pointed to many of the same types of organization and budgetary problems that the GAO had found in previous studies of the FAA, including excessive paperwork requirements, lax inspection standards, faulty follow-through on safety problems, and inadequate staff for inspections and enforcement. The GAO based its report on a review of FAA records and surveys, as well as interviews with FAA inspectors.

The GAO cited problems with relying on FAA records. For example, it noted that the agency's databases did not distinguish between major and minor violations of safety or security regulations. The GAO also said that more than half of the FAA inspectors it surveyed said they did not initiate enforcement measures to correct problems—especially minor problems— either because the FAA forced them to fill out too much paperwork or because the inspectors disagreed with the agency's reporting requirements. As a result, the GAO said, FAA information on safety compliance was "incomplete and of limited use in providing early warning of potential risks and in targeting inspection resources to the greatest risks."

The level of FAA enforcement of safety regulations also varied from region to region. For example, the GAO found that in fiscal year 1996 one FAA region filed legal actions in two-thirds of cases involving security violations, while another region filed legal actions in only one-fourth of similar cases. These types of differences led to "perceived inconsistencies" in the agency's response to regulatory violations, the GAO stated.

FAA attorneys routinely reduced the level of fines and suspensions that inspectors had recommended for safety and security violations, partly because they did not have enough resources to prosecute all the cases brought to them. Between fiscal years 1990 and 1996, for example, FAA attorneys reduced the level of recommended suspensions in more than half of 11,658 cases of violations, the GAO reported.

To correct these and similar problems the GAO issued several recommendations, including requiring that FAA inspectors report all safety and security violations and that they be given guidance on how to distinguish between major and minor violations. GAO said the FAA's enforcement resources should be targeted on the cases "with the greatest potential impact on aviation safety and security."

The Department of Transportation—the FAA's parent organization—filed objections to many of the GAO observations and conclusions. The department said, for example, that the overall record of the aviation industry was a better indicator of safety standards than the FAA records cited by the GAO.

Other GAO Reports

In an April 24 report to Congress entitled "Aviation Security: Implementation of Recommendations Is Under Way, but Completion Will Take Several Years," the GAO said the FAA and other federal agencies were making progress in implementing some of the fifty-seven recommendations put forth by the White House Commission on Aviation Safety and Security. Known as the Gore Commission because it was chaired by Vice President Al Gore, that panel in 1996 and 1997 recommended sweeping changes in aviation regulations, including installation of an expensive new computer system for the nation's outdated air traffic control network. (Gore Commission, Historic Documents of 1997, p. 116)

The GAO report tracked implementation of five major Gore Commission recommendations that Congress also mandated in the 1996 Federal Aviation Reauthorization Act (PL 104–205). The FAA, its sister agencies, and the airlines were working on all the recommendations but had fallen behind several of the target dates. For example, the GAO noted that none of the nation's airlines had implemented a controversial passenger "profiling" system by the end of 1997, as had been proposed. Under the system, airlines would compare passenger lists against computer profiles of the types of passengers who might pose security risks, such as a passenger with no luggage who purchased a ticket with cash at the last minute before takeoff. Civil liberties groups and some organizations representing Arab Ameri-

cans had objected to the profiling recommendation. The GAO said three major carriers began using the system early in 1998 and other major carriers were to follow suit later in the year.

In another report, issued June 2, the GAO faulted FAA slowness in carrying out recommendations, made between 1995 and 1997 by the National Research Council and an FAA advisory committee, for improving air safety in adverse weather conditions. The GAO convened a panel of aviation safety experts who concluded that the FAA had failed to provide the necessary leadership to carry out the recommendations, had failed to improve coordination of weather-related operations with other agencies, was not providing adequate training or guidance on weather-related issues to key people such as air traffic controllers and pilots, and had allocated insufficient funding for programs to improve air safety in adverse weather conditions.

The FAA took a beating on similar issues during an August 27 hearing of the National Transportation Safety Board (NTSB). That hearing reviewed the January 9, 1997, crash near Detroit of a Comair EMB-120 turboprop plane; all twenty-nine people aboard were killed in the crash, which was blamed on heavy ice buildup. NTSB Chairman James E. Hall and other safety board officials strongly criticized the FAA for not ordering airlines to use new de-icing procedures that had been developed in recent years.

FAA Safety Steps in 1998

In response to criticisms from other agencies and to events that demonstrated lapses in aviation safety and security, the FAA took several major steps during 1998. One formerly obscure issue that suddenly hit the headlines involved the flammability of airplane insulation. Aviation experts said insulation may have helped spread a fire in the Swiss Air Flight 111 plane (a McDonnell-Douglas MD-11) that crashed into the Atlantic Ocean near Halifax, Nova Scotia, on September 2, killing all 229 persons on board. A month later, the FAA said it was developing new standards for airplane insulation and was recommending that airlines replace existing insulation during regular maintenance.

There also were continuing repercussions during the year from investigations into the July 18, 1996, crash of TWA Flight 800 near Long Island, New York, in which all 230 persons on board were killed. The crash apparently was caused by an explosion in the plane's center fuel tank. Although the exact cause of the explosion was still under investigation, the NTSB was focusing on wiring in the plane's fuel-monitoring system. In April the board recommended the rewiring of hundreds of planes. In May, after an inspection showed faulty wiring in a Boeing 737 jet, the FAA ordered immediate wiring inspections of all Boeing 737's that had flown more than 40,000 hours. The inspections turned up dozens of cases of damaged wiring; the planes were allowed to return to service after the wiring had been repaired. Aviation experts praised the FAA for its prompt action in that case. (TWA Flight 800 investigations, Historic Documents of 1997, p. 780)

Also in May—one month after a near-collision of two planes over New York's LaGuardia Airport—the FAA ordered additional training of all air traffic controllers. A controller was faulted for allowing the planes to approach within twenty feet of each other.

Following is the executive summary of the report, "Weaknesses in Inspection and Enforcement Limit FAA in Identifying and Responding to Risks," issued March 30, 1998, by the General Accounting Office:

Purpose

The Federal Aviation Administration (FAA) regulates and monitors the safety and security of air transportation and air commerce, an effort supported by the aviation industry through training and self-monitoring programs. Both the agency and the industry have come under increased scrutiny since the fatal crashes of ValuJet Flight 592 in May 1996 and TWA Flight 800 in July 1996. The public has demanded better government oversight of aviation safety and security, and congressional hearings have focused on FAA's training of inspectors, targeting of inspection resources, and use of enforcement actions.

The Senate Committee on Commerce, Science, and Transportation and its Subcommittee on Aviation, which oversee FAA, asked GAO [General Accounting Office] to respond to the following two questions: (1) What were the outcomes of FAA's inspection process in fiscal years 1990 through 1996? (2) What were the outcomes of FAA's enforcement process during this period? To respond to these questions, GAO analyzed FAA's inspection and enforcement data for fiscal years 1990 through 1996 and in February and March 1997 conducted nationwide surveys of 600 safety inspectors and 175 security special agents who perform inspections for FAA. GAO also interviewed safety and security inspectors in two FAA regions, managers in all FAA programs that conduct inspections, and regional counsels in all nine FAA regions.

Background

FAA's aviation safety and security programs provide for the initial certification, periodic surveillance, and inspection of airlines, airports, repair stations, and other aviation entities, as well as of pilots and mechanics. These inspections are intended not only to detect actual violations but also to serve as part of an early warning system for identifying potential systemwide threats to aviation safety and security. Safety inspections range from a visual check by an individual FAA inspector of a pilot or an aircraft at the gate (ramp inspection) or during a flight (en route inspection) to a special in-depth inspection of an entity (airline) or a facility (repair station) that may last a week or longer and involve a team of inspectors. Security inspections typically range from a daily spot-check of an airport's security by a pair of inspectors to a comprehensive annual inspection involving larger teams systematically checking an airport's compliance with all applicable security regulations and requirements. When safety and security inspectors identify violations, agencywide guidance requires that such violations be investigated and appropriately addressed, and program office guidance requires that violations be reported in their respective program office's database for tracking the results of inspections.

FAA's enforcement program affords a range of options for responding to violations of aviation safety and security regulations, from providing training or issuing warning notices to imposing penalties, such as fines or suspensions of operating certificates, called certificate actions. Although FAA has long depended on the willingness of certificate holders to adhere to regulatory requirements, it has, since 1990, increased its emphasis on gaining compliance through cooperative rather than punitive means.

At the end of fiscal year 1996, FAA had about 3,000 inspection staff predominately based in the agency's nine regions. These inspectors worked in five FAA program offices with a budget of $535 million. Two of these offices followed up on reports of violations by opening nearly 90 percent of the enforcement cases and were, therefore, the focus of GAO's review: The Flight Standards Service (Flight Standards), which oversees aviation safety, had a budget of $322 million in fiscal year 1996, and the Office of Civil Aviation Security (Security) had a budget of $67 million to oversee the security of the nation's airports and air carriers and monitor the transportation of hazardous materials by air. When Flight Standards inspectors find problems (which include but are not limited to violations), they are required to enter their findings into a database for tracking the results of inspections. Security inspectors, called special agents, are required to report violations in one of two databases. In addition to tracking the results of inspections, these Flight Standards and Security databases track all activities performed by inspectors. Inspectors in both programs generally choose whether to open enforcement cases. FAA's field and regional program offices decide whether to handle these cases through administrative actions, such as warning notices; legal actions, such as fines or suspensions of operating certificates; or no action. If legal actions are chosen, the cases are handled by FAA regional or headquarters legal staff, who negotiate many of the final penalties.

The aviation community shares the responsibility for ensuring aviation safety and security. Many airlines, repair stations, and aviation companies conduct internal reviews and/or have quality assurance programs to foster and monitor their own compliance with FAA's regulations. In addition, some airlines and pilots participate in voluntary self-disclosure programs or partnership programs with FAA to identify and correct violations without being penalized.

Results in Brief

While there are no direct measures of the aviation industry's compliance with aviation safety and security regulations, the results of FAA's inspections provide both an indirect measure of the industry's compliance and an early warning of potential safety and security problems. In fiscal years 1990 through 1996, nearly 96 percent of the 2 million inspections conducted by Flight Standards and Security resulted in no reports of problems or violations. GAO questions whether this rate is a meaningful measure of the aviation industry's compliance with regulations for several reasons. First, many inspectors do not report all problems or violations they observe. In addition, many inspections are not thorough or structured enough to detect many violations. Finally, FAA's inspection tracking systems do not distinguish major from minor violations. FAA's information on compliance in the aviation industry is thus incomplete and of limited use in providing early warning of potential risks and in targeting inspection resources to the greatest risks.

During fiscal years 1990 through 1996, FAA inspectors opened nearly 110,000 enforcement cases to follow up on reports of violations from their inspections and from noninspection sources. Forty-five percent of the 110,000 enforcement cases were initiated as a result of inspections conducted by FAA. FAA inspectors also followed up on reports of violations from outside sources, such as police reports and public complaints, which accounted for 41 percent of the enforcement cases opened. In the remaining 14 percent of the cases, FAA inspectors followed up on violations reported by other FAA personnel, such as air traffic controllers who reported instances when aircraft deviated from their assigned flight altitudes. Inspectors exercised discretion in opening enforcement cases in response to reported problems and violations; not all reported problems or violations resulted in enforcement cases. When compliance could be gained informally, for example, many inspectors did not open cases. The amount of paperwork and the time needed to reenter inspection results in a separate enforcement database also discouraged inspectors from opening cases.

FAA resolved almost 121,000 enforcement cases during this same period, using administrative actions (46 percent), legal actions (34 percent), or no action (19 percent). The resolution could not be determined for 1 percent of the enforcement cases because of missing data. When resolving cases through legal action, FAA's legal staff generally negotiated lower penalties than the agency's inspection staff had recommended, reducing fines in 80 percent of the civil penalties closed and suspension days in 58 percent of the certificate actions settled. FAA legal staff told us that they do not have the legal resources to litigate all cases and that penalties were lowered for many reasons, including insufficient evidence to support certain charges and precedents for lower penalties set in prior cases. The impact of FAA's enforcement actions on compliance is difficult to assess because FAA has not followed up on the aviation industry's implementation of corrective actions.

In part because FAA's enforcement database, like FAA's inspection databases, does not distinguish major from minor cases, FAA cannot readily set risk-based priorities for resolving enforcement cases. Both the sequence and the time for processing enforcement cases often depended on factors other than the cases' impact on aviation safety and security. In addition, workload, accused violators' requests for additional information about their cases, and statutes of limitation or other deadlines for initiating certain types of cases influenced the sequence and the time for processing enforcement cases.

Principal Findings

FAA's Inspection Activities

Overall, during fiscal years 1990 through 1996, 96 percent of Flight Standards' inspections and 91 percent of Security's inspections resulted in no reports of problems or violations. Both the underreporting of observed problems or violations and the reliance on unstructured inspections by individual inspectors may result in the underreporting of problems or violations. Despite guidance requiring them to enter all observed problems or violations into their respective office's inspection tracking system, 35 percent of the Flight Standards inspectors and 32 percent of the Security inspectors surveyed by GAO said that they reported half or fewer of the problems or violations they observed during inspections in fiscal year 1996, the year covered by the survey. In some cases, FAA inspectors interviewed did not agree on the agency's reporting requirements; in other cases, inspectors did not report violations if compliance could be achieved informally. In addition, Flight Standards does not specify minimum or key tasks to be accomplished during ramp and en route inspections, even though DOT's Inspector General has issued recommendations to this effect several times since 1992. GAO's recent review of repair stations suggests that more intensive, structured team inspections identify more safety problems than unstructured inspections by individual inspectors. Moreover, when Security began in fiscal year 1996 to combine comprehensive inspections requiring the completion of specified tasks with rigorous, unannounced tests of security directives, the rate of violations found during its inspections more than doubled, rising from 9 percent to 19 percent.

The lack of distinction between major and minor violations in FAA's inspection tracking systems, combined with incomplete information on the frequency of violations, hampers FAA in using the results of its inspections as an early warning system for identifying potential threats to aviation safety and security, as well as in allocating its inspection resources to the greatest potential threats. GAO reported 10 years ago that FAA needed to develop criteria for targeting safety inspections to airlines whose characteristics may indicate safety problems, and in February 1995 and April 1996, GAO identified serious problems with the quality of the data systems on which FAA's targeting depends. Although Flight Standards has developed a system for targeting its inspections, this system relies on the database whose accuracy is compromised by incomplete information. Because of these and other problems, inspectors are making limited use of this system.

FAA's Enforcement Activities

In fiscal years 1990 through 1996, FAA's inspections generated the largest percentage of violation reports that led to enforcement cases, followed by sources outside FAA, and then other sources within FAA. Other noninspection activities conducted by air traffic controllers and other FAA personnel can identify violations that result in violation reports and may lead to enforcement actions. Sources outside FAA included, for example, the police (21 percent), who filed reports when they arrested individuals carrying weapons through airport security checkpoints or using drugs on aviation-related jobs; the public (5 percent); and the aviation industry (4 percent).

Inspectors exercise discretion in opening enforcement cases. In fiscal years 1990 through 1996, Flight Standards opened about one enforcement case for every four inspections that identified problems (25,392 cases for 88,912 inspections with problems). This number is consistent with the fact that problems may but do not always include regulatory violations. It also reflects FAA's current emphasis on gaining voluntary compliance rather than pursuing formal enforcement cases. In addition, inspectors may not initiate cases because of burdensome paperwork and because prior cases were dropped or recommended penalties were lowered. For example, in response to our survey, well over half of the Flight Standards inspectors (66 percent) and Security inspectors (58 percent) said they do not initiate enforcement cases because doing so entails too much paperwork, especially for minor violations. In their view, the paperwork is not worth the effort for many violations. In addition, because the enforcement database is not linked to the program offices' inspection tracking systems, the results of inspections must be entered manually a second time for violations that result in enforcement cases. In Security, the number of enforcement cases opened (12,850) exceeded the number of inspections with reported violations (11,052). This difference reflects the fact that certain types of violations can result in cases against more than one air carrier. For example, one violation at an airport security checkpoint that serves several air carriers could lead to cases against all of the carriers. While the vast majority of Flight Standards inspectors and Security inspectors rated their own efforts at fostering compliance with the Federal Aviation Regulations in fiscal year 1996 as successful, fewer than one-third of these inspectors rated FAA's enforcement process as an excellent or good method for fostering compliance.

In resolving enforcement cases, FAA has increased its use of administrative actions, such as warning notices, and reduced its reliance on legal actions, such as fines and suspensions of operating certificates. Administrative actions, which closed 35 percent of FAA's enforcement cases in fiscal years 1990 through 1992, accounted for over half of the agency's enforcement actions closed in fiscal years 1994 through 1996. FAA's regions varied, sometimes substantially, in their use of enforcement actions. In fiscal year 1996, for example, Security used legal actions nearly two-thirds of the time in one region and less than one-fourth of the time in another region. Department of Transportation (DOT) and FAA officials attributed these differences broadly to differences in regional enforcement philosophies or to variations in workload, the entities overseen, and community standards and laws. We were unable to verify any specific links between these factors and the regional variations in enforcement actions. Such regional variations and the discretion exercised by inspectors and legal staff were cited by airline officials and private attorneys interviewed as contributing to perceived inconsistencies in FAA's response to regulatory violations.

FAA's legal staff frequently negotiated reductions in the penalties recommended by the inspection staff for both civil penalty cases and certificate actions. Attorneys reduced the recommended fines in about 80 percent of the 20,179 civil penalty cases closed during fiscal years 1990 through 1996, arriving at a median final penalty of 25 cents for each dollar proposed by the inspection staff, including dropping the fines altogether for one-third of the cases. Attorneys also reduced the recommended suspensions in 58 percent of the 11,658 certificate actions settled during the same period, accepting a median suspension of 30 days instead of the median 60 days recommended by inspectors. In 27 percent of the certificate action cases, they settled for no suspensions at all. In addition, although FAA assessed fines against all types of aviation operators, it suspended the operating privileges of small operators and individuals, but not of major or national air carriers. The regional counsels in FAA's nine regional offices offered a number of reasons for the lower penalties, including insufficient evidence for certain charges, precedents set in prior cases, limits on the violator's ability to pay, and difficulties in calculating appropriate penalties for multiple violations. FAA's legal offices also varied in the extent to which they reduced fines. For example, the median fine ranged from 13 cents to 50 cents on the recommended penalty dollar for Flight Standards cases in fiscal year 1996.

The order in which enforcement cases were processed was determined by the regions, not by FAA headquarters. Because FAA's enforcement tracking system does not distinguish major from minor cases, it provided little information on relative risk for the regions to use in setting processing priorities. The time taken to process enforcement cases varied with the type of enforcement action taken: On average, administrative actions took 5 months while the average time for legal actions ranged from 15 months to 3 years, depending on the type of case. In addition, factors other than risk—such as the regions' enforcement caseload, the actions of violators, and various deadlines for initiating cases—often dictated both the time and the sequence for processing cases.

Recent and proposed changes in FAA's enforcement processes could reduce the time needed to resolve cases and help FAA target its resources more effectively to the cases with the greatest potential impact on safety and security. For example, the use of warning tickets, recently pilot-tested by Flight Standards in one region, provided immediate feedback to violators on their noncompliance, and the use of streamlined procedures for handling weapons cases, adopted by Security in fiscal year 1995, has already reduced the processing time for these legal cases to around 4 months, substantially down from the average of a little over 2 years for other civil penalty cases. Refining and expanding the use of these procedures could help FAA target its legal resources more effectively.

Recommendations

To strengthen FAA's inspection and enforcement processes, GAO recommends that the Secretary of Transportation direct the FAA Administrator to take several actions, including the following:

- Revise FAA's order on compliance and enforcement to specify that FAA's inspection staff are required to report all observed problems and violations in their respective program office's database for tracking the results of inspections.
- Provide guidance to FAA's inspection staff on how to distinguish major from minor violations and to legal staff on how to identify major legal cases.
- Improve and integrate FAA's inspection and enforcement databases to (1) identify major violations and major legal cases; (2) target inspection and legal resources to the violations and enforcement cases with the greatest potential impact on aviation safety and security; and (3) link inspection and enforcement data so that violations can be tracked from their identification through their resolution.

This report includes other recommendations to improve the usefulness of FAA's databases and the coordination of FAA's inspection and enforcement efforts.

Agency Comments

DOT expressed concern about the report's negative portrayal of FAA's efforts to oversee compliance with the Federal Aviation Regulations. DOT attributed GAO's conclusions to the use of inappropriate performance measures and selectivity in reporting survey results. DOT suggested that the safety record of air carriers transporting passengers and GAO's survey data on inspectors' assessments of their own success in fostering compliance would be better measures of the industry's compliance than inspection results. DOT further objected to the report's focus on systems for tracking FAA's inspection and enforcement activity as a means of evaluating the effectiveness of the oversight system. DOT stated that analysis of data in these tracking systems is but one tool at its disposal for assessing risk. Although DOT did not comment explicitly on GAO's recommendations, DOT agreed that actions can be taken that will further strengthen its inspection programs, improve compliance with applicable requirements, and strengthen its analytical capability. DOT added that some actions have already been completed and other actions are under way to make improvements, such as expediting the processing of cases through the use of warning tickets and streamlined procedures for Security weapons cases.

GAO's report offers a balanced portrayal of FAA's enforcement activities by presenting all of the relevant information developed in the course of GAO's review and identifying many actions in progress to improve the agency's existing systems and procedures. GAO's methodology is appropriate. The report is based on nationwide surveys of inspectors and complex analyses of FAA's inspection and enforcement data undertaken after extensive coordination with cognizant FAA legal and program officials. GAO placed the resulting data in context through interviews with inspectors about their workload, their reporting of violations, and the factors they weigh in deciding whether to initiate enforcement cases. Interviews with regional counsels added perspective on the constraints faced in handling and settling cases. The report describes serious weaknesses in FAA's processes for detecting and addressing the industry's violations of aviation regulations. These weaknesses hinder FAA in reliably using inspection data to identify and correct safety and security problems. As the report states, there are no direct measures of the industry's compliance with safety and security regulations. Given the relatively rare occurrence of fatal air carrier crashes, GAO believes that inspection results and other indicators of safety problems are appropriate indirect measures of the industry's compliance with the regulations that can provide early warning of potential safety risks and some sense of the industry's compliance with the regulations. As air traffic increases in the next decade, FAA's inspections and other indicators will be critical to improving safety and avoiding the increase in fatal crashes that is projected if the current crash rate continues. As requested by DOT, GAO incorporated into the report survey data showing that the vast majority of inspectors rated their own efforts in fostering compliance with the regulations as moderately or very successful. GAO also included related data showing that over two-thirds of the inspectors surveyed rated FAA's enforcement process as no better than fair as a method of fostering compliance. GAO concurs with DOT's assertion that inspection tracking systems are but one tool for assessing risk; however, underreporting by inspection staff and other inaccuracies in the tracking systems impair the reliability of these systems for understanding historical and current trends, assessing systemwide risks, and allocating FAA's resources to best address these and other potential risks.

April

UN REPORT ON THE USE OF THE DEATH PENALTY IN THE U.S.
April 3, 1998

The United States, long accustomed to pointing out human rights abuses in other countries, received a taste of that medicine on April 3 when a United Nations investigator denounced U.S. practices in imposing the death penalty. The investigator, Bacre Waly Ndiaye, a Senegalese lawyer working for the UN Human Rights Commission, reported that imposition of the death penalty was often arbitrary and discriminatory in the United States. Ndiaye called for a U.S. moratorium on executions—a position echoed by the commission itself, which also suggested that all countries move to abolish the death penalty.

The U.S. Supreme Court in 1972 struck down the death penalty as "cruel and unusual" punishment, ruling that various states were arbitrary and capricious in their imposition of it. The Court reversed itself in 1976, saying the death penalty did not violate the Constitution if procedures were in place to guard against arbitrary and discriminatory application of it. As of 1998 thirty-eight states had adopted the death penalty in capital cases. Ndiaye reported that nearly 3,300 people were on death row as of late 1997. On December 19, 1998, Andrew Lauren Smith, convicted of murdering an elderly couple in South Carolina in 1983, became the five hundredth person executed in the United States since the reintroduction of the death penalty. (Court on the death penalty, Historic Documents of 1976, p. 489)

Although no international treaties or commitments expressly prohibited the use of the death penalty by member nations of the United Nations, the International Convention on Civil and Political Rights, adopted by the UN General Assembly in 1966, strongly discouraged use of the death penalty. The United States delayed signing that treaty until 1992, and when it expressed reservations intended to protect U.S. practices in imposing the death penalty, including the execution of juvenile offenders.

The UN Report

Ndiaye, a former staff member of Amnesty International, the international human rights organization headquartered in London, visited the

183

United States from September 21 to October 8, 1997, to gather material for his report. He noted, with apparent annoyance, that numerous federal and state officials refused to meet with him or cooperate with his investigation. He was able to meet with only one sitting governor, George W. Bush of Texas, and one former governor, Mario Cuomo of New York.

In his report, Ndiaye noted that the death penalty was becoming increasingly common in the United States, in part because states and the federal government were continually adding offenses for which it could be imposed. This was counter to an "international trend towards the progressive reduction" of the number of offenses carrying the possibility of the death penalty, he said.

Ndiaye bluntly denounced the death penalty, as practiced in the United States, as a "step backwards in the promotion and protection of the right to life." Ndiaye focused in particular on the execution of juveniles (those under the age of eighteen) and mentally retarded and insane people. Executing juveniles, he said, violated international law because it was prohibited by the International Convention on Civil and Political Rights; this was one of the issues on which the United States entered a reservation when it signed that treaty. Ndiaye noted that the only other nations allowing execution of juveniles were Iran, Nigeria, Pakistan, Saudi Arabia, and Yemen. Execution of mentally retarded and insane people—allowed in twenty-eight states—was "in contravention of relevant international standards," Ndiaye said.

Imposition of the death penalty in the various states was subject to "a significant degree of unfairness and arbitrariness," Ndiaye's report concluded. "Race, ethnic origin and economic status appear to be key determinants of who will, and who will not, receive a death penalty." Ndiaye cited no direct evidence of discriminatory use of the death penalty. Instead, he noted such circumstantial evidence as the facts that the overwhelming majority of judges and prosecutors were white, especially in the South, and that a disproportionate percentage of prisoners on "death row" (41 percent as of late 1997) were black. Ndiaye said he was distressed by a 1987 U.S. Supreme Court ruling, in McCleskey v. Kemp, *which rejected the use of statistical studies intended to show racial discrimination in the general application of the death penalty. That ruling, he said, "has had the effect of allowing the courts to tolerate racial bias because of the great difficulties defendants face in proving individual acts of discrimination in their cases."* (Court on death penalty and race, Historic Documents of 1987, p. 463)

Ndiaye also pointed to two aspects of the American judicial system that influenced use of the death penalty. First, he said, the common practice of electing judges at the local and state level—coupled with allowing judicial candidates to solicit campaign contributions from lawyers and the general public—may risk interfering with the independence and impartiality of the judiciary. Second, the common practice of excluding from juries in capital cases those people who oppose or express doubts about the death penalty jeopardizes "the right to a fair trial before an impartial jury" that represents "the community conscience as a whole."

In his recommendations, Ndiaye echoed a 1997 proposal by the American Bar Association for a moratorium on the use of the death penalty. The bar association had said states should stop using the death penalty until they had adopted procedures to ensure that it was carried out "fairly and impartially, in accordance with due process" and that the risk of executing innocent people was minimized. Along with a general moratorium on the death penalty, Ndiaye called on states to stop executing juvenile offenders and the mentally retarded, and he said states should continue to honor a "de facto" moratorium on executing women. Even before Ndiaye's report was made public, Texas became the first state since 1984 to execute a woman. Karla Faye Tucker, convicted of murdering two people with a pickax, was executed on February 3.

U.S. Response

The UN investigator's report brought bristling responses from U.S. officials. George E. Moose, the U.S. ambassador to the Human Rights Commission, called the report "severely flawed." In a speech to the commission in Geneva on April 15, Moose denied that the United States was violating international law or standards in the use of the death penalty, and he accused Ndiaye of excluding from his report "valuable and extensive information" supporting the U.S. position. Bill Richardson, the U.S. ambassador to the UN, said the report would "collect a lot of dust."

Sen. Jesse Helms, the North Carolina Republican who chaired the Foreign Relations Committee and was a leading congressional critic of the UN, described Ndiaye's work as part of "an absurd UN charade." Marc Thiessen, a spokesman for Helms, said: "With all the abuses in places like Burma, China, Cuba, and Iraq, to be wasting time and money to investigate the freest country in the world shows what a strange and distant planet the United Nations inhabits."

On the same day it released Ndiaye's report, the UN Human Rights Commission voted for the second year in a row to call on nations that still had the death penalty to observe a moratorium on its use, "with a view to completely abolishing" it. The commission vote was 26–13, with 12 abstentions. The United States was joined in opposition by such nations as China, Congo, and the Sudan.

Court Ruling on Death Penalty Appeals

The Supreme Court issued a ruling on December 14 that would reduce the ability of federal courts to overturn state death penalty sentences. By a 5–4 ruling in Calderon v. Coleman, *the Court set standards for federal judges to use in reviewing death penalty appeals based on alleged constitutional flaws in state court trials. The Court ruled that a federal judge could overturn a death penalty only by determining that the trial court made errors that clearly and substantially influenced the jury's verdict.*

The Court's ruling came in a California case in which Russell Coleman was convicted of a 1979 rape and murder. A federal judge overturned the verdict, citing inaccurate instructions from the state judge, and the Ninth U.S. Circuit Court of Appeals upheld that action. In overturning the actions of the lower federal courts, the Supreme Court said the federal judiciary can block a state court's death penalty only when finding that a defendant "was actually prejudiced by" the flaws in the state court case. The ruling was the latest in a series of high court decisions apparently intended to reduce the involvement of the federal judiciary in appeals of state death penalty cases.

Following are excerpts from a report released April 3, 1998, on use of the death penalty in the United States, as prepared by Bacre Waly Ndiaye, special rapporteur for the United Nations Commission on Human Rights:

[Section I omitted]

II. The General Context of the Death Penalty in the United States

37. Currently, 40 jurisdictions in the United States of America have death penalty statutes. Thirteen other jurisdictions do not. According to the information received, 3,269 persons are on death row, of whom 47.05 per cent are White, 40.99 per cent are Black, 6.94 per cent are Hispanic, 1.41 per cent are Native American, and 0.70 per cent are Asian. Of the total death row population, more than 98 per cent are male.

38. Since the death penalty was reinstated in 1976, 403 persons have been executed. There have been no federal executions since 1963. Out of these 403 executions, only 6 white persons have reportedly been executed for the murder of a black person. Texas has been responsible for more than 30 per cent of the executions, followed by Virginia (10.17 per cent) and Florida (9.68 per cent). It is reported that since the reinstatement of death penalty statutes, more than 47 persons have been released from death row because of later evidence of their innocence. . . .

39. One hundred and fourteen women have reportedly been sentenced to death from 1973 to June 1997. Of them 47 are on death row and 66 had their sentences either reversed or commuted to life imprisonment. Florida, North Carolina and Texas account for the highest imposition of female death sentences. Female executions have been rare. The last woman executed was in 1984 in North Carolina.

40. Nine juvenile offenders, individuals aged less than 18 at the time they committed the crime for which they were convicted, have been executed. . . .

III. Findings of the Special Rapporteur

A. Current practices in the application of the death penalty

1. Reintroduction of death penalty statutes and extension of the scope

44. The Special Rapporteur has observed a tendency to increase the application of the death penalty both at the state level, either by reinstating the death penalty or by increasing the number of aggravating circumstances, and at the federal level, where the scope of this punishment has recently been dramatically extended. . . .

2. Execution of juveniles

49. International law prohibits the imposition of a death sentence on juvenile offenders (those who committed the crime while under 18 years of age). The consensus of the international community in this respect is reflected in the wide range of international legal instruments. . . .

51. Out of the 38 states with death penalty statutes, 14 provide that 18 is the minimum age for execution. In 4 states, 17 is the minimum age, while in 21 other states, 16 is the minimum age. According to the information received, 47 offenders who committed the crimes before the age of 18 are currently on death row. At the federal level, the imposition of the death penalty on juvenile offenders is not permitted.

52. In *Thompson v. Oklahoma* (1988), the Supreme Court ruled that it was unconstitutional to impose the death penalty on a person who was under 16 years of age at the time of commission of the crime. In *Stanford v. Kentucky*, the Supreme Court ruled that it was constitutional to impose the death penalty on an offender who was aged 16 at the time of commission of the crime.

53. Although the United States of America has not executed any juvenile offenders while still under 18, it is one of the few countries, together with the Islamic Republic of Iran, Pakistan, Saudi Arabia and Yemen, to execute persons who were under 18 years of age at the time they committed the crime. Charles Rumbaugh was the first juvenile offender executed in the United States since the reinstatement of the death penalty in 1976. He was executed in Texas in September 1985. The last one, Christopher Burger, was executed in Georgia in December 1993. . . .

3. Executions of persons with mental retardation

57. According to information received from non-governmental sources, at least 29 persons with severe mental disabilities have been executed in the United States since the death penalty was reinstated in 1976. Twenty-eight capital jurisdictions are said to permit the execution of mentally retarded defendants. Eleven death penalty states, and the Federal Government, prohibit the execution of mentally retarded persons. 58. Because of the nature of mental retardation, mentally retarded persons are much more vulnerable to

manipulation during arrest, interrogation and confession. Moreover, mental retardation appears not to be compatible with the principle of full criminal responsibility. The Special Rapporteur believes that mental retardation should at least be considered as a mitigating circumstance. . . .

B. The administration of the death penalty

61. A death sentence may be imposed both at the federal and state levels. The majority of death penalty sentences are imposed at the state level. Each capital punishment state has its own statute and each state determines how the death penalty will be administrated within the state. However, only a very small proportion of murders result in a sentence of death.

62. It is to be noted that the small percentage of defendants who receive a death sentence are not necessarily those who committed the most heinous crimes. Many factors, other than the crime itself, appear to influence the imposition of a death sentence. Class, race and economic status, both of the victim and the defendant, are said to be key elements. It is alleged that those who are able to afford good legal representation have less chance of being sentenced to death. The influence of public opinion and political pressure cannot be disregarded either. In addition, racial attitudes of lawyers, prosecutors, juries and judges, although not necessarily conscious, are also believed to play a role in determining who will, or who will not, receive a death sentence. Supreme Court Justice Blackmun, in his dissenting opinion in *Callins v. Collins* (1994) made reference to this problem stating that "(. . .) the death penalty remains fraught with arbitrariness, discrimination, caprice and mistake". He also stated that "Even under the most sophisticated death penalty statutes, race continues to play a major role in determining who shall live and who shall die".

63. Allegations of racial discrimination in the imposition of death sentences are particularly serious in southern states, such as Alabama, Florida, Louisiana, Mississippi, Georgia and Texas, known as the "death penalty belt". The Special Rapporteur was informed that a discriminatory imposition of capital sentences may be favoured by the composition of the judiciary: in Alabama, only 1 of the 67 elected district attorneys is said to be black, and none of Georgia's 159 counties is reported to have a black district attorney. The majority of judges in these states are also reported to be white. . . .

1. The judiciary

69. Federal judges are appointed for life. At the state level, in only 6 of the 38 death penalty states are judges appointed for life by the state governor. In the other 32 states, judges are subject to election.

70. The possibility of elected or appointed judges is recognized in principle 12 of the Basic Principles on the Independence of the Judiciary, adopted by the Seventh United Nations Congress on the Prevention of Crime and the Treatment of Offenders in 1985 and endorsed by the General Assembly in resolutions 40/32 of 29 November 1985 and 40/146 of 13 December 1985. No matter what system is being used, the judiciary shall decide matters impartially,

without any restrictions, improper influences, inducements, pressures, threats or interferences, direct or indirect (principle 2).

71. Many sources have expressed concern as to whether the election of judges puts their independence at risk. In its concluding observations to the United States report, the Human Rights Committee expressed its concern about the impact which the current system of election of judges may, in a few states, have on the implementation of the rights provided under article 14 of the ICCPR [International Covenant on Civil and Political Rights]. . . .

V. Conclusions and Recommendations

"Where, after all, do universal rights begin? In small places, close to home—so close and so small that they cannot be seen on any maps of the world. . . . Unless these rights have meaning there, they have little meaning anywhere. Without concerned citizen action to uphold them close to home, we shall look in vain for progress in the larger world."—Eleanor Roosevelt

A. Concerning the use of the death penalty

140. The Special Rapporteur shares the view of the Human Rights Committee and considers that the extent of the reservations, declarations and understandings entered by the United States at the time of ratification of the ICCPR are intended to ensure that the United States has only accepted what is already the law of the United States. He is of the opinion that the reservation entered by the United States on the death penalty provision is incompatible with the object and purpose of the treaty and should therefore be considered void.

141. Not only do the reservations entered by the United States seriously reduce the impact of the ICCPR, but its effectiveness nationwide is further undermined by the absence of active enforcement mechanisms to ensure its implementation at state level.

142. The Special Rapporteur is of the view that a serious gap exists between federal and state governments, concerning implementation of international obligations undertaken by the United States Government. He notes with concern that the ICCPR appears not to have been disseminated to state authorities and that knowledge of the country's international obligations is almost non-existent at state level. Further, he is of the opinion that the Federal Government cannot claim to represent the states at the international level and at the same time fail to take steps to implement international obligations accepted on their behalf.

143. The Special Rapporteur is aware of the implications of the United States system of federalism as set out in the Constitution and the impact that it has on the laws and practices of the United States. At the same time, it is clear that the Federal Government in undertaking international obligations also undertakes to use all of its constitutionally mandated powers to ensure that the human rights obligations are fulfilled at all levels.

144. The Special Rapporteur questions the overall commitment of the Federal Government to enforce international obligations at home if it claimed not

to be in a position to ensure the access of United Nations experts such as special rapporteurs to authorities at state level. He is concerned that his visit revealed little evidence of such a commitment at the highest levels of the Federal Government.

145. The Special Rapporteur believes that the current practice of imposing death sentences and executions of juveniles in the United States violates international law. He further believes that the reintroduction of the death penalty and the extension of its scope, both at federal and at state level, contravene the spirit and purpose of article 6 of the ICCPR, as well as the international trend towards the progressive restriction of the number of offences for which the death penalty may be imposed. He is further concerned about the execution of mentally retarded and insane persons which he considers to be in contravention of relevant international standards.

146. The Special Rapporteur deplores these practices and considers that they constitute a step backwards in the promotion and protection of the right to life.

147. Because of the definitive nature of a death sentence, a process leading to its imposition must comply fully with the highest safeguards and fair trial standards, and must be in accordance with restrictions imposed by international law. The Special Rapporteur notes with concern that in the United States, guarantees and safeguards, as well as specific restrictions on capital punishment, are not being fully respected. Lack of adequate counsel and legal representation for many capital defendants is disturbing. The enactment of the 1996 Anti-terrorism and Effective Death Penalty Act and the lack of funding of PCDOs [post-conviction defender organizations] have further jeopardized the implementation of the right to a fair trial as provided for in the ICCPR and other international instruments.

148. Despite the excellent reputation of the United States judiciary, the Special Rapporteur observes that the imposition of death sentences in the United States seems to continue to be marked by arbitrariness. Race, ethnic origin and economic status appear to be key determinants of who will, and who will not, receive a sentence of death. As Justice Marshall stated in *Godfrey v. Georgia*, "The task of eliminating arbitrariness in the infliction of capital punishment is proving to be one which our criminal justice system—and perhaps any criminal justice system—is unable to perform".

149. The politics behind the death penalty, particularly during election campaigns, raises doubts as to the objectivity of its imposition. The Special Rapporteur believes that the system of election of judges to relatively short terms of office, and the practice of requesting financial contributions particularly from members of the bar and the public, may risk interfering with the independence and impartiality of the judiciary. Further, the discretionary power of the prosecutor as to whether or not to seek the death penalty raises serious concern regarding the fairness of its administration.

150. The process of jury selection may also be tainted by racial factors and unfairness. The Special Rapporteur notes with concern that people who are opposed to or have hesitations about the death penalty are unlikely to sit as

jurors and believes that a "death qualified" jury will be predisposed to apply the harshest sentence. He fears that the right to a fair trial before an impartial tribunal may be jeopardized by such juries. Moreover, he is convinced that a "death qualified" jury does not represent the community conscience as a whole, but only the conscience of that part of the community which favours capital punishment.

151. The high level of support for the death penalty, even if studies have shown that it is not as deep as is claimed, cannot justify the lack of respect for the restrictions and safeguards surrounding its use. In many countries, mob killings and lynchings enjoy public support as a way to deal with violent crime and are often portrayed as "popular justice". Yet they are not acceptable in any civilized society.

152. While acknowledging the difficulties that authorities face in fighting violent crime, he believes that solutions other than the increasing use of the death penalty need to be sought. Moreover, the inherent cruelty of executions might only lead to the perpetuation of a culture of violence.

153. The Special Rapporteur is particularly concerned by the current approach to victims' rights. He considers that while victims are entitled to respect and compassion, access to justice and prompt redress, these rights should not be implemented at the expenses of those of the accused. Courts should not become a forum for retaliation. The duty of the State to provide justice should not be privatized and brought back to victims, as it was before the emergence of modern States.

154. While the Special Rapporteur would hope that the United States would join the movement of the international community towards progressively restricting the use of the death penalty as a way to strengthen the protection of the right to life, he is concerned that, to the contrary, the United States is carrying out an increasing number of executions, including of juveniles and mentally retarded persons. He also fears that executions of women will resume if this trend is not reversed.

155. The Special Rapporteur wishes to emphasize that the use of the death penalty in violation of international standards will not help to resolve social problems and build a more harmonious society but, on the contrary, will contribute to exacerbated tensions between races and classes, particularly at a moment when the United States is proclaiming its intention to combat racism more vigorously.

156. In view of the above, the Special Rapporteur recommends the following to the Government of the United States:

(a) To establish a moratorium on executions in accordance with the recommendations made by the American Bar Association and resolution 1997/12 of the Commission on Human Rights;

(b) To discontinue the practice of imposing death sentences on juvenile offenders and mentally retarded persons and to amend national legislation in this respect to bring it into conformity with international standards;

(c) Not to resume executions of women and respect the de facto moratorium in existence since 1984;

(d) To review legislation, both at federal and state levels, so as to restrict
the number of offences punishable by death. In particular, the growing
tendency to reinstate death penalty statutes and the increase in the
number of aggravating circumstances both at state and federal levels
should be addressed in order not to contravene the spirit and purpose
of article 6 of the ICCPR and the goal expressed by the international
community to progressively restrict the number of offences for which
the death penalty is applied;

(e) To encourage the development of public defender systems so as to
ensure the right to adequate legal representation for indigent defendants;
to reinstate funding for legal resource centres in order to guarantee a
more appropriate representation of death row inmates, particularly in
those states where a public defender system does not exist. This would
also help to diminish the risk of executing innocent persons;

(f) To take steps to disseminate and educate government officials at all
levels as well as to develop monitoring and appropriate enforcement
mechanisms to achieve full implementation of the provisions of the
ICCPR, as well as other international treaties, at state level;

(g) To include a human rights component in training programmes for
members of the judiciary. A campaign on the role of juries could further aim at informing the public about the responsibilities of jurors;

(h) To review the system of election of members of the judiciary at state
level, in order to ensure a degree of independence and impartiality similar to that of the federal system. It is recommended that in order to
provide a greater degree of independence and impartiality that judges
be elected for longer terms, for instance 10 years or for life;

(i) In view of the above, to consider inviting the Special Rapporteur on the
independence of judges and lawyers to undertake a visit to the United
States;

(j) To develop an intensive programme aimed at informing state authorities about international obligations undertaken by the United States
and at bringing national laws into conformity with these standards; to
increase the cooperation between the Department of Justice and the
Department of State to disseminate and enforce the human rights
undertakings of the United States;

(k) To lift the reservations, particularly on article 6, and the declarations
and understandings entered to the ICCPR. The Special Rapporteur also
recommends that the United States ratify the Convention on the Rights
of the Child. He further recommends that the United States consider
ratifying the first and second Optional Protocols to the ICCPR.

B. Concerning killings by the police

157. The Special Rapporteur is concerned by the reports of violations of
the right to life as a result of excessive use of force by law enforcement offi-

cials which he received during his mission, and he will continue to monitor the situation closely.

158. While acknowledging that the police face extremely difficult situations in their daily work, authorities have an obligation to ensure that the police respect the right to life.

159. Preliminary recommendations to the Government of the United States include the following:

(a) All alleged violations of the right to life should be investigated, police officials responsible brought to justice and compensation provided to the victims. Further, measures should be taken to prevent recurrence of these violations;

(b) Patterns of use of lethal force should be systematically investigated by the Justice Department;

(c) Training on international standards on law enforcement and human rights should be included in police academies. This is particularly relevant because the United States has taken a leading role in training police forces in other countries;

(d) Independent organs, outside the police departments, should be put in place to investigate all allegations of violations of the right to life promptly and impartially, in accordance with principle 9 of the Principles on the Effective Prevention and Investigation of Extra-legal, Arbitrary and Summary Executions;

(e) In order to avoid conflict of interest with the local district attorney's office, special prosecutors should be appointed more frequently in order to conduct investigations into allegations of violations of the right to life, to identify perpetrators and bring them to justice. . . .

NATIONAL CANCER INSTITUTE
ON BREAST CANCER DRUG
April 6, 1998

Officials at the National Cancer Institute announced April 6 that the synthetic hormone tamoxifen, long used to treat women with breast cancer, had been found unexpectedly effective in preventing the disease in high-risk women. Results from clinical trials showed that tamoxifen had cut the risks of developing cancer by nearly half. In fact, the drug was so effective that the trials were ended fourteen months ahead of schedule so that women who had been receiving a placebo could begin taking tamoxifen.

Federal health officials were at once jubilant with the findings and cautious in their promises. Several adverse effects from the drug "make the very personal decision about taking tamoxifen complex," Richard Klausner, director of the National Cancer Institute, said at a news conference. Among those effects were a heightened risk of developing uterine cancer and life-threatening blood clots. Moreover, the clinical tests lasted less than five years, which meant that the drug might have delayed the onset of cancers, not prevented them altogether.

Breast cancer was the second most common cancer among women after lung cancer. Some 178,000 women were diagnosed with breast cancer in 1997, and 43,500 women died of the disease. The risk of a woman developing breast cancer increased with age and with certain other factors, such as having a mother, sister, or daughter with the disease. In a controversial move in 1997, the National Cancer Institute recommended that women in their forties get a mammogram, or breast X-ray, every one or two years to screen for cancer. It had long been recommended that only women over fifty receive annual mammograms. (Mammograms for women in their forties, Historic Documents of 1997, p. 142)

The tamoxifen announcement was just one in a series of apparent breakthroughs in the fight against cancer. In March the Centers for Disease Prevention and Control announced that the number of new cases of cancer was declining for the first time since the 1930s. The number of deaths was also down, continuing a decline that began earlier in the 1990s. Later in April, the drug maker Eli Lilly announced that preliminary tests of its synthetic hormone raloxifene showed that the drug could reduce the risk of breast cancer about as much as tamoxifen—but without increasing the risk of uterine cancer. In September the Food and Drug Administration approved the first "monoclonal antibody" for treating advanced breast cancers. A monoclonal antibody is a genetically engineered version of the body's own diseases fighters. The drug, Herceptin, was made by Genentech, Inc. (Cancer deaths, Historic Documents of 1996, p. 790)

The Tamoxifen Trials

Tamoxifen was a synthetic hormone in pill form; it was made by the Zeneca Pharmaceutical Group and marketed under the name Nolvadex. Tamoxifen interfered with the activity of estrogen, a female hormone, and slowed or stopped the growth of breast cancer cells in the body. It had been used since 1977 to treat women with advanced breast cancer and since 1985 to help prevent a recurrence of the original breast cancer and development of new cancer in breast cancer survivors. Although tamoxifen acted as an "anti-estrogen" in breast tissue, it behaved like an estrogen in many other parts of the body, and researchers hoped that it, like estrogen replacement therapy, might slow bone loss and lower blood cholesterol in postmenopausal women. Heart disease and osteoporosis were two of the most common illnesses among older women.

Because tamoxifen appeared to prevent new cancers in women who had already experienced breast cancer, the National Cancer Institute began clinical trials (known as the Breast Cancer Prevention Trial) in 1992 to determine if the drug would prevent cancer in women who had never been diagnosed with breast cancer but who were deemed to be at increased risk for the disease. Researchers also looked for evidence that the drug reduced the incidence of heart disease and bone fractures in these women. Altogether 13,388 women ages thirty-five and older were enrolled in the trial, which was expected to cost $50 million.

The participants in the trials were all at high risk of developing cancer through a combination of age, first-degree relatives with breast cancer, age at time of first menstrual period and first birth, and a diagnosis of breast lumps or tissues known to increase the chances of developing cancer. Women over age sixty and women with lobular carcinoma in situ, a condition that often led to breast cancer, were automatically qualified to participate. Participants were randomly divided into two groups. The first group was given a daily dosage of twenty milligrams of tamoxifen; the other group received a similar dosage of a placebo. Neither the participants nor their physicians knew whether they were taking the drug or the placebo.

The trials had been scheduled to last for at least another year, but on March 24 an independent monitoring group recommended that the participants be told what pill they had been taking. The reduction of risk in the tamoxifen group was so great, the monitors said, that continuing to with-

hold the drug from women taking the placebo and women in general at increased risk for breast cancer would be unethical. The National Cancer Institute concurred, and the decision was made public on April 6.

Results of the Trials

The trials were stopped because women on tamoxifen were diagnosed with 45 percent fewer cases of invasive breast cancer than were women on the placebo (85 cases compared with 154 cases). Eight women in the study had died from breast cancer—three taking tamoxifen, five taking the placebo. Moreover, the women taking tamoxifen had 47 bone fractures of the hip, wrist, and spine—all fractures associated with loss of bone density— compared with 71 among the women taking the placebo. Somewhat to the researchers' surprise, there was no difference in the number of heart attacks between the two groups.

Tamoxifen did increase the risk of three serious health conditions: endometrial cancer, or cancer of the lining of the uterus (33 cases among women taking the hormone compared with 14 cases in the placebo group); pulmonary embolisms, or blood clots in the lungs (17 for tamoxifen; 6 for the placebo), and deep vein thrombosis, or blood clots in major veins (30 for tamoxifen; 19 for the placebo). Compared with the incidence of breast cancer, however, these conditions were relatively rare and tamoxifen appeared to increase the risk only among women ages fifty and older. There were also indications that women taking tamoxifen might be at greater risk for developing cataracts, and there were several side effects from the drug, including hot flashes and vaginal discharges. Other less common side effects were menstrual irregularities, depression, loss of appetite, nausea, headaches, and fatigue. Treatments for most of these conditions were available.

At their news conference National Cancer Institute officials warned that many questions about the use of tamoxifen still needed to be answered. Although the drug appeared effective over four or five years, longer trials had not been completed, and so researchers could not say with certainty whether the drug actually prevented cancer or simply delayed its onset. Moreover, tamoxifen's effect, if any, on women who carried either of the two genes known to increase the risk of breast cancer was unknown. Leslie Ford of the National Cancer Institute said the institute was working on guidelines to help women and their doctors make appropriate decisions about using tamoxifen. But she added that a set of guidelines that applied to everyone was unlikely because each individual had to weigh the potential benefits and risks in the context of her own situation. There were some women who should not take tamoxifen. These included women who were pregnant or who wanted to continue taking birth control pills or hormone replacement therapy. Tamoxifen might not be safe for women who are obese, smoke, or have diabetes, hypertension, or past experience with blood clots—all conditions that might increase the risk of blood clots from the drug.

The Food and Drug Administration on October 29 approved the use of tamoxifen as a cancer preventative for high-risk women, but because of the life-threatening side effects, warned doctors and patients to weigh the benefits and risks carefully. "For the right patient . . . this represents a very good option," said FDA acting commissioner Michael Friedman. "But it is not universally beneficial and shouldn't be misused. The key here is to be an informed consumer." The National Cancer Institute said that about three million women between the ages of thirty-five and sixty were at high risk for developing breast cancer; another 26 million were at increased risk because they were age sixty or older.

Following are excerpts from a news conference held April 6, 1998, by the National Cancer Institute to announce that the synthetic hormone tamoxifen had been found to reduce the risk of breast cancer by 45 percent in healthy women at high risk for the disease:

[Richard] KLAUSNER: I'd like to thank everyone for coming. My name is Richard Klausner, and I'm the director of the National Cancer Institute.

The goal of preventing cancer has long been a hope, a dream and a central focus of the national cancer program. Prevention of course can take many forms—from tobacco cessation to other behavioral changes, to vaccines for infectious causes of cancer, to an entirely new field in which medicines specifically interfere with the biologic processes of cancer development.

For the past several years, the National Surgical Adjuvant Breast and Bowel Project, or NSABP, an NCI-funded national clinical trials organization has been carrying out a historic trial to determine whether woman at increased risk of developing breast cancer can prevent the development of that cancer by taking a well-known medicine, the anti-estrogen tamoxifen. More than 13,000 women who participated in this study have been our partners in this important research.

As with all of our clinical trials, an independent endpoint . . . review, safety, monitoring and advisory committee has regularly examined the data to monitor whether either unacceptable or unexpected toxicities have arisen or whether the trial has succeeded in answering the questions it has been designed to answer.

That committee met most recently on March 24th. They concluded that the question of whether tamoxifen can significantly reduce the incidence of breast cancer had been answered. And the answer is an unequivocal yes.

Nevertheless, there were, as you will hear here, adverse effects of tamoxifen, which may make the very personal decision about taking tamoxifen complex.

For all of these reasons, the committee recommended that the participants of the study be notified of the important results. It has been our commitment from the very beginning to the participants—to our partners—from the very start to notify them as soon as clear results had been achieved.

Last week, the NSABP leadership presented these recommendations and the data behind them to the NCI, and together we agreed to accept those recommendations of the independent advisory committee.

This morning we will share with you this information describing the study, its results, its implications, and to try to place this historic study in the context of our larger march to turn the power of science and research toward alleviating the threat of this dread disease. . . .

[Joseph] COSTANTINO [associate director, biostatistical center, National Surgical Adjuvant Breast and Bowel Project]: . . .

Good afternoon. It's my pleasure to review for you the findings of the breast cancer prevention trial. The trial involves 13,388 women who are at high risk for breast cancer. The study design was that of a placebo-controlled, randomized double-blind study. This means that women who are in the trial were randomized to receive identical-looking pills of either placebo or tamoxifen, and that they nor their doctors knew exactly what medication they were taking.

. . . Forty percent of the women were between the ages of 35 and 49. Thirty percent were between the ages of 50 and 59, and 30 percent were 60 years of age or older. The average follow-up time of the women in the trial is about four years. And about 57 percent of the women have been followed for at least 48 months. . . . The primary end point for the breast cancer prevention trial is invasive breast cancer. We have found that tamoxifen is highly effective for preventing cancer, not only invasive breast cancer, but also noninvasive breast cancer.

This slide provides the cumulative incidence of both noninvasive and invasive breast cancer. . . . The first panel deals with invasive breast cancer. . . .

In terms of the actual number of cases of events, in the placebo arm, there were 154 cases compared to only 85 cases in the tamoxifen arm. This represents a highly statistically significant reduction in breast cancer of about 45 percent. . . .

In terms of the number of cases of noninvasive breast cancer, there were 59 cases in the placebo arm, and 31 in the tamoxifen arm. This represents a statistically significant reduction of about 47 percent in the rate of noninvasive cancer. . . .

Tamoxifen is effective in women of all ages. . . .

In terms of the age groups, for those women who are under 49 years of age, the numbers represent—the numbers of invasive breast cancer were 59 versus 38 for those who were young. In the middle age group, the numbers were 46 versus 24. And for the older population, the numbers were 49 versus 23, a substantial reduction in every arm. Each of these differences that we've talked about by age are statistically significant.

In addition to the breast cancer findings, I would like to review the findings from several other end points that were studied in the trial. These outcomes, the first two that I would like to start with are heart disease and fractures.

These two end points were studied because tamoxifen is known to reduce blood lipid levels, which may affect the risk of heart disease. And tamoxifen is postulated to have an effect on osteoporosis.

. . . There were no differences between the two treatment arms in terms of either the overall events of heart disease or for any of the four categories of end points that were evaluated.

Overall, there were 59 events of heart disease in the placebo [group], compared to 61 in the tamoxifen [group].

On the other hand, for fractures, there are findings suggesting a beneficial affect of tamoxifen on bone mineral density. Three specific types of fractures were studied in the trial. They included fractures of the spine, fractures of the hip, and a type of wrist fractures. . . . These end points were chosen because these were the types of fractures that were felt to be most likely associated with osteoporosis.

Differences in the number of fractures were noted for all three end points. Overall, there were 71 fractures that occurred in the placebo group, compared to 47 that occurred in the tamoxifen group. And of these, 29 events were hip fractures. Twenty of those occurred in the placebo arm compared to only nine in the tamoxifen arm.

When the breast cancer prevention trial was planned, it was anticipated that there would be side affects from the treatment of tamoxifen. This information was known and available from the trials where tamoxifen was used to treat breast cancer patients. These risks include the types of risks that are associated with estrogen replacement therapy. Specifically, they are endometrial cancer and vascular events. . . .

I have discussed the benefits to you, now I would like to present some of the risks. There had been 57 cases of endometrial cancer shown here in the trial. Fourteen have occurred in the placebo [group], and 33 have occurred in the tamoxifen [group]. It is important to note that in the tamoxifen arm, all of these cases were early stage one, good prognosis cases, treated by hysterectomy. It is also important to note that the excess risk of endometrial cancer associated with tamoxifen is only evident in women who started therapy when they were at least age 50. Therefore, women who were under 50 when they stared to take tamoxifen were not at increased risk of endometrial cancer.

In addition to endometrial cancer, there have been numerous vascular events on the trial. Overall, there have been 70 vascular events occurring in the placebo [group], compared to 99 in the tamoxifen [group].

There were actually four types of vascular events that were studied in the trial. . . . The only one of these . . . that [was] statistically significant, however, was that associated with differences in pulmonary embolism. In this case, there were six cases of pulmonary embolism which occurred in the placebo group, and 17 in the tamoxifen arm, and two of the 17 in the tamoxifen arm died from their pulmonary embolism.

As in the case with the occurrence of endometrial cancer, it is again important to note that the excess risk of vascular events associated with the treatment of tamoxifen was only shown in women who began taking the drug after they were 50 years of age. Among those who were less than 50 years of age when they began taking therapy, there was no excess risk of vascular events. . . . This concludes my presentation of the findings from the breast cancer prevention trial. And this slide just summarizes some of the points I've just made.

First, among women at increased risk for breast cancer, tamoxifen prevented about half of the invasive and noninvasive breast cancer. And the drug is effective among women in all ages. For women under 50 years of age, there is no apparent increased risk of side effects.

For women over 50 years of age, the side effects include vascular events and endometrial cancer. And, of course, women who have had a hysterectomy would not experience the endometrial cancer risk.

[Leslie] FORD, associate director, Early Detection and Community Oncology Program, Division of Cancer Prevention, NCI]: Thank you, Joe. I've been given the challenge of trying to put these results into some context: What does this mean for women in this country and women in North America as it relates to the decision to potentially take tamoxifen to prevent breast cancer?

And what I would like to do is first, we've talked a lot about women at increased risk of breast cancer. And I'd like to describe to you what the risks were and what risk factors were taken into account and what the women in the BCPT [Breast Cancer Prevention Trial] actually looked like. . . .

One of the things that I think is often overlooked in our culture is that the risk of breast cancer increases significantly with age. So, at between 35 and 49, only about six women in a thousand in the general population would be expected to develop breast cancer, as opposed to our group of women, in which 32 cases in a thousand actually occurred.

For women 50 to 59, it's the difference between 13 cases in a thousand versus our population that had 37 cases per thousand. And then even in the women over 60 where we said that no additional risk was necessary, in fact the women that participated in the trial were about twice the minimum risk of the average 60 year old, with almost 40 cases per thousand expected.

Now what are these risk factors. You've heard a lot about age, but in the trial we determine risk based on a computerized model that . . . took into account, in addition to risk, such factors as the number of first degree relatives that had breast cancer; that's mothers, sisters and daughters, the number of biopsies that the woman might have had for suspicious lesions herself, whether any of these biopsies had a diagnosis of atypical hyperplasia or a preinvasive cancer called lobular carcinoma in situ, also what her age is when she started her periods and whether she had had any children and how old she was when those children were born. And a woman was eligible for the BCPT if her risk was at least as great as that of the average 60 year old woman.

. . . [T]his trial really does represent a historic milestone in our approach to breast cancer. We now are in a position to give women an option. We can now intervene prior to the detection of breast cancer and really reduce a woman's chance of developing the disease. But as with any medication, the decision to begin Tamoxifen therapy is a very complex one. There are no simple answers. And even for women that are at high risk for developing breast cancer, Tamoxifen may not be the appropriate choice.

There are risks, some serious associated with Tamoxifen therapy. But I think it's important to note that none of the risks were unanticipated, and none were greater than we thought they might be going into the trial. None were out of line with what women had been informed about at the beginning of this study.

Finally, I would like to put these numbers into some context. . . . [I]magine a thousand women between the ages of 35 and 49 who might meet the eligibility criteria for this trial, what could we expect over a five year period based on these results?

Without Tamoxifen, we would expect 31 cases of breast cancer to develop. And with Tamoxifen, 14 or 45 percent of these could be prevented. Also, with respect to noninvasive breast cancers, about 11 of the 15 expected cases could be prevented. And in this age group, we see no effect, no difference in the rate of endometrial cancers or vascular events that have occurred.

Next, however in women over 50-years-old, 50 and over, the picture is somewhat different and gets more complex. If you imagine all thousand of these women have a uterus, then they would all be at risk for endometrial cancer. In that situation, we might prevent 17 out of the 33 expected cases of breast cancer. Three out of the 10 expected cases of noninvasive breast cancer. But there could be as many as 12 more cases of endometrial cancer in our study, the difference between four and 16. And 10 more vascular events occurring, the difference between 12 and 22.

This is an overall picture of a thousand women [with a] uterus, obviously, if a woman has had a hysterectomy, this risk all but is eliminated. And that's why the decision to begin therapy becomes a complex one. We also know of risk factors for vascular events including obesity, hypertension and diabetes and smoking. And women need to be counseled about those risks before they would decide to take the therapy.

So finally, in conclusion, I think that Tamoxifen provides women at increased risk with a proven option to prevent breast cancer. Not all women are at increased risk for breast cancer, and the balance of benefits and risks varies by age and hysterectomy status. Finally, the choice to take Tamoxifen has to be a personal one. We are feverishly working to both analyze this data, and get more experience so we can better define what makes a woman at increased risk for breast cancer. The criteria used in this study did not include gene status or mutation status and we are looking at our data to help define whether Tamoxifen does work equally well in women that have a mutation in their breast cancer gene.

But in addition, there are other things that we'll be looking at to help us better define who is at risk of breast cancer and who is at risk for some of the unwanted side effects that come with Tamoxifen therapy, as well as with other hormone replacement therapies. The NCI and the NSABP will be developing tools that can assist women and their health care providers in decision making. . . .

KLAUSNER: Thank you Dr. Ford. . . . The results of this study . . . are remarkable. It is not often that we get to present results of the magnitude of a 45 percent reduction, certainly not in this disease. They tell us that breast cancer can be prevented as a proof of principle, but they are complex. There is not a simple take home message as you've heard. That Tamoxifen might prevent breast cancer as you heard, is based upon previous clinical observations, in this case from the treatment realm. That it works, fits with our deep understanding of the biology of estrogen and estrogen receptors and their role in breast cancer, and an enormous amount of scientific data about this drug. While it may be tempting to generalize, our conclusions from this study must stick to the data in the study.

For women whose predicted risks of breast cancer fit those of this study, they may have the option of taking Tamoxifen in order to reduce their risk of developing breast cancer with some confidence. But these women have only been followed for a certain amount of time, and there's much we don't know about how long the protection will last. . . .

This study provides an estimate of the magnitude of the reduction of the risk, and importantly, it also provides significant amounts of information about important and serious side effects, adverse effects of taking Tamoxifen. As you've heard, women need to discuss with their physicians in order to determine their own risks, which must be carefully determined for each individual. . . .

. . . This study is not an end. But it is a very propitious beginning. It tells us that it is possible to prevent breast cancer. . . .

NORTHERN IRELAND PEACE AGREEMENT
April 10, 1998

For the first time in several hundred years, there appeared to be a real possibility in 1998 that Catholics and Protestants in Northern Ireland might be ready to live with each other in peace and with a degree of mutual respect. Leaders of sectarian factions that had battled each other with words, bombs, and guns agreed on April 10 to settle their differences through the peaceful exercise of politics.

Northern Ireland voters overwhelmingly supported the agreement a month later. Even so, it faced many bumpy challenges during the year—including a political stalemate lasting nearly eight months over implementing key parts of the accord. Other obstacles were certain to arise before 2000, when final provisions of the accord were to go into effect. Two men who were crucial to the agreement, Protestant leader David Trimble and Catholic leader John Hume, were awarded the 1998 Nobel Peace Prize.

A Long and Bitter History

Enmity between the Irish and the English, and the Protestants and the Catholics, dated from the Middle Ages. In the thirteen counties of Northern Ireland—a province of Great Britain known collectively as Ulster—the ancient sectarian grievances were still very much alive at the close of the twentieth century. Most Protestants, who constituted a slim but shrinking majority, wished to remain part of the United Kingdom; this was called the "Unionist" position. Many Catholics yearned for a merger between Northern Ireland and the predominantly Catholic Republic of Ireland, which had gained its independence from Britain in 1922 after a bloody revolution; this was called the "Republican" or "Nationalist" position. These sectarian differences broke out into violence in 1969, setting off a seemingly endless cycle of shootings and bombings that by 1998 had killed at least 3,200 people, most of them civilians.

During those three decades of killing and escalating hatred, numerous cease-fires and peacemaking efforts offered glimmers of hope, always *extinguished by a new round of violence. U.S. president Bill Clinton directly intervened in 1994, granting a visa for a visit to the United States to Gerry Adams, head of the Sinn Fein political wing of the Irish Republican Army (IRA), the Catholic-dominated paramilitary faction that had taken up violence to secure a united Ireland. Clinton wanted to shore up the standing of Adams and others who appeared ready to forswear violence. In 1995, Clinton visited Northern Ireland and promised American help in the search for peace.* (Clinton visit, Historic Documents of 1995, p. 727)

In June 1996, former U.S. Senate majority leader George Mitchell opened negotiations, sponsored by the British and Irish governments, between leaders of various factions in Northern Ireland. Those talks dragged on with little progress until 1997, when the British Labour Party, headed by Tony Blair, ousted Prime Minister John Major and his Conservative Party. Commanding a huge majority in Parliament and a popular mandate, Blair made peace in Northern Ireland a top priority and visited Belfast on his first official trip outside London as prime minister. Northern Ireland's "troubles"—as residents called the violence and political discord—long had been Britain's most serious domestic problem. (Blair's victory, Historic Documents of 1997, p. 277)

One by one, obstacles to an agreement were cleared away. Pressure and persuasion from London, Dublin, and Washington played an important part. But the central factor appeared to be a growing realization among the leaders of Northern Ireland's disparate communities that violence was not working for anyone. Among those leaders were men who had served time in prison for murder but were now looking for new ways to achieve their goals.

In July 1997 the IRA declared a cease-fire, opening the way for Adams and his Sinn Fein colleagues to join the peace talks. Blair invited Adams to 10 Downing Street and met frequently with David Trimble, the leader of the Ulster Unionist Party, the largest of the hard-line Protestant factions.

Working against a self-imposed deadline, Mitchell and leaders representing eight of the ten Northern Ireland political parties settled down to an intense round of bargaining in Belfast early in April 1998. The final session went round the clock on April 9–10. At several key points when disputes threatened to halt the talks, Blair, Irish prime minister Bertie Ahern, and Clinton (speaking by telephone from Washington) offered reassurance to individual factional leaders and encouraged them to take bold steps for peace.

In the early morning hours of April 10, an exhausted Mitchell announced an agreement that—pending approval by voters in Northern Ireland and the Republic of Ireland—would transform the politics of the island. Speaking directly to the people of Northern Ireland, Mitchell said it was their choice whether the agreement would succeed or fail. "If you support this agreement, and if you also reject the merchants of death and the purveyors of hate, if you make it clear to your political leaders that you want them to make it work, it will," Mitchell said.

The agreement came on Good Friday, a symbolism that leaders of both sides were quick to point out. "The old Northern Ireland has died, and now, on Easter weekend, it is ready to rise again," said Seamus Mallon, a Catholic leader of the moderate Social Democratic and Labor Party.

A New Political Framework

There actually were two agreements signed on April 10: the prime agreement was among representatives of the eight Northern Ireland political parties that participated in the talks, plus Blair and Irish Prime Minister Bertie Ahern; the other was between Blair and Ahern, in which they pledged steps to help make the Northern Ireland agreement work.

The essence of the Northern Ireland agreement was an attempt to satisfy at least some of the diametrically opposing goals of the Republicans and the Unionists. For the Republicans, who wanted to join with the predominantly Catholic Irish Republic to the south, the accord established a North-South Ministerial Council to work on issues affecting all of Ireland, such as the environment, transportation, and tourism. For Unionists, who wanted to remain part of Britain and opposed a merger with the Irish Republic, the agreement called on Dublin to revoke its territorial claims to Northern Ireland. For both sides, the agreement established a new legislature, the Northern Ireland Assembly, which gradually would take over many of the responsibilities that had been held by the British government since 1972 when it imposed direct rule on the province. The assembly was intended to reflect the political and religious composition of Northern Ireland; the agreement established voting procedures to ensure that the rights of minorities parties would be respected.

The first major test of the agreement came in referendums in both Northern Ireland and the Republic of Ireland on May 22. Despite a vigorous campaign of opposition by hard-line Protestants in the North, voters in both regions overwhelmingly supported the accord: The "yes" vote was 94 percent in the Republic and 71 percent in Ulster. Supporters had hoped for an endorsement by at least 70 percent of Ulster voters, to show that the overwhelming majority of both Protestants and Catholics there favored the agreement.

The next step in carrying out the accord—elections June 25 for the 108 seats in the Northern Ireland Assembly—produced somewhat more ambiguous results. Trimble, who had been one of the most hard-line Protestant leaders before deciding on a path of compromise, lost significant support within his Ulster Unionist Party and among Protestants in general. Protestant opponents of the agreement won 28 seats, matching the total for Trimble's party and giving them nearly enough seats to block some major actions by the assembly under a weighted voting procedure. Even so, Trimble was elected the first minister of the Assembly and Mallon, a leader of moderate Catholics, was elected deputy first minister.

A Bombing, and Words of Peace

A sickening reminder that not everyone wanted compromise came August 15 when a massive bomb exploded in downtown Omagh, a town of about 25,000 people in the western part of Northern Ireland. The bombing killed 28 people and wounded more than 200, Catholics and Protestants alike. An IRA splinter group, calling itself the "Real IRA," claimed responsibility for the attack and said it would continue to use violence to block implementation of the April 10 peace agreement. The death toll was the highest of any single attack during the last three decades.

Ironically, the bombing appeared to have the opposite effect from what was intended. The brutal murder of civilians, so soon after a majority of both Catholics and Protestants voted for peace, horrified the population and gave new determination to the leaders who signed the agreement. Adams, himself a former IRA militiaman, denounced the bombing and said violence was "a thing of the past, over, done with, and gone."

Three weeks later, on September 3, Clinton visited Northern Ireland for the second time in his presidency and told enthusiastic crowds that they had made a "courageous" choice for peace. "For yourselves and all the world, in every act of genuine reconciliation, you renew confidence that decency can triumph over hatred," Clinton said at a large outdoor gathering in the historic town of Armagh.

Another symbolic step came November 26 when Blair became the first British prime minister to address the Irish parliament in Dublin. Recalling his own Irish heritage (his mother was born in Donegal county), Blair won a standing ovation when he put the centuries of Anglo-Irish discord, hatred, and violence in this perspective: "So much shared history, so much shared pain. And now, the shared hope of a new beginning."

Follow-up Negotiations

Reaching agreement and holding elections were just the starting points in what promised to be a prolonged period of making peace work in Northern Ireland. Within a few weeks of the agreement, it was clear that the most difficult immediate issue was the demand for Protestant and Catholic paramilitary forces to disarm—a process called "decommissioning." Each side insisted that paramilitary forces aligned with the other side had to be the first to disarm, a formula that for months threatened renewed deadlock in the peace process. Protestant leader Trimble, using his new powers as first minister, barred Sinn Fein leaders from participating in governmental meetings until the IRA began to disarm.

For nearly eight months, this dispute prevented the new political bodies envisioned in the April 10 accord from taking office. With the peace agreement seeming imperiled—and with the British and Irish governments bringing renewed pressure for compromise—Protestant and Catholic leaders on December 19 settled their differences, at least temporarily. The leaders reached agreement on how membership of a ten-person cabinet would be apportioned among Ulster's leading political parties (two seats were reserved Sinn Fein, for example), and on composition of the North-South Ministerial Council that would discuss issues of concern to both Northern Ireland and the Republic of Ireland.

The December 19 agreement was widely seen as a victory for Sinn Fein, which extracted several concessions on procedural points from the Protestant side. On the same day, one of the most violent Protestant paramilitary factions, the Loyalist Volunteer Force, gained a public relations coup when it turned in several dozen rifles, pistols, and other armaments. Local television showed technicians destroying the weapons, leading Trimble and other Protestants to demand that the IRA follow suit in turning over its arms.

Although it broke a damaging stalemate, the December 19 agreement did not resolve the underlying issues that had led to the months of discord. Most important, the deal did not directly address the question of when the IRA and the remaining Protestant paramilitary forces would disarm, and it did not identify the names of those who would represent the parties in the ten-member cabinet or in the North-South Ministerial Council. By postponing such issues, the December 19 agreement opened possibilities either for further compromises at a later date, or another series of deadlocks that could ruin Northern Ireland's Easter 1998 hopes for long-term peace.

> *Following are excerpts from two agreements signed April 10, 1998, in Belfast, Northern Ireland. The first agreement, called the "Agreement Reached in Multi-Party Negotiations," resulted from negotiations among representatives of Northern Ireland's major political parties and the prime ministers of Great Britain and the Republic of Ireland; the second agreement, called the "Agreement Between the Governments of the United Kingdom of Great Britain and Northern Ireland and the Government of Ireland," was signed by British prime minister Tony Blair and Irish prime minister Bertie Ahern:*

PRIMARY PEACE AGREEMENT

Declaration of Support

1. We, the participants in the multi-party negotiations, believe that the agreement we have negotiated offers a truly historic opportunity for a new beginning.

2. The tragedies of the past have left a deep and profoundly regrettable legacy of suffering. We must never forget those who have died or been injured, and their families. But we can best honour them through a fresh start, in which we firmly dedicate ourselves to the achievement of reconcili-

ation, tolerance, and mutual trust, and to the protection and vindication of the human rights of all.

3. We are committed to partnership, equality and mutual respect as the basis of relationships within Northern Ireland, between North and South, and between these islands.

4. We reaffirm our total and absolute commitment to exclusively democratic and peaceful means of resolving differences on political issues, and our opposition to any use or threat of force by others for any political purpose, whether in regard to this agreement or otherwise.

5. We acknowledge the substantial differences between our continuing, and equally legitimate, political aspirations. However, we will endeavour to strive in every practical way towards reconciliation and rapprochement within the framework of democratic and agreed arrangements. We pledge that we will, in good faith, work to ensure the success of each and every one of the arrangements to be established under this agreement. It is accepted that all of the institutional and constitutional arrangements—an Assembly in Northern Ireland, a North/South Ministerial Council, implementation bodies, a British-Irish Council and a British-Irish Intergovernmental Conference and any amendments to British Acts of Parliament and the Constitution of Ireland—are interlocking and interdependent and that in particular the functioning of the Assembly and the North/South Council are so closely interrelated that the success of each depends on that of the other.

6. Accordingly, in a spirit of concord, we strongly commend this agreement to the people, North and South, for their approval.

Constitutional Issues

1. The participants endorse the commitment made by the British and Irish Governments that, in a new British-Irish Agreement replacing the Anglo-Irish Agreement, they will:

(i) recognise the legitimacy of whatever choice is freely exercised by a majority of the people of Northern Ireland with regard to its status, whether they prefer to continue to support the Union with Great Britain or a sovereign united Ireland;

(ii) recognise that it is for the people of the island of Ireland alone, by agreement between the two parts respectively and without external impediment, to exercise their right of self-determination on the basis of consent, freely and concurrently given, North and South, to bring about a united Ireland, if that is their wish, accepting that this right must be achieved and exercised with and subject to the agreement and consent of a majority of the people of Northern Ireland;

(iii) acknowledge that while a substantial section of the people in Northern Ireland share the legitimate wish of a majority of the people of the island of Ireland for a united Ireland, the present wish of a majority of the people of Northern Ireland, freely exercised and legitimate, is to maintain the Union and, accordingly, that Northern Ireland's status as part of the United Kingdom reflects and relies upon that wish; and that it would be wrong to make any change in the status of Northern Ireland save with the consent of a majority of its people;

(iv) affirm that if, in the future, the people of the island of Ireland exercise their right of self-determination on the basis set out in sections (i) and (ii) above to bring about a united Ireland, it will be a binding obligation on both Governments to introduce and support in their respective Parliaments legislation to give effect to that wish;

(v) affirm that whatever choice is freely exercised by a majority of the people of Northern Ireland, the power of the sovereign government with jurisdiction there shall be exercised with rigorous impartiality on behalf of all the people in the diversity of their identities and traditions and shall be founded on the principles of full respect for, and equality of, civil, political, social and cultural rights, of freedom from discrimination for all citizens, and of parity of esteem and of just and equal treatment for the identity, ethos, and aspirations of both communities;

(vi) recognise the birthright of all the people of Northern Ireland to identify themselves and be accepted as Irish or British, or both, as they may so choose, and accordingly confirm that their right to hold both British and Irish citizenship is accepted by both Governments and would not be affected by any future change in the status of Northern Ireland.

2. The participants also note that the two Governments have accordingly undertaken in the context of this comprehensive political agreement, to propose and support changes in, respectively, the Constitution of Ireland and in British legislation relating to the constitutional status of Northern Ireland.

Draft Clauses/Schedules for Incorporation in British Legislation

1. (1) It is hereby declared that Northern Ireland in its entirety remains part of the United Kingdom and shall not cease to be so without the consent of a majority of the people of Northern Ireland voting in a poll held for the purposes of this section in accordance with Schedule 1.

(2) But if the wish expressed by a majority in such a poll is that Northern Ireland should cease to be part of the United Kingdom and form part of a united Ireland, the Secretary of State shall lay before Parliament such proposals to give effect to that wish as may be agreed between Her Majesty's Government in the United Kingdom and the Government of Ireland. . . .

Irish Government Draft Legislation to Amend the Constitution

. . . .

ii. the following Articles shall be substituted for Articles 2 and 3 of the English text:

"Article 2

It is the entitlement and birthright of every person born in the island of Ireland, which includes its islands and seas, to be part of the Irish nation. That is also the entitlement of all persons otherwise qualified in accordance with law to be citizens of Ireland. Furthermore, the Irish nation cherishes its special affinity with people of Irish ancestry living abroad who share its cultural identity and heritage.

Article 3

1. It is the firm will of the Irish nation, in harmony and friendship, to unite all the people who share the territory of the island of Ireland, in all the diversity of their identities and traditions, recognising that a united Ireland shall be brought about only by peaceful means with the consent of a majority of the people, democratically expressed, in both jurisdictions in the island. Until then, the laws enacted by the Parliament established by this Constitution shall have the like area and extent of application as the laws enacted by the Parliament that existed immediately before the coming into operation of this Constitution.
2. Institutions with executive powers and functions that are shared between those jurisdictions may be established by their respective responsible authorities for stated purposes and may exercise powers and functions in respect of all or any part of the island." . . .

Democratic Institutions in Northern Ireland

1. This agreement provides for a democratically elected Assembly in Northern Ireland which is inclusive in its membership, capable of exercising executive and legislative authority, and subject to safeguards to protect the rights and interests of all sides of the community.

The Assembly

2. A 108-member Assembly will be elected by PR(STV) [proportional representation] from existing Westminster constituencies.

3. The Assembly will exercise full legislative and executive authority in respect of those matters currently within the responsibility of the six Northern Ireland Government Departments, with the possibility of taking on responsibility for other matters as detailed elsewhere in this agreement.

4. The Assembly—operating where appropriate on a cross-community basis—will be the prime source of authority in respect of all devolved responsibilities.

Safeguards

5. There will be safeguards to ensure that all sections of the community can participate and work together successfully in the operation of these institutions and that all sections of the community are protected, including:

(a) allocations of Committee Chairs, Ministers and Committee membership in proportion to party strengths;
(b) the European Convention on Human Rights (ECHR) and any Bill of Rights for Northern Ireland supplementing it, which neither the Assembly nor public bodies can infringe, together with a Human Rights Commission;
(c) arrangements to provide that key decisions and legislation are proofed to ensure that they do not infringe the ECHR and any Bill of Rights for Northern Ireland;

(d) arrangements to ensure key decisions are taken on a cross-community basis;

(i) either parallel consent, i.e. a majority of those members present and voting, including a majority of the unionist and nationalist designations present and voting;

(ii) or a weighted majority (60%) of members present and voting, including at least 40% of each of the nationalist and unionist designations present and voting.

Key decisions requiring cross-community support will be designated in advance, including election of the Chair of the Assembly, the First Minister and Deputy First Minister, standing orders and budget allocations. In other cases such decisions could be triggered by a petition of concern brought by a significant minority of Assembly members (30/108).

(e) an Equality Commission to monitor a statutory obligation to promote equality of opportunity in specified areas and parity of esteem between the two main communities, and to investigate individual complaints against public bodies. . . .

Legislation

26. The Assembly will have authority to pass primary legislation for Northern Ireland in devolved areas, subject to:

(a) the ECHR and any Bill of Rights for Northern Ireland supplementing it which, if the courts found to be breached, would render the relevant legislation null and void;

(b) decisions by simple majority of members voting, except when decision on a cross-community basis is required;

(c) detailed scrutiny and approval in the relevant Departmental Committee;

(d) mechanisms, based on arrangements proposed for the Scottish Parliament, to ensure suitable co-ordination, and avoid disputes, between the Assembly and the Westminster Parliament;

(e) option of the Assembly seeking to include Northern Ireland provisions in United Kingdom-wide legislation in the Westminster Parliament, especially on devolved issues where parity is normally maintained (e.g. social security, company law).

27. The Assembly will have authority to legislate in reserved areas with the approval of the Secretary of State and subject to Parliamentary control.

28. Disputes over legislative competence will be decided by the Courts.

29. Legislation could be initiated by an individual, a Committee or a Minister. . . .

North/South Ministerial Council

1. Under a new British/Irish Agreement dealing with the totality of relationships, and related legislation at Westminster and in the Oireachtas [Irish Parliament], a North/South Ministerial Council to be established to bring

together those with executive responsibilities in Northern Ireland and the Irish Government, to develop consultation, co-operation and action within the island of Ireland—including through implementation on an all-island and cross-border basis—on matters of mutual interest within the competence of the Administrations, North and South.

2. All Council decisions to be by agreement between the two sides. Northern Ireland to be represented by the First Minister, Deputy First Minister and any relevant Ministers, the Irish Government by the Taoiseach [Irish prime minister] and relevant Ministers, all operating in accordance with the rules for democratic authority and accountability in force in the Northern Ireland Assembly and the Oireachtas respectively. Participation in the Council to be one of the essential responsibilities attaching to relevant posts in the two Administrations. If a holder of a relevant post will not participate normally in the Council, the Taoiseach in the case of the Irish Government and the First and Deputy First Minister in the case of the Northern Ireland Administration to be able to make alternative arrangements. . . .

British-Irish Council

1. A British-Irish Council (BIC) will be established under a new British-Irish Agreement to promote the harmonious and mutually beneficial development of the totality of relationships among the peoples of these islands.

2. Membership of the BIC will comprise representatives of the British and Irish Governments, devolved institutions in Northern Ireland, Scotland and Wales, when established, and, if appropriate, elsewhere in the United Kingdom, together with representatives of the Isle of Man and the Channel Islands.

3. The BIC will meet in different formats: at summit level, twice per year; in specific sectoral formats on a regular basis, with each side represented by the appropriate Minister; in an appropriate format to consider cross-sectoral matters.

4. Representatives of members will operate in accordance with whatever procedures for democratic authority and accountability are in force in their respective elected institutions.

5. The BIC will exchange information, discuss, consult and use best endeavours to reach agreement on co-operation on matters of mutual interest within the competence of the relevant Administrations. Suitable issues for early discussion in the BIC could include transport links, agricultural issues, environmental issues, cultural issues, health issues, education issues and approaches to EU [European Union] issues. Suitable arrangements to be made for practical co-operation on agreed policies.

6. It will be open to the BIC to agree common policies or common actions. Individual members may opt not to participate in such common policies and common action.

7. The BIC normally will operate by consensus. In relation to decisions on common policies or common actions, including their means of implementation, it will operate by agreement of all members participating in such policies or actions.

8. The members of the BIC, on a basis to be agreed between them, will provide such financial support as it may require.

9. A secretariat for the BIC will be provided by the British and Irish Governments in co-ordination with officials of each of the other members.

10. In addition to the structures provided for under this agreement, it will be open to two or more members to develop bilateral or multilateral arrangements between them. Such arrangements could include, subject to the agreement of the members concerned, mechanisms to enable consultation, co-operation and joint decision-making on matters of mutual interest; and mechanisms to implement any joint decisions they may reach. These arrangements will not require the prior approval of the BIC as a whole and will operate independently of it.

11. The elected institutions of the members will be encouraged to develop interparliamentary links, perhaps building on the British-Irish Interparliamentary Body.

12. The full membership of the BIC will keep under review the workings of the Council, including a formal published review at an appropriate time after the Agreement comes into effect, and will contribute as appropriate to any review of the overall political agreement arising from the multi-party negotiations.

British-Irish Intergovernmental Conference

1. There will be a new British-Irish Agreement dealing with the totality of relationships. It will establish a standing British-Irish Intergovernmental Conference, which will subsume both the Anglo-Irish Intergovernmental Council and the Intergovernmental Conference established under the 1985 Agreement.

2. The Conference will bring together the British and Irish Governments to promote bilateral co-operation at all levels on all matters of mutual interest within the competence of both Governments.

3. The Conference will meet as required at Summit level (Prime Minister and Taoiseach). Otherwise, Governments will be represented by appropriate Ministers. Advisers, including police and security advisers, will attend as appropriate.

4. All decisions will be by agreement between both Governments. The Governments will make determined efforts to resolve disagreements between them. There will be no derogation from the sovereignty of either Government.

5. In recognition of the Irish Government's special interest in Northern Ireland and of the extent to which issues of mutual concern arise in relation to Northern Ireland, there will be regular and frequent meetings of the Conference concerned with non-devolved Northern Ireland matters, on which the Irish Government may put forward views and proposals. These meetings, to be co-chaired by the Minister for Foreign Affairs and the Secretary of State for Northern Ireland, would also deal with all-island and cross-border co-operation on non-devolved issues. . . .

Rights, Safeguards and Equality of Opportunity
Human Rights

1. The parties affirm their commitment to the mutual respect, the civil rights and the religious liberties of everyone in the community. Against the background of the recent history of communal conflict, the parties affirm in particular:

- the right of free political thought;
- the right to freedom and expression of religion;
- the right to pursue democratically national and political aspirations;
- the right to seek constitutional change by peaceful and legitimate means;
- the right to freely choose one's place of residence;
- the right to equal opportunity in all social and economic activity, regardless of class, creed, disability, gender or ethnicity;
- the right to freedom from sectarian harassment; and
- the right of women to full and equal political participation.

United Kingdom Legislation

2. The British Government will complete incorporation into Northern Ireland law of the European Convention on Human Rights (ECHR), with direct access to the courts, and remedies for breach of the Convention, including power for the courts to overrule Assembly legislation on grounds of inconsistency.

3. Subject to the outcome of public consultation underway, the British Government intends, as a particular priority, to create a statutory obligation on public authorities in Northern Ireland to carry out all their functions with due regard to the need to promote equality of opportunity in relation to religion and political opinion; gender; race; disability; age; marital status; dependents; and sexual orientation. Public bodies would be required to draw up statutory schemes showing how they would implement this obligation. Such schemes would cover arrangements for policy appraisal, including an assessment of impact on relevant categories, public consultation, public access to information and services, monitoring and timetables.

4. The new Northern Ireland Human Rights Commission (see paragraph 5 below) will be invited to consult and to advise on the scope for defining, in Westminster legislation, rights supplementary to those in the European Convention on Human Rights, to reflect the particular circumstances of Northern Ireland, drawing as appropriate on international instruments and experience. These additional rights to reflect the principles of mutual respect for the identity and ethos of both communities and parity of esteem, and—taken together with the ECHR—to constitute a Bill of Rights for Northern Ireland. Among the issues for consideration by the Commission will be:

- the formulation of a general obligation on government and public bodies fully to respect, on the basis of equality of treatment, the identity and ethos of both communities in Northern Ireland; and
- a clear formulation of the rights not to be discriminated against and to equality of opportunity in both the public and private sectors.

New Institutions in Northern Ireland

5. A new Northern Ireland Human Rights Commission, with membership from Northern Ireland reflecting the community balance, will be established by Westminster legislation, independent of Government, with an extended and enhanced role beyond that currently exercised by the Standing Advisory Commission on Human Rights, to include keeping under review the adequacy and effectiveness of laws and practices, making recommendations to Government as necessary; providing information and promoting awareness of human rights; considering draft legislation referred to them by the new Assembly; and, in appropriate cases, bringing court proceedings or providing assistance to individuals doing so. . . .

Rights, Safeguards and Equality of Opportunity

Economic, Social and Cultural Issues

1. Pending the devolution of powers to a new Northern Ireland Assembly, the British Government will pursue broad policies for sustained economic growth and stability in Northern Ireland and for promoting social inclusion, including in particular community development and the advancement of women in public life. . . .

Decommissioning

1. Participants recall their agreement in the Procedural Motion adopted on 24 September 1997 "that the resolution of the decommissioning issue is an indispensable part of the process of negotiation", and also recall the provisions of paragraph 25 of Strand 1 above.

2. They note the progress made by the Independent International Commission on Decommissioning and the Governments in developing schemes which can represent a workable basis for achieving the decommissioning of illegally-held arms in the possession of paramilitary groups.

3. All participants accordingly reaffirm their commitment to the total disarmament of all paramilitary organisations. They also confirm their intention to continue to work constructively and in good faith with the Independent Commission, and to use any influence they may have, to achieve the decommissioning of all paramilitary arms within two years following endorsement in referendums North and South of the agreement and in the context of the implementation of the overall settlement.

4. The Independent Commission will monitor, review and verify progress on decommissioning of illegal arms, and will report to both Governments at regular intervals.

5. Both Governments will take all necessary steps to facilitate the decommissioning process to include bringing the relevant schemes into force by the end of June.

Security

1. The participants note that the development of a peaceful environment on the basis of this agreement can and should mean a normalisation of security arrangements and practices.

2. The British Government will make progress towards the objective of as early a return as possible to normal security arrangements in Northern Ireland, consistent with the level of threat and with a published overall strategy, dealing with:

(i) the reduction of the numbers and role of the Armed Forces deployed in Northern Ireland to levels compatible with a normal peaceful society;

(ii) the removal of security installations;

(iii) the removal of emergency powers in Northern Ireland; and

(iv) other measures appropriate to and compatible with a normal peaceful society.

3. The Secretary of State will consult regularly on progress, and the response to any continuing paramilitary activity, with the Irish Government and the political parties, as appropriate.

4. The British Government will continue its consultation on firearms regulation and control on the basis of the document published on 2 April 1998.

5. The Irish Government will initiate a wide-ranging review of the Offences Against the State Acts 1939-85 with a view to both reform and dispensing with those elements no longer required as circumstances permit.

Policing and Justice

1. The participants recognise that policing is a central issue in any society. They equally recognise that Northern Ireland's history of deep divisions has made it highly emotive, with great hurt suffered and sacrifices made by many individuals and their families, including those in the RUC [Royal Ulster Constabulary] and other public servants. They believe that the agreement provides the opportunity for a new beginning to policing in Northern Ireland with a police service capable of attracting and sustaining support from the community as a whole. They also believe that this agreement offers a unique opportunity to bring about a new political dispensation which will recognise the full and equal legitimacy and worth of the identities, senses of allegiance and ethos of all sections of the community in Northern Ireland. They consider that this opportunity should inform and underpin the development of a police service representative in terms of the make-up of the community as a whole and which, in a peaceful environment, should be routinely unarmed.

2. The participants believe it essential that policing structures and arrangements are such that the police service is professional, effective and efficient, fair and impartial, free from partisan political control; accountable, both under the law for its actions and to the community it serves; representative of the society it polices, and operates within a coherent and co-operative criminal justice system, which conforms with human rights norms. The participants also believe that those structures and arrangements must be capable of maintaining law and order including responding effectively to crime and to any terrorist threat and to public order problems. A police service which cannot do so will fail to win public confidence and acceptance. They believe that any such structures and arrangements should be capable of delivering a policing service, in constructive and inclusive partnerships with the community at all levels, and with the maximum delegation of authority and responsibility, consistent with the foregoing principles. These arrangements should be based on principles of protection of human rights and professional integrity and should be unambiguously accepted and actively supported by the entire community.

3. An independent Commission will be established to make recommendations for future policing arrangements in Northern Ireland including means of encouraging widespread community support for these arrangements within the agreed framework of principles reflected in the paragraphs above and in accordance with the terms of reference at Annex A. The Commission will be broadly representative with expert and international representation among its membership and will be asked to consult widely and to report no later than Summer 1999. . . .

AGREEMENT SIGNED BY BLAIR AND AHERN

The British and Irish Governments:

Welcoming the strong commitment to the Agreement reached on 10th April 1998 by themselves and other participants in the multi-party talks and set out in Annex 1 to this Agreement (hereinafter "the Multi-Party Agreement");

Considering that the Multi-Party Agreement offers an opportunity for a new beginning in relationships within Northern Ireland, within the island of Ireland and between the peoples of these islands;

Wishing to develop still further the unique relationship between their peoples and the close co-operation between their countries as friendly neighbours and as partners in the European Union;

Reaffirming their total commitment to the principles of democracy and non-violence which have been fundamental to the multi-party talks;

Reaffirming their commitment to the principles of partnership, equality and mutual respect and to the protection of civil, political, social, economic and cultural rights in their respective jurisdictions;

Have agreed as follows:

Article 1

The two Governments:

(i) recognise the legitimacy of whatever choice is freely exercised by a majority of the people of Northern Ireland with regard to its status, whether they prefer to continue to support the Union with Great Britain or a sovereign united Ireland;

(ii) recognise that it is for the people of the island of Ireland alone, by agreement between the two parts respectively and without external impediment, to exercise their right of self-determination on the basis of consent, freely and concurrently given, North and South, to bring about a united Ireland, if that is their wish, accepting that this right must be achieved and exercised with and subject to the agreement and consent of a majority of the people of Northern Ireland;

(iii) acknowledge that while a substantial section of the people in Northern Ireland share the legitimate wish of a majority of the people of the island of Ireland for a united Ireland, the present wish of a majority of the people of Northern Ireland, freely exercised and legitimate, is to maintain the Union and accordingly, that Northern Ireland's status as part of the United Kingdom reflects and relies upon that wish; and that it would be wrong to make any change in the status of Northern Ireland save with the consent of a majority of its people;

(iv) affirm that, if in the future, the people of the island of Ireland exercise their right of self-determination on the basis set out in sections (i) and (ii) above to bring about a united Ireland, it will be a binding obligation on both Governments to introduce and support in their respective Parliaments legislation to give effect to that wish;

(v) affirm that whatever choice is freely exercised by a majority of the people of Northern Ireland, the power of the sovereign government with jurisdiction there shall be exercised with rigorous impartiality on behalf of all the people in the diversity of their identities and traditions and shall be founded on the principles of full respect for, and equality of, civil, political, social and cultural rights, of freedom from discrimination for all citizens, and of parity of esteem and of just and equal treatment for the identity, ethos and aspirations of both communities;

(vi) recognise the birthright of all the people of Northern Ireland to identify themselves and be accepted as Irish or British, or both, as they may so choose, and accordingly confirm that their right to hold both British and Irish citizenship is accepted by both Governments and would not be affected by any future change in the status of Northern Ireland.

Article 2

The two Governments affirm their solemn commitment to support, and where appropriate implement, the provisions of the Multi-Party Agreement. In particular there shall be established in accordance with the provisions of the Multi-Party Agreement immediately on the entry into force of this Agreement, the following institutions:

(i) a North/South Ministerial Council;

(ii) the implementation bodies referred to in paragraph 9 (ii) of the section entitled "Strand Two" of the Multi-Party Agreement;

(iii) a British-Irish Council;

(iv) British-Irish Intergovernmental Conference. . . .

UN SECRETARY GENERAL ON CONFLICT IN AFRICA
April 16, 1998

United Nations Secretary General Kofi Annan on April 16 presented an unusually blunt assessment of conflict and political failure in sub-Saharan Africa since the colonial era ended in the 1950s and 1960s. Annan, the UN's first leader to come from the region, said the entire world—Africans included—was to blame for the dozens of wars, a tendency toward repressive and corrupt governments, and halting economic development on the continent. Annan called for a new demonstration of political will to reverse these trends on the part of Africans, countries outside the region, multinational corporations, and others interested in Africa's future.

The UN Security Council passed several resolutions later in the year endorsing the key elements of Annan's report. The council paid special attention to Annan's proposals for an international effort to curb arms trafficking in Africa, instructing various UN agencies to redouble enforcement of arms embargoes in areas of conflict. Annan's report also won cautious praise from some quarters that were implicitly criticized in it. For example, the United States welcomed the report; State Department spokesman James P. Rubin called it a "thoughtful, comprehensive document that will contribute importantly to the international debate on how to best promote peace and development in sub-Saharan Africa."

Despite the eloquence of its call for peace and political pluralism, Annan's report appeared to have little immediate impact on daily life in Africa. Cross-border and internal conflicts flared throughout sub-Saharan Africa during the year, and for every step forward in the region there appeared to be at least one step backward some place else. Such was the case in the contrasting events in two of the continent's biggest and most important countries: Nigeria, which moved slowly toward a political opening following the death of its military dictator, General Sani Abacha; and the Democratic Republic of the Congo (formerly Zaire), which in the year after the ouster of dictator Mobutu Sese Seko seemed to be sliding back into repression, corruption, and civil war. (Congo conflict, Historic Documents of 1997, p. 877)

Annan's report came just a few weeks after President Clinton completed a widely heralded tour of African nations intended to highlight positive trends in the region. Clinton praised a "new generation" of African leaders who, he said, were trying to respond to the needs of their people. (Clinton African tour, p. 159)

Annan's Report

In an institution famed for reliance on diplomatic niceties and vaporous language, Annan's report was extraordinary for its clear and direct analysis of what had gone wrong in Africa during the four decades since independence from the colonial powers. A Ghanaian diplomat who had spent most of his career in various UN agencies, Annan spared no nation or institution from blame for the wars, political incompetence, and economic failures that had troubled nearly every country in sub-Saharan Africa. Delivering his report to the Security Council on April 16, Annan said he had been guided by "a commitment to honesty and clarity." The Security Council—in a September 25, 1997, meeting attended by the foreign ministers of member nations—had asked Annan for a report on Africa.

Annan divided his report into two main sections. One dealt with the causes of conflict in Africa and the other described corrective actions that Africans and outsiders could take.

Perhaps the boldest statement in the entire report was Annan's assertion that Africans had to recognize their own failures in the years since independence. Most African leaders, as well as many intellectuals both in Africa and outside the region, had insisted for years that colonialism was primarily at fault for the continent's modern-day problems. According to this reasoning, the great colonial powers (primarily France, Germany, Great Britain, and Belgium) had divided Africa along arbitrary lines, plundered the region's wealth, and left a legacy of arbitrary rule that Africans were unable to escape. Moreover, this argument continued, the great powers of the modern age were interested in Africa only for its natural resources and were reluctant to devote more than token funds to help develop sound economic and political systems. During the cold war, Western powers and the Soviet bloc used Africa as an ideological battleground, each side sponsoring political leaders and guerrilla factions for its own purposes. After the cold war, Africa was neglected by the rest of the world—except for multinational corporations, arms dealers, and others who sought quick profits there.

In his report, Annan said these criticisms of Africa's legacy were valid, but they did not fully explain why so much of Africa continued to be impoverished and embroiled in conflict. "More than three decades after African countries gained their independence, there is a growing recognition among Africans themselves that the continent must look beyond its colonial past for the causes of current conflicts," Annan said. "Today, more than ever, Africa must look at itself."

The root of many of the region's problem, Annan said, was what he called "the nature of political power" since independence. "It is frequently the case that political victory assumes a 'winner-takes-all' form with respect to wealth and resources, patronage, and the prestige and prerogatives of office," he said. "When there is insufficient accountability of leaders, lack of transparency in regimes, inadequate checks and balances, non-adherence to the rule of law, absence of peaceful means to change or replace leadership, or lack of respect for human rights, political control becomes excessively important, and the stakes become dangerously high." These factors were especially acute—and conflict was virtually inevitable—in situations where rival communities believed that "their security, perhaps their very survival, can be ensured only through control of state power," he said.

Annan recited a grim list of the consequences of political failures in Africa. Between 1970 and 1998, he said, more than thirty wars had been fought in Africa, "the vast majority" of which originated within one nation. In 1996 fourteen of the fifty-three African countries engaged in armed conflict, "accounting for more than half of all war-related deaths worldwide and resulting in more than eight million refugees, returnees, and displaced persons."

Preventing Conflict

Along with his powerful examination of failures in Africa, Annan insisted that positive alternatives were possible. "For too long, conflict in Africa has been seen as inevitable or intractable, or both," he told the Security Council. "It is neither."

In his report, Annan presented a detailed review of the failures and success of past efforts, by Africans themselves and by outside forces, to deal with the region's problems, and he outlined numerous steps for the future. In general, Annan said past attempts to fix Africa's problems had been too limited and halting and had been plagued by the same kinds of self-interested disagreements that had caused the problems in the first place.

Annan devoted much of the report to an analysis of peacemaking and peacekeeping efforts by the United Nations and other international organizations. He noted that many such efforts had failed because peacekeepers were brought in before warring parties had reached a fundamental political agreement, or the countries supplying the peacekeeping forces could not agree about the purpose or desired outcome of the mission. Annan traced the failure of the 1993 peacekeeping mission in Somalia, noting that, as a consequence, leading UN member nations were reluctant to intervene in the genocidal war in Rwanda a year later. As a result, he said, "hundreds of thousands of lives were lost in the course of the genocide that was perpetrated in the full view of the international community." (Rwandan genocide, p. 614)

Annan described a series of steps the United Nations could take to try to ensure the success of its peacekeeping missions, or to help missions mounted by other organizations or regional groups of nations. A peacekeeping force can be effective, he said, if it is "deployed with a credible deterrent capacity, equipped with appropriate resources, and backed by sufficient political will." Curtailing conflict in Africa also meant reducing the supply of weapons in the region, he said. One of the most effective means, he added, would be for international identification and control of arms dealers who had been profiting from African wars.

To improve chances of long-term stability and prosperity in Africa, Annan called for sweeping changes in foreign aid programs and in the fundamental economic and political systems in the region. The wealthy industrialized nations and multilateral agencies such as the World Bank needed to realize that many African countries were swamped by debt from loans they received decades previously for economic development, Annan said. Lenders should speed up forgiveness of those loans. In turn, he said, African nations needed to take more seriously the need for economic reforms, such as eliminating inefficient and corrupt state-run monopolies and encouraging competition. Annan said it was also time for Africans to look at democracy as an ongoing process in which free elections could lead to the transfer of power, not just the seizing of power by one faction after one set of elections.

Security Council Follow-up

On May 28 the UN Security Council established a "working group" to review Annan's report and make recommendations for carrying out its recommendations. Later in the year, the council adopted several resolutions and statements endorsing specific sections of the report and instructing UN agencies to take actions to put recommendations into effect.

On September 16 the council adopted Resolution 1196 establishing procedures for enforcing future UN arms embargoes, such as ones the council had imposed to curb fighting in Angola and Sierra Leone. Two months later, on November 19, the council adopted Resolution 1208, outlining several steps for improving UN refugee programs and Resolution 1209, encouraging arms-producing nations to halt weapons shipments to wartorn regions in Africa.

> *Following are excerpts from the report, "The Causes of Conflict and the Promotion of Durable Peace and Sustainable Development in Africa," submitted to the UN Security Council and General Assembly by Secretary General Kofi Annan, followed by the text of a statement about the report Annan gave to the Security Council; both were released April 16, 1998:*

UN REPORT ON CONFLICT IN AFRICA

I. Introduction

1. On 25 September 1997, the Security Council convened at the level of Foreign Ministers to consider the need for a concerted international effort to pro-

mote peace and security in Africa. The Council observed that despite the progress achieved by some African States the number and intensity of armed conflicts on the continent remained a matter of grave concern, requiring a comprehensive response. The Council requested that I submit a report regarding the sources of conflict in Africa, ways to prevent and address those conflicts, and how to lay the foundation for durable peace and economic growth following their resolution. In accordance with the wishes of the Council, and because the scope of the challenge extends beyond the purview of the Security Council alone, I hereby submit this report not only to the Security Council but also to the General Assembly and other components of the United Nations system that have responsibilities in Africa, including the Bretton Woods institutions.

2. Africa as a whole has begun to make significant economic and political progress in recent years, but in many parts of the continent progress remains threatened or impeded by conflict. For the United Nations there is no higher goal, no deeper commitment and no greater ambition than preventing armed conflict. The prevention of conflict begins and ends with the promotion of human security and human development. Ensuring human security is, in the broadest sense, the cardinal mission of the United Nations. Genuine and lasting prevention is the means to achieve that mission.

3. Conflict in Africa poses a major challenge to United Nations efforts designed to ensure global peace, prosperity and human rights for all. Although the United Nations was intended to deal with inter-State warfare, it is being required more and more often to respond to intra-State instability and conflict. In those conflicts the main aim, increasingly, is the destruction not just of armies but of civilians and entire ethnic groups. Preventing such wars is no longer a matter of defending States or protecting allies. It is a matter of defending humanity itself.

4. Since 1970, more than 30 wars have been fought in Africa, the vast majority of them intra-State in origin. In 1996 alone, 14 of the 53 countries of Africa were afflicted by armed conflicts, accounting for more than half of all war-related deaths worldwide and resulting in more than 8 million refugees, returnees and displaced persons. The consequences of those conflicts have seriously undermined Africa's efforts to ensure long-term stability, prosperity and peace for its peoples.

5. By not averting these colossal human tragedies, African leaders have failed the peoples of Africa; the international community has failed them; the United Nations has failed them. We have failed them by not adequately addressing the causes of conflict; by not doing enough to ensure peace; and by our repeated inability to create the conditions for sustainable development. This is the reality of Africa's recent past. It is a reality that must be confronted honestly and constructively by all concerned if the people of Africa are to enjoy the human security and economic opportunities they seek and deserve. Today, in many parts of Africa, efforts to break with the patterns of the past are at last beginning to succeed.

6. It is my aspiration, with this report, to add momentum to Africa's renewed quest for peace and greater prosperity. The report strives to do so by

offering an analysis of conflicts in Africa that does justice to their reality and seeks answers in their sources. It strives to do so by proposing realistic and achievable recommendations which, in time, may reduce if not entirely end those conflicts. It aims to summon the political will of Africans and non-Africans alike to act when action is so evidently needed—the will without which no level of assistance and no degree of hope can make the difference between war and peace in Africa.

II. The Sources of Conflict

7. Africa is a vast and varied continent. African countries have different histories and geographical conditions, different stages of economic development, different sets of public policies and different patterns of internal and international interaction. The sources of conflict in Africa reflect this diversity and complexity. Some sources are purely internal, some reflect the dynamics of a particular sub-region, and some have important international dimensions. Despite these differences the sources of conflict in Africa are linked by a number of common themes and experiences.

A. Historical legacies

8. At the Congress of Berlin in 1885, the colonial Powers partitioned Africa into territorial units. Kingdoms, States and communities in Africa were arbitrarily divided; unrelated areas and peoples were just as arbitrarily joined together. In the 1960s, the newly independent African States inherited those colonial boundaries, together with the challenge that legacy posed to their territorial integrity and to their attempts to achieve national unity. The challenge was compounded by the fact that the framework of colonial laws and institutions which some new States inherited had been designed to exploit local divisions, not overcome them. Understandably, therefore, the simultaneous tasks of State-building and nation-building preoccupied many of the newly independent States, and were given new momentum by the events that followed the outbreak of secessionist fighting in the Congo. Too often, however, the necessary building of national unity was pursued through the heavy centralization of political and economic power and the suppression of political pluralism. Predictably, political monopolies often led to corruption, nepotism, complacency and the abuse of power. The era of serious conflict over State boundaries in Africa has largely passed, aided by the 1963 decision of the Organization of African Unity (OAU) to accept the boundaries which African States had inherited from colonial authorities. However, the challenge of forging a genuine national identity from among disparate and often competing communities has remained.

9. The character of the commercial relations instituted by colonialism also created long-term distortions in the political economy of Africa. Transportation networks and related physical infrastructure were designed to satisfy the needs of trade with the metropolitan country, not to support the balanced growth of an indigenous economy. In addition to frequently imposing unfavourable terms of trade, economic activities that were strongly skewed towards extractive industries and primary commodities for export stimulated

little demand for steady and widespread improvements in the skills and educational levels of the workforce. The consequences of this pattern of production and exchange spilled over into the post-independence State. As political competition was not rooted in viable national economic systems, in many instances the prevailing structure of incentives favoured capturing the institutional remnants of the colonial economy for factional advantage.

10. During the cold war the ideological confrontation between East and West placed a premium on maintaining order and stability among friendly States and allies, though super-Power rivalries in Angola and elsewhere also fuelled some of Africa's longest and most deadly conflicts. Across Africa, undemocratic and oppressive regimes were supported and sustained by the competing super-Powers in the name of their broader goals but, when the cold war ended, Africa was suddenly left to fend for itself. Without external economic and political support, few African regimes could sustain the economic lifestyles to which they had become accustomed, or maintain the permanent hold on political power which they had come to expect. As a growing number of States found themselves internally beset by unrest and violent conflict, the world searched for a new global security framework.

11. For a brief period following the end of the cold war, the international community was eager to exercise its newly acquired capacity for collective decision-making. Beginning in the early 1990s, the Security Council launched a series of ambitious peacekeeping and peacemaking initiatives in Africa and elsewhere. Despite a number of important successes, the inability of the United Nations to restore peace to Somalia soured international support for conflict intervention and precipitated a rapid retreat by the international community from peacekeeping worldwide. An early and direct consequence of this retreat was the failure of the international community, including the United Nations, to intervene to prevent genocide in Rwanda. That failure has had especially profound consequences in Africa. Throughout the continent, the perception of near indifference on the part of the international community has left a poisonous legacy that continues to undermine confidence in the Organization.

B. Internal factors

12. More than three decades after African countries gained their independence, there is a growing recognition among Africans themselves that the continent must look beyond its colonial past for the causes of current conflicts. Today more than ever, Africa must look at itself. The nature of political power in many African States, together with the real and perceived consequences of capturing and maintaining power, is a key source of conflict across the continent. It is frequently the case that political victory assumes a "winner-takes-all" form with respect to wealth and resources, patronage, and the prestige and prerogatives of office. A communal sense of advantage or disadvantage is often closely linked to this phenomenon, which is heightened in many cases by reliance on centralized and highly personalized forms of governance. Where there is insufficient accountability of leaders, lack of

transparency in regimes, inadequate checks and balances, non-adherence to the rule of law, absence of peaceful means to change or replace leadership, or lack of respect for human rights, political control becomes excessively important, and the stakes become dangerously high. This situation is exacerbated when, as is often the case in Africa, the State is the major provider of employment and political parties are largely either regionally or ethnically based. In such circumstances, the multi-ethnic character of most African States makes conflict even more likely, leading to an often violent politicization of ethnicity. In extreme cases, rival communities may perceive that their security, perhaps their very survival, can be ensured only through control of State power. Conflict in such cases becomes virtually inevitable.

C. External factors

13. During the cold war, external efforts to bolster or undermine African Governments were a familiar feature of super-Power competition. With the end of the cold war, external intervention has diminished but has not disappeared. In the competition for oil and other precious resources in Africa, interests external to Africa continue to play a large and sometimes decisive role, both in suppressing conflict and in sustaining it. Foreign interventions are not limited, however, to sources beyond Africa. Neighbouring States, inevitably affected by conflicts taking place within other States, may also have other significant interests, not all of them necessarily benign. While African peacekeeping and mediation efforts have become more prominent in recent years, the role that African Governments play in supporting, sometimes even instigating, conflicts in neighbouring countries must be candidly acknowledged.

D. Economic motives

14. Despite the devastation that armed conflicts bring, there are many who profit from chaos and lack of accountability, and who may have little or no interest in stopping a conflict and much interest in prolonging it. Very high on the list of those who profit from conflict in Africa are international arms merchants. Also high on the list, usually, are the protagonists themselves. In Liberia, the control and exploitation of diamonds, timber and other raw materials was one of the principal objectives of the warring factions. Control over those resources financed the various factions and gave them the means to sustain the conflict. Clearly, many of the protagonists had a strong financial interest in seeing the conflict prolonged. The same can be said of Angola, where protracted difficulties in the peace process owed much to the importance of control over the exploitation of the country's lucrative diamond fields. In Sierra Leone, the chance to plunder natural resources and loot Central Bank reserves was a key motivation of those who seized power from the elected Government in May 1997.

E. Particular situations

15. In addition to the broader sources of conflict in Africa that have been identified, a number of other factors are especially important in particular sit-

uations and subregions. In Central Africa, they include the competition for scarce land and water resources in densely populated areas. In Rwanda, for example, multiple waves of displacement have resulted in situations where several families often claim rights to the same piece of land. In African communities where oil is extracted, conflict has often arisen over local complaints that the community does not adequately reap the benefit of such resources, or suffers excessively from the degradation of the natural environment. In North Africa, the tensions between strongly opposing visions of society and the State are serious sources of actual and potential conflict in some States. . . .

V. Summoning the Necessary Political Will

104. With sufficient political will—on the part of Africa and on the part of the international community—peace and development in Africa can be given a new momentum. Africa is an ancient continent. Its lands are rich and fertile enough to provide a solid foundation for prosperity. Its people are proud and industrious enough to seize the opportunities that may be presented. I am confident that Africans will not be found wanting, in stamina, in determination, or in political will. Africa today is striving to make positive change, and in many places these efforts are beginning to bear fruit. In the carnage and tragedy that afflicts some parts of Africa, we must not forget the bright spots or overlook the achievements.

105. *What is needed from Africa.* With political will, rhetoric can truly be transformed into reality. Without it, not even the noblest sentiments will have a chance of success. Three areas deserve particular attention. First, Africa must demonstrate the will to rely upon political rather than military responses to problems. Democratic channels for pursuing legitimate interests and expressing dissent must be protected, and political opposition respected and accommodated in constitutional forms. Second, Africa must summon the will to take good governance seriously, ensuring respect for human rights and the rule of law, strengthening democratization, and promoting transparency and capability in public administration. Unless good governance is prized, Africa will not break free of the threat and the reality of conflict that are so evident today. Third, Africa must enact and adhere to the various reforms needed to promote economic growth. Long-term success can be achieved only if African Governments have the political will to enact sound economic policies, and to persevere in their implementation until a solid economic foundation has been established.

106. *What is needed from the international community.* Political will is also needed from the international community. Where the international community is committed to making a difference, it has proved that significant and rapid transformation can be achieved. With respect to Africa, the international community must now summon the political will to intervene where it can have an impact, and invest where resources are needed. New sources of funding are required, but so too is a better use of existing resources and the enactment of trade and debt measures that will enable Africa to generate and

better reinvest its own resources. Concrete action must be taken, as it is in deeds rather than in declarations that the international community's commitment to Africa will be measured. Significant progress will require sustained international attention at the highest political levels over a period of years. To maintain the momentum for action in support of Africa, I call upon the Security Council to reconvene at ministerial level on a biennial basis so as to assess efforts undertaken and actions needed. I also urge that consideration be given to the convening of the Security Council at summit level within five years, for this purpose.

VI. Conclusions

107. In this report I set out to provide a clear and candid analysis of the sources of conflicts in Africa and the reasons why they persist. I have recommended actions and goals that are both realistic and achievable, to reduce conflict and in time help to build a strong and durable peace. I have urged Africans and non-Africans alike to summon the political will to rise to the challenge which together we must all confront. The time is long past when anyone could claim ignorance about what was happening in Africa, or what was needed to achieve progress. The time is also past when the responsibilities for producing change could be shifted on to other shoulders. It is a responsibility that we must all face. The United Nations stands ready to play its part. So must the world. So must Africa.

STATEMENT BY UN SECRETARY GENERAL

On 25 September 1997, the Security Council convened at the ministerial level to consider the need for a renewed and concerted international effort to promote peace and security in Africa. The Council requested that I submit a report on the sources of conflict in Africa and how they may best be addressed. I am pleased to submit that report today.

Allow me, however, to begin by expressing my deepest gratitude to the members of the Security Council for taking this unprecedented step for Africa. Of course, not all of Africa is in crisis; not all of Africa is facing conflict. Indeed, Africa itself has begun to make significant economic and social progress in recent years. But by showing the Council's concern for Africa's remaining conflicts, you have signalled your readiness to further that progress and make it last for all of Africa.

The report that I present today is guided, above all, by a commitment to honesty and clarity in analysing and addressing the challenge of conflict in Africa. For too long, conflict in Africa has been seen as inevitable or intractable, or both. It is neither.

Conflict in Africa, as everywhere, is caused by human action, and can be ended by human action. This is the reality that shames us for every conflict that we allow to persist, and emboldens us to believe that we can address and resolve every conflict that we choose to confront.

For the United Nations there is no higher goal, no deeper commitment and no greater ambition than preventing armed conflict so that people everywhere can enjoy peace and prosperity. In Africa, as elsewhere, the United Nations increasingly is being required to respond to intra-State instability and conflict. In those conflicts, the main aim, to an alarming degree, is the destruction not of armies but of civilians and entire ethnic groups.

Preventing such wars is no longer a question of defending States or protecting allies. It is a question of defending humanity itself.

Since 1970, Africa has had more than 30 wars fought on its territory, the vast majority of which have been intra-State in origin. Fourteen of Africa's 53 countries were afflicted by armed conflicts in 1996 alone. These accounted for more than half of all war-related deaths worldwide, resulting in more than 8 million refugees, returnees and displaced persons. The consequences of these conflicts have seriously undermined Africa's efforts to ensure long-term stability, prosperity and peace for its peoples.

No one—not the United Nations, not the international community, not Africa's leaders—can escape responsibility for the persistence of these conflicts.

Indeed, colossal human tragedies have taken place in Africa over the last decade—tragedies that could and should have been prevented. Not enough was done to address the causes of conflict. Not enough was done to ensure a lasting peace. Not enough was done to create the conditions for sustainable development. This is the reality of Africa's recent past. It is a reality that must be confronted honestly and constructively by all concerned if the people of Africa are to enjoy the human security and economic opportunities they seek and deserve.

Today in many parts of Africa, efforts to break with these past patterns are at last beginning to succeed. It is my aspiration that this report add momentum to Africa's renewed quest for peace and greater prosperity.

The report strives to do so by offering an analysis of Africa's conflicts that does justice to their reality and seeks answers in their sources. It strives to do so by proposing realistic and achievable recommendations which, over time, may reduce if not entirely end Africa's conflicts. And it aims to summon the political will of Africans and non-Africans alike to act when action so evidently is needed—the will without which no level of assistance and no degree of hope can make the difference between war and peace in Africa.

The sources of conflict in Africa are as varied and complex as the continent itself. In this report, I have sought to identify the kinds of actions that most effectively and most lastingly may address those conflicts and resolve them.

The significance of history and of factors external to Africa cannot be denied. But more than three decades after African countries gained their independence, there is a growing recognition among Africans that the continent must look beyond its colonial past for the sources and the solutions to its current conflicts.

The proposals that I set forth today require, in some cases, new ways of thinking about conflict in Africa. In others, they require new ways of acting.

Whether in peacekeeping, humanitarian assistance or post-conflict peace-building, genuine and sustainable progress depends on three critical factors: a clear understanding of the challenge; the political will to respond to that challenge; and the resources necessary to provide the adequate response.

Equally important is the understanding that peace and development remain inextricably linked—one feeding on the other, enabling the other and securing the other. The renunciation of violence as a means of gaining and holding power is only the beginning. Then must follow a renewed commitment to national development founded on sober, sound and uncorrupted economic policies.

A number of African States have made good progress in recent years, but others continue to struggle. Poor economic performance and inequitable development have resulted in a near-permanent economic crisis for some States, greatly exacerbating internal tensions and greatly diminishing the government's capacity to respond to those tensions.

Good governance is now more than ever the condition for the success of both peace and development. It is no coincidence that Africa's renaissance has come at a time when new and more democratic forms of government have begun to emerge and take root.

What we have learned over the last decades is that with political will, rhetoric can truly be transformed into reality. Without it, not even the noblest sentiments will have a chance of success. With sufficient political will—on the part of Africa and on the part of the international community—peace and development in Africa can be given a new momentum.

Africa is an ancient continent. Its lands are rich and fertile enough to provide a solid foundation for prosperity. Its people are proud and industrious enough to seize the opportunities that may be presented. I am confident that Africans will not be found wanting—in stamina, in determination or in political will.

Africa today is striving to make positive change, and in many places these efforts are beginning to bear fruit. In the carnage and tragedy that afflicts some parts of Africa, we must not forget the bright spots or overlook the achievements that have been made. What is needed is for those achievements to grow and multiply throughout Africa.

Three areas deserve particular attention. First, Africa must demonstrate the political will to rely upon political rather than military responses to problems. Democratic channels for pursuing legitimate interests and expressing dissent must be protected, and political opposition respected and accommodated in constitutional forms.

Second, Africa must summon the political will to take good governance seriously—ensuring respect for human rights and the rule of law, strengthening democratization and promoting transparency and capability in public administration. Unless good governance is prized, Africa will not break free of the threat and the reality of conflict which are so evident today.

Third, Africa must enact and adhere to the various reforms needed to promote economic growth. Long-term success can only be achieved if African governments have the political will to enact sound economic policies, and to persevere in their implementation until a solid economic foundation has been established.

Political will is also needed from the international community. Where the international community is committed to making a difference, it has proven that significant and rapid transformation can be achieved. With respect to Africa, the international community must now summon the will to intervene where it can have an impact, and invest where resources are needed.

New sources of funding are required, but so too is a better use of existing resources and the enactment of trade and debt relief measures that will enable Africa to generate and better reinvest its own resources. Concrete steps must be taken and I have made a number of concrete recommendations towards this end.

Let us never forget that it is the persistence of poverty that is impeding the full promise of peace for all of Africa's peoples. Alleviating poverty must be the first aim of all our efforts. Only then—only when prosperity and opportunity become real—will every citizen, young or old, man or woman, have a genuine and lasting stake in a peaceful future for Africa—politically, economically and socially.

In this report, I set out to provide a clear and candid analysis of the sources of Africa's conflicts and why they persist. I have recommended actions and goals to reduce conflict and in time help to build a strong and durable peace. I have urged Africans and non-Africans alike to summon the political will to rise to the challenge which together we must all confront.

The time is long past when one could claim ignorance about what was happening in Africa, or what was needed to achieve progress. The time is also past when the responsibility for producing change could be shifted on to other shoulders. It is responsibility that we all must face.

Allow me to conclude by saying that the United Nations not only seeks but welcomes this responsibility. For we wish, above all, that this report will mark a new beginning in the relations between the United Nations and Africa.

Let us make that beginning. Today. Together.

FEDERAL PROSECUTORS ON THE "UNABOMBER" CASE
April 28, 1998

Theodore J. Kaczynski, a former mathematics professor who turned his grievances against society into a seventeen-year bombing campaign, admitted in 1998 that he was the "Unabomber" who had killed three people and injured more than two dozen others. On January 22 Kaczynski pleaded guilty to federal murder charges. On May 4 a federal judge sentenced him to four life sentences plus thirty years in prison, without the possibility of parole.

Kaczynski planted his first bomb in 1978 and continued bombing, with periodic interruptions, until 1995. His early targets were at universities and airlines, resulting in the designation "unabomb." In later years Kaczynski mailed bombs to computer stores, university professors, and corporate officials—all targets of his stated rage against technology and other aspects of modern society.

An intense nationwide effort by the Federal Bureau of Investigation to track down the Unabomber succeeded only after Kaczynski apparently felt the urge to explain himself. In 1995 Kaczynski mailed a lengthy "manifesto" to newspapers. At the urging of the Justice Department, the Washington Post *and* New York Times *published the document, which was seen by Kaczynski's younger brother, David. David Kaczynski noted similarities between the manifesto and other writings by Theodore, and he described to federal agents the remote cabin in rural Montana where his brother lived.* (Unabomber manifesto, Historic Documents of 1995, p. 600)

David Kaczynski on August 20 received a $1 million reward from the government for providing the information that led to the Unabomber's arrest. He said he would put the money in a trust to benefit the victims of his brother's crimes. But in the closing hours of the 1998 session, Congress failed to act on a proposal to allow Kaczynski to receive the reward tax-free. Unless Congress acted, he would have to pay an estimated $355,000 in taxes before turning the money over to the victims.

In an April 28 sentencing memorandum for the judge in the case, federal prosecutors rejected Kaczynski's contention—as stated in his "manifesto"— that his actions represented a political protest against society as a whole. Rather, prosecutors said, Kaczynski was "a man who chose to repeatedly inflict violence and kill to gratify his own hatred" of everyone but himself. Kaczynski showed no remorse, prosecutors said, and likely would resume his murderous course if he was ever released back into society.

The Unabomber Campaign

Theodore Kaczynski was born in Chicago in 1942; he grew up in the city and in suburban Evergreen Park. Kaczynski graduated from high school two years early and, at age sixteen, entered Harvard University on a scholarship. He received bachelor's and master's degrees from Harvard and then a Ph.D. from the University of Michigan. In June 1967 Kaczynski joined the faculty of the University of California at Berkeley as an assistant professor of mathematics, but he left after only two years. In 1971 Kaczynski and his brother David purchased a small plot of land in Lincoln, Montana; later, Theodore built the 10 foot by 12 foot cabin in which he was to live for most of the time until his arrest.

Kaczynski planted his first bomb in the spring of 1978 on the campus of Northwestern University in Evanston, Illinois; it injured a security guard who opened a suspicious package. Kaczynski injured another person at the same university a year later when he left a bomb in a box. Other bombs mailed during the next six years to universities, airlines, and computer stores injured several people and led to heightened security around the country.

The bombing campaign led to its first death on December 11, 1985, when Hugh Campbell Scrutton, owner of computer store in Sacramento, opened a box containing a bomb filled with shrapnel. Working in his Montana cabin, Kaczynski continued perfecting his bombs but did not mail any for six years between mid-1987 and mid-1993, apparently fearing detection. His last two bombs were killers. One, mailed to the suburban New Jersey home of New York City advertising executive Thomas Mosser, exploded on December 10, 1994, killing Mosser in the presence of his family. Kaczynski mailed his last bomb to the Sacramento offices of the California Forestry Association. On April 24, 1995, the association's president, Gilbert P. Murray, opened the package containing the bomb and was immediately killed.

Two months later, Kaczynski mailed his rambling 35,000-word "manifesto" to numerous news organizations, demanding that it be printed in full. That act led to his eventual undoing when it alerted David Kaczynski to the possibility that his brother might be the Unabomber.

Based on information provided by David Kaczynski, federal agents raided Theodore Kaczynski's rustic Montana cabin on April 3, 1996, detained Kaczynski, and discovered dozens of items used to build bombs, along with technical manuals about chemicals and explosives. Agents also

*discovered journals Kaczynski had kept since 1969 describing his hatred
of society in general and detailing his bombing campaign.*

*Federal prosecutors charged Kaczynski with the three California murders, and a trial was scheduled for January 1998 in Sacramento, where
two of the Unabomber's victims died. As the trial date neared, Kaczynski
and his court-appointed lawyers sparred over tactics. The lawyers, hoping
to avoid the death penalty, wanted to portray Kaczynski as mentally ill;
Kaczynski maintained that he was sane and refused to participate in any
defense based on his mental state.*

*During the night of January 7—just before the scheduled start of his
trial—Kaczynski reportedly tried, and failed, to hang himself in his jail
cell. At the opening session of the trial on January 8, one of Kaczynski's
lawyers announced that her client wanted to represent himself. Judge Garland E. Burrell Jr. then ordered a psychiatric examination of Kaczynski,
which concluded that he was competent to stand trial. Burrell then rejected
Kaczynski's petition to represent himself.*

*Faced with a stated determination by prosecutors to seek the death
penalty, Kaczynski ultimately agreed to plead guilty to thirteen federal
charges involving bombing attacks in California, Connecticut, and New
Jersey. By acknowledging his guilt, in court on January 22, Kaczynski
avoided death but this guaranteed that he would be incarcerated for the rest
of his life.*

*The lifetime prison sentence came at a dramatic court hearing on May
4, when victims and relatives of victims spoke of the suffering Kaczynski
had caused. Susan Mosser described the events of December 10, 1994, when
her husband, Thomas Mosser, opened a package that exploded and drove
nails and razor blades into his body. "Please keep this creature out of society forever," she asked the judge, referring to Kaczynski. "Bury him so far
down he'll be closer to hell, because that's where the devil belongs."*

*Kaczynski himself spoke briefly, denouncing prosecutors who, he said,
had discredited him by misrepresenting his political views. "I ask only
that people reserve judgment on me and the Unabomber case," Kaczynski
said. "At a later time I will respond at length."*

*Following are excerpts from the sentencing memorandum presented April 28, 1998, by federal prosecutors to the U.S. District
Court for the Eastern District of California, in the case of United
States of America v. Theodore John Kaczynski, in which the government argued that Kaczynski should be sentenced to life in
prison for his crimes as the "Unabomber":*

Introduction

On January 22, 1998, Kaczynski pled guilty to 13 federal bombing offenses
resulting in the death of three men and serious injuries to two others. During
his plea colloquy Kaczynski acknowledged responsibility for a series of 16

bombings that occurred between May 25, 1978, and April 24, 1995, throughout the United States. Ex.1.

The plea agreement entered into by the parties calls for a sentence of life imprisonment without possibility of release and an order of restitution for the full loss caused by defendant's wrongful conduct. The offenses of conviction, as well as the applicable Sentencing Guideline provisions, require the imposition of mandatory sentences of life imprisonment.

Because this case was resolved by a plea bargain, the public and the defendant's victims continue to have a strong interest in having a full and accurate factual record in an open proceeding, so that the public may take full measure of the seriousness of the defendant's crimes and the harm they caused to the community. Therefore, notwithstanding the mandatory sentence, the United States files this memorandum to make clear that the defendant deserves the sentence that the Court is required to impose, to emphasize the harm that the defendant caused to victims and their families, and to dispel any notion that the defendant acted for any purpose other than satisfying his personal animosity. In addition, this memorandum provides a basis for the government's request that this Court make recommendations to the Bureau of Prisons regarding the terms and conditions of Kaczynski's confinement.

The seriousness of Kaczynski's crimes, his lack of remorse for his actions, and continuing threat he poses to the public, require that he be removed from society for the rest of his life. In addition, Kaczynski should be ordered to pay restitution to the survivors of his crimes in an amount commensurate with the harm he has inflicted on them, and should be ordered to disgorge any monies paid to him, or on his behalf, for writings, interviews or other information, as set forth in the plea agreement. *See* 18 U.S.C. 3681(a). Finally, this Court should recommend that the Bureau of Prisons incarcerate Kaczynski in a maximum security facility so that his activities can be monitored to prevent any future acts of violence or intimidation. *See* 18 U.S.C. Section 3621(b)(4)(B).

A. The Harm Wrought by Kaczynski

Kaczynski stands convicted of intentionally taking the lives of three men and grievously wounding two others. In imposing judgment, this Court should consider that "just as the murderer should be considered an individual, so too the victim is an individual whose death represents a unique loss to society and in particular to his family." *Payne v. Tennessee*, 501 U.S. 808, 825 (1991). Moreover, "[t]he affront to humanity of [the] brutal Murders such as (the defendant] committed is not limited to its impact on the victim or victims; a victim's community is also injured, and in particular the victim's family suffers shock and grief of a kind difficult to imagine for those who have not shared a similar loss." *Booth v. Maryland*, 482 U.S. 496, 515 (1987)(dissenting opinion).

Those who have been left to bear witness to Kaczynski's actions may choose to address the Court, as is their right under Fed. R. Crim. P. 32(c)(3)(E). We are simply presenting the Court with a "quick glimpse of the li[ves] that [Kaczynski] chose to extinguish." *Payne*, 501 U.S. at 830 (concurring opinion), quoting *Mills v. Maryland*, 486 U.S. 367, 397 (1988)(dissenting opinion).

Gilbert Murray

Gilbert Murray was a Marine Corps veteran of the Vietnam War and a graduate of the University of California, Berkeley. A life-long forester, he was the president of the California Forestry Association when, on April 24, 1995, he was killed at age 46 by a package bomb sent to his office by Kaczynski. The bomb so badly destroyed Gil Murray's body, that his family was allowed only to see and touch his feet and legs, below the knees, as a final farewell.

Gilbert Murray left behind a wife, two sons, a family who loved him, and many friends, colleagues, and co-workers. His wife, Connie, was introduced to Gil by her best friend, Jan Tuck, Gil's sister, when she was 16 years old. Connie and Gil began dating a few months after they met. The following year, Gil enlisted in the Marine Corps, and the two were married when Gil returned from his tour of duty in Vietnam. According to his wife, Connie, Gil "was in love with this Earth" and felt that he had been entrusted with a small patch of it to safeguard and protect. He was known as a voice of calm and reason in a highly contentious field and a man who worked hard to build bridges between differing camps. Above all, he was a dedicated father and husband, a man who "treasured" his family.

Together Connie and Gil raised two sons, Wil and Gib. Wil was 18 at the time of Gil's murder; Gib was just two weeks past his 16th birthday. Gil was always active in his sons' lives. He taught them to ski at an earlier age, watched and coached them in athletic leagues, and when they were in High School, went to their basketball, baseball and football games, even re-scheduling meetings to attend. At Gil's funeral, Wil told the congregation that his father was "the greatest man I ever met. He loved my mom, my brother and me more than life itself. He was always there for us. We always came first." For Connie Murray, her deepest regret comes from the realization that each of her sons will never know their father on an equal footing, as one adult to another.

Shortly before Gil Murray's death, his son Wil had been accepted to Cornell University where he had been recruited for the football team. There was much discussion in the family over whether they could afford to send their son to an Ivy League school which did not offer athletic scholarships. On the Sunday before Gil died, the Murray family met and decided that they would find a way to finance the education. One of the last images that Connie had of her husband was his throwing out all the catalogues for other schools that had accepted Wil. Gil was murdered the next day. Left without the family's provider, and emotionally unable to be far away from home at such a difficult time, Wil did not attend Cornell.

Thomas Mosser

Thomas Mosser was a Navy Veteran of the Vietnam war and worked for the public relations firm of Burson-Marsteller, for 25 years. He had recently been promoted to general manager of the parent company, Young and Rubicam, Inc., and had been away on a business trip. On December 9, 1994, he returned home to his family in New Jersey. Earlier that day, the postman delivered the package that had been mailed to him by Kaczynski. Thomas Mosser's wife, Susan, brought the package inside the house and placed it on a table by the front door. The package lay unopened overnight in the Mosser home only a few feet from where Thomas' daughters played with their friends.

The following day, December 10, was meant to be a special day for the Mosser household. It was the unofficial commencement of the holiday season, a time when Thomas devoted all of his time to his family, and the day when the family had planned to go out together to buy a Christmas tree. That morning, Thomas took the mail that had accumulated during his trip, including the package sent to him by Kaczynski, into the kitchen to open. His wife and 15-month-old daughter, Kelly, joined him, while another daughter, Kim, slept in her room nearby. Seconds before Thomas opened the package, Kelly scurried out of the kitchen and Susan followed her. Thomas opened the package; the ensuing blast drove shrapnel into his body, leaving a gaping hole in his head, opening up his body, and piercing his organs with nails. He died at age 50, on the floor of his own home, his wife at his side trying in vain to aid and comfort him.

Thomas Mosser left behind a wife, a son, three daughters, a family that loved him, and many friends, colleagues, and co-workers. The Christmas season is always a painful reminder of their loss. Last year, Kelly, who had only been 15 months old when her father was murdered, returned from Sunday school with a question for her mother. "Is God coming back from heaven?" she asked. When told God would indeed return, Kelly asked "Could he bring Daddy back with him?"

Hugh Scrutton

Hugh Scrutton was a native of Sacramento and a graduate of the University of California, Davis. He had traveled the world, devoted time to art, literature, and gardening and at age 38 was running his own computer rental business in Sacramento. Around noontime on December 11, 1985, he stepped out of his business and walked into the parking lot behind his store. There he stopped to try and pick up what looked like a wooden plank with nails protruding from it laying on the ground. In reality, the object was a bomb that Kaczynski had disguised and planted outside his store. Hugh Scrutton's simple act of courtesy trying to remove what looked like a potential hazard to others, cost him his life. Kaczynski had rigged the concealed bomb to detonate when it was moved, and when Hugh started to lift the wood, the bomb exploded, severing his right hand and driving shrapnel deep into his heart. He died at age 38, in the parking lot of the business he had only recently started, with a co-worker and a caring passerby trying desperately to save him.

Friends recall Hugh as a man who embraced life, a gentle man with a sense of humor who had traveled around the world, climbed mountains, and studied languages. He cared about politics, was "fair and kind" in business, and was remembered as "straightforward, honest, and sincere." He left behind his mother, sister, family members, a girlfriend who loved him dearly, and a circle of friends and colleagues who respected and cared for him.

The survivors

Other individuals narrowly survived Kaczynski's attacks. Charles Epstein, a professor of pediatrics and a renowned researcher in prenatal disorders, was maimed and injured when, in the quiet of his family home, he opened the carefully disguised package bomb that Kaczynski had mailed to him. A husband and father, accomplished musician, as well as a physician who has dedicated his life to healing others, Dr. Epstein suffered permanent injuries to his hand, arm, face, and hearing. Dr. Epstein underwent weeks of emergency and reconstructive surgery, as well as medical treatment that continues to this day.

David Gelernter, a professor of computer science, was maimed and injured in his office at Yale University, when he too opened a package bomb sent to him by Kaczynski. Dr. Gelernter narrowly escaped death from the explosion, surviving only because he managed to stagger down five flights of steps and across a street to a nearby medical clinic where he was rushed to the trauma unit of a local hospital. A husband and father, as well as a noted teacher and writer, Dr. Gelernter suffered permanent injuries to his hand, arm, body, and sight. Dr. Gelernter underwent weeks of emergency and reconstructive surgery, as well as medical treatment that continues to this day.

Numerous other individuals were injured by Kaczynski's bombs. Gary Wright was injured by the bomb Kaczynski planted in the parking lot of a Salt Lake City computer store. He suffered lacerations and puncture wounds to his face, hands, arms, shoulder, and legs, and underwent surgery to remove shrapnel. Nicklaus Suino, an assistant to Professor James McConnell at the University of Michigan, was hospitalized when he opened the package bomb Kaczynski mailed to McConnell. John Hauser, then an Air Force Captain and graduate student at U.C. Berkeley, was seriously wounded by a bomb Kaczynski planted in a university computer room. Dr. Hauser suffered permanent injuries, ending his career as an Air Force pilot and his dream of becoming an astronaut, and underwent weeks of surgery to repair the damage from the blast. Diogenes Angelakos, who died last year from cancer, was a distinguished Professor at U.C. Berkeley when he was injured by a bomb Kaczynski planted in a break room on the U.C. Berkeley campus. He was hospitalized and underwent surgery, suffering permanent injuries to his hand. Janet Smith was injured when she opened a package bomb Kaczynski mailed to the professor she worked for. She was hospitalized and underwent surgery for her injuries. Percy Wood was the President of United Airlines when he was injured in his family home by a book bomb Kaczynski mailed to him. He was hospitalized and underwent surgery for injuries to his hand, legs, and face. Eighteen passengers and crew members were treated for smoke inhalation when the flight of their passenger airliner was aborted by a fire started by one of Kaczynski's bombs in the cargo compartment. John G. Harris was a student at Northwestern University when he was injured by a disguised bomb placed in a university work room by Kaczynski. Officer Terry Marker was injured while examining the contents of a concealed bomb Kaczynski had left in a University campus parking lot.

Many people were placed directly in harm's way by Kaczynski's bombs. Only chance prevented the death and injury of many of the victims, family members and co-workers, such as the wife and daughters of Thomas Mosser and Gilbert Murray's colleagues at the California Forestry Association. Many of Kaczynski's bombs were left in heavily trafficked areas—the parking lot behind Hugh Scrutton's store, the student workrooms at Berkeley and North-western—and easily could have killed or injured many others.

The harm Kaczynski brought about is not limited to the physical injuries he inflicted. By his actions, Kaczynski forced family members and co-workers to witness the slaying or wounding of loved ones, friends, and colleagues. In addition, while hiding behind an alias, Kaczynski intimidated individuals and the public with letters, threatening two noted scholars for pursuing academic research, taunting one of the men he had maimed, bringing the nation's air traffic to standstill on a holiday weekend by a threat to bring down a jetliner, and coercing newspapers into publishing his turgid theories on society's shortcomings. His acts of terrorism deprived countless individuals of their sense of security in their homes, workplaces, and communities.

Kaczynski's Culpability

"Deeply ingrained in our legal tradition is the idea that the more purposeful is the criminal conduct, the more serious is the offense, and, therefore, the more severely it ought to be punished." *Tison v. Arizona*, 481 U.S. 137, 156 (1986). The purposefulness of Kaczynski's conduct is evident from the circumstances of the crimes themselves. Each offense entailed considerable preparation and planning, from the design and construction of the homemade bombs to their clandestine implementation. And every step in the commission of these offenses allowed substantial opportunity for reflection on the consequences. That the crimes continued unabated over the course of nearly two decades should dispel any uncertainty as to their deliberate nature.

In addition to what we may rightfully infer from the cruel details of these crimes, Kaczynski's own writings provide a stark account, in his own words, of his purposes and intentions. Thousands of pages of Kaczynski's handwritten and typed documents were found during the April 1996 search of his cabin; the documents include Kaczynski's self-styled "autobiography" chronicling his life to the age of 27, a daily journal for the days thereafter, and numerous handwritten entries and notes detailing plans for the bombings, the construction and placement of bombs, and Kaczynski's own reactions to the aftermath of his crimes. The earliest entry in these writings is 1969 and the latest is dated February 1996. Combined, these writings provide a detailed picture of Kaczynski's life and his motivation for becoming a serial killer.

Kaczynski killed out of hatred

In June of 1995, late in his bombing career, Kaczynski sent a manuscript (which came to be known as the 'Unabomb Manifesto') to newspapers under the alias 'FC' espousing an ideological basis for his crimes. He claimed that he "had to kill people" to get a "message before the public" that technology was destroying mankind. Ex. 2. While Kaczynski adopted the pretense that he was killing for the greater good of society, two points are clear from the writings seized from his home. First, his desire to kill preceded by several years any serious concerns about technology. Second, he wanted to kill not out of some altruistic sense that he would thereby benefit society, but, in his own words, out of "personal revenge" and without "any kind of philosophical or moralistic justification." Ex. 3.

Kaczynski's writings contain extensive meditations on his hatred of people, his ideology and motivations, and his intent to kill his victims. In his autobiography Kaczynski recounts that he first formed a desire to kill while still a graduate student at the University of Michigan in 1966, years before he made his way to Montana and adopted his isolated lifestyle. He immediately began to plan how he would murder: "My first thought was to kill somebody I hated and then kill myself before the cops could get me." Ex. 4. He quickly rejected this plan, however, in favor of one that would allow him to commit multiple murders and spare his own life:

> But, since I now had new hope, I was not ready to relinquish life so easily. So I thought, "I will kill, but I will make at least some effort to avoid detection, so that I can kill again."

Id.

According to his own writings, Kaczynski's decision to live a wilderness lifestyle was made in part to further his murderous plans:

> Then I thought, "Well, as long as I am going to throw everything up anyway, instead of having to shoot it out with the cops or something, . . . I will go up to Canada, take off into the woods with a rifle, and try to live off the country. If that doesn't work out, and if I can get back to civilization before I starve, then I will come back here and kill someone I hate."

Id.

Over the ensuing years, Kaczynski came to despise many people, including those who interfered with the solitude he craved or came to represent for him certain aspects of modern technological and industrial society. Thus, his journals are filled with expressions of hatred often expressed in terms of some ill-defined need for "revenge" and plans to injure a varied group of individuals, from campers and snowmobilers who found their way into the national forest near his home, to a woman who had spurned his advances. In describing this abundant hatred, Kaczynski wrote: "I often had fantasies of killing the kind of people whom I hated (e.g. government officials, police, computer scientists, behavioral scientists, the rowdy type of college students who left their piles of beer-cans in the Arboretum, etc., etc., etc.) and I had high hopes of eventually committing such crimes." Ex. 5.

Kaczynski's culpability lies in his decision to act on his "fantasies of killing." For Kaczynski, violence was never the result of momentary rage or a response to provocation; rather it was the culmination of a plan worked out over a number of-years. He described his motivation as "not hot rage, but a cold determination to get my revenge" (Ex. 6) and often wrote of his resolve to act on his hatred:

> Thus, when I had a fantasy of revenger had very little comfort from it, because I was all too clearly aware that I had had many previous fantasies of revenge, and nothing had ever come of any of them. This was very frustrating and humiliating. Therefore I became more and more determined that some day I would actually take revenge on some of the people that I hated.

Ex. 7. And while Kaczynski wrote extensively on a need for revenge, he was less articulate in explaining what he was seeking revenge for. Instead, his writings simply reveal that his hatred extended to virtually anyone who irritated him or represented some aspect of society he disagreed with. Kaczynski did, however, give considerable thought to how he would exact a plan of revenge, and was clear-eyed enough to admit (at least to himself) that he was not acting for anyone's gratification but his own. In April, 1971, before he embarked on his serial bombing campaign, Kaczynski recorded the following in his journal:

> My motive for doing what I am going to do is simply personal revenge. I do not expect to accomplish anything by it. Of course, if my crime (and my reasons for committing it) gets any public attention, it may help to stimulate public interest in the technology question and thereby improve the chances of stopping technology before it is too late; but on the other hand most people will probably be repelled by my crime, and the opponents of freedom may use it as a weapon to support their arguments for control over human behavior. I have no way of knowing whether my action will do more good than harm. I certainly don't claim to be an altruist or to be acting for the "good" (whatever that is) of the human race. I act merely from a desire for revenge.

Ex. 8. Throughout his furtive journal entries Kaczynski conceded that his motivation to kill grew out of a "personal grievance" against society, bereft of any genuine belief that his actions would lessen what he viewed to be the negative impact of technology on others. Indeed, he noted that he would not plan his crimes and "take such risks from a pure desire to benefit my fellow man." Ex. 9. Even the causes Kaczynski later extolled in his manuscript, such as the preservation of the wilderness, he at times ridiculed in his private entries:

> I believe in nothing . . . I don't even believe in the cult of nature-worshipers or wilderness-worshipers. (I am perfectly ready to litter in parts of the woods that are of no use to me—I often throw cans in logged-over areas or in places much frequented by people; I don't find wilderness particularly healthy physically; I don't hesitate to poach.)

Ex. 10.

Kaczynski seems to have prided himself in acting outside moral boundaries. He boasted that from an early age he had "never had any interest in or respect for morality, ethics, or anything of the sort." Ex. 11. Indeed, Kaczynski bragged in his autobiography:

> The fact that I was able to admit to myself that there was no logical justification for morality illustrates a very important trait of mine . . . I have much less tendency to self-deception than most people. . . . Thus, I tended to feel that I was a particularly important person and superior to most of the rest of the human race. . . . It just came to me as naturally as breathing to feel that I was someone special.

Ex. 12.

Kaczynski's journals also reflect that he worked at overcoming inhibitions against committing crimes, striving to develop what he called "the courage to behave irresponsibly." Ex. 4. Thus, in a journal entry dated December 1972 he wrote:

> About a year and a half ago, I planned to murder a scientist—as a means of revenge against organized society in general and the technological establishment in particular . . . Unfortunately, I chickened out. I couldn't work up the nerve to do it. The experience showed me that propaganda and indoctrination have a much stronger hold on me than I realized. My plan was such that there was very little chance of my getting caught. I had no qualms before I tried to do it, and I thought I would have no difficulty. I had everything well prepared. But when I tried to take the final, irrevocable step, I found myself overwhelmed by an irrational, superstitious fear—not a fear of anything specific, merely a vague but powerful fear of committing the act. I cannot attribute this to a rational fear of being caught. I made my preparations with extreme care, and I figured my chances of being caught were less than, say, my chances of being killed in an automobile accident within the next year. I am not in the least nervous when I get into my car. I can only attribute my fear to the constant flood of anticrime propaganda to which one is subjected. . . .

Ex. 13, 14.

As early as 1975, Kaczynski took the first tentative steps on his destructive path. In the summer of that year he engaged in various acts of vandalism, including putting sugar in the gas tanks of various vehicles and vandalizing trailers and camps in Montana. In an act of a more deadly nature, he strung wire at neck height across roads frequented by motorcyclists. These acts continued over several summers and were a prelude to Kaczynski's coming bombing attacks.

Kaczynski's terrorism began in 1978. The history of his bombings reveal a patient and methodical killer. In May of that year he left Montana and returned to Chicago where he lived and worked for approximately a year. He noted in his journal that his biggest reason for returning to Chicago in 1978 was to "more safely attempt to murder a scientist, businessman, or the like" (Ex. 15) and explained:

> In Montana, if I went to the city to mail a bomb to some big shot, [a Montana neighbor] would doubtless remember that I rode [the] bus that day. In the anonymity of the big city I figured it would be much safer to buy materials for a bomb, and mail it.

Ex. 16.

Around the same time, he wrote of his continuing determination to overcome any compunction against committing crimes and realize his "ambition":

> As a result of indoctrination since childhood, I had strong inhibitions against doing these things, and it was only at the cost of great effort that I overcame the inhibitions. I think that perhaps I could now kill someone (and I don't mean just set a booby trap having only a fractional chance of success), under circumstances where there was very little chance of getting caught . . . My ambition is to kill a scientist, big businessman, government official, or the like. I would also like to kill a Communist.

Ex. 3, 17.

Kaczynski's writings track his progress in realizing his "ambition." They also reflect his appreciation for the gravity and unlawfulness of his conduct. For example, Kaczynski classified many of his writings by their incriminating nature, and left catalogues designating which writings were the most damning, designating some to be burned and others to be buried. Ex. 18. These entries illustrate how well he grasped the legal significance of his actions, as when he noted that that certain journal passages detailed events "past [the] statute of limitations." Ex. 19. They also reveal his concern for his public image, with Kaczynski describing other passages as "embarrassing, not dangerous," or simply "very bad public relations." Id.

Kaczynski wrote some documents in code, others in Spanish, and concealed carbon copies of his later public "FC" missives deep within a storage container in the loft of his home. Many journal entries recount daily activities in plain English text and then revert to coded text, often in Spanish, as the subject matter moves to criminal acts. Some entries explicitly recognize the incriminating nature of the contents, as in this notebook entry where he wrote:

> [M]y motive for keeping these notes separate from the others is the obvious one. Some of my other notes contain hints of crime, but no actual accounts of felonies. But these notes must be very carefully kept from everyone's eyes. Kept separate from the other notes they make a small compact packet, easily concealed.

Ex. 20.

It is apparent that Kaczynski understood, indeed relished, the damage and suffering he was inflicting. In his journals he carefully monitored news accounts of his attacks and graphically rated their success, often by describing in detail the extent of the injuries his victims suffered. He also collected newspaper or magazine articles concerning his bombings, particularly those with photographs of bleeding victims or grieving family members, as souvenirs or trophies of his accomplishments. Eg. Ex. 21, 22.

Kaczynski has no remorse for his crimes

Kaczynski's own words demonstrate that he had neither remorse for his conduct nor empathy for his victims. When he planted his first bomb in May of 1978 at the University of Illinois, Chicago Circle Campus, he documented how he selected the name of the victim at random from the ranks of professors engaged in technical fields, and, when the bomb would not fit in a campus mailbox, left the bomb in a parking lot near a science building in the hope that a student in a scientific field would find the package and "blow his hands off or get killed." Ex. 15. In his journal he boasted: "I have not the least feeling of guilt about this—on the contrary, I am proud of what I did." Id.

In May 1979, just prior to returning to Montana, Kaczynski placed his second bomb on a table located in the Technological Institute at Northwestern University. A researcher was badly injured when he attempted to pick up the device, but not badly enough to suit Kaczynski. In a journal entry, Kaczynski stated:

> I figured the bomb was probably not powerful enough to kill (unless one of the lead pellets I put in it happened to penetrate a vital organ). But I had hoped that the victim would be blinded or have his hands blown off or be otherwise maimed . . . maybe he would have had burns in the eyes if his glasses hadn't momentarily retarded the flow of hot gasses. Well, at least I put him in the hospital, which is better than nothing. But not enough to satisfy me . . . . I wish I knew how to get hold of some dynamite.

Ex. 23.

Kaczynski's writings chronicle his emotions during his subsequent crimes. In November of 1979 Kaczynski tried to "blow up an airliner" and "kill a lot of business people," (Ex. 24) but failed. He noted in his journal that "unfortunately plane not destroyed, bomb too weak" and sought consolation in the thought that "at least it gave them a good scare." Ex. 25. Next, in June of 1980, after he mailed the bomb that injured Percy Wood in his own home, he recorded that "after complicated preparations I succeeded in injuring the pres of United A.L." Ex. 26. Around this time he noted in his journal:

> Guilty feelings? Yes, a little. Occasionally I have bad dreams in which the police are after me. Or in which I am threatened with punishment from some super natural source. Such as the devil. But these dont (sic) occur often you enuf (sic) to be a problem. I am definitely glad to have done what I have.

Ex. 27.

Kaczynski then returned his attention to universities, and in October of 1981 planted a firebomb at the University of Utah, but was disappointed with the result:

> last fall I attempted a bombing and spent nearly three hundred bucks just for travel expenses, motel, clothing for disguise, etc. aside from cost of materials for bomb. And then the thing failed to explode. Damn. This was the firebomb found in U. of Utah Business School outside door of room containing some computer stuff.

Ex. 28.

In May of 1982, when a bomb he sent wounded Janet Smith, a professor's secretary, he lamented:

> May about 1982 I sent a bomb to a computer expert named Patrick Fischer. His secretary opened it. One newspaper said she was in hospital? In good condition? With arm and chest cuts. Other newspaper said bomb drove fragments of wood into her flesh. But no indication that she was permanently disabled. Frustrating that I cant seem to mak[e] lethal bomb.

Ex. 29.

A few months later he traveled to U.C. Berkeley and planted another firebomb, this time injuring Professor Diogenes Angelakos. Again Kaczynski registered disappointment:

> According to newspaper, vice chairman of computer-sci. dept. picked it up. He was considered to be 'out of danger of losing any fingers', but would need further surgery for bone and tendon damage in hand. Apparently pipebomb went off but did not ignite gasoline. I dont understand it. Frustrated.

Ex. 30.

Kaczynski set no bombs for three years. His journals reflect that he used this sabbatical to experiment with more deadly bombs. His return was marked by renewed ferocity. In May of 1985 he set a bomb in the same building where he had injured Professor Angelakos. A graduate student, then Air Force Captain John Hauser, was seriously injured when the bomb exploded with such force that it left an exact imprint of his Air Force Academy ring embedded in the workshop wall. Kaczynski followed the news accounts closely, recording the descriptions of "blood all over the place" and Hauser's "mangled" arm. Ex. 31. While he confided to himself some unease over maiming a "father of 2 kids" he later reflected that he "just got over it" and even "laughed at the idea of having any compunction about crippling an airplane pilot." Id.

Around the time that he placed this bomb, Kaczynski mailed a bomb to the Boeing Corporation in Auburn, Washington. Unbeknownst to Kaczynski, this bomb was successfully rendered safe by police after several employees had handled it. Kaczynski could only record his disappointment: "Outcome of Boeing bomb unknown . . . . Seems inexplicable it was designed and built with such care that malfunction seems highly improbable."

Ex. 32. He sent the next bomb to a University of Michigan Professor James McConnell. When the bomb injured the Professor's assistant, Nicklaus Suino, Kaczynski noted only scientific detachment: "Only minor injuries to McConnells (sic) assistant. Deflagrated, did not detonate. Must be either pipe was a little weak or loading density of explosive a shade too high at failure."

Ex. 33.

Later that year, Kaczynski rejoiced when he killed his first victim. "Excellent . . . humane way to eliminate somebody" and "very good results" (Ex. 34,

35) was how he described his murder of Hugh Scrutton, who died in the parking lot of his Sacramento store when Kaczynski's bomb tore his hand from his body and drove shrapnel into his heart.

In February of 1987, Kaczynski placed the bomb that injured Gary Wright in Salt Lake City. Kaczynski noted that while the bomb detonated, the results "were not enough to satisfy" him. Ex. 36. Kaczynski was more concerned with the sketch of a suspect circulated after the bombing. He noted in his journals, "Description (several versions) . . . The 'composite drawing' did not show any beard, although it did show a small mustache." Id.

Apparently alarmed by the possibility of an eyewitness, Kaczynski was silent for nearly six years. In his April 1995, letter to the *New York Times*, Kaczynski explained these periods of apparent inactivity:

> Our early bombs were too ineffectual to attract much public attention or give encouragement to those who hate the system. We found by experience that gunpowder bombs, if small enough to be carried inconspicuously, were too feeble to do much damage, so we took a couple of years off to do some experimenting. We learned how to make pipe bombs that were powerful enough, and we used these in a couple of successful bombings as well as in some unsuccessful ones. Unfortunately we discovered that these bombs would not detonate *consistently*. . . . So we went back to work, and after a long period of experimentation we developed a type of bomb that does not require a pipe, but is set off by a detonating cap that consists of a chlorate explosive packed into a piece of small diameter copper tubing . . . we used bombs of this type to blow up the genetic engineer Charles Epstein and the computer specialist David Gelernter.

Ex. 37, 38.

By 1993, Kaczynski no longer accepted the risk of detection involved in placing bombs, so he concentrated on designing and sending mail bombs. In June he traveled to Sacramento and mailed bombs to Dr. Epstein in Tiburon and Dr. Gelernter in New Haven. Though he critically injured both recipients, Kaczynski was only partially satisfied:

> I sent these devices during June, 1993. They detonated as the should have. The effect of both of them was adequate, but no more than adequate.

Ex. 39.

Kaczynski thereafter ensured that his next attacks were fatal. He modified his designs to improve fragmentation and inserted additional screws, paneling nails, and even bits of razor blades into the bombs to serve as enhanced shrapnel. In December of 1994 he traveled to San Francisco and mailed a package bomb to Thomas Mosser in New Jersey. Mosser opened the package in the kitchen of his home. The bomb detonated, spraying shrapnel with such force that nails penetrated walls and metal kitchen pans. Mosser died on the floor of his kitchen with his wife and children nearby. Kaczynski noted his satisfaction in his journal, recording that the bomb "gave a totally satisfactory result." Ex. 40. Kaczynski later bragged about his technical innovation in one of his letters to the newspapers:

We did use a chlorate pipe bomb to blow up Thomas Mosser because we happened to have a piece of light-weight aluminum pipe that was just right for the job. The Gelernter and Epstein bombings were not fatal, but the Mosser bombing was fatal even though a smaller amount of explosive was used. We think this was because the type of fragmentation material that we used in the Mosser bombing is more effective . . . .

Ex. 41.

In April of 1995, Kaczynski sent a bomb addressed to William Dennison at the California Forestry Association (CFA) in Sacramento. On April 24, Gilbert Murray opened the package at the CFA and was killed by the blast and shrapnel. Several co-workers narrowly escaped harm as the force of the blast sent shrapnel and fragments through the walls of the building. In a later letter from "FC" to the *New York Times*, Kaczynski expressed no qualms about missing his mark at the CFA: "We have no regret about the fact that our bomb blew up the 'wrong' man, Gilbert Murray, instead of William N. Dennison, to whom it was addressed."

Ex. 42.

Around this time Kaczynski also took to taunting victims, law enforcement, and the public in a series of letters. These letters were designed not only to instill fear, but also to thwart investigators. For example, in April of 1995 he sent a letter to one of his previous targets, David Gelernter, mocking him for having opened the package Kaczynski had sent him two years earlier:

People with advanced degrees aren't as smart as they think they are. If you'd had any brains you would have realized that there are a lot of people out there who resent bitterly the way techno-nerds like you are changing the world and you wouldn't have been dumb enough to open an unexpected package from an unknown source.

Ex. 43.

Kaczynski explained the subterfuge in his journal:

In a letter say that, 'scientists consider themselves very intelligent because they have advanced diplomas (advanced degrees) but they are not as intelligent as they think because they opened those packages.' This will make it seem as though I have no advanced degree.

Ex. 44.

Kaczynski sent letters to Nobel laureates Phillip Sharp and Richard Roberts threatening them that "It would be beneficial to your health to stop your research in genetics." Ex. 45, 46. He sent a letter to a newspaper threatening to blow up an airliner out of the Los Angeles International Airport. The threat paralyzed air travel until Kaczynski wrote another letter saying:

Note. Since the public has a short memory we decided to play one last prank to remind them who we are. But no, we haven't tried to plant a bomb on an airliner (recently).

Ex. 47.

Kaczynski used fear to manipulate the public into considering his views. He threatened the public with "bombs much bigger" than any made before, offering to desist from further "terrorism" only if his manuscript was published in the newspapers. Ex. 48. At the request of law enforcement, the manuscript was published in September of 1995.

Kaczynski poses a future threat to society

Kaczynski's crimes were conceived and carried out with inventive cunning. Kaczynski crafted his bombs by hand, producing sophisticated lethal contraptions without the benefit of electricity or modern facilities. He experimented with different homemade explosive charges, often creating mixtures from household products, designed and perfected electrical initiating systems for bombs, and fashioned bomb components out of scrap materials. See eg. Ex. 49-55. He tested prototypes and plotted the force and distance of fragments and shrapnel to measure their effective killing zones. Kaczynski contrived ways to deceive his unsuspecting targets, designing books that exploded upon opening, test equipment that detonated when lifted by the handle, and bombs disguised in packages fashioned to look like research papers.

Kaczynski also labored methodically on his bombs, combining patience with stealth and eluding detection for nearly twenty years. When assembling his bombs, he wore gloves and manually sanded all parts to remove fingerprints. Ex. 56-83. He carefully chose stamps for his mail bombs, checking to make sure they bore no indented writing, and even soaked his stamps in a home-made solution in the hopes of removing trace evidence. Ex. 84-87. He went as far as to insert false evidence into his bombs to misdirect investigators, lacing human hair he collected from a public restroom in a bus station on tape used to construct the device. Ex. 88. He carefully sealed and weighed packages to determine the appropriate postage, hereby avoiding interaction with postal clerks. He researched names to select victims and fictitious return addresses, charted bus schedules to plan his attacks, and wore disguises to purchase materials and mail bombs. Ex. 89. Kaczynski also made plans for flight in the event the authorities identified him, charting escape routes through the Montana wilderness and designating secret hiding places and burying food and ammunition on map locations disguised in manner so that only he would recognize them.

And while Kaczynski had claimed in his 1995 letters to the press that he would forswear terrorism if his manuscript were published, it is clear he had no intention of halting the violence.

Instead, at the time of his arrest in April of 1996, Kaczynski was preparing for more lethal attacks. When agents searched his cabin they found all the materials necessary for the construction of several more bombs. Kaczynski had stockpiled in excess of 40 pipes, many individually wrapped and bearing coded notations, and nearly 200 feet of the copper tubing of the type he had used in approximate 411 increments as detonators in many of his previous bombs. He also had chemicals arranged on shelves, some in raw form and others in individually marked containers mixed to the specifications of his explosive charges.

The array of materials Kaczynski had in inventory speaks volumes as to his future plans. He had 23 identical initiating devices of the sort he had perfected over the years in other bombs, as well as a fully constructed pivot switch of the same configuration that he had used in three of his last four bombs. He also had a number of timing devices, a rigged alarm clock, an anti-movement ball switch, spools of wire, reserves of solder, ammunition, and even specially designated nails and screws for use as shrapnel. His home also had his work bench with all the tools necessary for his craft, as well as a wide variety of books that included textbooks on chemistry and electrical circuitry, and even an FBI manual on fingerprinting.

The most disconcerting discovery during the search was that Kaczynski had already completed another bomb. It was, by any standard, a powerful weapon, fully-armed and virtually identical in design to that which killed Gilbert Murray. The weapon was intended to kill people, as the outside of the bomb cylinder was covered with a mosaic of individual lead squares, a trademark of an anti-personnel device, since the lead pellets create a lethal zone of some distance when the bomb is detonated. The device was disguised in a package with a label describing it as a "Newell Channel Reamer," a mechanical tool commonly used in the aircraft industry. The package was ready for delivery, lacking only an address.

Finally, as a chilling reminder of the purpose of all this material, Kaczynski kept handwritten lists of potential victims with their home or work addresses as well as maps of various cities with these locations circled. See eg. Ex. 90.

From what can be discerned from the search of his home, it also appears that Kaczynski's weaponry was not limited exclusively to bombs. For example, agents discovered a completely homemade, operable handgun, as well as a corresponding written description of its creation and purpose, all of which further demonstrates the resourcefulness that Kaczynski was able to summon to further his murderous intent:

> a few days ago I finished making a twenty two caliber pistol. This took me a long time, for a year and a half, thereby preventing me from working on some other projects I would have liked to carry out. Gun works well and I get as much accuracy out of it as I'd expect for an inexperienced pistol shot like me. It is equipped with improvised silencer which does not work as well as I hoped. At a guess it cuts noise down to maybe one third. It is said that it is easy for machinist to make a gun, but of course I did not have machine tools, but only a few files, hacksaw blades, small vice, a rickety hand drill, etc. I took the barrel from an old pneumatic pistol. I made the other parts out of several metal pieces. Most of them come from the old abandoned cars near here. I needed to make the parts with enough precision but I made them well and I'm very satisfied. I want to use the gun as a homicide weapon.

Ex. 91.

Furthermore, while it is clear that Kaczynski plotted and carried out his crimes alone, he also contemplated recruiting others to join in his plans.

Among the many documents found in his cabin were "how to" guides he had prepared—a handwritten manual recounting step by step how to construct improvised bombs with detailed instructions on how to avoid detection by the FBI or police and a handwritten document entitled "How to Hit an Exxon Exec" detailing with chilling precision the step by step process one can undertake to send a package bomb to a corporate official.

Ex.92.

There were also copies of correspondence sent to other organizations, such as letters to radical environmental groups "Earth First!" and "Live Wild or Die", offering secret codes for communicating and seeking an audience for his "strategy for revolutionaries seeking to destroy the industrial system."

The history of Kaczynski's conduct demonstrates that he has both the capacity and willingness to dedicate years of his life to plan murders and elude detection. If released back into society, he would kill again.

C. Sentencing Recommendation

1. Imposition of Mandatory Life Sentence

The nature and circumstances of the offenses justify the life sentence the Court is required to impose. Kaczynski's repeated crimes were the considered acts of a man who chose to repeatedly inflict violence and kill to gratify his own hatred. Furthermore "any sentencing authority must predict a convicted person's probable future conduct when it engages in the process of determining what punishment to impose." *Jurek v. Texas*, 428 U.S. 262, 275 (1976). Kaczynski's abiding hatred of everyone but himself, coupled with his lack of remorse for his conduct, gives no cause to believe he could ever rejoin society as anything other than a killer. Justice therefore requires that he spend the remainder of his days imprisoned.

2. Restitution and Forfeiture

Pursuant to 18 U.S.C. Section 3663 and the Plea Agreement in this case, the Court should order restitution to the individuals, and in the amounts, identified in the Presentence Investigation Report. In addition, in accordance with the plea agreement (p. 4, Paragraph D.) and 18 U.S.C. Section 3681, this Court should order that Kaczynski forfeit all or any part of proceeds received or to be received by him for writings, interviews, memorabilia or other information for restitution or other distribution to the victims of his crimes.

3. Recommendation to the Bureau of Prisons That Defendant Be Placed in a Maximum Security Institution

In light of Kaczynski's continuing desire to kill and his evident resourcefulness, there remains the threat that Kaczynski could continue his lethal preoccupation behind prison walls. See, e.g. *United States v. Hamrick*, 43 F.3d 877, 878-79 (4th Cir. 1994) (en banc) (while in federal prison, defendant built "five improvised bombs" and later built and sent from state prison a bomb capable of producing "1000 degree fireball" to U.S. Attorney). Accordingly, pursuant to 18 U.S.C. Section 3621(b)(4)(B), the United States requests that in addition to imposing a sentence of life imprisonment without release, this Court recommend to the Bureau of Prisons that Kaczynski be incarcerated in a maximum security facility where he can be closely monitored to prevent any future acts of violence or intimidation.

Respectfully submitted,
PAUL L. SEAVE
United States Attorney

By:
STEPHEN P. FRECCERO
ROBERT J. CLEARY
J. DOUGLAS WILSON
R. STEVEN LAPHAM
Special Attorneys to the United States Attorney General

HUD REPORT ON HOUSING THE NATION'S POOREST FAMILIES
April 28, 1998

The economic boom of the late 1990s was not easing life for the nation's poorest families, according to two studies released in 1998. The studies showed that a growing number of the "poorest of the poor" were having to spend most of their limited incomes on housing, leaving them with inadequate resources for food, clothing, and other essentials of modern life. Millions of the "working poor," the studies found, were barely scraping by on minimum-wage jobs, even as the nation's supply of housing they could afford was shrinking.

The Department of Housing and Urban Development (HUD) on April 28 released one study, "Rental Housing Assistance—the Crisis Continues." On June 15 the Center on Budget and Policy Priorities, a liberal nonprofit research and advocacy group, issued a similar report entitled, "In Search of Shelter: The Growing Shortage of Affordable Rental Housing." Together, the two reports painted a bleak picture of how the nation's poorest citizens had failed to benefit from economic prosperity. The reports were the latest in a series of studies that had documented housing shortages for the poor. (Rental housing shortages, Historic Documents of 1996, p. 167)

The reports may have helped spur congressional action on housing issues during 1998. Congress passed legislation revamping federal public housing policy, and it gave HUD its biggest budget increase in a decade— including substantially increased funding for housing aid to poor families.

The Affordable Housing Gap

The two reports traced several trends in housing for low-income Americans during the 1980s and 1990s, a period that produced escalating federal budget deficits, growing public reluctance to spend tax dollars on social programs, a brief recession at the turn of the decades, and then sustained economic expansion that curbed the deficits. Taken together, these economic, fiscal, and political forces contributed to a series of factors that made it more difficult for the poor to find affordable housing: despite mod-

est increases in the minimum wage, the incomes of the working poor failed to keep pace with inflation; housing costs at all economic levels outstripped the overall rate of inflation, hitting the poor the hardest because they spent a greater portion of their income on housing than other Americans; private developers were converting inner-city housing units once occupied by the poor into "gentrified" apartments and condominiums for the middle- and upper-classes; the government was demolishing thousands of dilapidated public housing units and replacing few of them; there was little economic incentive for developers to create housing that the poor could afford; and, starting in 1995, the Republican-led Congress for the first time in decades stopped adding new public housing assistance measures.

Both studies used numerous indicators to demonstrate how poor Americans were having trouble finding housing. Perhaps the broadest measure was the finding in the HUD report that 5.3 million "very low income" families that did not receive government housing assistance spent more than half their incomes on housing or lived in severely substandard housing. The study described these families as "worst case needs." By the government's definition, affordable housing should consume only about 30 percent of a family's income.

About one-fourth of the "worst case needs" were the working poor: families with at least one member earning the minimum wage at a full-time job. "Full-time work should provide a family with an income sufficient to afford a decent place to live," the study said. But about 1.4 million households with a full-time worker still could not find adequate housing.

The study by the Center on Budget and Policy Priorities noted that in 1970 the nation had a surplus of low-cost housing units for the poor, but in succeeding years the number of poor people grew as the number of affordable housing units shrank. By 1995, the report said, 10.5 million American families had incomes below the federally defined poverty level ($12,000 for a family of three), but there were only 6.1 million affordable housing units for them. As a consequence, the poor were having to spend much greater portions of their limited incomes than other Americans on housing—as much as 60 percent in many cases.

At least one trend cited in both studies was sure to catch the attention of members of Congress: the low-income housing shortage, once confined primarily to the cities, was spreading to the suburbs. The HUD study noted that about one-third of the "worst case needs" families—or about 1.8 million households—lived in suburban areas. Moreover, this "suburbanization" of the housing shortage for the poor was growing at a faster rate than the overall rate nationally, the study said.

Congressional Action

HUD used the reports to support Clinton administration positions on several key housing issues in Congress, most importantly the overall funding levels for the department. The report said the findings showed a "clear and compelling need for Congress to provide greater support for Federal housing assistance." Cuomo said the report also backed the administration position that public housing assistance should be geared primarily toward the nation's poorest citizens. Several congressional Republican leaders had advocated shifting aid away from the poor and toward moderate-income families.

Congress responded to the housing shortage in two major pieces of legislation, both enacted in October, near the end of the 1998 session. In one case, Congress ended a three-year stalemate on federal housing policy by passing a bill to revise the nation's public housing programs. Signed into law (PL 105–276) by Clinton, the bill represented a compromise between the administration's position that housing aid should be targeted to the poor and the view of many Republicans that middle-income Americans should receive a greater share of federal housing aid. The bill required that at least 40 percent of public housing units and 75 percent of Section 8 vouchers (used to help pay the rent in private apartments) be reserved for the "very poor" (defined as those whose incomes were less than 30 percent of the median income in the local area).

The easing of the federal budget crunch in 1998 also gave Congress room to expand housing assistance for the first time since 1995. An appropriations bill (PL 105–276) containing fiscal 1999 appropriations for HUD gave the department $24.3 billion, a 14 percent increase over the previous year. On October 6, the day the House approved the measure, HUD issued a statement saying the bill put the agency "back in business." Among its provisions, the bill provided funding for 90,000 new Section 8 housing vouchers, most of which were reserved for families moving off the welfare rolls as a result of the 1996 welfare reform law. The bill also included substantial funding increases for programs to revitalize and replace public housing units.

Following is the executive summary of the report, "Rental Housing Assistance—The Crisis Continues," issued April 28, 1998, by the Department of Housing and Urban Development:

This Congressionally mandated report documents four major findings:

- The persistence of a housing affordability crisis for very-low-income renters despite the robust economic growth of the 1990s.
- A reduction in the stock of affordable rental housing and the elimination of new Federal rental assistance, beginning in 1995.
- A sharp increase in needs for rental housing assistance among the working poor.
- The increased suburbanization of housing needs.

These findings have significant implications for Federal housing policy. To begin to ameliorate this severe housing crisis, Congress should resume the expansion of Federal tenant-based rental assistance targeted to those with the most severe needs. In addition, Congress should expand programs like HOME and the Low Income Housing Tax Credit which subsidize the construction and rehabilitation of affordable rental housing. Finally, Congress should to the maximum extent possible continue to focus scarce Federal public and assisted housing opportunities on those households with the most severe housing needs, while still fostering a greater income mix in public and assisted housing developments.

Major Findings

Finding 1: Despite robust economic growth between 1993 and 1995, the number of very-low-income renters with worst case housing needs remained at an all-time high—5.3 million.

- In 1995, 5.3 million very-low-income renters without housing assistance paid over half their income for housing or lived in severely substandard housing. Households with worst case needs are defined as unassisted renters with incomes below 50 percent of the local median who pay more than half of their income for rent or live in severely substandard housing. Renters with incomes below 50 percent of area median income are called "very-low-income" renters.
- Households with the lowest incomes are most likely to have worst case needs. Almost 70 percent of unassisted renters with extremely low incomes had worst case housing needs in 1995. In this report, renters with incomes below 30 percent of area median income are called "extremely-low-income" renters. Nationally, 30 percent of median income approximates the poverty level, but the definition of extremely low income is adjusted for geographical differences. As a national average in 1998, "extremely low income" means less than $13,590 for a family of four or less than $10,872 for a two-person family.

Finding 2: The stock of rental housing affordable to the lowest income families is shrinking, and Congress has eliminated funding for new rental assistance since 1995.

- Between 1993 and 1995, there was a loss of 900,000 rental units affordable to very-low-income families, a reduction of 9 percent. There was an even greater reduction—16 percent—in the number of units affordable for "extremely-low-income" renters.
- Federal housing policy has done little to ameliorate these problems. Since 1995, Congress has denied Administration requests for new rental assistance and ceased funding for new incremental rental assistance to serve families with worst case needs. This is a historic reversal of Federal housing policy, which had continuously expanded Federal rental assistance in every year prior to 1995. From 1978 through 1982, an aver-

age of 224,000 additional households were provided Federal rental assistance each year. The average number of new households getting assistance dropped to approximately 146,000 during the 1980s and early 1990s.

Finding 3: The fastest growth in worst case needs in the 1990s was among working families.

- Full-time work should provide a family with an income sufficient to afford a decent place to live. In fact, having a low-paid job is increasingly unlikely to lift a family out of poverty or resolve worst case housing needs. Between 1991 and 1995, worst case needs rose by 265,000, or 24 percent, for renters with annual earnings of at least one full-time worker at the minimum wage. By 1995, there were 1.4 million such households with worst case needs.

Finding 4: One of every three households with worst case needs now lives in the suburbs.

- While the greatest numbers of worst case needs are in central cities, a large and fast-growing number live in the suburbs. The first half of the 1990s saw a suburbanization of worst case needs as more than 1.8 million of the 5.3 million households with worst case needs—or one of every three—lived in the suburbs in 1995. Suburban worst case needs grew by 9 percent from 1991 to 1995.

Supplementary Findings

Finding 5: The most serious housing needs are concentrated among households with the lowest incomes.

- Almost 4 million of the 5.3 million households with worst case needs have extremely low incomes—below 30 percent of median. Almost 7 of every 10 such households pay more than one-half their income for rent or live in severely inadequate housing when they are not assisted.

- The frequency of worst case needs declines sharply as income rises. Only 26 percent of unassisted renters with incomes between 31 and 50 percent of median have worst case needs and fewer than 5 percent of renters with incomes between 51 and 80 percent of median experience such problems.

Finding 6: Of the 12.5 million persons in households with worst case needs, almost 1.5 million are elderly and 4.5 million are children. The number of adults with disabilities in households with worst case needs is estimated between 1.1 and 1.4 million.

- From 1993 to 1995, there was a surge in the number of very-low-income single individuals who are not elderly, even as the overall number of very-low-income households declined slightly. Importantly, the likelihood of having worst case needs also grew among non-elderly singles.

Although the American Housing Survey does not measure disabilities directly, many of these individuals with worst case needs have disabilities.

- It is clear that both single individuals with disabilities and other households with a disabled member face substantial and growing housing problems. The number of adults with disabilities living in households with worst case needs is estimated at between 1.1 and 1.4 million in 1995.

- More than 2.1 million families with children had worst case problems in 1995. Among the 2.1 million families with children who had worst case problems, 930,000 had income from either Aid to Families with Dependent Children (AFDC) or Supplemental Security Income (SSI).

- More than 1 million elderly households had worst case problems in 1995.

Finding 7: Worst case needs continue to shift to the West.

- The number of very-low-income renters in the West continued to increase between 1993 and 1995, while dropping in other regions. The West had the highest percentage of very-low-income renters with acute housing needs, 42 percent, compared with 32 percent in the South, 33 percent in the Midwest, and 39 percent in the Northeast. The result is that the number of Western households with worst case needs reached a record 1.56 million in 1995.

- The mismatch between available extremely-low-rent units and extremely-low-income renters is large and getting larger in all four census regions. Shortages are worst in the West, however, where in 1995 for every 100 extremely-low-income renters there were only 31 units that were either already occupied by extremely-low-income renters or vacant and for rent, compared with the nationwide figure of 44 units per 100 renters.

Policy Implications

The findings of this report suggest that economic growth alone will not ameliorate the record-level housing needs among families with limited incomes. Not even families working full-time at the minimum wage can afford decent quality housing in the private rental market. The report also makes it clear that housing needs are not just found in big cities but increasingly in the suburbs as well.

The report suggests a clear and compelling need for the Congress to provide greater support for Federal housing assistance—by expanding both tenant-based rental assistance and programs that create and rehabilitate more affordable housing units. And Congress should act carefully in reforming the income targeting rules for public and assisted housing programs to balance the goals of achieving a greater income mix in public and assisted housing developments and providing assistance to families with the most severe housing needs.

New Housing Assistance

- **103,000 New Vouchers:** The Administration has asked Congress to fund 103,000 new housing assistance vouchers, including 50,000 welfare-to-work vouchers to help welfare recipients get and keep jobs. This report documents the need for those vouchers to reduce the overall number of families and individuals with worst case needs and to provide the portable housing assistance critical for a successful transition to work.

- **Ending the Delay on Reissuing Vouchers:** Congress should end immediately its cost-saving requirement placed on local housing authorities to hold for three months rental subsidies returned by families leaving the program. This practice reduces by 40,000 the number of subsidies in circulation and thus the number of families receiving housing assistance.

- **Expanding Production of Affordable Housing Through HOME and the Low Income Housing Tax Credit:** The Administration is also seeking to expand tools to build and rehabilitate affordable housing. HUD's FY 1999 budget includes increased funding for the HOME program, along with a new HOME Bank, a loan guarantee feature that would allow communities to leverage up to five times their Federal grants for larger scale housing investments. In addition, the Administration is proposing a substantial expansion of the Low Income Housing Tax Credit that would create 180,000 new affordable rental units over the next five years.

Careful Income Targeting of Federal Housing Assistance

Congress is considering legislation that will determine the income levels of households who will be admitted to public housing and to receive Section 8 rental assistance. The Clinton administration and U.S. Department of Housing and Urban Development (HUD) strongly support the transformation of public and assisted housing developments into healthier, mixed-income communities. But policymakers must be careful not to exclude poor families altogether from these housing developments, nor to reduce unnecessarily the numbers of families with worst case needs who can be served by Federal housing programs. This report shows that this goal can be achieved while still continuing to serve families who are working but who have low incomes and serious housing needs. . . .

FEDERAL REPORT ON
TEENAGE PREGNANCY
April 30, 1998

The birthrate among American teenagers fell 12 percent between 1991 and 1996, according to a federal report, reversing an upward trend that had prevailed from 1986 to 1991. In 1996 there were fifty-five live births for every one thousand women ages fifteen through nineteen. This rate was down 4 percent from 1995 and 12 percent from 1991, when the rate was sixty-two. The birthrate also declined for younger teenagers. The report said that the rate was falling because teenagers were less active sexually than they had been and because more of those who were sexually active were using contraception. "This report shows that our concerted efforts to reduce teen pregnancy is succeeding," Donna E. Shalala, secretary of health and human services, said in a press announcement. "The federal government, the private sector, parents, and caregivers are all helping send the same message: Don't become a parent until you are truly ready to have a child."

The report, released April 30 by the National Center for Health Statistics, said that the birthrate was declining among both older and younger teenagers, among all races, and in every state. The teenage birthrate in 1996 was higher than it had been at its lowest point in the early 1980s, but it was well below its historical highs in the 1950s. The highest recorded teenage birthrate was 96.3 in 1957. Still some 500,000 teenagers gave birth every year, and unlike most of their counterparts in 1957, most of the teenage mothers in 1996 were unmarried.

Teenage pregnancy was worrisome because many teenagers, married or otherwise, were not prepared emotionally or financially to bear and raise children. According to many studies, teenage mothers generally obtained less prenatal care than older mothers, were more likely to smoke, and were less likely to gain the recommended weight during pregnancy. As a result, babies born to teenage mothers were more likely to have low birth weight, which could lead to a variety of developmental problems. Teenage mothers were also less likely than other teenagers to finish school, thus reducing their options for economic self-sufficiency. Children of teenage mothers were also more likely than other children to drop out of school, commit crimes, and go on welfare.

Other reports issued later in the year confirmed various findings in the April report. For the first time in the 1990s a majority of high school students said they had not yet had sexual intercourse, according to a federal survey. Another federal survey found that the number of teenage mothers with more than one child had dropped substantially. In October the Alan Guttmacher Institute reported that the rate of teenage pregnancies had dropped to its lowest level in two decades. The teenage pregnancy rate included abortions and miscarriages as well as live births.

Highlights of the Report

Among the highlights of the report from the National Center for Health Statistics were these findings:

- *Overall the birthrate for women ages fifteen to nineteen fell from a high of 62.1 live births per 1,000 women in 1991 to 54.7 in 1996. Altogether teenagers in this age group had 494,272 babies in 1996. This was the lowest birthrate (and number of births) since 1988, when the rate was 53.0. In 1996 the birthrate for women aged fifteen through seventeen was 34.0; the rate for eighteen- and nineteen-year old women was 86.5.*

- *Hispanic teenagers had the highest birthrates in 1996; they were followed, in descending order, by African-Americans, American Indians, whites, and Asian-Americans. Birthrates for black teenagers dropped to their lowest level ever recorded, from 115.5 in 1991 to 91.7 in 1996. The rate among Hispanic teenagers was stable, at about 107, from 1991 through 1995 and then declined by 5 percent in 1996 to 101.6. These rates were more than double the rate for whites, which stood at 48.4 in 1996.*

- *The birthrate among girls ages fourteen and under also declined, from 1.4 in 1991 to 1.2 in 1996, a decrease of 14.3 percent. The rate for whites stayed the same, while the rate for blacks dropped by more than 20 percent. The birthrate among girls of Hispanic origin increased 8.3 percent over the five-year period, from 2.4 in 1991 to 2.6 in 1996.*

- *The vast majority of teenage mothers in 1996 were unmarried—84 percent of the fifteen- through seventeen-year-olds and 71 percent of the eighteen- and nineteen-year-olds. In 1950 only 23 percent of the younger teenage mothers and 9 percent of the older ones were unmarried. The report said the sharp increase reflected both the dramatic increase in the teenage birthrate, especially in the 1980s, and a decline in marriage among the teenagers since the mid-1970s.*

- *Teenage birthrates declined in every state between 1991 and 1995, but the amounts varied widely. Vermont had the lowest rate in 1995 at*

28.6 percent, and it also had one of the largest declines, 27.1 percent. The District of Columbia had the highest rate at 105.5, followed by Mississippi at 80.5. Because black and Hispanic teenagers had substantially higher birthrates than whites, states with relatively high proportions of black and Hispanic residents tended to have higher teenage birthrates.

The report also said that the underlying teenage pregnancy rate was declining, a trend supported by the findings of the Alan Guttmacher Institute, a nonprofit research group concerned with reproduction. In a report released in October the institute said that the rate had dropped from 117 pregnancies per 1,000 women ages fifteen through nineteen in 1990 to 101 in 1995. Another study by the National Center for Health Statistics, released in December, found that the rate of teenagers having second births had dropped by 21 percent between 1991 and 1996. Seventeen percent of teenage mothers gave birth to a second child in 1996, down from 22 percent in 1991. Still, 90,000 of the 500,000 teenage births were second children.

Reasons Behind the Decline

As the teenage birthrate began to increase in the 1980s, parents, school and community organizations, and local and state health and social services offices embarked on a variety of efforts to prevent teenage pregnancies, ranging from sex education to after-school programs and abstinence counseling. Community controversies frequently erupted over the extent and content of sex education in schools. Such controversies heightened after the outbreak of the AIDS epidemic, when many schools began teaching children about safe sex and the use of condoms. Many parents and conservative and religious organizations said such teachings were implicitly condoning, if not actually encouraging, teenage sexual activity.

Although no one could say with certainty, it appeared that both abstinence and greater use of contraception were responsible for declining births among teenagers. Stephanie Ventura, one of the authors of the two reports from the National Center for Health Statistics, attributed the decline in second births to the increased use of long-lasting contraceptives such as Norplant, which is implanted in the arm and can prevent pregnancy for up to five years, and Depo-Provera, which is injected once every three months. Ventura said that 25 percent of the teenage mothers who already had a child were using these contraceptives, compared with only about 5 percent of teens without children. The reliable, longer-lasting contraceptives also appeared to be particularly popular among black women. "My sense of why the black teens' birthrate is declining the fastest is that they are the most likely to use long-lasting contraceptives," said Jacqueline E. Darroch, senior vice president for research at the Alan Guttmacher Institute.

"We believe abstinence has played the central role in what's happening," a spokeswoman for Focus on the Family told the New York Times. *There*

were strong indications that more and more teenagers were refraining from sexual intercourse. A national survey of more than sixteen thousand teens in grades nine through twelve found that 48.4 percent said they were sexually active in 1997, compared with 54.1 percent in 1991. The Youth Risk Behavior Survey was conducted every two years by the federal Centers for Disease Control and Prevention. Isabel Sawhill, president of the National Campaign to Prevent Teen Pregnancy, said she thought that "more kids" were realizing "it's okay not to have sex—that, in fact, it may even be cool." Sawhill's group had also done research showing that parents could help prevent teenage pregnancy by talking openly with their children about sex and about their own values and by supervising their children's after-school and dating activities.

Following are excerpts of a report entitled, "Teenage Births in the United States: National and State Trends, 1990–96," written by Stephanie J. Ventura, Sally C. Curtin, and T. J. Mathews and issued April 30, 1998, by the National Center for Health Statistics in the Department of Health and Human Services:

Overview

Every year in America almost 500,000 teenagers give birth. Most are unmarried and many are not ready for the emotional, psychological, and financial responsibilities and challenges of parenthood. Teenage childbearing has important health and social consequences for these young women, their babies, and their families. Recently, the teenage birth rate has declined in all States. Rates for black teenagers have dropped more than for any other population group. Contributing to this decline are indications that teenagers today are less likely to be sexually active, and sexually active teenagers are more likely to use contraception. This publication presents the latest statistics as well as trends on the important topic of teenage childbearing in the United States. Data are from the National Center for Health Statistics' (NCHS) National Vital Statistics System.

Patterns of teen childbearing can be examined in terms of numbers and rates of births. The numbers indicate how many teenagers gave birth in a given year. The teenage birth rate is defined as the number of births to a group of 1,000 teenagers. Rates among different population groups can be compared because they are all computed on the basis of 1,000 women. The number of births to teenagers is affected by both the birth rate (the proportion of teens giving birth) and the number of teenaged women in the population. Therefore, trends in the birth rate and the number of births are not necessarily the same. To measure *pregnancies*, data on live births must be combined with information on induced abortion and fetal loss. Because abortion and fetal loss statistics are not as current as live birth statistics, this report focuses on trends births, with a brief discussion of pregnancy trends.

Teenage Birth Rate Declines in 90's;
Reverses Trend of the Late 80's

The U.S. birth rate for teenagers in 1996 was 54.7 live births per 1,000 women aged 15–19 years, down 4 percent from 1995 (56.8). The teenage birth rate has declined since 1991 when the rate was 62.1, an overall decline of 12 percent. These recent declines reverse the 24-percent rise in the teenage birth rate from 1986 to 1991.

Teenage Birth Rate in 90's
Higher Than in Early 80's

Despite the recent declines, however, the rate for 1996 is still higher than it was during the early to mid-1980's (50–53 per 1,000), when the rate was at its lowest point. The teenage birth rate was substantially higher in the 1950's and early 1960's than it is now. The highest recorded teenage birth rate was 96.3 in 1957.

Most Teenage Mothers Are Unmarried

The issues in teenage childbearing are different now than in past decades. Most teenagers giving birth prior to 1980 were married, whereas most teenagers giving birth recently are unmarried. The percent unmarried among teenage mothers 15–17 tears more than tripled between 1950 and 1996, rising from 23 percent to 84 percent; among older teenage mothers, the percent unmarried in 1996 (71 percent) was nearly 8 times the percent in 1950 (9 percent).

The increases in the proportion of teenage mothers who are unmarried reflect the convergence of two important demographic trends:

- Sharply increasing birth rate among unmarried teenagers especially during the 1980's
- Decline in marriage among teenagers since the mid-1970's

It is important to note, however, that while most teenage births are non-marital, the majority of births to unmarried women are not to teenagers.

Teenage Birth Rates and Pregnancy Rates Fall

The teenage birth rate describes the number of births in a given year to a group of 1,000 teenagers. Thus, on average in 1996 (preliminary data), 55 out of 1,000 women aged 15–19 had a baby. Total teenage pregnancies include live births combined with estimates of induced abortions and fetal losses. Abortion and fetal loss data are not as current as the data on live births. According to the most recent estimates, the teenage pregnancy rate for 1994 was 108 pregnancies per 1,000 women aged 15–19 years, nearly twice the birth rate in that year (58.9). The pregnancy rate declined 8 percent from 1991 to 1994 and has continued to fall since 1994. This is based on the continued decline in the teenage birth rate and preliminary data that indicate a drop in abortions among teenagers since 1994.

Births and Birth Rates Decline
for Younger and Older Teenagers

While teenage childbearing patterns differ considerably by age, rates for all age groups have declined in the 1990's, with greater declines for younger than for older teenagers.

Teenagers Under 15 Years

The birth rate in 1996 for teenagers under 15 years of age was 1.2 births per 1,000 young women 10–14 years of age. This rate has fallen since 1991, when the rate was 1.4. The number of young women under 15 years of age who had a baby in 1996 was 11,242. This number has fallen in recent years; in 1991–95, there were 12,000 to 13,000 births each year to young women aged 10–14 years. The decline in the number of births to very young teenagers has occurred despite the increase in the number of teenagers in this age group.

Rates and Numbers Fall for Teenagers
15–17 and 18–19 Years

The birth rate for teenagers 15–17 years was 34.0 per 1,000 in 1996, 12 percent lower than in 1991 (39.7). Half of the recent decline occurred between 1995 and 1996. The rate for older teenagers 18–19 years dropped 8 percent from 94.4 per 1,000 in 1991 to 86.5 in 1996; the decline between 1995 and 1996 was 3 percent. Despite the recent declines, however, the birth rates for younger and older teenagers are still higher than they were in the early to mid-1980's.

Overall, the number of births to teenagers 15–19 years declined by 5 percent between 1991 (519,577) and 1996 (494,272). This decline resulted from the 12-percent drop in the teenage birth rate, which more than compensated for the 8-percent increase in the number of women aged 15–19 years. The decline in the number of births to teenagers in the 1990's followed a period of increase during the late 1980's, when the number increased 13 percent from 1986 to 1990. As is true for the teenage birth rate, the number of births to teenagers was substantially higher several decades ago. The number peaked in 1970, when there were 644,708 births to women aged 15–19 years, nearly one-third more than the number reported in 1996.

Rates for Black Teenagers at Record Lows

Teenage birth rates for ages 15–19 years dropped 5–12 percent between 1991 and 1996 for white, American Indian, Asian or Pacific Islander, and Hispanic women. The largest declines since 1991 by race were for black women. The overall rate for black teenagers 15–19 years fell 21 percent between 1991 and 1996, to the lowest rate ever recorded, 91.7 per 1,000. The rate for Hispanic teenagers changed little between 1991 and 1995, before declining 5 percent between 1995 and 1996.

Black teenagers experienced the most substantial reductions in rates for teenagers in both age groups 15–17 and 18–19 years. The rate for young black teenagers, 15–17 years, declined 23 percent between 1991 and 1996, while the rate for older black teenagers, 18–19 years, fell 16 percent. Despite the sharp decline in the rates for black teenagers, their birth rates and the rates for Hispanic teenagers remain higher than for other groups. Hispanic teenagers now have the highest teenage birth rates.

Serious Health Consequences for Teenage Childbearing

Teenage mothers are much less likely than older women to receive timely prenatal care and more likely to have no care at all. Teenage mothers are also more likely to smoke and less likely to gain adequate weight during pregnancy. As a consequence of these and other factors, babies born to teenagers are at greatly elevated risk of low birthweight (less than 2,500 grams or 5 lb 8 oz), of serious and long-term disability, and of dying during the first year of life.

Teenage Birth Rates Vary Greatly by State

State-level birth rates for teenagers vary substantially. In 1995, the most recent year for which State-specific rates can be calculated, rates varied from 28.6 (Vermont) to 105.5 (District of Columbia). Some of the differences in overall rates by State reflect differences in the composition of the teenage populations by race and Hispanic origin. Given that birth rates for Hispanic and black teenagers are more than double the rates for non-Hispanic white teenagers, States with relatively high proportions of Hispanic and/or black teenagers in their populations would be expected to have higher overall teenage birth rates. In comparing teenage birth rates across States, it is important to keep these compositional differences in mind.

Rates Decline for All States

Birth rates for teenagers 15–19 years declined between 1991 and 1995 in all States and the District of Columbia, echoing the national trends during this time. (Declines in 5 States were not statistically significant.) The reductions in State-specific teenage birth rates reflect and in many cases exceed those reported for the country as a whole. While the U.S. rate fell 8 percent between 1991 and 1995, rates fell by 8.0 percent or more in 33 States. Rates dropped by 12.0 percent or more in 12 States; declines in 5 States exceeded 16.0 percent. While the decline in the teenage birth rate varied among States, States with both high and low teenage birth rates were successful in achieving reductions.

Declines in Sexual Activity and Increases in Condom Use Are Key Factors

The declines—for the country and for the States—in birth rates for teenagers since 1991 likely reflect a combination of demographic and behavioral factors. According to the 1995 National Survey of Family Growth

(NSFG), conducted by NCHS, the proportion of teenagers who are sexually experienced has stabilized, reversing the steady increases over the past two decades. Moreover, teenagers are now more likely to use contraceptives at first intercourse, especially condoms. In addition, some teenagers, particularly black teenagers, are using injectable and implant contraceptives. Similar changes in sexual experience for teenage males have been reported in the National Survey of Adolescent Males. Initial results from the National Longitudinal Study on Adolescent Health, a congressionally mandated survey of students in grades 7 through 12, suggest that a feeling of personal connection to home, family, and school is essential for protecting young people from a vast array of risky behaviors, including sexual activity.

May

EUROPEAN COMMISSION
PRESIDENT ON THE "EURO"
May 5, 1998

*Betting that the benefits of expanded economic integration would out-
weigh the risks, the leaders of eleven European countries in 1998 took irrev-
ocable steps toward creation of a single currency and monetary system. The
leaders agreed on a timetable under which the eleven nations would lock
their exchange rates together on December 31, 1998. On January 1, 1999,
the "euro" would become a unified currency for financial and accounting
purposes, such as transactions in stocks and bonds. At the same time, the
European Central Bank, headquartered in Frankfurt, Germany, would take
over monetary policy for the eleven countries. During the first six months
of 2002, euro coins and bills gradually would replace national currencies,
such as the franc, the mark, and the lira.*

*The introduction of the euro was expected to have an enormous impact
on the world economy, if not immediately, certainly over the course of a few
years. "Euroland," as the participating nations were informally known,
constituted a joint trading bloc larger than the United States. The eleven
Euroland nations would be bound together by common monetary policies
and by procedures that would force them to adopt similar fiscal policies.
Moreover, the euro was expected to become a reserve currency rivaling the
U.S. dollar—in effect creating a bipolar situation in which anyone looking
for a "safe" place to invest would have a choice of two competitive currencies. Some U.S. observers worried that the euro might weaken the dollar and
drive up interest rates.*

*The eleven countries participating in the introduction of the euro were
Austria, Belgium, Finland, France, Germany, Ireland, Italy, Luxembourg,
the Netherlands, Portugal, and Spain. Three members of the European
Union—Britain, Denmark, and Sweden—opted not to participate in the
euro, at least at the beginning. Greece wanted to participate but did not
meet the stringent fiscal requirements that had been established to ensure
that weak economies would not drag down the others.*

A Long March Toward Unity

Creation of the euro was one of the latest, and in many respects the single most important, of a series of efforts since World War II to bind European nations together. Many European leaders believed that unifying the continent economically—and eventually politically—was the only way to prevent another world war from originating on European soil.

The first step toward a united Europe came in 1953 with the creation of the six-member European Coal and Steel Community, led by France and Germany. Five years later, the Treaty of Rome laid out the broader vision of a European Community (EC), with a common market in which people, goods, and services could move freely, without national tariffs and with few other restraints. Throughout the next three decades, additional countries joined the EC, and concrete steps added new elements of unity to Europe (for example, member nations adopted common customs, immigration, and agricultural policies).

The collapse of the Soviet Union gave new impetus to the idea of true unity within Europe, and in 1991 European leaders, meeting in Maastricht, the Netherlands, signed a treaty calling for economic and monetary union and pledging new steps toward political unity. In 1993 the twelve nations then belonging to the EC transformed themselves into the European Union (EU)—a true common market with no barriers to the movement of people and goods from one member nation to another. Austria, Finland, and Sweden joined the EU in 1995, bringing the total number of nations involved to fifteen. (Maastricht Treaty, Historic Documents of 1991, p. 843)

All these steps over four decades involved political and economic risk, and in many cases came only after wrenching debates within member nations. Some countries—most notably Great Britain—were much less eager than others to give up elements of national sovereignty or submit to unified decision making.

Only two countries—Denmark and France—submitted the euro issue to the voters. Danish voters rejected participation, and French voters approved it by a narrow margin. In other countries, parliaments acted to approve participation—leading some commentators to wonder about the wisdom of taking such an important step without popular mandates.

Leading Up to the Euro

The idea for a common European currency was first proposed seriously in 1968 by Raymond Barre, the French prime minister, who suggested it as a counter to the growing dominance of the United States and its dollar. Many European leaders and theorists paid lip service to the suggestion in subsequent years, but it was not until the negotiations at Maastricht that the proposition of a united European currency began to approach reality. Led by German Chancellor Helmut Kohl, European leaders agreed at that summit on a plan to make the euro a reality by the turn of the century. As the plan evolved over the next few years, it required members to meet specific targets on key economic indicators. In effect, the Europeans were establishing a central authority they could blame for the controversial austerity measures many nations had to take, including raising taxes and cutting government subsidies and social programs.

The key indicator for admission to Euroland was the level of a country's budget deficit. Under the rules stemming from the Maastricht treaty, no country could join the united currency unless its governmental budget deficit was less than 3 percent of gross domestic product as of May 1998. Virtually every one of the nations wanting to join the euro made painful cutbacks to reach that figure. In some cases the cutbacks caused civil strife, such as a lengthy transport strike in France at the end of 1995. Several countries were able to reach the 3 percent figure only with the magic of accounting gimmicks that cost no money but made the books look better; Germany, for example, changed its method of figuring the debt of its health care system. (French strike, Historic Documents of 1995, p. 228)

The economic pain was real in many cases, however, and several governments were voted out of office in the mid-to-late 1990s, at least partly because of the euro-induced austerity. Among them, the conservative Gaullist Party fell from power in France in 1997, and Kohl himself was defeated for reelection in 1998. (German elections, p. 815)

Meeting in Brussels on May 2, EU leaders officially declared that eleven nations had met the necessary criteria for participation in the euro. But the meeting—called to demonstrate solidarity at the outset of such a momentous step—also displayed residual elements of the nationalistic bickering that had plagued Europe for hundreds of years. France held up appointment of the key official in the new European monetary union—the president of the European Central Bank—because it wanted a Frenchman at the helm. Led by Germany, most other countries had settled on a Dutch candidate, Wim F. Duisenberg. In the end, France forced a compromise under which Duisenberg would step down from the post in 2002 in favor of a French nominee, most likely Jean-Claude Trichet. That deal appeared to be in jeopardy by the end of 1998, when Duisenberg told journalists he might not quit in 2002.

Locking Currency Rates

The final step toward making the euro a reality came on December 31, when the finance ministers from the eleven Euroland countries met in Brussels to define the actual value of the euro. The ministers fixed the value of the euro in relation to each of their national currencies; those values would remain locked together until the national currencies were phased out in 2002.

As set by the ministers, the euro was to be equal to 6.56 French francs, 1.96 German marks, and 1,936.27 Italian lira. The euro opened trading on January 4, 1999, the first business day of the year, at a value of approximately $1.17 in U.S. dollars.

Even as the finance ministers were meeting and popping champagne corks in celebration, tens of thousands of workers at banks and financial markets around the world were busy reprogramming computers to convert the prices of European stocks and bonds into euros. Much of this activity took place in London, the leading financial center of Europe, despite the fact that the British government had opted not to participate in the euro. Euro-enthusiasm gained momentum in many parts of the continent at the turn of the year. Even though the euro currency would not be available for three years, many shops and restaurants began quoting prices in euros as well as the local currency.

Expected Impact of the Euro

Before a single euro was traded, the impact of a united European monetary policy was made clear. The newly elected German chancellor, Gerhard Schroeder, began agitating in October for a united cut in interest rates to spur economic growth across Europe. Some European nations had been cutting interest rates unilaterally, and the United States Federal Reserve Board cut rates three times during 1998. Central bankers in Germany and elsewhere at first rejected Schroeder's call for a unified reduction. But in a surprising and unified move on December 3, all eleven central banks of Euroland announced a coordinated cut in interest rates. At its final meeting of the year, on December 22, the European Central Bank announced technical details for interest rates to take effect in late January 1999.

The coordinated interest cut demonstrated how the eleven Euroland nations could set aside their differences to act for what they perceived as the common good—the original theory behind European integration. European Union officials said that, over time, the euro would force additional cooperative steps that would strengthen the economies of all the participating nations. For example, European Commission President Jacques Santer told an audience in Chicago on May 6 that introduction of the euro would encourage common policies to deregulate telecommunications and utilities markets, following similar steps in the United States during the 1990s. Optimists also noted that the financial markets appeared to have faith in the euro; by 1998 the currencies of the affected European countries were as stable as at any point in years.

Skeptics pointed to a number of stumbling blocks in the way of common economic and monetary policies. They noted that the eleven Euroland nations had histories, traditions, and economic situations that would make it difficult for their leaders to achieve consensus on specific actions once the euro was in place. The skeptics noted, for example, that a common currency meant that the eleven nations would have to adopt a one-size-fits-all monetary policy—even when that size did not fit some of its members. If inflation and unemployment were high in some countries but low in others, the European Central Bank would have to establish a unified monetary policy that might help some of those countries and harm others. The very

*rules under which the bank was to operate seemed to guarantee such a con-
flict: under its charter, the bank was to focus its monetary policies solely on
keeping inflation in check, rather than on promoting economic growth. At
the end of 1998 the new German government was continuing to press the
bank to stimulate job growth.*

*Bound by such rules as the limit on budget deficits, national govern-
ments also would have less flexibility to adopt taxation and spending policies geared to the specific circumstances of their individual economies. The
result, critics said, could be aggravated political turmoil in Europe as frustrated voters found their influence was subservient to an unelected European Central Bank.*

> *Following are excerpts from a speech delivered May 5, 1998, by
> Jacques Santer, president of the European Commission, to the
> Conference on "Whither Globalism: A World in Crisis," spon-
> sored by the Economic Strategy Institute in Washington, D.C.:*

Globalization is a fact. While the world is shrinking it is a mistake to think
that globalisation is withering: we are increasingly interdependent, we trade,
we invest, we are on-line, and borders also beyond the European Union and
its Single Market become invisible as reality is being overtaken by a virtual
world. Europeans and Americans tend to say that it "takes two to tango" but,
while that may be true in Trans Atlantic terms, globalization involves a "line
dance" of more than two partners moving in step.

As Washington insiders will have noticed in the *Washington Post*, an "emu"
is a large flightless fast-running Australian bird and a "euro" a large reddish
Australian kangaroo. After this week-end, we can add to the dictionary that
the euro is a large European currency that is ready to fly.

The key events of particular relevance to globalisation that are unfolding
in Europe are threefold:

- the introduction of the single currency, the euro, as of January 1, 1999
- fostering structural changes by further liberalising the EU's [European
  Union's] internal market, and finally
- preparing for the most spectacular enlargement in the EU's history.

Let me start with the euro.

Last week-end, the European Heads of State and Government nominated
the 11 Member States that will participate in the euro as of the 1st of January
1999.

This means that exchange rates between the participating currencies will
be irrevocably fixed between each other and relative to the euro. From this
date onwards, the euro will be our single currency and be used in the banking system, in wholesale financial and capital markets and can be used by the
private sector.

The clear legal principles which underlie the introduction of the euro rule out any speculation in currencies of the participating countries in the three-year transition period that will run until the 1st of January 2002, when bank notes and coins in euro will be introduced. During that period, the Deutsche Mark, for instance, is a subdivision of the euro very much as the dime is a subdivision of the dollar.

The euro will change the economic landscape, in Europe and abroad.

- The future euro zone is roughly comparable in size and economic weight to the United States. It will cover 300 million inhabitants and account for almost 20% of world GDP [gross domestic product] and of world trade—comparable to the United States.
- The euro zone is designed to have a high degree of stability. The European Central Bank will guarantee inflation between 0 and 2%. The Member States participating in the euro have committed themselves to a high degree of fiscal discipline.
- The stability performance of the euro zone countries is already a fact, with average inflation well below 2% and estimated fiscal deficits in 1998 of 2.4%, set to go down to 2% in 1999. This has helped putting economic growth back on track: having climbed to 2.5% in 1997, growth is expected to increase to a healthy 3% this year for the euro zone. Next year, it will increase again.

The introduction of the euro will have a globally positive economic impact.

- It will contribute to spurring economic growth, and will therefore indirectly stimulate job creation. The euro is therefore helpful for job creation, rather than the contrary as is sometimes suggested. We should however not be complacent: the euro will not solve Europe's structural unemployment problems as such, which we are tackling at the same time.
- The euro will also have a profound microeconomic effect on the functioning of Europe's internal market. It removes transaction costs and completely eliminates currency fluctuations and currency risk. This facilitates trade, investment and travel in the euro zone, and will drive prices downwards through greater competition. The potential for these benefits is illustrated by the simple fact that more than 60% of our trade is between ourselves.
- In the financial sector, the potentially positive impact of the euro is especially large. The combined volume of bonds, stocks and bank assets in the euro zone is already almost as high as in the United States, so future opportunities are enormous:
  - For instance, stock market capitalisation in the euro zone at the end of 1997 was only 44% of GDP compared to 139% in the United States.
  - Another typical example with large potential is the market for venture capital, where the stock market capitalisation of venture capital markets in Europe is still only 1% of that on the NASDAQ market. The big

unknown is the euro's international impact. Will it become a truly international currency? Performing the role of unit of account? Means of payment and reserve currency?

- According to some estimates, the euro's share in trade invoicing could rise to 35% of world trade.
- The introduction of the euro also is likely to lead to portfolio shifts in the reserves of central banks. According to some estimates, some giving the euro a share of 25% or more of global foreign exchange reserves in the medium-term. Similar effects can be expected for the euro's role in private portfolios.

What will the euro mean for the International Monetary System? Several people qualify the introduction of the euro as the most important change in the International Monetary System since the breakdown of the Bretton Woods system in 1971. Some indicators point in the direction of a shared monetary leadership for the euro and the dollar, such as:

- the decoupling of long-term interest rates between the United States and Europe, or
- the role of "safe haven" which both the dollar and European currencies have played in the Asian crisis.

In this context, a stable euro alongside the dollar can play a useful role as a catalyst for the development of trade and investment world-wide.

Ladies and gentlemen, this brings me to the wider significance of the introduction of the euro.

Let me be clear: I see the introduction of the euro as the most important step since the Treaty of Rome was signed in 1957.

- with the euro, Europe's single market will be strengthened irrevocably
- with the euro, economic fundamentals in Europe will be healthier than they have been for three decades
- with the euro, our integration process will receive an immeasurable boost in new areas of policy.

The euro also has important benefits for Americans:

- First of all, the euro will soon be here and it will be in very good shape. US business should urgently start preparing for it.
- Secondly, the euro, as a stable currency, will be beneficial for the economic, financial, monetary and, ultimately, peaceful political integration of the European continent.
- Thirdly, a successful euro is good for the United States: it facilitates business, it creates opportunities for American companies and provides stability on the European Continent.
- Finally, some people believe that the euro might become a threat for the dollar. Let me assure you, that is not our intention. We are not seeking protectionism or a game of competitive devaluations. The euro will reinforce the global system of trade, capital and investment.

Ladies and gentlemen, I already indicated to you the importance of the euro for our internal market process. But globalisation goes further. While the European single market has already created huge advantages in terms of growth and jobs, we can do better. This is why we launched a Single Market Action Plan with the goal of achieving significant progress by 1 January 1999. Let me cite three major issues:

- First, the further liberalisation of the network industries
  - telecommunications growing by 8% per year,
  - electricity where 50% of national markets will be opened up to competition by the end of the century,
  - gas and postal services.
- Second, the creation of an environment which is conducive to innovation and to a wide diffusion of new technologies, such as
  - the protection of intellectual property rights,
  - the promotion of collaboration between businesses and higher education institutions and
  - the encouragement of cross-border collaboration.
- Lastly, the information society, which opens up millions of new opportunities and challenges. I am confident that we are starting to see emerge in Europe the information industry dynamics that have driven the United States economy for the last few years.

These steps towards globalisation also matter in view of another historic process: that of the European Union's enlargement to the East.

The Union has grown from Six to Fifteen Member States since its inception in 1957, but the historic decision taken by the European Council in Luxembourg last December opened the doors for a further enlargement, the most ambitious ever, from fifteen to twenty six or more. Just over a month ago, on 30 and 31 March the accession process and negotiations were formally launched.

I should emphasise the opportunities offered to the United States by the enlarged European Union that will eventually cover 480 million people. It will increase the size of the single market and simplify and enhance access to the current candidate countries.

The potential benefits of this process, also for US companies, are enormous:

- The US currently accounts for 20% of the EU's trade with the rest of the world but only between 2 and 10% for the candidate countries. Over 50% of the stock of foreign FDI in the EU comes from the US, some $46 bn in 1995. For the candidate countries, the US FDI in 1995 was less than $1.5 bn.
- Secondly, where there is currently a single trade regime for the EU and a different regime for each of the candidates, the latter will be subsumed into the former. The average weighted industrial tariff levels of the candidate countries are in general higher than the 3.6% average for the EU.

Thus, in most cases, accession will lead to US firms facing lower tariffs in the new member countries than before.

- Finally, the same rules covering national treatment which apply in the existing EU will also apply in the acceding countries. This will bring substantial benefits to US operators who have established themselves in the EU.

The enlarged European Union is and will remain fully committed to the multilateral trading system as embodied in the rules of the WTO. We consider this is one of the main pillars of the globalisation process. This is why the European Union is looking for a new, comprehensive round of WTO trade negotiations.

The WTO Ministerial meeting taking place in two weeks time should pave the way for a decision in 1999 to launch negotiations in 2000. There is strong support for a new round and the Ministerial should harness this, so that a new round can be launched at the start of the new Millenium.

The European Union and the United States bear a major responsibility for the world trading system. Our two-way trade is traditionally strong and balanced, exceeding more than 100 billion dollars either way, and our overall trade and investment relationship exceeds one trillion dollars. But we can do more bilaterally to facilitate trade:

- removing red tape in terms of double testing or double certification, or by
- bringing our regulatory systems closer together.

Bilateral successes should however not obscure the need to make progress in the multilateral context.

But, Ladies and gentlemen, globalisation goes further, much further, than trade and investment alone.

Let me cite four examples where the co-operation between the European Union and the United States should be deepened.

- The first is information technology, and especially electronic commerce. It is estimated that, by the year 2000, 200 billion dollars worth of business will take place over the Internet. This is 1000 times the 1995 figure. The Internet is borderless. As with other global issues, we have to sit together and see how we can avoid chaos and confusion without handcuffing electronic commerce.
- A second issue concerns the Asian crisis. Europe and the US will have to absorb more Asian exports. This may lead to protectionist pressures. That is why the European Union and the Asian countries agreed a "trade and investment pledge" to keep markets open at the ASEM Summit one month ago in London. We hope that this pledge can be taken up and endorsed by all at the G8 Summit in Birmingham in 10 days time. The lack of transparency and weakness of financial systems in Asia have demonstrated the need to pay attention to issues such as good governance.
- I would like to extend this line of reasoning, and this is my third point, to the way in which we approach development and the Third World. We

increasingly believe that trade, private investment and development co-operation are the closely interrelated tools needed for improved management of global issues such as environment, health, sustainable development and poverty reduction. This is why in our approach to development we want to involve all parties, public and private.

- Sustainable development brings me to my fourth, and last issue concerning globalisation where I see a clear scope for EU-US co-operation, and that is the issue of climate change. Climate change is the biggest single environmental challenge facing us. Kyoto was a historic step forward. The industrial nations, as major emitters of greenhouse gases, have a special responsibility in ensuring that Kyoto commitments are met. At the Birmingham G8 Summit, we will therefore discuss how we can take this process so as to achieve real progress at the next Climate Change meeting in Buenos Aires in November.
  - Signing the Kyoto Protocol within the next year is the first step; the EU already did so last week.
  - Secondly, we should all immediately make significant reductions in greenhouse gas emissions. National domestic measures should be the main means of meeting commitments. We, the EU and US have to take the lead if we want to bring in others. We will discuss at Birmingham how we can best ensure that flexibility mechanisms such as emissions-trading and the clean development mechanism can deliver real additional reductions, over and beyond national action.
  - If we want to mitigate the adverse effects of climate change effectively, we will need action on a truly global scale, involving, over time, the developing countries. How best to do this is another major issue for Birmingham. The key word here is differentiation. We should expect the more advanced countries to take on legally binding commitments sooner than the less developed ones.

The United States and the European Union must lead the way now. Our children will not forgive us if we fail to do this.

Ladies and gentlemen, the European Union and the United States have enormous responsibilities. Our actions will contribute to shaping the international business environment at the Start of the Millennium.

I was proud to co-sign the New Transatlantic Agenda [NTA] with President Clinton in 1995. We have accomplished a good deal by working together on each of the NTA's elements. Our common efforts in the former Yugoslavia, in the Middle East and on economic liberalisation, and the successful Trans Atlantic Business Dialogue (TABD) are but a few examples.

As our joint commitment shows, we share many values and principles. We should therefore not work at cross-purposes but pool our ideas and resources. Fortunately, we agree more than we disagree.

Globalisation poses opportunities and challenges many of which can successfully be met, but only if we work together. . . .

REMARKS ON DISINTERNMENT AT THE TOMB OF THE UNKNOWNS
May 14, 1998

The Tomb of the Unknowns at Arlington National Cemetery—one of the most venerated locations in the United States—suddenly became embroiled in controversy in 1998. News reports suggested that the government had botched a decision leading to the internment of the remains of an unknown American serviceman from the Vietnam War. An investigation by the Pentagon led to a decision by Secretary of Defense William S. Cohen to disinter the remains. The subsequent examination of the remains using recently developed technology produced an identification of the "unknown" serviceman. The remains were those of an air force pilot, Lieutenant Michael J. Blassie, whose jet crashed in South Vietnam in May 1972. Blassie's remains were shipped to his hometown of St. Louis, where he was buried July 11.

Congress in 1921 approved the creation of a ceremonial tomb for an unknown soldier at the Memorial Amphitheater in Arlington National Cemetery, across the Potomac River from Washington, D.C. The remains from an unidentified soldier killed in France were placed in the tomb on November 11, 1921, with President Warren G. Harding presiding. The simple inscription on the tomb was: "Here rests in honored glory an American soldier known but to God." President Dwight D. Eisenhower in 1958 officiated at the internment of unidentified servicemen from World War II and the Korean War alongside the original tomb.

The Tomb of the Unknowns became one of the most important symbols of the American military and also one of the most popular tourist attractions in the nation's capital region. Honor guards representing the military services protected the tomb around the clock; for many Americans, witnessing the ceremony of the changing of the guards was an emotional and patriotic experience.

A Faulty Judgment

Early in the 1980s the Reagan administration decided the time had come to add the remains of an unknown serviceman from the Vietnam War.

But the administration faced a problem: while some 2,000 Vietnam-era servicemen were still unaccounted for, the military had recovered very few remains that it could not identify. In 1984 the Pentagon selected a set of remains known as X–26. The remains originally had been labeled as "BTB [believed to be] Blassie, Michael Joseph," because they were presumed to have been taken from the area of An Loc, Vietnam, where his plane had crashed on May 11, 1972. But in 1980 that identification of the remains was removed, and the X–26 label was applied, when a military board—the Armed Services Graves Registration Office—determined that the skeletal fragments appeared not to match Blassie's physical characteristics. As the sole "unknown" representative of the Vietnam War, the X–26 remains were interred at the Tomb of the Unknowns on Memorial Day, May 28, 1984, with President Ronald Reagan presiding.

The X–26 remains rested peacefully, and anonymously, at the Tomb of the Unknowns from 1984 until January 1998, when the CBS news magazine "60 Minutes" alleged that the military had designated the remains as unknown because of pressure from veterans groups to add a Vietnam-era serviceman to the honored position at the Tomb of the Unknowns. Cohen immediately ordered a investigation, headed by senior Defense Department officials. Those officials announced April 27 that they had found no reason to question the earlier decision to relabel the remains as unknown. However, they recommended that Cohen order the X–26 remains disinterred so they could be examined by mitochondrial DNA testing, a relatively new technique that could match bone samples with those from the maternal line of the deceased.

Cohen announced on May 7 that he was accepting the panel's recommendations because "we must honor our commitment to attempt to locate and identify the remains of all Americans lost in combat." Cohen on May 14 presided over a ceremony at the Tomb of the Unknowns during which the steel casket containing the Vietnam remains was removed from the marble and granite tomb. On June 30 the Pentagon announced that a DNA examination had determined that the remains were those of Lieutenant Blassie.

On July 11 Blassie was buried again at the Jefferson Barracks National Cemetery just south of St. Louis. This time his grave was marked with a simple tombstone giving his name and air force rank, dates of birth and death, and the inscription "Beloved son and brother." Blassie's mother and four siblings attended the burial ceremony, as did Cohen, other Pentagon officials, and hundreds of veterans and well-wishers. One World War II veteran in attendance, Stewart Piper, told the New York Times: *"I see this ceremony as a real plus to our government and to his family. For his family, to find out the truth. And for the government, it shows that the country could admit it made a mistake and do the right thing."*

Pentagon officials said it appeared likely that the space at the Tomb of the Unknowns for a Vietnam-era serviceman would not be filled again, since advances in technology held out the promise that all any remains from the war that were recovered in the future could be identified.

Following is the text of remarks by Defense Secretary William S. Cohen on May 14, 1998, at a ceremony at the Tomb of the Unknowns at Arlington National Cemetery, during which the remains of the "unknown" serviceman from the Vietnam War were disinterred:

To gather on this site always quickens our hearts and stirs our national pride. We disturb this hallowed ground with profound reluctance. And we take this step only because of our abiding commitment to account for every warrior who fought and died to preserve the freedoms that we cherish.

If advances in technology can ease the lingering anguish of even one family, then our path is clear. And so we yield today to the promise of science with the hope that the heavy burden of doubt may be lifted from a family's heart.

But we are not here simply as grateful beneficiaries of modern technology. Instead, our purpose is timeless. We gather to show our deep gratitude for the sacrifices of our warriors, including those who died unknown and unsung on distant battlefields. And that gratitude extends in particular to all of the families of our fallen heroes who have joined us here today.

Of the millions of visitors to this spiritual place, only a small number actually come to visit a specific gravesite. To the great majority of sojourners, those who lie under these green hills are unknown. And yet thousands are drawn here each week in quiet reverence to honor the service and the sacrifice of our dead.

As we live yet another day under the freedom for which their lives were given, we give thanks to them once again today. And far from diminishing the sanctity of this cemetery and this tomb, our actions today serve to recommit ourselves to the principles of freedom and democracy which this sacred ground represents.

May God continue to embrace our nation and all who rest here.

THE RESIGNATION OF PRESIDENT SUHARTO OF INDONESIA
May 21, 1998

President Suharto, who ruled Indonesia with an iron hand for thirty-two years, was forced from power in 1998 following violent student demonstrations. Suharto's fall, in the fourth most populous nation in the world, was one of the most dramatic consequences of the severe economic crisis that shook many East Asian countries starting in 1997. Indonesia's economy was battered by a severe drought, near-collapse of the country's currency and banking system, and the flight of foreign capital. Millions of Indonesians were thrown into poverty, laying the groundwork for political upheaval in what had been one of the world's most tightly controlled societies.

By the end of 1998, Suharto's hand-picked successor, B. J. Habibie, had been forced to call legislative elections for 1999, leading to the selection of a president. Although Indonesia nominally was a republic, the country had not experienced anything resembling a free election since the 1950s.

The fall of Suharto exposed deep societal divisions in Indonesia that had been kept in check during nearly four decades of dictatorship by Suharto and his predecessor, Sukarno. Composed of more than 17,000 islands stretching across the South Pacific, Indonesia was an artificial creation of nineteenth-century Dutch colonialism. Nearly 90 percent of the country's 201 million people were Muslim, but the islands featured a diverse patchwork of ethnic groups that had little in common. Ethnic Chinese controlled much of the economy and so were feared and hated by those in other ethnic groups. Many Indonesians and outside experts suggested that, without strong leadership from Jakarta, Indonesia might ultimately disintegrate into ethnic warfare, possibly leading to the creation of numerous ethnic-based countries.

Background to Suharto's Fall

Indonesia was one of the East Asian countries hardest hit by the financial crisis that started in Thailand in the summer of 1997. A currency cri-

sis exposed weak banking systems and widespread corruption in Thailand, South Korea, Indonesia, the Philippines, and other countries that had boomed during the 1970s and 1980s with the aid of foreign investment. In Indonesia, the currency (the rupiah) collapsed, falling more than two-thirds in value against the U.S. dollar. Banks folded, and huge corporations closed or scaled back their operations, forcing millions of people out of work. This man-made disaster was made worse by a severe drought that sharply curtailed production of rice and other food staples. (Asian financial crisis, Historic Documents of 1997, p. 832)

In October 1997 Suharto turned to the International Monetary Fund (IMF), the World Bank, and other international financial sources for help in shoring up the economy. The IMF offered a $40 billion aid package, but on the condition that Suharto initiate reforms in the country's corrupt business system, along with austerity measures to cut a ballooning government deficit. Suharto, his cronies, and members of his family owned major corporations that controlled much of the Indonesian economy. Various estimates put Suharto's personal worth in the billions of dollars, making him one of the world's richest men.

Suharto at first accepted the IMF conditions, but by late 1997—as the rupiah and stock market continued to fall—it was clear that he was refusing to carry out the mandated reforms and austerity programs. In January 1998 IMF managing director Michel Camdessus took the unusual step of flying to Jakarta to pressure Suharto in person. On January 15 the two men signed an agreement mandating further reforms, including specific steps to dismantle monopolies controlled by Suharto's friends and family members.

Despite statements by Camdessus and other world figures insisting that Suharto would carry out his promises, the latest IMF agreement failed to halt the slide in stock prices and the value of the rupiah. By late January riots broke out over rising food prices. In the midst of this economic crisis and growing unrest, Suharto stood for reelection in the rubber-stamp national assembly. On March 10 he won a seventh five-year term unopposed. The next day, when Suharto took the oath of office for his new term, students began protesting at universities across the country. The student protests continued for weeks, and early in May the students were joined by thousands of the poor and unemployed angered by skyrocketing prices for fuel and food.

Suharto left the country on May 9 for a week-long visit to Egypt but returned after a violent battle between students and police in Jakarta on May 12 that killed six students. The May 12 clash set off a week-long series of riots, principally in Jakarta. Mobs attacked and burned businesses and office buildings, including those owned by Suharto's family and friends. By May 16 more than five hundred people had been killed in the rioting.

Suharto's support from the political and military establishment crumbled quickly as the rioting intensified. On May 18 his hand-picked speaker of the parliament, Harmoko, called on Suharto to resign. Suharto offered a compromise, promising to call elections "as soon as possible" and then step down once a new parliament was in place. This last-minute, half-hearted attempt at compromise failed to stem the protests, and within two days Suharto's entire inner circle of supporters was calling on him to resign. Suharto appealed to several leading intellectuals and opposition figures to join a "reform committee," but they refused.

Suharto on May 21 finally heeded the demands of the street protesters and his friends, announcing from the presidential palace that he was resigning immediately. Suharto acknowledged the public protests only indirectly, noting the "aspirations of our peoples to institute reforms" and expressing "deep sorrow if there were mistakes, failures, or shortcomings."

Habibie, an engineer, former cabinet minister, and longtime friend of Suharto who had served as vice president only since March, immediately took the oath of office as president. Habibie later told reporters he would be able to handle the responsibilities of the presidency because he had learned "from the master."

The Post-Suharto Era

Suharto's resignation immediately reduced the violent public protests and brought a measure of renewed political stability. But in a country accustomed to having decisions made at the top, the sudden lack of an authoritative hand created new uncertainties. Many analysts viewed Habibie as a transitional figure without a political constituency of his own and with no public mandate to run a country in deep crisis. Habibie tried to put his own stamp on government, shuffling the Suharto cabinet and assuring his citizens and foreign investors that he would carry out promised economic reforms.

Habibie at first brushed aside student demands for immediate elections, saying he intended to serve out the rest of Suharto's five-year term. Under continuing pressure, Habibie gradually gave way on the election issue and agreed to call legislative elections in 1999. On December 3, the government announced plans for elections for a new parliament, called the House of Representatives, on June 7, 1999. This would be followed on August 29, 1999, by a meeting of the People's Consultative Assembly, which had authority under the constitution to elect a president.

The government's move toward elections followed renewed outbreaks of violence in November, resulting both from the political weakness in Jakarta and continuing economic decline. Street battles on November 13— the worst since the May rioting—killed five people and injured more than one hundred others. Inflation, unemployment, bankruptcies, and crime were all on the rise, and by the end of 1998 few Indonesians were able to see any indications that their lives were getting better.

On December 15 the IMF announced that it was continuing to pump money into the Indonesian economy, which, it said, "has remained on the stabilization path under the most difficult circumstances." Inflation had eased and there was "marked progress" in easing food shortages, the IMF noted. But the IMF stated that Indonesia still faced many structural chal-lenges left over from the days of Suharto's dictatorship, including reform-ing the nation's systems of banking and corporate ownership.

Following is the text of a statement by President Suharto of Indonesia announcing his resignation from office on May 21, 1998, followed by the oath of office taken by B. J. Habibie to suc-ceed Suharto. Both texts are as translated from the Javanese:

SUHARTO RESIGNATION

Holy greetings, ladies and gentlemen, fellow citizens. In the past few days I have followed with great care the development of our national situation, especially the aspirations of our peoples to institute reforms across the boards, across all aspects of our life and our nation.

Based on my understanding, with regard to these aspirations, and pushed by the conviction that these reforms will necessarily be executed in a con-stitutional and orderly manner for the unity and security of our nation, more-over, to cultivate the continuation of our national development, I have already announced the formation of our reform committee, as well as the reshuffling of our cabinet.

Nevertheless, it appears that the reality until today that the reform com-mittee cannot be realized because there is a lack of consensus with regard to the formation of a committee. In our desire to execute those reform program in the manner just outlined, I find that the inability to form this reform com-mittee, hence, the reshuffling of the cabinet is no longer necessary.

With respect to these aforementioned developments, I believe that it has become extremely difficult for me to continue the leadership of this country and to cultivate the development of our country. Therefore, respecting the foundations of our 1945 constitution, and while deeply taking into account the opinions and analysis of the leadership of Parliament and leadership of the various fashions, I have decided to hereby declare that I withdraw from my position as the president of this republic of Indonesia. Effective immedi-ately with my issuing this statement as of today, May 21st, 1998.

The statement of my withdrawal from the presidency of the Republic of Indonesia, I deliver to all of you, leaders of the houses of Parliament, as well as to the Upper House. I delivered the statement to the Parliament this morn-ing.

In keeping with chapter eight of our 1945 constitution, the vice president of the Republic of Indonesia, Professor, Dr. B. J. Habibie, will continue the term of the presidency from 1998 to 2003.

With regard to the help and the support of our society during my leader-ship of this country and this republic, I express my deepest gratitude and express my deepest sorrow if there were mistakes, failures or shortcomings.

With start of today, cabinet number seven to the cabinet to the ministers I also express my gratitude and thanks.

Because it is not currently possible to execute the swearing-in in front of Parliament, to avoid a vacuum of leadership of the country, the vice president will at this very moment undertake the swearing-in ceremony to the presidency of this country.

HABIBIE'S OATH OF OFFICE

Based on chapter nine of our 1945 constitution, in anticipation of accepting the position of the presidency, I declare that I will undertake all constitutional mandates, which concludes to swear under religious dictate for the God almighty, I hereby swear that I will fulfill all obligations of the presidency of the Republic of Indonesia with as great a care and fairness and justice to sustain and protect our constitution and to carry out all law and regulation, and to dedicate myself to our country, and our nation and our peoples.

U.S. REPORT ON WAR-TIME NEUTRAL NATIONS
June 2, 1998

Supposedly "neutral" nations provided strategic material that helped Nazi Germany prolong World War II and were paid with gold and other assets looted by the Nazis from occupied lands. These were central conclusions of a detailed report issued June 2 by the Clinton administration as part of its effort to complete the historical record of how Germany financed the war. The administration created a diplomatic furor in 1997 when it released the first report in the series; that report focused on the role of Swiss banks in accepting looted assets from the Nazis and financing Hitler's war machine. (Historic Documents of 1997, p. 257)

Focus on Five Neutrals

The U.S. report released June 2 provided detailed information on the wartime actions of five major neutral nations: Argentina, Portugal, Spain, Sweden, and Turkey. As was the 1997 report on Switzerland, the 1998 report was prepared by U.S. historians at the State Department and other agencies, under the direction of Stuart E. Eizenstat, undersecretary of state for economic, business, and agricultural affairs. In releasing the 1998 report, Eizenstat described the U.S. historical review "as a sort of cleansing process" for all countries a half-century after the war.

The 1998 report said four of the neutral nations actively traded with Germany during the war, in some cases providing vital raw materials for the Nazi war machine. Portugal and Spain sold Germany large quantities of wolfram, which is used in the production of tungsten; Sweden shipped to Germany high-quality iron ore (essential for steel production) and components for ball bearings; and Turkey sold chromite ore, which is essential for the production of chromium. Of the five neutrals examined in the report, only Argentina did not provide substantial amounts of militarily important material to Germany—largely because it was prevented from doing so by the Allied naval blockade.

The report said that the Allies (principally the United States and Great Britain) made numerous attempts to convince the neutral nations to enter the war against Germany, or at least to halt their strategic exports to the Nazis. These efforts met with little success until late in the war, usually because the neutrals were reluctant to give up lucrative trade deals with the Germans and they feared German reprisals should they halt the trade. In addition, the Allies had other priorities. In the case of Portugal, for example, Washington and London "placed greater importance" on gaining access to military bases on the Portuguese Azores islands than on forcing the Portuguese to halt their exports of wolfram, the report said.

The study said Germany paid the neutral countries about $500 million for their vital supplies. Of that total, about $300 million were in Nazi gold. The study estimated that $240 million of the $300 million had been looted from occupied countries.

The neutrals' trade with Germany certainly "sustained" the Nazi war effort, the study said. But the study drew no definitive conclusions about how long that trade helped prolong the war or whether the neutrals could have halted the war if they had collectively cut off Germany's supply of vital materiel. Eizenstat quoted the memoirs of Albert Speer, Hitler's armaments minister, who recalled telling the German leader in 1943 that—should Turkey cut off the supply of chromite—Germany would have to stop producing planes, tanks, artillery shells, and other essential items within a few months.

Eizenstat noted that other actions of the neutrals would appear to be inconsistent with their standing as nonbelligerents. Sweden, for example, allowed German troops to cross its borders thousands of times, and Spain sent a division to fight with the Germans against Russia. On the other hand, all five neutrals accepted refugees from occupied lands, in some cases many more than did the United States. The report noted that Argentina—despite its pro-Nazi regime—accepted between 25,000 and 45,000 European Jews; even at the low figure, Argentina was more generous than the United States, which took in only 21,000 European refugees during the war. Eizenstat said the U.S. position on refugees was "largely one of indifference."

Much of the 1998 report dealt with the generally unsuccessful postwar attempts by the United States and Britain to convince these five neutral nations to turn over gold, other precious metals, artwork, and similar valuables they had obtained from Nazi Germany during the war. Once again, broader military and diplomatic considerations often overrode these efforts. Ultimately, four of the five nations turned over a total of $18.5 million of the estimated $240 million in looted gold they had received from the Nazis. Sweden was the most cooperative, turning over $15 million. The Allies used the money for humanitarian programs and for partial compensation of individuals and businesses whose assets had been looted by the Nazis.

In the case of Turkey, for example, the report said that in the immediate aftermath of the war, the United States did not press seriously for the return *of Nazi gold held by Ankara. By 1946 Washington was more concerned with bolstering Turkey against possible communist threats than with forcing the government there to hand over Nazi gold. Turkey was the only one of the five neutrals mentioned in the report that never turned any Nazi valuables over to the Allies after the war.*

Ustasha Leaders

The 1998 Eizenstat report provided new details on how leaders of the Croatian Ustasha regime escaped following the war, possibly taking with them millions of dollars worth of looted assets. The fascist Ustasha regime was widely considered a puppet of Nazi Germany and was responsible for the wartime deaths of as many as 700,000 Serbs, Jews, and others. Ustasha leader Ante Pavelic escaped to Austria, where he was captured by British authorities and released when he turned over millions of Swiss francs. Pavelic and key aides then took refuge in the College of San Girolamo degli Illirici, just outside the Vatican walls in Rome, before fleeing to Argentina in 1948. These refugees were aided by a number of "Ustasha priests," the report said. The report said U.S. records showed no evidence that Vatican leaders supported or even knew about the Ustasha activity at the college, but given the location of the college, "troubling questions remain." More information about the issue might be available in archives stilled sealed at the Vatican, in Croatia, and at other locations, the report said.

Although the United States knew that Pavelic was hiding in Rome, the report said, Washington did nothing to bring him to justice. One reason was that by 1947 relations had soured between the United States and Marshal Tito, the new leader of Yugoslavia, which incorporated Croatia.

Swiss Study

The Swiss government on May 25 issued its own report on the role of the Swiss National Bank and Swiss private banks in financing the German war effort. A commission of historians headed by Jean-François Bergier estimated that Swiss banks handled some $440 million in gold from the Nazi Reichsbank before and during the war; the 1998 value of that gold would be about $4 billion. Of the $440 million, the commission said, an estimated $316 million was looted from the vaults of countries occupied by Germany. Both these figures were slightly higher than comparable U.S. estimates. The Swiss National Bank was the primary transfer point for Nazi gold, although private banks conducted transactions for the Nazi regime as well.

The Bergier commission dismissed recent arguments by some Swiss officials that wartime Swiss bankers could not have been expected to know the origins of the Nazi gold. In fact, the commission said, there was no doubt that the Swiss National Bank knew at the time that the Nazis had stolen the gold. Research showed, the commission said, that during the war "attentive citizens could read in the Swiss press exactly where the gold which the Reichsbank was circulating came from." The commission noted that Swiss bank officials considered melting down looted gold from the Nazis to disguise its origin but ultimately decided that the idea was impractical.

The commission said Swiss banks also handled gold that Nazis stole from Jews who were forced into concentration camps. Wedding rings, dental fillings, dinner plates, and other items taken from Jews were melted into ingots and incorporated into Germany's gold reserves. The 1998 Eizenstat report estimated the value of this "victims' gold" at around $40 million, at wartime rates. The Bergier commission said it traced $134,000 worth of such gold that went into Swiss banks.

Swiss Bank Accounts

In a related issue, two major private Swiss banks agreed on August 12 to pay $1.25 billion over three years to Holocaust survivors and the families of Holocaust victims. In return, officials in New York City and several states dropped threats to mount an economic boycott against the Swiss banks. The August 12 agreement was an attempt to resolve legal claims against the banks that had been filed by Jewish groups and lawyers representing thousands of Holocaust victims. The plaintiffs had claimed that the Swiss banks held billions of dollars worth of assets belonging to European Jews who suffered during the Holocaust.

At year's end, the banks and the Jewish groups had not settled on a plan for distributing the $1.25 billion. In addition, the Swiss government and the Swiss National Bank refused to participate in the settlement.

The August 12 agreement was the latest stage in a three-year controversy over Jewish assets in Swiss banks. Under pressure from international Jewish groups, the Swiss Bankers Association had agreed in 1995 and 1996 to turn over to Holocaust survivors an estimated $30 million to $40 million held in secret accounts since the World War II era. Those accounts had been opened by European Jews—or trustees acting on their behalf—who hoped to protect their money from the Nazis. Swiss banks in 1997 began publishing the names on thousands of bank accounts that had been dormant since 1945. A commission headed by former U.S. Federal Reserve Bank chairman Paul Volker was reviewing nearly 8,000 claims against the dormant accounts.

Several major European insurance companies also were negotiating during 1998 with groups representing Holocaust victims. These negotiations were trying to resolve claims on insurance policies taken out by Jews who perished in the Holocaust.

Washington Conference

An international conference in Washington on December 1–3, sponsored by the U.S. government, produced agreement on steps to return works of arts stolen by the Nazis to their rightful owners. Representatives of forty-four nations at the conference adopted a set of eleven "Principles with Respect to Nazi-Confiscated Art." Among the principles were plans to open archives by museums and governments, take international steps to authen-

ticate stolen art works and determine from whom they were stolen, and negotiate for compensation of valid claims.

Museum officials and other specialists attending the conference estimated that tens of thousands of artworks stolen by the Nazis remained unaccounted for, and that many of those pieces were in the collections of museums and private individuals. A major development at the Washington conference was a pledge by Valery Kulishov, director of restitution for the Russian culture ministry, to review claims by individuals whose artworks were stolen by Nazi and Soviet forces during World War II.

> *Following is the executive summary of the report, "U.S. and Allied Wartime and Postwar Relations and Negotiations with Argentina, Portugal, Spain, Sweden, and Turkey on Looted Gold and German External Asserts and U.S. Concerns about the Fate of the Wartime Ustasha Treasury," released June 2, 1998, by the State Department:*

Allied Relations and Negotiations with Argentina

Argentina, alone among the American Republics, pursued a neutrality in World War II that the United States perceived as not only failing to support the Allies but as actually sympathizing politically with the Axis and ignoring Nazi penetration of Argentina until the War was nearly over. Although Argentina had a history of close ties with Britain and there was considerable sympathy for the Allies among the Argentine public and some political parties, the government became increasingly dominated during the War by pro-Axis leaders, particularly after the overthrow of civilian authority and the establishment of a military regime in June 1943. The Argentine Government did not sever diplomatic and commercial relations with Nazi Germany until January 1944, refused to cooperate in U.S.-led economic warfare measures, permitted Argentina to become the center of Axis espionage and propaganda activities in South America, and even conspired to overthrow the governments of other South American nations and replace them with pro-Axis authoritarian regimes. The United States viewed the accession to power in February 1944 of General Edelmiro Farrell as representing the final triumph of the pro-Axis faction in the Argentine military and consequently refused to recognize the Farrell government.

During the War, Argentina ignored Allied recommendations and declarations to end all financial interaction, direct or indirect, with Nazi Germany. The Allies became particularly concerned about the operation within Argentina of subsidiaries of Germany's leading firms, including I.G. Farben, Staudt and Co., and Siemens Schuckert. These firms maintained links with Germany throughout the War and supported major Nazi espionage operations in Latin America.

On the other hand, Argentine exports to the United States and especially Britain (which depended on Argentine beef to help feed its population) rose dramatically during the War, essentially doubling their prewar volume. This fact reflected the convergence of two important factors: the willingness of Argentine producers to expand their exports, and the strength of prewar and wartime ties between Argentina and Britain in particular.

The Allied wartime blockade made it impossible for Argentina to provide substantial amounts of exports to Germany, which up until then had been one of its principal trading partners. The Argentine capital of Buenos Aires, however, was one of the principal Latin American ports from which goods valuable even in small quantities, such as platinum, palladium, drugs, and other chemicals, were smuggled to the Axis. The State Department instituted a contraband control program as one aspect of a broader State Department-Board of Economic Warfare effort that also included the management of U.S. exports to Argentina with the aim of denying Argentine trade and financial interaction with Germany and persuading Argentina not to serve as a base for Axis subversion.

Despite these efforts, the United States and its Allies were never able to mount effective measures to counter what the United States viewed as Nazi economic penetration of Argentina, in part because of differing views within the U.S. Government and, more importantly, because of even greater differences with the British Government. The State and Treasury Departments viewed the Argentine situation differently, with Treasury continually pressing for more aggressive action—a pattern often matched in U.S. policy-making toward the other wartime neutrals, especially Switzerland. State deplored Argentine policies but favored a more cautious diplomatic approach that would not alienate other Latin American countries and would lay the foundation for postwar solidarity among the American Republics and closer ties with the United States. For its part Britain did not share the U.S. concerns about Argentina but rather viewed Argentine neutrality as advantageous to the Allied cause, as it safeguarded from German attack the Argentine shipments of meat and other exports needed to sustain the embattled British population. The United States could not, even with high-level appeals to Prime Minister Churchill, persuade Britain to break its relations with Argentina or support strong sanctions against it. Argentina did not play a significant role in sustaining the Nazi war effort.

The United States found it difficult to extend its Safehaven program to Argentina. Argentina's insistence on a neutrality that deviated sharply from its neighbors' policies and could not be justified by an Axis security threat, combined with the known pro-Axis proclivities of certain Argentine leaders, gave rise to U.S. suspicions—never substantiated—that Argentina was a safehaven (indeed a willing one) for German gold and other assets. The Safehaven efforts in Argentina, mounted in late 1944 and into 1945, foundered on the strains between the United States and Argentina and the absence of official relations after the Farrell regime came to power in early 1944.

The Act of Chapultepec of 1945, the cornerstone agreement for postwar security and cooperation among the American Republics, recognized the fight of each Republic of the Western Hemisphere, including the United States, to dispose of German property within its own respective jurisdiction and retain the proceeds. Since the Farrell regime adopted the Chapultepec agreement when it finally declared war on the Axis at the end of March 1945, the Allies could not lawfully lay claim to German assets in Argentina. Instead, once U.S.-Argentine relations were resumed, the Treasury Department worked out a "replacement program" under which Argentina would, like other American Republics, eliminate Axis firms by liquidation, expropriation, and forced sale. As was also true in the other American Republics, including the United States, the proceeds from the liquidation or takeover of German assets in Argentina were never subject to postwar Allied control or disposition to aid the victims of Nazism.

In February 1946 the United States published its Argentine Blue Book, in which it sought to provide evidence of the pro-Axis policies pursued by Argentine governments during the War and to demonstrate the continuing potential for Argentina to become a base for a resurgent Nazism. The Blue Book confirmed that the Argentine Government asserted no control over German firms until its declaration of war against the Axis in March 1945, and reported systematic attempts to distribute or dissipate assets of German firms in Argentina. Although publication of the Blue Book gave rise to considerable anti-American public sentiment, and may have helped to elect Juan Peron President of Argentina, it actually fostered improved cooperation with the Enemy Property Board, established by the Argentine Replacement Program to take control of and liquidate German assets. By the end of 1946 U.S. relations with Argentina began to improve, and the onset of the Cold War renewed U.S. desire for hemispheric alignment, contributing to the improvement in U.S.-Argentine relations.

The Treasury Department made its final Safehaven reports regarding Argentina in May 1946, estimating German assets at $200 million but also concluding that Argentina had not become a haven for looted gold or assets. Although U.S. Safehaven investigations in Argentina were never pressed vigorously and did not include a review of the records of the Argentine Central Bank, documents were obtained by the U.S. Embassy in Buenos Aires that allowed the conclusion to be drawn that no gold in Argentina had come from Axis sources. Nor were any caches of gems or art treasures looted by Germans officially uncovered in Argentina. (A U.S. Government examination in 1997 of selected records released by the Argentine Central Bank found no evidence that any gold was acquired by the Argentine Central Bank from Europe between August 1942 and the end of the war, but the records also contain no information about the origin of any gold the Bank received prior to August 1942.) In the wake of the resumption of friendly relations with Argentina, the Embassy notified Washington in early 1947 that all German assets were lawfully the property of the Argentine Government. Although the Enemy Property Board had at one time stated that the proceeds from Argentina's Replacement Program would be deposited in accounts intended to reimburse wartime losses incurred by the United Nations, no negotiations regarding the distribution of the proceeds of liquidated assets were undertaken.

Although the United States had become aware during World War II of an extensive commercial relationship between Argentina and Switzerland, which often included payments for exports in gold, the Treasury Department made a determination in December 1946 that the current status of U.S.-Argentine relations precluded any investigation of rumored Argentine acquisition of gold and that no negotiation over the restitution of any gold could be conducted. In light of that determination, the State Department approved in June 1947 a shipment of gold from Argentina to the Federal Reserve Bank. In October 1947 a Treasury Department undertaking to purchase Argentine gold at the Federal Reserve Bank resulted in inquiries to Argentina regarding the origin of the gold and whether any had possibly been looted by Germany. Although Argentina provided some assurances that none of the gold had come from Germany, a complete investigation was put aside by U.S. officials in the interest of not jeopardizing the development of better relations with Argentina. Improving U.S.-Argentine relations and fully integrating Argentina into the postwar hemispheric solidarity system had by then become important U.S. policy goals.

Allied Relations and Negotiations with Portugal

During the War, Portugal practiced what Dean Acheson, then Assistant Secretary of State, described as "classical legal neutrality," balancing its trade as much as possible with each side. Germany and the Allies waged an economic war to lure Portugal to their side through a combination of threats and lucrative trade deals. The Allies began this economic war with some advantages, most notably a centuries-old Anglo-Portuguese alliance, coupled with close economic and trade relations (Britain was Portugal's leading trade partner), as well as Portugal's dependence on U.S. petroleum, coal, and chemical supplies. Germany, Portugal's second largest trade partner, also enjoyed significant advantages, particularly after its occupation of France gave it a direct overland route to the Iberian Peninsula, through which it could both supply Portugal with greater quantities of imports than the Allies and pose a military threat if Portugal attempted to curtail exports important to the German war effort.

Honoring its historic alliance with Britain, Portugal allowed Britain to trade and receive credit backed by the pound, allowing Britain to obtain vital goods at a time when it was short on gold and escudos. By 1945 Britain owed Portugal over $322 million under this arrangement. Portugal provided the Axis less formal but also advantageous trade facilities, permitting Germany and Italy to incur sizable debts in their clearing agreements with Portugal and advancing them significant amounts of escudos in government and private contracts. Deficits under the Portuguese clearing agreement with Germany averaged between 13 and 23.5 Reichsmarks ($59 million) between 1943 and 1944. A 1945 Allied study noted that, as a result of these arrangements, Germany never lacked escudos during the War.

The heated competition between the belligerents for its important resources greatly benefited Portugal's economy and generated huge profits for its businesses and banks. Although the Allies took a far greater share of Portugal's strategic goods during the War than the Axis did, Portugal exported one material to Germany without which, the Allies believed, Germany could not continue to fight: wolfram, which when processed into the extremely hard metal tungsten had myriad vital industrial and military uses. Allied officials predicted in 1944 that if Germany were deprived of wolfram, its machine-tool industry would virtually shut down within three months. Portugal was Europe's leading producer of wolfram, and while the Allies had easier access to sources in the Latin America and the Far East, Germany was dependent upon Portugal and Spain for the bulk of its supplies. The Allies' objective was to purchase enough of this vital ore to satisfy Portugal's export demands and prevent as much as possible from going to the enemy. Portuguese merchants also were an important source of vital smuggled commodities to the Axis, including industrial diamonds and platinum from Africa and Latin America.

Germany and Portugal negotiated secret agreements in accordance with which Portugal exported an average of over 2,000 metric tons of wolfram to Germany annually between 1941 and mid-1944, about 60 percent of Germany's estimated minimum industrial requirement, which the Allies estimated to be 3,500 tons annually. Portuguese Prime Minister Salazar commented to the British Ambassador in February 1944 that denying wolfram to Germany "would reduce her power of endurance, and the war would be accordingly shortened."

In January 1944 the Allies began to pressure Salazar to embargo all wolfram sales, but Portugal resisted, defending its right as a neutral to sell to anyone and fearing that any reduction in its exports would prompt Germany to attack Portuguese shipping, bomb Portuguese cities, or even launch an invasion from occupied France across Spain (which was neutral but under Franco's leadership, sympathetic to Nazi Germany). The Allies could have used the threat of an oil embargo to compel Portugal to end the trade with Germany, but they placed greater importance on negotiating access to military bases on the Azores. Portugal granted Britain access to these bases in October 1943 and extended such access to the United States a year later. On the eve of the D-Day invasion in June 1944, after Britain and the United States threatened economic sanctions, the Portuguese Government imposed a complete embargo on wolfram exports to both sides.

Germany paid for its Portuguese imports with German goods and escudos, as well as gold (most of which came through Switzerland) and Swiss francs purchased with gold. The Allies determined that after 1942 much of this German gold was looted, and warned all neutrals in early 1944 that they would not honor these transactions. The Bank of Portugal began to dispose of large amounts of German gold in 1943, and the Allies estimated that the Bank sold or traded 34 to 45 tons of gold by February 1945. Estimates of the total amount of looted gold received by Portugal ranged from 44.9 tons ($50.5 million), the amount of looted gold the Allies estimated Portugal had received after 1942, to the State Department estimate of 94.8 tons (including 20.1 tons of Belgian gold) ($106.6 million). According to the same State Department report, however, only the 20.1 tons of looted Belgian gold had been purchased by Portugal directly from German accounts in Switzerland; the other 74.7 tons of gold ($84 million) had been sold to Portugal by Switzerland, which had previously purchased it from Germany. Portugal did not respond to Allied requests for information on its secret gold transactions.

Negotiations with Portugal for the restoration of looted gold and the disposition of German external assets began in September 1946 and eventually stretched into the late 1950s. The talks were held away from Washington and by the late 1940s were conducted on the Allied side by diplomatic representatives assigned to the Embassies in Lisbon. Allied investigators estimated that there were $36.8 million in German assets in Portugal at War's end, although this figure was considered tentative. They demanded that the assets be liquidated and the proceeds delivered to them as reparations to help war refugees and rebuild Europe. In February 1947 the two sides agreed on a division of the proceeds from liquidation, giving the first $4 million to the International Refugee Organization, $9.2 million to Portugal for its own wartime claims against Germany, and the remainder to the Allies as reparations. Portugal refused to implement the plan until the two sides could reach agreement on the restitution of looted gold, but the plan's terms became the basis for all subsequent negotiations.

While the Allies had evidence that Portugal acquired a significant amount of looted gold through private sources and smuggling, they agreed to form a joint investigative committee with Portugal to review only records at the Bank of Portugal in order to resolve the dispute over gold. The Portuguese investigators, however, dragged out the work of the committee and refused to allow their Allied counterparts to review the Bank's actual records. Based on this limited investigation, the Allies concluded that Portugal had received between 38.45 and 43.95 tons ($43.349.4 million) of looted gold. The Allied investigators could not trace the origins of about 8.3 tons of gold ($9.3 million); no effort was made to determine if it was non-monetary gold stolen from the Nazis' victims. In November 1947 the Allies demanded that 38.331 tons ($43.1 million) be returned to its original owners. The Portuguese, however, contested all but 3.9 tons ($4.5 million), claiming they had purchased all the gold in a "good faith" belief that the Germans had not looted it. Consequently they refused to relinquish any without compensation.

In 1949 the Portuguese agreed to begin liquidating German assets and keep the proceeds in a blocked account while the gold negotiations continued. As the negotiations dragged into the 1950s, the value of the German assets depreciated and the liquidation process was slowed by complex procedures and Portuguese delays. The Allies had lost some negotiating leverage with Portugal when the United States unblocked Portuguese assets in the United States in August 1948. The U.S. Joint Chiefs of Staff also feared that the impasse might jeopardize what it considered the more important strategic goals of continued U.S. access to air bases on the Azores, talks on which had resumed as early as June 1947, and integrating Portugal into postwar Western Europe, goals which would be secured by membership in NATO.

The negotiations were further complicated by the Allies' efforts to integrate West Germany into the Western alliance, which raised difficult issues over how Germany would honor reparations commitments made by the Allies after the War and handle Portuguese claims for wartime damages. Consequently, by July 1951, the State Department recommended accepting a Portuguese offer from July 1948 to turn over to the Tripartite Gold Commission 3.9 tons of Dutch gold for which Portugal would be fully reimbursed out of the proceeds of liquidation.

Intermittent negotiations continued for several years as Portugal demanded that West Germany be brought into the negotiations. In the interim, the United States, Britain, and France fulfilled Portugal's contribution to the $25 million Reparations Fund out of their portion of Switzerland's payments in implementation of its agreement with the Allies. (Portugal did not repay the Allies specifically for the Allies' payment to the Reparations Fund on its behalf.) Finally, in October 1958 the United States, Britain, France, Portugal, and West Germany reached an agreement, and in December 1959 Portugal delivered $552,000 to the Allies and 3.998 tons of gold ($4.5 million) to the Tripartite Gold Commission. In addition, Germany paid Portugal about $13.7 million to reimburse it for the gold and to cover its wartime damage claims, for which Germany received still-unliquidated German assets in Portugal.

Allied Relations and Negotiations with Spain

Although Spanish General Franciso Franco declared Spain neutral in 1939, he was openly sympathetic to the Axis powers, which helped bring him to power, and only gradually abandoned his inclination to join the Axis. Spain supplied Germany with critical commodities, intelligence, and even some troops—the Blue Division—for the Eastern Front. By 1943, however, Spain had gradually adopted a more honestly neutral policy, largely in response to Allied economic warfare, the growing strength of Allied armed forces especially in North Africa and the Mediterranean, and the reversals experienced by Germany from 1942 onward. Nonetheless, Spain's strategic location and its supply routes to North Africa and South America gave Germany a conduit for important wartime materials, which Franco continued to supply. Private Spanish merchants were also Germany's principal source of vital commodities smuggled from Latin America and Africa, including industrial diamonds and platinum.

Wolfram was a major component of Spanish exports to Germany. As the second largest producer of this critical commodity (after Portugal), Spain sold Germany over 1,100 metric tons annually between 1941 and 1943, providing more than 30 percent of Germany's industrial requirements, and which, when combined with Portuguese sales to Germany, accounted for at least 90 percent of Germany's wartime wolframs needs, which the Allies estimated to be 3,500 tons annually. Allied economic warfare efforts against Spain were generally unsuccessful in the early years of the War. The Allied objective was to purchase enough of the ore to satisfy Spain's export demands and prevent it from increasing its trade with the enemy. The Franco regime combined desultory trade negotiations with the Allies and secret agreements with Germany to ensure the continued delivery of critical war supplies. In January 1944 the Spanish Minister for Industry and Commerce defended Spain's agreements with Germany, noting that Spain felt it "impossible" to deny Germany a commodity which "had a very high value in wartime." The Allies hesitated to act decisively against Spain for fear of driving Franco more fully into the Axis camp, but in January 1944 the Allies imposed an oil embargo on Spain.

In negotiations with Spain during the embargo, Britain favored a compromise that would allow Spain to resume wolfram exports to Germany at the 1943 level, but the United States continued to demand a complete ban. Finally in May 1944, as Germany's defeat became more certain, Spain agreed to limit exports of wolfram to Germany. Secretary of State Cordell Hull believed that if he had had "wholehearted British support," he would have achieved the objective of a complete ban on Portuguese wolfram exports to Germany. The Allies soon learned that senior members of Franco's Cabinet cooperated with Germany in smuggling more than 800 tons through July 1944 in violation of the agreement. Spain's exports of wolfram to Nazi Germany ended with the closing of the Franco-Spanish border in August 1944.

The American-led Safehaven program encountered resistance in the U.S. Embassy in Madrid. Intelligence operations to gain information about Spain's wartime support for Germany were undermined as U.S. Ambassador Carlton Hayes preferred a less aggressive attitude toward Franco and his government. Britain was less interested in the postwar political goals of Safehaven than in negotiating a trade agreement with Spain and ensuring the flow of Spanish goods to Britain in the postwar period.

In May 1945, just before V-E Day, in response to an Allied request, Spain issued a decree freezing all assets with Axis interests. The Allies estimated German external assets in Spain at the end of the War at about $95 million. American experts using some captured German documents conservatively estimated in 1946 that between February 1942 and May 1945 Spain acquired about 123 tons of gold worth nearly $140 million (over $1.2 billion in today's values): 11 tons directly from Germany and German-occupied territories, 74 tons from the German account at the Swiss National Bank, and about 38 tons directly from the Swiss National Bank, which the Allies believed included some looted gold (about $376 million in today's values). U.S. estimates indicated that 72 percent of the gold, worth approximately $100 million, acquired by Spain had been looted by Germany from the nations it occupied. Other reports of Spanish gold acquisitions included an SSU intelligence report that trucking gold from Switzerland to Spain became necessary by late 1942 because Germany could not pay for Spanish goods in any other manner; a War Department report that 203 tons of German gold were trucked from Switzerland to the Spanish Foreign Exchange Institute between January 1942 and February 1944; and a German diplomatic report that SOFINDUS, a large German State-owned enterprise in Spain, acquired about 83 tons of gold bars from Switzerland in 1943.

Protracted postwar Allied negotiations with Spain over the restitution of monetary gold and the application of external German assets for reparations began in Madrid in September 1946. The Allied-Spanish negotiations were more intermittent and lengthier than the Allied-Swiss and Allied-Swedish negotiations which had preceded them. In October 1946 Spain agreed to turn over to the Allies an estimated $25 million in official and semi-official German assets. In January 1948 Spain insisted on separating the negotiations over assets and gold, declaring that it would restitute any looted gold but would not sign an agreement that did not include a reciprocal claim for Spain's lost Civil War gold. The two sides agreed in May to a complex formula for liquidating private German assets (then estimated at $20-23 million) in which Spain would get about 24 percent and the Inter-Allied Reparations Agency about 76 percent of the proceeds. None of the proceeds was slated for the $25 million fund for non-repatriable victims of Nazism, as envisioned in the January 1946 Allied Reparations Agreement, because the Allied negotiators believed the fund would be fully subscribed by the amounts obtained from Switzerland, Sweden, and Portugal.

The two sides signed a separate agreement in May 1948 that Spain would return $114,329 (101.6 kilograms) out of about $30 million in looted Dutch gold that the Allies had identified at the Spanish Foreign Exchange Institute and be allowed to keep the remainder. This portion was the only gold that Spain had purchased directly from the Banco Aleman Transatlantico, a German institution, and the Allies claimed that under the terms of Bretton Woods Resolution VI only the original purchaser of the gold from Germany was liable for its return. The Allies publicly acknowledged that Spain had not been aware at the time it acquired the gold that it had been looted. In addition to the 101.6 kilograms of looted gold, Spain turned over to the Allies $1.3 million in gold bars and coins it had seized from German State properties at the end of the War.

The Allied-Spanish negotiations coincided with Allied efforts to ostracize the Franco regime. The Allies explored ways short of direct intervention to end the Franco regime and allow the Spanish people to choose freely a new government. During these years Spain was excluded from the United Nations, pending a UN review of wartime Spanish support for the Axis, as well as from the emerging Western Alliance, and most governments around the world downgraded their diplomatic relations with the Franco regime. Economic sanctions against Spain were under consideration but were ultimately excluded by the Allies for fear of exacerbating tensions that could bring about another civil war or allow Communism to gain a foothold in Spain. By 1948 the United States had concluded that these attempts at isolating Spain were counterproductive and were detrimental to the Spanish economy. As a result, with the signing of the May 1948 agreements, the United States released over $64 million in assets frozen since the War and informed Spain that it would allow it to use its remaining gold as collateral for private loans.

In 1950 the Federal Reserve Bank of New York held $50 million worth of gold as collateral for loans by Chase National Bank of New York (now Chase

Manhattan) and National City Bank (now Citibank) to the Spanish Foreign Exchange Institute. Part of the collateral consisted of looted gold Spain had purchased from Switzerland and Portugal during the War. Both the State Department and the Treasury Department ruled that, pursuant to postwar Allied restitution policy, the gold was considered "tainted only in the hands of the first purchaser." Thus Switzerland (not Spain) was held legally responsible for providing this quantity of gold to the TGC. At the request of Citibank, the looted gold Spain used to collateralize its loan was resmelted into "good delivery" bars by the U.S. Assay Office. In 1951 Spain collateralized a $10 million dollar extension of one of the loans using gold, including $2.6 million in looted gold that it had bought directly from the German account at the Swiss National Bank and had never revealed to the Allies. Both Treasury and State allowed the Federal Reserve to accept the looted bars, arguing that since Spain had negotiated the May 1948 Allied-Spanish accord on looted gold "in good faith" they would not consider them looted.

In 1951 Spain halted the distribution of German assets in an effort to garner a larger percentage and gain West Germany's assurance that it would not hold Spain responsible for compensating German owners of liquidated property. Intermittent negotiations continued until 1957, when Spain agreed to turn unliquidated assets over to Germany and Germany agreed not to hold Spain liable for compensation. This opened the way for an Allied-Spanish agreement in which Spain turned over the money it had blocked since 1951 in exchange for $1 million liquidated after that date. The total value of funds derived from German assets in Spain and disbursed by the IARA amounted to about $32.8 million, taking into consideration the fluctuation of the value of the peseta in the 1950s as a result of Spain's severe economic problems, stemming from the devastation of the Spanish Civil War and World War II. Altogether Spain received at least $5.3 million in liquidation proceeds.

By 1950 the Allies joined the U.S. effort to normalize relations with Spain, and the assets negotiations were subordinated to efforts to integrate Spain into the Western economic and military framework and provide Spain with substantial economic and military assistance—even though it was to remain formally outside the Western Alliance until its accession to NATO and the European Community in the post-Franco 1980s.

Allied Relations and Negotiations with Sweden

Sweden's neutrality in World War II was maintained at some cost to its independence and through considerable economic and military concessions to Nazi Germany. The Swedish Government sought to balance these accommodations by retaining, as best as its diplomats could manage, Sweden's traditional political and economic ties with the Western democracies. The British and, within the U.S. Government, the State Department and the President were inclined to sympathize with Sweden's plight (surrounded as it was by Axis powers or occupied countries) and understand its cautious relationship with Germany. There was considerable concern among the Allies, however, that Sweden went too far in accommodating the Nazi regime. U.S. and

British economic warfare experts generally felt that the German war effort depended on Swedish iron ore and ball-bearings and Soviet oil, and that without these materials, the War would come to a halt. Not only was the quantity of iron ore important, but the high quality of the Swedish ore made steel making more efficient, and the use of Swedish ships for transport eased delivery problems for Germany.

The Allied blockade of Europe and Germany's counter blockade of the waterway into the Baltic prevented all but the minimum of critical items like oil reaching Sweden from the West. Allied diplomacy through much of the War aimed at curtailing Swedish exports to Germany and reducing Sweden's more practical assistance to Germany's military operations on the northern front. Although these efforts did not, in the end, significantly constrain the German war industry in 1943 and 1944, an Allied-Swedish trade agreement of September 1943 did eventually bring about a progressive, substantial curtailment of Swedish commerce with Germany. Under the agreement, the United States and Britain agreed to allow an increase in exports to Sweden, including oil and rubber, in exchange for which Sweden agreed to cancel the transit of German military materiel and troops across Sweden, further reduce iron ore exports, end Swedish naval escorting of German sips in the Baltic, and reduce ball-bearing exports. The unremitting Allied diplomatic pressure and the crumbling of the Nazi war effort moved Sweden gradually to reduce and ultimately to end its trade with Germany. All Swedish trade with Germany halted completely in November 1944.

The U.S. military particularly deplored Sweden's continued critically important exports of iron ore and ball-bearings to Germany and its tolerance for the transit of German soldiers and war materials across Sweden and through the Baltic under Swedish naval protection. During the last half of 1943 and the early months of 1944, the United States sought to cripple Germany's ability to continue the War by carrying out a concentrated and costly bombing campaign against ball-bearing production in Germany combined with trade negotiations, including preclusive purchasing arrangements, intended to cut off Swedish ball-bearings to Germany. The U.S. bombing campaign reduced German ball-bearing production, but German industrial countermeasures and improvisations warded off any serious consequences. Moreover, the September 1943 agreement, which halted exports of ball-bearings, neglected to impose restrictions on exports of high-quality steel used to manufacture ball-bearings and appears to have allowed Sweden to provide Germany with ball-bearing steel, largely offsetting the drop in the Swedish export of finished ball-bearings. These efforts did not, therefore, significantly constrain the German war industry in 1943 and 1944.

After the tide of battle on the eastern front had irreversibly shifted following German defeats at Stalingrad and Kursk in the winter and summer of 1943, the Soviet Union took the lead in suggesting a more active role for Sweden in the War, such as the establishment of Allied air bases in Sweden. This idea was taken up at the Moscow Conference of Foreign Ministers in October 1943 and by Roosevelt, Stalin, and Churchill at the Tehran Conference in

November 1943. Although the Allies did not decide to call on Sweden to declare war on Germany, Churchill believed that the War might be brought to an early end if Sweden and Turkey entered it on the Allied side in order to confront Hitler on additional fronts.

With the end of the War, Sweden demonstrated a ready willingness to cooperate with the Allies' Safehaven program. The Swedish Government's Foreign Capital Control Office, which had adopted tightened exchange control regulations in November 1944, made great progress in identifying German properties and eliminating German influences from Sweden's economy. Allied estimates of looted gold sold to Sweden by Germany ranged between $18.5 million and $22.7 million. In March 1946 British, French, and U.S. officials met to discuss Swedish gold movements during the War. They concluded that the Swedish gold reserves had increased but were unable to determine if this was due to looted gold. In at least one instance, the Germans had attempted to sell gold looted from Belgium to Sweden, but the Swedes had apparently refused to buy.

Even before the postwar negotiations began with Sweden for the restitution of looted gold and the liquidation and application of external German assets to war reparations in Europe, the Allies found themselves at an important disadvantage. Sweden would not agree that the Allies could claim or dispose of German assets and property outside Germany, and the Allies could not agree to the use of economic sanctions against Sweden should negotiations over restitution and assets break down. In place of legal arguments based on Allied assumption of supreme authority in Germany, the negotiators cited the desperate plight of a devastated Europe and appealed to Swedish compassion. Negotiations in Washington moved swiftly from the start of their talks in late May 1946 until agreement was reached in early July. Sweden undertook to distribute more than $66 million in liquidated German assets as reparations, including a special $36 million fund at the Riksbank to forestall disease and unrest in Germany and to finance purchases essential for the German economy. It also agreed to restitute more than $8 million in gold to make up for that amount of Belgian monetary gold sold to Sweden during the War. Allied-Swedish negotiations regarding 8.6 kilograms of Dutch gold ($9.7 million), which began after the July 1946 accord, dragged on until 1955, with the Swedish negotiators arguing that the gold had been acquired before the January 1943 London Declaration on looted gold. In April 1955, after Swedish and Dutch officials met in Washington and the Dutch claim was proved conclusive, Sweden transferred about $6.8 million in gold to the TGC.

The U.S. negotiators informed Under Secretary of State for Economic Affairs Will Clayton that the July 1946 accord with Sweden was generally quite successful. The negotiations had none of the bitterness of the Swiss negotiations and resulted in the achievement of American Safehaven objectives. The agreement called for a 73-27 split in German external assets, which was an improvement over the 50-50 split of such assets with Switzerland. Within the State Department, critics acknowledged that the accord was better than that with Switzerland and as good as could have been expected in the absence of a willingness to resort to economic sanctions. The critics believed it was defective, however, because of its complexity (it consisted of 30 separate undertakings), because it reflected Sweden's rejection of the Allied assumption of supreme legal authority over German assets outside Germany and made Sweden's allocations of assets "voluntary contributions," and because its allocation of part of the liquidation proceeds to a fund for Germany to purchase essential commodities was more accurately a measure to benefit the Swedish economy.

The July 1946 Allied-Swedish accord proved to be as complicated as its critics warned, and its implementation stretched over the next eight years. Although Sweden was prompt in providing more than $12 million to the Intergovernmental Committee for Refugees for the succor of the non-repatriable victims of Nazism and $36 million was used in Sweden and elsewhere for essential commodities for occupied Germany, Swedish negotiators haggled with the Allies and the Inter-Allied Reparations Agency until 1955 over how to distribute the remaining $18 million for reparations. The promised payment of $8 million in gold to the Tripartite Gold Commission was delayed by Sweden until December 1949. Another $10 million in gold claimed by the Netherlands was not turned over to the TGC until 1955.

Allied Relations and Negotiations with Turkey

Turkey began World War II bound to Britain and France by the military alliance of October 1939, moved to non-belligerency in June 1940 after the fail of France, and adopted a policy of "active neutrality" in the spring of 1941 after German occupation of the Balkans and the conclusion of a German-Turkish Treaty of Friendship in June 1941. During most of the War, Turkey sough to balance the needs and expectations of Germany and the Axis on the one hand, and those of Britain and the United States on the other. Turkey took no overt action against Germany, which strictly observed Turkey's territorial integrity, and carried on extensive commerce with Germany, particularly the export of critical chromite ore for the Nazi war effort. American experts evaluated chromite ore, which could be converted to chromium, as one of the few raw materials that were essential for the German war industry and for which there were no adequate sources within German territory.

In October 1941 Germany concluded an important trade agreement with Turkey that provided for an exchange of Turkish raw materials, especially chromite ore, for German war materiel, together with iron and steel products and other manufactured goods, in order to draw Turkey further into the Axis orbit. At the same time, Turkey maintained its friendly relations with Britain and the United States, which provided Turkey with modern military equipment to upgrade its obsolete and ineffective armed forces, and both Allies sought to minimize the effect of Turkey's exports to Germany by preclusively buying its products, particularly chromite.

The United States and Britain began providing Lend-Lease military equipment to Turkey in 1941. Initially such aid was intended to maintain British influence with Turkey and keep it neutral. As the War progressed, much of the

Lend-Lease military aid was in fact from the United States, although it was American policy to defer somewhat to Britain on Turkey and maintain British influence there. At their January 1943 Conference at Casablanca, President Roosevelt and Prime Minister Churchill considered seeking to bring Turkey into the War, and Britain was assigned the lead in negotiating Turkey's move toward belligerency. The Soviet Union urged the immediate entry of Turkey into the War during the October Tripartite Foreign Ministers Conference in Moscow in October 1943, and in November 1943 at the Tehran Conference. Roosevelt, Churchill, and Stalin called for Turkey's entry into the War by the end of the year. Allied military experts foresaw no likely threat to Turkey from Germany in the last months of 1943 or any time in 1944, but they judged that Turkish intervention in the War could provoke German retaliation. During 1943 and into 1944, Turkey continued to receive British-U.S. military assistance but resisted entry into the War. When Turkish leaders made their nation's entry into the War contingent upon massive military assistance and a significant Allied military presence, Britain and the United States in February 1944 abandoned their aid program to Turkey.

After Turkey concluded the trade agreement with Germany in October 1941, which provided for major quantities of German military equipment in exchange for a significant portion of Turkish exports, especially chromite ore, the Allies undertook to redirect Turkey's German-oriented commerce, A preclusive purchasing program, in which the U.S. Commercial Corporation had the pre-eminent role but Britain look the lead, aimed particularly at preventing Turkish chromite exports going to Germany. President Roosevelt's proposed warning to Turkey in March 1944 that its chromite exports were keeping Germany in the War confirmed German Munitions Minister Albert Speer's assessment of November 1943 that much of Germany's manufacture of armaments would come to a halt within 10 months if Turkey's chromite exports to Germany were ended. British-U.S. pressure, persuasion, and preclusive purchasing did not succeed until early 1944 when it was supplemented by threats to apply to Turkey the same economic warfare measures earlier used against other neutrals. Turkey halted the export of chromite to Germany in April 1944 and suspended all commercial and diplomatic relations with Germany in August 1944. Turkey finally declared war on Germany in late February 1945 on the eve of the convening of the San Francisco Conference establishing the United Nations.

U.S. experts estimated that Turkey, while not a major recipient of gold from Germany during World War II, received as much as $10 to $15 million in gold, much of it probably for its chromite exports. After the War $3.4 million in Belgian monetary gold looted by Germany was traced to Turkey. In addition, two German banks with branches in Istanbul, the Deutsche Bank and the Dresdner Bank, took advantage of the high prices on the Turkish free gold market to sell looted gold provided by the Reichsbank in return for foreign currency, particularly Swiss francs. Some of the gold provided by the Reichsbank came from the infamous "Melmer account" in which the SS deposited the gold jewelry, coins, bars, and dental fillings robbed from its victims at the killing centers and concentration camps. Profits from the banks' Turkish gold trade were used to finance not only Germany's diplomatic, espionage, and propaganda activities in Turkey, but also the operations of various other Axis and "Axis friendly" Legations. Other German gold acquired by Turkey during and after the War included coins and ingots from the account of German Foreign Minister Joachim Ribbentrop at the Reichsbank, which had been stocked with gold looted from occupied Europe.

Turkey's last-minute shift from the status of a wartime neutral to that of an ally vitiated Allied efforts to gain Turkish support for the Safehaven program to locate German external assets and prevent their use for a Nazi resurgence. Within the U.S. Government, the State Department favored a less stringent approach toward Turkey regarding Safehaven than did the Treasury Department—a recurring pattern with respect to Safehaven and immediate postwar restitution objectives. The British and U.S. Ambassadors in Istanbul argued against treating Turkey as anything but an ally when it came to searching for looted gold. This position was persuasive in Washington, and the United States subsequently dropped any plans to request Turkey to provide detailed information about its gold supply.

The Allies conducted formal negotiations with Turkey over the restitution of looted monetary gold and the application of liquidated German external assets to the reconstruction of Europe. Allied experts estimated total German assets in Turkey at over $51 million in 1945 and possibly as much as $71 million in 1946. Turkey was willing to discuss assets with the Allies but insisted that they be applied to the settlement of Turkish war claims against Germany before the remainder might be shared with the Allies.

The Allied efforts to obtain agreements with Turkey in 1946 for the restitution of gold and return of German external assets were never pressed with vigor and were overshadowed by a major change in relations between and among the Allies and with Turkey. Although State Department policy papers identified no important U.S. national interests in Turkey as late as mid-1945, during the following year, in the wake of threatening Soviet gestures toward the Dardanelles and the Soviet-Turkish border, the United States quickly came to see Turkey as a cornerstone of the emerging Western strategy of containment. The enunciation of the Truman Doctrine in March 1947 to include not only Greece but also Turkey was followed in July by the signing of an aid agreement with Turkey worth $150 million.

The U.S.-Turkish aid agreement of July 1947 doomed negotiations with Turkey over gold and assets. In that month Turkey was willing to return more than $3.4 million in gold, but was unwilling to accept further Allied demands for information. Eventually Turkey failed to return any monetary gold; nor did any proceeds from liquidated German external assets ever reach the Allies. The status of Turkey as an ally rather than a neutral threw the negotiations off the course that the United States had envisioned at the outset. By 1953 the Allies abandoned further efforts to obtain from Turkey the restitution of gold or the application of external assets to the victims of Nazi Germany. In contrast to other wartime neutral nations, Turkey, an 11th hour ally, returned no looted gold to the Tripartite Gold Commission, and turned over no money either to the International Refugee Organization for the support of refugees or to the Inter-Allied Reparations Agency for reparations.

The Fate of the Wartime Ustasha Treasury

The so-called independent state of Croatia, established on April 10, 1941, as part of the German conquest and dismemberment of the Kingdom of Yugoslavia, was denounced by the U.S. Government. Throughout World War II, it was U.S. policy to avoid any action that might imply acknowledgment of the Croatian protectorate, and to support the guerrilla forces seeking to overthrow the German-backed regime.

The Fascist Ustasha political movement in power in wartime Croatia carried out a murderous campaign aimed at Serbs, Jews, and others. As many as 700,000 victims, mostly Serbs, may have died in the camps. The Ustasha Croat campaign started with the internment of 35,000 to 40,000 Croatian Jews in the spring and summer of 1941, followed by the deportation of remaining Jews to Germany in 1942 and 1943. Only a few thousand Croatian Jews escaped after first finding temporary sanctuary in the Italian portion of the Croatian protectorate.

The Ustasha regime in Croatia accumulated a treasury that apparently included valuables stolen from the dispossessed and deported Jewish and Sinti-Romani victims of the ethnic cleansing campaign. A variety of wartime and postwar U.S. intelligence reports confirm a Ustasha regime treasury of some size, but no authoritative quantification proved possible. Nor was it ever clear how much came from Croatian Jewish victims—although one U.S. intelligence report speculated that it might be as much as $80 million in gold, mostly coins. Official and postwar information does confirm that the Croatian regime transferred gold to Switzerland toward the end of the War, and at least 980 kilograms of gold (worth about $1 million), taken by the Croat officials from the Sarajevo branch of the Yugoslav National Bank in 1941, was transferred to the Swiss National Bank in 1944. In July 1945 the Swiss National Bank returned the gold to the new Yugoslav Government.

After the Ustasha regime collapsed at the end of the War, its leader, Ante Pavelic, and some companions fled to the British zone of occupation of Austria from where, according to intelligence reports, he escaped or was released after surrendering some or all of a quantity of gold he had brought from Croatia. Intelligence reports vary widely in the amount of gold Pavelic brought— $600,000, $5-$6 million, or even $35 million. None of the information on the amount or makeup of the gold Pavelic was carrying or turned over to the British, some of which has the quality of legend, has been confirmed. What is known is that no gold was reported by British authorities to have been recovered, and none was turned over to the Tripartite Gold Commission for restitution. Pavelic made his way to Rome, where he arrived in early 1946.

U.S. and British intelligence reports agree that the College of San Girolamo degli Illirici in Rome served as a place of refuge and support for the Croatian refugees. San Girolamo, which is located outside the walls of the Vatican and pays Italian State taxes, provided living quarters for Croatian priests studying at the Vatican. After the War, it was the reported center of an extensive and effective underground that assisted Ustasha fugitives, including Ante Pavelic, to flee from Europe to South America. Pavelic hid in Rome at various locations from 1946 until his flight to Argentina in November 1948 without any decisive action by the U.S. or British authorities to apprehend him and make him available for a war crimes trial.

A prime mover of the Ustasha activity in Rome was Father Krunoslav Dragonovic, secretary of the College of San Girolamo. Taking advantage of his contacts inside the International Red Cross, Dragonovic helped Ustasha fugitives emigrate illegally to South America by providing temporary shelter and false identity documents, and by arranging onward transport, primarily to Argentina. In the late 1940s and early 1950s, the U.S. Army Counter Intelligence Corps and the Ustashi collaborated in running a "rat line," an escape route for defectors or informants who had come to Austria from the Soviet zone of Germany or from Soviet bloc countries. In 1951 the anti-Communist informer and Nazi war criminal Klaus Barbie escaped to South America over the rat line. Some intelligence reports indicate that gold from the Ustasha treasury may have been used to finance the postwar underground activities involving Father Dragonovic at San Girolamo. There is no evidence in U.S. archives that the Vatican leadership knew of or gave support to the Ustasha activities outside its walls, but, given the location of the College, troubling questions remain.

The postwar fate of Croatian Ustasha fugitives, with or without portions of their wartime treasury, depended to a significant extent upon U.S. as well as British policies regarding Croatian Ustasha war criminals and escapees. In the first postwar months, U.S. and British policy was to turn over to the new Yugoslav Government of Marshal Tito anyone for whom the Yugoslavs could make a prima facie case of collaboration with the Nazis. This policy began to change in 1946 as the prisoner of war camps emptied. The standards for turning over Croatian prisoners of war steadily rose, and few were returned to Yugoslavia by late 1946. By May 1947 the U.S. Government became convinced that the Yugoslav Government was meting out unduly harsh treatment to its political enemies and perverting justice. U.S.-Yugoslav relations had cooled as a result of the Yugoslav regime's hostile actions, including harassment of U.S. Embassy personnel and accusations of espionage, the arrest and trial of Yugoslav employees of the Embassy on charges of espionage, attacks on unarmed U.S. aircraft over Yugoslavia, Yugoslav efforts to annex Trieste, and Yugoslav unwillingness to settle outstanding claims of American citizens for confiscated property. In addition, the U.S. and British intelligence services were relying increasingly on former Ustashi as sources of information and were consequently reluctant to antagonize these informants by extraditing their leaders to Yugoslavia. As a result, the policy of surrendering Ustashi was ended—a policy with which the British concurred. Even when the Allies learned the precise location of Ante Pavelic, the leader of the murderous Ustashi regime, they refrained from taking any action to bring him to justice.

U.S. official records provide only an imperfect understanding of the fate of the Croatian Ustasha treasury and the uses to which it may have been put. Evidence presented by the Croatian delegation to the December 1997 London Conference on Nazi Gold gives encouragement that more can be learned from Croatian sources. The bizarre circumstances attending the movement of Croatian State gold to Switzerland during the War and the flight of Ustasha leaders to Austria at War's end as well as the underground activities of Ustasha priests in Rome give rise to the hope that more information on the fate of Croatian Ustasha gold, including any possible victim gold, may come from the records of the Swiss National Bank and the British occupation forces and intelligence organizations, as well as from the archives of the Vatican and the Croatian State Archives.

CALIFORNIA INITIATIVE
ON BILINGUAL EDUCATION
June 2, 1998

California voters on June 2 ended the state's three-decade experiment with bilingual education. Voters overwhelmingly approved a ballot initiative, Proposition 227, ordering public schools to teach classes in English. The initiative, which took effect at the opening of the 1998–1999 school year, allowed non–English-proficient students—the vast majority of whom were Hispanic—to take only one year of classes in their native languages before transferring to English-only instruction.

Proposition 227 was the most important manifestation of growing dissatisfaction around the country with bilingual education, a process that gave students instruction in their native languages before moving to classes in English. Critics, including sponsors of Proposition 227, said bilingual education failed tens of thousands of students who never became proficient in English because they spent years taking classes in their native languages.

Bilingual Education

Beginning in the 1960s, educators and politicians prescribed bilingual education as the best way of aiding the educational progress of non–English-speaking students. The theory was that children of immigrants would take classes in their native languages at the same time they were learning English; after a few years, these students would be proficient enough in English to move into all-English classrooms.

The movement for bilingual education received its most important boost in 1974, when the U.S. Supreme Court ruled in Lau v. Nichols *that schools needed to give special help to students who did not speak English. The Court offered no specific education plan, leaving it up to each state to design a curriculum to help its non–English-speaking students. As of 1998 eleven states, including California, mandated the availability of bilingual education; most other states allowed individual school districts to offer bilingual programs. The federal government offered limited funding for bilingual education programs.*

California became the proving ground for bilingual education—and its programs became the biggest and most important in the nation—simply because the state had more immigrant children than any other. By 1998 there were an estimated 1.4 million school children in California who were not proficient in English—nearly half of all such students in the United States. The overwhelming majority of non–English-speaking students, both in California and nationally, were Hispanic.

As with many experimental educational programs, bilingual education spawned fierce emotions, both pro and con. Supporters insisted that bilingual education gave non–English-speaking children an opportunity for advancement they would never receive in English-only schools. Supporters acknowledged that many bilingual programs failed to provide adequate education, but insisted that was because most school districts never adequately funded or supported the effort. In fact, supporters said, the majority of Hispanic students were not enrolled in bilingual education classes because there were not enough classes for them.

Opponents noted that many students spent years in bilingual programs before transferring to English classes, and that despite bilingual education the national drop-out rate for Hispanic immigrant students was nearly four times that for blacks and more than five times that for whites. Critics also complained that bilingual education substantially increased costs; for example, to attract bilingual teachers California and other states paid them bonuses, often several thousand dollars a year.

The California Vote

Proposition 227 was developed by Ronald K. Unz, a wealthy software developer from the Silicon Valley, north of San Jose. Unz said he was responding to concerns of Mexican-Americans who did not want their children forced into bilingual education classes. Unz helped finance a grassroots campaign on behalf of Proposition 227. Chief opponents of the proposition were civil rights and education groups. The opponents were joined by all four Democratic and Republican candidates for governor in the June 2 primary, including the eventual winner of the gubernatorial election, Democrat Gray Davis, and most of the state's major newspaper editorial pages.

Declaring that English "is the national public language of the United States of America" and California, Proposition 227 said all California public school children "shall be taught in English as rapidly and effectively as possible." The proposition essentially abolished California's established system of bilingual education. In its place, Proposition 227 allowed school districts to set up "sheltered English immersion" classes, in which the curriculum was designed for students who were just learning English. Under normal circumstances, students could be assigned to these "sheltered English immersion" classes for no more than one school year before moving to English-only classes. Proposition 227 allowed parents, under very limited circumstances, to petition schools for bilingual education for their children.

California voters gave Proposition 227 overwhelming support, adopting it by a statewide margin of 69 percent to 31 percent. According to exit polls, the proposition was endorsed by two-thirds of white voters, 57 percent of Asian-American voters, 48 percent of black voters, and 37 percent of Hispanic voters. Public opinion polls conducted before the vote had estimated that nearly half of Hispanics—presumably the primary beneficiaries of bilingual education—would support Proposition 227.

Immediately after the outcome of the vote was announced, a coalition of civil rights and education groups filed suit in federal court to block implementation of Proposition 227, charging that it discriminated against Hispanics and other minorities. U.S. District Court Judge Charles Legge, in San Francisco, rejected that challenge on July 15, effectively allowing Proposition 227 to go into effect at the beginning of the 1998–1999 school year under regulations adopted by the state board of education.

Also in 1998, school boards in Chicago and Denver voted to limit students to a maximum of three years in bilingual education programs. Several other districts around the country, however, acted to expand bilingual education programs, often by introducing native-language programs for kindergarten students. Support for bilingual programs remained strong among many leading educators. Rudy Crew, chancellor of the New York City school district, the nation's biggest, told the New York Times *that bilingual education "should be strengthened," not abandoned.*

House Bill

The success of Proposition 227 gave encouragement to conservatives in the U.S. House of Representatives who sought to reduce federal involvement in bilingual education. Led by California Republican Frank Riggs, conservatives pushed legislation (HR 3892) converting all federal bilingual education funding into block grants administered by the states. The bill imposed two conditions intended to restrict state options on bilingual education: students could attend bilingual programs supported by federal funds for no more than three years, and 90 percent of federal grants would have to be spent on English-language programs.

Over the opposition of the Clinton administration, the House passed HR 3892 on September 10 by a 221–189 vote, with all but ten Republicans supporting the measure and all but fourteen Democrats opposing it. The Senate gave the issue no serious consideration during 1998.

Following is the text of Proposition 227, adopted June 2, 1998, by the voters of California, limiting bilingual education in that state:

PROPOSED LAW

SECTION 1. Chapter 3 (commencing with Section 300) is added to Part 1 of the Education Code, to read:

Chapter 3. English Language Education for Immigrant Children

Article 1. Findings and Declarations

300. The People of California find and declare as follows:

(a) Whereas, The English language is the national public language of the United States of America and of the State of California, is spoken by the vast majority of California residents, and is also the leading world language for science, technology, and international business, thereby being the language of economic opportunity; and

(b) Whereas, Immigrant parents are eager to have their children acquire a good knowledge of English, thereby allowing them to fully participate in the American Dream of economic and social advancement; and

(c) Whereas, The government and the public schools of California have a moral obligation and a constitutional duty to provide all of California's children, regardless of their ethnicity or national origins, with the skills necessary to become productive members of our society, and of these skills, literacy in the English language is among the most important; and

(d) Whereas, The public schools of California currently do a poor job of educating immigrant children, wasting financial resources on costly experimental language programs whose failure over the past two decades is demonstrated by the current high drop-out rates and low English literacy levels of many immigrant children; and

(e) Whereas, Young immigrant children can easily acquire full fluency in a new language, such as English, if they are heavily exposed to that language in the classroom at an early age.

(f) Therefore, It is resolved that: all children in California public schools shall be taught English as rapidly and effectively as possible.

Article 2. English Language Education

305. Subject to the exceptions provided in Article 3 (commencing with Section 310), all children in California public schools shall be taught English by being taught in English. In particular, this shall require that all children be placed in English language classrooms. Children who are English learners shall be educated through sheltered English immersion during a temporary transition period not normally intended to exceed one year. Local schools shall be permitted to place in the same classroom English learners of different ages but whose degree of English proficiency is similar. Local schools shall be encouraged to mix together in the same classroom English learners from different native-language groups but with the same degree of English fluency. Once English learners have acquired a good working knowledge of English, they shall be transferred to English language mainstream classrooms. As much as possible, current supplemental funding for English learn-

ers shall be maintained, subject to possible modification under Article 8 (commencing with Section 335) below.

306. The definitions of the terms used in this article and in Article 3 (commencing with Section 310) are as follows:

(a) "English learner" means a child who does not speak English or whose native language is not English and who is not currently able to perform ordinary classroom work in English, also known as a Limited English Proficiency or LEP child.

(b) "English language classroom" means a classroom in which the language of instruction used by the teaching personnel is overwhelmingly the English language, and in which such teaching personnel possess a good knowledge of the English language.

(c) "English language mainstream classroom" means a classroom in which the pupils either are native English language speakers or already have acquired reasonable fluency in English.

(d) "Sheltered English immersion" or "structured English immersion" means an English language acquisition process for young children in which nearly all classroom instruction is in English but with the curriculum and presentation designed for children who are learning the language.

(e) "Bilingual education/native language instruction" means a language acquisition process for pupils in which much or all instruction, textbooks, and teaching materials are in the child's native language.

Article 3. Parental Exceptions

310. The requirements of Section 305 may be waived with the prior written informed consent, to be provided annually, of the child's parents or legal guardian under the circumstances specified below and in Section 311. Such informed consent shall require that said parents or legal guardian personally visit the school to apply for the waiver and that they there be provided a full description of the educational materials to be used in the different educational program choices and all the educational opportunities available to the child. Under such parental waiver conditions, children may be transferred to classes where they are taught English and other subjects through bilingual education techniques or other generally recognized educational methodologies permitted by law. Individual schools in which 20 pupils or more of a given grade level receive a waiver shall be required to offer such a class; otherwise, they must allow the pupils to transfer to a public school in which such a class is offered.

311. The circumstances in which a parental exception waiver may be granted under Section 310 are as follows:

(a) Children who already know English: the child already possesses good English language skills, as measured by standardized tests of English vocabulary comprehension, reading, and writing, in which the child scores at or above the state average for his or her grade level or at or above the 5th grade average, whichever is lower; or

(b) Older children: the child is age 10 years or older, and it is the informed belief of the school principal and educational staff that an alternate course of educational study would be better suited to the child's rapid acquisition of basic English language skills; or

(c) Children with special needs: the child already has been placed for a period of not less than thirty days during that school year in an English language classroom and it is subsequently the informed belief of the school principal and educational staff that the child has such special physical, emotional, psychological, or educational needs that an alternate course of educational study would be better suited to the child's overall educational development. A written description of these special needs must be provided and any such decision is to be made subject to the examination and approval of the local school superintendent, under guidelines established by and subject to the review of the local Board of Education and ultimately the State Board of Education. The existence of such special needs shall not compel issuance of a waiver, and the parents shall be fully informed of their right to refuse to agree to a waiver.

Article 4. Community-Based English Tutoring

315. In furtherance of its constitutional and legal requirement to offer special language assistance to children coming from backgrounds of limited English proficiency, the state shall encourage family members and others to provide personal English language tutoring to such children, and support these efforts by raising the general level of English language knowledge in the community. Commencing with the fiscal year in which this initiative is enacted and for each of the nine fiscal years following thereafter, a sum of fifty million dollars ($50,000,000) per year is hereby appropriated from the General Fund for the purpose of providing additional funding for free or subsidized programs of adult English language instruction to parents or other members of the community who pledge to provide personal English language tutoring to California school children with limited English proficiency.

316. Programs funded pursuant to this section shall be provided through schools or community organizations. Funding for these programs shall be administered by the Office of the Superintendent of Public Instruction, and shall be disbursed at the discretion of the local school boards, under reasonable guidelines established by, and subject to the review of, the State Board of Education.

Article 5. Legal Standing and Parental Enforcement

320. As detailed in Article 2 (commencing with Section 305) and Article 3 (commencing with Section 310), all California school children have the right to be provided with an English language public education. If a California school child has been denied the option of an English language instructional curriculum in public school, the child's parent or legal guardian shall have legal standing to sue for enforcement of the provisions of this statute, and if successful shall be awarded normal and customary attorney's fees and actual damages, but not punitive or consequential damages. Any school board member or other elected official or public school teacher or administrator who

willfully and repeatedly refuses to implement the terms of this statute by providing such an English language educational option at an available public school to a California school child may be held personally liable for fees and actual damages by the child's parents or legal guardian.

Article 6. Severability

325. If any part or parts of this statute are found to be in conflict with federal law or the United States or the California State Constitution, the statute shall be implemented to the maximum extent that federal law, and the United States and the California State Constitution permit. Any provision held invalid shall be severed from the remaining portions of this statute.

Article 7. Operative Date

330. This initiative shall become operative for all school terms which begin more than sixty days following the date on which it becomes effective.

Article 8. Amendment

335. The provisions of this act may be amended by a statute that becomes effective upon approval by the electorate or by a statute to further the act's purpose passed by a two-thirds vote of each house of the Legislature and signed by the Governor.

Article 9. Interpretation

340. Under circumstances in which portions of this statute are subject to conflicting interpretations, Section 300 shall be assumed to contain the governing intent of the statute.

STATEMENTS ON THE STRIKE
BY GENERAL MOTORS UNIONS
June 5, 1998

Union workers struck two General Motors (GM) plants in Flint, Michigan, in June, forcing a shutdown of nearly all GM production in North America for much of the summer. Settlement of the strike on July 28 was generally considered a draw, with both management and labor claiming some gains in the face of huge financial losses.

The GM strike was the most important of several major actions during the year in which organized labor sought to challenge cost-cutting moves by major corporations. Unions posted gains in strikes against such major corporations as Northwest Airlines, U.S. West, and Bell Atlantic. None of the 1998 strikes, however, represented anywhere near the kind of clear victory that Teamsters won in their 1997 strike against the United Parcel Service. (UPS strike, Historic Documents of 1997, p. 628)

Striking for Job Security

The principal issue in the 1998 GM strike was the one that had most bedeviled organized labor in the United States for nearly two decades: job security in an era when major corporations were under intense stockholder pressure to cut costs and generate higher profits. Members of the United Auto Workers (UAW) in the industrial Midwest feared that General Motors—the world's biggest manufacturing corporation—was intending to accelerate its trends of buying more parts from nonunion suppliers and shifting jobs to low-wage, nonunion factories in the South and overseas. General Motors insisted that it had no choice but to streamline its operations. Once the dominant automaker in the world, GM's market share declined steadily from the 1970s through the 1990s, and it was generally considered the world's least efficient automaker.

The 1998 strike took place against a backdrop of strained relations between the UAW and General Motors. The union had struck GM plants nearly two dozen times since 1990 over a host of issues. By comparison, GM's two major domestic rivals, Ford and Chrysler, enjoyed comparative peace with the union; Ford had cultivated good relations with the UAW and had not faced a strike in a dozen years.

Two GM actions in Flint sparked the strike. In February the company sharply scaled back promises to the union to invest $300 million in the Flint Metal Fabricating Facility (a metal-stamping plant), arguing that workers were unwilling to step up production quotas. Then during the Memorial Day weekend, the company removed from the plant expensive stamping dies for a new line of full-size pickup trucks. Worried that the company was planning to curtail production at the plant, or perhaps close it altogether, 3,400 UAW workers struck the metal-stamping plant on June 5. A week later 5,000 workers at a nearby GM sparkplug and speedometer factory joined the strike.

The strikes at those key facilities quickly forced GM to suspend production at other plants as supplies of parts dwindled. By late June all but two of the company's twenty-nine manufacturing plants in North America were closed. GM eventually laid off 189,000 workers as the Flint strike dragged on, and the company's suppliers laid off thousands more.

In a war of words throughout the summer, each side portrayed the strike as representing life-and-death issues. Union officials said they were determined to prevent the company from continuing what they called an "America Last" strategy: shifting its production overseas and leaving hundreds of thousands of American workers unemployed. Company executives said the company could not survive without achieving the kinds of production efficiencies that had enabled Ford, Chrysler, and Japanese automakers to eat into GM's market share.

One indication of the bitter nature of the strike was GM's decision to file suit against the union, charging that the UAW was pursuing a "national" strike in violation of a contract between the two sides. The UAW denied the charge and insisted that the strike, while raising issues of national consequence, had been called because of the local concerns of its two Flint affiliates. The suit was the company's first against the union in several decades, and it clearly contributed to a hardening of positions. Arbitration on the suit continued on a parallel track with negotiations on the underlying issues in the strike.

Despite its poisoning effect on labor-management relations, the GM suit may have helped bring the strike to a close. In late July union leaders reportedly became concerned that an arbitrator might rule against them on some issues. Negotiations picked up, and GM returned the dies to the Flint plant. On July 28 the two sides announced an agreement that was ratified two days later by workers at both plants. Workers in Flint began returning to their jobs almost immediately, and within several weeks all GM plants that had been idled were back to full production.

A "Lose-Lose" Outcome

The agreement gave each side some of what it had wanted, but not enough for either side to be able to claim victory. Harvey Katz, professor of labor relations at Cornell University, told the New York Times *that the result could be described as a "lose-lose draw." Most analysts said neither side had gained enough to justify the enormous costs: workers lost an estimated $1 billion in wages (some of which they made up with strike and unemployment benefits), and the company lost an estimated $3 billion worth of production, before taxes. The strike could have been worse for the company, since two of the nearly eight weeks represented GM's standard summer shut-down period for retooling in anticipation of a new model year.*

In addition to forcing the company to return the dies to the Flint metal-stamping plant, the union won a company promise to invest $180 million to upgrade production facilities at the plant. GM also agreed not to sell or close the Flint auto parts plant and two brake factories in Dayton, Ohio, before January 2000. The company gained an average 15 percent increase in production quotas at the stamping plant. For example, welders would be required to step up the number of units they worked on, but the agreement did not reverse a standing practice under which many workers could draw eight hours pay each day for as little as five or six hours work. GM also bought labor peace for at least a year at the two Flint plants and at parts factories in Dayton and Indianapolis.

Many of the same issues involved in the Flint strike would be on the table again when the national UAW contract with General Motors expired in September 1999. Labor analysts predicted that negotiations toward a new contract would be difficult, and union leaders warned their members to start saving in anticipation of a national strike.

GM Restructuring

A week after the strike ended, GM executives announced a series of moves intended to make the company more competitive. Each of the moves had been in the planning stages before the strike, and each was expected to heighten the union's concern about the company's long-range plans for employing union workers in North America.

On August 3 GM announced plans to spin off its giant auto parts subsidiary, Delphi Automotive Systems, into an independent subsidiary. The sell-off would take place in two stages in 1999. Delphi employed about 200,000 employees worldwide, including 50,000 UAW members in the United States. The sale would make GM the last of the "big three" automakers to abandon a strategy of "vertical integration": producing most of the parts and components for automobiles and trucks within one company. UAW representatives expressed concern that the sale of Delphi was yet another step in GM's campaign to reduce its reliance on union labor.

On August 4 GM said it was abandoning a decades-long company policy of encouraging its automotive divisions—Buick, Cadillac, Chevrolet, Oldsmobile, and Pontiac-GMC—to compete with each other, as well as with other automotive companies. Instead, marketing efforts for these divisions would be combined, just as Ford and Chrysler had done previously with their name-brand divisions.

Finally, on August 5 GM chairman and chief executive officer John F. Smith Jr. said the company was committed to building new assembly plants in North America. The new plants, to be built over a period of many years, would be more efficient than existing plants and would rely more heavily on outside suppliers. Smith said the company would not lay off workers as it built these plants but would instead cut back its overall employment by not replacing workers as they retired or left the company. UAW representatives said they were pleased that the company planned to invest in the United States, rather than overseas, but they expressed concern that GM was intending to cut back overall employment and would increase its reliance on nonunion suppliers.

General Motors announced on October 12 that it had lost $809 million in the third quarter, during which much of its North American operations had been curtailed by the strike. Overall, the company said, the strike cost it $2.4 billion in after-tax losses, some of which would be recouped by speeded-up production later in the year. Longer-term damage to the company was difficult to assess. During the strike, company officials worried that thousands of once-loyal GM customers would turn to other companies for new cars and trucks; company studies reportedly showed that once customers shopped around, most never returned.

Following are texts of a statement by the United Auto Workers announcing a strike by local 659 against the Flint, Michigan, Metal Fabricating plant; and a statement by Donald E. Hackworth, vice president and group executive in charge of General Motors North American car production; both are dated June 5, 1998:

UNITED AUTO WORKERS' STATEMENT

UAW Vice President Richard Shoemaker and Region 1C Director Ruben Burks announced today that negotiations at UAW Local 659 at the Flint Metal Fabricating facility have not produced a tentative settlement, making a strike unavoidable.

"The UAW has tried hard to resolve serious health and safety, production standards and subcontracting issues at Local 659 to no avail because General Motors continues to drag their feet in addressing clear and repeated violations of long-standing contract obligations," Shoemaker said.

UAW President Stephen P. Yokich said, "It's a sad state of affairs that we have these continuous problems with General Motors, but we are able to work out problems with Ford and Chrysler."

"UAW members at Flint Metal Fab have been working too long in unsafe working conditions, such as being exposed to hazardous chemicals on the job," Shoemaker continued, adding, "in addition, members are exposed to excessive and potentially damaging noise levels and dangerous working conditions in the operation of mobile equipment."

"At the same time, the corporation takes work and jobs from this plant by hiring contractors to perform our work and by sending out the work of building and repairing dies," he added.

"This situation is further complicated by the presence of hundreds of unresolved grievances on other issues important to the membership, as well as the refusal of the corporation to live up to written commitments made in previous national and local negotiations," Shoemaker declared.

"In addition to the problems at Local 659, long-standing issues at the Delphi East facility also remain unresolved despite our best efforts. We have issued a 'five-day notice' to the corporation regarding Local 651 in an effort to focus increased attention on that situation as well. If ongoing negotiations at Delphi East fail to produce a resolution of the issues, the notice will expire at 7 p.m. on June 11, 1998."

"What makes this situation more troubling," Shoemaker added, "Is that in the same way GM is ignoring our national and local contracts, they are also ignoring their 'social contract' with America, by transferring jobs, technology and capital from the U.S. to Thailand, Mexico, China and elsewhere."

"At a time when the corporation is making record profits and its top executives are being rewarded with excessive compensation, it is unjustifiable that GM's workers are being forced by management to face hazardous working conditions and serious threats to their job security," Shoemaker stated.

"The rising tide of success once floated the rowboats and skiffs of the workers as well as the yachts of the top executives," Shoemaker said, adding, "But it is obviously no longer true that the success of the corporation is being shared at all levels."

"Indeed, it's a sad sight for most Americans to see a corporation so closely associated with the creation of a prosperous middle-class now doing so much to tear it down, especially here in Flint."

"If GM has their way, the Flint community could lose about 11,000 jobs in the next two years, a devastating blow to a community that has been loyal to GM for decades," Shoemaker noted.

"This situation in Flint is a dramatic example of GM's 'America Last' strategy in which the corporation is attempting to radically downsize its American workforce in favor of exploiting less than poverty level wages in other countries," Shoemaker stated.

"Apparently, GM believes this somehow justifies ignoring the agreements made with this union," Shoemaker declared, concluding, "It's not acceptable to us and we don't think it should be acceptable to this community either."

GENERAL MOTORS' STATEMENT

GM is committed to the U.S., its customers and employees. As proof, GM is investing $2.1 billion in the U.S. in the five years 1997–2001. That's more than we're investing in the rest of the world combined. And in Genesee County, where GM has several operations, GM is investing $1.5 billion. That money is being spent on exciting new product programs, and on a manufacturing infrastructure that will help GM become more flexible, productive and competitive. There is no doubt that the U.S. remains the cornerstone of GM's global strategy.

GM didn't invent globalization. It is fundamental to our business and a fact of life. The Daimler/Chrysler merger is just one more example of this. We cannot choose to invest only in the U.S. or overseas: GM must do both to remain strong, especially here in the U.S.

While discussions at the Flint Metal Center include subjects such as production standards, sub-contracting and health and safety, they are not the primary issues. In fact, for the first five months of this year, the plant has seen a 54 percent improvement in recordable injuries. Quoting the UAW/GM Health and Safety Audit of 1997, "auditors were very impressed with the efforts of the plant leadership in their efforts to provide all employees of the Flint Metal Center with a safe, clean environment."

The real issues are the non-competitive work practices at this plant that do not allow the equipment to reach its designed output. We are not expecting these employees to operate any differently than we operate at any other facilities with similar equipment and processes.

UN ON NUCLEAR TESTS
BY INDIA AND PAKISTAN
June 6, 1998

Breaking a moratorium of nearly a quarter-century and raising the prospect of a nuclear arms race on the Indian subcontinent, India conducted nuclear tests in May, and its rival and neighbor, Pakistan, followed suit. The nuclear tests brought widespread international condemnation, including the imposition of economic sanctions against both countries.

The development also raised serious questions about the viability of international agreements intended to curtail the spread of nuclear weapons. Among those agreements was a worldwide ban on nuclear tests that had been signed by many nations but had not yet gone into effect. The treaty was pending in the U.S. Senate, which indefinitely postponed action on it following the Indian and Pakistani tests. (Comprehensive Test Ban Treaty, Historic Documents of 1995, p. 234)

By the end of the year, India and Pakistan had taken modest steps to ease the crisis. But the fact remained that the two countries had unsettled the political and military balance in one of the most volatile regions in the world. It was widely assumed that India's tests were intended as a deterrent to China, which many Indian leaders saw as the country's greatest threat, rather than Pakistan. India and Pakistan had fought three wars since 1947, when the subcontinent was partitioned in the wake of the end of British colonialism. The most contentious issue between India and Pakistan involved Kashmir, a mostly Muslim province divided between the two nations in 1947.

Back-to-Back Testing

India, which had last tested a nuclear device in 1974, sparked the 1998 furor on May 11 by conducting three underground nuclear tests in a desert area in the northwest of the country. Prime Minister Atai Bihari Vajpayee, leader of the Hindu Nationalist Party, revealed the tests in a matter-of-fact announcement describing the three types of devices involved.

Several dozen governments issued statements denouncing the tests, among them the Clinton administration, which called the move "deeply disappointing." United Nations Secretary General Kofi Annan expressed "deep regret" at India's action. Russia was one of the few major powers not registering a protest, apparently in an effort to maintain cordial ties between the two countries. The most ominous protest came from Pakistan, which said it was reserving the right to conduct its own tests.

Rebuffing international calls for a halt to further testing—including a direct appeal from Clinton—India conducted two more tests on May 13. International experts expressed concern that India said one of its tests was of a "thermonuclear" device, an apparent reference to plans to develop a powerful hydrogen bomb.

Pakistan responded on May 28 by conducting five underground nuclear tests in a desert region in the southwest of the country. "Today, we have evened the score with India," Pakistan's prime minister, Nawaz Sharif, said in a televised address shortly after the tests were conducted. "Today, God has given us the opportunity to take critical steps in the country's defense. We have become a nuclear power." Sharif said Pakistan was following India's example by installing nuclear warheads on medium-range missiles. Experts said such missiles would be capable of striking targets in northern and central India, but many observers said Sharif's claim about installing warheads on missiles probably was more propaganda than reality.

Sharif's announcement sparked celebrations among Pakistanis, thousands of whom surged into city streets. Hours before the announcement, the government had invoked martial law, apparently as a precautionary measure in the event that India responded with force to the Pakistani tests.

Two days later Pakistan announced that it had conducted another nuclear test, which officials described as the last of a series. "We have proved our credibility," a foreign ministry spokesman said in announcing that test.

Pakistan's tests were met with distressed, even angry reactions from many world capitals. President Clinton, who had sent senior aides to Islamabad and had personally implored Sharif by telephone not to follow India's lead, immediately imposed economic sanctions, as required by U.S. law. The UN Security Council on June 6 condemned the tests by both India and Pakistan and called on both countries to halt their nuclear weapons programs.

The Indian and Pakistani tests left Israel as the only country that was known to possess nuclear weapons but had not declared itself as a nuclear weapons state. Israel reportedly developed a nuclear weapons capability during the 1970s but had never openly conducted a test. Iran, Iraq, and North Korea were among nations that had actively sought to develop nuclear weapons but, as of 1998, were presumed not to have succeeded in acquiring a capability that could be put to use.

Among numerous other issues, India's first tests raised questions in Washington about why U.S. intelligence agencies had not discovered preparations for the tests. Some Republicans in Congress alleged an "intelligence failure," which they blamed on the Clinton administration. The critics noted that the Indian government, upon taking office just two months earlier, had signaled its intention to reconsider the country's two-decade moratorium on nuclear testing. The Clinton administration had been able, through diplomacy, to head off Indian plans for a nuclear test in December 1995 when intelligence agencies uncovered preparations for it.

Although both India and Pakistan rejected international criticism of their actions, each took steps in subsequent weeks to respond to that criticism and to reassure the other nation. Both nations announced a moratorium on further tests. India offered to sign a mutual agreement with Pakistan promising not to be the first to use nuclear weapons against each other, and Pakistan offered to negotiate a bilateral ban on further nuclear tests.

Sanctions Imposed

Under U.S. law, Clinton was required to impose economic and military sanctions against both India and Pakistan because of their tests. Legislation passed by Congress in 1994 (known as the Glenn amendment, after its sponsor, Ohio senator John Glenn) required a cut-off of all U.S. economic and military aid, except for humanitarian and food aid, and sales of military equipment and supplies to countries that conducted nuclear tests or sold a nuclear device to another country. The law allowed the president to delay the sanctions for thirty days but gave him no other discretionary power to waive the sanctions.

Just two hours after India announced its second set of tests on May 13, Clinton said he was imposing the sanctions against India required by the Glenn amendment. The United States gave India little direct aid, but its action effectively blocked more than $1.1 billion in loans for India pending before the International Monetary Fund (IMF) and the World Bank.

Clinton imposed sanctions against Pakistan immediately after its tests were announced. Pakistan—its economy battered by heavy external debt, a weakened banking system, and rampant corruption—was heavily dependent on aid and loans from the World Bank, the IMF, and countries such as the United States.

On June 12 the foreign ministers of the Group of Eight (G-8)—the world's leading industrialized nations—formally called for a suspension of international lending to India and Pakistan. The G-8 ministers called on both countries to halt nuclear testing and refrain from installing nuclear weapons on missiles.

Within a matter of weeks after Clinton imposed the sanctions, administration officials began consulting with congressional leaders about the possibility of giving the president discretion to modify the sanctions if that would help U.S. diplomatic efforts with India and Pakistan. Testifying before a House subcommittee on July 13, Karl F. Inderfuth, assistant secretary of state for South Asian affairs, said loosening some sanctions might encourage India and Pakistan to take such steps as renouncing further tests. Inderfuth also noted that the sanctions had a "disproportionate effect" on Pakistan because it was more dependent on foreign aid than was India.

Congress in October gave Clinton authority to modify the sanctions, and he did so on November 6. In a letter to the prime ministers of both countries, Clinton said he was waiving most of the economic aid sanctions against them. Clinton left in place several restrictions on military aid and the U.S. veto of loans for development projects by the World Bank and other international banks.

Administration officials said Clinton acted because both Pakistan and India were taking steps to ease the crisis they had created with their tests. Officials also said the administration was becoming increasingly worried about the impact of sanctions on Pakistan's already weak economy. With U.S. support, the IMF announced on November 25 that it was resuming loans to Pakistan. The fund had been holding up about $1.3 billion in aid for Pakistan because of the nuclear tests.

Further Negotiations

One of the positive steps cited by Clinton was a resumption of face-to-face meetings between senior Indian and Pakistani officials. The first of these sessions came in late July during a meeting in Colombo, Sri Lanka, of the South Asian Association for Regional Cooperation. The two prime ministers held one brief, unproductive meeting on July 29, and their foreign ministers met three times but failed to settle any differences. As it had been for a half-century, Kashmir was the principal issue of contention. Pakistan demanded direct talks on the status of the territory, a demand India rejected. Although these meetings produced no agreements, U.S. officials and other observers said it was good to have the two sides talking to each other. The foreign ministers held another round of meetings in Islamabad in mid-October but reached no agreement other than to hold another series of talks in February 1999.

In late September both prime ministers addressed the opening session of the UN General Assembly and expressed a willingness to sign the Comprehensive Test Ban Treaty in 1999. If they followed through on that pledge, North Korea would be the only nation potentially affected by the treaty that refused to sign it. Under its provisions, the treaty would not go into effect until it had been signed by all forty-four nations with nuclear reactors.

India and Pakistan also agreed to participate in international negotiations toward a treaty banning production of fissile material used for nuclear weapons. International negotiators said such a treaty had the potential to blunt the spread of nuclear weapons to other countries.

In a statement to parliament on December 15 Indian prime minister Vajpayee insisted his country would continue work on nuclear weapons material and on intermediate-range missiles capable of carrying nuclear weapons. Vajpayee said India was committed to a "minimum credible nuclear deterrent" and would oppose any international agreements placing India at a "technological disadvantage" with its adversaries.

Despite that rhetoric, U.S. officials said they remained hopeful that India and Pakistan both could be persuaded to accept international agreements limiting further development of their nuclear arsenals. The New York Times *quoted one U.S. official as saying Vajpayee was trying to develop a consensus within his country for a halt to nuclear testing.*

Following is the text of United Nations Security Council resolution 1172, adopted June 6, 1998, condemning the nuclear tests conducted by India and Pakistan in May 1998, and calling on both countries to halt their nuclear weapons programs:

The Security Council,

Reaffirming the statements of its President of 14 May 1998 (S/PRST/1998/12) and of 29 May 1998 (S/PRST/1998/17),

Reiterating the statement of its President of 31 January 1992 (S/23500), which stated, *inter alia* that the proliferation of all weapons of mass destruction constitutes a threat to international peace and security,

Gravely concerned at the challenge that the nuclear tests conducted by India and then by Pakistan constitute to international efforts aimed at strengthening the global regime of non-proliferation of nuclear weapons, and also gravely concerned at the danger to peace and stability in the region,

Deeply concerned at the risk of a nuclear arms race in South Asia, and determined to prevent such a race,

Reaffirming the crucial importance of the Treaty on the Non-Proliferation of Nuclear Weapons and the Comprehensive Nuclear Test Ban Treaty for global efforts towards nuclear non-proliferation and nuclear disarmament,

Recalling the Principles and Objectives for Nuclear Non-Proliferation and Disarmament adopted by the 1995 Review and Extension Conference of the Parties to the Treaty on the Non-Proliferation of Nuclear Weapons, and the successful outcome of that Conference,

Affirming the need to continue to move with determination towards the full realization and effective implementation of all the provisions of the Treaty on the Non-Proliferation of Nuclear Weapons, and welcoming the determination of the five nuclear-weapon States to fulfil their commitments relating to nuclear disarmament under Article VI of that Treaty,

Mindful of its primary responsibility under the Charter of the United Nations for the maintenance of international peace and security,

1. *Condemns* the nuclear tests conducted by India on 11 and 13 May 1998 and by Pakistan on 28 and 30 May 1998;

2. *Endorses* the Joint Communiqué issued by the Foreign Ministers of China, France, the Russian Federation, the United Kingdom of Great Britain

and Northern Ireland and the United States of America at their meeting in Geneva on 4 June 1998 (S/1998/473);

3. *Demands* that India and Pakistan refrain from further nuclear tests and in this context calls upon all States not to carry out any nuclear weapon test explosion or any other nuclear explosion in accordance with the provisions of the Comprehensive Nuclear Test Ban Treaty;

4. *Urges* India and Pakistan to exercise maximum restraint and to avoid threatening military movements, cross-border violations, or other provocations in order to prevent an aggravation of the situation;

5. *Urges* India and Pakistan to resume the dialogue between them on all outstanding issues, particularly on all matters pertaining to peace and security, in order to remove the tensions between them, and encourages them to find mutually acceptable solutions that address the root causes of those tensions, including Kashmir;

6. *Welcomes* the efforts of the Secretary-General to encourage India and Pakistan to enter into dialogue;

7. *Calls upon* India and Pakistan immediately to stop their nuclear weapon development programmes, to refrain from weaponization or from the deployment of nuclear weapons, to cease development of ballistic missiles capable of delivering nuclear weapons and any further production of fissile material for nuclear weapons, to confirm their policies not to export equipment, materials or technology that could contribute to weapons of mass destruction or missiles capable of delivering them and to undertake appropriate commitments in that regard;

8. *Encourages* all States to prevent the export of equipment, materials or technology that could in any way assist programmes in India or Pakistan for nuclear weapons or for ballistic missiles capable of delivering such weapons, and welcomes national policies adopted and declared in this respect;

9. *Expresses* its grave concern at the negative effect of the nuclear tests conducted by India and Pakistan on peace and stability in South Asia and beyond;

10. *Reaffirms* its full commitment to and the crucial importance of the Treaty on the Non-Proliferation of Nuclear Weapons and the Comprehensive Nuclear Test Ban Treaty as the cornerstones of the international regime on the non-proliferation of nuclear weapons and as essential foundations for the pursuit of nuclear disarmament;

11. *Expresses* its firm conviction that the international regime on the non-proliferation of nuclear weapons should be maintained and consolidated and recalls that in accordance with the Treaty on the Non-Proliferation of Nuclear Weapons India or Pakistan cannot have the status of a nuclear-weapon State;

12. *Recognizes* that the tests conducted by India and Pakistan constitute a serious threat to global efforts towards nuclear non-proliferation and disarmament;

13. *Urges* India and Pakistan, and all other States that have not yet done so, to become Parties to the Treaty on the Non-Proliferation of Nuclear

Weapons and to the Comprehensive Nuclear Test Ban Treaty without delay and without conditions;

14. *Urges* India and Pakistan to participate, in a positive spirit and on the basis of the agreed mandate, in negotiations at the Conference on Disarmament in Geneva on a treaty banning the production of fissile material for nuclear weapons or other nuclear explosive devices, with a view to reaching early agreement;

15. *Requests* the Secretary-General to report urgently to the Council on the steps taken by India and Pakistan to implement the present resolution;

16. *Expresses* its readiness to consider further how best to ensure the implementation of the present resolution;

17. *Decides* to remain actively seized of the matter.

SOUTHERN BAPTISTS
ON WOMEN AND THE FAMILY
June 9, 1998

The Southern Baptist Convention, which represented America's largest Protestant denomination, in June adopted language calling on wives to "submit graciously" to their husbands. Delegates to the convention's annual meeting, in Salt Lake City, included the language in a 250-word statement on the family. The statement was incorporated into the "Baptist Faith and Message," a formulation of basic beliefs for the sixteen million members of the church.

President Bill Clinton, one of several top political leaders belonging to the church, threw up his hands and said, "What can I do?" when asked about the church statement. Other critics, including some Southern Baptist members, were more vocal in denouncing the church position, saying it misrepresented the Bible and ran counter to current cultural and social trends.

The Southern Baptist Convention was by far the largest of several Baptist groups in the United States. Conservatives took over the church in 1979 and in subsequent years staked out positions on social and religious questions that annoyed moderate members and ministers. Several national and regional splinter groups had broken away from the Southern Baptist Convention, and by 1998 few moderate Southern Baptist representatives bothered to attend the church's annual convention.

Statement on the Family

The underlying beliefs of the Southern Baptist Convention were contained in the Baptist Faith and Message, formulated in 1925 and amended in 1963. The church did not have a formal "creed," and so its members were free to accept or reject the Baptist Faith and Message. Employees of the Southern Baptist Convention were required to accept the document, however.

Reflecting widespread concern among conservatives about such issues as abortion, divorce, and homosexuality, delegates to the church's 1997 con-

vention requested a statement on the role of the family. A seven-member committee of church leaders drafted a statement for consideration by delegates to the 1998 meeting. Two members of the committee were women; both were wives of prominent church officials.

The four-paragraph statement said God had created the family "as the foundational institution of human society," and it described the family in traditional terms as a husband, wife, and children. Although declaring that husband and wife "are of equal worth before God," the statement laid out clear and separate roles for the two marriage partners. The husband's role was "to provide for, to protect, and to lead his family," the statement said. "A wife is to submit herself graciously to the servant leadership of her husband even as the church willingly submits to the headship of Christ," the statement added. The wife was to respect her husband "and serve as his helper in managing the household and nurturing the next generation."

Anthony Jordan, executive director of the Baptist General Convention of Oklahoma and chairman of the committee that drafted the statement on family, told the church's delegates it represented "in unequivocal terms the clear teaching of Scripture." Jordan said the language was grounded in Paul's letter to the Ephesians (chapter five, verse twenty-two), which said: "Wives, submit to your husbands."

The two women who served on Jordan's committee both said they accepted the language and believed they should "submit" to their husbands. "'Submit is not a negative word," said Mary Mohler, wife of Al Mohler, president of the Southern Baptist Theological Seminary in Louisville, Kentucky. "It may be a politically incorrect word. It may not be a popular word. But it is a biblically correct word and that is what counts." Dorothy Patterson, wife of Paige Patterson, the newly elected president of the Southern Baptist Convention, said she accepted the Bible's injunction to accept her husband's authority even "when I know he's wrong. I just have to do it and then he stands accountable at the judgment."

When the convention took up the proposed statement, Tim Owings, of the First Baptist Church in Augusta, Georgia, offered an amendment saying that the husband and wife "are to submit graciously to each other." Owings said his amendment reflected another verse from Ephesians: "Submit to one another out of reverence for Christ." Another amendment, offered by Dennis Wyles of the First Baptist Church in Huntsville, Alabama, would have expanded the definition of a family to include single adults, childless couples, widows, and widowers. Delegates overwhelmingly rejected both proposed amendments by a show of hands and then adopted the family statement by acclamation.

Adoption of the statement marked the third year in a row that the Southern Baptist Convention had generated controversy with its positions at annual meetings. In 1996 the church infuriated many Jewish groups when it established a missionary service to evangelize Jews. In 1997 the church called a boycott of films and other entertainment products of the Disney Corporation because of the firm's alleged support of homosexuality.

Also at their 1998 meeting, the Southern Baptists adopted a resolution condemning the theology of the Church of Jesus Christ of Latter-Day Saints, headquartered in Salt Lake City. Baptist delegates knocked on doors in the Salt Lake City area attempting to evangelize local Mormons.

Opposition to the Statement

The Southern Baptist position on the family was front-page news and the subject of heated debate around the country, including at many churches the following Sunday. Baptist ministers and parishioners who did not accept the teachings of the Southern Baptist Convention denounced the statement.

Bruce Prescott, pastor of the Easthaven Baptist Church in Houston, Texas, told the Houston Chronicle: *"I have not found a lady in my church who was happy with that statement. One said she didn't want to be a Southern Baptist anymore." David Albert Farmer, pastor of the University Baptist Church in North Baltimore, Maryland, said from his pulpit that the Southern Baptist Convention was engaging in "attempted brainwashing." Farmer said: "We cannot stand for this. We need to be affirming women and encouraging them to think and act for themselves as spiritual beings loved by the God who created them." Farmer's church was part of the Alliance of Baptists, a moderate group that broke away from the Southern Baptist Convention in 1987.*

Some critics said the Southern Baptist Convention statement was part of a broader effort by the church to impose its politically conservative views on society as a whole. "We are seeing one particular interpretation of the Scripture that is being manipulated for political purposes" said Rev. C. Welton Gaddy, executive director of the Interfaith Alliance, a broad organization of several dozen religious denominations. The church's statement on the family "in effect takes the social agenda of the religious right and elevates it to a litmus test on what it means to be a Baptist. And as a Baptist, I resent that," Gaddy told the Washington Post.

The controversy did not faze church leaders who had drafted the statement on women. "America has been engulfed by a tidal wave of moral relativism and we quite happily confess that we are moral absolutists," said Richard Land, president of the Southern Baptist Ethics and Religious Liberty Commission. "Some things are always wrong and some things are always right. That automatically puts us in direct confrontation with this culture. We're not trying to be politically correct, but biblically correct."

Women in the Military

Just one day before the Southern Baptist Convention took its conservative position on the role of women in the family, the Clinton administration resolved—for the time being—a debate over mixing men and women in the military. Secretary of Defense William S. Cohen announced on June 8 that men and women would continue to be trained together in the air force, army, and navy, but that the services would separate them in their living quarters.

A committee headed by former senator Nancy Kassebaum Baker in December 1997 had recommended that the military segregate men and women in basic training. Cohen had appointed the committee in the wake of several sex scandals in the military. One month after that committee issued its report, another Pentagon panel—the Defense Advisory Committee on Women in the Services—took an opposite approach. That committee said it found widespread support within the military for training men and women together. All-male training programs fostered "more negative and prejudicial attitudes toward women," the committee said. (Women in the military, Historic Documents of 1997, p. 657)

Seeking to resolve the conflicting advice from the two committees, Cohen said each of the military services should provide greater security and privacy for female trainees, but integrated training would continue in three of the services. The Marine Corps was the only service that segregated the sexes for basic training and in living quarters.

One of the most highly publicized military sex scandals involved Sergeant Major Gene C. McKinney, the army's top enlisted man. Six women, all white, had accused McKinney, a black, of sexual harassment and intimidation. A court martial on March 13 found McKinney not guilty on eighteen charges of sexual misconduct and guilty on one charge of obstruction of justice. Three days later the military jury sentenced McKinney to a one-step reduction in rank and a formal reprimand, allowing him to retire from the army with an honorable discharge. (McKinney case, Historic Documents of 1997, p. 656)

> *Following is the text of "The Family," a section added to the "Baptist Faith and Message" on June 9, 1998, by the annual meeting of the Southern Baptist Convention:*

XVIII. The Family

God has ordained the family as the foundational institution of human society. It is composed of persons related to one another by marriage, blood or adoption.

Marriage is the uniting of one man and one woman in covenant commitment for a lifetime. It is God's unique gift to reveal the union between Christ and His church, and to provide for the man and the woman in marriage the framework for intimate companionship, the channel for sexual expression according to biblical standards, and the means for procreation of the human race.

The husband and wife are of equal worth before God, since both are created in God's image. The marriage relationship models the way God relates to His people. A husband is to love his wife as Christ loved the church. He has the God-given responsibility to provide for, to protect, and to lead his family. A wife is to submit herself graciously to the servant leadership of her husband even as the church willingly submits to the headship of Christ. She, being in the image of God as is her husband and thus equal to him, has the God-given responsibility to respect her husband and to serve as his helper in managing the household and nurturing the next generation.

Children, from the moment of conception, are a blessing and heritage from the Lord. Parents are to demonstrate to their children God's pattern for marriage. Parents are to teach their children spiritual and moral values and to lead them, through consistent lifestyle example and loving discipline, to make choices based on biblical truth. Children are to honor and obey their parents.

Gen. 1:26–28; 2:18–25; 3:1–20; Ex. 20:12; Deut. 6:4–9; Josh. 24:15; 1 Sam. 1:26–28; Ps. 78:1–8; 127; 128; 139:13–16; Prov. 1:8; 5:15–20; 6:20–22; 12:4; 13:24; 14:1; 17:6; 18:22; 22:6,15; 23:13–14; 24:3; 29:15,17; 31:10–31; Eccl. 4:9–12; 9:9; Mal. 2:14–16; Matt. 5:31–32; 18:2–5; 19:3–9; Mark 10:6–12; Rom. 1:18–32; 1 Cor. 7:1–16; Eph. 5:21–33; 6:1–4; Col. 3:18–21; 1 Tim. 5:14; 2 Tim 1:3–5; Titus 2:3–5; Heb. 13:4; 1 Pet. 3:1–7.

FTC CHAIRMAN ON
CORPORATE MERGERS
June 16, 1998

Some of the biggest and most important companies in the world decided to join forces during 1998, apparently deciding that merging was a more certain route to higher profits and stock prices than competition. Giants of the oil, communications, banking, chemical, pharmaceutical, and auto industries helped make 1998 the busiest year ever for corporate mergers.

Regulators in the United States and Europe were kept busy trying to keep up with the flood of mergers. The Federal Trade Commission (FTC) reported that it received information on 4,728 business mergers during the fiscal year ending September 30, three times as many as at the beginning of the 1990s. The FTC believed the deals it reviewed were worth more than $1 trillion. News reports said the total value of all mergers announced around the world during the year topped $2 trillion.

Analysts said most of the mergers were motivated by the booming U.S. economy, heightened international competitiveness, and a desire by corporate managers to take advantage of the economies of scale possible when two companies merged. The mergers of oil companies were spurred by an additional factor: oil prices were at the lowest point in decades, making it difficult to maintain corporate profits and stock values.

Testifying before the Senate Judiciary Committee on June 16, Federal Trade Commission Chairman Robert Pitofsky said most recent mergers appeared to be "motivated by fundamental developments in the rapidly changing economy and reflect more traditional corporate goals of efficiency and competitiveness." By contrast, Pitofsky noted that many mergers during the 1980s were the work of "corporate raiders" who bought and dismantled companies for short-term gain.

In a year of record-setting mergers, the biggest of all was announced on December 1: Oil giant Exxon Corp. said it would merge with the Mobil Corp. in a deal valued at $81 billion. If approved by regulators, the new company—Exxon Mobil Corp.—would put back together the two biggest pieces of John D. Rockefeller's Standard Oil Co. trust, which was split apart by the Supreme Court in 1911.

Another mega-deal proposed to reunite major pieces of "Ma Bell," the old American Telephone and Telegraph Co. which was divided by a federal court ruling in 1984. SBC Corporation, which controlled local telephone service in California, Texas, and six other states, planned to merge with Ameritech, the telephone company for five big states in the Midwest. Announced in May, that merger had an estimated value of $62 billion. If approved by regulators, the merger would create a giant company controlling more than one-third of all local telephone lines in the United States.

In several cases, major merger deals came all at once, apparently by coincidence. Such was the case on November 23, when a half-dozen important mergers were made public, including a plan by Deutsche Bank to acquire Bankers Trust for an estimated $10 billion. The rush of merger announcements came to a brief pause in August when world financial markets plummeted because of financial turmoil in Russia. (Russian economy, p. 601)

The Big Deals

Mergers announced during 1998 involved some of the corporate names most familiar to consumers. In many cases the corporate names were the results of previous mergers; the result often was a confusing stew of acronyms and hyphenated titles. For the most part, the major mergers of 1998 were between companies in similar lines of business. By the late 1990s corporate managers appeared to have shunned the practice—popular during the 1960s—of creating giant conglomerates that incorporated industries with little or nothing in common. Many of those conglomerates proved unmanageable and had since fallen apart.

Except for its enormous scope, the Exxon-Mobil merger was typical in many respects of those announced during the year. Corporate leaders said they hoped that a bigger, unified company would be more competitive than two big companies; that one company would be better able to take risks and exploit opportunities, such as exploring for oil in remote locations; that two companies could merge their "back-office" operations (such as accounting and computer services), affording big savings in overhead; and that one big company would be more attractive to investors, thus keeping stock prices high.

Two other oil giants, the British Petroleum Co. (BP) and Amoco Corp., offered similar explanations in August for their $48 billion merger. That merger received unusually quick approval from federal regulators. The FTC announced on December 30 that it was allowing the merger to proceed, on the condition that the two companies sell 134 gas stations in eight markets and allow more than 1,600 gas station franchises in thirty markets to switch to other brands.

In sheer dollar terms, the second biggest merger of the year was the proposed marriage of two financial services companies: Citicorp, one of the nation's biggest banking firms, and Travelers Group Inc., one of the largest insurance companies. Announced in April, that deal was estimated to be worth about $70 billion. Officials of both companies said they wanted to *provide one-stop shopping for financial services, enabling consumers to turn to just one company for checking accounts, loans, insurance policies, and similar services.*

The Citicorp-Travelers merger generated as much controversy as any of the mega-mergers of the year, for two reasons. First, the merger could not go forward unless Congress amended a 1933 law (the Glass-Steagall Act) intended to keep banking, securities, and insurance companies separate. The House in May approved legislation (HR 10) amending Glass-Steagall, but the measure died in the Senate. Consumer advocates also were worried about the impact on consumers of a merger between two such companies. The Consumer Federation of America questioned whether such mergers would reduce the number of companies consumers could turn to for competitive prices on financial services. The consumer group said it feared that consumers might feel pressured to buy all their financial services at just one company; for example, to get a bank loan a consumer might come under pressure to buy an insurance policy from another branch of the same firm.

Three other major bank mergers were announced during the year. They involved NationsBank Corp. and BankAmerica Corp., announced April 13, at a value of $60 billion; Banc One Corp. and First Chicago Bank/NBD Corp., also announced April 13, at a value of $30 billion; and Norwest Corp. and Wells Fargo & Co., announced June 8, at a value of $34 billion.

Two major deals during the year involved purchases of U.S. companies by foreign firms. On May 7 the German automaker Daimler-Benz announced that it was acquiring Chrysler Corp. for $39 billion. In December, Scottish Power announced that it would acquire PacifiCorp, a utility company headquartered in Portland, Oregon, for $13 billion. The latter deal was the first purchase of an important U.S. utility by an overseas company.

Several dozen mergers and acquisitions during 1998 involved the new an exploding world of commerce on the Internet. By far the most important was a three-part deal, announced in November, in which America Online Inc. (AOL), the world's biggest Internet service, purchased Netscape Communications Corp., the developer of one of the two dominant software "browsers" for viewing material on the Internet. The deal was worth $4.2 billion in stock. As part of the deal, AOL entered into marketing agreements with Sun Microsystems, another major software developer.

Government Scrutiny

All the mergers planned during 1998 were subject to some form of government scrutiny. In the United States, the Federal Trade Commission had responsibility for reviewing all mergers to make sure they did not reduce competition; the Justice Department reviewed mergers for antitrust implications. The Federal Communications Commission (FCC) reviewed mergers of telephone and other telecommunications companies, and the Federal Reserve Board and other banking regulators reviewed mergers of banks and financial services firms. In addition, individual states had the opportunity to challenge mergers that affected their citizens. Mergers of international corporations faced scrutiny from regulators overseas. In some cases European regulators were tougher than those in the United States because they took into consideration such social issues as how many people would be put out of work by a proposed merger.

Federal regulators quickly approved the vast majority of U.S. mergers. Only a handful faced intense scrutiny. The FCC served notice that one such case would be the proposed SBC-Ameritech merger. FCC chairman William E. Kennard on May 11 issued a curt three-sentence statement in reaction to the merger: "The bottom line question is: Is this merger going to create competition or will it be a non-aggression pact? The Telecom Act [the 1996 Telecommunications Act, PL 104–104] was all about opening markets for competition. SBC and Ameritech must show us that this merger will serve the public interest and enhance competition." In October and December the FCC conducted hearings on that merger and the proposed mergers of Bell Atlantic with GTE Corporation and AT&T with Tele-Communications Inc. (a cable television provider).

Opposition by the FTC forced the cancellation of one of the most controversial mergers: Lockheed Martin's attempted takeover of the Northrup Grumman Corp. The merger would have created by far the nation's biggest defense contractor, and the FTC argued it would have reduced the government's ability to get competitive bids for its weapons systems. Each of the companies involved in that failed merger was itself the result of a previous merger: Lockheed Martin was formed by the 1995 merger of Lockheed and Martin Marietta; Northrup and Grumman corporations merged in 1994 to form Northrup Grumman.

During fiscal 1998, the FTC said it negotiated twenty-three consent agreements to resolve its concerns about anticompetitive aspects of various mergers. The agency also won three preliminary injunctions in federal court against proposed mergers. One case involved proposed mergers of the nation's four largest pharmaceutical wholesalers into two companies. The FTC successfully challenged those mergers as weakening competition in the drug wholesale market. In six other cases companies that intended to merge dropped their plans after the FTC expressed opposition.

The Justice Department on October 23 filed suit to block Northwest Airlines from acquiring a controlling stake in Continental Airlines. The department said the deal would hinder competition and lead to higher ticket prices. However, the government did not seek a restraining order to prevent the airlines from completing the merger—raising the question of whether the deal would go ahead before the case reached court.

Despite the potential social and economic impact of the mergers, there were few voices of opposition or criticism during the year. One of the most outspoken was Ralph Nader, the consumer advocate who headed Public Citizen. Nader said top corporate executives were promoting mergers for their own profit—not for the good of their companies. Noting that many execu-

*tives had stock options that could balloon in value when companies
swapped stock, Nader said the mergers "are driven not by sound economic
judgment as much as bonanzas for the men at the top."*

*Nader and other critics noted that, while senior executives received
windfalls from the deals, thousands of low-level employees often received
pink slips. When companies touted the economies of scale to be achieved in
mergers, that meant cutting jobs. Citicorp, for example, initially
announced that its proposed merger with Travelers would result in only
modest layoffs. But on December 16 the company announced plans to eliminate about 10,400 jobs worldwide, or 6 percent of its workforce.*

*Some criticism of the mega-mergers also came from organizations rep-
resenting small companies that wanted to stay small. An example was the
Independent Bankers Association of America, which represented small
community banks. The association expressed concern that the Citicorp-
Travelers merger could accelerate the trend to giant nationwide banks—
swamping the smaller banks, most of them located in small towns.*

> *Following is the text of a statement, "Mergers and Corporate
> Consolidation in the New Economy," given to the Senate Judi-
> ciary Committee on June 16, 1998, by Robert Pitofsky, chair-
> man of the Federal Trade Commission:*

Mr. Chairman and Members of the Committee, I am pleased to present the
Statement of the Federal Trade Commission on Mergers and Corporate Consolidation in the New Economy. The subject is one immediately familiar to us
because the Commission, along with the Antitrust Division of the Department of Justice, has a statutory responsibility to review the competitive
implications of almost every large merger that is proposed.

Recently, merger review has been an extremely daunting and challenging
task. The number of mergers reported to the antitrust agencies under the
Hart-Scott-Rodino ("HSR") Act has increased dramatically from 1,529 filings
in fiscal year 1991 to an estimated 4,500 in fiscal year 1998. It has been predicted that the market value of merger transactions this year could exceed $2
trillion, compared to $600 billion for the peak year (1989) during the merger
wave of the 1980's. Although antitrust requires a highly case-specific analysis, over the course of reviewing almost 20,000 transactions in the last seven
years, we have been able to gain valuable insight into the forces that drive
mergers. HSR regulations require merging companies to provide certain studies, analyses and reports that evaluate the proposed transaction. In many
cases, the companies supplement those documents with "white papers" prepared for the antitrust agencies that offer their reasons for a particular transaction. These documents, as well as other evidence gathered in our investigations, reveal a number of factors that underlie the growth in mergers and
acquisitions. This statement will touch on some of the economic forces and

corporate motivations underpinning this merger phenomenon, what it means for the competitiveness of the U.S. economy, and the appropriate governmental response.

I. Market Conditions and Corporate Responses

Why has the pace of consolidations increased so dramatically in the last few years? Are mergers today different in character from those of a decade ago? We believe it is fair to say that the current merger wave is significantly different from the "junk bond"-fueled mergers of the 1980's. Some of those mergers involved the acquisition of unrelated businesses that were targeted for their break-up value or designed to generate cash for corporate raiders. Today's mergers are more likely to be motivated by fundamental developments in the rapidly changing economy and reflect more traditional corporate goals of efficiency and competitiveness. Among the more prominent factors are the following:

Globalization of competition. Many of the largest and most important product markets for American consumers have become much more global in scope—automobiles, computers, pharmaceuticals, and commercial aircraft, to name just a few. A merger may enhance a firm's ability to compete in foreign markets by providing rapid access to an established distribution system, knowledge of local markets, economies of scale, and complementary products.

Deregulation. Many mergers are taking place in industries undergoing or anticipating deregulation. In the 1980's, the Commission reviewed a substantial number of mergers in the natural gas industry, which was then undergoing deregulation. Now, deregulatory changes are taking place in electricity, telecommunications, and banking and financial services. Deregulation often engenders structural change and more competition. Mergers may enable firms to acquire quickly the assets and other capabilities needed to expand into new product or geographic markets. Deregulation also facilitates market entry across traditional industry lines. For example, banks seek to provide other financial services, and other firms seek to serve markets traditionally served by banks. Firms increasingly seek to provide a bundle of services that cross industry lines as regulatory constraints are lowered. We see that happening in several deregulating industries such as financial services, telecommunications, and public utilities. Consequently, we can expect to see a number of cross-industry mergers.

Industry downsizing and consolidation. While this probably was a more important factor several years ago, a number of mergers continue to be associated with industry downsizing and consolidation. That is particularly true in some defense industries. With lower procurement levels and fewer new projects on the horizon, companies have sought to rationalize or reduce capacity through merger.

Downsizing and consolidation also are significant forces in the health care industry. Changes in health care practices, such as shorter hospital stays, may result in excess capacity in some hospitals. A merger may enable two hospitals to eliminate unneeded capacity and operate more efficiently. Structural changes also are occurring in health care as firms seek not only to become more efficient but to meet broader public policy goals, such as increasing the cost effectiveness of health care, increasing the quality of care, and providing diversity of choice. This, too, can lead to mergers that cross traditional industry lines.

Technological change. Economic progress is often driven by innovation and technological change, and mergers may be a response to that change or contribute to it. In a fast-moving, technology-driven economy, a merger may enable a firm to acquire quickly the technology or other capabilities to enter a new market or to be a stronger competitor. The communications industry is a good example. Other mergers may be driven by a desire to consolidate research and development resources to produce a greater research capability. Some pharmaceutical mergers fit that mold.

Strategic mergers. Many mergers, perhaps more than in some years past, involve direct competitors and appear to be motivated by "strategic" considerations. Firms are increasingly concerned about being number one or a strong number two in their markets, or perhaps even dominant. That drive can lead to mergers intended to boost market share, eliminate competitors, or acquire an important supplier of inputs needed by competitors. In these types of mergers we may be concerned that a firm has acquired a dominant position. In addition, a concentrated market can make it easier to collude. These mergers also require close scrutiny.

Financial market conditions. Low interest rates and low inflation have produced a favorable climate for investment, and that is reflected in the booming stock market. One result of the above-described emphasis on strategic combinations is that relatively fewer mergers today are financed with cash or debt, as compared to the 1980's. Today, more companies are financing mergers through exchanges of stock. To the extent that a company's improved performance is reflected in higher stock values, its managers may be more willing to acquire another corporation or be acquired by another corporation through the exchange of stock.

II. How Does the Merger Wave Affect Consumers and the U.S. Economy?

Some mergers can harm competition. The harm to competition, in turn, can harm consumers in many ways—higher prices, restricted supply of products, lower quality goods and services, less variety from which to choose, and less innovation for the future. In addition, less competition may dampen the incentives to be efficient, and economic performance will suffer. A fundamental goal of the Clayton Act, including its Hart-Scott-Rodino provisions, therefore, is to prevent harm to competition by stopping anticompetitive mergers before they take place. The Commission's efforts to achieve this goal during the current merger wave explains why the Commission now devotes over two-thirds of its competition mission resources to merger enforcement, compared to about fifty percent a few years ago. We believe those resources are well spent and produce significant dividends in protecting American consumers from competitive abuses and keeping the U.S. economy strong and competitive.

But current resources are inadequate to the task. Despite a three-fold increase in merger activity since 1991, the total workyears budgeted for the Commission's competition mission have remained essentially flat. We have tried to keep pace by being more efficient and working longer hours, and by shifting resources from non-merger enforcement. We are now stretched to the limit. Merger analysis has become increasingly sophisticated and fact-intensive to ensure that we understand the competitive implications of each transaction. We must examine the possible anticompetitive consequences as well as the potential efficiencies and procompetitive benefits of the transaction. This analysis produces better decisions, but it also is more resource-intensive. Consequently, more resources are needed for both the FTC and the Antitrust Division to do our job of ensuring a competitive American economy.

Although we have found that the majority of mergers do not appear to harm competition, we are able to make that determination only after reviewing the facts of each transaction. We must be able to do that quickly and accurately. We believe we have been quite successful under the circumstances. For example, of the 3,702 transactions filed under HSR in fiscal year 1997, roughly 70% were reviewed very quickly and allowed to proceed before the end of the statutory 30-day waiting period; that is, they were granted "early termination." Approximately 14% of the transactions raised enough issues to proceed beyond the initial review stage and were assigned to either the Commission or the Antitrust Division for further substantive review. In the past year, 4.5% raised questions serious enough to warrant a request for additional information ("second request") from either the Commission or the Antitrust Division. These are the most intensive investigations and require major resources. Almost half of those transactions resulted in enforcement action or abandonment due to antitrust concerns. In fiscal 1997, the Commission and the Antitrust Division challenged a total of 52 mergers through court or administrative actions and settlement proceedings, and an additional seven transactions were abandoned before formal enforcement action was announced. Over the past three fiscal years (1995–1997), Commission action has resulted in an average of 32 transactions per year either challenged or abandoned. Although the number of problematic mergers is small in relation to the total, the consequences of anticompetitive mergers can be enormous. For example, enforcement action in one case alone—the proposed merger of Staples and Office Depot—saved consumers an estimated $1.1 billion over five years.

III. The Antitrust Agencies' Response

Given the tremendous numbers of recent mergers, it is appropriate to ask whether the antitrust agencies are doing enough to prevent anticompetitive mergers. We believe the level of enforcement has been appropriate. To the extent the mergers not challenged are procompetitive, consumers benefit and companies can be more competitive in both domestic and international marketplaces. We should be concerned about the relatively small but important number of mergers that pose a serious threat to competition and to consumers. We believe we have been successful in distinguishing between the mergers that should be allowed to proceed, and those that raise significant concerns. We review transactions efficiently, we promptly give the green light to those that clearly are not anticompetitive, and we challenge those that present a serious threat to competition and consumers. Furthermore, we place great emphasis on implementing an effective remedy when we find reason to believe that a merger will be anticompetitive.

Forward-looking analysis. The dynamics of the new economy make it especially important that merger analysis be rigorous and forward-looking. In fact, the Commission held a series of public hearings in 1995–96 to address precisely whether antitrust analysis should be modified in light of competitive conditions in the new high-tech, global marketplace. Some of the issues considered were whether antitrust analysis recognized the international nature of competition, merger review in industries that were downsizing, the standards for strategic alliances and joint ventures, and evaluation of cost-savings or efficiency claims.

The hearings produced a comprehensive report and a general consensus that antitrust policy is on the right course. This consensus reflects the basic fact that the antitrust laws have been and continue to be sufficiently flexible to accommodate new economic learning and a changing business environment. Court decisions and the agencies' guidelines demonstrate that our interpretation and application of those laws have changed with the times. Merger analysis has moved from strict reliance on structure-based presumptions that focused largely on market share data to a sophisticated analysis that takes account of the dynamic nature of competition in the real world. The analysis recognizes that competition in many markets is global. Thus, antitrust analysis takes account of competition from imports, and it recognizes the need for U.S. firms to be competitive in world markets.

As we undertake this analysis, we find there is little inconsistency or conflict between the goal of the antitrust laws to protect U.S. consumers and competition in domestic markets, on the one hand, and the imperatives of global competition on the other. Competition in world markets and competition at home go hand in hand—one benefits the other. Likewise, efforts to increase efficiency and competitiveness transcend national boundaries. A merger that produces a stronger competitor in a global market could very well have procompetitive benefits in the United States, and those efficiencies will be taken into account. Further, if a merger does create a competitive problem in a domestic market, antitrust remedies are targeted to the specific competitive problem; we make every effort not to interfere with the remainder of the transaction. A Commission order may require a partial divestiture, or licensing of technology, and the remainder of the merger is allowed to proceed. In most cases it is not necessary to block a merger entirely.

Thus, the Commission's enforcement decisions recognize that the principles of merger analysis must be applied with sharp attention to the dynamics of competition in the new economy. It is important to take a careful look at how firms compete in the marketplace, and how a merger might affect that competition. The following are some examples of our analytic focus:

- *Identifying new markets and new methods of competition.* It is important to recognize new markets and new forms of competition, and identify what firms act as a competitive constraint on others. For example, in the proposed merger of Staples and Office Depot, many people thought that the relevant market for antitrust analysis would consist of all stores that sell office supplies. However, Staples and Office Depot had created a new market segment called office supply "superstores" that provided a bundle of products and services unavailable from other retailers. Extensive evidence, much of it from the companies' own documents and from their pricing behavior, showed that other retailers were not a competitive constraint on the pricing of Staples and Office Depot. The district court agreed that office supply superstores constituted a separate market for purposes of antitrust analysis. Because the merging companies were the two largest of only three firms in that market, the court found that the merger would be anticompetitive and granted the Commission's motion to enjoin the transaction.
- *Innovation competition.* Our examination of innovation markets is another example of paying close attention to the dynamics of new competition. Research and development—innovation—is the lifeblood of our economy. It produces new products and services, and it can greatly affect the competitive landscape of markets in the future. In fact, it is a way that firms compete for future market position.

Some mergers can enhance R&D efforts by combining complementary talents or technologies. Some of those mergers can enable a firm to gain market entry with a new product and interject new competition. Other mergers, however, can restrict R&D efforts and lessen competition. A recent example is the merger of Ciba-Geigy and Sandoz, two pharmaceutical giants based in Switzerland but with far-reaching global operations. Both companies were developing gene therapy treatments for various forms of cancer and other serious illnesses. These research efforts held significant promise for new treatments within the next few years. But, Ciba-Geigy and Sandoz were the only two firms with the bundle of patent rights and technology needed to develop products in this promising new area.

The Commission's concern with the Ciba-Geigy merger was that it would enable Ciba-Geigy to gain monopoly control over competing patents and other important technologies and, therefore, the power to preclude development and commercialization of these new products by other companies. The Commission therefore challenged the merger but allowed it to proceed with the condition that Ciba-Geigy license certain intellectual property to other firms so that the race to develop and commercialize these important new products could continue.

- *Evolving forms of business organization.* We may observe a variety of complex business relationships as firms enter into new markets. Many of these affiliations bring together businesses from different industries and nations. Firms may find the need to enter into strategic alliances with competitors, suppliers, or customers, or combinations of those entities. Examples include joint ventures and holding companies, which we already see in the financial sector as banks and insurance companies seek to affiliate. It will be important to sort through those relationships to determine their competitive significance.
- *Mergers in deregulating markets.* It is not unusual to see an increase in merger activity in deregulating markets as firms seek out new opportunities. In most cases, that is healthy for competition. However, we must also watch for mergers that may enable firms to retain market power they enjoyed under their prior sheltered existence. Such mergers obviously can frustrate the goals of deregulation and deprive consumers of the benefits of competition. Current concerns about the state of competition in certain sectors of the airline industry are a vivid reminder of the importance of close antitrust scrutiny as industries restructure under deregulation. More rigorous application of antitrust principles to airline mergers in the 1980's could have prevented the levels of market concentration we now see in certain airline hubs across the country.

Deregulating markets can be affected in several different ways through mergers. One, of course, is through a merger with a direct competitor. That was the case in the airline industry, and we would expect to see a number of horizontal mergers to occur in industries now undergoing or anticipating deregulation, such as electricity, telecommunications, and banking and financial services. We are prepared to review those mergers to the extent they are within our jurisdiction.

The goals of deregulation also can be frustrated by mergers that result in the elimination of a potential future competitor—a firm that is not yet in the market but is poised to enter and provide new competition. An example is a merger the Commission challenged in 1995, involving the proposed acquisition of a likely entrant into the natural gas pipeline market in the Salt Lake City area. The natural gas industry had undergone substantial deregulation and was offering new competitive opportunities for consumers. The potential entrant already was having a positive effect on the market through its efforts to line up customers before constructing new pipeline facilities. Enforcement action preventing the acquisition preserved the benefits of deregulation for industrial customers in the Salt Lake City area.

It is also important to take a close look at the strategic implications of vertical mergers in the new market environment. While many, if not most, vertical mergers are likely to be efficiency-enhancing, such as by joining complementary assets, some vertical mergers can be anticompetitive. For example, by acquiring the supplier of a critical input for which there are few or no alternatives, a firm may be able to raise the input costs of its rivals or foreclose entry. Two recent examples serve to illustrate this point.

The first is the merger of Time Warner and Turner Broadcasting. Both companies were major producers of video programming for distribution on cable television. In addition, Time Warner was a major operator of cable television systems, as was TCI, which held a significant interest in Turner Broadcasting. At the time, deregulation of the telecommunications industry promised to interject new competition for cable television, as telephone companies and others sought to use new technology to deliver video programming through alternative channels. The merger, however, threatened to give the combined entity control over competition and entry conditions in both the video programming and cable distribution markets. As a result, the Commission issued a consent order that prohibits Time Warner from discriminating against rivals at either level of the market.

Another recent example is the proposed merger of PacifiCorp and The Energy Group. PacifiCorp is a significant generator of electric power in the western United States. It sought to acquire certain coal mines that were the only source of fuel for several generating plants owned by competitors. By controlling a critical supply of coal, PacifiCorp could raise its rivals' costs and effectively boost the wholesale price of electricity during certain periods. Had that acquisition taken place, the goals of electric power deregulation in California could have been frustrated and consumers would have faced higher prices.

- *Focus on high technology.* The importance of high technology in the American economy cannot be overstated. High technology markets are marked by creativity, rapid change, and growth. It is precisely these characteristics that may allow anti-competitive behavior to have a more significant impact on a market. We recognize that many mergers may be beneficial to the advancement and commercialization of technology, but some mergers can be harmful. The rapid pace of technological change can appear to obviate competitive concerns because any market power will be short-lived, but that is not always the case. Entry into some high-technology markets can be difficult, and it can be made more difficult by incumbents with market power. It is important to maintain a climate that is conducive to innovation and competition. That requires a carefully balanced approach. Accordingly, the Commission devotes substantial resources to understanding and evaluating issues in this area.

A recent example is the enforcement action involving Digital Equipment Corporation's sale of microprocessor assets to Intel. The microprocessor at issue was Digital's Alpha chip, regarded by many as the fastest microprocessor in the world. It is the closest present substitute for Intel's Pentium chip for computers running the Windows NT operating system. Intel today is the dominant producer of microprocessors, and Digital is one of the few other innovation competitors in the design and development of high-performance microprocessors. The transaction would have given Intel sole control over the production of the Alpha chip and enabled Intel to block this competitive alternative to Intel's Pentium.

As a result of the Commission's investigation, Digital agreed to a consent order that will require it to license Alpha technology to certain Commission-approved producers of microprocessors or semiconductor products. The order will ensure the continued availability of the Alpha chip as a competitive alternative.

Another example is a case involving software used to automate the design of integrated circuits, or "microchips." The software, called "routing" software, is used to map out the connections between the millions of miniature electronic components within a microchip. The acquiring company, Cadence Design Systems, was the leading supplier of a complementary product that microchip designers used in conjunction with routing software. The evidence indicated that Cadence's acquisition of the routing software would give it an incentive to foreclose competition from competing developers of routing software, which needed to interface with Cadence's product. The Commission's consent order requires Cadence to allow other software developers to participate in Cadence software design programs on a non-discriminatory basis, to ensure compatibility of their products.   .

Finally, as an illustration of the fact that technological change cannot always be counted on to resolve competitive problems, there are continuing concerns about the state of competition in cable television markets. Our investigations show that alternative technologies for delivering video programming have not yet had a significant restraining effect on cable television rates. Since most local cable markets are franchised monopolies, antitrust has limited application in preventing higher prices. However, some communities authorize multiple franchises to serve their consumers, thereby permitting competition. Mergers in those situations are something we can address, and we have. Most recently, Commission action preserved competition between cable systems in two cities in New Jersey.

- *Recognition of efficiencies.* It also is important to recognize and give proper weight to the potential efficiency effects of mergers. With dynamic competition in a global setting, efficient firms will be in the best position to compete. One result of the Commission's 1995–96 hearings on competition policy in the new high-tech, global marketplace was a revision of the joint DOJ/FTC 1992 Horizontal Merger Guidelines to explain in greater detail how the agencies will analyze merger-generated efficiencies in assessing the overall competitive effects of a merger. The question of merger efficiencies need not be reached unless it appears that the merger may pose a serious threat to competition. When merger efficiencies are relevant, the Commission gives serious consideration to valid, substantiated claims of merger-specific efficiencies.
- *A balanced approach.* Another important principle is that the agencies use a balanced, carefully focused approach, and we do. First, of course,

the agencies must direct their enforcement resources at mergers that pose a serious threat to competition and to consumers. Two cases illustrating the importance of strong antitrust enforcement have already been mentioned: the proposed mergers of Ciba-Geigy/Sandoz, and Staples/Office Depot. In the first, enforcement action preserved competition in the race to develop life-saving treatments for cancer and other diseases. In the second, enforcement action saved consumers from paying substantially higher prices as a result of the merger—an estimated $1.1 billion over five years.

These cases demonstrate some of the many benefits of carefully focused merger enforcement: direct savings for consumers, business customers, and taxpayers; preservation of rivalry in innovation of products—some life-saving—for the future; and maintenance of open markets by preserving competitive opportunities for new firms. Importantly, the Commission devotes a major portion of its investigative resources to six high-priority economic sectors that affect millions of consumers and taxpayers: information and technology, health care, pharmaceuticals, defense, energy, and consumer goods and services. Increasingly, we leverage our resources by cooperating closely with state antitrust enforcers. They have been very supportive of Commission enforcement actions, as in the Staples case.

The other part of the equation is that antitrust should not intervene when it is not necessary. An example is the merger of Boeing and McDonnell Douglas. Although the merger would give Boeing control over 60 percent of the market for commercial airliners and leave only one major competitor, the evidence from the Commission's extensive investigation showed that McDonnell Douglas was no longer a significant competitive force in the market, and there was little likelihood that it would regain that status. Thus, although market concentration data suggested that a merger of Boeing and McDonnell Douglas would raise competitive concerns, a careful review of the evidence indicated that the merger would not significantly lessen competition.

- *Minimizing burdens.* The Commission also recognizes that it is important to minimize burdens on business as we conduct this essential review. Since the majority of mergers do not raise anticompetitive concerns, they should be reviewed quickly and allowed to proceed. We have taken several recent steps to reduce burdens. Last year, we adopted five new rules to exempt certain mergers from the Hart-Scott-Rodino reporting and waiting period requirements. Our experience showed that those kinds of transactions were very unlikely to raise competitive concerns. The new HSR exemptions reduced the reporting requirement by about seven to ten percent and resulted in a significant saving of filing fees and other reporting costs for companies engaging in those transactions, as well as a saving of resources for the antitrust agencies in processing and reviewing those filings. While adoption of additional exemptions may be possible, we must proceed cautiously. The fact-specific nature of merger analysis makes it very difficult to determine beforehand which transactions are not likely to raise competitive concerns.

The agencies also have worked on process improvements—ways to make merger review faster and more efficient. We have expedited the process, called "clearance," through which we decide which agency will review a particular merger. The agencies have also adopted a more streamlined joint model request for additional information, and we implemented a "quick look" investigative process that permits an investigation to be terminated if certain threshold information indicates that the merger is not likely to be anticompetitive.

- *Continued evaluation of antitrust standards.* Plainly, the antitrust agencies must continue to be forward-looking in their antitrust analysis, and must do so with efficiency and sophistication. In that regard, another observation from our review of marketplace behavior is that companies increasingly are entering into strategic alliances and joint ventures that are something less than a complete merger. That phenomenon is occurring in a number in industries, including high-tech markets, and a number of joint ventures are international. These ventures may involve, for example, joint research and development, joint manufacturing, marketing agreements, or joint distribution arrangements. While we would expect many of those ventures to be procompetitive, certain concerns inevitably arise whenever competitors collaborate. The need for further study of this issue is another outgrowth of the Commission's global competition hearings. As a result of those hearings, the Commission formed a task force to study the competitive implications of joint ventures and other forms of competitor collaboration, with the goal of providing additional antitrust guidance to firms and practitioners. That task force has completed its hearings and is in the process of preparing recommendations to the Commission. We, of course, are collaborating with the Antitrust Division in that effort.
- *Adequate resources.* Finally, it is important to ensure that agency resources are adequate to accomplish both parts of our job—to conduct a timely review of transactions to distinguish ones that are not anticompetitive, and to challenge those that are. The American public and American businesses are entitled to prompt and effective antitrust enforcement. We are doing that job, but with too few resources. As noted before, the workyears budgeted for the maintaining competition mission have been essentially flat since 1991. Mr. Klein's testimony indicates that the Antitrust Division is facing similar constraints. We are making every effort to keep pace with the surge of merger activity, but our resources currently are stretched to the limit.

IV. Conclusion

In summary, we appreciate this Committee's attention to the dramatically increasing level of merger activity that has enveloped our country over the past several years, and the opportunity to share with you our views of important issues pertaining to recent mergers and consolidations. We believe that many of these mergers are the result of fundamental economic changes in both our economy and world markets, and that they are, for the most part, beneficial to the economy and to consumers. At the same time, it is critically important to review each of these transactions to ensure that competition, and consumers, will not be harmed. The Federal Trade Commission embraces that challenge and the important responsibility to protect American consumers.

GAO REPORT ON
WELFARE REFORM
June 18, 1998

Two years after Congress enacted a sweeping reform of U.S. welfare laws, the number of Americans receiving welfare had dropped sharply and a growing number of former welfare recipients were finding work. President Bill Clinton and congressional leaders trumpeted the 1996 welfare reform law as a success. Nevertheless, questions remained about the impact of welfare changes on children and their families and the fate of former welfare recipients when the economic boom of the 1990s slowed. (Welfare reform law, Historic Documents of 1996, p. 450)

In a comprehensive report to Congress on June 18, the General Accounting Office (the investigative arm of Congress) said the new law appeared to be having the desired effect of encouraging welfare recipients to find work and become more self-sufficient. On August 5 the Clinton administration sent Congress another detailed report describing how the federal and state governments were implementing the law. That report said that, as of March 1998, 8.9 million Americans were receiving welfare, representing 3.1 percent of the total population—the lowest level since 1969.

The 1996 welfare reform law (PL 104–193) eliminated the decades-old concept that needy Americans with children were entitled to government aid. The law created new block grants to the states—called Temporary Assistance for Needy Families. The word temporary was an important one, intended to symbolize the end of welfare as a permanent source of support for those in need. States were required to impose work requirements on adults receiving welfare. With few exceptions, adults could receive assistance for no more than two years, and families could receive welfare for no more than five years. In addition to the aid cutoffs, the law provided several incentives to help states reduce their welfare rolls, including increased spending on child care subsidies and health care coverage for welfare mothers who go to work.

Studies conducted independently of the government raised troubling questions about the impact of welfare reform. On July 27, the New York

354

Times *reported unpublished Census Bureau statistics showing that the welfare recipients who had found work tended to be those who were the most employable and that whites had left the welfare rolls much more rapidly than had blacks and Hispanics. As a result, the newspaper reported, blacks outnumbered whites on the welfare rolls for the first time. Those who remained on welfare were concentrated in the poorest urban neighborhoods, where they lacked access to the job growth that tended to be centered in the suburbs. Many of those still on welfare had severe medical or mental problems that posed obstacles to their ever finding employment.*

On August 12, the Washington Post *reported that many states were working aggressively to prevent people from getting on welfare—even to the point, according to some critics, of discouraging people with legitimate needs for welfare assistance. "They are pushing people out the door too fast," the* Post *quoted Sister Jane Albert Mehrens, program director of the Catholic Community Services in Leavenworth, Kansas.*

GAO Report

The GAO reported to Congress on its review of how welfare reform had been implemented in seven states that were chosen because they represented the nation as a whole in demographic terms: California, Connecticut, Louisiana, Maryland, Oregon, Texas, and Wisconsin. Some of those states had reformed their welfare systems to emphasize job placement even before the 1996 national welfare reform law.

In general, the GAO found that the law appeared to be working as intended. Welfare offices were being transformed into job placement centers; applicants often were encouraged to begin looking for jobs as soon as they applied for assistance; adults with mental and physical impairments, and those caring for small children, were less likely than before to be exempted from work requirements; and states were enforcing time limits on cash assistance. States and localities were devising creative ways to help ease recipients off the welfare rolls and into productive employment, often by providing services or funding for child care, transportation, and medical care.

The GAO illustrated these trends with numerous statistics. For example, it noted that in the seven states the proportion of adults required to work as a condition of receiving welfare rose from 44 percent in 1994 to 65 percent in 1997. In many cases, former welfare recipients were able to earn substantially more from jobs than from welfare. Combining those earnings with food stamps, the earned income tax credit, subsidized child care, and other "transitional" programs enabled some families to move above the federal poverty level. Even so, the GAO said, many former welfare families were still hard-pressed, especially those living in areas with high housing costs or in jurisdictions that limited post-welfare assistance to one year. (Housing report, p. 253)

Although the GAO report answered many questions about how welfare reform was working in the early years, it raised many questions about longer-term issues. The biggest question involved the economy. The GAO said the economic boom of the 1990s had been one of the main reasons welfare reform had been so successful in moving recipients into jobs. With the national unemployment rate below 5 percent, welfare recipients in many areas were having little difficulty finding jobs, often at pay levels well above the minimum wage. The GAO said it was too early to know how the welfare-to-work programs would perform once the economy went into recession, or what would happen to the millions remaining on welfare who had severe mental or medical disabilities that interfered with finding and holding a job.

GAO noted that nineteen states had taken advantage of a provision of the welfare law allowing them to lower the five-year limit on how long families could receive welfare. Connecticut set one of the strictest time limits— twenty-one months—but allowed six-month extensions for recipients who demonstrated "good faith" in meeting work requirements but had been unable to find employment.

GAO also said it was too early to answer numerous questions about the impact of welfare reform on families that had been receiving welfare. Among those questions: How many people returned to the welfare rolls after once leaving the program? How economically stable were families once they left welfare? How did children fare after their parents lost welfare assistance because they did not comply with new work requirements? GAO said states were using various methods to answer these questions by tracking families once they left welfare. Some of the early results showed, for example, that welfare recipients sometimes went through two or three job placements before being able to hold a job that kept them off welfare. But the agency said it could not yet draw national conclusions on these questions.

Administration Report

The Clinton administration on August 5 sent Congress what it described as its "first annual report" on welfare reform. Although Clinton had signed the new welfare law in August 1996, major provisions did not take effect until July 1, 1997. In general, the report described the early experience of welfare reform in glowing terms, saying it "has helped millions of families make the successful transition from welfare to work."

The report said the number of welfare recipients nationally had declined from an all-time high of 14.4 million in March 1994 to 8.9 million in March 1998, a drop of 37 percent. A later report from the Department of Health and Human Services said the number of recipients had dropped to 8.4 million as of June 30, 1998. The report also said that 1.7 million adults who had received welfare in 1996 were employed a year later. State spending on welfare and related programs also had declined by about 18 percent between 1994 and the end of 1997, the report said.

Some congressional Republican leaders objected to Clinton's claims of credit for the success of welfare reform. They noted that the 1996 law was drafted primarily by Republicans in the House of Representatives and that Clinton had signed the bill, with some reluctance, after a heated internal debate among his advisers.

"Welfare to Work" Programs

A key feature of the 1996 law was its encouragement of new types of "welfare-to-work" programs that helped recipients find productive employment. Perhaps the broadest effort was directed by a nonprofit organization, the Welfare to Work Partnership, headed by Eli J. Segal, a former Clinton adviser. Between early 1997 and late 1998, the partnership had received commitments from 7,500 companies across the country to recruit, train, and hire welfare recipients. The partnership said those firms had hired tens of thousands of welfare recipients; in most cases the recipients took low-pay, entry-level jobs, but starting in mid-1998 the partnership was working with major corporations to match welfare recipients with better-paying, white-collar jobs.

In one surprising development, many firms reported that job turnover was much lower among former welfare recipients than other employees. For example, the United Parcel Service said it had hired 10,400 former welfare recipients, most for part-time jobs paying an average of $8.50 per hour. Turnover among those employees was substantially lower than among the rest of the company's nonskilled workforce, offsetting the extra costs to the company of training and counseling the former welfare recipients.

Following is the executive summary from the report, "Welfare Reform: States Are Restructuring Programs to Reduce Welfare Dependence," submitted to Congress June 18, 1998, by the General Accounting Office:

Purpose

The Personal Responsibility and Work Opportunity Reconciliation Act of 1996 (P.L. 104–193) made sweeping changes to the nation's cash assistance program for needy families with children. Title I of the law replaced the Aid to Families With Dependent Children (AFDC) program with fixed block grants to the states to provide Temporary Assistance for Needy Families (TANF) and ended the entitlement of families to assistance. In fiscal year 1996, AFDC paid benefits of over $20 billion in combined state and federal funds to a nationwide caseload that averaged about 4.6 million families a month. As specified by the new law, the goals of TANF include ending welfare dependence by promoting job preparation, work, and marriage; preventing and reducing the incidence of out-of-wedlock pregnancies; encouraging the formation and maintenance of two-parent families; and providing states increased flexibility to help them achieve these goals. Among other provisions, the law requires that, to avoid financial penalties, states must impose work requirements for adults, meet steadily rising requirements for the percentage of adults that must participate in work activities, and enforce a 5-year lifetime limit on receiving federal assistance.

At the request of the Chairmen of the Senate Committee on Finance and the House Committee on Ways and Means' Subcommittee on Human Resources, this report (1) describes states' efforts to require and encourage welfare recipients and potential recipients to assume greater personal responsibility, (2) examines how states are providing services to support the objectives of TANF, and (3) reviews early reported data to assess states' progress in achieving program objectives.

Background

Welfare reform gives states flexibility to design their own programs and strategies for achieving program goals, including how to help welfare recipients move into the workforce. At the same time, states must meet federal requirements that emphasize the importance of work for those receiving assistance. To avoid federal financial penalties, in fiscal year 1997 states must ensure that adult recipients in 25 percent of all their TANF families and 75 percent of their TANF two-parent families are engaged in work activities. These rates increase in subsequent years. To be counted in states' participation rates, adults must participate a specified minimum numbers of hours per week in work activities, such as unsubsidized employment, on-the-job training, job search and job readiness assistance, community service, and vocational educational training. If adults fail to participate as required, states must reduce their cash assistance and may terminate assistance for the entire family. The Department of Health and Human Services (HHS) is the primary federal agency providing oversight of states' welfare programs. HHS' responsibilities include developing regulations and assessing penalties for noncompliance with the law.

Because many states had already begun experimenting with changing their AFDC programs through waivers of federal law, states were at different stages of implementing their reform efforts when the federal legislation was enacted. For example, Oregon implemented its welfare reform program statewide under waivers in mid-1996, while California did not enact welfare reform legislation until mid-1997.

To obtain information for this request, GAO selected seven states for in-depth tracking on the basis of various program indicators and demographic characteristics: California, Connecticut, Louisiana, Maryland, Oregon, Texas, and Wisconsin. In these states, GAO collected and analyzed program data as well as interviewed state and local officials and members of community advisory committees and advocacy groups. In addition, to provide information on other states—and on all 50 states, when data were available—GAO analyzed data collected by HHS and other organizations. In developing the methodology for this study, GAO consulted with its Welfare Reform Advisory Committee, which is composed of 11 experts in this field.

Results in Brief

Consistent with the thrust of the federal welfare reform law, states are moving away from a welfare system focused on entitlement to assistance to one that emphasizes finding employment as quickly as possible and becoming more self-sufficient. In the seven states GAO visited, welfare offices are generally being transformed into job placement centers, and in some instances applicants are expected to engage in job search activities as soon as they apply for assistance. Adults with mental and physical impairments and those caring for small children are less likely than before to be exempt from participating in work activities, and adults who fail to participate as required are more likely to have their family's assistance terminated. In the states GAO reviewed, the average proportion of adult recipients required to participate in work activities increased from 44 percent in 1994 to 65 percent in 1997. In addition, to reinforce the expectation that welfare is temporary, states have established time limits on receiving cash assistance—in some cases shorter than 5 years—and have modified various policies to help make welfare recipients financially better off if they obtain jobs than if they do not. States also have devised strategies to reduce the need for monthly cash assistance, such as providing one-time, lump-sum payments in lieu of monthly payments and enhancing their efforts to reduce the number of out-of-wedlock pregnancies.

States also have modified their programs to better support welfare recipients in becoming more self-sufficient. In their efforts to change the culture of welfare offices, states are expanding welfare workers' roles by shifting their priorities from determining eligibility and cash assistance levels to helping recipients obtain work and become more self-sufficient. At the same time, states are using some of the additional budgetary resources available under the welfare reform law to enhance support services, such as transportation and child care, for recipients participating in work activities and poor families who have found jobs and left the welfare rolls. In addition, states are working to enhance their capacity to treat physical and mental health problems. In Oregon, state officials estimated that about 50 percent of the welfare caseload requires drug or alcohol treatment. Moreover, some states have given local administrative entities greater flexibility to design welfare-to-work programs tailored to the needs of their recipients. Implementing all these changes has not been quick or easy: among the most challenging and widespread implementation issues reported by the states have been training staff to perform their new roles and finding ways to involve recipients with multiple barriers to participation, such as mental and physical health problems and low literacy levels, in work activities.

Nationwide, welfare dependence has decreased. Welfare caseloads decreased by 30 percent between January 1994 and September 1997—and decreased by a larger percentage each year during this period. In addition, GAO's analysis showed that the seven states reviewed have generally increased their job placement rates. While these results are promising, it is too early to draw definitive conclusions about the success of states' programs because it is uncertain how states' programs will perform as more recipients leave welfare for work and states face increasing proportions of recipients with multiple problems, or if the current strong economy undergoes a major downturn. Moreover, little is known about program impacts, such as the effect the programs have had on the well-being of children and families. Future monitoring of states' programs will need to focus on areas such as job retention and earnings progression, children's welfare, and family stability.

Principal Findings

States' Policies Are Shifting Emphasis from Entitlement to Self-Sufficiency

States have modified their policies to require and encourage welfare recipients and potential recipients to seek work and become more self-sufficient. For example, in all seven of the states GAO visited, the proportion of recipients assigned to job placement activities—as opposed to education or training activities—was substantially higher in 1997 than in 1994, and the proportion assigned to job placement activities more than quadrupled in Connecticut and Louisiana during this time. All seven states now require nonexempt recipients to participate in work activities immediately upon applying for assistance or as soon as possible thereafter. In addition, five of the seven states have strengthened their sanctions by adopting provisions for terminating the assistance of the entire family for noncompliance with work requirements.

As part of an effort to "make work pay," 42 states have changed their policies relating to the treatment of earned income from those previously in effect under AFDC to permit recipients to keep more of their monthly cash assistance payments or retain them for longer periods once they begin working. Nearly all states have increased the amount of assets or the value of a vehicle that recipients can own and still remain eligible for cash assistance. The asset and vehicle limits under the AFDC program were widely considered to be too low, creating barriers to families' efforts to become more self-sufficient.

States also have adopted varying time limits on the receipt of cash assistance. Nineteen states have established policies to terminate assistance for some families sooner than the 5 years specified by the federal law, but these states generally have also adopted policies to extend assistance beyond these limits in certain circumstances. For example, recipients in Connecticut can receive 6-month extensions to the state's 21-month time limit if they have made a good faith effort to comply with work requirements but have been unable to find employment. Tracking the time families receive cash assistance poses significant challenges for many states, given their need to upgrade their automated information systems to collect all of the data required for such an undertaking. While states have set time limits on eligibility for cash assistance, they generally have not used their flexibility under TANF to reduce cash assistance levels or deny eligibility to specific groups of people, except for convicted drug felons.

In addition, states are pursuing various strategies to reduce the need for welfare. As of November 1997, 30 states had reported that they were using "diversion," a major new strategy that seeks to divert some applicants from monthly cash assistance by providing other forms of assistance, such as one-time, lump-sum payments; support services such as child care or Medicaid; and assistance with job search. To enhance the collection of child support, the welfare law requires states to reduce the amount of families' cash assistance by at least 25 percent for noncooperation with child support enforcement requirements. Sixteen states have adopted stronger provisions that call for terminating families' entire cash assistance payments on this basis. Finally, recognizing the strong link between teenage childbearing and welfare dependence, states are enhancing existing pregnancy prevention programs, especially for teens. Strategies being used by our case study states include abstinence education, stronger enforcement of statutory rape laws, and male involvement programs.

States Are Enhancing Support Services for Recipients

As states seek to expand the number of adults participating in work activities, they have generally expanded the roles of welfare workers to better support the work focus of their programs. Workers' new responsibilities vary but include such tasks as motivating clients to seek work, exploring the potential for diversions, and collecting more information about applicants and recipients to determine what they need to facilitate self-sufficiency. Training workers to perform these broader responsibilities has been especially challenging because of the need to help workers change their perspectives and help them cope with workload pressures. For example, Oregon responded to such challenges, in part, by streamlining paperwork for determining eligibility to allow staff more time for new responsibilities.

As a result of their large, recent caseload declines, most states have more budgetary resources for their welfare programs under the TANF funding formula than they would have had under prior law, under which funding was tied to caseload size. The seven states GAO reviewed are using some of the additional available budgetary resources to provide services to help families address barriers to employment. For example, these states are using a range of approaches to help recipients obtain reliable transportation, such as providing funding for rural transportation systems, enlisting volunteers to provide transportation for recipients, and providing funds for vehicle repairs. Some states have enhanced services by providing mentors or making case management available to those who have left welfare for jobs. As the most readily employable recipients leave welfare, states and localities are concerned that they will face a more difficult to serve population. In response to such concerns, Baltimore added a social service component to its welfare reform program, and Oregon placed counselors on site to provide mental health and substance abuse services. In addition, the seven states GAO visited have used federal and state funding to increase overall expenditures for their fiscal year 1997 child care subsidy programs for TANF and other low-income families, with increases over fiscal year 1996 expenditures ranging from about 2 percent in Maryland to 62 percent in Louisiana.

As welfare reform has provided states greater flexibility, some of GAO's case study states, in turn, have given local administrative entities greater flexibility to design programs tailored to the needs of their recipients. While policies regarding eligibility and cash assistance levels in these states continue to be set at the state level, local administrative entities now have more flexibility to customize their policies for moving recipients from welfare to work. To promote local accountability, these states are using methods such as creating financial incentives and establishing performance measures that focus more on desired outcomes. For example, California's welfare reform law stipulates that counties are to receive financial bonuses on the basis of their cost savings from recipients leaving welfare because of employment that lasted at least 6 months, increased earnings by recipients because of employment, and diversion of applicants from welfare for at least 6 months.

Welfare Dependence Has Decreased, But Little Is Known About Impacts on Families

While the number of families receiving cash assistance nationwide decreased 30 percent between January 1994 and September 1997, more than two-thirds of this decrease has occurred since January 1996. GAO estimated that three of the case study states more than doubled their job placement rates from 1995 to 1997, and two of them increased their rates by more than 70 percent. In addition, the seven states generally have increased the percentages of families participating in welfare-to-work programs under TANF compared with their prior welfare-to-work programs. While all seven states reported that they would meet their required TANF all-families participation rates for fiscal year 1997, two states reported that they would not meet their required rates for two-parent families.

In many states, favorable economic conditions appear to have facilitated implementation of "work first" approaches. It is not yet known, however, how states' welfare reform programs will perform under weaker economic conditions. In addition, as indicated by states that have experienced large caseload reductions, many of the remaining recipients have multiple problems that interfere with their ability to work. So far, little is known about how effective states will be in helping these families become more self-supporting.

Despite early indications of progress toward key goals of welfare reform, much remains unknown about how families fare after leaving welfare with respect to economic stability and child and family well-being. However, some states have efforts under way to obtain information on such topics. For example, Maryland is tracking a random sample of families that have exited welfare to provide information on topics including employment and earnings, welfare recidivism, and receipt of foster care. In addition, concerned about the importance of having national data on the impacts of states' welfare reforms, the Congress included provisions in the welfare reform law that direct HHS to conduct research on the benefits, costs, and effects of state programs funded under TANF, as well as mandate that the Bureau of the Census expand a national survey of families to permit an evaluation of the law's impacts.

Comments from HHS and the States

GAO obtained comments on a draft of this report from HHS and the seven case study states. HHS and the states generally agreed with the report's findings and provided additional technical information that GAO incorporated in the report as appropriate.

HUD REPORT ON THE STATE OF THE CITIES

June 19, 1998

After decades of decline, America's cities were on the mend at the close of the twentieth century—but many of them continued to lose population and faced severe shortages of adequate jobs, education, and housing. Those were the good news–bad news conclusions of a "State of the Cities" report issued June 19 by the federal Department of Housing and Urban Development (HUD).

The report was part of a campaign by the Clinton administration to focus congressional attention on the needs of the cities and the nation's less fortunate citizens. A companion HUD report documented the continuing decline in availability of affordable housing for the poor. The reports—coupled with prospects for the government's first budget surplus in nearly three decades—may have helped convince Congress to give HUD a significant budget boost for fiscal year 1999. (Housing report, p. 253)

Urban Renewal

The HUD report documented how the booming economy of the 1990s, along with other trends, had helped revitalize many of the nation's large cities. Urban employment levels were up, crime and poverty were down, visitors were coming back to inner cities, and most city governments were operating with balanced budgets—all in stark contrast to the gloom of the three previous decades, which lead to widespread fears that American cities were dead or dying.

The surge of new job opportunities in the cities was one of the most encouraging trends produced by overall improvements in the nation's economy. The report noted, for example, that the unemployment rate in central cities dropped to 5.3 percent in March 1998 from 8.2 percent five years earlier. Using another measure, during the same period the number of city residents with jobs rose by 10.4 percent; that rate was twice the increase in the inner city labor force, "suggesting that many previously unemployed adults were finding jobs," the report said. The report also noted that employers were adding all types of jobs in cities, including the low-skill jobs most in demand for inner-city residents with limited education.

With employment on the rise, crime and poverty were declining in most cities, the report said. The drop in poverty rates was especially noteworthy among black residents, who historically had been the poorest urban residents. Between 1993 and 1996, the report said, the central city poverty rate among blacks fell from 35.8 percent to 31 percent, the lowest level in twenty-two years.

Cities once again were becoming places that people wanted to visit. The report noted that Baltimore, Cleveland, Denver, San Antonio, Seattle, and Washington, D.C. were among the cities that experienced a "renaissance" as tourist centers with sports, entertainment, and cultural attractions.

The report noted that the extent of all these trends varied from city to city. Some cities in the Southwest and Northwest were in much better shape, according to all economic and social indicators, than many of the older industrial cities of the Northeast and Midwest. But even the latter cities were sharing in many of the improvements that, just a few years before, might have seemed unlikely.

Urban Negatives

Despite the definite upswing, most urban cities still were at a disadvantage when compared with their suburban neighbors, the report said. Particularly in the case of the older industrial cities, middle-class families continued to flee to the suburbs, most often because of high crime rates and poor schools in the cities. Poverty remained much higher in the cities than in the suburbs and tended to be concentrated in black and Hispanic neighborhoods.

The improving economy and decades of social programs had not eliminated what the HUD report called the three "opportunity gaps": the lack of adequate jobs, education, and housing for inner-city residents. The shortage of jobs was especially critical for those with few skills or little education. The HUD report quoted a U.S. Conference of Mayors study predicting that, in seventy-four urban counties, there could be two job-seekers for each available low-skill job that became available in the next five years. One factor in this job shortage was the requirement under the 1996 welfare reform law for able-bodied welfare recipients to find work; the mayors' study estimated that over five years some 353,000 former welfare recipients would be unable to find low-skill jobs. Tens of thousands of low-skill jobs were being created in the suburbs, but the report noted that inner-city residents often lacked the transportation to get to those jobs. (Welfare reform, Historic Documents of 1996, p. 450)

Urban school systems continued to face a host of problems—such as high drop-out rates, crumbling school buildings, drugs, and violence in the schools—that made it difficult for them to provide the type of education that would enable inner-city youths to escape poverty. Also, millions of inner-city residents could not afford or find decent housing. The report cited figures from HUD's companion housing study, including an estimate that more than five million low-income Americans paid more than 50 percent of their income in rent or lived in substandard housing.

The problems of America's cities did not develop overnight, the report noted, and so correcting them would take a long-term effort. The report called on Congress to work with the administration to "reinvent the way the Federal Government does business in the cities." New, streamlined federal programs would help states, cities, and private businesses create better jobs, educational opportunities, and housing in the cities, the report stated.

Following are excerpts from "The State of the Cities: 1998," a report issued June 19, 1998, by the federal Department of Housing and Urban Development:

Executive Summary

In early 1997, President Clinton asked the U.S. Department of Housing and Urban Development (HUD) to examine two questions. First, as we come to the close of a century that saw the rise of many of America's great cities, what is the state of those cities today? And second, what more can the Clinton-Gore Administration do to prepare our cities to meet the economic and social challenges of the future?

In response last year, HUD's 1997 *State of the Cities* report found both cause for optimism and reason for concern. The good news was that after two decades of decline, America's cities were on the rebound. A strong national economy—combined with the innovation of a new breed of mayors and the success of the Administration's targeted first-term urban agenda—left many cities fiscally and economically stronger than they had been in years. The bad news was that these same cities faced several structural challenges—on concentrated and growing poverty, on the job disparity between cities and suburbs, and on middle-class migration from the cities—that could eventually undermine the long-term success of urban America. This report finds that these problems didn't happen overnight, and they won't be solved overnight—but they must be addressed if America is going to thrive in the 21st century.

This second annual report, *The State of the Cities 1998*, picks up where last year's report left off. It does so at a time of renewed appreciation for the role cities play in our national success.

As the President noted in his 1998 State of the Union Address, "Cities are the vibrant hubs of great metropolitan regions." This fact was illustrated in a recent report by the U.S. Conference of Mayors and the National Association of Counties, which showed that metropolitan areas have generated 86 percent of the Nation's total economic growth since 1992, 84 percent of all jobs—and are home to 85 percent of our people. Perhaps more than ever, the fates of city and suburb are closely tied.

It is now—when the economy is humming, our communities are growing, our Federal budget is balanced, and our Nation is at peace—that we should examine the state and fate of America's cities. How America responds to the challenges articulated in this report will depend in large measure on how Congress responds to an Administration budget that goes a long way toward meeting those challenges. This report has three main findings:

- Finding #1: Driven by a robust national economy, cities are fiscally and economically the strongest they've been in a decade.
- Finding #2: Despite recent gains, cities still face the triple threat of concentrated poverty, shrinking populations, and middle-class flight that began two decades ago.
- Finding #3: Cities face three fundamental opportunity gaps—in jobs, education, and housing—that are critical to reducing poverty and attracting and retaining middle-class families.

These three findings and President Clinton's response to each are outlined in more detail below.

Finding #1: Driven by a robust national economy, cities are fiscally and economically the strongest they've been in a decade.

Time magazine recently said that "the U.S. now enjoys what in many respects is the healthiest economy in its history, and probably that of any Nation, ever." Driven by a prudent strategy of fiscal accountability balanced with targeted investments, the national economy is experiencing an unprecedented run of economic expansion. The budget deficit had 11 zeroes at the beginning of 1993, but the budget is now in surplus, with surpluses projected for the next 5 years. More than 16 million new jobs have been created in the past 5 years, and unemployment is at a 28-year low. Since 1993, incomes have been growing for all income groups but fastest for those at the bottom of the income ladder. And low interest rates combined with steady economic growth last year produced the highest homeownership rate in history.

While significant gaps remain, cities now are sharing in America's economic comeback:

- National economic progress is steady and strong.
  - The economy has produced 16 million new jobs and record low unemployment. Incomes are rising, particularly among those at the bottom of the economic ladder.
  - Regional economies, with cities at their center, are now the primary engines of national prosperity.
- Jobs are growing and unemployment is falling in central cities.
  - Central city employment is on the rise. Between 1993 and 1998, the number of employed workers living in central cities increased by 10.4 percent, or by almost 3.7 million people.
  - Central city unemployment rates have fallen. Unemployment in central cities fell to an average of 5.3 percent in March 1998, down from 8.2 percent in March 1993. In some cities—such as Austin, Charlotte,

Phoenix, and San Jose, for example—unemployment is now under 4 percent.

- Increased job opportunities in the cities. From 1991 to 1994, only 13 percent of the new low-skilled jobs were created in central cities. From 1994 to 1995, that number jumped to 34 percent.
- Central city poverty rates are falling. Poverty rates for central cities have fallen from 21.5 percent in 1993 to 19.6 percent in 1996. For African-Americans, who have historically experienced high rates of poverty, central city poverty rates have fallen from 35.8 percent in 1993 to 31.0 percent in 1996—the lowest level in 22 years.

- Cities are improving as places to live.
  - Many downtowns are experiencing a new renaissance as centers of tourism, sports, entertainment, and the arts. Cities as diverse as Baltimore, Cleveland, Denver, San Antonio, Seattle, and Washington, D.C., are becoming new destinations for tourists and residents of the larger regions.
  - Virtually every city in America has a stronger balance sheet today than it did a decade ago. A recent survey by the National League of Cities found that two-thirds of participating cities reported that they "were better able to meet city financial needs" in fiscal year 1997 than in the previous year—and all but 3 of the 77 largest cities had investment-grade bond ratings that enabled them to borrow funds at favorable rates.
  - Crime rates—particularly for violent crime—have plummeted for 6 years straight. Nationwide, violent crime dropped an estimated 27 percent between 1991 and 1997 and by 19 percent in large cities between 1993 and 1997. During the first 6 months of 1997 alone, the rate dropped by 6 percent.
  - Public perceptions are changing. In a recent survey by Money magazine, the Washington, D.C., metro area was listed as the most "livable" community on the East coast—countering the trends over the past 10 years, when small towns often received the most attention. And U.S. News and World Report recently called attention to the growing number of "smart cities" that are leaner more strategic, and more focused on sustainable growth.

- Homeownership is on the rise.
  - City homeownership rates are at their highest level in 15 years. While there is still more work to do to reduce the homeownership gap between central cities and suburbs, half of all central city households owned homes in 1997—representing an increase of approximately 1 million new homeowners since 1994.

Administration Response: The President plans to continue on the course of fiscal prudence, in three ways: (1) by preserving any budget surpluses until Social Security is reformed for the 21st century; (2) by adhering to a strategy of targeted investments in America's people and communities;

and (3) by continuing to reinvent and streamline the Federal Government to be a better, more effective partner for America's communities.

Finding #2: Despite recent gains, cities still face the triple threat of concentrated poverty, shrinking populations, and middle-class flight that began two decades ago.

- Central cities' share of metropolitan populations continues to decline. Although most central cities continue to grow slowly, only 11 of the 30 largest cities in 1970 have more people in them today than two decades ago. These population losses frequently translate into a shrinking municipal tax base. Population changes often reflect regional variation. While older industrial cities in the Northeast and Midwest—including Philadelphia, Washington, Detroit, and Chicago—continue to see their populations shrink, more "elastic cities" in the West, such as Las Vegas, Albuquerque, and Phoenix, continue their sharp population climb.

- Middle-class families are still leaving central cities. Since 1970, nearly 6 million middle-income and affluent families have left central cities. At the same time, between 1985 and 1995, the number of high-income families (defined as 150 percent of median) that located in suburbs grew by 16 percent, compared with just 2 percent for central cities. When asked why people are leaving cities, two answers most commonly cited are the poor quality of urban schools and the relatively high rates of urban crime.

- Poverty in cities is higher than in the suburbs. While overall poverty rates have dropped, poverty is more concentrated in distressed urban areas. Despite a drop in central city poverty rates between 1993 and 1996, 1 in every 5 urban families lived in poverty in 1996, compared with fewer than 1 in 10 suburban families. And there is a growing dichotomy in rates of minority poverty. While the rate of African-American poverty is at its lowest level in history, poverty in cities disproportionately affects minority populations—72 percent of the poor in cities are minority.

- Poverty remains highly concentrated in certain neighborhoods. The persistence of discrimination in the housing market leads to discrimination in our cities. Even if people are not poor themselves, they are likely to live in tracts of concentrated poverty. Indeed, almost one in four African-American and Hispanic residents of central cities live in census tracts where more than 40 percent of their neighbors are poor, compared with only 3 percent of the white urban population. Such high-poverty areas are often plagued by severe social dysfunctions such as violent crime and drug abuse, as well as family problems such as teenage pregnancy.

Administration Response: A three-part strategy concentrated on using incentives to bring jobs and businesses back to central cities, improving urban schools, and promoting homeownership and affordable housing is articulated in detail in the following section.

Finding #3: Cities face three fundamental opportunity gaps—in jobs, education, and housing—that are critical to reducing poverty and attracting and retaining middle-class families.

(A) Cities Face a Jobs Gap

While more jobs are being created in cities, there is still a sizable but manageable mismatch between the number of low-skilled jobs and the number of low-skilled urban residents who need work. The coordinated efforts of all levels of government, along with the private sector, are needed to address this challenge.

- The challenge facing America's cities. While projecting job gaps is difficult, one effort to do so is a forthcoming report from the U.S. Conference of Mayors (USCM). With job forecasts prepared by Regional Financial Associates, the USCM projects that there could be two job seekers for each low-skilled job in 74 urban counties over the next 5 years, with substantial variation among areas. This report further estimates that across these 74 urban areas, the number of current welfare recipients who will need jobs over the next five years could exceed the growth in low-skilled jobs by 353,000.

Projections of these job gaps vary; in any case, the challenge is to create the kinds of jobs needed in the places where people need them most and to help urban residents take advantage of these job opportunities. This challenge is not insurmountable. For example, in the period 1991 to 1994, only 13 percent of the new low-skilled jobs were created in central cities, compared with 34 percent from 1994 to 1995.

- Minority youth unemployment remains high. The unemployment rate for minority youth (ages 16 to 19) was 26 percent in central cities in May 1998—five times the Nation's overall unemployment rate.
- There is a wider wage gap. While progress has been made on the wage gap over the past few years, we haven't regained what we lost over the past 20 years. Over the past two decades, earnings inequality widened as the inflation-adjusted wages of low-skilled workers declined and the wages of high-skilled workers increased. According to a recent report by the U.S. Department of Labor, from 1982 to 1996, the inflation-adjusted hourly wages of workers in the top one-tenth of the workforce increased from $24.80 to $25.74 an hour while wages for workers in the bottom one-tenth of the workforce fell from $6.28 to $5.46. Adjusting for benefits added further to the growth of earnings inequality.
- People can't get to the jobs. Transportation to entry-level jobs in the suburbs is a substantial barrier. In Boston, for example, 98 percent of welfare recipients live within one-quarter mile of a bus route or other mass transit stop, but only 58 percent of potential entry-level jobs in the Boston metro area are within 1 mile of mass transit.
- The lack of affordable child care hits central cities hard. Safe and affordable child care is necessary to allow parents to work. However, nationwide, only 10 percent of the families who qualify for Federal child care assistance receive help. Many cities have tens of thousands of families on waiting lists for child care assistance.

Administration Response: The President's budget includes several important initiatives aimed at reducing the low-skilled jobs gap by creating jobs where people live and by connecting people to the places where jobs are being created. To create jobs, the President has proposed a new Community Empowerment Fund, administered by HUD, which will help create an estimated 280,000 jobs alone. He has also proposed increased funding for Community Development Financial Institutions Fund and creation of a second round of Empowerment Zones. And he has proposed extending the welfare-to-work tax credit, the work opportunity tax credit, and the brownfields tax incentive.

In addition to these budget initiatives, the President has called on the private sector to expand its efforts in response to welfare reform. In May 1998, he challenged the private Welfare to Work Partnership to double its number of business partners to 10,000 and to double the number of people these businesses hire from the welfare rolls to 270,000 in 1998.

To connect welfare recipients to jobs, the President has proposed $283 million for 50,000 Welfare-to-Work Housing Vouchers. His Access to Jobs transportation initiative to help welfare recipients and other low-income workers get to their jobs was recently enacted as part of the Transportation Equity Act for the 21st century (TEA21)—the reauthorization of ISTEA2. In addition, the President recently released the first round of 49 Welfare-to-Work competitive grants from the U.S. Department of Labor to help local communities move the hardest to place welfare recipients into employment. Welfare-to-Work funds are also being provided to local communities through formula grants to States, which are in turn administered by local Private Industry Councils.

The President has proposed other job support and workforce development initiatives that would enhance employment opportunities. He has proposed a $250 million Youth Opportunity Areas Initiative to increase employment for out-of-school youth in high-poverty areas. In addition, the President has proposed investing more than $20 billion over 5 years in a new Child Care Initiative to expand the availability, affordability, and quality of child care. The President also has proposed a G.I. Bill for America's Workers to consolidate and streamline activities in the Job Training Partnership Act and empower adults to make better choices for job training services.

(B) Cities Face an Education Gap

Urban schools are failing to prepare an alarming number of America's children to meet the challenges of the new high-technology economy, and—disproportionately—minority children are paying the highest price. In many cases, the poorest schools are serving the children with the greatest needs, and have the fewest resources—both financial and functional—to do so. More than 81 percent of urban schools have a student population that is at least 70 percent poor and 50 percent minority. In addition, many urban schools have trouble recruiting teachers to keep class sizes small and teaching quality high—and too many schools have seen standards erode as systems of "social promotion" graduate students who lack basic skills.

- Basic achievement is lagging—especially in high-poverty inner-city schools. In both 1994 and 1996, 60 percent of the children in urban school districts failed to achieve basic levels of competency in reading and math on the National Assessment of Educational Progress. For children in high-poverty urban schools, outcomes were even worse: 77 percent failed to achieve basic competency levels in reading, and 67 percent failed to achieve basic levels of competency in math.
- Low graduation rates in urban high schools. In the Nation's 20 largest urban school districts, more than half of all students never graduate. For millions of urban youth, finishing high school and attending college seems an impossible dream—this in an era demanding high skills for high wages.
- School violence is concentrated in large urban schools. Though school violence is not just an urban problem, violent attacks and fights are much more common in city schools, especially large ones, than they are in suburban schools. In a national survey, 1,800 urban schools reported more than 5,400 fights in which weapons were used during the 1996-97 school year.
- Many urban schools are crumbling. A sizable proportion of urban schools are literally falling apart. A recent General Accounting Office (GAO) study found that 38 percent of central city schools (serving more than 5.5 million students) had at least one inadequate building and two-thirds (with more than 10 million students) had at least one inadequate building feature, such as a roof or plumbing.

Administration Response: Urban education is a major priority in the President's budget. Proposed initiatives include the creation of Education Opportunity Zones to direct $1.5 billion over 5 years to low-achieving school districts in high-poverty areas; Federal tax credits to pay interest on an estimated $22 billion in School Modernization Bonds to rebuild and repair schools; $413 million for America Reads, a national campaign to increase children's literacy; $140 million for High Hopes to launch a national effort to help young people prepare for post-secondary education; and $7.3 billion over 5 years to raise educational achievement by hiring new and reducing class size in grades 1 to 3.

With so many of the better jobs in today's economy requiring post-secondary education, Administration policies, including HOPE Scholarships and Lifetime Learning Credits, the largest Pell Grant in history, and universal eligibility for subsidized loans, have made financial access to post-secondary education possible for everyone.

(C) Cities Face a Housing Gap

The Nation's affordable housing crisis has reached record levels, especially in central cities. At the same time, while homeownership is at its highest level ever, the central city homeownership rate continues to lag significantly behind the suburbs.

- Urban homeownership—including middle-class homeownership—lags behind the suburbs. Homeownership rates are 70 percent in suburbs but just 50 percent in cities. According to data from the 1995 American Housing Survey presented in the Harvard University Joint Center for Housing Studies' annual report, The State of the Nation's Housing 1997, central city residents of all income levels are less likely to own a home than suburban residents with similar incomes. The Harvard report found, for example, that among moderate-income households, 71.3 percent of suburban residents own a home compared with just 51.8 percent of central city residents at the same income level.
- Racial discrimination at all income levels adds to the urban homeownership gap. The Harvard University Joint Center data also document that African-American and Hispanic households of all income levels are less likely to own a home than white households of the same income group. This racial gap persists, even among households with incomes that are 20 to 50 percent higher than area median. While 78.3 percent of white households in this income group owned homes, the share for African-Americans is only 62.7 and for Hispanics, only 64.5 percent. Home Mortgage Disclosure Act (HMDA) data show substantial differentials in the mortgage denial rates between whites and minorities—and between city and suburban residents. The Harvard study concludes that such differentials result in part from "prejudicial lending and housing market practices still plagu(ing) some areas of the country."
- Worst case housing needs are at a record high. Despite robust economic growth, between 1993 and 1995, a record 5.3 million very low-income renters paid more than 50 percent of their income for rent or lived in substandard quality housing—commonly referred to as "worst case housing needs."
- Central cities are hardest hit. Households with severe housing problems are disproportionately found in central cities: 18 percent of central city renters—a total of 2.8 million families—have severe housing problems.
- Worst case needs increasingly affect the working poor. Between 1991 and 1995, worst case needs for families with at least one person earning a full-time paycheck rose by 265,000 families—an increase of 24 percent.
- There has been a sharp decline in affordable housing. Between 1993 and 1995, there was a loss of 900,000 rental units affordable to very low income families—a reduction of 9 percent. There was an even greater reduction of 16 percent in the number of units affordable to extremely low-income renters, who are people earning less than 30 percent of an area median income.
- Congress has provided no new housing vouchers to families on the waiting list for housing assistance since 1994. Until then, for as long as housing records have been kept—no matter what state the economy was in or who occupied the Oval Office—America had always increased its supply of affordable housing.

- Homelessness continues to plague our Nation's cities. Driven by a lack of affordable housing, inadequate access to decent jobs, and a myriad of problems ranging from mental illness and substance abuse to domestic violence and outdated or non-existent job skills, homelessness continues to be a challenge to cities across the Nation. Best estimates suggest that 600,000 men, women, and children are homeless on any given day, with several times that many persons experiencing homelessness each year.

Administration Response: The President's budget includes a range of proposals to expand homeownership, expand rental housing assistance, and reduce homelessness. These include an additional 100,000 Section 8 housing assistance rental vouchers; a new HOME Bank that will expand the use of HUD's successful HOME housing block grant funds; another round of Home-ownership Zones; record amount of funding for Homeless Assistance programs; a 40 percent expansion of the Low-Income Housing Tax Credit; increased promotion of Fair Lending; expansion of the Federal Housing Administration (FHA) loan limits, which will enable central city mixed-income development to help attract more middle-class families back to central cities; and a 73 percent increase in funding for fair housing education and enforcement.

Building Safe, Secure, and Sustainable Communities

In addition to closing opportunity gaps in the areas of jobs, housing and education, the President's FY 99 budget includes several important initiatives that will strengthen the environment and improve the quality of life in our cities. These include cleaning up and redeveloping brownfields; improving access to health care; continuing support for local efforts to prevent and reduce crime; and ensuring that there is a level playing field and equal opportunity for immigrants and minorities.

Conclusion

In our cities, we still see America's greatest problems. The great progress we've made in the past few years causes us to believe we can solve the remaining problems if we direct sufficient attention, commitment, and resources to doing so.

After more than two decades of wrenching change that undermined both the economic and social foundations of America's cities, 1998 finds most cities as financially strong as they have been in years. America's central cities—and the metropolitan areas that surround them—have helped fuel the most aggressive economic expansion in our Nation's history. Jobs, home-ownership, and consumer confidence are all up. Crime, unemployment, and inflation are all down.

At the same time, many of the old challenges remain—poverty, middle-class flight, and shrinking populations. The divisions in urban America are still strong, but they are no longer strictly black and white. Urban America today is Korean, Dominican, Mexican, and Latvian, among many others—the greatest influx of new immigrants in nearly 100 years. Today, more than 100 languages are spoken in Los Angeles schools, and 140 different racial and ethnic groups live in Detroit and Wayne County, Michigan, alone. The complexity of this new melting pot casts a light on three serious but surmountable gaps facing cities at the turn of the 21st century—namely, how we work, how we are educated, and how and where we live.

The primary observation of the President's "One America" Race Initiative—that the great unfinished work of democracy is the creation of a true union, a single society—takes on new urgency as well. Thirty years ago, there were 10 people working for every 1 person living on Social Security. Within 10 years, there will be just three people working for every one person living on Social Security—and those three people are more likely than ever before to speak a different language at home or come from a different country. At a time when fewer than 50 urban school districts are educating nearly half of our minority population we had better be sure as a Nation that our people are trained and educated to carry the workload in the 21st century. By default, we must be more unified than ever before. Our common future depends on it.

With this new urgency comes new opportunities. Our economic success has given us two great gifts. First, it has helped show us what is possible. For example, since 1994, we've added 1 million new homeowners in urban America. The combination of a good economy and a national homeownership strategy supported the success. This report identifies serious remaining challenges and at the same time, offers answers which have a proven track record.

The second great gift is that our strong economy has created a unique window of opportunity to address the challenges that face us, and the President has moved aggressively into that window—proposing the most wide-ranging budget for cities in more than a decade. This program will go a long way toward addressing the challenges articulated in this report. It is a program that recognizes that government alone cannot solve every problem, that it must be a good partner with the private sector. Ultimately, it is a program that recognizes we will only succeed if we are together—not city or suburb, not black or white, not rich or poor—but One America.

Rarely has the Nation ever been better positioned to tackle the challenges of rebuilding and re-energizing our nation's proud cities. If we are not now ready to take on these challenges when the budget is in surplus, unemployment is at record lows and the stock market is at record highs, when will we be ready?

Alternatively, if we have the courage and foresight—both as a Nation and on Capitol Hill—to address these challenges head-on and to enact many of the ideas and FY 1999 budget initiatives proposed by the President, we can ensure that America's cities have not only a proud past but a bright future. And we don't have a moment to waste. Our cities and their people are waiting. . . .

Part Two: Closing the Opportunity Gaps

Only a few years ago it seemed as if the Federal Government, hamstrung by exploding deficits and paralyzed by a crisis of public confidence in government itself, might withdraw completely and leave cities to fend for themselves. President Clinton has offered a new approach, one that is firmly committed to cities, but charts a smarter, more effective role for the Federal Government.

This Administration recognizes that Washington cannot pay for everything, should not regulate everything, and must not hand down mandates. Rather, the Federal role is more appropriately defined first as establishing broad national goals and priorities, and second as effectively providing the resources that States and local governments need to address the urgent challenges facing our cities. Discarding top-down approaches to urban policy, the Clinton-Gore Administration has adopted the ideas of mayors, faith and community leaders, businesses, and others in forging a genuine partnership between Washington and our Nation's cities and metropolitan areas. A strategy of community empowerment focuses on creating opportunity, demanding responsibility, and promoting a sense of community.

Accordingly, the Administration has worked within the Executive branch and with Congress to reinvent the way the Federal Government does business in cities, creating a new generation of programs and streamlined regulations that tear down barriers to opportunity. Vice President Gore's Partnership for Reinventing Government is helping to ensure that these programs work as they were intended and provide a level of service, efficiency, accountability, and competence that the American people have a right to expect.

President Clinton's urban agenda reflects a new consensus around some old ideas about how to build stronger communities. It involves moving beyond "business as usual" to provide important new types of assistance to cities, with particular emphasis on helping communities weave together disparate Federal programs, as well as regional problem solving that responds to the way we live and the way our economy functions.

Key Components

The Administration's urban agenda is built around the following components:

Closing the Jobs Gap

- Boost business investment and job creation in central cities and connect people to work opportunities, improve workforce preparedness and job skills, and increase access to child care.

Closing the Education Gap

- Encourage school reform through education opportunity zones and other initiatives, repair and modernize school facilities, and reduce class sizes with 100,000 new teachers.

Closing the Housing Gap

- Expand homeownership; reduce worst case housing needs by increasing the supply of affordable housing; fight housing discrimination; expand assistance to homeless people; and restore and rebuild public housing.

Building Safe, Healthy, and Sustainable Communities

- Strengthen the environment; continue crime-prevention efforts; improve access to health care; and ensure a fair deal for immigrants.

Moving Beyond Business as Usual

- Streamline Federal programs; encourage cooperation among urban and suburban communities to address regional concerns; and promote the development and wide application of technology in cities. . . .

SUPREME COURT ON HIV INFECTION AS A DISABILITY
June 25, 1998

A divided Supreme Court ruled on June 25 that people infected with the virus that causes AIDS (acquired immunodeficiency syndrome) may be protected from discrimination under the federal Americans with Disabilities Act (ADA) even though they show no outward symptoms of the disease. It was the first time that the Court had issued a ruling related to AIDS, for which no cure has yet been found. It was also the first time the Court had made any ruling related to the scope of the landmark federal law protecting the disabled from discrimination.

The ADA, enacted in 1990, barred discrimination in employment and public accommodations, including such services as medical care, against people with disabilities that substantially limited their ability to perform "major life activities." People with full-blown cases of AIDS have always been considered disabled under the law, but the question whether people infected with asymptomatic HIV (human immunodeficiency virus) met the definition of disabled under the ADA had never been tested. Although the Court's ruling in the case of Bragdon v. Abbott *addressed the relatively narrow issue of whether reproduction was a major life activity under the ADA, its finding that HIV infection was "an impairment" under the ADA "from the moment of infection" suggested that a majority of the justices favored a broad interpretation of disability.*

AIDS activists hailed the decision, saying that it could lead to improved public health. If people no longer had to fear losing their jobs if they turned out to be HIV-positive, these activists argued, more people might get tested, and more of those who were found to be HIV-positive might then take precautions to prevent the disease from spreading. Others said the decision could have a positive affect on those Americans who suffered from diabetes, epilepsy, and other diseases that have no outward symptoms. The Court "sent a very strong signal to the lower courts" to interpret the meaning of disability broadly, one advocate for a disability rights group said.

A Limitation on the Ability to Reproduce

The case arose in 1994 when a Maine dentist, Randon Bragdon, refused to fill a cavity for Sidney Abbott in his office because she was HIV-infected; Abbott had disclosed her infection on a new patient information form. Bragdon offered to treat Abbott at a local hospital for the same fee, but she would have had to pay additional hospital fees. She refused and filed a lawsuit against Bragdon, claiming that he had illegally discriminated against her under the ADA.

Abbott's legal argument turned on her assertion that her HIV infection was a disability because it imposed a substantial limitation on a major life activity, namely, her ability to bear children. Women who carry the HIV infection can transmit the virus to their sexual partners as well as to their unborn children. Bragdon argued that the ability to reproduce was not a major life activity under the ADA in the same sense that walking, seeing, and hearing were. He also argued that he had a right to deny treatment to protect his own health. The ADA allows doctors to refuse to treat patients if their condition "poses a direct threat to the health or safety of others."

The Court decided, 5–4, that HIV infection was a disability under the ADA and that reproduction was a major life activity. "In light of the immediacy with which the virus begins to damage the infected person's white blood cells and the severity of the disease, we hold it is an impairment from the moment of infection," Justice Anthony M. Kennedy wrote for the majority. The majority, Kennedy wrote, had "little difficulty" concluding that reproduction was a major life activity under the ADA. "Reproduction and the sexual dynamics surrounding it are central to the life process itself," he wrote.

The question then was whether the HIV infection was "a substantial limitation" on Abbott's ability to reproduce. A positive finding would qualify Abbott to be protected from discrimination under the ADA. Again, the majority answered affirmatively. "Conception and childbirth are not impossible for an HIV victim but, without doubt, are dangerous to public health. This meets the definition of a substantial limitation," Kennedy wrote. He was joined by Justices John Paul Stevens, David H. Souter, Ruth Bader Ginsburg, and Stephen G. Breyer.

Writing in dissent, Chief Justice William H. Rehnquist rejected the notion that reproduction was a major life activity in the sense that breathing and walking were. "No one can deny that reproductive decisions are important in a person's life. But so are decisions as to who to marry, where to live, and how to earn one's living," Rehnquist wrote. But, he said, these important functions were not the same as the activities intended by the ADA, which he defined as "repetitively performed and essential in the day-to-day existence of a normally functioning individual."

Even if reproduction were defined as a major life activity, Rehnquist continued, he disagreed that HIV imposed a substantial limitation on a woman's ability to reproduce. "While individuals infected with HIV may choose not to" conceive and bear a child, "there is no support in language, logic, or our case law for the proposition that such voluntary choices constitute a 'limit' on one's own life activities," he said. Justices Sandra Day O'Connor, Antonin Scalia, and Clarence Thomas also dissented.

The decision was not a clear-cut victory for Abbott because the Court did not decide the discrimination question, that is, whether Bragdon was justified in refusing to treat Abbott in his office on the ground that her infection imposed a significant risk to his own health. Because the scope of the appeal itself did not permit the justices to review this question, Kennedy said, they were sending the case back to the appeals court for further consideration. He added that evidence on the risk to Bragdon should be limited to "objective, scientific information," rather than the determination of individual practitioners. In its brief supporting Abbott, the Justice Department said that the federal Centers for Disease Control and Prevention had found that the risk of HIV being transmitted "in the dental context" was "so low as to be unquantifiable," an opinion supported by the American Medical Association. In his dissent, however, Rehnquist noted that patients had transmitted the HIV virus to health care providers on forty-two documented occasions, which could qualify as objective information justifying Bragdon's refusal to treat Abbott in other than a hospital setting. Bragdon's position was supported by the American Dental Association.

A Decision About More Than "Dentists' Chairs"

AIDS activists hailed the decision; one called it "the most important legal victory for people with HIV in the history of the epidemic." According to the Centers for Disease Control, between 650,000 and 900,000 Americans were infected with HIV; another 242,000 had full-blown AIDS. Several said the ruling could actually improve public health by encouraging more people to seek testing. Many people who suspected that they might have the infection avoided being tested for fear of losing their jobs or their homes. Others said the ruling was an indication of how much attitudes about the deadly disease had changed since the epidemic began. "It reflects that this country has come a long way from moving from simply fear of this disease to a more realistic understanding," Chai Feldman, a Georgetown University law professor, told the Washington Post. *(AIDS epidemic, p. 878)*

Others applauded the majority for their broad interpretation of the ADA. "This isn't just about dentists' chairs," said Matthew Coles, director of the American Civil Liberties Union AIDS project. "Most of the courts have been giving extremely technical readings of the act and restricting" its reach, he said, but this decision is "about everything the Americans with Disabilities Act covers."

People with conditions such as diabetes and epilepsy were heartened by the Court's decision to view a person with no outward signs of a disease as disabled. "I've had insulin-dependent diabetes for eighteen years," said Michael Greene, chairman of the American Diabetes Association's legal advocacy committee. "You couldn't tell from looking at me that I have a noncurable, major disease. In that sense, I'm similar to an HIV person who's nonsymptomatic." The decision emphasizes that people need to be treated fairly, he continued, that employers must accommodate the need for workers with diabetes to eat regularly, test their blood sugar, and give themselves insulin shots. Couples being treated for infertility might also come under the protection of the ADA. A spokesperson for the National Infertility Association said the Court's definition of reproduction as a major life activity meant that employers would have to make work schedule accommodations to permit infertile couples to receive treatment.

Groups representing employers were generally not pleased with the ruling. It "just throws the statute wide open," said one. "It's anybody's guess how far [employers] can be pushed" to accommodate their workers, said another, referring specifically to infertility treatments.

Following are excerpts from the majority and minority opinions in the case of Bragdon v. Abbott, *handed down by the Supreme Court on June 25, 1998, in which the Court ruled that an HIV-infected woman with no symptoms was covered by the Americans with Disabilities Act, which barred discrimination against the disabled in employment and public accommodations:*

No. 97–156

| Randon Bragdon, Petitioner
v.
Sidney Abbott et al. | On writ of certiorari to the
United States Court of Appeals
for the First Circuit |

[June 25, 1998]

JUSTICE KENNEDY delivered the opinion of the Court.

We address in this case the application of the Americans with Disabilities Act of 1990 (ADA), 42 U.S.C. § 12101 et seq., to persons infected with the human immunodeficiency virus (HIV). We granted certiorari to review, first, whether HIV infection is a disability under the ADA when the infection has not yet progressed to the so-called symptomatic phase; and, second, whether the Court of Appeals, in affirming a grant of summary judgment, cited sufficient material in the record to determine, as a matter of law, that respondent's infection with HIV posed no direct threat to the health and safety of her treating dentist.

I

Respondent Sidney Abbott has been infected with HIV since 1986. When the incidents we recite occurred, her infection had not manifested its most serious symptoms. On September 16, 1994, she went to the office of petitioner Randon Bragdon in Bangor, Maine, for a dental appointment. She disclosed her HIV infection on the patient registration form. Petitioner completed a dental examination, discovered a cavity, and informed respondent of his policy against filling cavities of HIV-infected patients. He offered to perform the work at a hospital with no added fee for his services, though respondent would be responsible for the cost of using the hospital's facilities. Respondent declined.

Respondent sued petitioner under state law and § 302 of the ADA, . . . alleging discrimination on the basis of her disability. The state law claims are not before us. Section 302 of the ADA provides:

> "No individual shall be discriminated against on the basis of disability in the full and equal enjoyment of the goods, services, facilities, privileges, advantages, or accommodations of any place of public accommodation by any person who . . . operates a place of public accommodation." . . .

The term "public accommodation" is defined to include the "professional office of a health care provider." . . .

A later subsection qualifies the mandate not to discriminate. It provides:

> "Nothing in this subchapter shall require an entity to permit an individual to participate in or benefit from the goods, services, facilities, privileges, advantages and accommodations of such entity where such individual poses a direct threat to the health or safety of others." . . .

The United States and the Maine Human Rights Commission intervened as plaintiffs. After discovery, the parties filed cross-motions for summary judgment. The District Court ruled in favor of the plaintiffs, holding that respondent's HIV infection satisfied the ADA's definition of disability. . . . The court held further that petitioner raised no genuine issue of material fact as to whether respondent's HIV infection would have posed a direct threat to the health or safety of others during the course of a dental treatment. . . .

The Court of Appeals affirmed. It held respondent's HIV infection was a disability under the ADA, even though her infection had not yet progressed to the symptomatic stage. . . . The Court of Appeals also agreed that treating the respondent in petitioner's office would not have posed a direct threat to the health and safety of others. . . .

II

We first review the ruling that respondent's HIV infection constituted a disability under the ADA. The statute defines disability as:

> "(A) a physical or mental impairment that substantially limits one or more of the major life activities of such individual;
> "(B) a record of such an impairment; or
> "(C) being regarded as having such impairment." . . .

We hold respondent's HIV infection was a disability under subsection (A) of the definitional section of the statute. In light of this conclusion, we need not consider the applicability of subsections (B) or (C).

Our consideration of subsection (A) of the definition proceeds in three steps. First, we consider whether respondent's HIV infection was a physical impairment. Second, we identify the life activity upon which respondent relies (reproduction and child bearing) and determine whether it constitutes a major life activity under the ADA. Third, tying the two statutory phrases together, we ask whether the impairment substantially limited the major life activity. In construing the statute, we are informed by interpretations of parallel definitions in previous statutes and the views of various administrative agencies which have faced this interpretive question.

A

The ADA's definition of disability is drawn almost verbatim from the definition of "handicapped individual" included in the Rehabilitation Act of 1973, 29 U.S. C. § 706(8)(B), and the definition of "handicap" contained in the Fair Housing Amendments Act of 1988, 42 U.S. C. § 3602(h)(1). Congress' repetition of a well-established term carries the implication that Congress intended the term to be construed in accordance with pre-existing regulatory interpretations. In this case, Congress did more than suggest this construction; it adopted a specific statutory provision in the ADA directing as follows:

> Except as otherwise provided in this chapter, nothing in this chapter shall be construed to apply a lesser standard than the standards applied under title V of the Rehabilitation Act of 1973 . . . or the regulations issued by Federal agencies pursuant to such title." . . .

The directive requires us to construe the ADA to grant at least as much protection as provided by the regulations implementing the Rehabilitation Act.

1

The first step in the inquiry under subsection (A) requires us to determine whether respondent's condition constituted a physical impairment. The Department of Health, Education and Welfare (HEW) issued the first regulations interpreting the Rehabilitation Act in 1977. The regulations are of particular significance because, at the time, HEW was the agency responsible for coordinating the implementation and enforcement of § 504. The HEW regulations, which appear without change in the current regulations issued by the Department of Health and Human Services, define "physical or mental impairment" to mean:

> "(A) any physiological disorder or condition, cosmetic disfigurement, or anatomical loss affecting one or more of the following body systems: neurological; musculoskeletal; special sense organs; respiratory, including speech organs; cardiovascular; reproductive, digestive, genito-urinary; hemic and lymphatic; skin; and endocrine; or

"(B) any mental or psychological disorder, such as mental retardation, organic brain syndrome, emotional or mental illness, and specific learning disabilities." . . .

In issuing these regulations, HEW decided against including a list of disorders constituting physical or mental impairments, out of concern that any specific enumeration might not be comprehensive. The commentary accompanying the regulations, however, contains a representative list of disorders and conditions constituting physical impairments, including "such diseases and conditions as orthopedic, visual, speech, and hearing impairments, cerebral palsy, epilepsy, muscular dystrophy, multiple sclerosis, cancer, heart disease, diabetes, mental retardation, emotional illness, and . . . drug addiction and alcoholism."

In 1980, the President transferred responsibility for the implementation and enforcement of § 504 to the Attorney General. The regulations issued by the Justice Department, which remain in force to this day, adopted verbatim the HEW definition of physical impairment quoted above. In addition, the representative list of diseases and conditions originally relegated to the commentary accompanying the HEW regulations were incorporated into the text of the regulations.

HIV infection is not included in the list of specific disorders constituting physical impairments, in part because HIV was not identified as the cause of AIDS until 1983. [Medical citations omitted.] HIV infection does fall well within the general definition set forth by the regulations, however.

The disease follows a predictable and, as of today, an unalterable course. Once a person is infected with HIV, the virus invades different cells in the blood and in body tissues. . . . Although the body does produce antibodies to combat HIV infection, the antibodies are not effective in eliminating the virus. . . .

The initial stage of HIV infection is known as acute or primary HIV infection. In a typical case, this stage lasts three months. . . .

After the symptoms associated with the initial stage subside, the disease enters what is referred to sometimes as its asymptomatic phase. The term is a misnomer, in some respects, for clinical features persist throughout, including lymphadenopathy, dermatological disorders, oral lesions, and bacterial infections. Although it varies with each individual, in most instances this stage lasts from 7 to 11 years. . . . It was once thought the virus became inactive during this period, but it is now known that the relative lack of symptoms is attributable to the virus' migration from the circulatory system into the lymph nodes. The migration reduces the viral presence in other parts of the body, with a corresponding diminution in physical manifestations of the disease. The virus, however, thrives in the lymph nodes. . . .

In light of the immediacy with which the virus begins to damage the infected person's white blood cells and the severity of the disease, we hold it is an impairment from the moment of infection. As noted earlier, infection with HIV causes immediate abnormalities in a person's blood, and the infected person's white cell count continues to drop throughout the course of the disease, even when the attack is concentrated in the lymph nodes. In light of these facts, HIV infection must be regarded as a physiological disorder with a constant and detrimental effect on the infected person's hemic and lymphatic systems from the moment of infection. HIV infection satisfies the statutory and regulatory definition of a physical impairment during every stage of the disease.

2

The statute is not operative, and the definition not satisfied, unless the impairment affects a major life activity. Respondent's claim throughout this case has been that the HIV infection placed a substantial limitation on her ability to reproduce and to bear children. Given the pervasive, and invariably fatal, course of the disease, its effect on major life activities of many sorts might have been relevant to our inquiry. Respondent and a number of *amici* make arguments about HIV's profound impact on almost every phase of the infected person's life. In light of these submissions, it may seem legalistic to circumscribe our discussion to the activity of reproduction. We have little doubt that had different parties brought the suit they would have maintained that an HIV infection imposes substantial limitations on other major life activities.

From the outset, however, the case has been treated as one in which reproduction was the major life activity limited by the impairment. It is our practice to decide cases on the grounds raised and considered in the Court of Appeals and included in the question on which we granted certiorari. We ask, then, whether reproduction is a major life activity.

We have little difficulty concluding that it is. As the Court of Appeals held, "[t]he plain meaning of the word 'major' denotes comparative importance" and "suggest[s] that the touchstone for determining an activity's inclusion under the statutory rubric is its significance." Reproduction falls well within the phrase "major life activity." Reproduction and the sexual dynamics surrounding it are central to the life process itself.

While petitioner concedes the importance of reproduction, he claims that Congress intended the ADA only to cover those aspects of a person's life which have a public, economic, or daily character. The argument founders on the statutory language. Nothing in the definition suggests that activities without a public, economic, or daily dimension may somehow be regarded as so unimportant or insignificant as to fall outside the meaning of the word "major." The breadth of the term confounds the attempt to limit its construction in this manner. . . .

. . . Petitioner advances no credible basis for confining major life activities to those with a public, economic, or daily aspect. In the absence of any reason to reach a contrary conclusion, we agree with the Court of Appeals' determination that reproduction is a major life activity for the purposes of the ADA.

3

The final element of the disability definition in subsection (A) is whether respondent's physical impairment was a substantial limit on the major life activity she asserts. The Rehabilitation Act regulations provide no additional guidance.

Our evaluation of the medical evidence leads us to conclude that respondent's infection substantially limited her ability to reproduce in two independent ways. First, a woman infected with HIV who tries to conceive a child imposes on the man a significant risk of becoming infected. The cumulative results of 13 studies collected in a 1994 textbook on AIDS indicates that 20% of male partners of women with HIV became HIV-positive themselves, with a majority of the studies finding a statistically significant risk of infection.

Second, an infected woman risks infecting her child during gestation and childbirth, i.e., perinatal transmission. Petitioner concedes that women infected with HIV face about a 25% risk of transmitting the virus to their children. Published reports available in 1994 confirm the accuracy of this statistic. . . .

Petitioner points to evidence in the record suggesting that antiretroviral therapy can lower the risk of perinatal transmission to about 8%. The Solicitor General questions the relevance of the 8% figure, pointing to regulatory language requiring the substantiality of a limitation to be assessed without regard to available mitigating measures. We need not resolve this dispute in order to decide this case, however. It cannot be said as a matter of law that an 8% risk of transmitting a dread and fatal disease to one's child does not represent a substantial limitation on reproduction.

The Act addresses substantial limitations on major life activities, not utter inabilities. Conception and childbirth are not impossible for an HIV victim but, without doubt, are dangerous to the public health. This meets the definition of a substantial limitation. The decision to reproduce carries economic and legal consequences as well. There are added costs for antiretroviral therapy, supplemental insurance, and long-term health care for the child who must be examined and, tragic to think, treated for the infection. The laws of some States, moreover, forbid persons infected with HIV from having sex with others, regardless of consent. [Citations omitted.]

In the end, the disability definition does not turn on personal choice. When significant limitations result from the impairment, the definition is met even if the difficulties are not insurmountable. For the statistical and other reasons we have cited, of course, the limitations on reproduction may be insurmountable here. Testimony from the respondent that her HIV infection controlled her decision not to have a child is unchallenged. In the context of reviewing summary judgment, we must take it to be true. We agree with the District Court and the Court of Appeals that no triable issue of fact impedes a ruling on the question of statutory coverage. Respondent's HIV infection is a physical impairment which substantially limits a major life activity, as the ADA defines it. In view of our holding, we need not address the second question presented, i.e., whether HIV infection is a *per se* disability under the ADA.

[Parts B and C omitted]

III

The petition for certiorari presented three other questions for review. The questions stated:

> "3. When deciding under title III of the ADA whether a private health care provider must perform invasive procedures on an infectious patient in his office, should courts defer to the health care provider's professional judgment, as long as it is reasonable in light of then-current medical knowledge?
>
> "4. What is the proper standard of judicial review under title III of the ADA of a private health care provider's judgment that the performance of certain invasive procedures in his office would pose a direct threat to the health or safety of others?
>
> "5. Did petitioner, Randon Bragdon, D.M.D., raise a genuine issue of fact for trial as to whether he was warranted in his judgment that the performance of certain invasive procedures on a patient in his office would have posed a direct threat to the health or safety of others?"

Of these, we granted certiorari only on question three. The question is phrased in an awkward way, for it conflates two separate inquiries. In asking whether it is appropriate to defer to petitioner's judgment, it assumes that petitioner's assessment of the objective facts was reasonable. The central premise of the question and the assumption on which it is based merit separate consideration.

Again, we begin with the statute. Notwithstanding the protection given respondent by the ADA's definition of disability, petitioner could have refused to treat her if her infectious condition "pose[d] a direct threat to the health or safety of others." . . . The ADA defines a direct threat to be "a significant risk to the health or safety of others that cannot be eliminated by a modification of policies, practices, or procedures or by the provision of auxiliary aids or services." . . .

The ADA's direct threat provision stems from the recognition in *School Bd. of Nassau Cty. v. Arline* (1987) of the importance of prohibiting discrimination against individuals with disabilities while protecting others from significant health and safety risks, resulting, for instance, from a contagious disease. . . .

The existence, or nonexistence, of a significant risk must be determined from the standpoint of the person who refuses the treatment or accommodation, and the risk assessment must be based on medical or other objective evidence. As a health care professional, petitioner had the duty to assess the risk of infection based on the objective, scientific information available to him and others in his profession. His belief that a significant risk existed, even if maintained in good faith, would not relieve him from liability. To use the words of the question presented, petitioner receives no special deference simply because he is a health care professional. . . .

Our conclusion that courts should assess the objective reasonableness of the views of health care professionals without deferring to their individual judgments does not answer the implicit assumption in the question presented, whether petitioner's actions were reasonable in light of the available medical evidence. In assessing the reasonableness of petitioner's actions, the views of public health authorities, such as the U.S. Public Health Service, CDC, and the National Institutes of Health, are of special weight and authority. The views of these organizations are not conclusive, however. A health care professional who disagrees with the prevailing medical consensus may refute it by citing a credible scientific basis for deviating from the accepted norm.

We have reviewed so much of the record as necessary to illustrate the application of the rule to the facts of this case. For the most part, the Court of Appeals followed the proper standard in evaluating the petitioner's position and conducted a thorough review of the evidence. . . .

A further illustration of a correct application of the objective standard is the Court of Appeals' refusal to give weight to the petitioner's offer to treat respondent in a hospital. Petitioner testified that he believed hospitals had safety measures, such as air filtration, ultraviolet lights, and respirators, which would reduce the risk of HIV transmission. Petitioner made no showing, however, that any area hospital had these safeguards or even that he had hospital privileges. His expert also admitted the lack of any scientific basis for the conclusion that these measures would lower the risk of transmission. Petitioner failed to present any objective, medical evidence showing that treating respondent in a hospital would be safer or more efficient in preventing HIV transmission than treatment in a well-equipped dental office.

We are concerned, however, that the Court of Appeals might have placed mistaken reliance upon two other sources. In ruling no triable issue of fact existed on this point, the Court of Appeals relied on the 1993 CDC Dentistry Guidelines and the 1991 American Dental Association Policy on HIV. This evidence is not definitive. . . .

[Discussion of evidence omitted.]

We conclude the proper course is to give the Court of Appeals the opportunity to determine whether our analysis of some of the studies cited by the parties would change its conclusion that petitioner presented neither objective evidence nor a triable issue of fact on the question of risk. In remanding the case, we do not foreclose the possibility that the Court of Appeals may reach the same conclusion it did earlier. A remand will permit a full exploration of the issue through the adversary process.

The determination of the Court of Appeals that respondent's HIV infection was a disability under the ADA is affirmed. The judgment is vacated, and the case is remanded for further proceedings consistent with this opinion.

It is so ordered.

JUSTICE STEVENS, with whom JUSTICE BREYER joins, concurring.

The Court's opinion demonstrates that respondent's HIV infection easily falls within the statute's definition of "disability." Moreover, the Court's discussion in Part III of the relevant evidence has persuaded me that the judgment of the Court of Appeals should be affirmed. . . .

There are not, however, five Justices who agree that the judgment should be affirmed. . . . Because I am in agreement with the legal analysis in JUSTICE KENNEDY's opinion, in order to provide a judgment supported by a majority, I join that opinion even though I would prefer an outright affirmance.

JUSTICE GINSBURG, concurring.

HIV infection, as the description set out in the Court's opinion documents, has been regarded as a disease limiting life itself. The disease inevitably pervades life's choices: education, employment, family and financial undertakings. It affects the need for and, as this case shows, the ability to obtain health care because of the reaction of others to the impairment. No rational legislator . . . would require nondiscrimination once symptoms become visible but permit discrimination when the disease, though present, is not yet visible. I am therefore satisfied that the statutory and regulatory definitions are well met. . . .

I further agree . . . that it is wise to remand, erring, if at all, on the side of caution. By taking this course, the Court ensures a fully informed determination whether respondent Abbott's disease posed "a significant risk to the health or safety of [petitioner Bragdon] that [could not] be eliminated by a modification of policies, practices, or procedures. . . ."

CHIEF JUSTICE REHNQUIST, with whom JUSTICE SCALIA and JUSTICE THOMAS join, and with whom JUSTICE O'CONNOR joins as to Part II, concurring in the judgment in part and dissenting in part.

I

Is respondent—who has tested positive for the human immunodeficiency virus (HIV) but was asymptomatic at the time she suffered discriminatory treatment—a person with a "disability" as that term is defined in the Americans with Disabilities Act of 1990 (ADA)? [Definition of "disability" omitted; see majority opinion.] It is important to note that whether respondent has a disability covered by the ADA is an individualized inquiry. . . .

Petitioner does not dispute that asymptomatic HIV-positive status is a physical impairment. I therefore assume this to be the case, and proceed to the second and third statutory requirements for "disability."

According to the Court, the next question is "whether reproduction is a major life activity." That, however, is only half of the relevant question. As mentioned above, the ADA's definition of a "disability" requires that the major life activity at issue be one "of such individual." The Court truncates the question, perhaps because there is not a shred of record evidence indicating that, prior to becoming infected with HIV, respondent's major life activities included reproduction (assuming for the moment that reproduction is a major life activity at all). At most, the record indicates that after learning of her HIV status, respondent, whatever her previous inclination, conclusively decided that she would not have children. There is absolutely no evidence that, absent the HIV, respondent would have had or was even considering having children. Indeed, when asked during her deposition whether her HIV infection had in any way impaired her ability to carry out any of her life functions, respondent answered "No." . . .

But even aside from the facts of this particular case, the Court is simply wrong in concluding as a general matter that reproduction is a "major life activity." Unfortunately, the ADA does not define the phrase "major life activities." But the Act does incorporate by reference a list of such activities contained in regulations issued under the Rehabilitation Act. The Court correctly recognizes that this list of major life activities "is illustrative, not exhaustive," but then makes no attempt to demonstrate that reproduction is a major life activity in the same sense that "caring for one's self, performing manual tasks, walking, seeing, hearing, speaking, breathing, learning, and working" are.

Instead, the Court argues that reproduction is a "major" life activity in that it is "central to the life process itself." In support of this reading, the Court focuses on the fact that " 'major' " indicates " 'comparative importance,' " . . . ignoring the alternative definition of "major" as "greater in quantity, number, or extent." It is the latter definition that is most consistent with the ADA's illustrative list of major life activities.

No one can deny that reproductive decisions are important in a person's life. But so are decisions as to who to marry, where to live, and how to earn one's living. Fundamental importance of this sort is not the common thread linking the statute's listed activities. The common thread is rather that the activities are repetitively performed and essential in the day-to-day existence of a normally functioning individual. They are thus quite different from the series of activities leading to the birth of a child. Both respondent and the United States as *amicus curiae* argue that reproduction must be a major life activity because regulations issued under the ADA define the term "physical impairment" to include physiological disorders affecting the reproductive system. If reproduction were not a major life activity, they argue, then it would have made little sense to include the reproductive disorders in the roster of physical impairments. This argument is simply wrong. There are numerous disorders of the reproductive system, such as dysmenorrhea and endometriosis, which are so painful that they limit a woman's ability to engage in major life activities such as walking and working. And, obviously, cancer of the various reproductive organs limits one's ability to engage in numerous activities other than reproduction.

But even if I were to assume that reproduction is a major life activity of respondent, I do not agree that an asymptomatic HIV infection "substantially limits" that activity. The record before us leaves no doubt that those so infected are still entirely able to engage in sexual intercourse, give birth to a child if they become pregnant, and perform the manual tasks necessary to rear a child to maturity. While individuals infected with HIV may choose not to engage in these activities, there is no support in language, logic, or our case law for the proposition that such voluntary choices constitute a "limit" on one's own life activities.

The Court responds that the ADA "addresses substantial limitations on major life activities, not utter inabilities." I agree, but fail to see how this assists the Court's cause. Apart from being unable to demonstrate that she is utterly unable to engage in the various activities that comprise the reproductive process, respondent has not even explained how she is less able to engage in those activities.

Respondent contends that her ability to reproduce is limited because "the fatal nature of HIV infection means that a parent is unlikely to live long enough to raise and nurture the child to adulthood." But the ADA's definition of a disability is met only if the alleged impairment substantially "limits" (present tense) a major life activity. Asymptomatic HIV does not presently limit respondent's ability to perform any of the tasks necessary to bear or raise a child. Respondent's argument, taken to its logical extreme, would render every individual with a genetic marker for some debilitating disease "disabled" here and now because of some possible future effects.

In my view, therefore, respondent has failed to demonstrate that any of her major life activities were substantially limited by her HIV infection.

II

While the Court concludes to the contrary as to the "disability" issue, it then quite correctly recognizes that petitioner could nonetheless have refused to treat respondent if her condition posed a "direct threat." . . .

I agree with the Court that "the existence, or nonexistence, of a significant risk must be determined from the standpoint of the person who refuses the treatment or accommodation," as of the time that the decision refusing treatment is made. I disagree with the Court, however, that "[i]n assessing the reasonableness of petitioner's actions, the views of public health authorities . . . are of special weight and authority." Those views are, of course, entitled to a presumption of validity when the actions of those authorities themselves are challenged in court, and even in disputes between private parties where Congress has committed that dispute to adjudication by a public health authority. But in litigation between private parties originating in the federal courts, I am aware of no provision of law or judicial practice that would require or permit courts to give some scientific views more credence than others simply because they have been endorsed by a politically appointed public health authority (such as the Surgeon General). In litigation of this latter sort, . . . the credentials of the scientists employed by the public health authority, and the soundness of their studies, must stand on their own. . . .

Applying these principles here, it is clear to me that petitioner has presented more than enough evidence to avoid summary judgment on the "direct threat" question. In June 1994, the Centers for Disease Control and

Prevention published a study identifying seven instances of possible transmission of HIV from patients to dental workers. While it is not entirely certain whether these dental workers contracted HIV during the course of providing dental treatment, the potential that the disease was transmitted during the course of dental treatment is relevant evidence. One need only demonstrate "risk," not certainty of infection. . . . Given the "severity of the risk" involved here, i.e., near certain death, and the fact that no public health authority had outlined a protocol for *eliminating* this risk in the context of routine dental treatment, it seems likely that petitioner can establish that it was objectively reasonable for him to conclude that treating respondent in his office posed a "direct threat" to his safety.

In addition, petitioner offered evidence of 42 documented incidents of occupational transmission of HIV to healthcare workers other than dental professionals. The Court of Appeals dismissed this evidence as irrelevant because these health professionals were not dentists. But the fact that the health care workers were not dentists is no more valid a basis for distinguishing these transmissions of HIV than the fact that the health care workers did not practice in Maine. At a minimum, petitioner's evidence was sufficient to create a triable issue on this question, and summary judgment was accordingly not appropriate.

JUSTICE O'CONNOR, concurring in the judgment in part and dissenting in part.

I agree with THE CHIEF JUSTICE that respondent's claim of disability should be evaluated on an individualized basis and that she has not proven that her asymptomatic HIV status substantially limited one or more of her major life activities. In my view, the act of giving birth to a child, while a very important part of the lives of many women, is not generally the same as the representative major life activities of all persons—"caring for one's self, performing manual tasks, walking, seeing, hearing, speaking, breathing, learning, and working"—listed in regulations relevant to the Americans with Disabilities Act of 1990. Based on that conclusion, there is no need to address whether other aspects of intimate or family relationships not raised in this case could constitute major life activities; nor is there reason to consider whether HIV status would impose a substantial limitation on one's ability to reproduce if reproduction were a major life activity.

I join in Part II of THE CHIEF JUSTICE's opinion concurring in the judgment in part and dissenting in part, which concludes that the Court of Appeals failed to properly determine whether respondent's condition posed a direct threat. Accordingly, I agree that a remand is necessary on that issue.

SUPREME COURT ON THE ATTORNEY-CLIENT PRIVILEGE
June 25, 1998

By a 6–3 vote, the Supreme Court ruled on June 25 that attorney-client privilege, which protects the confidentiality of information a client gives to his or her attorney, remains in place after the client dies. The immediate effect of the ruling was to allow attorney James Hamilton to withhold from Independent Counsel Kenneth W. Starr notes that Hamilton had taken in a meeting with White House aide Vincent W. Foster Jr. just days before Foster committed suicide. But the ruling was seen as having a far broader impact, according to the legal associations and others who supported Hamilton. Permitting posthumous disclosure, they argued, would discourage clients from confiding in their attorneys for fear of losing their reputation or harming their survivors, thus eroding a fundamental and long-standing principle of the American legal system.

The ruling was a defeat for Starr, who had sought the notes in his investigation of possible wrongdoing by President Bill Clinton and first lady Hillary Rodham Clinton. But Starr carried the day on two other instances in which he sought to compel testimony. On July 17 members of the Secret Service were called to testify before the federal grand jury investigating Clinton's affair with former White House intern Monica Lewinsky. The president's bodyguards began their testimony after Chief Justice William H. Rehnquist refused to delay the questioning until the full Supreme Court could determine whether the guards were entitled to what the Department of Justice called a "protective function privilege." On July 28 a federal appeals court ruled that the traditional attorney-client privilege did not extend to the president's discussions with attorneys employed in the White House. That meant that several senior White House aides, including presidential confidant Bruce R. Lindsey, would have to appear before the grand jury.

Posthumous Confidentiality

Like so much else that happened in Washington in 1998, the attorney-client privilege case, Swidler & Berlin v. United States, *had its origins in the investigation of President Clinton by the independent counsel's office. In July 1993 Foster, a former law partner of Hillary Clinton's, was White House deputy counsel and was apparently concerned about the firings of seven career White House travel office employees in May 1993. Critics of the president said the sudden firings in the "Travelgate" affair appeared aimed at benefiting the travel business of presidential friend Harry Thomasson, and they suspected that the first lady was behind the firings. Foster went to see Hamilton on a Sunday morning and began by asking whether the conversation would be protected by the attorney-client privilege. Hamilton said later that he had assured Foster it was, and during the two-hour conversation Hamilton took three pages of notes. Nine days later Foster committed suicide.*

In early 1996, after a White House memo surfaced in which Foster was quoted as saying that Hillary Clinton wanted the travel office fired, Starr subpoenaed Hamilton's notes, arguing that the information would help him determine whether White House officials had committed perjury, obstruction of justice, or other federal crimes in their accounts of the firings. Hamilton, a partner in the Washington firm of Swidler & Berlin, challenged the subpoena, arguing that without his promise of confidentiality to Foster the conversation would never have occurred and there would have been no notes to argue about later. A federal district court judge agreed with Hamilton in December 1996, but on appeal a divided three-judge appeals court ruled in August 1997 that the attorney-client privilege did not apply after the client's death. Except for so-called testamentary cases, when courts have required lawyers to reveal their clients' wishes in order to resolve disputed wills, no federal court had ever before granted an exemption from the attorney-client privilege.

The appeals court ruling sent a tidal wave through legal circles. The American Bar Association (ABA), the National Association of Criminal Defense Lawyers, and two other national organizations of lawyers filed briefs asking the Supreme Court to reverse the appeals court decision. In its brief the ABA disagreed with Starr's contention that when clients seek advise from lawyers, they do not much care what happens to the information after they are dead. On the contrary, the ABA brief said, hundreds of thousands, perhaps millions of people contemplating their own deaths might have "secrets and confidences that, if revealed, would be at the least highly embarrassing to themselves or their friends and loved ones." These people might want the aid of an attorney in sorting matters out before their deaths, but might forgo legal assistance for fear the information would not remain confidential. Among the other groups seeking a reversal was the American Psychiatric Association, which in 1996 had won a Supreme Court decision recognizing a privilege between patients and their psychotherapists. (Patients' privilege, Historic Documents of 1996, p. 388)

The Supreme Court took the case on an expedited basis, hearing arguments on June 8, 1998, and issuing its decision just seventeen days later.

In an opinion written by Rehnquist, the majority acknowledged that attorney-client privilege was supported by "the great body" of case law. "Knowing that communications will remain confidential even after death encourages the client to communicate freely and frankly with counsel," Rehnquist wrote. Even if clients had no reason to fear criminal prosecution, they might still be concerned about "reputation, civil liability, or possible harm to family and friends." On that basis, Rehnquist continued, the independent counsel had not made a "sufficient showing" that the long-established privilege should be overturned in the Foster case. He left open the question whether a defendant in a criminal case could override the privilege if necessary to protect his or her constitutional rights.

In a dissent joined by Justices Antonin Scalia and Clarence Thomas, Justice Sandra Day O'Connor argued that the risks of harming someone's interests by disclosing confidential conversations with his or her attorney were "greatly diminished" after death, while the costs of recognizing an absolute privilege were "inordinately high." In support of that argument, she cited a number of cases in which confessions to a crime had been shielded by attorney-client privilege, sometimes even when disclosure would have exonerated an innocent defendant.

Starr expressed disappointment in the decision but promised to continue the investigation "as thoroughly and expeditiously as possible." His report to Congress outlining eleven possible grounds for impeachment of the president contained no mention of the travel office matter, nor had his office filed any indictments by the end of the year in connection with the firings. (Starr report, p. 632, background, p. 564)

Privilege for Aides and Secret Service Officers

Claims that White House attorneys and Secret Service officers assigned to protect the president were entitled to a privilege allowing them not to testify to the federal grand jury investigating Clinton's affair with Lewinsky were on much shakier legal ground—a fact Starr noted when he complained that the challenges to his subpoenas were intended only to delay his investigation. The White House had invoked both executive privilege and attorney-client privilege to prevent White House deputy counsel Lindsey from having to testify. But on May 5 the presiding judge, Norma Holloway Johnson, ruled against the president. In a sealed opinion she wrote that Starr's interests in obtaining information in a criminal investigation outweighed the president's interests in maintaining the confidentiality of White House conversations. The White House then dropped its executive privilege claim, but appealed the ruling on the attorney-client privilege.

On July 27 a three-judge federal appeals court ruled 2–1 that the "public interest in honest government and in exposing wrongdoing by government officials" precluded extending the attorney-client privilege to government lawyers, including those in the White House. "With respect to investigations of federal criminal offenses, and especially offenses committed by those in government, government attorneys stand in a far dif-

ferent position from members of the private bar. Their duty is not to defend clients against criminal charges and it is not to protect wrongdoers from public exposure," but to ensure that the laws of the country were faithfully executed.

White House counsel Charles F. C. Ruff said the ruling had implications beyond the immediate circumstances of the case itself. "The practical result of the court's decision is that the president and all other government officials will be less likely to receive full and frank advice about their official obligations and duties from government attorneys," he said.

The claim of a "protective function privilege" for Secret Service officers guarding the president was made by the organization's parent agency, the Treasury Department, and the Justice Department. They argued that if the president's bodyguards could be compelled to testify about what they heard and observed in the vicinity of the president, the president might try to distance himself from his guards on occasion and thus put his safety in danger. On June 22 Johnson dismissed the claim, saying that it had no basis in the Constitution and was not even a logical argument, an opinion that was affirmed by a unanimous three-judge appeals panel, which upheld Johnson's decision on July 7. The "greatest danger to the president arises when he is in public," the three judges wrote, "yet the privilege presumably would have its greatest effect when he is in the White House or in private meetings. . . . [W]e suspect that even with a protective function privilege in place, conscience might impel a president to distance himself from Secret Service agents when engaging in wrongful conduct, as might a simple desire for privacy at other times."

The Justice Department then appealed to Chief Justice Rehnquist to delay the agents' testimony until the full Supreme Court, which was in recess until October, could hear the case. In refusing the request on July 17, Rehnquist said testimony by agents would not cause "irreparable harm " to the relationship between the president and his bodyguards. Rehnquist predicted that the full court would uphold the lower courts, but said if it did not, "disclosure of past events will not affect the President's relationship with his protectors in the future."

Lindsey and several Secret Service agents eventually testified before the grand jury, and the independent counsel used parts of that testimony to support charges that the president had obstructed justice and abused his constitutional powers in his efforts to cover up his affair with Lewinsky.

Following are excerpts from the majority and dissenting opinions in the case of Swidler & Berlin v. United States, in which the Supreme Court ruled 6–3 on June 25, 1998, that a client's conversations with his or her attorney were protected from disclosure even after the client's death:

No. 97–1192

Swidler & Berlin and James Hamilton, Petitioners v. United States	On writ of certiorari to the United States Court of Appeals for the District of Columbia Circuit

[June 25, 1998]

CHIEF JUSTICE REHNQUIST delivered the opinion of the Court.

Petitioner, an attorney, made notes of an initial interview with a client shortly before the client's death. The Government, represented by the Office of Independent Counsel, now seeks his notes for use in a criminal investigation. We hold that the notes are protected by the attorney-client privilege.

This dispute arises out of an investigation conducted by the Office of the Independent Counsel into whether various individuals made false statements, obstructed justice, or committed other crimes during investigations of the 1993 dismissal of employees from the White House Travel Office. Vincent W. Foster, Jr., was Deputy White House Counsel when the firings occurred. In July, 1993, Foster met with petitioner James Hamilton, an attorney at petitioner Swidler & Berlin, to seek legal representation concerning possible congressional or other investigations of the firings. During a 2-hour meeting, Hamilton took three pages of handwritten notes. One of the first entries in the notes is the word "Privileged." Nine days later, Foster committed suicide.

In December 1995, a federal grand jury, at the request of the Independent Counsel, issued subpoenas to petitioners Hamilton and Swidler & Berlin for, *inter alia*, Hamilton's handwritten notes of his meeting with Foster. Petitioners filed a motion to quash, arguing that the notes were protected by the attorney-client privilege and by the work product privilege. The District Court, after examining the notes *in camera*, concluded they were protected from disclosure by both doctrines and denied enforcement of the subpoenas.

The Court of Appeals for the District of Columbia Circuit reversed. *In re Sealed Case* (1997). While recognizing that most courts assume the privilege survives death, the Court of Appeals noted that holdings actually manifesting the posthumous force of the privilege are rare. Instead, most judicial references to the privilege's posthumous application occur in the context of a well recognized exception allowing disclosure for disputes among the client's heirs. It further noted that most commentators support some measure of posthumous curtailment of the privilege. The Court of Appeals thought that the risk of posthumous revelation, when confined to the criminal context, would have little to no chilling effect on client communication, but that the costs of protecting communications after death were high. It therefore concluded that the privilege was not absolute in such circumstances, and that instead, a balancing test should apply. It thus held that there is a posthumous exception to the privilege for communications whose relative importance to particular criminal litigation is substantial. While acknowledging that uncertain privileges are disfavored, the Court of Appeals determined that the uncertainty introduced by its balancing test was insignificant in light of existing exceptions to the privilege. The Court of Appeals also held that the notes were not protected by the work product privilege.

The dissenting judge would have affirmed the District Court's judgment that the attorney-client privilege protected the notes. He concluded that the common-law rule was that the privilege survived death. He found no persuasive reason to depart from this accepted rule, particularly given the importance of the privilege to full and frank client communication.

Petitioners sought review in this Court on both the attorney-client privilege and the work product privilege. We granted certiorari (1998), and we now reverse.

The attorney-client privilege is one of the oldest recognized privileges for confidential communications. *Upjohn Co. v. United States* (1981); *Hunt v. Blackburn* (1888). The privilege is intended to encourage "full and frank communication between attorneys and their clients and thereby promote broader public interests in the observance of law and the administration of justice." *Upjohn.* The issue presented here is the scope of that privilege; more particularly, the extent to which the privilege survives the death of the client. Our interpretation of the privilege's scope is guided by "the principles of the common law . . . as interpreted by the courts . . . in the light of reason and experience." Fed. Rule Evid. 501; *Funk v. United States* (1933).

The Independent Counsel argues that the attorney-client privilege should not prevent disclosure of confidential communications where the client has died and the information is relevant to a criminal proceeding. There is some authority for this position. One state appellate court, *Cohen v. Jenkintown Cab Co.* (Pa. Super. 1976), and the Court of Appeals below have held the privilege may be subject to posthumous exceptions in certain circumstances. In *Cohen,* a civil case, the court recognized that the privilege generally survives death, but concluded that it could make an exception where the interest of justice was compelling and the interest of the client in preserving the confidence was insignificant.

But other than these two decisions, cases addressing the existence of the privilege after death—most involving the testamentary exception—uniformly presume the privilege survives, even if they do not so hold. [Citations omitted.] In *John Doe Grand Jury Investigation* [1990], for example, the Massachusetts Supreme Court concluded that survival of the privilege was "the clear implication" of its early pronouncements that communications subject to the privilege could not be disclosed at any time. The court further noted that survival of the privilege was "necessarily implied" by cases allowing waiver of the privilege in testamentary disputes.

Such testamentary exception cases consistently presume the privilege survives. [Citations omitted.] They view testamentary disclosure of communications as an exception to the privilege: "[T]he general rule with respect to confidential communications . . . is that such communications are privileged during the testator's lifetime and, also, after the testator's death unless sought to be disclosed in litigation between the testator's heirs." [*United States v.*] *Osborn* [CA9 1977]. The rationale for such disclosure is that it furthers the client's intent.

Indeed, in *Glover v. Patten* (1897), this Court, in recognizing the testamentary exception, expressly assumed that the privilege continues after the individual's death. The Court explained that testamentary disclosure was permissible because the privilege, which normally protects the client's interests, could be impliedly waived in order to fulfill the client's testamentary intent.

The great body of this caselaw supports, either by holding or considered dicta, the position that the privilege does survive in a case such as the present one. Given the language of Rule 501, at the very least the burden is on the Independent Counsel to show that "reason and experience" require a departure from this rule.

The Independent Counsel contends that the testamentary exception supports the posthumous termination of the privilege because in practice most cases have refused to apply the privilege posthumously. He further argues that the exception reflects a policy judgment that the interest in settling estates outweighs any posthumous interest in confidentiality. He then reasons by analogy that in criminal proceedings, the interest in determining whether a crime has been committed should trump client confidentiality, particularly since the financial interests of the estate are not at stake.

But the Independent Counsel's interpretation simply does not square with the caselaw's implicit acceptance of the privilege's survival and with the treatment of testamentary disclosure as an "exception" or an implied "waiver." And the premise of his analogy is incorrect, since cases consistently recognize that the rationale for the testamentary exception is that it furthers the client's intent. There is no reason to suppose as a general matter that grand jury testimony about confidential communications furthers the client's intent.

Commentators on the law also recognize that the general rule is that the attorney-client privilege continues after death. [Citations omitted.] Undoubtedly, as the Independent Counsel emphasizes, various commentators have criticized this rule, urging that the privilege should be abrogated after the client's death where extreme injustice would result, as long as disclosure would not seriously undermine the privilege by deterring client communication. . . . But even these critics clearly recognize that established law supports the continuation of the privilege and that a contrary rule would be a modification of the common law. . . .

Despite the scholarly criticism, we think there are weighty reasons that counsel in favor of posthumous application. Knowing that communications will remain confidential even after death encourages the client to communicate fully and frankly with counsel. While the fear of disclosure, and the consequent withholding of information from counsel, may be reduced if disclosure is limited to posthumous disclosure in a criminal context, it seems unreasonable to assume that it vanishes altogether. Clients may be concerned about reputation, civil liability, or possible harm to friends or family. Posthumous disclosure of such communications may be as feared as disclosure during the client's lifetime.

The Independent Counsel suggests, however, that his proposed exception would have little to no effect on the client's willingness to confide in his attorney. He reasons that only clients intending to perjure themselves will be chilled by a rule of disclosure after death, as opposed to truthful clients or those asserting their Fifth Amendment privilege. This is because for the latter group, communications disclosed by the attorney after the client's death purportedly will reveal only information that the client himself would have revealed if alive.

The Independent Counsel assumes, incorrectly we believe, that the privilege is analogous to the Fifth Amendment's protection against self-incrimination. But as suggested above, the privilege serves much broader purposes. Clients consult attorneys for a wide variety of reasons, only one of which involves possible criminal liability. Many attorneys act as counselors on personal and family matters, where, in the course of obtaining the desired advice, confidences about family members or financial problems must be revealed in order to assure sound legal advice. The same is true of owners of small businesses who may regularly consult their attorneys about a variety of problems arising in the course of the business. These confidences may not come close to any sort of admission of criminal wrongdoing, but nonetheless be matters which the client would not wish divulged.

The contention that the attorney is being required to disclose only what the client could have been required to disclose is at odds with the basis for the privilege even during the client's lifetime. In related cases, we have said that the loss of evidence admittedly caused by the privilege is justified in part by the fact that without the privilege, the client may not have made such communications in the first place. This is true of disclosure before and after the client's death. Without assurance of the privilege's posthumous application, the client may very well not have made disclosures to his attorney at all, so the loss of evidence is more apparent than real. In the case at hand, it seems quite plausible that Foster, perhaps already contemplating suicide, may not have sought legal advice from Hamilton if he had not been assured the conversation was privileged.

The Independent Counsel additionally suggests that his proposed exception would have minimal impact if confined to criminal cases, or, as the Court of Appeals suggests, if it is limited to information of substantial importance to a particular criminal case. However, there is no case authority for the proposition that the privilege applies differently in criminal and civil cases, and only one commentator ventures such a suggestion. . . . In any event, a client may not know at the time he discloses information to his attorney whether it will later be relevant to a civil or a criminal matter, let alone whether it will be of substantial importance. Balancing *ex post* the importance of the information against client interests, even limited to criminal cases, introduces substantial uncertainty into the privilege's application. For just that reason, we have rejected use of a balancing test in defining the contours of the privilege.

In a similar vein, the Independent Counsel argues that existing exceptions to the privilege, such as the crime-fraud exception and the testamentary exception, make the impact of one more exception marginal. However, these exceptions do not demonstrate that the impact of a posthumous exception would be insignificant, and there is little empirical evidence on this point. The established exceptions are consistent with the purposes of the privilege, while a posthumous exception in criminal cases appears at odds with the goals of encouraging full and frank communication and of protecting the client's interests. A "no harm in one more exception" rationale could contribute to the general erosion of the privilege, without reference to common law principles or "reason and experience."

Finally, the Independent Counsel, relying on cases such as *United States v. Nixon* (1974) and *Branzburg v. Hayes* (1972), urges that privileges be strictly construed because they are inconsistent with the paramount judicial goal of truth seeking. But both *Nixon* and *Branzburg* dealt with the creation of privileges not recognized by the common law, whereas here we deal with one of the oldest recognized privileges in the law. And we are asked, not simply to "construe" the privilege, but to narrow it, contrary to the weight of the existing body of caselaw.

It has been generally, if not universally, accepted, for well over a century, that the attorney-client privilege survives the death of the client in a case such as this. While the arguments against the survival of the privilege are by no means frivolous, they are based in large part on speculation—thoughtful speculation, but speculation nonetheless—as to whether posthumous termination of the privilege would diminish a client's willingness to confide in an attorney. In an area where empirical information would be useful, it is scant and inconclusive.

Rule 501's direction to look to "the principles of the common law as they may be interpreted by the courts of the United States in the light of reason and experience" does not mandate that a rule, once established, should endure for all time. But here the Independent Counsel has simply not made a sufficient showing to overturn the common law rule embodied in the prevailing caselaw. Interpreted in the light of reason and experience, that body of law requires that the attorney client privilege prevent disclosure of the notes at issue in this case. The judgment of the Court of Appeals is

Reversed.

JUSTICE O'CONNOR, with whom JUSTICE SCALIA and JUSTICE THOMAS join, dissenting.

Although the attorney-client privilege ordinarily will survive the death of the client, I do not agree with the Court that it inevitably precludes disclosure of a deceased client's communications in criminal proceedings. In my view, a criminal defendant's right to exculpatory evidence or a compelling law enforcement need for information may, where the testimony is not available from other sources, override a client's posthumous interest in confidentiality.

We have long recognized that "[t]he fundamental basis upon which all rules of evidence must rest—if they are to rest upon reason—is their adaptation to the successful development of the truth." *Funk v. United States* (1933). In light of the heavy burden that they place on the search for truth, see *United States v. Nixon* (1974), "[e]videntiary privileges in litigation are not favored, and even those rooted in the Constitution must give way in proper circumstances," *Herbert v. Lando* (1979). Consequently, we construe the scope of privileges narrowly. We are reluctant to recognize a privilege or read an existing one expansively unless to do so will serve a "public good transcending the normally predominant principle of utilizing all rational means for ascertaining truth." *Trammel v. United States* (1980).

The attorney-client privilege promotes trust in the representational relationship, thereby facilitating the provision of legal services and ultimately the administration of justice. See *Upjohn Co. v. United States* (1981). The systemic benefits of the privilege are commonly understood to outweigh the harm caused by excluding critical evidence. A privilege should operate, however, only where "necessary to achieve its purpose," see *Fisher v. United States* (1976), and an invocation of the attorney-client privilege should not go unexamined "when it is shown that the interests of the administration of justice can only be frustrated by [its] exercise," *Cohen v. Jenkintown Cab Co.* (Pa. Super. (1976)).

I agree that a deceased client may retain a personal, reputational, and economic interest in confidentiality. But, after death, the potential that disclosure will harm the client's interests has been greatly diminished, and the risk that the client will be held criminally liable has abated altogether. Thus, some commentators suggest that terminating the privilege upon the client's death "could not to any substantial degree lessen the encouragement for free disclosure which is [its] purpose." . . . This diminished risk is coupled with a heightened urgency for discovery of a deceased client's communications in the criminal context. The privilege does not "protect disclosure of the underlying facts by those who communicated with the attorney," *Upjohn*, and were the client living, prosecutors could grant immunity and compel the relevant testimony. After a client's death, however, if the privilege precludes an attorney from testifying in the client's stead, a complete "loss of crucial information" will often result. . . .

As the Court of Appeals observed, the costs of recognizing an absolute posthumous privilege can be inordinately high. See *In re Sealed Case* (CADC 1997). Extreme injustice may occur, for example, where a criminal defendant seeks disclosure of a deceased client's confession to the offense. . . . In my view, the paramount value that our criminal justice system places on protecting an innocent defendant should outweigh a deceased client's interest in preserving confidences. Indeed, even petitioner acknowledges that an exception may be appropriate where the constitutional rights of a criminal defendant are at stake. An exception may likewise be warranted in the face of a compelling law enforcement need for the information. . . . Given that the complete exclusion of relevant evidence from a criminal trial or investigation may distort the record, mislead the factfinder, and undermine the central truth-seeking function of the courts, I do not believe that the attorney-client privilege should act as an absolute bar to the disclosure of a deceased client's communications. When the privilege is asserted in the criminal context, and a showing is made that the communications at issue contain necessary factual information not otherwise available, courts should be permitted to assess whether interests in fairness and accuracy outweigh the justifications for the privilege.

A number of exceptions to the privilege already qualify its protections, and an attorney "who tells his client that the expected communications are absolutely and forever privileged is oversimplifying a bit." [Quoting Court of Appeals opinion.] In the situation where the posthumous privilege most frequently arises—a dispute between heirs over the decedent's will—the privilege is widely recognized to give way to the interest in settling the estate. This testamentary exception, moreover, may be invoked in some cases where the decedent would not have chosen to waive the privilege. For example, "a decedent might want to provide for an illegitimate child but at the same time much prefer that the relationship go undisclosed." [Quoting Court of Appeals opinion.] Among the Court's rationales for a broad construction of the posthumous privilege is its assertion that "[m]any attorneys act as counselors on personal and family matters, where, in the course of obtaining the desired advice, confidences about family members or financial problems must be revealed . . . which the client would not wish divulged." That reasoning, however, would apply in the testamentary context with equal force. Nor are other existing exceptions to the privilege—for example, the crime-fraud exception or the exceptions for claims relating to attorney competence or compensation—necessarily consistent with "encouraging full and frank communication" or "protecting the client's interests." Rather, those exceptions reflect the understanding that, in certain circumstances, the privilege " 'ceases to operate' " as a safeguard on "the proper functioning of our adversary system." See *United States v. Zolin* (1989).

Finally, the common law authority for the proposition that the privilege remains absolute after the client's death is not a monolithic body of precedent. Indeed, the Court acknowledges that most cases merely "presume the privilege survives," and it relies on the case law's "implicit acceptance" of a continuous privilege. Opinions squarely addressing the posthumous force of the privilege "are relatively rare." And even in those decisions expressly holding that the privilege continues after the death of the client, courts do not typically engage in detailed reasoning, but rather conclude that the cases construing the testamentary exception imply survival of the privilege. . . . Moreover, as the Court concedes, there is some authority for the proposition that a deceased client's communications may be revealed, even in circumstances outside of the testamentary context. California's Evidence Code, for example, provides that the attorney-client privilege continues only until the deceased client's estate is finally distributed, noting that "there is little reason to preserve secrecy at the expense of excluding relevant evidence after the estate is wound up and the representative is discharged." [Citation omitted.] And a state appellate court has admitted an attorney's testimony concerning a deceased client's communications after "balanc[ing] the necessity for revealing the substance of the [attorney-client conversation] against the unlikelihood of any cognizable injury to the rights, interests, estate or memory of [the client]." See *Cohen*. The American Law Institute, moreover, has recently recommended withholding the privilege when the communication "bears on a litigated issue of pivotal significance" and has suggested that courts "balance the interest in confidentiality against any exceptional need for the communication." . . . ("[I]f a deceased client has confessed to criminal acts that are later charged to another, surely the latter's need for evidence sometimes outweighs the interest in preserving the confidences").

Where the exoneration of an innocent criminal defendant or a compelling law enforcement interest is at stake, the harm of precluding critical evidence that is unavailable by any other means outweighs the potential disincentive to forthright communication. In my view, the cost of silence warrants a narrow exception to the rule that the attorney-client privilege survives the death of the client. Moreover, although I disagree with the Court of Appeals' notion that the context of an initial client interview affects the applicability of the work product doctrine, I do not believe that the doctrine applies where the material concerns a client who is no longer a potential party to adversarial litigation.

Accordingly, I would affirm the judgment of the Court of Appeals. Although the District Court examined the documents *in camera*, it has not had an opportunity to balance these competing considerations and decide whether the privilege should be trumped in the particular circumstances of this case. Thus, I agree with the Court of Appeals' decision to remand for a determination whether any portion of the notes must be disclosed.

With respect, I dissent.

SUPREME COURT ON DECENCY IN THE ARTS
June 25, 1998

By an 8–1 vote, the Supreme Court upheld a federal law allowing the National Endowment for the Arts (NEA) to consider general standards of decency when deciding which arts projects to fund. The law had been challenged as a violation of free speech, but the Court majority said that the law was only "advisory" and did not prohibit the endowment from funding works of art that might be considered pornographic, sacrilegious, or otherwise indecent.

The ruling brought to a close, at least momentarily, a battle that had been running since 1989, when NEA-funded exhibits that included the work of two controversial artists led to passage of a law in 1990 requiring the NEA to take into consideration "general standards of decency and respect for the diverse beliefs and values of the American public." In deeming that this language was merely advisory, the Court managed to avoid directly answering the question whether a law explicitly directing the agency to fund only those projects that met a decency test would violate the First Amendment protections of free speech. In her majority opinion, Justice Sandra Day O'Connor indicated that it would; a law that imposed a "penalty," that is, denial of funding, "on disfavored viewpoints" would violate the First Amendment, she wrote.

Although he concurred with the outcome, Justice Antonin Scalia took exception to O'Connor's reasoning. The Court's opinion, Scalia said, sustained the constitutionality of the 1990 law "by gutting it." Joined by Justice Clarence Thomas, Scalia argued that the law in fact did amount to what is called "viewpoint discrimination" and that such discrimination was permissible when a federal agency was determining how to distribute limited federal funding. The free expression of a particular viewpoint is not abridged, Scalia maintained, just because the federal government refuses to underwrite it. In the lone dissent, Justice David H. Souter argued that the 1990 law was both a directive and a violation of the First Amendment.

NEA chairman William J. Ivey said the endowment was pleased with the decision. Reaction in the arts community ranged from outright condemnation to concerns that the decision would undermine both public and private support for art of all kinds. Ironically, even as the Court was handing down its decision on June 25, the House Appropriations Committee was approving a $98 million dollar appropriation for the NEA for fiscal 1999, the same amount the NEA had received in fiscal 1998. The committee action virtually ensured that congressional conservatives would be unsuccessful in any efforts to reduce or even eliminate funding for the endowment.

The Government's Relation to Artistic Expression

Since 1965 the NEA had distributed more than $3 billion in grants to individuals and organizations, such as symphony orchestras, theaters, and museums. Federal support for the arts was viewed as an important source of funding in its own right, as well as a stimulus to elicit financial support for the arts from corporations, individuals, and nonprofit organizations. Over the years a handful of the agency's 100,000 grants had triggered public controversy, none more so than two grants made in 1989. One grant was used by a local arts institute to support an exhibit of the works of the late Robert Mapplethorpe, known for his homoerotic and sadomasochistic photographs; the other was used by a contemporary arts center to support the work of Andres Serrano, creator of "Piss Christ," a photograph of a crucifix in a jar of urine.

After several members of Congress condemned the photographs as pornographic and sacrilegious, Congress in 1989 prohibited the NEA from underwriting projects that would be considered obscene, sadomasochistic, or homoerotic. In 1990 that ban was dropped in favor of language directing the NEA chairman to take into account in awarding grants not only artistic excellence and merit but also general standards of decency and respect for the diverse beliefs and values of the American people. On December 14 the National Council on the Arts, which advised the NEA chairman, voted not to impose standards of decency on panelists who recommend arts grants. Instead, the council told panel members that "by virtue of your backgrounds and diversity you represent general standards of decency—you bring that with you."

The case before the Supreme Court, National Endowment for the Arts v. Finley, *began in 1990 when the NEA denied grants to Karen Finley and three other performance artists. The four went to court contesting the denials. After Congress enacted the so-called decency standard, the four artists amended their complaint to challenge the constitutionality of the congressional language. Although all four submitted revised grant applications that the NEA approved, they continued with their suit. Both a federal district court and a federal appeals court ruled in favor of the artists. The appeals court said the decency language was vague and constituted discrimination against a particular viewpoint.*

The Supreme Court majority overruled the lower courts on both scores. The decency clause imposed "no categorical requirement" on NEA funding decisions, O'Connor wrote, and the language of the clause "stands in sharp contrast to congressional efforts to prohibit the funding of certain classes of speech." In short, O'Connor said, the majority did "not perceive a realistic danger" that the decency clause threatened First Amendment values. Nor was the clause unconstitutionally vague. It "merely adds some imprecise considerations to an already subjective selection process," O'Connor maintained.

In his sharply worded opinion concurring only in the judgment and not O'Connor's opinion, Scalia said that decency clause should be "evaluated as written, rather than as distorted by the agency it was meant to control. By its terms, it establishes content- and viewpoint-based criteria upon which grant applications are to be evaluated. And that is perfectly constitutional." Scalia argued that the decency clause did not abridge free speech. "Those who wish to create indecent and disrespectful art are as unconstrained now as they were before" the clause was enacted, he said. "They are merely deprived of the additional satisfaction of having the bourgeoisie taxed to pay for it."

Souter, the only justice in dissent, agreed with Scalia that the clause was directive rather than advisory, but disagreed on its constitutionality. The clause "mandates viewpoint-based decisions in the disbursement of governmental subsidies," he said, which he said was a violation of the First Amendment. "The Court's conclusions that the proviso is not viewpoint based, that it is not a regulation, and that the NEA may permissibly engage in viewpoint-based discrimination, are all patently mistaken," he said.

Reaction to the decision was mixed. House Speaker Newt Gingrich said the ruling "vindicated the right of the American people not to pay for art that offends their sensibilities." NEA chairman Ivey said the decision was "an endorsement of the endowment's mission to nurture the excellence, vitality, and diversity of the arts and a reaffirmation of the agency's discretion in funding the highest quality art in America."

Most artists who voiced a public opinion about the decision said it would have a chilling effect not only on their work but on funding from both public and private sources. Finley, whose performances often involved smearing her nude body with chocolate to illustrate abuse of women, wanted to know who was going to decide what was decent and what wasn't. "The witch hunt can happen anywhere," she told the New York Times *as she prepared for her new show "The Return of the Chocolate-Smeared Woman." Playwright David Rabe said he was not surprised by the decision. He saw it as "a recent manifestation of a fundamental hatred of art, of anything that does not coddle the public, that is not entertainment."*

Federal Arts Funding

Congressional funding for the NEA was much less contentious in 1998 than it had been in previous years. When Republicans won control of Con-

gress in 1994, they promised to eliminate the arts endowment. In 1995 they succeeded in cutting the agency's financing by 40 percent. But efforts by House conservatives to phase out funding for the endowment altogether failed in the Senate in both 1995 and 1996.

In 1997 Congress adopted several changes designed to minimize the chances that federal tax money would fund art projects that many taxpayers might find offensive. Those changes undercut the position of the most ardent foes of the endowment, and desire to avoid controversy during the 1998 election year apparently finished the job. By a vote of 253–173, the House on July 21 agreed to give $98 million to the endowment in fiscal 1999. The Senate approved a higher amount, but conceded to the $98 million in a House-Senate conference. The money was included in an omnibus appropriations bill (HR 4328—PL 105–277), approved in the final days of the session. "The old debate over the existence of the NEA finally has given way to a more thoughtful dialogue about the appropriate level of federal arts funding in America," Ivey, the endowment's new chairman, said in statement issued after the House vote in July.

Following are excerpts from the majority, concurring, and dissenting opinions in the case of National Endowment for the Arts v. Finley, in which the Supreme Court ruled 8–1 on June 25, 1998, upholding the constitutionality of a federal law allowing the National Endowment for the Arts to consider standards of decency when making its awards:

No. 97–371

| National Endowment for the Arts, et al., Petitioners *v.* Karen Finley et al. | On writ of certiorari to the United States Court of Appeals for the Ninth Circuit |

[June 25, 1998]

JUSTICE O'CONNOR delivered the opinion of the Court. (JUSTICE GINSBURG joins all but Part II–B of this opinion.)

The National Foundation on the Arts and Humanities Act, as amended in 1990, requires the Chairperson of the National Endowment for the Arts (NEA) to ensure that "artistic excellence and artistic merit are the criteria by which [grant] applications are judged, taking into consideration general standards of decency and respect for the diverse beliefs and values of the American public." 20 U.S.C. § 954(d)(1). In this case, we review the Court of Appeals' determination that § 954(d)(1), on its face, impermissibly discriminates on the basis of viewpoint and is void for vagueness under the First and Fifth Amendments. We conclude that § 954(d)(1) is facially valid, as it neither inherently interferes with First Amendment rights nor violates constitutional vagueness principles.

I

A

With the establishment of the NEA in 1965, Congress embarked on a "broadly conceived national policy of support for the . . . arts in the United States," . . . pledging federal funds to "help create and sustain not only a climate encouraging freedom of thought, imagination, and inquiry but also the material conditions facilitating the release of . . . creative talent." . . . The enabling statute vests the NEA with substantial discretion to award grants; it identifies only the broadest funding priorities, including "artistic and cultural significance, giving emphasis to American creativity and cultural diversity," "professional excellence," and the encouragement of "public knowledge, education, understanding, and appreciation of the arts." . . .

Applications for NEA funding are initially reviewed by advisory panels composed of experts in the relevant field of the arts. Under the 1990 Amendments to the enabling statute, those panels must reflect "diverse artistic and cultural points of view" and include "wide geographic, ethnic, and minority representation," as well as "lay individuals who are knowledgeable about the arts." § § 959(c)(1)-(2). The panels report to the 26-member National Council on the Arts (Council), which, in turn, advises the NEA Chairperson. The Chairperson has the ultimate authority to award grants but may not approve an application as to which the Council has made a negative recommendation. . . .

Since 1965, the NEA has distributed over three billion dollars in grants to individuals and organizations, funding that has served as a catalyst for increased state, corporate, and foundation support for the arts. Congress has recently restricted the availability of federal funding for individual artists, confining grants primarily to qualifying organizations and state arts agencies, and constraining sub-granting. By far the largest portion of the grants distributed in fiscal year 1998 were awarded directly to state arts agencies. In the remaining categories, the most substantial grants were allocated to symphony orchestras, fine arts museums, dance theater foundations, and opera associations.

Throughout the NEA's history, only a handful of the agency's roughly 100,000 awards have generated formal complaints about misapplied funds or abuse of the public's trust. Two provocative works, however, prompted public controversy in 1989 and led to congressional revaluation of the NEA's funding priorities and efforts to increase oversight of its grant-making procedures. The Institute of Contemporary Art at the University of Pennsylvania had used $30,000 of a visual arts grant it received from the NEA to fund a 1989 retrospective of photographer Robert Mapplethorpe's work. The exhibit, entitled *The Perfect Moment*, included homoerotic photographs that several Members of Congress condemned as pornographic. Members also denounced artist Andres Serrano's work *Piss Christ*, a photograph of a crucifix immersed in urine. Serrano had been awarded a $15,000 grant from the Southeast Center for Contemporary Art, an organization that received NEA support.

When considering the NEA's appropriations for fiscal year 1990, Congress reacted to the controversy surrounding the Mapplethorpe and Serrano photographs by eliminating $45,000 from the agency's budget, the precise amount contributed to the two exhibits by NEA grant recipients. Congress also enacted an amendment providing that no NEA funds "may be used to promote, disseminate, or produce materials which in the judgment of [the NEA] may be considered obscene, including but not limited to, depictions of sadomasochism, homoeroticism, the sexual exploitation of children, or individuals engaged in sex acts and which, when taken as a whole, do not have serious literary, artistic, political, or scientific value." ... The NEA implemented Congress' mandate by instituting a requirement that all grantees certify in writing that they would not utilize federal funding to engage in projects inconsistent with the criteria in the 1990 appropriations bill. That certification requirement was subsequently invalidated as unconstitutionally vague by a Federal District Court, *Bella Lewitzky Dance Foundation v. Frohnmayer* (CD Cal. 1991), and the NEA did not appeal the decision....

... Congress debated several proposals to reform the NEA's grant-making process when it considered the agency's reauthorization in the fall of 1990. The House rejected the Crane Amendment, which would have virtually eliminated the NEA, and the Rohrabacher Amendment, which would have introduced a prohibition on awarding any grants that could be used to "promote, distribute, disseminate, or produce matter that has the purpose or effect of denigrating the beliefs, tenets, or objects of a particular religion" or "of denigrating an individual, or group of individuals, on the basis of race, sex, handicap, or national origin." Ultimately, Congress adopted the Williams/Coleman Amendment, a bipartisan compromise between Members opposing any funding restrictions and those favoring some guidance to the agency. In relevant part, the Amendment became § 954(d)(1), which directs the Chairperson, in establishing procedures to judge the artistic merit of grant applications, to "tak[e] into consideration general standards of decency and respect for the diverse beliefs and values of the American public."

The NEA has not promulgated any official interpretation of the provision, but in December 1990, the Council unanimously adopted a resolution to implement § 954(d)(1) merely by ensuring that the members of the advisory panels that conduct the initial review of grant applications represent geographic, ethnic, and aesthetic diversity. John Frohnmayer, then Chairperson of the NEA, also declared that he would "count on [the] procedures" ensuring diverse membership on the peer review panels to fulfill Congress' mandate.

B

The four individual respondents in this case, Karen Finley, John Fleck, Holly Hughes, and Tim Miller, are performance artists who applied for NEA grants before § 954(d)(1) was enacted. An advisory panel recommended approval of respondents' projects, both initially and after receiving Frohnmayer's request to reconsider three of the applications. A majority of the Council subsequently recommended disapproval, and in June 1990, the NEA informed respondents that they had been denied funding. Respondents filed suit, alleging that the NEA had violated their First Amendment rights by rejecting the applications on political grounds, had failed to follow statutory procedures by basing the denial on criteria other than those set forth in the NEA's enabling statute, and had breached the confidentiality of their grant applications through the release of quotations to the press, in violation of the Privacy Act of 1974. Respondents sought restoration of the recommended grants or reconsideration of their applications, as well as damages for the alleged Privacy Act violations. When Congress enacted § 954(d)(1), respondents, now joined by the National Association of Artists' Organizations (NAAO), amended their complaint to challenge the provision as void for vagueness and impermissibly viewpoint based.

The District Court denied the NEA's motion for judgment on the pleadings [1992], and, after discovery, the NEA agreed [in 1993] to settle the individual respondents' statutory and as-applied constitutional claims by paying the artists the amount of the vetoed grants, damages, and attorney's fees.

The District Court then granted summary judgment in favor of respondents on their facial constitutional challenge to § 954(d)(1) and enjoined enforcement of the provision. The court rejected the argument that the NEA could comply with § 954(d)(1) by structuring the grant selection process to provide for diverse advisory panels. The provision, the court stated, "fails adequately to notify applicants of what is required of them or to circumscribe NEA discretion." Reasoning that "the very nature of our pluralistic society is that there are an infinite number of values and beliefs, and correlatively, there may be no national 'general standards of decency,' " the court concluded that § 954(d)(1) "cannot be given effect consistent with the Fifth Amendment's due process requirement." Drawing an analogy between arts funding and public universities, the court further ruled that the First Amendment constrains the NEA's grant-making process, and that because § 954(d)(1) "clearly reaches a substantial amount of protected speech," it is impermissibly overbroad on its face. The Government did not seek a stay of the District Court's injunction, and consequently the NEA has not applied § 954(d)(1) since June 1992.

A divided panel of the Court of Appeals affirmed the District Court's ruling. (CA9 1996). The majority agreed with the District Court that the NEA was compelled by the adoption of § 954(d)(1) to alter its grant-making procedures to ensure that applications are judged according to the "decency and respect" criteria. The Chairperson, the court reasoned, "has no discretion to

ignore this obligation, enforce only part of it, or give it a cramped construction." Concluding that the "decency and respect" criteria are not "susceptible
to objective definition," the court held that § 954(d)(1) "gives rise to the danger of arbitrary and discriminatory application" and is void for vagueness
under the First and Fifth Amendments. In the alternative, the court ruled that
§ 954(d)(1) violates the First Amendment's prohibition on viewpoint-based
restrictions on protected speech. Government funding of the arts, the court
explained, is both a "traditional sphere of free expression" and an area in
which the Government has stated its intention to "encourage a diversity of
views from private speakers." Accordingly, finding that § 954(d)(1) "has a
speech-based restriction as its sole rationale and operative principle" and
noting the NEA's failure to articulate a compelling interest for the provision,
the court declared it facially invalid. . . .

We granted certiorari (1997) and now reverse the judgment of the Court of
Appeals.

II

A

Respondents raise a facial constitutional challenge to § 954(d)(1), and
consequently they confront "a heavy burden" in advancing their claim. . . . To
prevail, respondents must demonstrate a substantial risk that application of
the provision will lead to the suppression of speech.

Respondents argue that the provision is a paradigmatic example of viewpoint discrimination because it rejects any artistic speech that either fails to
respect mainstream values or offends standards of decency. The premise of
respondents' claim is that § 954(d)(1) constrains the agency's ability to fund
certain categories of artistic expression. The NEA, however, reads the provision as merely hortatory, and contends that it stops well short of an absolute
restriction. Section 954(d)(1) adds "considerations" to the grant-making
process; it does not preclude awards to projects that might be deemed "indecent" or "disrespectful," nor place conditions on grants, or even specify that
those factors must be given any particular weight in reviewing an application. Indeed, the agency asserts that it has adequately implemented §
954(d)(1) merely by ensuring the representation of various backgrounds and
points of view on the advisory panels that analyze grant applications. . . . We
do not decide whether the NEA's view—that the formulation of diverse advisory panels is sufficient to comply with Congress' command—is in fact a reasonable reading of the statute. It is clear, however, that the text of § 954(d)(1)
imposes no categorical requirement. The advisory language stands in sharp
contrast to congressional efforts to prohibit the funding of certain classes of
speech. When Congress has in fact intended to affirmatively constrain the
NEA's grant-making authority, it has done so in no uncertain terms. . . .

Furthermore, like the plain language of § 954(d), the political context surrounding the adoption of the "decency and respect" clause is inconsistent
with respondents' assertion that the provision compels the NEA to deny

funding on the basis of viewpoint discriminatory criteria. The legislation was a bipartisan proposal introduced as a counterweight to amendments aimed at eliminating the NEA's funding or substantially constraining its grant-making authority. . . . [T]he criteria in § 954(d)(1) inform the assessment of artistic merit, but Congress declined to disallow any particular viewpoints. . . .

In contrast, the "decency and respect" criteria do not silence speakers by expressly "threaten[ing] censorship of ideas." Thus, we do not perceive a realistic danger that § 954(d)(1) will compromise First Amendment values. As respondents' own arguments demonstrate, the considerations that the provision introduces, by their nature, do not engender the kind of directed viewpoint discrimination that would prompt this Court to invalidate a statute on its face. Respondents assert, for example, that "[o]ne would be hard-pressed to find two people in the United States who could agree on what the 'diverse beliefs and values of the American public' are, much less on whether a particular work of art 'respects' them"; and they claim that " '[d]ecency' is likely to mean something very different to a septegenarian in Tuscaloosa and a teenager in Las Vegas." The NEA likewise views the considerations enumerated in § 954(d)(1) as susceptible to multiple interpretations. . . . Accordingly, the provision does not introduce considerations that, in practice, would effectively preclude or punish the expression of particular views. Indeed, one could hardly anticipate how "decency" or "respect" would bear on grant applications in categories such as funding for symphony orchestras.

Respondents' claim that the provision is facially unconstitutional may be reduced to the argument that the criteria in § 954(d)(1) are sufficiently subjective that the agency could utilize them to engage in viewpoint discrimination. Given the varied interpretations of the criteria and the vague exhortation to "take them into consideration," it seems unlikely that this provision will introduce any greater element of selectivity than the determination of "artistic excellence" itself. And we are reluctant, in any event, to invalidate legislation "on the basis of its hypothetical application to situations not before the Court." *FCC v. Pacifica Foundation* (1978). . . .

We recognize, of course, that reference to these permissible applications would not alone be sufficient to sustain the statute against respondents' First Amendment challenge. But neither are we persuaded that, in other applications, the language of § 954(d)(1) itself will give rise to the suppression of protected expression. Any content-based considerations that may be taken into account in the grant-making process are a consequence of the nature of arts funding. The NEA has limited resources and it must deny the majority of the grant applications that it receives, including many that propose "artistically excellent" projects. The agency may decide to fund particular projects for a wide variety of reasons, "such as the technical proficiency of the artist, the creativity of the work, the anticipated public interest in or appreciation of the work, the work's contemporary relevance, its educational value, its suitability for or appeal to special audiences (such as children or the disabled), its service to a rural or isolated community, or even simply that the work could increase public knowledge of an art form." As the dissent below noted, it would be "impossible to have a highly selective grant program without denying money to a large amount of constitutionally protected expression." The "very assumption" of the NEA is that grants will be awarded according to the "artistic worth of competing applications," and absolute neutrality is simply "inconceivable." . . .

Respondents do not allege discrimination in any particular funding decision. (In fact, after filing suit to challenge § 954(d)(1), two of the individual respondents received NEA grants.) Thus, we have no occasion here to address an as-applied challenge in a situation where the denial of a grant may be shown to be the product of invidious viewpoint discrimination. If the NEA were to leverage its power to award subsidies on the basis of subjective criteria into a penalty on disfavored viewpoints, then we would confront a different case. . . . In addition, as the NEA itself concedes, a more pressing constitutional question would arise if government funding resulted in the imposition of a disproportionate burden calculated to drive "certain ideas or viewpoints from the marketplace." Unless and until § 954(d)(1) is applied in a manner that raises concern about the suppression of disfavored viewpoints, however, we uphold the constitutionality of the provision. . . .

B

Finally, although the First Amendment certainly has application in the subsidy context, we note that the Government may allocate competitive funding according to criteria that would be impermissible were direct regulation of speech or a criminal penalty at stake. So long as legislation does not infringe on other constitutionally protected rights, Congress has wide latitude to set spending priorities. In the 1990 Amendments that incorporated § 954(d)(1), Congress modified the declaration of purpose in the NEA's enabling act to provide that arts funding should "contribute to public support and confidence in the use of taxpayer funds," and that "[p]ublic funds . . . must ultimately serve public purposes the Congress defines." § 951(5). And as we held in *Rust [v. Sullivan* (1991)], Congress may "selectively fund a program to encourage certain activities it believes to be in the public interest, without at the same time funding an alternative program which seeks to deal with the problem in another way." In doing so, "the Government has not discriminated on the basis of viewpoint; it has merely chosen to fund one activity to the exclusion of the other."

III

The lower courts also erred in invalidating § 954(d)(1) as unconstitutionally vague. Under the First and Fifth Amendments, speakers are protected from arbitrary and discriminatory enforcement of vague standards. The terms of the provision are undeniably opaque, and if they appeared in a criminal statute or regulatory scheme, they could raise substantial vagueness concerns. It is unlikely, however, that speakers will be compelled to steer too far clear of any "forbidden area" in the context of grants of this nature. [Citations omitted.] We recognize, as a practical matter, that artists may conform their speech to what they believe to be the decision-making criteria in order to acquire funding. But when the Government is acting as patron rather than as sovereign, the consequences of imprecision are not constitutionally severe.

In the context of selective subsidies, it is not always feasible for Congress to legislate with clarity. Indeed, if this statute is unconstitutionally vague, then so too are all government programs awarding scholarships and grants on the basis of subjective criteria such as "excellence." [Citing statutes establishing the Congressional Award Program, National Endowment for the Humanities, Fulbright grants, and grant programs by the Departments of Education and Energy.] To accept respondents' vagueness argument would be to call into question the constitutionality of these valuable government programs and countless others like them.

Section 954(d)(1) merely adds some imprecise considerations to an already subjective selection process. It does not, on its face, impermissibly infringe on First or Fifth Amendment rights. Accordingly, the judgment of the Court of Appeals is reversed and the case is remanded for further proceedings consistent with this opinion.

It is so ordered.

JUSTICE SCALIA, with whom JUSTICE THOMAS joins, concurring in the judgment.

"The operation was a success, but the patient died." What such a procedure is to medicine, the Court's opinion in this case is to law. It sustains the constitutionality of 20 U.S.C. § 954(d)(1) by gutting it. The most avid congressional opponents of the provision could not have asked for more. I write separately because, unlike the Court, I think that § 954(d)(1) must be evaluated as written, rather than as distorted by the agency it was meant to control. By its terms, it establishes content- and viewpoint-based criteria upon which grant applications are to be evaluated. And that is perfectly constitutional.

I

The Statute Means What It Says

Section 954(d)(1) provides:

"No payment shall be made under this section except upon application therefor which is submitted to the National Endowment for the Arts in accordance with regulations issued and procedures established by the Chairperson. In establishing such regulations and procedures, the Chairperson shall ensure that—

"(1) artistic excellence and artistic merit are the criteria by which applications are judged, taking into consideration general standards of decency and respect for the diverse beliefs and values of the American public."

The phrase "taking into consideration general standards of decency and respect for the diverse beliefs and values of the American public" is what my grammar-school teacher would have condemned as a dangling modifier. . . . Even so, it is clear enough that the phrase is meant to apply to those who do the judging. The application reviewers must take into account "general standards of decency" and "respect for the diverse beliefs and values of the American public" when evaluating artistic excellence and merit. . . .

This is so apparent that I am at a loss to understand what the Court has in mind (other than the gutting of the statute) when it speculates that the statute is merely "advisory." General standards of decency and respect for Americans' beliefs and values must (for the statute says that the Chairperson "shall ensure" this result) be taken into account . . . in evaluating all applications. This does not mean that those factors must always be dispositive, but it *does* mean that they must always be considered. The method of compliance proposed by the National Endowment for the Arts (NEA)— selecting diverse review panels of artists and nonartists that reflect a wide range of geographic and cultural perspectives—is so obviously inadequate that it insults the intelligence. A diverse panel membership increases the odds that, if and when the panel takes the factors into account, it will reach an accurate assessment of what they demand. But it in no way increases the odds that the panel will take the factors into consideration—much less *ensures* that the panel will do so, which is the Chairperson's duty under the statute. . . .

The "political context surrounding the adoption of the 'decency and respect' clause" . . . does not change its meaning or affect its constitutionality. . . . It is evident in the legislative history that § 954(d)(1) was prompted by, and directed at, the public funding of such offensive productions as Serrano's "Piss Christ," the portrayal of a crucifix immersed in urine, and Mapplethorpe's show of lurid homoerotic photographs. Thus, . . . it is perfectly clear that the statute was meant to disfavor—that is, to discriminate against—such productions. Not to ban their funding absolutely, to be sure (though as I shall discuss, that also would not have been unconstitutional); but to make their funding more difficult. . . .

II

What the Statute Says Is Constitutional

The Court devotes so much of its opinion to explaining why this statute means something other than what it says that it neglects to cite the constitutional text governing our analysis. The First Amendment reads: "Congress shall make no law . . . *abridging* the freedom of speech" (emphasis added). . . . With the enactment of § 954(d)(1), Congress did not abridge the speech of those who disdain the beliefs and values of the American public, nor did it abridge indecent speech. Those who wish to create indecent and disrespectful art are as unconstrained now as they were before the enactment of this statute. *Avant-garde artistes* such as respondents remain entirely free to *épater* [spite] *les bourgeois*; they are merely deprived of the additional satisfaction of having the bourgeoisie taxed to pay for it. . . .

Section 954(d)(1) is no more discriminatory, and no less constitutional, than virtually every other piece of funding legislation enacted by Congress. "The Government can, without violating the Constitution, selectively fund a program to encourage certain activities it believes to be in the public interest, without at the same time funding an alternative program. . . ." *Rust v. Sullivan* (1991). . . . It takes a particularly high degree of chutzpah for the NEA to contradict this proposition, since the agency itself discriminates—and is required by law to discriminate—in favor of artistic (as opposed to scientific, or political, or theological) expression. . . .

The nub of the difference between me and the Court is that I regard the distinction between "abridging" speech and funding it as a fundamental divide, on this side of which the First Amendment is inapplicable. The Court, by contrast, seems to believe that the First Amendment, despite its words, has some ineffable effect upon funding, imposing constraints of an indeterminate nature which it announces . . . are not violated by the statute here—or, more accurately, are not violated by the quite different, emasculated statute that it imagines. . . .

Finally, what is true of the First Amendment is also true of the constitutional rule against vague legislation: it has no application to funding. . . .

* * *

In its laudatory description of the accomplishments of the NEA, the Court notes with satisfaction that "only a handful of the agency's roughly 100,000 awards have generated formal complaints." The Congress that felt it necessary to enact § 954(d)(1) evidently thought it much *more* noteworthy that *any* money exacted from American taxpayers had been used to produce a crucifix immersed in urine, or a display of homoerotic photographs. It is no secret that the provision was prompted by, and directed at, the funding of such offensive productions. Instead of banning the funding of such productions absolutely, which I think would have been entirely constitutional, Congress took the lesser step of requiring them to be disfavored in the evaluation of grant applications. The Court's opinion today renders even that lesser step a nullity. For that reason, I concur only in the judgment.

JUSTICE SOUTER, dissenting.

The question here is whether the italicized segment of this statute is unconstitutional on its face: "artistic excellence and artistic merit are the criteria by which applications [for grants from the National Endowment for the Arts] are judged, *taking into consideration general standards of decency and respect for the diverse beliefs and values of the American public.* "20 U.S.C. § 954(d) (emphasis added). It is.

The decency and respect proviso mandates viewpoint-based decisions in the disbursement of government subsidies, and the Government has wholly failed to explain why the statute should be afforded an exemption from the fundamental rule of the First Amendment that viewpoint discrimination in the exercise of public authority over expressive activity is unconstitutional. The Court's conclusions that the proviso is not viewpoint based, that it is not a regulation, and that the NEA may permissibly engage in viewpoint-based discrimination, are all patently mistaken. Nor may the question raised be answered in the Government's favor on the assumption that some constitutional applications of the statute are enough to satisfy the demand of facial constitutionality, leaving claims of the proviso's obvious invalidity to be dealt with later in response to challenges of specific applications of the discriminatory standards. This assumption is irreconcilable with our long standing and sensible doctrine of facial overbreadth, applicable to claims brought under the First Amendment's speech clause. I respectfully dissent. . . .

SUPREME COURT ON THE
LINE-ITEM VETO
June 25, 1998

The Supreme Court on June 25 declared unconstitutional a cumbersome procedure Congress had enacted in 1996 to give presidents a form of "line-item veto" over individual items in spending bills. The Court's ruling ended a brief experiment intended to strengthen the president's hand in curbing the congressional spending appetite. Proponents of a line-item veto said they would try to find another way to resurrect the idea, but the advent in 1998 of a balanced budget undermined the political urgency that had originally impelled Congress to give up part of its cherished spending power.

The governors of forty-four states had some form of line-item veto power, enabling them to cancel individual items in a spending bill without having to veto the entire measure. Numerous presidents since Ulysses S. Grant had expressed a desire for the power, but it was not until the burgeoning deficits under the presidency of Ronald Reagan that the idea gained any measurable support on Capitol Hill. Republican candidates for the House of Representatives made the line-item veto a cornerstone of their "Contract with America" platform in 1994. The Contract was a ten-point manifesto signed by 367 Republican candidates that pledged reform of Democratic policies and defined Republican legislative priorities. When Republicans took control of both houses of Congress in 1995, they moved to follow through on their pledge, and Congress enacted a version of the line-item veto in 1996. (Contract with America, Historic Documents of 1994, p. 374)

Even before the Supreme Court invalidated the line-item veto, it had become clear that the procedure, by itself, was not likely to be a cure-all for chronic budget deficits. Clinton was careful to use his new power sparingly, especially after his first vetoes provoked howls of protest from Capitol Hill. For the most part, the president avoided vetoing spending items sponsored by members of Congress with power to influence his top legislative priorities. By 1998 there also was little evidence that the prospect of a line-item veto had encouraged members of Congress to curb spending on "pork barrel" projects that benefited their constituencies.

The "Enhanced Recission"

The line-item veto struck down by the Supreme Court involved a complex procedure that Congress had crafted in hopes of getting around the need for a constitutional amendment on the issue. It was widely acknowledged that Congress could not give the president a full-scale line-item veto except by amending the constitution. So Congress tried a short-cut, called the "enhanced recission." A recission was a time-honored procedure allowing a president to tell Congress that he was planning not to spend certain sums that had been appropriated, and Congress could overturn his recission by passing legislation by majority vote. Under the new "enhanced recission" procedure, Congress would pass its normal appropriations bills and send them to the president for his signature. Within five days after signing a spending bill, the president could, in effect, "cancel" individual spending items, as well as narrowly focused tax breaks and new entitlement programs. To restore the spending or tax provision, Congress would have to pass a "disapproval" bill, which itself would be subject to a presidential veto. Congress could then overturn that veto with a two-thirds vote of both chambers.

After Congress approved the line-item veto in 1996 (PL 104–130), Clinton used it between August and December of 1997 to cancel eighty-two spending and tax items. For the most part, Clinton vetoed narrow pork barrel projects benefiting limited constituencies. Congress allowed most of Clinton's vetoes to stand without challenge, but in February 1998 it overrode one set of vetoes involving thirty-eight projects in a military construction bill (PL 105–45). (Clinton's use of the veto, Historic Documents of 1997, p. 611)

A handful of members of Congress, led by Sen. Robert C. Byrd, D-W.Va., in 1996 filed a legal challenge to the veto law. The Supreme Court in 1997 threw out that challenge on procedural grounds, arguing that the legislators did not have the standing to sue because they had not been harmed personally by use of the veto.

The successful challenge to the line-item veto law came from Clinton's first use of it: his attempts to block a provision to help New York state finance its Medicaid program and of a capital gains tax break for farmer-owned cooperatives. Plaintiffs claiming they had been harmed by Clinton's vetoes included New York City, its hospital system and hospital workers, and the Snake River Potato Growers Inc. in Idaho. The cases of Clinton v. City of New York *and* Snake River Potato Growers Inc. v. Rubin *were subsequently consolidated, to help assure that at least one plaintiff would have standing under the Constitution.*

On February 12, 1998, U.S. District Court Judge Thomas F. Hogan, in Washington, ruled in favor of the plaintiffs, declaring the veto law was unconstitutional. Hogan's ruling went straight to the Supreme Court for review. The high court held a hearing on the issue April 27; during that session several justices expressed skepticism about the government's claim that the line-item veto law was constitutional.

The Court Decision

In a 6–3 ruling, the Supreme Court struck down the line-item veto law as violating Article I, section 7 of the Constitution, which established the requirement for the enactment of laws, and Article I, section 1, which defined the separate powers of the three branches of government. Justice John Paul Stevens wrote the majority opinion, in which he was joined by Chief Justice William H. Rehnquist and Justices David H. Souter, Clarence Thomas, and Ruth Bader Ginsburg. Justice Anthony Kennedy wrote a separate concurring opinion. Justices Antonin Scalia, Stephen G. Breyer, and Sandra Day O'Connor dissented and said they would have upheld the law as constitutional.

In effect, Stevens said Congress had been too clever when it enacted the complicated "enhanced recission" procedure for a line-item veto. Under this procedure, Stevens said, the president was unilaterally changing the text of a bill after he had signed it into law. The Constitution "is silent on the subject of unilateral presidential action that either repeals or amends part of duly enacted statutes," Stevens said—and on such an important issue constitutional silence is "equivalent to an express prohibition." If Congress wanted to give the president the power to change the text of statutes after enactment, it would have to do so by amending the Constitution, Stevens wrote.

In his concurring opinion, Justice Kennedy heaped scorn on Congress for attempting to hand its constitutional responsibilities over to the president. Noting that Congress had resorted to the line-item veto because of its own inability to control spending, Kennedy wrote: "Failure of political will does not justify unconstitutional remedies. Abdication of responsibility is not part of the constitutional design."

Scalia, in his minority opinion, insisted the veto law was "entirely in accord" with the Constitution and did not violate the separation of powers or the procedures for enacting laws. Scalia rejected the majority's argument that the law represented a substantial difference from the long-standing practice of presidential rescissions of spending items. "There is not a dime's worth of difference between Congress's authorizing the president to cancel a spending item and Congress's authorizing money to be spent on a particular item at the president's discretion," Scalia wrote.

Congressional Reaction

The Court's ruling came in the context of political circumstances that had changed substantially since Congress debated and approved the line-item veto in 1995 and 1996. The biggest change was in the budgetary situation. By 1998 an expanding economy had helped narrow the chronic federal budget deficit, and fiscal year 1998 produced the first surplus in nearly thirty years. As a result, the original urgency for giving the president more power to cut spending had diminished. Moreover, some Republican proponents of a line-item veto had been stung by Clinton's veto of spending items for their states or districts.

Under these circumstances, few members of Congress expressed a deep sense of regret when the Court overturned the veto. Several proponents, including Sen. John McCain, R-Ariz., said they would try again to craft line-item veto legislation that would meet the Supreme Court's test of constitutionality. One of their proposals was for Congress to pass its appropriations bills as usual but then break each of them into hundreds, or even thousands, of separate pieces of legislation for review by the president. This would allow the president to pick and choose items to veto, just as he did any other piece of legislation. Even proponents acknowledged that this type of procedure was so complex and fraught with political controversy that Congress was unlikely ever to adopt it.

Senator Byrd and other opponents of the line-item veto hailed the Supreme Court decision. Waving a copy of the Constitution before reporters, an excited Byrd said: "This is a great day for the Constitution of the United States of America. . . . The liberties of the American people have been assured. God save this honorable court."

In a statement, Clinton called the Court's decision "a defeat for all Americans." Overturning the veto had deprived presidents of "a valuable tool for eliminating waste in the federal budget," he said.

Following are excerpts from the majority, concurring, and dissenting opinions in Clinton v. City of New York, *in which the Supreme Court on June 25, 1998, struck down as unconstitutional the Line Item Veto Act of 1996, which gave the president the power to "cancel" individual spending or tax items:*

No. 97–1374

William J. Clinton, President of the United States, et al., Appellants *v.* City of New York et al.	On appeal from the United States District Court for the District of Columbia

[June 25, 1998]

JUSTICE STEVENS delivered the opinion of the Court.

The Line Item Veto Act (Act) 2 U.S.C. § 691 et seq., was enacted in April 1996 and became effective on January 1, 1997. The following day, six Members of Congress who had voted against the Act brought suit in the District Court for the District of Columbia challenging its constitutionality. On April 10, 1997, the District Court entered an order holding that the Act is unconstitutional. *Byrd v. Raines.* In obedience to the statutory direction to allow a direct, expedited appeal to this Court, see § §692(b)–(c), we promptly noted probable jurisdiction and expedited review (1997). We determined, however, that the Members of Congress did not have standing to sue because they had not "alleged a sufficiently concrete injury to have established Article III standing, *Raines v. Byrd* (1997); thus, in . . . light of [the] overriding and time-honored concern about keeping the Judiciary's power within its proper constitutional sphere," we remanded the case to the District Court with instructions to dismiss the complaint for lack of jurisdiction.

Less than two months after our decision in that case, the President exercised his authority to cancel one provision in the Balanced Budget Act of 1997 and two provisions in the Taxpayer Relief Act of 1997. Appellees, claiming that they had been injured by two of those cancellations, filed these cases in the District Court. That Court again held the statute invalid (1998), and we again expedited our review (1998). We now hold that these appellees have standing to challenge the constitutionality of the Act and, reaching the merits, we agree that the cancellation procedures set forth in the Act violate the Presentment Clause, Art. I, § 7, cl. 2, of the Constitution.

I

We begin by reviewing the canceled items that are at issue in these cases.

Section 4722(c) of the Balanced Budget Act

Title XIX of the Social Security Act, as amended, authorizes the Federal Government to transfer huge sums of money to the States to help finance medical care for the indigent. In 1991, Congress directed that those federal subsidies be reduced by the amount of certain taxes levied by the States on health care providers. In 1994, the Department of Health and Human Services (HHS) notified the State of New York that 15 of its taxes were covered by the 1991 Act, and that as of June 30, 1994, the statute therefore required New York to return $955 million to the United States. The notice advised the State that it could apply for a waiver on certain statutory grounds. New York did request a waiver for those tax programs, as well as for a number of others, but HHS has not formally acted on any of those waiver requests. New York has estimated that the amount at issue for the period from October 1992 through March 1997 is as high as $2.6 billion.

Because HHS had not taken any action on the waiver requests, New York turned to Congress for relief. On August 5, 1997, Congress enacted a law that resolved the issue in New York's favor. Section 4722(c) of the Balanced Budget Act of 1997 identifies the disputed taxes and provides that they "are deemed to be permissible health care related taxes and in compliance with the requirements" of the relevant provisions of the 1991 statute.

On August 11, 1997, the President sent identical notices to the Senate and to the House of Representatives canceling "one item of new direct spending," specifying § 4722(c) as that item, and stating that he had determined that "this cancellation will reduce the Federal budget deficit." He explained that § 4722(c) would have permitted New York "to continue relying upon impermissible provider taxes to finance its Medicaid program" and that "[t]his preferential treatment would have increased Medicaid costs, would have treated

New York differently from all other States, and would have established a costly precedent for other States to request comparable treatment."

Section 968 of the Taxpayer Relief Act

A person who realizes a profit from the sale of securities is generally subject to a capital gains tax. Under existing law, however, an ordinary business corporation can acquire a corporation, including a food processing or refining company, in a merger or stock-for-stock transaction in which no gain is recognized to the seller; the seller's tax payment, therefore, is deferred. If, however, the purchaser is a farmers' cooperative, the parties cannot structure such a transaction because the stock of the cooperative may be held only by its members; thus, a seller dealing with a farmers' cooperative cannot obtain the benefits of tax deferral.

In § 968 of the Taxpayer Relief Act of 1997, Congress amended § 1042 of the Internal Revenue Code to permit owners of certain food refiners and processors to defer the recognition of gain if they sell their stock to eligible farmers' cooperatives. The purpose of the amendment, as repeatedly explained by its sponsors, was "to facilitate the transfer of refiners and processors to farmers' cooperatives." The amendment to § 1042 was one of the 79 "limited tax benefits" authorized by the Taxpayer Relief Act of 1997 and specifically identified in Title XVII of that Act as "subject to [the] line item veto."

On the same date that he canceled the "item of new direct spending" involving New York's health care programs, the President also canceled this limited tax benefit. In his explanation of that action, the President endorsed the objective of encouraging "value-added farming through the purchase by farmers' cooperatives of refiners or processors of agricultural goods," but concluded that the provision lacked safeguards and also "failed to target its benefits to small-and-medium-size cooperatives."

II

Appellees filed two separate actions against the President and other federal officials challenging these two cancellations. The plaintiffs in the first case are the City of New York, two hospital associations, one hospital, and two unions representing health care employees. The plaintiffs in the second are a farmers' cooperative consisting of about 30 potato growers in Idaho and an individual farmer who is a member and officer of the cooperative. The District Court consolidated the two cases and determined that at least one of the plaintiffs in each had standing under Article III of the Constitution.

Appellee New York City Health and Hospitals Corporation (NYCHHC) is responsible for the operation of public health care facilities throughout the City of New York. If HHS ultimately denies the State's waiver requests, New York law will automatically require 10 NYCHHC to make retroactive tax payments to the State of about $4 million for each of the years at issue. This contingent liability for NYCHHC, and comparable potential liabilities for the other appellee health care providers, were eliminated by § 4722(c) of the Balanced Budget Act of 1997 and revived by the President's cancellation of that provision. The District Court held that the cancellation of the statutory protection against these liabilities constituted sufficient injury to give these providers Article III standing.

Appellee Snake River Potato Growers, Inc. (Snake River) was formed in May 1997 to assist Idaho potato farmers in marketing their crops and stabilizing prices, in part through a strategy of acquiring potato processing facilities that will allow the members of the cooperative to retain revenues otherwise payable to third-party processors. At that time, Congress was considering the amendment to the capital gains tax that was expressly intended to aid farmers' cooperatives in the purchase of processing facilities, and Snake River had concrete plans to take advantage of the amendment if passed. Indeed, appellee Mike Cranney, acting on behalf of Snake River, was engaged in negotiations with the owner of an Idaho potato processor that would have qualified for the tax benefit under the pending legislation, but these negotiations terminated when the President canceled § 968. Snake River is currently considering the possible purchase of other processing facilities in Idaho if the President's cancellation is reversed. Based on these facts, the District Court concluded that the Snake River plaintiffs were injured by the President's cancellation of § 968, as they "lost the benefit of being on equal footing with their competitors and will likely have to pay more to purchase processing facilities now that the sellers will not [be] able to take advantage of section 968's tax breaks."

On the merits, the District Court held that the cancellations did not conform to the constitutionally mandated procedures for the enactment or repeal of laws in two respects. First, the laws that resulted after the cancellations "were different from those consented to by both Houses of Congress." Moreover, the President violated Article I "when he unilaterally canceled provisions of duly enacted statutes." As a separate basis for its decision, the District Court also held that the Act "impermissibly disrupts the balance of powers among the three branches of government."

III

As in the prior challenge to the Line Item Veto Act, we initially confront jurisdictional questions. [Stevens rejected several arguments by the government contending that the plaintiffs lacked standing to bring the suits. First, he rejected an argument that the act authorized only "individuals," not corporations, to invoke its provision for expedited review. "There is no plausible reason," Stevens wrote, "why Congress would have intended to provide for such special treatment of actions filed by natural persons and to have precluded entirely jurisdiction over comparable cases brought by corporate persons."]

We are also unpersuaded by the Government's argument that appellees' challenge to the constitutionality of the Act is nonjusticiable. . . .

In both the New York and the Snake River cases, the Government argues that the appellees are not actually injured because the claims are too speculative and, in any event, the claims are advanced by the wrong parties. We find no merit in the suggestion that New York's injury is merely speculative because HHS has not yet acted on the State's waiver requests. The State now has a multibillion dollar contingent liability that had been eliminated by § 4722(c) of the Balanced Budget Act of 1997. The District Court correctly concluded that the State, and the appellees, "suffered an immediate, concrete injury the moment that the President used the Line Item Veto to cancel section 4722(c) and deprived them of the benefits of that law." . . .

We also reject the Government's argument that New York's claim is advanced by the wrong parties because the claim belongs to the State of New York, and not appellees. Under New York statutes that are already in place, it is clear that both the City of New York and the appellee health care providers will be assessed by the State for substantial portions of any recoupment payments that the State may have to make to the Federal Government. . . .

The Snake River farmers' cooperative also suffered an immediate injury when the President canceled the limited tax benefit that Congress had enacted to facilitate the acquisition of processing plants. . . .

IV

The Line Item Veto Act gives the President the power to "cancel in whole" three types of provisions that have been signed into law: "(1) any dollar amount of discretionary budget authority; (2) any item of new direct spending; or (3) any limited tax benefit." 2 U.S.C. § 691(a). It is undisputed that the New York case involves an "item of new direct spending" and that the Snake River case involves a "limited tax benefit" as those terms are defined in the Act. It is also undisputed that each of those provisions had been signed into law pursuant to Article I, § 7, of the Constitution before it was canceled.

The Act requires the President to adhere to precise procedures whenever he exercises his cancellation authority. In identifying items for cancellation he must consider the legislative history, the purposes, and other relevant information about the items. See 2 U.S.C. § 691(b). He must determine, with respect to each cancellation, that it will "(i) reduce the Federal budget deficit; (ii) not impair any essential Government functions; and (iii) not harm the national interest." § 691(a)(A). Moreover, he must transmit a special message to Congress notifying it of each cancellation within five calendar days (excluding Sundays) after the enactment of the canceled provision. See § 691(a)(B). It is undisputed that the President meticulously followed these procedures in these cases.

A cancellation takes effect upon receipt by Congress of the special message from the President. See § 691b(a). If, however, a "disapproval bill" pertaining to a special message is enacted into law, the cancellations set forth in that message become "null and void." The Act sets forth a detailed expedited procedure for the consideration of a "disapproval bill," see § 691d, but no such bill was passed for either of the cancellations involved in these cases. A majority vote of both Houses is sufficient to enact a disapproval bill. The Act does not grant the President the authority to cancel a disapproval bill, see § 691(c), but he does, of course, retain his constitutional authority to veto such a bill.

The effect of a cancellation is plainly stated in § 691e. . . . With respect to both an item of new direct spending and a limited tax benefit, the cancellation prevents the item "from having legal force or effect." 2 U.S.C. § § 691e(4)(B)–(C). . . .

In both legal and practical effect, the President has amended two Acts of Congress by repealing a portion of each. "[R]epeal of statutes, no less than enactment, must conform with Art. I." *INS v. Chadha* (1983). There is no provision in the Constitution that authorizes the President to enact, to amend, or to repeal statutes. Both Article I and Article II assign responsibilities to the President that directly relate to the lawmaking process, but neither addresses the issue presented by these cases. The President "shall from time to time give to the Congress Information on the State of the Union, and recommend to their Consideration such Measures as he shall judge necessary and expedient. . . ." Art. II, § 3. Thus, he may initiate and influence legislative proposals. Moreover, after a bill has passed both Houses of Congress, but "before it become[s] a Law," it must be presented to the President. If he approves it, "he shall sign it, but if not he shall return it, with his Objections to that House in which it shall have originated, who shall enter the Objections at large on their Journal, and proceed to reconsider it." Art. I, § 7, cl. 2. His "return" of a bill, which is usually described as a "veto," is subject to being overridden by a two-thirds vote in each House.

There are important differences between the President's "return" of a bill pursuant to Article I, § 7, and the exercise of the President's cancellation authority pursuant to the Line Item Veto Act. The constitutional return takes place before the bill becomes law; the statutory cancellation occurs after the bill becomes law. The constitutional return is of the entire bill; the statutory cancellation is of only a part. Although the Constitution expressly authorizes the President to play a role in the process of enacting statutes, it is silent on the subject of unilateral Presidential action that either repeals or amends parts of duly enacted statutes.

There are powerful reasons for construing constitutional silence on this profoundly important issue as equivalent to an express prohibition. The procedures governing the enactment of statutes set forth in the text of Article I were the product of the great debates and compromises that produced the Constitution itself. Familiar historical materials provide abundant support for the conclusion that the power to enact statutes may only "be exercised in accord with a single, finely wrought and exhaustively considered, procedure." *Chadha*. Our first President understood the text of the Presentment Clause as requiring that he either "approve all the parts of a Bill, or reject it in toto." What has emerged in these cases from the President's exercise of his statutory cancellation powers, however, are truncated versions of two bills that passed both Houses of Congress. They are not the product of the "finely wrought" procedure that the Framers designed. . . .

V

The Government advances two related arguments to support its position that despite the unambiguous provisions of the Act, cancellations do not amend or repeal properly enacted statutes in violation of the Presentment Clause. First, relying primarily on *Field v. Clark* (1892), the Government contends that the cancellations were merely exercises of discretionary authority granted to the President by the Balanced Budget Act and the Taxpayer Relief Act read in light of the previously enacted Line Item Veto Act. Second, the Government submits that the substance of the authority to cancel tax and spending items "is, in practical effect, no more and no less than the power to 'decline to spend' specified sums of money, or to 'decline to implement' specified tax measures." Neither argument is persuasive.

In *Field v. Clark*, the Court upheld the constitutionality of the Tariff Act of 1890. That statute contained a "free list" of almost 300 specific articles that were exempted from import duties "unless otherwise specially provided for in this act." Section 3 was a special provision that directed the President to suspend that exemption for sugar, molasses, coffee, tea, and hides "whenever, and so often" as he should be satisfied that any country producing and exporting those products imposed duties on the agricultural products of the United States that he deemed to be "reciprocally unequal and unreasonable...." The section then specified the duties to be imposed on those products during any such suspension. The Court provided this explanation for its conclusion that § 3 had not delegated legislative power to the President [excerpt from opinion omitted]....

This passage identifies three critical differences between the power to suspend the exemption from import duties and the power to cancel portions of a duly enacted statute. First, the exercise of the suspension power was contingent upon a condition that did not exist when the Tariff Act was passed: the imposition of "reciprocally unequal and unreasonable" import duties by other countries. In contrast, the exercise of the cancellation power within five days after the enactment of the Balanced Budget and Tax Reform Acts necessarily was based on the same conditions that Congress evaluated when it passed those statutes. Second, under the Tariff Act, when the President determined that the contingency had arisen, he had a duty to suspend; in contrast, while it is true that the President was required by the Act to make three determinations before he canceled a provision, those determinations did not qualify his discretion to cancel or not to cancel. Finally, whenever the President suspended an exemption under the Tariff Act, he was executing the policy that Congress had embodied in the statute. In contrast, whenever the President cancels an item of new direct spending or a limited tax benefit he is rejecting the policy judgment made by Congress and relying on his own policy judgment....

The Government's reliance upon other tariff and import statutes, discussed in *Field*, that contain provisions similar to the one challenged in *Field* is unavailing for the same reasons. Some of those statutes authorized the President to "suspen[d] and discontinu[e]" statutory duties upon his determination that discriminatory duties imposed by other nations had been abolished....

The cited statutes all relate to foreign trade, and this Court has recognized that in the foreign affairs arena, the President has "a degree of discretion and freedom from statutory restriction which would not be admissible were domestic affairs alone involved." *United States v. Curtiss-Wright Export Corp.* (1936). . . . More important, when enacting the statutes discussed in *Field*, Congress itself made the decision to suspend or repeal the particular provisions at issue upon the occurrence of particular events subsequent to enactment, and it left only the determination of whether such events occurred up to the President. The Line Item Veto Act authorizes the President himself to effect the repeal of laws, for his own policy reasons, without observing the procedures set out in Article I, § 7. The fact that Congress intended such a result is of no moment. Although Congress presumably anticipated that the President might cancel some of the items in the Balanced Budget Act and in the Taxpayer Relief Act, Congress cannot alter the procedures set out in Article I, § 7, without amending the Constitution.

Neither are we persuaded by the Government's contention that the President's authority to cancel new direct spending and tax benefit items is no greater than his traditional authority to decline to spend appropriated funds. The Government has reviewed in some detail the series of statutes in which Congress has given the Executive broad discretion over the expenditure of appropriated funds. . . . The critical difference between this statute and all of its predecessors, however, is that unlike any of them, this Act gives the President the unilateral power to change the text of duly enacted statutes. None of the Act's predecessors could even arguably have been construed to authorize such a change.

VI

. . . [T]he profound importance of these cases makes it appropriate to emphasize three points.

First, we express no opinion about the wisdom of the procedures authorized by the Line Item Veto Act. Many members of both major political parties who have served in the Legislative and the Executive Branches have long advocated the enactment of such procedures for the purpose of "ensur[ing] greater fiscal accountability in Washington." [Citing 1996 conference report.] The text of the Act was itself the product of much debate and deliberation in both Houses of Congress and that precise text was signed into law by the President. We do not lightly conclude that their action was unauthorized by the Constitution. We have, however, twice had full argument and briefing on the question and have concluded that our duty is clear.

Second, although appellees challenge the validity of the Act on alternative grounds, the only issue we address concerns the "finely wrought" procedure commanded by the Constitution. We have been favored with extensive debate about the scope of Congress' power to delegate law-making authority, or its functional equivalent, to the President. The excellent briefs filed by the parties and their *amici curiae* have provided us with valuable historical information that illuminates the delegation issue but does not really bear on the narrow issue that is dispositive of these cases. Thus, because we conclude that the Act's cancellation provisions violate Article I, § 7, of the Constitution, we find it unnecessary to consider the District Court's alternative holding that the Act "impermissibly disrupts the balance of powers among the three branches of government."

Third, our decision rests on the narrow ground that the procedures authorized by the Line Item Veto Act are not authorized by the Constitution. The Balanced Budget Act of 1997 is a 500-page document that became "Public Law 105–33" after three procedural steps were taken: (1) a bill containing its exact text was approved by a majority of the Members of the House of Representatives; (2) the Senate approved precisely the same text; and (3) that text was signed into law by the President. The Constitution explicitly requires that each of those three steps be taken before a bill may "become a law." Art. I, § 7. If one paragraph of that text had been omitted at any one of those three stages, Public Law 105–33 would not have been validly enacted. If the Line Item Veto Act were valid, it would authorize the President to create a different law—one whose text was not voted on by either House of Congress or presented to the President for signature. Something that might be known as "Public Law 105-33 as modified by the President" may or may not be desirable, but it is surely not a document that may "become a law" pursuant to the procedures designed by the Framers of Article I, § 7, of the Constitution.

If there is to be a new procedure in which the President will play a different role in determining the final text of what may "become a law," such change must come not by legislation but through the amendment procedures set forth in Article V of the Constitution.

The judgment of the District Court is affirmed.

It is so ordered.

JUSTICE KENNEDY, concurring.

A nation cannot plunder its own treasury without putting its Constitution and its survival in peril. The statute before us, then, is of first importance, for it seems undeniable the Act will tend to restrain persistent excessive spending. Nevertheless, for the reasons given by JUSTICE STEVENS in the opinion for the Court, the statute must be found invalid. Failure of political will does not justify unconstitutional remedies.

I write to respond to my colleague JUSTICE BREYER, who observes that the statute does not threaten the liberties of individual citizens, a point on which I disagree. . . . Liberty is always at stake when one or more of the branches seek to transgress the separation of powers.

. . . [The Framers] used the principles of separation of powers and federalism to secure liberty in the fundamental political sense of the term, quite in addition to the idea of freedom from intrusive governmental acts. The idea and the promise were that when the people delegate some degree of control to a remote central authority, one branch of government ought not possess the power to shape their destiny without a sufficient check from the other two. In this vision, liberty demands limits on the ability of any one branch to influence basic political decisions. . . .

It follows that if a citizen who is taxed has the measure of the tax or the decision to spend determined by the Executive alone, without adequate control by the citizen's Representatives in Congress, liberty is threatened. Money is the instrument of policy and policy affects the lives of citizens. The individual loses liberty in a real sense if that instrument is not subject to traditional constitutional constraints.

The principal object of the statute, it is true, was not to enhance the President's power to reward one group and punish another, to help one set of taxpayers and hurt another, to favor one State and ignore another. Yet these are its undeniable effects. The law establishes a new mechanism which gives the President the sole ability to hurt a group that is a visible target, in order to disfavor the group or to extract further concessions from Congress. The law is the functional equivalent of a line item veto and enhances the President's powers beyond what the Framers would have endorsed.

It is no answer, of course, to say that Congress surrendered its authority by its own hand; nor does it suffice to point out that a new statute, signed by the President or enacted over his veto, could restore to Congress the power it now seeks to relinquish. That a congressional cession of power is voluntary does not make it innocuous. The Constitution is a compact enduring for more than our time, and one Congress cannot yield up its own powers, much less those of other Congresses to follow. Abdication of responsibility is not part of the constitutional design. . . .

JUSTICE SCALIA, with whom JUSTICE O'CONNOR joins, and with whom JUSTICE BREYER joins as to Part III, concurring in part and dissenting in part.

Today the Court acknowledges the " 'overriding and time-honored concern about keeping the Judiciary's power within its proper constitutional sphere.' " It proceeds, however, to ignore the prescribed statutory limits of our jurisdiction by permitting the expedited-review provisions of the Line Item Veto Act to be invoked by persons who are not "individual[s]," 2 U.S.C. § 692; and to ignore the constitutional limits of our jurisdiction by permitting one party to challenge the Government's denial *to another party* of favorable tax treatment from which the first party might, but just as likely might not, gain a concrete benefit. In my view, the Snake River appellees lack standing to challenge the President's cancellation of the "limited tax benefit," and the constitutionality of that action should not be addressed. I think the New York appellees have standing to challenge the President's cancellation of an "item of new direct spending"; I believe we have statutory authority (other than the expedited-review provision) to address that challenge; but unlike the Court I find the President's cancellation of spending items to be entirely in accord with the Constitution.

I

[Scalia concluded that none of the plaintiffs except Mike Cranney qualified as "individuals" under the expedited review provision of the act. However, he said that "in light of the public importance of the issues involved," the Court should exercise its certiorari power to review both cases.]

II

[Scalia argued at length that the Snake River appellees lacked standing to bring the case. He disputed the Court's conclusion that "harm to one's bargaining position" could amount to "a legally cognizable injury." In any event, he said, "Snake River has presented no evidence to show that it was engaged in bargaining, and that that bargaining was impaired by the President's cancellation of § 968."]

III

. . . I turn, then, to the crux of the matter: whether Congress's authorizing the President to cancel an item of spending gives him a power that our history and traditions show must reside exclusively in the Legislative Branch. . . .

Insofar as the degree of political, "law-making" power conferred upon the Executive is concerned, there is not a dime's worth of difference between Congress's authorizing the President to cancel a spending item, and Congress's authorizing money to be spent on a particular item at the President's discretion. And the latter has been done since the Founding of the Nation. From 1789–1791, the First Congress made lump-sum appropriations for the entire Government—"sum[s] not exceeding" specified amounts for broad purposes. [Citations omitted.] From a very early date Congress also made permissive individual appropriations, leaving the decision whether to spend the money to the President's unfettered discretion. In 1803, it appropriated $50,000 for the President to build "not exceeding fifteen gun boats, to be armed, manned and fitted out, and employed for such purposes as in his opinion the public service may require." President Jefferson reported that "[t]he sum of fifty thousand dollars appropriated by Congress for providing gun boats remains unexpended. The favorable and peaceable turn of affairs on the Mississippi rendered an immediate execution of that law unnecessary." Examples of appropriations committed to the discretion of the President abound in our history. During the Civil War, an Act appropriated over $76 million to be divided among various items "as the exigencies of the service may require." During the Great Depression, Congress appropriated $950 million "for such projects and/or purposes and under such rules and regulations as the President in his discretion may prescribe," and $4 billion for general classes of projects, the money to be spent "in the discretion and under the direction of the President." The constitutionality of such appropriations has never seriously been questioned. . . .

Certain Presidents have claimed Executive authority to withhold appropriated funds even *absent* an express conferral of discretion to do so. In 1876, for example, President Grant reported to Congress that he would not spend money appropriated for certain harbor and river improvements, because "[u]nder no circumstances [would he] allow expenditures upon works not clearly national," and in his view, the appropriations were for "works of purely private or local interest, in no sense national." President Franklin D. Roosevelt impounded funds appropriated for a flood control reservoir and levee in Oklahoma. President Truman ordered the impoundment of hundreds of millions of dollars that had been appropriated for military aircraft. President Nixon, the Mahatma Ghandi of all impounders, asserted at a press conference in 1973 that his "constitutional right" to impound appropriated funds was "absolutely clear." Our decision two years later in *Train v. City of New York* (1975) proved him wrong, but it implicitly confirmed that Congress may confer discretion upon the executive to withhold appropriated funds, even funds appropriated for a specific purpose. . . .

The short of the matter is this: Had the Line Item Veto Act authorized the President to "decline to spend" any item of spending contained in the Balanced Budget Act of 1997, there is not the slightest doubt that authorization would have been constitutional. What the Line Item Veto Act does instead—authorizing the President to "cancel" an item of spending—is technically different. But the technical difference does *not* relate to the technicalities of the Presentment Clause, which have been fully complied with; and the doctrine of unconstitutional delegation, which is at issue here, is preeminently not a doctrine of technicalities. The title of the Line Item Veto Act, which was perhaps designed to simplify for public comprehension, or perhaps merely to comply with the terms of a campaign pledge, has succeeded in faking out the Supreme Court. The President's action it authorizes in fact is not a line-item veto and thus does not offend Art. I, § 7; and insofar as the substance of that action is concerned, it is no different from what Congress has permitted the President to do since the formation of the Union.

IV

I would hold that the President's cancellation of § 4722(c) of the Balanced Budget Act as an item of direct spending does not violate the Constitution. Because I find no party before us who has standing to challenge the President's cancellation of § 968 of the Taxpayer Relief Act, I do not reach the question whether that violates the Constitution.

For the foregoing reasons, I respectfully dissent.

JUSTICE BREYER, with whom JUSTICE O'CONNOR and JUSTICE SCALIA join as to Part III, dissenting.

I

I agree with the Court that the parties have standing, but I do not agree with its ultimate conclusion. In my view the Line Item Veto Act does not violate any specific textual constitutional command, nor does it violate any implicit Separation of Powers principle. Consequently, I believe that the Act is constitutional.

II

I approach the constitutional question before us with three general considerations in mind. *First*, the Act represents a legislative effort to provide the President with the power to give effect to some, but not to all, of the expenditure and revenue-diminishing provisions contained in a single massive appropriations bill. And this objective is constitutionally proper. . . .

Second, the case in part requires us to focus upon the Constitution's generally phrased structural provisions, provisions that delegate all "legislative" power to Congress and vest all "executive" power in the President. The Court, when applying these provisions, has interpreted them generously in terms of the institutional arrangements that they permit. . . .

Third, we need not here referee a dispute among the other two branches. . . .

These three background circumstances mean that, when one measures the *literal* words of the Act against the Constitution's literal commands, the fact that the Act may closely resemble a different, literally unconstitutional, arrangement is beside the point. To drive exactly 65 miles per hour on an interstate highway closely resembles an act that violates the speed limit. But it does not violate that limit, for small differences matter when the question is one of literal violation of law. No more does this Act literally violate the Constitution's words. . . .

III

The Court believes that the Act violates the literal text of the Constitution. A simple syllogism captures its basic reasoning:

> Major Premise: The Constitution sets forth an exclusive method for enacting, repealing, or amending laws.
> Minor Premise: The Act authorizes the President to "repea[l] or amen[d]" laws in a different way, namely by announcing a cancellation of a portion of a previously enacted law.
> Conclusion: The Act is inconsistent with the Constitution.

I find this syllogism unconvincing, however, because its Minor Premise is faulty. When the President "canceled" the two appropriation measures now before us, he did not *repeal* any law nor did he amend any law. He simply *followed* the law, leaving the statutes, as they are literally written, intact. . . .

IV

Because I disagree with the Court's holding of literal violation, I must consider whether the Act nonetheless violates Separation of Powers principles—principles that arise out of the Constitution's vesting of the "executive Power" in "a President," U.S. Const., Art. II, § 1, and "[a]ll legislative Powers" in "a Congress," Art. I, § 1. There are three relevant Separation of Powers questions here: (1) Has Congress given the President the wrong kind of power, i.e., "non-Executive" power? (2) Has Congress given the President the power to "encroach" upon Congress' own constitutionally reserved territory? (3) Has Congress given the President too much power, violating the doctrine of "nondelegation?" These three limitations help assure "adequate control by the citizen's representatives in Congress," upon which JUSTICE KENNEDY properly insists. And with respect to this Act, the answer to all these questions is "no."

A

Viewed conceptually, the power the Act conveys is the right kind of power. It is "executive".... [A]n exercise of that power "executes" the Act. Conceptually speaking, it closely resembles the kind of delegated authority—to spend or not to spend appropriations, to change or not to change tariff rates—that Congress has frequently granted the President, any differences being differences in degree, not kind.

The fact that one could also characterize this kind of power as "legislative," say, if Congress itself (by amending the appropriations bill) prevented a provision from taking effect, is beside the point....

If there is a Separation of Powers violation, then, it must rest, not upon purely conceptual grounds, but upon some important conflict between the Act and a significant Separation of Powers objective.

B

The Act does not undermine what this Court has often described as the principal function of the Separation of Powers, which is to maintain the tripartite structure of the Federal Government—and thereby protect individual liberty—by providing a "safeguard against the encroachment or aggrandizement of one branch at the expense of the other." *Buckley v. Valeo* (1976)....

[O]ne cannot say that the Act "encroaches" upon Congress' power, when Congress retained the power to insert, by simple majority, into any future appropriations bill, into any section of any such bill, or into any phrase of any section, a provision that says the Act will not apply.... Congress also retained the power to "disapprov[e]," and thereby reinstate, any of the President's cancellations. And it is Congress that drafts and enacts the appropriations statutes that are subject to the Act in the first place—and thereby defines the outer limits of the President's cancellation authority....

Nor can one say that the Act's basic substantive objective is constitutionally improper, for the earliest Congresses could have, and often did, confer on the President this sort of discretionary authority over spending....

Nor can one say the Act's grant of power "aggrandizes" the Presidential office. The grant is limited to the context of the budget. It is limited to the power to spend, or not to spend, particular appropriated items, and the power to permit, or not to permit, specific limited exemptions from generally applicable tax law from taking effect. These powers ... resemble those the President has exercised in the past on other occasions. The delegation of those powers to the President may strengthen the Presidency, but any such change in Executive Branch authority seems minute when compared with the changes worked by delegations of other kinds of authority that the Court in the past has upheld. [Citations omitted.]

C

The "nondelegation" doctrine represents an added constitutional check upon Congress' authority to delegate power to the Executive Branch. And it raises a more serious constitutional obstacle here. . . . [I]n Chief Justice Taft's . . . familiar words, the Constitution permits only those delegations where Congress "shall lay down by legislative act an *intelligible principle* to which the person or body authorized to [act] is directed to conform." *J. W. Hampton [Jr., & Co. v. United States* (1938)] (emphasis added).

The Act before us seeks to create such a principle in three ways. The first is procedural. The Act tells the President that, in "identifying dollar amounts [or] . . . items . . . for cancellation" . . . he is to "consider," among other things, "the legislative history, construction, and purposes of the law which contains [those amounts or items, and] . . . any specific sources of information referenced in such law or . . . the best available information. . . ."

The second is purposive. The clear purpose behind the Act, confirmed by its legislative history, is to promote "greater fiscal accountability" and to "eliminate wasteful federal spending and . . . special tax breaks." [Quoting conference report.]

The third is substantive. The President must determine that, to "prevent" the item or amount "from having legal force or effect" will "reduce the Federal budget deficit; . . . not impair any essential Government functions; and . . . not harm the national interest."

The resulting standards are broad. But this Court has upheld standards that are equally broad, or broader. [Citations omitted.]

Indeed, the Court has only twice in its history found that a congressional delegation of power violated the "nondelegation" doctrine. [Summary of *Panama Refining Co. v. Ryan* (1935) and *Schechter Poultry Corp. v. United States* (1935) omitted.]

The case before us . . . is limited to one area of government, the budget, and it seeks to give the President the power, in one portion of that budget, to tailor spending and special tax relief to what he concludes are the demands of fiscal responsibility. Nor is the standard that governs his judgment, though broad, any broader than the standard that currently governs the award of television licenses, namely "public convenience, interest, or necessity." (emphasis added). To the contrary, (a) the broadly phrased limitations in the Act, together with (b) its evident deficit reduction purpose, and (c) a procedure that guarantees Presidential awareness of the reasons for including a particular provision in a budget bill, taken together, guide the President's exercise of his discretionary powers. . . .

V

In sum, I recognize that the Act before us is novel. In a sense, it skirts a constitutional edge. But that edge has to do with means, not ends. The means chosen do not amount literally to the enactment, repeal, or amendment of a law. Nor, for that matter, do they amount literally to the "line item veto" that the Act's title announces. Those means do not violate any basic Separation of Powers principle. They do not improperly shift the constitutionally foreseen balance of power from Congress to the President. Nor, since they comply with Separation of Powers principles, do they threaten the liberties of individual citizens. They represent an experiment that may, or may not, help representative government work better. The Constitution, in my view, authorizes Congress and the President to try novel methods in this way. Consequently, with respect, I dissent.

SUPREME COURT ON
SEXUAL HARASSMENT
June 26, 1998

In an attempt to clarify what had become a confusing and sometimes contradictory body of law, the Supreme Court used its decisions in a pair of cases to set out new standards for employers to meet in defending themselves in sexual harassment suits. The rulings held that employers could be held responsible for the misconduct of their supervisors even if the employers were unaware of the misconduct. At the same time, the Court outlined steps that employers could take to avoid liability in such cases.

Whether and under what circumstances employers were legally responsible for sexual harassment in the workplace had been an issue since 1986, when the Supreme Court handed down its first ruling in the area. In that case, Meritor Savings Bank v. Vinson, *the Court unanimously held that "severe and pervasive" sexual harassment that created an "abusive working environment" amounted to discrimination on the basis of sex in violation of Title VII of the Civil Rights Act of 1964. To successfully bring suit under Title VII, however, a plaintiff had to show that the employer was aware of or should have been aware of the misconduct and did nothing to stop it. Title VII claims generally could not be brought against individual supervisors.*

As a result, two lines of rulings grew up around sexual harassment cases. "Quid pro quo" harassment occurred when a supervisor conditioned some tangible job action, such as a raise, promotion, or demotion, on the employee's acquiescence or resistance to a sexual advance. Courts generally considered employers automatically liable in these situations because theoretically the supervisor could not take the job action without the approval of his superiors. The second line of rulings involved a work environment in which supervisors subjected employees to crude comments and unwanted touching but made no specific sexual demands or job threats, or, if demands were made, did not follow through on the threats. Plaintiffs generally had to show some degree of fault on the employer's part to prevail in these "hostile environment" cases.

438

Confusion over the liability issue increased throughout the 1990s as the number of sexual harassment cases increased. Some of the increase was spurred by the dramatic accusations of sexual harassment brought against Clarence Thomas during his Supreme Court confirmation hearings in 1991. Even though Thomas steadfastly denied the allegations, many women were subsequently emboldened to complain either to their employers or in court about offensive behavior on the job. Congress added incentives for bringing sexual harassment claims when it revised Title VII in 1991 to allow plaintiffs to recover compensatory and punitive damages, not just back pay and attorneys' fees. (Thomas confirmation hearings, Historic Documents of 1991, p. 551)

Recent out-of-court settlements might also have encouraged more women to sue. The automaker Mitsubishi agreed to pay $34 million to settle a harassment case brought by female employees of a factory in Illinois. In a proposed settlement of another case, the investment firm Smith, Barney had agreed to pay hundreds of thousands of dollars to women who said they had been harassed and to spend $15 million on antiharassment training programs.

The lower court rulings in the two cases before the Court in 1998 illustrated the legal confusion that often surrounded sexual harassment claims. In Faragher v. City of Boca Raton, *the federal district judge found three possible rationales for holding the city liable for the hostile work environment created for Faragher by two of her supervisors at her lifeguard job at a city beach. The federal appeals court rejected all three rationales and threw out the case.*

In Burlington Industries, Inc. v. Ellerth, *the district court judge said Burlington was not liable for the misconduct of its supervisor, who allegedly made repeated sexually suggestive remarks to Ellerth and made unmistakable sexual propositions to her at least twice, once during a promotion interview. But the federal appeals court in the case reinstated Ellerth's suit in a decision that produced eight opinions among twelve judges. The full appeals court also asked the Supreme Court to "bring order to the chaotic case law in this important field of practice."*

In the two decisions, adopted by identical 7–2 votes, the Court majority tried to do just that by drawing clear standards stating when employers could be held liable and what they had to do to avoid that liability. In coordinated opinions written by Justices David H. Souter and Anthony M. Kennedy, the Court held that employers could be held vicariously liable for the sexual harassment of their employees by supervisors. No longer would employees have to show that their employer knew or should have known about the harassment and failed to stop it.

At the same time, the Court said, employers could escape liability for the actions of their supervisors if they could show that they had taken "reasonable care" to prevent or correct any harassment, including establishing an effective complaint procedure, and that the employee had failed to use that procedure.

The decisions were widely applauded by civil rights organizations and employer groups. "It's a tremendous victory for women," said Kathy Rodgers, executive director of the National Organization for Women's Legal Defense Fund. The pair of rulings "makes it clear to employers what they have to do to protect themselves from being sued," said Stephen Bokat, vice president and general counsel for the U.S. Chamber of Commerce.

A Hostile Work Environment

The two cases before the Court involved hostile work environment claims. Beth Faragher worked part-time as a lifeguard at a Boca Raton beach where she and other female lifeguards were subjected to lewd comments, sexual come-ons, and physical gropes by two supervisors. The women never made a formal complaint about the actions of the supervisors, although Boca Raton had a written policy prohibiting sexual harassment. They talked informally about the harassment with another male supervisor, who never discussed the situation with his superiors. Faragher brought suit after quitting her job.

Kim Ellerth also quit before she filed suit against her former employer, Burlington Industries. She claimed that one of her supervisors had made crude and suggestive sexual remarks to her. On one occasion, when she gave him no encouragement, he warned her that he could make her life "very hard or very easy at Burlington." Despite the implied threat, Ellerth was never passed over for a raise or promotion, and her initial reason for quitting did not mention the harassment. Ellerth said she knew that Burlington had an antiharassment policy, but she did not tell her immediate supervisor about their boss's misconduct because he would have been obliged to report it to both men's superiors, and Ellerth apparently was worried that she might lose her job.

Both the city of Boca Raton and Burlington argued that they could not be held liable for actions of their supervisors that they knew nothing about. In addition, Burlington argued that Ellerth had not been hurt by the harassment because she had not been passed over for promotions or raises during her time with the company.

It was clear that Souter and Kennedy had coordinated the drafting of their opinions in the two cases not only from their remarks in announcing the decisions, but in the identical language the justices used to lay out the new standard. That standard imposed indirect or vicarious liability on employers for sexual harassment caused by a supervisor whenever any tangible employment action resulted. An employer could also be held liable if the employee did not suffer any visible consequence. In those cases, an employer could defend against the liability by showing that it "exercised reasonable care to prevent and correct promptly any sexually harassing behavior" and that the employee "unreasonably failed to take advantage of any preventive or corrective opportunities provided by the employer or to avoid harm otherwise."

The rulings did not require employers to establish antiharassment policies, but made it clear that employers would be wise to put such policies in place. An employee's failure to use a company's established complaint procedure would generally be enough to "satisfy the employer's burden of defense." The rule reiterated, however, that no defense was available to an employer "when the supervisor's harassment culminates in a tangible employment action, such as discharge, demotion, or undesirable reassignment."

Applying the new standard in the Faragher case, the Court reversed the appeals court decision in favor of the city and reinstated the district court judgment that the city was liable for damages under Title VII. Souter said that the evidence of the sexual harassment against Faragher was "undisputed" and that the city had failed to tell employees about its antiharassment policy or to provide a way to bypass supervisors in registering complaints.

The Ellerth case also presented the Court with an opportunity to distinguish between a hostile work environment and a quid pro quo claim. The majority held that such distinctions were, in Kennedy's words, "helpful, perhaps, in making a rough demarcation" between the two types of cases, but "beyond this are of limited utility." Under the new standard, Kennedy said, if the job threat was carried out, the violation of Title VII was automatically established. If the threat was not carried out, as it was not in Ellerth's case, then the plaintiff had to show that threats were sufficiently severe to create a hostile work environment. Because Ellerth had made such a showing, Kennedy continued, she was entitled to proceed to trial against Burlington, where the company would have an opportunity to present an affirmative defense.

The two dissenting justices in the cases were Thomas and Justice Antonin Scalia. Surprisingly, perhaps, because of his personal involvement in earlier harassment allegations, Thomas wrote the dissent, arguing that employers should be liable "if, and only if, the plaintiff proves that the employer was negligent in permitting the supervisor's conduct to occur."

According to news reports in the days following the decisions, corporate lawyers and human resource directors immediately began to review their company's harassment policies to be sure that they could defend against future sexual harassment claims. Susan Meisinger, senior vice president of the Society for Human Resource Management in Alexandria, Virginia said the Court's "message to employers is . . . to make sure it's not just written policy but [that] it reflects the actual practice in the workplace. You need a vibrant, real policy of no tolerance with an avenue for people to complain if they feel they have been harmed."

William Kilberg, a Washington attorney, concurred. "These decisions give employers a road map," he said. "You have to have a policy and then regularly remind people of its existence. And you should create some easy mechanism, like a hot line, for employees to file complaints."

Other Court Decisions on Harassment

The Court issued two other important decisions on sexual harassment during its 1997–1998 term. In the case of Oncale v. Sundowner Offshore Services, Inc., *the Court unanimously held that sexual harassment of a member of one sex by a member of the same sex was covered under Title VII of the Civil Rights Act of 1964. Writing for the Court, Justice Scalia said that the plaintiff had to show that the behavior was "so objectively offensive as to alter the 'conditions' of the victim's employment." In determining whether the harassment had occurred, he continued, courts should consider both common sense and social context: "A professional football player's working environment is not severely or pervasively abusive, for example, if the coach smacks him on the buttocks as he heads onto the field—even if the same behavior would reasonably be experienced as abusive by the coach's secretary (male or female) back at the office."*

In the case of Gebser v. Lago Vista Independent School District, *the Court ruled, 5–4, that school districts were not liable under federal law for sexual harassment of a student by a teacher unless a ranking school official knew about and was "deliberately indifferent" to the misconduct. The suit was brought under Title IX of the Education Amendments of 1972, which prohibited sexual discrimination by school districts that receive federal funds. In agreeing with the lower courts that the school district could not be held liable unless it knew about the conduct, Justice Sandra Day O'Connor said that a stricter standard would "frustrate" the purposes of Title IX. The law was intended to equalize treatment of boys and girls in sports and other school programs. Writing for the four dissenters, Justice John Paul Stevens argued that the ruling in fact thwarted the purpose of Title IX by encouraging school districts to "insulate themselves from knowledge about this sort of conduct."*

> *Following are excerpts from the majority and dissenting opinions in* Faragher v. City of Boca Raton *and* Burlington Industries, Inc. v. Ellerth, *issued by the Supreme Court June 26, 1998, by identical 7–2 votes, in which the Court ruled that employers could be held vicariously liable for sexual harassment of their employees by company supervisors and laid out steps the employers could take to defend against such liable claims:*

No. 97–282

Beth Ann Faragher, Petitioner	On writ of certiorari to the United
v.	States Court of Appeals for the
City of Boca Raton	Eleventh Circuit

[June 26, 1998]

JUSTICE SOUTER delivered the opinion of the Court.

This case calls for identification of the circumstances under which an employer may be held liable under Title VII of the Civil Rights Act of 1964 as amended, 42 U.S.C. § 2000e *et seq.*, for the acts of a supervisory employee whose sexual harassment of subordinates has created a hostile work environment amounting to employment discrimination. We hold that an employer is vicariously liable for actionable discrimination caused by a supervisor, but subject to an affirmative defense looking to the reasonableness of the employer's conduct as well as that of a plaintiff victim.

I

Between 1985 and 1990, while attending college, petitioner Beth Ann Faragher worked part time and during the summers as an ocean lifeguard for the Marine Safety Section of the Parks and Recreation Department of respondent, the City of Boca Raton, Florida (City). During this period, Faragher's immediate supervisors were Bill Terry, David Silverman, and Robert Gordon. In June 1990, Faragher resigned.

In 1992, Faragher brought an action against Terry, Silverman, and the City, asserting claims under Title VII, 42 U.S.C. § 1983, and Florida law. So far as it concerns the Title VII claim, the complaint alleged that Terry and Silverman created a "sexually hostile atmosphere" at the beach by repeatedly subjecting Faragher and other female lifeguards to "uninvited and offensive touching," by making lewd remarks, and by speaking of women in offensive terms. The complaint contained specific allegations that Terry once said that he would never promote a woman to the rank of lieutenant, and that Silverman had said to Faragher, "Date me or clean the toilets for a year." Asserting that Terry and Silverman were agents of the City, and that their conduct amounted to discrimination in the "terms, conditions, and privileges" of her employment . . . Faragher sought a judgment against the City for nominal damages, costs, and attorney's fees.

Following a bench trial, the United States District Court for the Southern District of Florida found that throughout Faragher's employment with the City, Terry served as Chief of the Marine Safety Division, with authority to hire new lifeguards (subject to the approval of higher management), to supervise all aspects of the lifeguards' work assignments, to engage in coun-

seling, to deliver oral reprimands, and to make a record of any such discipline. (1994). Silverman was a Marine Safety lieutenant from 1985 until June
1989, when he became a captain. Gordon began the employment period as a
lieutenant and at some point was promoted to the position of training captain. In these positions, Silverman and Gordon were responsible for making
the lifeguards' daily assignments, and for supervising their work and fitness
training.

The lifeguards and supervisors were stationed at the city beach and
worked out of the Marine Safety Headquarters, a small one-story building
containing an office, a meeting room, and a single, unisex locker room with a
shower. Their work routine was structured in a "paramilitary configuration,"
with a clear chain of command. Lifeguards reported to lieutenants and cap-
tains, who reported to Terry. He was supervised by the Recreation Superintendent, who in turn reported to a Director of Parks and Recreation, answer-
able to the City Manager. The lifeguards had no significant contact with
higher city officials like the Recreation Superintendent.

In February 1986, the City adopted a sexual harassment policy, which it
stated in a memorandum from the City Manager addressed to all employees.
In May 1990, the City revised the policy and reissued a statement of it.
Although the City may actually have circulated the memos and statements to
some employees, it completely failed to disseminate its policy among employees of the Marine Safety Section, with the result that Terry, Silverman, Gordon, and many lifeguards were unaware of it.

From time to time over the course of Faragher's tenure at the Marine
Safety Section, between 4 and 6 of the 40 to 50 lifeguards were women. During that 5-year period, Terry repeatedly touched the bodies of female employees without invitation, would put his arm around Faragher, with his hand on
her buttocks, and once made contact with another female lifeguard in a
motion of sexual simulation. He made crudely demeaning references to
women generally, and once commented disparagingly on Faragher's shape.
During a job interview with a woman he hired as a lifeguard, Terry said that
the female lifeguards had sex with their male counterparts and asked
whether she would do the same.

Silverman behaved in similar ways. He once tackled Faragher and
remarked that, but for a physical characteristic he found unattractive, he
would readily have had sexual relations with her. Another time, he pan-
tomimed an act of oral sex. Within earshot of the female lifeguards, Silverman
made frequent, vulgar references to women and sexual matters, commented
on the bodies of female lifeguards and beachgoers, and at least twice told
female lifeguards that he would like to engage in sex with them.

Faragher did not complain to higher management about Terry or Silverman. Although she spoke of their behavior to Gordon, she did not regard
these discussions as formal complaints to a supervisor but as conversations
with a person she held in high esteem. Other female lifeguards had similarly
informal talks with Gordon, but because Gordon did not feel that it was his
place to do so, he did not report these complaints to Terry, his own supervi-

sor, or to any other city official. Gordon responded to the complaints of one lifeguard by saying that "the City just [doesn't] care."

In April 1990, however, two months before Faragher's resignation, Nancy Ewanchew, a former lifeguard, wrote to Richard Bender, the City's Personnel Director, complaining that Terry and Silverman had harassed her and other female lifeguards. Following investigation of this complaint, the City found that Terry and Silverman had behaved improperly, reprimanded them, and required them to choose between a suspension without pay or the forfeiture of annual leave.

On the basis of these findings, the District Court concluded that the conduct of Terry and Silverman was discriminatory harassment sufficiently serious to alter the conditions of Faragher's employment and constitute an abusive working environment. The District Court then ruled that there were three justifications for holding the City liable for the harassment of its supervisory employees. First, the court noted that the harassment was pervasive enough to support an inference that the City had "knowledge, or constructive knowledge" of it. Next, it ruled that the City was liable under traditional agency principles because Terry and Silverman were acting as its agents when they committed the harassing acts. Finally, the court observed that Gordon's knowledge of the harassment, combined with his inaction, "provides a further basis for imputing liability on [sic] the City." The District Court then awarded Faragher one dollar in nominal damages on her Title VII claim.

A panel of the Court of Appeals for the Eleventh Circuit reversed the judgment against the City. (1996). Although the panel had "no trouble concluding that Terry's and Silverman's conduct . . . was severe and pervasive enough to create an objectively abusive work environment," it overturned the District Court's conclusion that the City was liable. The panel ruled that Terry and Silverman were not acting within the scope of their employment when they engaged in the harassment, that they were not aided in their actions by the agency relationship, and that the City had no constructive knowledge of the harassment by virtue of its pervasiveness or Gordon's actual knowledge.

In a 7-to-5 decision, the full Court of Appeals, sitting en banc, adopted the panel's conclusion. (1997). Relying on our decision in *Meritor Savings Bank, FSB v. Vinson* (1986), and on the Restatement (Second) of Agency § 219, the court held that "an employer may be indirectly liable for hostile environment sexual harassment by a superior: (1) if the harassment occurs within the scope of the superior's employment; (2) if the employer assigns performance of a nondelegable duty to a supervisor and an employee is injured because of the supervisor's failure to carry out that duty; or (3) if there is an agency relationship which aids the supervisor's ability or opportunity to harass his subordinate."

Applying these principles, the court rejected Faragher's Title VII claim against the City. First, invoking standard agency language to classify the harassment by each supervisor as a "frolic" unrelated to his authorized tasks, the court found that in harassing Faragher, Terry and Silverman were acting outside of the scope of their employment and solely to further their own per-

sonal ends. Next, the court determined that the supervisors' agency relationship with the City did not assist them in perpetrating their harassment. . . .
Because neither Terry nor Silverman threatened to fire or demote Faragher,
the court concluded that their agency relationship did not facilitate their
harassment.

The en banc court also affirmed the panel's ruling that the City lacked constructive knowledge of the supervisors' harassment. The court read the District Court's opinion to rest on an erroneous legal conclusion that any harassment pervasive enough to create a hostile environment must a fortiori also
suffice to charge the employer with constructive knowledge. Rejecting this
approach, the court reviewed the record and found no adequate factual basis
to conclude that the harassment was so pervasive that the City should have
known of it, relying on the facts that the harassment occurred intermittently,
over a long period of time, and at a remote location. In footnotes, the court
also rejected the arguments that the City should be deemed to have known of
the harassment through Gordon, or charged with constructive knowledge
because of its failure to disseminate its sexual harassment policy among the
lifeguards.

Since our decision in *Meritor*, Courts of Appeals have struggled to derive
manageable standards to govern employer liability for hostile environment
harassment perpetrated by supervisory employees. While following our
admonition to find guidance in the common law of agency, as embodied in the
Restatement, the Courts of Appeals have adopted different approaches. [Cita-
tions omitted.] We granted certiorari to address the divergence (1997), and
now reverse the judgment of the Eleventh Circuit and remand for entry of
judgment in Faragher's favor.

II

Under Title VII of the Civil Rights Act of 1964, "[i]t shall be an unlawful
employment practice for an employer . . . to fail or refuse to hire or to discharge any individual, or otherwise to discriminate against any individual
with respect to his compensation, terms, conditions, or privileges of employment, because of such individual's race, color, religion, sex, or national origin.". . . [I]n *Meritor* we held that sexual harassment so "severe or pervasive"
as to " 'alter the conditions of [the victim's] employment and create an abusive working environment' " violates Title VII.

. . . [I]n Harris [v. Forklift Systems, Inc. (1993)], we explained that in order
to be actionable under the statute, a sexually objectionable environment must
be both objectively and subjectively offensive, one that a reasonable person
would find hostile or abusive, and one that the victim in fact did perceive to
be so. We directed courts to determine whether an environment is sufficiently
hostile or abusive by "looking at all the circumstances," including the "frequency of the discriminatory conduct; its severity; whether it is physically
threatening or humiliating, or a mere offensive utterance; and whether it
unreasonably interferes with an employee's work performance." . . . A recur-

ring point in these opinions is that "simple teasing," offhand comments, and isolated incidents (unless extremely serious) will not amount to discriminatory changes in the "terms and conditions of employment."

These standards for judging hostility are sufficiently demanding to ensure that Title VII does not become a "general civility code." Properly applied, they will filter out complaints attacking "the ordinary tribulations of the workplace, such as the sporadic use of abusive language, gender-related jokes, and occasional teasing." . . . We have made it clear that conduct must be extreme to amount to a change in the terms and conditions of employment, and the Courts of Appeals have heeded this view. [Citations omitted.]

While indicating the substantive contours of the hostile environments forbidden by Title VII, our cases have established few definite rules for determining when an employer will be liable for a discriminatory environment that is otherwise actionably abusive. . . .

B

The Court of Appeals identified, and rejected, three possible grounds drawn from agency law for holding the City vicariously liable for the hostile environment created by the supervisors. It considered whether the two supervisors were acting within the scope of their employment when they engaged in the harassing conduct. The court then enquired whether they were significantly aided by the agency relationship in committing the harassment, and also considered the possibility of imputing Gordon's knowledge of the harassment to the City. Finally, the Court of Appeals ruled out liability for negligence in failing to prevent the harassment. Faragher relies principally on the latter three theories of liability.

1

A "master is subject to liability for the torts of his servants committed while acting in the scope of their employment." Restatement § 219(1). This doctrine has traditionally defined the "scope of employment" as including conduct "of the kind [a servant] is employed to perform," occurring "substantially within the authorized time and space limits," and "actuated, at least in part, by a purpose to serve the master," but as excluding an intentional use of force "unexpectable by the master." § 228(1).

Courts of Appeals have typically held, or assumed, that conduct similar to the subject of this complaint falls outside the scope of employment. . . . In so doing, the courts have emphasized that harassment consisting of unwelcome remarks and touching is motivated solely by individual desires and serves no purpose of the employer. For this reason, courts have likened hostile environment sexual harassment to the classic "frolic and detour" for which an employer has no vicarious liability. . . .

The proper analysis here, then, calls not for a mechanical application of indefinite and malleable factors set forth in the Restatement, but rather an enquiry into the reasons that would support a conclusion that harassing behavior ought to be held within the scope of a supervisor's employment, and the reasons for the opposite view. . . .

In the case before us, a justification for holding the offensive behavior within the scope of Terry's and Silverman's employment was well put in Judge Barkett's dissent: "[A] pervasively hostile work environment of sexual harassment is never (one would hope) authorized, but the supervisor is clearly charged with maintaining a productive, safe work environment. The supervisor directs and controls the conduct of the employees, and the manner of doing so may inure to the employer's benefit or detriment, including subjecting the employer to Title VII liability." It is by now well recognized that hostile environment sexual harassment by supervisors (and, for that matter, co-employees) is a persistent problem in the workplace. . . . An employer can, in a general sense, reasonably anticipate the possibility of such conduct occurring in its workplace, and one might justify the assignment of the burden of the untoward behavior to the employer as one of the costs of doing business, to be charged to the enterprise rather than the victim. . . . [D]evelopments like this occur from time to time in the law of agency.

Two things counsel us to draw the contrary conclusion. First, there is no reason to suppose that Congress wished courts to ignore the traditional distinction between acts falling within the scope and acts amounting to what the older law called frolics or detours from the course of employment. Such a distinction can readily be applied to the spectrum of possible harassing conduct by supervisors. . . .

The second reason goes to an even broader unanimity of views among the holdings of District Courts and Courts of Appeals thus far. Those courts have held not only that the sort of harassment at issue here was outside the scope of supervisors' authority, but, by uniformly judging employer liability for coworker harassment under a negligence standard, they have also implicitly treated such harassment as outside the scope of common employees' duties as well. . . .

2

The Court of Appeals also rejected vicarious liability on the part of the City insofar as it might rest on the concluding principle set forth in § 219(2)(d) of the Restatement, that an employer "is not subject to liability for the torts of his servants acting outside the scope of their employment unless . . . the servant purported to act or speak on behalf of the principal and there was reliance on apparent authority, or he was aided in accomplishing the tort by the existence of the agency relation." Faragher points to several ways in which the agency relationship aided Terry and Silverman in carrying out their harassment. She argues that in general offending supervisors can abuse their authority to keep subordinates in their presence while they make offensive statements, and that they implicitly threaten to misuse their supervisory powers to deter any resistance or complaint. Thus, she maintains that power conferred on Terry and Silverman by the City enabled them to act for so long without provoking defiance or complaint.

The City, however, contends that § 219(2)(d) has no application here. It argues that the second qualification of the subsection, referring to a servant "aided in accomplishing the tort by the existence of the agency relation," merely "refines" the one preceding it, which holds the employer vicariously liable for its servant's abuse of apparent authority. But this narrow reading is untenable; it would render the second qualification of § 219(2)(d) almost entirely superfluous. . . .

We therefore agree with Faragher that in implementing Title VII it makes sense to hold an employer vicariously liable for some tortious conduct of a supervisor made possible by abuse of his supervisory authority, and that the aided-by-agency-relation principle embodied in § 219(2)(d) of the Restatement provides an appropriate starting point for determining liability for the kind of harassment presented here. Several courts, indeed, have noted what Faragher has argued, that there is a sense in which a harassing supervisor is always assisted in his misconduct by the supervisory relationship. . . . The agency relationship affords contact with an employee subjected to a supervisor's sexual harassment, and the victim may well be reluctant to accept the risks of blowing the whistle on a superior. When a person with supervisory authority discriminates in the terms and conditions of subordinates' employment, his actions necessarily draw upon his superior position over the people who report to him, or those under them, whereas an employee generally cannot check a supervisor's abusive conduct the same way that she might deal with abuse from a co-worker. When a fellow employee harasses, the victim can walk away or tell the offender where to go, but it may be difficult to offer such responses to a supervisor. . . . Recognition of employer liability when discriminatory misuse of supervisory authority alters the terms and conditions of a victim's employment is underscored by the fact that the employer has a greater opportunity to guard against misconduct by supervisors than by common workers; employers have greater opportunity and incentive to screen them, train them, and monitor their performance.

In sum, there are good reasons for vicarious liability for misuse of supervisory authority. That rationale must, however, satisfy one more condition. We are not entitled to recognize this theory under Title VII unless we can square it with *Meritor's* holding that an employer is not "automatically" liable for harassment by a supervisor who creates the requisite degree of discrimination. . . . [W]e think there are two basic alternatives, one being to require proof of some affirmative invocation of that authority by the harassing supervisor, the other to recognize an affirmative defense to liability in some circumstances, even when a supervisor has created the actionable environment.

There is certainly some authority for requiring active or affirmative, as distinct from passive or implicit, misuse of supervisory authority before liability may be imputed. . . .

But neat examples illustrating the line between the affirmative and merely implicit uses of power are not easy to come by in considering management behavior. . . . Judgment calls would often be close, the results would often seem disparate even if not demonstrably contradictory, and the temptation to litigate would be hard to resist. We think plaintiffs and defendants alike would be poorly served by an active-use rule.

The other basic alternative to automatic liability would avoid this particular temptation to litigate, but allow an employer to show as an affirmative defense to liability that the employer had exercised reasonable care to avoid harassment and to eliminate it when it might occur, and that the complaining employee had failed to act with like reasonable care to take advantage of the employer's safeguards and otherwise to prevent harm that could have been avoided. This composite defense would, we think, implement the statute sensibly. . . .

Although Title VII seeks "to make persons whole for injuries suffered on account of unlawful employment discrimination," *Albemarle Paper Co. v. Moody* (1975), its "primary objective," like that of any statute meant to influence primary conduct, is not to provide redress but to avoid harm. As long ago as 1980, the Equal Employment Opportunity Commission (EEOC), charged with the enforcement of Title VII, 42 U.S.C. § 2000e–4, adopted regulations advising employers to "take all steps necessary to prevent sexual harassment from occurring, such as . . . informing employees of their right to raise and how to raise the issue of harassment," and in 1990 the Commission issued a policy statement enjoining employers to establish a complaint procedure "designed to encourage victims of harassment to come forward [without requiring] a victim to complain first to the offending supervisor." EEOC Policy Guidance on Sexual Harassment (Mar. 19, 1990). It would therefore implement clear statutory policy and complement the Government's Title VII enforcement efforts to recognize the employer's affirmative obligation to prevent violations and give credit here to employers who make reasonable efforts to discharge their duty. Indeed, a theory of vicarious liability for misuse of supervisory power would be at odds with the statutory policy if it failed to provide employers with some such incentive.

The requirement to show that the employee has failed in a coordinate duty to avoid or mitigate harm reflects an equally obvious policy imported from the general theory of damages, that a victim has a duty "to use such means as are reasonable under the circumstances to avoid or minimize the damages" that result from violations of the statute. *Ford Motor Co. v. EEOC* (1982). An employer may, for example, have provided a proven, effective mechanism for reporting and resolving complaints of sexual harassment, available to the employee without undue risk or expense. If the plaintiff unreasonably failed to avail herself of the employer's preventive or remedial apparatus, she should not recover damages that could have been avoided if she had done so. If the victim could have avoided harm, no liability should be found against the employer who had taken reasonable care, and if damages could reasonably have been mitigated no award against a liable employer should reward a plaintiff for what her own efforts could have avoided.

In order to accommodate the principle of vicarious liability for harm caused by misuse of supervisory authority, as well as Title VII's equally basic policies of encouraging forethought by employers and saving action by objecting employees, we adopt the following holding in this case and in *Burlington Industries, Inc. v. Ellerth,* also decided today. An employer is subject to vicarious liability to a victimized employee for an actionable hostile environment created by a supervisor with immediate (or successively higher) authority over the employee. When no tangible employment action is taken, a defending employer may raise an affirmative defense to liability or damages, subject to proof by a preponderance of the evidence. The defense comprises two necessary elements: (a) that the employer exercised reasonable care to prevent and correct promptly any sexually harassing behavior, and (b) that the plaintiff employee unreasonably failed to take advantage of any preventive or corrective opportunities provided by the employer or to avoid harm otherwise. While proof that an employer had promulgated an antiharassment policy with complaint procedure is not necessary in every instance as a matter of law, the need for a stated policy suitable to the employment circumstances may appropriately be addressed in any case when litigating the first element of the defense. And while proof that an employee failed to fulfill the corresponding obligation of reasonable care to avoid harm is not limited to showing an unreasonable failure to use any complaint procedure provided by the employer, a demonstration of such failure will normally suffice to satisfy the employer's burden under the second element of the defense. No affirmative defense is available, however, when the supervisor's harassment culminates in a tangible employment action, such as discharge, demotion, or undesirable reassignment. Applying these rules here, we believe that the judgment of the Court of Appeals must be reversed. The District Court found that the degree of hostility in the work environment rose to the actionable level and was attributable to Silverman and Terry. It is undisputed that these supervisors "were granted virtually unchecked authority" over their subordinates, "directly controll[ing] and supervis[ing] all aspects of [Faragher's] day-to-day activities." It is also clear that Faragher and her colleagues were "completely isolated from the City's higher management." The City did not seek review of these findings. While the City would have an opportunity to raise an affirmative defense if there were any serious prospect of its presenting one, it appears from the record that any such avenue is closed. The District Court found that the City had entirely failed to disseminate its policy against sexual harassment among the beach employees and that its officials made no attempt to keep track of the conduct of supervisors like Terry and Silverman. The record also makes clear that the City's policy did not include any assurance that the harassing supervisors could be bypassed in registering complaints. Under such circumstances, we hold as a matter of law that the City could not be found to have exercised reasonable care to prevent the supervisors' harassing conduct. Unlike the employer of a small workforce, who might expect that sufficient care to prevent tortious behavior could be exercised informally, those responsible for city operations could not reasonably have thought that precautions against hostile environments in any one of many departments in far-flung locations could be effective without communicating some formal policy against harassment, with a sensible complaint procedure. . . .

3

The Court of Appeals also rejected the possibility that it could hold the City liable for the reason that it knew of the harassment vicariously through the knowledge of its supervisors. We have no occasion to consider whether this was error, however. We are satisfied that liability on the ground of vicarious knowledge could not be determined without further factfinding on remand, whereas the reversal necessary on the theory of supervisory harassment renders any remand for consideration of imputed knowledge entirely unjustifiable (as would be any consideration of negligence as an alternative to a theory of vicarious liability here).

III

The judgment of the Court of Appeals for the Eleventh Circuit is reversed, and the case is remanded for reinstatement of the judgment of the District Court.

It is so ordered.

JUSTICE THOMAS, with whom JUSTICE SCALIA joins, dissenting.

For the reasons given in my dissenting opinion in *Burlington Industries v. Ellerth*, absent an adverse employment consequence, an employer cannot be held vicariously liable if a supervisor creates a hostile work environment. Petitioner suffered no adverse employment consequence; thus the Court of Appeals was correct to hold that the City is not vicariously liable for the conduct of Chief Terry and Lieutenant Silverman. Because the Court reverses this judgment, I dissent.

As for petitioner's negligence claim, the District Court made no finding as to the City's negligence, and the Court of Appeals did not directly consider the issue. I would therefore remand the case to the District Court for further proceedings on this question alone. I disagree with the Court's conclusion that merely because the City did not disseminate its sexual harassment policy, it should be liable as a matter of law. The City should be allowed to show either that: (1) there was a reasonably available avenue through which petitioner could have complained to a City official who supervised both Chief Terry and Lieutenant Silverman, or (2) it would not have learned of the harassment even if the policy had been distributed. Petitioner, as the plaintiff, would of course bear the burden of proving the City's negligence.

No. 97–569

Burlington Industries, Inc., Petitioner *v.* Kimberly B. Ellerth	On writ of certiorari to the United States Court of Appeals for the Seventh Circuit

[June 26, 1998]

JUSTICE KENNEDY delivered the opinion of the Court.

We decide whether, under Title VII of the Civil Rights Act of 1964 as amended, 42 U.S.C. § 2000e *et seq.*, an employee who refuses the unwelcome and threatening sexual advances of a supervisor, yet suffers no adverse, tangible job consequences, can recover against the employer without showing the employer is negligent or otherwise at fault for the supervisor's actions.

I

Summary judgment was granted for the employer, so we must take the facts alleged by the employee to be true. The employer is Burlington Industries, the petitioner. The employee is Kimberly Ellerth, the respondent. From March 1993 until May 1994, Ellerth worked as a salesperson in one of Burlington's divisions in Chicago, Illinois. During her employment, she alleges, she was subjected to constant sexual harassment by her supervisor, one Ted Slowik.

In the hierarchy of Burlington's management structure, Slowik was a mid-level manager. Burlington has eight divisions, employing more than 22,000 people in some 50 plants around the United States. Slowik was a vice president in one of five business units within one of the divisions. He had authority to make hiring and promotion decisions subject to the approval of his supervisor, who signed the paperwork. According to Slowik's supervisor, his position was "not considered an upper-level management position," and he was "not amongst the decision-making or policy-making hierarchy." Slowik was not Ellerth's immediate supervisor. Ellerth worked in a two-person office in Chicago, and she answered to her office colleague, who in turn answered to Slowik in New York.

Against a background of repeated boorish and offensive remarks and gestures which Slowik allegedly made, Ellerth places particular emphasis on three alleged incidents where Slowik's comments could be construed as threats to deny her tangible job benefits. In the summer of 1993, while on a business trip, Slowik invited Ellerth to the hotel lounge, an invitation Ellerth felt compelled to accept because Slowik was her boss. When Ellerth gave no encouragement to remarks Slowik made about her breasts, he told her to "loosen up" and warned, "[y]ou know, Kim, I could make your life very hard or very easy at Burlington."

In March 1994, when Ellerth was being considered for a promotion, Slowik expressed reservations during the promotion interview because she was not "loose enough." The comment was followed by his reaching over and rubbing her knee. Ellerth did receive the promotion; but when Slowik called to announce it, he told Ellerth, "you're gonna be out there with men who work in factories, and they certainly like women with pretty butts/legs."

In May 1994, Ellerth called Slowik, asking permission to insert a customer's logo into a fabric sample. Slowik responded, "I don't have time for you right now, Kim—unless you want to tell me what you're wearing." Ellerth told Slowik she had to go and ended the call. A day or two later, Ellerth called Slowik to ask permission again. This time he denied her request, but added something along the lines of, "are you wearing shorter skirts yet, Kim, because it would make your job a whole heck of a lot easier."

A short time later, Ellerth's immediate supervisor cautioned her about returning telephone calls to customers in a prompt fashion. In response, Ellerth quit. She faxed a letter giving reasons unrelated to the alleged sexual harassment we have described. About three weeks later, however, she sent a letter explaining she quit because of Slowik's behavior.

During her tenure at Burlington, Ellerth did not inform anyone in authority about Slowik's conduct, despite knowing Burlington had a policy against sexual harassment. In fact, she chose not to inform her immediate supervisor (not Slowik) because "'it would be his duty as my supervisor to report any incidents of sexual harassment.'" On one occasion, she told Slowik a comment he made was inappropriate.

In October 1994, after receiving a right-to-sue letter from the Equal Employment Opportunity Commission (EEOC), Ellerth filed suit in the United States District Court for the Northern District of Illinois, alleging Burlington engaged in sexual harassment and forced her constructive discharge, in violation of Title VII. The District Court granted summary judgment to Burlington. The Court found Slowik's behavior, as described by Ellerth, severe and pervasive enough to create a hostile work environment, but found Burlington neither knew nor should have known about the conduct. There was no triable issue of fact on the latter point, and the Court noted Ellerth had not used Burlington's internal complaint procedures. Although Ellerth's claim was framed as a hostile work environment complaint, the District Court observed there was a quid pro quo "component" to the hostile environment. Proceeding from the premise that an employer faces vicarious liability for quid pro quo harassment, the District Court thought it necessary to apply a negligence standard because the quid pro quo merely contributed to the hostile work environment. The District Court also dismissed Ellerth's constructive discharge claim.

The Court of Appeals en banc reversed in a decision which produced eight separate opinions and no consensus for a controlling rationale. [Summary of various opinions omitted.]

The disagreement revealed in the careful opinions of the judges of the Court of Appeals reflects the fact that Congress has left it to the courts to determine controlling agency law principles in a new and difficult area of federal law. We granted certiorari to assist in defining the relevant standards of employer liability (1998).

II

At the outset, we assume an important proposition yet to be established before a trier of fact. It is a premise assumed as well, in explicit or implicit terms, in the various opinions by the judges of the Court of Appeals. The premise is: a trier of fact could find in Slowik's remarks numerous threats to retaliate against Ellerth if she denied some sexual liberties. The threats, however, were not carried out or fulfilled. Cases based on threats which are carried out are referred to often as *quid pro quo* cases, as distinct from bothersome attentions or sexual remarks that are sufficiently severe or pervasive to create a hostile work environment. The terms *quid pro quo* and hostile work environment are helpful, perhaps, in making a rough demarcation between cases in which threats are carried out and those where they are not or are absent altogether, but beyond this are of limited utility.

Section 703(a) of Title VII forbids

"an employer—
"(1) to fail or refuse to hire or to discharge any individual, or otherwise to discriminate against any individual with respect to his compensation, terms, conditions or privileges of employment, because of such individual's . . . sex." 42 U.S.C. § 2000e-2(a)(1).

"*Quid pro quo*" and "hostile work environment" do not appear in the statutory text. The terms appeared first in the academic literature; found their way into decisions of the Courts of Appeals; and were mentioned in this Court's decision in *Meritor Savings Bank, FSB v. Vinson* (1986).

In *Meritor*, the terms served a specific and limited purpose. There we considered whether the conduct in question constituted discrimination in the terms or conditions of employment in violation of Title VII. We assumed, and with adequate reason, that if an employer demanded sexual favors from an employee in return for a job benefit, discrimination with respect to terms or conditions of employment was explicit. Less obvious was whether an employer's sexually demeaning behavior altered terms or conditions of employment in violation of Title VII. We distinguished between *quid pro quo* claims and hostile environment claims, and said both were cognizable under Title VII, though the latter requires harassment that is severe or pervasive. The principal significance of the distinction is to instruct that Title VII is violated by either explicit or constructive alterations in the terms or conditions of employment and to explain the latter must be severe or pervasive. The distinction was not discussed for its bearing upon an employer's liability for an employee's discrimination. On this question *Meritor* held, with no further specifics, that agency principles controlled.

Nevertheless, as use of the terms grew in the wake of *Meritor*, they acquired their own significance. The standard of employer responsibility turned on which type of harassment occurred. If the plaintiff established a *quid pro quo* claim, the Courts of Appeals held, the employer was subject to vicarious liability. [Citations omitted.] The rule encouraged Title VII plaintiffs to state their claims as *quid pro quo* claims, which in turn put expansive pressure on the definition. The equivalence of the *quid pro quo* label and vicarious liability is illustrated by this case. The question presented on certiorari is whether Ellerth can state a claim of *quid pro quo* harassment, but the issue of real concern to the parties is whether Burlington has vicarious liability for Slowik's alleged misconduct, rather than liability limited to its own negligence. The question presented for certiorari asks:

> "Whether a claim of *quid pro quo* sexual harassment may be stated under Title VII . . . where the plaintiff employee has neither submitted to the sexual advances of the alleged harasser nor suffered any tangible effects on the compensation, terms, conditions or privileges of employment as a consequence of a refusal to submit to those advances?"

We do not suggest the terms *quid pro quo* and hostile work environment are irrelevant to Title VII litigation. To the extent they illustrate the distinction between cases involving a threat which is carried out and offensive conduct in general, the terms are relevant when there is a threshold question whether a plaintiff can prove discrimination in violation of Title VII. When a plaintiff proves that a tangible employment action resulted from a refusal to submit to a supervisor's sexual demands, he or she establishes that the employment decision itself constitutes a change in the terms and conditions of employment that is actionable under Title VII. For any sexual harassment preceding the employment decision to be actionable, however, the conduct must be severe or pervasive. Because Ellerth's claim involves only unfulfilled threats, it should be categorized as a hostile work environment claim which requires a showing of severe or pervasive conduct. . . . For purposes of this case, we accept the District Court's finding that the alleged conduct was severe or pervasive. The case before us involves numerous alleged threats, and we express no opinion as to whether a single unfulfilled threat is sufficient to constitute discrimination in the terms or conditions of employment.

When we assume discrimination can be proved, however, the factors we discuss below, and not the categories *quid pro quo* and hostile work environment, will be controlling on the issue of vicarious liability. That is the question we must resolve.

III

We must decide, then, whether an employer has vicarious liability when a supervisor creates a hostile work environment by making explicit threats to alter a subordinate's terms or conditions of employment, based on sex, but does not fulfill the threat. We turn to principles of agency law, for the term "employer" is defined under Title VII to include "agents." 42 U.S.C. § 2000e(b). In express terms, Congress has directed federal courts to interpret Title VII based on agency principles. Given such an explicit instruction, we conclude a uniform and predictable standard must be established as a matter of federal law. . . .

As *Meritor* acknowledged, the Restatement (Second) of Agency (1957) is a useful beginning point for a discussion of general agency principles. Since our decision in *Meritor*, federal courts have explored agency principles, and we find useful instruction in their decisions, noting that "common-law principles may not be transferable in all their particulars to Title VII." The EEOC has issued Guidelines governing sexual harassment claims under Title VII, but they provide little guidance on the issue of employer liability for supervisor harassment. . . .

A

Section 219(1) of the Restatement sets out a central principle of agency law:

> "A master is subject to liability for the torts of his servants committed while acting in the scope of their employment."

An employer may be liable for both negligent and intentional torts committed by an employee within the scope of his or her employment. Sexual harassment under Title VII presupposes intentional conduct. While early decisions absolved employers of liability for the intentional torts of their employees, the law now imposes liability where the employee's "purpose, however misguided, is wholly or in part to further the master's business." . . . [Quoting Prosser and Keeton on Torts.]

The general rule is that sexual harassment by a supervisor is not conduct within the scope of employment.

B

Scope of employment does not define the only basis for employer liability under agency principles. In limited circumstances, agency principles impose liability on employers even where employees commit torts outside the scope of employment. The principles are set forth in the much-cited § 219(2) of the Restatement:

> "(2) A master is not subject to liability for the torts of his servants acting outside the scope of their employment, unless:
> "(a) the master intended the conduct or the consequences, or
> "(b) the master was negligent or reckless, or
> "(c) the conduct violated a non-delegable duty of the master, or
> "(d) the servant purported to act or to speak on behalf of the principal and there was reliance upon apparent authority, or he was aided in accomplishing the tort by the existence of the agency relation."

See also § 219, Comment e (Section 219(2) "enumerates the situations in which a master may be liable for torts of servants acting solely for their own purposes and hence not in the scope of employment").

Subsection (a) addresses direct liability, where the employer acts with tortious intent, and indirect liability, where the agent's high rank in the company makes him or her the employer's alter ego. None of the parties contend Slowik's rank imputes liability under this principle. There is no contention, furthermore, that a nondelegable duty is involved. So, for our purposes here, subsections (a) and (c) can be put aside.

Subsections (b) and (d) are possible grounds for imposing employer liability on account of a supervisor's acts and must be considered. Under subsection (b), an employer is liable when the tort is attributable to the employer's own negligence. Thus, although a supervisor's sexual harassment is outside the scope of employment because the conduct was for personal motives, an employer can be liable, nonetheless, where its own negligence is a cause of the harassment. An employer is negligent with respect to sexual harassment if it knew or should have known about the conduct and failed to stop it. Negligence sets a minimum standard for employer liability under Title VII; but Ellerth seeks to invoke the more stringent standard of vicarious liability.

Subsection 219(2)(d) concerns vicarious liability for intentional torts committed by an employee when the employee uses apparent authority (the apparent authority standard), or when the employee "was aided in accomplishing the tort by the existence of the agency relation" (the aided in the agency relation standard). As other federal decisions have done in discussing vicarious liability for supervisor harassment, we begin with § 219(2)(d).

C

As a general rule, apparent authority is relevant where the agent purports to exercise a power which he or she does not have, as distinct from where the agent threatens to misuse actual power. . . . In the usual case, a supervisor's harassment involves misuse of actual power, not the false impression of its existence. Apparent authority analysis therefore is inappropriate in this context. . . .

D

We turn to the aided in the agency relation standard. In a sense, most workplace tortfeasors are aided in accomplishing their tortious objective by the existence of the agency relation: Proximity and regular contact may afford a captive pool of potential victims. Were this to satisfy the aided in the agency relation standard, an employer would be subject to vicarious liability not only for all supervisor harassment, but also for all co-worker harassment, a result enforced by neither the EEOC nor any court of appeals to have considered the issue. [Citations omitted.] The aided in the agency relation standard, therefore, requires the existence of something more than the employment relation itself.

At the outset, we can identify a class of cases where, beyond question, more than the mere existence of the employment relation aids in commission of the harassment: when a supervisor takes a tangible employment action against the subordinate. Every Federal Court of Appeals to have considered the question has found vicarious liability when a discriminatory act results in a tangible employment action. [Citations omitted.] In *Meritor,* we acknowledged this consensus. . . . Although few courts have elaborated how agency principles support this rule, we think it reflects a correct application of the aided in the agency relation standard.

In the context of this case, a tangible employment action would have taken the form of a denial of a raise or a promotion. The concept of a tangible employment action appears in numerous cases in the Courts of Appeals discussing claims involving race, age, and national origin discrimination, as well as sex discrimination. Without endorsing the specific results of those decisions, we think it prudent to import the concept of a tangible employment action for resolution of the vicarious liability issue we consider here. A tangible employment action constitutes a significant change in employment status, such as hiring, firing, failing to promote, reassignment with significantly different responsibilities, or a decision causing a significant change in benefits. . . .

When a supervisor makes a tangible employment decision, there is assurance the injury could not have been inflicted absent the agency relation. A tangible employment action in most cases inflicts direct economic harm. As a general proposition, only a supervisor, or other person acting with the authority of the company, can cause this sort of injury. A co-worker can break a co-worker's arm as easily as a supervisor, and anyone who has regular contact with an employee can inflict psychological injuries by his or her offensive conduct. . . . But one co-worker (absent some elaborate scheme) cannot dock another's pay, nor can one co-worker demote another. Tangible employment actions fall within the special province of the supervisor. The supervisor has been empowered by the company as a distinct class of agent to make economic decisions affecting other employees under his or her control.

Tangible employment actions are the means by which the supervisor brings the official power of the enterprise to bear on subordinates. A tangible employment decision requires an official act of the enterprise, a company act. The decision in most cases is documented in official company records, and may be subject to review by higher level supervisors. . . . The supervisor often must obtain the imprimatur of the enterprise and use its internal processes. . . .

For these reasons, a tangible employment action taken by the supervisor becomes for Title VII purposes the act of the employer. Whatever the exact contours of the aided in the agency relation standard, its requirements will always be met when a supervisor takes a tangible employment action against a subordinate. In that instance, it would be implausible to interpret agency principles to allow an employer to escape liability, as *Meritor* itself appeared to acknowledge.

Whether the agency relation aids in commission of supervisor harassment which does not culminate in a tangible employment action is less obvious. Application of the standard is made difficult by its malleable terminology, which can be read to either expand or limit liability in the context of supervisor harassment. On the one hand, a supervisor's power and authority invests his or her harassing conduct with a particular threatening character, and in this sense, a supervisor always is aided by the agency relation. . . . On the other hand, there are acts of harassment a supervisor might commit which might be the same acts a co-employee would commit, and there may be some circumstances where the supervisor's status makes little difference.

It is this tension which, we think, has caused so much confusion among the Courts of Appeals which have sought to apply the aided in the agency relation standard to Title VII cases. The aided in the agency relation standard, however, is a developing feature of agency law, and we hesitate to render a definitive explanation of our understanding of the standard in an area where other important considerations must affect our judgment. In particular, we are bound by our holding in *Meritor* that agency principles constrain the imposition of vicarious liability in cases of supervisory harassment. See *Meritor* ("Congress' decision to define 'employer' to include any 'agent' of an employer, 42 U.S.C. § 2000e(b), surely evinces an intent to place some limits on the acts of employees for which employers under Title VII are to be held responsible"). Congress has not altered *Meritor*'s rule even though it has made significant amendments to Title VII in the interim. . . .

Although *Meritor* suggested the limitation on employer liability stemmed from agency principles, the Court acknowledged other considerations might be relevant as well. . . . For example, Title VII is designed to encourage the creation of antiharassment policies and effective grievance mechanisms. Were employer liability to depend in part on an employer's effort to create such procedures, it would effect Congress' intention to promote conciliation rather than litigation in the Title VII context and the EEOC's policy of encouraging the development of grievance procedures. To the extent limiting employer liability could encourage employees to report harassing conduct before it becomes severe or pervasive, it would also serve Title VII's deterrent purpose. As we have observed, Title VII borrows from tort law the avoidable consequences doctrine, and the considerations which animate that doctrine would also support the limitation of employer liability in certain circumstances.

In order to accommodate the agency principles of vicarious liability for harm caused by misuse of supervisory authority, as well as Title VII's equally basic policies of encouraging forethought by employers and saving action by objecting employees, we adopt the following holding in this case and in *Faragher v. Boca Raton*, also decided today. An employer is subject to vicarious liability to a victimized employee for an actionable hostile environment created by a supervisor with immediate (or successively higher) authority over the employee. When no tangible employment action is taken, a defending employer may raise an affirmative defense to liability or damages, subject to proof by a preponderance of the evidence. The defense comprises two necessary elements: (a) that the employer exercised reasonable care to prevent and correct promptly any sexually harassing behavior, and (b) that the plaintiff employee unreasonably failed to take advantage of any preventive or corrective opportunities provided by the employer or to avoid harm otherwise. While proof that an employer had promulgated an antiharassment policy with complaint procedure is not necessary in every instance as a matter of law, the need for a stated policy suitable to the employment circumstances may appropriately be addressed in any case when litigating the first element of the defense. And while proof that an employee failed to fulfill the corresponding obligation of reasonable care to avoid harm is not limited to showing any unreasonable failure to use any complaint procedure provided by the employer, a demonstration of such failure will normally suffice to satisfy the employer's burden under the second element of the defense. No affirmative defense is available, however, when the supervisor's harassment culminates in a tangible employment action, such as discharge, demotion, or undesirable reassignment.

IV

Relying on existing case law which held out the promise of vicarious liability for all *quid pro quo* claims, Ellerth focused all her attention in the Court of Appeals on proving her claim fit within that category. Given our explanation that the labels *quid pro quo* and hostile work environment are not controlling for purposes of establishing employer liability, Ellerth should have an adequate opportunity to prove she has a claim for which Burlington is liable.

Although Ellerth has not alleged she suffered a tangible employment action at the hands of Slowik, which would deprive Burlington of the availability of the affirmative defense, this is not dispositive. In light of our decision, Burlington is still subject to vicarious liability for Slowik's activity, but Burlington should have an opportunity to assert and prove the affirmative defense to liability.

For these reasons, we will affirm the judgment of the Court of Appeals, reversing the grant of summary judgment against Ellerth. On remand, the District Court will have the opportunity to decide whether it would be appropriate to allow Ellerth to amend her pleading or supplement her discovery.

The judgment of the Court of Appeals is affirmed.

It is so ordered.

JUSTICE GINSBURG, concurring in the judgment.

I agree with the Court's ruling that "the labels quid pro quo and hostile work environment are not controlling for purposes of establishing employer liability." I also subscribe to the Court's statement of the rule governing employer liability, which is substantively identical to the rule the Court adopts in *Faragher v. Boca Raton.*

JUSTICE THOMAS, with whom JUSTICE SCALIA joins, dissenting.

The Court today manufactures a rule that employers are vicariously liable if supervisors create a sexually hostile work environment, subject to an affirmative defense that the Court barely attempts to define. This rule applies even if the employer has a policy against sexual harassment, the employee knows about that policy, and the employee never informs anyone in a position of authority about the supervisor's conduct. As a result, employer liability under Title VII is judged by different standards depending upon whether a sexually or racially hostile work environment is alleged. The standard of employer liability should be the same in both instances: An employer should be liable if, and only if, the plaintiff proves that the employer was negligent in permitting the supervisor's conduct to occur.

I

Years before sexual harassment was recognized as "discriminat[ion] ... because of ... sex," 42 U.S.C. § 2000e-2(a)(1), the Courts of Appeals considered whether, and when, a racially hostile work environment could violate Title VII. In the landmark case *Rogers v. EEOC* (1971), cert. denied (1972), the Court of Appeals for the Fifth Circuit held that the practice of racially segregating patients in a doctor's office could amount to discrimination in " 'the terms, conditions, or privileges' " of employment, thereby violating Title VII. (Quoting 42 U.S.C. § 2000e-2(a)(1)). The principal opinion in the case concluded that employment discrimination was not limited to the "isolated and distinguishable events" of "hiring, firing, and promoting" (opinion of Goldberg, J.). Rather, Title VII could also be violated by a work environment "heavily polluted with discrimination," because of the deleterious effects of such an atmosphere on an employee's well-being.

Accordingly, after *Rogers*, a plaintiff claiming employment discrimination based upon race could assert a claim for a racially hostile work environment, in addition to the classic claim of so-called "disparate treatment." A disparate treatment claim required a plaintiff to prove an adverse employment consequence and discriminatory intent by his employer. A hostile environment claim required the plaintiff to show that his work environment was so pervaded by racial harassment as to alter the terms and conditions of his employment. . . . This is the same standard now used when determining whether sexual harassment renders a work environment hostile. See *Harris v. Forklift Systems, Inc.* (1993) (actionable sexual harassment occurs when the workplace is "*permeated* with discriminatory intimidation, ridicule, and insult") (emphasis added).

In race discrimination cases, employer liability has turned on whether the plaintiff has alleged an adverse employment consequence, such as firing or demotion, or a hostile work environment. If a supervisor takes an adverse employment action because of race, causing the employee a tangible job detriment, the employer is vicariously liable for resulting damages. This is because such actions are company acts that can be performed only by the exercise of specific authority granted by the employer, and thus the supervisor acts as the employer. If, on the other hand, the employee alleges a racially hostile work environment, the employer is liable only for negligence: that is, only if the employer knew, or in the exercise of reasonable care should have known, about the harassment and failed to take remedial action. [Citations omitted.] Liability has thus been imposed only if the employer is blameworthy in some way. [Citations omitted.]

This distinction applies with equal force in cases of sexual harassment. When a supervisor inflicts an adverse employment consequence upon an employee who has rebuffed his advances, the supervisor exercises the specific authority granted to him by his company. His acts, therefore, are the company's acts and are properly chargeable to it. . . .

If a supervisor creates a hostile work environment, however, he does not act for the employer. As the Court concedes, a supervisor's creation of a hostile work environment is neither within the scope of his employment, nor part of his apparent authority. Indeed, a hostile work environment is antithetical to the interest of the employer. In such circumstances, an employer should be liable only if it has been negligent. That is, liability should attach only if the employer either knew, or in the exercise of reasonable care should have known, about the hostile work environment and failed to take remedial action.

Sexual harassment is simply not something that employers can wholly prevent without taking extraordinary measures—constant video and audio surveillance, for example—that would revolutionize the workplace in a manner incompatible with a free society. Indeed, such measures could not even detect incidents of harassment such as the comments Slowik allegedly made to respondent in a hotel bar. The most that employers can be charged with, therefore, is a duty to act reasonably under the circumstances. . . .

Under a negligence standard, Burlington cannot be held liable for Slowik's conduct. Although respondent alleged a hostile work environment, she never contended that Burlington had been negligent in permitting the harassment to occur, and there is no question that Burlington acted reasonably under the circumstances. The company had a policy against sexual harassment, and respondent admitted that she was aware of the policy but nonetheless failed to tell anyone with authority over Slowik about his behavior. Burlington therefore cannot be charged with knowledge of Slowik's alleged harassment or with a failure to exercise reasonable care in not knowing about it.

II

Rejecting a negligence standard, the Court instead imposes a rule of vicarious employer liability, subject to a vague affirmative defense, for the acts of supervisors who wield no delegated authority in creating a hostile work environment. This rule is a whole-cloth creation that draws no support from the legal principles on which the Court claims it is based. Compounding its error, the Court fails to explain how employers can rely upon the affirmative defense, thus ensuring a continuing reign of confusion in this important area of the law.

In justifying its holding, the Court refers to our comment in *Meritor Savings Bank, FSB v. Vinson* (1986), that the lower courts should look to "agency principles" for guidance in determining the scope of employer liability. The Court then interprets the term "agency principles" to mean the Restatement (Second) of Agency (1957). The Court finds two portions of the Restatement to be relevant: § 219(2)(b), which provides that a master is liable for his servant's torts if the master is reckless or negligent, and § 219(2)(d), which states that a master is liable for his servant's torts when the servant is "aided in accomplishing the tort by the existence of the agency relation." The Court appears to reason that a supervisor is aided . . . by . . . the agency relation" in creating a hostile work environment because the supervisor's "power and authority invests his or her harassing conduct with a particular threatening character."

Section 219(2)(d) of the Restatement provides no basis whatsoever for imposing vicarious liability for a supervisor's creation of a hostile work environment. Contrary to the Court's suggestions, the principle embodied in § 219(2)(d) has nothing to do with a servant's "power and authority," nor with whether his actions appear "threatening." Rather, as demonstrated by the Restatement's illustrations, liability under § 219(2)(d) depends upon the plaintiff's belief that the agent acted in the ordinary course of business or within the scope of his apparent authority. In this day and age, no sexually harassed employee can reasonably believe that a harassing supervisor is conducting the official business of the company or acting on its behalf. Indeed, the Court admits as much in demonstrating why sexual harassment is not committed within the scope of a supervisor's employment and is not part of his apparent authority.

Thus although the Court implies that it has found guidance in both precedent and statute . . . its holding is a product of willful policymaking, pure and simple. The only agency principle that justifies imposing employer liability in this context is the principle that a master will be liable for a servant's torts if the master was negligent or reckless in permitting them to occur; and as noted, under a negligence standard, Burlington cannot be held liable.

The Court's decision is also in considerable tension with our holding in *Meritor* that employers are not strictly liable for a supervisor's sexual harassment. Although the Court recognizes an affirmative defense . . . it provides shockingly little guidance about how employers can actually avoid vicarious liability. Instead, it issues only Delphic pronouncements and leaves the dirty work to the lower courts:

> "While proof that an employer had promulgated an anti-harassment policy with complaint procedure is not necessary in every instance as a matter of law, the need for a stated policy suitable to the employment circumstances may appropriately be addressed in any case when litigating the first element of the defense. And while proof that an employee failed to fulfill the corresponding obligation of reasonable care to avoid harm is not limited to showing any unreasonable failure to use any complaint procedure provided by the employer, a demonstration of such failure will normally suffice to satisfy the employer's burden under the second element of the defense."

What these statements mean for district courts ruling on motions for summary judgment—the critical question for employers now subject to the vicarious liability rule—remains a mystery. Moreover, employers will be liable notwithstanding the affirmative defense, *even though they acted reasonably,* so long as the plaintiff in question fulfilled her duty of reasonable care to avoid harm. In practice, therefore, employer liability very well may be the rule. But as the Court acknowledges, this is the one result that it is clear Congress did not intend.

The Court's holding does guarantee one result: There will be more and more litigation to clarify applicable legal rules in an area in which both practitioners and the courts have long been begging for guidance. It thus truly boggles the mind that the Court can claim that its holding will effect "Congress' intention to promote conciliation rather than litigation in the Title VII context." All in all, today's decision is an ironic result for a case that generated eight separate opinions in the Court of Appeals on a fundamental question, and in which we granted certiorari "to assist in defining the relevant standards of employer liability."

*   *   *

Popular misconceptions notwithstanding, sexual harassment is not a free-standing federal tort, but a form of employment discrimination. As such, it should be treated no differently (and certainly no better) than the other forms of harassment that are illegal under Title VII. I would restore parallel treatment of employer liability for racial and sexual harassment and hold an employer liable for a hostile work environment only if the employer is truly at fault. I therefore respectfully dissent.

NEWS CONFERENCE IN CHINA
BY CLINTON AND JIANG
June 27, 1998

The communist leaders of China took significant steps to open their country's closed political system in the early months of 1998. Against the advice of many in the United States, President Bill Clinton visited China for eight days in late June and early July, praising the leadership for market-based economic reforms and expressing optimism that China was headed toward democracy. His visit was the first by an American president since Chinese leaders crushed a pro-democracy movement in Beijing's Tiananmen Square in June 1989. Clinton was reciprocating a visit to the United States in late 1997 by Chinese president Jiang Zemin. (Jiang visit, Historic Documents of 1997, p. 728)

China on October 5 signed the International Covenant on Civil and Political Rights, a United Nations treaty intended to promote open societies. But in late October the government launched a crackdown against democracy advocates, including several who had tried to form the country's first opposition political party. The ferocity of the attack seemed to end any hopes that democracy was about to blossom there.

Chinese and western analysts said the year's events demonstrated once again that the communist leaders in Beijing could accept token levels of dissent, but nothing that might pose any conceivable threat to their power. The crackdown toward the end of the year threw the country's dissidents off balance and frustrated those in the West who had been pressing the Chinese leadership for reform.

The Clinton Visit

President Clinton's visit to China came during a year in which his dealings with China faced intense domestic political pressure on two fronts. First, critics questioned whether his approach of quiet diplomacy was having any impact on the Chinese leaders. Republicans in Congress also continued to voice suspicions about China's alleged attempt to influence the 1996 elections through questionable campaign donations to Democrats.

Some Republicans tried to link the campaign finance issue with what they said was administration indifference to improper sales of high technology to China. Republicans also accused the administration of playing down China's role in supplying some of the technology that enabled Pakistan to test nuclear weapons in late May. Key Republicans, and even some Democrats, demanded that he cancel the visit. (Technology transfer issue, p. 976; nuclear weapons tests, p. 326)

The administration angered many critics in March when it dropped what had been an annual campaign for a resolution by the United Nations Human Rights Commission condemning Chinese repression. For seven straight years, the United States had lost its drive for such a resolution, but Washington had used the annual debate to highlight concerns about the lack of human and political rights in China.

By April news reports from China seemed to indicate that the government was relaxing its grip. Students, college professors, and dissidents said they were sensing a new willingness by the government to tolerate open discussion of such sensitive topics as human rights and political freedoms. China in April released Wang Dan, one of the country's most prominent political prisoners, and allowed him to fly to exile in the United States.

Clinton defended his policies and his planned trip in a June 11 speech at the National Geographic Society in Washington. "Seeking to isolate China will not free one more political dissident, will not open one more church to those who wish to worship, will do nothing to encourage China to live by the laws it has written," Clinton said. "Instead, it will limit our ability to advance human rights and religious and political freedoms."

Arriving in China on June 25, Clinton spent a day visiting historic sites and watching oriental pageantry in the central city of Xian. On June 27 he flew to Beijing and was met with a military ceremony in Tiananmen Square, the site of the government's bloody suppression of protesters. In keeping with diplomatic custom, Clinton made no public comment at that ceremony.

Clinton had been in the capital just a few hours when the Chinese government gave him what may have been the biggest surprise of the trip: an opportunity to address a news conference with Jiang that was broadcast live across the country. There was no advance notice of the broadcast, and so only a tiny fraction of Chinese saw it. But the event at the Great Hall of the People offered a highly unusual opportunity for any Chinese to hear a foreign leader speak freely about issues in their country.

In his opening statement, Clinton used the forum to explain his reasons for carrying on an active diplomacy with China—but he also spoke directly about the differing views between the United States and China on many issues. On perhaps the most sensitive issue of all, the 1989 Tiananmen Square massacre, Clinton said the two countries "still disagree about the meaning" of that event. "I believe, and the American people believe, that the use of force and the tragic loss of life was wrong," Clinton said, as

Jiang stood nearby. "I believe, and the American people believe, that freedom of speech, association, and religion are, as recognized by the UN charter, the right of people everywhere and should be protected by their governments." Clinton took some of the edge off his comments by noting that the United States had "painful moments" in its own history, and that China faced "enormous challenges" on many fronts.

In response, Jiang repeated a standard Chinese formulation that the 1989 "political disturbances" left the government no choice but to act to protect the country's stability and efforts at economic reform." . . . [H]ad the Chinese government not taken the resolute measures, then we could not have enjoyed the stability that we are enjoying today," he said. Clinton countered that guaranteeing individual freedoms was a better and more certain way of ensuring political stability.

Clinton had other opportunities to speak directly to the Chinese people. On June 29 the government allowed the broadcast of the president's speech, followed by a question-and-answer session, at Beijing University. On June 30 Clinton appeared on a radio call-in program, broadcast by Shanghai Radio 990. The calls were screened, and callers asked about such issues as education, library exchanges, and automobile emissions—topics the president was happy to discuss at length. The next day he was interviewed by the government's main television network; he praised what he called "a genuine movement toward openness and freedom in China."

Even as Clinton's trip proceeded, however, Chinese authorities seemed unable to avoid customary restrictions on political freedom. The government denied visas to three journalists accredited to Radio Free Asia (the U.S. government's station that broadcast to Asian nations), and it prevented several Chinese dissidents from meeting with journalists accompanying Clinton.

Clinton wound up his trip on July 3 in Hong Kong, the former British colony that had been returned to China one year earlier. The president praised the entrepreneurial spirit of the people of Hong Kong who, under British rule, had made their city one of the economic powerhouses of Asia. In a private meeting, Clinton pressed the Chinese-appointed chief executive of Hong Kong, Tung Chee-hwa, to resume a move toward democracy that the British had encouraged during their last years in power there. (Hong Kong transfer, Historic Documents of 1997, p. 501)

Sounding an optimistic note, Clinton also used his last day in China to praise the country's leaders, specifically Jiang and the new prime minister, Zhu Rongji. Asked whether China could develop a democracy, Clinton said: "Oh yes, I believe there can be, and I believe there will be. And what I would like to see is the present government—headed by this president and this premier who are clearly committed to reform—ride the wave of change and take China fully into the twenty-first century and basically dismantle the resistance to it."

Clinton's trip appeared to disarm his Republican critics at home, most of whom praised his forthright statements on democracy and human rights. "I think the president did a pretty good job talking on Chinese radio and TV," House Speaker Newt Gingrich told reporters. "It's less expensive to be friends than enemies."

Cracking Down on Dissent

Just three months after Clinton left China, his parting words of optimism were made to seem premature. China's signing on October 5 of the UN Covenant on Civil and Political Rights was quickly overshadowed by reports of another crackdown on dissent. Leading democracy activists were put under round-the-clock surveillance or held for questioning. Some were arrested, and several journals and institutes that sought to foster political dialogue were closed.

On December 2 the government stepped up its attack on dissidents, arresting and pressing criminal charges against two men—Xu Wenli of Beijing and Qin Yongmin of Wuhun, a city in central China—who had been part of an effort to start an opposition political party, the China Democratic Party. The two men were among China's best-known dissidents, and each had spent years in prison for espousing their views. The arrests sparked an international protest from human rights groups and other countries, to which China responded that Xu had engaged in activities "damaging to national security."

Other arrests followed, and by late December Xu and three colleagues had been given long prison terms for subversion and similar crimes. Xu was sentenced to thirteen years, Qin Yongmin to twelve years, Wang Youcai to eleven years, and Zhang Shanguang to ten years. In contrast to the vague charges against the others, Zhang faced a specific accusation, that he illegally gave intelligence information "to hostile foreign organizations and persons." That charge apparently was a reference to an interview Zhang gave to Radio Free Asia in March, during which he described anti-tax protests by farmers in Hunan province.

The government-controlled media publicized the charges against the dissidents, an unusual move that observers said was intended to discourage others who might consider expressing dissent. The government also published rules warning film directors, other artists, and computer software developers that they faced prison terms if they tried to "overthrow state power." On December 29 the government also sentenced to prison two dissidents who had moved to New York but had slipped back into China to help promote the China Democratic Party.

Human rights groups and other countries, including the United States, denounced the crackdown on dissidents. In a December 21 statement, the State Department said the United States "deeply deplores" the convictions of the dissidents.

The Chinese government defended the arrests as necessary to protect stability and national security. Jiang was quoted by government media as saying that "any factors that could jeopardize our stability must be annihilated in the early stages."

469

Jiang's statement served as a reminder that the Communist Party's will-ingness to tolerate dissent had definite limits. Most Western analysts agreed that, in allowing any degree of political openness, the government did not have in mind allowing a movement toward a liberal democracy.

Following are excerpts from a news conference given by Chinese president Jiang Zemin and U.S. president Bill Clinton on June 27, 1998, at the Great Hall of the People in Beijing, China:

President Jiang: Ladies and gentlemen, just now I've held official talks with President Clinton. The two sides have held an extensive and in-depth exchange of views on China-U.S. relations and the major international and regional issues. The talks were positive, constructive, and productive.

The successful exchange of visits between the two heads of state of China and the United States marks a new stage of growth for China-U.S. relations. This not only serves the common interests of China and the United States, but also will be of important significance to promoting peace, stability, and prosperity in the Asia Pacific and the world at large.

Peace and the development are the main themes of contemporary times. In the new historical conditions, the common interests between China and the United States are increasing, not decreasing. The foundation for cooperation between the two countries is reenforcing, not weakening.

Both sides believe that China and the United States, as the permanent members of the U.N. Security Council, should continue to work together to promote peace and security in the world and the Asia Pacific in particular, to ease and eliminate all kinds of tensions and to prevent the proliferation of weapons of mass destruction, to strengthen the efforts in protecting the environment, combating international crime, drug trafficking, and international terrorism. Our two sides have agreed to further step up cooperation and the dialogue between the two countries on major international issues.

China-U.S. relations are improving and growing. The cooperation between the two sides in many areas has made important progress. President Clinton and I have decided that China and the United States will not target the strategic nuclear weapons under their respective control at each other. This demonstrates to the entire world that China and the United States are partners, not adversaries.

I hereby wish to reiterate that since the very first day when China came into possession of nuclear weapons, China has undertaken not to be the first to use nuclear weapons under any circumstances.

President Clinton and I have reached a broad range of agreements and consensus on further increasing exchanges in cooperation between China and the United States in all areas in our bilateral relations. We have agreed to take positive steps to promote the growth of the mutually beneficial economic cooperation and trade between China and the United States and to expand the exchanges and the cooperation between the two countries in the energy, environment, scientific, educational, cultural, health, legal, and the military fields; and also to enhance the people-to-people exchanges and friendship.

We have also agreed to enhance the consultations and the cooperation between China and the United States on the issues of disarmament, arms control, and non-proliferation. And we have issued joint statements on the BWC protocol on the question of the antipersonnel land mines and on the question of South Asia.

The Taiwan question is the most important and the most sensitive issue at the core of China-U.S. relations. We hope that the U.S. side will adhere to the principles set forth in the three China-U.S. joint communiqués and the joint China-U.S. statement, as well as the relevant commitments it has made in the interest of a smooth growth of China-U.S. relations.

The improvement and the growth of China-U.S. relations have not come by easily. It is the result of the concerted efforts of the governments and people of our two countries. So we should all the more treasure this good result.

As China and the United States have different social systems, ideologies, values, and culture traditions, we have some difference of views on certain issues. However, they should not become the obstacles in the way of the growth of China-U.S. relations. The world is a colorful one. The development parts of the countries in the world should be chosen by the people of the countries concerned.

China and the United States should view and handle the bilateral relations from a long-term and strategic perspective. We should promote the growth of China-U.S. relations in the spirit of mutual respect, equality, mutual benefit, seeking common ground while putting aside differences, and developing cooperation. I believe that through the concerted efforts of both sides, we will make constant progress in the direction of building a constructive, strategic partnership between China and the United States oriented towards the 21st century.

President Clinton: Thank you, Mr. President. And I also thank the Chinese people for their warm welcome to me, to my family, and to our delegation.

Over the past five years, President Jiang and I have met seven times. Mr. President, your leadership is helping us to transform our nations' relationship for the future. Clearly, a stable, open, prosperous China, shouldering its responsibilities for a safer world is good for America. Nothing makes that point better than today's agreement not to target our nuclear missiles at each other. We also agreed to do more to shore up stability in Asia, on the Korean Peninsula, and the Indian subcontinent. I reaffirmed our long-standing one China policy to President Jiang and urged the pursuit of cross-strait discussions recently resumed as the best path to a peaceful resolution. In a similar vein, I urged President Jiang to assume a dialogue with the Dalai Lama in return for the recognition that Tibet is a part of China and in recognition of the unique cultural and religious heritage of that region.

I welcome the progress we made today in non-proliferation, including China's decision to actively study joining the Missile Technology Control Regime, our joint commitment not to provide assistance to ballistic missile programs in South Asia, and President Jiang's statement last week that China will not sell missiles to Iran.

We also welcome the steps China recently has taken to tighten nuclear export controls, to strengthen controls on the export of chemicals that can be turned into weapons, and to work jointly with us to strengthen the Biological Weapons Convention.

As the President said, we are also working together against international crime, drug trafficking, alien smuggling, stepping up our scientific cooperation, which already has produced remarkable breakthroughs in areas including the fight against birth defects like spina bifida. We're helping to eradicate polio and working to predict and to mitigate national disasters. And perhaps most important over the long run, we are committed to working together on clean energy to preserve our natural environment, a matter of urgent concern to both our nations.

I am also very pleased by our cooperation on rule of law programs, from training lawyers and judges to providing legal assistance to the poor.

President Jiang and I agree on the importance of China's entry into the World Trade Organization. I regret we did not make more progress on this front, and we must recommit ourselves to achieving that goal on strong terms. We agree that we need to work together to avoid another round of destablizing currency devaluations in the region and to restore economic growth.

As you can see, we are working together in many areas of cooperation. We have developed a relationship of openness and candor. When we differ, as we do from time to time, we speak openly and honestly in an effort to understand our differences and, if possible, to work toward a common approach to resolving them.

It is well known that the principal area of our difference in recent years has been over human rights questions. America recognizes and applauds China's economic and social transformation, which has expanded the rights of its citizens by lifting hundreds of millions from poverty, providing them greater access to information, giving them village elections, greater freedom to travel and to choose their own jobs, and better education for their children.

As I said again to President Jiang, we Americans also firmly believe that individual rights, including the freedom of speech, association, and religion are very important, not only to those who exercise them, but also to nations whose success in the 21st century depends upon widespread individual knowledge, creativity, free exchange, and enterprise.

Therefore, we welcome China's decision to sign the International Covenant on Civil and Political Rights, the recent release of several prominent political dissidents, the recent visit China graciously accorded American religious leaders, and the resumption of a human rights dialogue between China and the United States.

Earlier this morning, during my official welcome, I could hear and see the many echoes of China's past and the call of its promising future, for Tiananmen Square is an historical place. There, 100 years ago, China's quest for constitutional government was born. There, in 1919, young people rallied against foreign occupation and launched a powerful movement for China's political and cultural renewal. There, in 1976, public mourning for Zhou Enlai led to the Cultural Revolution's end and the beginning of your remarkable transformation. And there, nine years ago, Chinese citizens of all ages raised their voices for democracy.

For all of our agreements, we still disagree about the meaning of what happened then. I believe, and the American people believe, that the use of force and the tragic loss of life was wrong. I believe, and the American people believe, that freedom of speech, association, and religion are, as recognized by U.N. Charter, the right of people everywhere and should be protected by their governments.

It was to advance these rights that our Founding Fathers in our Declaration of Independence pledged our lives, our fortunes, our sacred honor. Fifty years ago, the U.N. recognized these rights as the basic freedoms of people everywhere.

The question for us now is how shall we deal with such disagreements and still succeed in the important work of deepening our friendship and our sense of mutual respect.

First, we Americans must acknowledge the painful moments in our own history when fundamental human rights were denied. We must say that we know, still, we have to continue our work to advance the dignity and freedom and equality of our own people. And, second, we must understand and respect the enormous challenges China has faced in trying to move forward against great odds with a clear memory of the setbacks suffered in past periods of instability.

Finally, it is important that whatever our disagreements over past action, China and the United States must go forward on the right side of history for the future sake of the world. The forces of history have brought us to a new age of human possibility, but our dreams can only be recognized by nations whose citizens are both responsible and free.

Mr. President, that is the future America seeks to build with China, in partnership and honest friendship.

Tomorrow, Hillary and I will visit the Great Wall. The wall's builders knew they were building a permanent monument, even if they were unable to see it finished in their lifetimes. Likewise, we know we are building a friendship that will serve our descendants well, even if we, ourselves, will not see its full development across the next century and into the new millennium. Our friendship may never be perfect—no friendship is. But I hope it will last forever. . . .

Q: My question to President Jiang and also to President Clinton is, we know that there were four dissidents in Xian who were arrested earlier and three were released, and one of them is still under detainment. And I would like to know if you talked about the issue. And what about the rest of the 2,000 dissidents who are being reported as still under imprisonment right now in China? Can both of you elaborate on that? Thank you.

President Jiang: In our talks just now, President Clinton raised this issue. We adopt an attitude of extending very warm welcome to the visit to China by President Clinton.

As for the matter you raised, I think you are referring to the incident in Xian, and I think in China there is no question that there is no restriction whatsoever on the coverage and interview by the reporters and the correspondents within the scope of law. But as for some activities that have been detrimental or have prejudiced the security, then the local authorities should take measures to deal with them, and it is also understandable.

As for the question you raised, actually, I do not have very detailed information in this regard. But as for the latter part of your question concerning 2,000 dissidents, I think in China we have our laws. And in China's constitution, it is clearly stipulated that the Chinese citizens have the freedom of speech, but any law-breaking activities must be dealt with according to law. I think this is true in any country of rule of law. And I think China's judicial departments will deal with the matter according to law.

Q: I want to ask that I believe that the vast majority of the correspondents and the reporters are willing to promote the friendship between China and the United States through President Clinton's visit to China this time. However, before President Clinton's visit, I read some reports from some media and newspapers saying—alleging China had been involved in so-called political contributions in the United States. I really think it very absurd and ridiculous, and I think they are sheer fabrications. China can never do such a thing and China never interferes in other country's internal affairs.

President Jiang: Actually, at the talks this morning, President Clinton also asked me of this question. And I told him that after hearing of such an allegation we conducted very earnest investigation into the matter. And the results of the investigation shows that there was never such a thing.

Recently, in my meetings with many foreign visitors and visiting leaders of other countries, I often said to them that as countries in the world have different social systems and values, it is something that should be allowed that they may have different understandings about one fact. And this actually, itself, is a representation and the manifestation of democracy.

However, what is important is that the fact itself should not be distorted.

I'm sorry I've taken up too much of the time, and I now invite President Clinton to say a few words.

President Clinton: Well, we did discuss the questions you raised. And, of course, I made my views known about the recent detentions yesterday. On the larger question you raised, I actually made a couple of specific and practical suggestions about how we might take our dialogue farther there.

There are some people who are incarcerated now for offensives no longer on the books in China, reflecting real progress in present Chinese practice, and the Chinese, in my view—we should acknowledge that. But the question then arises is there some way that these people might be released? Is there some procedure through which we could move? There are some people imprisoned for non-violent activities in June of '89. Is there something that could be done there?

There are some other practical things we discussed, which I think it would be premature to ask the Chinese government to make a statement on now because we just have had these discussions. But I want to say to all of you that the atmosphere—whatever your position on these issues is, and particularly if you agree with me, I think you should at least appreciate the fact that we now have an atmosphere in which it is possible for us to be open and honest and in great detail about this; and that there are legitimate and honest differences in the way we look at this. But I believe that we are making progress, and I believe that we will make more.

I remember the things that I specified in my statement about that. You can see that neither one of us are shy about being strong about how we believe about this. And I think that we have them in the public debate now, we have them in the private discussions, and we just have to keep pushing forward in trying to work through it. . . .

Q: My question is to President Jiang. At his opening statement, President Clinton expressed appreciation of the achievements made by the Chinese government in respecting human rights. At the same time, he also said that China and the United States also had difference of views over this matter. So my question is, what is the position of the Chinese government on the human rights issue?

President Jiang: China and the United States have differences of views and also have common ground on the human rights issue. More than 2,000 years ago, a great thinker of China's Han Dynasty, Dong Zhongshu, once said, "Of all the living things nurtured between heaven and the Earth, the most valuable is human beings." So the Chinese nation always respects and maintains the dignity and rights of the people. Today the Chinese government solemnly commits itself to the promotion and the protection of human rights and fundamental freedoms.

The United States is the most developed country in the world, with a per capita GDP approaching $30,000 U.S. dollars, while China is a developing country with a population of 1.2 billion, with a per capita GDP of less than $700 U.S. dollars. As the two countries differ in social system, ideology, historical tradition and cultural background, the two countries have different means and ways in realizing human rights and fundamental freedoms. So it's nothing strange that we may have some difference of views over some issues.

China stresses that the top priority should be given to the right to subsistence and the right to development. Meanwhile, efforts should be made to strengthen democracy and the legal system building, and to protect the economic, social, cultural, civil and the political rights of the people.

I listened very carefully to what President Clinton said just now, and I noticed that he made mention of the political disturbances happened in

Tiananmen in 1989 and he also told the history of Tiananmen and told of the things that happened in Tiananmen.

With regard to the political disturbances in 1989, the Chinese people have long drawn a historical conclusion. During my visit to the United States last year and also on many international occasions, I have stated our position that with regard to the political disturbances in 1989, had the Chinese government not taken the resolute measures, then we could not have enjoyed the stability that we are enjoying today.

China is a socialist country in which its people are masters of the nation. The Chinese people can elect their own representatives to the people's congresses through direct or indirect means, and they can fully express their views and exercise their political rights. In the two decades since the reform and opening up program was started, the National People's Congress of China has adopted more than 320 laws and acts; thus, constantly strengthening the legal protection of the democracy, fundamental freedoms, and the various rights enjoyed by the Chinese people. Over the past two decades, another 200 million people in China were lifted out of poverty.

No country's human rights situation is perfect. Since the founding of new China, the fundamental changes and the tremendous achievements that have been achieved, that have been scored in the human rights conditions in China are for all to see.

I'd like to know whether President Clinton will have anything more to add.

President Clinton: I would like to add a comment. First of all, I think this debate and discussion today has been a healthy thing and a good thing. Secondly, I think to understand the priority that each country attaches to its own interpretation of this issue of human rights, you have to understand something of our history.

The Chinese who are here understand better than I the price paid over time at various moments in history for disruption and upheaval in China, so there is an understandable desire to have stability in the country. Every country wants stability.

Our country was founded by people who felt they were abused by royal powers—by people in power, and they wanted to protect their personal liberties by putting limits on government. And they understood—they understood clearly—that any system, because human beings are imperfect, any system can be abused.

So the question for all societies going forward into the 21st century is, which is the better gamble? If you have a lot of personal freedom, some people may abuse it. But if you are so afraid of personal freedom because of the abuse that you limit people's freedom too much, then you pay, I believe, an even greater price in a world where the whole economy is based on ideas and information and exchange and debate, and children everywhere dreaming dreams and feeling they can live their dreams out.

So I am trying to have a dialogue here that will enable both of us to move forward so that the Chinese people will get the best possible result. I believe stability in the 21st century will require high levels of freedom.

President Jiang: I'm sorry, I have to take up an additional five minutes. So I'd like to say a few words on Dalai Lama. President Clinton is also interested in this question, in Dalai Lama. Actually, since the Dalai Lama left in 1959, earthshaking changes have taken place in Tibet.

First, the system of bureaucracy has forever become bygones. Though it is unfortunate that the disappearance of this bureaucracy was much later than the demise of bureaucracy in Europe before Renaissance. And the more than one million serfs under the rule of the Dalai Lama were liberated. In 1990 when I was in Tibet I went to visit the liberated serfs. And now the system of national autonomy is in practice in Tibet and the people there, they have their Tibetan autonomous region government.

Since I came to work in the central government I have urged the rest of the 29 provinces, municipalities and autonomous regions to assist Tibet in its development—even including those provinces that are not very developed, such as Qinghai Province. So altogether, nearly 8 billion RMB-yuan financial resources were raised and already 62 projects have been completed in Tibet.

As for the freedom of religious belief, there is fierce stipulations in our constitution for the protection of religious belief and this also includes in Tibet. And we have also spent a lot of money in renovating the lamasis and temples in Tibet. And we have spent $100 million RMB-yuan and one ton of gold in renovating the Budala Palace.

Just now President Clinton also mentioned the Tibetan issue and the dialogue with the Dalai Lama. Actually, as long as the Dalai Lama can publicly make the statement and a commitment that Tibet is an inalienable part of China and he must also recognize Taiwan as a province of China, then the door to dialogue and negotiation is open. Actually, we are having several channels of communications with the Dalai Lama. So I hope the Dalai Lama will make positive response in this regard.

Finally, I want to emphasize that according to China's constitution, the freedom of religious belief in Tibet, and also throughout China, is protected. But as the President of the People's Republic of China and as a communist member, a member of the communist party, I myself am an atheist. But this will by no means affect my respect for the religious freedom in Tibet.

But still, I have a question. That is, during my visit to the United States last year, and also during my previous visits to other European countries, I found that although the education in science and technology have developed to a very high level, and people are now enjoying modern civilization, but still quite a number of them have a belief in Lamaism. So this is a question that I'm still studying and still looking into. I want to find out the reason why.

I think President Clinton is a strong defender of the American interests and I am a strong defender of the Chinese interests. But despite that, we still can have very friendly exchanges of views and discussions. And I think that is democracy. And I want to stress that, actually, there are a lot of areas in which we can learn from each other.

If you agree, we will finish this.

President Clinton: I agree, but I have—you have to let me say one thing about the Dalai Lama.

First, I agree that Tibet is a part of China, an autonomous region of China. And I can understand why the acknowledgment of that would be a precondition of dialogue with the Dalai Lama. But I also believe that there are many, many Tibetans who still revere the Dalai Lama and view him as their spiritual leader.

President Jiang pointed out that he has a few followers of Tibetan Buddhism, even in the United States and Europe. But most of his followers have not given up their own religious faith. He has followers who are Christians—supporters—excuse me—not followers, supporters—who are Christians, who are Jews, who are Muslims, who believe in the unity of God and who believe he is a holy man.

But, for us, the question is not fundamentally religious; it is political. That is, we believe that other people should have the right to fully practice their religious beliefs, and that if he, in good faith, presents himself on those terms, it is a legitimate thing for China to engage him in dialogue.

And let me say something that will perhaps be unpopular with everyone. I have spent time with the Dalai Lama. I believe him to be an honest man, and I believe if he had a conversation with President Jiang, they would like each other very much.

July

RUMSFELD COMMISSION ON MISSILE THREATS
July 15, 1998

A commission of military experts—including several former top U.S. government officials—warned in 1998 that the United States could be vulnerable to missile attacks early in the twenty-first century from North Korea and other countries. The commission, chaired by former defense secretary Donald H. Rumsfeld, said in a July 15 report that the United States might have little or no warning of such an attack.

The commission report directly touched on one of the most important national security disputes between Republican congressional leaders and the Clinton administration. Republicans in both chambers had been pressing for higher funding of experimental programs to counter a foreign missile attack on the United States, and they had demanded that the Clinton administration move more quickly to put such defenses in place. Although the Rumsfeld commission made no specific recommendations on the missile defense issue, Republicans successfully used the commission findings to get more money for these programs. However, Republicans failed during 1998 to speed up administration decision making on the issue.

The Rumsfeld Commission

Congress in 1996 mandated the creation of a commission to examine the potential threats to the United States from ballistic missiles held by, or under development in, foreign countries. Nominated by congressional leaders, commission members included two retired air force generals, several leading civilian military experts, and former senior government officials, including former CIA director James R. Woolsey and former Defense Department and State Department official Paul D. Wolfowitz.

During 1998 the commission interviewed about two dozen current and former national security officials and visited several U.S. military bases. The panel gave congressional leaders and the administration a 307-page classified report on July 14 and released a 27-page unclassified version on July 15.

The core findings of the commission report were that so-called rogue nations, such as North Korea, were moving to build long-range ballistic missiles and that Washington might have far less warning of a missile attack than U.S. intelligence estimates had predicted. The threat to the United States "is broader, more mature and evolving more rapidly than has been reported in estimates and reports by the intelligence community," the panel said. Long-range ballistic missiles could be used to deliver nuclear, chemical, or biological weapons—as well as conventional weapons.

Because of a variety of factors, the commission said, a nation such as Iran or North Korea could be capable of inflicting "major destruction" on the United States "within about five years" of deciding to acquire long-range ballistic missiles. (The commission put this time period at ten years for Iraq, because of damage to that country's infrastructure during and after the Persian Gulf War). It was also possible that the United States might have "little or no warning" before such an attack, the panel said. The official U.S. estimate was that the United States was unlikely to face threats from these countries until about 2010, and that Washington probably would have adequate warning of any such attacks. (United Nations confrontations with Iraq, p. 934)

The commission noted that, in the post-cold war era, nations such as North Korea found it much easier than before to obtain the necessary technology and material for ballistic missiles and weapons of mass destruction. Some European allies had become less vigilant in guarding against sales of weapons material to these nations. In addition, Russia and other former Soviet republics were selling Soviet military technology for cash for their hard-pressed economies. News reports also quoted commission members as warning that North Korea, India, and other countries were moving their weapons development programs to underground sites, thus evading the spy satellites that provided much of U.S. intelligence information.

Within weeks of the Rumsfeld panel report reaching Capitol Hill, Iran and North Korea conducted missile tests that reinforced fears about their intentions. U.S. officials said on July 22 that Iran had successfully tested a missile with a range of about 800 miles—enough to make it capable of hitting targets in Israel, Saudi Arabia, and elsewhere in the Middle East. Administration sources said it was likely that Iran purchased the missile and related technology from North Korea.

On August 31 North Korea tested a three-stage, medium-range ballistic missile that flew over northern Japan. That test unnerved Japan and prompted a demand from Washington that North Korea halt its ballistic missile program. North Korea spurned that appeal, announcing on December 25 that it was prepared to continue testing missiles and that it was "foolish" for Washington to expect a change on North Korean policy. Throughout 1998 the two countries were engaged in a related dispute over the status of a 1994 accord under which North Korea agreed to freeze work on its nuclear weapons program in return for international aid for its civilian nuclear power program. Intelligence satellites uncovered evidence of a giant underground industrial center, which U.S. officials believed was intended for secret production of nuclear weapons. At year's end, efforts were still under way to negotiate an independent inspection of the site.

Most of the Rumsfeld report dealt with nations that were attempting to acquire ballistic missiles and weapons of mass destruction for the first time. But the panel also warned that the United States needed to remain vigilant about Russia and China, two nations that already possessed long-range missiles and nuclear warheads. The political future of both those nations was uncertain, the panel said.

The commission also reported on the nuclear weapons and ballistic missile programs of India and Pakistan. Although neither nation was hostile to the United States, the panel said weapons development in both country threatened stability throughout South Asia. India in May conducted its first nuclear tests since 1974, an action that prompted Pakistan to conduct its first nuclear test ever, setting off an international uproar and threatening a nuclear arms race in the region. (India-Pakistan nuclear testing, p. 326)

Administration Response

The administration's chief rebuttal came in a July 15 letter to congressional leaders from George J. Tenet, the director of Central Intelligence. Tenet said the administration took seriously the threat of missile attack and was constantly monitoring developments in countries such as North Korea. As a result of work by the Rumsfeld commission, he said, the intelligence community was "looking at some issues differently" than in the past.

Tenet said the intelligence community stood by its assessments that direct missile threats to the United States from North Korea, Iraq, Iran, and similar countries were still years away. He argued that those countries appeared more interested in developing medium-range ballistic missiles that would threaten their immediate neighbors than in longer-range missiles capable of hitting the United States.

Other officials said that commission members and administration analysts had looked at the same intelligence information but had drawn different conclusions. The commission disputed that contention, arguing that the United States was suffering from "intelligence gaps" that made it impossible for Washington to know exactly what countries such as North Korea and Iran were doing.

Congressional Action

With its pessimistic warnings, the Rumsfeld commission report gave political muscle to Republican arguments on the antimissile defense issue. House Speaker Newt Gingrich, a strong supporter of building an antimissile defense, said the Rumsfeld report had reached "a very sobering conclusion." Gingrich, along with other Republicans, said the report added urgency to their demands that the administration work with Congress toward an early decision on an antimissile system.

The Republicans used the report later in 1998 to secure increased spending on antimissile projects: a total of $4.5 billion during fiscal year 1999. By 1998 the Defense Department had spent more than $50 billion on such programs since the Reagan administration launched its Strategic Defense Initiative (often referred to as "Star Wars").

Republicans failed in 1998 to force the Clinton administration to speed up decision making on deploying a nationwide defense against missiles. Under a 1996 agreement, the administration was working on a limited antimissile defense system and planned to decide in 2000 whether to deploy a system by 2003. That decision was to be based on the world security situation as of 2000. Senate Republicans pushed for legislation repudiating the administration plan and, instead, declaring a U.S. policy of deploying an antimissile defense as soon as it was technologically possible. Democrats twice in 1998 blocked that legislation through filibusters. The Joint Chiefs of Staff had sided with the administration on the matter, sending Congress a letter in April calling a surprise missile attack an "unlikely development."

Following are excerpts from the unclassified executive summary of the report to Congress by the Commission to Assess the Ballistic Missile Threat to the United States, made public July 15, 1998:

II. Executive Summary

A. Conclusions of the Commissioners

The nine Commissioners are unanimous in concluding that:

- Concerted efforts by a number of overtly or potentially hostile nations to acquire ballistic missiles with biological or nuclear payloads pose a growing threat to the United States, its deployed forces and its friends and allies. These newer, developing threats in North Korea, Iran and Iraq are in addition to those still posed by the existing ballistic missile arsenals of Russia and China, nations with which we are not now in conflict but which remain in uncertain transitions. The newer ballistic missile-equipped nations' capabilities will not match those of U.S. systems for accuracy or reliability. However, they would be able to inflict major destruction on the U.S. within about five years of a decision to acquire such a capability (10 years in the case of Iraq). During several of those years, the U.S. might not be aware that such a decision had been made.
- The threat to the U.S. posed by these emerging capabilities is broader, more mature and evolving more rapidly than has been reported in estimates and reports by the Intelligence Community.
- The Intelligence Community's ability to provide timely and accurate estimates of ballistic missile threats to the U.S. is eroding. This erosion has

roots both within and beyond the intelligence process itself. The Community's capabilities in this area need to be strengthened in terms of both resources and methodology.

- The warning times the U.S. can expect of new, threatening ballistic missile deployments are being reduced. Under some plausible scenarios— including re-basing or transfer of operational missiles, sea- and air-launch options, shortened development programs that might include testing in a third country, or some combination of these—the U.S. might well have little or no warning before operational deployment.

Therefore, we unanimously recommend that U.S. analyses, practices and policies that depend on expectations of extended warning of deployment be reviewed and, as appropriate, revised to reflect the reality of an environment in which there may be little or no warning.

B. The Commission and Its Methods

The Commissioners brought to their task the perspectives of former senior policymakers from outside the Intelligence Community, who have decades of experience and a variety of views as users of the Intelligence Community's products. We shared an informed understanding of intelligence processes. In making our assessment, we took into account not only the hard data available, but also the often significant gaps in that data. We had access to both data and experts drawn from the full array of departments and agencies as well as from sources throughout the Intelligence Community. We also drew on experts from outside that Community and on studies sponsored by the Commission. Our aim was to ensure that we were exposed to a wide range of opinion and to the greatest possible depth and breadth of analysis.

We began this study with different views about how to respond to ballistic missile threats, and we continue to have differences. Nevertheless, as a result of our intensive study over the last six months we are unanimous in our assessment of the threat, an assessment which differs from published intelligence estimates.

This divergence between the Commission's findings and authoritative estimates by the Intelligence Community stems primarily from our use of a somewhat more comprehensive methodology in assessing ballistic missile development and deployment programs. We believe that our approach takes more fully into account three crucial factors now shaping new ballistic missile threats to the United States:

- Newer ballistic missile and weapons of mass destruction (WMD) development programs no longer follow the patterns initially set by the U.S. and the Soviet Union. These programs require neither high standards of missile accuracy, reliability and safety nor large numbers of missiles and therefore can move ahead more rapidly.
- A nation that wants to develop ballistic missiles and weapons of mass destruction can now obtain extensive technical assistance from outside sources. Foreign assistance is not a wild card. It is a fact.

Nations are increasingly able to conceal important elements of their ballistic missile and associated WMD programs and are highly motivated to do so.

C. New Threats in a Transformed Security Environment

The Commission did not assess nuclear, biological and chemical weapons programs on a global basis. We considered those countries about which we felt particular reason to be concerned and examined their capabilities to acquire ballistic missiles armed with weapons of mass destruction.

All of the nations whose programs we examined that are developing long range ballistic missiles have the option to arm these, as well as their shorter-range systems, with biological or chemical weapons. These weapons can take the form of bomblets as well as a single, large warhead.

The knowledge needed to design and build a nuclear weapon is now widespread. The emerging ballistic missile powers have access to, or are pursuing the acquisition of, the needed fissile material both through domestic efforts and foreign channels.

As our work went forward, it became increasingly clear to us that nations about which the U.S. has reason to be concerned are exploiting a dramatically transformed international security environment. That environment provides an ever-widening access to technology, information and expertise that can be and is used to speed both the development and deployment of ballistic missiles and weapons of mass destruction. It can also be used to develop denial and deception techniques that seek to impede U.S. intelligence gathering about the development and deployment programs of those nations.

1. Geopolitical Change and Role for Ballistic Missiles

A number of countries with regional ambitions do not welcome the U.S. role as a stabilizing power in their regions and have not accepted it passively. Because of their ambitions, they want to place restraints on the U.S. capability to project power or influence into their regions. They see the acquisition of missile and WMD technology as a way of doing so.

Since the end of the Cold War, the geopolitical environment and the roles of ballistic missiles and weapons of mass destruction have both evolved. Ballistic missiles provide a cost-effective delivery system that can be used for both conventional and non-conventional weapons. For those seeking to thwart the projection of U.S. power, the capability to combine ballistic missiles with weapons of mass destruction provides a strategic counter to U.S. conventional and information-based military superiority. With such weapons, these nations can pose a serious threat to the United States, to its forward-based forces and their staging areas and to U.S. friends and allies.

Whether short or long range, a successfully launched ballistic missile has a high probability of delivering its payload to its target compared to other means of delivery. Emerging powers therefore see ballistic missiles as highly effective deterrent weapons and as an effective means of coercing or intimidating adversaries, including the United States.

2. Russia

With regard to Russia, the principal cloud over the future is lingering political uncertainty. Despite enormous changes since the break-up of the Soviet Union, Russia is in an uncertain, in some ways precarious, transition. It may succeed in establishing a stable democracy allied with the West in maintaining peace and extending freedom. Or it may not. Or it might be torn by internal struggles for an extended period. In its present situation, accurate U.S. intelligence estimates are difficult to make.

Russia continues to pose a ballistic missile threat to the United States, although of a different character than in the past. The number of missiles in its inventory is likely to decline further compared with Cold War levels in that large numbers of Soviet strategic missiles deployed in the 1970s and 1980s are scheduled to be retired. Still, Russian ballistic missile forces continue to be modernized and improved, although the pace of modernization has been slowed from planned schedules by economic constraints. The Russian ballistic missile early warning system and nuclear command and control system have also been affected by aging and delays in planned modernization. In the context of a crisis growing out of civil strife, present early warning and command and control (C2) weaknesses could pose a risk of unauthorized or inadvertent launch of missiles against the United States.

With the Cold War ended, the likelihood of a deliberate missile attack on the U.S. from Russia has been greatly lessened but not entirely eliminated. However, Russia's leaders issued a new national security policy in 1993 that places greater reliance on nuclear deterrence, very likely in response to Russia's economic difficulties and decline in its conventional military capabilities. At the same time, the risk of an accident or of a loss of control over Russian ballistic missile forces—a risk which now appears small—could increase sharply and with little warning if the political situation in Russia were to deteriorate.

Also, quite apart from these risks, Russia poses a threat to the U.S. as a major exporter of enabling technologies, including ballistic missile technologies, to countries hostile to the United States. In particular, Russian assistance has greatly accelerated Iran's ballistic missile program.

3. China

As in the case of Russia, China's future is clouded by a range of uncertainties. China, too, is going through a transition, but one which has been going on for 20 years. The improvement in Sino-U.S. relations, interrupted in 1989, has resumed. Although the U.S. and China are developing a more cooperative relationship, significant potential conflicts remain, and China is less constrained today by fear of Russia than it once was by fear of the Soviet Union. Taiwan is an obvious potential flashpoint. Others could arise as China pursues its drive for greater influence in Asia and the Western Pacific. Even now China has conflicts with several of its neighbors, some of which could involve the U.S. in a confrontation.

China is modernizing its long range missiles and nuclear weapons in ways that will make it a more threatening power in the event of a crisis. China's 1996 missile firings in the Taiwan Strait, aimed at intimidating Taiwan in the lead-up to its presidential election, provoked a sharp confrontation with the United States. For example, during this crisis a pointed question was posed by Lt. Gen. Xiong Guang Kai, a frequent spokesman for Chinese policy, about U.S. willingness to trade Los Angeles for Taipei. This comment seemed designed to link China's ballistic missile capabilities with its regional priorities.

China also poses a threat to the U.S. as a significant proliferator of ballistic missiles, weapons of mass destruction and enabling technologies. It has carried out extensive transfers to Iran's solid-fueled ballistic missile program. It has supplied Pakistan with a design for a nuclear weapon and additional nuclear weapons assistance. It has even transferred complete ballistic missile systems to Saudi Arabia (the 3,100-km-range CSS-2) and Pakistan (the 350-km-range M-11).

The behavior thus far of Russia and China makes it appear unlikely, albeit for different reasons—strategic, political, economic or some combination of all three—that either government will soon effectively reduce its country's sizable transfer of critical technologies, experts or expertise to the emerging missile powers.

4. Countries With Scud-Based Missile Infrastructures

The basis of most missile developments by emerging ballistic missile powers is the Soviet Scud missile and its derivatives. The Scud is derived from the World War II-era German V-2 rocket. With the external help now readily available, a nation with a well-developed, Scud-based ballistic missile infrastructure would be able to achieve first flight of a long range missile, up to and including intercontinental ballistic missile (ICBM) range (greater than 5,500 km), within about five years of deciding to do so. During several of those years the U.S. might not be aware that such a decision had been made. Early production models would probably be limited in number. They would be unlikely to meet U.S. standards of safety, accuracy and reliability. But the purposes of these nations would not require such standards. A larger force armed with scores of missiles and warheads and meeting higher operational standards would take somewhat longer to test, produce and deploy. But meanwhile, even a few of the simpler missiles could be highly effective for the purposes of those countries.

The extraordinary level of resources North Korea and Iran are now devoting to developing their own ballistic missile capabilities poses a substantial and immediate danger to the U.S., its vital interests and its allies. While these nations' missile programs may presently be aimed primarily at regional adversaries, they inevitably and inescapably engage the vital interests of the U.S. as well. Their targeted adversaries include key U.S. friends and allies. U.S. deployed forces are already at risk from these nations' growing arsenals. Each of these nations places a high priority on threatening U.S. territory, and each is even now pursuing advanced ballistic missile capabilities to pose a direct threat to U.S. territory.

North Korea. There is evidence that North Korea is working hard on the Taepo Dong 2 (TD-2) ballistic missile. The status of the system's development cannot be determined precisely. Nevertheless, the ballistic missile test infrastructure in North Korea is well developed. Once the system is assessed to be ready, a test flight could be conducted within six months of a decision to do so. If North Korea judged the test to be a success, the TD-2 could be deployed rapidly. It is unlikely the U.S. would know of such a decision much before the missile was launched. This missile could reach major cities and military bases in Alaska and the smaller, westernmost islands in the Hawaiian chain. Lightweight variations of the TD-2 could fly as far as 10,000 km, placing at risk western U.S. territory in an arc extending northwest from Phoenix, Arizona, to Madison, Wisconsin. These variants of the TD-2 would require additional time to develop and would likely require an additional flight test.

North Korea has developed and deployed the No Dong, a medium range ballistic missile (MRBM) using a scaled-up Scud engine, which is capable of flying 1,300 km. With this missile, North Korea can threaten Japan, South Korea, and US bases in the vicinity of the DPRK. North Korea has reportedly tested the No Dong only once, in 1993. The Commission judges that the No Dong was operationally deployed long before the U.S. Government recognized that fact. There is ample evidence that North Korea has created a sizable missile production infrastructure, and therefore it is highly likely that considerable numbers of No Dongs have been produced.

In light of the considerable difficulties the Intelligence Community encountered in assessing the pace and scope of the No Dong missile program, the U.S. may have very little warning prior to the deployment of the Taepo Dong 2.

North Korea maintains an active WMD program, including a nuclear weapon program. It is known that North Korea diverted material in the late 1980s for at least one or possibly two weapons. North Korea's ongoing nuclear program activity raises the possibility that it could produce additional nuclear weapons. North Korea also possesses biological weapons production and dispensing technology, including the capability to deploy chemical or biological warheads on missiles.

North Korea also poses a major threat to American interests, and potentially to the United States itself, because it is a major proliferator of the ballistic missile capabilities it possesses—missiles, technology, technicians, transporter-erector-launchers (TELs) and underground facility expertise—to other countries of missile proliferation concern. These countries include Iran, Pakistan and others.

Iran. Iran is placing extraordinary emphasis on its ballistic missile and WMD development programs. The ballistic missile infrastructure in Iran is now more sophisticated than that of North Korea, and has benefited from broad, essential, long-term assistance from Russia and important assistance from China as well. Iran is making very rapid progress in developing the Shahab-3 MRBM, which like the North Korean No Dong has a range of 1300 km. This missile may be flight tested at any time and deployed soon thereafter.

We judge that Iran now has the technical capability and resources to demonstrate an ICBM-range ballistic missile, similar to the TD-2 (based on scaled-up Scud technology) within five years of a decision to proceed—whether that decision has already been made or is yet to be made.

In addition to this Scud-based long range ballistic missile program, Iran has acquired and is seeking major, advanced missile components that can be combined to produce ballistic missiles with sufficient range to strike the United States. For example, Iran is reported to have acquired engines or engine designs for the RD-214 engine, which powered the Soviet SS-4 MRBM, and to have an interest in even more advanced engines. A 10,000 km-range Iranian missile could hold the U.S. at risk in an arc extending northeast of a line from Philadelphia, Pennsylvania, to St. Paul, Minnesota.

Iran has also developed a solid-fueled rocket infrastructure and produces short range rockets, and also is seeking long range missile technology from outside sources, purportedly for a space launch vehicle. Both contribute directly to Iran's ballistic missile technology base. Iran is known to rely heavily on imports of missile technology from foreign sources, particularly Russia and North Korea. These imports have allowed Iran's missile programs to proceed swiftly, and they can be incorporated into Iran's domestic infrastructure as well.

Iran is developing weapons of mass destruction. It has a nuclear energy and weapons program, which aims to design, develop, and as soon as possible produce nuclear weapons. The Commission judges that the only issue as to whether or not Iran may soon have or already has a nuclear weapon is the amount of fissile material available to it. Because of significant gaps in our knowledge, the U.S. is unlikely to know whether Iran possesses nuclear weapons until after the fact. While Iran's civil nuclear program is currently under International Atomic Energy Agency (IAEA) safeguards, it could be used as a source of sufficient fissile material to construct a small number of weapons within the next ten years if Iran were willing to violate safeguards. If Iran were to accumulate enough fissile material from foreign sources, it might be able to develop a nuclear weapon in only one to three years. Iran also has an active chemical weapon development and production program, and is conducting research into biological weapons.

Iraq. Iraq has maintained the skills and industrial capabilities needed to reconstitute its long range ballistic missile program. Its plant and equipment are less developed than those of North Korea or Iran as a result of actions forced by UN Resolutions and monitoring. However, Iraq has actively continued work on the short range (under 150 km) liquid- and solid-fueled missile programs that are allowed by the Resolutions. Once UN-imposed controls are lifted, Iraq could mount a determined effort to acquire needed plant and equipment, whether directly or indirectly. Such an effort would allow Iraq to pose an ICBM threat to the United States within 10 years. Iraq could develop a shorter range, covert, ship-launched missile threat that could threaten the United States in a very short time.

Iraq had a large, intense ballistic missile development and production program prior to the Gulf War. The Iraqis produced Scuds, and then modified Scud missiles to produce the 600 km range Al Hussein and 900 km range Al Abbas missiles. The expertise, as well as some of the equipment and materials from this program remain in Iraq and provide a strong foundation for a revived ballistic missile program.

Prior to the invasion of Kuwait in 1990, Iraq could have had nuclear weapons in the 1993–1995 time frame, although it still had technical hurdles to overcome. After the invasion of Kuwait, Iraq began a crash program to produce a nuclear device in six to nine months based on highly enriched uranium removed from the safeguarded reactor at Tuwaitha. Iraq has the capability to reconstitute its nuclear weapon program; the speed at which it can do so depends on the availability of fissile material. It would take several years to build the required production facilities from scratch. It is possible that Iraq has hidden some material from U.N. Special Commission (UNSCOM) inspection, or that it could acquire fissile material abroad (e.g., from another "rogue" state.) Iraq also had large chemical and biological weapons programs prior to the war, and produced chemical and biological warheads for its missiles. Knowledge, personnel, and equipment related to WMD remain in Iraq, so that it could reconstitute these programs rapidly following the end of sanctions.

India. India is developing a number of ballistic missiles from short range to those with ICBM-class capabilities, along with a submarine-launched ballistic missile (SLBM) and a short range, surface ship-launched system. India has the infrastructure to develop and produce these missiles. It is aggressively seeking technology from other states, particularly Russia. While it develops its long range ballistic missiles, India's space-launch vehicles provide an option for an interim ICBM capability. India has detonated several nuclear devices and it is clear that it is developing warheads for its missile systems. India has biological and chemical weapons programs. Since the Pakistani nuclear tests, India has announced its intention to increase its spending on missiles and nuclear weapons.

India's program to develop ballistic missiles began in 1983 and grew out of its space-launch program, which was based on Scout rocket technology acquired from the United States. India currently has developed and deployed the Prithvi short range ballistic missile (SRBM), and is developing longer range, liquid- and solid-fueled missiles. They include the Prithvi II SRBM, the Agni, Agni-Plus and Agni-B IRBMs, a sea-launched ballistic missile and an SLBM, the Sagarika.

India detonated a nuclear device in 1974, conducted a test series in May 1998, and it is clear that it is developing warheads for its missile systems. Indian leaders recently declared that India has developed nuclear weapons for deployment on the Prithvi SRBM and the Agni Plus MRBM.

India has acquired and continues to seek Russian, U.S., and Western European technology for its missile programs. Technology and expertise acquired from other states, particularly from Russia, are helping India to accelerate the development and increase the sophistication of its missile systems. For example, Russian assistance is critical to the development of the Indian SLBM and its related submarine. But India is rapidly enhancing its own missile science and technology base as well. Many Indian nationals are educated and work in the U.S., Europe, and other advanced nations; some of the knowledge thereby acquired returns to the Indian missile program. While India continues to benefit from foreign technology and expertise, its programs and industrial base are now sufficiently advanced that supplier control regimes can affect only the rate of acceleration in India's programs. India is in a position to supply material and technical assistance to others.

Pakistan. Pakistan's ballistic missile infrastructure is now more advanced than that of North Korea. It will support development of a missile of 2,500-km range, which we believe Pakistan will seek in order to put all of India within range of Pakistani missiles. The development of a 2,500-km missile will give Pakistan the technical base for developing a much longer range missile system. Through foreign acquisition, and beginning without an extensive domestic science and technology base, Pakistan has acquired these missile capabilities quite rapidly. China and North Korea are Pakistan's major sources of ballistic missiles, production facilities and technology.

Pakistan currently possesses nuclear-capable M-11 SRBMs acquired from China, and it may produce its own missile, the Tarmuk, based on the M-11. In 1998, Pakistan tested the 1300 km Ghauri MRBM, a version of the North Korean No Dong, and we believe Pakistan has acquired production facilities for this missile as well.

Pakistan possesses nuclear weapons that employ highly-enriched uranium and in May 1998 conducted its first nuclear weapon test series. A new Pakistani nuclear reactor has been completed that could be used for the production of plutonium. In addition to its nuclear weapons, Pakistan has biological and chemical weapons programs. Chinese assistance has been crucial to Pakistan's nuclear weapons program.

India and Pakistan are not hostile to the United States. The prospect of U.S. military confrontation with either seems at present to be slight. However, beyond the possibility of nuclear war on the subcontinent, their aggressive, competitive development of ballistic missiles and weapons of mass destruction poses three concerns in particular. First, it enables them to supply relevant technologies to other nations. Second, India and Pakistan may seek additional technical assistance through cooperation with their current major suppliers—India from North Korea, Iran and Russia; Pakistan from North Korea and China—because of the threats they perceive from one another and because of India's anxieties about China, combined with their mounting international isolation. Third, their growing missile and WMD capabilities have direct effects on U.S. policies, both regional and global, and could significantly affect U.S. capability to play a stabilizing role in Asia.

D. A New Non-Proliferation Environment

Since the end of the Cold War a number of developments have made ballistic missile and WMD technologies increasingly available. They include:

- A number of nations have chosen not to join non-proliferation agreements.
- Some participants in those agreements have cheated.
- As global trade has steadily expanded, access has increased to the information, technology and technicians needed for missile and WMD development.
- Access to technologies used in early generations of U.S. and Soviet missiles has eased. However rudimentary compared to present U.S. standards, these technologies serve the needs of emerging ballistic missile powers.
- Among those countries of concern to the U.S., commerce in ballistic missile and WMD technology and hardware has been growing, which may make proliferation self-sustaining among them and facilitate their ability to proliferate technology and hardware to others.

Some countries which could have readily acquired nuclear weapons and ballistic missiles—such as Germany, Japan and South Korea—have been successfully encouraged not to do so by U.S. security guarantees and by non-proliferation agreements. Even though they lack such security guarantees, other countries have also joined non-proliferation agreements and abandoned development programs and weapons systems. Some examples are Argentina, Brazil, South Africa and the former Soviet republics of Belarus, Kazakhstan and Ukraine.

1. Increased Competence of and Trade Among Emerging Ballistic Missile Powers

Conversely, there are other countries—some of which are themselves parties to various non-proliferation agreements and treaties—that either have acquired ballistic missile or WMD capabilities or are working hard to do so. North Korea, Iran and Iraq, as well as India and Pakistan, are at the forefront of this group. They now have increased incentives to cooperate with one another. They have extensive access to technology, information and expertise from developed countries such as Russia and China. They also have access through commercial and other channels in the West, including the United States. Through this trade and their own indigenous efforts, these second-tier powers are on the verge of being able to provide to one another, if they have not already done so, the capabilities needed to develop long range ballistic missiles.

2. U.S. as a Contributor to Proliferation

The U.S. is the world's leading developer and user of advanced technology. Once it is transferred by the U.S. or by another developed country, there is no way to ensure that the transferred technology will not be used for hostile purposes. The U.S. tries to limit technology transfers to hostile powers, but history teaches that such transfers cannot be stopped for long periods. They can only be slowed and made more costly, and even that requires the cooperation of other developed nations. The acquisition and use of transferred technologies in ballistic missile and WMD programs has been facilitated by foreign student training in the U.S., by wide dissemination of technical information, by the illegal acquisition of U.S. designs and equipment and by the relaxation of U.S. export control policies. As a result, the U.S. has been and is today a major, albeit unintentional, contributor to the proliferation of ballistic missiles and associated weapons of mass destruction.

3. Motives of Countries of Concern

Recent ballistic missile and nuclear tests in South Asia should not be viewed as merely a sharp but temporary setback in the expanding reach of nonproliferation regimes. While policymakers may try to reverse or at least contain the trends of which these tests are a part, the missile and WMD programs of these nations are clearly the results of fundamental political calculations of their vital interests. Those nations willing and able to supply dangerous technologies and systems to one another, including Russia, China and their quasi-governmental commercial entities, may be motivated by commercial, foreign policy or national security interests or by a combination thereof. As noted above, such countries are increasingly cooperating with one another, perhaps in some instances because they have reciprocal needs for what one has and the other lacks. The transfer of complete missile systems, such as China's transfer to Saudi Arabia, will continue to be available. Short of radical political change, there is every reason to assume that the nations engaged in these missile and WMD development activities will continue their programs as matters of high priority.

4. Readier Market Access to Technology

In today's increasingly market-driven, global economy, nations so motivated have faster, cheaper and more efficient access to modern technology. Commercial exchanges and technology transfers have multiplied the pathways to those technologies needed for ballistic missiles and weapons of mass destruction. These pathways reduce development times and costs, lowering both technical and budget obstacles to missile development and deployment.

Expanding world trade and the explosion in information technology have accelerated the global diffusion of scientific, technical and industrial information. The channels, both public and private, legal and illegal, through which technology, components and individual technicians can be moved among nations have increased exponentially.

5. Availability of Classified Information and Export-Controlled Technology

Those trends in the commercial sector have been accompanied, and in many ways accelerated, by an increased availability of classified information as a result of:

- Lax enforcement of export controls.
- Relaxation of U.S. and Western export controls.

- Growth in dual-use technologies.
- Economic incentives to sell ballistic missile components and systems.
- Extensive declassification of materials related to ballistic missiles and weapons of mass destruction.
- Continued, intense espionage facilitated by security measures increasingly inadequate for the new environment.

Extensive disclosure of classified information, including information compromising intelligence sources and methods. Damaging information appears almost daily in the national and international media and on the Internet.

E. Alternative Ballistic Missile Launch Modes

In evaluating present threats, it is misleading to use old patterns of development as guides. The history of U.S. and Soviet missile and WMD development has become irrelevant. Approaches that the U.S. considered and specifically rejected on grounds of safety, reliability, accuracy and requirements for high volume production are in many cases well suited to nations less concerned about safety and able to meet their needs with only a few, less accurate, less reliable weapons. Analytical approaches the Intelligence Community could realistically rely on in the past need to be restudied and reevaluated in light of this newer model.

The Commission believes the U.S. needs to pay attention to the possibility that complete, long range ballistic missile systems could be transferred from one nation to another, just as China transferred operational CSS-2s to Saudi Arabia in 1988. Such missiles could be equipped with weapons of mass destruction.

One nation's use of another nation's territory also needs to be considered. The U.S. did this during the Cold War, and the Soviet Union tried to do it in Cuba in the early 1960s. For example, if Iran were to deploy ballistic missiles in Libya, it could reduce the range required to threaten the U.S. as well as Europe. Given the existing patterns of cooperation we have already seen, both testing by one country on the territory of another and deriving data from other-country tests are also distinct possibilities.

Sea launch of shorter range ballistic missiles is another possibility. This could enable a country to pose a direct territorial threat to the U.S. sooner than it could by waiting to develop an ICBM for launch from its own territory. Sea-launching could also permit it to target a larger area of the U.S. than would a missile fired from its home territory. India is working on a sea launch capability. Air launch is another possible mode of delivering a shorter range missile to U.S. territory.

The key importance of these approaches is that each would significantly shorten the warning time of deployment available to the United States.

F. Erosion of Warning

Precise forecasts of the growth in ballistic missile capabilities over the next two decades—tests by year, production rates, weapons deployed by year, weapon characteristics by system type and circular error probable

(CEP)—cannot be provided with confidence. Deception and denial efforts are intense and often successful, and U.S. collection and analysis assets are limited. Together they create a high risk of continued surprise.

The question is not simply whether we will have warning of an emerging capability, but whether the nature and magnitude of a particular threat will be perceived with sufficient clarity in time to take appropriate action.

Concealment, denial and deception efforts by key target countries are intended to delay the discovery of strategically significant activities until well after they had been carried out successfully. The fact that some of these secret activities are discovered over time is to the credit of the U.S. Intelligence Community. However, the fact that there are delays in discovery of those activities provides a sharp warning that a great deal of activity goes undetected.

Both technical and human intelligence are inherently more difficult to collect in those countries where the United States has limited access, which includes most of the ballistic missile countries of concern. The U.S. is not able to predict and anticipate with confidence the behavior and actions of emerging ballistic missile powers and their related political decision-making.

Their ballistic missile programs often do not follow a single, known pattern or model, and they use unexpected development patterns. These are not models of development the U.S. follows or that intelligence analysts expect to see. For example, Pakistan's test launch in April 1998 of its Ghauri medium range ballistic missile (MRBM)—its version of the North Korean No Dong—could not be predicted on the basis of any known pattern of technical development either for MRBMs generally or Pakistan in particular. Similarly, North Korea's decision to deploy the No Dong after what is believed to be a single successful test flight is another example. Based on U.S. and Russian experience, the Intelligence Community had expected that a regular test series would be required to provide the confidence needed before any country would produce and deploy a ballistic missile system. Yet North Korea deployed the No Dong.

The Commission believes that the technical means of collection now employed will not meet emerging requirements, and considerable uncertainty persists whether planned collection and analysis systems will do so.

G. Methodology

In analyzing the ballistic missile threat, the Commission used an expanded methodology. We used it as a complement to the traditional analysis in which a country's known program status is used to establish estimates of its current missile capabilities. We believe this expanded approach provides insights into emerging threats that the prevailing approaches used by the Intelligence Community may not bring to the surface.

To guide our assessment of the ballistic missile threat to the United States we posed three questions:

- What is known about the ballistic missile threat, including the domestic infrastructure of a ballistic missile power; the efforts of a power to acquire foreign technology, materials and expertise; and the scale, pace and progress of its programs?

- What is not known about the threat in each of those three categories?
- Can a power intent on posing a ballistic missile threat to any part of the United States, including the use of but not limited to ICBM-range missiles, use the open market, the black market and/or espionage to secure the needed technology and expertise and then carry out its program in ways that will minimize the interval between the time the U.S. becomes aware of the threat and the fielding of that capability?

In seeking answers to these questions, the Commission familiarized itself with the current state of knowledge as well as the depth of analytic capability within the Intelligence Community related to ballistic missile and WMD threats. The Commission used its broad access to individuals, special compartmented intelligence and special access programs. It consulted with experts in the broader government and private analytic and policy communities. It reviewed the strengths, weaknesses and vulnerabilities of current and planned human and technical collection efforts and capabilities, especially in light of the increasingly sophisticated means and methods available to target countries to hide from U.S. intelligence collection. It reviewed with scientists, engineers and program managers from the public and private sectors the technical issues associated with the design, development and testing of ballistic missiles and the means and methods available to the emerging ballistic missile powers to meet the challenges associated with long range ballistic missile development and testing.

The Commission analyzed the available information in order to develop an understanding of the threat from three perspectives:

- We examined the known size and quality of the deployed forces, the doctrine and the command and control systems that govern the forces and the availability of weapons of mass destruction to arm the forces. We reviewed the infrastructure supporting the programs and the extent of past and present foreign assistance available to those programs from Russia, China and other countries, including the West.
- We examined the ways in which the programs of emerging ballistic missile powers compared with one another. For example, we traced the development histories of the related programs of North Korea, Iran, Iraq and Pakistan and the relationships among them. This comparison helped in identifying the similarities between programs, the extent to which each had aided one another in overcoming critical development hurdles and, importantly, the pace at which a determined country can progress in its program development.
- We reviewed the resources ("inputs") available and the ways in which they provide indicators of the prospects for successful missile development.

By integrating these perspectives, we were able to partially bridge a significant number of intelligence gaps. Emphasizing inputs makes two important contributions to the analysis. Inputs include domestic opportunity costs, the foreign technology and expertise sought and obtained, the urgency with which facilities are constructed both above and below ground and the willingness to absorb cost and time penalties in order to hide activities from detection by U.S. intelligence. Attention to inputs across all elements of a program helps develop an understanding of the scale and scope of a program before traditional output indicators, such as testing and production rates, can be observed and evaluated. When combined with observed outputs and the application of engineering judgments, the understanding of the scale and scope of a program that this provided helped us to measure the probable pace and magnitude of a program and its potential products. We were then able to make what we believe to be reasonably confident estimates of what the various programs can achieve.

Rather than measuring how far a program had progressed from a known starting point, the Commission sought to measure how close a program might be to demonstrating the first flight of a long range ballistic missile. This approach requires that analysts extrapolate a program's scope, scale, pace and direction beyond what the hard evidence at hand unequivocally supports. It is in sharp contrast to a narrow focus on the certain that obscures the almost-certain. The approach helps reduce the effects of denial and deception efforts. When strategically significant programs were assessed by narrowly focusing on what is known, the assessments lagged the actual state of the programs by two to eight years and in some cases completely missed significant programs.

We chose to focus on what is left to be accomplished in the programs of potentially threatening ballistic missile powers and alternative paths they can follow to attain their goals. We reviewed program histories and current activities, including foreign assistance, to determine whether a ballistic missile program acquired the means to overcome its identified problems. We considered the multiple pathways available for completing its development given the combination of expertise and technology available to it and the circumstances in which it is operating. This approach accepts as a basic premise that a power determined to possess a long range missile, knowing that the U.S. is trying to track its every action but aware of American intelligence methods and sources, will do its best to deny information and to deceive the U.S. about its actual progress.

Because of these options available to emerging ballistic missile powers, the Commission, unanimously recognizing that missile development and deployment now follows new models, strongly urges the use of an expanded approach to intelligence that assesses both inputs and outputs in other countries' ballistic missile programs. We believe this approach is needed in order to capture both sooner and more accurately the speed and magnitude of potential ballistic missile proliferation in the post-Cold War world and to assess, in time, the various threats this proliferation poses to the United States.

The Commission's key judgments are derived from applying this methodology and examining the evidence in light of the individual and collective experience of the nine Commissioners.

H. Summary

Ballistic missiles armed with WMD payloads pose a strategic threat to the United States. This is not a distant threat. Characterizing foreign assistance as a wild card is both incorrect and misleading. Foreign assistance is pervasive, enabling and often the preferred path to ballistic missile and WMD capability.

A new strategic environment now gives emerging ballistic missile powers the capacity, through a combination of domestic development and foreign assistance, to acquire the means to strike the U.S. within about five years of a decision to acquire such a capability (10 years in the case of Iraq). During several of those years, the U.S. might not be aware that such a decision had been made. Available alternative means of delivery can shorten the warning time of deployment nearly to zero.

The threat is exacerbated by the ability of both existing and emerging ballistic missile powers to hide their activities from the U.S. and to deceive the U.S. about the pace, scope and direction of their development and proliferation programs. Therefore, we unanimously recommend that U.S. analyses, practices and policies that depend on expectations of extended warning of deployment be reviewed and, as appropriate, revised to reflect the reality of an environment in which there may be little or no warning. . . .

BUDGET OFFICE ON THE BUDGET SURPLUS
July 15, 1998

A generation-long era of federal budget deficits came to an end in 1998, when the government showed a budget surplus of $70 billion for the fiscal year ending September 30. It was the first surplus since 1969; when measured against the overall economy the surplus was the biggest since 1956. Three decades of red ink had ballooned the federal debt by $3.5 trillion; as of 1998 the debt stood at $5.4 trillion.

The end of deficits—at least for the time being—did not end partisan bickering in Washington over how to spend tax dollars. Congressional action on a budget for fiscal 1999 was as messy as anyone could remember, signaling the prospect that the politics of budget surpluses could be just as unpleasant as the politics of budget deficits.

In celebrating a new era of black ink, many Washington politicians chose to ignore two important factors that were largely responsible for the surpluses for fiscal 1998 and those projected for several succeeding years. First, a booming economy was generating higher tax revenues than had been anticipated. A sharp economic downturn could rapidly transform surpluses into deficits. Second, surpluses in the Social Security trust fund and Postal Service operations masked an actual deficit in the government's operating accounts. Technically, Social Security and the Postal Service were "off-budget" and should not be counted in the total budget picture. Excluding a combined $99 billion surplus in those two accounts, the government's operating budget for fiscal 1998 ran a deficit of $29 billion, according to the Congressional Budget Office (CBO).

Years of Deficits

Until 1998, the federal government's books had dripped red ink for nearly three decades. The last budget surplus was $3.2 billion for fiscal year 1969, made possible by a temporary 10 percent income tax surcharge used by President Lyndon Johnson to help pay for the Vietnam War, which raged during the 1960s. Deficits were small during the administrations of Richard Nixon and his successor Gerald Ford but grew starting in fiscal 1975 with the oil price shocks caused by an Arab oil embargo and the nation's worst economic downturn since the Great Depression. Through the presidency of Jimmy Carter, as inflation was the number one economic challenge, deficits averaged around $50 billion annually. That was a large amount of money, to be sure, but still manageable when compared to the overall economy.

It was during the presidency of Ronald Reagan that the government became expert in the art of big-time deficit spending. Reagan in 1981 prodded Congress to enact the biggest tax cut in U.S. history, arguing that the move would stimulate the economy. At the same time, spending shot up because of the president's massive increases in defense spending and the inability of the White House and Capitol Hill to agree on how to keep other federal spending in check. The annual deficit crept over $100 billion in 1982, and then over $200 billion in fiscal 1983, before leveling off at around $150 billion during the economic expansion in the remaining Reagan years. A recession in the middle of the Bush presidency pushed the deficit to previously unimagined heights: a record $292 billion in fiscal 1992. Projections at the time put future deficits at $400 billion or more unless dramatic action was taken to cut spending or boost tax revenues.

President Bill Clinton had the good fortune of taking office just as the recession was ending and the economy was beginning the longest uninterrupted period of growth in U.S. history. The booming economy generated tax revenues to slash the deficit on a steady curve, even while Clinton and Congress struggled to restrain spending. Congress in 1993 enacted a $500 billion deficit-reduction plan of budget cuts and tax increases developed by Clinton and the Democrats, who then had the majority on Capitol Hill; not a single Republican voted for it. Clinton later claimed this package helped stimulate the economic boom of the 1990s. (1993 budget plan, Historic Documents of 1993, p. 181)

A watershed on the budget front occurred in late 1995, when House Republican leaders—eager to exercise their power as the new majority party on Capitol Hill—forced three temporary shutdowns of much of the federal government in an ill-fated attempt to pressure Clinton on budget issues. Public reaction against the Republicans helped guarantee Clinton's reelection in 1996 and reminded the Republicans that compromise often produced better results than confrontation. As a result, Washington's annual budget debates in 1996 and 1997 were among the least contentious in years. In 1997 Clinton and the Republicans reached a series of agreements calling for a balanced budget by fiscal 2002. The agreements established rigid budget "caps" that would limit the room for future Congresses to increase spending on most programs. (1995 budget impasse, Historic Documents of 1995, p. 737; 1996 budget issues, Historic Documents of 1996, p. 147; 1997 budget issues, Historic Documents of 1997, p. 602)

A Looming Surplus

At the beginning of 1998, government budget analysts estimated that the deficit for fiscal 1998, ending September 30, would be somewhere between $2 billion and $10 billion. Private analysts were more optimistic, estimating a surplus of between $20 billion and $40 billion. In his State of the Union speech and follow-up budget, Clinton laid down a marker for how prospective surpluses should be handled: "Save Social Security first," he said. Clinton's budget proposal for fiscal 1999 was the first balanced budget sent to Congress since 1971, when President Nixon delivered overly optimistic spending and revenue projections. (Clinton State of the Union speech, p. 38)

As spring approached, and as the economy continued to roar ahead, government analysts adopted the more optimistic posture of their private counterparts, though with caution. In fact, Republicans in April criticized the CBO for excessive caution in suggesting that the surplus would range from $8 billion to $18 billion. By May, Clinton and Republicans already were sparring over what to do with a surplus that the White House was then estimating at $39 billion. Clinton stood by his demand that any surpluses be set aside to bolster Social Security, while Republicans bickered among themselves over such options as returning the surplus to the taxpayers as a tax cut or using it to pay down the national debt.

On July 15 the CBO presented a new forecast putting the fiscal year 1998 surplus at $63 billion. The CBO projected that the surplus would rise to $80 billion in fiscal 1999 and to $251 billion by fiscal 2008—assuming no major change in government spending and tax policies and no serious economic downturn. Taking away the cushion of surpluses in the Social Security trust fund, CBO said the true budget figure for fiscal 1998 would be a $41 billion deficit, giving way to surpluses starting in fiscal 2002.

On September 30, the last day of the fiscal year, Clinton hosted a celebration at the White House to announce a surplus for fiscal 1998 projected at nearly $70 billion. Clinton said his 1993 balanced-budget plan deserved much of the credit for the surplus because it helped stimulate the economy. Administration aides gleefully resurrected statements from Republicans in 1993 predicting that the president's budget plan would doom the economy.

For their part, Republicans insisted they deserved much of the credit for the surplus because the economy continued to grow after their takeover of Congress. Many observers outside the confines of Washington gave more credit to the anti-inflation, pro-growth policies of the Federal Reserve Board under the chairmanship of Alan Greenspan.

Final figures for fiscal 1998, released October 29, showed the overall surplus reached $70 billion. When surpluses in the Social Security trust fund and Postal Service operations were stripped away, however, the fiscal year actually ended with a $29 billion deficit.

Another Budget Fiasco

Any thoughts that an era of surpluses would produce budget harmony in Washington were dashed by the year's deliberations. For starters, Congress was unable, for the first time since the modern congressional process was established in 1974, to adopt a budget resolution for the forthcoming fiscal year (1999). Budget resolutions were intended to set overall guidelines for individual committees to respect when writing their spending legislation. But the two chambers—both under Republican control—passed resolutions that were so divergent that no serious attempt was made to reconcile them. The main issues were cutting taxes and figuring out how to pay for it; the House Republican leadership wanted much deeper tax cuts than most Senate Republicans could accept.

In the meantime, Congress neglected action on its meat-and-potatoes legislation: the thirteen appropriations bills that actually allocated spending for fiscal 1999. At the October 1 start of the new fiscal year, only five of the bills had been enacted into law. Rushing to get out of town so they could hit the campaign trail, legislators in October dumped the remaining eight bills into a giant "omnibus" measure totaling about $500 billion. Details of this bill were negotiated in a week-long series of private meetings in mid-October between a handful of senior Republican leaders and White House aides. Rank-and-file members of Congress had little influence on the deliberations.

Despite Clinton's perceived political weakness because of the pending impeachment inquiry involving his affair with former White House intern Monica Lewinsky, the White House got its way on most major points of contention. Clinton ultimately won even more money for discretionary spending programs, such as education, than he had requested in his original budget in February. The Republicans also dropped their plans for a major tax cut and for numerous social policy measures on abortion and other issues popular with conservatives. The bill included $21 billion in supplemental spending for items such as increased defense spending, U.S. contributions to the UN peacekeeping mission in Bosnia, fixing government computers so they could recognize the year 2000, and providing relief for distressed farmers. That $21 billion package was financed out of the projected fiscal surplus, despite Clinton's pledge to save that money for Social Security. Negotiators managed to avoid the spending caps from the 1997 budget agreements by declaring this extra $21 billion as "emergency" funding.

The massive budget package angered many on Capitol Hill, especially conservative Republicans who believed their leaders had sold out their principles on such issues as taxes. Others bemoaned the fact that they had only a vague idea of what was in the forty-pound measure of nearly 4,000 pages. Even supporters of the bill admitted that the process by which it had been written messy, or, as House Appropriations Chairman Bob Livingston bluntly said, "Ugly." But in the larger political scene, anger with the details of the bill had to take a back seat to Clinton's amazing performance in thwarting congressional leaders who were contemplating his impeachment.

> *Following are excerpts from a report to Congress, "The Economic and Budget Outlook For Fiscal Years 1999–2008: A Preliminary Update," released by the Congressional Budget Office July 15, 1998:*

The Congressional Budget Office (CBO) projects that the federal budget for fiscal year 1998 will record a total surplus of $63 billion, or 0.8 percent of gross domestic product (GDP). If current policies remain unchanged, the surplus is expected to rise to $80 billion in 1999 and reach no billion (nearly 2 percent of GDP) by 2008. Excluding the surplus in Social Security and the net outlays of the Postal Service (both of which are legally classified as off budget), CBO's new projections show an on-budget deficit of $41 billion in 1998, which gives way to surpluses in 2002 and in 2005 through 2008.

The budget outlook has improved significantly in the past six months. Unexpectedly strong revenue collections by the Treasury in the first nine months of fiscal year 1998 are the major reason that CBO has gone from projecting a small deficit last January to estimating a surplus of $63 billion today. The strength of 1998 revenues, together with a slightly more optimistic economic outlook, also forms the basis for increases in CBO's projections of the surplus for 1999 through 2008.

Determining the degree to which this year's unanticipated revenues should carry over into projections of future revenues is difficult at this time because the reasons for the increase are still largely unknown. In January, CBO projected that 1998 revenues would total $1,665 billion. By March, revenue collections to date suggested that the total would reach $1,680 billion. Based on collections through June, CBO believes that 1998 revenues will total $1,717 billion. New economic data explain less than $7 billion of the increase in the projection since January, while new legislation is responsible for $1 billion. That leaves $45 billion, almost all in revenues from individual income taxes, to be explained by other factors.

At this point, analysts can only speculate about the sources of income that produced the added revenues in 1998 and their implications for revenue growth in future years. Certain explanations of the sources of the additional income would suggest that projections of revenues should be adjusted by growing amounts over time. But others point to temporary factors and would suggest an adjustment that fades away over several years. After assessing the possible causes, CBO has chosen a middle path: it has assumed that the factors producing the additional revenues in 1998 will continue to add a similar amount to revenues in future years.

Changes in the economic outlook also boost surpluses projected over the next decade. A smaller expected decline in corporate profits as a share of

GDP increases projected revenues, and slightly lower real long-term interest rates after 2000 reduce interest payments on the national debt. A reduction in the projected rate of inflation—which holds down required cost-of-living increases, the growth of Medicare costs, nominal interest rates, and assumed increases in discretionary spending after 2002—significantly lowers projected outlays in the longer term. But lower inflation does not have a major impact on the surplus because it also slows the growth of taxable incomes, leading to a reduction in projected tax revenues that offsets the reduction in outlays.

CBO now expects lower outlays in 1998 than it projected in March, but that decrease largely reflects temporary factors that are not expected to reduce spending in the future. Legislation enacted since March has lowered projected surpluses by a few billion dollars a year—primarily reflecting higher spending for transportation programs.

The Economic Outlook

The economy has continued to grow at a healthy pace, with low unemployment and subdued inflation. CBO projects that growth will slow over the next few years and that the unemployment and inflation rates will gradually rise. . . . The current outlook is not dramatically different from CBO's last economic projections, made in January, but small increases in real growth, somewhat lower inflation, profits that account for a larger share of GDP, and lower real long-term interest rates significantly affect the budget's projected bottom line. exclude capital gains on inventories.

The Forecast for 1998 and 1999

The growth of real GDP is likely to slow to 2 percent for the rest of calendar year 1998 and early 1999, down from the 4 percent pace set during 1997 and the first quarter of 1998. Factors contributing to the slowdown include a continuation of the recent increase in the real trade deficit, a pickup in inflation, and weaker profits.

Demand for U.S.-produced goods and services has been dampened by events overseas. The economic contraction in Asia stemming from that region's currency crisis was the major reason for the slowdown in demand, but an already strong dollar and the slowly growing demand in Europe also contributed to stagnating real exports and accelerating import growth. The outlook is for continued strength of the dollar and weak demand growth overseas, which make it likely that foreign trade will continue to depress demand for U.S. goods into 1999.

The underlying rate of inflation—the increase in the consumer price index (CPI) excluding energy and food prices—is forecast to rise slightly over the next year and a half because of strong upward pressure on wages and a partial dissipation of the factors that have been dampening price growth for several years. Growth of the overall CPI on a year-over-year basis was 1.7 percent in June, but that measure is distorted by the sharp drop in petroleum prices this year. The underlying rate of inflation was 2.2 percent through

June. CBO's forecast assumes that the underlying rate will increase slowly to 2.7 percent by the end of 1999. Because energy prices are expected to remain steady, the forecast growth rate for the overall CPI is similar.

Some factors that have held down CPI growth over the past two or three years will continue to have an effect. For example, import prices are expected to continue declining in 1998 (in part because of the Asian crisis), and the Bureau of Labor Statistics will institute more changes to the CPI that will reduce its growth by about 0.2 percentage points in 1999 and later years. However, import price deflation is expected to fade during 1999. In addition, medical care inflation, which grew relatively slowly and dampened overall inflation in the past two years, is forecast to bounce back from its 1997 low of 2.6 percent to more than 4 percent a year during the next 18 months.

Corporate profits, which have stagnated since the third quarter of last year, will remain under pressure through 1999. Rising wages and an expected increase in the growth of employee benefits will push the growth of total compensation higher at the same time that sales growth slows. Thus, costs per unit of output will rise more rapidly over the next year and a half than in 1997. Some of those costs will be passed on in the form of higher prices, but some will be absorbed through lower profits.

The anticipated rise in inflation may lead to higher interest rates, but any increase is likely to be mild and temporary. If the Federal Reserve Board is uncertain about the pervasiveness of the slowdown in economic activity, an increase in inflation may prompt it to raise short-term rates by the end of the year. Long-term rates may also pick up slightly. However, if economic growth slows to a 2 percent rate for 1999, short-term interest rates will probably ease back to their current levels by the end of that year.

The Projection for 2000 Through 2008

CBO does not forecast cyclical economic effects beyond two years. Instead, it calculates a range of estimates for the medium-term path of the economy that reflect the possibility of booms and recessions. CBO then presents the middle of that range as its baseline projection of the economy for 2000 through 2008. Over that period, CBO expects real GDP to grow at an average rate of 2.2 percent a year, the CPI to increase at an average rate of 2.5 percent, and short-term interest rates to average 4.5 percent.

The small variations in real GDP growth and other variables during that period . . . do not stem from any assumptions about cyclical effects in those years. The slight drop in the projected growth rate of real GDP between 2002 and 2008 reflects a demographic assumption that growth of the labor force will slow in line with slower growth of the working-age population and an assumption that growth of investment will return to a lower, long-term trend. In order to achieve the projected average values assumed over the 2000-2008 period without having a misleadingly sudden drop at the end of 1999, CBO phases in reductions in inflation, interest rates, and profits as a share of GDP over the first few years of the projection period. . . .

Uncertainty of the Outlook

One source of errors in predicting the future performance of the economy is data on its recent performance. Reported data on GDP and the components of national income are regularly revised, sometimes by quite large amounts. Because forecasts necessarily depend on the economic data that are currently available, the likelihood of revisions to those data increases the uncertainty of any forecast.

In addition, there is a risk that future events will cause a significant divergence from the path laid out in the new forecast. The economy could be more adversely affected by the Asian crisis than CBO assumes; the tightness of the labor market could cause a significant jump in the rate of inflation (such as the increase of 3 percentage points that occurred in the 1960s); or the stock market could drop precipitously. Conversely, the Asian crisis could have little additional effect on the United States; productivity growth might remain higher than CBO anticipates, which would permit a continuation of rapid noninflationary growth and stronger profits; or labor force participation rates might again increase rapidly, easing pressures on the labor market for a few years. Such alternative outcomes could have a substantial effect on the budget, increasing or decreasing its bottom line by $100 billion or more in a single year.

The Budget Outlook

In March, CBO projected that the total federal budget would show a surplus of $8 billion in fiscal year 1998—the first surplus in almost 30 years—but warned that the final budget numbers for the year could quite easily show a small deficit or a larger surplus. With actual spending and revenues reported for three-quarters of the fiscal year, a surplus this year is now virtually certain, and CBO has boosted its projection of that surplus to $63 billion. . . . Moreover, the improvement in the budget outlook for 1998—primarily associated with higher-than-anticipated revenues—seems likely to carry over to future years as well. Assuming that policies remain unchanged, CBO projects that the surplus will generally increase over the next 10 years, reaching $251 billion (1.9 percent of GDP) in 2008. . . .

Although the total budget is expected to show a healthy surplus in 1998, CBO expects that there will still be an on-budget deficit. On-budget revenues (which by law exclude revenues earmarked to Social Security) are projected to be $41 billion less than on-budget spending (which excludes spending for Social Security benefits and administrative costs and the net outlays of the Postal Service, but includes general fund interest payments to the Social Security trust funds). By 2002, and in 2005 through 2008, the budget will be balanced even when off-budget revenues and spending are excluded from the calculation. . . .

Current Revenue Projections for 1998 Through 2008

CBO projects that revenues will grow about 3.5 percentage points faster than the economy in 1998, reaching 20.5 percent of GDP—a post-World War

II high. In 1999, revenues are projected to grow only slightly faster than the economy and will equal 20.6 percent of GDP. . . . After that, revenues are expected to decline gradually as a percentage of GDP through 2003 (when they will equal 19.8 percent) and then grow at the same rate as the economy through 2008. Despite the decline (as a percentage of GDP) from the 1999 high point, the 19.8 percent level projected for revenues in 2003 through 2008 is equal to the level attained in 1997. Thus, even with tax cuts in the Taxpayer Relief Act of 1997 that reduce revenues by an estimated 0.3 percent of GDP a year, revenues are projected to equal a larger share of GDP than in any post-war year before 1997. . . .

Although CBO assumes that the unexplained increase in 1998 revenues carries over into 1999—thus boosting revenues to an all-time high of 20.6 percent of GDP—the projected growth rate of revenues drops sharply, from 8.7 percent in 1998 to 4.9 percent in 1999. That drop is attributable in part to economic factors—the growth in taxable incomes is projected to slow to 4.1 percent in 1999, down from 5.8 percent in 1998. The rest comes from assuming that the unexplained revenue effect will not increase in 1999. If, instead, that effect increased substantially, revenues would rise at a much faster rate. However, if the unexplained revenues resulted largely from temporary factors in 1998, the rate of growth of revenues in 1999 would decline even more precipitously.

Even if revenues continue to grow rapidly in 1999, CBO believes the rate of growth will eventually slow. Because of the scheduled tax cuts provided by the Taxpayer Relief Act, and because corporate profits are expected to fall as a share of GDP, CBO projects that over the next 10 years, the average growth rate of revenues will be slightly lower than the growth rate of the economy. Revenues are projected to grow at the same rate as GDP from 2003 through 2008. During that period, individual income taxes will grow faster than GDP because individual income tax brackets are indexed for inflation but not for changes in real income, which boosts the effective tax rate as real income grows. But excise taxes grow more slowly than GDP because many rates are fixed in nominal terms.

Current Outlay Projections for 1998 Through 2008

In dollar terms, total outlays are projected to grow from $1,654 billion in 1998 to $2,303 billion in 2008. But as a percentage of GDP, they are projected to decline throughout the period—from 19.7 percent of GDP in 1998 to 17.9 percent in 2008.

Net interest, which was the fastest-growing category of spending in the 1980s, is now projected to decline from $244 billion (2.9 percent of GDP) in 1998 to $140 billion (1.1 percent of GDP) in 2008 as projected surpluses reduce the stock of debt held by the public by $1.4 trillion. . . . Discretionary spending is projected to increase from $552 billion to $657 billion over that period but to shrink relative to the size of the economy—from 6.6 percent of GDP to 5.1 percent. By contrast, mandatory spending is expected to increase both in nominal terms (from $942 billion to $1,626 billion) and as a percentage of GDP (from 11.2 percent to 12.6 percent). That increase comes from both means-tested and non-means-tested programs, with Medicaid and Medicare leading the way. . . .

Conclusion

An unexpected increase in revenues in 1998 has virtually ensured that the total federal budget will be balanced for the first time in almost 30 years, and nothing currently visible on the horizon seems to threaten a return to deficits in the near term if policies remain unchanged. However, if any of a number of assumptions that CBO has made turn out to be off the mark, budget outcomes could be quite different than projected even if there are no changes in policy. For instance, if CBO's economic projections prove to be just a little too optimistic, surpluses could be much lower than anticipated, while a recession similar to that of the early 1990s could even produce a deficit. Likewise, surpluses could be lower than projected if the factors that produced the unexpected revenues in 1998 fade away quickly. Of course, it is also possible that the economy will be more robust than expected or that the unexplained revenue effect will grow over time, in which case the budget outlook is much brighter than CBO currently projects. In the face of those uncertainties, the current budget projections represent CBO's estimate of the middle of the range of likely outcomes.

REMARKS AT SERVICE FOR SLAIN CAPITOL POLICEMEN
July 28, 1998

A deranged man carrying a revolver burst into the U.S. Capitol on July 24 and fatally shot two Capitol Police officers before succumbing to wounds from return fire. Prosecutors charged Russell Eugene Weston Jr. with two counts of murdering a federal police officer. A court-appointed psychiatrist told a federal court on December 4 that Weston was not yet mentally fit to stand trial. Weston had not entered a plea because of his mental condition.

The incident was the most serious violent attack on the Capitol in more than four decades. The slain men—Officer Jacob J. Chestnut, fifty-eight, and Detective John M. Gibson, forty-two—were the first Capitol policemen ever killed by hostile fire in the line of duty. Both men had been on the force for eighteen years.

A Brief Terror

It was 3:40 p.m. on a warm Friday afternoon. The House of Representatives had just finished debate on a controversial health care measure. Suddenly, according to statements by law enforcement officers and a security videotape, a man later identified as Weston rushed into a first-floor entrance of the House side of the Capitol and walked through a metal detector, setting it off. Weston allegedly pointed a .38 caliber revolver at the head of Chestnut and shot him point-blank before Chestnut could respond. Chestnut collapsed in front of two visitors to whom he had been giving directions.

Officer Douglas B. McMillan, who was nearby, fired at Weston, apparently hitting him in the arms. One or more stray bullets struck a nearby visitor, Angela Dickerson, injuring her in the face and shoulder.

Despite his wounds, Weston ran down a hallway behind a screaming woman who was trying to find cover. The two ran through a door marked "Private," leading to the office suite of Majority Whip Tom DeLay, a Texas Republican. At the doorway, Weston confronted Gibson, who pushed the woman aside. Before Gibson was able to draw his pistol, Weston shot him in the chest. The two men exchanged gunfire, and both fell to the floor bleeding from their wounds.

Republican senator Bill Frist of Tennessee, a former heart surgeon and trauma-care specialist, rushed to the scene and worked to stabilize Chestnut and Weston, both of whom were bleeding profusely. Frist may have saved Weston's life, and he rode with Weston in an ambulance to D.C. General Hospital.

The shootings terrified hundreds of tourists and employees at the Capitol, many of whom had taken cover in doorways and under desks. Capitol policemen rounded up several dozen tourists who were near the scene, questioned them and took names and addresses before letting them go.

Chestnut died shortly after he was taken to George Washington University Medical Center; Gibson was pronounced dead on arrival at Washington Hospital Center. Both officers were married, with children.

Honors for Chestnut and Gibson

Both chambers of Congress passed resolutions honoring Chestnut and Gibson for their service of protecting the Capitol and the people who worked and visited there. Early in the morning of July 28 the flag-draped caskets of the officers were placed under the Rotunda of the Capitol. Thousands of visitors somberly paid their respects during the day. At mid-afternoon President Bill Clinton, Vice President Al Gore, and the leaders and members of both the House and Senate attended an emotional memorial service in the vast Rotunda chamber, flanked by statues and paintings of America's heroes and historic scenes.

Chestnut and Gibson were the twenty-fourth and twenty-fifth individuals honored with memorials at the Capitol; all the others were presidents, influential members of Congress, other high-ranking officials, and military heroes. The officers' grieving families were seated by their caskets.

In their tributes, the nation's leaders said Chestnut and Gibson had given their lives to protect the nation's freedom. "As much as any soldier who ever landed on a beach, last week the gatekeepers of our Capitol became the front-line guardians of our freedom," said Gore, who, as a senator and later as vice president, had known both men. "In defending each citizen's right to cross through that doorway in safety, they were defending democracy itself at its core."

Clinton said Chestnut and Gibson represented hundreds of thousands of police officers across the land who are prepared to give their lives to protect other citizens. "They make it seem so ordinary, so expected, asking for no awards or acknowledgment, that most of us do not always appreciate—indeed most of the time we do not even see their daily sacrifice," Clinton said. "Until crisis reveals their courage, we do not see how truly special they are. And so they walk humbly."

Both officers were buried with honors at Arlington National Cemetery: Gibson on July 30 and Chestnut on July 31. Senior members of Congress attended funeral services for both men; many wept, along with the families.

Weston's Background

Weston, forty-one at the time of the shootings, had been an unemployed drifter, living for several years in a remote cabin in Montana. In a twist of fate, Weston's one-room cabin in the hamlet of Rimini, Montana, was only about forty miles from the rustic cabin where Theodore Kaczynski, the confessed "Unabomber," assembled the bombs that he mailed to corporate executives and college campuses, killing three people and wounding more than two dozen others. Both men also had grown up in Illinois. (Unabomber sentencing, p. 233)

According to news reports, statements by law enforcement officials, and affidavits filed with the U.S. District Court in Washington, Weston had been deranged for many years. He was diagnosed as a paranoid schizophrenic in 1984—a finding that entitled him to Social Security disability benefits. Weston was arrested in Helena, Montana, in 1991 on a charge of selling narcotics, but the charge was dropped. Local law enforcement officials said Weston came to their attention on several occasions for delusional behavior, but never anything violent. In 1993 Weston moved to the cabin in Rimini that had been purchased the year before by his sister.

Neighbors in Montana and others who knew him told reporters that Weston was obsessed with a number of bizarre beliefs: that he was cloned at birth (indeed, that everyone was cloned); that the Central Intelligence Agency and other government agencies had spied through television satellite dishes and had planted land mines at his cabin; and that his "friend," President Clinton, had been responsible for the assassination of President Kennedy because Kennedy had stolen Clinton's "girlfriend," Marilyn Monroe. Even so, neighbors described him as "harmless," especially when he was taking his medication.

In 1996 the Secret Service investigated comments Weston made about Clinton, but reportedly determined that he did not pose a threat to the president. Weston drove to CIA headquarters in Virginia that summer and offered his services to the spy agency. He reportedly told security officials that he was receiving government signals through television and radio.

In October 1996 Weston was confined to the state psychiatric hospital in Warm Springs, Montana, after he allegedly threatened a resident of Helena. Doctors released him after fifty-two days and insisted that he seek further treatment in his home state of Illinois. Weston reportedly received some treatment at a community mental health center in Waterloo, Illinois, near his father's home.

In June 1998 Weston went to Illinois for one of his periodic visits with his father in Valmeyer, but left on July 23 after a dispute with his father. Law enforcement officials said he drove straight to Washington in a 1983 red Chevrolet pickup truck, parked at the foot of Capitol Hill, then went to the Capitol and started shooting.

At a hearing on December 4, U.S. District Judge Aimed G. Sullivan revealed portions of a psychiatric report saying Weston was mentally unfit to stand trial on the murder charges. The report, by government psychia-

trist Sally C. Johnson—who had also examined Kaczynski—said that with "adequate treatment" Weston might become well enough to stand trial. Weston was confined to a wheelchair at the hearing, apparently still recovering from the gunshot wounds he received at the Capitol.

Protecting the Capitol

The July 24 incident was the most violent at the Capitol since March 1, 1954, when three supporters of Puerto Rican nationalists pulled guns in the House visitors' gallery and fired at least two dozen shots onto the floor. Six people, including five House members, were wounded in that shooting.

Security at the Capitol was tightened in the subsequent decades, usually in response to overseas terrorism against the United States or minor incidents at the Capitol itself. By the 1980s all visitors were required to go through metal detectors and submit handbags and packages to searches. Concrete barriers were put in place to prevent car or truck bombs from reaching the Capitol (although adjacent congressional office buildings were easy targets for these types of attacks). Security officials repeatedly pressed for additional measures, such as installing a fence around the Capitol grounds or building a visitors center beneath the East Front of the Capitol. Over the years, these proposals were rejected because of concerns about cost and hindering public access to the symbolic center of the country's democracy, the "People's House."

The shooting quickly brought an end to the years of debate. As part of an "omnibus" appropriations bill for fiscal 1999 (PL 105–277), Congress in October set aside $207 million to beef up security at the Capitol, including construction of the long-discussed underground visitors center. Advocates said the center would provide a central access point to the Capitol, thus making it easier for police to screen visitors. Congress also approved substantial pay raises for the nearly 1,300 members of the Capitol Police force.

> *Following are remarks made July 28, 1998, at the memorial service held at the U.S. Capitol for Capitol Police Officer Jacob J. Chestnut and Detective John M. Gibson:*

Sen. Trent Lott (R-Miss.), Senate Majority Leader:

Members of the Chestnut family, members of the Gibson family, and members of the Capitol Police Force of the United States of America, this is truly a very emotional moment for the United States Congress family.

We share the pain and the suffering of this family. We struggle to find a way to express our feeling of grief and sorrow and appreciation at the same time.

These two men have proven that they are the very best of friends, because they have paid the ultimate price.

In this room, there are murals, pictures, statues of the great men and women in our country's history. Today, we honor two men that should rightly be recognized in this hall of heroes.

We've had presidents lie in repose here, generals, members of Congress, unknown soldiers. But it's appropriate today that we honor these two men who did their job, who stood the ground and defended freedom, this very room, and all of our lives, and that we honor them here with these heroes.

Abraham Lincoln, in his most famous speech, said it best when he said that there's very little that we could say to add or detract from the moment and the sacrifice that these men have given. But we must try to express our love and our appreciation.

At the top of this dome is a statute. Many argue about its symbolism. But it stands for the spirit of freedom. And today, the spirit of freedom is in this room because of these men. And it will continue to live in this building, in our hearts and as we maintain freedom and liberty for future generations.

The monument for these two heroes, J. J. (sic) Gibson—J. J. Chestnut and John Gibson—is the monument of freedom that is so exemplified by this building.

On behalf of the Congress and the Senate and the American people, we extend to you our sympathy, our love and our appreciation.

Rep. Newt Gingrich (R-Ga.), Speaker of the House of Representatives:

I wish that I could say to the two wives who are here and to the children who are here that their fathers were going to come through the door.

I wish that we could say that terrible things did not happen. But we can't. The most we can do is come together as a remarkable extended family, really from all across the country—as people have called in, people who are watching now, people who are concerned, people who have visited the Capitol, people who see this as their centerpiece of freedom—and try to reach out to the wives, to the children, to all of the relatives who are here, to say that your personal loss is shared by a remarkable number of people. That in the case of Officer Chestnut, there were so many people, who everyday, walked right past that door—including me, my staff, most of the leadership on the House side—to say of Officer Gibson, there are so many people, as you know, who literally believe that they today would be dead, except that he sacrificed his life for theirs, and to try to extend to you some of our love, our concern and our caring.

But in addition, I wanted to suggest to you that in passing your husbands and your fathers had, in fact, brought together this nation, that their devotion to duty, their sacrifice to defend freedom, their commitment of their life—both on a daily basis and at the crisis that occurred on Friday—has, in fact, reminded millions and million of people that while this is the center of freedom in world and this building is the centerpiece of freedom in our constitutional system it only lasts as long as there is courage.

And so, in part, on behalf of the family of freedom worldwide, on behalf of all Americans, and on behalf of the congressional family, I want to say to both families that your sacrifice is a painful but real building block of freedom, and that for the rest of your lives, you will, in fact, know from people you see all around the country and all around the world that your husbands and your fathers did not die in vain. They, in fact, died in duty to the very freedom that each of us cherishes.

Albert Gore, Vice President of the United States:

Today, we honor two watchmen who guarded not just a building, but an ideal—men who lived and labored not only to keep our democracy free from harm, but to keep it free and open to all our people.

So many times, upon entering this building, I've been greeted by Officer Chestnut standing proudly at his post. So many times as I have walked through this Rotunda, I've been accompanied and guarded by Detective Gibson and the protective detail on which he served.

And I know I'm alone among those who are here today in thinking how fragile is the safety and security we take for granted, how thin the blue line these brave men and women have drawn for us here in the Capitol and in every American community.

Soon, two new names will be inscribed on the Law Enforcement Memorial less than a mile from here. But future generations will owe these men a debt outlasting any monument.

As much as any soldier who ever landed on a beach, last week, the gatekeepers of our Capitol became the front-line guardians of our freedom. In defending each citizen's right to cross through that doorway in safety, they were defending democracy itself at its core.

It is written in the scripture that "Whosoever will be great among you, let him be your minister, and whoever will be chief among you, let him be your servant, even as the son of man came not be ministered unto, but to minister and to give his life as ransom for many."

I believe it is men like John Gibson and J. J. Chestnut who are, in a sense, ministers of our democracy, and who, by virtue of their extraordinary sacrifice, are rightly honored here today as chief among us.

They also remind us that, for all those who suffer and die for righteousness sake, theirs is the kingdom of God.

Let me say to the Gibson and the Chestnut families, we know nothing can lift your loss. We do not forget that, for you, each day forward the sacrifice will go on.

But I hope there is comfort, and I know there is pride and truth in the poet's words, "How sleep the brave who sink to rest by all their country's which is blessed?" God bless you and God bless America.

William J. Clinton, President of the United States:

To the Chestnut and Gibson families, my fellow Americans.

The Bible defines a good life thusly. "To love justice, to do mercy, and to walk humbly with thy God."

Officer J. J. Chestnut and Detective John Gibson loved justice. The story of what they did here on Friday in the line of duty is already a legend.

It is fitting that we gather here to honor these two American heroes, here in this hallowed chamber that has known so many heroes, in this Capitol they gave their lives to defend.

And we thank their families for enduring the pain and extra burden of joining us here today. For they remind us that what makes our democracy strong is not only what Congress may enact or a president may achieve.

Even more, it is the countless individual citizens who live our ideals out every day; the innumerable acts of heroism that go unnoticed. And especially, it is the quiet courage and uncommon bravery of Americans like J. J. Chestnut and John Gibson, and indeed every one of the 81 police officers who just this year have given their lives to ensure our domestic tranquillity.

John Gibson and J. J. Chestnut also did mercy in giving their lives to save the lives of their fellow citizens. We honor them today. And in so doing we honor also the hundreds of thousands of other officers, including all of their comrades, who stand ready every day to do the same.

They make it seem so ordinary, so expected, asking for no awards or acknowledgment, that most of us do not always appreciate—indeed, most of the time we do not even see their daily sacrifice.

Until crisis reveals their courage, we do not see how truly special they are. And so they walked humbly.

To the Gibsons, to Evelyn, Kristin, Jack and Danny; to the Chestnuts, Wendy, Joseph, Janice, Janet, Karen and William; to the parents, the brothers and siblings and friends here, you always knew that John and J. J. were special. Now, the whole world knows as well.

Today, we mourn their loss and we celebrate their lives. Our words are such poor replacements for the joys of family and friends, the turning of the seasons, the rhythms of normal life that should rightfully have been theirs.

But we offer them to you from a grateful nation, profoundly grateful that in doing their duty, they saved lives, they consecrated this house of freedom, and they fulfilled our Lord's definition of a good life. They loved justice. They did mercy.

Now and forever, they walk humbly with their God.

Gary L. Abrecht, Chief, United States Capitol Police:

There is no easy way to absorb the tragic events of last Friday. For all of us, it is difficult to comprehend why someone would commit such an egregious act in the building which is at the core of our democracy. The American people hold a unique reverence for the United States Capitol. Its soaring dome and marble columns exemplify the strength of our nation. When we look at this grand building, our hearts swell with pride. Today, our hearts are heavy with sorrow.

When Officer Jacob Chestnut and Detective John Gibson lost their lives, it was in the defense of this building and all those who work and visit here. They selflessly sacrificed their lives so that others may live. We could not have asked any more of them. They would not have given any less for us.

The men and women of the United States Capitol Police are committed to continuing to serve with the level of dedication, professionalism and bravery exhibited by these two fine officers.

We understand that there are those who seek to disrupt the national legislative process or come here to commit acts of violence. It is important that those individuals understand that there are other officers like J. J. and John who are determined to fill the breach and hold tight the thin blue line which protects our Congressional community and allows the public to safely visit their seat of government.

It is therefore fitting that we gather in the Rotunda of this great building to remember the lives of the officers who made the ultimate sacrifice defending it. While what we say here will soon be forgotten, the memory of the heroic actions of Officer Jacob Chestnut and Detective John Gibson will become as timeless as the building in which they died.

To the Gibson and the Chestnut families, you have our deepest sympathy and our never-ending gratitude.

August

GAO ON FOOD SAFETY
August 6, 1998

The Clinton administration and outside experts stepped up pressure on Congress during 1998 to give government agencies more power to ensure food safety. Although saying that the U.S. food production system probably was the safest in the world, public health experts and consumer advocates had been arguing for several years that Americans were facing increasing risks from foodborne illness. They cited such factors as the growing popularity of fresh fruits and vegetables, many of which could contain dangerous bacteria if not properly handled; an increasing dependence on imported foods (especially fruits, vegetables, and seafood) produced under conditions not subject to U.S. inspection; and the introduction into the U.S. food system of new types of pathogens that often were difficult to detect.

Organizations representing the food industry questioned whether these factors were posing serious dangers to the foods Americans consumed. Their strenuous opposition to new government mandates helped block several major food safety proposals on Capitol Hill, most importantly President Bill Clinton's request for legislation allowing the Agriculture Department to impose fines on food processors who repeatedly violate safety standards.

In addition to disputing approaches to food safety, the food industry and its critics argued about the extent of the problem of foodborne illness. The General Accounting Office (GAO), the investigative arm of Congress, estimated that as many as 9,000 Americans died annually from contaminated food and that the total economic cost of foodborne illness was between $7 billion and $37 billion. Industry officials said these figures were exaggerated.

While legislation on the issue languished on Capitol Hill, the Clinton administration took several steps of its own. The Food and Drug Administration (FDA) required warning labels on fresh fruit and vegetable juices, and the FDA and the Agriculture Department proposed new rules for the safe handling and transportation of fresh eggs in shells. The Agriculture Department also moved ahead with its plan, announced in 1996, requiring

U.S. meat and poultry plants to adopt new a safety system called Hazard Analysis and Critical Control Points; as of January 1998, the 300 largest plants, which produced about 90 percent of federally inspected meat and poultry, were required to have this system in place. Smaller plants were to adopt the systems in 1999 and 2000. The Department of Health and Human Services created a national computer network to help public health laboratories identify causes of foodborne illness. President Bill Clinton established an interagency council to coordinate federal food safety programs. (Meat safety systems, Historic Documents of 1996, p. 414; Clinton food safety proposals, Historic Documents of 1997, p. 690)

A More Unified Approach

Two major reports released in August challenged key features of the U.S. food safety systems. Both reports were commissioned by Congress. The first report, "Food Safety: Opportunities to Redirect Federal Resources and Funds Can Enhance Effectiveness," was released August 6 by the GAO. The second report, "Ensuring Safe Food from Production to Consumption," released August 20, came from a committee representing the Institute of Medicine and the National Research Council, both of which were associated with the National Academy of Sciences.

Both reports cited problems in the existing U.S. food safety system and made recommendations for improvements. Two of the most important areas cited in the reports were:

- Meat and poultry inspections. *The Agriculture Department employed 7,000 inspectors who, by law, were still using the "look-touch-and-smell" system to detect problems with meat and poultry carcasses at U.S. processing plants. The system helped guarantee the overall quality of meat but did not enable detection of bacterial contamination— the most serious health threat in food. The GAO noted that the annual cost of these inspections exceeded $270 million. Both reports said existing laws mandating an inspection of every meat and poultry carcass were outdated. Instead, they said, the Agriculture Department should have latitude to spend money on more sophisticated methods of detecting bacterial contamination. The GAO also suggested that the Agriculture Department could help small processing plants pay the cost of converting to the new Hazard Analysis and Critical Control Points system. In response, the Agriculture Department defended its procedures, saying that its inspectors were conducting appropriate evaluations to uncover risks at meat and poultry plants.*
- The federal inspection system. *The federal government's system of monitoring food safety was fragmented, the result of decades of piecemeal legislation that directed individual agencies to respond to individual problems. Twelve federal agencies had responsibilities for various food types; for example, eggs in their shells were monitored by the FDA, but processed eggs were under the purview of the Agriculture Department. Both reports called for a more unified approach. Echoing*

its recommendations of previous years, the GAO suggested giving one federal agency authority to supervise all food inspection programs. The committee from the Institute of Medicine and the National Research Council offered a similar proposal for putting one high-level official in charge of all food safety programs, similar to the "drug czar" who supervised antinarcotics efforts. (Previous GAO proposal, Historic Documents of 1997, p. 693)

In response, President Clinton on August 25 created an interagency council to supervise the twelve agencies with food safety responsibilities. The new Council on Food Safety was co-chaired by the heads of three agencies: the Agriculture Department, the Health and Human Services Department, and the White House Office of Science and Technology Policy. Clinton asked the council to develop, by early 1999, a "comprehensive strategic plan" for improved food safety efforts. In addition, Clinton gave the council ongoing chores, such as coordinating the annual budget requests for all twelve food safety agencies.

Agriculture Secretary Dan Glickman noted that Clinton was able establish the Council on Food Safety on his own authority by signing an executive order. Creating a unified agency, as proposed by the GAO, would require legislation by Congress—something that was uncertain, at best, he said.

Industry groups made it clear during 1998 that they would staunchly oppose any effort to establish such an agency. John R. Cady, president of the National Food Processors Association, said a unified agency could use "unbridled authority" to put a company out of business "for the slightest reason." Members of Congress also expressed doubts that the twelve existing food safety agencies would be willing to give up their powers to a single agency—or that the congressional committees with oversight responsibilities for those agencies would be willing to give up their influence, either.

Consumer advocates took a wait-and-see approach to Clinton's new Council on Food Safety. Caroline Smith DeWaal, director of food safety for the Center for Science in the Public Interest, said creation of the council could be a useful step toward "a more rational food safety system." But she expressed concern that federal agencies might use the council as a way to protect their own powers by blocking proposals to create a single food safety office.

Inspecting Imported Food

A dramatic increase in the proportion of food coming from outside the United States spurred interest in protecting Americans against contamination of imported food. In a report to Congress released May 11, the GAO said federal agencies needed more authority and resources to ensure the safety of the millions of food items imported into the United States every year. The GAO cited in particular the FDA, which had jurisdiction over imported fruit, vegetables, seafood, and processed food items. In 1997 the FDA had been able to inspect only 1.7 percent of the 2.7 million food ship-

ments under its jurisdiction—down from 8 percent in 1992, the GAO said. The agency had only 112 inspectors for imported food.

Rather than hiring thousands of FDA inspectors to examine every imported box of strawberries or broccoli, the GAO said the FDA should have the same authority as the Agriculture Department to inspect the food regulatory systems in countries that exported to the United States. Agriculture Department inspectors regularly reviewed overseas meat-processing plants and as of 1998 had approved meat imports from thirty-six countries. Michael Friedman, FDA deputy commissioner, praised the GAO report as "a wake-up call to Congress to pass legislation to help ensure the safety of imported foods."

As with the proposal for a single food safety agency, the suggestion of giving more power to the FDA to inspect imported food faced strong opposition from the U.S. food industry. The Grocery Manufacturers Association, the United Fresh Fruit and Vegetable Association, and other industry organizations said further government regulation was unnecessary. Instead, they said, the government should develop better scientific methods to detect and destroy harmful organisms in the food supply.

Following are excerpts from the General Accounting Office report, "Food Safety: Opportunities to Redirect Federal Resources and Funds Can Enhance Effectiveness," presented August 6, 1998 to the House Budget Committee:

Background

Foodborne illness in the United States is extensive and expensive. The incidence of foodborne illness is estimated to range from 6.5 million to 81 million cases each year and result in as few as 500 to as many as 9,100 related deaths annually. In terms of medical costs and productivity losses, foodborne illness costs the nation between $7 billion and $37 billion annually, according to USDA's estimates.

Public health officials believe that the risk of foodborne illness has been increasing over the last 20 years. Trends in the incidence of foodborne illness in the United States are linked, at least in part, to changes in Americans' eating habits. For example, Americans today consume more raw fruits and vegetables than they did in the past and in some cases may mishandle them by not washing them. While this change in diet has many health benefits, the mishandling of these foods and other foods, such as undercooking and/or improperly refrigerating meat and poultry, may also contribute to the spread of foodborne illnesses.

The scientific community has recognized that preventing contamination is the key to reducing the risk of foodborne illness. However, FSIS [Food Safety and Inspection Service] conducts organoleptic meat and poultry inspections of each and every meat and poultry carcass in order to fulfill current program requirements for carcass-by-carcass inspections in slaughtering plants. While these inspections fulfill the requirements, they primarily identify defects in quality but do not detect microbial contamination.

However, as the threat of microbial contamination has increased, a Hazard Analysis and Critical Control Point (HACCP) system has come to be considered the best approach currently available for ensuring safe food because it focuses on preventing contamination rather than on detecting it once it has occurred. The HACCP system (1) identifies hazards and assesses the risks associated with each phase of food production, (2) determines the critical points where the identified hazards can be controlled, and (3) establishes procedures to monitor these critical control points.

In January 1998, FSIS began to require meat and poultry plants to implement HACCP systems. Implementation is expected to take 3 years, starting with the nation's 300 largest slaughtering plants, which account for 75 percent of all meat and poultry slaughter production. In 2000, this system will be fully implemented and will have reached very small plants—those with fewer than 10 employees. The HACCP system requires FSIS' verification that a plant's overall system—not just the individual control points—is working. This verification relies on, among other things, microbial and other types of testing of product samples taken at various times throughout production. These tests contribute to verifying whether the plants meet food safety standards and alert the plants to deficiencies in the slaughtering process.

In addition to carcass-by-carcass slaughter inspections, FSIS inspects meat- and poultry-processing plants at least once per day during each operating shift. Its current inspection program practice for processing plants is labor-intensive and is not based on the health risk that a plant poses. Processing plants' operations can include the simple cutting and packaging of meat and poultry, grinding, complex canning procedures, or the preparation of ready-to-eat products.

Multiple agencies share the responsibility for ensuring the safety of the nation's food supply. In fact, 12 different federal agencies located within six federal entities are involved: HHS' [Department of Health and Human Services'] Food and Drug Administration and Centers for Disease Control and Prevention (CDC); USDA's FSIS, Agricultural Marketing Service (AMS), Animal and Plant Health Inspection Service (APHIS), Agricultural Research Service (ARS), and Grain Inspection, Packers, and Stockyards Administration; the Department of Commerce's National Marine Fisheries Service (NMFS); the Department of the Treasury's U.S. Customs Service and Bureau of Alcohol, Tobacco, and Firearms; the Environmental Protection Agency (EPA); and the Federal Trade Commission.... This structure necessitates extensive coordination to minimize duplication of effort, prevent gaps in regulatory coverage, and avoid conflicting actions. Our past reviews have shown inconsistencies and differences between agencies' approaches and enforcement authorities that undercut overall efforts to ensure a safe food supply. In the past, we have recommended a single food safety agency to correct the problems created by this fragmented system.

In addition to the more than $1 billion provided for routine food safety activities, the administration's food safety initiatives increased funding for federal food safety efforts by $43 million in fiscal year 1998 and requested $101 million for fiscal 1999. These funds went to various agencies—some of which previously did not have any food safety activities—to target efforts for collaborating on food safety priorities in six areas: (1) enhance surveillance of foodborne illnesses and build an early warning system; (2) improve the assessment of the risks associated with exposure to foodborne pathogens; (3) improve coordination among local, state, and federal health authorities; (4) improve the efficiency and effectiveness of seafood, fruits and vegetables, and other FDA inspections; (5) develop educational messages for a variety of audiences, such as consumers and schoolchildren, on the hazards associated with handling food; and (6) research methodologies for, among other things, more rapid and accurate identification and characterization of foodborne hazards. These areas represent important and specific food safety activities that, in many cases, existed prior to the initiatives but had difficulty obtaining funding through their agencies' processes for setting budget priorities. . . .

Funds for Food Safety Inspection Resources Could Be Spent More Effectively

A significant area in which food safety funds could be spent more effectively is inspection resources. Most of the $271 million—over one-fourth of the food safety budget—spent annually on FSIS' organoleptic, carcass-by-carcass slaughter inspections could be spent more effectively on other food safety activities that better address food safety risks. Once HACCP is fully implemented, the funds could become available through the Congress's (1) authorizing FSIS to impose user fees on meat and poultry plants for carcass-by-carcass slaughter inspections, (2) eliminating the legislatively mandated requirement for these federal inspections and allowing slaughter plants to hire their own inspectors, or (3) combining the above options—permitting the slaughter plants to either pay the user fees for federal inspections or hire their own inspectors. In addition, if daily inspections of the processing plants—at an annual cost of about $109 million—were replaced by inspections based on health risk, an undetermined amount of funds could be made available. All or part of the funds made available through the implementation of revisions to food safety inspections could be redirected to other food safety priorities.

Resources from Carcass-by-Carcass Slaughter Inspections Could Be Spent More Effectively

Currently, FSIS spends about $271 million annually on inspectors who are present at each slaughter plant nationwide every day that it is in operation. These inspectors, under current FSIS rules and regulations, inspect each carcass—over 8 billion birds and livestock annually—for visible defects, such as lesions and diseases. Under the traditional organoleptic inspection system, an inspector has about 2 seconds per bird, at the fastest line speeds, to determine whether the carcass meets federal standards for wholesomeness.

We previously reported that with the introduction of the HACCP system, the traditional system of organoleptic meat and poultry inspections of each meat and poultry carcass will become obsolete for improving the safety of meat and poultry because it does not prevent microbial contamination. Moreover, experts have recognized that post-mortem organoleptic inspections on every carcass must be changed because (1) they waste resources and cannot detect microbial pathogens, (2) the animal diseases for which they were originally designed have been eradicated in many countries, and (3) they result in unnecessary cross-contamination because the hands-on inspection techniques used virtually ensure that contamination spreads from one carcass to another. However, this type of inspection may be useful to slaughter plants, since it primarily provides an assurance of quality, such as ensuring that feathers are removed and that tumors and blood clots are not present. While these conditions do not generally threaten human health, they affect the quality of the product.

Because the organoleptic inspections of slaughtered animals primarily help to ensure quality rather than food safety, these inspections are foremost in the slaughter plants' interest. Therefore, as we previously reported, it may be appropriate to charge user fees to cover the cost of these activities. Historically, FSIS has sought but never received the authority to charge user fees for all of its inspection activities. FSIS is requesting user fees again in its fiscal year 1999 budget for all inspection activities. Although the Congress has decided in the past that it is not appropriate to impose user fees for all food safety inspections, the Congress, as a first option, may consider it appropriate to authorize user fees for the federal organoleptic, carcass-by-carcass inspection of slaughtered animals after FSIS has fully implemented the new science- and risk-based HACCP inspection system. If this authority were granted and used, most of the $271 million that FSIS currently spends on these inspections could be recovered.

As a second option, the Congress could amend the mandated requirement for federal carcass-by-carcass inspections by stipulating that after a slaughter plant has operated under a HACCP system for a period of time, the plant could conduct its own carcass-by-carcass slaughter inspections, with appropriate FSIS oversight. Alternatively, as we previously recommended, the Congress could revise the meat and poultry acts to provide FSIS with the flexibility and discretion to target its inspection resources to meet the most serious food safety risks.

Finally, the Congress could provide for a combination of the first two options. That is, a plant could (1) pay a user fee to FSIS, adjusted periodically to reflect FSIS' increased costs, and use FSIS inspectors for carcass-by-carcass slaughter inspections or (2) hire its own employees to do these inspection activities with the appropriate FSIS oversight.

Resources from Daily Processing Plant Inspections Could Be Spent More Effectively

In prior work, we reported on the opportunity to more effectively use federal food safety resources by adopting a risk-based approach rather than the approach currently used by FSIS, which requires daily inspections at all processing plants. This inflexible, labor-intensive approach costs an estimated $109 million annually. Under FSIS' current approach, an inspector must visit each meat and poultry processing plant every 8-hour operating shift to perform a number of tasks, such as monitoring the cleanliness of the workers' bathrooms and ensuring that the canning process operates under the right temperatures and pressures. An undetermined amount of funds could be made available by adopting a risk-based approach to determine the appropriate frequency for these inspections and to allow for more substantial inspections, if needed, when they do occur. Funds made available from this new approach could then be redirected to other food safety priorities.

Developing a risk-based system to determine the frequency of daily inspections would result in fewer inspections but also in inspections that are more closely tied to risk. Our past work pointed out the inefficiencies of FSIS' daily inspection of all 5,900 meat- and poultry-processing plants (or once per shift if a plant operates more than one 8-hour shift) with the same frequency and intensity of inspection regardless of the processing plant's public health risk and compliance history. In fiscal year 1997, the annual cost associated with inspectors traveling between processing plants on daily "patrol assignments," which averaged three to six plants per day, was $6 million. Under a risk-based approach, some of these inspections would occur less frequently because they would be based on the risk that specific food products pose to public health and the plants' past inspection histories.

Opportunities Exist to Redirect Budget Resources to More Effective Uses

If FSIS changes its current approach to carcass-by-carcass slaughter inspections, all or part of the $271 million annually spent on these inspections could be redirected to other federal food safety activities that better reduce the threat of foodborne illness. In prior work, we identified a number of food safety concerns that could be addressed, such as the following:

- FSIS could help to install HACCP inspection systems at the smallest meat and poultry slaughter and processing plants. Since industry will bear most of the installation cost for these new systems and the smallest plants have a smaller volume over which to spread this cost, these plants will be disproportionately affected by the cost of the new inspection systems.
- FDA could increase the frequency of its inspections of other U.S. food-processing plants, such as nonmeat soup plants, cereal manufacturers, and canned fruit and vegetable processors. Currently, FDA inspects such plants under its jurisdiction only once in 10 years, on average. These

inspections are not based on the health risks that these plants pose, but rather on available resources. FDA officials informed us that if they had increased resources, FDA could increase the frequency of inspections of high-, moderate-, and low-risk firms, in that order. In general, the inspections of lower-risk firms would be based on the availability of resources.

- FDA could improve its oversight of imported foods by assisting foreign countries in developing equivalent food safety systems or it could use the funds to improve its oversight of imported foods at ports of entry.

In addition to these actions, the food safety agencies may have other priorities for the use of the funds that are made available from organoleptic slaughter inspections of meat and poultry plants or by basing the frequency of meat- and poultry-processing plant inspections on risk. For example, an ARS official stated that FDA could use additional funding to support an ongoing surveillance system of food animals. This system samples tissue from food animals that have been treated with antibiotics. The system monitors (1) the buildup of antibiotic tolerances in animals and (2) the mutation of pathogens due to antibiotic treatment. The health concern is antibiotic resistance to pathogens in humans as a result of consuming these food animals.

National Food Safety Initiatives Identified Weaknesses, But the Fragmented Structure Persists

The national food safety initiatives were announced by the President for fiscal years 1998-99 and provided additional funds for identified weaknesses. These initiatives have improved some food safety activities. However, the initiatives do not address the fundamental problem of the system—its fragmented structure. In fact, for certain food safety activities, the initiatives intensified the need for coordination among the loosely networked group of federal food safety agencies.

Initiatives Identified Weaknesses and Provided Additional Funds

For fiscal year 1998, the administration's initiative received $43 million for specific food safety activities to improve the nation's food safety system. Prior to the initiative, these activities had competed with other agency priorities for funding. The $43 million in funding was aimed at, among other things, (1) improving a nationwide early-warning system for foodborne illnesses, (2) increasing seafood safety inspections, and (3) expanding research, training, and education in food safety. Under the initiative for fiscal year 1999, the administration has requested $101 million to build upon the food safety efforts in the 1998 initiative and to enhance the safety of imported and domestic fruits and vegetables, among other things.

CDC used initiatives funding to improve its monitoring of foodborne illnesses and will expand its surveillance locations throughout the country to eight. This program, now known as FoodNet, provides national data to better identify illnesses associated with foods; these data allow for more informed decisions about dealing with microbial contamination. Prior to FoodNet, CDC had very limited information on the extent of foodborne illnesses. Since this surveillance effort was undertaken, for example, CDC has learned that the incidence of one pathogen, Campylobacter, is far more frequent than previously known. Policymakers can now use this information to direct research and other activities to reduce illnesses from this pathogen.

Initiatives Do Not Address Fragmented Structure of the Food Safety System

While these food safety initiatives have addressed, and intend to address, some targeted problems, they do not effectively deal with the underlying fragmentation in the federal food safety system. As we have reported, past efforts to correct deficiencies in the federal inspection system for food safety have fallen short, in part because they did not address the fundamental problems in the system. Agencies operate under different regulatory approaches, have widely disparate budgets and staffs, and lack the flexibility needed to respond to changing consumption patterns and emerging food safety issues. These agencies' efforts are hampered by laws that were designed to address safety concerns in specific foods in a piecemeal fashion, typically in response to particular health threats or economic crises.

In addition, this fragmentation may have impeded the effective implementation of some of the activities funded through the food safety initiatives. For example, the initiatives for fiscal years 1998-99 included about $15.7 million to FSIS, FDA, and the Cooperative State Research, Education, and Extension Service, among other agencies, to jointly develop a national campaign to educate the public about the safe handling of fruits and vegetables. However, this effort excluded EPA, which is spending about $230,000 in fiscal year 1998 and about $400,000 in fiscal 1999 to develop and distribute its own brochure to educate the public about pesticides and foods. While EPA attempted to coordinate its educational brochure with the other agencies, significant differences over the message still occurred. According to USDA and FDA officials and consumer groups, EPA's message implied that there are risks associated with eating fruits and vegetables treated with pesticides. These groups said that EPA's message contradicted USDA's advice to eat more fruits and vegetables. At the same time, the other agencies' effort developed a message that discussed the safe handling of fruits and vegetables and encouraged their consumption. In March 1998, after receiving comments from other agencies and the public on its draft brochure as published in the Federal Register, EPA began revising its brochure to reflect the concerns of the other agencies and advised us that it is still in that process.

Even when an activity under the initiatives has been designed to address a fragmentation problem, there is no assurance that it will be successful. For example, in January 1997, the President's Food Safety Initiative (Food Safety From Farm to Table: A National Food Safety Initiative) proposed improving seafood inspection activities by consolidating seafood inspections under one agency by October 1998. Under the proposal, NMFS' voluntary fee-for-service seafood inspection program would be moved to FDA. Progress on this consolidation has been slow because some of the necessary legislative changes are still being drafted. As of May 1998, NMFS officials told us that they have drafted legislation, in conjunction with FDA, to transfer the program to FDA but budget issues have delayed the legislation from being sent to the Office of Management and Budget for its review and approval. Consequently, the Congress has not had the opportunity to decide on the proposed legislation. Commerce's fiscal year 1999 budget request does not show NMFS' program as part of Commerce's fiscal 1999 budget, because Commerce assumed that legislation to transfer the program would be enacted during fiscal 1998. In addition, neither FDA's fiscal year 1999 budget nor its initiative funds provide for transferring NMFS' program to FDA, which has primary responsibility for seafood inspections. FDA officials told us that they did not include the transfer in their fiscal year 1999 budget request because they had not received the legislative authority to charge the user fees that are associated with NMFS' inspection program. . . .

JAPANESE PRIME MINISTER
ON ECONOMIC CRISIS
August 7, 1998

The Japanese economy, which had been lagging for nearly eight years, fell into deep recession in 1998, threatening to undermine the chances for economic recovery in the rest of Asia and helping destabilize financial markets worldwide. The economic decline in Japan was the steepest since World War II; it caused the downfall of the Japanese government in July, bringing to office a new prime minister—the sixth to hold the office during the decade.

The Japanese economy had been suffering since 1990, when the so-called bubble burst: The country's overheated securities and real estate markets collapsed, sending thousands of speculators into bankruptcy and creating mountains of bad debt based on loans that were no longer worth anywhere near their face value. For eight years the government took modest steps to deal with the situation but until 1998 consistently refused to mandate painful economic reforms.

In terms of numbers, the Japanese recession was not as severe as some that had buffeted the United States in previous years, including those in 1982–1983 and 1990–1991. In a country where citizens had been virtually guaranteed jobs for life, the unemployment rate peaked in 1998 at 4.4 percent—a modest figure when compared to the 7 percent unemployment rates registered during some U.S. recessions. Despite years of a weakened economy, Japan did not experience a real recession—defined as two consecutive quarters of negative economic growth—until 1998, when the economy slid backward by 2.2 percent.

Japan's economic slide provoked intense domestic and international concern for two reasons. The recession exposed fundamental problems in the ways Japan had done business for many years, most notably the lack of government oversight of the banking industry. The recession also occurred in the midst of the broader Asian economic crisis that was triggered in 1997 by similar problems in other East Asian countries. (Asian financial crisis, p. 722; Historic Documents of 1997, p. 832)

Recovery Plans

Exacerbating the economic crisis was the reluctance of Japan's political leaders to take bold steps to deal with the situation. A succession of Japanese governments had unveiled a series of economic packages during the decade, spending or promising to spend more than $800 billion to stimulate the economy. The Bank of Japan, the country's central bank, lowered interest rates to 1 percent or less. These actions may have slowed the pace of the economic downturn, but they did not reverse the general direction, and they did not address fundamental problems that experts said needed to be corrected. Throughout 1998 financial analysts and world leaders, including American president Bill Clinton, called on the Japanese government to reduce subsidies and government protections for inefficient industries, reform the secretive banking system, and lift trade barriers that artificially limited imports.

The Japanese government acknowledged that flawed policies and practices by the government and private business had contributed to the recession. In a report released December 28, the Economic Planning Agency pointed in particular to the government's unwillingness to deal with the flood of bad loans that emerged in 1990. The government hoped an economic recovery would solve the problem, the report said, but when the recovery failed to materialize, the debt crisis worsened, compounding effects of the earlier failures to take action. The report also acknowledged problems such as excessive secrecy in the financial system and the inability or unwillingness by banks to deal with bad loans.

The government of Prime Minister Ryutaro Hashimoto announced a stimulus package on April 24. It included $59 billion in public works projects and $31 billion in temporary income tax cuts to spur consumer spending, along with tax incentives to help banks dispose of problem loans. The Hashimoto government announced another plan on July 3; it called for establishing government-run "bridge banks" that would take over the assets of insolvent financial institutions.

Ten days later the voters rebuked the Liberal Democratic Party in parliamentary elections, forcing the Hashimoto government out of office. The election results caused an unusually open squabble within the party, which needed the support of minority parties to retain control of the lower house of parliament, the Diet. Keizo Obuchi, Hashimoto's foreign minister, emerged as the new party leader and on July 30 took over as prime minister. Obuchi had little experience in financial or economic affairs, and so he selected Kichi Miyazawa to be his finance minister. Miyazawa had held the post in the late 1980s and had served as prime minister from 1991 to 1993. The appointment of Miyazawa helped reassure skeptical financial markets, although many observers said his monetary policies during the 1980s had helped create the speculative "bubble" that burst in the early 1990s.

Obuchi announced two stimulus measures during his first five months in office. The first, revealed August 7, included about $40 billion worth of *corporate and individual tax cuts and an estimated $69 billion in public spending projects. The second plan, made public November 17, included the same elements but with a much bigger total price tag: about $200 billion in loans, tax cuts, and public works investments. Obuchi called the November program "the first step to put the Japanese economy on a recovery orbit within a couple of years."*

By the end of 1998 most international financial experts were expressing cautious optimism that the Japanese economy could begin a turnaround in 1999 or 2000 at the latest. The International Monetary Fund (IMF), for example, on December 20 projected that Japan's negative growth rate for 1999 would be about –0.5 percent, a substantial improvement over the –2.2 percent rate in the fiscal year covering most of 1998. The IMF said the stimulus packages announced in April by the Hashimoto government and in November by the Obuchi government were promising. Nevertheless, the IMF said there still was significant "uncertainty" about how fully the government would implement its programs and how much direct effect they would have on the economy.

Financial analysts and political observers said this uncertainty stemmed from several factors. First, the Japanese people apparently did not believe that the numerous tax cuts offered by the government would be permanent, and so they tended to put more money into savings rather than consumption, which had been the primary goal of the cuts. Second, much of the proposed public spending was put in the hands of local authorities who were unable to develop projects with any meaningful impact on the economy. Third, despite Obuchi's statements that the government was committed to reform, it was far from clear that his government was prepared to carry out such steps as tightening regulation of the banking industry. Finally, the proposals did little to counter what everyone understood was Japan's most important problem: the mountain of bad debt held by the banks.

The Banking Crisis

Ever since the collapse of speculative investments in 1990, Japan had been unable to deal with—or even to determine the actual extent of—the enormous number of bad loans held by Japanese banks. In the first half of 1998 estimates of the total amount of bad loans ranged in the vicinity of $400 billion. As the extent of the problem became more apparent, unofficial estimates of the total gradually crept higher, to $550 billion, then $700 billion, then $1 trillion. The one common factor in all the estimates was that no one really knew, or was willing to acknowledge, exactly how many bad loans Japanese banks held and what the face value of those loans might be. Despite its size and global importance, the Japanese banking system was one of the most secretive in the world, and government regulation of the banks was notoriously weak and poorly enforced, with little public accounting of the results.

As the economic crisis deepened, many banks reportedly resorted to questionable accounting gimmicks in hopes of disguising the true extent of their problem portfolios. Analysts said some banks were even extending credit to customers who were unable to make payments on bad loans—in effect temporarily bailing out those customers but putting them even deeper in debt.

Despite the seriousness of the problem, the government was reluctant to close troubled banks or even to force banks to liquidate bad loans. The Hashimoto government's plan for government-funded "bridge banks" to help private banks deal with their loans was a modest step but had no significant impact. Some analysts said the government was actually making the problem worse by encouraging banks to continue making bad loans in hopes of stimulating the economy.

During the last quarter of 1998 the Obuchi government announced it would nationalize two of the country's biggest debt-ridden banks: the Long-Term Credit Bank of Japan, which held nearly $40 billion worth of loans termed "unrecoverable" or "questionable"; and the Nippon Credit Bank Ltd., which held about $32 billion worth of problem loans. In both cases the government said it would attempt to liquidate bad loans and then sell the banks on the open market. In a statement about the December 13 takeover of Nippon Credit Bank, Obuchi said the government would "continue to take all possible measures to protect depositors, maintain order in the financial system, and stabilize financial markets, both in Japan and abroad."

Effect on Other Countries

Japan's recession contributed to financial turmoil all over the world. With the second biggest economy in the world, Japan's actions—or inaction—in dealing with its recession had automatic effects on financial markets and economies everywhere. The impact was greatest on other Asian countries, which depended on Japan as their major source of capital and as the most important customer for their exports. The Japanese downturn worsened the collapse of other Asian economies in 1997; by the same token, the general Asian financial crisis hindered Japan's efforts to resurrect its economy.

In Washington, officials worried that the Japanese recession might undermine U.S. economic growth, which in 1998 was in its seventh consecutive year. Of particular concern to the Clinton administration was the ever-widening U.S. trade deficit with Japan. As its economy shrunk, Japan reduced its imports from the United States and other countries. During the first half of 1998 the Japanese yen dropped precipitously against the dollar, boosting the competitiveness of Japanese exports to the United States, further widening the trade imbalance.

The fall of the yen was a major concern of world leaders. By the middle of June, the yen had dropped to its lowest point in years: one dollar bought 146.22 yen. On June 17 the United States and Japan jointly intervened in currency markets by selling dollars and buying yen, to bolster the Japanese currency. Officials in both countries said they were concerned that con-

*tinued weakening of the yen would worsen the overall Asian economic sit-
uation by damaging the competitiveness of exports by South Korea,
Indonesia, the Philippines, and other Asian countries.*

*Ironically, the yen recovered during the turmoil that shook world finan-
cial markets in August and September as a result of instability in Russia.
The yen rose sharply against the dollar in September and continued rising,
at a more moderate pace, through the end of the year, when it stood at
113.57 to the dollar.* (Russian economy, p. 601)

*Following are excerpts from the first major policy speech by
Keizo Obuchi to the Diet, delivered August 7, 1998, after being
elected Japanese prime minister:*

Introduction

Recently appointed as Prime Minister, I have shouldered a heavy responsibility, and as such, I feel strongly that in facing up to the serious situation
currently confronting our country, losing courage today would spell complete defeat tomorrow. You have my assurance that I will commit myself,
body and soul, to addressing affairs of state.

The most important issues of the moment are the prolonged stagnation
of the economy and the loss of confidence in our financial system. The
recent Upper House elections made clear that above and beyond all else, the
people of Japan regard the economic situation as extremely critical, and
want an economic recovery as soon as possible. Giving serious attention to
this call from the people, I have designated my Cabinet as a "Cabinet for
Economic Revival," and will move forward decisively. The greatest way in
which Japan can contribute to Asia and the world is through the sound functioning of the Japanese financial system and the revitalization of the Japanese economy.

The most important element in overcoming the current critical state of the
national economy will be the crystallization of the wisdom of the people. To
this end, I have decided to establish a Strategic Economic Council under my
direct jurisdiction for consideration centering around members of the private
sector and economic specialists. Then, I myself will make the final decisions
and implement the policies which emerge. I will also lend an ear directly to
the voices of the people of Japan—workers and managers of small and
medium enterprises, as well as others—and create as many opportunities as
possible to explain my own views.

Contemporary Japan stands at a major juncture, faced with rapid progress
in terms of the aging of society, a falling birth rate, computerization and inter-
nationalization. The people of Japan have begun to have concerns about the
future of our economy and society. Politics must dispel these fears, give the
people dreams and hopes, and should be trusted by the people. To break free
from the current imbroglio and build a prosperous and secure society, I will

move policies quickly into place on the basis of political leadership, simultaneously clarifying where responsibility lies.

I ask for the support of the people of Japan and members of the Diet in this endeavor.

Resolution to Restore the Japanese Economy

It is of highest priority to address the non-performing loan problem decisively in order to reconstruct the Japanese economy. The government will put the so-called Bridge Bank scheme into operation. It will also see to it that the organization and procedure will be established for the prompt and smooth settlement of the relationship between creditors and debtors of collateralized real estate underlying bad loans as soon as possible on the basis of the Comprehensive Plan for Financial Revitalization. Therefore, we have already submitted the necessary bills to the current Diet session, and the related bills are also proposed by members of the Diet. I will tackle with the issue of the disposal of non- performing loans by financial institutions on the basic principle that depositors are protected and financial revitalization is achieved as quickly as possible. I would like to ask understanding and cooperation for the prompt approval of these bills.

The flow of funds is like the blood of society, and the financial institutions that are responsible for its circulation assumes the role of the heart. A partial failure in the financial sector, therefore, might lead to a systemic crisis. I would never let a systemic crisis occur. Public funds will be used to revitalize the financial system in the course of implementing the Comprehensive Plan for Financial Revitalization. In this context, the Cabinet as a whole will handle this issue in a responsible way so that the people of Japan would understand its necessity. On the other hand, it is necessary that financial institutions adopt the internationally accepted level of disclosure and boldly engage themselves in their own reorganization and restructuring. The management of failed financial institutions should assume responsibility for the failure of their companies, and further, their strict responsibilities under civil and criminal codes should be investigated. Also, it goes without saying that while sufficient consideration should be paid to the sound borrowers in good faith, the responsibilities of vicious borrowers should be strictly pursued. With the view to letting our country have a strong "heart" and have "blood" circulated to every limb in the future, I will work on revitalization of the financial system while continuing to aggressively cope with the credit crunch. The Financial System Reform, aimed at eliminating "barriers" among financial institutions and promoting the creation of a market and a system that are user-friendly and in which people have confidence is an important initiative also in the context of enhancing the international use of the yen. I will continue to promote it.

The stagnation of the economy is serious. Looking straight at such situation, I have decided to suspend the Fiscal Structural Reform Act for the time being, and will submit a bill to the next Ordinary Diet Session to this effect. Also, the basic guidelines for the budget requests for FY 1999 will be set on the premise that the Fiscal Structural Reform Act be suspended with a view to clearly explaining to the Japanese people and to the international community that all possible efforts will be taken toward economic recovery under political leadership. (In consideration of the future generations, we cannot deny the necessity of the fiscal structural reform in the medium- and long-term. Under the current situation, it is not allowed to postpone the settlement of the long-term liabilities of the former National Railway and the fundamental reform of the National Forestry Operations, including their debt program. I would like to ask the cooperation for the prompt approval of the bills that are carried over from the previous Diet session.

Furthermore, I will prepare a second supplementary budget of total projects over 10 trillion yen for this fiscal year so that fiscal spending can be continued without interruption into the fiscal year in order to promptly bring back the economy to its recovery path. In doing so, I will review public investments, considering their effect on economic recovery and focusing on areas indispensable for Japan in the 21st century, free from the traditional approach.

To promote economic structural reform, it will be absolutely crucial to strengthen the economy from the supply side, working to redress the structure of high industrial costs while boosting medium- to long-term growth. Using as a guide the process by which the United States and some European countries have rebuilt their economies since the 1980s, I will promote measures for deregulation, administrative reform, privatization of the public sector and tax system reform. In addition, I will stimulate research and development so that new industries will spring up vigorously through the constant concentration of human resources, capital and technology around outstanding ideas. I will create a society where foreign companies will move into Japan drawn by our attractive business environment. I will also push forward strongly with the fostering and promotion of venture companies and other new businesses.

With regard to taxation, I will implement permanent tax reductions which in total substantially exceed 6 trillion yen, while foreseeing a fundamental review of the tax system to construct a better one consistent with the future of our country, as well as paying utmost consideration to the economic recovery. As to personal income tax, I will reduce the maximum combined level of tax rates of individual income tax and inhabitants tax to 50%, with a view to unleashing work incentive of Japanese people. Considering the current economic situation, I do not think that the environment surrounding us will allow us to bring down the taxation threshold. I aim at the reduction in individual income tax amounting to 4 trillion yen. With regard to corporate income tax, I will bring down the effective rate to approximately 40%, after conducting a comprehensive deliberation on the matter so that Japanese companies can compete in the international market. The revision of taxation on personal income will be implemented starting from January next year and that of taxation on corporate income from next fiscal year. I will proceed with the preparations so that the related bills can be submitted to the next

Ordinary Diet Session. As for the funding of the tax reduction, I will make use of deficit financing bonds for the time being, while thorough retrenchment, disposal of national property, and other efforts are being made. I believe that this should be considered in a long run in relation to the situation of economic revitalization and the progress of administrative and fiscal reform.

The employment situation is currently looking extremely bleak. All possible measures will be taken to secure employment. In addition, in order to dispel uncertainty over employment prospects, improvement of the employment environment and capacity-building measures will be actively promoted in line with changes in the industrial structure and employment practices. This will create an environment which allows diverse working styles in accordance with people's individual wishes. Moreover, in order to expand and create employment, a reliable high- speed information and communications network will be constructed and user technology will be developed to create new industries in promising growth areas such as information and communications, medical care and welfare, and the environment. At the same time, I will also push forward strongly to strengthen the foundations of small and medium enterprises, which absorb around 80% of Japan's employment, and to innovate their management methods.

Through the implementation of the measures mentioned above, I am determined to take my utmost effort, at the risk of the Cabinet's life, to bring the Japanese economy to its recovery path within a year or two.

Realizing a Better Society and Promoting Structural Reform

Given factors such as economic and social globalization, and the swift aging of Japanese society paralleled by a falling birth rate, my mission is to transform Japan's social system, developed with a mass-production modern industrial society in mind, into one that is appropriate for the age of knowledge in the 21st century. I will carry out a number of reforms, bearing in mind the basic tenets promoted by the Hashimoto Cabinet.

In terms of administrative reform, based on the Basic Law for the Reform of Central Government Ministries and Agencies, passed at the last Ordinary Diet Session, my target is to submit, under political leadership, the necessary legislation to the Diet as early as next April, aiming to launch the transition to the new regime in January 2001. I will not retract this schedule. At the same time, I will trim down central government ministries and agencies through the creation of independent administrative corporations, a complete review of the business conducted by existing ministries and agencies, and by promoting the decentralization of power and deregulation based on a transfer from administration centering on prior regulation to that based on ex post facto checks. Through these efforts, I will seek to shorten the payroll of government officials by 20% and to cut costs by 30% over the next decade. I will also further promote the decentralization of power while clarifying the division of roles and the cost burden between central and local government, submitting to the next Ordinary Diet Session, for example, bills related to the Decentralization Promotion Plan. I will also encourage local governments to enhance their capacities and to engage in administrative reform. This will be extremely significant also in terms of revitalizing regional communities and ensuring the balanced development of national territory. Another important challenge will be realizing administration which is open to the public. I ask for your cooperation in the early approval of the Information Disclosure Act which remains under deliberation. In addition, I hope to see the early approval of the political reform-related bills and the National Civil Servants Ethics Bill, drafted by Diet members and proposed at the last Diet session, in order to garner the trust of the people in both administration and in politics, which stands in the position of leadership to direct administration. . . .

Foreign Policy

Domestic and foreign policy are two sides of the same coin. Despite the difficult situation in which the country currently finds itself, to live up to our internationally-perceived responsibilities, Japan will play a positive and sincere role in line with our standing in the international community in order to ensure Japanese security and to achieve world peace.

Japan-U.S. relations continue to be the cornerstone of Japan's foreign policy. It is vital to build strong and amicable bilateral relations across a wide range of areas such as security and the economy. It is also crucial for the two countries to work together on the various issues facing the international community. Subject to the approval of the Diet, I am hoping to have the opportunity to hold a Summit meeting with President Clinton in September. In addition, passing and approving the legislative package related to the Guidelines for U.S.- Japan Defense Cooperation, still under deliberation, as well as resolving the issues involving Okinawa, where U.S. facilities and areas are concentrated, continue to be important tasks for the new Cabinet. With the understanding and cooperation of Okinawa Prefecture, the Government will do its utmost toward implementing the content of the SACO Final Report and stimulating the local economy.

In terms of improving Japan-Russia relations, I will build on the results achieved by former Prime Minister Ryutaro Hashimoto to strengthen relations in various areas and, at the same time, do my best to see a peace treaty signed by the year 2000 based on the Tokyo Declaration and thereby completely normalize Japan-Russia relations. If possible, I would like to visit the Russian Federation myself this fall.

The peace and stability of the Asia-Pacific region are the foremost objectives of Japan's foreign policy. Accordingly, basing its efforts on the IMF-centered international framework, Japan has responded seriously to the turmoil of the currency and financial markets of the Asian countries which has caused uncertainty not only in the region but throughout the world economy. Japan will continue to play a leading role toward the economic recovery of the Asian countries, providing all possible assistance.

This year marks the 20th anniversary of the Treaty of Peace and Friendship between Japan and the People's Republic of China, and President Jiang Zemin is scheduled to visit Japan this September. As nations bearing responsibility for the stability and prosperity of the Asia-Pacific region as a whole, Japan and China must extend their relationship to further develop dialogue and exchange beyond merely bilateral ties, but with an eye also to the international community. In terms of relations with the Republic of Korea, with President Kim Dae Jung to visit Japan this fall, we will seek to build a new Japan-Korea partnership toward the 21st century and also will continue to work toward the conclusion of a fisheries agreement. Looking to North Korea, we will seek to rectify the anomalous relations between Japan and North Korea, in a manner conducive to the peace and stability of the Korean Peninsula and in close contact with the Republic of Korea and other countries concerned, while seeking to resolve the various outstanding issues.

Contributing to the peace and stability of the international community is also a vital task. Recently, in the Republic of Tajikistan, four people met untimely deaths, among them, Mr. Yutaka Akino, a Japanese citizen who had been dispatched there during my tenure as Minister for Foreign Affairs. One cannot find sufficient words to describe our sorrow at this most tragic incident, and I can only offer my deepest sympathies for the bereaved. I will intensify Japan's continuing efforts for making the Convention on the Safety of United Nations and Associated Personnel enter into effect as soon as possible, in order to provide a means of ensuring the safety of personnel taking part in United Nations peacekeeping activities and to make sure that the sacrifice of the four people was not made in vain. Moreover, recalling the precious sacrifice of Messrs. Nakata and Takata in Cambodia, I would like to make a financial contribution to the United Nations as, so to speak, an Akino Fund toward measures for the safety of United Nations personnel.

The Republic of India and the Islamic Republic of Pakistan recently conducted nuclear tests. As the only country that has experienced nuclear bombings, Japan has observed the Three Nuclear Principles and has continued to promote policies for nuclear disarmament and non- proliferation. As such, we find those acts completely unacceptable. Japan has seized every possible opportunity to express our views to the international community. We will continue to support and strengthen the non- proliferation regime, promote nuclear disarmament and take initiatives in the international community in advancing a practical approach in order to realize a nuclear-weapon-free world, above all, by holding the Conference on Urgent Actions for Nuclear Non- Proliferation and Disarmament to be established at the end of August. Japan will work to conclude the so-called "Anti-Personnel Landmine Ban Treaty" as soon as possible so that this treaty can enter into force at the earliest possible timing. Moreover, to ensure that the United Nations fulfills a role in line with the demands of the time, the reforms of the United Nations must be realized, including Japan becoming a permanent member of the Security Council.

Foreign policy results cannot be achieved simply through government efforts. With the understanding and the support of the people of Japan, I will push forward with my personal motto of foreign policy that moves hand-in-hand with the Japanese people.

Conclusion

Japan's economy and society still have strong fundamentals. In recent years, our foreign asset balance has outweighed foreign debt, with net assets well in the black at around a high 120 trillion yen. Extensive personal financial assets supported by high savings rates stand at around 1,200 trillion yen, and annual GDP is more than 500 trillion yen, both on a scale which places Japan second in the world. These figures would suggest that Japan's economic fundamentals are extremely robust. Japan also enjoys good social order, with education and work ethics both at extremely high levels. Japan in fact has very strong social foundations as well. I would call on the people of Japan to have more confidence and pride in their country.

With such strong foundations, if Japan can overcome the current difficult circumstances, it will once again surge forward powerfully. I believe that by establishing faith today in our country, we can ensure our peace of mind for tomorrow.

As we stand on the verge of the 21st century, I believe that the kind of country we should be aiming for is one which is not only economically prosperous but also has the trust of the international community, or in other words, a rich country which also has virtue. To ensure that the new era brings a bright world rich in hope for ourselves and future generations, I am resolved to bring together the wisdom of the people to build the next era, based on the creed of hard hands and a soft heart. I will lead the way in this endeavor, devoting my full strength to the task of remaking Japan into a country in which the people can believe and which offers them peace of mind.

I humbly ask for the support and cooperation of the people of Japan and members of the Diet.

GAO ON YEAR 2000 COMPUTER CRISIS
August 13, 1998

The prospect that millions of computers and computer-assisted products would fail on January 1, 2000, became a major worry of government officials, private businesses, and individuals around the world by 1998. Called the Y2K crisis (for "Year 2000"), or the "Millennium Bug," the problem stemmed from the fact that many computers, computer systems, and computerized items such as cars and telephones were programmed to recognize only two digits for the year, rather than four. At the time of development, the cost of computer memory to program four digits was prohibitably expensive, so most computer systems went with just two. Unless they were fixed or reprogrammed, the computers might stop functioning or begin spewing out inaccurate information once the year 2000 arrived.

In the early 1990s, computer experts started pointing out the massive problems that could be caused by the failure of computers that handled billions of financial transactions, ran air traffic control systems and public utility networks, and controlled traffic lights and hundreds of other aspects of daily life. By the mid-1990s many government agencies and private businesses were working to fix their computer systems so they could recognize the year 2000, but it was not until 1998 that "Y2K" became a household word and that action to head off massive computer failures reached a fever pitch. Thousands of individuals were stockpiling food, gasoline, and other supplies in expectation of widespread computer crashes. Makers of portable electrical generators were unable to keep up with the demand from consumers who feared power outages. The Federal Reserve Board was planning to keep an extra $50 billion in cash on hand at the end of 1999 to meet the demands of people anticipating a collapse of the banking system. Some economists predicted that computer failures in 2000 could cause a recession, or at least contribute to one. (Year 2000 crisis, Historic Documents of 1997, p. 534)

President Bill Clinton in February appointed a White House task force called the Year 2000 Conversion Council, headed by John A. Koskinen, to supervise programs to fix the thousands of computer systems used by the federal government and to help coordinate similar efforts in the private sector. Clinton on July 14 gave his first speech on the issue, urging increased cooperation between the government and business. Clinton said he had told "every member of my Cabinet that the American people have a right to expect uninterrupted service from the government, and I expect them to deliver."

Making computers Y2K compliant turned out to be very costly. The Office of Management and Budget estimated in November 1998 that the federal government would spend at least $6.4 billion updating its computers. Congress in October appropriated $3.35 billion for Y2K programs in fiscal 1999; the spending was included in a massive omnibus spending bill (PL 105–277). The government's cost was tiny compared to the impact on the private sector. The GartnerGroup, a consulting firm specializing in the Y2K issue, on October 7 gave a Senate committee estimates that fixing Y2K problems would cost $150 billion to $225 billion in the United States and between $300 billion and $600 billion worldwide.

By the end of 1998 the Clinton administration reported that government and industry were working hard to prevent widespread computer disruptions in 2000. White House officials said they had concluded that there probably would be no large-scale disruptions in banking, power-generation, and telecommunications services, but localized failures of computer systems were possible.

The biggest potential for massive computer crashes was overseas, according to experts in the government and private industry. Many other countries were said to be well behind the United States in working to make sure computers would function properly in 2000.

Fixing Government Computers

The U.S. government focused on the Y2K problem for two reasons. First, government computers were responsible for much of the daily functioning of life in the United States, such as writing Social Security checks, supervising the nation's banking system, and monitoring the flights of airplanes. Second, the U.S. government had a high proportion of out-of-date computers operating on obsolete software programs that did not recognize the year 2000.

Many individual government agencies began working on their own computer systems by the mid-1990s, and the White House established a March 31, 1999, deadline for agencies to have all their most important systems "Y2K compliant"—able to function properly in 2000. The White House identified 7,649 federal computer systems as "mission-critical"; in other words, they were vital to the functioning of essential services provided by the government.

Some agencies moved much more quickly than others, according to a series of reports issued by the General Accounting Office (GAO), the investigative arm of Congress. The GAO told Congress throughout 1997 and

1998 that the Social Security Administration, for example, was making good progress in fixing its computers while the departments of defense, energy, health and human services, justice, transportation, and the Treasury were behind schedule in many areas. Testifying before a House subcommittee on August 13, Joel C. Willemssen, director of civil agencies information systems for the GAO, said there was a "high risk that critical services provided by the government and the private sector could be severely disrupted by the year 2000 computing crisis."

Several members of Congress who had taken a particular interest in the Y2K issue were critical of administration efforts. Rep. Steve Horn, R-Calif., issued several report cards during the year that said the administration was failing to meet the Y2K challenges. In his November 23 report, Horn gave the administration a "D" grade overall; he assigned "F" grades to the energy and health and human services departments.

Despite such criticisms, the individual agencies said they were working as quickly as possible to fix their computers. John Hamre, the deputy defense secretary, told reporters on October 14 that the Pentagon would have all its mission-critical systems Y2K-compliant well before the start of 2000. "We can't use the excuse that we can't defend the country because our computers went down" on January 1, 2000, he said.

Clinton announced on December 28 that the Social Security Administration had updated all its computer systems that generated Social Security and Supplemental Security Income payments to more than 48 million Americans. "The millennium bug will not delay our payment of a single Social Security check by a single day," he said. Also on December 28, White House officials said they had determined that 61 percent of the government's critical computer systems had passed tests showing they were Y2K compliant—a jump from the 27 percent in that status one year before. Another 30 percent of the critical federal computer systems had been updated but were still being tested at the end of 1998, the White House added.

Despite the progress at the federal level, the GAO and other observers expressed concern about the slow response of some state and local governments. States were responsible for administering many federal programs—such as welfare, food stamps, and Medicaid—as well as their own programs in the social services, transportation, highway safety, and other areas. Some states, such as New York, appeared to have dealt with many of their important computer systems, while others were still struggling to confront their problems. The GartnerGroup said local governments were even further behind, putting "at risk" the ability of governments at all levels to communicate with each other in 2000.

Private Industry

The differing pace of progress among federal and state agencies was mirrored in the private sector. Y2K experts said many companies, and some industries generally, appeared to have their computer problems *under control, but others were struggling with the consequences of not having acted sooner.*

There appeared to be a general consensus among experts that the banking industry was one of the best prepared to deal with the Y2K issue. By the end of 1998 giant international banks with thousands of offices and small community banks alike had come close to completing work to update their computer systems—often under intense pressure from federal and state regulators. The Federal Financial Examinations Council, which set banking standards, reported that as of October 31, 1998, approximately 96 percent of the more than 20,000 banks, thrift institutions, and savings and loans nationwide had made "satisfactory" progress in meeting or exceeding deadlines for Y2K upgrades.

At the other end of the scale were such important sectors as the electric, oil, and gas industries. Throughout the year influential columnists for computer magazines and other experts predicted that national or regional power-generating networks would fail in January 2000 because the utility industry would not finish its Y2K updates in time.

In May 1998 the Energy Department asked the North American Electric Reliability Council to coordinate Y2K programs in the electric power-generating and transmission industry. The council was a nationwide umbrella organization representing nearly all major electric utilities in the nation. The council reported that as of October 31, 1998, only 36 percent of the 188 largest power suppliers had completed updating and testing their computer systems. Most of those suppliers said their systems would be Y2K compliant by July 1999.

The oil and natural gas industry also was slow in updating its computer systems. According to results of a survey conducted by the President's Council on Year 2000 Conversion, only 19 percent of oil and gas producers, refiners, and transmission systems had completed work on their business computer systems and associated software, as of August 1998.

Government officials and other Y2K experts said another area of concern was small business. A high proportion of the 24 million small and medium-size industrial firms, retail establishments, and service enterprises were said to be lagging behind in updating their computer systems. Surveys showed that many small business owners and operators did not understand the consequences of computer failures in 2000, were unwilling to spend the money needed to fix their computer systems, or were simply waiting until January 2000 to find out what might go wrong. The Small Business Administration and private organizations were working to educate small business people about the need to fix their computers well before January 2000.

The President's Council noted that businesses and individuals at all levels needed to be aware that fixing their own computers would not guarantee that they were safe for 2000. As an example, the council said a small grocery store might have updated all its cash registers and computerized inventory systems well ahead of January 2000—but the store still could be vulnerable if its suppliers had failed to fix their systems in time.

To encourage the spread of information about Y2K issues, the Clinton administration requested, and Congress in October approved, legislation (PL 105–271) providing limited liability protection for businesses and organizations that shared information about their Y2K compliance efforts. The bill barred, with few exceptions and in cases of fraud, the use in court of a company's Y2K "readiness disclosure statement" to prove the accuracy of the company's assertions about how it was dealing with the problem.

Following are excerpts of testimony, "Year 2000 Computing Crisis: Strong Leadership and Partnerships Needed to Mitigate Risk of Major Disruptions," delivered August 13, 1998, by Joel C. Willemssen, director of Civil Agencies Information Systems for the General Accounting Office, to the Subcommittee on Government Management, Information and Technology of the House Committee on Government Reform and Oversight:

The public faces a high risk that critical services provided by the government and the private sector could be severely disrupted by the Year 2000 computing crisis. Financial transactions could be delayed, flights grounded, power lost, and national defense affected. Moreover, America's infrastructures are a complex array of public and private enterprises with many interdependencies at all levels. These many interdependencies among governments and within key economic sectors could cause a single failure to have adverse repercussions. Key economic sectors that could be seriously affected if their systems are not Year 2000 compliant include information and telecommunications; banking and finance; health, safety, and emergency services; transportation; power and water; and manufacturing and small business.

The information and telecommunications sector is especially important. In testimony in June, we reported that the Year 2000 readiness of the telecommunications sector is one of the most crucial concerns to our nation because telecommunications are critical to the operations of nearly every public-sector and private-sector organization. For example, the information and telecommunications sector (1) enables the electronic transfer of funds, the distribution of electrical power, and the control of gas and oil pipeline systems, (2) is essential to the service economy, manufacturing, and efficient delivery of raw materials and finished goods, and (3) is basic to responsive emergency services. Reliable telecommunications services are made possible by a complex web of highly interconnected networks supported by national and local carriers and service providers, equipment manufacturers and suppliers, and customers.

In addition to the risks associated with the nation's key economic sectors, one of the largest, and largely unknown, risks relates to the global nature of the problem. With the advent of electronic communication and international commerce, the United States and the rest of the world have become critically dependent on computers. However, there are indications of Year 2000 readiness problems in the international arena. For example, in a June 1998 informal World Bank survey of foreign readiness, only 18 of 127 countries (14 percent) had a national Year 2000 program, 28 countries (22 percent) reported working on the problem, and 16 countries (13 percent) reported only awareness of the problem. No conclusive data were received from the remaining 65 countries surveyed (51 percent).

The following are examples of some of the major disruptions the public and private sectors could experience if the Year 2000 problem is not corrected.

- Unless the Federal Aviation Administration (FAA) takes much more decisive action, there could be grounded or delayed flights, degraded safety, customer inconvenience, and increased airline costs.
- Aircraft and other military equipment could be grounded because the computer systems used to schedule maintenance and track supplies may not work. Further, the Department of Defense (DOD) could incur shortages of vital items needed to sustain military operations and readiness.
- Medical devices and scientific laboratory equipment may experience problems beginning January 1, 2000, if the computer systems, software applications, or embedded chips used in these devices contain two-digit fields for year representation.
- According to the Basle Committee on Banking Supervision—an international committee of banking supervisory authorities—failure to address the Year 2000 issue would cause banking institutions to experience operational problems or even bankruptcy.

Recognizing the seriousness of the Year 2000 problem, on February 4, 1998, the President signed an executive order that established the President's Council on Year 2000 Conversion led by an Assistant to the President and composed of one representative from each of the executive departments and from other federal agencies as may be determined by the Chair. The Chair of the Council was tasked with the following Year 2000 roles: (1) overseeing the activities of agencies, (2) acting as chief spokesperson in national and international forums, (3) providing policy coordination of executive branch activities with state, local, and tribal governments, and (4) promoting appropriate federal roles with respect to private-sector activities.

Much Work Remains to Correct
the Federal Government's Year 2000 Problem

Addressing the Year 2000 problem in time will be a tremendous challenge for the federal government. Many of the federal government's computer systems were originally designed and developed 20 to 25 years ago, are poorly documented, and use a wide variety of computer languages, many of which are obsolete. Some applications include thousands, tens of thousands, or even millions of lines of code, each of which must be examined for date-format problems.

The federal government also depends on the telecommunications infrastructure to deliver a wide range of services. For example, the route of an electronic Medicare payment may traverse several networks—those operated by the Department of Health and Human Services, the Department of the Treasury's computer systems and networks, and the Federal Reserve's Fedwire electronic funds transfer system. In addition, the year 2000 could cause problems for the many facilities used by the federal government that were built or renovated within the last 20 years and contain embedded computer systems to control, monitor, or assist in operations. For example, building security systems, elevators, and air conditioning and heating equipment could malfunction or cease to operate.

Agencies cannot afford to neglect any of these issues. If they do, the impact of Year 2000 failures could be widespread, costly, and potentially disruptive to vital government operations worldwide. Nevertheless, overall, the government's 24 major departments and agencies are making slow progress in fixing their systems. In May 1997, the Office of Management and Budget (OMB) reported that about 21 percent of the mission-critical systems (1,598 of 7,649) for these departments and agencies were Year 2000 compliant.

A year later, in May 1998, these departments and agencies reported that 2,914 of the 7,336 mission-critical systems in their current inventories, or about 40 percent, were compliant. Unless progress improves dramatically, a substantial number of mission-critical systems will not be compliant in time.

In addition to slow governmentwide progress in fixing systems, our reviews of federal agency Year 2000 programs have found uneven progress. Some agencies are significantly behind schedule and are at high risk that they will not fix their systems in time. Other agencies have made progress, although risks continue and a great deal of work remains. The following are examples of the results of some of our recent reviews.

- Earlier this month, we testified about FAA's progress in implementing a series of recommendations we had made earlier this year to assist FAA in completing overdue awareness and assessment activities. These recommendations included assessing how the major FAA components and the aviation industry would be affected if Year 2000 problems were not corrected in time and completing inventories of all information systems, including data interfaces. Officials at both FAA and the Department of Transportation agreed with these recommendations, and the agency has made progress in implementing them. In our August testimony, we reported that FAA had made progress in managing its Year 2000 problem and had completed critical steps in defining which systems needed to be corrected and how to accomplish this. However, with less than 17 months to go, FAA must still correct, test, and implement many of its mission-critical systems. It is doubtful that FAA can adequately do all of this in the time remaining. Accordingly, FAA must determine how to ensure continuity of critical operations in the likely event of some systems' failures.

- In October 1997, we reported that while SSA [Social Security Adminis-
  tration] had made significant progress in assessing and renovating mission-critical mainframe software, certain areas of risk in its Year 2000
  program remained. Accordingly, we made several recommendations to
  address these risk areas, which included the Year 2000 compliance of
  the systems used by the 54 state Disability Determination Services that
  help administer the disability programs. SSA agreed with these recommendations and, in July 1998, we reported that actions to implement
  these recommendations had either been taken or were underway. Further, we found that SSA has maintained its place as a federal leader in
  addressing Year 2000 issues and has made significant progress in
  achieving systems compliance. However, essential tasks remain. For
  example, many of the states' Disability Determination Service systems
  still had to be renovated, tested, and deemed Year 2000 compliant.
- Our work has shown that much likewise remains to be done in DOD and
  the military services. For example, our recent report on the Navy found
  that while positive actions have been taken, remediation progress had
  been slow and the Navy was behind schedule in completing the early
  phases of its Year 2000 program. Further, the Navy had not been effectively overseeing and managing its Year 2000 efforts and lacked complete and reliable information on its systems and on the status and cost
  of its remediation activities. We have recommended improvements to
  DOD's and the military services' Year 2000 programs with which they
  have concurred.

In addition to these examples, our reviews have shown that many agencies
had not adequately acted to establish priorities, solidify data exchange agreements, or develop contingency plans. Likewise, more attention needs to be
devoted to (1) ensuring that the government has a complete and accurate picture of Year 2000 progress, (2) setting governmentwide priorities, (3) ensuring that the government's critical core business processes are adequately
tested, (4) recruiting and retaining information technology personnel with
the appropriate skills for Year 2000-related work, and (5) assessing the
nation's Year 2000 risks, including those posed by key economic sectors. I
would like to highlight some of these vulnerabilities, and our recommendations made in April 1998 for addressing them.

- First, governmentwide priorities in fixing systems have not yet been
  established. These governmentwide priorities need to be based on such
  criteria as the potential for adverse health and safety effects, adverse
  financial effects on American citizens, detrimental effects on national
  security, and adverse economic consequences. Further, while individual
  agencies have been identifying mission-critical systems, this has not
  always been done on the basis of a determination of the agency's most
  critical operations. If priorities are not clearly set, the government may
  well end up wasting limited time and resources in fixing systems that
  have little bearing on the most vital government operations. Other enti-

ties have recognized the need to set priorities. For example, Canada has established 48 national priorities covering areas such as national defense, food production, safety, and income security.

- Second, business continuity and contingency planning across the government has been inadequate. In their May 1998 quarterly reports to OMB, only four agencies reported that they had drafted contingency plans for their core business processes. Without such plans, when unpredicted failures occur, agencies will not have well-defined responses and may not have enough time to develop and test alternatives. Federal agencies depend on data provided by their business partners as well as services provided by the public infrastructure (e.g., power, water, transportation, and voice and data telecommunications). One weak link anywhere in the chain of critical dependencies can cause major disruptions to business operations. Given these interdependencies, it is imperative that contingency plans be developed for all critical core business processes and supporting systems, regardless of whether these systems are owned by the agency. Our recently issued guidance aims to help agencies ensure such continuity of operations through contingency planning.
- Third, OMB's assessment of the current status of federal Year 2000 progress is predominantly based on agency reports that have not been consistently reviewed or verified. Without independent reviews, OMB and the President's Council on Year 2000 Conversion have little assurance that they are receiving accurate information. In fact, we have found cases in which agencies' systems compliance status as reported to OMB has been inaccurate. For example, the DOD Inspector General estimated that almost three quarters of DOD's mission-critical systems reported as compliant in November 1997 had not been certified as compliant by DOD components. In May 1998, the Department of Agriculture reported (USDA) 15 systems as compliant, even though these were replacement systems that were still under development or were planned for development. (The department plans to remove these systems from compliant status in its next quarterly report.)
- Fourth, end-to-end testing responsibilities have not yet been defined. To ensure that their mission-critical systems can reliably exchange data with other systems and that they are protected from errors that can be introduced by external systems, agencies must perform end-to-end testing for their critical core business processes. The purpose of end-to-end testing is to verify that a defined set of interrelated systems, which collectively support an organizational core business area or function, will work as intended in an operational environment. In the case of the year 2000, many systems in the end-to-end chain will have been modified or replaced. As a result, the scope and complexity of testing—and its importance—is dramatically increased, as is the difficulty of isolating, identifying, and correcting problems. Consequently, agencies must work early and continually with their data exchange partners to plan

and execute effective end-to-end tests. So far, lead agencies have not been designated to take responsibility for ensuring that end-to-end testing of processes and supporting systems is performed across boundaries, and that independent verification and validation of such testing is ensured. We have set forth a structured approach to testing in our recently released exposure draft.

In our April 1998 report on governmentwide Year 2000 progress, we made a number of recommendations to the Chair of the President's Council on Year 2000 Conversion aimed at addressing these problems. These included

- establishing governmentwide priorities and ensuring that agencies set agencywide priorities,
- developing a comprehensive picture of the nation's Year 2000 readiness,
- requiring agencies to develop contingency plans for all critical core business processes,
- requiring agencies to develop an independent verification strategy to involve inspectors general or other independent organizations in reviewing Year 2000 progress, and
- designating lead agencies responsible for ensuring that end-to-end operational testing of processes and supporting systems is performed.

We are encouraged by actions the Council is taking in response to some of our recommendations. For example, OMB and the Chief Information Officers Council adopted our guide providing information on business continuity and contingency planning issues common to most large enterprises as a model for federal agencies. However, as we recently testified before this Subcommittee, some actions have not been initiated—principally with respect to setting national priorities and end-to-end testing.

State and Local Governments
Face Significant Year 2000 Risks

State and local governments also face a major risk of Year 2000-induced failures to the many vital services—such as benefits payments, transportation, and public safety—that they provide. For example,

- food stamps and other types of payments may not be made or could be made for an incorrect amount,
- date-dependent signal timing patterns could be incorrectly implemented at highway intersections, and safety severely compromised, if traffic signal systems run by state and local governments do not process four-digit years correctly, and
- criminal records (i.e., prisoner release or parole eligibility determinations) may be adversely affected by the Year 2000 problem.

Recent surveys of state Year 2000 efforts have indicated that much remains to be completed. For example, a July 1998 survey of state Year 2000 readiness conducted by the National Association of State Information

Resource Executives, Inc., found that only about one-third of the states reported that 50 percent or more of their critical systems had been completely assessed, remediated, and tested.

In a June 1998 survey conducted by USDA's Food and Nutrition Service, only 3 and 14 states, respectively, reported that the software, hardware, and telecommunications that support the Food Stamp Program, and the Women, Infants, and Children program, were Year 2000 compliant. Although all but one of the states reported that they would be Year 2000 compliant by January 1, 2000, many of the states reported that their systems are not due to be compliant until after March 1999 (the federal government's Year 2000 implementation goal). Indeed, 4 and 5 states, respectively, reported that the software, hardware, and telecommunications supporting the Food Stamp Program, and the Women, Infants, and Children program would not be Year 2000 compliant until the last quarter of calendar year 1999, which puts them at high risk of failure due to the need for extensive testing.

State audit organizations have also identified significant Year 2000 concerns. For example, (1) Illinois' Office of the Auditor General reported that significant future efforts were needed to ensure that the year 2000 would not adversely affect state government operations, (2) Vermont's Office of Auditor of Accounts reported that the state faces the risk that critical portions of its Year 2000 compliance efforts could fail, and (3) Florida's Auditor General has issued several reports detailing the need for additional Year 2000 planning at various district school boards and community colleges. State audit offices have also made recommendations, including the need for increased oversight, Year 2000 project plans, contingency plans, and personnel recruitment and retention strategies.

Federal/State Data Exchanges Critical to Delivery of Services

To fully address the Year 2000 risks that states and the federal government face, data exchanges must also be confronted—a monumental issue. As computers play an ever-increasing role in our society, exchanging data electronically has become a common method of transferring information among federal, state, and local governments. For example, SSA exchanges data files with the states to determine the eligibility of disabled persons for disability benefits. In another example, the National Highway Traffic Safety Administration provides states with information needed for driver registrations. As computer systems are converted to process Year 2000 dates, the associated data exchanges must also be made Year 2000 compliant. If the data exchanges are not Year 2000 compliant, data will not be exchanged or invalid data could cause the receiving computer systems to malfunction or produce inaccurate computations.

Our recent report on actions that have been taken to address Year 2000 issues for electronic data exchanges revealed that federal agencies and the states use thousands of such exchanges to communicate with each other and other entities. For example, federal agencies reported that their mission-critical systems have almost 500,000 data exchanges with other federal agencies, states, local governments, and the private sector.

To successfully remediate their data exchanges, federal agencies and the states must (1) assess information systems to identify data exchanges that are not Year 2000 compliant, (2) contact exchange partners and reach agreement on the date format to be used in the exchange, (3) determine if data bridges and filters are needed and, if so, reach agreement on their development, (4) develop and test such bridges and filters, (5) test and implement new exchange formats, and (6) develop contingency plans and procedures for data exchanges.

At the time of our review, much work remained to ensure that federal and state data exchanges will be Year 2000 compliant. About half of the federal agencies reported during the first quarter of 1998 that they had not yet finished assessing their data exchanges. Moreover, almost half of the federal agencies reported that they had reached agreements on 10 percent or fewer of their exchanges, few federal agencies reported having installed bridges or filters, and only 38 percent of the agencies reported that they had developed contingency plans for data exchanges.

Further, the status of the data exchange efforts of 15 of the 39 state-level organizations that responded to our survey was not discernable because they were not able to provide us with information on their total number of exchanges and the number assessed. Of the 24 state-level organizations that provided actual or estimated data, they reported, on average, that 47 percent of the exchanges had not been assessed. In addition, similar to the federal agencies, state-level organizations reported having made limited progress in reaching agreements with exchange partners, installing bridges and filters, and developing contingency plans. However, we could draw only limited conclusions on the status of the states actions because data were provided on only a small portion of states' data exchanges.

To strengthen efforts to address data exchanges, we made several recommendations to OMB. In response, OMB agreed that it needed to increase its efforts in this area. For example, OMB noted that federal agencies had provided the General Services Administration with a list of their data exchanges with the states. In addition, as a result of an agreement reached at an April 1998 federal/state data exchange meeting, the states were supposed to verify the accuracy of these initial lists by June 1, 1998. OMB also noted that the General Services Administration is planning to collect and post information on its Internet World Wide Web site on the progress of federal agencies and states in implementing Year 2000 compliant data exchanges.

In summary, federal, state, and local efforts must increase substantially to ensure that major service disruptions do not occur. Greater leadership and partnerships are essential if government programs are to meet the needs of the public at the turn of the century.

U.S. OFFICIALS ON EMBASSY BOMBINGS IN AFRICA
August 13, 1998

Bombings at the U.S. embassies in Kenya and Tanzania on August 7 killed more than 250 people, wounded thousands more, and provided yet another reminder that U.S. outposts overseas were easy targets for terrorists. The Clinton administration quickly fingered Usama bin Laden, a wealthy exiled Saudi Arabian, as the mastermind of the bombings. On August 20, U.S. warships launched missiles against a remote mountain compound in Afghanistan that reportedly served as bin Laden's headquarters. The United States also attacked a pharmaceutical plant in the Sudan that was said to be a source of chemical weapons for the terrorists. (Attacks in Afghanistan and Sudan, p. 586)

A federal grand jury in New York on November 4 returned a multiple-count indictment against bin Laden and Mohammad Atef, a man described as bin Laden's "military commander." The indictment charged the men in connection with the embassy bombings and other attacks against U.S. interests. That same day the U.S. government offered a reward of up to $5 million for information leading to the conviction of bin Laden and Atef. The government offered similar rewards for information about several of bin Laden's associates.

The bombing at the U.S. embassy in Nairobi, Kenya, killed 247 people, 12 of whom were Americans; more than 4,000 people, the vast majority of whom were Kenyan civilians, were wounded. Eleven people were confirmed dead as a result of a nearly simultaneous bombing at the U.S. embassy in Dar Es Salaam, Tanzania; one man was missing and presumed dead as of the end of 1998. None of the 12 fatalities was an American. An estimated 85 people were wounded in the Dar Es Salaam bombing, many of whom were Americans.

The bombings were the latest in a series of terrorist attacks against U.S. diplomatic and military personnel in the Middle East and eastern Africa. The bloodiest attacks occurred in 1983, when a car bomb destroyed the U.S. embassy in Beirut, Lebanon, killing 17 Americans, followed by the truck-

bombing of a U.S. Marine Corps barracks, killing 241 servicemen and injuring about 80 others. (Lebanon bombings, Historic Documents of 1983, p. 933)

At a ceremony on August 13 marking the arrival back in the United States of the bodies of ten of the Americans killed in the Nairobi bombing, President Bill Clinton said the U.S. government would locate and bring to justice those who were responsible for the bombings "no matter what it takes."

A Day of Terror

The August 7 bombings occurred nearly simultaneously at the U.S. embassies in Nairobi and Dar Es Salaam, 300 miles apart. At about 10:30 a.m., a small truck drove into a parking lot in downtown Nairobi between the U.S. embassy and two other buildings. One of the men in the truck demanded that a guard lift a gate barring the entrance to a parking garage beneath the embassy; when the guard refused, one man in the truck began shooting at the embassy and the other man threw a grenade at several cars parked in the lot. A few seconds later, the bomb exploded, blowing out all windows and callapsing walls and ceilings at the embassy and the adjacent 21-story Cooperative Bank Building. Flying glass and metal killed or injured dozens of occupants. The greatest impact was at another building adjacent to the embassy, called the Ufundi Cooperative House, which housed offices and a secretarial school. The bomb reduced that building to a pile of rubble.

The vast majority of those killed and wounded in the Nairobi attack were Kenyan civilians who had no connection with the U.S. embassy. Twelve American employees and 32 Kenyan employees of the embassy were among the 247 killed. The disaster overwhelmed Kenyan hospitals, which ran short of blood and other supplies to treat the thousands of wounded. Prudence Bushnell, the U.S. ambassador to Kenya, received minor cuts from flying glass. At the time of the bombing she was meeting with a Kenyan government official at the bank building next door.

At almost exactly the same time, a truck carrying a bomb pulled in front of the U.S. embassy in Dar Es Salaam, the seaside capital of Tanzania. The truck was stopped at a concrete wall surrounding the embassy when the bomb exploded, causing severe structural damage to the embassy and damaging buildings and automobiles several blocks away. Of the eleven people confirmed dead as a result of the explosion, five were embassy security guards. U.S. officials said some of the force of the explosion was absorbed by a water-tank truck parked in front of the embassy; if that truck had not been there, many more people might have been killed.

Most of those wounded in the attacks were treated locally, but the United States flew twenty-four of the most seriously wounded victims to the U.S. army hospital in Landstuhl, Germany. The State Department announced November 6 that all twenty-four had survived and that some of them had subsequently been transferred to hospitals in the United States.

In the weeks after the bombing, the State Department temporarily closed or curtailed operations at embassies and other facilities in more than a dozen countries. Officials said the department was taking precautionary steps in the event that terrorists planned further strikes against U.S. interests.

Embassy Security Lapses

The embassies in Africa were similar to scores of U.S. diplomatic compounds: they were office buildings on busy streets in the middle of capital cities. Fences surrounded both buildings, but only unarmed guards protected the parking lots. Neither building met key security standards for U.S. embassies established by a State Department commission in 1985 following the bombings of U.S. outposts in Lebanon. Moreover, the State Department had not considered either embassy as particularly subject to terrorist threats. The department rated the threat to the embassy in Kenya at a "medium" level and the embassy in Tanzania at a "low" level.

The State Department acknowledged on August 12 that Ambassador Bushnell had repeatedly appealed to the department for heightened security at the Nairobi embassy for the short term and, for the longer term, a new embassy that met current security standards. Bushnell in December 1997 sent a cable to the department citing numerous security concerns about the embassy building, including its location at a busy intersection. Bushnell in May 1998 sent a follow-up cable directly to Albright. In both cases, Bushnell's appeals were endorsed by the U.S. Central Command, the Pentagon's division responsible for East Africa and the Middle East.

Patrick F. Kennedy, the assistant secretary of state for administration, said the State Department had shared Bushnell's concerns and promised security improvements at the existing building but had rejected her appeal for a new embassy for financial reasons. "We did the very best we could, given what we had" in the budget, Kennedy said, noting that other building projects were deemed to be higher priority. Even if the department had granted Bushnell's request for a new embassy, the necessary planning and construction for it would have taken several years, Kennedy added.

In September President Clinton asked Congress to appropriate $1.8 billion for emergency security improvements at dozens of embassies, consulates, and other diplomatic posts around the world. Congress in late October approved the bulk of Clinton's request with unusual speed; $1.4 billion for diplomatic security was included in a fiscal 1999 "emergency" supplemental spending bill (PL 105–277). Of that amount, $1 billion was earmarked for security improvements at existing facilities and $200 million was set aside for new embassies in Nairobi and Dar Es Salaam.

Bin Laden's Role

Two men allegedly involved in the Nairobi bombing were captured almost immediately and provided information that enabled the United States to cite bin Laden as the man who had planned and financed both of the bombings.

One of the men was Mohammed Rashed Daoud Al-'Owhali, an alleged occupant of the truck that delivered the bomb to the Nairobi embassy. Al-'Owhali reportedly had planned to die in the explosion but instead ran from the scene before the bomb went off. He was hospitalized with a minor cut; two days later he was arrested and gave investigators key information about the plot, including the bin Laden connection. The FBI flew Al-'Owhali to New York, and on August 27 he was charged with the murder of the twelve Americans killed in the Kenya bombing, with conspiracy to commit murder, and with the use of weapons of mass destruction.

Another break in the case came on the day of the bombing when authorities in Pakistan arrested Mohammad Sadeek Odeh, who reportedly acknowledged taking part in planning the Nairobi bombing. A week after the bombing Pakistan turned Odeh over to U.S. authorities, who immediately flew him to Nairobi, where he was taken into custody by Kenyan authorities. News reports quoted Pakistani officials as saying Odeh claimed he was one of seven men who had helped plan the bombing and had then flown to Karachi just before the event. Odeh reportedly told Pakistani authorities that the bombing had been financed by bin Laden. The FBI flew Odeh to New York and on August 28 charged him with twelve counts of murder and conspiracy to commit murder.

As of the end of 1998 U.S. officials were seeking a half-dozen other men suspected of participating in the bombings. The State Department was offering rewards of up to $5 million for information leading to the arrest or conviction of each of them.

Bin Laden was the chief target of the U.S. search, described as the most intense worldwide manhunt in U.S. history. Bin Laden made no secret of his hatred of the United States and his determination to attack U.S. interests whenever possible. In August 1996 he called for Islamic holy strikes against the American military. On February 23, 1998, he broadened that call, saying American civilians should be killed, as well. The State Department on August 21 issued a report accusing bin Laden and his organization—known as al Qaeda, or "the base"—of numerous terrorist attacks since 1992 against Americans and U.S. allies.

The Associated Press on December 24 reported that bin Laden had told officials in Afghanistan that he had not been involved in the embassy bombings. Even so, bin Laden reportedly said: "I don't regret what happened there." Bin Laden also told an interviewer for ABC News that he had not been present when the United States attacked his headquarters in Afghanistan.

Following are excerpts from statements by Secretary of Defense William S. Cohen, Secretary of State Madeleine K. Albright, and President Bill Clinton at Andrews Air Force Base in Maryland on August 13, 1998, during a ceremony marking the return to the United States of the bodies of ten Americans killed in the August 7, 1998, bombing at the U.S. embassy in Nairobi, Kenya:

Secretary Cohen: Mr. President, Mrs. Clinton, Secretary Albright, members of Congress, General Shelton, members of the Joint Chiefs, Janet, distinguished guests, ladies and gentlemen, and especially families and friends of those we honor today.

This is a moment of profound sadness and grief—for the families whose loved ones have been torn from their embrace, for the many friends and colleagues whose lives they have enriched, and for our nation, whose cause they so courageously served.

Justice Oliver Wendell Holmes Jr. once spoke words that give us strengthen today. "Alas," he said, "we cannot live our dreams. We're lucky enough if we can give a sample of our best and if, in our hearts, we can feel it's been nobly done."

We borrow this moment to express our sorrow and gratitude both to the families who are gathered here and to these fallen heroes, who lived their dreams, giving more than a sample of their best—both as soldiers and diplomats. They endured hardship and yet they served quietly and proudly.

They knew the dangers of their profession, yet risked life and limb for us all. They lived with action and passion. They were the best that America has to offer. They were the better angels of our nature.

I consider the men and women in uniform to be ambassadors of goodwill as well as warriors, carrying our values and virtues wherever they are deployed. But today is a stark reminder that America's ambassadors diplomats and their staffs are granted no exemption from danger while serving on the front lines of democracy. On behalf of America's armed forces, I want to recognize all who serve in our embassies, consulates and compounds abroad. The freedoms that we cherish are stronger, our nation is more secure because of who you are and what you do.

The 12 Americans and the 245 Kenyans and Tanzanians were taken from us in a violent moment by those who traffic in terror and rejoice in the agony of their victims.

We pledge here today that neither time nor distance can bend or break our resolve to bring to justice those who have committed these unspeakable acts of cowardice and horror. We will not rest and we'll never retreat from this mission.

This tragedy has cost us precious lives, and there's no expression of grief and no vow for justice that can lift the pain of this day. But we can never allow terrorists to diminish our determination to press on with the inspiring work of those who have been taken from us.

Their sudden loss must only strengthen our sense of purpose. They did not serve and they did not sacrifice, they did not give their lives so that we could walk away from this new world that they were helping to build for others.

We must ensure that the torch of freedom always burns brighter than the fires of hate and that we continue to be an America worthy of the ultimate price that they have paid.

These sons and daughters of America were of a manner pure with lofty purpose. Six days ago they left us, lifted beyond this mortal veil, having given more than a sample of their best.

Along with their families, we now bid them farewell with reverence and respect, and knowing in our hearts that their work was nobly done. May God continue to embrace our nation and may he open up his arms to these heroes there on high where they shall dwell forever.

Secretary Albright: Mr. President and Mrs. Clinton, Secretary Cohen, members of the Cabinet, General Shelton and leaders of our armed forces, distinguished members of Congress, excellencies from the diplomatic corps—on behalf of the State Department family, thank you all for being here to share our sorrow, determination and pride. Above all I want to welcome the family members and friends of our fallen colleagues and loved ones. We will miss them and grieve for them.

We are proud of these fine Americans. They were our best. Their memory and our love for them lives on.

We are mindful that the same explosions that caused their deaths killed many more Kenyans and Tanzanians, including at least 42 foreign service nationals who worked with great dedication for the identical causes that we do.

We are deeply saddened by this tragedy. We pray for all those who were murdered and for the speedy restoration to health of those who were injured. We pray that the burdens of grief will be tempered by the affection of so many who knew and worked with those who have been lost.

At the same time, we must act to prevent such outrages in the future. The plague of terror has claimed victims on every continent. The people of every continent must unite in defeating terror and the world must understand what terror can and cannot do.

Terror can turn life to death, laughter to tears and shared hopes to sorrowful memory. It can turn a building to rubble, but it cannot change America's determination to lead or to strive with others to build a world where there is more hope and prosperity, freedom and peace.

Make no mistake, terror is the tool of cowards. It is not a form of political expression, and certainly not a manifestation of religious faith.

It is murder, plain and simple. And those who perpetrate it, finance it or otherwise support it must be opposed by all decent people.

Rest assured, America will continue to be present around the world wherever we have interests to defend, friends to support, and work to do. America will not be intimidated. We will maintain our commitments to the people of Africa. We will do all we can to protect our diplomatic and military peoples around the world.

We will do everything possible to see that those responsible for last week's bombings are held accountable. America's memory is long; our reach is far; our resolve unwavering and out commitment to justice unshatterable.

To the families, let me say I know that words are not enough. Love is the most wonderful gift in life, and times like this also the most painful.

The loss you have suffered is without measure.

We're all diminished for those we remember today reflected the strength and diversity of our country. They were the kind of unpretentious, but remarkable, people who represent America in diplomatic outposts around the world—people doing their jobs day in and day out, working for peace, strengthening democracy, healing the ill, helping those in need, winning friends for America.

Above all, they were builders, doers, good people who acted out of hope and with the conviction that what will be can be made better than what has been.

This has been a mission of pride and sorrow. I am honored to bring them home to America. It is beyond our power to turn the clock back to before last Friday.

We cannot alter the past. We cannot bring back the ones we love. But we can choose what they chose—to be animated not by fear, but by hope; to define ourselves not by what we are against, but by what we are for; to acknowledge the presence of evil in this world, but never lose sight of the good; to endure terrible blows, but never give in to those who would have us give us up or turn away from our responsibilities or abandon our principles or surrender our faith. By so doing, we can ensure that the perpetrators of the bombings will be foiled in whatever purpose they may have had, and that America will continue to stand tall and straight and strong in the world.

May our fallen colleagues and loved ones be forever honored, for we will never cease to be proud of them. May they rest in peace, for we will never forget them. And may their deaths inspire us to be fully worthy of freedom, which we hold in solemn and sacred trust for our generation and generations yet to come.

Thank you and God bless you all.

President Clinton: To the members of the families here, Secretary Albright, Secretary Cohen, members of the Cabinet, members of Congress, leaders of the armed forces, members of the diplomatic corps, friends—and we say a special appreciation to the representatives here from Kenya and Tanzania—every person here today would pray not to be here, but we could not be anywhere else, for we come to honor 12 proud sons and daughters who perished half a world away but never left America behind, who carried with them the love of their families, the respect of their countrymen, and above all, the ideals for which America stands.

They perished in the service of the country for which they gave so much in life. To their families and friends, the rest of your fellow Americans have learned a little bit about your loved ones in the past few days.

Of course, we will never know them as you did or remember them as you will—as a new baby, a proud graduate, the beaming bride or groom, a reassuring voice on the phone from across the ocean, a tired, but happy traveler at an airport, bags stuffed with gifts, arms outstretched. Nothing can bring them back, but nothing can erase the lives they lead, the difference they made, the joy they brought.

We can only hope that, even in grief, you can take pride and solace in the gratitude all the rest of us have for the service they gave. The men and women who serve in our embassies all around this world, through hard work that is not always fully appreciated and not even understood by many of their fellow Americans—they protect our interests and promote our values abroad. They are diplomats and doctors and drivers, bookkeepers and technicians and military guards. Far from home, they endure hardships, often at great risk. These 12 Americans came from diverse backgrounds. If you see their pictures, you know they are a portrait of America today and of America's tomorrow. But as different as they were, each of them had an adventurous spirit, a generous soul. Each relished the chance to see the world and to make it better. They were a senior diplomat I had the honor to meet twice and his son who proudly worked alongside him this summer; a budget officer; a wife and mother who had just spent her vacation caring for her aged parents; a State Department worker who looked forward to being back home with a new grandson; a foreign service officer born in India who became an American citizen and traveled the world with her family for her new country; a Marine sergeant, the son of very proud parents; an Air Force sergeant who followed in her own father's footsteps; an epidemiologist who loved her own children and worked to save Africa's children from disease and death; an embassy administrator who married a Kenyan and stayed in close touch with her children back in America; a foreign service officer and mother of three children, including a baby girl; a foreign service member, who was an extraordinarily accomplished jazz musician and devoted husband; an Army sergeant, a veteran of the Gulf War, a husband, a father, who told his own father that if anything ever happened to him, he wanted his ashes scattered in the Pacific off Big Sur, because that was where he had met his beloved wife. What one classmate said to me of his friend today, we can say of all of them—they were what America is all about. We also remember today the Kenyans and Tanzanians who have suffered a great loss. We are grateful for your loved ones who worked alongside us in our embassies. And we are grateful for your extraordinary efforts and great pain in the wake of this tragedy. We pray for the speedy recovery of all the injured, Americans and Africans alike. No matter what it takes, we must find those responsible for these evil acts and see that justice is done.

There may be more hard road ahead, for terrorists target America because we act and stand for peace and democracy, because the spirit of our country is the very spirit of freedom. It is the burden of our history and the bright hope of the world's future.

We must honor the memory of those we mourn today by pressing the cause of freedom and justice for which they lived.

We must continue to stand strong for freedom on every continent. America will not retreat from the world and all its promises nor shrink from our responsibility to stand against terror and with the friends of freedom everywhere.

We owe it to those we honor today. As it is written, their righteous deeds have not been forgotten. Their glory will not be blotted out. Their bodies were buried in peace, but their names shall live forever.

Sergeant Jesse Nathan Aliganga, Julian Bartley Sr., Julian Bartley Jr., Jean Dalizu, Molly Huckaby Hardy, Sergeant Kenneth Hobson, Prabhi Guptara Kavaler, Arlene Kirk, Dr. Mary Louise Martin, Ann Michelle O'Connor, Senior Master Sergeant Sherry Lynn Olds, Uttamlal "Tom" Shah.

May they find peace in the warm embraced of God. And may God give peace to those who love them and bless their beloved country.

PRESIDENT CLINTON'S
GRAND JURY TESTIMONY
August 17 and September 21, 1998

The worst political scandal to hit Washington since Watergate in the early 1970s erupted into public view in January with allegations that President Bill Clinton had lied under oath to cover up his extramarital affair with Monica S. Lewinsky, a former White House intern. In December Clinton became only the second American president ever impeached by the House of Representatives, which charged him with perjury and obstruction of justice. In the intervening months the American public was exposed to intimate, graphic details of the president's personal life as well as the wrenching experience of listening to the president admit that he had deliberately misled his family, his aides, his Cabinet, and the American people. Throughout Clinton repeatedly insisted that he had not committed perjury or obstructed justice and maintained his determination to serve out the remainder of his term, which would expire on January 20, 2001.

Although few observers expected the Senate to convict the president when it took up the matter early in 1999, the events leading up to the president's impeachment had already taken a toll. Clinton's personal conduct undermined any moral authority he had as president and sullied his place in history, while the political struggle to hold him publicly accountable further poisoned an already harshly partisan atmosphere in Washington, possibly weakening the institution of the presidency itself, and heightened the mistrust and cynicism with which the American public regarded its government.

Ironically, the Republicans who pursued impeachment, rather than Clinton, suffered the most immediate political damage. Polls throughout the year showed that although most Americans disapproved of Clinton's conduct, a substantial majority of them supported his performance as president and did not want him removed from office. Ignoring those clear signals in their eagerness to inflict as much damage as possible on the man many of them considered to be their political nemesis, House Republican leaders pressed ahead anyway. The price was high: a loss of five seats in the midterm elections and the resignation of two top House leaders.

The Unfolding of a Scandal

Some finding of wrongdoing on the president's part may have been almost inevitable. For nearly four years Clinton had been under scrutiny in two separate legal investigations. Since August 1994 independent counsel Kenneth W. Starr had been investigating Clinton and his wife, Hillary Rodham Clinton, in connection with their involvement in a complicated Arkansas land deal known as Whitewater. Starr had also expanded his probe to look into allegations involving the firing of the staff of the White House travel office shortly after Clinton took office and the possible illegal misuse of confidential FBI files.

Clinton was also the defendant in a sexual harassment suit brought against him in February 1994 by Paula Corbin Jones. Jones had accused the president of requesting oral sex from her in a Little Rock hotel room when he was governor of Arkansas and she was a minor state functionary. Clinton's attorneys had fought off the case until May 1997, when the Supreme Court ruled that a sitting president was not immune to a civil suit for a personal action alleged to have occurred before he took office. Hoping to show at the trial, scheduled for May 1998, that Clinton's alleged conduct with Jones was part of a broader pattern of sexual harassment, Jones's attorneys compiled a list of women whose names had been linked publicly and privately with Clinton's over the years. Lewinsky's name was on that list. (Supreme Court ruling, Historic Documents of 1997, p. 290)

Arguing that she had no information relevant to the Jones case, Lewinsky filed a sworn affidavit on January 7 in which she denied ever having sexual relations with Clinton. Lewinsky, however, had told several friends about her affair with the president, which began in November 1995, when she was twenty-two and working in the White House legislative affairs office, and continued sporadically through 1996 and early 1997. One of her confidants was Linda R. Tripp, a former White House employee whom Lewinsky had met at the Pentagon, where they were both working. Unbeknownst to Lewinsky, Tripp had taped several of the conversations in which Lewinsky described her sexual relations with Clinton and said that Clinton had urged her to lie about it. Lewinsky was recorded urging Tripp, herself a witness in the Jones case, to lie to the court about her knowledge of Lewinsky's affair with the president.

The two investigations were linked, according to Starr, when Tripp turned the tapes over to the independent counsel's office. She subsequently agreed to wear a "body wire" recorder at a January 16 meeting she arranged with Lewinsky at a suburban Virginia hotel. With FBI agents monitoring every word, Tripp got Lewinsky once again to say that the president had urged her to lie about their affair and again asked Tripp to lie about it.

Later the same day prosecutors from Starr's office confronted Lewinsky with the tapes and sought her cooperation in their investigation of the president. Starr also used the tapes to persuade Attorney General Janet

Reno to recommend to the three-judge "special division" that oversees the jurisdiction of independent counsels that Starr be permitted to investigate the Lewinsky affair. That permission was quickly granted. Unaware that Starr had confronted Lewinsky, President Clinton in a sworn deposition on January 17 told Jones's attorneys that he had never had sexual relations with Lewinsky—a denial he repeatedly publicly after the Washington Post *broke the news of the alleged affair and the possible perjury on January 21. On January 26, the day before he was scheduled to give the annual State of the Union address, Clinton looked directly into the television cameras, wagged his finger, and said, "I want to say one thing to the America people. I want you to listen to me. I'm going to say this again. I did not have sexual relations with that woman, Miss Lewinsky. I never told anyone to lie. Not a single time. Never. These allegations are false. And I need to go back to work for the American people."*

At the same time Clinton and the White House mounted a counterattack on Starr. Hillary Clinton referred to Starr scathingly as a "politically motivated prosecutor" allied with "right-wing opponents of my husband" to try to drive the president from office. "It's obvious, I think, to the American people," Clinton said at a news conference on April 30, that the Starr investigation "has been a hard, well-financed, vigorous effort over a long period of time" to discredit the president by any means available. For the remainder of the year the White House and Starr's office traded charges of unethical conduct, illegal leaks to news organizations, and other underhanded behavior.

Throughout the spring and summer Starr called a steady stream of White House aides and Lewinsky friends before a federal grand jury in Washington, issuing a series of subpoenas for those who refused to testify voluntarily. The White House failed in several efforts to block Starr from taking testimony from key officials, when federal courts rejected claims of executive privilege and attorney-client privilege. A unique assertion that secret service agents guarding the president enjoyed a "protective function privilege" that allowed them to refuse to testify about the president's movements also failed. The one case the president did win was the Jones sexual harassment case. On April 1 Federal Judge Susan Webber Wright threw out the suit, ruling that there were "no genuine issues for trial." (In November Clinton agreed to settle the case, giving Jones $850,000 in return for her pledge not to appeal the dismissal.) (Rulings on privilege, p. 393)

By mid-July the only two key people who had not appeared before Starr's grand jury were Lewinsky and Clinton. Starr subpoenaed Clinton on July 17—it was the first time a sitting president had been subpoenaed to appear before a federal grand jury. Clinton's lawyers stalled for time, but on July 28, after months of negotiation, Starr and Lewinsky finally reached agreement on a deal giving Lewinsky immunity in return for her grand jury testimony. On July 29 Clinton agreed to testify voluntarily. Starr withdrew his subpoena, thus averting any potential clash over whether a sitting president could be forced to testify. (In another unprecedented move,

Clinton also agreed to a blood test, which was used to determine that his DNA matched that of stains on a blue dress that Lewinsky wore at one of their encounters.) Appearing before the grand jury on August 6, Lewinsky acknowledged that she and the president had had an affair, but insisted that he had never told her to lie about it.

Clinton's turn before the grand jury came August 17, when he testified from the White House through a remote television arrangement. That evening Clinton appeared on national television to tell the American people that he had misled them. "I did have a relationship with Miss Lewinsky that was not appropriate. In fact it was wrong," the president said. But he denied that he had done anything illegal and he lashed out at Starr for pursuing a politically inspired investigation into what were essentially private matters. "Even presidents have private lives," Clinton said. "It is time to stop the pursuit of personal destruction and the prying into private lives and get on with our national life."

It was a challenge that went unheeded. Three weeks later, on September 9, Starr delivered a massive report to the U.S. House of Representatives setting out eleven grounds for possible impeachment. The Republican-dominated House voted to release the report to the public on September 11; the report was immediately posted on the Internet. Ten days later the House Judiciary Committee released videotapes of Clinton's grand jury testimony, which was immediately aired on all major television networks. On October 8 the full House authorized its Judiciary Committee to proceed with an impeachment inquiry.

Clinton's Explanations: Legalistic and Literal

Previous presidents had given sworn testimony in legal proceedings, but Clinton was the first to give evidence to a grand jury investigating alleged criminal conduct of the president himself. Under the unique arrangement, Clinton was questioned for four hours by attorneys from the independent counsel's office, including Starr, Robert Bittman, and Solomon L. Wisenberg, in the White House Map Room. The president's private attorney David E. Kendall was also present. The questions and the president's answers were transmitted through closed circuit television to a nearby federal courthouse, where the grand jurors watched on two large television screens. Jurors could also call in with questions that were then relayed to the president.

As he had in his deposition in the Jones case, Clinton gave narrow, literal, and legalistic answers to most of the questions. He began with a prepared statement in which he acknowledged "inappropriate intimate contact" with Lewinsky but said it "did not constitute sexual relations as I understood that term to be defined" at his January deposition. He refused to provide any specific details about the intimate contact, and he avoided directly answering many questions. "It depends on what the meaning of the word 'is' means," he said in response to a question about his January denial that he was having an affair with Lewinsky. "If 'is' means 'is and never has been,' that's one thing. If it means, 'there is none,' that was a completely true statement."

If Republicans had hoped that the release of the videotaped testimony would further damage the president's standing with the public, they miscalculated. Clinton's personal ratings, which had fallen considerably after his August 17 address to the nation and then declined further after the release of the Starr report, began to recover immediately after the videotape was aired. The president's job approval ratings remained high, at about 60 percent, and the polls showed that a majority of people did not want Clinton forced from office. According to a New York Times/CBS News Poll *conducted September 22–23, 65 percent of those surveyed did not want Congress to hold impeachment hearings; 78 percent said Starr's investigation was not worth the time and money.*

Following are the text of President Bill Clinton's address to the nation August 17, 1998, admitting that he had an inappropriate relationship with Monica S. Lewinsky, and excerpts from his grand jury testimony given the same day but made public September 21, 1998:

CLINTON'S ADDRESS TO THE NATION

Good evening.

This afternoon, in this room, from this chair, I testified before the Office of Independent Counsel and the grand jury.

I answered their questions truthfully, including questions about my private life, questions no American citizen would ever want to answer.

Still, I must take complete responsibility for all my actions, both public and private. And that is why I am speaking to you tonight.

As you know, in a deposition in January, I was asked questions about my relationship with Monica Lewinsky. While my answers were legally accurate, I did not volunteer information.

Indeed, I did have a relationship with Ms. Lewinsky that was not appropriate. In fact, it was wrong. It constituted a critical lapse in judgment and a personal failure on my part for which I am solely and completely responsible.

But I told the grand jury today, and I say to you now that at no time did I ask anyone to lie, to hide or destroy evidence or to take any other unlawful action.

I know that my public comments and my silence about this matter gave a false impression. I misled people, including even my wife. I deeply regret that.

I can only tell you I was motivated by many factors. First, by a desire to protect myself from the embarrassment of my own conduct.

I was also very concerned about protecting my family. The fact that these questions were being asked in a politically inspired lawsuit, which has since been dismissed, was a consideration too.

In addition, I had real and serious concerns about an independent counsel investigation that began with private business dealings 20 years ago, dealings, I might add, about which an independent federal agency found no evidence of any wrongdoing by me or my wife over two years ago.

The independent counsel investigation moved on to my staff and friends, then into my private life. And now the investigation itself is under investigation.

This has gone on too long, cost too much and hurt too many innocent people.

Now, this matter is between me, the two people I love most—my wife and our daughter—and our God. I must put it right, and I am prepared to do whatever it takes to do so.

Nothing is more important to me personally. But it is private, and I intend to reclaim my family life for my family. It's nobody's business but ours.

Even presidents have private lives. It is time to stop the pursuit of personal destruction and the prying into private lives and get on with our national life.

Our country has been distracted by this matter for too long, and I take my responsibility for my part in all of this. That is all I can do.

Now it is time—in fact, it is past time—to move on.

We have important work to do—real opportunities to seize, real problems to solve, real security matters to face.

And so tonight, I ask you to turn away from the spectacle of the past seven months, to repair the fabric of our national discourse and to return our attention to all the challenges and all the promise of the next American century.

Thank you for watching. And good night.

CLINTON'S GRAND JURY TESTIMONY

Robert Bittman: Mr. President, we are first going to turn to some of the details of your relationship with Monica Lewinsky that follow up on your deposition that you provided in the Paula Jones case, as was referenced, on January 17th, 1998.

The questions are uncomfortable, and I apologize for that in advance. I will try to be as brief and direct as possible.

Mr. President, were you physically intimate with Monica Lewinsky?

Mr. Bittman, I think maybe I can save the—you and the grand jurors a lot of time if I read a statement, which I think will make it clear what the nature of my relationship with Ms. Lewinsky was and how it related to the testimony I gave, what I was trying to do in that testimony. . . .

Q: Absolutely. Please, Mr. President.

Clinton: When I was alone with Ms. Lewinsky on certain occasions in early 1996 and once in early 1997, I engaged in conduct that was wrong.

These encounters did not consist of sexual intercourse. They did not constitute sexual relations as I understood that term to be defined at my January 17th, 1998, deposition. But they did involve inappropriate intimate contact. These inappropriate encounters ended, at my insistence, in early 1997. I also had occasional telephone conversations with Ms. Lewinsky that included inappropriate sexual banter.

I regret that what began as a friendship came to include this conduct, and I take full responsibility for my actions. While I will provide the grand jury whatever other information I can, because of privacy considerations affecting my family, myself, and others, and in an effort to preserve the dignity of the office I hold, this is all I will say about the specifics of these particular matters. I will try to answer, to the best of my ability, other questions including questions about my relationship with Ms. Lewinsky; questions about my understanding of the term: "sexual relations," as I understood it to be defined at my January 17th, 1998, deposition; and questions concerning alleged subornation of perjury, obstruction of justice, and intimidation of witnesses.

That, Mr. Bittman, is my statement. . . .

["Sexual Relations"]

Q: Let us then move to the definition [of sexual relations] that was provided you during your deposition [in the Paula Jones case]. . . .

Clinton: I can tell you what my understanding of the definition is, if you want me to. . . . My understanding of this definition is it covers contact by the person being deposed with the enumerated areas [genitalia, anus, groin, breast, inner thigh or buttocks], if the contact is done with an intent to arouse or gratify. That's my understanding of the definition.

Q: What did you believe the definition to include and exclude? What kinds of activities?

Clinton: I thought the definition included any activity by the person being deposed, where the person was the actor and came in contact with those parts of the bodies with the purpose or intent or gratification, and excluded any other activity. For example, kissing is not covered by that, I don't think.

Q: Did you understand the definition to be limited to sexual activity?

Clinton: Yes, I understood the definition to be limited to, to physical contact with those areas of the bodies with the specific intent to arouse or gratify. That's what I understood it to be.

Q: What specific acts did the definition include, as you understood the definition on January 17, 1998?

Clinton: Any contact with the areas there mentioned, sir. . . . If the person being deposed contacted those parts of another person's body with an intent to arouse or gratify, that was covered. . . .

Q: [In the Paula Jones deposition] your attorney, Mr. Bennett, objected to any questions about Ms. Lewinsky. . . . I will read the portion that I am referring to. . . . "Counsel is fully aware that Ms. Lewinsky has filed, has an affidavit which they are in possession of saying that there is absolutely no sex of any kind in any manner, shape or form, with President Clinton". . . .

Clinton: Well, actually, in the present tense that is an accurate statement. . . .

Q: And do you remember in the deposition that Mr. Bennett asked you about that. This is at the end of the—towards the end of the deposition. And you indicated, he asked you whether the statement that Ms. Lewinsky made in her affidavit was—

Clinton: Truthful.

Q:—true. And you indicated that it was absolutely correct.

Clinton: I did. . . . I believe at the time that she filled out this affidavit, if she believed that the definition of sexual relationship was two people having intercourse, then this is accurate. And I believe that is the definition that most ordinary Americans would give it.

If you said Jane and Harry have a sexual relationship, and you're not talking about people being drawn into a lawsuit and being given definitions, and then a great effort to trick them in some way, but you are just talking about people in ordinary conversations, I'll bet the grand jurors, if they were talking about two people they know, and said they have a sexual relationship, they meant they were sleeping together; they meant they were having intercourse together.

So, I'm not at all sure that this affidavit is not true and was not true in Ms. Lewinsky's mind at the time she swore it out.

Q: Did you talk with Ms. Lewinsky about what she meant to write in her affidavit?

Clinton: I didn't talk to her about her definition. I did not know what was in this affidavit before it was filled out specifically. I did not know what words were used specifically before it was filled out, or what meaning she gave to them. But I'm just telling you that it's certainly true what she says here. . . .

Q: Do you agree with me that if [Bennett] misled Judge Wright in some way that you would have corrected the record and said, excuse me, Mr. Bennett, think the judge is getting a misimpression by what you're saying?

Clinton: Mr. Bennett was representing me. I wasn't representing him. And I wasn't even paying much attention to this conversation, which is why, when you started asking me about this, I asked to see the deposition, I was focusing on my answers to the questions. And I've told you what I believe about this deposition, which I believe to be true. And it's obvious, and I think by your questions you have betrayed that the Jones lawyers' strategy in this case had nothing to do with uncovering or proving sexual harassment.

By the time this discovery started, they knew they had a bad case on the law and they knew what our evidence was. They knew they had a lousy case on the facts. And so their strategy, since they were being funded by my political opponents, was to have this dragnet of discovery. They wanted to cover everybody. And they convinced the Judge, because she gave them strict orders not to leak, that they should be treated like other plaintiffs in other civil cases, and how could they ever know whether there had been any sexual harassment, unless they first knew whether there had been any sex.

And so, with that broad mandate limited by time and employment in the federal or state government, they proceeded to cross the country and try to turn up whatever they could; not because they thought it would help their case. By the time they did this discovery, they knew what this deal was in their case, and they knew what was going to happen. And Judge Wright subsequently threw it out. . . .

[Lewinsky Meetings]

Q: If I could summarize your testimony [on the number of times you were alone with Lewinsky], approximately five times you saw her before she left the White House, and approximately nine times after she left the employment of the White House?

Clinton: I know there were several times in '97. I've told you that I've looked at my calendar and I tell you what I think the outer limits are. I would think that would sound about right. . . .

Q: Do you believe that Ms. Lewinsky was at the White House and saw you on December 28th, 1997?

Clinton: Yes, sir, I do.

Q: And do you remember talking with Ms. Lewinsky about her subpoena that she received for the Paula Jones case on that day?

Clinton: I remember talking with Ms. Lewinsky about her testimony, or about the prospect that she might have to give testimony. And she, she talked to me about that. I remember that.

Q: And you also gave her Christmas gifts, is that not correct, Mr. President?

Clinton: That is correct. They were Christmas gifts and they were going-away gifts. She was moving to New York taking a new job, starting a new life. And I gave her some gifts.

Q: And you actually requested this meeting, is that not correct?

Clinton: I don't remember that, Mr. Bittman, but it's quite possible that I invited her to come by before she left town. But usually when we met, she requested the meetings. . . .

Q: You mentioned that you discussed her subpoena in the Paula Jones case. Tell us specifically, what did you discuss?

Clinton: No, sir, that's not what I said. I said, my recollection is I knew by then, of course, that she had gotten a subpoena. And I knew that she was, therefore, was slated to testify. And she mentioned to me—and I believe it was at this meeting.

She mentioned—I remember a conversation about the possibility of her testifying. I believe it must have occurred on the 28th.

She mentioned to me that she did not want to testify. So, that's how it came up. Not in the context of, I heard you have a subpoena, let's talk about it. She raised the issue with me in the context of her desire to avoid testifying, which I certainly understood; not only because there were some embarrassing facts about our relationship that were inappropriate, but also because a whole lot of innocent people were being traumatized and dragged through the mud by these Jones lawyers . . . and since she didn't know Paula Jones and knew nothing about sexual harassment, and certainly had no experience with that, I, I clearly understood why she didn't want to be a part of it. . . .

Q: Did anyone, as far as you knew, know about your embarrassing, inappropriate intimate relationship that you had with Ms. Lewinsky?

Clinton: At that time, I was unaware that she had told anyone else about it. But if, if I had known that, it would not have surprised me.

Q: Had you told anyone?

Clinton: Absolutely not.

Q: Had you tried, in fact, not to let anyone else know about this relationship?

Clinton: Well, of course.

Q: What did you do?

Clinton: Well, I never said anything about it, for one thing. And I did what people do when they do the wrong thing. I tried to do it where nobody else was looking at it.

Q: How many times did you do that?

Clinton: Well, if you go back to my statement, I remember there were a few times in '96, I can't say with any certainty. There was once in early '97. After she left the White House, I do not believe I ever had any inappropriate contact with her in the rest of '96. There was one occasion in '97 when, regrettably, that we were together for a few minutes, I think about 20 minutes, and there was inappropriate contact. And after that, to the best of my memory and belief it did not occur again. . . .

Q: Getting back to your meeting with Ms. Lewinsky on December 28, you are aware that she's been subpoenaed. You are aware, are you not, Mr. President, that the subpoena called for the production of, among other things, all the gifts that you had given Ms. Lewinsky? You were aware of that on December 28th, weren't you?

Clinton: I'm not sure. And I understand this is an important question. I did have a conversation with Ms. Lewinsky at some time about gifts, the gifts I'd given her. I do not know whether it occurred on the 28th, or whether it occurred earlier. I do not know whether it occurred in person or whether it occurred on the telephone. I have searched my memory for this, because I know it's an important issue. . . .

The reason I'm not sure it happened on the 28th is that my recollection is that Ms. Lewinsky said something to me like, what if they ask me about the gifts you've given me. That's the memory I have. That's why I question whether it happened on the 28th, because she had a subpoena with her, request for production. And I told her that if they asked her for gifts, she'd have to give them whatever she had, that that's what the law was. . . . And I think, Mr. Bittman, it must have happened before then, because—either that, or Ms. Lewinsky didn't want to tell me that she had the subpoena, because that was the language I remember her using. . . .

Q: Mr. President, if your intent was, as you have earlier testified, that you didn't want anybody to know about this relationship you had with Ms. Lewinsky, why would you feel comfortable giving her gifts in the middle of discovery in the Paula Jones case?

Clinton: Well, sir, for one thing, there was no existing improper relationship at that time. I had, for nearly a year, done my best to be a friend to Ms. Lewinsky, to be a counselor to her, to give her good advice, and to help her. She had, for her part, most of the time, accepted the changed circumstances. She talked to me a lot about her life, her job ambitions, and she continued to give me gifts. And I felt that it was a right thing to do to give her gifts . . . .

[Currie's Role]

Q: After you gave her the gifts on December 28th, did you speak with your secretary, Ms. Currie, and ask her to pick up a box of gifts that were some compilation of gifts that Ms. Lewinsky would have—

Clinton: No, sir, I didn't do that.

Q:—to give to Ms. Currie?

Clinton: I did not do that.

Q: When you testified in the Paula Jones case, this was only two-and-a-half weeks after you had given her these six gifts, you were asked, at page 75 in your deposition, lines 2 through 5, "Well, have you ever given any gifts to Monica Lewinsky?" And you answer, "I don't recall." And you were correct. You pointed out that you actually asked them, for prompting, "Do you know what they were?"

Clinton: I think what I meant there was—don't recall what they were, not that I don't recall whether I had given them. And then if you see, they did give me these specifics, and I gave them quite a good explanation here. . . . I had no interest in not answering their questions about these gifts. I do not believe that gifts are incriminating, nor do I think they are wrong, I think it was a good thing to do. I'm not, I'm still not sorry I gave Monica Lewinsky gifts. . . .

[Currie Testimony]

Q: Let me ask you about the meeting you had with Betty Currie at the White House on Sunday, January 18 of this year, the day after your deposition. First of all, you didn't—Mrs. Currie, your secretary of six-some years, you never allowed her, did you, to watch whatever intimate activity you did with Ms. Lewinsky, did you?

Clinton: No, sir, not to my knowledge.

Q: And as far as you know, she couldn't hear anything either, is that right?

Clinton: There were a couple of times when Monica was there when I asked Betty to be places where she could hear, because Monica was upset and I—this was after there was—all the inappropriate contact had been terminated.

Q: No, I'm talking . . . about the times that you actually had the intimate contact.

Clinton: She was—I believe that—well, first of all, on that one occasion in 1997, I do not know whether Betty was in the White House after the [Feb. 28] radio address in the Oval Office complex. I believe she probably was, but

I'm not sure. But I'm certain that someone was there. I always—always someone was there. In 1996, I think most of the times that Ms. Lewinsky was there, there may not have been anybody around except maybe coming in and out, but not permanently so. I—that's correct. I never—I didn't try to involve Betty in that in any way.

Q: Well, not only did you not try to involve her, you specifically tried to exclude her and everyone else, isn't that right?

Clinton: Well, yes. . . .

Q: So, if Ms. Currie testified that you approached her on the 18th, or you spoke with her and you said, you were always there when she was there, she wasn't, was she? That is, Mrs. Currie?

Clinton: She was always there in the White House, and I was concerned—let me back up and say . . . . I was more concerned about the times after [the final sexual encounter] when Ms. Lewinsky was upset, and I wanted to establish at least that I had not—because these questions were—some of them were off the wall. Some of them were way out of line, I thought.

And what I wanted to establish was that Betty was there at all other times in the complex, and I wanted to know what Betty's memory was about what she heard, what she could hear. And what I did not know was—I did not know that. And I was trying to figure out, and I was trying to figure out in a hurry because I knew something was up.

Q: So, you wanted . . . to check her memory for what she remembered, and that is—

Clinton: That's correct.

Q:—whether she remembered nothing, or whether she remembered an inappropriate intimate relationship?

Clinton: Oh, no, no, no, no. No. I didn't ask her about it in that way. I asked her about what the—what I was trying to determine was whether my recollection was right and that she was always in the office complex when Monica was there, and whether she thought she could hear any conversations we had, or did she hear any.

And then I asked her specifically about a couple of times when—once when I asked her to remain in the dining room, Betty, while I met with Monica in my study. And once when I took Monica in the, the small office Nancy Hernreich occupies right next to Betty's and talked to her there for a few minutes. That's my recollection of that. . . .

Q: If Ms. Currie testified that these were not really questions to her, that they were more like statements, is that not true?

Clinton: Well, I can't testify as to what her perception was. I can tell you this. I was trying to get information in a hurry. I was downloading what I remembered. I think Ms. Currie would also testify that I explicitly told her, once I realized that you were involved in the Jones case—you, the Office of Independent Counsel—and that she might have to be called as a witness, that she should just go in there and tell the truth, tell what she knew, and be perfectly truthful. So, I was not trying to get Betty Currie to say something that was untruthful. I was trying to get as much information as quickly as I could.

Q: What information were you trying to get from her when you said, I was never alone with her, right?

Clinton: I don't remember exactly what I did say with her. That's what you say I said.

Q: If Ms. Currie testified to that, if she says you told her, I was never alone with her, right?. . . .

Clinton: Mr. Bittman, just a minute. I was never alone with her, right, might be a question. And what I might have meant by that is, in the Oval Office complex. . . .

[Endorsing Lewinsky's Testimony]

Solomon Wisenberg: Mr. President, I want to, before I go into a new subject area, briefly go over something you were talking about with Mr. Bittman. The statement of your attorney, Mr. Bennett, at Paula Jones deposition, "Counsel is fully aware"—it's page 54, line 5—"Counsel is fully aware that Ms. Lewinsky has filed, has an affidavit which they are in possession of saying that there is absolutely no sex of any kind in any manner, shape or form, with President Clinton." That statement is made by your attorney in front of Judge Susan Webber Wright, correct?

Clinton: That's correct.

Q: That statement is a completely false statement. Whether or not Mr. Bennett knew of your relationship with Ms. Lewinsky, the statement that there was "no sex of any kind in any manner, shape or form, with President Clinton," was an utterly false statement. Is that correct?

Clinton: It depends on what the meaning of the word "is" is. If the—if he—if "is" means is and never has been that is not—that is one thing. If it means there is none, that was a completely true statement.

But, as I have testified, and I'd like to testify again, this is—it is somewhat unusual for a client to be asked about his lawyer's statements, instead of the other way around. I was not paying a great deal of attention to this exchange. I was focusing on my own testimony.

And if you go back and look at the sequence of this, you will see that the Jones lawyers decided that this was going to be the Lewinsky deposition, not the Jones deposition. . . . But that is not how I prepared for it. That is not how I was thinking about it. And I am not sure, Mr. Wisenberg, as I sit here today, that I sat there and followed all these interchanges between the lawyers. I'm quite sure that I didn't follow all the interchanges between the lawyers all that carefully.

And I don't really believe, therefore, that I can say Mr. Bennett's testimony or statement is testimony and is imputable to me. I didn't—I don't know that I was even paying that much attention to it. . . .

Q: You are the President of the United States and your attorney tells a United States District Court Judge that there is no sex of any kind, in any way, shape or form, whatsoever. And you feel no obligation to do anything about that at that deposition, Mr. President?

Clinton: I have told you, Mr. Wisenberg, I will tell you for a third time. I am not even sure that when Mr. Bennett made that statement that I was concentrating on the exact words he used. Now, if someone had asked me on that day, are you having any kind of sexual relations with Ms. Lewinsky, that is, asked me a question in the present tense, I would have said no. And it would have been completely true. . . .

Q: I just want to make sure I understand, Mr. President. Do you mean today that because you were not engaging in sexual activity with Ms. Lewinsky during the deposition that the statement of Mr. Bennett might be literally true?

Clinton: No, sir. . . . I wasn't trying to give you a cute answer, that I was obviously not involved in anything improper during a deposition. I was trying to tell you that generally speaking in the present tense, if someone said that, that would be true. But I don't know what Mr. Bennett had in his mind. I don't know. I didn't pay any attention to this colloquy that went on. I was waiting for my instructions as a witness to go forward I was worried about my own testimony. . . .

[Jordan's Role]

Q: If Mr. Jordan has told us that he visited you in the Residence on the night of the 19th [Dec. 19, 1997], after a White House holiday dinner, to discuss Monica Lewinsky and her subpoena with you, do you have any reason to doubt it?

C: No. . . .

Q: If Mr. Jordan has told us that he spoke with you over the phone within about an hour of Monica receiving her subpoena, and later visited you that very day, the night at the White House, to discuss it, again you'd have no reason to doubt him, is that correct?

Clinton: I've already—I believe I've already testified about that here today, that I had lots of conversations with Vernon. I'm sure that I had lots of conversations with him that included comments about this. And if he has a specific memory of when I had some conversation on a certain day, [I] would be inclined to trust his memory over mine, because under the present circumstances my head's probably more cluttered than his, and my schedule is probably busier. He's probably got better records.

Q: And when Mr. Jordan met with you at the Residence that night, sir, he asked you if you'd been involved in a sexual relationship with Monica Lewinsky, didn't he?

Clinton: I do not remember exactly what the nature of the conversation was. I do remember that I told him that there was no sexual relationship between me and Monica Lewinsky, which was true. . . .

Q: Mr. President, if Mr. Jordan has told us that he had a very disturbing conversation with Ms. Lewinsky that day, then went over to visit you at the White House, and that before he asked you the question about a sexual relationship, related that disturbing conversation to you, the conversation being that Ms. Lewinsky had a fixation on you and thought that perhaps the First Lady would leave you at the end of—that you would leave the First Lady at the end of your term and come be with Ms. Lewinsky, do you have any reason to doubt him that it was on that night that that conversation happened?

Clinton: All I can tell you, sir, is I, I certainly don't remember him saying that. Now, he could have said that because, as you know, a great many things happened in the ensuing two or three days. And I could have just forgotten it. But I don't remember him ever saying that.

Q: At any time?

Clinton: No, I don't remember him saying that. What I remember was that he said that Monica came to see him, that she was upset that she was going to have to testify, that he had referred her to a lawyer. . . .

Q: That is something that one would be likely to remember, don't you think, Mr. President?

Clinton: I think I would, and I'd be happy to share it with you if I did. I only had one encounter with Ms. Lewinsky, I seem to remember, which was somewhat maybe reminiscent of that. But not that, if you will, obsessive, if that's the way you want to use that word. . . .

Q: Mr. President, you swore under oath in the Jones case that you didn't think anyone other than your lawyers had ever told you that Monica Lewinsky had been subpoenaed. . . . Here's the testimony, sir:

"Question—we've gone over it a little bit before: 'Did anyone other than your attorneys ever tell you that Monica Lewinsky had been served with a subpoena in this case?' Answer, 'I don't think so.' " Now, this deposition was taken just three-and-a-half weeks after, by your own testimony, Vernon Jordan made a trip at night to the White House to tell you, among other things, that Monica Lewinsky had been subpoenaed and was upset about it. Why did you give that testimony under oath in the Jones case, sir?

Clinton: Well, Mr. Wisenberg, I think you have to—again, you have to put this in the context of the flow of questions, and I've already testified to this once today, I will testify to it again. My answer to the next question, I think, is a way of finishing my answer to the question and the answer you've said here. I was trying to remember who the first person, other than Mr. Bennett— I don't think Mr. Bennett—who the first person told me that, who told me Paula Jones had, I mean, excuse me, Monica Lewinsky had a subpoena. And I thought that Bruce Lindsey was the first person. And that's how I was trying to remember that.

Keep in mind, sort of like today, these questions are being kind of put at me rapid-fire. But, unlike today, I hadn't had the opportunity to prepare at this level of detail. . . . Several of my answers are somewhat jumbled. But this is an honest attempt here—if you read both these answers, it's obvious they were both answers to that question you quoted, to remember the first person, who was not Mr. Bennett, who told me. And I don't believe Vernon was the first person who told me. I believe Bruce Lindsey was.

Q: Let me read the question, because I want to talk about the first person issue. The question on line 25 of page 68 is, "Did anyone other than your attorneys ever tell you that Monica Lewinsky had been served with a subpoena in this case?" Answer, "I don't think so." You would agree with me, sir, that the question doesn't say, the question doesn't say anything about who was the first person. It just says, did anyone tell you. Isn't that correct?

Clinton: That's right. And I said Bruce Lindsey, because I was trying to struggle with who—where I had heard this. And they were free to ask a follow-up question, and they didn't. . . .

Q: If Vernon Jordan has told us that you have an extraordinary memory, one of the greatest memories he's ever seen in a politician, would that be something you would care to dispute?

Clinton: No, I do have a good memory. At least, I have had a good memory in my life. . . . Now, I have been shocked, and so have members of my family and friends of mine, at how many things that I have forgotten in the last six years, I think because of the pressure and the pace and the volume of events in the president's life, compounded by the pressure of your four-year inquiry, and all the other things that have happened, I'm amazed there are lots of times when I literally can't remember last week. . . .

Q: If he's told us that he notified you around January 7th, when [Lewinsky] signed her affidavit, and that you generally understood that it would deny a sexual relationship, do you have any reason to doubt that?

Clinton: No.

Q: . . . And yet when you were asked, sir, at the Jones deposition about Vernon Jordan, and specifically about whether or not he had discussed the lawsuit with you, didn't reveal that to the Court. . . . This is your answer, or a portion of it: "I knew that he met with her. I think Betty suggested that he meet with her. Anyway, he met with her. I, I thought that he talked to her about something else."

Why didn't you tell the Court, when you were under oath and sworn to tell the truth, the whole truth, and nothing but the truth, that you had been talking with Vernon Jordan about the case, about the affidavit, the lawyer, the subpoena?

Clinton: Well, that's not the question I was asked. I was not asked any question about—I was asked, "Has it ever been reported to you that he met with Monica Lewinsky and talked about this case." I believe—I may be wrong about this—my impression was that at the time, I was focused on the meetings. I believe the meetings he had were meetings about her moving to New York and getting a job. I knew at some point that she had told him that she needed some help, because she had gotten a subpoena. I'm not sure I know whether she did that in a meeting or a phone call. And I was not, I was not focused on that.

I know that, I know Vernon helped her to get a lawyer, Mr. Carter. And I, I believe that he did it after she had called him, but I'm not sure. But I knew that the main source of their meetings was about her move to New York and her getting a job.

Q: Are you saying, sir, that you forgot when you were asked this question that Vernon Jordan had come on December 19th, just three-and-a-half weeks before, and said that he had met that day, the day that Monica got the subpoena?

Clinton: It's quite possible—it's a sort of a jumbled answer. It's quite possible that I had gotten mixed up between whether she had met with him or talked to him on the telephone in those three and a half weeks.

Again, I say, sir, just from the tone of your voice and the way you are asking questions here, it's obvious that this is the most important thing in the world, and that everybody was focused on all the details at the time. But that's not the way it worked. I was, I was doing my best to remember. . . .

[Clinton's Responsibility]

Q: Mr. President, the next series of questions are from the grand jurors. And let me tell you that the grand jurors want you to be more specific about the inappropriate conduct. The first question was, one of the grand jurors has said that you referred to what you did with Ms. Lewinsky as inappropriate contact; what do you mean by that?

Clinton: . . . . What I meant was, and what they can infer that I meant was, that I did things that were—when I was alone with her, that were inappropriate and wrong. But that they did not include any activity that was within the definition of sexual relations that I was given by Judge Wright in the deposition. I said that I did not do those things that were in that, within that definition, and I testified truthfully to that. And that's all I can say about it. . . .

Q: Well, I have a question regarding your definition then. And my question is, is oral sex performed on you within that definition as you understood it, the definition in the Jones—

Clinton: As I understood it, it was not, no. . . .

Q: If a person touched another person, if you touched another person on the breast, would that be, in your view, and was it within your view, when you took the deposition, within the definition of sexual relations?

Clinton: If the person being deposed?

Q: Yes.

C:—in this case, me, directly touched the breast of another person, with the purpose to arouse or gratify, under that definition that would be included.

Q: Only directly, sir, or would it be directly or through clothing?

C: Well, I would—I think the common sense definition would be directly. That's how I would infer what it means.

Q: If the person being deposed kissed the breast of another person, would that be in the definition of sexual relations as you understood it when you were under oath in the Jones case?

Clinton: Yes, that would constitute contact. I think that would. If it were direct contact, I believe it would. I—maybe I should read it again, just to make sure. Because this basically says if there was any direct contact with an intent to arouse or gratify, if that was the intent of the contact, then that would fall within the definition. That's correct.

Q: So, touching, in your view then and now—the person being deposed touching or kissing the breast of another person would fall within the definition?

Clinton: That's correct, sir.

Q: And you testified that you didn't have sexual relations with Monica Lewinsky in the Jones deposition, under that definition, correct?

Clinton: That's correct, sir.

Q: If the person being deposed touched the genitalia of another person, would that be—and with the intent to arouse the sexual desire, arouse or gratify, as defined in [the operative definition in the Jones case], would that be, under your understanding then and now sexual relations? . . .

Clinton: Yes, it would. If you had a direct contact with any of these places in the body, if you had direct contact with intent to arouse or gratify, that would fall within the definition.

Q: So, you didn't do any of those three things—with Monica Lewinsky?

Clinton: You are free to infer that my testimony is that I did not have sexual relations, as I understood this term to be defined.

Q: Including touching her breast, kissing her breast, or touching her genitalia?

Clinton: That's correct. . . .

Q: Oral sex, in your view, is not covered, correct?

Clinton: If performed on the deponent.

Q: Is not covered, correct?

Clinton: That's my reading of this number (1).

Q: And you are declining to answer the hypothetical about insertion of an object. I need to inform you, Mr. President—we'll go on, at least for now. But I need to inform you that the grand jury will consider your not answering the questions more directly in their determination of whether or not they are going to issue another subpoena. . . .

[Lying to Staff]

Q: Do you recall denying any sexual relationship with Monica Lewinsky to the following people: Harry Thomasson, Erskine Bowles, Harold Ickes, [John] Podesta, Mr. Blumenthal, Mr. Jordan, Ms. Betty Currie? Do you recall denying any sexual relationship with Monica Lewinsky to those individuals?

Clinton: I recall telling a number of those people that I didn't have, either I didn't have an affair with Monica Lewinsky or didn't have sex with her. And I believe, sir, that—you'll have to ask them what they thought. But I was using those terms in the normal way people use them. You'll have to ask them what they thought I was saying. . . .

Did I hope that I would never have to be here on this day giving this testimony? Of course. But I also didn't want to do anything to complicate this matter further. So, I said things that were true. They may have been misleading, and if they were I have to take responsibility for it, and I'm sorry.

Q: After January 21st when the [*Washington*] *Post* article broke and said that Judge Starr was looking into this, you knew that they might be witnesses. You knew that they might be called into a grand jury, didn't you?

Clinton: That's right. I think I was quite careful what I said after that. I may have said something to all these people to that effect, but I'll also—whenever anybody asked me any details, I said, look, I don't want you to be a witness or I turn you into a witness or give you information that could get you in trouble. I just wouldn't talk. I, by and large, didn't talk to people about this.

Q: If all of these people—let's leave out Mrs. Currie for a minute. Vernon Jordan, Sid Blumenthal, John Podesta, Harold Ickes, Erskine Bowles, Harry Thomasson, after the story broke, after Judge Starr's involvement was known on January 21st, have said that you denied a sexual relationship with them. Are you denying that?

Clinton: No.

Q: And you've told us that you—

Clinton: I'm just telling you what I meant by it.

[Job for Lewinsky]

Q: Did you, on or about January the 13th, 1998, Mr. President, ask Erskine Bowles to ask John Hilley if he would give a recommendation for Monica Lewinsky?

C: In 1998?

Q: Yes. On or about January 13th, 1998, did you ask Erskine Bowles, your Chief of Staff, if he would ask John Hilley to give a recommendation for Monica Lewinsky?

Clinton: At some point, sir, I believe I talked to Erskine Bowles about whether Monica Lewinsky could get a recommendation that was not negative from the Legislative Affairs Office. I believe I did. . . . I do not know what the date was. At some point I did talk to him. . . .

My recollection is, sir, that Ms. Lewinsky was moving to New York, wanted to get a job in the private sector; was confident she would get a good recommendation from the Defense Department; and was concerned that because she had been moved from the Legislative Affairs Office, transferred to the Defense Department, that her ability to get a job might be undermined by a bad recommendation from the Legislative Affairs Office.

So, I asked Erskine if we could get her a recommendation that just was at least neutral, so that if she had a good recommendation from the Defense Department it wouldn't prevent her from getting a job in the private sector. . . .

Q: And who was it that asked you to do that on Monica Lewinsky's behalf?

Clinton: I think she did. You know, she tried for months and months to get a job back in the White House, not so much in the West Wing but somewhere in the White House complex, including the Old Executive Office Building. And she talked to Marsha Scott, among others.

She very much wanted to come back. And she interviewed for some jobs but never got one.

She was, from time to time, upset about it. And I think what she was afraid of is that she couldn't get a—from the minute she left the White House she was worried about this. That if she didn't come back to the White House and work for awhile and get a good job recommendation, that no matter how well she had done at the Pentagon it might hurt her future employment prospects.

Well, it became obvious that, you know, her mother had moved to New York. She wanted to go to New York. She wasn't going to get a job in the White House. So, she wanted to get a job in the private sector, and said, I hope that I won't get a letter out of the Legislative Affairs Office that will prevent my getting a job in the private sector. And that's what I talked to Erskine about. Now, that's my entire memory of this.

[Hiding the Gifts]

Q: All right. I want to go back briefly to the December 28th conversation with Ms. Lewinsky. I believe you testified to the effect that she asked you, what if they ask me about gifts you gave me. My question to you is, after that statement by her, did you ever have a conversation with Betty Currie about gifts, or picking something up from Monica Lewinsky?

Clinton: I don't believe I did, sir. No.

Q: You never told her anything to this effect, that Monica has something to give you?

Clinton: No, sir. . . .

Q: And so you have no knowledge that, or you had no knowledge at the time, that Betty Currie went and picked up, your secretary went and picked up from Monica Lewinsky items that were called for by the Jones subpoena and hid them under her bed? You had no knowledge that anything remotely like that was going to happen?

Clinton: I did not. I did not know she had those items, I believe, until that was made public.

Q: And you agree with me that that would be a very wrong thing to do, to hide evidence in a civil case, or any case? Isn't that true?

Clinton: Yes. I don't know that, that Ms. Currie knew that that's what she had at all. But—

Q: I'm not saying she did. . . .

Q: Did you ever say anything like that, you can always say that you were coming to see Betty or bringing me letters? Was that part of any kind of a, anything you said to [Lewinsky] or a cover story, before you had any idea she was going to be part of Paula Jones?

Clinton: I might well have said that.

Q: Okay.

Clinton: Because I certainly didn't want this to come out, if I could help it. And I was concerned about that. I was embarrassed about it. I knew it was wrong. And, you know, of course, I didn't want it to come out. But—

Q: But you are saying that you didn't say anything—I want to make sure I understand. Did you say anything like that once you knew or thought she might be a witness in the Jones case? Did you repeat that statement, or something like it to her?

Clinton: Well, again, I don't recall, and I don't recall whether I might have done something like that, for example, if somebody says, what if the reporters ask me this, that or the other thing. I can tell you this: In the context of whether she could be a witness, I have a recollection that she asked me, well, what do I do if I get called as a witness, and I said you have to get a lawyer. And that's all I said. And I never asked her to lie.

Q: Did you tell her to tell the truth?

Clinton: Well, I think the implication was she would tell the truth. I've already told you that I felt strongly that she could issue, that she could execute an affidavit that would be factually truthful, that might get her out of having to testify. . . .

[Getting a Job]

Q: I want to go back to a question about Vernon Jordan. I want to go back to late December and early January, late December of '97 and early January of '98. During this time, Mr. President, you are being sued for sexual harassment by a woman who claims, among other things, that others got benefits that she didn't because she didn't [have] sex [with] you. While this is happening, your powerful friend, Vernon Jordan, is helping to get Monica Lewinsky a job and a lawyer. He's helping to get a job and a lawyer for someone who had some kind of sex with you, and who has been subpoenaed in the very case, the Jones case. Don't you see a problem with this? Didn't you see a problem with this?

Clinton: No. . . . I don't think it was wrong to be helping her. Look—

Q: A subpoenaed witness in a case against you?

Clinton: Absolutely. Look, for one thing, I had already proved in two ways that I was not trying to influence her testimony. I didn't order her to be hired at the White House. I could have done so. I wouldn't do it. She tried for months to get in. She was angry. Secondly, after I—

Q: Wasn't she kept—

Clinton: After I terminated the improper contact with her, she wanted to come in more than she did. She got angry when she didn't get in sometimes. I knew that that might make her more likely to speak, and I still did it because I had to limit the contact.

And, thirdly, let me say, I formed an opinion really early in 1996 . . . once I got into this unfortunate and wrong conduct, that when I stopped it, which I knew I'd have to do and which I should have done a long time before I did, that she would talk about it. Not because Monica Lewinsky is a bad person. . . . But I knew that the minute there was no longer any contact, she would talk about this. She would have to. She couldn't help it. It was, it was a part of her psyche. So, I had put myself at risk, sir. I was not trying to buy her silence or get Vernon Jordan to buy her silence. I thought she was a good person. She had not been involved with me for a long time in any improper way, months, and I wanted to help her get on with her life. It's just as simple as that . . .

[Defining Sex]

Q: Well, the grand jury would like to know, Mr. President, why it is that you think that oral sex performed on you does not fall within the definition of sexual relations as used in your deposition.

C: Because that is—if the deponent is the person who has oral sex performed on him, then the contact is with—not with anything on that list, but with the lips of another person. It seems to be self-evident that that's what it is. And I thought it was curious.

Let me remind you, sir, I read this carefully.... And I had to admit under this definition that I'd actually had sexual relations with Gennifer Flowers. Now, I would rather have taken a whipping than done that, after all the trouble I'd been through with Gennifer Flowers....

Q: Would you have been prepared, if asked by the Jones lawyers, would you have been prepared to answer a question directly asked about oral sex performed on you by Monica Lewinsky?

Clinton: If the Judge had required me to answer it, of course, I would have answered it. And I would have answered it truthfully....

CLINTON ON RAIDS AGAINST "TERRORIST" SITES
August 20, 1998

Retaliating for the August 7 terrorist bombings of the U.S. embassies in Kenya and Tanzania, the United States on August 20 launched cruise missile attacks against locations in Afghanistan and the Sudan. In announcing the strikes, President Bill Clinton said the bombing targets in those countries were linked to the terrorists who were responsible for the embassy bombings. (Embassy bombings, p. 555)

The U.S. attacks caused serious damage to the targets but did not harm the man said by the U.S. officials to have been the mastermind of the embassy bombings: exiled Saudi millionaire Usama bin Laden. Bin Laden reportedly lived in a remote Afghanistan camp hit by the U.S. missiles, but he was not harmed. In the months after the air strikes he continued to denounce the United States and call for Islamic retaliation against the United States. In November a grand jury in New York indicted bin Laden and an associate on dozens of charges of murder stemming from the embassy bombings.

The August 20 attack was the third time since the mid-1980s that the United States had launched a major military assault in response to alleged terrorism. In April 1986 the Reagan administration bombed Libyan targets—including one of the homes of Libyan leader Mu'ammar al-Qadhafi— in retaliation for the bombing of a disco in Berlin that killed one U.S. servicemen and one Turkish citizen, with more than two hundred injured. In June 1993, after receiving reports that the Iraqi government had attempted to assassinate former president George Bush during a visit to Kuwait, the Clinton administration bombed sites in Baghdad. (U.S. airstrikes against Libya, Historic Documents of 1986, p. 347)

Clinton administration officials said the United States took unilateral action to respond to the 1998 embassy bombings because it was clear that the governments that hosted terrorist organizations would not take any steps to punish those responsible for the bombings. Administration officials also said the United States was hoping to deter future terrorist attacks. However, Secretary of State Madeleine K. Albright was among senior U.S. officials who warned that the U.S. struggle against terrorism was a new kind of war—"the war of the future," she called it—and one that likely would persist for many years. Thomas R. Pickering, the undersecretary of state for political affairs, said of the U.S. air strikes: "We do not expect that these strikes will in themselves end the threat [of terrorism], but they are important because they clearly show that we are in this for the long haul."

The Targets

Approximately seventy-five cruise missiles launched from U.S. warships in the Arabian Sea and the Red Sea hit three targets in Afghanistan and one in the Sudan. The Afghan targets were three camps, located in the rural mountains southeast of the capital city, Kabul, that U.S. officials said were used by terrorists: a base camp named Zhawar Kili al Badr, a training camp, and a support camp. U.S. officials said bin Laden lived at the base camp. It was unclear whether bin Laden was present at the time of the missile attack; in any event, he was not harmed. Afghan officials gave conflicting estimates of the number of people killed in the attack, ranging from a low of twenty-one to a high of more than fifty. The attack caused heavy damage to the buildings at all three camps, according to U.S. intelligence observations.

U.S. officials said the attack on the Afghan camps was timed to disrupt a meeting of terrorists scheduled to take place there August 20. It was possible, the officials said, that bin Laden had called the meeting to plan future attacks against U.S. interests overseas.

The U.S. target in the Sudan was a factory located just north of the capital, Khartoum. U.S. officials said the factory was owned by bin Laden or his associates and produced precursor chemicals for the deadly nerve gas called "VX." The Sudanese government insisted the plant produced medicines, both for humans and animals. Sudan's president, Omar Hassan al-Bashir, said the plant was the source of about half the country's medicines. The missile attack destroyed much of the plant but left the surrounding neighborhood unscathed. Sudanese officials said ten people were wounded in the attack.

World Reaction

Support for the attacks came from close U.S. allies, especially Israel, Britain, and Germany. Even the French government, which often distanced itself from U.S. policy toward the Middle East, said the United States had the right to respond to terrorism. Leaders of several Arab nations with close ties to the United States—including Egypt, Jordan, and Saudi Arabia—were circumspect, apparently wishing to avoid taking a position.

Ironically, the most intense initial criticism came from two sources with little in common: a handful of Republicans on Capitol Hill and anti-American Islamic factions in the Middle East. Sen. Dan Coats, R-Ind., crit-

icized Clinton, suggesting that the president was taking military action to divert attention away from his legal troubles in the Monica Lewinsky affair. Just three days before the attack, Clinton's grand jury testimony in the Lewinsky case had been aired on television. After attending closed-door briefings from senior U.S. military and intelligence officials, most of Clinton's critics supported the attacks as a necessary strike against terrorism. Leaders in Iran, Iraq, Libya, the Sudan, and several other Arab countries also cited the Lewinsky affair in denouncing Clinton. (Lewinsky case, pp. 564, 632, 695, 950)

Anti-American street demonstrations took place throughout the Arab world, particularly in countries that had strained relations with Washington. On the day of the missile attacks, the State Department issued a warning to Americans traveling or living abroad that they should be alert to the possibility of retaliation by terrorists. Americans should exercise "much greater caution than usual," the State Department said, and should avoid large crowds and other situations where anti-American sentiments were expressed.

Questions About the Sudan Factory

In justifying the attack on the chemical factory in Sudan, the Clinton administration cited evidence that the factory had produced the chemical "Empta," which had no known use other than as a component of the VX nerve gas. VX was one of the most deadly chemical agents; a tiny amount placed on the skin or inhaled was capable of killing a human within a matter of minutes. Early in 1998 a U.S. intelligence agent had obtained a sample of soil from the vicinity of the Sudanese plant. A chemical analysis determined that the soil contained traces of Empta. It was that analysis that U.S. officials cited in determining that the plant produced chemical weapons. U.S. officials also said they had evidence that scientists from Iraq had worked at the factory, called Al Shifa Pharmaceutical Industries.

In the weeks after the attack, U.S. statements about the plant were called into question by news reports and statements from individuals claiming to have first-hand knowledge of operations at the plant. News organizations quoted Tom Carnaffin, a British mechanical engineer who said he worked at the plant for nearly four years until 1996, as saying the facility was used to mix medicines and lacked the space or equipment to produce chemical weapons. Other observers quoted in news reports cast doubt on U.S. assertions that the plant was a tightly guarded facility financed by bin Laden. Chemical industry experts also said the U.S. analysis of the soil sample from near the plant could have been mistaken; Empta was said to have some similarities to commonly used fungicides.

In an extensive report in its September 21 editions, the New York Times *quoted some administration officials as saying that the U.S. intelligence analysis of the Al Shifa plant was flawed. Other officials, however, insisted that the United States had adequate information on which to base a judgment that the plant was used to produce dangerous chemical weapons.*

Following is the text of a speech by President Bill Clinton on August 20, 1998, in which he discussed U.S. air strikes earlier that day against alleged terrorist sites in Afghanistan and the Sudan:

Good afternoon. Today I ordered our Armed Forces to strike at terrorist-related facilities in Afghanistan and Sudan because of the imminent threat they presented to our national security.

I want to speak with you about the objective of this action and why it was necessary. Our target was terror. Our mission was clear—to strike at the network of radical groups affiliated with and funded by Osama bin Laden, perhaps the preeminent organizer and financier of international terrorism in the world today.

The groups associated with him come from diverse places, but share a hatred for democracy, a fanatical glorification of violence, and a horrible distortion of their religion to justify the murder of innocents. They have made the United States their adversary precisely because of what we stand for and what we stand against.

A few months ago, and again this week, bin Laden publicly vowed to wage a terrorist war against America, saying—and I quote—"We do not differentiate between those dressed in military uniforms and civilians. They're all targets. Their mission is murder and their history is bloody."

In recent years, they killed American, Belgian and Pakistani peacekeepers in Somalia. They plotted to assassinate the President of Egypt and the Pope. They planned to bomb six United States 747s over the Pacific. They bombed the Egyptian embassy in Pakistan. They gunned down German tourists in Egypt.

The most recent terrorist events are fresh in our memory. Two weeks ago, 12 Americans and nearly 300 Kenyans and Tanzanians lost their lives, and another 5,000 were wounded when our embassies in Nairobi and Dar es Salaam were bombed. There is convincing information from our intelligence community that the bin Laden terrorist network was responsible for these bombings.

Based on this information, we have high confidence that these bombings were planned, financed, and carried out by the organization bin Laden leads.

America has battled terrorism for many years. Where possible, we've used law enforcement and diplomatic tools to wage the fight. The long arm of American law has reached out around the world and brought to trial those guilty of attacks in New York and Virginia and in the Pacific. We have quietly disrupted terrorist groups and foiled their plots. We have isolated countries that practice terrorism. We've worked to build an international coalition against terror.

But there have been, and will be, times when law enforcement and diplomatic tools are simply not enough, when our very national security is challenged, and when we must take extraordinary steps to protect the safety of our citizens. With compelling evidence that the bin Laden network of terrorist groups was planning to mount further attacks against Americans and other freedom-loving people, I decided America must act.

And so, this morning, based on the unanimous recommendation of my national security team, I ordered our Armed Forces to take action to counter an immediate threat from the bin Laden network. Earlier today, the United States carried out simultaneous strikes against terrorist facilities and infrastructure in Afghanistan. Our forces targeted one of the most active terrorist bases in the world. It contained key elements of the bin Laden network's infrastructure and has served as a training camp for literally thousands of terrorists from around the globe. We have reason to believe that a gathering of key terrorist leaders was to take place there today, thus underscoring the urgency of our actions.

Our forces also attacked a factory in Sudan associated with the bin Laden network. The factory was involved in the production of materials for chemical weapons.

The United States does not take this action lightly. Afghanistan and Sudan have been warned for years to stop harboring and supporting these terrorist groups. But countries that persistently host terrorists have no right to be safe havens.

Let me express my gratitude to our intelligence and law enforcement agencies for their hard, good work. And let me express my pride in our Armed Forces who carried out this mission while making every possible effort to minimize the loss of innocent life.

I want you to understand, I want the world to understand, that our actions today were not aimed against Islam, the faith of hundreds of millions of good, peace-loving people all around the world, including the United States. No religion condones the murder of innocent men, women and children. But our actions were aimed at fanatics and killers who wrap murder in the cloak of righteousness; and in so doing, profane the great religion in whose name they claim to act.

My fellow Americans, our battle against terrorism did not begin with the bombing of our embassies in Africa; nor will it end with today's strike. It will require strength, courage and endurance. We will not yield to this threat. We will meet it, no matter how long it may take. This will be a long, ongoing struggle between freedom and fanaticism; between the rule of law and terrorism. We must be prepared to do all that we can for as long as we must.

America is and will remain a target of terrorists precisely because we are leaders; because we act to advance peace, democracy and basic human values; because we're the most open society on Earth; and because, as we have shown yet again, we take an uncompromising stand against terrorism.

But of this I am also sure. The risks from inaction to America and the world would be far greater than action, for that would embolden our enemies, leaving their ability and their willingness to strike us intact. In this case, we knew before our attack that these groups already had planned further actions against us and others.

I want to reiterate: The United States wants peace, not conflict. We want to lift lives around the world, not take them. We have worked for peace—in Bosnia, in Northern Ireland, in Haiti, in the Middle East and elsewhere. But in this day, no campaign for peace can succeed without a determination to fight terrorism. Let our actions today send this message loud and clear: There are no expendable American targets. There will be no sanctuary for terrorists. We will defend our people, our interests and our values. We will help people of all faiths, in all parts of the world, who want to live free of fear and violence. We will persist and we will prevail.

Thank you. God bless you, and may God bless our country.

CANADIAN SUPREME COURT ON QUEBEC INDEPENDENCE
August 20, 1998

Voters in Quebec—Canada's second most populous province—signaled again in 1998 that they were not yet ready to declare their independence from Canada. A provincial election on November 30 produced a virtual dead-heat between political parties in the French-majority province who wanted independence and those who wanted to remain within the Canadian federation. The results forced separatists to shelve plans for a referendum on independence, at least for the time being.

Quebecers had rejected independence in referenda in 1980 and 1995— the latter vote by a narrow margin of only 52,000 votes of 5 million cast. The separatist party, Parti Quebecois, had hoped that a convincing victory in 1998 provincial elections would pave the way for a third independence referendum, perhaps in 1999. The separatists, led by Premier Lucien Bouchard, managed to retain control of the provincial government in the November 30 elections, but they fell behind the antiseparatist Liberal Party in the popular vote.

The province of Quebec in 1998 had 7 million residents, about 82 percent of whom were native French speakers. Ever since Britain ousted France as the colonial power in Canada in 1759, French-speaking Quebecers had resented the political and economic power of English-speaking Canadians. Sentiment in Quebec for independence from Canada began to pick up in the 1960s. Saying they were treated as second-class citizens, French separatists likened their cause to the civil rights movement for blacks in the United States. The separatist movement scored its initial victory in 1976 when the Parti Quebecois gained control of the Quebec provincial government for the first time. Four years later, 60 percent of Quebecers rejected independence in a referendum. But another vote in October 1995 showed Quebec voters almost evenly divided: 50.56 percent against independence and 49.44 percent for it.

The three decades of debate over independence had wearied most Canadians and Quebecers. Perhaps the most telling argument by those opposing independence was the economic impact of the separatist movement. Scores of major companies had pulled out of Quebec during the 1980s and 1990s because of the political uncertainty there and the Quebec government's rules limiting the use of English in everyday commerce.

Court Ruling

After the 1995 independence referendum, the Canadian government asked the country's Supreme Court for an advisory opinion—called a "reference"—on the question of whether Quebec could secede unilaterally. The nine-judge court on August 20 gave a unanimous Solomon-like answer of both "no" and "yes."

No, the court said, Quebec could not constitutionally secede just by declaring independence. "Democracy means more than simple majority rule" within a province, the court said, because Canada had a federal system of government that had several responsibilities, including protecting the rights of minorities.

But if the majority of Quebec voters were to declare in a referendum that they wanted to secede, the federal government would have an obligation to negotiate with the province on the terms of secession. "A clear majority vote in Quebec on a clear question in favor of secession would confer democratic legitimacy on the secession initiative which all the other participants in the Confederation would have to recognize," the court said.

If such a majority were to emerge in a referendum, the court added, there would have to be "principled negotiation" among all parties to the Canadian constitution, including the federal government and the nine other provinces. The results would be subject to the same procedures as any other amendment to the constitution: approval by the federal parliament and at least seven provinces.

Implicitly rebuking separatist leaders who had played down the complexities of secession, the court said negotiations following an independence referendum "would undoubtedly be difficult. While negotiators would have to contemplate the possibility of secession, there would be no absolute entitlement to it and no assumption that an agreement reconciling all relevant rights and obligations would actually be reached." It was even possible that negotiations could reach an impasse, the court said, adding that it did not want to speculate "as to what would then transpire."

In fact, the prospect of an impasse was more than a theoretical possibility. Throughout the 1980s and 1990s federal and provincial leaders had tried to negotiate various ways of satisfying the yearning of many Quebecers for independence—and of people in other provinces for more autonomy from Ottawa—while keeping the federation whole. Negotiated agreements in 1987 and 1992 both held promise of compromise, but neither was implemented because of opposition in one or more of the provinces. Several other efforts failed to produce any lasting agreement of substance. (Negotiation attempts, Historic Documents of 1990, p. 367)

Advocates on both sides of the Quebec independence issue claimed to be pleased by the court ruling. Canadian prime minister Jean Chretien, a Quebecer who fervently opposed independence, praised the court for "bringing clarity to certain fundamental rules" for how the secession issue should be handled. Jacques Brassard, Quebec's minister for intergovernmental affairs and a hard-line separatist, insisted the ruling had given an "uncompromising reaffirmation" of the province's right to independence.

The court's ruling played a modest role in the Quebec provincial elections three months later. Separatist forces successfully used the ruling to bolster their argument that the federal government would have no choice but to negotiate with Quebec should the province vote for independence. That was an argument with some attraction for Quebecers who wanted independence but only as a result of peaceful talks with the government in Ottawa.

Quebec Election

Both sides on the Quebec independence issue agreed that 1998 was to be a pivotal year. Bouchard, the fiery Quebec pro-independence premier, called parliamentary elections for the end of November because he believed his Parti Quebecois could score a resounding victory and then lead the province to independence through a third, and final, referendum as early as 1999. Anti-independence forces were just as determined and optimistic that they could stop Bouchard; they coalesced under a newly refashioned Liberal Party under the leadership of Jean Charest.

Both men were charismatic politicians who had served in the federal cabinet of Prime Minister Brian Mulroney, then changed political affiliation, and returned to the provincial politics of Quebec. Bouchard was from Jonquiere, an area northeast of Quebec City that was a hotbed of the independence movement. Charest hailed from Sherbrooke in the Eastern Townships, just north of the border with Vermont—an area with one of the heaviest concentration of English-speakers in Quebec.

Both Bouchard and Charest said the election would be a referendum on a referendum. A strong Parti Quebecois victory would mean that the voters wanted to be able to vote directly on independence, Bouchard said. A victory by the Liberals would mean that voters were tired of the independence movement and wanted to remain within Canada, Charest said.

The voters handed a surprise to both men. They gave Bouchard another term in office, largely because the method of apportioning parliamentary districts (called "ridings") favored his Parti Quebecois. But they gave Charest and his party a tiny plurality in the popular vote: 43.7 percent for the Liberals to 42.7 for the Parti Quebecois. A third party that opposed independence, Action Democratique, polled 11.8 percent, apparently drawing much of its support from disaffected Parti Quebecois supporters.

Charest declared a "moral victory" and claimed that the vote had spoken clearly against staging another referendum. Bouchard at first said he was still keeping his options open on the issue, but then quickly shelved any further talk of holding a referendum in the near future. The voters, he acknowledged, "are not prepared to give us the correct conditions for a referendum right now."

In the weeks immediately after the election, Bouchard turned to another issue to stoke the secessionist fires: negotiating a "social union" compact between the ten provinces and the federal government. Bouchard and other provincial leaders in August had proposed an agreement under which the federal government would not impose new social spending programs on the provinces without their consent. Leaders of Quebec and several other provinces had been angered by what they saw as the Ottawa government's habit of mandating new programs but failing to provide any money for them.

Following the November 30 election, Bouchard insisted that the federal government reach an agreement with the provinces on social program spending by February 1999. Chretien said he was willing to negotiate with the provinces on the issue but was unwilling to give up the federal government's authority over social programs that affected all Canadians.

Following are excerpts from a decision issued by the Supreme Court of Canada on August 20, 1998, answering questions posed to the court on the possibility of secession by the province of Quebec:

Pursuant to s. 53 of the *Supreme Court Act,* the Governor in Council referred the following questions to this Court:

Question 1: Under the Constitution of Canada, can the National Assembly, legislature or government of Quebec effect the secession of Quebec from Canada unilaterally?

Question 2: Does international law give the National Assembly, legislature or government of Quebec the right to effect the secession of Quebec from Canada unilaterally? In this regard, is there a right to self-determination under international law that would give the National Assembly, legislature or government of Quebec the right to effect the secession of Quebec from Canada unilaterally?

Question 3: In the event of a conflict between domestic and international law on the right of the National Assembly, legislature or government of Quebec to effect the secession of Quebec from Canada unilaterally, which would take precedence in Canada? . . .

The reference questions are justiciable and should be answered. They do not ask the Court to usurp any democratic decision that the people of Quebec may be called upon to make. The questions, as interpreted by the Court, are strictly limited to aspects of the legal framework in which that democratic decision is to be taken. Since the reference questions may clearly be interpreted as directed to legal issues, the Court is in a position to answer them. The Court cannot exercise its discretion to refuse to answer the questions on a pragmatic basis. The questions raise issues of fundamental public importance and they are not too imprecise or ambiguous so as not to permit a proper legal answer. Nor has the Court been provided with insufficient information regarding the present context in which the questions arise. Finally, the Court may deal on a reference with issues that might otherwise be considered not yet "ripe" for decision.

[(1) omitted]

(2) Question 1

The Constitution is more than a written text. It embraces the entire global system of rules and principles which govern the exercise of constitutional authority. A superficial reading of selected provisions of the written constitutional enactment, without more, may be misleading. It is necessary to make a more profound investigation of the underlying principles animating the whole of the Constitution, including the principles of federalism, democracy, constitutionalism and the rule of law, and respect for minorities. Those principles must inform our overall appreciation of the constitutional rights and obligations that would come into play in the event that a clear majority of Quebecers votes on a clear question in favour of secession.

The Court in this Reference is required to consider whether Quebec has a right to unilateral secession. Arguments in support of the existence of such a right were primarily based on the principle of democracy. Democracy, however, means more than simple majority rule. Constitutional jurisprudence shows that democracy exists in the larger context of other constitutional values. Since Confederation, the people of the provinces and territories have created close ties of interdependence (economic, social, political and cultural) based on shared values that include federalism, democracy, constitutionalism and the rule of law, and respect for minorities. A democratic decision of Quebecers in favour of secession would put those relationships at risk. The Constitution vouchsafes order and stability, and accordingly secession of a province "under the Constitution" could not be achieved unilaterally, that is, without principled negotiation with other participants in Confederation within the existing constitutional framework.

Our democratic institutions necessarily accommodate a continuous process of discussion and evolution, which is reflected in the constitutional right of each participant in the federation to initiate constitutional change. This right implies a reciprocal duty on the other participants to engage in discussions to address any legitimate initiative to change the constitutional order. A clear majority vote in Quebec on a clear question in favour of secession would confer democratic legitimacy on the secession initiative which all of the other participants in Confederation would have to recognize.

Quebec could not, despite a clear referendum result, purport to invoke a right of self-determination to dictate the terms of a proposed secession to the other parties to the federation. The democratic vote, by however strong a majority, would have no legal effect on its own and could not push aside the principles of federalism and the rule of law, the rights of individuals and minorities, or the operation of democracy in the other provinces or in Canada as a whole. Democratic rights under the Constitution cannot be divorced from constitutional obligations. Nor, however, can the reverse proposition be accepted: the continued existence and operation of the Canadian constitutional order could not be indifferent to a clear expression of a clear majority of Quebecers that they no longer wish to remain in Canada. The other provinces and the federal government would have no basis to deny the right of the government of Quebec to pursue secession should a clear majority of the people of Quebec choose that goal, so long as in doing so, Quebec respects the rights of others. The negotiations that followed such a vote would address the potential act of secession as well as its possible terms should in fact secession proceed. There would be no conclusions predetermined by law on any issue. Negotiations would need to address the interests of the other provinces, the federal government and Quebec and indeed the rights of all Canadians both within and outside Quebec, and specifically the rights of minorities.

The negotiation process would require the reconciliation of various rights and obligations by negotiation between two legitimate majorities, namely, the majority of the population of Quebec, and that of Canada as a whole. A political majority at either level that does not act in accordance with the underlying constitutional principles puts at risk the legitimacy of its exercise of its rights, and the ultimate acceptance of the result by the international community.

The task of the Court has been to clarify the legal framework within which political decisions are to be taken "under the Constitution" and not to usurp the prerogatives of the political forces that operate within that framework. The obligations identified by the Court are binding obligations under the Constitution. However, it will be for the political actors to determine what constitutes "a clear majority on a clear question" in the circumstances under which a future referendum vote may be taken. Equally, in the event of demonstrated majority support for Quebec secession, the content and process of the negotiations will be for the political actors to settle. The reconciliation of the various legitimate constitutional interests is necessarily committed to the political rather than the judicial realm precisely because that reconciliation can only be achieved through the give and take of political negotiations. To the extent issues addressed in the course of negotiation are political, the courts, appreciating their proper role in the constitutional scheme, would have no supervisory role.

(3) Question 2

The Court was also required to consider whether a right to unilateral secession exists under international law. Some supporting an affirmative answer did so on the basis of the recognized right to self-determination that belongs to all "peoples". Although much of the Quebec population certainly shares many of the characteristics of a people, it is not necessary to decide the "people" issue because, whatever may be the correct determination of this issue in the context of Quebec, a right to secession only arises under the principle of self-determination of people at international law where "a people" is governed as part of a colonial empire; where "a people" is subject to alien subjugation, domination or exploitation; and possibly where "a people" is denied any meaningful exercise of its right to self-determination within the state of which it forms a part. In other circumstances, peoples are expected to achieve self-determination within the framework of their existing state. A state whose government represents the whole of the people or peoples resident within its territory, on a basis of equality and without discrimination, and respects the principles of self-determination in its internal arrangements, is entitled to maintain its territorial integrity under international law and to have that territorial integrity recognized by other states. Quebec does not meet the threshold of a colonial people or an oppressed people, nor can it be suggested that Quebecers have been denied meaningful access to government to pursue their political, economic, cultural and social development. In the circumstances, the "National Assembly, the legislature or the government of Quebec" do not enjoy a right at international law to effect the secession of Quebec from Canada unilaterally.

Although there is no right, under the Constitution or at international law, to unilateral secession, the possibility of an unconstitutional declaration of secession leading to a de facto secession is not ruled out. The ultimate success of such a secession would be dependent on recognition by the international community, which is likely to consider the legality and legitimacy of secession having regard to, amongst other facts, the conduct of Quebec and Canada, in determining whether to grant or withhold recognition. Even if granted, such recognition would not, however, provide any retroactive justification for the act of secession, either under the Constitution of Canada or at international law.

(4) Question 3

In view of the answers to Questions 1 and 2, there is no conflict between domestic and international law to be addressed in the context of this Reference.

September

YELTSIN AND CLINTON ON RUSSIAN ECONOMIC CRISIS
September 2, 1998

Weak and divided political leadership, a poor harvest, and the Soviet-era legacy of waste and corruption were some of the factors that pushed the Russian economy to the brink of collapse in 1998. Western governments and aid agencies offered billions of dollars worth of loans to help Russia move toward a free market, but that money failed to prevent private investors from pulling even more billions of dollars out of Russia once they lost confidence in the country's haphazard economic reforms.

President Boris Yeltsin had three different governments during the year, each unable to develop a credible plan to keep the economy on an even keel. The most reform-minded of the three took a series of bold steps in August to devalue the ruble and freeze debt payments; that move backfired and hastened the country's economic slide.

Each of Yeltsin's governments was caught in an impossible squeeze. On the one hand, international investors, both public and private, were pressing for continued economic reforms and government spending cutbacks. The International Monetary Fund (IMF) and other lenders were particularly insistent that the Kremlin begin a serious effort to collect taxes and curtail unproductive subsidies of state-run enterprises. But domestically, the government faced directly opposite pressure from the communist-led opposition in parliament, labor unions, and many segments of the general public to resort to the old ways of keeping the economy going—printing more money, bailing out inefficient industries, and boosting wages.

The IMF worked feverishly during much of the year to develop international support for the Russian economy. After those efforts failed to halt the economic crisis, the IMF concluded that Russia's troubles were essentially political in nature. Writing in the October 3 issue of the Economist *magazine, the IMF's deputy managing director, Stanley Fischer, said the key lesson about the Russian crisis was that "successive governments have been too weak to implement their desired policies."*

Leading to the Collapse

The Russian financial collapse of 1998 was the result of nearly eight years of a halting, hit-or-miss transition from the command economy of the Soviet era to a free market with many leftover elements of communism. Throughout those years, Yeltsin had trouble winning public support for his reform measures, many of which had painful consequences for average Russians. Often it appeared that the chief beneficiaries were the few eager capitalists who seemed to understand how to benefit from a free market system; many Russians derisively called them the "oligarchs" and voiced suspicions that all of Yeltsin's moves were intended to make them richer.

In the early years of the decade, Russia's chief economic problem had been hyperinflation. The collapse of the communist system and the opening of free markets forced prices up and the value of the ruble down. By 1992 inflation reached 1,500 percent on an annual basis. Inflation gradually subsided in the middle part of the decade as Russians became more accustomed to the vagaries of the marketplace. Yeltsin won reelection in 1996, defeating an aggressive challenge by the resurrected Communist Party. (Yeltsin election, Historic Documents of 1996, p. 430)

Twin events in the second half of 1997 helped to undermine Russia's fragile economic stability. The first was the worldwide financial crisis that started in Thailand and spread to much of southeast Asia, then to other emerging market economies. The "contagion" effect of the Asian crisis ultimately reached Russia when nervous investors began looking for safer places to put their money. The resulting capital flight forced Russian banks and the government to offer increasingly higher interest rates (reaching as high as 200 percent) to attract investors back. A companion shock was the continuing slide of world prices for oil and natural gas, Russia's chief exports. (Asian financial crisis, p. 722)

By early 1998 many foreign investors had pulled out of Russia, sending the stock market tumbling and making it virtually impossible for hard-pressed businesses to obtain new capital. The capital flight also forced the government to rely on agencies such as the IMF for money to finance its gigantic debt because the country's currency reserves were dwindling.

Yeltsin's First Change of Government

As the Russian financial picture worsened—and as rumors spread that Yeltsin was out of touch with daily affairs—Yeltsin on March 23 dramatically fired several of his key aides, including Viktor S. Chernomyrdin, who had served as prime minister since December 1992. A former chairman of the Gazprom natural gas monopoly, Chernomyrdin had been a cautious but steady proponent of economic reform and an important link between the Russian government and the Clinton administration. Yeltsin said he shook up his cabinet "in an effort to make economic reforms more energetic and effective, to give them a political push, a new impulse." On

March 30 Yeltsin said he would not run for president again when his term expired in 2000.

As Chernomyrdin's replacement, Yeltsin appointed Sergei Kiriyenko, the young and relatively obscure minister for fuel and energy programs. The communist-dominated lower house of parliament, the Duma, refused to confirm Kiriyenko's appointment for nearly a month. The parliament finally gave way and approved Kiriyenko on April 24, only after Yeltsin threatened to call new elections.

The new government took some of its boldest steps to stem the tide in late May, when the ruble was coming under intense pressure. On May 26, the Kremlin pared government spending by 12 percent. The next day, the Central Bank tripled interest rates to 150 percent, hoping to encourage investors to buy ruble-based securities.

The actions in May temporarily stabilized the situation, but within weeks key economic indicators were again weakening, and the government was once more forced to consider alternatives to devaluing the ruble. The Kiriyenko government renewed previous appeals to the IMF for a new financing package.

Under pressure from the Clinton administration, the IMF in mid-July put together a package intended to bolster the Russian financial posture and prevent remaining private investors from panicking and withdrawing their money. An agreement reached on July 13 provided for $17.1 billion in new loans; when added to previous commitments by the IMF and other lenders, that brought the total two-year commitment to $22 billion.

The IMF board approved the $17.1 billion loan package on July 21 but reduced the planned first installment (from $5.6 billion to $4.8 billion) as a signal of dissatisfaction with the Russian government's failure to follow through on previous reform pledges. The IMF also was attempting to give Yeltsin additional ammunition in its campaign to get a reform package through the communist-controlled parliament.

The first installment reached Russia at the end of July, but it provided only a short-lived respite for the Russian economy. By the second week of August, nervous foreign investors were again pulling money out of Russia, threatening to push the country's banks into bankruptcy because they lacked the cash to pay overseas creditors. The parliament went into its summer recess without approving the government's reform plan. George Soros, an influential financier and currency trader, heightened international fears about Russia with a statement that the country's finances had reached a "terminal" stage. Then over the August 15–16 weekend the Kiriyenko government appealed to the IMF and Western lenders for another emergency bailout. The request was turned down.

A Bold Gamble

On August 17 Kiriyenko announced that the government was taking several drastic, risky steps to prevent an economic collapse. The government *would allow the ruble to float against foreign currencies within a much broader band than previously (effectively devaluing the currency by as much as 50 percent); delay payments for 90 days on foreign debts, most of which were owed by Russian banks; and restructure the terms of an estimated $60 billion domestic market in government bonds.*

These moves heightened the already developing sense of panic among Russians, millions of whom tried to exchange rubles for dollars before their currency fell even further. Some international financial experts said Kiriyenko's moves might stabilize the situation, but many overseas investors who had not already pulled their money out of Russia quickly rushed to do so. IMF managing director Michel Camdessus said it was becoming increasingly urgent that the Russian government follow through on its promised reforms, most notably increasing tax collections. The popular view in Moscow and other Russian cities appeared to be that Yeltsin's government was merely bailing out a dozen commercial banks who had helped him with his 1996 reelection.

Each of the government's steps represented a gamble, both domestically and internationally. Yeltsin's aides said the government had reached a point where it had to do something to staunch the flow of money out of the country. Officials were said to have worried that panicky Russians might take to the streets to topple the government—just as students had done a few months earlier in Indonesia. (Indonesian crisis, p. 284)

Much of the international concern was focused on the ninety-day moratorium on foreign debt payments, a move that many observers interpreted as a de facto default. Kiriyenko insisted that the government was not allowing banks to default but was merely giving them breathing space to find new sources of money.

At first international financial markets took the Kremlin moves in stride, but within a few days the reality of Russia's sinking economic position shook investors all over the world. Concern about Russia was a major factor in a sudden dive in stock markets in the United States and other countries at the end of August. The slide continued until early October, when the markets recovered and marched upward, with only a few brief interruptions, through the end of the year. Meanwhile, investors continued pulling their money out of Russia, and the ruble rapidly lost its value against the dollar and other foreign currencies.

Another Change of Governments

With the Russian economy seemingly on the verge of collapse, Yeltsin once again intervened with a surprise shake-up of his government. On the evening of August 23, after the sports news had been presented, Russian television newscasters announced that Yeltsin had dumped Kiriyenko as prime minister and was reinstalling Chernomyrdin.

Yeltsin's latest course reversal resulted in another period of political uncertainty. In follow-up negotiations aimed at winning parliament's endorsement of Chernomyrdin, Yeltsin agreed to give up some of his vast presidential powers, including his right to appoint all cabinet ministers. Yeltsin promised Western lenders, including the IMF and the United States, that economic reforms would continue. But Yeltsin's physical appearance, in a rare television interview on August 28, fanned widespread rumors that he was seriously ill.

Predictions that Chernomyrdin would win easy approval in parliament proved wrong. After a heated debate on August 31, the parliament rejected his nomination. That move came on the eve of a planned visit to Moscow by President Bill Clinton, and it was a major rebuke to Yeltsin.

Clinton spent two days in Moscow—September 1–2—meeting with Yeltsin, Chernomyrdin (who was still acting prime minister), and other officials. The meetings produced no major agreements or policy advances, although Clinton and Yeltsin did sign a pledge under which the United States and Russia would notify each other in advance of any launchings of ballistic missiles.

Clinton told an audience of students at Moscow University on September 1 that Russia had no "painless solutions" to its economic crisis but had to persevere on the course toward free markets. Clinton's specific prescriptions were the same ones that Western nations, the IMF, and private economists had been giving for nearly eight years: fair and consistent tax collections, protection of private property rights, and an end to government bailouts "for a privileged few." Those steps did not represent an "American agenda" for Russia but rather were "the imperatives of the marketplace" that any nation could ignore only at its peril, he said.

At a news conference with Yeltsin September 2, Clinton said he would favor additional Western aid to Russia—but only if economic reforms stayed on track. "If there is a clear movement toward reform, I'll do everything I can to accelerate outside support of all kinds," he said.

Another New Government

A little more than a week after Clinton left Russia, Yeltsin blinked in his confrontation with the parliament over a new government. Unable to win confirmation of Chernomyrdin, Yeltsin relented on September 10 and agreed to name as prime minister Yevgeny M. Primakov, who had been the foreign minister in the Chernomyrdin and Kiriyenko governments. A former journalist and Middle East specialist, Primakov had been a confidante of the last leader of the Soviet Union, Mikhail S. Gorbachev. Primakov had no experience in economic matters, but many Russians and foreign observers expressed hope that he might introduce an element of stability into Russia's increasingly volatile politics.

The parliament confirmed Primakov as prime minister on September 11. Although he said Russia would not return to the "command and administrative system" of the Soviet era, Primakov appointed several communists to key government posts, and he failed to articulate any clear program for getting Russia out of its financial crisis. IMF officials insisted they would not release $4.3 billion in pending loans for Russia until Primakov *developed an economic plan that took decisive steps to close the budget deficit and continue economic reforms.*

After less than a month in office the Primakov government appealed to the United States and western European nations for several hundred million dollars worth of food aid. The worst harvest since 1953 had sharply depleted Russia's food stocks—a disaster compounded by the country's lack of hard currency to buy food for its people on the world market. The United States promised to provide about 3.1 million metric tons of food—but only under conditions guaranteeing that the aid would be distributed fairly. Then, on November 4, the Russian government announced that it would not have enough money to make payments on about $17 billion in foreign debts due in 1999.

In the midst of these crisis developments, Russia's political establishment suffered a profound shock on November 20 when one of the most prominent reformist politicians was murdered by an unknown assailant. Galina Starovoitova, a legislator and a former aide to Yeltsin, was shot to death in the entrance of her St. Petersburg apartment. The killing deeply angered and troubled many Russians, particularly Starovoitova's liberal reformers who saw it as a sign of increasing instability and lawlessness.

Under continuing pressure from the IMF to develop an economic plan, Primakov finally won parliamentary approval of an austerity budget on December 24. It called for none of the spending on new social programs that communists had demanded, and it was based on the expectation of additional loans from the West and a refinancing of the $17 billion in foreign debt that was due in 1999. As of the end of 1998 the Primakov government had not completed negotiations with overseas private lenders and governments to reschedule its debts. On December 29 the government failed to make a $362 million payment that it owed to private lenders on debt held over from the old Soviet regime.

Following are excerpts from a joint news conference in Moscow on September 2, 1998, by Russian president Boris Yeltsin and U.S. president Bill Clinton:

President Yeltsin: Distinguished ladies and gentlemen, the official visit of the President of the United States Bill Clinton to Russia is coming to an end. We have had intensive, productive negotiations. We have managed to discuss a wide range of topical issues. I would like to emphasize the exchanges were sincere and keen. The dialogue was marked by the spirit of mutual understanding.

Responsibility of our two countries for maintaining and strengthening peace and stability is obvious. That is why we have paid special attention to the discussion of the entire spectrum of security issues in the world.

The discussion has included the implementation of international and bilateral treaties and agreements concerning the weapons of mass destruction, as well as the elaboration of common approaches to dealing with the threat of nuclear weapons proliferation and their delivery means.

Unfortunately, this is not the only major task the humanity struggles to resolve. That is why President Clinton and I have discussed global threats and challenges. Our positions on this issue have coincided and this closeness of approaches is reflected in the joint statement on common security changes on the threshold of the 21st century. I consider this document to be a significant step towards strengthening strategic partnership between Russia and the United States.

We have also had substantial talks on the most topical international issues. And there are quite a few such issues. I'll put it frankly; here our approaches have not always completely coincided. Russia rejects the use of power methods as a matter of principle. Conflicts of today have no military solutions, be it in Kosovo or around Iraq or Afghanistan or others. Also we do not accept the NATO centrism idea for the new European security architecture. Nevertheless, our talks have been conducive to greater mutual understanding on these issues.

Of course, we could not do without discussing economy problems. Current dimensions of our economic relations should be brought up to a qualitatively new level. We shall have to suffer through much blood, sweat, and tears before new forms of business cooperation worthy of our two great powers are found, reforms that would be able to withstand volatile circumstances. There exist quite a few opportunities for this. These are mentioned in our joint statement on economic issues.

In conclusion, I would like to say—and I hope Bill will agree with me—the summit was a success. This meeting, the 15th in a row, confirmed once again when Presidents of Russia and the United States join their efforts, no issue is two big for them.

Thank you for your kind attention.

President Clinton: Thank you very much, Mr. President, for your hospitality and for giving Hillary and me and our team the chance to come to Moscow again.

Over the past five years I have been in this great, historic city in times of bright hope and times of uncertainty. But throughout, I have witnessed the remarkable transformation of this nation to democracy and to a more open economy. We all know that this meeting comes at a challenging time for the Russian people. But I don't believe anyone could ever have doubted that there would be obstacles on Russia's road to a vibrant economy and a strong democracy. I don't—also believe that anyone can seriously doubt the determination of the Russian people to build a brighter, better, stronger future.

Russia is important to America. Our economies are connected; we share values, interests and friendship. We share security interests and heavy security responsibilities. In our discussions, President Yeltsin and I spoke about Russia's options for stabilizing its economy and restoring confidence. I reaffirmed America's strong view that Russia can move beyond today's crisis and create growth and good jobs, but only if it carries forward with its transformation, with a strong and fair tax system, greater rule of law, dealing forthrightly with financial institutions, having regulation that protects against abuses, and yes, developing an appropriate safety net for people who are hurt during times of change.

President Yeltsin reaffirmed his commitment to reform, and I believe that is the right commitment. The answer to the present difficulties is to finish the job that has been begun, not to stop it in mid-stream or to reverse course. This is a view I will reaffirm when I meet today with leaders of the Duma and the Federation Council. America and the international community are, I am convinced, ready to offer further assistance if Russia stays with the path of reform.

We discussed also at length common security concerns. We've reached an important agreement to increase the safety of all our people, an arrangement under which our countries will give each other continuous information on worldwide launches of ballistic missiles or space-launched vehicles detected by our respective early warning systems. This will reduce the possibility of nuclear war by mistake or accident, and give us information about missile activity by other countries.

We've also agreed to remove from each of our nuclear weapons program approximately 50 tons of plutonium—enough to make literally thousands of nuclear devices. Once converted, this plutonium can never again be used to make weapons that become lethal in the wrong hands. Our experts will begin meeting right away to finalize an implementation plan by the end of this year.

I'd like to say in passing, I'm very grateful for the support this initiative received in our Congress. We have four members of Congress here with us today, and I especially thank Senator [Pete] Domenici [R-N.M.] for his interest in this issue.

Next let me say I look forward to, and hope very much that the Russian Duma will approve START II so that we can negotiate a START III agreement that would cut our levels of arsenals down to one-fifth of Cold War levels. I think that would be good for our mutual security and good for the Russian economy. . . .

This has been a full agenda, a productive summit. Again, let me say that I have great confidence that the people of this great nation can move through this present difficult moment to continue and complete the astonishing process of democratization and modernization that I have been privileged to witness at close hand over the last five and a half years. . . .

Q. A question to both Presidents. Prior to meeting, many experts, politicians, and public at large believed that your meeting is futile. Nobody needs it. No results will be produced due to the known difficulties both in Russia and America. I understand now you're trying to make the case it's the other way around, the situation is different. So what was the psychological atmosphere to your talks, bearing in mind this disbelief in the success, this skeptical approach?

And, second, are we, Russia and U.S., partners right now, or still contenders? And today, bidding farewell, Boris Yeltsin and Bill Clinton, are they still friends? Thank you.

President Yeltsin: I will start with your last question. Yes, we stay friends and the atmosphere since the beginning of the talks until the end was a friendly one. I would say it was very considerate and there were no discontents during the talks that we had.

And this brings my conclusion that since we did not have any differences, in my opinion, there will be no differences also in our activities, in what we do bilaterally. Of course, that goes without saying. This is very logical.

Now, in response to those skeptical observers who alleged, and continue to do so, that they don't believe, I've been always saying, no, on the contrary—we need to repeat it—we do believe we do that in order to remove the tension, and each time, having those meetings, we've been able to do something to alleviate the tension. This is what really matters. We've been doing that, removing that tension. And this time again we have removed part of the tension one more time.

President Clinton: Well, first of all, I think it's important to answer your question of what happened from the point of view of the Russian people and then from the point of view of the American people.

You ask if we're still friends. The answer to that is, yes. You ask if Russia and the United States have a partnership. I think the plain answer to that is, yes, even though we don't always agree on every issue. I can tell you from my point of view this was a successful meeting on the national security issues, because I think establishing this early warning information sharing is important and I know that the destruction of this huge volume of plutonium is important. And it also might be important to the Russian economy. It can be . . . a national security plus.

Now, on the domestic economic issues, from the point of view of America, it was important to me to come here just to say to the President and to his team and to the Duma leaders I will see later and the Federation Council leaders that I know this is a difficult time, but there is no shortcut to developing a system that will have the confidence of investors around the world. These are not American rules or anybody else's rules. These are—in a global economy, you have to be able to get money in from outside your country and keep the money in your country invested in your country.

And if the reform process can be completed, then I for one would be strongly supportive of greater assistance to Russia from the United States and the other big economic powers, because I think we have a very strong vested interest in seeing an economically successful Russia that is a full partner across the whole range of issues in the world. I also think it's good for preserving Russia's democracy and freedom.

So, from my point of view, saying that we support reform and saying we will support those who continue it was in itself a reason to come. . . .

President Yeltsin: I would like to add just for one second, please, just two words here. We have put it on paper. We have decided to set up on the territory of Russia a joint center of control over the missile launches. For the first time this has been done. This is exceptionally important.

Q. President Yeltsin, yesterday President Clinton spoke of the painful steps that Russia will have to take and the need to play by the rules of international economics. What difficult steps are you prepared to take? And are you committed to play by these rules of international economics?

And to President Clinton, the world stock market seems very fragile right now. How can the United States withstand all these outside pressures?

President Clinton: Do you want me to go first?

I think the answer to your question about what we can do that's best for our economy is really twofold. The first thing we have to do is to do our very best to make the right decisions at home. You know, we have to stay with the path of discipline that has brought us this far in the last five and a half years, and we have to make the investments and decisions that we know will produce growth over the long run for the American economy. Whether it's in education, or science and technology, we have to do the things that send the signal that we understand how the world economy works and we intend to do well in it. But the most important thing is sticking with sound economic policy. Now, in addition to that, it is important that more and more Americans, without regard to party, understand that we are in a global economy and it's been very good to the United States over the last five and half years—about 30 percent of our growth has come from exports—but that we at this particular moment in history, because of our relative economic strength have an extra obligation to try to build a system for the 21st century where every person in every country who is willing to work hard has a chance to get a just reward for it.

And that means that we have to—in my opinion, that means that we have to continue to contribute our fair share to the International Monetary Fund. It means that we have to do everything we can to support our friends in Russia who believe that we should continue to reform. It means that [Treasury] Secretary [Robert] Rubin's upcoming meeting with the Finance Minister of Japan, former Prime Minister Miyazawa, is profoundly important. Unless Japan begins to grow again, it's going to be difficult for Russia and other countries to do what they need to do. It means, in short, that America must maintain a leadership role of active involvement in trying to build an economic system that rewards people who do the right thing. And that's in our best interest.

So I think this is a terribly important thing. The volatility in the world markets, including in our stock market, I think is to be expected under these circumstances. The right thing to do is to try to restore growth in the economies of the world where there isn't enough growth now, and to continually examine whether the institutions we have for dealing with problems are adequate to meet the challenges of today and tomorrow. And we are aggressively involved in both those activities.

President Yeltsin: Naturally, we face problems basically of our own. We have not been able to do many things over the past time when we started our reforms. And still we need to conclude our reforms, to bring them to completion, and consequently, to get results.

We are not saying that we count solely on the support from outside—no. One more time I will reiterate this no. So let your mass media not spread the word to the effect that allegedly we would count solely on the support from the West. And to this end, we have gathered together here by no means. What we need from the United States is political support to the effect that the United States is in favor of reforms in Russia. This is what we really need, and then all the investors who would like to come to the Russian reformed market will do so, will come with their investments. And this is what we really need now. This is what is lacking—investments. This is first and foremost.

Certainly, we ought to fight our expenditures pattern and mismanagement. This is the second issue which, to us, is one of the most important issues. And we have been adopting accordingly the measures which need to be taken— like we have adopted the program of stabilization measures; in other words, those measures which will result in stabilization of our reforms. Stabilization—I believe that such measures and such a program will work, promptly, over the coming two years it will produce results.

Q. I'd like to pose a question to the President of the United States, Mr. Clinton. One gets the impression that some politicians in the United States right now like to somehow frighten Russia. On the other hand, we are aware of the fact that you are never afraid of Russia, yourself, and you did everything possible so that people in the U.S. would not be afraid of Russia. Now, on the results of these talks, tell us please your belief—what is the basis of your belief that our country will get back to its feet and that Russian-U.S. relations have promising prospects? Thank you.

President Clinton: Well, my belief that Russian-U.S. relations have promising prospects has been supported by the agreements we have made in the security and foreign policy areas. My belief that Russia will get back on its feet is based on my observation that in Russian history every time outsiders counted the Russian people out, they turned out to be wrong. And this is a very big challenge, but, I mean, a country that rebuffed Napoleon and Hitler can surely adjust to the realities of the global marketplace.

Now, what has to be done? The reason I wanted to come here—and, to be fair, let me back up and say, I don't think there are many people in America who are afraid of Russia anymore. I think there are some people in America who question whether I should come at this moment of great economic and political tension for the country. But I don't think it's because they want something bad to happen to Russia. I think, by and large, the American people wish Russia well and want things to go well for Russia, and like the fact that we are partners in Bosnia and that we've reduced our nuclear arsenals so much and that we've reduced our deficit establishment and that we've found other ways to cooperate in space, for example. I think most Americans like this very, very much.

So let me go back to the economic question. I believe whether you succeed and how long it takes you to succeed in restoring real growth to the Russian economy depends upon President Yeltsin's ability to persuade the Duma to support his formation of a government which will pursue a path of reform with a genuine sensitivity to the personal dislocation of the people who have been hurt. And here's where I think the World Bank and other institutions can come in and perhaps help deal with some of the fallout, if you will, of the reform process.

But I think if other political forces in Russia try to force the President to abandon reform in midstream or even reverse it, what I think will happen is even less money will come into Russia, and even more economic hardship will result. I believe that because that is, it seems to me, the unwavering experience of every other country.

That does not mean you should not have a social safety net. It does not mean you have to make the same domestic decisions that the United States or Great Britain or France or Sweden or any other country has made. You have to form your own relationship with this new economic reality. But I still believe that unless there is a manifest commitment to reform, the economy will not get better.

So I support President Yeltsin's commitment in that regard. And I think—my conviction that it will get better is based on my reading of your history. How long it will take to get better depends a lot more on you and what happens here than anything else we outsiders can do, although if there is a clear movement toward reform, I'll do everything I can to accelerate outside support of all kinds.

Q. Sir, you were just speaking of the challenges that we face as a nation. And one is the reaction since your admission of a relationship with Ms. Lewinsky—given you any cause for concern that you may not be as effective as you should be in leading the country?

President Clinton: No, I've actually been quite heartened by the reaction of the American people and leaders throughout the world about it. I have acknowledged that I made a mistake, said that I regretted it, asked to be forgiven, spent a lot of very valuable time with my family in the last couple of weeks and said I was going back to work. I believe that's what the American people want me to do, and based on my conversations with leaders around the world, I think that's what they want me to do, and that is what I intend to do.

As you can see from what we're discussing here, there are very large issues that will affect the future of the American people in the short run and over the long run. There are large issues that have to be dealt with now in the world and at home. And so I have been quite encouraged by what I think the message from the American people has been and what I know of the message from leaders around the world has been. And I'm going to do my best to continue to go through this personal process in an appropriate way, but to do my job, to do the job I was hired to do. And I think it very much needs to be done right now.

Q. The question has to do with the relationship between Russia and NATO. I understand you had time to discuss this issue with the U.S. President. It's known that the next NATO summit will take place in Washington, where important decisions will be taken regarding the European security architecture. How do you think this relation should evolve in the future?

President Yeltsin: Yes, we have discussed with President Clinton the question concerning the relationship between Russia and NATO. We're not running away from the position which has been that we are against NATO expanding eastward. We believe this is a blunder, a big mistake, and one day this will be a historic error.

Therefore, at this point in time, what we necessarily would like to do is to improve relations so that there be no confrontation. Therefore, we have signed an agreement between Russia and NATO. And in accordance with that agreement we want to do our job. However, no way shall we allow anybody to transgress that agreement, bypass that agreement, or, generally speaking, put aside it. No, this will not happen. . . .

We still are in favor of being cautious with regards to NATO. We don't have any intentions to move towards the West, ourselves; we don't intend to create additional forces. We're not doing that, and we're not planning to do that. This is what really matters.

President Clinton: I would like to say one word about that. We obviously, President Yeltsin and I, have a disagreement about whether it was appropriate for NATO to take on new members or not. But I think there is a larger reality here where we are in agreement, and I would like to emphasize it.

Russia has made historic commitments in the last few years to essentially redefine its greatness, not in terms of the territorial dominance of its neighbors, but instead, of constructive leadership in the region and in the world. The expansion of NATO, therefore, should be seen primarily as nations interested in working together to deal with common security problems, not to be ready to repel expected invasions. . . .

UN TRIBUNAL ON GENOCIDE BY RWANDAN OFFICIALS
September 4, 1998

Four years after the massacre of hundreds of thousands of people in Rwanda, an international tribunal in 1998 found three former Rwandan officials guilty of charges of genocide—mass killings or attacks on broad ethnic and national groups. Among the three was the Rwandan prime minister at the time of the killings, Jean Kambanda, who pleaded guilty to six genocide-related charges and was sentenced to life in prison. Kambanda was the first person ever punished for committing genocide, which was made an international crime under the Genocide Convention of 1948.

The UN-sponsored court, the International Criminal Tribunal for Rwanda, had come under international criticism for its slowness in acting on the cases of more than two dozen persons charged with genocide and other crimes in connection with the Rwandan massacres. UN officials said they hoped that Kambanda's guilty plea on May 1, coupled with his detailed testimony on how the massacres were planned, would allow a faster pace of prosecutions. Created in November 1994 by the UN Security Council, the tribunal conducted its proceedings in Arusha, Tanzania.

Just a week before Kambanda pleaded guilty, the current government of Rwanda executed twenty-two people for their role in the 1994 massacres. The executions followed trials in local courts that were strongly criticized by human rights groups.

The events of the Rwandan genocide stemmed from the historic enmity between two of the most important ethnic groups in eastern Africa: the Hutus and the Tutsis. After four years of sporadic fighting, the two groups reached a peace agreement early in 1994. But on April 6, 1994, an airplane carrying Rwanda's president, Juvenal Habyarimana, a Hutu moderate, was shot down and Habyarimana was killed.

Two days later, Hutu extremists killed Rwandan prime minister Agathe Uwilingiyimana, took over the government and military, murdered ten members of a Belgian peacekeeping force, and launched a broad attack on the country's Tutsi minority. For three months the Hutu forces hunted down and killed Tutsi men, women, and children. Thousands of moderate Hutus who opposed the killings also were murdered. According to UN estimates, the death toll exceeded 500,000.

In mid-July 1994, Tutsi rebels, with support from several neighboring countries, counterattacked, drove the Hutu militants from power, and established a new Tutsi-led government in Rwanda. Nearly one million Hutus took refugee in neighboring countries, including Zaire, where they were gathered in enormous camps. The UN and other relief agencies provided food and medicine to the refugee camps, but Hutu militants dominated the camps and used them as bases for cross-border raids against the new Tutsi government in Rwanda. The Hutu refugees in turn were attacked by Tutsi forces from Rwanda. Some of those Tutsi fighters participated in the rebellion that in May 1997 ousted President Mobutu Sese Seko from power in Zaire. (Overthrow of Mobutu, Historic Documents of 1997, p. 877)

The 1994 massacres in Rwanda represented one of the world's great tragedies of the half-century following World War II. Despite widespread reporting of the events in Rwanda, the United Nations took no effective action to intervene—in part because of the reluctance of the United States and other Western nations to get involved. During a trip to Africa in 1998, President Bill Clinton apologized to survivors of the massacres for the failure by the United States to act. (Massacres, Historic Documents of 1994, p. 541, and Historic Documents of 1996, p. 809; Clinton apology, p. 159)

The Kambanda Case

A banker and economist, Kambanda was a leader of the Democratic Popular Movement, a Hutu political party in Rwanda. On April 8, 1994— the day they took over the government—Hutu militants chose Kambanda as chairman of the government's Council of Ministers, a post equivalent to prime minister. He served in that position until Tutsi guerrillas overthrew the Hutu government July 17, 1994. Kambanda then fled to Zaire and later moved to Nairobi, Kenya, where he was arrested in October 1997 on genocide charges.

On May 1, 1998, Kambanda pleaded guilty to six charges of genocide, conspiracy to commit genocide, direct and public incitement to commit genocide, complicity in genocide, and two counts of crimes against humanity.

In his guilty plea, Kambanda acknowledged that during his tenure as prime minister he had played a role in the murder of Rwandans. Specifically, Kambanda admitted helping distribute weapons to Hutu forces and encouraging the Hutu population to attack Tutsi civilians (as well as any moderate Hutus who opposed the killings).

Kambanda admitted chairing a meeting on May 3, 1994, in the town of Kibuye, where local officials asked him to help save Tutsi children who were hiding at a hospital. Kambanda refused the request, and later that day the children were killed by Hutu militia.

Arguing for leniency for his client, Kambanda's lawyer, Oliver Michael Inglis, told the court September 3 that Kambanda had been merely a "puppet" who was installed in office by Hutu militants. Kambanda had no choice but to follow the lead of the militants, Inglis said, because he feared for the safety of his family if he refused their demands.

UN prosecutors rejected that contention, noting that Kambanda had traveled throughout Rwanda inciting his fellow Hutus to attack Tutsis. By imposing the life sentence September 4, the three-judge tribunal appeared to side with the prosecution's claim that Kambanda was responsible for his own actions.

Between the time of his May 1 guilty plea and his September 4 sentencing, Kambanda reportedly gave UN prosecutors approximately ninety hours of testimony detailing how the 1994 massacres were planned and carried out. Prosecutors said Kambanda's information would help them prepare their cases against two dozen other defendants who had been charged in connection with the Rwandan massacres.

The life sentence imposed on Kambanda was the maximum allowed under international law. Human rights advocates and spokesmen for survivors of the Rwandan massacres expressed satisfaction with Kambanda's conviction—although several massacre survivors said they wished he could have been executed.

Other Genocide Cases

The UN tribunal on September 2 found another Rwandan official, Jean-Paul Akayesu, guilty of nine charges stemming from the 1994 massacres. Akayesu had been the mayor of the town of Taba in central Rwanda. After a lengthy trial, the tribunal ruled that Akayesu had ordered the execution of several Tutsi residents of his own town, as well as eight Tutsis from the neighboring town of Runda. The tribunal found that in several cases Akayesu participated in killings, tortures, and beatings.

Defense lawyers had argued that Akayesu initially tried to stop the killings and had no control over the Hutu militants. Akayesu said he was forced to flee Rwanda in May 1994. His lawyers said they would appeal the conviction to a higher UN court based at The Hague, Netherlands.

On December 14 the UN tribunal received a guilty plea on four genocide-related charges from Omar Serushago, who had been a regional leader of the Hutu militia forces known as the "Interahamwe." Both Akayesu and Serushaga were to face sentencing in 1999.

> *Following are excerpts from the judgment handed down September 4, 1998, by the International Criminal Tribunal for Rwanda in the case of Jean Kambanda, who had served as prime minister of Rwanda from April 8 to July 17, 1994, and had pleaded guilty to six genocide-related charges:*

I. The Proceedings

A. Background

1. Jean Kambanda was arrested by the Kenyan authorities, on the basis of a formal request submitted to them by the Prosecutor on 9 July 1997, in accordance with the provisions of Rule 40 of the Rules of Procedure and Evidence (the "Rules"). . . .

2. On 16 October 1997, an indictment against the suspect Jean Kambanda, prepared by the Office of the Prosecutor, was submitted to Judge Yakov Ostrovsky, who confirmed it, issued a warrant of arrest against the accused and ordered his continued detention.

3. On 1 May 1998, during his initial appearance before this Trial Chamber, the accused pleaded guilty to the six counts contained in the indictment, namely genocide, conspiracy to commit genocide, direct and public incitement to commit genocide, complicity in genocide, crimes against humanity (murder), punishable under Article 3 (a) of the Statute and crimes against humanity (extermination), punishable under Article 3 (b) of the Statute.

4. After verifying the validity of his guilty plea, particularly in light of an agreement concluded between the Prosecutor, on the one hand, and the accused and his lawyer, on the other, an agreement which was signed by all the parties, the Chamber entered a plea of guilty against the accused on all the counts in the indictment. . . .

[Section II omitted.]

III. Case on Merits

38. . . . [T]he Trial Chamber proceeds to consider all relevant information submitted by both parties in order to determine an appropriate sentence in terms of Rule 100 of the Rules.

A. Facts of the Case

39. Together with his 'guilty' plea, Jean Kambanda submitted to the Chamber a document entitled "Plea Agreement between Jean Kambanda and the OTP [Office of the Prosecutor]", signed by Jean Kambanda and his defence counsel, Oliver Michael Inglis, on 28 April 1998, in which Jean Kambanda makes full admissions of all the relevant facts alleged in the indictment. In particular:

> (i) Jean Kambanda admits that there was in Rwanda in 1994 a widespread and systematic attack against the civilian population of Tutsi, the purpose of which was to exterminate them. Mass killings of hundreds of thousands of Tutsi occurred in Rwanda, including women and children, old and young who were pursued and killed at places where they had sought refuge i.e. prefectures, commune offices, schools, churches and stadiums.
> (ii) Jean Kambanda acknowledges that as Prime Minister of the Interim Government of Rwanda from 8 April 1994 to 17 July 1994, he was head of the 20 member Council of Ministers and exercised *de jure* authority and

control over the members of his government. The government determined and controlled national policy and had the administration and armed forces at its disposal. As Prime Minister, he also exercised de jure and *de facto* authority over senior civil servants and senior officers in the military.

(iii) Jean Kambanda acknowledges that he participated in meetings of the Council of Ministers, cabinet meetings and meetings of *prefets* where the course of massacres were actively followed, but no action was taken to stop them. He was involved in the decision of the government for visits by designated ministers to prefectures as part of the government's security efforts and in order to call on the civilian population to be vigilant in detecting the enemy and its accomplices. Jean Kambanda also acknowledges participation in the dismissal of the *prefet* of Butare because the latter had opposed the massacres and the appointment of a new *prefet* to ensure the spread of massacre of Tutsi in Butare.

(iv) Jean Kambanda acknowledges his participation in a high level security meeting at Gitarama in April 1994 between the President, T. Sindikubwabo, himself and the Chief of Staff of the Rwandan Armed Forces (FAR) and others, which discussed FAR's support in the fight against the Rwandan Patriotic Front (RPF) and its "accomplices", understood to be the Tutsi and Moderate Hutu.

(v) Jean Kambanda acknowledges that he issued the Directive on Civil Defence addressed to the *prefets* on 25 May 1994 (Directive No. 024-0273, disseminated on 8 June 1994). Jean Kambanda further admits that this directive encouraged and reinforced the Interahamwe who were committing mass killings of the Tutsi civilian population in the prefectures. Jean Kambanda further acknowledges that by this directive the Government assumed the responsibility for the actions of the Interahamwe.

(vi) Jean Kambanda acknowledges that before 6 April 1994, political parties in concert with the Rwanda Armed Forces organized and began the military training of the youth wings of the MRND [National Movement for Democracy and Development] and CDR political parties (Interahamwe and Impuzamugambi respectively) with the intent to use them in the massacres that ensued. Furthermore, Jean Kambanda acknowledges that the Government headed by him distributed arms and ammunition to these groups. Additionally, Jean Kambanda confirms that roadblocks manned by mixed patrols of the Rwandan Armed Forces and the Interahamwe were set up in Kigali and elsewhere as soon as the death of President J. B. Habyarimana was announced on the Radio. Furthermore Jean Kambanda acknowledges the use of the media as part of the plan to mobilize and incite the population to commit massacres of the civilian Tutsi population. That apart, Jean Kambanda acknowledges the existence of groups within military, militia, and political structures which had planned the elimination of the Tutsi and Hutu political opponents.

(vii) Jean Kambanda acknowledges that, on or about 21 June 1994, in his capacity as Prime Minister, he gave clear support to Radio Television Libre des Mille Collines (RTLM), with the knowledge that it was a radio station whose broadcasts incited killing, the commission of serious bodily or mental harm to, and persecution of Tutsi and moderate Hutu. On this occasion, speaking on this radio station, Jean Kambanda, as Prime Minister, encouraged the RTLM to continue to incite the massacres of the Tutsi civilian population, specifically stating that this radio station was "an indispensable weapon in the fight against the enemy."

(viii) Jean Kambanda acknowledges that following numerous meetings of the Council of Ministers between 8 April 1994 and 17 July 1994, he as Prime Minister, instigated, aided and abetted the *Prefets, Bourgmestres*, and members of the population to commit massacres and killings of civilians, in particular Tutsi and moderate Hutu. Furthermore, between 24 April 1994 and 17 July 1994, Jean Kambanda and Ministers of his Government visited several prefectures, such as Butare, Gitarama (Nyabikenke), Gikongoro, Gisenyi and Kibuye to incite and encourage the population to commit these massacres including by congratulating the people who had committed these killings.

(ix) Jean Kambanda acknowledges that on 3 May 1994, he was personally asked to take steps to protect children who had survived the massacre at a hospital and he did not respond. On the same day, after the meeting, the children were killed. He acknowledges that he failed in his duty to ensure the safety of the children and the population of Rwanda.

(x) Jean Kambanda admits that in his particular role of making public engagements in the name of the government, he addressed public meetings, and the media, at various places in Rwanda directly and publicly inciting the population to commit acts of violence against Tutsi and moderate Hutu. He acknowledges uttering the incendiary phrase which was subsequently repeatedly broadcast, "you refuse to give your blood to your country and the dogs drink it for nothing." (*Wima igihugu amaraso imbwa zikayanywera ubusa*).

(xi) Jean Kambanda acknowledges that he ordered the setting up of roadblocks with the knowledge that these roadblocks were used to identify Tutsi for elimination, and that as Prime Minister he participated in the distribution of arms and ammunition to members of political parties, militias and the population knowing that these weapons would be used in the perpetration of massacres of civilian Tutsi.

(xii) Jean Kambanda acknowledges that he knew or should have known that persons for whom he was responsible were committing crimes of massacre upon Tutsi and that he failed to prevent them or punish the perpetrators. Jean Kambanda admits that he was an eye witness to the massacres of Tutsi and also had knowledge of them from regular reports of prefets, and cabinet discussions.

Judgement

40. In light of the admissions made by Jean Kambanda in amplification of his plea of guilty, the Trial Chamber, on 1st May 1998, accepted his plea and found him guilty on the following counts:

(1) By his acts or omissions described in paragraphs 3.12 to 3.15, and 3.17 to 3.19 of the indictment, Jean Kambanda is responsible for the killing of and the causing of serious bodily or mental harm to members of the Tutsi population with intent to destroy, in whole or in part, an ethnic or racial group, as such, and has thereby committed **GENOCIDE,** stipulated in Article 2(3)(a) of the Statute as a crime, and attributed to him by virtue of Article 6(1) and 6(3), and punishable in reference to Articles 22 and 23 of the Statute of the Tribunal.

(2) By his acts or omissions described in paragraphs 3.8, 3.9, 3.13 to 3.15 and 3.19 of the indictment, Jean Kambanda did conspire with others, including Ministers of his Government, such as Pauline Nyiramasuhuko, Andre Ntagerura, Eliezer Niyitegeka and Edouard Karemera, to kill and to cause serious bodily or mental harm to members of the Tutsi population, with intent to destroy in whole or in part, an ethnic or racial group as such, and has thereby committed **CONSPIRACY TO COMMIT GENOCIDE,** stipulated in Articles 2(3)(b) of the Statute as a crime, and attributed to him by virtue of Article 6(1) and punishable in reference to Articles 22 and 23 of the Statute of the Tribunal.

(3) By his acts or omissions described in paragraphs 3.12 to 3.14 and 3.19 of the indictment, Jean Kambanda did directly and publicly incite to kill and to cause serious bodily or mental harm to members of the Tutsi population, with intent to destroy, in whole or in part, an ethnic group as such, and has thereby committed **DIRECT AND PUBLIC INCITEMENT TO COMMIT GENOCIDE,** stipulated in Article 2(3)(c) of the Statute as a crime, and attributed to him by virtue of Article 6(1) and 6(3),which is punishable in reference to Articles 22 and 23 of the Statute of the Tribunal.

(4) By his acts or omissions described in paragraphs 3.10, 3.12 to 3.15 and 3.17 to 3.19 of the indictment, which do not constitute the same acts relied on for counts 1,2 and 3 Jean Kambanda was complicit in the killing and the causing of serious bodily or mental harm to members of the Tutsi population, and thereby committed **COMPLICITY IN GENOCIDE** stipulated in Article 2(3)(e) of the Statute as a crime, and attributed to him by virtue of Article 6(1) and 6(3), which is punishable in reference to Articles 22 and 23 of the Statute of the Tribunal.

(5) By his acts or omissions described in paragraphs 3.12 to 3.15 and 3.17 to 3.19 of the indictment, Jean Kambanda is responsible for the murder of civilians, as part of a widespread or systematic attack against a civilian population on ethnic or racial grounds, and has thereby committed a **CRIME AGAINST HUMANITY,** stipulated in Article 3(a) of the Statute as a crime, and attributed to him by virtue of Article 6(1) and 6(3), which is punishable in reference to Articles 22 and 23 of the Statute of the Tribunal.

(6) By his acts or omissions described in paragraphs 3.12 to 3.15, and 3.17 to 3.19 of the indictment, Jean Kambanda is responsible for the extermination of civilians, as part of a widespread or systematic attack against a civilian population on ethnic or racial grounds, and has thereby commit-

ted a **CRIME AGAINST HUMANITY,** stipulated in Article 3(b) of the Statute as a crime, and attributed to him by virtue of Article 6(1) and 6(3), which is punishable in reference to Articles 22 and 23 of the Statute of the Tribunal.

B. Factors Relating to Sentence

41. Article 23(1) of the Statute stipulates that penalties imposed by the Trial Chamber shall be limited to imprisonment and that in the determination of imprisonment, the Trial Chamber shall have recourse to the general practice regarding prison sentences in the Court s of Rwanda. The Trial Chamber notes that the Death sentence which is proscribed by the Statute of the ICTR [International Criminal Tribunal for Rwanda] is mandatory for crimes of this nature in Rwanda. Reference to the Rwandan sentencing practice is intended as a guide to determining an appropriate sentence and does not fetter the discretion of the judges of the Trial Chamber to determine the sentence. In determining the sentence, the Court shall, in accordance with the Rules of Procedure, take into account such factors as the gravity of the crime and the individual circumstances of Jean Kambanda.

(i) Gravity of the Crime

42. In the brief dated 10 August 1998 and in her closing argument at the hearing, the Prosecutor stressed the gravity of the crimes of genocide, and crimes against humanity. The heinous nature of the crime of genocide and its absolute prohibition makes its commission inherently aggravating. The magnitude of the crimes involving the killing of an estimated 500,000 civilians in Rwanda, in a short span of 100 days constitutes an aggravating fact.

43. Crimes against Humanity are as aforementioned conceived as offences of the gravest kind against the life and liberty of the human being.

44. The crimes were committed during the time when Jean Kambanda was Prime Minister and he and his government were responsible for maintenance of peace and security. Jean Kambanda abused his authority and the trust of the civilian population. He personally participated in the genocide by distributing arms, making incendiary speeches and presiding over cabinet and other meetings where the massacres were planned and discussed. He failed to take necessary and reasonable measures to prevent his subordinates from committing crimes against the population. Abuse of positions of authority or trust is generally considered an aggravating factor.

(ii) Individual Circumstances of Jean Kambanda: Personal Particulars

45. Jean Kambanda was born on 10 October 1955 at Mubumbano in the Prefecture of Butare. He has a wife and two children. He holds a Diploma d'Ingenieur Commercial and from May 1989 to April 1994, he worked in the Union des Banques Populaires du Rwanda rising to the position of Director of the network of those banks. He was Vice President of the Butare Section of the MDR [Democratic Republican Movement] and member of its Political

Bureau. On 9 April 1994, he became Prime Minister of the Interim Government. The Prosecutor has not proved previous criminal convictions, if any, of Jean Kambanda.

(iii) Mitigating Factors

46. Defence Counsel has proffered three factors in mitigation: Plea of guilty; remorse, which he claims is evident from the act of pleading guilty; and co-operation with the Prosecutor's office.

47. The Prosecutor confirms that Jean Kambanda has extended substantial co-operation and invaluable information to the Prosecutor. The Prosecutor requests the Trial Chamber to regard as a significant mitigating factor, not only the substantial co-operation so far extended, but also the future co-operation when Jean Kambanda testifies for the prosecution in the trials of other accused.

48. The Plea Agreement signed by the parties expressly records that no agreements, understandings or promises have been made between the parties with respect to sentence which, it is acknowledged, is at the discretion of the Trial Chamber.

49. The Prosecutor however disclosed that Jean Kambanda's co-operation has been recognised by significant protection measures that have been put in place to alleviate any concerns that he may have, about the security of his family.

50. According to the Prosecutor, Jean Kambanda had expressed his intention to plead guilty immediately upon his arrest and transfer to the Tribunal, on 18 July 1997. Jean Kambanda declared in the Plea Agreement that he had resolved to plead guilty even before his arrest in Kenya and that his prime motivation for pleading guilty was the profound desire to tell the truth, as the truth was the only way to restoring national unity and reconciliation in Rwanda. Jean Kambanda condemned the massacres that occurred in Rwanda and considers his confession as a contribution towards the restoration of peace in Rwanda.

51. The Chamber notes however that Jean Kambanda has offered no explanation for his voluntary participation in the genocide; nor has he expressed contrition, regret or sympathy for the victims in Rwanda, even when given the opportunity to do so by the Chamber, during the hearing of 3 September 1998.

52. Both Counsel for Prosecution and Defence have urged the Chamber to interpret Jean Kambanda's guilty pleas as a signal of his remorse, repentance and acceptance of responsibility for his actions. The Chamber is mindful that remorse is not the only reasonable inference that can be drawn from a guilty plea; nevertheless it accepts that most national jurisdictions consider admissions of guilt as matters properly to be considered in mitigation of punishment. "A prompt guilty plea is considered a major mitigating factor."

53. In civil criminal law systems, a guilt plea may be favourably considered as a mitigating factor, subject to the discretionary faculty of a judge.

- "An admission of guilt demonstrates honesty and it is important for the International Tribunal to encourage people to come forth, whether already indicted or as unknown perpetrators."

54. The Chamber has furthermore been requested to take into account in favour of Jean Kambanda that his guilty plea has also occasioned judicial economy, saved victims the trauma and emotions of trial and enhanced the administration of justice.

55. The Trial Chamber finds that the gravity of the crime has been established and the mitigatory impact on penalty has been characterised.

56. The Trial Chamber holds the view that a finding of mitigating circumstances relates to assessment of sentence and in no way derogates from the gravity of the crime. It mitigates punishment, not the crime. In this respect the Trial Chamber adopts the reasoning of "Erdemovic" and the "Hostage" case cited therein.

- "It must be observed however that mitigation of punishment does not in any sense of the word reduce the degree of the crime. It is more a matter of grace than of defence. In other words, the punishment assessed is not a proper criterion to be considered in evaluating the findings of the court with reference to the degree of magnitude of the crime."

57. The degree of magnitude of the crime is still an essential criterion for evaluation of sentence.

58. A sentence must reflect the predominant standard of proportionality between the gravity of the offence and the degree of responsibility of the offender. Just sentences contribute to respect for the law and the maintenance of a just, peaceful and safe society.

59. The Chamber recalls as aforementioned that the Tribunal was established at the request of the government of Rwanda; and the Tribunal was intended to enforce individual criminal accountability on behalf of the international community, contribute in ensuring the effective redress of violence and the culture of impunity, and foster national reconciliation and peace in Rwanda. (Preamble, Security Council resolution 955(1994)).

60. In her submissions, although the Prosecutor sought a term of life imprisonment for Jean Kambanda, she requested that the Tribunal, in the determination of the sentence, take into consideration the guilty plea and the cooperation of Jean Kambanda with her office. The Defence Counsel in his submissions emphasised that Jean Kambanda was only a puppet controlled by certain military authorities and that his power was consequently limited. He thus submitted that the Tribunal, taking into account the guilty plea, Jean Kambanda's cooperation and willingness to continue cooperating with the Prosecutor, and the role Jean Kambanda could play in the process of national reconciliation in Rwanda, sentence him for a term of imprisonment not exceeding two years.

61. The Chamber has examined all the submissions presented by the Parties pertaining to the determination of sentence, from which it can be inferred:

(A) (i) Jean Kambanda has cooperated and is still willingly cooperating with the Office of the Prosecutor;

(ii) the guilty plea of Jean Kambanda is likely to encourage other individuals to recognize their responsibilities during the tragic events which occurred in Rwanda in 1994;

(iii) a guilty plea is generally considered, in most national jurisdictions, including Rwanda, as a mitigating circumstance;

(B) but that, however:

(v) the crimes for which Jean Kambanda is responsible carry an intrinsic gravity, and their widespread, atrocious and systematic character is particularly shocking to the human conscience;

(vi) Jean Kambanda committed the crimes knowingly and with premeditation;

(vii) and, moreover, Jean Kambanda, as Prime Minister of Rwanda was entrusted with the duty and authority to protect the population and he abused this trust.

62. On the basis of all of the above, the Chamber is of the opinion that the aggravating circumstances surrounding the crimes committed by Jean Kambanda negate the mitigating circumstances, especially since Jean Kambanda occupied a high ministerial post, at the time he committed the said crimes.

IV. Verdict

TRIAL CHAMBER I,

FOR THE FOREGOING REASONS,

DELIVERING its decision in public, inter partes and in the first instance;

PURSUANT to Articles 23, 26 and 27 of the Statute and Rules 100, 101, 102, 103 and 104 of the Rules of Procedure and Evidence;

NOTING the general practice of sentencing by the Courts of Rwanda;

NOTING the indictment as confirmed on 16 October 1997;

NOTING the Plea of guilty of Jean Kambanda on 1 May 1998 on the Counts of:

COUNT 1: Genocide (stipulated in Article 2(3)(a) of the Statute as a crime, and attributed to him by virtue of Article 6(1) and 6(3), and punishable in reference to Articles 22 and 23 of the Statute of the Tribunal);

COUNT 2: Conspiracy to commit genocide (stipulated in Articles 2(3)(b) of the Statute as a crime, and attributed to him by virtue of Article 6(1) and punishable in reference to Articles 22 and 23 of the Statute of the Tribunal);

COUNT 3: Direct and public incitement to commit genocide (stipulated in Article 2(3)(c) of the Statute as a crime, and attributed to him by virtue of Article 6(1) and 6(3), which is punishable in reference to Articles 22 and 23 of the Statute of the Tribunal);

COUNT 4: Complicity in genocide (stipulated in Article 2(3)(e) of the Statute as a crime, and attributed to him by virtue of Article 6(1) and 6(3), which is punishable in reference to Articles 22 and 23 of the Statute of the Tribunal);

COUNT 5: Crime against humanity (murder) (stipulated in Article 3(a) of the Statute as a crime, and attributed to him by virtue of Article 6(1) and 6(3), which is punishable in reference to Articles 22 and 23 of the Statute of the Tribunal);

COUNT 6: Crime against humanity (extermination) (stipulated in Article 3(b) of the Statute as a crime, and attributed to him by virtue of Article 6(1) and 6(3), which is punishable in reference to Articles 22 and 23 of the Statute of the Tribunal);

HAVING FOUND Jean Kambanda guilty on all six counts on 1 May 1998;

NOTING the briefs submitted by the parties;

HAVING HEARD the Closing Statements of the Prosecutor and the Defence Counsel;

IN PUNISHMENT OF THE ABOVEMENTIONED CRIMES,

SENTENCES Jean Kambanda

born on 19 October 1955 in Gishamvu Commune, Butare Prefecture, Rwanda

TO LIFE IMPRISONMENT

RULES that imprisonment shall be served in a State designated by the President of the Tribunal, in consultation with the Trial Chamber and the said designation shall be conveyed to the government of Rwanda and the designated State by the Registry;

RULES that this judgement shall be enforced immediately, and that until his transfer to the said place of imprisonment, Jean Kambanda shall be kept in detention under the present conditions.

Arusha, 4 September 1998,

Laïty Kama (Presiding Judge)
Lennart Aspegren (Judge)
Navanethem Pillay (Judge)

MARK McGWIRE ON BREAKING
THE HOME RUN RECORD
September 8, 1998

One of the premiere records in professional sports fell by the wayside in 1998—not once, but twice. Mark McGwire, the first baseman for the St. Louis Cardinals, hit his sixty-second home run of the season on September 8, breaking the record of sixty-one home runs set in 1961 by Roger Maris of the New York Yankees. A week later, Sammy Sosa of the Chicago Cubs—who had vied all season with McGwire for the coveted home run record—matched the total McGwire had achieved. McGwire ended the season with seventy home runs and Sosa ended with sixty-six.

The McGwire-Sosa chase of the home run crown helped excite public interest in major league baseball. Once known as the "national pastime," baseball was still suffering from damage resulting from a players' strike in 1994–1995 and public cynicism about escalating salaries paid by team owners to attract top stars. One team with a huge payroll, the New York Yankees, set several records for winning in 1998: the most victories in a modern-era regular season (114) and the most victories counting post-season games (125). The Yankees met the San Diego Padres in the World Series, winning four games to none.

Chasing a Record

George Herman "Babe" Ruth, the New York Yankees outfielder largely responsible in the 1920s and 1930s for making baseball the nation's most popular spectator sport, established a record in 1927 that, for many years, seemed destined to stand for all time: sixty home runs in one season. Despite numerous challenges to it by other great players, Ruth's record stood until 1961, when Maris—who also wore the Yankees' famed pin-striped uniform—hit sixty-one home runs.

The conservative baseball establishment was reluctant to set Ruth's record aside, however. In the official record books, Maris's achievement was marked with an asterisk, indicating that his sixty-one home runs had come in a season that had been extended to 162 games—eight more than during the era when Ruth played. Many baseball fans also begrudged Maris the title because he beat out a more popular teammate, Mickey Mantle. Maris died of cancer in 1985, somewhat embittered that baseball officials were so reluctant to acknowledge his record.

The decades after 1961 saw a leap forward in the overall quality of performance in baseball, along with most other professional sports. Players were in much better physical condition than their predecessors, and technological changes improved the equipment they used. Even so, no one seriously challenged either the Ruth or the Maris record until 1998.

McGwire was a likely candidate to tackle the record successfully. A big man (six foot five inches, 250 pounds), McGwire was one of baseball's most prolific home run hitters. He won the attention of baseball fans in 1987, his first year in the big leagues, when he hit forty-nine home runs— a record for a rookie. McGwire suffered a severe slump in 1991 and missed the better part of the 1993 and 1994 seasons due to injuries. He recovered in 1996, when he hit fifty-two home runs, an impressive accomplishment but far from the Maris record. Despite his demonstrated ability to hit home runs, McGwire was not among the superstars of baseball until 1998. His low-key, unassuming manner—and the fact that he played for teams outside the major media markets—kept him out of the spotlight reserved for the sport's most famous stars.

Sosa was a child of poverty in the Dominican Republic who overcame a seemingly endless series of hurdles to succeed in the major leagues. Unlike McGwire, he was not an overwhelmingly powerful hitter; before 1998, he had never hit more than forty home runs in a season. Even so, Sosa was a national hero in the Dominican Republic. He used his baseball wealth to help people back home, financing such civic projects as installing computers in public schools.

Through the first part of the season, a third man was in contention for the home run championship: Ken Griffey Jr. of the Seattle Mariners. Griffey fell behind McGwire and Sosa and ended the season with fifty home runs, a respectable total but not very glamorous in a record-setting season.

Sosa and McGwire battled neck-and-neck for the National League home run championship throughout the spring and summer. McGwire kept a few home runs ahead of his rival, until August 31, when Sosa caught up with him at fifty-five home runs. By that point is was all but certain that one or both of them would break the Maris record; it remained to be seen which one would do it first. The two men developed what appeared to be a friendly rivalry based on mutual respect. Sosa repeatedly said he expected McGwire to finish ahead: "He's the man," he said, in reference to McGwire when asked about the home run race. Both men played before sold-out crowds for much of the season.

In the kind of twist of fate, the record-breaking day came September 8, when McGwire's Cardinals played host to Sosa's Cubs. McGwire went into the game having tied the Maris record of sixty-one home runs; Sosa had fifty-eight. In the bottom of the fourth inning, Cubs pitcher Steve Traschel *served up a slider, which McGwire returned as a low line drive down the left field line that barely cleared the fence for home run number sixty-two. It was one of the shortest, least impressive home runs McGwire hit all year.*

In the excitement of the moment, McGwire forgot to touch first base as he began his celebratory circuit around the diamond. First base coach Dave McKay pointed at the bag, and McGwire returned for the obligatory step on the base before trotting on to second base, third base, and then home plate. At each base, he received a slap of congratulations from Cubs players. He raised his right arm and pointed his index finger in the air, claiming the number-one position. Sosa rushed in from right field to join in the celebration.

Perhaps the most impressive fact about McGwire's record was the pace at which he set it. McGwire hit his seventy home runs in 509 at-bats, a ratio of one home run for every 7.27 at-bats. By contrast, Ruth hit his sixty home runs in 540 at-bats in 1927, and Maris took 590 at-bats to hit his sixty-one home runs in 1961. When he was not hitting a home run during his time at bat, McGwire was likely to draw a base-on-balls from pitchers unwilling to give him a good pitch to hit. Pitchers walked him 162 times in 1998; that tied him with Ted Williams for second place, behind Ruth, who was walked a record 170 times in 1923. Along with many other home-run hitters, McGwire also struck out frequently. His 1998 total was 155.

Asked by a reporter if he might be able to break his own home run record, McGwire replied: "I don't know if I want to break my own record. I think I'd rather leave it as is."

After the season was over, baseball writers gave Sosa, rather than Mc-Gwire, one of the most coveted annual honors in baseball: the Most Valuable Player award for the National League. Sosa received 438 points to McGwire's 272 in the voting for the award, reflecting the vital help Sosa gave his team in reaching a spot in the National League championship series. McGwire's team was not in contention for post-season play.

McGwire's demolition of the Maris record was marred by one controversy. Late in the season a reporter noticed that McGwire kept a bottle of a muscle-building supplement, androstenedione, in his locker. The drug, which was intended to boost testosterone levels and thus build muscles, was legal under major league baseball rules even through it had been banned by the National Football League and the Olympics. McGwire said the nonprescription drug was "legal stuff," but many commentators noted that long-term use of the drug could cause liver and heart disease, and they questioned whether baseball should permit its use.

Ripken Takes a Rest

After the excitement of the McGwire-Sosa home run chase, there was still time in the 1998 season for baseball fans to savor the significance of another of the game's marquee records. Cal Ripken Jr., the Baltimore Orioles player who in 1995 had broken Lou Gehrig's record for consecutive games played, took himself out of the lineup on September 20. It was the first time since 1982 that Ripken sat out a game; he amassed a record of

2,632 consecutive games. (Ripken's record, Historic Documents of 1995, p. 588)

In breaking Gehrig's record, Ripken had almost single-handedly restored baseball's luster following the trauma of the 1994–1995 players' strike. A self-effacing man, Ripken seemed to embody the qualities of determination, fair play, and endurance that many baseball fans still wanted to associate with the game.

As the 1998 season neared its close, Ripken decided that the time had come to end his streak of consecutive games on his own terms. Moments before a home game against the Yankees, Ripken went to his team manager, Ray Miller, and said: "I think it's time." Miller placed a rookie, Ryan Minor, into Ripken's spot in the lineup. The hometown fans at Camden Yards realized the historic nature of the moment only when the revised lineup was announced, and they gave Ripken an emotional standing ovation. Ripken left his mark not just in the record books; there was general agreement that no baseball player in modern times had earned more respect and affection than the "Iron Man."

Following is the text of a news conference with baseball player Mark McGwire on September 8, 1998, following a game in which he hit his sixty-second home run of the season, setting a new major league baseball record:

Q: How does it feel to own the most prestigious record in sports?

Mark McGuire: Absolutely incredible. What can I say, I mean, I am almost speechless. I mean, I have been talking about this since January and I get to 61, it is one swing away and then next thing you know I hit a ball that all of a sudden disappeared on me. I tell you what, I totally believe in fate and I believe that is what happened this week and I thank the man upstairs.

Q: Tell us what happened on the turn on first.

Mark McGuire: Well, when I hit the ball, I thought it was a the line drive and I thought it was going to hit the wall, next thing you know, it disappeared. I looked up and Dave McKay was jumping up and sort of like, [motioned that I] missed one big thing, touch first base. So, I had to go back and touch it. Honestly, that is the first time that I think I missed. First time I have had to do that, but I will tell you what, I will always remember that and it was a sweet, sweet run around the bases.

Q: Do you have any idea how you have impacted the game?

Mark McGuire: I think so right now, I believe, yeah. I will tell you what, you know, the whole country has been involved in this. I think since after the All-Star break and it has just—people have been saying it is bringing the country together. So be it. I am happy to bring the country together.

Q: How does it feel sitting there with your bat next to Roger Maris's bat?

Mark McGuire: Well, as I went over to the box and talked to Roger's kids, I told them today when I met with the Hall of Fame they pulled out

Roger's bat that he hit his 61st home run with and I touched it. I touched it with my heart. Now I can honestly say that my bat will lie next to his and I am damn proud of it.

Q: What is your next goal?

Mark McGuire: My next goal? Sleep.

Q: Mark, we have heard so much about you opening up as a person and willing to talk and share your emotions. You are physically showing it a little bit right now. What was it like rounding the bases, Gaetti hugging you, Sammy hugging you, then meeting the Maris family again?

Mark McGuire: I honestly have to tell you I really have to see the tape because I really don't remember it. I was trying to imagine what it was going to feel like doing that and I sort of was telling myself, I think I will be floating. I have to look at the tape, but I just remember briefly shaking some of the player's hands and you know, signaling to the dugout and the Cubs and then after that, I just hope I didn't act foolish, but I mean this is history, so— can I say one thing? I talked to a good friend of mine today, Jim Corsey, so everybody in Boston, Jim Corsey does know me and thanks for giving me that hug over the phone today, Jim.

Mark McGuire: I told you I was going to talk to you after the game today.

Q: I know, congratulations. How are you going to celebrate tonight?

Mark McGuire: Well, I hope there is a lot of champagne on that flight to Cincinnati, so—I think everybody is going to be drinking except for the pilots.

Q: What does it mean to do it so fast, in the 145th game?

Mark McGuire: Was it that quick? I—I just—it has been awesome. I will tell you what, the last week and a half my stomach has been turning, my heart has been beating a million miles a minute. To do it that fast, I don't know, I just give thanks to the man upstairs and all of them; Roger Maris, Babe Ruth, everybody who is watching up there, what a feat.

Q: In your wildest dreams, Mark, did you ever imagine to break the record this quickly?

Mark McGuire: Not even. Not even a chance. I mean, I truly believed that if somebody got to 50 by September, they had an honest shot at doing it. I got to it pretty quickly.

Q: When you took the microphone after you hit the home run, you dedicated the home run to the people in St. Louis. Talk about how special it was to hit it here.

Mark McGuire: Well, I will tell you what, after yesterday doing what I did for my father and my son showing up just in time, I tell you what a perfect way to end the week by the last game in the home stand and hitting the 62nd for the city of St. Louis and all the great fans. I had a couple of milestones this year, hitting my 50th and 60th on the road. I really truly wanted to do it here. Really wanted to do it here, guys, and I did it. Thank you, St. Louis.

Q: What do you have to say to the Oakland As fans and—where you were in 1993, and 1994, you have been healthy, what do you have to say?

Mark McGuire: I have to thank everybody in the Bay Area for all the support they gave me. I started there. They have been through rocky times with me through my injuries, through my down year of hitting .201. They were behind me. And I truly believed the times that when I was down with the injuries, I truly believe it was for a reason and I think this is the reason I am sitting here talking to all you guys, so . . . .

Q: You have carried this with you since the winter, talking about it all year. Do you feel like a big weight has been lifted off your shoulders?

Mark McGuire: Yeah, I don't know happy the arch is, but the arch is off my back now.

Q: What kind of message does this send beyond baseball to the country?

Mark McGuire: I just think it puts baseball back on the map as the sport—it's America's pastime and you just look at everybody come out to the ballparks and you look at all the great players in the game of baseball, and it has been an exciting year. It is not over, and it is a—it is great, great time.

Q: Were you aware of how this whole process has evolved you as a person?

Mark McGuire: Oh, yeah, Yeah, it has. I mean, I don't know if I am going to sit here and talk about it, but we can talk later about that.

Q: You may have already been asked this, but talk about going into the stands to see the Maris family?

Mark McGuire: Yeah, I mean, it just—like I said, today when I touched and held Roger's bat that he hit his 61st with and I just put it against my heart and that is the first thing that came to my mind when I ran over there and I told all four of them and it just unbelievable, it was an unbelievable feeling.

Q: You have seen how the Maris's children have remembered their father's accomplishment. How will your son remember your accomplishment today?

Mark McGuire: I hope my son one day grows up and becomes a baseball player and breaks it.

Q: Have you gotten the ball yet?

Mark McGuire: No, I haven't. No, you know, whoever came on the field and gave me that ball, it wasn't the ball. So, it said official league. It didn't say National League. So I said: Here, take it back. So it wasn't the ball. So I haven't seen it yet.

Q: What number will it say at the Hall of Fame? I guess we will find out September 27th.

STARR REPORT TO CONGRESS
September 9 and 12, 1998

The third presidential impeachment inquiry in American history was set into motion on September 9, when independent counsel Kenneth W. Starr delivered a report to Congress that contained what Starr said was "substantial and credible evidence" that President Bill Clinton had committed impeachable offenses in his effort to cover up an extramarital affair with former White House intern Monica S. Lewinsky. The report laid out eleven charges against Clinton, including perjury, obstruction of justice, witness tampering, and abuse of power. Nearly overshadowing those charges, however, were Starr's graphic and detailed descriptions of the sexual encounters between Clinton and Lewinsky. The explicit descriptions, which read more like a bad pulp novel than a somber legal document, were regrettable but necessary, Starr said, to show that the president had lied under oath when he said that he had never had sexual relations with Lewinsky.

Legislators in both parties expressed outrage, shock, and deep disappointment with the president's behavior as described in the report, which was posted on the Internet at the same time that it became available to House members. Many legislators were also annoyed with Starr, saying that the independent counsel could have made his case without the seamy details—a point that the White House was quick to emphasize. "In the face of the President's admission of his relationship, the disclosure of lurid and salacious allegations can only be intended to humiliate the President and force him from office," a White House release said even before the report had been released. The White House reiterated its assertions that Starr was using whatever means he could to force the president from office.

Shortly before the report was made public September 11, Clinton offered his most contrite statements to date about his behavior. "I don't think there is a fancy way to say that I have sinned," he said at a White House prayer meeting, and for the first time he publicly apologized to Lewinsky and her family. At the same time, however, he said he would ask his attorneys to mount a "vigorous defense" against the Starr charges, "using all available, appropriate arguments."

*The two Democratic leaders of Congress, House Minority Leader Richard
A. Gephardt of Missouri and Senate Minority Leader Thomas Daschle of
South Dakota, warned the president and his aides in coordinated public
statements released September 14 that continued legalistic "hairsplitting"
would undermine support for the president. "The president and his advisers must accept that continued legal jousting serves no constructive purpose," Daschle said. "It simply stands in the way of what we need to do:
move forward and let common sense guide us in doing what it best for the
country."*

*The two Democrats asked Congress to move quickly to determine whether
and how to punish Clinton. Some legislators had already begun to explore
the possibility of censuring and perhaps fining the president for his misconduct. Republican leaders were eager to press ahead with a full-scale
impeachment inquiry that examined not only Clinton's conduct with
Lewinsky but also several other allegations against the president. Even
before formally voting to open an impeachment inquiry, the House Judiciary Committee decided to release the videotape of Clinton's secret grand
jury testimony, given August 17. The move to further embarrass Clinton
backfired, however. Although a majority of those surveyed continued to
believe that Clinton had lied under oath, polls taken the day after the tapes
were released showed the president's job rating had gone up six to nine
points since the tapes were aired.* (Clinton's grand jury testimony, p. 564;
Clinton impeachment inquiry, p. 695)

The Starr Investigation

*Starr's report to Congress was the culmination of a four-year investiga-
tion that began in August 1974 when the former solicitor general was hired
as an independent counsel to investigate Whitewater, a failed Arkansas
land deal that Clinton and his wife, Hillary Rodham Clinton, were involved
with when Clinton was governor of Arkansas. In subsequent months Starr
expanded his operations to look into the abrupt firing of White House travel
office personnel in 1993; the subsequent suicide of Vincent W. Foster Jr., a
close friend of the first family and a White House aide who played a role in
the firings; and administration requests in 1993 and 1994 for hundreds of
FBI files, including those of former Republican White House officials.
Starr's probes led to some notable indictments and convictions, including
that of Clinton's successor as governor, Jim Guy Tucker, and Hillary Clinton's former law partner and associate attorney general Webster L. Hubbell.
But the independent counsel never lodged any formal charges against Clinton in connection with any of those investigations.*

*Starr's investigation of the Lewinsky scandal arose not from any of his
ongoing investigations but from a suit brought by Paula Corbin Jones, who
alleged that Clinton had sexually harassed her when he was governor of
Arkansas and she was a minor state employee. Seeking to prove that Clinton had a history of preying on women, Jones's lawyers began to track
down women whose names had been connected with Clinton's. One of these*

was Lewinsky. According to Starr's office, the independent counsel was tipped off about the Lewinsky's affair with the president from Lewinsky confidant Linda R. Tripp, who said she had evidence that Lewinsky might have been offered a job in exchange for her silence in the Jones case. Clinton supporters later disputed Starr's version of these events, arguing that Starr's office had deliberately structured events to set up the president. Starr dismissed those allegations as an attempt by the White House to smear him by "innuendo and guilt by association."

Starr's report to Congress dealt solely with matters arising out of Clinton's relationship with Lewinsky. There were no findings pertaining to Whitewater, the deal that Starr was initially appointed to investigate. Nor did the report contain any material relating to the 1993 firing of White House travel office personnel or improper White House use of confidential FBI files. In the report, Starr said it had been his original intention to send to the House all findings at once, but as the information about the Lewinsky matter grew to overwhelming proportions, it was apparent, he said, that delay "would be unwise." Decisions about additional findings would be made "at the earliest practical time," the report said. At his appearance before the House Judiciary Committee on November 19, Starr acknowledged that he was no longer investigating the president in connection with either the travel staff firings or the FBI files, although he said other investigations were continuing. Starr's relentless pursuit of Clinton contributed to growing dissatisfaction with the law that authorized the Office of Independent Counsel (OIC); the law was scheduled to expire on June 30, 1999. (Independent counsel law, p. 905)

Starr Report Allegations

In the report, or referral, as it was formally called, the independent counsel listed eleven "possible grounds for impeachment," which the White House rebutted point-for-point in a document released September 12. The referral leveled charges against Clinton in four areas.

***Perjury.** The referral said that Clinton had lied numerous times, both in the civil deposition in a sexual harassment lawsuit brought by former Arkansas state employee Paula Corbin Jones and in testimony before a federal grand jury, about the nature of his relationship with Lewinsky and efforts to conceal the affair. During his deposition in the Jones case, Clinton denied that he had had a sexual relationship with Lewinsky. In his grand jury testimony, Clinton said that his statements, while misleading, were accurate and that he had not engaged in sex with Lewinsky as defined by Jones's lawyers. To show that Clinton had lied, the report detailed several encounters between Clinton and Lewinsky from November 15, 1995, to December 28, 1997.*

According to Lewinsky's testimony, the two never had sexual intercourse, but she had performed oral sex on the president nine times and he had touched her breasts and genitals during some of those encounters. Although a narrow, literal interpretation of the definition used by the Jones lawyers might not cover oral sex, Clinton's fondling of Lewinsky clearly fell within the scope of the definition, the referral said. The report further charged that Clinton was untruthful during his deposition when he said he could not recall whether he had ever been alone with Lewinsky or had exchanged gifts with her.

Obstruction of justice. *The referral said Clinton and Lewinsky had an understanding that they would deny their relationship and that she would lie under oath in the Jones case. Lewinsky originally signed an affidavit denying her affair with Clinton, but changed her story after she received a grant of immunity from Starr. According to the report, Clinton and Lewinsky also had an understanding to conceal gifts that they had given each other instead of turning them over to lawyers in the Jones suit. Although testimony on the matter conflicted, Starr said it was possible that Clinton had asked his personal secretary Betty Currie to retrieve gifts he had given to Lewinsky and to hide those gifts, which had been subpoenaed by Jones's attorneys. The "reasonable inference" from the evidence, the report said, was that the "President orchestrated or approved the concealment of gifts."* (Clinton grand jury testimony, p. 564)

The referral further said that Clinton attempted to impede investigators by helping Lewinsky find a job in New York at a time when she would have been a witness harmful to him if she had testified in the Jones case. Starr also said Clinton had not told the truth about discussions with his friend Vernon E. Jordan Jr., who tried to help Lewinsky find a job in New York.

Witness tampering. *The report charged that Clinton had improperly tampered with a potential witness by attempting to influence Currie's testimony before the grand jury. Starr also said Clinton deliberately lied to key staff members, knowing that they would repeat those falsehoods in their subsequent grand jury testimony.*

Abuse of constitutional authority. *In a catch-all charge, Starr said that since Clinton's deposition in the Jones case on January 17, his actions on the Lewinsky matter were inconsistent with his constitutional duty to faithfully execute the laws. Specifically, Starr said, the president had promised to cooperate with the investigation and then refused six invitations to testify voluntarily; he deliberately misled his senior aides, his Cabinet, and the American people about the affair; and he asserted executive privilege "all as part of an effort to hinder, impede, and deflect possibly inquiry by the Congress of the United States."*

The White House Rebuttal

In their rebuttal, Clinton's attorneys declared that as a matter of law Clinton had not done any of the things he was accused of. On the perjury charges, they said that OIC had to show that Clinton not only was wrong about his interpretation of sex as defined by the Jones lawyers at his deposition, but that he knew he was wrong and intentionally lied. All the independent counsel had shown, they said, was that Clinton gave "narrow answers to ambiguous questions." The rebuttal said that Clinton had acknowledged in his deposition that he and Lewinsky exchanged gifts and denied that the president had ever taken steps to conceal the gifts. Clinton's attorneys said that it was Lewinsky, not the president, who had asked Currie to retrieve the gifts. Nor did Clinton ever try to get Lewinsky a job in order to influence her testimony. Clinton's attorneys quoted the Starr report in which it acknowledged that there was "no evidence" of any "arrangement . . . explicitly spelled out."

Clinton's attorneys were scathing in their remarks castigating Starr's motives. "Any fair reader of the Referral," they wrote, "will easily discern that many of the lurid allegations . . . have no justification at all, even in terms of any OIC legal theory. . . . They are simply part of a hit-and-run smear campaign and their inclusion says volumes about the OIC's tactics and objectives. . . ." The president's conduct was wrong, the rebuttal said, and his efforts to keep his illicit affair from becoming public, while understandable, were also wrong, but the president's actions did not rise to the level of high crimes and misdemeanors required for impeachment. The report was "at bottom overreaching in an extravagant effort to find a case where there is none."

Public Release of the Report

Under the law authorizing the OIC, Starr was to report his findings of possible impeachable offenses to the House of Representatives, which would then decide whether to proceed with an impeachment inquiry. The House had not expected Starr's report for several more weeks, so the unannounced arrival on Capitol Hill of the 445-page report and thirty-six boxes of grand jury material, delivered about 4:00 p.m. September 9, caught most legislators off guard. "Nobody knows what to do. We've never done this before," an aide to House Minority Leader Richard A. Gephardt said.

Although Democratic and Republican leaders had pledged to consider any charges Starr might level in a spirit of bipartisanship, that resolve evaporated in the debate over when and how to release the report. Republican leaders announced September 10 that they would release the report and post it on the Internet simultaneously the next day, before anyone in Congress had had an opportunity to read it. Democrats argued that the president's attorneys should be given at least forty-eight hours to review the report before it was made public. "The House of Representatives is not the U.S. Postal Service," said John Conyers Jr., the ranking Democrat on the House Judiciary Committee. "We are not a delivery system for Kenneth W. Starr. . . . We cannot, we ought not, we should not release anything to anybody unless we know what it is we are releasing."

Concurring with Judiciary Committee Chairman Henry J. Hyde that "it is important that the American people learn the facts," the House voted, 363–63, on the morning of September 11 to disseminate the report immediately. By late afternoon, people across the country were reading the Starr report on the Internet, and portions of it were being read on radio and television. Some broadcasts warned that the material was unsuitable for children and might be offensive to some adults. Some television reporters were visibly embarrassed by the explicit sexual descriptions that they were reporting. Although people expressed a range of emotion, from embarrassment to outrage, polls taken in the days immediately after the report was released found that 59 percent of those surveyed thought that Congress had erred in releasing all the details.

Following are excerpts from the "Referral" submitted by Independent Counsel Kenneth W. Starr to the U.S. House of Representatives September 9, 1998, and released September 11, 1998, laying out eleven possible grounds for impeaching the president, followed by excerpts from President Bill Clinton's rebuttal to the Starr report, released September 12, 1998:

THE STARR REPORT

Pursuant to Section 595(c) of Title 28, the Office of Independent Counsel hereby submits substantial and credible information that President Clinton obstructed justice during the *Jones v. Clinton* sexual harassment lawsuit by lying under oath and concealing evidence of his relationship with a young White House intern and federal employee, Monica Lewinsky.

After a federal criminal investigation of the President's actions began in January 1998, the President lied under oath to the grand jury and obstructed justice during the grand jury investigation. There also is substantial and credible information that the President's actions with respect to Monica Lewinsky constitute an abuse of authority inconsistent with the President's constitutional duty to faithfully execute the laws.

There is substantial and credible information supporting the following eleven possible grounds for impeachment:

1. President Clinton lied under oath in his civil case when he denied a sexual affair, a sexual relationship, or sexual relations with Monica Lewinsky.

2. President Clinton lied under oath to the grand jury about his sexual relationship with Ms. Lewinsky.

3. In his civil deposition, to support his false statement about the sexual relationship, President Clinton also lied under oath about being alone with Ms. Lewinsky and about the many gifts exchanged between Ms. Lewinsky and him.

4. President Clinton lied under oath in his civil deposition about his discussions with Ms. Lewinsky concerning her involvement in the *Jones* case.

5. During the *Jones* case, the President obstructed justice and had an understanding with Ms. Lewinsky to jointly conceal the truth about their relationship by concealing gifts subpoenaed by Ms. Jones's attorneys.

6. During the *Jones* case, the President obstructed justice and had an understanding with Ms. Lewinsky to jointly conceal the truth of their relationship from the judicial process by a scheme that included the following means: (i) Both the President and Ms. Lewinsky understood that they would

lie under oath in the *Jones* case about their sexual relationship; (ii) the President suggested to Ms. Lewinsky that she prepare an affidavit that, for the President's purposes, would memorialize her testimony under oath and could be used to prevent questioning of both of them about their relationship; (iii) Ms. Lewinsky signed and filed the false affidavit; (iv) the President used Ms. Lewinsky's false affidavit at his deposition in an attempt to head off questions about Ms. Lewinsky; and (v) when that failed, the President lied under oath at his civil deposition about the relationship with Ms. Lewinsky.

7. President Clinton endeavored to obstruct justice by helping Ms. Lewinsky obtain a job in New York at a time when she would have been a witness harmful to him were she to tell the truth in the *Jones* case.

8. President Clinton lied under oath in his civil deposition about his discussions with Vernon Jordan concerning Ms. Lewinsky's involvement in the *Jones* case.

9. The President improperly tampered with a potential witness by attempting to corruptly influence the testimony of his personal secretary, Betty Currie, in the days after his civil deposition.

10. President Clinton endeavored to obstruct justice during the grand jury investigation by refusing to testify for seven months and lying to senior White House aides with knowledge that they would relay the President's false statements to the grand jury—and did thereby deceive, obstruct, and impede the grand jury.

11. President Clinton abused his constitutional authority by (i) lying to the public and the Congress in January 1998 about his relationship with Ms. Lewinsky; (ii) promising at that time to cooperate fully with the grand jury investigation; (iii) later refusing six invitations to testify voluntarily to the grand jury; (iv) invoking Executive Privilege; (v) lying to the grand jury in August 1998; and (vi) lying again to the public and Congress on August 17, 1998—all as part of an effort to hinder, impede, and deflect possible inquiry by the Congress of the United States.

The first two possible grounds for impeachment concern the President's lying under oath about the nature of his relationship with Ms. Lewinsky. The details associated with those grounds are, by their nature, explicit. The President's testimony unfortunately has rendered the details essential with respect to those two grounds, as will be explained in those grounds.

Jones v. Clinton

I. There is substantial and credible information that President Clinton lied under oath as a defendant in *Jones v. Clinton* regarding his sexual relationship with Monica Lewinsky.

(1) He denied that he had a "sexual relationship" with Monica Lewinsky.

(2) He denied that he had a "sexual affair" with Monica Lewinsky.

(3) He denied that he had "sexual relations" with Monica Lewinsky.

(4) He denied that he engaged in or caused contact with the genitalia of "any person" with an intent to arouse or gratify (oral sex performed on him by Ms. Lewinsky).

(5) He denied that he made contact with Monica Lewinsky's breasts or genitalia with an intent to arouse or gratify. . . .

On May 6, 1994, former Arkansas state employee Paula Corbin Jones filed a federal civil rights lawsuit against President Clinton claiming that he had sexually harassed her on May 8, 1991, by requesting her to perform oral sex on him in a suite at the Excelsior Hotel in Little Rock. . . .

On January 17, 1998, Ms. Jones' lawyers deposed President Clinton under oath with Judge Wright present and presiding over the deposition. . . .

The term "sexual relations" was defined: For the purposes of this deposition, a person engages in "sexual relations" when the person knowingly engages in or causes . . . contact with the genitalia, anus, groin, breast, inner thigh, or buttocks of any person with an intent to arouse or gratify the sexual desire of any person. . . . "Contact" means intentional touching, either directly or through clothing.

President Clinton answered a series of questions about Ms. Lewinsky, including:

Q: Did you have an extramarital sexual affair with Monica Lewinsky?

WJC: No. . . . I have never had sexual relations with Monica Lewinsky. I've never had an affair with her.

President Clinton reiterated his denial under questioning by his own attorney. . . .

Monica Lewinsky testified under oath before the grand jury that, beginning in November 1995, when she was a 22-year-old White House intern, she had a lengthy relationship with the President that included substantial sexual activity. She testified in detail about the times, dates, and nature of ten sexual encounters that involved some form of genital contact. . . . White House records corroborate Ms. Lewinsky's testimony in that the President was in the Oval Office area during the encounters. The records of White House entry and exit are incomplete for employees, but they do show her presence in the White House on eight of those occasions. . . .

Ms. Lewinsky testified that she and the President engaged in "phone sex" approximately fifteen times. The President initiated each phone sex encounter by telephoning Ms. Lewinsky. . . .

Ms. Lewinsky produced to OIC [Office of Independent Counsel] investigators a dress she wore during the encounter on February 28, 1997, which she believed might be stained with the President's semen. At the request of the OIC, the FBI Laboratory examined the dress and found semen stains.

At that point, the OIC requested a DNA sample from the President. On August 3, 1998, two weeks before the President's grand jury testimony, a White House physician drew blood from the President in the presence of a senior OIC attorney and a FBI special agent. Through the most sensitive DNA testing, RFLP testing, the FBI Laboratory determined conclusively that the semen on Ms. Lewinsky's dress was, in fact, the President's. The chance that the semen is not the President's is one in 7.87 trillion. . . .

During her relationship with the President, Monica Lewinsky spoke contemporaneously to several friends, family members, and counselors about the relationship. Their testimony corroborates many of the details of the sexual activity provided by Ms. Lewinsky to the OIC.

Sexual Relationship

II. There is substantial and credible information that President Clinton lied under oath to the grand jury about his sexual relationship with Monica Lewinsky. . . .

The President was largely aware [of the substantial body assembled by the OIC] before he testified to the grand jury on August 17, 1998. Not only did the President know that Ms. Lewinsky had reached an immunity agreement with this Office in exchange for her truthful testimony, but the President knew from public reports and his own knowledge that his semen might be on one of Ms. Lewinsky's dresses. . . .

The President admitted to an "inappropriate intimate" relationship, but he maintained that he had not committed perjury in the *Jones* case when he denied having a sexual relationship, sexual affair, or sexual relations with her. The President contended that he had believed his various statements in the *Jones* case to be legally accurate. He also testified that the inappropriate relationship began not in November 1995 when Ms. Lewinsky was an intern, as Ms. Lewinsky and other witnesses have testified, but in 1996.

During his grand jury testimony, the President was asked whether Monica Lewinsky performed oral sex on him and, if so, whether he had committed perjury in his civil deposition by denying a sexual relationship, sexual affair, or sexual relations with her. The President refused to say whether he had oral sex. Instead, the President said (i) that the undefined terms "sexual affair," "sexual relationship," and "sexual relations" necessarily require sexual intercourse, that he had not engaged in intercourse with Ms. Lewinsky, and that he therefore had not committed perjury in denying a sexual relationship, sexual affair, or sexual relations. . . .

In the foregoing testimony to the grand jury, the President lied under oath three times.

1. The President testified that he believed oral sex was not covered by any of the terms and definitions for sexual activity used at the *Jones* deposition. That testimony is not credible: At the *Jones* deposition, the President could not have believed that he was telling "the truth, the whole truth, and nothing but the truth" in denying a sexual relationship, sexual relations, or a sexual affair with Monica Lewinsky.

2. In all events, even putting aside his definitional defense, the President made a second false statement to the grand jury. The President's grand jury testimony contradicts Ms. Lewinsky's grand jury testimony on the question whether the President touched Ms. Lewinsky's breasts or genitalia during their sexual activity. There can be no contention that one of them has a lack of memory or is mistaken. On this issue, either Monica Lewinsky lied to the grand jury, or President Clinton lied to the grand jury. Under any rational view of the evidence, the President lied to the grand jury. . . .

First, Ms. Lewinsky's testimony about these encounters is detailed and specific. She described with precision nine incidents of sexual activity in which the President touched and kissed her breasts and four incidents involving contacts with her genitalia.

Second, Ms. Lewinsky has stated repeatedly that she does not want to hurt the President by her testimony. Thus, if she had exaggerated in her many prior statements, she presumably would have said as much, rather than adhering to those statements. She has confirmed those details, however, even though it clearly has been painful for her to testify to the details of her relationship with the President.

Third, the testimony of many of her friends, family members, and counselors corroborate her testimony in important detail. . . . These statements were made well before the President's grand jury testimony rendered these precise details important. Ms. Lewinsky had no motive to lie to these individuals (and obviously not to counselors). Indeed, she pointed out to many of them that she was upset that sexual intercourse had not occurred, an unlikely admission if she were exaggerating the sexual aspects of their relationship.

Fourth, a computer file obtained from Ms. Lewinsky's home computer contained a draft letter that referred in one place to their sexual relationship. The draft explicitly refers to "watching your mouth on my breast" and implicitly refers to direct contact with Ms. Lewinsky's genitalia. This draft letter further corroborates Ms. Lewinsky's testimony and indicates that the President's grand jury testimony is false.

Fifth, as noted above, the President's "hands-off" scenario—in which he would have received oral sex on nine occasions from Ms. Lewinsky but never made direct contact with Ms. Lewinsky's breasts or genitalia—is implausible. As Ms. Lewinsky herself testified, it suggests that she and the President had some kind of "service contract—that all I did was perform oral sex on him and that that's all this relationship was." But as the above descriptions and the [preceding] Narrative explain, the nature of the relationship, including the sexual relationship, was far more than that. . . .

3. Finally, the President made a third false statement to the grand jury about his sexual relationship with Monica Lewinsky. He contended that the intimate contact did not begin until 1996. Ms. Lewinsky has testified that it began November 15, 1995, during the government shutdown—testimony corroborated by statements she made to friends at the time. A White House photograph of the evening shows the President and Ms. Lewinsky eating pizza. White House records show that Ms. Lewinsky did not depart the White House until 12:18 a.m. and show that the President was in the Oval Office area until 12:35 a.m.

Ms. Lewinsky was still an intern when she says the President began receiving oral sex from her, whereas she was a full-time employee by the time that the President admits they began an "inappropriate intimate" relationship. . . .

Civil Deposition

III. There is substantial and credible information that President Clinton lied under oath during his civil deposition when he stated that he could not recall being alone with Monica Lewinsky and when he minimized the number of gifts they had exchanged. . . .

Substantial and credible information demonstrates that the President made three false statements under oath in his civil deposition regarding whether he had been alone with Ms. Lewinsky.

First, the President lied when he said "I don't recall" in response to the question whether he had ever been alone with Ms. Lewinsky. The President [subsequently] admitted to the grand jury that he had been alone with Ms. Lewinsky. It is not credible that he actually had no memory of this fact six months earlier, particularly given that they were obviously alone when engaging in sexual activity.

Second, when asked whether he had been alone with Ms. Lewinsky in the hallway in the Oval Office, the President answered, "I don't believe so, unless we were walking back to the back dining room with the pizza." That statement, too, was false: Most of the sexual encounters between the President and Ms. Lewinsky occurred in that hallway (and on other occasions, they walked through the hallway to the dining room or study), and it is not credible that the President would have forgotten this fact.

Third, the President suggested at his civil deposition that he had no specific recollection of being alone with Ms. Lewinsky in the Oval Office, but had a general recollection that Ms. Lewinsky may have brought him "papers to sign" on certain occasions when she worked at the Legislative Affairs Office.

This statement was false. Ms. Lewinsky did not bring him papers for official purposes. To the contrary, "bringing papers" was one of the sham "cover stories" that the President and Ms. Lewinsky had originally crafted to conceal their sexual relationship. The fact that the President resorted to a previously designed cover story when testifying under oath at the *Jones* deposition confirms that he made these false denials in a calculated manner with the intent and knowledge that they were false. . . .

The President stated in his civil deposition that he could not recall whether he had ever given any gifts to Ms. Lewinsky; that he could not remember whether he had given her a hat pin although "certainly, I could have"; and that he had received a gift from Ms. Lewinsky only "once or twice." In fact, the evidence demonstrates that they exchanged numerous gifts of various kinds at many points over a lengthy period of time. Indeed, on December 28, only three weeks before the deposition, they had discussed the hat pin. Also on December 28, the President had given Ms. Lewinsky a number of gifts, more than he had ever given her before.

A truthful answer to the questions about gifts at the *Jones* deposition would have raised further questions about the President's relationship with Monica Lewinsky. The number itself would raise questions about the relationship and prompt further questions about specific gifts; some of the specific gifts (such as . . . *Leaves of Grass*) would raise questions whether the relationship was sexual and whether the President had lied in denying that their relationship was sexual. Ms. Lewinsky explained the point: Had they admitted the gifts, it would "at least prompt [the *Jones* attorneys] to want to question me about what kind of friendship I had with the President and they would want to speculate and they'd leak it and my name would be trashed and he [the President] would be in trouble."

Clinton-Lewinsky Conversations

IV. There is substantial and credible information that the President lied under oath during his civil deposition concerning conversations he had with Monica Lewinsky about her involvement in the *Jones* case.

Ms. Lewinsky testified that she spoke three times to President Clinton about the prospect of testifying in the *Jones* lawsuit—once (December 17, 1997) after she was on the witness list and twice more (December 28, 1997, and January 5, 1998) after she had been subpoenaed. . . .

There is substantial and credible information that President Clinton lied under oath in his civil deposition in answering "I'm not sure" when asked whether he had talked to Ms. Lewinsky about the prospect of her testifying. In fact, he had talked to Ms. Lewinsky about it on three occasions in the month preceding his civil deposition, as Ms. Lewinsky's testimony makes clear. . . .

There is substantial and credible information that the President lied under oath in his civil deposition when he denied knowing that Ms. Lewinsky had received her subpoena at the time he had last talked to her. . . . In fact, he knew that she had been subpoenaed. Given that the conversation with Ms. Lewinsky occurred in the few weeks immediately before the President's civil deposition, he could not have forgotten the conversation. As a result, there is no plausible conclusion except that the President intentionally lied in this answer.

During the civil deposition, the President also falsely dated his last conversation with Ms. Lewinsky as "probably sometime before Christmas," which implied that it might have been before the December 19 subpoena. Because Ms. Lewinsky had been subpoenaed on December 19, that false statement about the date of the conversation was a corollary to his other false statement (that he did not know she had been subpoenaed at the time of their last conversation). . . .

Concealment of Evidence

V. There is substantial and credible information that President Clinton endeavored to obstruct justice by engaging in a pattern of activity to conceal evidence regarding his relationship with Monica Lewinsky from the judicial process in the *Jones* case. The pattern included:

(i) concealment of gifts that the President had given Ms. Lewinsky and that were subpoenaed from Ms. Lewinsky in the *Jones* case; and

(ii) concealment of a note sent by Ms. Lewinsky to the President on January 5, 1998.

From the beginning, President Clinton and Monica Lewinsky hoped and expected that their relationship would remain secret. They took active steps,

643

when necessary, to conceal the relationship. The President testified that "I hoped that this relationship would never become public." . . .

The uncontroverted evidence demonstrates that the President had given gifts to Ms. Lewinsky before December 28, 1997; that the President told Ms. Lewinsky on the phone on December 17, 1997, that he had more gifts for her; that Ms. Lewinsky met with the President at the White House on December 28; that on the 28th, Ms. Lewinsky was concerned about retaining possession of the gifts the President had previously given her because they were under subpoena; that on the 28th, the President gave several Christmas gifts to Ms. Lewinsky; and that after that meeting, Ms. Lewinsky transferred some gifts (including one of the new gifts) to the President's personal secretary, Ms. Currie, who stored them under her bed in her home. . . .

The testimony conflicts as to what happened when Ms. Lewinsky raised the subject of gifts with the President and what happened later that day. The President testified that he told Ms. Lewinsky that "you have to give them whatever you have." According to Ms. Lewinsky, she raised the possibility of hiding the gifts, and the President offered a somewhat neutral response.

Ms. Lewinsky testified that Betty Currie called her to retrieve the gifts soon after Ms. Lewinsky's conversation with the President. Ms. Currie says that she believes that Ms. Lewinsky called her about the gifts, but she says she has a dim memory of the events.

The central factual question is whether the President orchestrated or approved the concealment of the gifts. The reasonable inference from the evidence is that he did.

The witnesses disagree about whether Ms. Currie called Ms. Lewinsky or Ms. Lewinsky called Ms. Currie. That issue is relevant because Ms. Currie would not have called Ms. Lewinsky about the gifts unless the President directed her to do so. Indeed, because she did not know of the gifts issue, there is no other way that Ms. Currie could have known to make such a call unless the President told her to do so.

Ms. Lewinsky's testimony on the issue is consistent and unequivocal. In her February 1, 1998, handwritten statement, she wrote: "Ms. Currie called Ms. L later that afternoon a[nd] said that the Pres. had told her Ms. L wanted her to hold onto something for her." In her grand jury testimony, Ms. Lewinsky said that several hours after she left the White House, Ms. Currie called and said something along the lines of "The President said you have something to give me."

Ms. Currie's testimony is contrary but less clear. Ms. Currie has stated that Ms. Lewinsky called her, but her memory of the conversation, in contrast to Ms. Lewinsky's, generally has been hazy and uncertain. As to whether she had talked to the President about the gifts, for example, Ms. Currie initially said she had not, but then said that Ms. Lewinsky (who said that Ms. Currie had talked to the President) "may remember better than I. I don't remember."

Ms. Lewinsky's testimony makes more sense than Ms. Currie's testimony. First, Ms. Lewinsky stated that if Ms. Currie had not called, Ms. Lewinsky simply would have kept the gifts (and perhaps thrown them away). She would not have produced the gifts to Ms. Jones' attorneys. And she would not have given them to a friend or mother because she did not want to get anyone else involved. She was not looking for someone else to take them.

Also, Ms. Currie drove to Ms. Lewinsky's house to pick up the gifts. That was only the second time that Ms. Currie had ever gone there. More generally, the person making the extra effort (in this case, Ms. Currie) is ordinarily the person requesting the favor.

2. Even if Ms. Lewinsky is mistaken and she did call Ms. Currie first, the evidence still leads clearly to the conclusion that the President orchestrated this transfer. . . .

3. Even if the President did not orchestrate the transfer to Ms. Currie, there is still substantial evidence that he encouraged the concealment and non-production of the gifts by Ms. Lewinsky. The President "hoped that this relationship would never become public." The President gave Ms. Lewinsky new gifts on December 28, 1997. Given his desire to conceal the relationship, it makes no sense that the President would have given Ms. Lewinsky more gifts on the 28th unless he and Ms. Lewinsky understood that she would not produce all of her gifts in response to her subpoena. . . .

On January 4, 1998, Ms. Lewinsky left a book for the President with Ms. Currie. Ms. Lewinsky had enclosed in the book a romantic note that she had written, inspired by a recent viewing of the movie "Titanic." In the note, Ms. Lewinsky told the President that she wanted to have sexual intercourse with him, at least once.

On January 5, in the course of discussing her affidavit and possible testimony in a phone conversation with the President, Ms. Lewinsky says she told the President, "I shouldn't have written some of those things in the note." According to Ms. Lewinsky, the President said that he agreed and that she should not write those kinds of things on paper.

On January 15, President Clinton served responses to Ms. Jones' second set of document requests, which again asked for documents that related to "Monica Lewisky." The President stated that he had "no documents" responsive to this request.

The President remembered the book Ms. Lewinsky had given him about the Presidents and testified that he "did like it a lot." President Clinton testified that he did not recall a romantic note enclosed in the book or when he had received it.

The request for production of documents that the President received from Ms. Jones' attorneys called for all documents reflecting communications between him and Ms. Lewinsky. The note given to him by Ms. Lewinsky on January 5, 1998, fell within that category and would have been revealing about the relationship. Indeed, had the note been produced, the President might have been foreclosed from denying a sexual relationship at his deposition. Based on Ms. Lewinsky's testimony, there is substantial and credible information that the President concealed or destroyed this note at a time when such documents were called for by the request for production of documents.

False Affidavit

VI. There is substantial and credible information that (i) President Clinton and Ms. Lewinsky had an understanding that they would lie under oath in the *Jones* case about their relationship; and (ii) President Clinton endeavored to obstruct justice by suggesting that Ms. Lewinsky file an affidavit so that she would not be deposed, she would not contradict his testimony, and he could attempt to avoid questions about Ms. Lewinsky at his deposition.

Based on their conversations and their past practice, both the President and Ms. Lewinsky understood that they would lie under oath in the *Jones* case about their sexual relationship, as part of a scheme to obstruct justice in the *Jones* case. In pursuing this effort:

The President suggested that Monica Lewinsky file an affidavit, which he knew would be false;

The President had an interest in Ms. Lewinsky's false affidavit because it would "lock in" her testimony, allowing the President to deny the sexual relationship under oath without fear of contradiction;

Ms. Lewinsky signed and, on January 16, sent to the Court the false affidavit denying a sexual relationship with the President as part of a motion to quash her deposition subpoena;

The President's attorney used the affidavit to object to questions about Ms. Lewinsky at his January 17 deposition; and

When that failed, the President also lied under oath about the relationship with Ms. Lewinsky at his civil deposition, including by the use of "cover stories" that he and Ms. Lewinsky had devised. . . .

There is substantial and credible information that the President and Ms. Lewinsky reached an understanding that both of them would lie under oath when asked whether they had a sexual relationship (a conspiracy to obstruct justice or to commit perjury, in criminal law terms). Indeed, a tacit or express agreement to make false statements would have been an essential part of their December and January discussions, lest one of the two testify truthfully in the *Jones* case and thereby incriminate the other as a perjurer.

There also is substantial and credible information that President Clinton endeavored to obstruct justice by suggesting that Ms. Lewinsky file an affidavit to avoid her deposition, which would "lock in" her testimony under oath, and to attempt to avoid questions at his own deposition—all to impede the gathering of discoverable evidence in the *Jones v. Clinton* litigation.

During the course of their relationship, the President and Ms. Lewinsky also discussed and used cover stories to justify her presence in and around the Oval Office area.

The evidence indicates—given Ms. Lewinsky's unambiguous testimony and the President's lack of memory, as well as the fact that they both planned to lie under oath—that the President suggested the continued use of the cover stories even after Ms. Lewinsky was named as a potential witness in the *Jones* litigation. At no time did the President tell Ms. Lewinsky to abandon these stories and to tell the truth about her visits, nor did he ever indicate to her that she should tell the truth under oath about the relationship.

While the President testified that he could not remember such conversations about the cover stories, he had repeated the substance of the cover stories in his *Jones* deposition. The President's use of false cover stories in testimony under oath in his *Jones* deposition strongly corroborates Ms. Lewinsky's testimony that he suggested them to her on December 17 as a means of avoiding disclosure of the truth of their relationship.

Lewinsky Job Search

VII. There is substantial and credible information that President Clinton endeavored to obstruct justice by helping Ms. Lewinsky obtain a job in New York at a time when she would have been a witness against him were she to tell the truth during the *Jones* case.

The President had an incentive to keep Ms. Lewinsky from jeopardizing the secrecy of the relationship. That incentive grew once the Supreme Court unanimously decided in May 1997 that the case and discovery process were to go forward.

At various times during the *Jones* discovery process, the President and those working on his behalf devoted substantial time and attention to help Ms. Lewinsky obtain a job in the private sector. . . .

On October 1, the President was served with interrogatories asking about his sexual relationships with women other than Mrs. Clinton. On October 7, 1997, Ms. Lewinsky couriered a letter expressing dissatisfaction with her job search to the President. In response, Ms. Lewinsky said she received a late-night call from President Clinton on October 9, 1997. She said that the President told her he would start helping her find a job in New York.

The following Saturday, October 11, 1997, Ms. Lewinsky met with President Clinton alone in the Oval Office dining room from 9:36 a.m. until about 10:54 a.m. In that meeting, she furnished the President a list of New York jobs in which she was interested. Ms. Lewinsky mentioned to the President that she would need a reference from someone in the White House; the President said he would take care of it. Ms. Lewinsky also suggested to the President that Vernon Jordan might be able to help her, and President Clinton agreed. Immediately after the meeting, President Clinton spoke with Mr. Jordan by telephone.

According to White House Chief of Staff Erskine Bowles, at some time in the summer or fall of 1997, President Clinton raised the subject of Monica Lewinsky and stated that "she was unhappy where she was working and wanted to come back and work at the OEOB [Old Executive Office Building]; and could we take a look." Mr. Bowles referred the matter to Deputy Chief of Staff John Podesta.

Mr. Podesta said he asked Betty Currie to have Ms. Lewinsky call him, but heard nothing until about October 1997, when Ms. Currie told him that Ms. Lewinsky was looking for opportunities in New York. The Ambassador to the United Nations, Bill Richardson, said that Mr. Podesta told him that Ms. Currie had a friend looking for a position in New York.

According to Ms. Lewinsky, Ambassador Richardson called her on October 21, 1997, and interviewed her soon thereafter. She was then offered a position at the U.N. Ms. Lewinsky was unenthusiastic. During the latter part of October 1997, the President and Ms. Lewinsky discussed enlisting Vernon Jordan to aid in pursuing private-sector possibilities.

On November 5, 1997, Ms. Lewinsky met Mr. Jordan in his law office. Mr. Jordan told Ms. Lewinsky that she came "highly recommended." Ms. Lewinsky explained that she hoped to move to New York, and went over her list of possible employers. Mr. Jordan telephoned President Clinton shortly after the meeting.

Ms. Lewinsky had no contact with the President or Mr. Jordan for another month. On December 5, 1997, however, the parties in the *Jones* case exchanged witness lists. Ms. Jones's attorneys listed Ms. Lewinsky as a potential witness. The President testified that he learned that Ms. Lewinsky was on the list late in the day on December 6.

The effort to obtain a job for Ms. Lewinsky then intensified. On December 7, President Clinton met with Mr. Jordan at the White House. Ms. Lewinsky met with Mr. Jordan on December 11 to discuss specific job contacts in New York. Mr. Jordan gave her the names of some of his business contacts. He then made calls to contacts at MacAndrews & Forbes (the parent corporation of Revlon), American Express, and Young & Rubicam.

Mr. Jordan also telephoned President Clinton to keep him informed of the efforts to help Ms. Lewinsky. Mr. Jordan testified that President Clinton was aware that people were trying to get jobs for her, that Mr. Podesta was trying to help her, that Bill Richardson was trying to help her, but that she wanted to work in the private sector. . . .

On December 17, 1997, according to Ms. Lewinsky, President Clinton called her in the early morning and told her that she was on the witness list [in the *Jones* case], and they discussed their cover stories. On December 18 and December 23, she interviewed for jobs with New York-based companies that had been contacted by Mr. Jordan. On December 19, Ms. Lewinsky was served with a deposition subpoena by Ms. Jones's lawyers. On December 22, 1997, Mr. Jordan took her to her new attorney; she and Mr. Jordan discussed the subpoena, the *Jones* case, and her job search during the course of the ride. . . .

On Sunday, December 28, 1997, Monica Lewinsky and the President met in the Oval Office. During that meeting, the President and Ms. Lewinsky discussed both her move to New York and her involvement in the *Jones* suit.

On January 5, 1998, Ms. Lewinsky declined the United Nations offer. On January 7, 1998, Ms. Lewinsky signed the affidavit denying the relationship with President Clinton (she had talked on the phone to the President on January 5 about it). Mr. Jordan informed the President of her action. . . .

One can draw inferences about the party's intent from circumstantial evidence. In this case, the President assisted Ms. Lewinsky in her job search in late 1997, at a time when she would have become a witness harmful to him in the *Jones* case were she to testify truthfully. The President did not act halfheartedly. His assistance led to the involvement of the Ambassador to the United Nations, one of the country's leading business figures (Mr. Perelman), and one of the country's leading attorneys (Vernon Jordan).

The question, therefore, is whether the President's efforts in obtaining a job for Ms. Lewinsky were to influence her testimony or simply to help an ex-intimate without concern for her testimony. Three key facts are essential in analyzing his actions: the chronology of events, the fact that the President and Ms. Lewinsky both intended to lie under oath about the relationship, and the fact that it was critical for the President that Ms. Lewinsky lie under oath.

There is substantial and credible information that the President assisted Ms. Lewinsky in her job search motivated at least in part by his desire to keep her "on the team" in the *Jones* litigation.

Vernon Jordan and Lewinsky

VIII. There is substantial and credible information that the President lied under oath in describing his conversations with Vernon Jordan about Ms. Lewinsky.

President Clinton was asked during his civil deposition whether he had talked to Mr. Jordan about Ms. Lewinsky's involvement in the *Jones* case. The President stated that he knew Mr. Jordan had talked to Ms. Lewinsky about her move to New York, but stated that he did not recall whether Mr. Jordan had talked to Ms. Lewinsky about her involvement in the *Jones* case. The testimony was false. A lie under oath about these conversations was necessary to avoid inquiry into whether Ms. Lewinsky's job and her testimony were improperly related. . . .

Vernon Jordan testified that his conversations with the President about Ms. Lewinsky's subpoena were, in fact, "a continuing dialogue." When asked if he had kept the President informed about Ms. Lewinsky's status in the *Jones* case in addition to her job search, Mr. Jordan responded: "The two—absolutely."

On December 19, Ms. Lewinsky phoned Mr. Jordan and told him that she had been subpoenaed in the *Jones* case. Following that call, Mr. Jordan telephoned the President to inform him "that Monica Lewinsky was coming to see me, and that she had a subpoena"—but the President was unavailable. Later that day, at 5:01 p.m., Mr. Jordan had a seven-minute telephone conversation with the President:

I said to the President, "Monica Lewinsky called me up. She's upset. She's gotten a subpoena. She is coming to see me about this subpoena. I'm confident that she needs a lawyer, and I will try to get her a lawyer."

Later on December 19, after meeting with Ms. Lewinsky, Mr. Jordan went to the White House and met with the President alone in the Residence. Mr. Jordan testified: "I told him that Monica Lewinsky had been subpoenaed, came to me with a subpoena." According to Mr. Jordan, the President "thanked me for my efforts to get her a job and thanked me for getting her a lawyer."

According to Mr. Jordan, on January 7, 1998, Ms. Lewinsky showed him a copy of her signed affidavit denying any sexual relationship with the President. He testified that he told the President about the affidavit, probably in one of his two logged calls to the White House that day. . . .

In his civil deposition, the President stated that he had talked to Vernon Jordan about Ms. Lewinsky's job. But as the testimony of Mr. Jordan reveals, and as the President as much as conceded in his subsequent grand jury appearance, the President did talk to Mr. Jordan about Ms. Lewinsky's involvement in the *Jones* case—including that she had been subpoenaed, that Mr. Jordan had helped her obtain a lawyer, and that she had signed an affidavit denying a sexual relationship with the President.

Given their several communications in the weeks before the deposition, it is not credible that the President forgot the subject of their conversations during his civil deposition. His statements [Clinton had said: I knew that he met with her. I think Betty suggested that he meet with her. Anyway, he met with her. I, I thought that he talked to her about something else. I didn't know that—I thought he had given her some advice about her move to New York. Seems like that's what Betty said.] were more than mere omissions; they were affirmative misstatements. . . .

The President's motive for making false and misleading statements about this subject in his civil deposition was straightforward. If the President admitted that he had talked with Vernon Jordan both about Monica Lewinsky's involvement in the *Jones* case and about her job, questions would inevitably arise about whether Ms. Lewinsky's testimony and her future job were connected. Such an admission by the President in his civil deposition likely would have prompted Ms. Jones' attorneys to inquire further into the subject. And such an admission in his deposition would have triggered public scrutiny when the deposition became public.

Betty Currie's Testimony

IX. There is substantial and credible information that President Clinton endeavored to obstruct justice by attempting to influence the testimony of Betty Currie.

In a meeting with Betty Currie on the day after his deposition and in a separate conversation a few days later, President Clinton made statements to her that he knew were false. The contents of the statements and the context in which they were made indicate that President Clinton was attempting to influence the testimony that Ms. Currie might have been required to give in the *Jones* case or in a grand jury investigation. . . .

The President referred to Ms. Currie on multiple occasions in his civil deposition when describing his relationship with Ms. Lewinsky. As he himself recognized, a large number of questions about Ms. Lewinsky were likely to be asked in the very near future. The President thus could foresee that Ms. Currie either might be deposed or questioned or might need to prepare an affidavit.

The President called her shortly after the deposition and met with Ms. Currie the next day. The President appeared "concerned," according to Ms. Currie. He then informed Ms. Currie that questions about Ms. Lewinsky had been asked at the deposition.

The statements the President made to her on January 18 and again on January 20 or 21—that he was never alone with Ms. Lewinsky, that Ms. Currie could always hear or see them and that he never touched Ms. Lewinsky—were false, but consistent with the testimony that the President provided under oath at his deposition. The President knew that the statements were false at the time he made them to Ms. Currie. The President's suggestion that he was simply trying to refresh his memory when talking to Ms. Currie conflicts with common sense: Ms. Currie's confirmation of false statements could not in any way remind the President of the facts. Thus, it is not plausible that he was trying to refresh his recollection.

The President's grand jury testimony reinforces that conclusion. He testified that in asking questions of Ms. Currie such as "We were never alone, right" and "Monica came on to me, and I never touched her, right," he intended a date restriction on the questions. But he did not articulate a date restriction in his conversations with Ms. Currie.

Moreover, with respect to some aspects of this incident, the President was unable to devise any innocent explanation, testifying that he did not know why he had asked Ms. Currie some questions and admitting that he was "just trying to reconcile the two statements as best [he could]." On the other hand, if the most reasonable inference from the President's conduct is drawn—that he was attempting to enlist a witness to back up his false testimony from the day before—his behavior with Ms. Currie makes complete sense.

The content of the President's statements and the context in which those statements were made provide substantial and credible information that President Clinton sought improperly to influence Ms. Currie's testimony. Such actions constitute an obstruction of justice and improper influence on a witness.

Lying to Grand Jury Witnesses

X. There is substantial and credible information that President Clinton endeavored to obstruct justice during the federal grand jury investigation. While refusing to testify for seven months, he simultaneously lied to potential grand jury witnesses knowing that they would relay the falsehoods to the grand jury.

The President's grand jury testimony followed seven months of investigation in which he had refused six invitations to testify before the grand jury. During this period, there was no indication that the President would admit any sexual relationship with Ms. Lewinsky. To the contrary, the President vehemently denied the allegations.

Rather than lie to the grand jury himself, the President lied about his relationship with Ms. Lewinsky to senior aides, and those aides then conveyed the President's false story to the grand jury.

In this case, the President lied to, among others, three current senior aides—John Podesta, Erskine Bowles, and Sidney Blumenthal—and one former senior aide, Harold Ickes. The President denied any kind of sexual relationship with Monica Lewinsky; said that Ms. Lewinsky had made a sexual demand on him; and denied multiple telephone conversations with Monica Lewinsky. The President, by his own later admission, was aware that his aides were likely to convey the President's version of events to the grand jury.

The President's aides took the President at his word when he made these statements. Each aide then testified to the nature of the relationship between Monica Lewinsky and the President based on those statements—without knowing that they were calculated falsehoods by the President designed to perpetuate the false statements that the President made during his deposition in the *Jones* case.

The aides' testimony provided the grand jury a false account of the relationship between the President and Ms. Lewinsky. Their testimony thus had the potential to affect the investigation—including decisions by the OIC and grand jury about how to conduct the investigation (for example, whether to subpoena Secret Service agents) and whether to indict particular individuals. . . .

The President made the following misleading statements to his aides:

The President told Mr. Podesta that he had not engaged in sex "in any way whatsoever" with Ms. Lewinsky, "including oral sex."

The President told Mr. Podesta, Mr. Bowles, and Mr. Ickes that he did not have a "sexual relationship" with Ms. Lewinsky.

The President told Mr. Podesta that "when [Ms. Lewinsky] came by, she came by to see Betty [Currie]."

The President told Mr. Blumenthal that Ms. Lewinsky "came on to him and that he had told her he couldn't have sexual relations with her and that she threatened him."

The President told Mr. Blumenthal that he couldn't remember making any calls to Ms. Lewinsky other than once when he left a message on her answering machine.

During the President's grand jury testimony, the President admitted that his statements to aides denying a sexual relationship with Ms. Lewinsky "may have been misleading." The President also knew his aides likely would be called to testify regarding any communications with him about Ms. Lewinsky. And he presumably expected his aides to repeat his statements regarding Ms. Lewinsky to all questioners, including to the grand jury. Finally, he himself refused to testify for many months. The combination of the President's silence and his deception of his aides had the effect of presenting a false view of events to the grand jury.

The President says that at the time he spoke to his aides, he chose his words with great care so that, in his view, his statements would be literally true because he was referring only to intercourse.

That explanation is undermined by the President's testimony before the grand jury that his denials "may have been misleading" and by the contradictory testimony by the aides themselves—particularly John Podesta, who says that the President specifically denied oral sex with Ms. Lewinsky. Moreover, on January 24, 1998, the White House issued talking points for its staff, and those talking points refute the President's literal truth argument: The talking points state as the President's view the belief that a relationship that includes oral sex is "of course" a "sexual relationship."

For all of these reasons, there is substantial and credible information that the President improperly tampered with witnesses during the grand jury investigation.

Constitutional Duty

XI. There is substantial and credible information that President Clinton's actions since January 17, 1998, regarding his relationship with Monica Lewinsky have been inconsistent with the President's constitutional duty to faithfully execute the laws.

Before, during, and after his January 17, 1998, civil deposition, the President attempted to conceal the truth about his relationship with Ms. Lewinsky from the judicial process in the *Jones* case. Furthermore, the President has since lied under oath to the grand jury and facilitated the provision of false information to the grand jury by others.

The President also misled the American people and the Congress in his public statement of January 26, 1998, in which he denied "sexual relations" with Ms. Lewinsky. The President misled his Cabinet and his senior aides by denying the relationship to them. The Cabinet and senior aides in turn misled the American people and the Congress by conveying the President's denials and professing their belief in the credibility of those denials.

The President promised in January 1998 to cooperate fully with the grand jury investigation and to provide "more rather than less, sooner rather than later." At that time, the OIC was conducting a criminal investigation and was obligated to report to Congress any substantial and credible information that may constitute grounds for an impeachment.

The President's conduct delayed the grand jury investigation (and thereby delayed any potential congressional proceedings). He asserted, appealed, withdrew, and reasserted Executive Privilege (and asserted other governmental privileges never before applied in federal criminal proceedings against the government). The President asserted these privileges concerning the investigation of factual questions about which the President already knew the answers.

The President refused six invitations to testify voluntarily before the grand jury. At the same time, the President's aides and surrogates argued publicly that the entire matter was frivolous and that any investigation of it should cease.

After being subpoenaed in July, the President made false statements to the grand jury on August 17, 1998. That night, the President again made false statements to the American people and Congress, contending that his answers in his civil deposition had been "legally accurate." The President then made an implicit plea for Congress to take no action: "Our country has been distracted by this matter for too long."

The President has pursued a strategy of deceiving the American people and Congress in January 1998, delaying and impeding the criminal investigation for seven months, and deceiving the American people and Congress again in August 1998. . . .

CLINTON'S REBUTTAL

On May 31, 1998, the spokesman for Independent Counsel Kenneth W. Starr declared that the Office's Monica Lewinsky investigation "is not about sex. This case is about perjury, subornation of perjury, witness tampering, obstruction of justice. That is what this case is about." Now that the 450-page Referral to the United States House of Representatives Pursuant to Title 28, United States Code 595(c) is public, it is plain that "sex" is precisely what this four-and-a-half-year investigation has boiled down to. The Referral is so loaded with irrelevant and unnecessary graphic and salacious allegations that only one conclusion is possible: Its principal purpose is to damage the President.

The President has acknowledged and apologized for an inappropriate sexual relationship with Ms. Lewinsky, so there is no need to describe that relationship in ugly detail. No one denies that the relationship was wrong or that the President was responsible. The Referral's pious defense of its pornographic specificity is that, in the Independent Counsel's view: "The details are crucial to an informed evaluation of the testimony, the credibility of witnesses, and the reliability of other evidence. Many of the details reveal highly personal information; many are sexually explicit. This is unfortunate, but it is essential." This statement is patently false. Any fair reader of the Referral will easily discern that many of the lurid allegations, which need not be recounted here, have no justification at all, even in terms of any OIC [Office of the Independent Counsel] legal theory. . . . They are simply part of a hit-and-run smear campaign, and their inclusion says volumes about the OIC's tactics and objectives. . . .

Because presidential impeachment invalidates the will of the American people, it was designed to be justified for the gravest wrongs—offenses against the Constitution itself. In short, only "serious assaults on the integrity of the processes of government," and "such crimes as would so stain a president as to make his continuance in office dangerous to the public order," constitute impeachable offenses. The eleven supposed "grounds for impeachment" set forth in the section of the Referral called "Acts That May Constitute Grounds for an Impeachment" fall far short of that high standard, and their very allegation demeans the constitutional process. The document is at bottom overreaching in an extravagant effort to find a case where there is none.

Allegation I—Perjury in January 17, 1998, Deposition

. . . The OIC begins its catalogue of "acts that may constitute grounds for impeachment" with the allegation that "[t]here is substantial and credible information that President Clinton lied under oath as a defendant in *Jones v. Clinton* regarding his sexual relationship with Monica Lewinsky." The OIC contends that, for legal reasons, it must discuss its allegations of sexual activity in detail and then goes out of its way to supply lurid detail after lurid detail that are completely irrelevant to any legal claim, obviously hoping that the shock value of its footnotes will overcome the absence of legal foundation for the perjury allegation. . . .

By selectively presenting the facts and failing to set out the full context of the answers that it claims may have been perjurious, the OIC has presented a wholly misleading picture. This tactic is most pronounced in the OIC's astonishing failure to set out the initial definition of "sexual relations" presented by the Jones lawyers at President Clinton's deposition, two parts of which were eliminated by Judge Wright as being "too broad." The OIC also fails to mention that the Jones lawyers were fully able, and indeed were invited by President Clinton's counsel, to ask the President specific questions about his sexual encounters, but they chose not to do so. . . .

As any fair prosecutor would acknowledge, what the OIC dismisses as a mere "semantical defense" is, in fact, reflective of the great care the courts have taken to ensure that a witness is not charged with perjury except when the government can demonstrate a clear intent to provide false testimony. Thus, in any ordinary prosecutor's office, and surely in the chambers of the House Judiciary Committee, the definitions of such terms as "sexual affair," "sexual relations," and "sexual relationship" would be seen as vital to a determination whether some violation of law had occurred. The burden that must be met by the OIC extends beyond showing that the President was wrong on the semantics, it must also show that, because perjury is a specific intent crime, he knew he was wrong and intended to lie—something that the OIC could not begin to demonstrate. In fact, all the OIC has is a witness who gave narrow answers to ambiguous questions. . . .

The OIC argues that oral sex falls within the definition of sexual relations and that the President therefore lied when he said he denied having sexual relations. It is, however, the President's good faith and reasonable interpretation that oral sex was outside the special definition of sexual relations provided to him. The OIC simply asserts that it disagrees with the President's "linguistic parsing," and that reasonable people would not have agreed with him. This simply is not the stuff of which criminal prosecutions—and surely impeachment proceedings—are made. . . .

Allegation II—Perjury in August 17, 1998, Grand Jury Testimony

In its second allegation, the OIC contends that "[t]here is substantial and credible information that President Clinton lied under oath to the grand jury about his sexual relationship with Monica Lewinsky." . . .

1. The OIC first claims that the President testified falsely that he did not believe oral sex to be covered by any of the terms and definitions for sexual activity used at the *Jones* deposition. . . . Not content to accept his explana-

tion, the OIC makes the extraordinary (and factually unsupported) claim that the President committed perjury before the grand jury by lying not about some fact but about his belief about the meaning of certain words. The OIC then compounds this error by claiming as perjury the President's explanation of his understanding of the contorted definition of "sexual relations" in the *Jones* suit, as modified by the court.

This claim is quite stunning. The OIC charges the President with perjury, saying it is "not credible" that the President believed oral sex fell outside the definition he was given, even though it plainly did, and even though many commentators and journalists have stated that they believe that the definition of sexual relations in the *Jones* deposition did not include oral sex (performed on the President). . . .

It is beyond debate that false testimony provided as a result of confusion or mistake cannot as a matter of law constitute perjury. Moreover, if there is any doubt as to the falsity of testimony, the issue must be resolved in favor of the accused. . . . The OIC's very allegation that the President committed perjury by re-explaining his belief and interpretation to the grand jury is yet another indication of the extent of the OIC's overreaching in this Referral.

2. The OIC's next charge—that the President testified falsely when he contradicted Ms. Lewinsky's grand jury testimony on the question whether he touched Ms. Lewinsky's breasts or genitalia during their sexual activity—is substantially identical to the allegation contained in Allegation I, and cannot constitute perjury for the same reason. The critical issue here is not whether the testimony of the President and Ms. Lewinsky differ but whether there is any evidence that the President knowingly and intentionally gave false testimony. It is worthwhile to note, however, the inaccuracy of the OIC's assertion that "[t]here can be no contention that one of them has a lack of memory or is mistaken" about the details of their physical relationship.

3. The OIC's final allegation here is that the President made a false statement to the grand jury regarding the timing of the beginning of his relationship with Ms. Lewinsky. . . . As a legal allegation this claim is frivolous, because the statement by the President regarding the timing of the relationship (mid-November 1995 as opposed to January 1996) was utterly immaterial to the grand jury's investigation. . . . There is no conceivable way in which any statement by the President with regard to the date (within a few weeks) of the commencement of his relationship with Ms. Lewinsky could possibly have influenced the grand jury, and the OIC has of course not identified how the grand jury was "influenced" by this testimony. . . .

Allegation III—Meetings and Exchanging Gifts with Ms. Lewinsky

In its third allegation, the OIC makes various claims of perjury based on President Clinton's statements in the *Jones* deposition regarding whether he had been alone with Ms. Lewinsky in the Oval Office and in an adjacent hallway and whether he and Ms. Lewinsky had exchanged gifts. Like the other perjury allegations, the OIC fails to offer a credible case.

First and foremost, President Clinton did not deny meeting alone with Ms. Lewinsky at the White House nor deny that they exchanged gifts.

In essence, the OIC's complaint is that President Clinton was not more forthcoming, which is plainly not a ground for perjury, rather than that he knowingly lied under oath. . . . The transcript makes it clear that, when asked about particular gifts, the President honestly stated his recollection of the particular item.

Nor can President Clinton's testimony regarding whether he was alone with Ms. Lewinsky at various times and places constitute perjury. The Jones lawyers often failed to follow up on incomplete or unresponsive answers. Read as a whole, the deposition makes clear that the President acknowledged being alone with Ms. Lewinsky on some occasions. The Referral unfortunately mischaracterizes the testimony to suggest an absolute denial, for example, transforming a question about being alone with Ms. Lewinsky in the Oval Office (where the President did not recall engaging in improper contact) into being alone at all ("The President lied when he said 'I don't recall' in response to the question whether he had ever been alone with Ms. Lewinsky."). And, surprisingly since the Jones lawyers had been briefed by Ms. Tripp, the Jones lawyers never asked the President whether he was alone with Ms. Lewinsky in the study, where some of the alleged activity took place. They were free to ask specific follow-up questions about the nature and locale of any physical contact, and they did not do so. The OIC cannot now hold the President to blame for their failure.

Allegation IV—Discussions With Ms. Lewinsky About Potential Testimony

The Referral claims that in the following exchange in President Clinton's January 17 deposition in the *Jones* case he committed perjury:

Q: Have you ever talked to Ms. Lewinsky about the possibility that she might be asked to testify in this lawsuit?

A: I'm not sure and let me tell you why I'm not sure. Seems to me the last time she was there to see Betty before Christmas we were joking about how you-all, with the help of the Rutherford Institute, were going to call every woman I'd ever talked to and . . . ask them that, and so I said you would qualify, or something like that. I don't, I don't think we ever had more of a conversation than that about it. . . .

Q: What, if anything, did Monica Lewinsky say in response?

A: Nothing, that I remember. Whatever she said, I don't remember. Probably just some predictable thing.

This answer was literally accurate. The President described a joking conversation that he had with many women about the possibility that they might be subpoenaed by the Jones lawyers. He made clear that the recollection of the conversation with Ms. Lewinsky preceded the appearance of Ms. Lewinsky's name on the witness list (on December 5), ... In his grand jury testimony, additional details of a December 28 conversation with Ms. Lewinsky were provided by the President. The testimony that the Referral cites is not inconsistent—his first answer indicating he was referring to a conversation that occurred before she had been named a witness, and his August 17 testimony describing a conversation after she had been subpoenaed in mid-December. The fact that Ms. Lewinsky recalls additional conversations on the subject, all occurring after she had been named on the witness list, does not establish that the President's answer was inaccurate. This answer cannot possibly support a perjury charge.

Allegation V—Concealing Gifts and an Intimate Note

In its fifth allegation, the OIC contends that President Clinton obstructed justice by concealing gifts he had given to Ms. Lewinsky. This claim is wholly unfounded and simply absurd. On her December 28, [1997] visit, the President gave Ms. Lewinsky several holiday and going-away gifts. Ms. Lewinsky apparently testified that, during the visit, she raised a question about the *Jones* subpoena and suggested "put[ting] the gifts away outside of my house or somewhere or giv[ing] them to someone, maybe Betty." To this suggestion, the President, according to Ms. Lewinsky's reported testimony, responded with something like, "I don't know" or "Hmmm" or "there really was no response." President Clinton contradicts this testimony. But even if one accepts Ms. Lewinsky's testimony, "I don't know," "Hmmm" and silence do not constitute obstruction of justice.

Moreover, Ms. Lewinsky's testimony is contradicted by Ms. Currie, who testified that it was Ms. Lewinsky, not the President, who asked her to come get the gifts and keep them. . . .

The OIC's theory of concealment also is belied by Ms. Lewinsky's decision to turn over some, but not all, of the gifts she had received from the President to Ms. Currie; if the purpose of the exercise was to avoid having gifts in her possession at the time of the deposition (which of course would not have been proper), retaining some gifts made no sense. . . .

Ultimately, the only theory that does make sense is the truth, as testified to by the President and Ms. Currie and as supported by the fact that the President acknowledged giving Ms. Lewinsky gifts as early as his January 17, 1998, deposition. The President was unconcerned about the gifts he had given to Ms. Lewinsky because he frequently exchanges gifts with friends. That is why he gave her additional gifts on December 28 even though, according to her testimony, he knew the Jones lawyers were interested in them. . . .

The OIC also argues that the President obstructed justice in the *Jones* case by destroying an intimate note that Ms. Lewinsky included in a book she left for him on January 4, 1998. The OIC states in its Referral that the President was served with a document request from the Jones lawyers on December 16, 1997, that required him to produce this note to the Jones lawyers. The disingenuousness of this allegation is apparent on several levels.

As a preliminary matter, the President testified that he recalled receiving a book from Ms. Lewinsky, that he believed he had received it in December, and that he did not recall receiving an accompanying note. . . .

Second, the OIC asserts, without basis, that the President purposefully destroyed Ms. Lewinsky's note because he did not want to have to turn it over to the Jones lawyers. The OIC has absolutely no basis for assuming that the President was aware of the document request at the time he received the book. Thus, even assuming the President had received and discarded the note, his acts would not constitute obstruction of justice. . . .

Allegation VI—Concealment of the Relationship

In the sixth allegation, the OIC contends that there is substantial and credible information that: (i) President Clinton and Ms. Lewinsky had an understanding that they would lie under oath in the *Jones* case about their relationship; and (ii) President Clinton endeavored to obstruct justice by suggesting that Ms. Lewinsky file an affidavit so that she would not be deposed, she would not contradict his testimony, and he could attempt to avoid questions about Ms. Lewinsky at his deposition.

The essence of the OIC's argument is that, because the President and Ms. Lewinsky attempted to conceal the improper nature of their relationship while it was going on and because the President failed affirmatively to assure that each statement contained in the affidavit filed by Ms. Lewinsky was true, he therefore obstructed justice. The Referral fails even to allege facts that, if true, would constitute obstruction of justice under the law. . . .

The Referral alleges that during the course of their admittedly improper relationship, the President and Ms. Lewinsky concealed the nature of their relationship from others. This is hardly a remarkable proposition. The use of "cover stories" to conceal such a relationship, apart from any proceeding, is not unusual and not an obstruction of justice.

The Referral alleges only one specific statement that Ms. Lewinsky claims the President made to her regarding the substance of her testimony. Ms. Lewinsky testified that the President told her, "You know, you can always say you were coming to see Betty or that you were bringing me letters." As an initial matter, the President testified that he did not recall saying anything like that in connection with Ms. Lewinsky's testimony in the *Jones* case. But even if he did, neither of those two ambiguous statements would be false. And most importantly, as even the OIC concedes, the President never instructed her to lie. . . .

Finally, the OIC suggests that the President was "knowingly responsible" for a misstatement of fact to a federal judge because he failed to correct a statement made by his lawyer to the court in the *Jones* deposition. The President testified to the grand jury that the lawyers' argument at the start of the deposition "passed [him] by"; he also remarked that the statement of his lawyer might be literally true. The OIC distorts this response to suggest the President testified that he did not correct the statement at the January deposition because it might have been true. We do not believe the testimony would support that claim. . . .

Allegation VII—Job Search for Ms. Lewinsky

In its seventh allegation, the Referral contends that certain actions taken on behalf of Ms. Lewinsky in her job efforts amounted to obstruction of justice. The Referral acknowledges that the case for obstruction based on the job search is wholly circumstantial and that there is absolutely "no evidence" of any "arrangement . . . explicitly spelled out." Noting that the critical issue centers on the intent of the party providing the assistance, the Referral asks that "inferences be drawn" from the circumstantial evidence set forth in the Referral chronology.

But that chronology presents precious little in the way of Presidential involvement and nothing that supports an inference of any intent to obstruct justice by helping Ms. Lewinsky (to the limited extent he did) in her job efforts. It may be the OIC's view that the President should have cast Ms. Lewinsky off and refused to assist her in any way, simply because the *Jones* case was filed. Fortunately the law requires no such callous absurdity. . . .

There is no suggestion that he ever ordered or directed anyone to assist Ms. Lewinsky or asked anyone to give her special advantages or disadvantages because of their relationship or that he ever linked his relatively insubstantial assistance to a requirement that she act—or testify—in a certain way. The kinds of actions that are alleged simply do not constitute obstruction of justice. . . .

Allegation VIII—Conversations with Mr. Jordan

The OIC asserts in its eighth allegation that the President was "asked during his civil deposition whether he had talked to Mr. Jordan about Ms. Lewinsky's involvement in the *Jones* case" and that he "stated that he did not recall whether Mr. Jordan had talked to Ms. Lewinsky about her involvement in the *Jones* case." This account of the question and answer is simply false. The President was not asked that question, and he did not give that answer. . . .

Moreover, the OIC's 252-page Narrative does not identify reports to the President about conversations that Mr. Jordan had with Ms. Lewinsky in that time period—instead, it recounts only that, 10 days before the deposition, Mr. Jordan left word for the President that the affidavit was signed. The last passage on which the OIC relies simply asked whether the President had heard that Mr. Jordan and Ms. Lewinsky met to discuss the case; the President recounted his belief that the two had met to discuss the job search—about which the President readily acknowledged an awareness. The OIC's assertion that the President "did not recall whether Mr. Jordan had talked to Ms. Lewinsky about her involvement in the *Jones* case," is simply not supported by the testimony. This allegation is a fabrication by the OIC.

Allegation IX—'Witness Tampering'

In its ninth allegation, the OIC charges that President Clinton obstructed justice and improperly influenced a witness when he spoke with Ms. Currie the day after his deposition in the *Jones* case. The OIC's claims are wrong and, again, the product of extraordinary overreaching and pejorative conjecture—a transparent attempt to draw the most negative inference possible about lawful conduct.

The President's actions could not as a matter of law give rise to either charge because Ms. Currie was not a witness in any proceeding at the time he spoke with her: Her name had not appeared on any of the *Jones* witness lists; she had not been named as a witness in the *Jones* case; there were just two weeks of discovery left in the case; and there was no reason to suspect she would play any role in that case. The President had no reason to suspect that the OIC had embarked on a wholly new phase of its four-year investigation, one in which Ms. Currie would later be called by the OIC as a witness. To obstruct a proceeding or tamper with a witness, there must be both a witness and a proceeding. Here, there was neither. Despite the OIC's far-fetched suggestion to the contrary, there was no reason the President should not have spoken with Ms. Currie about Ms. Lewinsky. . . .

Allegation X—Refusal to Testify

The tenth allegation is premised on the OIC's misrepresentation of the facts. The assertion that "[the President] simultaneously lied to potential grand jury witnesses," "[w]hile refusing to testify for seven months" is a gross distortion of the Referral's own citations.

The statements to Presidential aides cited by the Referral were made either on the day the Lewinsky story broke (January 21, 1998) or within a few days of that date. Those statements were concurrent in time with the President's repeated public statements to the country denying sexual relations with Ms. Lewinsky. And they were virtually identical in substance. Having announced to the whole country on live television that he was not having sexual relations with Ms. Lewinsky, it is simply absurd to believe that he was somehow attempting to corruptly influence the testimony of aides when he told them virtually the same thing at the same time.

And in any event, the mere repetition of a public denial to these aides could not have affected the grand jury process. The elicited testimony was hearsay. The aides were not witnesses to any sexual activity, and they had no first-hand knowledge pertinent to the denials. Their testimony as to what they heard from the President was truthful—the President in no conceivable way sought to alter any other perceptions or information they might have had. . . .

Nor is there evidence that the President's statements constituted "witness tampering" in violation of section 1512. To make out such a violation, the government must show that the behavior knowingly occurred through one of the specific means set forth in the statute: intimidation, physical force, threats, misleading conduct or corrupt persuasion—with intent to influence testimony in a legal proceeding. . . . In fact, the President simply repeated to aides substantially the same statement he made to the whole country. There was no action here intended specifically to influence the grand jury through the testimony of Presidential aides. Under the OIC's theory, it could have subpoenaed to the grand jury any citizen who heard the President's denial and thus have created a new violation of law. . . .

The OIC suggests that the President's delay in acknowledging a relationship with Ms. Lewinsky somehow contributed to an obstruction of justice because it affected how the prosecutors would conduct the investigation. This claim is unfounded, as a matter of law. The President had no legal obligation to appear before the grand jury absent compulsion and every reason not to do so, given the OIC's tactics, illegal leaking, and manifest intent to cause him damage.

Allegation XI—Abuse of Power

As the Office of Independent Counsel itself acknowledges, from the very beginning, its investigation was focused on the prospect that the information it was gathering would be transmitted to the Congress. It is in this context, with the threat of impeachment on the horizon, that the OIC's last allegation of an abuse of power must be judged.

The OIC begins with the charge that the President's false denial that he had an improper relationship with Ms. Lewinsky—something that he has now admitted and apologized for—was itself an abuse of power because it served to deceive the American people. Implicit in this charge is the notion that any official, in any branch of the government, who makes a public statement about his own conduct, or indeed any other matter, that is not true may be removed from office. It would follow, therefore, that no official could mount a defense to impeachment, or to ethics charges, or to a criminal investigation while remaining in office, for anything other than an immediate admission of guilt will necessarily be misleading. . . .

The manifest desire to create improprieties where none exist and to transform personal misconduct into impeachable official malfeasance is evident also in the OIC's claim that the President's assertion of executive privilege was somehow unlawful. Oddly enough, the OIC finds abuse of power both in the assertion of the privilege and its withdrawal—surely evidence of an overwrought imagination or of a conceit that any legal position other than the OIC's is presumptively obstructive. In truth, the OIC's decision to invade the confidential relationship between the President and his most senior advisers and lawyers was unprecedented. It reflects a patent abuse of authority by the OIC and a wholesale abandonment of any prosecutorial judgment in a campaign to prevent the President from consulting meaningfully with his advisers. At bottom, the Independent Counsel seems to believe that, merely because he chooses to seek confidential information from the Office of the President, the President may not contest that demand without risking a charge that he is abusing his power. . . .

More importantly, the OIC's abuse-of-power allegation must necessarily rest on the assumption that the President initiated the executive privilege claim with intent to impede the OIC's investigation. Yet, the record is clear that it was only after extensive negotiations in which the White House offered to make available to the OIC factual information concerning the President's conduct and had its offer rejected out of hand, that the White House Counsel notified the President of the OIC's demands, explained the failed accommodation effort, and recommended that he invoke the privilege. Counsel gave that advice because he believed it important to protect the constitutional interests of the presidency. Thus, the President's decision to claim privilege was not the result of his own initiative, much less of any intent to obstruct the grand jury investigation, but rather was the result of his Counsel's advice.

Even more egregiously misleading is the claim that the President abused his power by "acquiescing" in the efforts of the Secret Service to assert a protective function privilege. First, the OIC characterizes that assertion as frivolous even though it reflected the judgment of the law enforcement professionals charged with protecting this and future presidents and was supported by former President Bush. Further, the OIC charges the President with abusing his power despite the fact that the OIC knew that he had nothing to do with the decision to assert the privilege or to pursue the appeal from [U.S. District] Judge [Norma Holloway] Johnson's decision. Indeed, the OIC itself had argued (in contesting the claim of the Secret Service in the district court) that the failure of the President to involve himself in the matter was itself a reason for the court to reject the Service's claim.

The OIC cannot have it both ways.

Last, the OIC charges that it was an abuse of power for the President, at a time when both his personal and official interests were in the balance, not to testify before the grand jury until August—surely a claim that must astound lawyers and laymen alike. Could the OIC truly be taking the position that any government official who is the subject of a criminal investigation must immediately come forward and testify at a prosecutor's whim or risk impeachment? To state the question is to answer it.

Conclusion

It has come down to this.

After four years, scores of FBI agents, hundreds of subpoenas, thousands of documents, and tens of millions of dollars. After hiring lawyers, accountants, IRS agents, outside consultants, law professors, personal counsel, ethics advisers, and a professional public relations expert. After impaneling grand juries and leasing office space in three jurisdictions, and investigating virtually every aspect of the President's business, financial, political, official and, ultimately, personal life, the Office of Independent Counsel has presented to the House a Referral that no prosecutor would present to any jury.

The President has admitted he had an improper relationship with Ms. Lewinsky. He has apologized. The wrongfulness of that relationship is not in dispute. And yet that relationship is the relentless focus of virtually every page of the OIC's Referral.

In 445 pages, the Referral mentions Whitewater, the failed land deal which originated its investigation, twice. It never once mentions other issues it has been investigating for years—matters concerning the firing of employees of the White House travel office and the controversy surrounding the FBI files. By contrast, the issue of sex is mentioned more than 500 times, in the most graphic, salacious and gratuitous manner.

The Office of Independent Counsel is asking the House of Representatives to undertake its most solemn and consequential process short of declaring war; to remove a duly, freely and fairly elected President of the United States because he had—as he has admitted—an improper, illicit relationship outside of his marriage. Having such a relationship is wrong. Trying to keep such a relationship private, while understandable, is wrong. But such acts do not even approach the Constitutional test of impeachment. . . .

The President did not commit perjury. He did not obstruct justice. He did not tamper with witnesses. And he did not abuse the power of the office of the Presidency.

ADVISORY BOARD REPORT
ON RACE RELATIONS
September 18, 1998

A presidential advisory board formed to initiate a nationwide dialogue on race in the United States gave its formal report to President Bill Clinton on September 18, making dozens of recommendations for improving race relations in the fields of education, health, law enforcement, affirmative action, and other areas. But civil rights groups and others quickly dismissed the board's report as little more than platitudes and empty rhetoric. Throughout its fifteen months of existence, the board had been criticized for a lack of focus and direction.

In accepting the report at a formal ceremony, Clinton acknowledged that some of the criticism might have been justified, but he also suggested that the critics had overblown expectations of what the panel could reasonably have been expected to accomplish. He also reminded his audience that the board's work was only a first step. "This board has raised the consciousness and quickened the conscience of America," the president said at a gathering of civil rights activists and others in the Old Executive Office Building. "They have moved us closer to our ideal. But we have more to do."

The president had launched the initiative on race in a commencement address at the University of California at San Diego in June 1997. In the first phase of that initiative Clinton envisioned a series of town meetings and other events in which ordinary Americans would "confront and work through" their feelings about race in all facets of American life. The seven-member advisory board, headed by the prominent historian John Hope Franklin, was charged with organizing those meetings and gathering information on matters of race from experts. (Clinton's race initiative, Historic Documents of 1997, p. 314)

The board made no real policy recommendations but offered modest steps in a variety of areas. The president had already incorporated several of these ideas into legislation, including asking for more money to reduce class sizes in elementary and secondary schools and increasing the amount of Small Business Administration loans that go to minority businesses.

These "are not a lot of bold, new, or exciting recommendations," said a spokesman for a Hispanic advocacy organization. "But it is important to understand that this is not the final step in the process. This stuff is hard."

By all accounts the board was slow to get organized and staffed. At their first public meeting, board members disagreed with each other over whether to focus primarily on black-white relations or to take a more balanced approach that would include issues of concern to Hispanics, Asian-Americans, American Indians, and other racial groups. The board was also criticized when it held a private meeting in Dallas in December to which only blacks were invited. Another meeting on ways to achieve racial diversity on college campuses was criticized because the board had not invited anyone opposed to affirmative action.

Clinton appeared at three town meetings and spoke of the need for a national dialogue on race in speeches and radio addresses. But there were reports that the White House staff squelched some ideas for speeches and appearances as too risky politically, and for most of 1998 the race initiative could not compete for attention against the investigation into Clinton's affair with Monica S. Lewinsky and his pending impeachment. Any disappointment that more was not accomplished during the year may have been deepened by the realization that Clinton was uniquely suited to undertake such an effort. A Southerner by birth with a large reservoir of good will among minorities and a lifelong interest in the subject, Clinton was also skilled at drawing people with divergent viewpoints into conversation.

Some of the board's members openly said they would have liked the board to be bolder in its recommendations. Thomas H. Kean, a former Republican governor of New Jersey, for example, said he would have directly challenged the news media and entertainment industry to end their racial stereotyping. The board's report simply asked that attention be paid to this problem.

The Board's Final Report

The panel stated flatly that its report was "not a definitive analysis of the state of race relations" in the United States. Rather, it was "an account of the Board's experiences and impressions" gleaned during its meetings with civil rights, religious, and corporate leaders around the country. The board looked at the role race played in several specific areas, namely, civil rights enforcement, education, poverty, employment, housing, stereotyping, the administration of justice, health care, and immigration. The report included all the recommendations the board made to the president after its formal meetings. Many had already been implemented or were awaiting congressional action. Many of the recommendations urged the president to improve data collection in a specific area (racial and ethnic discrimination, for example), to strengthen the laws intended to protect the rights of minorities, or to look more closely at particularly tenacious problems, such as income inequality and racial stereotyping.

It also urged the president to take four steps, which it said were "the most critical in developing a long-term strategy to advance race relations." First, and most important, the president should create a permanent "President's Council for One America" to continue the work of the panel. Second, the panel called for a multimedia public education program that would keep the American public informed about racial matters and increase the nation's understanding of racial and ethnic differences. Third, the panel asked Clinton to issue a call to action to leaders from all public and private sectors to work together "to make racial reconciliation a reality" in local communities. Fourth, the committee said that young people specifically should be encouraged to join the effort to build racial bridges.

The report concluded with a list of ten things that every American should do to promote racial reconciliation.

Update on the Kerner Commission Report

In 1968 a presidential commission, appointed by President Lyndon B. Johnson to look into the causes behind the urban rioting that had destroyed parts of several cities and led by former Illinois governor Otto Kerner, concluded that "our nation is moving toward two societies, one black, one white—separate and unequal." In March 1998 a group established to carry on the work of that commission said its prophecy had come to pass.

The report from the Milton S. Eisenhower Foundation noted major social, political, and economic gains that black Americans had made since the Kerner Commission report of 1968—a vibrant and expanding black middle class, significant increases in black-owned businesses, and growing numbers of elected officials at all levels of government. Nonetheless, the report said a troubling racial disparity continues: "The rich are getting richer, the poor are getting poorer and minorities are suffering disproportionately." Despite the lowest levels of unemployment in a generation, the report said, many adults in many inner cities did not work in a typical week; academic achievement among minority students in urban schools was unacceptably low, and one out of every three young black men was in prison, on parole, or on probation. "The private market has failed the inner city. The prison system is a symbol of discrimination. A class and racial breach is widening again as we begin the new millennium," the report said. The report called for the expansion of programs that have been shown to work, including the Head Start program, after-school programs, targeted job training, and community-sensitive policing strategies.

Critics said the report was overly pessimistic and too quick to blame racism for continuing economic disparities. "It is almost as if people want it to be 1963 all over again," author Jim Sleeper told the Washington Post. "It is almost like people take their moral bearing by fixing the old coordinates of racism firmly in place." Fred R. Harris, the co-author of the Eisenhower Foundation report and a member of the original Kerner Commission disagreed, pointing out that poverty had worsened over the thirty years and that the poor were disproportionately black and Hispanic. "Race *and poverty are intertwined, and each makes the other worse," he said. "You can't argue with the facts."*

> *Following is the text of the executive summary of a report entitled "One America in the 21st Century: Forging a New Future," presented September 18, 1998, to President Bill Clinton by his advisory board on the president's initiative on race, together with a section entitled "Ten Things Every American Should Do to Promote Racial Reconciliation":*

Executive Summary

One America in the 21st Century: Forging a New Future

Today, I ask the American people to join me in a great national effort to perfect the promise of America for this new time as we seek to build our more perfect union. . . . That is the unfinished work of our time, to lift the burden of race and redeem the promise of America.

—President Clinton, June 14, 1997

America's greatest promise in the 21st century lies in our ability to harness the strength of our racial diversity. The greatest challenge facing Americans is to accept and take pride in defining ourselves as a multiracial democracy. At the end of the 20th century, America has emerged as the worldwide symbol of opportunity and freedom through leadership that constantly strives to give meaning to democracy's fundamental principles. These principles—justice, opportunity, equality, and racial inclusion—must continue to guide the planning for our future.

On June 13, 1997, President William Jefferson Clinton issued Executive Order No. 13050 (the "Executive Order"), which created the Initiative on Race (the "Initiative") and authorized the creation of an Advisory Board to advise the President on how to build one America for the 21st century. The Board, consisting of Dr. John Hope Franklin (chairman), Linda Chavez Thompson, Reverend Dr. Suzan D. Johnson Cook, Thomas H. Kean, Angela E. Oh, Bob Thomas, and William F. Winter, was tasked with examining race, racism, and the potential for racial reconciliation in America using a process of study, constructive dialogue, and action.

Board members have spent the last 15 months seeking ways to build a more united and just America. They have canvassed the country meeting with and listening to Americans who revealed how race and racism have impacted their lives. Board meetings focused on the role race plays in civil rights enforcement, education, poverty, employment, housing, stereotyping, the administration of justice, health care, and immigration. Members have convened forums with leaders from the religious and corporate sectors.

This Report, a culmination of the Board's efforts, is not a definitive analysis of the state of race relations in America today. Board members had no independent authority to commit Federal resources to a particular problem, community, or organization. Rather, this Report is an account of the Board's experiences and impressions and includes all of the recommendations for action submitted by the Board to the President following its formal meetings. Many have already been implemented or are awaiting congressional action.

Chapter One—Searching for Common Ground

Throughout the year, the Board heard stories and shared experiences that reinforced its belief that we are a country whose citizens are more united than divided. All too often, however, racial differences and discrimination obstruct our ability to move beyond race and color to recognize our common values and goals. Common values include the thirst for freedom, desire for equal opportunity, and a belief in fairness and justice; collective goals are securing a decent affordable home, a quality education, and a job that pays decent wages. All people, regardless of race, want financial and personal security, adequate and available health care, and children who are healthy and well-educated. Chapter One discusses these shared goals and values and also describes how the Initiative used dialogue as a tool for finding common ground. Through One America Conversations, the Campus Week of Dialogue, Statewide Days of Dialogue, tribal leaders meetings, and the *One America Dialogue Guide*, the Initiative was able to spark dialogue across the country. The chapter also points to the importance of recruiting a cadre of leaders to provide strong leadership in the corporate, religious, and youth sectors of our society and provides examples of Promising Practices.

Chapter Two—Struggling with the Legacy of Race and Color

Chapter Two confronts the legacy of race in this country and in so doing, answers the question of whether race matters in America. Our Nation still struggles with the impact of its past policies, practices, and attitudes based on racial differences. Race and ethnicity still have profound impacts on the extent to which a person is fully included in American society and provided the equal opportunity and equal protection promised to all Americans. All of these characteristics continue to affect an individual's opportunity to receive an education, acquire the skills necessary to maintain a good job, have access to adequate health care, and receive equal justice under the law.

Americans must improve their understanding of the history of race in this country and the effect this history has on the way many minorities and people of color are treated today. Each minority group shares a common history of legally mandated and/or socially and economically imposed subordination to white European-Americans and their descendants. In this chapter, the experiences of American Indians and Alaska Natives, African Americans, Latinos, Asian Pacific Americans, and white immigrants are highlighted.

The lesson of this chapter is that the absence of both knowledge and understanding about the role race has played in our collective history continues to make it difficult to find solutions that will improve race relations, eliminate disparities, and create equal opportunities in *all* areas of American life. This absence also contributes to conflicting views on race and racial progress held by Americans of color and white Americans.

This is especially relevant in the context of race-conscious affirmative action programs. Lack of knowledge and understanding about the genesis and consequences of racial discrimination in America often make it difficult to discuss affirmative action remedies productively. It also obscures the significant progress made in the last two decades in eliminating racial disparities in the workplace and in educational institutions through the use of properly constructed affirmative action strategies.

Chapter Three—The Changing Face of America

In Chapter Three, the Board examines the changing face of America. The discussion of race in this country is no longer a discussion between and about blacks and whites. Increasingly, conversations about race must include all Americans, including, but not limited to, Hispanics, American Indians and Alaska Natives, and Asian Pacific Americans. Statistics show that by the year 2050, the population in the United States will be approximately 53 percent white, 25 percent Hispanic, 14 percent black, 8 percent Asian Pacific American, and 1 percent American Indian and Alaska Native. This represents a significant shift from our current demographics of 73 percent white, 12 percent black, 11 percent Hispanic, 4 percent Asian Pacific American, and 1 percent American Indian and Alaska Native.

Further complicating the discussions of race is the increasing amount of interracial marriages. Americans are marrying persons of a different race at consistently high rates. U.S. Census data show that 31 percent of nativeborn Hispanic husbands and wives, between ages 25 and 34, have white spouses. In the native-born Asian Pacific American category, 36 percent of the men and 45 percent of the women marry white spouses.

The complexities, challenges, and opportunities that arise from our growing diversity point to the need for a new language, one that accurately reflects this diversity. Our dialogue must reflect the steps being taken to close the gap in data reporting on America's less visible racial groups-American Indians, Alaska Natives, Native Hawaiians, and all of the subgroups of Asian Pacific Americans and Hispanics.

Chapter Four—Bridging the Gap

Chapter Four summarizes key facts and background information that emerged from each of the Board's formal meetings and the recommendations made to the President on civil rights enforcement, education, economic opportunity, stereotypes, criminal justice, health care, and the immigrant experience. The data show that although minorities and people of color have made progress in terms of the indicators used to measure quality of life, persistent barriers to their full inclusion in American society remain.

In the area of civil rights enforcement, the Board made the following recommendations:

- Strengthen civil rights enforcement.
- Improve data collection on racial and ethnic discrimination.
- Strengthen laws and enforcement against hate crimes.

Two of the early Board meetings focused on the role of education in helping to overcome racial disparities. These meetings stressed the importance of educating children in high-quality, integrated schools, where they have the opportunity to learn about and from each other. These meetings served as the basis for the following recommendations:

- Enhance early childhood learning.
- Strengthen teacher preparation and equity.
- Promote school construction.
- Promote movement from K–12 to higher education.
- Promote the benefits of diversity in K-12 and higher education.
- Provide education and skills training to overcome increasing income inequality that negatively affects the immigrant population.
- Implement the Comprehensive Indian Education Policy.

The Board analyzed the issue of economic opportunity through formal meetings on employment and poverty. Information gathered showed that a substantial amount of disparity remains between the economic prosperity of whites and most minority groups. Also, the Board found clear evidence of active forms of discrimination in employment, pay, housing, and consumer and credit markets. The Board made the following recommendations for correcting these disparities:

- Examine income inequality.
- Support supplements for Small Business Administration programs.
- Use the current economic boom to provide necessary job training and to increase the minimum wage.
- Evaluate anti-poverty program effectiveness.
- Provide a higher minimum wage for low-wage workers and their families.
- Improve racial data collection.
- Evaluate the effectiveness of job-training programs designed to reach minority and immigrant communities.
- Commission a study to examine American Indian economic development.
- Support the right of working people to engage in collective bargaining.

The U.S. Department of Housing and Urban Development convened a meeting for the Board on race and housing. Active forms of racial discrimination continue to plague our housing markets. According to current statistics, blacks and Hispanics are likely to be discriminated against roughly half of the time that they go to look for a home or apartment. The recommendations for addressing the disparities in the area of housing follow:

- Continue to use testing to develop evidence of continuing discrimination.
- Highlight housing integration efforts.
- Support the increase and targeting of Federal funds for urban revitalization.
- Support community development corporations.
- Promote American Indian access to affordable housing.

In one meeting, the Board addressed the issues surrounding negative racial stereotypes, which are the core elements of discrimination and racial division. Stereotypes influence how people of different races and ethnicides view and treat each other. The Board's recommendations on stereotypes, which follow, focus on using both public and private institutions and individuals to challenge policymakers and institutional leaders to examine the role stereotypes play in policy development, institutional practices, and our view of our own racial identity:

- Hold a Presidential event to discuss stereotypes.
- Institutionalize the Administration's promotion of racial dialogue.
- Convene a high-level meeting on the problem of racial stereotypes with leaders from the media.

At the Board meeting on race, crime, and the administration of justice, experts explained how racial disparities and prejudices affect the way in which minorities are treated by the criminal system. Examples of this phenomenon can be found in the use of racial profiling in law enforcement and in the differences in the rates of arrest, conviction, and sentencing between whites and minorities and people of color. These discoveries led to the following recommendations:

- Expand data collection and analysis.
- Consider restricting the use of racial profiling.
- Eliminate racial stereotypes and diversify law enforcement.
- Reduce or eliminate drug sentencing disparities.
- Promote comprehensive efforts to keep young people out of the criminal justice system.
- Continue to enhance community policing and related strategies.
- Support initiatives that improve access to courts.
- Support American Indian law enforcement.

The U.S. Department of Health and Human Services sponsored a meeting on race and health for the Board. Disparities in the treatment of whites and minorities and people of color by the health care system can be attributed to disparities in employment, income, and wealth. The Board made the following recommendations as a result of information received at this meeting:

- Continue advocating for broad-based expansions in health insurance coverage.
- Continue advocacy of increased health care access for underserved groups.

- Continue pushing Congress for full funding of the Race and Ethnic Health Disparities Initiatives.
- Increase funding for existing programs targeted to under served and minority populations.
- Enhance financial and regulatory mechanisms to promote culturally competent care.
- Emphasize the importance of cultural competence to institutions training health care providers.

The Carnegie Endowment for International Peace and the Georgetown University Law Center jointly sponsored a meeting for the Board that explored immigration and race. Evidence showed that race is the source of a fundamental rift in American society that affects immigrants and their experiences with discrimination. The Board issued the following recommendations as a result of the information it received in this meeting:

- Strongly enforce anti-discrimination measures on behalf of every racial and ethnic minority group.
- Back programs that would promote a clear understanding of the rights and duties of citizenship.
- Support immigrant-inclusion initiatives.

Chapter Five—Forging a New Future

Chapter Five calls for the continuation of the Initiative to complete the work already begun. The following elements are the most critical in developing a meaningful long-term strategy to advance race relations in the 21st century:

- **A President's Council for One America.** This year's effort has been vital in laying the foundation for the larger task that lies ahead. The creation of a President's Council for One America speaks to the need for a long-term strategy dedicated to building on the vision of one America. Its main function would be to coordinate and monitor the implementation of policies designed to increase opportunity and eliminate racial disparities.
- **A public education program using a multimedia approach.** A public education program could assist in keeping the American public informed on the facts about race in America, pay tribute to the different racial and ethnic backgrounds of Americans, and emphasize and highlight the common values we share as a racially diverse Nation.
- **A Presidential "call to action" of leaders from all sectors of our society.** A call to action should come from the President to leaders in State and local government and private sector organizations to address the racial and ethnic divides in their communities. Public/private partnerships can demonstrate leadership by working collaboratively to make racial reconciliation a reality in all communities across America.
- **A focus on youth.** Young Americans are this Nation's greatest hope for realizing the goal of one America. Young people must be engaged in

efforts to bridge racial divides and promote racial reconciliation. Organizations and groups that encourage the development of youth leaders must be supported.

This chapter also includes a brief discussion of other critical issues, such as environmental justice, media and stereotyping, and police misconduct, that the Advisory Board believes deserve further dialogue. Among these issues is affirmative action, which the Board believes remains an important tool among many for overcoming racial discrimination and promoting the benefits of diversity in education, employment, and other contexts.

Chapter Five concludes with the 10 suggestions on how Americans can help to build on the momentum that will lead our Nation into the 21st century as one America. . . .

Ten Things Every American Should Do to Promote Racial Reconciliation

One of the most striking findings from our work is that there are many Americans who are willing to accept that racial prejudice, privilege, and disparities are major problems confronting our Nation. Many of them told us that they would welcome concrete advice about what they should do. To fill that need, we offer a brief list of actions that individual Americans could take that would increase the momentum that will make us one America in the 21st century.

(1) **Make a commitment to become informed about people from other races and cultures.** Read a book, see a movie, watch a play, or attend a cultural event that will inform you and your family about the history and current lives of a group different than your own.

(2) **If it is not your inclination to think about race, commit at least 1 day each month to thinking about how issues of racial prejudice and privilege might be affecting each person you come in contact with that day.** The more that people think about how issues of race affect each person, the easier it will be for Americans to talk honestly about race and eliminate racial divisions and disparities.

(3) **In your life, make a conscious effort to get to know people of other races.** Also, if your religious community is more racially isolated than your local area, encourage it to form faith partnerships with racially different faith groups.

(4) **Make a point to raise your concerns about comments or actions that appear prejudicial, even if you are not the targets of these actions.** When people say or do things that are clearly racially biased, speak out against them, even if you are not the target. When people do things that you think *might be* influenced by prejudice, raise your concerns that the person or institution seriously consider the role that racial bias might play, even unconsciously.

(5) **Initiate a constructive dialogue on race within your workplace, school, neighborhood, or religious community.** The *One America*

Dialogue Guide provides some useful ideas about how to construct a dialogue and lists some organizations that conduct dialogues and can help with facilitation.

(6) **Support institutions that promote racial inclusion.** Watch television programs and movies that offer racially diverse casts that reflect the real world instead of those perpetuating an inaccurately segregated view of America. Support companies and nonprofit organizations that demonstrate a commitment to racial inclusion in personnel and subcontracting. Write the institutions to let them know of your support for what they are doing.

(7) **Participate in a community project to reduce racial disparities in opportunity and well-being.** These projects can also be good ways of getting to know people from other backgrounds.

(8) **Insist that institutions that teach us about our community accurately reflect the diversity of our Nation.** Encourage our schools to provide festivals and celebrations that authentically celebrate the history, literature, and cultural contributions of the diverse groups that comprise the United States. Insist that our children's schools textbooks, curricula, and libraries provide a full understanding of the contributions of different racial groups and an accurate description of our historic and ongoing struggle for racial inclusion. Insist that our news sources whether print, television, or radio—include racially diverse opinions, story ideas, analysis, and experts. Support ethnic studies programs in our colleges and universities so that people are educated and that critical dialogue about race is stimulated.

(9) **Visit other areas of the city, region, or country that allow you to experience parts of other cultures, beyond their food.** If you have an attitude that all people have histories, cultures, and contributions about which you could benefit from learning, it is usually not difficult to find someone who enjoys exposing others to their culture.

(10) **Advocate that groups you can influence (whether you work as a volunteer or employee) examine how they can increase their commitment to reducing racial disparities, lessening discrimination, and improving race relations.** Whether we are a member of a small community group or an executive of a large corporation, virtually everyone can attempt to influence a group to join the national effort to build one America.

GAO ON PROTECTING COMPUTER SECURITY
September 23, 1998

The importance of protecting the security of computer systems at government agencies and private businesses was becoming increasingly evident in the late 1990s. By 1998 numerous studies warned that increasing use of the Internet was making massive computer systems in both the public and private sectors vulnerable to attacks from "hackers" who broke into computers for political and other reasons or who simply enjoyed the thrill of damaging someone else's property.

A presidential commission in 1997 raised an alert on the potential for attacks on the nation's computer networks. The commission did not propose massive government programs but did call for greater public awareness of the danger posed by computer hackers and terrorists. President Bill Clinton issued an order in 1998 implementing some of the commission's recommendations, but the General Accounting Office (GAO) and other observers said the government needed to do more. (Commission study, Historic Documents of 1997, p. 711)

Scares at the Pentagon

Incidents in 1997 and 1998 provided a wake-up call for the Defense Department and other federal agencies on computer security matters. In June 1997 the Pentagon and the National Security Agency (NSA) conducted a joint project, called "Eligible Receiver," that tested vulnerabilities of the nation's electrical and telecommunications networks and the Pentagon's own unclassified computer systems. Both tests showed significant weaknesses. For example, NSA specialists were able to simulate widespread power blackouts caused by attacks on computer systems. The exercise also showed that, using retail computer systems and software available on the Internet, "hackers" could gain supervisory-level access to the computer systems at regional military commands, including the Pentagon's own National Military Command Center. Describing the exercise on June 10, 1998, to a Senate subcommittee, Ellie Padgett, deputy chief of the Office of

Defense Information Warfare in the NSA, said a similar, real-life attack on the Pentagon's computers probably could be carried out "by a handful of folks working together."

One real-life attack came in February 1998, when air force computer officials discovered that someone had gained unauthorized access to unclassified information systems at several air force bases around the country. It took Pentagon and law enforcement officials nearly a month to track down the culprits: two high school students in northern California, aided by another teenager in Israel. Officials said the trio caused no lasting, serious damage to Pentagon computers—but the attack clearly demonstrated that the military lacked the ability to closely monitor or head off computer intrusions.

Pentagon officials assured congressional committees that they were taking steps to shore up the systems that had been found deficient. Even so, the Pentagon insisted that its "classified" computer systems, including those that controlled nuclear weapons, were safe from outside penetration.

Presidential Directive

Clinton on May 22 signed Presidential Decision Directive 63, the first-ever presidential order aimed at dealing with threats to the security of the government's computer systems. The directive established numerous procedures for assessing and correcting computer vulnerabilities and mandated government-wide coordination of those efforts. The directive established a new high-level White House position, the National Coordinator for Security, Infrastructure Protection, and Counter-Terrorism, along with two offices to deal strictly with "critical infrastructure" issues. Clinton named Richard Clarke, a former senior State Department official, as the first national coordinator.

In addition to tracking computer security issues within the federal government, Clinton's directive ordered new efforts to promote cooperation between the government and private entities. Clarke told congressional committees that many of the steps mandated by the directive had been recommended in the 1997 report of the President's Commission on Critical Infrastructure Protection. The administration planned, within three years, to develop a comprehensive national plan to protect both public and private computer networks against deliberate attacks and accidental failures. The government would not mandate solutions, he said, but instead would say to counterparts in the private sector: "We're from Washington, and we understand some of the problems, and we're here to work with you to see what the answers might be."

However, Clarke said, the White House was not yet ready to endorse a key commission recommendation calling for increased spending on research and development for protecting computer systems. The commission had proposed doubling government spending in that area to $500 million in fiscal year 1999, with a 20 percent increase in each of the following five years. Clarke said the White House was reviewing the issue.

GAO Report

The GAO had issued numerous reports on computer security matters, beginning with a general assessment in September 1996 that was intended to bring the issue to the attention of members of Congress and senior officials of the executive branch. The GAO's report in September 1998 said the issue had received "increased visibility and attention" in the intervening two years, but much remained to be done to protect government computer systems.

In its follow-up report, the GAO emphasized the danger of computer attacks that could damage the government's "critical operations," such as air traffic control and tax collections, or that could result in disclosure of "sensitive information" in government files, such as military secrets or personal information about individual citizens. Although it was obvious that government computer systems were subject to attacks, the GAO said, the full extent of vulnerability was not yet apparent "because key areas of controls at many agencies have not yet been assessed."

Overall, the GAO called for improved government-wide coordination of computer security efforts, and it said the White House Office of Management and Budget (OMB) should provide that coordination. Commenting on the report, G. Edward DeSeve, acting deputy director for management of the OMB, expressed concern that an emphasis on White House supervision might "distract" officials at individual agencies from their own responsibilities. GAO countered that, rather than distracting the agencies, a greater White House role would remind the agencies that they were being held accountable for their actions on computer security matters.

To find solutions for security problems, the GAO studied practices at eight private companies and public agencies "known for their superior security programs." The GAO distilled its findings into sixteen specific "risk management" practices. In general, these practices emphasized coordinated approaches to making information security an "integral component" of an organization's everyday operations, the GAO said.

The GAO said the government was in the "early stage" of implementing Clinton's directive. As a result, the GAO said, it was "unclear" how the specifics would be put into action and how well the government's new efforts would be coordinated.

Several members of Congress said they were concerned that administration officials still were not taking the issue of computer security seriously enough. Sen. John Kyl, R-Ariz., who chaired the Senate Judiciary Subcommittee on Terrorism, Technology, and Government Information, expressed concern about the willingness of various government agencies to cooperate with each other. He cited in particular the FBI and the Defense Department, which in the past had differed on the relative priorities of law enforcement and national security. "Only recently have they been able to work together in a way that satisfies all the parties," Kyl said.

Following are excerpts from the report, "Information Security: Serious Weaknesses Place Critical Federal Operations and Assets at Risk," delivered to Congress September 23, 1998, by the General Accounting Office:

Purpose

Due to growing concerns about our government's reliance on inadequately protected information systems to support critical and sensitive operations, the Chairman and Ranking Minority Member of the Senate Committee on Governmental Affairs asked GAO to (1) evaluate the effectiveness of federal information security practices based on the results of recent audits and (2) review efforts to centrally oversee and manage federal information security. This report describes the results of that analysis and outlines management practices that could improve the effectiveness of federal agency security programs.

Background

Federal agencies rely on computers and electronic data to perform functions that are essential to the national welfare and directly affect the lives of millions of individuals. More and more, these functions, which include national defense, tax collection, benefits payments, and law enforcement, depend on automated, often interconnected, systems and on electronic data rather than on manual processing and paper records. This shift has resulted in a number of benefits so that information can now be processed quickly and communicated almost instantaneously among federal offices, departments, and outside organizations and individuals. In addition, vast amounts of useful data are at the disposal of anyone with access to a personal computer, a modem, and telephone.

However, the government's increasing reliance on interconnected systems and electronic data also increases the risks of fraud, inappropriate disclosure of sensitive data, and disruption of critical operations and services. The same factors that benefit federal operations—speed and accessibility—also make it possible for individuals and organizations to inexpensively interfere with or eavesdrop on these operations from remote locations for purposes of fraud or sabotage, or other malicious or mischievous purposes.

Threats of such actions are increasing, in part, because the number of individuals with computer skills is increasing and because intrusion, or "hacking," techniques have become readily accessible through media such as magazines and computer bulletin boards. In addition, natural disasters and inadvertent errors by authorized computer users can have negative consequences if information resources are poorly protected.

Gauging the level of risk is difficult because summary data on computer security incidents and related damage are incomplete. However, break-ins and damage of varying levels of significance have been acknowledged in both the public and private sectors, and media reports on intrusions, fraud, and sabotage abound. In a recent survey conducted by the Computer Security

Institute in cooperation with the Federal Bureau of Investigation, 64 percent of the 520 respondents, which were from both the private and public sectors, reported computer security breaches within the last 12 months—a 16 percent increase in security breaches over those reported in a similar survey in 1997. While many of the survey respondents did not quantify their losses, those that did cited losses totaling $136 million. In an October 1997 report entitled Critical Foundations: Protecting America's Infrastructures, the President's Commission on Critical Infrastructure Protection described the potentially damaging implications of poor information security from a national perspective, noting that computerized interaction within and among infrastructures has become so complex that it may be possible to do harm in ways that cannot yet be fully conceived.

To guard against such problems, federal agencies must take steps to understand their information security risks and implement policies and controls to reduce these risks, but previous reports indicate that agencies have not adequately met this responsibility. In September 1996, GAO reported that a broad array of federal operations were at risk due to information security weaknesses and that a common underlying cause was inadequate security program management. In that report, GAO recommended that the Office of Management and Budget (OMB) play a more proactive role in leading federal improvement efforts, in part through its role as chair of the Chief Information Officers (CIO) Council. Subsequently, in a February 1997 series of reports to the Congress, GAO designated information security as a new governmentwide high-risk area. More recently, in its March 31, 1998, report on the federal government's consolidated financial statements, GAO reported that widespread computer control deficiencies also contribute to problems in federal financial management because they diminish confidence in the reliability of financial management data.

Results in Brief

The expanded amount of audit evidence that has become available since mid-1996 describes widespread and serious weaknesses in the federal government's ability to adequately protect (1) federal assets from fraud and misuse, (2) sensitive information from inappropriate disclosure, and (3) critical operations, including some affecting public safety, from disruption. Significant information security weaknesses were reported in each of the 24 largest federal agencies, with inadequately restricted access to sensitive data being the most widely reported problem. This and the other types of weaknesses identified place critical government operations, such as national defense, tax collection, law enforcement, and benefit payments, as well as the assets associated with these operations, at great risk of fraud, disruption, and inappropriate disclosures. In addition, many intrusions or other potentially malicious acts could be occurring but going undetected because agencies have not implemented effective controls to identify suspicious activity on their networks and computer systems.

Individual agencies have not yet done enough to effectively address these problems. Specifically, agency officials have not instituted procedures for ensuring that risks are fully understood and that controls implemented to mitigate risks are effective. Implementing such procedures as part of a proactive, organization-wide security management program is essential in today's interconnected computing environments.

Similarly, agency performance in this area is not yet being adequately managed from a governmentwide perspective, although some important steps have been taken. The CIO Council, under OMB's leadership, designated information security as a priority area in late 1997 and, since then, has taken some steps to develop a preliminary strategy, promote awareness, and identify ways to improve a federal incident response program developed by the National Institute of Standards and Technology (NIST). In May 1998, Presidential Decision Directive (PDD) 63 on critical infrastructure protection was issued. PDD 63 acknowledged computer security as a national security risk and established several entities within the National Security Council, the Department of Commerce, and the Federal Bureau of Investigation to address critical infrastructure protection, including federal agency information infrastructures. At the close of GAO's review in August 1998, it was too early to determine how the Directive's provisions would be implemented and how they would relate to other ongoing efforts, such as those initiated by the CIO Council.

What needs to emerge is a coordinated and comprehensive strategy that incorporates the worthwhile efforts already underway and takes advantage of the expanded amount of evidence that has become available in recent years. The objectives of such a strategy should be to encourage agency improvement efforts and measure their effectiveness through an appropriate level of oversight. This will require a more structured approach for (1) ensuring that risks are fully understood, (2) promoting use of the most cost-effective control techniques, (3) testing and evaluating the effectiveness of agency programs, and (4) acting to address identified deficiencies. This approach needs to be applied at individual departments and agencies and in a coordinated fashion across government.

Principal Findings

Significant Weaknesses at 24 Major Agencies Place Critical Operations at Risk

Audit reports issued from March 1996 through August 1998 identified significant information security weaknesses in each of the 24 agencies covered by the analysis. The most widely reported type of weakness was poor control over access to sensitive data and systems. This type of weakness makes it possible for an individual or group to inappropriately modify or destroy sensitive data or computer programs or inappropriately obtain or disclose confidential information for malicious purposes, such as personal gain or sabotage. In today's increasingly interconnected computing environment, poor access controls can expose an agency's information and operations to attacks from remote locations all over the world by individuals with minimal computer and telecommunications resources and expertise.

These weaknesses place a broad range of critical operations and assets at great risk of fraud, misuse, and disruption. For example, weaknesses at the Department of Defense increase the vulnerability of various military operations that support the Department's warfighting capability, and weaknesses at the Department of the Treasury increase the risk of fraud associated with billions of dollars of federal payments and collections.

In addition, information security weaknesses place an enormous amount of highly sensitive data at risk of inappropriate disclosure. For example, weaknesses at agencies such as the Internal Revenue Service, the Health Care Financing Administration, the Social Security Administration, and the Department of Veterans Affairs place sensitive tax, medical, and other personal records at risk of disclosure.

As significant as these reported weaknesses are, it is likely that the full extent of control problems at individual agencies has not yet surfaced because key areas of controls at many agencies have not been assessed. In particular, agency managers, who are primarily responsible for ensuring adequate security, have not fully evaluated the adequacy of their computer-based controls. In addition, audits at most agencies have not yet fully covered controls associated with operating system software, which are critical to the security of all of the applications the systems support. In agencies where this control area was reviewed, weaknesses were always identified.

Improved Security Program Planning and Management Needed at Individual Agencies

Poor security program planning and management continue to be fundamental problems. Agencies have not yet developed effective procedures for assessing computer security risks, determining which risks are significant, assigning responsibility for taking steps to reduce risks, and ensuring that these steps remain effective. Security planning and management deficiencies were reported for 17 of the 24 agencies included in GAO's analysis and numerous recommendations have been made to address specific agency deficiencies.

To identify potential solutions to this problem, GAO studied the security management practices of eight organizations known for their superior security programs. These organizations included two financial institutions, a retailer, an equipment manufacturing company, a state university, a state agency, a regional electric utility, and a computer vendor. GAO found that these organizations managed their information security risks through a cycle of risk management activities, and it identified 16 specific practices that supported these risk management principles.

These practices involve (1) establishing a central security management focal point, (2) assessing risk, (3) selecting and implementing cost-effective policies and controls, (4) promoting awareness, and (5) continually evaluating and improving control effectiveness. They also emphasize the importance of viewing information security program management as an integral component of managing agency operations and of involving both program managers and technical experts in the process.

GAO published the findings from this study in the May 1998 executive guide Information Security Management: Learning From Leading Organizations, which has been endorsed by the Federal CIO Council. . . .

The security management practices described in GAO's executive guide are most likely to be successful if they are implemented as part of broader improvements to information technology management. Such improvements are underway across government due to specific information technology management reforms mandated by the Paperwork Reduction Act amendments of 1995 and the Clinger-Cohen Act of 1996.

Initiatives to Improve Central Coordination and Management Need to Provide a Comprehensive Strategy

Individual agencies are primarily responsible for the security of their information resources, but central management also is important to (1) ensure that federal executives understand risks to their operations, (2) monitor agency performance in mitigating these risks, (3) facilitate implementation of any needed improvements, and (4) address issues that affect multiple agencies. Under the Paperwork Reduction Act, this oversight responsibility lies with OMB.

Since September 1996 when GAO reported that OMB needed to strengthen its oversight of agency practices, the CIO Council, under OMB's leadership, has become a component of the administration's efforts to address federal information security problems and has taken some actions in this regard. Specifically, during 1997, the Council designated information security as one of six priority areas and, late in the year, established a Security Committee. Since then, the Committee has (1) developed a preliminary plan for addressing various aspects of the problem, (2) established links with other federal entities involved in security issues, (3) held a security awareness day for federal CIOs, deputy CIOs, and security officers, and (4) developed plans for reorienting the Federal Computer Incident Response Capability (FedCIRC), a program initiated by NIST to assist agencies in improving their security incident response capabilities and other aspects of their security programs.

In addition, OMB has continued to monitor selected agency system-related projects, many of which have significant security implications. However, neither OMB nor the CIO Council has yet developed a program for comprehensively overseeing and managing the security of critical federal operations by ensuring that agency programs are adequately evaluated and that the results are used to measure and prompt improvements, as recommended in GAO's September 1996 report.

Concurrent with OMB and CIO Council efforts during late 1997 and early 1998, the administration developed and issued PDD 63 in response to recommendations made by the President's Commission on Critical Infrastructure

Protection. The Directive acknowledges computer security risk as a national security risk, addresses a range of national infrastructure protection issues, and includes several provisions intended to ensure that critical federal computer, or "cyber-based," systems are protected from attacks by our nation's enemies. Also, it establishes a National Coordinator for Security, Infrastructure Protection, and Counter-Terrorism, who reports to the President through the Assistant to the President for National Security Affairs; a Critical Infrastructure Coordination Group; and a Critical Infrastructure Assurance Office within the Department of Commerce. The Directive outlines planned actions pertaining to federal information security, which include:

- requiring each federal department and agency to develop a plan for protecting its own critical infrastructure, including its cyber-based systems;
- reviewing existing federal, state, and local entities charged with information assurance tasks;
- enhancing collection and analysis of information on the foreign information warfare threat to our critical infrastructures;
- establishing a National Infrastructure Protection Center within the Federal Bureau of Investigation to facilitate and coordinate the federal government's investigation and response to attacks on its critical infrastructures;
- assessing U.S. Government systems' vulnerability to interception and exploitation; and
- incorporating agency infrastructure assurance functions in agency strategic planning and performance measurement frameworks.

Though some of these efforts have begun, at this early stage of implementation, it is unclear how the provisions outlined in the Directive will be implemented and how they will be coordinated with other related efforts, such as those of the CIO Council.

Conclusion

Since September 1996, the need for improved federal information security has received increased visibility and attention. Important efforts have been initiated to address this issue, but more effective actions are needed both at the individual agency level and at the governmentwide level. Many aspects of the recommendations GAO made in September 1996 are still applicable. In particular, a comprehensive governmentwide strategy needs to be produced. The CIO Council's efforts during late 1997 and the first half of 1998, as well as issuance of PDD 63 in May 1998, indicate that senior federal officials are increasingly concerned about information security risks, both to federal operations as well as to privately controlled national infrastructures, and are now moving to address these concerns. Coordinated efforts throughout the federal community, as envisioned by PDD 63, will be needed to successfully accomplish the objectives of these efforts and substantively improve federal information security. It is especially important that a governmentwide strategy be developed that clearly defines and coordinates the roles of new and existing federal entities in order to avoid inappropriate duplication of effort and ensure governmentwide cooperation and support.

Recommendation

GAO recommends that the Director of OMB and the Assistant to the President for National Security Affairs ensure that the various existing and newly initiated efforts to improve federal information security are coordinated under a comprehensive strategy. Such a strategy should

- ensure that executive agencies are carrying out the responsibilities outlined in laws and regulations requiring them to protect the security of their information resources;
- clearly delineate the roles of the various federal organizations with responsibilities related to information security;
- identify and rank the most significant information security issues facing federal agencies;
- promote information security risk awareness among senior agency officials whose critical operations rely on automated systems;
- identify and promote proven security tools, techniques, and management best practices;
- ensure the adequacy of information technology workforce skills;
- ensure that the security of both financial and nonfinancial systems is adequately evaluated on a regular basis;
- include long-term goals and objectives, including time frames, priorities, and annual performance goals; and
- provide for periodically evaluating agency performance from a governmentwide perspective and acting to address shortfalls.

Agency Comments and Our Evaluation

In commenting on a draft of this report, OMB's Acting Deputy Director for Management stated that OMB and the CIO Council, working with the National Security Council, have developed a plan to address the PDD 63 provision that the federal government serve as a model for critical infrastructure protection and to coordinate the new requirements of the PDD with the existing requirements of the various laws pertaining to federal information security. The comments further stated that the plan is to develop and promote a process by which government agencies can (1) identify and assess their existing security posture, (2) implement security best practices, and (3) set in motion a process of continued maintenance. Also described are plans for a CIO Council-sponsored interagency security assist team that will review agency security programs. Regarding our conclusion that many aspects of the recommendations in our September 1996 report are still applicable, OMB reiterated its concern that the 1996 report's "overemphasis on OMB's role could distract program managers in the Federal agencies from their primary responsibility for assuring information security." The full text of OMB's comments is reprinted in appendix III.

OMB's comments indicate that it, the CIO Council, and the National Security Council are moving to coordinate their responsibilities and beginning to develop the comprehensive strategy that is needed. Based on the description provided, the plans being developed include several key elements, most notably a means of evaluating agency performance. These plans were still being finalized at the close of our work and were not yet available for our review. Accordingly, we are not able to comment on their content, scope, and detail, or whether they will be effective in improving federal information security.

Regarding OMB's concern that we have overemphasized its role, we agree that agency managers are primarily responsible for the security of their operations. Increased attention and support from central oversight, if done effectively, should not distract agencies from their responsibilities in this area. On the contrary, active oversight of agency performance is more likely to have the effect of emphasizing the agency managers' accountability and providing more visibility for agencies that are achieving their information assurance goals as well as those that are falling short.

LIFTING OF DEATH THREAT AGAINST SALMAN RUSHDIE
September 24, 1998

The Iranian government on September 24 disavowed a 1989 decree that threatened British author Salman Rushdie with death because of his allegedly anti-Islamic writings in the book, The Satanic Verses. *The British government immediately restored diplomatic relations with Tehran.*

The lifting of the Iranian death penalty against Rushdie was one of the most visible signs of a gradual effort by President Mohammed Khatemi to improve his country's relations with the West. Khatemi was elected in 1997 over the opposition of the conservative Islamic clerics who still controlled the most important functions of Iran's government. In both 1997 and 1998 Khatemi made statements indicating that he wanted to improve Iran's image outside of the Islamic world, and he took hesitant steps toward better relations with the United States. (Khatemi election, Historic Documents of 1997, p. 284)

Lifting the Death Sentence

A prominent novelist, Rushdie had been living a life of seclusion and stealth since 1989, when Iran's spiritual leader at the time, Ayatollah Ruhollah Khomeini, issued a religious ruling (called a "fatwa") that demanded Rushdie's death. Khomeini and many other Islamic figures were angered by portions of Rushdie's surrealistic book that they said maligned Muhammed, the first prophet of Islam. A foundation associated with the Iranian government offered a $2.5 million bounty for whoever succeeded in killing Rushdie. Several translators who worked on the book were physically attacked.

The Indian-born Rushdie, who had lived in Great Britain for many years, went into hiding shortly after Khomeini issued the edict. He moved frequently and for nine years was guarded around the clock by officers of the British "Special Branch" military force. British Airways refused to accept Rushdie as a passenger, saying his presence on an airplane would endanger others.

Many Western leaders denounced the Iranian stance against Rushdie, saying it demonstrated the radical, antidemocratic nature of the regime in Tehran. Great Britain broke off diplomatic relations with Iran in protest. The United States, which had not had diplomatic relations with Iran since the 1979 seizure of the U.S. embassy in Tehran, added the Rushdie case to its long list of grievances against the Iranian government.

Khomeini's death in June 1989 did not make life easier for Rushdie. The ayatollah's successor, Ayatollah Ali Khamenei, said in 1993 that the fatwa against Rushdie was "irreversible." Rushdie "should be and will be executed," Khamenei said then. "It is the duty for all Muslims who have access to the mercenary to carry out the sentence."

Despite the continued death sentence, Rushdie gradually began making public appearances. By the mid-1990s he was no longer escorted by an armed military convoy.

Khatami's overwhelming election as president in 1997 appeared to signal a moderating trend in Iran, at least among the general public. Khatami succeeded in winning approval for his cabinet choices from the parliament, which was still dominated by hard-line Islamic clerics.

On September 22, 1998, during a visit to the United Nations in New York, Khatami signaled a new Iranian stance on Rushdie. He told journalists: "We should consider the Salman Rushdie issue as completely finished."

Two days later, Khatemi's foreign minister, Kamal Kharrazi, stood next to the British foreign secretary, Robin Cook, at a New York news conference and announced that the Iranian government would no longer seek to enforce the death penalty against Rushdie. "The government of the Islamic Republic of Iran has no intention, nor is it going to take any action whatsoever to threaten the life of the author of 'The Satanic Verses' or anybody associated with his work, nor will it encourage or assist anybody to do so," Kharrazi said. The government also disassociated itself from "any reward" that had been offered for the killing of Rushdie, he added.

Based on those assurances, Cook said the British government was restoring full diplomatic relations with Iran. Cook repeated previous British statements expressing regret for the offense that Rusdie's book caused Moslems.

An obviously relieved Rushdie told reporters he had received "unequivocal and emphatic" assurances from the British government that his life was no longer in serious jeopardy. "When you're so used to getting hard news—and by that I mean bad news—then news like this is almost unbelievable," he said. "It's like being told the cancer is gone. Well, the cancer's gone."

Despite Rushdie's euphoric statements, his case illustrated the continuing tensions in Iran. Less than a month after the government reversed course on the death sentence, militant Islamic groups insisted they would continue to seek the death penalty against Rushdie. A majority of members of parliament signed a statement insisting the fatwa against Rushdie was still valid, and several Iranian groups continued to offer financial rewards for whoever could claim credit for killing the author.

U.S.-Iranian Issues

Also during 1998, Khatami and U.S. officials took cautious steps toward an improved relationship. Even so, it was clear that a genuine warming of ties between the two long-time enemies was still in the future.

In an interview with Cable News Network on January 7, Khatami suggested a tentative step toward improved relations between Iran and the United States: the opening of cultural exchanges. "Nothing should prevent dialogue and understanding between two nations, especially between their scholars and thinkers," he said. "Right now I would recommend the exchange of professors, scholars, authors, journalists, and tourists."

At the same time, Khatami said he saw no need for direct relations with the U.S. government, "especially as the modern world is so diverse and plural that we can reach our objectives without any U.S. assistance." In response, the State Department issued a statement welcoming Khatami's suggestions for a "dialogue with the American people." But the State Department said the United States remained concerned about issues such as Iran's backing of terrorism, adding that improved relations between the two countries "will depend not upon what the government of Iran says but what it does."

On January 16 Ayatollah Khamenei appeared to endorse Khatami's overture, calling the president's television interview "very good." Even so, Khamenei denounced the United States in violent terms and said there was no need for a dialogue between the two countries.

In testimony before the Senate Foreign Relations Committee on May 14, the State Department's senior Middle East official said the United States was pleased with Khatami's initiatives and was receptive to improved relations with Tehran. But Martin S. Indyk, the assistant secretary of state for Near East affairs, noted that Khatami did not control the military, police, and security forces—the elements of the Iranian government responsible for the policies "of greatest concern to us." Indyk added: "If President Khatami is able to turn his constructive rhetoric into real changes in the areas of concern to us, that would lay the foundation for an appropriate response on our side, including better relations between our two countries." Indyk said the principle issues of concern to the United States were Iran's support of terrorism and opposition to the Middle East peace process, its effort to acquire long-range missiles and weapons of mass destruction, and its human rights abuses.

In a speech to the Asia Society in New York on June 17, Secretary of State Madeleine K. Albright emphasized the same issues in offering what she called a "roadmap" for improved relations between Washington and Tehran. Albright cited with approval several developments, such as Khatami's denunciation in January of terrorist attacks against Israeli citizens. "We are ready to explore further ways to build mutual confidence *and avoid misunderstandings," Albright said. "The Islamic Republic should consider parallel steps."*

Albright's overture was spurned by Tehran, at least for the time being. In an interview with the New York Times *on June 25, Iranian deputy foreign minister Mohammed Javad Zarif said, "the behavior of the United States" demonstrated that it was not ready for "a dialogue based on mutual respect." Then on September 22, during his visit to the United Nations in New York, Khatami told journalists that Iran was not ready for a direct dialogue with the United States until Washington took such steps as dropping its economic sanctions against Iran.*

> *Following is the text of statements made at a news conference at the United Nations in New York on September 24, 1998, by British foreign secretary Robin Cook and Iranian foreign minister Kamal Kharrazi concerning the lifting of the Iranian death threat against Salman Rushdie:*

British Foreign Secretary Cook: Dr Kharrazi and I had positive discussions about a range of international and bilateral issues of mutual interest and concern. On Afghanistan and Iraq, in particular, we found a lot of common ground. I passed on my condolences about the recent murder of Iranian diplomats and a journalist by the Taliban and reiterated my Government's strong condemnation of this outrage. We both agreed on the need to see a broad based government in Afghanistan and a negotiated settlement under UN/OIC [United Nations and the Organization of Islamic Countries] auspices. We also agreed on the need to combat terrorism. I repeated our condemnation of recent terrorist incidents inside Iran by the Mujaheddin-e-Khalq Organisation.

On the bilateral side we agreed to intensify the dialogue between our two countries and to explore further ways of developing practical co-operation, for example in combating drugs trafficking and in the provision of humanitarian assistance to refugees, an area in which Iran has borne a huge burden for many years.

During our meeting, we discussed the case of Salman Rushdie, which has long been a source of difference between us. I explained that Her Majesty's Government recognised the fundamental role of Islam in Iranian life and understood and regretted the offence that the book The Satanic Verses has caused to Muslims in Iran and elsewhere in the world. I confirmed that neither we nor any of our EU [European Union] partners condoned the content of Salman Rushdie's book The Satanic Verses, but believed in an individual's right to express his views freely in line with our belief in the right to freedom of expression, as enshrined in international law and the Universal Declaration of Human Rights. Dr Kharrazi and I agreed on the importance of the Islamic and Western worlds working together to prevent a 'clash of civilisations'.

During our discussion, I referred to various statements which some senior Iranian officials have previously made to the media, according to which the Islamic Republic of Iran's government would not send anyone to threaten the life of Salman Rushdie. I am delighted to say that His Excellency Dr Kharrazi has clarified the Iranian government's position on this and on the bounty on the life of the author of The Satanic Verses. These assurances should make possible a much more constructive relationship between the UK, and I believe the EU, with Iran, and the opening of a new chapter in our relations. Dr Kharrazi and I have, accordingly, agreed that we should upgrade the level of our diplomatic relations to Ambassadorial level.

Iranian Foreign Minister Karrazi: I too found my discussions with the Foreign Secretary very positive and we have identified a number of ways in which we can develop political and practical co-operation. We also identified a number of regional and international issues on which we would like to intensify our political discussions. I congratulated Mr Cook on the success of the peace process in Northern Ireland and passed on my government's condolences about the recent Omagh bombing, reaffirming the Government of the Islamic Republic of Iran's strong condemnation of terrorism in all its forms. We both agreed on the importance of basing our relations on the principle of non-interference in each other's internal affairs.

I told Mr Cook that the Government of the Islamic Republic of Iran remains firmly of the belief that the prevention of insults to religious values and beliefs will greatly contribute to mutual understanding and confidence between the Islamic world and Europe. I explained to Mr Cook the offence and distress the book The Satanic Verses had caused to Muslims throughout the world, and repeated the Government of the Islamic Republic of Iran's strong condemnation of this book. I stressed to Mr Cook that insults to our sacred Islamic values are under no circumstances acceptable to us or to Muslims world wide.

Senior Iranian officials have previously made clear our position on this issue. I reaffirmed that position. The Government of the Islamic Republic of Iran has no intention, nor is it going to take any action whatsoever to threaten the life of the author of The Satanic Verses or anybody associated with his work, nor will it encourage or assist anybody to do so. Accordingly the Government disassociates itself from any reward which has been offered in this regard and does not support it. Mr Cook has explained to me the British Government's strong desire to improve understanding between the Western and Islamic worlds, and that it no way condones or supports offence to religious sanctions and values, including those of Islam.

Like Mr Cook, I hope that we can now pursue a new, more constructive relationship between the Islamic Republic of Iran, the UK and the EU. We have, therefore, agreed that we are now able to upgrade our relations to Ambassadorial level.

October

HOUSE JUDICIARY COMMITTEE ON IMPEACHMENT
October 5 and December 12, 1998

After conducting a formal, post-election inquiry, the lame-duck House Judiciary Committee on December 11 and 12 approved four articles of impeachment against President Bill Clinton, charging him with two counts of perjury, obstruction of justice, and abuse of power. In a move that showed their animosity toward this particular president, Republicans included language in each of the articles that barred Clinton from ever again holding a federal elected or appointed office. A week later, on December 19, in one of the most dramatic days in American political history, the House adopted the four articles, making Clinton only the second president to be impeached. (Impeachment vote, p. 950)

The impeachment inquiry was set into motion September 9 when independent counsel Kenneth W. Starr sent a report to the House charging that Clinton had committed eleven potentially impeachable offenses in connection with his efforts to conceal his illicit affair with Monica S. Lewinsky, a former White House intern. Clinton had already acknowledged having an "inappropriate" relationship with Lewinsky and making "misleading" statements under oath. (Background, Clinton testimony, p. 564; Starr report, p. 632)

In recommending that Clinton be impeached, the House Judiciary Committee voted along straight party lines. Republicans argued that Clinton had committed perjury and obstructed justice in dereliction of his duty as president to take care that the laws be faithfully executed. Democrats countered that Clinton's actions to cover up his affair were the natural reactions of a man trying to avoid personal and public embarrassment and that they did not rise to the level of impeachable "high crimes and misdemeanors." Republicans said the distinction between personal actions and official conduct was a false one; perjury was legally wrong under either circumstance, and no one, including the president of the United States, was above the law.

These constitutional arguments were overshadowed by the political animosity that many House Republicans harbored toward Clinton. Led by

Newt Gingrich of Georgia, Republicans in 1994 had gained control of Congress vowing to enact a "Contract with America" that was based on balancing the budget, cutting capital gains taxes, boosting national defense spending, sharply curtailing welfare payments, and getting tough with criminals, among other measures. In the next three years, Clinton either managed to co-opt many of these issues, as he did with the balanced budget and welfare reform, or to block their enactment. Republicans were also frustrated that Clinton managed to pin the blame on them for forcing a shutdown of most of the federal government in late 1995.

Moreover, Republicans may not have totally forgiven the Democrats for mounting a lengthy investigation of President Ronald Reagan and several White House aides for their actions in the Iran-contra scandal in the 1980s. Conservative Republicans may also have remained bitter with the Democrats for defeating the nominations of several Republicans for Cabinet positions or court appointments. Prominent among these were former solicitor general Robert H. Bork, a conservative appeals court judge whose nomination for a seat on the Supreme Court was rejected in 1987, and former senator John Tower of Texas, whose nomination to be secretary of defense was defeated in 1989. Allegations of drinking and womanizing figured prominently in the Tower debate. (Bork defeat, Historic Documents of 1987, p. 717; Tower defeat, Historic Documents of 1989, p. 105)

In recommending Clinton's impeachment, the House Judiciary Committee in essence rubberstamped the Starr report. During its inquiry the committee uncovered no new evidence, and it called no witnesses with firsthand information of the events. The only significant witnesses to appear were Starr himself and a team of Clinton's lawyers who rebutted Starr's charges. Initial plans to call witnesses and to expand the inquiry into other areas of alleged presidential wrongdoing, including the failed Arkansas land deal known as Whitewater, were all dropped after the results of the November elections made it abundantly clear that the public wanted an end to the matter as soon as possible. Polls also showed that the public did not want Clinton impeached. But committee Republicans insisted on moving forward on the charges stemming from the Lewinsky scandal, and they turned all censure efforts aside.

Judiciary Committee Chairman Henry J. Hyde, of Illinois, maintained that the committee had acted appropriately. Its role was accusatory, he said, much like that of a grand jury. In Hyde's view, it was the responsibility of the Senate, which was scheduled to try the impeachment case early in 1999, to develop a full body of evidence, including taking testimony of witnesses. This view of the impeachment process was sharply disputed by Democrats, who called the House inquiry a "kangaroo court," and by several constitutional scholars, who feared the House handling of the Clinton impeachment was undercutting the chamber's importance in any future impeachment proceedings.

As Democrats were wont to note, the impeachment inquiry against Clinton bore little resemblance to that against Richard Nixon in 1974. In that case, the House Judiciary Committee spent several weeks behind closed doors sifting through evidence before meeting publicly to cast a bipartisan vote recommending impeachment of the president for his role in covering up the bungled attempt to wiretap the Democrats' national headquarters. Forced to turn over Oval Office tapes that proved his involvement, Nixon resigned rather than face certain impeachment by the full House.

The only other presidential impeachment inquiry occurred in 1868, when radical Republicans sought to get rid of Andrew Johnson, who was blocking their attempts to punish the South and limit the influence of southern politicians after the Civil War. In an atmosphere laden with partisan undertones, Johnson was impeached in the House but escaped conviction in the Senate by a single vote.

Opening the Impeachment Inquiry

Even before the formal debate on impeachment opened, the partisan disputes that characterized the Judiciary Committee proceedings were evident. Behind closed doors and by a party-line vote, the committee voted on September 21 to release the videotapes of Clinton's grand jury testimony and some 2,800 pages of printed material. Describing the meeting as "vigorously partisan," chairman Hyde said "there was a general view among Democrats not to reveal anything, and a general view among Republicans to reveal as much as possible." Hyde himself was the subject of another angry exchange after an on-line magazine, Salon, published a story revealing an affair Hyde, a married man, had had many years before with a married woman. Speaker Gingrich and other Republicans immediately demanded that the FBI investigate whether the White House had leaked the story.

After days of behind-the-scenes debates about procedure, the Judiciary Committee began its formal, public deliberations on October 5. A round of opening statements from each of the panel's twenty-one Republicans and sixteen Democrats laid out the arguments for and against impeachment that would be heard repeatedly in the following months. The gulf that separated the two parties was evident in their stated views of the president's conduct. Clinton's alleged lies under oath constituted "an assault on the rule of law" that threaten "our system of government," Hyde argued. Democrats maintained that impeachment should be reserved for high crimes against the state, not for making misleading statements about extramarital sex. "Under our constitutional system of government, if the president misbehaves in a way that does not impact on his official duties, the remedy still lies in the voting booth and not in a legislative takeover of the executive branch," said John Conyers Jr., of Michigan, the committee's ranking Democrat.

By straight party-line votes the committee then rejected two Democratic resolutions that sought to limit the time and scope of the inquiry and adopted the open-ended plan proposed by Republicans. Modeled on the plan the committee used in the Watergate impeachment inquiry, the resolution *set no limits on the scope of the inquiry or on the time for its completion. Hyde and Conyers were authorized jointly to subpoena witnesses and material. Matters on which Hyde and Conyers could not agree would be submitted to the full committee for decision. The Democratic alternatives would have limited the scope of the inquiry only to the Lewinsky matter and ended the inquiry by November 25.*

Following a curiously undramatic debate given the historic nature of the vote, the full House adopted House Resolution 581, directing the Judiciary Committee to open the impeachment inquiry, by a vote of 258–176 on October 8. Thirty-one Democrats joined all the Republicans in support of the resolution. A Democratic resolution to limit the scope and length of the inquiry was defeated by a vote of 198–236. The Judiciary Committee immediately put the inquiry on a back burner as Congress rushed to complete work on an omnibus appropriations bill before going home to campaign for the November elections.

Post-Election Deliberations

When the committee returned to Washington after the elections, the situation had changed dramatically. Instead of the twenty seats they had hoped to win, Republicans lost five seats, giving the GOP only a six-vote margin in the 106th Congress. Speaker Newt Gingrich, who had been credited with helping Republicans win control of the House in 1994, announced his resignation rather than face a challenge from within the party, and Republicans threatened to challenge several other members of the leadership. (Gingrich resignation, p. 799)

In that atmosphere Judiciary Committee Republicans were caught between the proverbial rock and a hard place. Support from rank-and-file Republicans for a full-blown investigation was dwindling not only because the public was opposed to it, but because the committee might not be able to finish such an investigation by the end of the year. Republicans wanted to avoid a House vote on impeachment in the 106th Congress, where their reduced numbers would work to the president's advantage. They also wanted to avoid the soap opera atmosphere that might develop if the committee sought testimony from Lewinsky and others. But committee Republicans could not simply drop the matter, partly because many of them sincerely believed that Clinton's actions amounted to impeachable offenses and partly because of pressure from hard-line Republicans both in and out of Congress who would not be content until Clinton was removed from office.

Uncertainty seemed to tinge the committee's sudden and short-lived diversions into campaign finance issues and sexual misconduct charges leveled against Clinton by former White House volunteer Kathleen Willey. In both cases the committee voted to subpoena witnesses but never called them. The inquiry's public hearings ranged from thoughtful if somewhat tangential discourses by judges and scholars on the definition of impeachable offenses to taking testimony from two convicted perjurers whose cases involved deceptions related to sex.

The one major witness the committee did hear was Starr, who appeared for twelve hours on November 19 to lay out his case against the president in person. The marathon hearing included a two-hour statement, cross-examination by lawyers for the committee and for the president, and questions from committee members. Starr's appearance probably did little to change any minds on the Judiciary Committee, but it did lead his special counsel for ethics to resign. Sam Dash, who had served as the Democratic counsel to the special Senate Watergate Committee, told Starr in a letter dated November 20 that he had "no right or authority" under the law authorizing independent counsels "to advocate for a particular position" on impeaching Clinton. By doing so in his appearance before the Judiciary Committee, Dash wrote, Starr had "unlawfully intruded" on Congress's power.

The president's attorneys were allowed to present witnesses during two days of hearings in early December. These witnesses included prosecutors, defense attorneys, constitutional scholars, and three former members of the Judiciary Committee who had voted to impeach President Nixon in 1974. These witnesses argued that Starr's case against Clinton was so weak that it never would have been brought to trial in a regular court room; that it would tie up the Senate for months; and that Clinton's transgressions, however immoral, hardly rose to the level of impeachable offenses.

Perhaps the committee's most damaging action against Clinton grew out of a letter the committee sent to Clinton's lawyers asking them to verify or deny eighty-one assertions Starr made in his report to Congress. Hyde said the purpose of the questions was to eliminate those areas that were not in dispute and concentrate on those that were. Some of the questions were fairly straightforward or technical in nature, such as asking whether the president called a certain person on a certain date. Others, however, asked Clinton to make very damaging admissions. The Clinton team's decision to answer these questions in the same carefully crafted, legalistic language that had marked the president's testimony and his defense before the Judiciary Committee deeply disappointed undecided Republican moderates. Several had called on Clinton to admit that he had lied under oath, even if those admissions placed him in greater jeopardy of criminal charges after he left office. Hyde permitted Democrats to offer a censure resolution in committee, which was easily defeated, and censure became a dead issue later when Republican leaders barred Democrats from offering a similar resolution on the House floor.

Committee Votes on Impeachment

After hours of summation by committee counsels and statements by each committee, the panel began to debate specific articles of impeachment on December 11. Only one Republican broke ranks to vote with the Democrats on one article of impeachment. Rep. Lindsey Graham of South Carolina said he gave the president "the benefit of the legal doubt" on one of the two articles charging Clinton with perjury.

The committee completed its work on December 12, after voting for a final article of impeachment and voting down the censure resolution offered by the Democrats. That resolution would have censured Clinton for "making false statements concerning reprehensible conduct" with Lewinsky. It also said that Clinton had "violated the trust of the people, lessened their esteem for the office of the President, and dishonored the presidency." All twenty-one Republicans and one Democrat, Robert C. Scott of Virginia, voted against censure.

Following are excerpts from remarks by members of the House Judiciary Committee on October 5, 1998, before the committee voted to begin a formal impeachment inquiry of President Bill Clinton, followed by excerpts from the committee report (H Rept 105–830), which accompanied the resolution of impeachment approved December 12, 1998:

COMMENTS BY JUDICIARY COMMITTEE MEMBERS

Chairman Henry J. Hyde, R-Ill.

. . . On Sept. 11, the Office of Independent Counsel transmitted materials to the House of Representatives that, in his opinion, constituted substantial and credible evidence that may constitute grounds for impeachment of the president of the United States. . . .

Today it's our responsibility and our constitutional duty to review those materials referred to us and recommend to the House of Representatives whether the matter merits a further inquiry. Let me be clear about this. We are not here today to decide whether or not to impeach Mr. Clinton. We are not here to pass judgment on anyone. We are here to ask and answer this one simple question: Based upon what we now know, do we have a duty to look further or to look away?

We are constantly reminded how weary America is of this whole situation, and I dare say most of us share that weariness. But we members of Congress took an oath that we would perform all of our constitutional duties, not just the pleasant ones. . . .

We are going to work expeditiously and fairly. When we have completed our inquiry, whatever the result, we will make our recommendations to the House. We will do so as soon as we can, consistent with principles of fairness and completeness.

I anticipate several objections to our procedures from our Democratic friends, the first of which deals with their demand that we establish first, before proceeding with any inquiry, what the standards are for impeachment. We don't propose, however, to deviate from the wise counsel of former Chairman Peter Rodino who during the Nixon impeachment inquiry, published a staff report rejecting the establishment of a particular standard for impeachment before inquiring into the facts of the case.

Let me quote from Chairman Rodino's report: "Delicate issues of basic constitutional law are involved. Those issues cannot be defined in detail in advance of full investigation of the facts. The Supreme Court of the United States does not reach out in the abstract to rule on the constitutionality of statutes or of conduct.

"Cases must be brought and adjudicated on particular facts in terms of the Constitution. Similarly, the House does not engage in abstract, advisory or hypothetical debates about the precise nature of conduct that calls for the exercise of its constitutional powers. Rather, it must await full development of the facts and understanding of the events to which those facts relate."

The 20th century has been referred to often as the American century. It is imperative we be able to look back at this episode with dignity and pride, knowing we have performed our duty in the best interests of the entire country. In this difficult moment in our history lies the potential for our finest achievement: proof that democracy works.

Ranking Democrat John Conyers Jr., Mich.

We meet today for only the third time in the history of our nation to consider whether or not to open an inquiry of impeachment against the president of the United States. For more than 200 years, we have been guided by that brilliant legacy of our Founding Fathers and of our Constitution, which, generation after generation, has helped us endure the difficult political and social questions that face us. . . .

This committee was called upon to consider the standard for impeachment of a president in 1974. And at the risk of dating myself, I remain the only member of the committee serving today who was there then. Our staff issued a report in February of that year that has become a model for scholars and historians alike. The report concluded that "impeachment is a constitutional remedy addressed to serious offenses against the system of government. And it is directed at constitutional wrongs that subvert the structure of government or undermine the integrity of office and even the Constitution itself."

Those words are as true today as they were in 1974. An impeachment is only for a serious abuse of official power or a serious breach of official duties. On that, the constitutional scholars are in overwhelming agreement.

The failure to even articulate a standard of impeachment against which the evidence can be measured, a step the 1974 committee took prior to any investigation, is not [the] only failure of this investigation into the president. The tactics of the investigation into the president have also, in my judgment, been an offense to the tradition of this great country and to the common sense of the American people. . . .

Our review of the evidence sent with the referral convinces many of us of one thing: There is no support for any suggestion that the president obstructed justice, or that he tampered with witnesses or abused the power of his office. . . . This is not Watergate; it is an extramarital affair. Americans know [that] and want to finish this.

And 99 percent of the facts are already on the table. The investigatory phase will be far less significant than in previous congressional inquiries. There are only a handful of witnesses that can provide us probative information, all of whom have been before the grand jury three, four, five and six times. . . .

The open-ended Republican proposal [is] a means for dragging this matter out well past the [November] elections. . . . There is no need for this investigation to be open-ended when we can, because of its limited factual predicate, close it down within six weeks. . . .

F. James Sensenbrenner Jr., R-Wis.

Today we begin a task second only in gravity to Congress' power to declare war. It is important at the outset to note that this debate is not about the fact that President Clinton had an affair with Monica Lewinsky and then lied about it to his family, his staff, his Cabinet and to the American public. It is about Judge Starr's finding that the president violated his oath "to tell the truth, the whole truth and nothing but the truth" in a successful attempt to defeat Paula Jones' civil-rights suit against him. . . .

The president denies all the allegations. Someone is lying, and someone is telling the truth. An impeachment inquiry is the only way to get to the bottom of this mess. . . .

Barney Frank, D-Mass.

. . . The chairman said we shouldn't look away, we should look further. I agree. What we shouldn't do, however, is adopt a resolution which says, "Let's look around. Let's see what we can find. Let's see if we can find something in Whitewater and the FBI files and the travel office and the campaign finance office." . . .

I don't think much of the job [Starr has] done, but he's there and he has that statutory responsibility and, therefore, I think we have to look at what he said. But let's look at what he said; let us not turn this into an impeachment inquiry in search of a high crime. Let's look at what Mr. Starr charged the president with and decide. . . .

Bill McCollum, R-Fla.

. . . This is not about jaywalking, it's not about driving under the influence. Those are not major crimes for which any president would be impeached.

But I would suggest to you that what it's about is whether or not we can sustain the constitutional form of our government without going forward at this point. It's about the separation of powers in the three branches of government: the legislative, the executive and judicial. It's about whether or not what the president may have done, if gone without punishment, without being impeached, without being removed from office, would undermine the judicial system, the third branch of our government. . . .

Even if it were only shown to us that the president of the United States lied under oath and committed perjury in the civil deposition he took or, even more seriously, before the grand jury when he testified just a month or so ago, if that is all that's proven, that's enough for us to impeach and enough for him to be thrown out of office. And if we were not to do that, I submit, it would undermine our constitutional system and destroy the foundation of our judicial system. . . .

Charles E. Schumer, D-N.Y.

. . . Whether you cite The Federalist Papers or legal scholars like Justice [Joseph] Story, the president's actions, while wrong and inappropriate and possibly illegal, are clearly not impeachable. . . .

I'd support a motion of censure or a motion to rebuke, as President Ford suggested yesterday, not because it is politically expedient to do but because the president's actions cry out for punishment and because censure or rebuke, not impeachment, is the right punishment.

It is time to move forward and not have the Congress and the American people endure a specter of what could be a yearlong focus on a tawdry, but not impeachable, affair. The world economy is in crisis and cries out for American leadership. . . . The American people cry out for us to solve the problems facing America like health care, education and ensuring that seniors have a decent retirement. This investigation, now it its fifth year, has run its course. It's time to move on.

George W. Gekas, R-Pa.

. . . Reviewing and re-reviewing the referral by the independent counsel . . . is a duty imposed upon us by statute and by the Constitution. In the referral, there are allegations, again, for the evaluation of this committee. I have had difficulty, for instance, in one allegation in which the independent counsel says, "The president repeatedly and unlawfully invoked the executive privilege to conceal evidence of his personal misconduct from the grand jury." . . . But that is not for me to conclude . . . simply because I have doubts about it. . . . I have to inquire further into what justification there is for the allegation. . . .

I am not yet satisfied that there's guilt or innocence with respect to the perjury allegations, but, by darn, it is worth a fuller inquiry by this body.

Howard L. Berman, D-Calif.

. . . Let's seek some common ground. First, every four years the people vote for president. This popular decision is a defining moment of our constitutional system. The people's vote is almost sacred and should not be altered except under the most extreme circumstances.

Secondly, the impeachment process is a constitutionally mandated procedure for undoing the people's will, but only when the president is found guilty of treason, bribery, or other high crimes and misdemeanors. Third, the impeachment process is not a legal proceeding. We are not a courtroom. The

impeachment process should not be used as a legislative vote of no confidence on the president's conduct or policies. We are not governed by a parliamentary system. . . .

The majority party has an obligation to recognize that "high crimes and
misdemeanors" has a meaning. All felonies are not high crimes and misdemeanors. All high crimes and misdemeanors are not felonies. Because of the
deference the Constitution gives to the person who wins a presidential Electoral College vote, the standard for impeachment is far more complicated and
subtle than a straight reading of a criminal statute. . . .

The minority party has an obligation to recognize that a Democratically
controlled Congress, at the urging of President Clinton, passed a statute that
allowed for the naming of an independent counsel by a three-judge panel. The
independent counsel was in turn given the approval by a Democratic attorney
general to pursue the Monica Lewinsky matter. . . .

I may . . . regret my vote for the independent counsel statute. But the fact
remains, no matter what I think, that statute is the law. . . . The same statute
requires the independent counsel to report what he believes are grounds for
impeachment to the House. It is our obligation to proceed to decide whether
the independent counsel's contentions are in fact grounds for impeachment. . . .

I suggest that whatever rules of procedure are adopted, our first order of
business is to resolve if the events portrayed in the Starr report's narrative
rise to the level of an impeachable offense. . . .

Howard Coble, R-N.C.

. . . A society founded upon the rule of law is one which values truth. Without it, we have no courts which will function. In its absence, we have no civil
society. This ultimately means that citizens in our republic, regardless of the
power they have or the position they hold, must make an obligatory commitment to observe the law. As Theodore Roosevelt once said, obedience to the
law is demanded as a right, not asked as a favor. . . .

Rick Boucher, D-Va.

. . . The rules we set, the process that we employ, the balances we achieve
to assure that the rights of all are protected and that the nation's interests are
served, will influence not just the course of this investigation but future
impeachment investigations, as well. . . .

Before the investigation phase of our work begins, we should establish a
shared understanding . . . of the fact that the framers of the Constitution did
not intend for impeachment to be a punishment for individual misconduct; of
the fact that they intended for impeachment to occur only when that misconduct is substantial and is so important to the functioning of the office of the
president that it is absolutely incompatible with our constitutional system of
government.

Our process will then require that the allegations of the independent counsel each be compared to the historical constitutional standard, and that only

those allegations that meet that threshold test become the subject of our formal inquiry. . . .

Lamar Smith, R-Texas

. . . The inquiry into the president's conduct must go on for one simple reason: The truth matters.

The president holds a public office we rightly regard as the most powerful in the world. The president serves as a role model for us and for our children. He influences the lives of millions of people. That is why no president should tarnish our values and our ideals. Actions do have consequences. The difference between right and wrong still exists, and honesty always counts.

We should not underestimate the gravity of the case against the president. When he put his hand on the Bible and recited his oath of office, he swore to faithfully uphold the laws of the United States—not some laws, all laws. . . .

Jerrold Nadler, D-N.Y.

The work of this committee during the Nixon impeachment investigation commanded the respect and the support of the American people. A broad consensus that Mr. Nixon had to go was developed precisely because the process was seen to be fair and deliberate. If our conduct in this matter does not earn the confidence of the American people, then any action we take, especially if we seek to overturn the result of a free election, will be viewed with great suspicion and could divide our nation for years to come. . . .

[In 1974] the committee stated the issue clearly: "The crucial factor is not the intrinsic quality of behavior but the significance of its effect upon our constitutional system or the functioning of government."

We should, therefore, first determine the standard we will use to determine what is an impeachable offense. As far as I am concerned, we could simply reaffirm the report of this committee adopted by the House in 1974.

Then we should inquire which of the 11 allegations, if proven to be true, would meet the standard and would be, therefore, impeachable offenses. Only then would it make sense to examine the evidence relating to those allegations, if any, determined to constitute impeachable offenses in order to determine whether there is sufficient evidence to justify going forward with formal impeachment proceedings. . . .

Elton Gallegly, R-Calif.

. . . In my 12 years in Congress, this is undoubtedly the most serious issue I've ever had to deal with and, without question, the most serious issue that any of us on this committee will likely ever have to deal with. . . . I would appeal to all my colleagues to concentrate on the facts. So far, this whole matter has been a contest of spin. . . . We should get back to the hard work of analyzing the evidence for the purpose of reaching a just result.

If at the end of our inquiry the facts do not support the charges, the president should be fully exonerated. On the other hand, if the facts support the allegations, we have a duty to move forward. . . .

Robert C. Scott, D-Va.

... I am not aware of any constitutional scholar who believes that all of the allegations before us are impeachable offenses, as intended by the framers of the Constitution. In fact, half of the leading authorities interviewed by the International Law Journal said that not only did none of the allegations reach that level, but also said that the question wasn't even close.

And so it is in that light that ... we ask to consider the standards of impeachment before we go further. And even if we don't adopt a standard, we should at least take a moment to consider the history in prior cases of impeachments, rather than simply blurt out unreasoned, partisan feelings about whether or not we want the president to continue in office. ...

Charles T. Canady, R-Fla.

... In the Nixon case, this committee never adopted a fixed definition or standard for impeachable offenses, not before the inquiry, not during the inquiry, not at the end of the inquiry. ... After the House had voted to commence an impeachment inquiry, the staff of the Judiciary Committee prepared a report on constitutional grounds for presidential impeachment.

But that report itself acknowledged that it offered "no fixed standards for determining whether grounds for impeachment exist." The staff recognized, as Mr. Hyde noted earlier, that judgments concerning application of the constitutional standard must await full development of the facts.

More importantly, the inappropriateness of attempts to articulate a fixed standard for impeachable offenses was recognized by the Founders. Alexander Hamilton in The Federalist No. 65, stated that, "Impeachment proceedings cannot be tied down by strict rules in the delineation of impeachable offenses." ...

Melvin Watt, D-N.C.

... There's nothing in our Constitution which mandates that Congress weigh in on the political judgment about whether the president should or should not resign. ... But what our Constitution does mandate us to do is to make a constitutional judgment based on a constitutional standard. ...

In meeting and honoring that mandate, it seems to me that the starting place should be putting politics aside and having a clear understanding of what our Founding Fathers and our historical precedents say the constitutional standard means. Without that, we have no standards and the process will become majority rule and partisan politics as usual. ...

Bob Inglis, R-S.C.

... The question is whether the truth matters, and there are some who seem to be saying that the truth really doesn't matter. It doesn't matter whether the president lied under oath ... whether the president obstructed justice ... whether the president tampered with witnesses.

Basically, I think what those people who would assert that have to be saying is that power is what matters, power unconstrained by principle. And the risk for us there is that that seems to me to be the sure prescription for tyranny and what the Founders wanted to avoid. They wanted a constitutional republic where power was constrained by truth. . . .

Zoe Lofgren, D-Calif.

. . . In England, impeachment was used as a tool by Parliament to tame the King. But it was altered when our Constitution was written because we don't need to tame the king. We have three branches of government that are ruled by laws. . . . George Mason and James Madison said on Sept. 8, 1787: ". . . We need to have a specific form of reference for the use of impeachment, and it is very limited. It is limited to those actions that are so serious, that so threaten our constitutional system of government that we may not wait for the next election to take action." Ben Franklin referred to it as "the alternative to assassination."

So we believe that before we begin chasing facts, we ought to know what is the relevance of the facts we are chasing? . . . We need a common understanding of what is an impeachable offense. . . .

Robert W. Goodlatte, R-Va.

. . . The charges against the president include perjury, witness tampering and obstruction of justice. These are serious charges, charges that cannot be wiped away by a mere wink and a nod, an apology, or someone's interpretation of the latest public opinion poll. The standard that we follow and the standard we teach our children is that no person is above the law, including the president of the United States. . . .

If we did not proceed with this inquiry of impeachment, the committee would be doing a grave disservice to our Constitution, our House of Representatives and our sacred trust with the American people.

Sheila Jackson-Lee, D-Texas

. . . The Founding Fathers included impeachment as a constitutional remedy because they were worried about presidential tyranny and gross abuse of power. They did not intend impeachment or the threat of impeachment to serve as a device for denouncing the president for private misbehavior or for transforming the United States into a parliamentary form of government in which Congress can vote no confidence in an executive whose behavior it dislikes. . . .

The framers of the Constitution never intended the availability of impeachment as a license for a fishing expedition. Never before has this House authorized a free-ranging, potentially endless investigation [into] a public official's private behavior or his behavior before he attained federal office. . . .

Steve Buyer, R-Ind.

. . . While acting in his role as commander-in-chief of the military, it is alleged that [the president] was on the telephone with a subcommittee chairman of the Appropriations Committee discussing sending troops to Bosnia when he had a subordinate perform a sex act upon him. . . .

While I recognize that the Uniform Code of Military Justice does not apply to the president, clearly his conduct, at a minimum, would be unbecoming of an officer and a gentleman. In the military, even a consensual relationship between a superior and a subordinate is unacceptable behavior, prejudicial to good order and discipline. . . .

Should we ask the members of the armed forces to accept a code of conduct that is higher for troops than for the commander in chief? . . .

Maxine Waters, D-Calif.

. . . Democracy is threatened when a fair legal process is sacrificed to appease the passions of a few. After all the pontificating, posturing and debating, let's think about what is happening to the rights of individuals. Let's take a look at the actions of the independent counsel, who appears to be gathering evidence by any means necessary. . . .

Let's have a review of what the majority has done to date. First, it dumped 445 pages of a report needlessly filled with explicit sexual details on the public. Next, they released the president's videotaped grand jury testimony along with more than 3,000 pages of similar materials. When that fizzled, the Republicans then released 4,600 pages of transcripts and other grand jury testimony.

The Republicans did this without giving the president the opportunity to review the materials prior to their release. . . . The power to impeach a president should not be casually used to remove a president, overturn an election, simply because we don't like him or his policies. . . .

Ed Bryant, R-Tenn.

. . . The president of our country has been accused of 11 counts of violating the provisions of our Constitution as defined by the standards "high crimes and misdemeanors," many of which if true, would have disastrous effects on our third branch of government, the judiciary. . . .

My experience as one of three former federal prosecutors on this panel has taught me that some matters cannot be rushed to judgment. Justice cannot be rushed. And we should not place arbitrary timetables on such an important task as this. . . . We must work as a committee to preserve the integrity of that third branch of government, the judiciary. We must also set an example that truth is what we seek, and lying, especially under oath, is not permissible. . . .

Martin T. Meehan, D-Mass.

. . . The committee should first ascertain reasonably specific constitutional standards for impeachment and then ask ourselves whether Ken Starr's best case against the president surpasses or falls short of that standard.

If we fail to ask ourselves this fundamental question at the beginning of our inquiry, we fail the American people. Prolonging an impeachment investigation that inflicts daily damage to our country, where the independent counsel's case on its face fell short of high crimes and misdemeanors, would be a wholesale abdication of our responsibility to pursue the public interest. . . .

The reality is that the committee already has all the evidence it needs to resolve the Lewinsky matter. . . . Leaving the timing and scope of this inquiry open-ended is certain to permit excursions into far-flung matters. . . .

Steve Chabot, R-Ohio

. . . Those who would urge an end to this inquiry before it even starts frequently argue that impeachable offenses are only those which result in an injury to the state. They contend that perjury, or at least perjury relating to sexual matters in a civil action that was subsequently dismissed, results only in an injury to a private litigant and is not impeachable. That argument is wrong. It is a misstatement of the historic record. . . .

Perjury has long been considered a crime against the state. By committing perjury, a person has interfered with the administration of justice. In 1890, the Supreme Court said in [*In Re Loney*] that, "Perjury is an offense against the public justice of the United States." . . .

As a crime against the state, perjury was directly described as a higher misdemeanor at its inception in 15th century England. . . .

When state governments were first being established in the early days of the American republic, perjury also was regularly listed in their constitutions as a "high crime or misdemeanor" or in some varied phrase of that nature. The Kentucky Constitution, ratified in 1792, for example, stated that, "Laws shall be made to exclude from suffrage . . . those who shall thereafter be convicted of bribery, perjury, forgery or other high crimes or misdemeanors." The House and the Senate have impeached federal judges for perjury. . . .

Bill Delahunt, D-Mass.

. . . I am profoundly disturbed at the thought that this committee would base its determination solely on the Starr referral. Never before in our history has the House proceeded with a presidential impeachment inquiry premised exclusively on the raw allegations of a single prosecutor, nor should it now. It is the committee's responsibility to conduct our own preliminary review to determine whether the information from the independent counsel is sufficient to warrant a full-blown investigation, and we have not done that.

If we abdicate that responsibility, we will turn the independent counsel statute into a political weapon with an automatic trigger aimed at every future president. And in the process, we will have turned the United States Congress into a rubberstamp. . . .

That is the difference between the two resolutions before us today: The majority version permits no independent assessment by the committee and asks us instead to accept the referral purely on faith. Our alternative ensures that there is a process, one that is orderly, deliberative and expeditious for determining whether the referral is a sound basis for an inquiry. . . .

Bob Barr, R-Ga.

. . . As we so quickly . . . forget in times of stability and prosperity, our system is a fragile one, a brief flicker of light in an otherwise dark march of human political history. If we drop our guard, even for a moment, and allow a president to demand citizens gratify his personal desires and let him place himself in the way of laws designed to prevent such conduct, that light will be greatly dimmed, if not snuffed out. . . .

We are witnessing nothing less than the symptoms of a cancer on the American presidency. If we fail to remove it, it will expand to destroy the principles that matter most to all of us. Any system of government can choose to perpetuate virtue or vice. If this president is allowed to use the presidency to gratify his personal desires in the same way a corrupt county or parish boss solicits money for votes, future occupants will, sadly, do the same. If the proposition that perjury is sometimes acceptable is allowed to stand, in the blink of an eye it will become acceptable in every case. . . .

The president of the United States controls at his fingertips the greatest arsenal of destructive power ever assembled in human history. . . . He is the singular individual charged with the constitutional duty of faithfully enforcing the laws, all the laws, of the United States. When evidence emerges that he would abuse that power or fail in that duty, it is a matter of gravest constitutional importance. If we fail to address such charges, we will soon be left standing dazed and befuddled among the smoldering ruins of a great democracy. . . . History is littered with the wreckage of nations whose leaders buried their heads in the sand as adversity appeared on the horizon. . . .

Robert Wexler, D-Fla.

. . . Impeachment is not about adultery; it is rooted in a constitutional standard that has met the test of time. It is about subversion of government. The president had an affair. He lied about it. He didn't want anyone to know about it. Does anyone reasonably believe that this amounts to subversion of government?

Does anyone reasonably believe that this is what the Founding Fathers were talking about? For more than 200 years since that convention in Philadelphia, Congress has never, never removed a president from office. Is this where we want to set the bar for future presidents? I plead with this committee to end this nonsense. We have real work to do for the people who sent us.

Bill Jenkins, R-Tenn.

. . . In my mind, the task, although painful, is simple. We're bound by the Constitution and the laws. We have information, we have evidence, we have recent precedents. These are ingredients that make up all the trials that have been conducted in the courts of our land for as long as we've been a nation. . . .

Our role today, and it's been said many times in this hearing, is elementary. It is much like a preliminary hearing. It is to determine if we should recommend to the House of Representatives whether an inquiry should take place. The burden required for this is far less than will be required at other stages, if any, of this proceeding. . . .

Steven R. Rothman, D-N.J.

. . . After a four-year investigation, the independent counsel Mr. Starr has presented the House with 11 allegations of presidential misconduct. Our goal should be to resolve these 11 charges without further delay. However, I will not give my consent to another blank-check, open-ended investigation of the president. That is not the role of our committee. It is not fair to the president, it is not fair to the country, and it is not in our national interest.

If Mr. Starr has more charges, let him bring them forth now, or else we should resolve these Lewinsky charges before the end of this year.

President Clinton engaged in a morally wrong relationship with Ms. Lewinsky and engaged in highly inappropriate conduct in trying to hide that relationship. He must be given an appropriate punishment that fits his offenses. . . .

Asa Hutchinson, R-Ark.

. . . I know many are saying, "This is not Watergate," and I agree. The facts are different. But are not the important questions the same? Is the rule of law less significant today than 25 years ago? Is unchecked perjury, if proven, less of a threat to our judicial system today than when Watergate was the example? In my judgment, these are not insignificant questions that our committee and the American people must answer. . . .

I do not know the conclusion of this matter. I do not have all the answers. But in my judgment, the first step is clear; we must seek out those answers. And based upon my own independent review of the evidence, it appears there exists reasonable cause to conduct a formal inquiry that is independent, that is fair and leads to a speedy resolution. . . .

Thomas M. Barrett, D-Wis.

. . . President Clinton's conduct was wrong, and he must be held accountable. But it would hurt our country in the long run to drag this matter out endlessly.

It's time, Mr. Chairman, therefore, for a focused and fair inquiry, and there must be finality to this process, for if there is one common thread tying the views of virtually every American together, it is this: The time has come to put this chapter of our history behind us and move on to the matters that affect the lives of citizens throughout our country.

Ed Pease, R-Ind.

. . . As a people, we share a heritage which provides a system for the determination of truth, where everyone who has an interest also has the opportunity to be heard. Our duty, as members, in the matter before us is to ensure that this heritage is sustained and enhanced here. It can only be so if we remain firm in our resolve to find the truth, no matter the political consequences. The Constitution provides our compass. I intend to follow it wherever it may take us. . . .

Christopher B. Cannon, R-Utah

. . . Our debate is just beginning as to whether [the president's] conduct . . . is so reckless as to justify impeachment. And yet my colleagues on the other side are demanding ad nauseam a clear standard for what constitutes an impeachable offense. They speak of the rule of law as requiring such a standard because they apparently misunderstand the meaning of the core concept of the rule of law. . . .

In opposition to the clarity necessary in criminal matters, the rule of law is simple; that no person or position or organization is above the law. Here we are burdened to determine, each according to his conscience, after the facts are as clear as we can make them, if the president's conduct falls short of the standard the Founding Fathers left intentionally vague. . . .

James E. Rogan, R-Calif.

. . . I enter these proceedings with no fixed conclusions as to whether the president committed potentially impeachable offenses. As a former gang-murder prosecutor and trial court judge, I know the presumption of innocence is not a courtesy we grant to the president; it is his as a matter of right. . . .

If this president or any president has engaged in marital indiscretions, this appropriately is the concern of a limited universe of people. . . . It is not the concern of the House Judiciary Committee, nor is it the concern of the Congress of the United States. . . .

However, it is both our purpose and our legal obligation to review the president's alleged conduct within the framework of the rule of law and whether such conduct violated his obligation to faithfully execute the law. This is a very critical distinction, because up until now, the heritage of American jurisprudence has been that no person is above the law. . . .

Theodore Roosevelt understood this when he said that "no man is above the law and no man is below it, nor do we ask any man's permission when we require him to obey it." His words are important because Roosevelt made no exception to this ideal for those who happen to share his party affiliation or his political agenda. Roosevelt knew the rule of law had to apply to all men, or it would apply to no man.

President Kennedy echoed that sentiment shortly before his death, when he said that "for one man to defy a law or court order he does not like is to invite others to do the same. This leads to a breakdown of all justice. Some societies respect the rule of force. America respects the rule of law." . . .

Lindsey Graham, R-S.C.

. . . Nobody can tell me yet whether this is part of a criminal enterprise or a bunch of lies that built upon themselves based on not wanting [to] embarrass your family. If that's what it is, about an extramarital affair with an intern, and that's it, I will not vote to impeach this president no matter if 82 percent of the people [at] home want me to, because we will destroy this country.

If it is about a criminal enterprise where the operatives of the president at every turn confront witnesses against him in illegal ways, threaten people, extort them, if there's a secret police unit in this White House that goes after women or anybody else that gets in the way of this president, that is Richard Nixon times 10, and I will vote to impeach him.

Mary Bono, R-Calif.

... There are too many questions that need to be answered. ... I would just like to know whether the president committed perjury ... obstructed justice ... [or] abused power. ... Without this process, none of us will ever know the answers to these questions, and without these answers, our country cannot put this issue behind us. ...

IMPEACHMENT REPORT AND DISSENT

Introduction

"Equal Justice Under Law." That principle so embodies the American constitutional order that we have carved it in stone on the front of our Supreme Court. The carving shines like a beacon from the highest sanctum of the Judicial Branch across to the Capitol, the home of the Legislative Branch, and down Pennsylvania Avenue to the White House, the home of the Executive Branch. It illuminates our national life and reminds those other branches that despite the tumbling tides of politics, ours is a government of laws and not of men. It was the inspired vision of our founders and framers that the Judicial, Legislative, and Executive branches would work together to preserve the rule of law.

But Equal Justice Under Law amounts to much more than a stone carving. Although we cannot see or hear it, this living, breathing force has real consequences in the lives of average citizens every day. Ultimately, it protects us from the knock on the door in the middle of the night. More commonly, it allows us to claim the assistance of the government when someone has wronged us—even if that person is stronger or wealthier or more popular than we are. In America, unlike other countries, when the average citizen sues the Chief Executive of our nation, they stand equal before the bar of justice. The Constitution requires the judicial branch of our government to apply the law equally to both. That is the living consequence of Equal Justice Under Law.

The President of the United States must work with the Judicial and Legislative branches to sustain that force. The temporary trustee of that office, William Jefferson Clinton, worked to defeat it. When he stood before the bar of justice, he acted without authority to award himself the special privileges of lying and obstructing to gain an advantage in a federal civil rights action in the United States District Court for the Eastern District of Arkansas, in a federal grand jury investigation in the United States District Court for the District of Columbia, and in an impeachment inquiry in the United States House of Representatives. His resistance brings us to this most unfortunate juncture.

So Equal Justice Under Law lies at the heart of this matter. It rests on three essential pillars: an impartial judiciary, an ethical bar, and a sacred oath. If litigants profane the sanctity of the oath, Equal Justice Under Law loses its protective force. Against that backdrop, consider the actions of President Clinton.

On May 27, 1997, the nine justices of the Supreme Court of the United States unanimously ruled that Paula Corbin Jones could pursue her federal civil rights actions against William Jefferson Clinton. . . . On December 11, 1997, United States District Judge Susan Webber Wright ordered President Clinton to provide Ms. Jones with answers to certain routine questions relevant to the lawsuit. Acting under the authority of these court orders, Ms. Jones exercised her rights—rights that every litigant has under our system of justice. She sought answers from President Clinton to help her prove her case against him, just as President Clinton sought and received answers from her.

President Clinton used numerous means to prevent her from getting truthful answers. On December 17, 1997, he encouraged a witness, whose truthful testimony would have helped Ms. Jones, to file a false affidavit in the case and to testify falsely if she were called to testify in the case. On December 23, 1997, he provided, under oath, false written answers to Ms. Jones's questions. On December 28, 1997, he began an effort to get the witness to conceal evidence that would have helped Ms. Jones. Throughout this period, he intensified efforts to provide the witness with help in getting a job to ensure that she carried out his designs. On January 17, 1998, President Clinton provided, under oath, numerous false answers to Ms. Jones's questions during his deposition. In the days immediately following the deposition, he provided a false and misleading account to another witness, Betty Currie, in hopes that she would substantiate the false testimony he gave in the deposition.

These actions denied Ms. Jones her rights as a litigant, subverted the fundamental truth-seeking function of the United States District Court for the Eastern District of Arkansas, and violated President Clinton's constitutional oath to preserve, protect and defend the Constitution of the United States and his constitutional duty to take care that the laws be faithfully executed. Beginning shortly after his deposition, President Clinton became aware that a federal grand jury empaneled by the United States District Court for the District of Columbia was investigating his actions before and during his civil deposition. President Clinton made numerous false statements to potential grand jury witnesses in hopes that they would repeat these statements to the grand jury. On August 17, 1998, President Clinton appeared before the grand jury by video and, under oath, provided numerous false answers to the questions asked. These actions impeded the grand jury's investigation, subverted the fundamental truth-seeking function of the United States District Court for the District of Columbia, and violated President Clinton's constitutional oath to preserve, protect and defend the Constitution of the United States and his constitutional duty to take care that the laws be faithfully executed. . . .

On October 8, 1998, the United States House of Representatives passed House Resolution 581 directing the Committee on the Judiciary to begin an inquiry to determine whether President Clinton should be impeached. As part of that inquiry, the Committee sent written requests for admission to him. On November 27, 1998, President Clinton provided, under oath, numerous false statements to this Committee in response to the requests for admission. These actions impeded the committee's inquiry, subverted the fundamental truth-seeking function of the United States House of Representatives in exercising the sole power of impeachment, and violated President Clinton's constitutional oath to preserve, protect and defend the Constitution of the United States and his constitutional duty to take care that the laws be faithfully executed.

By these actions, President Clinton violated the sanctity of the oath without which Equal Justice Under Law cannot survive. . . . He has disgraced himself and the high office he holds. His high crimes and misdemeanors undermine our Constitution. They warrant his impeachment, his removal from office, and his disqualification from holding further office. . . .

Explanation of Articles

Article I: Perjury in the Civil Case

On August 17, 1998, William Jefferson Clinton swore to tell the truth, the whole truth, and nothing but the truth before a federal grand jury of the United States. Contrary to that oath, William Jefferson Clinton willfully provided perjurious, false and misleading testimony to the grand jury concerning one or more of the following: (1) the nature and details of his relationship with a subordinate government employee; (2) prior perjurious, false and misleading testimony he gave in a federal civil rights action brought against him; (3) prior false and misleading statements he allowed his attorney to make to a Federal judge in that civil rights action; and (4) his corrupt efforts to influence the testimony of witnesses and to impede the discovery of evidence in that civil rights action. . . .

[T]he fact that he provided to the grand jury a half-true, incomplete and misleading statement as a true and complete characterization of his conduct (as required by the oath), and used that statement as a response to direct questions going to the heart of the investigation into whether he committed perjury and obstructed justice related to his deposition, constitutes a premeditated effort to thwart the investigation and to justify prior criminal wrongdoing. . . .

At the deposition of the President, his attorney Mr. [Robert] Bennett, in characterizing the affidavit of Monica Lewinsky in which she stated that she did not have sexual relations with the President, stated that sexual relations in that affidavit meant there is no sex of any kind in any manner, shape or form. The President would have the grand jury, and now the House of Representatives, believe that the purposely broad definition of sexual relations, meant to address the affidavit filed, and chosen by the court in the Jones case, meant something different than the same words in Ms. Lewinsky's affidavit, and that it took into account contorted and strained interpretations of words and meanings. It is unrealistic to contemplate that the President, at his deposition, honestly and without a desire to mislead, gave the meaning to the definition of sexual relations that he testified to before the grand jury. . . .

The [Office of Independent Counsel] proceeded to gather a substantial body of evidence proving that the President did indeed subvert the judicial system by lying under oath in his deposition and obstructing justice. This evidence includes Ms. Lewinsky's consistent and detailed testimony given under oath regarding 11 specific sexual encounters with the President, confirmation of the President's semen stain on Monica Lewinsky's dress, and the testimony of Monica Lewinsky's friends, family members and counselors to whom she made near contemporaneous statements about the relationship. Ms. Lewinsky's memory and accounts were further corroborated by her recollection of times and phone calls which were shown to be correct with entrance logs and phone records. . . .

As indicated, contrary to this compelling corroborated evidence, President Clinton testified before the grand jury that he did not have sexual relations with Ms. Lewinsky. The Committee has concluded that the President lied under oath in making this statement. The obligation to tell the truth, the whole truth, and nothing but the truth requires a complete answer and does not allow a deponent to hide behind twisted interpretations that a reasonable person would not draw. . . . Legal hairsplitting used to bypass the requirement of telling the complete truth directly challenges the deterrence factor of the nation's perjury laws, denying a citizen her right to a constitutional orderly disposition of her claims in a court of law. . . .

The President . . . testified that even under his strained and unrealistic interpretation of the definition of sexual relationship, intended to cover that term as used in Ms. Lewinsky's false affidavit, the touching of her breasts and genitalia would fall under that definition and thus would constitute sexual relations. While it is curious that the President would assert that oral sex would not constitute sexual relations, but the touching of breasts would constitute such relations, even under his tortured reconstruction of the definition, the President committed perjury. . . . Ms. Lewinsky testified under oath on several occasions that the President and she did engage in conduct that involved the touching of breasts and genitalia. . . .

The President did not have to answer untruthfully in the grand jury. The Constitution provided him with the opportunity to assert his Fifth Amendment right to refuse to respond, based on his opinion that a completely truthful answer would tend to incriminate him for prior acts of perjury and obstruction of justice. . . .

The Committee concluded that the President provided perjurious, false and misleading testimony to a Federal grand jury concerning prior perjurious, false and misleading testimony. . . .

The President did not believe that he had given truthful answers in his deposition testimony. If he had, he would not have related a false account of events to Betty Currie, his secretary, who he knew, according to his own statements in the deposition, might be called as a witness in the Jones case. He would not have told false accounts to his aides who, he admitted, he knew would be called to testify before the grand jury. . . . Rather than tell the complete truth, the President lied about his relationship, the cover stories, the affidavit, the subpoena and the search for a job for Ms. Lewinsky at his deposition. He then denied committing perjury at his deposition before the grand jury. The President thus engaged in a series of lies and obstruction, each one calculated to cover the one preceding it. . . .

The Committee concluded that the President provided perjurious, false, and misleading testimony to a Federal grand jury concerning prior false and misleading statements he allowed his attorney to make to a Federal judge in that civil rights action. . . .

At the President's deposition on January 17, 1998, an attorney for Paula Jones began to ask the President questions about his relationship with Ms. Lewinsky. Mr. Bennett objected to the innuendo of the questions and he pointed out that Ms. Lewinsky had signed an affidavit denying a sexual relationship with the President. Mr. Bennett asserted that this indicated there is no sex of any kind in any manner, shape or form, between the President and Ms. Lewinsky, and after a warning from Judge Wright he stated that, "I am not coaching the witness. In preparation of the witness for this deposition, the witness is fully aware of [Lewinsky's] affidavit, so I have not told him a single thing he doesn't know." . . . The President did not say anything to correct Mr. Bennett, even though he knew the affidavit was false. . . .

Later in the deposition, Mr. Bennett read the President the portion of Ms. Lewinsky's affidavit in which she denied having a sexual relationship with the President and asked the President if Ms. Lewinsky's statement was true and accurate. The President responded: "That is absolutely true." . . .

The Committee concluded that the President provided perjurious, false, and misleading testimony to a Federal grand jury concerning his corrupt efforts to influence the testimony of witnesses and to impede the discovery of evidence in that civil rights action. . . .

On December 19, 1997, Monica Lewinsky was served with a subpoena in connection with the case of *Jones v. Clinton*. The subpoena required her to testify at a deposition on January 23, 1998. The subpoena also required her to produce each and every gift given to her by President Clinton. On the morning of December 28, 1997, Ms. Lewinsky met with the President for about 45 minutes in the Oval Office. . . . At this meeting they discussed the fact that the gifts had been subpoenaed, including a hat pin, the first gift Clinton had given Lewinsky. Monica Lewinsky testified that at some point in this meeting she said to the President, " 'Well, you know, I—maybe I should put the gifts away outside my house somewhere or give them to someone, maybe Betty.' And he sort of said, I think he responded, 'I don't know' or 'Let me think about that.' And left that topic."

President Clinton provided the following explanation to the grand jury and this Committee regarding this conversation: "Ms. Lewinsky said something to me like, 'What if they ask me about the gifts you've given me?' but I do not know whether that conversation occurred on December 28, 1997, or earlier. Whenever this conversation occurred, I testified, I told her that if they asked her for gifts, she'd have to give them whatever she had. I simply was not concerned about the fact that I had given her gifts. Indeed, I gave her additional gifts on December 28, 1997." ...

It simply strains logic to believe the President would encourage Monica Lewinsky to turn over the gifts. To do so would have raised questions about their relationship and would have been contrary to all of their other efforts to conceal the relationship, including the filing of an affidavit denying a sexual relationship. ...

The record reflects that President Clinton attempted to influence the testimony of Betty Currie, his personal secretary, by coaching her to recite inaccurate answers to possible questions that might be asked of her if called to testify in the Paula Jones case. ...

The record reflects that President Clinton met with a total of five aides who would later be called to testify before the grand jury shortly after the President's deposition in the Paula Jones case and following a Washington Post story, published on January 21, 1998, which detailed the relationship between the President and Monica Lewinsky. During the meetings the President made untrue statements to his aides. ...

Article II: Perjury in the Civil Case

On December 23, 1997, William Jefferson Clinton, in sworn answers to written questions asked as part of a Federal civil rights action brought against him, willfully provided perjurious, false and misleading testimony in response to questions deemed relevant by a Federal judge concerning conduct and proposed conduct with subordinate employees. ...

According to the sworn testimony of Monica Lewinsky, she and the President had 11 [sic] sexual encounters, eight while she worked at the White House and two thereafter. The sexual encounters generally occurred in or near the Oval Office private study. ... According to Ms. Lewinsky, she performed oral sex on the President; he never performed oral sex on her.

The record indicates an agreement to deny the conduct and that a relationship existed between the President and Monica Lewinsky. ... The President lied in his deposition about his being alone or in certain locations with a subordinate federal employee who was a witness in the action brought against him. ...

The President lied in his deposition about his knowledge of gifts exchanged between himself and a subordinate federal employee who was a witness in the action brought against him. The record indicates that the President did present each of these items as gifts to Monica Lewinsky: 1. A lithograph; 2. A hatpin; 3. A large "Black Dog" canvas bag; 4. A large "Rockettes" blanket; 5. A pin of the New York skyline; 6. A box of "cherry chocolates"; 7. A pair of novelty sunglasses; 8. A stuffed animal from the "Black Dog"; 9. A marble bear's head; 10. A London pin; 11. A shamrock pin; 12. An Annie Lennox compact disc; 13. Davidoff cigars.

The record indicates that the President gave false and misleading testimony in his deposition when he responded "once or twice" to the question "has Monica Lewinsky ever given you any gifts?" The evidence shows that Ms. Lewinsky gave the President approximately a total of 38 gifts presented on numerous occasions. . . .

Monica Lewinsky was served with a subpoena on December 19, 1997, a subpoena that commanded her to appear for a deposition on January 23, 1998, and to produce certain documents and gifts. Monica Lewinsky talked to Vernon Jordan about it that day, and Mr. Jordan spoke to the President shortly thereafter. The President and Ms. Lewinsky met on December 28th and discussed the subpoena. . . .

When asked in the Jones deposition about his last meeting with Ms. Lewinsky, the President remembered only that she stopped by "probably sometime before Christmas" and he "stuck his head out [of the office], said hello to her." . . .

Article III: Obstruction of Justice

. . . President Clinton, using the powers of his high office, engaged personally and through his subordinates and agents, in a course of conduct or plan designed to delay, impede, cover up, and conceal the existence of evidence and testimony related to the duly instituted federal civil rights lawsuit of Jones v. Clinton and the duly instituted investigation of Independent Counsel Kenneth Starr.

Although the actions of President Clinton do not have to rise to the level of violating the federal statute regarding obstruction of justice in order to justify impeachment, some if not all of his actions clearly do. . . .

The Committee concluded that on or about December 17, 1997, William Jefferson Clinton . . . corruptly encouraged a witness in a Federal civil rights action brought against him to give perjurious, false and misleading testimony if and when called to testify personally in that proceeding. Prior to December 17, 1997, the record demonstrates that the President and Monica Lewinsky had discussed the use of fabricated stories to conceal their relationship. The record also reveals that the President revisited this same topic in a telephone conversation with Monica Lewinsky on December 17, 1997; in fact, she was encouraged to repeat these fabrications if called to testify in the Paula Jones case. . . .

The Committee concluded that on or about December 28, 1997, William Jefferson Clinton corruptly engaged in, encouraged, or supported a scheme to conceal evidence that had been subpoenaed in a Federal civil rights action brought against him. . . . The concealment and non-production of the gifts to the attorneys for Paula Jones allowed the President to provide false and misleading statements about the gifts at his deposition in the case of Jones v. Clinton. . . .

The Committee concluded that beginning on or about December 7, 1997, and continuing through and including January 14, 1998, William Jefferson Clinton intensified and succeeded in an effort to secure job assistance to a witness in a Federal civil rights action brought against him in order to corruptly prevent the truthful testimony of that witness. . . .

The Committee concluded that on or about January 18 and January 20-21, 1998, William Jefferson Clinton related a false and misleading account of events relevant to a Federal civil rights action brought against him to a potential witness in that proceeding, in order to corruptly influence the testimony of that witness [Currie]. . . .

The President's public apology occurred on August 17, 1998, during a nationally televised broadcast in which he confessed having made misleading statements about the nature of his relationship with Monica Lewinsky. It should be noted, however, that the apology was delivered [on the same day that] the FBI released its DNA report that linked the President (based on his blood sample) to a semen stain on one of Ms. Lewinsky's dresses. . . .

Article IV: Abuse of Power

The President abused his power by refusing and failing to respond to certain written requests for admission and willfully made perjurious, false, and misleading sworn statements in response to certain written requests for admission propounded to him by the Committee. . . .

On November 5, 1998, the Committee presented President Clinton with 81 requests for admission. The requests were made in order to allow the President to candidly dispute or affirm key sworn evidence before the Committee by admitting or denying certain facts. The President responded to the requests on November 27, 1998. After a thorough review . . . the Committee concluded that several of the President's answers to the 81 questions asked of him by the Committee are clearly perjurious, false, and misleading. . . . His answers are a continuation of a pattern of deceit and obstruction of duly authorized investigations. . . .

President Clinton made six public statements denying allegations that he had an improper sexual relationship with Monica Lewinsky or obstructed justice in the federal civil rights case of Jones v. Clinton. The Committee concluded that the public trust, which is held by the President of the United States, was deliberately abused by President Clinton when he made these false statements. . . .

The Committee concluded that President Clinton consciously misled several aides and Cabinet members knowing that they would repeat his false statements to the American public. These officials are all federally paid civil servants who have used their positions in the White House as a pulpit to repeat President Clinton's false statements to the American public. The Committee believes that use of these advisors in an attempt to mislead the American public and beat his criminal allegations was an abuse of the office of the

President and his position as head of the executive branch of government. The President's continued deceptions caused millions of tax dollars to be spent by not only the Office of Independent Counsel in its duly authorized investigation, but also by White House lawyers, communications employees and other government employees, who were utilized to help perpetuate the President's lies and defend him from his criminal conduct.

Minority Dissent

For only the second time in the history of our Nation, the House is poised to impeach a sitting President. The Judiciary Committee Democrats uniformly and resoundingly dissent.

We believe that the President's conduct was wrongful in attempting to conceal an extramarital relationship. But we do not believe that the allegations that the President violated criminal laws in attempting to conceal that relationship—even if proven true—amount to the abuse of official power, which is an historically rooted prerequisite for impeaching a President. Nor do we believe that the Majority has come anywhere close to establishing the impeachable misconduct alleged. . . .

Impeachment is like a wall around the fort of the separation of powers fundamental to our Constitution; the crack we put in the wall today becomes the fissure tomorrow, which ultimately destroys the wall entirely. This process is that serious. It is so serious the wall was not even approached when President Lincoln suspended the writ of habeas corpus, nor when President Roosevelt misled the public in the lend-lease program, nor when there was evidence that Presidents [Ronald] Reagan and [George] Bush gave misleading evidence in the Iran-contra affair. . . .

Without any independent examination of fact witnesses, this Committee essentially rubber-stamped a September 9th Referral from the Office of Independent Counsel (OIC).

That Referral contained largely unproven allegations based on grand jury testimony—often inadmissable hearsay evidence—which was never subject to cross examination. Indeed, the Committee's investigation of this material amounted to nothing more than simply releasing to the public the Referral and tens of thousands of accompanying pages of confidential grand jury material.

In this regard, we decry the partisanship that accompanied this sad three-month process at nearly every turn, and point out its unfortunate departure from the experience of Watergate in 1974.

WORLD BANK ON
ASIAN FINANCIAL CRISIS
October 6, 1998

A financial crisis that began in East Asia in mid-1997 threw countries around the world into economic recession and political turmoil by 1998. Japan, with the world's second biggest economy, was the most notable of several dozen countries that fell into recession. Economic upheaval helped precipitate the downfall of one of the world's most durable dictators, Indonesian president Suharto, and it heightened political instability in Russia. The "contagion" effect of the Asian financial crisis also contributed to the near-collapse of the economy of Brazil, the biggest in Latin America. The U.S. economy escaped relatively unscathed, although the New York financial markets fell sharply in late August following an economic setback in Russia. (Indonesian turmoil, p. 284; Japanese recession, p. 532; Russian crisis, p. 601; U.S. economic projections, p. 500; Asian financial crisis, Historic Documents of 1997, p. 832)

In a December 2 report, the World Bank estimated that thirty-six countries experienced "negative per capita growth" in 1998—in other words, their economies contracted. Those countries, the report said, accounted for more than 40 percent of the developing world's gross domestic product (GDP) and more than twenty-five percent of its population.

The bank reported that the five hardest-hit Asian countries—Indonesia, Malaysia, the Philippines, South Korea, and Thailand—suffered a combined decline of 8 percent in GDP during 1998. By contrast, the economies of those countries grew by an average of about 7 percent annually from 1981 through 1996. The World Bank, the International Monetary Fund (IMF), and most private economists acknowledged that the effects of the recession were more severe than they expected when the financial crisis emerged in 1997. "We did not anticipate the strength of this virus, which has struck far and wide, for instance attacking Latin America because Russia fell into trouble," IMF managing director Michel Camdessus told the annual combined meeting of the fund and the World Bank on October 6.

By the end of 1998 most economists were predicting a modest rebound for many countries during 1999, with economic growth expected to resume on a steady course from 2000 onward. There were some the positive signs: despite the turbulence, China continued to experience economic growth (the government reported a growth rate of nearly 8 percent in 1998); the economic picture was slowly improving in South Korea, Thailand, and several other countries that had been among the hardest-hit; and most countries were able during 1998 to ease some of the austerity measures that were imposed when the financial crisis first hit. Even so, some economists warned that continued sluggishness in Asia, especially Japan, could led to a worldwide recession as early as 1999.

In a year of extensive debate about the financial crisis, world leaders took few actions to head off another such crisis. One step came on October 30, when representatives of the "Group of Seven" leading industrialized nations endorsed a U.S.-sponsored plan to help countries battle attacks on their currencies and financial markets. Under the proposal, the IMF would create a fund of several billion dollars that would support countries when their markets came under speculative attacks because of unrelated events elsewhere. U.S. officials said the existence of such a fund might discourage speculators from attacking troubled currencies—such as they did with Thailand's baht in 1997—in hopes of making a quick profit.

Background to the Crisis

Throughout most of the 1980s and 1990s, the United States and the IMF lead a campaign demanding that the so-called emerging market countries open their economic systems to outside investment—a process called "liberalization." Many countries for years had imposed restrictions on the amounts and types of investments by foreigners in their economies, apparently fearing loss of control to outsiders. The Reagan, Bush, and Clinton administrations—with the active support of the IMF—pressured these countries to open their markets to trade and investments. When they complied, private investors quickly poured in billions of dollars. But when a currency crisis hit Thailand in mid-1997, investors just as quickly pulled their money out of Thailand and several other Asian countries, forcing them into an economic tailspin.

In many countries, the crisis was worsened by the lack of governmental regulation of banking and financial systems. Most Asian countries—even Japan and others with sophisticated economies—exercised little control over their banks, which often made risky loans to speculative enterprises. When the Asian economies turned sour, hundreds of Asian banks were left with billions of dollars in bad loans; by the end of 1998 some estimates put the total amount of bad loans held by Japanese banks as high as $1 trillion.

During the years of booming investment and economic growth, the IMF and other international agencies paid little attention to the flimsy regulatory environments in such countries. But once the Asian bubble burst, the IMF and the Clinton administration began putting a higher priority on the *importance of ensuring the soundness of financial and banking systems worldwide. "Transparency"—eliminating the excessive secrecy that encouraged corruption and unsound financial practices—suddenly became one of the IMF's chief criteria in its lending decisions.*

Debating Lessons Learned

Economic experts generally agreed, during 1998, about why the Asian crisis occurred. They cited a variety of contributing factors, including overvalued real estate markets, excessive amounts of short-term debt, weak banking regulations that permitted speculative lending, economically unsound "sweetheart deals" between governments and large corporations, and widespread corruption and cronyism in financial markets and major industries. In essence, many developing countries had been swamped with money from overseas investments without having the institutional safeguards in place to protect their economies from wild swings when something went wrong.

There was less agreement, however, about two issues. The first was whether the IMF and successive U.S. administrations had pushed developing countries too aggressively during the 1980s and 1990s to open their economies to foreign trade and investment. In late 1998 the World Bank—the IMF's sister institution, headquartered in Washington—joined a chorus of critics who said the IMF pushed developing countries into these types of foreign investments before their economies were strong enough to absorb the shock of sudden swings in the marketplace. The bank also said that developing countries should have been given more help to improve their regulation of banks and financial markets before accepting huge foreign investments. In its official responses to these criticisms, the IMF acknowledged that many developing countries lacked the institutional strengths to deal with huge flows of foreign capital—and the IMF said it was devoting more attention to the problem. But the monetary fund denied that it muscled developing countries to open their markets too rapidly during the 1980s and 1990s.

The second issue was whether the IMF and the Clinton administration prescribed the right policies, starting in late 1997, to help Asian countries start the process of economic recovery. In particular, the World Bank and other critics questioned whether the IMF was correct in forcing the Asian countries to raise interest rates and adopt austerity measures that slashed government spending. Such policies helped deepen the recessions in these countries by forcing thousands of companies into bankruptcy and throwing millions of people out of work, the World Bank said. The bank's chief economist, Joseph E. Stiglitz, noted that as many as 75 percent of the firms in Indonesia were bankrupt by the middle of 1998. "You know, you can't have a country perform with 75 percent of its firms in bankruptcy," he said.

Instead, the World Bank said in a December report that keeping interest rates low might have helped revive the ailing economies more quickly. Ail-

ing countries also should have been given more support to expand their "social safety nets" to reduce the impact of unemployment, the bank said.

IMF officials defended their approach, saying that a gradual turn-around in most Asian economies during the last half of 1998 was evidence that high interest rates and government austerity programs had worked. Currencies had stabilized, interest rates returned to more "normal" levels, and the worst of the recession appeared to be over, IMF officials said.

The IMF also rejected the World Bank's suggestion that interest rates should have been kept low right after the crisis broke. Doing that, the IMF said, might have created steep inflation and frightened off investors, damaging the economies of developing countries even more. At a news conference in September, IMF chief economist Michael Mussa said: "Those who argue that monetary policy should have been eased rather than tightened in those economies [the Asian countries in 1997] are smoking something that is not entirely legal."

IMF officials also said some of their steps early in the crisis—especially a severe austerity program prescribed for Thailand in August 1997—were taken before the full extent of the financial crisis was apparent. Writing in the Economist *magazine's October 3 edition, IMF deputy managing director Stanley Fischer said that "less fiscal contraction would have been recommended" for Thailand if the IMF had realized at the time that the rest of Asia, including Japan, was heading into recession.*

The Clinton administration, which had helped foster the policies under debate between the IMF and the World Bank, attempted to step in as a mediator. In an October 4 speech to the annual meeting of the two institutions, Treasury Secretary Robert E. Rubin said the IMF and the World Bank should "put aside institutional rivalries unbefitting public institutions with the same shareholders. The IMF and World Bank must evolve to meet the new demands of the global economy. All of us must work together."

The Crisis and the Poor

In numerous speeches and reports during the year, World Bank officials sought to focus attention on the impact of the economic crisis on the poor, who usually were the first to suffer. In its economic report issued December 2, the World Bank said more than 25 million people in Indonesia and Thailand could fall back into poverty. "We are seeing poverty increase overnight, undoing the slow progress that has been taking place year by year," World Bank chief economist Stiglitz said. By late 1998 senior IMF officials were making similar statements, noting that social upheavals in countries such as Indonesia had been greater than expected because the recession was worse than anyone had anticipated.

Addressing the World Bank-IMF annual meeting on October 6, World Bank president James Wolfensohn sought to focus world attention on the social consequences of the economic crisis. He asked delegates—among them the world's finance ministers and central bank presidents—to recall "dark, searing images of desperation, hopelessness, and decline. Of people who once had hope, but have it no more" because of the previous year's financial crisis.

Wolfensohn said the World Bank had participated in IMF programs to help stabilize the financial picture in most of the countries hardest hit by the economic crisis. But he said ensuring long-term stability meant more than simply restoring interest and currency exchange rates. "If we do not have the capacity to deal with social emergencies, if we do not have longer-term plans for solid institutions, if we do not have greater equity and social justice, there will be no political stability," he said. "And without political stability no amount of money put together in financial packages will give us financial stability."

Wolfensohn noted that the financial crisis came at the same time that many countries were suffering from the effects of severe weather, in some cases the result of the periodic "el niño" weather pattern in the Pacific Ocean. China and Bangladesh were hit by damaging floods, while serious droughts hit dozens of countries, including Indonesia and Russia; the latter two were forced to increase their food imports at a time when they were hard-pressed to pay for them. In late 1998 Russia turned to Europe and the United States for food donations, an extremely embarrassing position for a country that still considered itself a superpower.

In many Asian countries, the most wrenching impact of the economic crisis was the sudden growth of unemployment. From Japan to Thailand, workers traditionally had what amounted to guaranteed, lifetime jobs; the periodic waves of unemployment that hit Western nations were virtually unknown in Asia. When the crisis hit in 1997 and continued through 1998, millions of businesses folded and even giant conglomerates were forced to lay off thousands of workers. A report issued December 2 by the UN's International Labor Organization showed that unemployment levels doubled or even tripled in many Asian countries. The organization cited the following official unemployment statistics, for example: in Thailand from 2.2 percent early in 1997 to 6.0 percent in late 1998; in South Korea from 2.3 percent in October 1997 to 8.4 percent a year later; and in Indonesia from 4.9 percent in August 1997 to 15.0 percent a year later. Actual unemployment levels probably were much higher than these official statistics showed, the labor organization said.

Following are excerpts from a speech, "The Other Crisis," delivered October 6, 1998, by James D. Wolfensohn, president of the World Bank, to the bank's board of governors at the combined annual meeting of the bank and the International Monetary Fund:

We all recognize that we meet under the shadow of a global crisis. We come here in a united endeavor to protect the common welfare, to listen to ideas from all quarters, to reach out to friends and critics alike to find new solutions. We must embrace the bold. . . .

Twelve months ago, we were reporting global output that grew by 5.6 per-cent—the highest rate in twenty years. Twelve months ago, East Asia was stumbling, but no one was predicting the degree of the fall. Twelve months ago, South Asia, home to 35 percent of the world's poor, was still nuclear test-free, and seemed set to enjoy future years of 6 percent growth. Perhaps more. Twelve months ago, developing countries as a whole were on a path toward strong growth over the next decade. Twelve months ago, there was optimism about Russia with its strong reformist team.

And then came a year of turmoil and travail.

East Asia, where estimates suggest that more than 20 million people fell back into poverty last year, and where, at best, growth is likely to be halting and hesitant for several years to come. Russia, beset by economic and polit-ical crisis—caught between two worlds, two systems, comfortable with nei-ther. Japan, the world's second largest economy, so crucial to East Asian recovery, with a government committed to economic reform, and yet still in recession, with a profound impact not just in Asia but around the world. Nuclear tests in India and Pakistan. War threatened in Eritrea and Ethiopia. Terrorist bombs in Kenya and Tanzania.

And all this compounded by the impact of El Niño—the worst in history—with its full devastating force falling most heavily on the poor. In Bangladesh, floods that kept two-thirds of the nation under water for more than two months, setting back many of the recent social and economic gains. In China, flooding of the Yangtze River region, with an estimated 3,500 deaths, 5 mil-lion homes destroyed, and 200 million lives dislocated.

Mr. Chairman, I have spoken in the past about images of hope—of people from the slums of Brazil to the rural villages of Uganda, from the Loess plateau in China to the hundreds of thousands of women who are finding their dignity through microcredit. People empowered to take charge of their destinies.

But today I have other memories. Dark, searing images of desperation, hopelessness, and decline. Of people who once had hope, but have it no more.

The mother in Mindanao, pulling her child out of school, haunted by the fear that he will never return. The family in Korea, with a mid-size scrap metal business, made destitute through lack of credit. The father in Jakarta, paying a money lender three times in interest what he can make that day, falling deeper and deeper into debt. Not knowing how he will ever work him-self free. The child in Bangkok, now condemned to work the streets, a child no longer. . . .

We talk of financial crisis while in Jakarta, in Moscow, in Sub- Saharan Africa, in the slums of India, and the barrios of Latin America, the human pain of poverty is all around us.

The Financial Crisis

Mr. Chairman, we must address this human pain. We must go beyond financial stabilization. We must address the issues of long-term equitable growth, on which prosperity and human progress depend. We must focus on the institutional and structural changes needed for recovery and sustainable development. We must focus on the social issues.

We must do all this. Because if we do not have the capacity to deal with social emergencies, if we do not have longer term plans for solid institutions, if we do not have greater equity and social justice, there will be no political stability. And without political stability, no amount of money put together in financial packages will give us financial stability.

And so in response to the current crisis, we at the Bank have been focusing on putting in place the short- and the long-term measures for sustained recovery. . . .

Mr. Chairman, we have learned that while the establishment of appropriate macroeconomic plans with effective fiscal and monetary policies is essential in every respect, financial plans alone are not sufficient.

We have learned that when we ask governments to take the painful steps to put their economies in order we can create enormous tension. It is people not governments that feel pain.

When we redress budget imbalances, we must recognize that programs to keep children in school may be lost, that programs to ensure health care for the poorest may be lost, that small and medium enterprises, which provide income to their owners and employment to many, may be starved of credit, and fail.

We have learned, Mr. Chairman, that there is a need for balance. We must consider the financial, the institutional, and the social, together. We must learn to have a debate where mathematics will not dominate humanity, where the need for often drastic change can be balanced with protecting the interests of the poor. Only then will we arrive at solutions that are sustainable. Only then will we bring the international financial community and local citizens with us.

Mr. Chairman, there has been much talk leading up to and within these meetings of a new global financial architecture. That talk reflects a growing sentiment that there is something wrong with a system in which even countries that have pursued strong economic policies over a period of years are battered by international financial markets, where workers within those countries will be thrown out of work, where their children's education will be interrupted, their hopes and dreams destroyed.

I believe that in the more than half century that has elapsed since the creation of the new economic architecture in the aftermath of World War II, our international economic institutions have served us well. No, they have not solved all our problems. But we are far better off with them than we would have been without them. . . .

But Mr. Chairman, we cannot pretend that all is well. We cannot close our eyes to the fact that the crisis has exposed weaknesses and vulnerabilities that we must address. We must be bold but we must also be realistic. We will not devise a new architecture in two days, or even two weeks. But neither can we afford a lost decade like the one that afflicted Latin America in the aftermath of its crisis in the early 1980s. Too much is at stake, too many people's lives. . . .

What we can do here and now is this: We can identify what needs to be done. We can recognize the problems. We can clarify our objectives. We can work to reach consensus. The problems are too big, their consequences too important, to be guided by the pat answers of the past, or the fads or ideologies of the day. We must make a collective commitment to join together to build something better. Let me suggest a three-pillared approach.

The first pillar must be prevention: We must understand the causes of the crises, and work to create economic structures that make them less frequent and less severe.

The second pillar must be response: No matter how successful we are in the first task, there will be crises. We need to devise more effective ways of responding to the crises, ways that entail a better sharing of the burden, ways that do not entail such pain on workers and small businesses, and other innocent victims.

The third pillar must be safety nets: No matter how successful we are in devising fair and efficient responses—and it is clear that we have a long way to go—there will be innocent victims. Unemployment rates will rise. We must do a much better job of ensuring that these innocent victims are protected. . . .

The New Approach

Mr. Chairman, when we look at the pace and the depth of global change over the last twelve months, we, like all of you in this room, are concerned about what are the lessons we should learn from these experiences. We like all of you are asking, what can we do differently in the future to try and avoid these shifts in the economic and socio-political landscape? What is it that we have observed?

We see that in today's global economy countries can invest in education and health, can put the macroeconomic fundamentals in place, can build modern communications and infrastructure, can do all this, but, if they do not have an effective financial system, if they do not have adequate regulatory supervision or adequate bankruptcy laws, if they do not have effective competition and regulatory laws, if they do not have transparency and accounting standards, their development is endangered and will not last.

We see that in today's global economy countries can move toward a market economy, can privatize, can break up state monopolies, can reduce state subsidies, but if they do not fight corruption and put in place good governance, if they do not introduce social safety nets, if they do not have the social and political consensus for reform, if they do not bring their people with them, their development is endangered and will not last.

We see that in today's global economy, countries can attract private capital, can build a banking and financial system, can deliver growth, can invest in people—some of their people—but if they marginalize the poor, if they marginalize women and indigenous minorities, if they do not have a policy of inclusion—their development is endangered and will not last.

We see, Mr. Chairman, that in a global economy, it is the totality of change in a country that matters.

Development is not just about adjustment. Development is not just about sound budgets and fiscal management. Development is not just about education and health. Development is not just about technocratic fixes.

Development is about getting the macroeconomics right—yes; but it is also about building the roads, empowering the people, writing the laws, recognizing the women, eliminating the corruption, educating the girls, building the banking systems, protecting the environment, inoculating the children.

Development is about putting all the component parts in place—together and in harmony.

The need for balanced development is true for East Asia and Russia. It is true for Africa. It is true for Latin America, for the Middle East, for the transition economies of Central and Eastern Europe and Eurasia. It is true, Mr. Chairman, for us all.

The notion that development involves a totality of effort—a balanced economic and social program—is not revolutionary, but the fact remains that it is not the approach that we in the international community have been taking.

While we have had some extraordinary success over the many years with individual programs and projects, too often we have not related them to the whole. Too often we have been too narrow in our conception of the economic transformations that are required—while focusing on macroeconomic numbers, or on major reforms like privatization, we have ignored the basic institutional infrastructure, without which a market economy simply cannot function. Rather than incentives for wealth creation, there can be misplaced incentives for asset stripping.

Too often we have focused too much on the economics, without a sufficient understanding of the social, the political, the environmental, and the cultural aspects of society.

We have not thought adequately about the overall structure that is required in a country to allow it to develop in an integrated fashion into the type of economy that is chosen by its people and its leadership. We have not thought sufficiently about the vulnerabilities—those parts of an economy that can bring all the building blocks tumbling down. Or about sustainability—what it takes to make social and economic transformation last. Without that, we may build a new international financial architecture. But it will be a house built on sand.

Mr. Chairman, let me suggest a concept that may help us address some of these concerns.

The IMF has an overall framework that it reviews annually with its client countries—a framework that finance ministers—all of us—use to evaluate the macroeconomic performance of each country.

Today, in the wake of crisis, we need a second framework, one that deals with the progress in structural reforms necessary for long-term growth, one that includes the human and social accounting, that deals with the environment, that deals with the status of women, rural development, indigenous people, progress in infrastructure, and so on. . . .

And so in our discussions at the Bank, we have developed and are experimenting with a new approach. One that is not imposed by us on our clients but developed by them with our help. An approach that would move us "beyond projects," to think instead much more rigorously about what is required for sustainable development in its broadest sense.

Mr. Chairman, we need a new development framework.

What might countries look for in such a development framework?

First, the framework would outline the essentials of good governance—transparency, voice, the free flow of information, a commitment to fight corruption, and a well-trained, properly remunerated civil service.

Second, it would specify the regulatory and institutional fundamentals essential to a workable market economy—a legal and tax system that guards against caprice, secures property rights, and that ensures that contracts are enforced, that there is effective competition and orderly and efficient processes for resolving judicial disputes and bankruptcies, a financial system that is modern, transparent, and adequately supervised, with supervision free of favor, and with internationally recognized accountancy and auditing standards for the private sector.

Third, our framework would call for policies that foster inclusion—education for all, especially women and girls. Health care. Social protection for the unemployed, elderly, and people with disabilities. Early childhood development. Mother and child clinics that will teach health care and nurture.

Fourth, our framework would describe the public services and infrastructure necessary for communications and transport. Rural and trunk roads. Policies for livable cities and growing urban areas, so that problems can be addressed with urgency—not in twenty-five years when they become overwhelming. And alongside an urban strategy, a program for rural development that provides not only agricultural services, but capacity for marketing and for financing and for the transfer of knowledge and experience.

Fifth, our framework would set forth objectives to ensure environmental and human sustainability—so essential to the long-term success of development and the future of our shared planet—water, energy, food security—issues that must also be dealt with at the global level. And we must ensure that the culture of each country is nurtured and enriched so that development is firmly based and historically grounded. All of these five, of course, within a supportive and effective macroeconomic plan and open trade relations.

This may not be a comprehensive list. It will of course vary from country to country depending on the views of government, parliamentary assemblies, and civil society. But I would submit it gets at the essentials.

Mr. Chairman, we must learn from the past. How a framework is developed and applied is as important as the contents of the framework.

Ownership matters. Countries and their governments must be in the driver's seat, and, in our experience, the people must be consulted and involved.

Participation matters—not only as a means of improving development effectiveness as we know from our recent studies, but as the key to long-term sustainability and to leverage.

We must never stop reminding ourselves that it is up to the government and its people to decide what their priorities should be. We must never stop reminding ourselves that we cannot and should not impose development by fiat from above—or from abroad.

Mr. Chairman, in our discussions at the Bank we ask each other a simple series of questions.

What if it were possible for governments to join together with civil society, with the private sector, to decide on long-term national priorities? What if it were possible for donors to then come in and coordinate their support, with countries in the driver's seat, with local ownership and local participation? What if it were possible for these strategies to look five, ten, twenty years ahead so that development could really take root and grow and could be monitored on an ongoing basis? Too ambitious some will say. Too utopian. But what if I told you it is already happening?

In El Salvador today, there is a national peace commission, born of civil war, which together with civil society, the private sector, and the government, is drawing up a list of national priorities—so that those priorities can extend beyond the life of one government and become part of a national consensus for the future. And the same thing is happening in Guatemala and is being considered elsewhere in Latin America. . . .

Mr. Chairman, hubris should not allow us to think we at the Bank or in the donor community can be the cartographers. But we can be important catalysts.

What I am proposing is that over the next couple of years we bring a new perspective in working with interested governments in drawing up holistic frameworks that sharpen strategic vision. We would like to find two countries in each region of the world that we could work with to test this idea. And we will report to you all at the end of that time.

We must work with our partners in the donor community to see how it is that together with the participant countries we can develop coordinated strategies, joint missions, and joint objectives, so that we can put an end to the duplication that wastes precious resources and leaves tempers and clients frayed.

Within our institution we must build on the work we have already begun to move from a project-by-project approach, to an approach that looks at the totality of effort necessary for country development, that takes the long view, that asks of every project—how does this fit into the bigger picture? How can this be scaled up to cover the country? How can this be rolled out over time—five, ten, twenty years, so that it is not only fully owned by countries and participated in, but that it becomes sustainable and part of the strategy and fabric of that society's overall development?

In some cases we will go beyond national strategies to regional strategies to better reap the benefits of economies of scale. And we must think also of global strategies to achieve global public goods—not only the often discussed need for a cleaner environment, but also the international economic environment, the instability that is of such concern today, and the knowledge that we are increasingly recognizing as a key to successful development.

Mr. Chairman, what we are talking about is a new approach to development partnership.

It is a partnership led by governments and parliaments of the countries, influenced by the civil society of those countries, and joined by the domestic and international private sectors, and by bilateral and multilateral donors. It is a partnership that can look at measurable goals with much better marked road maps for development achievement. Critically, it is a partnership where we in the donor community must learn to cooperate with each other, must learn to be better team players capable of letting go.

Let me assure you, Mr. Chairman that we in the Bank Group are committed to such a partnership. To putting issues of turf behind us. What matters is not who leads, or who follows, who has their name on a project or who is anonymous. What matters is that we join together to get the job done. . . .

Conclusion

Mr. Chairman, this year the headlines have been full of the financial crises. This year we are asking ourselves how we can prevent the financial crises of the future. This year we are focusing on financial architecture, corporate restructuring, and building strong safety nets as part of both crisis prevention and crisis resolution. This year we are waking up to the fact that we do not have all the answers.

Let us not stop at financial analysis. Let us not stop at financial architecture. Let us not stop at financial sector reforms.

Now is our chance to launch a global debate on the architecture—yes—but also on the foundations of development. Now is our chance to show that we can take a broader and more balanced view. Now is our chance to recognize that there is a silent crisis looming on the horizon.

A crisis of world population that will add 3 billion more people to the planet over the next twenty-five years. A crisis of global water that will see 2 billion people suffering from chronic water shortages by 2025. A crisis of urbanization that will mean that urban populations will treble over the next thirty years. That by the year 2020 two-thirds of Africa's population will live in cities—cities that today have no economic growth. A crisis of food security that will mean that over the next thirty years food production will have to double.

A human crisis, Mr. Chairman. A human crisis from which the developed world will not be able to insulate itself. A human crisis that will not be resolved unless we address the fundamental issue of the essential interdependence of the developed and the developing worlds. A human crisis that will not be met unless we begin to take a holistic approach both to development and to how we respond to crisis—looking at the financial, the social, the political, the institutional, the cultural, and the environmental aspects of society—together.

Mr. Chairman, the poor cannot wait on our deliberations. The poor cannot wait while we debate new architecture. The poor cannot wait until we wake up—too late—to the fact that the human crisis affects us all.

The child on the streets of Bangkok needs to go back to school. The mother in the slums of Calcutta needs to survive through childbirth. The father in the village in Mali needs to be able to see beyond today.

As markets tumble and the poverty numbers soar, all of us in this room have a shared responsibility and a shared interest in promoting prosperity in developing and emerging markets. As markets tumble and the poverty numbers soar, all of us in this room have a shared responsibility to put in place policies that can help these countries work their way out of crisis.

In the end, Mr. Chairman, we succeed or we suffer together. We owe it to our children to recognize now that their world is one world linked by communications and trade, linked by markets, linked by finance, linked by environment and shared resources, linked by common aspirations.

If we act now with realism and with foresight, if we show courage, if we think globally and allocate our resources accordingly, we can give our children a more peaceful and equitable world. One where poverty and suffering will be reduced. Where children everywhere will have a sense of hope.

This is not just a dream—this is our responsibility.

FEDERAL REPORT ON SCHOOL SAFETY

October 14, 1998

A rapid succession of shootings in schools during a few months from late 1997 through the spring of 1998 caught the public's attention and heightened fears among parents and educators about the safety of American schools. Despite evidence showing that schools were safe—and that serious violence in schools was on the decline—the mass killings by troubled teenage boys created the public perception that students and teachers could no longer feel safe at school.

President Bill Clinton described the shootings as evidence of a "changing culture" that made violence seem to be a normal, even acceptable part of everyday life. During 1998 the Clinton administration issued a stream of studies and reports on school violence, culminating in the government's first "Annual Report on School Safety." That report summarized the previous studies and recommended specific steps school systems could take to improve safety. The report was released October 14, one day before a White House conference during which Clinton proposed a series of initiatives, including tough discipline policies and programs to keep drugs and guns out of schools.

A Spate of In-School Killings

The killings at schools in 1997–1998 did not represent a new trend: students armed with guns and knives had been killing teachers and classmates throughout American history, and juvenile crime had become more violent during the 1980s with an epidemic in the use of crack cocaine in urban areas. According to some accounts, the number of in-school killings reached a peak in the 1992–1993 school year, when about fifty students and teachers were killed.

Congress in 1990 passed "gun-free school zones" legislation making it a felony for anyone to carry a gun within 1,000 feet of any school; that law was struck down by the Supreme Court in 1995 as an unconstitutional infringement on state rights. In 1994 Congress approved the Gun-Free

*Schools Act, which required school systems to expel for one year any stu-
dent caught with a firearm at school.* (Gun-free zones, Historic Documents
of 1995, p. 183)

*Tougher laws, an improved economy, and other factors helped lead to a
reduction in the overall rate of juvenile crime during the latter part of the
1990s. Between 1994 and 1996, the number of juveniles arrested for violent
crimes dropped by 12 percent; the number of juveniles arrested for murder
declined by 30 percent.*

*Such statistics fell by the wayside of public debate as a series of unre-
lated killings in small-town schools during the 1997–1998 school year
shook the nation. The killings began October 1, 1997, in Pearl, Mississippi,
when sixteen-year-old Luke Woodham killed his mother, then went to his
high school, where he shot nine students; two of them died, including his
former girlfriend. Two months later, on December 1, fourteen-year-old
Michael Carneal shot and killed three students and wounded five others
while they were praying in a high school lobby in West Paducah, Kentucky.*

*Perhaps the most sensational incident occurred March 24, 1998, when two
boys in Jonesboro, Arkansas—Mitchell Johnson, age thirteen, and Andrew
Golden, age eleven—set off a false fire alarm at their middle school and then,
from a nearby woods, opened fire with high-powered rifles on students and
teachers gathered outside the building. Four students and one teacher were
killed; nine students and a teacher were wounded. This shooting provoked the
greatest sense of outrage and soul-searching nationally because the boys were
so young and had acted deliberately—not on the spur of the moment.*

*On April 24, 1998, in Edinboro, Pennsylvania, fourteen-year-old Andrew
Wurst allegedly shot and killed a middle-school science teacher and wounded
two students during a graduation dance. Finally, on May 21, 1998, fifteen-
year-old Kipland P. "Kip" Kinkel shot and killed his parents at home and
later opened fire in his high school cafeteria in Springfield, Oregon. Two
students were killed and twenty-two others were injured in the rampage.*

*In several of the cases, friends and police officials said the students who
committed the crimes had been fascinated with guns and violence and had
some kind of grievance against their parents, their teachers, or their classmates. Most of the students had been in trouble previously and had given
some type of warning about their plans. Most of the youths stole the guns
they used from parents or relatives.*

*Two days after the Oregon shootings, President Clinton used his weekly
radio address to express his and the nation's shock. Clinton said Americans needed to understand that the school shootings "are more than isolated
incidents. They are symptoms of a changing culture that desensitizes our
children to violence; where most teenagers have seen hundreds or even thousands of murders on television, in movies, and in video games before they
graduate from high school; where too many young people seem unable or
unwilling to take responsibility for their actions; and where all too often,
everyday conflicts are resolved not with words, but with weapons, which,
even when illegal to possess by children are all too easy to get."*

The shootings sparked national debates about a variety of school safety and juvenile justice issues. In some cases local officials charged the youths involved as adults. Among them, Carneal, in West Paducah, Kentucky, pleaded guilty to a murder charge and faced a sentence of life in prison with the possibility of parole after twenty-five years. Laws in other states required that the youths be charged as juveniles, making it likely that they would be released from detention centers after a few years. During the 1990s, many states had lowered or even eliminated the minimum age at which juveniles could be charged with capital offenses; the shooting sprees in 1997–1998 accelerated this trend, despite a concern expressed by many experts that juveniles thrown into adult prisons could be beaten, raped, and turned into hardened criminals. Many schools also moved to tighten security by hiring police guards, installing metal detectors at school entrances, and strictly enforcing regulations barring weapons on school property.

Federal Reports on School Violence

Even before the 1997–1998 killing sprees began, the Clinton administration initiated a series of studies of violence and safety issues in schools. A major purpose of the studies was to improve the accuracy of information about nationwide trends in school violence. Most previous reports on the subject were hampered by different standards for reporting crimes among the nation's thousands of schools and local jurisdictions.

The first study released in 1998 by the Clinton administration was "Violence and Discipline Problems in U.S. Public Schools, 1996–97." Commissioned by the Departments of Education and Justice and released in March, the study reported results from a survey of 1,234 principals and disciplinarians at elementary, middle, and high schools. This survey found that the vast majority of schools—nine out of ten nationally—did not experience any serious or violent crimes during the 1996–1997 school year, such as robbery, fights with weapons, murders, or rapes. Serious crimes were more common in urban schools, and the crime rate was much greater in high schools than in elementary schools. With few exceptions, officials in the survey said their schools had "zero tolerance" policies banning weapons, drugs, and alcohol on school property.

The Education and Justice departments in April released another study, "Students' Reports of School Crime: 1989 and 1995," based on surveys of students in those years. This study found that the percentage of students saying they had been victims of crime at school was about the same in 1995 (14.6 percent) as in 1989 (14.5 percent). While the percentage of students saying they had been the victim of a violent crime (such as a physical attack) remained low (fewer than one in twenty-five students), there was a statistically significant increase in this percentage between 1989 and 1995.

In October 1998 the Departments of Education and Justice released a broader report, "Indicators of School Crime and Safety, 1998," which included information from the surveys of principals and students, as well as results from surveys of teachers and other statistical studies. In gen-

eral, the studies showed that serious and violent crimes were unusual in American schools and that there had not been a sudden upsurge in school violence during the 1990s. The reports showed that young people were much more likely to experience violent crime away from school, especially at home. During the two school years between 1992 and 1994, for example, 7,357 children were murdered in the United States. Only 63 of them were killed at school; most murders of children were committed at home.

These studies supplied the background information for the administration's first "Annual Report on School Safety," released at the October White House conference. That report said that "schools should not be singled out as especially dangerous places." Most schools are safe, the report said, adding: "In fact, a child is more likely to be a victim of violent crime in the community or at home than in school." The report also reviewed what it called "a decline in school crime and a reduction in the percentage of students carrying weapons to school."

Even so, the report said there was "a substantial amount of crime" in the schools, and further steps were necessary to reduce it. The report outlined a series of steps that school officials, community leaders, parents, and others could take to develop a "comprehensive school safety plan."

> *Following is a statement issued October 14, 1998, by the Departments of Education and Justice announcing the release of the first "Annual Report on School Safety," followed by the executive summary from the report:*

In the first effort to present an accurate and comprehensive picture of the nature and scope of crime and violence on school property, the U.S. Departments of Education and Justice's "Annual Report on School Safety" shows declining overall school crime, a stable victimization rate of serious violent crime and a reduction in the number of students carrying weapons to school. However, the report also details crimes in school against both teachers and students, points to a growing gang presence in schools, and notes that more students today are fearful in schools than in the past.

"This comprehensive report proves that the vast majority of America's schools are still among the safest places for young people to be," said U.S. Secretary of Education Richard W. Riley. "We can also take some satisfaction that the tough measures to keep guns out of schools are having a real impact. Even one incident of crime in a school is too many, and I especially worry about the increasing presence of gangs in school. I encourage parents, educators and entire communities to use this report as a tool to help them find solutions to address this important issue in a comprehensive way that best meets their local needs."

"All of us must take the issue of school safety seriously," said Attorney General Janet Reno. "We cannot rest until every child is safe at school and in the community."

In addition to findings on the nature and extent of school crime nationwide and in states and cities, the report presents steps for schools, parents, businesses, communities and elected officials to use to develop and implement their own comprehensive school safety plan and lists resources that schools and communities can use to obtain more information about school crime and safety issues. It also describes model programs that reflect proven solutions that schools across the nation are using to address a wide variety of issues that can lead to incidents of school violence.

Specific findings of the Annual Report on School Safety show that:

- **Schools are basically safe places.** 43% of schools reported no incidents of crime. Ninety percent of schools reported no incidents of serious violent crime (defined as physical attack or fight with a weapon, rape, robbery, murder or suicide). 47% reported at least one less serious or nonviolent crime, and ten percent reported one or more incidents of serious violent crime.

- **Despite recent occurrences, schools should not be singled out as especially dangerous places in a community.** Most school crime is theft, not serious violent crime. In 1996, theft accounted for 62% of all crime against students at school. In 1996, about 26 of every 1,000 students (ages 12–18) were victims of serious violent crimes away from school in contrast to about 10 of every 1,000 students at school or going to and from school.

- **Homicides in school are extremely rare events.** While the number of multiple-victim homicide events at schools has increased from two in 1992–93 to six in 1997–98, and the number of victims has increased from four in 1992–1993 to 16 in 1997–98, the overall number of violent deaths of students at school has remained steady.

- **Teachers' concern about their own safety are not without foundation.** On average from 1992–1996, as reported by teachers in public and private schools, approximately 30 violent crimes and 46 thefts occurred for every 1,000 teachers.

- **Students in school today are not significantly more likely to be victimized than in previous years.** The overall school crime rate declined between 1993–1996 from 164 to 128 school-related crimes for every 1,000 students (ages 12–18). Crime victimization outside of school declined from about 140 to 117 crimes for every 1,000 students during the same time period.

- **Fewer students are bringing weapons to school and there are consequences for those who do.** Between 1993–1997 there was an overall decline from 12% to nine percent among students in grades 9–12 who reported carrying a weapon to school in the previous month. In 1996–97, states and territories expelled 6,093 students for bringing firearms to school.

- **Some conditions, including the presence of gangs in schools, make students and teachers more vulnerable to school crime.** Between 1989 and 1995 the percentage of students who reported street gangs present at their schools increased from 15 to 28%, with increases reported in urban, suburban and rural schools.

- **A majority of schools nationwide are implementing some type of security measure on their campuses.** Measures range from zero tolerance policies for firearms, alcohol and drugs to controlled access to school buildings and grounds to requiring visitors to sign in before entering school facilities. In 1996–97, 96% of public schools reported having some type of security measure in place.

In addition, the new statistical study referenced in the Annual Report on School Safety, Indicators of School Crime and Safety 1998, is the first in a series of annual reports on school crime and safety from the National Center for Education Statistics and the Bureau of Justice Statistics. This report presents the latest available data on school crime and student safety and describes the characteristics of the victims of these crimes.

Executive Summary

Most schools are safe. In fact, a child is more likely to be a victim of violent crime in the community or at home than at school. In particular, homicides in school are extremely rare events. However, violence does occur in schools, endangering students and teachers and compromising the learning environment. We must not tolerate any school violence. This report provides a description of the nature and extent of crime and violence on school property, and presents information on how schools and communities can work together to prevent and address school violence.

The data in this report show a decline in school crime and a reduction in the percentage of students carrying weapons to school. At the same time, the data indicate a substantial amount of crime, including violent crime, against both students and teachers. It is also very important to note that students are more fearful at school today than in the past. These conditions highlight the importance of accurately measuring incidents of school crime so that we can improve our school environments and make them safer places.

Schools are responding to the challenge posed by school crime in many ways. They are implementing zero-tolerance policies, increasing school security, and implementing formal school violence prevention or reduction programs. Many schools are working with communities to successfully reduce school crime and violence by adopting a strategy that takes into account the specific safety problems experienced by the school and then identifies appropriate interventions. This problem-solving approach requires the school and community to collaborate to develop and implement a comprehensive school safety plan.

Steps for developing and implementing a comprehensive school safety plan are described in this report: (1) establish school-community partnerships; (2) identify and measure the problem; (3) set and measure the problem; (4) identify appropriate research-based programs and strategies; (5) implement the comprehensive plan; (6) evaluate the plan; and (7) revise the plan on the basis of the evaluation. The report also provides information on what schools, students, parents, business leaders, law enforcement and juvenile justice agencies, and elected officials and government agencies can do to contribute to the creation of safer schools.

Despite recent tragedies that received national attention, schools should not be singled out as especially dangerous places. Rather, schools should be the focus of community collaborations that create safe learning environments for all students.

LEADERS ON IMPLEMENTING THE MIDDLE EAST PEACE AGREEMENT
October 23, 1998

During a few weeks in late 1998, Israeli and Palestinian leaders were able to set aside differences that, for nearly two years, had blocked implementation of historic peace agreements signed in 1993 and 1995. Under U.S. pressure, Israeli prime minister Benjamin Netanyahu and Palestinian leader Yasir Arafat on October 23 signed an agreement pledging to carry out provisions of their previous accords. One month later, Israel turned over to Palestinian control about 200 square miles of territory on the West Bank of the Jordan River—the first Israeli territorial concession since early 1997. But underlying differences between Israel and the Palestinians, coupled with political divisions within Israel, prevented any further progress for the rest of the year. By mid-December, the peace process was back on hold pending elections in Israel called for May 1999.

Israeli prime minister Yitzhak Rabin and Arafat, the chairman of the Palestine Liberation Organization (PLO), in 1993 signed a "Declaration of Principles" to settle Israeli-Palestinian issues by the end of the century. This agreement was widely referred to as the "Oslo accord" because it was negotiated under the auspices of the Norwegian government. In September 1995 Rabin and Arafat signed a detailed follow-up agreement at the White House in Washington calling for Israel to turn control of much of the West Bank over to Palestinians. Five weeks after he signed the latter agreement, Rabin was assassinated by an Israeli extremist. (Rabin assassination, Historic Documents of 1995, p. 689; Washington peace agreement, Historic Documents of 1995, p. 622; Oslo accord, Historic Documents of 1993, p. 747)

Rabin's assassination set in motion a series of events leading to elections in Israel and the formation in 1996 of a new right-of-center government headed by Netanyahu, who had bitterly opposed the original 1993 peace agreement. Even so, Netanyahu said he would honor the agreements, and in 1997 he carried out a controversial transfer to Palestinian control of the West Bank city of Hebron. But a later withdrawal scheduled for March 1997 was postponed because of disputes between the Israelis and the Pales-

tinians. For the remainder of 1997 and the early months of 1998, the peace process was essentially deadlocked.

The Wye Negotiations

Moving to revive the peace process, the Clinton administration in 1998 offered new proposals on the central issue of how much land Israel would turn over to the Palestinians. The administration proposed that Israel hand over 13 percent of West Bank territory, fulfilling the first two stages of promises made in the 1993 and 1995 peace accords. The Palestinians readily accepted that proposal, but Netanyahu balked, saying any pullback from more than 9 percent of the West Bank would damage Israeli security.

A stalemate over the issue continued until late September, when the administration sponsored two rounds of talks between Arafat—first at UN headquarters in New York and then at the White House. Those sessions helped produce a general agreement that 3 percent of the land turned over to the Palestinians would be designated a "nature preserve" where Palestinians would not live; this bridged most of the gap between the 9 percent and 13 percent figures.

Key questions remained unresolved, however, most notably the central issue of whether Arafat and Netanyahu could trust each other enough to strike a deal and then adhere to it. To get answers to those questions, Clinton summoned the two leaders and their aides to negotiations held at a rural conference center in Wye, Maryland, east of Washington.

For nine days and nights, the leaders argued and negotiated, with U.S. officials—including Clinton—serving as mediators. In the early morning hours of October 23, Arafat and Netanyahu reached a broad agreement. Netanyahu agreed to withdraw Israeli troops from an additional 13 percent of West Bank territory and to turn over to Palestinian control about 14 percent of West Bank territory that had been jointly controlled, to release 750 Palestinians held in Israeli jails, to establish "safe passage" corridors for Palestinians traveling from the West Bank to the Gaza strip, and to allow the opening of a Palestinian airport that had been built in Gaza.

For his part, Arafat agreed to convene a meeting of the Palestine National Council to revoke language in the PLO charter that called for the destruction of Israel and to take new steps to combat Palestinian terrorism and weapons trafficking. To give Israel assurance that the Palestinians were keeping their promises, Clinton agreed to formalize existing procedures under which the Central Intelligence Agency would monitor arrests of terrorists and similar matters.

At the last minute, just as the leaders were reaching final agreement, Netanyahu raised a final obstacle by demanding that Clinton release from prison Jonathan J. Pollard, a former U.S. Navy intelligence analyst who was serving a life sentence on charges of spying against the United States on behalf of Israel. Clinton promised to review the Pollard case—which had been reviewed previously at Israel's request—but it was certain that U.S.

intelligence agencies would remain adamantly opposed to releasing Pollard.

The agreement marked the first time that a right-of-center Israeli prime minister had signed a document turning over land that many Israelis considered part of "Great Israel." In signing the 1978 Camp David accords, Prime Minister Menachem Begin, leader of the rightist Likud Party, had agreed to return the Sinai Peninsula to Egypt. But that was territory captured in a military conquest and did not have the same historical or emotional significance for Israel as the West Bank. The Oslo peace accords had been signed by Rabin, the leader of the Labor Party, which for years had accepted the concept of trading land for peace. (Camp David agreement, Historic Documents of 1978, p. 605)

Participants in the negotiations at Wye cited two factors as key to the agreement: Clinton's dogged determination to clinch a deal and an emotional appeal for peace from Jordan's King Hussein. Israelis and Palestinians both gave Clinton credit for spending nearly ninety hours in grueling negotiations, often late at night. The president, they said, sat with Arafat and Netanyahu, taking notes on a legal pad and offering suggestions to bridge their differences.

Clinton also asked Hussein, who had been undergoing treatment for cancer at the Mayo Clinic, to join the negotiations. Late at night on October 22 the ailing king addressed the Israeli and Palestinian delegations and, according to participants, eloquently urged them to consider the historical importance of setting aside their differences. Hussein repeated much of that statement during his remarks at a White House signing ceremony the next day: "There has been enough destruction, enough death, enough waste, and it's time that together, we occupy a place beyond ourselves, our peoples, that is worthy of them under the sun, the descendants of the children of Abraham—Palestinians and Israelis coming together."

Post-Agreement Posturing

In the weeks after the Wye conference, both Arafat and Netanyahu tried to emphasize to their constituencies the concessions they had won from the other side. Both leaders also used hard-line rhetoric to warn of the consequences should the other side fail to follow through on the agreement: Arafat threatened a Palestinian uprising if Israel failed to carry out its West Bank withdrawals, and Netanyahu threatened to suspend the withdrawals if the PLO failed to crack down on terrorists. One Israeli journalist, Nahum Barnea, a columnist for the Yediot Ahronot *newspaper, gave this wry summary of the two leaders' positions: "Both of them tried to obtain support for the agreement by promising to violate it."*

For nearly a month the Israelis and the PLO haggled over details of the Wye agreement, including the names of the Palestinians to be released from jail and the exact location of West Bank lands to be turned over to the Palestinians. Arafat also antagonized Netanyahu and many Israelis with veiled threats to declare an independent Palestinian state in May 1999—the orig-

inal date for completion of "final status" negotiations under the Oslo peace agreement.

The inevitable terrorist attack derailed the process for a few days; on November 6 a car bomb exploded in Jerusalem, injuring twenty-four people but killing only the bombers. Netanyahu's Cabinet suspended its consideration of the Wye agreement in protest but grudgingly approved the accord a few days later.

The Israeli parliament approved the first withdrawal on November 17. The final tally—seventy-five in favor, nineteen opposed, nine abstentions, and sixteen absences—masked the deep divisions within the parliament, especially in the right-of-center parties. Only half the members representing Netanyahu's coalition government voted for the withdrawal, and seven Cabinet members either voted "no" or walked out in protest. Netanyahu made no effort to present the Wye agreement as a triumph for Israel; instead he offered it to the parliament as a realistic, if unpleasant, deal that might help buy peace and security for Israel.

The first Israeli withdrawal under the Wye agreement took place November 20. It was a relatively low-key affair involving the transfer of sparsely settled land containing twenty-eight towns and villages in the northern part of the West Bank around the city of Jenin. The total transfer from joint Israeli-Palestinian control to sole Palestinian control involved about 200 square miles. Even after the withdrawal, Israel still had sole control over 71 percent of the West Bank, including key strategic areas and most of the Jewish settlements that had been erected in the previous three decades.

In conjunction with the withdrawal, Israel released 250 Palestinian prisoners. Arafat had wanted the release to include men who had been charged with terrorism and political crimes, but most of those released were common criminals.

Another event of symbolic importance for the Palestinians occurred November 24, with the opening of Gaza International Airport in the PLO-controlled Gaza Strip. The airport had been completed in 1997, with aid from several Arab and European countries, but had been sitting unused for more than a year because of the stalemate in the peace process. Officially, the Palestinian Authority administered the airport, but Israel supervised flight schedules and routes. Israel also controlled security operations at the airport and had the right to search aircraft, passengers, and baggage.

The United States on November 30 sponsored an international conference in Washington, where several nations and aid agencies pledged to increase their financial support to the Palestinian Authority by $3 billion over the next five years. Addressing the conference, Clinton said he would ask Congress to boost U.S. aid to the Palestinians by $400 million over that five-year period, nearly doubling the $500 million that had been planned. The pledges of additional aid came despite recurring reports of corruption and mismanagement of previous aid programs by the Palestinian Authority. Several donor nations had been pressing Arafat to improve the authority's administrative procedures.

Israeli Backlash

Netanyahu's ability to win cabinet and parliamentary approval of the Wye agreement did not guarantee him political peace at home. Even before he returned from Washington, right-wing politicians were threatening to pull out of his coalition government. By early December Netanyahu was scrambling frantically to keep his coalition intact; while he scrambled further progress on implementing the Wye agreement was put on hold.

With Israel absorbed in political turmoil, Clinton arrived in the Middle East to witness the revocation of the anti-Israel language in the PLO charter. On December 14 Clinton watched as several hundred members of the Palestine National Council raised their hands to vote to revoke thirty-three articles in the PLO's 1964 charter that had called for the "elimination of Zionism in Palestine" and denied Israel's right to exist. The council had voted in 1996 to cancel anti-Israel articles in the charter, but the Netanyahu government had demanded another vote specifying exactly which articles were no longer valid.

In an emotional speech to the Palestinian leaders, gathered at a hall in Gaza City, Clinton said: "I am profoundly proud to be the first American president to address the Palestinian people in a city governed by Palestinians." Clinton praised the Palestinians for making the "choice for peace" represented by the 1993 Oslo accords and "because through all the tough times since, when in your own mind you had 100 good reasons to walk away, you didn't. . . . You still can raise your hand and stand and lift your voice for peace."

Clinton's presence at the PLO meeting was widely seen as of enormous symbolic importance. By attending the session, the president was stamping American approval on what was, in effect, the final step in the transformation of the PLO from a guerrilla organization to a governing body. Many Israelis worried that Clinton was throwing U.S. support behind the Palestinians in the fragile balance of power in the Middle East. Despite U.S. assurances to the contrary, these Israelis said they believed Clinton's presence at the PLO meeting signaled a weakening of the "special relationship" between the United States and Israel.

Domestic Israeli politics prevailed the next day, December 15, when Clinton and his aides met for about ninety minutes with Netanyahu and Arafat at an Israeli air base in an attempt to win agreement on carrying out the next steps of the Wye accord. Claiming that the Palestinians had failed to follow through on their commitments, Netanyahu would not relent from his refusal to carry out further land transfers to the Palestinians. A clearly frustrated Clinton insisted that "I have achieved what I came here to achieve," but he returned to Washington without new promises from either the Israelis or the Palestinians.

Five days later, on December 20, Netanyahu's cabinet formally endorsed a freeze on land transfers, effectively halting all further progress on the Wye agreement. The cabinet also demanded numerous concessions by the

Palestinians before any more land transfers would be carried out. The next day, the Israeli parliament agreed to dissolve the Netanyahu government, pending new elections to be held in the spring of 1999. One effect of that action was to halt any progress under the Wye agreement until Israel's voters had decided on new leadership for their country.

Following are excerpts from statements made at the White House on October 23, 1998, by U.S. president Bill Clinton, Israeli prime minister Benjamin Netanyahu, Palestinian leader Yasir Arafat, and Jordan's King Hussein, in connection with the signing of the "Wye Memorandum" to implement provisions of previous peace agreements between Israel and the Palestinians:

President Bill Clinton: After some very difficult negotiations, very long, dare I say, quite sleepless, the Israelis and Palestinians here have reached an agreement on issues over which they have been divided for more than 17 months. This agreement is designed to rebuild trust and renew hope for peace between the parties. Now both sides must build on that hope, carry out their commitments, begin the difficult, but urgent journey toward a permanent settlement.

Over the last nine days I have witnessed extraordinary efforts on behalf of peace. I thank our team, beginning with its head, the Secretary of State, who showed remarkable creativity, strength and patience. I thank the Vice President for his interventions. I thank my good friend, Sandy Berger; our Director of Central Intelligence, George Tenet, who had an unusual, almost unprecedented role to play because of the security considerations; our Special Middle East Coordinator, Dennis Ross, who was a young man with no gray hair when all this began. I thank all the other outstanding members of our delegation.

I thank Prime Minister Netanyahu, who stood so firmly for the security of his citizens and of his country, and of the impressive members of his Cabinet and administration. I thank Chairman Arafat, who tenaciously defended the interests of his people, and the very impressive members of his team as well. In the end, after all the twists and turns and ups and downs, all their late and ultimately sleepless nights, both reaffirmed their commitment to the path of peace. And for that, the world can be grateful.

And finally, let me thank His Majesty King Hussein, whose courage, commitment, wisdom, and, frankly, stern instruction at appropriate times, were at the heart of this success. Your Majesty, we are all profoundly in your debt.

This agreement is good for Israel's security. The commitments made by the Palestinians were very strong, as strong as any we have ever seen. They include continuous security cooperation with Israel and a comprehensive plan against terrorism and its support infrastructure.

This agreement is good for the political and economic well-being of Palestinians. It significantly expands areas under Palestinian authority to some

40 percent of the West Bank. It also offers the Palestinian people new economic opportunities, with an airport and industrial zone, soon safe passage between Gaza and the West Bank, and in time a seaport. The Palestinian people will be able to breathe a little easier and benefit from the fruits of peace.

Most importantly, perhaps, this agreement is actually good for the peace process itself. For 18 months, it has been paralyzed, a victim of mistrust, misunderstanding and fear. Now, ordinary Israelis and Palestinians once again can become partners for peace.

To bolster this effort, Chairman Arafat will invite members of the Palestinian National Council and other important political entities to reaffirm his prior commitments and their support for the peace process. I have agreed to address that meeting, several weeks hence, and to underscore the values of reconciliation, tolerance and respect, and my support for those commitments and this process.

People around the world should be heartened by this achievement today. These leaders and those with whom they work have come a very long way. The Israeli and Palestinian peoples, whose bitter rivalry in this century has brought so much suffering to both sides, have moved yet another step closer toward fulfilling the promise of the Oslo Accords; closer to the day when they can live peacefully as true neighbors, with security, prosperity, self-governance, cooperation and eventually, God willing, genuine friendship.

No doubt, as peace gains momentum, forces of hate, no matter how isolated and disparate, will once again lash out. They know this, the leaders, and they are prepared to face it. Staying on the path of peace under these circumstances will demand even greater leadership and courage.

The work at Wye River shows what can happen when the will for peace is strong. But let me say once again to all the rest of you—everyone who is tempted to handicap every little twist and turn over the last nine days, you need to know one overwhelming thing: The Prime Minister and the Chairman, and the members of their delegation who supported this process, even when there were things about it they did not agree with, are quite well aware that the enemies of peace will seek to extract a price from both sides. They are quite well aware that in the short run, they themselves may have put themselves at greater risk. But by pledging themselves to the peaceful course for the future, to the same values and, ultimately, to the same enemies, they have given both Israelis and Palestinians a chance to have the future we all want for our children and our children's children.

Every effort will have to be exerted to ensure the faithful implementation of this agreement—not because the parties do not want to do so, but because the agreement covers many things, was developed over many days, involved many discussions and sleepless nights. It will test whether the Palestinian people are prepared to live in peace, recognizing Israel's permanence, legitimacy and a common interest in security. It will tell us whether Israelis want to help build a strong Palestinian entity that can fulfill the aspirations of its people and provide both real security and real partnership for Palestinians and Israelis.

The United States is determined to be of whatever help we can to both sides in their endeavors. I will consult with Congress to design a package of aid to help Israel meet the security costs of redeployment, and help the Palestinian Authority meet the economic costs of development. I hope we will have support from Republicans and Democrats in that endeavor.

With respect to Mr. Pollard, I have agreed to review this matter seriously, at the Prime Minister's request. I have made no commitment as to the outcome of the review. Ultimately, the parties will have to translate the gains of Wye River into renewed efforts to secure a just and lasting peace. For as big a step as today is - and after 17 months, it is a very large step, indeed—it is just another step along the way. Therefore, perhaps as important as any other statement to be made today, let me say how grateful I am that the Prime Minister and the Chairman have agreed to begin permanent status talks upon ratification of this agreement.

I have agreed to convene the two leaders at an appropriate time to seek to complete these talks. We have all agreed to try to do it under circumstances which permit more sleep at night.

Let me say that no agreement can wipe away decades of distrust. But I think these last several days have helped each side to get a better understanding of the other's hopes and fears, a better feel for all they have in common, including on occasion, thank the Lord, a good sense of humor.

The future can be bright for Israelis and Palestinians if they maintain the will for peace. If we continue to work together, the next generation will grow up without fear. Israel can have the genuine security and recognition it has sought for so long. The Palestinian people can, at long last, realize their aspirations to live free in safety, in charge of their own destiny.

So, on behalf of all the people of the United States, let me say to the Israeli and Palestinian peoples, salaam—shalom—peace be with you in the hard and hopeful days ahead. We value our friendship and we thank you for your trust, for giving us the opportunity to walk this road with you.

Now it is my privilege to introduce Prime Minister Netanyahu. Let me say, I was, once again, extraordinarily impressed by the energy, the drive, the determination, the will, the complete grasp of every detailed aspect of every issue that this Prime Minister brought to these talks. He showed himself willing to take political risks for peace, but not to risk the security of his people. And as a result, this agreement embodies an enormous increase in the security of the people of Israel. . . .

Prime Minister Benjamin Netanyahu: . . . Today's a day when Israel and our entire region are more secure. Now, this has required sacrifice from both sides, and reaching into what Lincoln called, "the better nature of mankind." This is an important moment to give a secure and peaceful future for our children and the children of our neighbors, the Palestinians. We have seized this moment.

I'm asking all people of goodwill, of honesty and candor, I'm asking all of them to join us in support for this important step for a secure future, a future of peace.

We are more secure today because, for the first since the signing of the Oslo Accords, we will see concrete and verifiable commitments carried out. Our Palestinian partners will join us in fighting terrorism. They will follow a detailed and systematic plan to fight terrorists and their infrastructure; to jail killers that have so far roamed at large; to stop vitriolic incitement; and above all, finally, after 35 years, to cancel the articles in the Palestinian Charter which call for the destruction of Israel.

This means that our world today will be safer for our children and for our neighbors' children. But it has been said here, and it's true, that we are just at the beginning, or maybe at the middle, of the road to a permanent peace. We will soon embark on negotiations for a permanent peace settlement between our two peoples. Now, I guarantee you it will not be easy and it will not be simple and it will be, Mr. President, despite your best wishes, sleepless. I guarantee you.

Mr. Chairman, I guarantee that to you, too.

But I am today brimming with some confidence—and not overconfidence—simply because we have overcome tremendous challenges and achieved success for both sides—not at the expense of one side and the benefit of the other, but success and advantage and progress for both sides. And that fills me with the confidence that we are able to tackle the larger challenges that still await us and that still await our two peoples.

There are so many people that I could thank in the American delegation. . . .

But I want to especially thank President Clinton. He is—if I can borrow a cliché—he is a warrior for peace. I mean, he doesn't stop. He has this ability to maintain a tireless pace and to nudge and prod and suggest. and use a nimble and flexible mind to truly explore the possibilities of both sides, and never just of one side. That is a great gift, I think a precious and unique one. And it served us well.

So I thank you, Mr. President, for serving us and the cause of peace well. I thank you, too, for your boundless optimism, without which these qualities cannot come into effect. You needed a lot of optimism.

I want to thank Chairman Arafat. Mr. Chairman, you're cooperation was invaluable. And I want to thank you, personally, once again, for the kind wishes you extended me on a birthday that I shall never forget. Thank you very much. . . .

I want to thank King Hussein, who visited us twice. And, Your Majesty, you gave us an unforgettable and inspiring example of courage and humanity, and it moved me deeply. It moved every one of our people and our delegates deeply, and I thank you for that.

Thank you very much.

President Clinton: . . . Just as I was able to say a thank-you to Prime Minister Netanyahu, let me say to Chairman Arafat, I thank you. I thank you for turning away from violence toward peace. I thank you for embracing the idea that Palestinians and Israelis can actually share the land of our fathers together. I thank you for believing that the home of Islam and Judaism and Christianity can surely be the home of people who love one God and respect every life God has created. And I thank you for decades and decades and decades of tireless representation of the longing of the Palestinian people to be free, self-sufficient, and at home. . . .

Chairman Yasir Arafat: . . . This is an important and a happy day, a day of achievement that we will always remember with optimism and hope. It is true that whatever we achieved is only temporary, that has been late. But our agreement in the Wye River underscores that the peace process is going ahead, and that whatever we agreed upon in Madrid, Oslo, and in Washington and Cairo is being implemented on the same bases that have been agreed to, and that we will never go back. We will never leave the peace process, and we will never go back to violence and confrontation. No return to confrontation and violence.

Please allow me to mention in this connection, first and foremost, to direct my talk to Mr. Bill Clinton for the long hours which he exerted during the past 10 days, particularly those 24 hours that he spent continuously, where he was always alert and understanding, creative in order to bring back history between the cousins—this friendliness that had been separated through wars and destruction and violence for many years. . . .

This reconciliation between the two peoples, the Palestinian and the Israeli people, will not divert this path and will go through negotiations on the table and go through tanks, grenades and barbed wires. We have achieved today a large step, but it is important—my co-partner, Mr. Netanyahu—it is important in establishing the peace process because this is the peace of courageous people.

The implementation of the Security Council resolutions 242 and 338 and the principle of land for peace, achievement of political rights of the Palestinian people, and putting every effort possible in the service of achieving security for all, particularly for the Israeli people—all this will bring us to begin at once and quickly in the negotiations of the final solution that will try to achieve just and peaceful permanent peace in order to complement what takes place also on the Syrian and the Lebanese paths very soon.

What we achieved together with the leading and effective role of President William Clinton and his U.S. team is something, if fully and sincerely implemented, will open the door before the Palestinian and Israeli people for more achievements, more hope, and more optimism not only for ourselves, but also for the Middle East regions as a whole.

Once again, I'm saying that it is a big step that came late, but it is, indeed, an important one because it will allow the return of 13 percent of the Palestinian land on the West Bank to the Palestinian people, to their sovereignty, and will allow to double the area where the Palestinian Authority will enjoy full-fledged authority and sovereignty. Yes, indeed, it is a step that will allow to the Palestinian airplanes to fly to and from the Gaza International Airport, carrying visitors and merchandise, carrying to the whole world the Palestinian flowers and fresh fruit.

It will also open the door to build the Gaza seaport and the realization of the Palestinian dream of geographic unification between the regions of the Palestinian land in the Bank and Gaza through a secured area. It will also allow the achievement of real happiness for hundreds of the prisoners of Palestinians in the Israeli jails, and also for the families everywhere, liberating them. And I will never forget this, in fact, for Mr. Netanyahu, with the assistance of King Hussein and President Clinton.

I say they will be liberated outside their cells, to where there is freedom and participation in the completion of what we started of a peace process and building their free land, with their heads held high and proud.

I led those children during our struggle for freedom, and they gave their freedom and their lives for the sake of the land. However, they adopted the peace process, adopted peace and stood by peace, while they were in the jails. And now, they are joining us in our peace process for the sake of peace. It is the peace of courageous people.

We have succeeded in the agreement to stop all the unilateral actions that would undermine the final solution and bring about a difficult climate for negotiations on peace. With this agreement, we begin the final solution negotiations, which we will take very seriously, and commitment in order to achieve it on its stipulated times in all the agreements we signed together, which is the 4th of May 1999. . . .

We are quite certain that we will stand together here in this place which is at high level forum, and under the guardianship of President Clinton, in order to announce the achievement of permanent peace between the Palestinian and the Israeli peoples, that we have completed the solution of all issues—the return of the land, the status of Jerusalem, the status of the settlements, the final frontiers, and the return of refugees, and the just distribution of order and security, and good relations with our neighbors, and that we have achieved freedom and independence and security for all.

We will begin a new era of new relations based on equality, mutual feelings and cooperation between two independent, neighboring countries enjoying security and openness with their neighbors, in a regional framework that would bring about peace, justice, and stability for all.

Mr. President—President Clinton; Your Majesty King Hussein; my co-partner, Mr. Netanyahu; Mr. Al Gore; ladies and gentlemen, I talked in hope and optimism about the future, which I hope will be achieved together through sincere and accurate achievement of whatever we agreed upon. But I would like to, certain in honesty and sincerity, that we are fully committed to whatever is required from us in order to achieve real security and constant peace for every Israeli person and for the Israeli people. We will not forget our duties as we underline our rights.

I am quite confident that I'm talking in the name of all Palestinians when I assure you that we are all committed to the security of every child, woman and man in Israel. Here we have come to a detailed agreement, and we are committed to play our independent role to keep security. And we will achieve whatever we promise here.

I will do everything I can so that no Israeli mother will be worried if her son or daughter is late coming home, or any Israeli would be afraid when they heard an explosion. It is true that nobody can secure 100 percent results of security for all Palestinians and all Israelis. But I am proud that we were able to work together and we will be able to do more together, with assistance of all our friends all over the world, in America and in Europe, and with great commitment to achieve much more in the years ahead—yes, indeed.

Ladies and gentlemen, we want achievement of the peace of courageous people to end this long suffering in order to build an independent nation having a lot of democracy and caring for his children. We want a school and education for every child and young man. We want a job for every man and woman, and a modern medical clinic and a hospital, and a small house as well, where everybody feels comfortable and where laughter is heard of happy, healthy kids. We want that and more for our neighbors and co-partners, the Israeli people, and the Arabs. . . .

And at last, I would like to direct my talk to Mr. Netanyahu and his colleagues, to say today we have achieved a great positive agreement. We have to continue that together very soon and to implement it quite sincerely in reality.

Your security is our security. Your security is our security, and peace for your children and our children. And we will work together through the peace process and negotiations, even though they are difficult, in order to achieve a final solution. We will not retreat, we will not go back to violence or confrontation. And we, together, will be the leaders in order that peace would prevail on our land and the land of our neighbors. And peace be with you all. . . .

King Hussein: Mr. President; Mr. Vice President; Ms. Albright, Secretary of State; my friend, Sandy Berger; and, of course, all our friends here and all our friends who played such a vital part in the last few days in which I was privileged to be an observer and one who sought to give courage to the process that was ongoing—George Tenet. And as the President said, Dennis has lost his black hair and replaced it to grey; I've lost all mine and even my eyebrows. But this is part of the life in which we live. And I was privileged to be with you all. And no matter what, I would have been. If I had an ounce of strength, I would have done my utmost to be there, and to help in any way I can.

By the way, many in our part of the world and different parts of the world have written me off. But I have a lot of faith in God, and I believe that one lives one's destiny. And as far as I'm concerned, my morale is the highest it has ever been. And this has been a shot in the arm for me, what you have accomplished today, President Arafat and Prime Minister Netanyahu.

I recall in discovering past events over many years, and one thing that remained with me throughout those many years was a total commitment to the cause of peace. We quarrel, we agree; we are friendly, we are not friendly. But we have no right to dictate through irresponsible action or narrow-mindedness the future of our children and their children's children. There has been enough destruction. Enough death. Enough waste. And it's time that, together, we occupy a place beyond ourselves, our peoples, that is worthy of them under the sun, the descendants of the children of Abraham.

Palestinians and Israelis coming together. I have attended, sir, previous occasions here, and, of course, you, Mr. President, together with the late Prime Minister Yitzhak Rabin, were my partners four years ago in the Washington Declaration, and later on when the state of peace was finalized in our weekend in Jordan and in Aqaba. I don't think we might have given you as much hard work, or less sleep than you have been subjected to of late. But what I found this time, and what really gives me hope and confidence, is that that same chemistry, after the first meeting between Prime Minister Netanyahu and President Arafat, is there.

I think that we passed a crossroad. We have made our commitment to the welfare and happiness and security and future of our peoples in all the times to come. And now our partners are numerous, and we wish them every success in their endeavors and we'll do everything we can to help them.

I think such a step as is concluded today will inevitably trigger those who want to destroy life, destroy hope, create fear in the hearts and minds of people, trigger in them their worst instincts. They will be skeptical on the surface, but if they can, they will cause damage, wherever they are and wherever they belong. Let's hope that the overwhelming majority of us—those who are committed to the future, those who know what responsibilities they hold now—will be able, through steady progress and a determined combined joint effort, be able to thwart their aims and their objectives and move—and maybe, God willing, witness the dawn that we are always seeking of a comprehensive peace in our entire region.

Mr. President, I have had the privilege of being a friend of the United States and Presidents since late President Eisenhower. Throughout all the years that have passed, I have kept in touch. But on the subject of peace, the peace we are seeking, I have never—with all due respect and all the affection that I held for your predecessors—have known someone with your dedication, clear-headedness, focus and determination to help resolve this issue in the best possible way.

Mr. President, permit me to say what I feel—I was mentioning it more than once in the last few days. You have the tolerance and the patience of Job, and you are the subject of our admiration and respect. And we hope that you will be with us as we see greater successes and as we help our brethren and our friends move ahead towards a better tomorrow.

On behalf of Noor and for those colleagues of mine from Jordan, thank you all for your great kindness. And thank you, our Israeli friends and this very fine delegation, for all your contributions and efforts. And, obviously, my pride is limitless in the efforts and in the commitment of President Arafat and his colleagues.

I think we are moving. We are not marking time, but we are moving in the right direction. I believe that very sincerely. And may God bless our efforts. Thank you very much.

REPORT OF SOUTH AFRICAN TRUTH COMMISSION

October 29, 1998

A commission appointed by the South African government issued a report on October 29 that concluded that the country's former white minority government, black organizations that were allied with the government, and groups that battled the government for three decades all committed human rights abuses, including killing civilians. The Truth and Reconciliation Commission, headed by Archbishop Desmond Tutu, called on all elements of society to face up to the country's brutal past during the last three decades of apartheid—the domination of blacks, Asians, and other ethnic groups by the white minority.

The commission encountered numerous obstacles in its work, which took more than two and a half years, including 160 hearings around the country. The chief obstacles included legal challenges, the refusal of nearly all major figures from the apartheid era to cooperate with its investigations, and the fact that the former ruling National Party had destroyed many important government and party records. The commission was particularly indignant about the records-destruction, calling it an effort to protect guilty parties by wiping out the country's "social memory."

Just before the 3,500-page report was to be released, the commission faced a final hurdle from the governing African National Congress (ANC). The party filed suit to block release of the report because it included descriptions of human rights abuses by ANC officials. A court threw out that challenge October 28.

In his foreword, Tutu acknowledged that the report represented the best version of the truth that the commission could assemble given its limited mandate and time. "It is not and cannot be the whole story, but it provides a perspective on the truth about a past that is more extensive and more complex than any one commission could, in two and a half years, have hoped to capture," he wrote. Tutu had received the Nobel Peace Prize in 1984 in recognition of his struggle against apartheid.

In addition to its findings concerning human rights abuses, the commission report recommended several steps to compensate those who suf-

fered under apartheid. These included imposing a "wealth tax" and asking companies listed on the South African Stock Exchange to donate one percent of their market capitalization.

The report came four years after the nation's first universal elections brought to power a black-majority regime headed by Nelson Mandela. Those four years had been full of stress and turmoil, and much of the excitement of the transition from apartheid had diminished. By 1998 many South Africans of all races viewed the report as an unwanted reminder of an unpleasant past. Even so, Tutu tried to persuade his countrymen that the document presented an opportunity to clean the slate for a fresh start on the nation's future. "Fellow South Africans, accept this report as a way, an indispensible way, of healing, where we have looked the beast in the eye." (South African elections, Historic Documents of 1994, p. 247)

Tutu predicted that many South Africans would be unhappy with the report, and he was right. In accepting the report, Mandela—an old friend of Tutu's—pointedly noted "all its imperfections" and added: "Many of us would have reservations about aspects of what is contained in these five volumes." Later, however, Mandela defended the report when his deputy president and likely successor, Thabo Mbeki, criticized the report's findings that the ANC had been guilty of human rights violations during its fight against apartheid.

Numerous officials of the former white government also complained about aspects of the report, saying the commission was biased and was attempting only to humiliate former government officials. F. W. de Klerk, the last white minority president, said he had concluded that the Truth and Reconciliation Commission was determined to implicate "entire generations" of whites in human rights abuses.

The White Minority Regime

The commission found that the "preponderance of responsibility" for killings, tortures, and other human rights violations of the apartheid era rested with the white minority government, its security forces, and black organizations that cooperated with the government. By the 1970s, the report said, the apartheid regime was using "institutionalized violence" as its primary means of intimidating blacks and confronting the African National Congress and other anti-apartheid groups.

The commission said the State Security Council, which included the president and the heads of major government security services, explicitly authorized "gross violations of human rights" in the battle to retain power. The government hunted down and punished its opponents, whether they were in South Africa or in neighboring countries, the commission said. In many cases, security forces acted directly to kill or torture opponents; in other cases, the government provided funding, training, and weapons to foreign and domestic groups.

The most senior former government official cited directly in the report was P. W. Botha, who served as prime minister and then as president from

1978 to 1989—generally considered the period of the government's most violent repression of the black majority. The commission said Botha, as chairman of the State Security Council, had overall responsibility for the government's violence against its opponents. Botha had signed documents ordering that apartheid opponents be "eliminated" and "neutralized." Such orders could only have meant that Botha wanted those people killed, the commission said. The panel found that Botha had personally ordered the 1988 bombing of Khotso House (the headquarters of the South African Council of Churches), which injured twenty-one people, and the 1982 bombing of the ANC's headquarters in London.

Botha repeatedly refused to testify at commission hearings on his actions, despite several concessions made by the commission because of his ill health. Ultimately, the commission went to court to compel his testimony—a step that angered many conservative whites who accused the panel of engaging in a witch hunt. A judge in August held Botha in contempt and required him to pay a fine or spend a year in jail. The case was on appeal at the end of 1998.

The most important white political leader whose actions were not detailed in the report released on October 29 was F. W. de Klerk, the president who freed Mandela from prison and oversaw the transition to majority rule. The commission had included in its report a section discussing charges that de Klerk had covered up the involvement of the heads of two government security services in two fatal bombings in the late 1980s. De Klerk insisted he became aware of the role of those officials only years after the bombings; he filed suit to force the commission to withdraw its conclusion that he had been an accessory after the fact. Rather than delay release of the entire report while de Klerk's suit was pending, the commission blacked out the relevant section in the report.

The ANC and Its Allies

For Mandela and his associates in the government, undoubtedly the most painful portions of the report dealt with human rights abuses by the ANC and its allies in the struggle against apartheid. ANC leaders had acknowledged that the organization—especially its paramilitary wing, the Umkhonto weSizwe, known as MK—had killed and tortured hundreds of people, including civilians, between 1961 and 1990. But some ANC officials were angered that the commission listed such abuses alongside crimes committed by the government; the effect, they said, was to equate the excesses of those fighting oppression with those fighting to maintain oppression.

The commission directly addressed that issue, noting that the conflict over apartheid "was neither initiated by nor in the interests of the ANC." Even so, the commission said, the ANC needed to account "for the many hundreds of people killed or injured by its members in the conflict."

The commission drew particular attention to the ANC's use of land mines and other hidden explosives, some of which were clearly aimed at civilian populations. Regardless of the justification given by the ANC, the commission said, "the people who were killed or injured by such explosions were all victims of gross violations of human rights perpetuated by the ANC."

The Inkatha Freedom Party

Some of the most damning information in the report concerned the Inkatha Freedom Party, the Zulu-based political organization headed by Chief Mangosuthu Buthelezi. For many years Buthelezi and his party were the principal black opponents of the ANC. According to the report, by the late 1980s Inkatha had aligned itself with the white government through a policy of "covert collaboration." Inkatha received "direct financial and logistical assistance from the highest echelons" of the white government, the report said, and its paramilitary forces launched attacks against the ANC and its allies.

The commission detailed Inkatha "attacks and massacres" from 1983 through the elections in 1994, most of them against ANC members and supporters. Some of the bloodiest attacks initiated by Inkatha were in the Transvaal region in the early 1990s, when apartheid was in the process of being dismantled. The commission gave details about the brutal practice of "necklacing": placing a gasoline-soaked automobile tire around a victim's neck and then setting it afire. The commission said Buthelezi, as head of Inkatha and as the former minister of police for the KwaZulu province, was accountable for human rights abuses committed by Inkatha forces.

Buthelezi and other top Inkatha officials refused to cooperate with the Truth and Reconciliation Commission. The Inkatha Freedom Party issued a statement saying it was "disgusted and alarmed" by the commission's report.

Winnie Mandela

Perhaps the most famous person directly implicated in murder in the commission report was Mandela's former wife, Winnie Madikizela-Mandela. During the late 1980s, when her husband was imprisoned by the white government and she was president of the ANC Women's League, Madikizela-Mandela ran a youth organization, the Mandela United Football Club, in the black township of Soweto outside Johannesburg.

The commission said that members of the club were involved in "at least" eighteen killings, as well as torture, assaults, and arson. Madikizela-Mandela was aware of these events and did nothing to stop them, the commission said, and so she was "politically and morally responsible" for gross human rights violations. The commission implicated Madikizela-Mandela directly in eight killings, including that of Stompie Seipei, whose decomposed body was found in 1989. The commission said Madikizela-Mandela "in all probability" was aware of the murder and had failed to prevent it. Two of Madikizela-Mandela's associates testified that she participated in the killing of Seipei.

Granting Amnesty

A committee composed of commission members but independent of the full panel, had the troublesome responsibility of determining who should be granted amnesty from legal prosecution for crimes committed during the struggle over apartheid. The committee received more than 7,000 applications for amnesty from government officials, ANC guerrillas, and others. By the end of 1998 the committee had rejected more than 4,000 of those amnesty requests and had about 2,600 cases pending.

The committee's most controversial step was a blanket amnesty granted in December 1997 to thirty-seven ANC officials, including deputy president Mbeki and four other members of Mandela's cabinet. In the case of those officials, the committee waived its standard procedures under which amnesty applicants were required to acknowledge specific acts they had committed and then attend hearings at which they could be questioned by victims and family members. Instead, the committee accepted general statements from the officials acknowledging responsibility for the actions of ANC members under their supervision.

The granting of amnesty for the ANC officials generated widespread protests, including from Tutu that the committee had given them preferential treatment. Acting on a complaint from the full commission, a judge in May voided the amnesties and returned the ANC cases to the amnesty committee for a more detailed review.

Following are excerpts from the Findings and Conclusions, volume 5, chapter 6, of the "Report of the South African Truth and Reconciliation Commission," issued October 29, 1998:

Introduction

1 The Promotion of National Reconciliation and Unity Act (the Act) was a contested piece of legislation. Its passage through cabinet and Parliament and its final form mirror the many different interests, fears and perspectives in South African society.

2 The new government settled on a compromise. Focusing not only on those violations committed by the former state, the Act chose instead to focus on violations committed by *all* parties to the conflict. It eschewed notions of vengeance or retribution, and instead created a mechanism for the granting of amnesty for politically motivated actions, providing full individual disclosure was made.

3 It is the view of the Truth and Reconciliation Commission (the Commission) that the spirit of generosity and reconciliation enshrined in the founding Act was not matched by those at whom it was mainly directed. Despite amnesty provisions extending to criminal and civil charges, the white community often seemed either indifferent or plainly hostile to the work of the Commission, and certain media appear to have actively sought to sustain this

indifference and hostility. With rare individual exceptions, the response of the former state, its leaders, institutions and the predominant organs of civil society of that era, was to hedge and obfuscate. Few grasped the olive branch of full disclosure.

4 Even where political leaders and institutional spokespersons of the former state claimed to take full responsibility for the actions of the past, these sometimes seemed to take the form of ritualised platitudes rather than genuine expressions of remorse. Often, it seemed to the Commission, there was no real appreciation of the enormity of the violations of which these leaders and those under them were accused, or of the massive degree of hurt and pain their actions had caused.

5 In making its findings, the Commission drew on a wide range of evidence. Apart from over 21,000 statements on violations of human rights, it considered the evidence contained in numerous submissions, amnesty applications and other documents to which it had access. . . .

Primary Finding

77 On the basis of the evidence available to it, the primary finding of the Commission is that: the predominant portion of gross violations of human rights was committed by the former state through its security and law-enforcement agencies.

Moreover, the South African state in the period from the late 1970s to early 1990s became involved in activities of a criminal nature when, amongst other things, it knowingly planned, undertook, condoned and covered up the commission of unlawful acts, including the extra-judicial killings of political opponents and others, inside and outside South Africa.

In pursuit of these unlawful activities, the state acted in collusion with certain other political groupings, most notably the Inkatha Freedom Party (IFP). . . .

Findings on the State and Unlawful Activities

. . .

101 Arising from the above [summary of testimony], and from evidence presented in Volume Two of this report, the Commission makes the following findings in respect of the state's involvement in gross violations of human rights during the period 1960–94:

The Commission endorses the position in international law that apartheid as a form of systematic racial discrimination and separation constituted a crime against humanity.

Within this context, the Commission finds that:

- the state—in the form of the South African government, the civil service and its security forces—was, in the period 1960–94 the primary perpetrator of gross violations of human rights in South Africa, and from 1974, in Southern Africa.
- In the application of the policy of apartheid, the state in the Commission's mandate period was increasingly authoritarian in nature and

intolerant of dissent. This was manifested, inter alia, in a host of legislative measures which severely abridged the principles of the rule of law and limited the right of the people of South Africa to free political activity.

- The development of an authoritarian political order in the mandate period was facilitated by a culture of impunity which emerged as a result of legislative and other measures by the state, and by the failure, largely as a consequence of state pressure, of organs of civil society—political parties, the mass media, faith, business, legal, medical and other groups—to observe and adhere to the codes and standards of conduct integral to their professions.
- In the application of the policy of apartheid, the state in the period 1960–90 sought to protect the power and privilege of a racial minority. Racism therefore constituted the motivating core of the South African political order, an attitude largely endorsed by the investment and other policies of South Africa's major trading partners in this period. A consequence of this racism was that white citizens in general adopted a dehumanising position towards black citizens, to the point where the ruling order of the state ceased to regard them as fellow citizens and largely labelled them as "the enemy." This created a climate in which gross atrocities committed against them were seen as legitimate.

As a consequence of these factors, the Commission finds that the state perpetrated, among others, the following types of gross violations of human rights in South and/or Southern Africa:

- torture, including not only the intentional infliction of pain but also detention without trial and solitary confinement;
- abduction, involving the forcible and illegal removal or capture of people, often from beyond the borders of South Africa;
- severe ill treatment including sexual assault, abuse or harassment, the imposition of restrictions on individuals in the form of banning and banishment orders, the deliberate withholding of medical attention, food and water, the destruction of homes or offices through arson or sabotage, and the mutilation of body parts;
- the unjustified use of deadly force in situations where lesser measures would have been adequate to control demonstrations or detain or arrest suspects;
- the deliberate manipulation of social divisions in society with the intention of mobilising one group against another, resulting, at times, in violent clashes;
- the arming, funding and training of foreign nationals for military operations against sovereign governments in the region;
- incursions across South Africa's borders with the intention of killing or abducting opponents living outside of South Africa;
- judicial killings, involving the execution of opponents for offences of a political and not a criminal nature;

- extra-judicial killings in the form of state-planned and executed assassinations, attempted killings, disappearances, abductions and so-called 'entrapment killings', where individuals were deliberately enticed into situations;
- The covert training, arming or funding of offensive paramilitary units or hit squads for deployment internally against opponents of the government.

Finding on Former President PW Botha

102 Mr PW Botha presided as executive head of the former South African government (the government) from 1978 to 1984 as Prime Minister, and from 1984 to 1989 as Executive State President. Given his centrality in the politics of the 1970s and 1980s, the Commission has made a finding on the role of former the State President:

During the period 1978–1989, according to submissions made to, and findings made by, the Commission, gross violations of human rights and other unlawful acts were perpetrated on a wide scale by members of the former South African Police (SAP) and the former South African Defence Force (SADF), among others. Such violations included:

- the deliberate unlawful killing, and attempted killing, of persons opposed to the policies of the government, within and outside South Africa;
- the widespread use of torture and other forms of severe ill treatment against such persons;
- the forcible abduction of such persons who were resident in neighbouring countries;
- covert logistical and financial assistance to organisations opposed to the ideology of the ANC and other liberation movements both within and outside of South Africa, enabling those organisations to commit gross human rights violations on a wide scale within and beyond the borders of this country;
- acts of arson and sabotage against the property of persons and organisations opposed to the government, within and outside of the country.

During the period 1979–89, Mr PW Botha chaired the State Security Council (SSC), established to advise the government on national security issues which were, or were perceived to be, a threat to the government. Under his leadership, the SSC—

- placed great pressure on the government's security forces to engage robustly against organisations and persons opposed to the government, in their perceived onslaught against the government;
- used language in its meetings and recommendations that was highly ambiguous and was interpreted by persons with access to the meetings, their minutes and recommendations, as authorising the killing of people;

- failed to recommend to the government that appropriate steps be taken against members of the security forces who were involved in or who were suspected of being involved in gross violations of human rights, thus contributing to the prevailing culture of impunity;
- recommended that the government impose states of emergency, under which gross violations of human rights committed against persons opposed to the government increased, and assisted the government in the implementation of the states of emergency;
- recommended the adoption of principles of counter-revolutionary warfare which led to the increased deployment of special units of the SADF in support of the SAP in South Africa, resulting in a shift of focus in policing from arresting and charging opponents of the government to eliminating opponents and their bases;
- recommended that the government support covert projects aimed at opposing and destabilising the governments of neighbouring countries which were supportive of liberation movements;
- recommended that the government support covert projects to help destabilise and oppose organisations and people opposed to the government.

As a consequence, the SSC created a political climate that greatly facilitated the gross violation of human rights, and in which such violations occurred on a wide scale.

Mr Botha was responsible for ordering former Minister of Law and Order Adriaan Vlok and former Police Commissioner Johan van der Merwe unlawfully to destroy Khotso House in Johannesburg, (a building occupied by organisations considered by Botha to be a threat to the security of the government), thereby endangering the lives of people in and around the building. This decision greatly enhanced the prevailing culture of impunity and facilitated the further Gross violation of human rights by senior members of the security forces.

For the reasons set out above and by virtue of his position as head of state and chairperson of the SSC, Botha contributed to and facilitated a climate in which the above gross violations of human rights could and did occur, and as such is accountable for such violations.

Finding on Former State President FW de Klerk

[These findings were blacked out in the version of the report released October 29, 1998.]

Findings on the Destruction of Documents by the Former State

. . . The following is a summary of the Commission's finding with regard to this issue:

The former government deliberately and systematically destroyed state documentation over a number of years. This process began in 1978, when classified records were routinely destroyed, supposedly in order to safeguard state security. By the 1990s the process of destruction of records and documents had become a co-ordinated endeavour, sanctioned by the cabinet, with the aim of denying a new government access to incriminating evidence and sanitising the history of the apartheid era. . . .

The Commission finds the following official bodies responsible for the destruction of documents: the cabinet of the former government, the NIS, the Security Branch of the SAP, and the SADF.

Findings on the Role of Allies of the State

The Homelands

106 As has been stated above, the state was not acting alone in its strategies involving gross human rights violations. It had the active and passive support of numerous other elements in society. One of these was the white electorate which returned the National Party to power in one election after another. Others were the institutional creations of the apartheid system and the political parties that operated largely within these creations. The homeland or bantustan system gave rise to a set of semi-autonomous security and law-enforcement structures and such political groupings as the Inkatha Freedom Party.

107 So-called independent and semi-autonomous homelands emerged on the political landscape of South Africa in the 1970s and 1980s. From the outset, they were sites of steadily escalating resistance and repression. All forms of human rights abuse (torture, extra-judicial killings, unjustifiable use of deadly force etc) which occurred within so-called white South Africa were also found in the homelands arena. Indeed, such factors as a lack of public attention or scrutiny, little media interest and weak civil society structures, created an environment in the homelands that was even more conducive to gross violations of human rights than the wider South African society.

108 In consequence, human rights were grossly violated on a vast scale. The great majority of those who suffered human rights abuses in South Africa in the mandate period were the victims of black perpetrators, acting in many cases as surrogates for the South African government. Nowhere is this more true than in Natal and KwaZulu. It is for this reason that the IFP is the only homeland-based party and the KwaZulu Police (KZP) the only homeland security structure singled out by the Commission for specific findings.

109 Before focusing on those two entities, the Commission has made the following general finding on the homelands system:

The former state's policy of establishing ethnically separate reservations lay at the core of its policy of territorial and political separation on the basis of race. The policy was an extension of a colonially established practice of 'divide and rule' and had the dual aim of seeking to inhibit or divert the struggle by Africans for democratic rights inside South Africa while simultaneously protecting and preserving the economic and social privileges of the white minority.

The administrations and governments that presided over the various homelands were, accordingly, a cornerstone of the state's policy of apartheid in that they purported to grant full political, social and economic rights to black cultural and linguistic groupings, but only within defined limited geographic and ethnically exclusive enclaves. Economically, they remained nonviable, which left them little choice but to collaborate with the South African state on security and related matters, and function as extensions of that state and as instruments of its security forces. This does not, however, exonerate them or their leaders from responsibility for the gross violation of human rights perpetrated in the homelands.

Homeland governments implemented systems of rural local government and administration which led to widespread abuses and gross violations of human rights, as did the implementation of civil codes by chiefs and headmen.

Homeland governments were responsible for the establishment of police forces and, in the case of the "independent" homelands such as Transkei and Ciskei, defence forces characterised by incompetence, brutality, and political bias. In particular, they—

- displayed bias and partiality towards members and supporters of the homeland governments, both through acts of commission, when they worked openly with pro-homeland government vigilantes and/or covert armed groups, and through acts of omission when they failed to protect or serve those who did not support the homeland governments;
- were responsible for large numbers of killings and attempted killings as well as acts of incitement and conspiracy to kill, severe ill treatment, abduction, torture and arson, the victims of which were almost exclusively non-supporters of homeland government;
- were involved in covering up crimes committed by supporters of the homeland governments. These practices included neglecting basic investigative procedures and deliberately tampering with evidence.

In KwaZulu specifically, the homeland government and police force (KZP) were responsible for:

- ensuring that suspects in matters of political violence were concealed, often for lengthy periods, in SADF and other training camps;
- issuing false police certificates and identity documents to supporters of the homeland governments who were involved in political violence, in order to prevent their arrest and conviction and to facilitate their continued criminal activity;
- taking part in killings and purporting to investigate the very cases in which they had been involved as perpetrators;
- collaborating with members of the SAP's Security Branch and SADF military intelligence (MI) section in covert activities and projects aimed at destabilising popular opposition to state and homeland government authority.

The Commission finds the homeland security forces accountable not only for the gross human rights violations perpetrated by their members but also for those perpetrated by members and supporters of the homeland governments' ruling parties, as a result of the security forces' failure to act against such members and supporters. That failure engendered a climate of impunity that facilitated such gross violations of human rights.

At a political level, the Commission finds that accountability for the gross human rights violations cited above rests jointly with the South African government and the governments of the homelands.

Findings on the Inkatha Freedom Party

. . . 121 The formal finding of the Commission in regard to the IFP is set out below:

During the period 1982–94, the Inkatha Freedom Party, known as Inkatha prior to July 1990 (hereinafter referred to as "the organisation") was responsible for gross violations of human rights committed in the former Transvaal, Natal and KwaZulu against:

- persons who were perceived to be leaders, members or supporters of the UDF, ANC, South African Communist Party (SACP) and COSATU;
- persons who were identified as posing a threat to the organisation;
- members or supporters of the organisation whose loyalty was doubted.

It is a further finding of the Commission that such violations formed part of a systematic pattern of abuse which entailed deliberate planning on the part of the organisation.

The Commission based this finding on the following actions of the IFP:

- speeches by the IFP president, senior party officials and persons aligned to the organisation's ideology, which had the effect of inciting supporters of the organisation to commit acts of violence;
- arming the organisation's supporters with weapons in contravention of the Arms and Ammunition, and Explosives and Dangerous Weapons Acts;
- mass attacks by supporters of the organisation on communities inhabited by persons referred to above, resulting in death and injury and the destruction and theft of property;
- killing of leaders of the political organisations and persons referred to above;
- collusion with the South African government's security forces to commit the violations referred to above;
- entering into a pact with the SADF to create a paramilitary force for the organisation, which was intended to and did cause death and injury to the persons referred to above;
- establishing hit squads within the KZP and the special constable structure of the SAP to kill or cause injury to the persons referred to above;
- under the auspices of the self-protection unit project, training large numbers of the organisation's supporters with the specific objective of

preventing, by means of violence, the holding of elections in KwaZulu-Natal in April 1994, under a Constitution which did not recognise the organisation's demands for sovereignty. In order to achieve this objective, the KwaZulu government and its KwaZulu Police structures were subverted;

- conspiring with right-wing organisations and former members of the South African government's security forces to commit acts which resulted in loss of life or injury in order to achieve the objective referred to above;
- creating a climate of impunity by expressly or implicitly condoning gross human rights violations and other unlawful acts committed by members or supporters of the organisation.

Chief MG Buthelezi served simultaneously as President of the IFP and as the Chief Minister of the KwaZulu government and was the only serving Minister of Police in the KwaZulu government during the entire thirteen-year existence of the KwaZulu Police. Where these three agencies are found to have been responsible for the commission of gross human rights, Chief Mangosuthu Buthelezi is held by this Commission to be accountable in his representative capacity as the leader, head or responsible Minister of the parties concerned. . . .

Finding on the "Third Force"

126 The early 1990s saw unprecedented levels of violence: more people died in political conflict during this time than for the whole of the earlier mandate period. Numerous allegations were made that a "hidden hand" or "third force" was involved in orchestrating and fomenting such violence in order to derail the negotiation process. This "third force" was seen to involve covert units of the security forces acting in concert with other individuals or groupings, such as the IFP and various right-wing paramilitary structures. . . .

129 While little evidence exists of a centrally directed, coherent and formally constituted "third force," on the basis of the above:

The Commission finds that a network of security and ex-security force operatives, often acting in conjunction with right-wing elements and/or sectors of the IFP, fomented, initiated, facilitated and engaged in violence which resulted in gross violations of human rights, including random and targeted killings.

The Commission finds that such networks had established "partnerships" during the 1980s with pro-government individuals or groups at a local level which then acted in concert to perpetrate such violations. The Commission finds further that the sanction of illegal activities by security force operatives during the 1980s provided the basis for their continuation in the 1990s.

The Commission finds that such networks, at times, functioned with the active collusion and/or knowledge of senior security force personnel, and that the former government, either deliberately or by omission, failed to take sufficient steps to put an end to such practices.

The Commission also finds that the success of 'third force' attempts to generate violence was at least in part a consequence of extremely high levels of political intolerance, for which both the liberation movements and other structures such as the IFP are held to be morally and politically accountable.

The Liberation Movements

130 This section includes the Commission's findings on the ANC, PAC, UDF and on ANC national executive member, Ms Winnie Madikizela-Mandela.

131 In reviewing the activities of the ANC and PAC, the Commission endorsed the position in international law that the policy of apartheid was a crime against humanity and that both the ANC and PAC were internationally recognised liberation movements conducting legitimate struggles against the former South African government and its policy of apartheid.

132 Nonetheless, as indicated previously, the Commission drew a distinction between a "just war" and "just means" and has found that in terms of international conventions, the ANC and its organs (the National Executive Council, the National Working Committee, the Revolutionary Council, the Secretariat and its armed wing, MK, as well as the PAC and its armed formations Poqo and APLA, committed gross violations of human rights in the course of their political activities and armed struggles, for which they are morally and politically accountable.

133 The Commission also wishes to note that the fact that the Commission makes a more detailed finding and comments more extensively on the ANC than on the PAC should not be interpreted as suggesting that the Commission finds it to have been more responsible for gross violations of human rights than the PAC. This is not the case. Instead, what it reflects is the far greater degree of openness to the Commission of the ANC than the PAC. The ANC made two full submissions to the Commission, answered its questions on the exile camps and made available to the Commission its various enquiry reports into alleged human rights abuses in exile. By contrast, the PAC offered very little by way of information on any of its activities, including exile abuses, and supplied no documentation.

134 The Commission has taken note that of the three main parties to the armed struggle—the state, the ANC and the PAC—only the ANC signed the Geneva Convention in regard to the conduct of wars of national liberation, and made the most conscious effort to conduct its armed struggle within the framework of international humanitarian law. While actions were undertaken which violated the ANC's guidelines—and the Commission has made adverse findings on them—the Commission acknowledges that it was in general not ANC policy to target civilians. By contrast, the PAC consciously targeted certain categories of civilians, and whites in general, and the Commission has made findings in this regard.

135 The Commission acknowledges the comparative restraint with which the ANC conducted its armed struggle, at least in terms of its identification of targets, and the fact that the ANC leadership instructed its MK cadres to

abandon the landmine campaign when it became clear that innocent civilians were being killed and hurt by it.

Findings on the African National Congress

Violations Committed in the Course of the Armed Struggle

136 The ANC has accepted responsibility for all actions committed by members of MK under its command in the period 1961 to August 1990. In this period there were a number of such actions—in particular the placing of limpet and landmines—which resulted in civilian casualties. Whatever the justification given by the ANC for such acts—misinterpretation of policy, poor surveillance, anger or differing interpretations of what constituted a "legitimate military target"—the people who were killed or injured by such explosions are all victims of gross violations of human rights perpetrated by the ANC. While it is accepted that targeting civilians was not ANC policy, MK operations nonetheless ended up killing fewer security force members than civilians.

With regard to actions committed during the armed struggle, the Commission makes the following findings:

- while it was ANC policy that the loss of civilian life should be 'avoided', there were instances where members of MK perpetrated gross violations of human rights in that the distinction between military and civilian targets was blurred in certain armed actions, such as the 1983 Church Street bombing of the SAAF headquarters, resulting in gross violations of human rights through civilian injury and loss of life.
- in the course of the armed struggle there were instances where members of MK conducted unplanned military operations using their own discretion, and, without adequate control and supervision at an operational level, determined targets for attack outside of official policy guidelines. While recognising that such operations were frequently undertaken in retaliation for raids by the former South African government into neighbouring countries, Such unplanned operations nonetheless often resulted in civilian injury and loss of life, amounting to gross violations of human rights. The 1985 Amanzimtoti shopping centre bombing is regarded by the Commission in this light.
- in the course of the armed struggle the ANC, through MK, planned and undertook military operations which, though intended for military or security force targets, sometimes went awry for a variety of reasons, including poor intelligence and reconnaissance. The consequences in these cases, such as the Magoo's Bar and Durban Esplanade bombings, were gross violations of human rights in respect of the injuries to and loss of lives of civilians.
- while the Commission acknowledges the ANC's submission that the former South African government had itself by the mid-1980s blurred

the distinction between military and "soft" targets by declaring border areas "military zones" where farmers were trained and equipped to operate as an extension of military structures, it finds that the ANC's landmine campaign in the period 1985–87 in the rural areas of the northern and eastern Transvaal cannot be condoned, in that it resulted in gross violations of the human rights of civilians, including farm labourers and children, who were killed or injured. The ANC is held accountable for such gross violations of human rights.

- individuals who defected to the state and became informers and/or members who became state witnesses in political trials and/or became askaris were often labelled by the ANC as collaborators and regarded as legitimate targets to be killed. The Commission does not condone the legitimisation of such individuals as military targets and finds that the extra-judicial killings of such individuals constituted gross violations of human rights.

The Commission finds that, in the 1980s in particular, a number of gross violations of human rights were perpetrated not by direct members of the ANC or those operating under its formal command, but by civilians who saw themselves as ANC supporters. In this regard, the Commission finds that the ANC is morally and politically accountable for creating a climate in which such supporters believed their actions to be legitimate and carried out within the broad parameters of a "people's war" as enunciated by the ANC.

Gross Violations of Human Rights Committed by the ANC in Exile

. . . On the basis of the evidence available to it, the Commission finds that the ANC, and particularly its military structures responsible for the treatment and welfare of those in its camps, were guilty of gross violations of human rights in certain circumstances and against two categories of individuals, namely suspected "enemy agents" and mutineers.

The Commission finds that suspected "agents" were routinely subjected to torture and other forms of severe ill treatment and that there were cases of such individuals being charged and convicted by tribunals without proper attention to due process, sentenced to death and executed. The Commission finds that the human rights of the individuals so affected were grossly violated. Likewise, the Commission finds that the failure to communicate properly with the families of such victims constituted callous and insensitive conduct.

The Commission also finds that all so-called mutineers who were executed after conviction by military tribunal, irrespective of whether they were afforded proper legal representation and due process or not, suffered a gross violation of their human rights.

With regard to allegations of torture and severe ill treatment, the Commission finds that although torture was not within ANC policy, the Security Department of the ANC routinely used torture to extract information and confessions from those being held in camps, particularly in the period 1979-

89. The Commission has taken note of the various forms of torture detailed by the Motsuenyane Commission, namely the deliberate infliction of pain, severe ill treatment in the form of detention in solitary confinement, and the deliberate withholding of food and water and/or medical care, and finds that they amounted to gross violations of human rights.

The Commission further finds that adequate steps were not taken in good time against those responsible for such violations.

Gross Violations of Human Rights Committed by the ANC After Its Unbanning

138 While the Commission accepts that the violent conflict which consumed the country in the post-1990 period was neither initiated by nor in the interests of the ANC, the ANC must nonetheless account for the many hundreds of people killed or injured by its members in the conflict. While the ANC leadership has argued that its members were acting in self-defence, it is the Commission's view that at times the conflict assumed local dynamics in which proactive revenge attacks were carried out by both sides. This situation was exacerbated by high levels of political intolerance among all parties, including the ANC. Further, the Commission contends that the leadership should have been aware of the consequences of training and arming members of SDUs in a volatile situation in which they had little control over the actions of such members.

The Commission therefore finds that in the period 1990–94, the ANC was responsible for:

- killings, assaults and attacks on political opponents including members of the IFP, PAC, Azapo and the SAP;
- contributing to a spiral of violence in the country through the creation and arming of self-defence units (SDUs). Whilst acknowledging that it was not the policy of the ANC to attack and kill political opponents, the Commission finds that in the absence of adequate command structures and in the context of widespread state-sponsored or -directed violence and a climate of political intolerance, SDU members often "took the law into their own hands" and committed gross violations of human rights.

The Commission takes note that the political leadership of the African National Congress and the command structure of Umkhonto weSizwe has accepted political and moral responsibility for all the actions of its members in the period 1960–94 and therefore finds that the leadership of the ANC and MK must take responsibility, and be accountable, for all gross violations of human rights perpetrated by its membership and cadres in the mandate period.

Findings in Regard to Mrs Winnie Madikizela-Mandela and the Mandela Football Club

The Commission finds that Ms Madikizela-Mandela was central to the establishment and formation of the Mandela United Football Club, which later developed into a private vigilante unit operating around Ms Madikizela-

Mandela and from her houses in both Orlando West and Diepkloof. The Commission finds that the community anger against Ms Madikizela-Mandela and the Football club manifested itself in the burning of the Mandela home in Orlando West in July 1988, which led to political, community and church leaders requesting that she disband the football club.

The Commission further finds that the Mandela United Football Club was involved in a number of criminal activities including killing, torture, assaults and arson in the community. It is the Commission's view that Ms Madikizela-Mandela was aware of the criminal activity and the disquiet it caused in the community, but chose deliberately not to address the problems emanating from the Football Club. The Commission finds that those who opposed Ms Madikizela-Mandela and the Mandela United Football Club, or dissented from them, were branded as informers, and killed. The labelling by Ms Madikizela-Mandela of opponents as informers created the perception that they were legitimate targets. It is the finding of this Commission that Ms Madikizela-Mandela had knowledge of and/or participated in the activities of Club members, and/or that they were authorised and/or sanctioned by her.

The Commission finds that Ms Madikizela-Mandela failed to account to community and political structures. Further that she is accountable, politically and morally, for the gross violations of human rights committed by the Mandela United Football Club. The Commission finds further that Mrs Madikizela-Mandela herself was responsible for committing such gross violations of human rights.

Findings in Regard to the Pan Africanist Congress

139 Within the context of the international position on apartheid and the recognition of the PAC as a liberation movement, the Commission makes the following findings:

Violations committed by Poqo in the early 1960s. While the Commission takes note of the explanation tendered by the PAC that its activities in the early 1960s need to be understood in the context of the "land wars of the time," it nevertheless finds that the PAC and Poqo were responsible for the commission of gross violations of human rights through Poqo's campaign to liberate the country. This unleashed a reign of terror, particularly in the Western Cape townships. In the course of this campaign, the following groups suffered gross violations of their human rights:

- members of the police, particularly those living in black townships;
- the so-called 'Katangese', dissident members of the PAC who opposed the campaign and were subjected to physical attacks and assassinations by other Poqo members;
- representatives of traditional authority in the homelands, that is, chiefs and headmen;
- white civilians in non-combat situations.

The Commission finds the PAC accountable for such violations.

Gross violations of human rights committed by the PAC during its armed struggle.

140 While the PAC proclaimed a military strategy of a protracted people's war, which involved the infiltration of guerrillas into the country to conduct rural guerrilla warfare and attacks in the townships, in actuality the primary target of its operations were civilians. This was especially so after 1990 when, in terms of its 'Year of the Great Storm' campaign, the PAC/APLA targeted whites at random, and white farmers in particular.

The Commission finds that the targeting of civilians for killing was not only a gross violation of human rights of those affected but a violation of international humanitarian law. The Commission notes but rejects the PAC's explanation that its killing of white farmers constituted acts of war for which it has no regrets and apologies. To the contrary, the Commission finds PAC action directed towards both civilians and whites to have been a gross violation of human rights for which the PAC and APLA leadership are held to be morally and politically responsible and accountable.

Gross violations of human rights committed by the PAC against its own members.

The Commission finds that numbers of members of the PAC were extra-judicially killed in exile, particularly in camps in Tanzania, by APLA cadres acting on the instructions of its High Command, and that members inside the country branded as informers or agents, and those who opposed PAC policies, were also killed. All such actions constituted instances of gross violations of human rights for which the PAC and APLA are held to be responsible and accountable. . . .

Finding in Respect of IFP Office-Bearers

145 The IFP submitted a list of over 400 alleged office-bearers who, according to the IFP, had been deliberately targeted and killed by structures of the ANC and its affiliates. The IFP's submission made it clear that it believed that the killings were part of a deliberate pattern of behaviour on the part of the ANC—or in the words of the IFP, "serial killing". The Durban office of the Commission conducted an intensive investigation into those incidents that occurred in former Natal and KwaZulu and produced an extremely detailed and comprehensive report. . . .

150 . . . [I]nvestigations reveal that ANC, UDF or MK structures were responsible for the killing of seventy-six IFP office-bearers during the period 1985 to 1994. In only two of the incidents did the perpetrators hold leadership positions in the UDF, ANC or MK. In eight of the incidents, the killings were administered by people's courts and it was not possible to establish whether IFP members had been targeted because of their IFP membership. However, given the history of the conflict, it would seem safe to assume that membership of the IFP would have been a factor.

The Commission finds that, in seventy-six incidents, the deceased were deliberately targeted because of the fact that they held positions within the IFP. The killings of the IFP office-bearers amount to a systematic pattern of abuse, entailing deliberate planning, and constitute gross violations of human rights for which the respective local structures of the UDF, ANC and MK are held accountable.

Civil Society

... 151 The Commission sought and received a number of submissions from organisations representing specific sectors of civil society. These sectors, while generally not directly involved in gross violations of human rights, were structurally part of an overall system designed to protect the rights and privileges of a racial minority. Many, such as the media and organised religion, exerted immense influence, not least of which was their capacity to influence the ideas and morals of generations of South Africans. In a society organised not only along lines of race but of class as well, professional bodies representing lawyers and doctors were frequently seen to be the custodians of scientific knowledge and impartiality. As such, their failure to oppose the injustice around them vociferously and actively, contributed in no small way to an ethos and climate that supported the status quo and isolated those who did oppose injustice.

152 It should be noted that in almost every sector, complicity relates both to the continuing perpetuation of race-based systems and structures and to a failure to speak out against the gross violations of human rights occurring throughout the society.

153 The Commission also notes that within these sectors, there were pockets of individuals, sometimes organised into formal structures, that did indeed resist apartheid and other injustices, and sometimes paid dearly for their stance. Many of these structures were isolated by the mainstream bodies and were frequently cast as "fringe" elements. There were not many who chose this path. Had their number been greater, and had they not been so harassed and isolated by both government and the professions, the moral bankruptcy of apartheid would have been more quickly and starkly exposed. To their credit, most representatives of the various civil society sectors who appeared before the Commission acknowledged their omissions and failures and apologised for them. ...

Conclusion

162 The findings outlined above, to a greater or lesser extent, touch *all* the major role-players who were party to the conflict that enveloped South Africa during its mandate period. No major role-player emerges unscathed although, as already stated, a distinction must be made between those who fought for and those who fought against apartheid. There are many who will reject these findings and argue that they fail to understand the complexities and historical realities of the time, and of the motives and perspectives of those who perpetrated gross violations of human rights. In this regard it needs to be firmly stated that, while the Commission has attempted to convey some of these complexities and has grappled with the motives and perspectives of perpetrators in other sections of this report, it is not the Com-

mission's task to write the history of this country. Rather, it is the Commission's function to expose the violations of all parties in an attempt to lay the basis for a culture in which human rights are respected and not violated.

163 It should also be noted—as will be obvious from the content above—that the Commission's findings have focused mainly on events and violations that occurred *inside* South Africa in the 1960–94 period. There are obvious and good reasons for that, but it represents something of a historical distortion. It is the view of the Commission that, in terms of the gross violations of human rights, most of these occurred not internally, but *beyond the borders* of South Africa, in some of the poorest nations of the world. It was the residents of the Southern African region who bore the brunt of the South African conflict and suffered the greatest number of individual casualties and the greatest damage to their countries' economies and infrastructure.

164 Finally, in the context of a society moving towards reconciliation, South Africans need to acknowledge this country's divided history and its regional burden; to understand the processes whereby all, citizens included, were drawn in and are implicated in the fabric of human rights abuse, both as victims and perpetrators—at times as both.

165 The primary task of the Commission was to address the moral, political and legal consequences of the apartheid years. The socio-economic implications are left to other structures—the Land Commission, the Gender Commission, the Youth Commission and a range of reform processes in education, social welfare, health care, housing and job creation. Ultimately, however, because the work of the Commission includes reconciliation, it needs to unleash a process that contributes to economic developments that redress past wrongs as a basis for promoting lasting reconciliation. This requires *all those who benefited from apartheid,* not only those whom the Act defines as perpetrators, to commit themselves to the reconciliation process.

JOHN GLENN'S RETURN TO SPACE ON SHUTTLE MISSION
October 31, 1998

John Glenn, the first American astronaut to orbit the earth and the man many considered the last authentic American hero, achieved another superlative in 1998. At age seventy-seven, he became the oldest person ever in space. In his final months as a U.S. senator from Ohio, Glenn spent nine days in late October and early November aboard the space shuttle Discovery.

Glenn's second journey into space was the most heavily publicized space mission in years. For many Americans, it also was a nostalgic trip down memory lane, a reminder of the early 1960s when Glenn helped restore the self-confidence of a nation shaken by the tensions of the cold war and the early lead the Soviet Union had taken in space.

Six astronauts shared Glenn's encore visit to space, including the first Japanese female in space, Chiaki Mukai. All seven astronauts, including Glenn, conducted scientific experiments on what was to be the last shuttle mission before the National Aeronautic and Space Administration (NASA) began launching components of an international space station. (Space station launch, p. 929)

Glenn Background

Glenn was a forty-year-old Marine Corps lieutenant colonel and one of the original seven U.S. astronauts when he rode into space February 20, 1962, aboard Friendship 7, *a cramped Mercury space capsule. Glenn orbited the Earth just three times on a mission lasting five hours. He was only the third person to orbit the Earth in space (the Soviet Union already had sent two cosmonauts around the globe), and his exploit was an exhilarating experience for Americans. His boyish grin, freckles, and apparent modesty endeared Glenn to the nation and made him an instant hero. Playing down his own role, Glenn later said the importance of his flight was that it "came at a time when we [the United States] desperately needed a success, and it was a success."*

NASA did not offer Glenn a second chance to go into space; one report held that President John F. Kennedy was so concerned about Glenn's value as a national hero that he feared risking him on another space mission. Glenn retired from the astronaut corps and in 1964 made his first attempt at elected office. He ran for the U.S. Senate as a Democrat from his native Ohio, but he slipped and fell in a bathroom, injuring an inner ear, and was forced to withdraw before the primary election. Glenn went into business and ran again for the Senate in 1970, losing the primary. He finally won a Senate seat in 1974.

Ohio voters traditionally were reluctant to allow senators to serve more than one or two terms, but Glenn won reelection three times. He developed a reputation as a hard-working legislator who avoided center stage and enjoyed tackling the details of such complex issues as arms control and nuclear nonproliferation. Glenn ran for the Democratic presidential nomination in 1984 against Vice President Walter Mondale, but he was not an effective campaigner and withdrew during the primaries.

Throughout his public career, Glenn never made a secret of his desire to return to space. In the mid-1990s, as he contemplated closing out his Senate career, Glenn began appealing to NASA for another space mission. He offered himself as a "guinea pig" for space experiments about aspects of the aging process (such as bone and muscle deterioration) that might have beneficial results for senior citizens. His years in Washington had taught him a few things about lobbying the federal government, and he had no need to send NASA a resume and personal references. Even so, he had to be persistent to overcome initial skepticism at the space agency about the value of Glenn's suggested experiments. On January 16, NASA administrator Daniel S. Goldin announced his decision to grant Glenn his wish, referring to the senator as "the most tenacious human being on the face of the planet." Although still a senator, Glenn spent much of 1998 preparing for his space mission, originally scheduled for early October.

An Encore Mission

There was no shortage of skeptics who criticized Glenn's return to space as a publicity gimmick by NASA. Some commentators also suggested that the administration was offering Glenn a reward for defending President Bill Clinton and Vice President Al Gore during 1997 Senate hearings on campaign finance abuses in the 1996 elections. Young Americans, who had not experienced the euphoria surrounding Glenn's first mission thirty-six years earlier, were puzzled by the sudden uproar in 1998 over a return trip to space by the senator.

When the date for Glenn's mission approached, the skepticism faded into the background as millions of Americans felt a renewed sense of excitement from the early days of the space age. On television, the Internet, and in newspapers and magazines, black-and-white images of John Glenn the youthful astronaut of 1962 suddenly appeared alongside new color photographs of an aging man undergoing intensive training at the Johnson Space Center in Houston.

On October 29 President Clinton, members of Congress, and several of Glenn's former astronaut colleagues joined a crowd estimated at 250,000 at the Kennedy Space Center and surrounding areas for the launching of the Discovery mission. After two brief delays, the shuttle lifted off at 2:19 p.m. as NASA announcer Lisa Malone exclaimed: "Lift off of Discovery with a crew of six astronaut heroes and one American legend." Later in the day, in his first radio communication with mission control, an excited Glenn paraphrased his 1962 reaction to zero-gravity: "A trite old statement: zero-G and I feel fine."

On the third day of the mission, October 31, Glenn and mission commander Curtis Brown answered questions posed by school students, among them several students at John Glenn High School in Glenn's home town, New Concord, Ohio. Several students asked about such practical matters as eating and sleeping in space, but many of the questions concerned science and the experiments Glenn was conducting. The next day, Glenn and Brown conducted their first full-scale news conference during the mission. With more than fifty years experience as a pilot, Glenn admitted he had "snuck up" to the pilot's seat in the shuttle cockpit "to see how it feels." Glenn said he spent much of his time conducting research projects and undergoing tests, including giving numerous samples of blood.

Discovery returned safely November 7 after 134 orbits of the planet, a journey of 3.6 million miles. At a news conference the following day, Glenn stood in front of a giant photograph of himself in 1962 and declared that he was "probably 95 or 98 percent back to normal."

Throughout his public career, Glenn was famous for his rambling, fact-filled answers to reporters' questions. But at that first news conference after the flight, he gave an eloquent answer when an elderly reporter asked if the shuttle flight showed that there was hope for "people of my generation." Glenn responded: "There is a lot of hope. You should run your life not by the calendar but how you feel, and what your interests are and ambitions. Old folks have dreams and ambitions too, like everybody else. Don't sit on a couch someplace, that's my attitude."

NASA officials said they were pleased with the publicity bonanza that Glenn's flight had reaped for the space program. On the day Discovery returned to Earth, NASA administrator Goldin told the legion of reporters at the landing site: "Don't wait for Senator Glenn's third launch before you come back."

Glenn and his six Discovery colleagues were honored with a ticker-tape parade down Broadway in New York City on November 16, but the turnout was a modest echo of the enormous celebration that New York had put on for Glenn the first time, in March 1962.

In December Glenn made a final round of appearances back in Ohio before retiring from the Senate. NASA said preliminary results of Glenn's experiments aboard Discovery would be released in 1999.

Following are excerpts from a question-and-answer session given October 31, 1998, by Discovery mission commander Curtis Brown and Sen. John Glenn, D-Ohio, and school children from Ohio and Virginia:

Okay, Okay, Curt/John, this is Kathy. I do just want to warn you that your 5th grade teacher, Miss Smith, has joined us here in Columbus and she has got a paper on her lap; I think she is going to be grading your questions. Here comes the first one for you now.

[The first questions were posed by students assembled at the Center of Science and Industry in Columbus, Ohio.]

Senator Glenn, were you more nervous being the first American to orbit the Earth or to be the oldest man ever in space?
[Sarah Ravely, Holleh Moheimani, Janara Walker—Whetstone High School]

Senator Glenn: Well I think they are both great things to participate in and I had a wonderful time the first time. I think I was probably more nervous back in those days because we did not know much about spaceflight in those days; we were sort of feeling our way and finding out what would happen to the human body in space and now we are putting the whole thing to work for everybody up here so I think I was a little more nervous the first time.

Commander Brown, how fast can the spaceship go?
[Jessica Davis, Amber Whitney, Laura Stereff, Gloria Minard—Delta Middle School]

Commander Brown: Well, it can go pretty fast; actually as we lifted off, we had it wide open and it kept accelerating until it ran out of gas; but right now we are traveling about 17,500 miles per hour; to put it in terms—if you were five miles away from something, every second you would travel you would travel that five miles. So, if it were five miles to get to school, in one second you would be there.

Senator Glenn, how has technology advanced since Freedom 7?
[Jeremy Fry, DJ Danhauer, Kristopher Bechtel, Brock Burkholder—Delta Middle School]

Senator Glenn: Well, it is hardly even comparable because it has advanced so much, and we are learning so much. We point out all the time that it is a benefit to people right there on Earth to all the things we are learning. The science is not just learning how to do this, how to get into space. Out of the 83 different research experiments we have on board on this particular flight and they are designed for a whole bunch of different things on the body and medical things and material matters and new medicines that are being experimented with and a whole bunch of things that benefit everybody right there. So it has changed a great deal since way back in those days in '62.

Commander Brown, when blasting off, do you actually feel the inertia? Do you feel like we often see on TV when the faces are distorted?
[Mubarak Abdurraqib, David Tynan, Keith Smith—Whetstone High School]

Commander Brown: Well, first of all we astronauts, we don't really refer to it as blasting off because that sounds pretty uncontrollable. During the launch we call it launching; during the launch you don't really have the distortion on your faces, that is more for the movies, I think. But we do feel the acceleration of the Orbiter, it is a very amazing vehicle; we jump off the launch pad and accelerate right up to 2-1/2 G's which means you would weight 2-1/2 times what you weight here on Earth. By the time we get up to orbital speed, we're up to around 3 G's which means if you weighed 100 pounds on the ground, you would weigh 300 pounds during that ascent, so we do feel the G's at acceleration, but it doesn't distort our face or anything.

Senator Glenn, would microgravity lessen the effects of certain types of joint pain?
[Scott Gordon, Jack Gaynor, Jordon Given, Jared Bruner—Delta Middle School]

Senator Glenn: I think it would because when you no longer have the same kind of pressure on those joints quite a lot of pain should be much lessened. You know we are studying a lot of things up here trying to—now one of the experiments I started out on yesterday was on OSTEO; it is an experiment that looks into bone structure and so on. We hope to learn a lot that will benefit a lot of people right on Earth.

Senator Glenn, do you feel younger when you are in space?
[Jeff Butz, Matt Lewis, Dawn VanDyke, Jessica Burger—Delta Middle School]

Senator Glenn: I guess I feel young all the time. That is the reason I volunteered to come up here. But it is a great place up here and I am having a great time and of course, I am the oldest on the trip here. But we are getting along fine and I guess it is an advantage up here for older folks because in zero G you can move around much more easily. I have been bumping my head a lot on things as I float around here, but that is all right, that is par for the course up here. It is a great thing; we just came over Florida a few minutes ago here and looking down on that and all the Bahama Islands just laid out like on a map is just absolutely beautiful, so that is enough to keep you young up here if you were not when you got here.

Senator Glenn, is it difficult to eat and swallow food?
[Sarin Chhevy, Alysia Stevenson—Briggs High School]

Senator Glenn: Difficult to eat and swallow food? No, in fact back in 1962 that is one of the things that the people thought might be very difficult and I was to eat some food on that flight just to see if I could swallow and now we have all kinds of food. I think there are 42 kinds of food and drinks we have here. Each person can pick their own menu coming up here. It is quite easy to swallow, but you have to be quite careful you don't let the food get loose or it floats all over the place. Yesterday I was eating a little bit of oatmeal for breakfast and some of it got loose and instead of falling down on my chest as it would have on Earth, it came up and stuck right in the middle of my glasses. So, you have to learn how to eat and drink a little differently up here and don't let things get loose or they will float all over the place. . . .

Senator Glenn, do you think space travel will have a positive effect on people with osteoporosis or other degenerative diseases?
[Binh Nguyen, Edwayne Howard, T.J. Seabrooks—Columbus Alternative High School, Brookhaven High School, Columbus Academic High School]

Senator Glenn: Yes, I think we can learn a lot about these diseases and I really do. We are just doing some experiments on that now. I mentioned OSTEO, the experiment we are dealing with here a few minutes ago that shows how different cells combine or break down and I think that can have a possible very big effect on medical experiments into the future. . . .

Senator Glenn, does your family support you going back into space?
[Becky Tanner, Danielle Pacey, Lindsey McCulloch, Erin Brehm—Delta Middle School]

Senator Glenn: Yes, although I must say my wife, Annie, was a little bit dubious about the whole project when we were starting out. But as she sat in on some of the classes and learned more about what we were trying to do, the experiments trying to run, and the benefit they will be to everybody on Earth, why she became very enthusiastic about this, particularly my part. You know we have some 34 million Americans that are over 65 right now and that is due to go up to about 100 million over the next 50 years. The same thing is going on all over the world; it has been called "the graying of nations." So the more we can learn about some of the problems of the elderly and some of the similarities between younger astronauts up here and older folks like me where there may be a correlation between body activities, we can learn more about what causes some of these things to happen. So, Annie has become very enthusiastic about this as well as the other members of the family also.

[The following questions were posed by students assembled at the Newseum in Arlington, Virginia.]

Commander Brown, how are everyday experiences, such as sneezing, different in a microgravity environment?
[Emily Gould, Ronald Holsey, Elaine Mermick—Montgomery Blair High School]

Commander Brown: Well there is a number of things that are different; every day activities that you take for granted on Earth once you come to the weightless environment are actually more difficult or more fun sometimes depending on how you look at them. On Earth if you ever drop anything or let go of anything, it will fall to the floor; up here in space if you drop something or let go of something, it will float away and you will not be able to find it for a while. But as for sneezing and those kinds of things—with seven people here in the Orbiter that is kind of a small compartment so if you get ready to sneeze, we definitely recommend putting your hand over your mouth because as you know, that stuff will not fall to the floor.

Senator Glenn, since you are experimenting to observe the effects of space on the elderly, what about observing the effects of space travel on the young?

[Susannah Rosenblatt, Kyle Casazza, Andy Miller—Thomas Jefferson High School for Science & Technology]

Senator Glenn: Well, I think we will get around to that sometime. But you know you have to be careful because you know we are talking for younger people, really young people we would be talking about their bones being formed and their bodies changing very rapidly as part of the growth process and up here that might be interfered with rather drastically. So I think we have to be rather careful on that, but perhaps that will be looked into sometime in the future. That is not an easy area to get into. Now I am at the other end of the spectrum here where bones and things like that are breaking down and we are trying to find out why things like that occur. But it is a good question and maybe sometime they will send younger people up, but I think they would have to be very, very careful before they do that.

Commander Brown, what experiments should be done on the International Space Station that may have potential benefits for mankind?

[Douglas Merrell, Paul Merrell, Craig Neely—Thomas Jefferson High School for Science & Technology]

Commander Brown: That is a very good question. We are right on the verge of launching the elements of the Space Station and starting to assemble the Station. The things that we are going to do up there are going to be very beneficial to the folks on Earth. We are going to do similar things that we do here on the Shuttle; however, on the Station we will be able to leave the experiments running for weeks and months and even years. It is kind of like going on a camping trip; if you go there and get all settled in, about the time you start to enjoy yourself you have to pack up and go home. And that is the problem with the Shuttle compared with the Space Station. Once we get here and get all organized and start doing our science, producing it, it is time to pack up and go home. Whereas the Station will always continue research for many, many months; so that is one of our big benefits with the Station.

Senator Glenn, what role do you think America's youth should play in the development of the space program? How should they get involved?

[Bladimir Castillo, Matthew Smith, Claudia Cabrera—Montgomery Blair High School]

Senator Glenn: Well, I think the youth should play a very major role because the future belongs to all the young people today and what we are learning is of benefit to all the people today, I mean into the future. So, I am glad to see so many people interested in what is going on. I think some of the interest has come from things like TV programs that are fiction like Star Trek and things like that, but you know I find when I go around talking to schools and places like that most of the young people are tremendously interested in space and they know a lot more about it than most of their parents do as a matter of fact because they have followed it closer and learned more about it in school. Much of what we will learn in the future will come from space. There will be a tremendous benefit to all the young people today.

Commander Brown, what foods do you eat and do you enjoy them?
[David Umoren, Sabrina Mack, Khadijah Dark—H.D. Woodson]

Commander Brown: Actually there are a lot of foods we can pick from, the foods I picked on my flight, one of our favorites is shrimp cocktail. We had that actually last night at dinner; we had some beefsteak, some spaghetti and meat sauce, teriyaki chicken, and for dessert we had some applesauce, some pudding, and some candy. So, we have a large variety of food and it's a long way from the first flight of Senator Glenn's—so we got much, much better food. As for do we enjoy them—that is one of the more fun times of the Orbiter life is when we all get together on mid deck and put our food together and tell stories and enjoy ourselves during the evening meal.

Senator Glenn, how do you feel about being part of a scientific experiment as compared to being a pioneer in space travel?
[Bernice Mireku, Katy Califa, Mary Anne Anderson—Montgomery Blair High School]

Senator Glenn: Well, I like both of them and back in the days when we were just going up for the first time and I was taking part in that, it was a brand new experience. And this time around we are on a different area of research. I am just glad to see things progress this far over these last 36 years. As we go across, I am looking out the window right now at the horizon way off some 2,000 miles away, I guess from this altitude we are at up here. It is a great experience to get up here and look down like this, but the major thing is all the research we are doing is of benefit to everybody right there on the ground. That is the main thing. I want to make sure we say hello to everybody around Washington we know and at the Newseum. I was there not long ago at a program; that is quite a place you have there, glad they could use that as a center for this kind of communication. Also, COSI in Columbus with Kathy Sullivan where we were at a little while ago. They are probably still listening. I am just glad we had a chance to get so many young people on today and answer a few questions. I wish you all could be up here with us and experience some of this, and look out and just see this; participate in doing some of the research we are involved in also.

Commander Brown, what impact has the space exploration had on the environment?
[Tiffany Thomas, Felicia Comfort, Jessica Rucker, Le'kia King—H.D. Woodson]

Commander Brown: I think the space business has had a big impact on our environment and how we live our everyday life. A perfect example is just last week we were worried about Hurricane Mitch, a very, very strong hurricane down in the Caribbean. It wasn't that many years ago that we didn't have any satellites that were up in space to look down and give us warning and help us prepare and hopefully save a lot of lives from the impending storm. So that is a perfect example of our space exploration. Also, our farmers these days worry about their crops and their yields. We now have satellites up in space that can look down on these crops and help us determine if they are getting the right amount of fertilizer; if they are getting the right amount of water, and what their yield is going to be—so those kinds of things have a huge impact into our every day lives. And the funny part about this is that people don't realize that without the space program that would not have come about.

Senator Glenn, are you concerned that the bone loss, which results from being in space, will be permanent because an older person cannot regenerate bones as well?
[Christian Cloke, Naomi Gottlieb-Miller, Joseph Lee—Montgomery Blair High School]

Senator Glenn: Yes, I am concerned about it, but I am concerned mainly that we do the research on it that we are doing up here so we can look into how we can prevent that sort of thing. I think the length of time that we are going to be up on this flight, just about 9 days, is not enough that my bones will weaken to the point where it will be a danger to me. But they are measuring that very, very carefully. We had very specific measurements of my bone and structure and everything several times over, repeated several times. We will do that postflight also to see exactly what the effect has been. So that is one of the purposes of this flight is to see whether there is as much change in the body of older persons as there is in the younger people who are the rest of the crew up here now. We have a long history at NASA in the data bank of younger people and this will be the first addition of someone older like myself to that. I think that eventually we will probably send more older folks up to continue this, so that a real data base, my being just a data point of one. I think look more to this in the future and I think my main task is to make sure we get back that good information so we can see the benefit of the value of it so we can then make the decision to send more older folks up and get a real data base that can lead on to medical studies that can be of benefit to everyone.

(for both) How does microgravity affect your ability to comprehend/process information?
[Shaheer Hussam, Karita Sharma, Justin Moran—Thomas Jefferson High School for Science & Technology]

Commander Brown: I don't think it really has that much effect on how to comprehend or understand; process information. But I use an example—it is kind of like riding in a car as a passenger reading a book and trying to concentrate on the book. There are a lot of things around you happening and a lot of things going by the windows, lot of people may be talking in the car.

Those kinds of things do affect how your space operations happen so you have to be focused and concentrate and be very attentive to what you are doing up here.

Senator Glenn: It is a very good question; one that the scientists have been looking into. One of the experiments I will be dealing with is cognitive responses. On a computer I will be measured on my reaction times and how they compare with all the many times I ran through the same thing on the ground; how well I remember things over a period of time. It is a test that takes about 25 minutes to run and we did it many times on the ground and now we will do it many times up here while we are in flight. I will do the same thing when I get back to Houston to see how the changes, what changes were in flight and postflight also. So, it is called cognitive response—reaction time, memory time, and comprehensive time—so that is one of the things we are looking at.

[The following questions were posed by students at John Glenn High School, New Concord, Ohio.]

Commander Brown, you probably grew up looking up to men like John Glenn. How does it feel to work with such an American hero?
[Jeremy Parrish, Jeff Moffitt, Kyle Cunningham—John Glenn High School]

Commander Brown: You put it right. When I was growing up, Senator Glenn was definitely one of my heroes. I was pretty young at that time, but as we grew up obviously the history books and the events of the times you understood how that all got started and Senator Glenn was a big part of that. How does it feel to work with Senator Glenn? Well, I think I speak for the whole crew, it has been our pleasure and we are honored to have him aboard. But he is one of the crew members and he has been very professional and energetic and motivated. He has done some fantastic work in the last few days and I expect the same out of him in the next 7. As of right now, he is a member of the crew and we are all teammates and you know it takes a team to get a job done and we are having a good team up here.

Senator Glenn, who were your influences in your childhood and why? Do you consider yourself a positive influence on today's youth?
[J. Kane Nick Thomas, Paul Steinberger—John Glenn High School]

Senator Glenn: . . . .[T]here were many people who had an influence on my life and I think the main thing is to just take them seriously, study as hard as you can and then you are ready for whatever opportunities occur. I was lucky to have some good opportunities in my life time, this being one of them. I had the background to make the most out of it, that is the most important thing.

Senator Glenn, with all the experiments being performed, we've been told that you have 21 leads hooked to you, some with needles—how has this affected your mobility? Do you feel any pain?
[Sarah Felde, Larissa Chisnar, Renee Morrow—John Glenn High School]

Senator Glenn: Well, I don't have the 21 leads yet; we are just going to start that at our next sleep period. I do have 21, they will measure electroencephalogram, your brain waves, eye movements; EKG, your heart recordings; and body core temperature, a whole bunch of things. There are 21 different measurements being made. Now that is all contained, being recorded in a little machine that is on a strap around your waist; you just float around with it. It doesn't really hurt your mobility, but it is a funny thing to look at because to look at it you are looking at some kind of bug with all this head net on and all the different leads that come off of your head. But it is not that uncomfortable; I think it would be more comfortable here in space than when it was tested down on the ground where you had to try and sleep several different nights with all that rigged on. I think it will probably be better up here. But we will have that; I will be running those experiments over the next several days repeating them over and over. . . .

Senator Glenn, was it worth waiting 36 years to be able to fly in space again?
[Jamie Archer, Andy Winner, Jennie Troendly—John Glenn High School]

Senator Glenn: Yes, a one word answer, I guess, I should stop there. It was indeed; you know I wanted to go up again back then and wasn't permitted to do so back in the old days, so I had always hoped to go again. As I got older, I thought that would lessen my chances ever going up again, but going back about 4 years ago is when we got in some of these possibilities of doing some aging studies here and the National Institute of Aging got behind it as well as NASA and set up the projects that they thought would be of benefit. I was able to qualify physically for this so I feel very fortunate to be able to come up again. Things are so different now than they were back then, but it is a very worthwhile experience and my answer is yes it was worth waiting for. Yes, it certainly was. Not just as a personal experience, but also in looking forward to some of the research we are going to do that is going to benefit everybody back there on Earth, benefit all of us into the future. Before we run out of time here, let me wish y'all at John Glenn High the very, very best . We will be seeing you back there one of these days. I am sure I will be back in New Concord, maybe we can come out and talk to all of you in person there one of these days. . . .

November

UN REPORT ON DAMAGE FROM HURRICANE MITCH
November 3, 1998

Two major hurricanes pounded parts of the Caribbean and Central America in the fall of 1998, killing thousands of people and causing billions of dollars worth of damage. The four nations that were hardest hit—the Dominican Republic, Haiti, Honduras, and Nicaragua—already were among the most impoverished in the western hemisphere. The storms caused so much damage that experts said it would be years, possibly even a decade or more in some cases, before the affected nations could recover.

The 1998 hurricane season was one of the most severe in memory. U.S. officials said there were fourteen named storms between June and November; ten were hurricanes, of which three were major hurricanes (with winds in excess of 110 miles per hour, capable of causing major damage). The most concentrated period was thirty-five days starting August 19, when there were ten named storms. Among those storms was Tropical Storm Charley, which hit just north of Corpus Christi, Texas, on August 22, dumping as much as eighteen inches of rain on the Rio Grande valley and causing extensive flooding, especially around Del Rio, Texas. Four days later, Hurricane Bonnie caused considerable damage in North Carolina.

Especially in the Caribbean and Central America, the devastation of natural disasters was made worse by the works of man. Deforestation of mountains helped create rivers of water that inundated scores of villages, many of them in floodplains. Poorly constructed roadways, bridges, and buildings were unable to stand up to the ravages of storms.

Hurricane Georges

A category four hurricane, Georges swept across the northern Caribbean and the Gulf of Mexico September 20–22. Georges attacked the eastern Caribbean islands of St. Kitts and Nevis, Antigua, and Barbuda, then hit the U.S. Virgin Islands and Puerto Rico. Heavy winds and flooding caused moderate damage in all those areas. St. Kitts was the most seriously affected, largely because of damage to its tourism industry.

Georges landed next on the large island of Hispaniola, divided between Haiti in the west and the Dominican Republic in the east. Heavy winds, floods, and mud slides destroyed roads, bridges, and entire communities in both countries. The Dominican Republic suffered the greatest damage. Relief organizations and the U.S. Agency for International Development reported that several hundred thousand residents of the Dominican Republic were forced from their homes, nearly all roads and most bridges were damaged, and 90 percent of the agricultural sector suffered major losses.

Casualty estimates varied according to agencies, but by mid-October the most reliable estimates appeared to be that the storm had killed about 150 people in Haiti and 200 to 300 people in the Dominican Republic. International aid officials complained that the government in the Dominican Republic had ignored warnings about the hurricane and refused to alert the population—a factor that could have contributed to the death toll.

Georges hit Cuba on September 23–24, then made landfalls in the Florida Keys and the Gulf states of Mississippi, Alabama, and Louisiana. The storm dropped as much as thirty inches of rain on parts of the Gulf Coast, causing massive floods and triggering tornadoes. Few people were killed in the United States, but property damage was estimated in the hundreds of millions of dollars.

Hurricane Mitch

Georges would have been considered a serious hurricane in any year, but its devastation paled in comparison with Mitch, which struck Central America and the Gulf of Mexico a month later. Mitch was a category five hurricane, the most powerful type possible. At its peak October 26–27 Mitch had sustained winds of 180 miles an hour, with gusts up to 200 miles an hour. It tied Camille, of 1969, as the fourth strongest Atlantic hurricane of the century.

Mitch formed in the southern Caribbean as a tropical storm on October 17, then developed into a hurricane that moved westward across Central America. Mitch brought torrential rains that caused massive floods and mud slides, especially in Honduras and Nicaragua. After moving into the Pacific Ocean, Mitch regenerated as a tropical storm and turned eastward, crossing over the Gulf of Mexico and hitting South Florida on November 4–5.

U.S. officials called Mitch the deadliest hurricane since a storm that struck the Antilles in 1780 killing more than 20,000 people. Depending on the estimate, Mitch was responsible for as many as 10,000 deaths, and the storm forced an estimated 3 million people to flee their homes. Jerry Jarrell, of the U.S. National Hurricane Center, said the destruction caused by Mitch was "of Biblical proportions" not because of the winds—which had calmed by the time the storm hit Central America on October 29—but because the storm stalled over the region "and dumped feet, not inches, of rain in a mountainous area."

Honduras suffered the brunt of the storm, primarily because of flooding. On December 2 the Honduran government published an estimated death toll of more than 5,600, with another 8,000 still missing. Aid officials and journalists reported that both figures might be inflated, however, because the Honduran government had no accurate means of counting the dead and missing. Nearly 2 million Hondurans had been displaced in the immediate aftermath of the storm; as of early December an estimated 300,000 of them were still living in temporary shelters.

Mitch destroyed or severely damaged much of the infrastructure that made Honduras a civilized society. Roads, bridges, schools, water and sewer systems, and at least 70,000 houses were destroyed. The government planned to reopen the school system in February 1999, but thousands of classrooms were destroyed and hundreds of others were still occupied in December by people needing temporary shelter. The Honduran government estimated total damage at more than $4 billion. One of the few bright spots for Honduras was that most of the nation's staple crops, such as beans and corn, suffered only modest damage because they were grown on high ground.

The damage in neighboring Nicaragua was modest only in comparison with the tragedy of Honduras. Floods and mud slides caused extensive damage, particularly in the northwestern section of the country. The single most damaging mud slide was caused when rains filled the crater of Casitas volcano in western Nicaragua; the crater's wall collapsed, sending a giant tide of mud down the mountainside, burying two towns and several villages and killing an estimated 1,500 people. As of mid-November, the national emergency commission estimated that more than 2,800 people had died, and more than 31,000 houses had been destroyed. The government assessed total damage at about $1.5 billion.

El Salvador and Guatemala also suffered extensive damage from floods and mud slides caused by Mitch. In El Salvador, the death toll was estimated at 200 to 400, with about 10,000 houses destroyed. Guatemala estimated its death toll at about 250 people, with approximately 19,000 houses destroyed or heavily damaged. In both countries hundreds of roads and bridges were destroyed.

In all the affected countries, one of the long-term effects of the storm was expected to be the loss of jobs. Agricultural production was the most severely affected. In Guatemala and Honduras nearly all the banana and coffee crops—the nations' chief exports—were destroyed.

Tens of thousands of Central Americans fled their homes before, during, and after Mitch pounded the region. Many made their way to the United States. The Clinton administration announced December 30 that an estimated 150,000 Hondurans and Nicaraguans who had illegally sought refuge in the United States following the hurricane would be allowed to stay for up to eighteen months. Another 500,000 Salvadorans and Guatemalans would be allowed to stay until March 1999, when the government would begin deportation proceedings against them if they remained in the United States. Administration officials said they were giving more generous treatment to refugees from Honduras and Nicaragua because those countries had been hardest hit by the storm.

Relief Efforts

Government and private relief agencies from the United States and many other countries pumped hundreds of millions of dollars worth of aid into Caribbean and Central American nations devastated by Georges and Mitch. By December, U.S. government relief efforts totaled nearly $50 million for Haiti and the Dominican Republic and $263 million for Central America. By mid-November more than five thousand U.S. military personnel were aiding rescue and reconstruction efforts in Central America. The United Nations in December appealed for international contributions of $153 million for aid to be channeled to Central American nations through various UN humanitarian and relief agencies.

Many nations and international agencies also announced plans to forgive or relax payment requirements on debts owed by some of the affected nations, especially Honduras and Nicaragua. Even before Mitch, both countries had accumulated relatively large international debts that they were struggling to pay off. According to some estimates, about one-third of Nicaragua's exports went to pay off foreign debt totaling about $6 billion. The United States was among countries pledging debt relief; in December Washington canceled $40 million in past loans owed by the Honduran government. The "Paris Club," an international consortium of lender nations, on December 10 announced plans to defer payments by Honduras and Nicaragua on several billion dollars worth of loans until long-term arrangements could be made to reduce those debts.

Following are excerpts from "UN Honduras Situation Report No. 1," issued November 3, 1998, by the United Nations Hurricane Mitch Information Center:

Situation

General

Since Monday October 26, 1998, when Mitch first hit northeast Honduras, the floods have peaked affecting all of the country's 18 Provinces. According to official estimates, this disaster situation is unprecedented, and exceeds the combined effects of all previous floods and hurricanes in the country's history, in human, economic and social terms. Relief workers indicate that at least 1.5 million people are suffering from the impact of very severe flooding and landslides. Villages have been completely destroyed and losses in the agricultural sector are extensive. Government actions have been taken to alleviate the situation of many communities, but leaving, nevertheless, vast needs for international assistance.

Effects on Humans

At least 1.5 million persons are affected, of which more than 560,000 have been displaced. Death estimates have already reached 5,000, and are expected to exceed 10,000 eventually. Considering the age structure of the Honduran population, most of these will probably be youth and children.

As water levels recede, a serious public health hazard—reflected mainly in the lack of access to potable water—is becoming an overriding concern. UN agencies have appealed for commonly accepted priority requirements, namely shelter materials, food, blankets, as well as support for community coping mechanisms.

Infrastructure

- **Bridges:** At last count, COPECO [the Honduran Committee for Emergency Contingencies] has confirmed that 93 bridges were destroyed. Another 75 bridges have been damaged. A bridge destroyed in the southern region supported a fuel pipeline, which has led to rationing of gasoline in Tegucigalpa and the central region. News that communication through the main road linking the two largest cities—Tegucigalpa and San Pedro Sula—has been restored, create some hope that shortages of fuel and other commodities may be overcome in the central region soon.
- **Roads:** Most major cities are isolated by land. The country is also isolated from its neighbors and will probably remain so for weeks. Throughout the country roads have been submerged under water or cut off by landslides. The full extent of the damage to the roads has thus not been assessed yet. Distribution of food supplies, rescue operations, transportation, and commercial distribution is severely limited. The number of destroyed bridges and the severity of the damage to the road and water supply systems is a near-fatal blow to the economy, and presents the potential for heightening shortages of food, water and fuel in the next few weeks.
- **Ports:** The international airport in San Pedro Sula is still under water. Tegucigalpa, La Ceiba, and Roatan international airports are open after several days of inactivity. Information on the situation of seaports is less well known but is expected to be bad, especially for those ports on the Caribbean coast.
- **Buildings:** The level of damage to buildings and other infrastructure is uncertain, but widespread damage is reported in cities where the press and assistance workers have been able to access. In Tegucigalpa, for example, this includes government offices (The Ministry of Education was totally flooded), hospitals (the Social Security hospital was flooded up to the third floor), schools, as well as many commercial buildings.
- **Households:** The current estimate for destroyed households nationwide reaches 10,000, and another 20,000 are flooded or damaged. These estimates are expected to increase substantially, as the full extent of the damage is still unknown, especially for non-communicated areas.

Social Sector

- **Health:** Relief workers estimate that in addition to death casualties, an indeterminate number of injured persons exist in the country. A large number of health workers are part of the affected populations. Reserve medicines have been used to cope with emergencies. The social Security hospital in Tegucigalpa is out of services and the public hospital in San Lorenzo is totally damaged. Several health units in rural areas are out of service due to lack of electricity and potable water, as well as infrastructure damage. The required investment to repair and restore health services is estimated at about US$ 10 million. Sewage and solid waste disposal systems are insufficient thereby making the implementation of emergency programs a priority. The main diseases reported are common cold, bronchitis, pneumonia, diarrhea, skin infections, conjunctivitis, and depressive anxiety. An increase in vector-transmitted diseases is foreseen, mainly dengue, malaria, leptospirosis, water and food transmitted diseases, especially if sanitary measures are not taken into consideration in shelters and by affected population.

- **Other public services:** Potable water systems in most of the large cities are out of service. Only the San Pedro Sula and Juticalpa systems are working, and only at 50% capacity. The extension of electricity services damage is uncertain. The capital required to repair the potable water systems in the country is estimated by SANAA [National System of Aqueducts] to reach $300 million. Sewage systems have been damaged and garbage disposal has been suspended in the larger cities. This creates the potential for further health hazards and epidemic outbreaks.

- **Communications:** International access is limited. Phone services were initially restricted, but are being gradually restored. The extent of damage is not clear, although it is evident that communications in flooded areas has been hampered.

- **Education:** The infrastructure and educational facilities of schools throughout the country is precarious. The Ministry of Education was flooded with waters reaching offices on the second floor. The level of damage on educational records, information systems, equipment and other materials is critical. The whole education system in the country is expected to experience a compete restructuring as a consequence of the disaster situation. Regular education activities are not expected to be restored for at least a few more weeks.

Productive Sectors

- **Agriculture and food security:** President Flores indicated that more than 70% of agricultural production has been lost. Export crops have been severely hit. Expert sources report that the full banana crop is lost. The oil palm crop is over 60% lost, especially young replacement plantations. Substantial losses have also been reported in melon and pineapple crops. The coffee harvest,—that was just starting—will suffer losses. This in turn will result in significant economic losses as coffee is Honduras' main source of foreign exchange. Livestock loss is estimated to reach up to 75%. Major losses are reported in the fishing industry sector, particularly shrimp cultivation. Basic staple crops (maize, beans, rice) have been seriously affected which will impact food security of all of the population of Honduras in the coming months. The overall effect of these damages to the economy are difficult to measure now, but will be substantial as the export capacity of the country has been severely affected, with the implications for lost jobs, foreign exchange, and reduction in tax collections by the government.

- **Industry/commerce:** The maquiladora sector, located primarily in the northern Sula Valley was not seriously hurt. Most of the factories are reported back in operation.
- **Financial sector:** The cumulative impact of all losses in the productive and commercial sectors will seriously affect the banking and financial sectors. This involves the slowing down of financial activities because of hampered production, and the precarious situation faced by many farmers and agro-industries with bank loans. Somewhat offsetting some of these effects will be the collection of insurance benefits by some industries, especially from machinery and equipment insurance.
- **Tourism:** The tourism infrastructure has suffered considerably. But the impact of cancellations for the imminent high season, especially in the Bay Islands, will have the most adverse effect on this sector.

Macro Impact

Emin Barjum, the President of the Central Bank, stated: " . . . According to preliminary estimates, the drop of the GDP for 1998 and 1999 will be about 7% and 8%, respectively, from previous GDP growth estimates for these years. . . ." This would take the country to a GDP growth of 0–1%, effectively wiping out any hopes for an improvement of the economic condition of Honduras, already one of the poorest countries in the Western Hemisphere.

National Response

Institutional Arrangements

COPECO is the Permanent Contingency Commission. It started working immediately to coordinate rescue and relief operations.

- A newer Commission with a wider mandate was installed on October 30th to organize assistance. Responsibilities were assigned to different Ministers and key government officials by province. The Ministries of Foreign Affairs and SETCO are coordinating all international aid.

In addition to actions for immediate relief and rescue operations, several government agencies are currently assessing the extent of the damage and making estimates of the needs for reconstruction and rehabilitation of the country's infrastructure.

Municipalities: Are working with civil society in organizing self-support groups.

Local NGO's [non-governmental organizations]: Are assisting in organizing food distribution in shelters. At local level diverse assistance actions are being taken, including aid to senior citizens, handicapped, etc.

On-Site International Response

UN System

From the very beginning, the UN system has responded quickly to provide assistance to government agencies involved in relief and rescue operations. This has included emergency food and water supplies, clothing, and logistical support. . . .

The UN was in a position to respond swiftly with food relief assistance with existing inventories. There is however technical constraints related to inappropriate capacity for food preparation in the shelters under current conditions. There are limited food-assistance supplies that can be used and more are being sought in the international community. Other supplies in the country such as the strategic food-security reserves of the government are also limited and likely to be damaged in part. Food assistance programs also need a complex and expensive logistical transportation system.

Innovative and creative alternative approaches are being sought to ensure that the minimum caloric intake of 1780–1800 is provided to the affected populations. An estimated 45 million rations are needed for sustain for three months the 500,000 people who have been affected by the hurricane.

Specific actions taken by UN agencies to contribute to Honduras emergency relief efforts:

- Food: Over 400,000 persons attended for four days from October 25, 1998.
- Water: About 65,000 persons attended for five weeks starting October 26, 1998.
- Clothing: 2,150 blankets for women and children; 150 rain kits for municipality relief workers.
- Logistical support: Assistance to ministry of Health to establish an operations center
- Support to organization and functioning of health brigades in Tegucigalpa
- Immediate technical assistance for the evaluation and disaster management in the health sector.
- Fuel (5,000 gallons) for transport at Health Ministry . . .
- Support to transport of food to the northern region for 340,000 persons (CODER)
- Support to transport of food and clothing in Tegucigalpa and the southern region. . . .
- Computer system for registry and coordination of international assistance to the health sector.

An Office of Coordination of Humanitarian Affaires (OCHA) mission is already in the country to make an assessment of emergency needs.

Bilateral Donors

- Cayman Islands (clothing and medicine)
- Colombia (rubber boats)
- Germany (food supplies)
- Great Britain (Evaluation mission and aid for Guanaja)
- Italy (food supplies)
- Japan (tents and potable water equipment)
- Japan, Spain and Switzerland (cooking kits)
- Spain (pasta boxes)
- Sweden (substantial assistance funds)
- Switzerland (Clorox, US$ 500,000 in assistance funds)
- USA (food supplies, funds, plastic rolls and Clorox pills)

International NGO's

- Care (food supplies)

Assistance

Priority Relief Needs

A main concern for the UN is contributing to solve the problem of water supply in the country. Efforts to facilitate the task of SANAA (the public water supply institution) are under way. The UN will provide support to increase from 10-25 the number of trucks distributing water in the capital. Studies are being carried out to evaluate the needs for pipes and other equipment to restore the water distribution systems. Funds are also urgently needed to build temporary bridges to restore communications, as 93 bridges are reported to have been destroyed nationwide.

Immediate relief supply is required for three months (shelter, food, etc.) for 500,000 displaced people.

Reconstruction

As estimates of the damage to infrastructure are still incomplete, it is difficult to make an assessment of the capital flows in international cooperation needed to start rebuilding the country's infrastructure. Some have expressed that at least US$1,000 million will be needed for reconstruction, although this figure may increase in the coming days.

An UNDP/ECLAC [UN Development Program] mission is to arrive shortly to carry out a comprehensive assessment of the damages.

A FAO [Food and Agriculture Organization] mission will assess the impact on the productive sector of the country, with emphasis on the food security situation, as a consequence of the disaster.

Several World Bank missions are in the country, assessing the extent of the damages and the long term financing needed for the country's reconstruction.

An Interamerican Development Bank mission is also in the country assessing the damages and the needs of the country for financing of the reconstruction process.

Other information

A state of emergency was declared in the country to prevent looting and other illegal activities. A curfew is in effect throughout the country from 8:00 PM to 6:00 AM for at least 15 days.

The pubic government apparatus is expected to be back to work on November 3, after a two-day break given by the authorities for public workers to deal with family and community situations. . . .

SPEAKER GINGRICH ON
RESIGNATION FROM CONGRESS
November 6, 1998

Newt Gingrich, the aggressively partisan Republican who led his party to a stunning 1994 electoral victory that gave them control of Congress, suffered an equally stunning fall from personal power just four years later. Gingrich gambled that voters would reward Republicans in the 1998 midterm elections for pursuing the impeachment of President Bill Clinton, but they chose instead to reduce the Republican majority in the House. Facing an internal challenge from his own party, Gingrich chose to surrender rather than fight. Gingrich announced November 6 that he would not seek a third term as Speaker of the House of Representatives and would resign the congressional seat from Georgia to which he had just been reelected for the eleventh time.

Robert Livingston, a Louisiana Republican who had helped push Gingrich from power, quickly consolidated support within the party to succeed Gingrich. But just six weeks later—even before he had been elected Speaker—Livingston dramatically announced his own resignation. As the House was about to impeach Clinton because of charges relating to his affair with Monica Lewinsky, Livingston was forced to acknowledge his own past marital infidelities, and so he joined Gingrich in leaving Congress for the good of his party. (Livingston resignation, p. 951)

This extraordinary turn of events capped one of the most tumultuous years in the two centuries of Washington politics. Despite his impending impeachment, Clinton remained highly popular; his adversaries in the House Republican leadership were the ones thrown into disarray.

Gingrich: Rise and Fall

Few figures in twentieth century American politics were more polarizing than Newt Gingrich. Fellow conservative Republicans admired his devotion to conservative ideology and his combative, hard-edged attacks on Democrats. Democrats loathed him for the same reasons, and they successfully portrayed Gingrich to the general public as a partisan extremist. For most of his four years as Speaker, Gingrich was the nation's most unpopular political figure.

Gingrich first came to national attention in 1989, when—as a backbench Republican—he raised questions about the ethics of House Speaker Jim Wright, a Texas Democrat. An investigation based on Gingrich's allegations found that Wright had violated House rules in transactions concerning royalties for a book he had written. Wright became the first Speaker to resign from Congress, and Gingrich was an instant hero among his fellow Republicans. (Wright resignation, Historic Documents of 1989, p. 239)

In October 1993 Robert H. Michel, the House Republican leader, announced his intention not to seek reelection. Gingrich was the overwhelming choice to succeed him. For the 1994 midterm elections, Gingrich crafted a politically brilliant strategy centered around a series of popular campaign pledges, including a balanced budget, welfare reform, tax cuts, and term limits for members of Congress. Gingrich put these pledges into a "Contract with America," signed by nearly all Republican candidates for the House. Democrats, who had controlled Congress for forty years, were especially vulnerable in 1994 because of Clinton's failed effort to enact a complex health care reform plan. The Gingrich strategy worked: Republicans took control of both houses of Congress (even though Senate Republicans had distanced themselves from the Contract with America), and Gingrich was suddenly the most powerful politician in the land.

The seeds of Gingrich's eventual downfall were planted in his first year in office. First, several Democrats sought to give Gingrich a taste of the medicine he had administered to Wright. They filed complaints with the House ethics committee alleging improprieties in a $4.5 million book deal he had signed and in his use of tax-exempt donations to promote a partisan course he sponsored in Georgia colleges. Perhaps more importantly, Gingrich failed to translate his Contract with America into law. The House passed parts of the agenda contained in the contract, but the Senate failed to follow through on much of it. By late 1995 it was clear that the contract had been a better election-year gimmick than a recipe for legislation.

In the fall of 1995 Gingrich made the first of several serious miscalculations that would prove his undoing. Believing that the public was ready for a confrontation over the federal budget deficit, Gingrich forced repeated shutdowns of much of the federal government. Rather than rallying to his call for fiscal austerity, the public reacted with alarm. Gingrich was forced to retreat in his budget battle with Clinton. The president's sudden ability to face down the Republicans helped ensure his reelection in 1996. The Republicans lost nine seats in the House, but retained control of both chambers of Congress. (Budget battles, Historic Documents of 1995, p. 737)

In the meantime, the ethics investigation of Gingrich found numerous violations of House rules and federal tax laws. As he began his second term as Speaker, in January 1997, Gingrich was forced to undergo the humiliating experience of being reprimanded by the full House and ordered to *pay a $300,000 fine.* (Ethics investigations, Historic Documents of 1996, p. 838; Historic Documents of 1997, p. 3)

Six months later a group of renegade House Republicans discussed how to force Gingrich from the Speakership. Their plot folded when Gingrich and his lieutenants discovered it, but the episode drew attention to deepening divisions within the party. Many of the hard-line conservatives Gingrich had helped bring into the House had become disenchanted with his leadership. Battered by the budget battle, the ethics inquiry, and Clinton's reelection, Gingrich by 1997 had lost much of the partisan edge that his fellow conservatives had admired in earlier years. Gingrich had discovered that passing legislation in so fractious an institution as Congress meant having to compromise with the opposition—a concept he had spurned when he had no leadership responsibilities and that some of his fellow conservatives still rejected. Republicans of all ideological stripes were frustrated that Gingrich had become so controversial that he was a drag on the party. Many senior Republicans, including committee chairmen, chafed at numerous procedural restrictions Gingrich imposed upon them.

Also in 1997, congressional Republican leaders reached agreement with Clinton on a blueprint for reaching a balanced budget by 2002. In one sense, the agreement represented a high point for the Republicans because it meant Clinton and the Democrats had accepted a key component of the 1994 Contract with America. But the agreement also deprived Republicans of what for years had been one of their most potent issues against "tax and spend" Democrats. Many observers said the Republicans no longer seemed to have much of an agenda that could capture public attention. (Balanced budget agreement, Historic Documents of 1997, p. 602)

Gingrich in 1998

The sudden emergence in January 1998 of a sex scandal involving Clinton and a former White House intern at first appeared to be a political gift to the Republicans. With midterm elections looming, Clinton once again seemed vulnerable. During the first half of the year, while Clinton was engaged in legal battles with Independent Counsel Kenneth W. Starr, most Republicans held their fire but quietly laid plans for taking political advantage of the situation. Gingrich was uncharacteristically silent on the sex scandal until April, when he promised he would mention it in every speech "as long as I am Speaker."

As the scandal progressed, Republicans began talking more openly about the possibility of impeachment. When the independent counsel presented a report of his findings to the House Judiciary Committee in September, the House Republican leadership was ready to take on the president, both through the impeachment process and at the ballot box.

Despite opinion polls showing Clinton's continuing popularity, Gingrich calculated that voters would reward Republicans for pursuing the president on the Lewinsky scandal. As late as election day, November 2, Gingrich was confidently predicting that Republicans would pick up as many as twenty House seats; Senate Republicans were hoping to pick up the five seats they needed for a sixty-vote "filibuster-proof" majority. But the voters had other ideas. They dealt Republicans a setback in both chambers of Congress. Republicans lost five seats in the House—narrowing their margin of majority to just six seats—and they managed only to hold onto their five-seat majority in the Senate. Not since 1934 had a party out of the White House lost seats in an off-year election.

Gingrich and some of his fellow Republican leaders tried to put the best face on the election results, but the actions of other Republicans came closer to demonstrating the truth of the situation. On November 5 Livingston, who had been Gingrich's hand-picked chairman of the powerful Appropriations Committee, told Gingrich he was considering challenging his mentor for the Speakership; Livingston publicly announced his challenge the following day. Several key House leaders who had pledged Gingrich continuing support suddenly changed their minds, most importantly Bill Archer of Texas, chairman of the Ways and Means Committee.

From his home in Roswell, Georgia, Gingrich frantically called several dozen House Republicans and discovered that his support was slipping away. Then in two conference calls with his closest supporters, Gingrich announced that he would step down as Speaker and leave Congress when his current term ended in January 1999. Several Republicans who participated in those calls said Gingrich referred to his colleagues as "cannibals" and blamed the news media for focusing on his troubles and preventing voters from hearing the Republican "message." One Republican said Gingrich expressed the hope that his resignation would help "purge some of the poison" in the party.

In a written statement announcing his decision, Gingrich alluded to the party's internal problems that had led to his downfall. "I urge my colleagues to pick leaders who can both reconcile and discipline, who can work together and communicate effectively," he said.

Reaction to Gingrich's Fall

For the most part, Republicans responded to Gingrich's announcement with a combination of surprise and relief. Even those who had been among his strongest supporters seemed to acknowledge that Gingrich has lost much of his effectiveness and the time had come for someone else to lead. Rep. Sherwood Boehlert, R-N.Y., who had often strayed from the party line on key issues, said members who participated in the conference calls with Gingrich had expressed "shock and surprise" at Gingrich's announcement, but also had expressed appreciation to him "for leading us to the Promised Land."

Livingston, whose challenge had been the final straw in toppling the Speaker, offered this summary of Gingrich's problems: "Revolutionizing takes some talents, many talents. My friend, Newt Gingrich, brought those talents to bear, put the Republicans in the majority. Day-to-day governing takes others."

Some Republicans said Gingrich was merely the victim of a divided party. "It wasn't a problem with leadership. It was a problem of follower-ship," said Mike Parker, of Mississippi, who was about to retire from the House. "We had all these people [in the House] who couldn't get along."

Many Democrats used Gingrich's fall from power as an opportunity to remind voters why he had been so unpopular. House Minority Leader Richard A. Gephardt, of Missouri, expressed hope that "whoever succeeds Newt Gingrich as Speaker will immediately begin the process of repairing the damage that was wrought on this institution over the last four years."

At a November 9 dinner sponsored by GOPAC, a Republican political action committee, Gingrich delivered what many observers called his "valedictory" address. He said he had stepped down as Speaker to spare his party further turmoil. "It became clear to me that if I were to remain in the House I would be an excuse for divisiveness and factionalism," Gingrich told his fellow Republicans. "The ideas are too big, the issues are too important for any one person to put their office above the good of the country and the party."

Gingrich urged Republicans to unite behind Livingston as Speaker. Republicans were prepared to do just that until, on December 19, Livingston also stepped from power once his past marital infidelities became public knowledge.

Following is the text of a written statement by Rep. Newt Gingrich, R-Ga., released November 6, 1998, announcing his intention to step down as Speaker of the House of Representatives, followed by excerpts from a speech delivered November 9, 1998, by Gingrich at a dinner sponsored by GOPAC, a Republican political action committee:

GINGRICH'S RESIGNATION AS SPEAKER

Today I have reached a difficult personal decision. I will not be a candidate for the speaker of the 106th Congress.

The Republican conference needs to be unified, and it is time for me to move forward where I believe I still have a significant role to play for our country and our party.

My party will have my full support, and I will do all I can to help us win in 2000.

I urge my colleagues to pick leaders who can both reconcile and discipline, who can work together and communicate effectively. They have my prayers and my thoughts as they undertake this task.

I want to thank everyone whose friendship and support has made these years enjoyable. Marianne and I are grateful to the citizens of Georgia who gave us the wonderful opportunity to represent them and to my Republican colleagues who became our extended family.

Thank you and God bless you.

GINGRICH'S GOPAC SPEECH

You know, it was a tremendous honor to become the first Republican Speaker since 1954. And it was, if anything, an even greater honor to be the first Republican Speaker to be reelected since 1928.

As speaker, I've had the privilege of leading the People's House which I believe is the centerpiece of freedom on the entire planet. . . . Let me say without apology that as speaker, I sought to aggressively lead toward our goals and our vision.

We never had a big majority, but we always stood for big ideas. And that is what made us different.

And let me say that if every Republican will pull together with Bob Livingston [R-La.], these big ideas will continue to move us forward. This is another step in the right direction. If all of us work in the right way for the year 2000, I think that this party will be stronger, that we will achieve more and that we can build on the foundation of three consecutive elections, the first in 70 years to be won by the House Republican party.

And let me say, and I hope we can drive this home to every Republican, every conservative and every taxpayer in this country— the image of a President Al Gore and a Democratic Congress should be more than enough to unify us in two years of very diligent hard work.

Because our ideas are so important, our majority is so vital and the challenge of the year 2000 is so important, I had to make a decisive choice between my own interests and what I believe to be the more important cause of the country and my party. On Friday, it became clear to me that if I were to remain in the House, I would be an excuse for divisiveness and factionalism.

The ideas are too big, the issues are too important for any one person to put their office above the good of the country and the party. That is why I announced my retirement on Friday. I had worked 40 years, since I was a 15 years high school freshman in 1958 to achieve a House Republican majority. Through GOPAC and the National Republican Congressional Campaign Committee, I had criss-crossed the country for candidates for 20 years. In the week before the election, I was in 14 states. So when I thank my family, I mean it. . . .

Precisely because I owe so much to so many hard workers, I believe that both in the House and as a party, we need new energy, new teamwork, and a willingness to work together as one team. As for me, public office is not the same as public service. There are many avenues for a public life beyond the speakership. Marianne and I will continue to work as active citizens in every way that we can.

I'm encouraged to stay active by the example of my father's 27 years in the United States Army defending freedom. Dad's generation has been captured in the movie *Saving Private Ryan*. My father knew from World War II, Korea, and Vietnam that freedom takes courage, responsibility, and effort. As a child of the United States Army, the words "duty, honor, country" came to have deep meaning for me. Precisely because of that army tradition of subordinating yourself to the larger cause and the higher calling, it was easy to make Friday's decision.

I had to ask what was right for my country, for my party, and only then for myself.

So now, as Marianne and I look forward, we must ask: What is our duty as citizens? I believe it is first to recognize and remind people how much we Republican have achieved. President Ronald Reagan cut taxes and regulations, reestablished the entrepreneurial spirit of job creation, created 15 years of job growth. And the truth is, we are living today in a Reagan prosperity.

President Reagan reestablished the pride of the American people in their own country, their own history, and their own traditions. President rebuilt the American military and defeated the Soviet empire.

And it was, as President Reagan said, a truly evil empire. President Bush helped manage the collapse of the Soviet empire without a war. President Bush assembled 27 nations to decisively defeat Iraq in a four-day ground campaign.

Then, in 1994, the House Republicans created a totally positive campaign message—a message which appeared in *TV Guide* with no pictures and with no attacks on President Clinton or the Democrats. This is the original "Contract with America."

We promised to get a vote on 10 items. The original contract is tiny print that's totally positive, and says near the side: "A campaign promise is one thing; a signed contract is quite another."

And this contract made 10 commitments and said we get a vote on all 10; did not say we could pass all 10, 'cause we knew we couldn't. Two of them were constitutional amendments that took 290 votes. But we voted, not in the first 100 days as we promised, but as Dick Armey reminded me, in the first 93 days, on every single item, and we passed all but one of them. . . . Let me also remind you, we did a lot more than the contract. One of the things I'm proudest of that I think in the long run will do more to change Washington and more to get beyond the lobbyist than everything done by Common Cause in 30 years, was the simple act of creating the Thomas system at the Library of Congress so that every bill introduced in the House, every debate, every committee report, every hearing shows up on the Internet. And one of the proudest days I had in the last Congress was when Chairman Bill Archer [R-Texas] stood on the floor of the House, introduced the tax bill, and announced the website it was available at within 30 seconds and that afternoon 200,000 citizens accessed the entire tax bill without a lobbyist, without paying for it and without cutting down any trees for the paper. . . .

You know, it's important to remember that in this city, no one wants to recognize that when we became a majority in January 1995, the projection for the deficits after the 1991, 1993 tax increase, after the Democrats so-called deficit reduction, the projection of the deficits over the next 11 years was $3,100,000,000,000 of additional debt. Today, the projection is for a surplus of $1,600,000,000,000.

And I think we Republicans have to establish a couple of principals. First, that surplus belongs to the American taxpayer, not the Washington bureaucrat.

Second, let's be honest with the American people. If you leave a trillion dollars sitting around Washington, D.C., the liberals are going to spend it. So let's get it back home at a rate faster than Al Gore and [Sen.] Teddy Kennedy [D-Mass.] can invent new bureaucracies.

And there's a very practical first goal. And that is to use a large part of the surplus to save Social Security by creating a personal Social Security savings account for every worker who pays the FICA tax. This is a great historic opportunity, and I hope the president will not flinch from joining with Republicans in saving Social Security. We have an opportunity, if we use part of the surplus intelligently right now, to create savings accounts where the poorest worker in Washington, D.C., when they go to work and they pay a FICA tax, will automatically get a savings account with a tax free build up of interest over their working lifetime.

You save Social Security for my mother and my mother-in-law, without raising taxes and without cutting benefits; you improve and strengthen Social Security for the baby boomers; and you guarantee that their children have a savings account that no Washington politician can touch and no Washington politician can ever use. And you do it in a way which eliminates class warfare in America because every citizen who works becomes a saver and an investor and we ought to do it now. . . . And I think the second principle is simple. The American people are overtaxed and if there's a surplus it belongs to them, and we should return it as tax cuts. And I believe that there are frankly three very obvious tax cuts. First, we should eliminate the penalty on work after 65 years of age. It is exactly wrong in the information age to discourage people who are going to live longer from staying active, and we ought to simply eliminate all penalties on work after 65.

Second, we should pass a capital gains tax cut at once—of another five percent, to continue economic growth. It will actually pay for itself in the first several years, and if you scored it accurately, it probably pays for itself permanently, as Alan Greenspan has suggested, when he said it was the most destructive tax we have. But the world economy is teetering and we need the American economy strong enough to pull the world out of a recession. And we should pass a tax cut early next year, and I hope the president will propose, since he's advising the Japanese to cut taxes, it wouldn't hurt for him to advise the Americans to cut taxes, and let's cut taxes ourselves.

And third, we should eliminate completely the death tax. It is a socially destructive tax. . . . Finally, I want to say, we need a national debate as Americans, not Republicans or Democrats, as Americans. A national debate, and a very simple proposition. The proposition was brought Dwight Eisenhower back from Europe in 1952. And I'll say it bluntly, my side of it. The United States has no choice except to lead the world because there is no replacement.

We need to lead the world in terms of the financial system, because the truth is if we weren't trying to keep the financial system operating, it would have crashed probably two or three times in the last four years. And that doesn't mean we're doing it all right. And it doesn't mean that I approve of everything that's being done. But we had better be thinking about it, because if we're not thinking about it, there is no one on the planet with the prestige and the impact to solve the problem of how you deal with what has become a totally different world. Real time, worldwide, 24 hours a day, trillions of dollars in transactions dwarfing any government system. A different world than we had even 20 years ago. And we had better be prepared to lead in it, because no one else can.

Second, we need to have a big debate in this country about whether we're going to be in the world market, or whether we're going to see the world collapse into oligarchy and protectionism. We have had a very, very good run for 50 years because we have been in the world. We have traded worldwide. We have bought worldwide. We have the lowest consumer prices in the world. We are the largest exporter in the world. The world has been good to us and we have been good to the world. But somebody needs to stand up and say, you go to your home town and find how many jobs are going to die if we end up in a protectionist world. You go to your communities and find out how much poorer are we going to be 10 years from now if we go back to Smoot Hauley. And we need to be able to look people in the eye and say, those of you who want your children to live in a poorer country, in a poorer world with more divisions, fine. You are for that kind of protectionism.

But those of you who believe that with the right investment in science, the right reform of education, the right tax code, the right litigation reforms, the United States can compete anywhere in the world with anyone if we have a government that's prepared to be tough minded in its negotiation, then we want to open the world market to give our children and grandchildren and even richer future with even greater choices. And that's a very major part of our leadership.

But there's a third part of leadership, and I think we Republicans are particularly positioned over the last half century to insist on it. We are the only country capable of providing military security on a worldwide basis. Remember I said earlier, the world is dangerous.

Well, whether it's bin Laden and the terrorists or Saddam Hussein and biological and chemical and nuclear weapons or the North Koreans trying to test a multi-stage missile, the world is dangerous. And somebody ought to have the courage to tell the truth to the American people. We do not today have a national missile defense system. If one missile were fired by one dictator or one terrorist or one Russian silo were taken over by one group, and they fired one weapon of mass destruction at an American city, our satellites could report the launch. We'd have 30 minutes of warning, and we do not tonight have anything which could stop that missile. It is dereliction beyond belief.

And in fact, it's worst than that. Our liberal friends will tell you that we have a treaty with the Soviet Union which blocks us from defending America. Now I want to ask you how bad your fantasy life has to be that you think that a treaty with a country which died in 1991 is more important than stopping an Iraqi missile in 1999?

Let me just say, that I think there are two principles in defense without a doubt. First, that the American people and our allies and our troops in the field, deserve a worldwide system that involves the best intelligence, the best prevention, the best missile defense that science and engineering can design, not the best that the lawyers and diplomats will tolerate. And we owe it to our children to defend them.

And second, the young man—maybe I feel this particularly strongly because of the years my dad served his country—the young man or woman has the courage and the patriotism to serve in the uniform of the United States of America, they deserve the best equipment, the best training and overwhelming force to win decisively with minimum loss of American lives.

Let me just close by pointing out to all of you, particularly those of you who have been around awhile and who've been out campaigning for many years. We've actually come a long way—in governorships, in the Senate, in the House, in county commissions, the mayor of New York, the mayor of Los Angeles. It's amazing how far this party has come in the last 25 years. Some days we have setbacks, some days we do better. But the long term general direction, I believe is very positive. I'm convinced that if we reach out to all of the American people in every neighborhood, share with them our vision and our values, offer common sense specific solutions, we can have a remarkable future for our children and our grandchildren.

Let me just say to all of you that with your help, as I leave public office and rejoin the ranks of active citizenship, the venue changes and the cause lives on.

Thank you, good luck, and God bless you.

ATTORNEY GENERAL ON ANTIABORTION VIOLENCE
November 9, 1998

A surge of violence and attacks against abortion providers in 1998 raised renewed concerns among law enforcement officials and abortion-rights activists about the activities of antiabortion extremists. The most serious incidents during the year were the January 29 bombing of a Birmingham, Alabama, clinic that killed a security guard, and the October 23 murder of Barnett Slepian, a well-known abortion doctor in the Buffalo, New York, area.

Largely in response to the Slepian murder, Attorney General Janet Reno on November 9 announced the establishment of a federal task force to investigate violence at abortion clinics and related facilities nationwide. Reno also announced an offer of a $500,000 reward for information leading to the arrest and conviction of Slepian's killer.

Antiabortion Violence

In a news conference November 9, Reno listed a series of attacks and threats against abortion clinics—most of them in southern and border states. During the summer, she said, about twenty clinics in Florida, Louisiana, and Texas had been attacked with stink bombs made with isobutyric acid. In the fall, two clinics in North Carolina were the targets of arson and attempted bombings. In late October and early November clinics in Indiana, Kansas, Kentucky, and Tennessee received threatening letters falsely claiming to contain elements of the deadly anthrax nerve gas; two of the clinics also received packages containing fake bombs.

"These attacks and others seek to undermine a woman's basic constitutional right—the right to reproductive health care," Reno said. "And while some people may oppose that right, no one should ever use violence to impede it."

Reno announced the formation of a special investigative group, the National Task Force on Violence Against Health Care Providers, to investigate possible connections between the various attacks on abortion clinics.

Reno said the task force also would help local officials in their investiga-
tions of anticlinic violence, identify clinics that might be at risk, and coor-
dinate other activities to prevent violence against abortion clinics and
other types of health care facilities. The task force was to include represen-
tatives from the Justice Department, FBI, and other federal agencies.

The task force was an expanded version of an investigative effort that
Reno created in 1994 after an abortion doctor was murdered near a clinic
in Pensacola, Florida. That task force operated until 1996 and brought
twenty-seven criminal cases and seventeen civil cases. One job of the ear-
lier task force was to determine whether there was a national conspiracy
to attack abortion clinics; the task force reported that it was unable to iden-
tify such a conspiracy. While refusing to say in 1998 whether she believed
such a conspiracy existed, Reno said the government would "leave no stone
unturned in trying to find any connection" between the various attacks on
abortion providers.

Also in 1994 Congress enacted a law, the Free Access to Clinic Entrances
act (known as FACE), which made it a federal crime to obstruct the
entrances of abortion clinics and to use force or threats to injure or inter-
fere with clinic employees or patients. (Access law, Historic Documents of
1994, p. 313)

By late 1998 Justice Department officials said they believed that the
access law and the work of the earlier task force had contributed to a
decline in violence against abortion clinics in 1994 and 1995. However,
they said antiabortion violence had been on the rise again since 1996,
including the bombings of twelve abortion clinics in 1997.

On January 29, 1998, Robert "Sandy" Sanderson, an off-duty police offi-
cer employed as a security guard, was killed in a bomb explosion at an
abortion clinic in Birmingham, Alabama; a clinic nurse also was severely
wounded by the bomb, which was laced with hundreds of nails that tore
into her and cost her an eye. Federal officials in July launched a massive
manhunt for Eric Robert Rudolph, the suspect in that case, who was
believed to be hiding in the Appalachian mountains. The Justice Depart-
ment on October 14 also charged Rudolph in connection with three bomb-
ings in the Atlanta area, including an attack on an abortion clinic and the
July 1996 bombing at the city's Olympic Park during the summer
Olympics. The department offered a $1 million reward for information
leading to the arrest and conviction of Rudolph. (Olympic bombing, Historic
Documents of 1996, p. 445)

The Slepian Murder

Slepian was killed on the evening of October 23 by a rifle shot fired
through the kitchen window of his home in Amherst, New York, a suburb of
Buffalo. One of the most prominent abortion doctors in upstate New York,
Slepian for years had been the target of abuse by antiabortion protesters.

Investigators said Slepian's murder bore several similarities to nonfa-
tal attacks between 1994 and 1997 against other abortion doctors in west-

ern New York and Canada. In those cases, rifle shots were fired at the doctors through windows in their homes. The previous attacks all took place in late October or early November, leading investigators to believe they might have been related to the Canadian holiday Remembrance Day (similar to Veterans Day in the United States), which some antiabortion groups used to commemorate children who had been aborted.

Federal officials were searching for James Charles Koop, a resident of northern Vermont and a prominent antiabortion protester, whose car allegedly was seen near Slepian's house at the time of the shooting. Officials said Koop was being sought as a material witness in the case.

Late-Term Abortions

During 1998 antiabortion forces failed for the second time in two years to win enactment of federal legislation banning a controversial late-term abortion procedure. Both chambers of Congress in 1997 and 1998 had passed legislation prohibiting a procedure in which a fetus was partially delivered before being aborted. Abortion opponents called the procedure "infanticide" and used graphic descriptions of it in an effort to rally the public against abortion in general. Others, including President Bill Clinton, said the procedure occasionally was necessary to protect the life or health of the mother.

Clinton vetoed the abortion ban in both 1997 and 1998, and both times Congress failed to overturn his veto. The closest vote took place in the Senate on September 19, when supporters of the ban gathered sixty-four votes to overturn the veto, just three votes short of the required two-thirds majority.

On March 23 the Supreme Court took its first action ever on the late-term abortion question, letting stand a lower court ruling that overturned an Ohio law prohibiting the procedure. A federal appeals court had ruled that the Ohio law contained such a broad restriction on the procedure that it had the effect of prohibiting nearly all abortions during the second trimester of a pregnancy.

Twenty-one other states had passed legislation banning late-term abortions. However, the Ohio law was unusual in its wording, and so the Supreme Court's stance on it, in a 6–3 decision, was not generally seen as indicating how the Court might act if presented with a case involving the underlying issue of late-term abortions.

Bishops Step Up Antiabortion Crusade

One of the pillars of the antiabortion community, the Roman Catholic Church, escalated its campaign against abortion, euthanasia, and physician-assisted suicide. At its semiannual meeting November 18, the National Conference of Roman Catholic Bishops overwhelmingly adopted a detailed statement urging all Catholics—including religious leaders, private citizens, and public officials—to speak out against what were described as "attacks on innocent human life."

In keeping with teachings of the church, the bishops had routinely taken positions opposing abortion, but they had never before declared that Catholics had a duty to press that view in the public arena. "As chief teachers of the church, we must therefore explain, persuade, correct and admonish those in leadership positions who contradict the Gospel of life through their actions and policies," the bishops said in their statement. The statement also appealed to those in public life, saying: "We urge those Catholic officials who choose to depart from Church teaching on the inviolability of human life in their public life to consider the consequences for their own spiritual well-being, as well as the scandal they risk by leading others into serious sin."

The bishops adopted the document, entitled "Living the Gospel of Life: A Challenge to American Catholics," by a vote of 217–30. Some bishops expressed reservations about taking such an assertive stance, but the majority clearly embraced the view of William Cardinal Keeler, archbishop of Baltimore, who described the statement as a "theology of persuasion." A few bishops took a more combative stance, among them Bernard Cardinal Law, archbishop of Boston, who said the governor and both senators of Massachusetts were "wrong" to support abortion, while "only I am right" in opposing it.

Following are excerpts from a news conference held November 9, 1998, by Attorney General Janet Reno and other U.S. law enforcement officials to announcement the formation of a National Task Force on Violence Against Health Care Providers:

Attorney General Janet Reno: Last month, Americans everywhere were outraged over the death of Dr. Barnett Slepian. While standing in his kitchen in Amherst, New York, Dr. Slepian was shot by a high-powered rifle fired through his window. Sadly, this was not the first such shooting. There were others. And it was just one more act of violence in a series of savage attacks against providers of reproductive health care.

Over the summer, about 20 clinics in Florida, Louisiana and Texas were attacked with acid. This fall, two clinics in North Carolina were the victims of arson and attempting bombings. And just last week, clinics in Indiana, Tennessee, Kansas and Kentucky were sent letters falsely claiming to contain anthrax.

These attacks and others seek to undermine a woman's basic constitutional right—the right to reproductive health care. And while some people may oppose that right, no one should ever use violence to impede it.

Since I became attorney general, I have been very concerned about this issue. That's why in 1994 I established a task force to investigate whether a national conspiracy existed. While that task force developed several successful criminal cases, it did not develop evidence sufficient to prosecute a national conspiracy.

Two years later, the efforts of the task force were taken over by the Civil Rights Division, which continued the work of prosecuting clinic violence cases. In addition, local working groups were set up by U.S. attorneys across the country.

To date, these efforts have made a difference. Since 1994, we have brought 27 criminal cases and 17 civil cases. But in light of the recent increase in clinic violence, we are taking new steps.

Today I am announcing the creation of the National Task Force Against Violence Against Health Care Providers. Its mission is very important. First, it will lead a national investigative effort, focusing on connections that may exist between individuals engaged in these acts.

Secondly, it will assist local officials in the investigation and prosecution of clinic violence.

Third, it will identify at-risk clinics and develop ways to make those clinics more secure.

Fourth, it will establish a centralized national database for all information on clinic violence.

Fifth, it will assist the many working groups already hard at work across the country.

And sixth, it will oversee a program to train law enforcement on the best ways to handle clinic cases. Two training sessions are already scheduled for December.

As part of our stepped-up effort, today I have also directed all U.S. attorneys to convene their local working groups to assess the security needs of clinics in their communities.

The National Clinic Violence Task Force will be led by the head of the Civil Rights Division, Bill Lann Lee. It will be staffed by attorneys from the Civil Rights and Criminal Divisions, as well as agents from the FBI, ATF, U.S. Marshal Service and the U.S. Postal Service. And it will work closely with state and local officials in deciding how best to proceed with each incident.

Treasury Secretary Robert Rubin will be represented on the task force by Assistant Secretary Elizabeth Bresee. And Mr. Lee will consult with her concerning his oversight of the task force.

Today I am announcing a reward of $500,000 for information leading to the arrest and conviction of the person or persons responsible for the murder of Dr. Slepian. Anyone with information or tips in that shooting should call 1-800-281-1184. That's 1-800-281-1184.

One thing must be very, very clear: There is no excuse for this violence. And working together with state and local law enforcement, we will do everything we can to prevent it. . . . I would now like to introduce the deputy director of the FBI, Robert Bryant.

Robert Bryant, Deputy Director of the FBI: America cannot tolerate violence, whether it is violence on the street, violence in the workplace or violence to health care providers. America has seen over the last several months buteric acid attacks in the South—from Florida to Texas. In middle America, anthrax threat letters have been received from Ohio to Kansas. And doctors have been shot at and wounded in Canada and the United States.

The attorney general just announced a task force to address this violence, which will not be tolerated.

This task force is set up to prevent and stop violence. The FBI will be joining the Department of Justice, and our federal, state and local agencies and our Canadian colleagues to ensure that all Americans have safe access to health service providers as well as any other lawfully protected activity.

FBI special agents and analysts—including those experienced in criminal and civil investigations of the Freedom of Access to Clinic Entrances, or better known as the FACE Act—also experienced in domestic terrorism matters and in matters involving weapons of mass destruction as they relate to abortion clinics will join with the attorney general's task force.

The concrete steps that will be taken—the FBI personnel will oversee ongoing FBI investigations of violence directed against abortion providers and/or threats of violence directed toward the same, and it will integrate all FBI intelligence information together with details from investigations, including the FACE and other databases.

I would just like to say in closing that this task force and the FBI are dedicated to the prevention of violence and to ensure the protection of constitutional rights.

GERMAN CHANCELLOR ON
HIS LEGISLATIVE PLANS
November 10, 1998

Helmut Kohl, the longest serving Western democratic leader in modern history, lost a bid in September to serve a fifth term as chancellor of Germany. After sixteen years in office, Kohl, leader of the right-of-center Christian Democratic Party, was ousted by Gerhard Schroeder, governor of Lower Saxony and the leader of the left-of-center Social Democratic Party. Schroeder took office October 27, heading a coalition government that included the environmentalist Green Party.

Kohl entered office in 1982 as a lightly regarded party functionary, but in time he assembled an enormous legacy equaled by few leaders in the post-World War II era. He oversaw the unification of West and East Germany in 1990, maintained and even expanded Germany's role as the chief economic and political powerhouse of Europe, and led the way toward the economic integration of Europe.

But in the end, most observers agreed, Kohl simply overreached. He promised too much at the time of German unification, and his failure to deliver on those promises contributed to an economic malaise that fueled voter dissatisfaction in 1998. Kohl also tried to stay in office too long. Many Germans, including thousands of longtime Christian Democrats, believed that sixteen years in office was long enough, and they were ready for a change.

The victorious Schroeder's biggest challenge, once in office, was to follow through on his campaign promises to do something about Germany's high unemployment rate, which was hovering around 11 percent. He pressed the new European Central Bank for interest rate cuts and called for an alliance between business and labor to create more jobs. (European interest rates, p. 271)

Schroeder's victory meant that the four largest countries in Europe all had left-of-center governments for the first time in decades. In the previous two years, voters in France, Great Britain, and Italy had ousted conservative governments and replaced them with social democratic parties.

Schroeder and the new British prime minister, Tony Blair, sought to model their appeal after Bill Clinton's centrist approach in the United States. Blair promised a "New Britain." Schroeder campaigned on a slogan of the "New Middle." (Blair victory, Historic Documents of 1997, p. 277)

Kohl's Legacy

The unification of Germany was the central achievement of Kohl's tenure. Since the end of World War II, Germany had been divided into two sectors separated by concrete, steel, and ideological barriers: the West, at first dominated by the victorious allies of the war but later a forward-looking, confident democracy that developed the most vibrant economy in Europe; and the East, a dictatorship under the thumb of the Soviet Union with a backwards economy barely able to feed and clothe its citizens.

All that changed in 1989 when a reformist Soviet leader, Mikhail Gorbachev, relaxed Moscow's grip on Eastern Europe and the citizens of Berlin began tearing down the infamous wall that separated them. Seizing a historic opportunity, Kohl flew to Moscow and won a landmark agreement from Gorbachev. The Soviets would allow the unification of the two Germanies, and West Germany would pay for the repatriation of 380,000 Soviet troops based in East Germany. The two Germanies were formally reunited on October 3, 1990, and Kohl was a hero. (Fall of the Berlin Wall, Historic Documents of 1989, p. 625; Treaty on German unification, Historic Documents of 1990, p. 599; Unification ceremony, Historic Documents of 1990, p. 681)

In the euphoria of the moment, Kohl planted the seeds of an economic and social upheaval that would prove his undoing in 1998. He promised West Germans that unification would be virtually cost-free, most important that they would not have to pay additional taxes for it. He promised East Germans that they would soon enjoy the high standard of living of their Western compatriots. One of Kohl's most costly gestures was to allow East Germans to exchange their nearly worthless currency for West German marks on a one-for-one basis. Many critics said Kohl could not keep his promises and still maintain strong economic growth, and they were proved right. By the late 1990s unification was costing Germany more than $100 billion annually, Kohl was forced to raise taxes to pay for it, and Germans on both sides of the former border were feeling economic stress.

The pain of unification was most noticeable in the east, where hundreds of antiquated factories had been closed. East Germans who had lived under communism for nearly a half-century suddenly found themselves having to compete in a modern, capitalist economy. Billions of dollars worth of business and government investments in the east helped ease the situation but could not totally overcome the social and economic costs of integrating two substantially different societies.

Even before unification, West Germany had developed an expensive welfare system and a culture of government-mandated benefits for workers (including medical care and lengthy vacations). The Bonn government also heavily subsidized inefficient industries, just to keep them afloat. West Germany could afford to pay for those comforts, but a united Germany could not.

By 1998 the unemployment rate in the former East Germany was 17 percent, about double that in the west, and many East Germans were angry and disillusioned. The growth of fringe political parties was one of the results. The former East German Communist Party, renamed the Party of Democratic Socialism, enjoyed a spurt of popularity, as did several right-wing nationalist parties.

Despite warning signs, Kohl pressed ahead with plans to seek reelection in 1998. Many of his supporters said he should have stepped aside in favor of his deputy, Wolfgang Schauble, ranked in the polls at the time as the country's most popular politician, but Kohl clearly enjoyed being the "Chancellor of German Unity."

Schroeder's Rise to Power

Schroeder was born into poverty in Lower Saxony on April 7, 1944, just a year before the end of World War II. His father was one of millions of German soldiers killed in the war. Schroeder worked his way through school, dabbling in the left-wing politics that swept German universities in the late 1960s and early 1970s; at one point he referred to himself as a "Marxist." Schroeder earned a law degree in 1976, at age thirty-two. An accomplished debater and orator, he won a seat in the West German parliament in 1980. Ten years later he was elected premier of Lower Saxony, an industrial region, but was forced to share power with the Green Party in a coalition government. Four years later he won an outright majority in the provincial assembly and ousted the Greens from his government.

During his two decades in politics, before winning the chancellorship, Schroeder changed his political outlook from the leftist approach of his college days to a pragmatic liberalism. He developed friendships with wealthy corporate executives and learned to appeal to both the working and business classes.

Schroeder's reelection victory in 1994, at the same time Kohl was winning a fourth term as chancellor, established him as the leading candidate to lead the Social Democratic Party. The party's losing candidate against Kohl in 1994—Oskar Lafontaine—remained as chairman, and during 1998 was still widely considered the dominant power within the party. Lafontaine's political views were considerably to the left of Schroeder's, a difference that many observers predicted would become troublesome as time passed.

Schroeder ran a media-savvy campaign in 1998, portraying himself as representing a new postwar generation that was ready to take over from Kohl's generation, which had grown to adulthood in the World War II era. His campaign slogan was the "New Middle," a concept he only vaguely outlined as a pragmatic course between pure capitalism and the discredited socialism that had ruined East Germany.

Unemployment was his chief campaign issue; in every speech he lam-
basted Kohl for allowing millions of Germans to lose their jobs. But
Schroeder offered few specific remedies for the country's economic ills. His
one prescription for easing unemployment was to convene negotiations
involving business, labor unions, and the government—a tactic Kohl had
tried in 1996 with little apparent success.

When German voters went to the polls September 27, a majority clearly
had concluded that Schroeder was right in calling for a change. Schroeder's
Social Democrats won 40.9 percent of the vote, giving them 299 seats in
parliament, shy of a majority in the 638-member Bundestag, the lower
house of parliament.

Kohl's Christian Democrats captured only 35.2 percent of the vote, a drop
of six percentage points since the 1994 elections. Kohl, who had gone into
the election as the underdog, was philosophical about his defeat: "It was a
great time. We achieved a lot. But as democrats, we accept the decision of
the voters. Life goes on." A tearful Kohl stepped down as party leader on
November 7, turning the reins over to Schauble.

Despite his reported disdain for the Greens, Schroeder turned to them as
his coalition partner. The Greens had won 6.7 percent of the vote, giving
them 47 seats in parliament—enough to constitute a working majority
when added to the Social Democrats' total. Schroeder named Joschka Fis-
cher, a leader of the Greens, as his foreign minister and Lafontaine as his
finance minister.

Schroeder took office October 27, after he had reached agreement with the
Greens on a legislative agenda including income tax cuts, the phasing out
of nuclear power plants, and making it easier for foreign workers to obtain
German citizenship. Schroeder also promised that he would maintain
Kohl's foreign policies—reassuring foreign leaders who had been concerned
about the pacifist views of the Greens.

In his first major policy speech to parliament November 10, Schroeder
offered few specifics about how he would steer Germany into economic
growth with reduced unemployment. Following through on his chief cam-
paign promise, he proposed an "Alliance for Jobs"—a conclave of business,
labor, and government to discuss job creation. Schroeder acknowledged that
Germany's extensive social security protections had been costly and had
crippled the economy, but he said his government would reverse modest
cutbacks that Kohl's government had initiated in requirements for sick pay,
pensions, and job security in the private sector.

Schroeder would be the chancellor to finish a plan initiated by Kohl to
move the seat of German government back to Berlin in 1999; the West Ger-
man government had been headquartered in Bonn since the end of World
War II. Signifying the significance of the move, Schroeder began referring
to Germany as the "Berlin Republic."

Schauble, who had taken the unfamiliar position as a Christian Demo-
cratic leader in opposition, dismissed Schroeder's speech. "I have not found
anything of the new center, but plenty of the old left, and even more confu-
sion," he told Schroeder. "Your speech was remarkably vague."

During his first two months in office, Schroeder struggled to put specific policies behind his campaign rhetoric. Among the challenges he encountered was a deep division within his own party. Social Democrats on the right called for deep tax cuts and reductions in welfare state requirements to spur business investment; Lafontaine and others on the left pressed for European-wide cuts in interest rates and government-sponsored programs to create jobs. An initial meeting of Schroeder's Alliance for Jobs negotiations on December 7 produced general agreement on the need for reforms in social programs and taxation—but no specifics on how to implement or pay for those reforms. Schroeder called another meeting for early 1999.

Following are excerpts from the inaugural speech in the Bundestag on November 10, 1998, by German chancellor Gerhard Schroeder:

For the first time in the Federal Republic's history the electorate have with their direct votes brought about a change of government. They have authorized the Social Democrats and Alliance 90/The Greens to lead Germany into the next millennium.

This change is a manifestation of democratic normality and of a greater democratic self-awareness.

We can be proud that the people in Germany have clearly rejected radical right-wing and xenophobic tendencies.

I wish once again to thank my predecessor, Dr. Helmut Kohl, for his work and the dignified manner in which he handed over the chancellorship.

Huge tasks lie ahead. The people expect better policies for Germany. We know that economic efficiency is the beginning of everything. And we shall have to modernize government and industry, restore and underpin social justice, develop the European house economically, socially and politically in such a way that the common currency will be successful, press ahead with restoring Germany's inner unity, and above all ensure that unemployment is reduced, that existing jobs are preserved and new ones created.

For this we need new companies, new products, new markets. We need faster innovation, better training, and tax and contribution policies which take the strain off labour. This government will face up to this problem. And it will mobilize the country's creative energies. The starting conditions are anything but favourable. The previous government has by no means left us a well-ordered household.

A first look at the ledger has revealed the seriousness of the situation. The federal debt has been pushed well beyond a trillion marks. The current budget carries an interest burden of more than 80 billion marks. In other words, every fourth mark of federal tax revenue has to be set aside for interest payments.

Budgetary risks running into billions were ignored. Revenue assessments were too high, expenditure assessments too low. For years the budget was balanced merely by one-off adjustments the effective of which have quickly vanished. The tremendous burdens on the budget, the serious structural problems, were simply put off until the future.

According to our new assessment, annual borrowing in the medium term will have to be put at up to 20 billion marks more than envisaged in the financial plan.

This I cannot and will not accept. So let me say right away that this financial burden we have inherited forces us to adopt a resolute policy of consolidation.

Structural adjustments will be unavoidable. All items of federal expenditure will have to be examined. Government action must be more accurately geared to our objectives and be made more economically efficient.

The misuse of public funds must be stopped. We will concentrate subsidies and social benefits more than hitherto on the genuinely needy.

The citizens of this country don't expect us to accomplish everything in a short time, but they have a right to expect us not just to talk but to act to ensure that policies are again geared to people's needs.

We said we did not want to do everything differently but to do many things better. We will abide by this motto. . . .

This change of government is also a change of generation in the life of our nation. Our country is now being increasingly shaped by a generation who have had no direct experience of the Second World War.

It would be dangerous to interpret this as abandoning our historical responsibility. Every generation leaves a mortgage for posterity. No one can claim to be exonerated because they were born after the Nazi terror.

To some people this change of generation is a tremendous challenge. A glance at the government benches or this parliament as a whole shows how the great majority of us have been politically formed. Their biographies are those of people who have led a democratic life.

We have experienced and played an active part in the cultural transformation following the restoration years. Many of us were involved in the civil rights movements of the seventies and eighties. The former civil rights groups from the GDR, who together with East German Social Democrats directed the peaceful revolution in the East, are represented in this government.

This generation upholds the tradition of public spirit and individual courage. They have grown up rebelling against authoritarian structures, testing new social and political models.

Now it is they, and with them the nation, who are called upon to form a new political covenant, to do away with the stagnation and speechlessness into which the previous government led our country.

We are putting in their place a policy designed to encourage people to assume greater responsibility for their actions. This is what we mean by the New Centre.

We will pursue this course on the basis of partnership. Everyone, whether at home or abroad, can rely on this government to meet its social and political responsibility.

The hopes placed in us are almost overpowering, but a government cannot bring about the necessary improvements alone. Everyone must help. And the greater the number of people who participate through their initiative and achievements in the task of reforming our society, the better our chance of accomplishing it.

The people of Germany have no shortage of creative energy. We will help them release that energy.

Our most urgent and grievous problem continues to be mass unemployment. It leads to emotional distress and the collapse of social structures. It deprives some of hope and fills others with fear. In addition, it is costing the country 170 billion marks a year.

The government is fully aware that one of the main reasons for its election is that it is expected to take effective steps to reduce unemployment. We are facing up to this challenge.

Every measure, every instrument will be checked to see whether it safeguards existing jobs or creates new ones. And we want the extent to which we are succeeding in reducing unemployment to be judged at any time, not only after four years.

The tax reform we will be starting in the next few days will be the first step. We won't spend another 16 years discussing the need for such reforms or the pros and cons for the interest groups.

We will actually carry out the tax reform. This will also make government credible again.

The reform will be based on our awareness of economic necessity. It combines modern pragmatism with a keen sense of social fairness.

The main emphasis will be on relieving the burden on those in employment and their families and on small and medium-sized companies. We intend to increase their investment potential.

Both together will help reduce unemployment, create new jobs and safeguard existing ones.

Our tax reform will provide relief totaling 57 billion marks. After counter-financing the net reduction for citizens and companies is 15 billion marks.

Income tax rates will be considerably lowered, child benefit increased.

Taking the legislative period as a whole, the tax reform will bring annual net tax relief of 2,700 marks a year for an average family with two children. We will plug loopholes and eliminate unjustified concessions and thus ensure a fairer distribution of tax burdens.

We will also thoroughly reform the company tax. Company income will be eventually taxed at a maximum rate of 35 per cent. We are now creating the statutory framework for this. We are thus easing the burden on small and medium-sized business, which has a key role to play in creating jobs.

But to those who have been throwing strident accusations at us in the recent weeks I would say: You cannot have low, simple tax rates as in the United States and keep the large number of exemptions we have in Germany.

That is not the name of the game.

We shall at long last subject the use of economic resources to market economy reason. Hence we shall immediately embark on the path of ecological tax and contribution reform.

By doing so we are carrying out a long overdue reversal of policy. Nature and energy as finite and thus scarce commodities will be made more expensive in order to make labour, of which there is plenty, cheaper.

Let me repeat once again: The aim is not to tap another source of public revenue.

By taxing energy we are following the example of our neighbours in Denmark, the Netherlands and Austria. We are solving the problems of modern society with the means of modern society.

We will use the energy tax revenue to reduce statutory non-wage labour costs. And through the incentives created by the energy tax we are encouraging the creation of new jobs in viable, future-oriented technologies. . . .

Together with the energy industry and the environmental associations we shall be looking for new ways of supplying the country with energy. Nuclear energy is socially unacceptable. By the same token it does not make economic sense either. We will therefore phase it out in an orderly fashion.

But phasing out is not the government's main consideration. It is more concerned with adopting a future-oriented energy supply concept. The proportion of nuclear energy will be reduced step by step and ultimately replaced. This will be a huge investment programme which will also create new jobs. . . .

[L]et us be under no illusions. Tackling unemployment is an epochal challenge and to meet it will require the cooperation of all social players.

There is no one single solution to the problem. Fiscal policy, reductions in non-wage labour costs, investments in the future and collective bargaining, they all must fit together. Only if the economic players pull in harness can more jobs be created on a sustainable basis.

Here the German employers have the same responsibility as the unions and relevant social organizations.

I invite them all to join in an Alliance for Jobs. I am pleased to be able to tell you that the first meeting of this Alliance, which is conceived as a permanent forum to combat unemployment, is to take place early in December. Those concerned are, I now know, keen to take up my invitation and to meet their responsibilities. I expect the participants to cast off old habits of mind, perceptions of vested interests.

I look forward to discussions that will allow an unbiased appraisal of the situation and fair solutions based on a spirit of give and take.

In many areas we can already see successful Alliances for Jobs at work: in neighbouring countries but also very often at the company level. German entrepreneurs with a sense of social responsibility and hard-working shop stewards endowed with sound commercial sense have made people abroad realize that the modern codetermination we have evolved in Germany has a great deal to offer.

The Alliance for Jobs is the right place for broaching urgent issues. We need to consider, for instance, how changes in taxes and contributions might provide greater leeway in the area of collective bargaining. What are the implications of targeting social benefits more directly to those most in need?

What scope can we create for investment? What is the potential of new instruments such as invested wages? What gains can more flexible working hours bring?

I also want us to seize the unique opportunity offered by the new political constellations in Europe. With this Government, the fight against unemployment can finally be tackled also at the European level.

With its tax reform, reductions in non-wage labour costs and a crash programme to get young people into work, the Government is already making a strong and constructive contribution to the success of the Alliance even as preparations get under way. I trust the other economic players will follow suit.

People rightly expect us to live up to our responsibilities and grasp the opportunities held out by an Alliance for Jobs in a Europe that believes in social commitment.

No one is looking for patent recipes but all of us have a duty to do our best. And that means cooperation, confidence and faith in the future. . . .

Let there be no misunderstanding: our economy produces the resources that are needed to finance the welfare state. What we cannot afford is injustice or a policy of doing nothing. There is no need to ask our citizens to prepare for "blood, sweat and tears". They have demonstrated that they are ready to share and to give.

Surely it was only thanks to the drive and solidarity shown by people in both East and West Germany that—although much remains to be done—such remarkable feats have been achieved in rebuilding the economy in the new Länder. And let me state plainly: we are going to need that solidarity also in the years ahead. To reduce the transfer payments to the new Länder would be to jeopardize what has already been achieved. Equal living standards in East and West are clearly still a long way off.

In concrete terms that means the 1993 Solidarity Pact will remain the financial backbone of economic reconstruction. . . .

The Government will . . . cancel the measures enacted to the detriment of the pensioners by the previous government. I call them "measures" and not "a reform". Reform is something that still lies ahead of us. . . .

This then must be the New Centre's flagship national project: the ecological renewal of our country in a spirit of solidarity, with a modern, social market economy our goal.

That is why we want the pensions system to truly reflect solidarity between the generations, not just between occupational groups. We want a meaningful contract between the generations, not a contract that penalizes work.

It is on these lines that we will table a bill in the Bundestag to reform the pensions system based on solidarity and social reality.

At the same time we make a three-fold pledge:

- We will guarantee today's pensioners their pensions, and at any rate ensure that their often already modest pensions will not be reduced.

- To those now paying into the national insurance scheme we will guarantee effective pension entitlements in line with earnings.
- To those now entering working life we will guarantee that the reformed pension system will be a transparent, future-oriented insurance package.

This package will be made up of four different parts:

- the national insurance scheme;
- company pension schemes
- private pension schemes, for which e.g. tax incentives will be provided by the state;
- participation of employees in their companies' productive capital and profits. . . .

Realism teaches us for instance that the immigration to Germany which has taken place over the past decades is irreversible. We invited these immigrants to come and they are here to stay. And today we say these people in our midst are not strangers. It is those who propagate hatred and xenophobia who have become the strangers in our midst.

To them we respond with a resolute policy for integration.

For far too long those who have come to work here, who pay their taxes and abide by our laws have been told they are just "guests". But in truth they have for years been part of German society.

This Government will modernize the law on nationality. That will enable those living permanently in Germany and their children born here to acquire full rights of citizenship.

No one who wants to be a German citizen should have to renounce or deny his foreign roots. That is why we will also allow dual nationality.

Integration clearly requires the full and active commitment of those who are to be integrated. But we will reach out a hand to those who live and work here and pay their taxes so they may be encouraged to participate fully in the life of our democracy. This is responding positively to the realities in Europe. . . .

With the help of their friends and allies the Germans have been reunited in peace and self-determination. We remain unreservedly committed to the Western Alliance and the European Union.

Today we are democrats and Europeans—not because we have to be, but because we want to be. . . .

Berlin is also the city that for tormentuous decades was divided by the East-West conflict. Though we Germans are happy that it has been overcome, we are equally well aware that the end of the Cold War has by no means yet brought world peace.

The dramatic transformation in global politics has triggered new instabilities and violent conflicts in many regions, also on our doorstep in Europe. The misery of refugees, scarce resources and the destruction of the environment in the countries of the South are a dangerous breeding-ground for new conflicts.

In view of such risks, but above all in view of the opportunities for international cooperation, the world is expecting us more than ever before to meet our obligations within the context of our alliances. We will remain a reliable partner in Europe and the world.

We owe a great deal to our friendship with the United States of America—indeed no less than peace and our freedom.

I will not attempt to deny that some of those sitting here in the German Bundestag today—and even some who are now members of the Government—did not always agree with what our American partners did and proposed, above all at the height of the arms race during the Cold War. And they were not alone in the Western world in so thinking.

But it is that same generation which was influenced more by John F. Kennedy's visit to Berlin and his commitment to the freedom of West Berlin than by almost any other event in post-war history.

Authors have referred to this generation as the "children of the American zone". They grew up with American culture and American products. The critical distance of the "children" grew into a partnership of adults. The friendship with America was not forced on that generation, but offered to them, by American democracy and culture. It is a friendship based on mutual understanding and ever better mutual knowledge. It is a friendship that has stood the test of time and is not facing any severe test. We guarantee it not only for the sake of continuity or loyalty to the Alliance, but as a result of the trust that could only be built up through talking to one another and feeling for one another.

We stand by our commitments within the Atlantic Alliance. We want to develop and use the instruments of the Common Foreign and Security Policy to enable Europe to act at long last in international politics. Our friends in the United States are waiting for this with impatience.

German foreign policy is and shall remain peace policy. In this context, we are expressly committed to cooperating in peacemaking and peacekeeping missions. That applies particularly to the situation in South-Eastern Europe. . . .

We will offer separate units to the United Nations for peacekeeping measures. The Government is actively committed to maintaining the United Nations' monopoly to use force and to strengthening the role of its Secretary-General. We will pursue the opportunity of becoming a permanent member of the UN Security Council if a joint European seat cannot be achieved.

We do not presume to play the role of a leading power or to take political initiatives in crisis situations without liaising with our partners.

We are interested in good cooperation world-wide and our foreign economic relations should also serve peace and the process of democratization.

The third pillar of our foreign policy is to strengthen and develop foreign cultural policy. This is essential, especially under the conditions of globalization. . . .

European Monetary Union is an irreversible fact. The euro will enable us to make prices and services fully comparable. It means that the time when nations went their own way is gone for good. That applies for example to the further development of ecological tax reform. It can only be successful within a European context.

The common currency must be a success. That means it must be, and remain, stable.

We do not call into question the emphasis on the stability of Europe's future monetary policy.

But we want to have a discussion on interest policy, a discussion the President of the Bundesbank also described as "desirable". The independence of the Bundesbank and of the European Central Bank will of course be respected and safeguarded.

This independence follows from the Bundesbank Act and from Article 107 of the Maastricht Treaty. It is enshrined there because it is necessary from a practical point of view, and it serves stability. . . .

We regard Germany in Europe as our project for the future. Together, with the social modernizers in neighbouring countries, we are this project's vanguard. This opportunity to build together a modern Europe based on a social market economy and ecological responsibility is one we will boldly accept.

We are not making promises that cannot be kept. But we can and we want to instil courage in others: the courage for a new civility, the courage for more partnership, but also the courage to be optimistic and to be curious about the future.

I recall Willy Brandt, who, in the policy statement of his reform alliance to this parliament in 1973, cited the "vital civic spirit" which was at home in what he, too, called the "new political centre".

Helmut Schmidt said in front of this House in 1976, at a time when the economic situation was equally difficult, that the Government was above all banking on the hard work, intelligence and sense of responsibility of the German people.

I am consciously following on from that idea. And I am sure: We will make it. Because we trust in Germany's vitality.

UN SECRETARY GENERAL
ON WAR IN KOSOVO
November 12, 1998

Kosovo, long considered the tinderbox of the Balkans, erupted into a brutal civil war in 1998 that displaced an estimated 300,000 civilians. The fighting forced Western nations, including the United States, to scramble for a diplomatic solution in hopes of heading off a broader conflict that might engulf the entire region.

Kosovo was a province of Serbia, one of two federations (along with Montenegro) remaining in the Federal Republic of Yugoslavia following the breakup of Yugoslavia in the early 1990s. The ethnic makeup of Kosovo made it a strong candidate for the kind of sectarian conflict that had engulfed two other former Yugoslavian territories, Croatia in 1991 and Bosnia from 1992 to 1995. Of the two million residents of Kosovo, about 90 percent were ethnic Albanian. Most of the others were ethnic Serbs, who controlled the political and security establishments in the province with the help of the Serbian-dominated Yugoslav government in Belgrade. For years, analysts had feared that all-out war in Kosovo could spill over into neighboring Albania and Macedonia, and possibly even into Greece and Turkey. (Croatian conflict, Historic Documents of 1991, p. 372; Bosnia conflict, Historic Documents of 1996, p. 816)

An underground Albanian guerrilla movement for the independence of Kosovo launched an offensive in February, provoking a series of counterattacks by Serbian authorities. By year's end, dozens of ethnic Albanian villages had been destroyed, and an estimated 300,000 civilians had fled their homes and taken refuge elsewhere in Kosovo or in other countries as far away as Great Britain. Estimates of the number killed in the fighting during 1998 ranged from a low of 500 to a high of about 2,000.

The United Nations and Western powers, led by the United States, issued numerous warnings early in 1998 but did not intervene with decisive diplomatic action until the fall. By that time the Serbian authorities in Belgrade had achieved much of their apparent aim of destroying a vast segment of the Albanian community in Kosovo. Restoring the dozens of vil-

lages and reviving the local economy would take years and millions of dollars in aid.

The conflict put the outside world in a bind. The scale of Serbian atrocities against the Kosovar Albanians was so enormous that the international community was compelled to take action. At the same time, there was little international support for allowing Kosovo to become an independent Albanian state, as the vast majority of Kosovar Albanians seemed to want. If the Albanians in Kosovo gained independence, Western officials believed, dozens of ethnic groups throughout Europe might be encouraged to demand independence—a recipe for unending conflict on the continent where two world wars started during the twentieth century. Madeleine K. Albright, the U.S. secretary of state, gave this formula for the West's diplomatic posture on Kosovo: "We want Serbia out of Kosovo, not Kosovo out of Serbia."

Background to the Kosovo Conflict

The Albanians in Kosovo had enjoyed a significant degree of autonomy from Serbia until 1989, when Slobodan Milosevic—then the president of Serbia, later the president of the Federal Republic of Yugoslavia—asserted Belgrade's political and security control over the province. That action helped energize a latent independence movement among Kosovar Albanians. Throughout the 1990s, as conflict raged elsewhere in the former Yugoslavia, world leaders watched Kosovo warily, hoping against an outbreak of fighting there as well. In 1982 U.S. president George Bush sent a small military contingent to neighboring Macedonia as a warning against a Serbian offensive against the Kosovar Albanians. That tactic may have helped delay the onset of fighting in Kosovo, but it was not enough to prevent it altogether.

The trigger for the fighting in 1998 came in February when the Kosovo Liberation Army (KLA), an armed pro-independence guerrilla group, launched attacks on Serbian security positions in Kosovo and succeeded in occupying much of the countryside. The KLA received much of its military support from the government of Albania. The offensive set in motion a seesaw chain of events in which the Kosovar Albanians gained ground, triggering a furious counterattack from the Serbian police and military, and then a renewed offensive by the Albanians. By the middle of the year the KLA claimed to control about 40 percent of Kosovo—most of it in areas of small villages and in the central mountains of the province.

The fighting drove thousands of civilians from their homes and destroyed much of the province's agriculture-based economy. From the perspective of most outsiders, the destruction was brutal and senseless. But the opposing sides each saw an advantage in the conflict. For the KLA, the intensity of the Serbian counterattacks helped harden public support for the independence movement; by the middle of 1998 most Kosovar Albanians appeared willing to accept nothing short of independence. But the Milosevic regime in Belgrade also appeared to take satisfaction from its ability to demolish Albanian communities and force the residents into exile.

Other countries and international organizations condemned the fighting and called for peace talks. The UN Security Council on March 31 passed the first of three resolutions on Yugoslavia during 1998; resolution 1160 condemned "excessive force" by the Serbian police and "all acts of terrorism" by the KLA, demanded that outside parties stop supplying weapons to either side in Kosovo, and suggested a "meaningful dialogue" to settle outstanding political issues. A "contact group" of Western nations, including the United States, also issued a series of proposals for ending the fighting and establishing peace talks between the Serbs and the Kosovar Albanians.

On July 19, less than two weeks after a July 8 statement by the contact group, Serbia launched its most massive and sustained offensive. The offensive was originally described as a move to regain government control over major roads in the province, but it soon became clear that Serbian forces were determined to destroy dozens of villages that had been KLA strongholds and regain territory the guerrillas had claimed.

The principle tactic of the Serbian police and military was to shell ethnic Albanian villages with artillery until the civilians fled. Serbian forces then moved into the villages to burn houses, shops, farms, and fields to prevent the civilians from returning. Often, the military bulldozed whatever buildings survived the fires. Meanwhile, the security forces gave weapons to ethnic Serbs under the guise of helping them protect themselves from the Albanians, but in reality this was aimed at encouraging vigilante groups. By early August the Serbian offensive had succeeded in recovering much of the territory that had been claimed by the KLA.

During much of the fighting it was difficult for journalists and international monitors to determine exactly what was happening in the rural countryside. Serbian security forces routinely prevented outsiders from entering areas of their operations. Reports of atrocities often were delayed by days or weeks, by which time eyewitnesses usually had fled the scene. Representatives of human rights organizations spent weeks trying to piece together fragmentary information about mass killings in isolated areas.

On August 3, with the fighting in one of its most intense stages, State Department spokesman James P. Rubin announced in Washington that NATO ambassadors had approved the use of military force—most likely air strikes—against Serbia to try to halt the offensive. Rubin said diplomatic reports had indicated that Kosovo was "on the edge of a humanitarian catastrophe."

The NATO threat had little immediate impact. The Serbian offensive continued unabated for nearly two months, while the Western powers debated what kind of action, if any, to take. During the late summer and early fall of 1998 at least 200,000 people were forced from their homes; an estimated 50,000 of them were living in the open air, protected only by plastic sheets.

The UN Security Council on September 23 adopted its second resolution of the year on Kosovo. Resolution 1199 repeated demands of the earlier resolution for an immediate halt to the fighting and laid most of the responsibility for Kosovo's hardships on the Yugoslav government in Belgrade.

In late September reports emerged of a series of massacres of Albanian civilians in villages in central Kosovo. One confirmed report revealed that on September 26 eighteen civilians—including children, women, and elderly people—had been shot, and in some cases mutilated, near the village of Gornje Obrinje. The reports helped stiffen the resolve of Western leaders to take more decisive action.

By early October the Serbian offensive had accomplished much of its apparent mission of terrorizing civilians in the countryside. On October 4 there were reports that Yugoslav president Milosevic had ordered Serbian military units to halt the offensive and return to their barracks.

On October 5 UN Secretary General Kofi Annan gave the Security Council a strongly worded report expressing his personal outrage at the "mass killings" and destruction in Kosovo. "I reiterate my utter condemnation of such wanton killing and destruction," Annan said. "It is clear beyond any reasonable doubt that the great majority of such acts have been committed by security forces in Kosovo acting under the authority of the Federal Republic of Yugoslavia." The Yugoslav government had the right, under international law, to respond to violence within its territory, he added. "However, this can in no way justify the systematic terror inflicted on civilians these past few days and weeks."

U.S. Mediation

U.S. special envoy Richard C. Holbrooke flew to Belgrade on October 5 for a series of negotiations with Milosevic. Holbrooke had been the principal architect of the 1995 agreement that ended the fighting in Bosnia; Milosevic's acquiescence had made the Bosnia agreement possible.

Over the course of a week, Holbrooke and Milosevic hammered out an agreement for implementing key provisions of UN Security Council Resolution 1199. The agreement provided for a cease-fire in Kosovo to be monitored by an international force of 2,000 "verifiers" and NATO reconnaissance flights. The agreement also called for new negotiations between the Serbs and the Kosovar Albanians, leading toward a restoration of local autonomy. Christopher Hill, the U.S. ambassador to Macedonia, for months had been trying to formulate a political agreement on Kosovo.

Holbrooke announced his agreement with Milosevic in Belgrade on October 13. He said Milosevic had accepted the agreement two days earlier, the same day that NATO ambassadors had authorized specific air strikes against Serbia if Milosevic did not accept a cease-fire. In his negotiations Holbrooke did not deal directly with the Kosovar Albanians; he said most of the burden of peace rested with the Milosevic regime.

Milosevic on October 15 signed a related agreement with NATO allowing the reconnaissance flights by unarmed NATO planes over Kosovo, and on October 16 he signed an agreement with the Organization for Security and Cooperation in Europe, the umbrella group of fifty-four countries that had the task of verifying Yugoslav compliance with Security Council resolutions on Kosovo. In the October 16 agreement Milosevic accepted the pres-

ence of the 2,000 unarmed "compliance verifiers," who were to report their findings to the Security Council.

The significance of the role played by NATO's threat of air strikes against Yugoslavia was subject to dispute. Clinton administration officials insisted that Milosevic accepted Holbrooke's demands for a cease-fire primarily because he feared a NATO attack. They noted that Milosevic had consistently followed a pattern of pushing for military gains until the West threatened to intervene militarily, and then he backed down. Skeptics said it was doubtful that Milosevic really feared NATO air strikes; they noted that NATO for months had debated the proper course of action and that some NATO members had been reluctant to attack Yugoslavia.

In any event, NATO was forced to extend for nearly two weeks its deadline for Milosevic to comply with the cease-fire agreement. It was not until October 27 that NATO representatives determined that Serbian forces had withdrawn to the extent that they were in "substantial compliance" with the agreement. Although NATO dropped an immediate threat of air attack, it maintained an "activation order" that kept NATO warplanes on alert in case the alliance decided that Milosevic was backtracking on his promises and needed another reminder.

With the conflict quieted, at least for the moment, the UN Security Council in November turned its attention to an effort to punish those responsible for atrocities during the war. On November 17 the council adopted resolution 1203 demanding that Milosevic allow a UN war crimes tribunal to conduct an investigation in Kosovo. Milosevic had refused to allow the tribunal into Kosovo on the grounds that what happened there was an "internal matter" outside the UN's jurisdiction.

Secretary General Annan told the Security Council in a November 12 report that the human rights situation in Kosovo had not significantly improved since the agreements negotiated by Holbrooke. "Retaliatory and armed action, torture and ill-treatment, arbitrary detention, forced disappearances, harassment and discriminatory treatment are widely reported," he Annan said.

A Renewed Offensive

Despite several low-level battles, the cease-fire agreed to by Milosevic remained intact until mid-December, when Yugoslav troops battled with Kosovo guerrillas trying to smuggle arms across the border from Albania. About three dozen guerrillas died in that clash; several Serb civilians were killed by gunmen during the following week, possibly in retaliation. The incidents demonstrated that the KLA was continuing to recruit and arm guerrillas for a renewed battle against the government and that the government was determined to respond.

A broad government response came on December 24 when Serbian military forces broke the cease-fire with an assault by tanks and other armored vehicles on an area of north-central Kosovo. The guerrillas repelled the assault, but four days of fighting ensued, raising new questions about the *willingness of either side to accept a peaceful settlement. International monitors were pouring into Kosovo as the year ended, with a plan of reaching a total of 2,000 by January 1999.*

Following are excerpts from a report submitted November 12, 1998, by UN Secretary General Kofi Annan to the UN Security Council describing the situation in Kosovo:

IV. Situation in Kosovo

5. This section of the report is based on information provided by the Chairman-in-Office of OSCE [Organization for Security and Cooperation in Europe], the European Union, NATO (annex II), the Kosovo Diplomatic Observer Mission and individual Member States. It also draws upon the report of a United Nations mission to the Federal Republic of Yugoslavia that visited the region from 17 to 27 October 1998 (hereinafter referred to as the United Nations mission; see sect. V), as well as contributions provided by the Office of the United Nations High Commissioner for Refugees and the United Nations High Commissioner for Human Rights.

Political framework

6. The accord reached by the President of the Federal Republic of Yugoslavia, Slobodan Milosevic, and the United States Special Envoy, Richard Holbrooke, on 13 October 1998, as well as the agreements signed in Belgrade on 15 October 1998 between the Federal Republic of Yugoslavia and NATO, and on 16 October 1998 between the Federal Republic of Yugoslavia and OSCE, have contributed towards defusing the immediate crisis situation in Kosovo and have created more favourable conditions for a political settlement.

7. The authorities of the Federal Republic of Yugoslavia welcomed the Agreement of 16 October establishing the Kosovo Verification Mission and indicated their readiness to cooperate fully with the Mission. They pledged to ensure full freedom of movement for the Kosovo Verification Mission monitors and undertook to inform them of possible dangers. The Minister of the Interior of Serbia, in particular, indicated the Government's intention to inform the Mission promptly of all incidents that might occur in the region excluding, however, incidents that the authorities might classify as "criminal activity".

8. Government officials informed the United Nations mission that they were considering holding elections in Kosovo in about nine months. The Kosovo Executive Council, that is, the local administration established by the Government, had recently became functional, albeit with no Kosovo Albanian participation. The Deputy Prime Minister of the Federal Republic of Yugoslavia indicated to the United Nations mission the need for joint national and international efforts to address the humanitarian situation in Kosovo and

pledged to promote active cooperation with humanitarian organizations on the ground to that end.

9. The Kosovo Albanian leaders, in their contacts with the United Nations mission, expressed reservations about the 13 October accord and the 16 October agreement, although they appreciated the fact that Kosovo was no longer considered to be exclusively an internal problem of the Federal Republic of Yugoslavia. They still insisted on their right to self-determination and signalled their continuing wish for an international armed presence on the ground.

10. The position of Kosovo Albanian paramilitary units remained unclear. The authorities of the Federal Republic of Yugoslavia expressed concern that members of those units might try to provoke the police and military in Kosovo and trigger a reaction from the Government. The Kosovo Albanian leaders indicated, with various degrees of certainty, that Kosovo Albanian paramilitary units would respect the 13 October accord by and large. Nonetheless, they could not rule out the possibility that some small splinter armed groups might continue attacks, thus giving the authorities of the Federal Republic of Yugoslavia a pretext for violent retaliation.

Recent military situation

11. Both the parties to the conflict and the international observers on the ground acknowledge that the military situation has stabilized recently and that, despite some serious but isolated incidents, there has been no major fighting since 1 October. Many local people indicated to the United Nations mission that the situation had improved in the two weeks following the cease-fire, although several villages had reportedly been destroyed recently by the Serbian police. Tensions persist, however, in many areas dominated by Kosovo Albanian paramilitary units, with guerrilla-style attacks on police and military positions and frequent reports of sporadic gunfire exchanges and shelling by Government forces.

12. Between 28 September and 19 October 1998, the Ministry of the Interior reported a total of 117 attacks of varying intensity, in which a total of 10 policemen were killed and 22 were injured. Seven members of the Yugoslav army were also reported killed and two injured during the incidents. The demarcation between police and Kosovo Albanian paramilitary units was not always clear at the time of the visit of the United Nations mission; in some cases their respective positions were only several hundred metres apart. Accordingly, in almost all cases, it was difficult to determine which side had initiated hostilities.

13. Recent attacks by Kosovo Albanian paramilitary units have indicated their readiness, capability and intention to actively pursue the advantage gained by the partial withdrawal of the police and military formations. Reports of new weapons, ammunition and equipment indicate that the capacity of those units to resupply themselves is still fairly good.

14. The army and police presence in Kosovo has been significantly reduced since early October. The presence and disposition of the remaining

Government forces indicate a strategy based on containing pockets of resistance and on control of high ground and the main arterial routes in areas dominated by Kosovo Albanian paramilitary units. Tripwires and anti-personnel mines have reportedly been laid at the approaches to some police positions as an early warning measure. Since 27 October, there has been a continued withdrawal of the Serbian security forces from Kosovo and numerous checkpoints and fortified positions have been dismantled. The Serbian police retain control over key roads. Mobile police checkpoints have been established on major roads in some areas.

15. Kosovo Albanian paramilitary units are asserting their own authority to supplant that of the Serbian police in areas from which the police have withdrawn, and have established their own checkpoints on a number of secondary roads.

16. While the ceasefire is generally holding, there are continued reports of sporadic violations, including armed provocations against police and police harassment of ethnic Albanians. The presence of Kosovo Albanian paramilitary units is reportedly on the increase in several areas, and they appear to be responsible for some of the reported violations, including attacks on civilians. Serbian police raised security measures around a coal mine and power plant outside Pristina following an attack by Kosovo Albanian paramilitary units on 3 November in which three Serbian workers were injured.

17. Kosovo Albanian paramilitary units denied access to Kosovo Diplomatic Observer Mission teams to some areas, requesting a letter from their political representative. On 5 November, a clearly marked OSCE vehicle was fired on as it drove close behind a Federal Republic of Yugoslavia military convoy between Suva Reka and Stimlje.

Security

18. The overriding concern of both ethnic Serbs and Albanians is the security of their families. While the Serbian authorities told the United Nations mission that they needed a large police presence in designated parts of Kosovo to protect ethnic Serbs living in the province and to ensure that at least main highways remained safe and free for travel, the Kosovo Albanian representatives stated that police units were used as another arm of the military, intent on intimidating local Albanians. Police and military personnel have occupied some village homes, making their owners' return impossible. Furthermore, many deserted villages have a presence of some five to eight police, who remain purportedly to prevent or give early warning of attempts by Kosovo Albanian paramilitary units to reoccupy territory previously taken by Government forces. This presence was cited almost universally by the internally displaced persons as the primary reason for people not returning to their homes.

19. Government authorities informed the mission that they had established local police units with Kosovo Albanian participation in some 100 "secured" villages. The only ethnic Albanian police officers met by the mission were three elderly officers involved in food distribution near Dakovica.

Humanitarian situation

20. As of mid-October, the United Nations High Commissioner for Refugees (UNHCR) estimated that some 200,000 persons were still displaced inside Kosovo. The number of people who had fled to other areas was estimated at 42,000 in Montenegro, 20,500 in Albania, 3,000 in the former Yugoslav Republic of Macedonia, 10,000 in Bosnia and Herzegovina and some 20,000 in Serbia. In 11 European countries recently surveyed by UNHCR, the total number of applications by asylum-seekers from the Federal Republic of Yugoslavia increased from 11,000 in the first quarter of 1998 to 28,000 in the third. Some 80 to 90 per cent of the applicants are asylum-seekers from Kosovo.

21. Significant progress was made in the return of displaced persons in Kosovo following the ceasefire and the 13 October accord. UNHCR estimates that up to 50,000 people have returned to their original villages, including 2,000 internally displaced persons from Montenegro. Since the military withdrawal on 27 October, thousands of displaced persons have returned to their villages. Many of the returnees whose houses were intact indicated that they would stay and would shelter neighbours who had lost their homes. Others are repairing homes to bring back their families. In some areas, villagers were preparing to plant the winter crop of wheat. Although there were some reports of harassment and obstruction by security forces, most returnees encountered few problems.

22. As of mid-October, people living in the open presented one of the major concerns to the international community. Of the 10,000 internally displaced persons estimated to be living under plastic sheeting before the 27 October military withdrawal, almost all had either returned to their villages or were staying with host families. There were still, however, a number of villages that remained deserted.

23. There are still many displaced families remaining with host families and in towns that have been untouched by the hostilities. This, in turn, has created problems. In many towns private dwellings are packed to three or four times their normal capacity, creating serious sanitary hazards.

24. UNHCR estimates that there are some 20,000 damaged houses, of which approximately 60 per cent are currently inhabitable. From 2 to 4 November, United Nations agencies, non-governmental organizations and the Kosovo Diplomatic Observer Mission conducted a village-by-village survey in order to get an accurate picture of the number of returnees and the condition of houses. The results of the survey are expected to help aid agencies in planning emergency shelter assistance and relief supplies. Preliminary indications are that some 370 villages have suffered varying degrees of damage. UNHCR, together with non-governmental organizations, is currently distributing 3,000 emergency shelter kits, pending a more systematic distribution of shelter materials upon completion of the inter-agency survey.

25. Access by humanitarian agencies to internally displaced persons has generally improved since the time of my previous report, although delays in

obtaining entry visas from the authorities of the Federal Republic of Yugoslavia for their staff and difficulties in obtaining radio licences persist.

26. The encouraging response from donors to the current United Nations Consolidated Inter-agency Appeal for Humanitarian Assistance to Kosovo has enabled United Nations humanitarian agencies to step up emergency assistance to the victims of the conflict. From 28 October to 4 November, UNHCR escorted multi-agency convoys that delivered relief aid for 208,700 people in various parts of Kosovo. Supplies came from UNHCR, the World Food Programme (WFP), Mercy Corps International, Children's Aid Direct, Catholic Relief Services and Oxfam. Convoys are currently running three times a day, six days a week.

27. The initiative of the authorities of the Federal Republic of Yugoslavia to establish distribution centres throughout Kosovo has been welcomed by United Nations agencies as a constructive step. However, many potential beneficiaries interviewed by the mission stressed that the decision to delegate management of the centres to the local police is likely to dissuade Albanian internally displaced persons from taking advantage of such facilities. In line with the United Nations principle that assistance should be delivered where it is most needed, most agencies have so far opted to continue to distribute aid mainly through the Mother Teresa Society, which has a wide network and enjoys the trust of the Albanian population. Since it is questionable whether any Serb in need in Kosovo would be in a position to use the Albanian-managed Mother Teresa centres, assistance to needy Serbs is channelled through the Yugoslav Red Cross Society.

28. The situation of refugees and internally displaced persons in Montenegro, which hosts the biggest number of internally displaced persons outside Kosovo, remains of concern. The decision by the Government of Montenegro to close its border to internally displaced persons from Kosovo on 11 September is still in force. The authorities have justified this decision on economic and security grounds, voicing particular concern about potential destabilization in Montenegro as a result of the situation in Kosovo.

29. With almost half of the Montenegrin population living under the poverty line and with refugees and internally displaced persons comprising up to 12 per cent of the total population, Montenegro may indeed face a lack of capacity to cope with the problem. Economic sanctions against the Federal Republic of Yugoslavia and the general downturn in Montenegro's economy have made it virtually impossible for the Government, through the local Red Cross, to continue on its own to provide comprehensive assistance to the 42,000 new arrivals from Kosovo, in addition to a refugee caseload of 25,000 from the former Yugoslavia. However, considerable assistance is being provided by the international community to these persons.

30. A recent assessment mission by the Food and Agriculture Organization of the United Nations (FAO) to the Federal Republic of Yugoslavia concluded that the conflict in Kosovo was affecting the agricultural sector through uncertain access by returnees to their land, the collapse of local cereal production, a shortage of farming equipment and a decline in

livestock. FAO will appeal for essential agricultural inputs to enable basic food production activities.

Mines

31. There have been many reports of mines being laid in Kosovo by both the Government forces and the Kosovo Albanian paramilitary units. The Deputy Chief of the General Staff of the Federal Republic of Yugoslavia asserted that the Yugoslav army had laid mines only on the borders with Albania and the former Yugoslav Republic of Macedonia, but not in the interior; that they were properly and accurately recorded in accordance with international conventions; and that the army was in a position to lift all mines without the assistance of the United Nations or other agencies. There are, however, some reports of small protective minefields being laid by police around their positions in central Kosovo. Reports of mined areas in the territories dominated by Kosovo Albanian paramilitary units are mostly undetailed.

32. Landmines and booby traps are becoming a growing problem in Kosovo, both for displaced persons returning to their homes and for humanitarian personnel. As internally displaced persons returned to their villages, several people were reportedly killed by anti-personnel mines or booby traps laid around houses, buildings and wells. Vehicle mines are also present on a number of dirt roads in the province. The reported presence of mines has restricted humanitarian access in several areas. This situation will be exacerbated by the onset of winter, when snow will cover traces of landmine locations. Humanitarian agencies have asked local communities to seek the assistance of Kosovo Albanian paramilitary units in removing landmines in the areas that they control. Efforts are under way to train relief staff in mine awareness and first aid. In the absence of a technical mine survey mission, the general uncertainty regarding mined areas poses a particular threat.

Human Rights

33. The Office of the United Nations High Commissioner for Human Rights continues its monitoring presence in Kosovo and reports regularly to the United Nations High Commissioner for Human Rights and the Special Rapporteur of the Commission on Human Rights, Jiri Dienstbier. From 21 to 29 October, the Special Rapporteur conducted his third visit to the Federal Republic of Yugoslavia. His report on human rights in Bosnia and Herzegovina, Croatia and the Federal Republic of Yugoslavia, including Kosovo, is contained in documents A/53/322 and Add.1.

34. Reports on the situation of human rights are consistent with the categories of serious violations of human rights that have characterized the crisis in Kosovo for many months. The human rights situation appears not to have changed significantly since the signing of the 16 October agreement. Violations have been attributed to Serbian security forces, Kosovo Albanian paramilitary units and village defence groups. Retaliatory and armed action, torture and ill-treatment, arbitrary detention, forced disappearances, harassment and discriminatory treatment are widely reported.

35. Religious and cultural monuments have been damaged and vandalized, both in conflict-affected areas and in urban areas where no fighting has taken place. In discussions with the Special Rapporteur and the staff of the Office of the United Nations High Commissioner for Human Rights, Government representatives in Pristina confirmed that in some locations Government forces had been responsible for deliberate and retaliatory destruction of property owned by Kosovo Albanians. Returning internally displaced persons and Government officials have also confirmed the practice of the "screening" of internally displaced persons, in which men are separated from women and children and then held for questioning for periods ranging from hours to several days. It is reported that many of those detained are beaten and ill-treated during interrogation.

36. The Serbian Ministry of Justice has also confirmed that more than 1,500 persons, including 500 in absentia, are currently being investigated under suspicion of involvement in anti-state activities and in activities of the Kosovo Albanian paramilitary units. Some persons have already been convicted and sentenced. Five cases of death in custody have been reported so far. The Office of the United Nations High Commissioner for Human Rights monitors these trials, the first of which began on 22 October in Prizren. The Serbian Minister of the Interior has observed that an amnesty law can be discussed only after a political agreement has been finalized, a census and elections held, and new organs of local government subsequently formed.

37. The need for independent investigations into alleged arbitrary executions gained renewed urgency with the discovery of additional concentrations of corpses in several locations in Kosovo. The United Nations mission also received reports of alleged extra-judicial killings and massacres at Gornje Obrinje, Klecka, Golubovac, Volujak, Malisevo, Rausic, Glogovac and Gremnik. As a result of efforts by the European Union and other international organizations, including OHCHR [Office of the United Nations High Commissioner for Human Rights], and initiatives by the Government of the Federal Republic of Yugoslavia, a group of Finnish forensic experts arrived in the Federal Republic of Yugoslavia on 20 October to assist the authorities in investigations into alleged arbitrary killings and mass graves. According to the Finnish Ministry for Foreign Affairs, the group also intended to carry out independent investigations as necessary. Unfortunately, the Government of the Federal Republic of Yugoslavia failed to cooperate fully with the International Tribunal for the Former Yugoslavia. A team of Tribunal officials, led by Chief Prosecutor Louise Arbour, was unable to visit Kosovo since the requested visas were not issued by the Federal Republic of Yugoslavia.

38. There are growing concerns as to the fate and whereabouts of the 140 to 150 civilians and police officers who are still missing after having been abducted by the Kosovo Albanian paramilitary units. The authorities of the Federal Republic of Yugoslavia report that 249 civilians and police have been abducted by Kosovo Albanian paramilitary units. The most recent of these cases involves two journalists of the state news agency, who went missing on 18 October; despite assurances about their well-being and imminent release,

reports now indicate that they have been "sentenced" to 60 days' imprisonment. During his visit to Kosovo, the Special Rapporteur has appealed for the release of all abductees. . . .

VI. Observations and Recommendations

46. I welcome the accord reached by the President of the Federal Republic of Yugoslavia and the United States Special Envoy on 13 October 1998 and the agreements of 15 October between the Federal Republic of Yugoslavia and NATO and of 16 October between the Federal Republic of Yugoslavia and the OSCE. I believe the establishment of the Kosovo Verification Mission can contribute to the peaceful settlement of the Kosovo crisis, and I call upon all parties concerned to cooperate with the mission. For its part, the United Nations will continue its humanitarian and human rights activities and will support the efforts of the Kosovo Verification Mission, regional organizations and individual Member States aimed at restoring peace and stability to the region. The complexity and the scope of tasks in Kosovo require coordinated and concerted efforts by all organisations on the ground. All United Nations agencies operating there will establish their lines of communication with the Kosovo Verification Mission to this end. Moreover, the United Nations is prepared to provide assistance to the Mission operation through the United Nations Logistics Base at Brindisi and the United Nations Staff College in Turin.

47. I also welcome the efforts of Christopher Hill of the United States of America, supported by European Union Envoy Wolfgang Petrisch of Austria, in promoting a political dialogue between the Serbian authorities and the representatives of the Albanian community in Kosovo and I call on all parties to cooperate with them in their endeavours.

48. While welcoming reports of the withdrawal of Government forces in Kosovo to agreed levels, I urge all the parties concerned to honour their commitments and to comply fully with the Security Council resolutions. In this regard, reports of the return of Kosovo Albanian paramilitary units to positions vacated by Government forces and particularly by their continued attacks against security forces and civilians are disturbing. This situation makes it all the more urgent that early deployment of Kosovo Verification Mission monitors take place, with a 24-hour presence in order to restore stability and confidence and to enable continuous verification of events on the ground.

49. I am also disturbed by the denial of cooperation on the part of the Government of the Federal Republic of Yugoslavia with the International Tribunal for the Former Yugoslavia. I urge the authorities of the Federal Republic of Yugoslavia to comply with the demands of the international community including, inter alia, paragraph 14 of Security Council resolution 1203 (1998).

50. Despite the beginning of the mass return of internally displaced persons to their homes, the situation on the ground indicates that their needs must be further addressed at the international, regional and local levels. In

this connection, the effective and well-established coordinating role played by UNHCR as the lead agency for humanitarian activities in Kosovo should be maintained and reflected in a formal agreement with OSCE. The coordinating role of UNHCR will be further reinforced by the larger involvement of the Office for the Coordination of Humanitarian Affairs in facilitation of coordination efforts and longer-term reconstruction and post-conflict development plans in Kosovo. More attention will also need to be paid to the humanitarian needs of refugees in Montenegro, as well as to those of the half a million refugees in Serbia.

51. Given the fact that legitimate personal security fears were the overriding obstacle to the return of internally displaced persons, political action to ensure real security to the people is a requisite for any solution to the humanitarian crisis. Such a process would be facilitated if the authorities of the Federal Republic of Yugoslavia were to extend guarantees to all returning civilians so as to avoid the blanket interrogation of male internally displaced persons. The issuance of appropriate amnesty legislation to permit this to happen would be crucial in this regard. Likewise, Kosovo Albanian paramilitary units must stop any armed actions to provoke the Federal Republic of Yugoslavia security forces and must put an immediate end to abductions and other violent activities.

52. The persistent fear expressed about returnees' security highlights the need to actively monitor the activities of and to train local police forces, particularly in the area of human rights. Unless this issue is addressed on an urgent basis, the return process will be seriously undermined by a lack of confidence in the ability or the desire of the local police to protect returnees. If requested and deemed appropriate, the United Nations Civilian Police Unit would be prepared to provide advice in this area. The Office of the High Commissioner for Human Rights will provide existing manuals and other training resources on the subject.

53. The establishment of a United Nations human rights sub-office in Kosovo will allow OHCHR to perform its expanded monitoring and promotional tasks in close cooperation with the Kosovo Verification Mission and UNHCR and other international and national institutions and organizations. Early, effective and coordinated action in cases of human rights abuses will be critical in building confidence for the return of refugees and displaced persons.

54. It is necessary to establish a capability to initiate a comprehensive and integrated mine action plan, including mine awareness, education, information, mine-marking and mine clearance. The United Nations Mine Action Centre will study the possibility of providing assistance in this area.

55. The immediate crisis in Kosovo should not overshadow the necessity to assess the medium-term rehabilitation and reconstruction needs of the Federal Republic of Yugoslavia. As conditions allow, the World Bank, the United Nations Development Programme and bilateral donors should play a major role in this process, particularly in post-conflict projects in Kosovo.

56. With regard to the issue of a first-hand capability to assess the situation

on the ground, it is recalled that subsequent to its request to me, the Security Council endorsed the establishment of the Kosovo Verification Mission by OSCE. Under the 16 October agreement between the Federal Republic of Yugoslavia and OSCE, the Kosovo Verification Mission has been assigned, inter alia, the responsibility of reporting to the Council. In my view, this should subsume the reporting on the situation in Kosovo from a political perspective, a function that the Secretariat has been carrying out with considerable difficulty, for lack of an independent presence on the ground in the past few months. It is quite obvious that any need that might have existed for such a presence has been superseded by the decision to establish the Kosovo Verification Mission. Taking this into account and having considered the options presented by Mr. de Mistura, I have decided against recommending a United Nations political presence in Kosovo, thus avoiding parallel reporting channels that might lead to confusion and overlapping in the field, as well as unnecessary financial expenditure. I consider it important at this stage, therefore, to develop clear channels of communication between the United Nations and OSCE on this issue. If necessary, short-term missions could be sent to the region to look into specific aspects at the Council's request. Should the future situation require an expanded United Nations presence on the ground, the Council could revert to this issue at a later stage.

57. In its resolution 1203 (1998), the Security Council requested me, in consultation with the parties concerned with the agreements signed in Belgrade on 16 October 1998 between the Federal Republic of Yugoslavia and OSCE, and on 15 October 1998 between the Federal Republic of Yugoslavia and NATO, to report regularly to the Council regarding implementation of that resolution. The agreement between the Federal Republic of Yugoslavia and OSCE, however, indicates that the latter will report directly to the Council. I suggest that OSCE and NATO report to the Council through me (as do the Stabilization Force and the Office of the High Representative), while I would continue to report to the Council on the humanitarian and human rights situation in Kosovo. As to the frequency of these reports, this should be determined in consultation with the Kosovo Verification Mission and NATO. It is my opinion, however, that under the present circumstances and in view of the stability achieved on the ground, quarterly reports would suffice, unless otherwise requested by the Council or necessitated by events in the area.

ATTORNEYS GENERAL ON
TOBACCO SETTLEMENT
November 16, 1998

*In the largest legal settlement in the nation's history, the four largest cig-
arette makers agreed to pay forty-six states and the District of Columbia
$206 billion over twenty-five years to compensate the states for Medicaid
funds used to treat smoking-related illnesses. The companies also agreed to
fund a $1.5 billion antismoking campaign, refrain from advertising and
marketing campaigns aimed at teenagers, and disband several tobacco-
related organizations that the attorneys general said were concealing damaging research from the public. Forty-six states and the District of
Columbia signed the agreement with Philip Morris, R. J. Reynolds, Brown
& Williamson, and Lorillard. The other four states had settled earlier with
the tobacco companies for a total of about $40 billion.*

*Despite its price tag, the settlement was somewhat of an anticlimax. In
June 1997 the tobacco companies had negotiated a settlement with the
attorneys general that would have paid the states $368.5 billion, sharply
restricted advertising and marketing to teenagers, and authorized the Food
and Drug Administration (FDA) to regulate tobacco. In return the cigarette
companies would have been protected from future state and class-action
lawsuits that might have ruined the companies financially had they been
successful. The settlement died in June 1998 when the tobacco companies
walked out after a Senate committee proposed placing even tougher measures on the companies.*

*Some three dozen states still had lawsuits pending against the compa-
nies and, rather than fight each one individually, eight attorneys general
approached the tobacco companies to see what might be salvaged from the
original settlement. The November agreement was the result. The public
health community was generally critical of the state settlement because it
did not demand enough of the companies. But others noted that Senate bill
died in part because the public health activists had refused to compromise.
"We can keep doing this state by state, winning and losing . . . and continuing to addict 3,000 kids a day. Or take a giant step now and get on with*

it," said Christine Gregoire, the attorney general of Washington and one of the primary negotiators of the settlement.

The Beginning of the 1990s Tobacco Wars

The settlement was the culmination of a multiyear struggle to reduce smoking in the United States, particularly among teenagers, and to force the tobacco companies to shoulder some of the smoking-related health costs that states had been carrying. Public sentiment against smoking had been growing for several years and was heightened in the early 1990s, when previously secret company documents revealed that the companies had long known about the health hazards of smoking, including the addictive nature of nicotine. Other documents also strongly suggested that the tobacco companies had deliberately targeted advertising and marketing at teenagers to ensure continuing generations of smokers. According to government statistics, 3,000 teenagers started smoking every day, and 1,000 of them were expected to die prematurely of smoking-related illnesses. (Targeted advertising, Historic Documents of 1994, p. 205)

The attack on cigarettes came from two directions. First, in 1995 the FDA proposed regulations to restrict advertising and marketing of cigarettes and smokeless tobacco. Among other things the regulations banned the sale of cigarettes to anyone under age eighteen; banned cigarette vending machines; barred tobacco companies from putting brand names and logos on caps, T-shirts, and other promotional items; and placed restrictions on cigarette ads in publications read by a significant number of teenagers. The FDA issued the regulations, which were made final in 1996, after asserting the authority to regulate the nicotine in tobacco as an addictive drug and cigarettes as a drug-delivery device. At about the same time, states began to file suit against the tobacco companies seeking to recoup the money they had spent under Medicaid to treat thousands of sick smokers. By 1997 dozens of states had either filed such suits or were taking the necessary steps to do so. (FDA regulations, Historic Documents of 1995, p. 670; Historic Documents of 1996, p. 589)

With White House participation, the tobacco companies and the state attorneys general in February 1997 began to explore the possibility of a settlement. Pressure on the big four companies increased in March when the Liggett Group, makers of Chesterfield and L&Ms among other brands, settled suits filed by twenty states. It was the first major defection the tobacco companies had suffered and was worsened by Liggett's admission as part of the settlement that smoking was addictive and caused cancer and other illnesses and that the tobacco industry had targeted advertising to underage smokers. The tobacco companies came under even more pressure in April, when a federal district court judge in North Carolina upheld the FDA's authority to regulate cigarettes as drug-delivery devices.

In June 1997 the tobacco companies and the state attorneys general signed off on a complex, multifaceted settlement. In exchange for immunity from state and class-action lawsuits and restrictions on individual *suits, the companies agreed to pay $368.5 billion to the states over twenty-five years and to pay additional fines if underage smoking did not decline by specified levels. They admitted that smoking was addictive and lethal, and they agreed to sharp constraints on advertising and selling tobacco products. The settlement was expected to raise the price of a pack of cigarettes by about sixty-five cents.* (Tobacco settlement, Historic Documents of 1997, p. 331)

Before the settlement could take effect, however, Congress had to incorporate it into draft legislation that then had to be debated, approved, and signed into law by the president. The settlement was immediately attacked from several sides. The public health community said it was not hard enough on the tobacco companies and did not go far enough in curbing teenage smoking. Tobacco growers were upset because the settlement did not include any protections for them. On April 1 the Senate Commerce Committee approved comprehensive tobacco legislation that raised the amount of money the tobacco companies would have to pay to $516 billion and did not give the companies immunity from future lawsuits. A week later the tobacco companies withdrew their support from the settlement and mounted a $40 million advertising campaign against the Senate legislation (S 1415), known as the McCain bill after its chief sponsor John McCain, R-Ariz.

That campaign sought to portray the comprehensive antitobacco legislation not as an effective means to curb teenage smoking but as a money grab by the government and a bonanza for trial lawyers. Senate Republicans, long the major beneficiaries of campaign funds from the tobacco companies, had reluctantly gone along with the legislation rather than risk voter backlash at the polls. But as public sentiment began to turn against the legislation, many Republicans began to speak out against it. Finally, on June 17, Republicans killed the bill in a series of procedural votes.

Two months later, a three-judge federal appeals panel in Richmond, Virginia, overturned the federal district court ruling and declared that the FDA did not have the authority to regulate cigarettes or smokeless tobacco. The FDA could not regulate tobacco products without explicit authorization from Congress, the panel ruled August 14. The Justice Department immediately said it would appeal the ruling to the full appeals court, and it seemed certain that the question would likely go to the Supreme Court for final resolution.

The Multistate Settlement

With its hand strengthened by those two victories, the tobacco companies renewed talks with the attorneys general from eight states that were proceeding with their lawsuits against the companies. Those talks resulted in the $206 billion settlement announced November 16 and finalized November 23 when all forty-six states that had not already settled with the companies earlier agreed to its terms.

While the tobacco companies did not have to pay out as much money in the multistate settlement as they would have under the earlier plan, they did not get one of the things they wanted most—protection from class-action and individual lawsuits. Still, according to one estimate the deal settled about 70 percent of the litigation risk facing the companies. It seemed likely that smokers would pay for most of the companies' costs through increased prices. R. J. Reynolds and Philip Morris both announced November 24 that they would raise the price of cigarettes by forty-five cents.

Public health activists said the multistate settlement was too soft on the companies. "Compared to what they were looking at essentially in every serious bill on the hill, they pulled off another coup," Sen. Ron Wyden, D-Ore., said of the tobacco companies. Others said that the public activists bore a large share of the blame for the collapse of the earlier settlement. "We brought the industry to the brink and these guys [the public health advocates] never knew when to cut the deal," said one attorney involved in the negotiations. "Now they're suffering the consequences." They also expressed concern about how the states would spend their settlement money. The settlement did not require the states to devote the money to health care or antismoking campaigns, and several state legislatures were already arguing over how to use the money.

An Upward Trend in Smoking Among Teenagers

Antismoking activists vowed to continue fighting for strong measures to curb smoking, especially among teenagers. Several studies released during the year showed that the problem was worsening. A report released by the federal Centers for Disease Prevention and Control (CDC) on April 2 found that while smoking was increasing among all teenagers, it had shot up nearly 80 percent among black teenagers between 1991 and 1997. The increase was worrisome because black teenagers had low rates of smoking in the 1970s and 1980s. According to the CDC study, 39.7 percent of white high school students smoked in 1997, up from 30.9 in 1991; 22.7 percent of black high school students smoked in 1997, up from 12.6 percent in 1991. Although the survey did not ask teenagers why they smoked, researchers speculated that cigarette marketing directed specifically at black youth was one of the factors behind the increase in black teenage smoking.

In his annual report, released April 27, Surgeon General David Satcher warned that increases in smoking among minorities could reverse declines in cancer that statisticians had been seeing in the past few years. That message was reinforced by a May 21 report from the CDC's Office of Smoking and Health finding that almost 36 percent of high school students developed a smoking habit while still in school, smoking at least one cigarette a day. Nearly 73 percent with a daily habit said they had tried to quit, but only 13.5 percent of them were successful. "That's strictly a testimony to the power of nicotine," said Michael Richness, director of the office.

Finally, a national survey of about 15,000 college students conducted by the Harvard School of Public Health found that smoking was on the rise, increasing from 22.3 percent in 1993 to 28.5 percent in 1997. Because college students were less likely to smoke than their peers who were not in college, the increase "signals great danger" for the health of the next generation, one of the report's authors said. That study was released November 17, the day after the multistate settlement was reached.

Following are the texts of two November 16, 1998, news releases from the National Association of Attorneys General; the first announced a multistate settlement of lawsuits brought against the four major tobacco companies and the second summarized the main points of that settlement, under which the states would receive $206 billion in compensation for Medicaid funds they had spent to treat smoking-related health problems:

TOBACCO SETTLEMENT PROPOSAL

A historic settlement proposal, that mandates the most significant legal reform in the tobacco industry and the largest financial recovery in the nation's history, was released today. The proposal was negotiated by a team of eight established by the state Attorneys General [AGs].

Under the settlement proposal, tobacco companies would agree to significant curbs on their advertising and marketing campaigns, fund a $1.5 billion anti-smoking campaign, open previously secret industry documents, and disband industry trade groups which Attorneys General maintain conspired to conceal damaging research from the public.

In announcing the settlement, the Attorneys General said it should be viewed as the beginning, not the end, of tobacco reform in this country. The Attorneys General said "this is litigation, not legislation. Congress should pass legislation to provide essential reforms—including full Food and Drug Administration authority over tobacco—we pledge to help them."

The settlement has numerous provisions aimed at protecting kids. In filing their lawsuits, state Attorneys General contended the industry was targeting children. In this nation, about 3,000 kids a day start smoking, and a third of them will die prematurely as a result of that decision.

Noting it would take years to complete all the state lawsuits and even longer to exhaust the inevitable appeals, the AGs said the settlement, "moves the fight out of courtroom and onto the streets so we can begin protecting kids now."

Under the settlement proposal, the tobacco industry would contribute $1.5 billion over the next five years for a national public education fund which would carry out a massive education and advertising campaign. It also would pay $250 million for a foundation dedicated to reducing teen smoking.

Other provisions in the settlement would ban cartoon characters in tobacco advertising, prohibit the industry from targeting youth in ads and marketing, prohibit billboards and transit advertising, and ban the sale and distribution of apparel, backpacks and other merchandise which bear brand-name logos and become, in effect, walking billboards.

The AGs said the settlement won't end youth smoking in America, but it does provide "realistic, workable steps to stop the addiction of our children."

Under the settlement, tobacco companies would pay the states more than $9 billion a year beginning in the year 2008. Total payments through the year 2025 would be $206 billion. This does not include settlements already reached with four other states totaling over $40 billion in the same period of time.

States spend billions each year on medical care for smoking related illnesses and the industry payments, which will be made in perpetuity, will relieve taxpayers of the costs from future smoking-related illnesses.

Terms of the settlement call for the industry to pay the states $12 billion in "up-front" money over five years.

The annual payments will be adjusted annually based on inflation and volume adjustments based on future sales of cigarettes.

More than 40 states sued tobacco companies, alleging, among other things, that the industry violated antitrust, and consumer protection laws. In addition, states alleged the companies conspired to withhold information about adverse health effects of tobacco, that they manipulated nicotine levels to keep smokers addicted and that they conspired to withhold less risk products from the market.

To settle the lawsuits, the industry has agreed to dozens of new restrictions and public health initiatives which are aimed at changing the way it does business. The Attorneys General said the ability to force a change in tobacco industry conduct was an important factor in their settlement decision. "Attorneys General must determine whether the economic and non-economic terms of this settlement are equal to or greater than the uncertain results they could achieve in court," they said.

The Attorneys General said they believe strong state cases against the tobacco industry led to the settlement proposal and that a national settlement will avoid a patchwork of reform which could result if each state individually pursued its lawsuit.

The industry would pay all attorney fees—both state and private counsel—and reimburse states for their costs.

Four states—Mississippi, Florida, Texas and Minnesota—already have settled with tobacco companies. The new settlement builds on the previous settlements and provides the most comprehensive package of public health reforms to date.

To ensure the industry lives up to the agreement, the settlement would be enforceable through consent decrees which will be entered in each state court. In addition, the industry will provide $50 million for an enforcement fund which states could use to pursue violations of the settlement.

The settlement proposal was negotiated with the industry by Attorneys General Drew Edmondson of Oklahoma, Mike Fisher of Pennsylvania, Christine Gregoire of Washington, Heidi Heitkamp of North Dakota, Dan Lungren of California, Mike Easley of North Carolina, Gale Norton of Colorado, and Dennis Vacco of New York.

The settlement proposal, that was negotiated over the last five months, now will be sent to all other Attorneys General for their review. It will not be final until agreed to by an as-yet unspecified number of states. A decision is expected November 23.

TOBACCO SETTLEMENT SUMMARY

The Foundation

Anti-smoking advertising campaigns are extremely effective when they are long-term, and consistently portray smoking as hazardous for adults and children alike, according to an article in the Annals of Internal Medicine.

The Settlement:

- Requires the industry each year for ten years to pay $25 million to fund a charitable foundation which will support the study of programs to reduce teen smoking and substance abuse and the prevention of diseases associated with tobacco use.
- The foundation will:
  - Carry out a nationwide, sustained advertising and education program to counter youth tobacco use and educate consumers about the cause and prevention of diseases associated with tobacco use.
  - Develop, disseminate and test the effectiveness of counter advertising campaigns.
  - Commission studies, fund research and publish reports on factors that influence youth smoking and substance abuse.
  - Track and monitor youth smoking and substance abuse with a focus on reasons for increases or failures to decrease tobacco and substance use rates.
- Creates an industry-funded $1.45 billion national public education fund for tobacco control.
- The fund is established to carry out a nationwide sustained advertising and education program to counter youth tobacco use and educate consumers about tobacco-related diseases.

Cartoon Characters

"[Tobacco] advertisements present images that appeal to children and youths and are seen and remembered by them. Concern has been expressed

that while smoking may not have had an immediate effect on smoking uptake, they may increase susceptibility to smoking, which over time translates into behavior."—Institute of Medicine.

The Settlement:

- Bans use of cartoons in the advertising, promotion, packaging or labeling of tobacco products.

Targeting Youth

"This young adult market, the 14-24 group . . . represent(s) tomorrow's cigarette business. As this 14-24 age group matures, they will account for a key share of the total cigarette volume for at least the next 25 years."— Presentation from C.A. Tucker, Vice President of Marketing, to the Board of Directors, RJR Industries, September 30, 1974.

The Settlement:

- Prohibits targeting youth in advertising, promotions, or marketing.
- Bans industry actions aimed at initiating, maintaining or increasing youth smoking.
- Requires companies to:
  - Develop and regularly communicate corporate principles which commit to complying with the Master Settlement Agreement and reducing youth smoking.
  - Designate executive level manager to identify ways to reduce youth access and consumption of tobacco.
  - Encourage employees to identify additional methods to reduce youth access and youth consumption.

Public Access to Documents and Court Files

"The American people deserve to know the truth about the tobacco industry's marketing practices. . . ."—U.S. Rep. Thomas Bliley.

The Settlement:

- Requires tobacco companies to open, at their expense, a Website which includes all documents produced in state and other smoking and health related lawsuits.
- Requires the industry to maintain the site for ten years in a user-friendly and searchable format (requires and index and other features to improve searchable access).
- Requires the industry to add, at its expense, all documents produced in future civil actions involving smoking and health cases.

Outdoor Advertising

"Tobacco companies spend more than $5 billion annually, or $13 million a day, on advertising and marketing campaigns."—Federal Trade Commission.

The Settlement:

- Bans all outdoor advertising, including: billboards, signs and placards in arenas, stadiums, shopping malls, and video game arcades.
- Limits advertising outside retail establishments to 14 square feet.
- Bans transit advertising of tobacco products.
- Allows states to substitute, for the duration of billboard lease periods, alternative advertising which discourages youth smoking.

Tobacco Merchandise

"Thirty percent of kids (12 to 17 years old), both smokers and non-smokers, own at least one tobacco promotional item, such as T-shirts, back-packs, and CD players."—Campaign for Tobacco-Free Kids.

The Settlement:

- Beginning July 1, 1999, bans distribution and sale of apparel and merchandise with brand-name logos (caps, T-shirts, backpacks, etc.).

Product Placement and Sponsorships

A document uncovered in the Minnesota case revealed how Phillip Morris provided products for use in movies as youth-oriented as "The Muppet Movie" and "Who Framed Roger Rabbit."

The Settlement:

- Bans payments to promote tobacco products in movies, television shows, theater productions or live performances, live or recorded music performances, videos and video games.
- Prohibits brand name sponsorship of events with a significant youth audience or team sports (football, basketball, baseball, hockey or soccer).
- Prohibits sponsorship of events where the paid participants or contestants are underage.
- Limits tobacco companies to one brand name sponsorship per year (after current contracts expire or after three years - whichever comes first).
- Bans tobacco brand names for stadiums and arenas.

Dissolution of Tobacco-Related Organizations

"The documents, considered as a whole, provide evidence that supports the state's assertions that defendants used CTR (Council for Tobacco Research) to mislead the public. . . ."—Honorable George Finkle, King County Superior Court Judge (Washington State).

The Settlement:

- Disbands the Council for Tobacco Research, the Tobacco Institute, and the Council for Indoor Air Research.

- Requires all records of these organizations that relate to any lawsuit to be preserved.
- Provides regulation and oversight of new trade organizations.

Financial Recovery for the States

The Settlement:

- Requires industry payments to the states in perpetuity, with the payments totaling $206 billion through the year 2025.
- Provides that distributions to states will be made based on formulas agreed to by Attorneys General.
- Requires annual payments by the industry to begin April 15, 2000.
- Provides that if all states participate in the settlement, annual payments will "ramp-up" beginning with a $4.5 billion payment on April 15, 2000. Ensuing April 15 payments will be at the following rates:
  - 2001: $5 billion
  - 2002–2003: $6.5 billion
  - 2004–2007: $8 billion
  - 2008–2017: $8.139 billion (plus $861 million to the strategic fund)
  - 2018 on: $9 billion
- Requires tobacco companies will pay "up front" payments of nearly $13 billion in the following amounts: $2.4 billion in 1998, $2.472 billion on January 10, 2000, $2.546 billion in 2001, $2.622 billion in 2002, and $2.701 billion in 2003.
- Requires the companies, on April 15, 2008 and on April 15 each year through 2017, to pay $861 million into a strategic contribution fund.
- Money from the fund will be allocated to states based on a strategic contribution formula developed by Attorneys General no later than June, 1999. The allocation formula will reflect the contribution made by states toward resolution of the state lawsuits against tobacco companies.

Enforcement

"At least 516 million packs of cigarettes per year are consumed by minors and at least half of those are illegally sold to minors."—Institute of Medicine in its book *Growing Up Tobacco Free.*

The Settlement:

- Provides Court Jurisdiction For Implementation and Enforcement
- If the court issues an enforcement order enforcing the agreement and a party violates that order, the court may order monetary, civil contempt or criminal sanctions to enforce compliance with the enforcement order.
- Key public health provisions of the agreement are included in consent decrees to be filed in each state.
- Settling states or tobacco companies may apply to the court to enforce the terms of the consent decree.

- Allows settling state AGs access to company documents, records and personnel to enforce the agreement.
- On March 31, 1999, the industry is directed to pay $50 million which will be used to assist settling states in enforcing and implementing the agreement and to investigate and litigate potential violations of state tobacco laws.

Free Samples

"Samples encourage experimentation by providing minors with a risk-free and cost-free way to satisfy their curiosity."—Institute of Medicine.

The Settlement:

- Free samples cannot be distributed except in a facility or enclosed area where the operator ensures no underage person is present.

Gifts Based on Purchases

"[T]eens save Marlboro Miles and Camel Cash coupons in order to acquire other types of goods. . . . My brother gets Camel Cash. He's got stacks and stacks of them to get hats or whatever."—The Institute of Medicine in its book *Growing up Tobacco Free.*

The Settlement:

- Bans gifts without proof of age.

Lobbying

"Big tobacco spent $28.8 million in 1996 and $35.5 million in 1997 and employed 208 lobbyists to lobby Congress. That is one lobbyist for every 2.5 members of Congress."—Public Citizen.

The Settlement:

- Tobacco companies prohibited from opposing proposed state or local laws or administrative rules which are intended to limit youth access to and consumption of tobacco products.
- The industry must require its lobbyists to certify in writing they have reviewed and will fully comply with settlement terms including disclosure of financial contributions regarding lobbying activities and new corporate culture principles;
- Prohibits lobbyists from supporting or opposing state, federal, or local laws or actions without authorization of the companies.

Prohibition on Agreements to Suppress Research

"Cigarettes kill more than 400,000 Americans every year. This figure represents more deaths than from AIDS, alcohol, car accidents, murders, suicides, drugs and fires—combined."—Campaign for Tobacco-Free Kids.

The Settlement:

- Prohibits manufacturers from jointly contracting or conspiring to:
  - Limit information about the health hazards from the use of their products;
  - Limit or suppress research into smoking and health; and
  - Limit or suppress research into the marketing or development of new products.
  - Prohibits the industry from making any material misrepresentations regarding the health consequences of smoking.
- Prohibits manufacturers from jointly contracting or conspiring to:
  - Limit information about the health hazards from the use of their products;
  - Limit or suppress research into smoking and health; and
  - Limit or suppress research into the marketing or development of new products.
- Prohibits the industry from making any material misrepresentations regarding the health consequences of smoking.

Minimum Pack Size

"As the price of a pack of cigarettes continues to increase, more merchants (in minority, white, poor, and middle-class communities alike) may begin selling singles as a way to continue to make profits from adult and minor customers who can no longer afford an entire pack."—From a study by the Public Health Foundation.

The Settlement:

- Limits minimum pack size to 20 cigarettes through December 31, 2001.
- Tobacco companies prohibited from opposing state legislation which bans the manufacture and sale of packs containing fewer than 20 cigarettes.

Cost Recovery and Attorney Fees

The Settlement:

- Requires the industry to reimburse states for costs, expenses and market rate for attorney fees.
- Requires the industry to pay for outside attorneys hired by the states.
  - Establishes two payment methods—liquidated fee agreement and arbitration.
  - Outside counsel can negotiate a liquidated fee agreement with the industry, and if accepted, would be paid from a $1.25 billion pool of money from the tobacco industry over four years.
  - If outside counsel rejects the liquidated fee process or cannot agree to an offer, they can go through arbitration.

- A three-member arbitration panel will be established with two permanent members and a member from the state represented by the outside counsel.
- The industry will pay whatever arbiters award, but timing of the payment will be subject to a $500-million-per-year cash flow cap.

APPEALS COURT ON AFFIRMATIVE ACTION IN PUBLIC SCHOOLS
November 19, 1998

Affirmative action programs continued to come under attack in 1998. Washington became the second state, after California, to ban the use of affirmative action programs by any state agency. The Clinton administration reduced or eliminated several federal affirmative action programs that were unlikely to meet the strict new standards set out by the Supreme Court in a 1995 case. The most far-reaching action, however, may have been a federal appeals court ruling that diversity was not a "compelling" reason for considering race in admissions to a public high school. In one major victory for the year, supporters of affirmative action decisively turned back a move in the House of Representatives to bar race-based admissions to all public colleges and universities.

Controversial from their beginnings in the 1960s, affirmative action programs embraced a variety of methods to help minorities and women overcome the effects of past discrimination and become full participants in the nation's educational and economic life. Courts ordered employers guilty of job discrimination to adopt such plans, and many other corporations set up voluntary programs to recruit, hire, and promote minorities and women. Federal, state, and local government programs ranged from mandates, such as requiring that a certain number of slots in a particular contract be filled by minorities and women, to outreach programs that simply encouraged employers to hire or contract with minorities.

Opponents argued that the programs meant that qualified white and male applicants were often passed over in favor of less-qualified minorities and women, resulting in "reverse discrimination." The marketplace should be colorblind, they said. Others argued that the programs were no longer necessary because the discrimination they had been designed to overcome had been largely eradicated.

New Federal Policy on Antidiscrimination Plans

In 1995 opponents won a major victory, when the Supreme Court in Adarand Constructors v. Peña *ruled that federal affirmative action plans*

*had to meet the Court's "strict scrutiny" test if they were to be found con-
stitutional. That test required that the programs serve a "compelling governmental interest" and be narrowly tailored to address past discrimination. A month later, President Bill Clinton endorsed affirmative action.
His admonition to "mend it, don't end it" firmed up his political support
among civil rights groups and women's organizations, even as federal
agencies were beginning to review their antidiscrimination plans to see
which ones might be in violation of the Court's* Adarand *ruling.* (Supreme
Court ruling, Historic Documents of 1995, p. 307; Clinton on affirmative
action, Historic Documents of 1995, p. 483)

*During the next two years, several federal affirmative action plans were
either eliminated or sharply curtailed. All programs that set aside a specific percentage of contracts or sum of money for minority-owned companies were ended, for example. On June 24, 1998, the White House
announced a new policy on letting procurement contracts that was
designed to meet the "strict scrutiny" test laid out in* Adarand. *Under the
revised policy small "disadvantaged" businesses competing for government
contracts would be given an advantage but only in those industries or
regions of the country where they were underrepresented.*

*Businesses owned by American Indians and Americans who were black,
Hispanic, or Asian were assumed to be disadvantaged; businesses owned
by whites, including women, would be eligible only if they could show
through a "preponderance of the evidence" that they were socially and economically disadvantaged. Eligible companies would be considered the low
bidder on a contract if their bid price was within 10 percent of the lowest
price bid by a nondisadvantaged company. To determine where discrimination still existed, the government surveyed more than seventy industries. According to that survey, which the White House said would be
updated periodically, minority businesses were underrepresented in truck-
ing and textile mills, for example, but there appeared to be no discrimination in agriculture or food manufacturing. General contracting was broken down by geographic region; minorities were found to be
underrepresented in the Middle Atlantic states, for example, but not in the
Pacific states.*

*In a statement issued by the White House, President Clinton said the
new policy was an example of his promise to "mend, not end" affirmative
action, adding that the policy "satisfies constitutional requirements while
targeting our efforts in areas where disparities still exist." The policy
received support from some civil rights groups. Rep. Maxine Waters,
D-Calif., chairman of the Congressional Black Caucus, said it would "provide opportunities for qualified minority businesses to compete openly
and fairly" for federal contracts. Others were less enthusiastic. Wade
Henderson, executive director of the Leadership Conference on Civil
Rights, said the new rules were "at best a mixed bag." Opponents of racial
preferences said the new policy was just more of the same. "Decisions will
still be made on the basis of ethnic background," said Rep. Charles T.*

Canady, R-Fla., who had introduced legislation to end federal affirmative action programs.

Washington Referendum on Affirmative Action

Washington became the second state in the nation to bar affirmative action programs in state programs, when 58 percent of the state's voters adopted "Initiative 200" on November 3. The ban, which prohibited "discriminating or granting preferential treatment," applied to hiring and contracting in every state and local government agency and to admissions to public schools and universities. It was modeled after California's Proposition 209, which was adopted in 1996. Legal challenges to that referendum had all failed. (California referendum adopted, Historic Documents of 1996, p. 759; California referendum upheld, Historic Documents of 1997, p. 183)

Washington's ballot initiative was sponsored by Ward Connerly, an African American businessman from Sacramento who was also a main sponsor of the California initiative. Connerly headed a group called the American Civil Rights Institute, which planned to press similar initiatives in future elections. It was unclear immediately after the election whether a court challenge to the Washington initiative would be mounted.

Racial Preferences Barred in Public High School

Controversy surrounding racial preferences in education admissions expanded from the public university realm to the public high school arena in 1998, when a federal appeals court ruled for the first time that a race-based admissions policy in a public high school was unconstitutional. In 1996 the Fifth Circuit Court of Appeals struck down a University of Texas policy that used racial preferences in admissions; the Supreme Court let that ruling stand without review.

The high school case involved the Boston Latin School, a prestigious public school and one of three magnet schools in the city requiring students to pass an achievement test to be admitted. The case, Wessmann v. Gittens, *had its beginning in 1974, when a federal court ordered busing to end desegregation. In 1975 the court required Boston Latin to set aside 35 percent of each entering class for black and Hispanic students; the First Circuit Court of Appeals upheld that requirement in 1976. The mandate was removed in 1987, but the Boston School Committee kept the policy in place until 1995, when it was challenged by the parent of a white applicant who had been denied admission even though her examination scores were higher than those of some of the black and Hispanic applicants who were accepted. That challenge was dismissed after the school agreed to change its policy and admit the applicant.*

Under the policy adopted for the 1997–1998 school year, half the students in the entering class were admitted strictly on the basis of their test scores and grade point averages; the other half were admitted in proportion to the percentage of their race in the remaining pool of applicants.

Thus, if there were ten slots to be filled and there were sixty whites, twenty blacks and twenty Hispanics in the remaining pool of one hundred applicants, then six of the slots would be filled by highest-rated whites remaining in the pool, two by the highest-rated blacks, and two by the highest-rated Hispanics—even if some students in one group ranked higher overall than students selected from the other two groups. A white applicant who would have been admitted if all slots were filled strictly on academic merit but who was rejected in favor of minority students sued.

In throwing out the admissions policy, the divided appeals court panel said that even if vestiges of past discrimination still existed in the city, the admissions policy was not designed narrowly enough to reach only those individual students who had actually been harmed by discrimination. Nor was ensuring racial diversity a "compelling" enough "governmental interest" to permit the school district to take race into account in its admissions policy. "We do not question the School Committee's good intentions," the court wrote, adding, however, that those good intentions could have "harmful consequences." The admissions policy, the court continued, "is, at bottom, a mechanism for racial balancing—and placing our imprimatur on racial balancing risks setting a precedent that is both dangerous to our democratic ideals and almost always constitutionally forbidden."

Although the ruling applied only to school districts in states that fell within the First Circuit's jurisdictions, it raised legal uncertainty over the validity of race-based admissions policies in public schools all over the country. Most school districts no longer applied strict racial quotas in their school systems, if they ever did, but many magnet schools, which tended to have more applicants than available slots, considered race in their admissions policy to ensure diversity among their students. "It's an issue of great frustration to school boards, because if there can be no consideration of race and ethnicity, many schools that have worked very hard over the years to become diverse will slide back to very segregated patterns," said Julie Underwood of the National School Boards Association.

House Vote on Affirmative Action

Advocates of affirmative action had won a victory during the year when the House of Representatives turned back a move to end racial preference programs at all public colleges and universities that accepted any federal funding. The language was offered by Rep. Frank Riggs, R-Calif., as an amendment to the Higher Education Act reauthorization. "I believe we must focus on equality of opportunity in this country, not mandate equality of results," Riggs said of his amendment that would have ended admissions preferences based on race, sex, ethnicity, or national origin.

Instead of serving as a defining issue between Republicans and Democrats, however, the amendment exposed deep fissures over the issue within the Republican Party. Members were split over ending what many considered to be special treatment with a political need to reach out to women and minorities. House Republican leaders supported the amendment, but they were opposed by J. C. Watts of Oklahoma, the only African American Republican in the House. Watts joined Rep. John Lewis, D-Ga., a noted civil rights leader, in a letter urging colleagues to vote against the amendment. It was defeated May 6 by a 171–249 vote, with fifty-five Republicans voting against it and only five Democrats voting in favor.

> *Following are excerpts from the decision in the case of* Wessmann v. Gittens, *in which the First Circuit Court of Appeals ruled 2–1 on November 19, 1998, that a race-based admissions policy for a public high school in Boston was a violation of the Constitution's equal protection clause:*

The City of Boston operates three renowned "examination schools," the most prestigious of which is Boston Latin School (BLS). The entrance points for admission to BLS occur principally at the seventh- and ninth-grade levels. In this litigation, plaintiff-appellant Henry Robert Wessmann, on behalf of his minor child, Sarah P. Wessmann, challenges the constitutionality of BLS's admissions policy (the Policy). The district court rebuffed Wessmann's challenge.... On appeal, we must decide whether the Policy, which makes race a determining factor in the admission of a subset of each year's incoming classes, offends the Constitution's guarantee of equal protection. We conclude that it does.

I. Background

. . . .

Over two decades ago, a federal district court adjudged the City of Boston (through its School Committee) to have violated the constitutional rights of African-American children by promoting and maintaining a dual public school system.... Although the court found the school system as a whole guilty of de jure segregation, no specific evidence was produced to suggest that BLS's examination-based admissions policy discriminated against anyone or that those responsible for running BLS intended to segregate the races.... Nonetheless, BLS exhibited some of the symptoms of segregation: an anomalously low number of African-American students attended the school, ... and the school had just changed its entrance testing methods pursuant to a consent decree settling charges that the earlier methods were themselves discriminatory.... These factors, combined with the City's inability to demonstrate that existing racial imbalances were not a result of discrimination, led the court to conclude that the City's examination schools (BLS included) were complicit in promoting and maintaining the dual system....

The remedy adopted by the district court, among other things, obligated BLS to ensure that at least 35% of each entering class would be composed of African-American and Hispanic students.... Relying on the *Keyes* presumption, we affirmed this set-aside as part of a comprehensive plan to ameliorate pervasive and persistent constitutional infirmities throughout the Boston public schools. . . .

The Boston school system began gradually to mend its ways. By 1987, systemic progress permitted us to conclude that, for all practical purposes, the School Committee had achieved unitariness in the area of student assignments. . . . We based our conclusion not only on the distribution of students throughout the City's schools, but also on the good faith demonstrated by school administrators in conforming with the demands of meaningful change. Because comparable improvement had not been accomplished in other areas, such as faculty and staff integration and the renovation of facilities, we instructed that federal court supervision of elements other than student assignment continue. . . . The district court thereupon relinquished control over student assignments, even while retaining active supervision over other aspects of the school system.

After 1987, the City's three examination schools—BLS, Boston Latin Academy, and the O'Bryant School—were no longer under a federal court mandate to maintain a 35% set-aside. Nevertheless, the School Committee remained committed to the policy until 1995, when a disappointed applicant challenged the set-aside's constitutionality. The district court granted injunctive relief directing the complainant's admission to BLS. . . .

Concerned that the number of African-American and Hispanic students admitted to the examination schools might drop precipitously without a predetermined set-aside, school officials began researching alternative admissions policies in hopes of finding one that might prevent that result without offending the Constitution. . . .

. . . To gain admission to one of Boston's three examination schools, a student must take a standardized test. Based on a mathematical formula that purports to predict academic performance, school hierarchs combine each applicant's test score with his or her grade point average, derive a composite score, rank all applicants accordingly, and proceed to assign individuals to the applicant pool for the examination school(s) in which they have indicated an interest. To be eligible for admission to any of the examination schools, an applicant must be in the qualified applicant pool (QAP), a group composed of those who rank in the top 50% of the overall applicant pool for that particular school.

Half of the available seats for an examination school's entering class are allocated in strict accordance with composite score rank order. The other half are allocated on the basis of "flexible racial/ethnic guidelines" promulgated as part of the Policy. To apply these guidelines, school officials first determine the relative proportions of five different racial/ethnic categories— white, black, Hispanic, Asian, and Native American—in the remaining pool of qualified applicants (RQAP), that is, the QAP for the particular school *minus* those persons already admitted on the basis of composite score rank order alone. They then fill the open seats in rank order, but the number of students taken from each racial/ethnic category must match the proportion of that category in the RQAP. Because the racial/ethnic distribution of the second group of successful applicants must mirror that of the RQAP, a member of a designated racial/ethnic group may be passed over in favor of a lower-ranking applicant from another group if the seats allotted for the former's racial/ethnic group have been filled.

Sarah Wessmann encountered such a fate. BLS had 90 available seats for the 1997 ninth-grade entering class. Based on her composite score, Sarah ranked 91st (out of 705) in the QAP. To fill the first 45 seats, the school exhausted the top 47 persons on the list (two aspirants declined in order to accept invitations from another examination school). Had composite scores alone dictated the selection of the remainder of the ninth-grade entering class, Sarah would have been admitted. But the racial/ethnic composition of the RQAP was 27.83% black, 40.41% white, 19.21% Asian, 11.64% Hispanic, and 0.31% Native American. Consequently, the Policy required school officials to allocate the final 45 seats to 13 blacks, 18 whites, 9 Asians, and 5 Hispanics. As a result, black and Hispanic students whose composite score rankings ranged from 95th to 150th displaced Sarah and ten other white students who had higher composite scores and ranks.

Acting to Sarah's behoof, her father sued a coterie of defendants (collectively, the School Committee), alleging that the Policy had defeated her candidacy and challenging its constitutionality. Following a 13-day bench trial, the district court held that the School Committee's interests in promoting a diverse student body and remedying vestiges of past discrimination were compelling, and that the means crafted by the School Committee to further these interests were not so expansive as to raise constitutional concerns. . . . This appeal ensued.

II. Analysis

We divide our analysis into four segments, beginning with the standards that govern our review, then addressing the general idea of "compelling governmental interests," and, finally, proceeding to consider seriatim the two justifications asserted by the School Committee in defense of the Policy.

A. Standards of Review.

The Supreme Court consistently employs sweeping language to identify the species of racial classifications that require strict scrutiny, . . . and the Policy fits comfortably within this rubric. We conclude, therefore, that strict scrutiny is the proper standard for evaluating the Policy. Hence, the Policy must be both justified by a compelling governmental interest and narrowly tailored to serve that interest in order to stand.

The School Committee's rejoinder—that the Policy is not a quota—is a non sequitur. We agree that the Policy does not constitute a quota—at least not in the literal sense of an unchanging set-aside—but that fact gains the School Committee little ground. At a certain point in its application process—specifically, during the selection of the second half of each incoming class—the Policy relies on race and ethnicity, and nothing else, to select a subset of entrants. Thus, whether the Policy is truly a quota or whether it is best described otherwise is entirely irrelevant for the purpose of equal protection analysis. Attractive labeling cannot alter the fact that any program which induces schools to grant preferences based on race and ethnicity is constitutionally suspect. . . .

The School Committee also asserts an entitlement to more lenient review because the Policy neither benefits nor burdens any particular group. Under the flexible guidelines, the argument goes, the racial/ethnic distribution of the entering classes will change yearly, and thus, there is no real preference for any single group.

This assertion leads nowhere, for the manner in which the Policy functions is fundamentally at odds with the equal protection guarantee that citizens will be treated "as individuals, not as simply components of a racial, religious, sexual or national class." *Miller* v. *Johnson* (1995) (citations and internal quotation marks omitted). Even though we may not know before the fact which individuals from which racial/ethnic groups will be affected, we do know that someone from some group will be benefitted and a different someone from a different group will be burdened. Because a court's obligation to review race-conscious programs and policies cannot be made to depend "on the race of those burdened or benefitted by a particular classification," *City of Richmond* v. *J.A. Croson Co.* (1989) (plurality op.), no more is exigible to bring strict scrutiny into play.

A remaining issue under this heading concerns our review of the district court's findings and conclusions. We accord deferential review to specific findings of fact emanating from a bench trial. . . . Here, however, because the issues advanced in this appeal—specifically, whether diversity and curing vestiges of past discrimination satisfy strict scrutiny—raise either questions of law or questions about how the law applies to discerned facts, our review is essentially plenary. . . .

B. Compelling Interests: An Overview.

The question of precisely what interests government may legitimately invoke to justify race-based classifications is largely unsettled. . . .

A few cases suggest (albeit in dictum) that remedying past discrimination is the only permissible justification for race-conscious action by the government. . . . But in certain milieus, some courts have accepted race-based taxonomies that are not linked to remedying past discrimination, particularly in settings such as law enforcement and corrections. . . .

In considering whether other governmental interests, beyond the need to heal the vestiges of past discrimination, may be sufficiently compelling to justify race-based initiatives, courts occasionally mention "diversity". At first blush, it appears that a negative consensus may be emerging on this point. . . .

We think that any such consensus is more apparent than real. In the education context, *Hopwood* is the only appellate court to have rejected diversity as a compelling interest, and it did so only in the face of vigorous dissent from a substantial minority of the active judges in the Fifth Circuit. See *Hopwood* v. *State of Texas*, (5th Cir. 1996). . . . The question that divided the Fifth Circuit centered on the precedential value of Justice Powell's controlling opinion in *Bakke*. The panel in *Hopwood* pronounced that opinion dead. The dissenting judges countered that the reports of *Bakke*'s demise were premature.

It may be that the *Hopwood* panel is correct and that, were the Court to address the question today, it would hold that diversity is not a sufficiently compelling interest to justify a race-based classification. It has not done so yet, however, and we are not prepared to make such a declaration in the absence of a clear signal that we should. . . . This seems especially prudent because the Court and various individual Justices from time to time have written approvingly of ethnic diversity in comparable settings, . . . or have noted that the issue remains open. . . .

As matters turn out, we need not definitively resolve this conundrum today. Instead, we assume *arguendo*—but we do not decide—that *Bakke* remains good law and that some iterations of "diversity" might be sufficiently compelling, in specific circumstances, to justify race-conscious actions. It is against this chiaroscuro backdrop that we address the School Committee's asserted "diversity" justification for the Policy. Thereafter, we turn to its alternate justification: that the Policy is an appropriate means of remediating the vestiges of past discrimination.

C. Diversity.

. . . .

By its terms, the Policy focuses exclusively on racial and ethnic diversity. Its scope is narrowed further in that it takes into account only five groups— blacks, whites, Hispanics, Asians, and Native Americans—without recognizing that none is monolithic. No more is needed to demonstrate that the School Committee already has run afoul of the guidance provided by the principal authority on which it relies: "The diversity that furthers a compelling state interest encompasses a far broader array of qualifications and characteristics of which racial or ethnic origin is but a single though important element" [*Bakke*]. A single-minded focus on ethnic diversity "hinder[s] rather than further[s] attainment of genuine diversity." Nor is the Policy saved because the student assignments that it dictates are proportional to the composition of the RQAP. . . .

When we articulated this concern at oral argument, the School Committee's able counsel responded that it is unnecessary for the Policy to consider other indicia of diversity because BLS historically has been diverse with respect to everything but race and ethnicity. . . .

If, as we are told, diversity has been attained in all areas other than race and ethnicity, then the School Committee's argument implodes. Statistics compiled for the last ten years show that under a strict merit-selection approach, black and Hispanic students together would comprise between

15% and 20% of each entering class, and minorities, *in toto*, would comprise a substantially greater percentage. Even on the assumption that the need for racial and ethnic diversity alone might sometimes constitute a compelling interest sufficient to warrant some type of corrective governmental action, it is perfectly clear that the need would have to be acute—much more acute than the relatively modest deviations that attend the instant case. In short, the School Committee's flexible racial/ethnic guidelines appear to be less a means of attaining diversity in any constitutionally relevant sense and more a means for racial balancing. The Policy's reliance on a scheme of proportional representation buttresses this appearance and indicates that the School Committee intended mainly to achieve a racial/ethnic "mix" that it considered desirable. . . .

We do not question the School Committee's good intentions. The record depicts a body that is struggling valiantly to come to terms with intractable social and educational issues. Here, however, the potential for harmful consequences prevents us from succumbing to good intentions. The Policy is, at bottom, a mechanism for racial balancing—and placing our imprimatur on racial balancing risks setting a precedent that is both dangerous to our democratic ideals and almost always constitutionally forbidden. . . . Nor does the School Committee's reliance on alleviating underrepresentation advance its cause. Underrepresentation is merely racial balancing in disguise—another way of suggesting that there may be optimal proportions for the representation of races and ethnic groups in institutions. . . .

D. Vestiges of Past Discrimination.

The School Committee endeavors, in the alternative, to uphold the Policy as a means of redressing the vestiges of past discrimination. The court below accepted this explanation. . . . We do not.

Governmental bodies have a significant interest in adopting programs and policies designed to eradicate the effects of past discrimination. . . . Before embarking on such projects, however, government actors must be able to muster a "strong basis in evidence" showing that a current social ill in fact has been caused by such conduct. . . .

The threshold problem that we confront in this instance is that the School Committee disclaims the necessity for such evidence. Its disclaimer rests on the premise that a decree issued in the quarter-century-old desegregation litigation mandates local authorities to remedy any racial imbalance occurring in the school system and thereby obviates the need for an independent showing of causation. This premise lacks force.

The decree in question was entered in 1994 by Judge Garrity, pursuant to our instructions in *Morgan* v. *Nucci*, . . . (1st Cir. 1987). The particular provision to which the School Committee refers is entitled "Permanent Injunction." It enjoins the School Committee "from discriminating on the basis of race in the operation of the public schools of the City of Boston and from creating, promoting or maintaining racial segregation in any school or other facility in the Boston public school system." Nothing in the plain language of this provision requires school officials to undertake any affirmative action, let alone to adopt a race-based classification (such as is contained in the Policy). Perhaps more important, the cited provision is not (as the School Committee would have it) a mandatory injunction. Rather, it operates as a negative injunction, forbidding the defendants from engaging in the acts that supported the original cause of action. As long as school officials do not engage in discrimination against minorities—and there is no evidence that such conduct persists at BLS—they have not violated the injunction. . . .

Because the 1994 decree turns out to be a blind alley, the School Committee must identify a vestige of bygone discrimination and provide convincing evidence that ties this vestige to the de jure segregation of the benighted past. . . . To meet this challenge, the School Committee cites an "achievement gap" between black and Hispanic students, on the one hand, and white and Asian students, on the other, and claims that this gap's roots can be traced to the discriminatory regime of the 1970s and before.

The scope of what social phenomena the law considers vestiges of past discrimination presents an open question. The presumptive vestiges are the well-known factors that the Supreme Court enumerated in *Green v. County Sch. Bd.* (1968) (mentioning student assignments, faculty, staff, facilities, transportation, and extra-curricular activities). Since *Green*, federal courts have recognized other permutations, including "quality of education.". . . What this means and how it is to be measured are difficult questions. Rather than entering that debate, we accept *arguendo* the School Committee's position that, in principle, a documented achievement gap may act as an indicator of a diminution in the quality of education. Even so, whether an achievement gap is a vestige of past discrimination depends on whether there is satisfactory evidence of a causal connection.

The court below short-circuited this inquiry. Citing Judge Garrity's 1994 order, the court reasoned that, once there has been a past judicial finding of institutional discrimination, no more evidence is needed to justify a policy that employs racial classifications. . . . The lower court was wrong.

There are times when a history of discrimination, in itself, may supply a powerful evidentiary predicate sufficient to justify some race-conscious action. . . .

In sum, whether past discrimination necessitates current action is a fact-sensitive inquiry, and courts must pay careful attention to competing explanations for current realities. . . . The mere fact that an institution once was found to have practiced discrimination is insufficient, in and of itself, to satisfy a state actor's burden of producing the reliable evidence required to uphold race-based action. . . .

Beyond history, the School Committee offers statistical and anecdotal evidence to satisfy its burden of demonstrating a strong evidentiary basis for the inauguration of remedial policies. The district court found the evidence favoring race-conscious remedies to be adequate, but the court's entire treatment of the subject comprises a lone paragraph composed of unrelievedly conclusory observations. . . . In the absence of specific findings, we could remand. Given the time constraints applicable to the case, we opt instead to exercise plenary review, taking the statistical and anecdotal evidence in the manner suggested by the School Committee. . . .

The centerpiece of the School Committee's showing consists of statistical evidence addressed to a persistent achievement gap at the primary school level between white and Asian students, on the one hand, and black and Hispanic students, on the other. One way to measure the achievement gap is in terms of relative performance on standardized tests. Over the years, whites and Asians have scored significantly higher, on average, than blacks and Hispanics. The School Committee theorizes that, because of this achievement gap, BLS receives fewer African-American and Hispanic applicants than otherwise might be the case, and even in comparison to this modest universe, an abnormally small number of black and Hispanic students qualify for admission. Accordingly, the Committee concludes that the statistics documenting the achievement gap, on their own, satisfy the "strong basis in evidence" requirement.

In mounting this argument, the School Committee relies heavily on a line of cases addressing affirmative action plans designed to remedy vestiges of past employment discrimination. . . . This reliance is mislaid. Fundamental differences distinguish the statistical inquiry involved in the employment discrimination context from the one proposed by the School Committee here. In employment discrimination cases, we know ex ante the locus of discrimination: it is the barrier to entry. Based on that premise, an appropriate statistical analysis compares the number of qualified minority applicants with those who gain entrance. The greater the disparity, the stronger the inference that discrimination is the cause of non-entry. . . .

In this case, the "barrier to entry" comparable to those in the employment discrimination cases is BLS's requirement of an entrance examination and the resultant composite score—and no one (least of all, the School Committee) claims that the examination or any component thereof is discriminatory in operation or effect, or that it would be discriminatory if it were used as the sole criterion for admission. . . .

With the admissions process eliminated as an illegitimate barrier to entry, the achievement gap statistics, by themselves, must specifically point to other allegedly discriminatory conduct in order to suggest a causal link between those discriminatory acts and the achievement gap. Unlike the focused inquiry characteristic of the employment discrimination cases, however, the raw achievement gap statistics presented in this case do not by themselves isolate any particular locus of discrimination for measurement. Without such a focus, the achievement gap statistics cannot possibly be said to measure the causal effect of any particular phenomenon, whether it be discrimination or anything else. . . . As such, the achievement gap statistics, by themselves, do not even eliminate the possibility that they are caused by what the Court terms "societal discrimination." *Shaw* v. *Hunt* (1996). . . . To be sure, gross statistical disparities at times may suffice to satisfy a state actor's burden of production. . . . But the achievement gap statistics adduced here fail to do so because it is unclear exactly what causative factors they measure.

The *Croson* Court relied on precisely this reasoning when it concluded, in the contractor context, that low minority membership in a local trade association "standing alone, cannot establish a prima facie case of discrimination." . . . The Court reasoned that there could be "numerous explanations for this dearth of minority participation, including past societal discrimination." . . . Therefore, if such statistics are to be at all probative of discrimination, they must link cause and effect variables in a manner which would permit such an inference. . . .

We do not propose that the achievement gap bears no relation to some form of prior discrimination. We posit only that it is fallacious to maintain that an endless gaze at any set of raw numbers permits a court to arrive at a valid etiology of complex social phenomena. Even strong statistical correlation between variables does not automatically establish causation. . . . On their own, the achievement gap statistics here do not even identify a variable with which we can begin to hypothesize the existence of a correlation. . . .

III. Conclusion

We do not write on a pristine page. The Supreme Court's decisions in *Croson* and *Adarand* indicate quite plainly that a majority of the Justices are highly skeptical of racial preferences and believe that the Constitution imposes a heavy burden of justification on their use. *Croson*, in particular, leaves no doubt that only solid evidence will justify allowing race-conscious action; and the unsystematic personal observations of government officials will not do, even if the conclusions they offer sound plausible and are cloaked in the trappings of social science. . . .

Our dissenting brother's valiant effort to read into *Croson* a broad discretion for government entities purporting to ameliorate past discrimination strikes us as wishful thinking. The *Croson* Court's own reference to the need for a "searching judicial inquiry," . . . suggest[s] an attitude that is antipathetic to those who yearn for discretion. And unless and until the Justices reconfigure their present doctrine, it is the job of judges in courts such as this to respect the letter and spirit of the Supreme Court's pronouncements.

We need go no further. While we appreciate the difficulty of the School Committee's task and admire the values that it seeks to nourish, noble ends cannot justify the deployment of constitutionally impermissible means. Since Boston Latin School's admissions policy does not accord with the equal protection guarantees of the Fourteenth Amendment, we strike it down. The judgment of the district court must therefore be reversed.

We are mindful that Henry Wessmann asks not only that we declare the Policy unconstitutional—which we have done—but also that his daughter, Sarah, be admitted to BLS forthwith. The School Committee, which has vigorously defended the Policy, has tacitly conceded that, if its defense fails, Sarah should be allowed to enroll at BLS. The circumstances of this case are unusual, for the school year is under way and Sarah Wessmann—who already has spent elsewhere the first year and some months of what normally would be a four-year matriculation at BLS—does not have the luxury of time that a remand would entail. We therefore direct the district court to enter a judgment, in appropriate form, that, *inter alia*, commands Sarah's admission to BLS without delay.

Reversed.

FBI REPORT ON CRIME
November 22, 1998

Serious crime declined for the sixth straight year in 1997, the Federal Bureau of Investigation said in its annual crime report. Three weeks later the FBI announced that the trend was continuing, with preliminary figures showing that serious crime had dropped another 5 percent in the first six months of 1998. "These decreases are real and go beyond a statistical blip. But we have not won the war on crime. We cannot let up even one minute," Attorney General Janet Reno cautioned November 22 when she released the FBI's Uniform Crime Reporting Program's annual publication, Crime in the United States, 1997.

At the same time that crime rates were going down, incarceration rates were continuing to climb. In June the Justice Department reported that 1.7 million Americans were in federal, state, and local prisons and jails, up from 1.1 million in 1990. Only Russia had a greater proportion of its people imprisoned. The U.S. incarceration rate was 645 people for each 100,000 population, six to ten times higher than in most other industrial nations.

Criminal experts said that crime and incarceration rates typically moved somewhat independently of each other. Incarceration rates were going up because of longer sentences, reduced use of parole, and increased arrests of parole violators. Keeping known criminals off the streets reduced crime somewhat, experts said, but the main reasons crime rates were dropping had more to do with the aging of the baby boom generation and the waning of the crack cocaine epidemic. More effective police strategies for keeping guns off the street were also important, these experts said. "If crime stayed down for the long term," Martin Horn, the Secretary of Corrections in Pennsylvania told the New York Times *in August, "then the incarceration rate might fall. But crime never does stay down for long."*

Continuing Decline in Crime Rate

Two complementary crime reports were issued annually by the federal government. The FBI's Crime in the United States, 1997 *was based on reports from 17,000 local and state law enforcement agencies. The National Crime*

Victimization Survey for 1997 was based on a survey of 43,000 households conducted by the Bureau of Justice Statistics. The survey covered many hundreds of thousands of crimes that were not serious enough to be included in the FBI report or that were not reported to law enforcement agencies. The Bureau of Justice Statistics estimated that only four of every ten crimes were reported.

According to the FBI report, 13.2 million violent and serious property crimes were reported in 1997, 2 percent fewer than in 1996. Overall, violent crime had fallen 15 percent in the last five years but was still four points higher than it had been ten years earlier. Murder and robbery were both down 7 percent from their 1996 levels, but rape and other sexual assaults remained about the same. All property crime categories—burglary, larceny-theft, and motor vehicle theft—registered declines.

The murder rate of 6.8 for every 100,000 people fell to its lowest level in thirty years. An estimated 18,209 people were murdered in 1997, 70 percent of them with guns. Nearly 50 percent of the victims knew their assailants; 30 percent of the murders resulted from arguments. Nineteen percent occurred in connection with other crimes such as robbery or arson. A total of 9,861 hate crimes were reported. Seventy percent of those were committed against people (the rest were against property), and about 60 percent were racially motivated.

Arrests for all criminal infractions totaled 15.3 million, a 1 percent increase from 1996. Drug abuse violations accounted for 1.6 million of those arrests. Larceny-theft and driving under the influence each accounted for another 1.5 million arrests.

The National Crime Victimization Survey largely corroborated the FBI's statistics. Nearly 35 million crimes, ranging from purse snatchings to rape, were committed against people in 1997, down from 37 million in 1996. About 50 percent of all crimes were committed by someone the victim knew. Of the total some 8.6 million crimes were violent—rape, assault, and robbery (because it was a survey of victims, this report did not include murder).

According to criminologists and other experts, the decrease in crime resulted from a number of factors, including the booming economy with its high employment rate, increased numbers of police, improved police-community relations, more effective crime prevention strategies, tougher gun control laws, and strict sentencing guidelines. But two factors were especially important. First, the baby boom generation, which represented about 25 percent of the population, was approaching middle age and was largely beyond the age at which most criminals commit crimes. Second, the use of crack cocaine, which had caused an upsurge in burglaries and violent crimes, was waning. Teen homicides, which skyrocketed in the late 1980s and early 1990s from the combination of crack cocaine and associated gang activity, dropped 16 percent in 1997, the fourth straight year of declines. Two researchers who studied the crack cocaine epidemic in New York City posited that today's youngsters were avoiding crack because of the devastation it had caused in their lives when they were children. "They clearly do not want to emulate their parents, older siblings, close relatives or other associates in their neighborhoods, who were enmeshed in crack," the two researchers told a conference of criminologists in New Orleans in December.

While welcoming the decline in crack cocaine use, experts cautioned that teenagers were still vulnerable. "There's still too much television and too little supervision after school, to much alienation and access to guns," said James Alan Fox, dean of the College of Criminal Justice at Northeastern University. "The teen population is rising, and the growth projections, particularly among blacks and Hispanics, show we will have more teens at risk." Legislation in Congress to beef up federal efforts to combat juvenile crime fell by the wayside in 1998, when the Gun Owners of American complained that a provision intended to heighten the federal government's ability to prosecute gang activity could actually be used to prosecute gun dealers.

Continuing Rise in the Incarceration Rate

With one major exception, incarceration rates in 1997 tended to follow trends set in earlier years. The number of women in prison or jail continued to grow at a faster rate than the number of men, but women still accounted for only 6.4 percent of all inmates. Violent crimes accounted for more than half of the growth among male prisoners, while drug crimes were the major source of growth among female prisoners. Blacks were imprisoned at eight times the rate of whites and nearly double the rate of Hispanics. More than 8 percent of all black men aged twenty-five to twenty-nine were in prison, compared with less than 3 percent of Hispanic men and less than 1 percent of white men in this age category. The South and West continued to have the highest incarceration rates. The fastest growth in 1997 occurred in California and Texas, followed by the federal prison system. Massachusetts, Virginia, and the District of Columbia all registered small declines in their incarceration rates.

The exception to the trend was in the growth of the jail rate, which had been growing at a slower pace than the prison rate. In 1997, however, the jail rate grew by 9.4 percent over 1996, double the growth in the prison rate. Jails usually housed suspects awaiting trial or persons convicted and sentenced to less than a year; prisons housed people serving longer sentences. Some experts warned that the growth in the jail rate presaged another big jump in the prison rate, because people sent to jail were those judges and prosecutors considered most likely to be convicted and sent on to prison for their alleged crimes. "Jail numbers are kind of a leading indicator" of future prison populations, Franklin Zimring, director of the Earl Warren Legal Institute at the University of California, Berkeley, told the New York Times.

Two studies released in 1997 revealed new data about drug and alcohol abuse among criminals. According to a report released by the National Center on Addiction and Substance Abuse at Columbia University, 80 percent *of all people behind bars were there because they had violated drug or alcohol laws, were high on drugs or alcohol when they committed their crimes, committed their crime to get money to support their habit, or had a history of drug or alcohol abuse. Alcohol usage, more than any illegal drug, was found to be closely associated with the commission of violent crimes such as murder, rape, and assault. Twenty percent of state prisoners convicted of violent crimes were under the influence of alcohol at the time of the crime, while 3 percent were high on crack or powder cocaine. Only 1 percent were high on heroin. The report also said that drug abuse was a major factor driving repeat offenders; 81 percent of state prison inmates with five or more convictions used drugs regularly, compared with 63 percent with two prior convictions and 41 percent who were in prison for the first time.*

A profile of jail inmates conducted by the Bureau of Justice Statistics found similar patterns. According to that survey, 62 percent of convicted jail inmates said they drank regularly (at least once a week for at least a month) and 64 percent said they used illegal drugs regularly, primarily marijuana. About 41 percent said they had been drinking at the time they committed their crime; 36 percent said they were one drugs. Overall, about six of every ten jail prisoners were high on drugs or alcohol or both when they committed their crimes.

"The most troublesome aspect of these grim statistics is that the nation is doing so little to change them," said Joseph Califano Jr., in a preface to the Columbia University report. Califano chaired the center at Columbia University and was secretary of health, education, and welfare under President Jimmy Carter. According to the report 840,000 federal and state prisoners needed substance abuse treatment in 1996, but fewer than 150,000 received any treatment before being released. "Failure to use the criminal justice system to get nonviolent drug and alcohol abusing offenders into treatment is irrational public policy, and a profligate use of public funds," Califano declared at a news conference on January 8. "Releasing drug and alcohol addicted inmates without treating them is tantamount to visiting criminals on our society at large."

> *Following is a press release issued November 22, 1998, by the Federal Bureau of Investigation that accompanied the release of its annual report,* Crime in the United States, 1997, *and summarized the data for 1997:*

The Federal Bureau of Investigation announced today that for the sixth consecutive year reported serious crime decreased in the United States. In 1997, reported serious crime, which includes both violent and property crimes, was estimated at nearly 13.2 million offenses, a decline of 2 percent from the 1996 level and 7 percent from the 1993 figures.

According to the FBI, the Uniform Crime Reporting (UCR) Program's final 1997 statistics which were released today revealed violent crime totals were down 3 percent and property crime totals declined 2 percent from 1996 levels.

By offense, the decline in violent crimes in 1997 from 1996 totals were murder and robbery, each 7 percent; aggravated assault, 1 percent; and forcible rape showed a slight decrease.

In 1997, the number of violent crimes was 15 percent below the 1993 level but 4 percent above the 1988 level.

Decreases in property crimes in 1997 from 1996 levels were motor vehicle theft, 3 percent; and burglary and larceny-theft, 2 percent each.

The Nation's crime experience ranged from a 3-percent decrease in cities overall to a 1-percent increase in the rural areas.

Crime in the United States, 1997, the FBI's annual report released today, contains the most current UCR crime data available. The statistics are based on a Crime Index of selected violent and property crimes submitted by more than 17,000 city, county, and state law enforcement agencies to the UCR Program. Estimates are included for nonreporting areas.

Summarized data from the 1997 edition include:

Crime Volume

The 1997 Crime Index total of approximately 13.2 million offenses represents a 2-percent decline from the 1996 total. Five- and 10-year comparisons show the 1997 national total has dropped 7 percent since 1993 and is 5 percent lower than in 1988.

The South had 40 percent of reported crime in 1997; the West, 24 percent; the Midwest, 22 percent; and the Northeast, 15 percent. Crime was down 5 percent in the Northeast, 2 percent in the South and West; and 1 percent in the Midwest.

Crime Rate

In 1997, the Crime Index rate of 4,923 offenses per 100,000 United States inhabitants was 3 percent lower than the 1996 rate. The crime rate was 10 percent below the 1993 rate and 13 percent lower than the 1988 figure.

Regionally, the Crime Index rate in the South was 5,547 offenses per 100,000 inhabitants; in the West, 5,335; in the Midwest, 4,572; and in the Northeast, 3,734. All regions reported rate declines from 1996 levels.

The Nation's metropolitan areas recorded a Crime Index rate of 5,325 offenses per 100,000 inhabitants; cities outside metropolitan areas recorded 5,207 offenses per 100,000 inhabitants; and rural counties, 2,064 per 100,000 inhabitants.

Violent Crime

There were an estimated 1.6 million violent crimes during 1997. The rate of 611 violent crimes for every 100,000 inhabitants was the lowest since 1987.

Data collected on weapons used in connection with violent crimes showed personal weapons (hands, fists, and feet) were used in 30 percent of all murders, robberies, and aggravated assaults, collectively. Firearms were used in another 27 percent.

All individual violent crimes showed declines in volume and rate from 1996 to 1997.

Property Crime

All property crime categories (burglary, larceny-theft, and motor vehicle theft) in 1997 decreased in volume and rate.

The estimated property crime total, 11.5 million offenses, was 2 percent lower than the 1996 total.

The 1997 property crime rate dropped 3 percent from the 1996 rate to 4,312 offenses per 100,000 population.

It is estimated that more than a $15 billion loss in stolen property occurred in 1997, an average loss per offense of $1,311.

Hate Crime

In 1997, a total of 9,861 hate crimes were reported; 5,898 were motivated by racial bias; 1,483 by religious bias; 1,375 by sexual-orientation bias; 1,083 by ethnic bias; 12 by disability bias; and 10 were multiple-bias offenses.

A total of 11,211 agencies covering nearly 223 million of the U.S. population participated in hate crime data collection.

Crimes against persons comprised 70 percent of the 9,861 offenses reported. Among the crimes against persons, intimidation accounted for 55 percent of the total; simple assault and aggravated assault accounted for 26 percent and 18 percent, respectively; murder and rape each accounted for less than 1 percent.

Crime Clearances

A 22-percent Crime Index clearance rate in 1997 was recorded by law enforcement agencies nationwide. The clearance rate for violent crimes was 48 percent; for property crimes, 18 percent.

Among the Crime Index offenses, murder had the highest clearance rate, 66 percent; burglary and motor vehicle theft the lowest, 14 percent each.

Clearances involving only juvenile offenders (under 18 years of age) accounted for 20 percent of the Crime Index offenses cleared; 12 percent of the violent crime clearances; and 23 percent of the property crime clearances.

Arrests

Law enforcement agencies made an estimated 15.3 million arrests for all criminal infractions, excluding traffic violations, in 1997, an increase of 1 percent over the previous year's figure. The highest estimated arrest counts were for drug abuse violations at approximately 1.6 million. Larceny-theft and driving under the influence arrests followed closely behind at nearly 1.5 million each. There were an estimated 1.4 million arrests for simple assaults. Relating the number of arrests to the total U.S. population, the rate was 5,752 arrests per 100,000 population.

From 1996 to 1997, adult arrests rose 1 percent while juvenile arrests decreased 1 percent. Violent crime arrests of juveniles decreased 4 percent and those of adults remained virtually the same.

Forty-five percent of all persons arrested in 1997 were under the age of 25. Of those arrested, 78 percent were male, and 67 percent were white.

Twenty-nine percent of all arrests were for drug abuse violations and alcohol-related offenses. Females and juveniles were most often arrested for the offense of larceny-theft. Males were most often arrested for drug abuse violations and driving under the influence.

Murder

The number of murders in 1997 was estimated at 18,209, which is 7 percent lower than the 1996 total and 26 percent lower than in 1993. The murder rate was 6.8 offenses per 100,000 inhabitants, the lowest measure since 1967.

Supplemental data received for 15,289 of the estimated murders showed that 77 percent of murder victims in 1997 were males and 88 percent were persons 18 years or older. The percentage of white and black murder victims was 48 and 49 percent, respectively.

According to data submitted on 17,272 murder offenders, 90 percent of the assailants were male, 87 percent were 18 years of age or older, 53 percent of the offenders were black, and 45 percent were white.

Forty-eight percent of murder victims knew their assailants. Among all female murder victims, 29 percent were slain by husbands or boyfriends, while 3 percent of the male victims were slain by wives or girlfriends.

Thirty-one percent of all murders were a result of arguments, and 19 percent resulted from felonious activities such as robbery, arson, and other crimes.

Firearms were the weapons used in approximately 7 out of every 10 murders reported.

Forcible Rape

There were an estimated total of 96,122 forcible rapes during 1997.

Approximately 70 of every 100,000 females in the country were reported rape victims in 1997, a rate that is 1 percent lower than in 1996.

Robbery

Robberies declined 7 percent in 1997 as compared to 1996 levels. The 1997 estimated robbery total was 497,950 or 186 robberies per 100,000 population nationwide.

Nearly $500 million in monetary loss was attributed to property stolen in connection with this offense. Bank robberies resulted in the highest average loss, $4,802 per offense; convenience store robberies the lowest, $576.

Street or highway robberies accounted for half of the offenses in this category.

Forty percent of all robberies were committed using firearms. Strong-arm tactics accounted for 38 percent.

Aggravated Assault

In 1997, it is estimated that over 1 million aggravated assaults were reported to law enforcement, a decline of 1 percent from the 1996 total.

Blunt objects or other dangerous weapons were used in 35 percent of aggravated assaults in 1997. Personal weapons such as hands, fists, and feet were used in 27 percent of reported incidents; firearms in 20 percent; and knives or cutting instruments in 18 percent.

Burglary

There were an estimated 2.4 million burglaries in 1997, with 2 of every 3 being residential in nature.

Sixty-six percent of all burglaries involved forcible entry, and 52 percent occurred during daylight hours. The average loss for residential burglaries was $1,305, and for nonresidential, $1,391.

Larceny-theft

Of the three property crime offenses (burglary, larceny-theft, and motor vehicle theft) collected, larceny-theft, with an estimated total of 7.7 million offenses, comprised 67 percent of the property crime total for the year.

It is estimated that over $4.5 billion in total dollar losses to victims nationwide occurred in 1997. Property loss averaged $585 per offense.

Thirty-six percent of the reported larcenies involved the theft of motor vehicle parts, accessories, and contents.

Motor Vehicle Theft

In 1997, an estimated 1.4 million motor vehicles were reported stolen, representing a 3-percent drop in motor vehicle thefts for the Nation and the lowest number since 1987.

Motor vehicle thefts declined 3 percent in the Nation and 5 percent in cities from 1996 levels.

The estimated average value of stolen motor vehicles at the time of theft was $5,416 per vehicle. The estimated total value of vehicles stolen nationwide was over $7 billion.

Arson

In 1997, a total of 81,753 arson offenses were reported, a 7-percent decline from the 1996 total.

With 49 percent of the reported incidents, structures were the most frequent targets of arsonists. Residential property was involved in 59 percent of the structural arsons during the year; 41 percent of these structural arsons were directed at single-family dwellings.

The monetary value of property damaged due to reported arsons averaged $11,294 per incident.

Persons under the age of 18 were involved in 46 percent of arson crimes cleared by law enforcement in 1997. Of the eight Crime Index offenses, arson had the highest percentage of juvenile involvement.

Law Enforcement Employees

A total of 13,339 city, county, and state police agencies submitting UCR data reported collectively employing 618,127 officers and 240,405 civilians in 1997. Reporting agencies provided law enforcement services to over 251 million U.S. inhabitants.

The average rate of full-time officers for every 1,000 inhabitants across the country was 2.5.

Geographically, the Northeastern States with 2.8 officers per 1,000 inhabitants had the highest rate of sworn officers to population.

UN REPORT ON THE GLOBAL AIDS EPIDEMIC
November 24, 1998

The war against the spread of the virus that causes acquired immune deficiency syndrome (AIDS) appeared to make little headway in 1998. According to the United Nations Programme on HIV/AIDS (UNAIDS), an estimated 33.4 million people worldwide were infected with human immunodeficiency virus (HIV) at the end of the year, a 10 percent increase from 1997. All but 5 percent of the 5.8 million new HIV infections occurred in Africa, Asia, and Eastern Europe. In some African countries nearly one in four adults had HIV or AIDS. Almost half the new infections were among young people in their peak productive and reproductive years. Women accounted for more than two-fifths of all HIV infections in people older than fifteen. In parts of the developing world the AIDS epidemic was turning increasing numbers of children into orphans, lowering life expectancy, and devastating economies.

Since 1981, when the epidemic first began, 47 million people had become infected worldwide and 14 million had died—2.5 million of them in 1998. AIDS killed more people in 1998 than any other infectious disease; malaria killed 1 million. In the United States, the number of deaths from AIDS continued to drop, largely as a result of new drug treatments. But the number of new HIV infections remained stable, at about 40,000 a year, indicating that efforts to stop the spread of the infection had hit a plateau.

AIDS experts and demographers said the figures were beginning to approach those of historic epidemics, such as the influenza epidemic of 1918–1919 that killed 20 million. "If HIV killed as rapidly as plague and influenza, the epidemic would be controlled by now," Peter Piot, head of the UNAIDS program, told the New York Times *in June when preliminary 1998 estimates were released. AIDS was an incurable disease that gradually weakened the immune system, making the person susceptible to opportunistic diseases such as tuberculosis; if left untreated, an infected person usually died within ten years of contracting HIV. The virus was typically transmitted through unprotected sexual intercourse or needles used by*

878

more than one person to inject drugs. Infected mothers could also transmit the disease to their children through infection at birth or through breast-feeding. The presence of other sexually transmitted diseases such as syphilis appeared to heighten the spread of the disease.

Portrait of an Epidemic Out of Control

The statistics compiled by the UNAIDS program and other agencies painted a gloomy picture of an epidemic that was out of control and beginning to reverse decades of development gains:

- *Seventy percent of the new HIV infections worldwide during 1998 occurred in sub-Saharan Africa, which was home to only 10 percent of the world's population. Nine of ten new infections in children under fifteen occurred in this region. In Botswana, Namibia, Swaziland, and Zimbabwe, 20 to 26 percent of adults between the ages of fifteen and fifty had AIDS or HIV. All told, an estimated 22.5 million people in sub-Saharan Africa had AIDS or HIV. Half of them were women.*
- *The next most afflicted area of the world was Asia, where 7 million people were infected. The UNAIDS program was particularly concerned by the apparent spread of the disease in China and India, the two most populous countries in the world. Once thought to have been confined primarily to urban sex workers and their clients and to intravenous drug users, the infection had spread not only in cities but rural areas as well.*
- *In Eastern Asia, Latin America, and the Caribbean, the disease remained concentrated in "marginalized" groups—primarily homosexual men and drug injectors who shared needles. Heterosexual transmission was becoming more prevalent in the Caribbean and in other areas where other sexually transmitted diseases were also on the rise.*
- *Children were increasingly falling victim to the disease. More children were contracting the disease from their mothers during birth or infancy. The number of children orphaned by the disease was on the rise, reaching 1.6 million children in 1997. Both factors put substantial stress on traditional family structures and other coping mechanisms.*
- *Life expectancy rates—one of the chief indicators of a country's development status—were declining significantly in several of the countries hardest hit by the AIDS epidemic. In nine African countries where 10 percent of more of the adults had HIV, life expectancy was now expected to fall to forty-seven years on average by 2010 or so. Without the AIDS epidemic the lifespan was projected to increase from about sixty years in the late 1990s to sixty-four years by 2010. In Botswana the lifespans of children born in the first decade of the twenty-first century were expected to be nearly thirty years shorter than they would have been absent the epidemic.*

Trends in the United States

The picture was not quite so grim in the United States, where effective drug treatments were widely available and prevention programs had been in place for several years. According to the National Center for Health Statistics, 16,865 Americans died from AIDS in 1997, down from 31,130 in 1996 and well below the 43,000 deaths that occurred in 1995, the peak year for AIDS deaths in the United States. The decline was attributed to the new combinations of drugs that were capable of slowing the progress of the disease.

Researchers were thrilled by the magnitude of the decline, but they quickly warned of a potential downside: when HIV-infected people lived longer, they had a greater chance of infecting others. "We have people who, in the past, might have been very ill, not able to be sexually active, who now are much more active and potentially could continue to pass on HIV," one AIDS expert said. They also noted that many people with AIDS could not afford these drugs, which cost about $15,000 a year on average.

Experts were also concerned that the number of new infections appeared stable, at about 40,000 a year, after having declined for several years. Homosexual men and drug users who shared needles continued to be the populations with the highest numbers of infection, but HIV infection was rising among women, minorities, and young people ages thirteen to twenty-four.

Researchers in the United States and elsewhere said that in the absence of a vaccine and affordable drug treatments, prevention was the best—and only—way to attack the epidemic. Speaker after speaker at the twelfth World AIDS Conference in Geneva, Switzerland, called for greater use of preventive measures that were known to work, including wide distribution of condoms, sex education, public information campaigns, and drug treatments to prevent transmission of the infection from a mother to her fetus or newborn child. Condom distribution, for example, had been shown very effective in slowing the transmission not only of HIV but of other sexually transmitted diseases. A sustained program to promote the use of condoms in Senegal had given that country one of the lowest AIDS and HIV rates in Africa; the number of people under age twenty-five who used condoms with nonregular sexual partners increased from 5 percent in 1990 to 40 percent for the women in 1997 and 65 percent of the young men.

Perhaps the biggest barriers to more effective prevention programs, health researchers said, were government and community leaders who often opposed such programs because they feared the controversy the programs might generate. In April, for example, the Clinton administration endorsed the use of needle exchange programs to slow the spread of HIV infection among drug users and their sex partners but refused to allocate any federal funds to the controversial programs. Ignorance and refusal to acknowledge or deal with the behavior that put people at risk for the disease also undermined the success of prevention programs. One myth traveling through black communities in the United States was that Magic John-

son, the basketball player forced to retire because of AIDS, had been cured.
(Prevention efforts, Historic Documents of 1997, p. 81)

Speaking at the world conference, Piot of the UNAIDS program warned that "it is time to embrace a new realism and new urgency in our efforts" to overcome complacency about the deadly disease. "This epidemic is out of control at the very time when we know what to do, and what to do now," he said.

Following are excerpts from the United Nations Programme on HIV/AIDS report, "AIDS Epidemic Update—December 1998," released November 24, 1998:

Anatomy of the Epidemic

Global Summary

By the end of 1998, according to new estimates from the Joint United Nations Programme on HIV/AIDS (UNAIDS) and the World Health Organization (WHO), the number of people living with HIV (the virus that causes AIDS) will have grown to 33.4 million, 10% more than just one year ago. The epidemic has not been overcome anywhere. Virtually every country in the world has seen new infections in 1998 and the epidemic is frankly out of control in many places.

More than 95% of all HIV-infected people now live in the developing world, which has likewise experienced 95% of all deaths to date from AIDS, largely among young adults who would normally be in their peak productive and reproductive years. The multiple repercussions of these deaths are reaching crisis level in some parts of the world. Whether measured against the yardstick of deteriorating child survival, crumbling life expectancy, overburdened health care systems, increasing orphanhood, or bottom-line losses to business, AIDS has never posed a bigger threat to development.

According to new UNAIDS/WHO estimates, 11 men, women and children around the world were infected per minute during 1998—close to 6 million people in all. One-tenth of newly infected people were under age 15, which brings the number of children now alive with HIV to 1.2 million. Most of them are thought to have acquired their infection from their mother before or at birth, or through breastfeeding.

While mother-to-child transmission can be reduced by providing pregnant HIV-positive women with antiretroviral drugs and alternatives to breastmilk, the ultimate aim must be effective prevention for young women so that they can avoid becoming infected in the first place. Unfortunately, when it comes to HIV infection, women appear to be heading for an unwelcome equality with men. While they accounted for 41% of infected adults worldwide in 1997, women now represent 43% of all people over 15 living with HIV and AIDS. There are no indications that this equalizing trend will reverse.

Altogether, since the start of the epidemic around two decades ago, HIV has infected more than 47 million people. And though it is a slow-acting virus that can take a decade or more to cause severe illness and death, HIV has already cost the lives of nearly 14 million adults and children.

An estimated 2.5 million of these deaths occurred during 1998, more than ever before in a single year.

AIDS and the Infectious Disease Picture

According to recent WHO estimates, malaria causes over I million deaths a year. In 1998, AIDS deaths totalled some 2.5 million. Both diseases are among the five top killers worldwide. However, it is important not to overlook the dynamics in this picture. Already in 1954, millions of people were dying annually of malaria. AIDS is a still-emerging epidemic whose death toll rises every year, while the ranks of the newly infected swell by some 16000 a day.

Tuberculosis, the second biggest infectious killer, is also on the rise, driven in large part by the HIV epidemic. Tuberculosis, the second biggest infectious killer, is also on the rise, driven in large part by the HIV epidemic. . . . Around 30% of all AIDS deaths result directly from tuberculosis.

While people undermined by HIV infection are more easily infected with the TB bacillus, many already harbour it from childhood. In either case, individuals with dual HIV/TB infection run a far greater risk than TB carriers who are HIV-negative that their tuberculosis will become active and potentially lethal. Worldwide, millions of people are already infected with both HIV and the tuberculosis bacillus, and the potential for further growth of co-infection in the developing countries is vast, given the crushing prevalence of TB carriers in the general population (some 30%) and the almost 6 million new HIV infections a year. Tackling the dual epidemics calls for stronger TB casefinding and treatment-tuberculosis can be cured with antibiotics regardless of whether the person is HIV-infected or not-in parallel with stronger AIDS prevention programmes to avert new HIV infections.

Regional roundup

Sub-Saharan Africa is home to 70% of the people who became infected with HIV this year. It is also the region in which four-fifths of all AIDS deaths occurred in 1998.

Africa, the global epicentre, continues to dwarf the rest of the world on the AIDS balance sheet. Since the start of the epidemic, 83% of all AIDS deaths so far have been in the region. Among children under 15, Africa's share of new 1998 infections was 9 out of 10. At least 95% of all AIDS orphans have been African. Yet only a tenth of the world's population lives in Africa south of the Sahara.

The sheer number of Africans affected by the epidemic is overwhelming. Since HIV began spreading, an estimated 34 million people living in sub-Saharan Africa have been infected with the virus. Some 11.5 million of those people have already died, a quarter of them children. In the course of 1998, AIDS will have been responsible for an estimated 2 million African— 5500 funerals a day. And despite the scale of death, today there are more Africans living with HIV than ever before: 21.5 million adults and a further 1 million children.

While no country in Africa has escaped the virus, some are far more severely affected than others. The bulk of new infections continue to be concentrated in East and especially in Southern Africa.

The southern part of the African continent holds the majority of the world's hard-hit countries. In Botswana, Namibia, Swaziland and Zimbabwe, current estimates show that between 20% and 26% of people aged 15–49 are living with HIV or AIDS. South Africa, which trailed behind some of its neighbours in HIV infection levels at the start of the 1990s, is unfortunately catching up fast: one in seven new infections on the continent this year are believed to be in this one country. Zimbabwe is especially hard-hit. There are 25 surveillance sites in the country where blood taken from pregnant women is tested anonymously as a way of tracking HIV infection. The most recent data, from 1997, show that in only 2 of these sites did HIV prevalence remain below 10%. In the remaining 23 sites, some 20–50% of all pregnant women were found to be infected. At least one-third of these women are likely to pass the infection on to their baby.

Other areas of the continent are far from immune. One in ten adults or more are HIV-infected in Central African Republic, Côte d'Ivoire, Djibouti and Kenya. In general, however, West Africa is less affected by HIV than Southern or East Africa, and some countries in Central Africa have also seen HIV remain relatively stable. Early and sustained prevention efforts can be credited with these lower rates in some cases-Senegal provides a good example. But elsewhere, where far less has been done to encourage safer sex, the reasons for the relative stability remain obscure. Research is under way to explain the differences between epidemics in various countries. These studies are looking into factors that may play some role, such as patterns of sexual networking, levels of condom use with different partners, and treatment of other sexually transmitted diseases (STDs), which if left untreated make it easier for HIV to pass through sexual intercourse.

Increasingly, the spotlight is on the spread of HIV through the **Asian continent,** especially in South Asia and East Asia. While rates remain low relative to some other regions, well over 7 million Asians are already infected and HIV is clearly beginning to spread in earnest through the vast populations of India and China.

India provides an interesting example of the shifting patterns of HIV.

- Until recently, it was commonly assumed that HIV infection in the world's second most populous nation was concentrated in urban sex workers and their clients and in drug injectors living in a few states. The last round of sentinel surveillance in antenatal clinics shows that in at least in five states, more than 1 % of pregnant women in urban areas are now infected.
- India's rural areas—home to 73% of the country's 930 million people— were thought to be relatively spared by the epidemic. Again, new stud-

ies show that at least in some areas, HIV has become worryingly common in villages as well as cities. A recent survey of randomly selected households in Tamil Nadu found that 2.1 % of the adult population living in the countryside had HIV, as compared with 0.7% of the urban population. For this small state, with its population of 25 million, the study findings suggest that there are close to half a million people already infected with HIV in Tamil Nadu. Considering that nearly 10% of the people surveyed had gonorrhoea, syphilis or another sexually transmitted disease, HIV clearly has fertile ground for further spread.

- The virus is firmly embedded in the general population, among women whose only risk behaviour is having sex with their own husbands. In a study of nearly 400 women attending STD clinics in Pune, 93% were married and 91% had never had sex with anyone but their husband. All of these women were infected with a sexually transmitted disease, and a shocking 13.6% of them tested positive for HIV.

In **Eastern Europe** and in **Latin America and the Caribbean,** infections are concentrated in marginalized groups though clearly not limited to them.

In Latin America the pattern of H[V spread is much the same as in industrialized countries. Men who have unprotected sex with other men and drug injectors who share needles are the focal points of infection. In Mexico studies suggest that up to 30% of men who have sex with men may be infected; among drug injectors in Argentina and Brazil the proportion may be close to half. While transmission through sex between men and women is on the rise, especially in Brazil, heterosexual HIV spread is especially prominent in the Caribbean. Prevalence rates of 8% among pregnant women have been reported from Haiti and one surveillance site in the Dominican Republic.

HIV continues to gallop through drug-injecting communities in **Eastern Europe** and **Central Asia.** A region which until the mid-1990s appeared to have been spared the worst of the epidemic, it now holds an estimated 270 000 people living with HIV. For the moment Ukraine remains the worst-affected country, though the Russian Federation, Belarus and Moldova have all registered enormous increases in the past few years. With HIV gaining new footholds as it penetrates new drug-user communities, the potential for continued spread through drugs and sex is undeniable given the known overlap between drug-injecting and sex-worker populations and the dramatic rises in other STDs. In the Russian Federation, for example, syphilis rates have shot up from around 10 cases per 100 000 people in the late 1980s to over 260 cases per 100 000 a decade later.

In **North America** and **Western Europe,** new combinations of anti-HIV drugs continue to reduce AIDS deaths significantly. For example, recently-published figures show that in 1997 the death rate for AIDS in the United States was the lowest in a decade—almost two-thirds below rates recorded just two years earlier, before combination therapy came into widespread use. However, because new infections continue to occur while antiretroviral drug cocktails keep already-infected people alive, the proportion of the population living with HIV has actually grown. This obviously increases the demands for care. In a number of less obvious ways, it adds to countries' prevention challenges.

During 1998, North America and Western Europe recorded no progress in reducing the number of new infections. The early dramatic rises in HIV were successfully reversed by the mid-to-late 1980s thanks to prevention campaigns that raised condom use among gay men from virtually zero to well over 50%. But over the last decade, the rate of new infections has remained stable instead of continuing to decrease. During 1998 alone, nearly 75 000 people became infected with HIV, bringing the total number of North Americans and Western Europeans living with HIV to almost 1.4 million.

Clearly, the epidemic is no longer out of control in these countries. Just as clearly, it has not been stopped. And at this stage the prevention challenges are greater than ever. One reason is that prevention efforts have already reached the easier-to-reach groups, such as the largely well-educated and well-organized white gay communities. Another reason is that HIV infections are increasingly concentrated in the poorer sectors of the population. In the USA, to take one example, HIV has become a disproportionate threat to US citizens of African origin. Although African-Americans represent only 13% of the total US population, they bear an undue share of American poverty, underemployment and inadequate health care access. African-Americans are now more than 8 times as likely as whites to have HIV. According to the Centers for Disease Control and Prevention (CDC), among black males national HIV prevalence is estimated to have reached 2% and AIDS has become the leading killer in the 25-44 age group. For black women in the same age group, AIDS takes second place as cause of death. The US administration has just announced a new $156 million federal effort for minority communities to help curb HIV spread through drug injecting and sex, and to help ensure access to antiretroviral drug therapy for those already living with HIV. . . .

A Health Crisis and Beyond

Invisible No Longer

For many years, AIDS was referred to as "the invisible epidemic". HIV makes its silent way through a population for many years before infections develop into symptomatic AIDS and become a cause of recurring illness and, finally, death. The virus thus spread stealthily for years before AIDS deaths were registered in any significant numbers.

In industrialized countries AIDS activists succeeded in raising the profile of the epidemic early on. But in the developing world where most men and women with HIV live, it is only now, two decades after the virus first started spreading, that the repercussions of AIDS are stripping off its cloak of invisibility.

In countries with mature epidemics—Uganda in East Africa, Zambia and Zimbabwe in Southern Africa, for example—AIDS is leaving highly-visible damage in its wake. Some doctors report that three-quarters of beds on hospital paediatric wards are occupied by children ill from HIV. Millions of adults have died. Most have left behind orphaned children. Many have left surviving partners who are infected and in need of care. Their families struggle to find money to pay for their funerals, and their employers must now train other staff to replace them.

Wiping out the Gains of Development

Together, the epidemic's visible and less-visible consequences constitute an urgent and massive threat to development.

Life Expectancy Crumbles

Life expectancy at birth is one of the key measures that policy-makers look at to assess human development. Because of the extra deaths from AIDS in children and young adults, this indicator is giving off alarm signals. According to a just-released report prepared by the United Nations Population Division in collaboration with UNAIDS and WHO, the epidemic will wipe out precious development gains by slashing life expectancy.

The impact on life expectancy is proportional to the severity of the local epidemic. In Botswana, for example, where more than 25% of adults are infected, children born early next decade can expect to live just past their 40th birthday. Had AIDS not been in the picture, they could have expected to live to the age of 70. Not surprisingly, between 1996 and 1997 Botswana dropped 26 places down the Human Development Index, a ranking of countries that takes into account wealth, literacy and life expectancy.

Taking the nine countries with an adult HIV prevalence of 10% or more (Botswana, Kenya, Malawi, Mozambique, Namibia, Rwanda, South Africa, Zambia and Zimbabwe), calculations show that AIDS will on average cost them 17 years of life expectancy. Instead of rising and reaching 64 years by 2010-2015, a gain which would be expected in the absence of AIDS, life expectancy will regress on average to 47 years.

Deteriorating Child Survival

The dismal decline in life expectancy is due not only to deaths of adults—most of them young or in early middle age—but also to child deaths. HIV is contributing substantially to rising child mortality rates in many areas of sub-Saharan Africa, reversing years of hard-won gains in child survival.

By 2005–2010, for example, 61 of every 1000 infants born in South Africa are expected to die before the age of one year. In the absence of AIDS, infant mortality would have been as low as 38 per 1000. With AIDS in the picture, the infant mortality rate in Namibia is projected to be 72 per 1000; without the epidemic the country could have expected a far lower rate of 45 per 1000.

Children on the Brink

Zimbabwe offers a frightening window onto orphanhood, another aspect of the epidemic's development impact. In this nation, where over a quarter of the 5.5 million adults are HIV-infected, AIDS is already pushing hundreds of thousands of children to the brink.

The government estimates that in two years' time 2400 Zimbabweans a week will be dying of AIDS. Most of those deaths will be in adults, and they will be concentrated in the young adult ages when people are building up their families. What is more, they may be disproportionately concentrated among single women whose death would leave a child with no parent at all: one recent study in a farming area showed that single mothers, many of them widowed by AIDS, were twice as likely to be HIV-infected as married women.

As early as 1992, a study in Zimbabwe's third largest city, Mutare, recorded that over 10% of children in the study area were orphaned, and that nearly one household in five had taken in orphans. By 1995, an enumeration in the same area showed that the proportion of children who were orphaned had grown to nearly 15%.

The number of children in need of care is rising just as AIDS is cutting into the number of intact families able to provide such care. Some 45% of those caring for orphans are grandparents; often they have no income of their own, and there is a limit to how many children they can take on without outside help. One orphan-support programme reports helping an 80-year-old grand-mother who lives with 12 children in a single room. Another has received a request for help from a widower with 9 dependents who has just inherited another 3 grandchildren to care for. A study of households headed by ado-lescents and children (some as young as 11) showed that while the over-whelming majority had lost both parents, most did have surviving relatives. However, in 88% of those cases, the relatives reported that they did not want to care for the orphans.

Children themselves are beginning to worry about orphanhood and to rec-ognize the importance of supporting needy children. A majority of children interviewed in one study said that if orphans' needs were not met they would become delinquent. Many said the children would drift into prostitution and onto the streets. They also worried about abuse and exploitation of orphans by relatives. With reason. Reports of sexual abuse of girls have risen rapidly in recent years in Zimbabwe, prompting the establishment of a special clinic at a major Harare hospital and an initiative to promote child-friendly courts. In a single rural district of Zimbabwe one study recorded nearly 400 cases of child sexual abuse, at least a quarter of them girls under the age of 12, and at least 10% of them orphans.

AIDS and Business: The Bottom Line Suffers

The onslaught of AIDS is denting the prospects for economic development too. In the hard-hit countries of Africa, the epidemic is decimating a limited pool of skilled workers and managers and eating away at the economy. With many economies in the region in flux, it is hard to determine exactly what the impact of HIV is on national economies as a whole. However, it is clear that businesses are already beginning to suffer.

In Zimbabwe, for instance, life insurance premiums quadrupled in just two years because of AIDS deaths. Some companies say that their health bills have doubled. Several report that AIDS costs absorb as much as one-fifth of company earnings. In Tanzania and Zambia, large companies have reported that AIDS illness and death cost more than their total profits for the year. In Botswana, companies estimate that AIDS-related costs will soar from under 1% of the wage bill now to 5% in six years' time, because of the rapid rise in infection in the last few years.

HIV—A Threat to the World's Young People

This year's World AIDS Campaign—"Young People: Force for Change"—was prompted in part by the epidemic's threat to those under 25 years old. Young people are disproportionately affected by HIV and AIDS. Around half of new HIV infections are in people aged 15–24, the range in which most people start their sexual lives. In 1998, nearly 3 million young people became infected with the virus, equivalent to more than five young men and women every minute of the day, every day of the year. And as HIV rates rise in the general population, new infections are increasingly concentrated in the younger age groups. A recent study in Malawi, for instance, found the annual rate of new HIV infections to be as high as 6% in teenage women, compared with under 1% in women over 35.

But the Campaign also highlights the power of young people. The future of the HIV epidemic lies in their hands. The behaviours they adopt now and those they maintain throughout their sexual lives will determine the course of the epidemic for decades to come. Young people will continue to learn from one another, but their behaviour will depend largely on the information, skills and services that the current generation of adults choose to equip their children with.

Research shows that young people adopt safer sexual behaviour provided they have the information, skills and means to do so. In Senegal, 40% of women under 25 and 65% of men used condoms with non-regular partners in 1997, compared with less than 5% for both sexes at the start of the decade. In fact, given the chance, young people are more likely to protect themselves than adults. In Chile, a 1996 study showed that condom use is highest among 15–18-year-olds, and similar patterns have been found in Brazil and Mexico.

Safer sexual behaviour is becoming the norm among young people in developed countries, too. In several studies in Western Europe, some 60% of young people are now using condoms the very first time they ever have sex—a six-fold increase since the early 1990s. Among young people in the United States, abstinence is becoming more common and condom use is rising significantly. Among high school students in 1997, 63% of boys reported that they had used a condom the last time they had sex, up from 55% six years earlier. For girls, condom use rose to 51% from 38% over the same period.

However, much remains to be done. In the USA, for example, 3 million adolescents a year contract a sexually transmitted disease, a clear indicator of unsafe sex. In developing countries, where the likelihood of encountering a partner infected with a sexually transmitted disease is high, STD infection rates in young people are often much higher.

Young people are vulnerable to HIV for many reasons—they do not know about HIV or STDs, or they know about them but do not know how to avoid infection. Those with the information may be unable to get hold of condoms, or may feel unable to discuss condom use with their partner. Young people, and especially girls, may be unable to defend themselves against unwanted sex. In the Democratic Republic of Congo, nearly a third of young women in a large study reported that they had been forced by their partners into first sex. Similar statistics on coerced sex are reported from many parts of the world.

What is more, adolescence is a time when many people experiment—not only with different forms of sex but with drugs. Apart from the HIV risk connected with needle-sharing, it is known that alcohol and other drugs can affect sexual behaviour and increase young people's risk of becoming infected with HIV or the other STDs. Excessive drinking, for example, diminishes inhibitions, increases aggression, diminishes the ability to use important information learnt about AIDS prevention, and impairs the capacity to make decisions about protection. . . .

What Drives the Epidemic?

The AIDS epidemic has unfolded very differently in different parts of the world, and among different populations. It is not always clear why HIV infection takes off in some places while rates in neighbouring countries remain stable over many years. However, there are several factors which clearly influence the shape of the epidemic. People on the move—escaping from abuse, or even just leaving their families in search of work—are especially likely to be exposed to infection. People whose daily existence is stressful and dangerous may not care about the long-term risks posed by HIV. People in conflict and refugee situations may have little control over their exposure to HIV, indeed even to sex. And the stigma that still attaches to HIV hinders people from protecting themselves and others from infection, or from seeking out care and support.

ATTORNEY GENERAL ON CAMPAIGN FINANCE INQUIRY
November 24, 1998

For the second year in a row, there was a lot of talk in Washington about problems with laws governing the financing of federal election campaigns. Also for the second year in a row, politicians and officials in Washington did little to correct those problems. Attorney General Janet Reno conducted two investigations of fundraising during the 1996 election by President Bill Clinton, Vice President Al Gore, and other Democrats but found no reason to appoint an independent counsel in the cases, as Republicans had demanded. Despite their often shrill rhetoric alleging abuses by Democrats, Senate Republican leaders killed bipartisan legislation that was intended to reform campaign finance laws.

Perhaps most telling, leaders of both political parties continued to engage in many of the same campaign finance practices they denounced when used by the other side. Congressional candidates raised and spent record amounts in 1998 for a midterm election—including millions of dollars worth of unregulated "soft money" donations to the political parties by corporations, labor unions, special interest groups, and wealthy individuals. Candidates and potential candidates for the presidential race in 2000 already were soliciting soft money contributions. Over the long term—unless Congress ultimately changed the laws—the chief outcome of two years of controversy was likely to be increased reliance by candidates on the same fundraising tactics that had generated the most controversy.

In any other year, the campaign finance issue might have dominated the headlines from Washington. But 1998 was the year of a sex scandal involving the president, and so the political squabbling over the arcane laws governing political fundraising and spending faded into the background. Polls showed that most Americans dismissed the issue as "business as usual" in the nation's capital. One effort that had the potential to heighten public interest in the issue—a report on hearings held during 1997 by the Senate Governmental Affairs Committee—was marginalized by partisan disagreements among committee members. (Background on 1996 campaign finance issue, Historic Documents of 1997, p. 822; Clinton scandal, p. 564, 632, 695, 950)

Reno's Investigations

The underlying controversy concerned the Clinton campaign's aggressive fundraising efforts in the 1996 campaign. Most of what Clinton, Gore, and other Democrats did to raise and spend money had been done before by candidates of both parties. The Democrats in 1996 merely took their fundraising to new levels. The Democrats used questionable tactics and accepted questionable contributions—some of which they promised to return after those donations became public. Clinton defended his party's fundraising efforts as necessary to counter the Republican Party's traditional advantage in raising campaign money.

Under pressure from Republicans, Attorney General Reno in 1997 investigated a series of telephone calls that Clinton and Gore had made from the White House complex soliciting contributions for the 1996 elections. Reno announced on December 2, 1997, that a detailed investigation had found no grounds to conclude that either man had violated the law— and she declined to call for appointment of an independent counsel to probe the matter further. Reno's decision infuriated Republicans, who had hoped that an independent investigation would expose a wide range of fundraising irregularities by the Democrats.

The Republicans had support for their position from Louis J. Freeh, the director of the Federal Bureau of Investigation. Freeh's position was widely known by late 1997, but his specific reasons for supporting a call for an independent counsel were not disclosed until July 15, 1998. That was when Sen. Fred Thompson, R-Tenn., who chaired an investigation of the 1996 campaign, revealed the general contents of a memorandum Freeh had sent Reno in November 1997 calling for appointment of an independent counsel. Quoting from language he said was in the document, Thompson said Freeh had argued that Reno misconstrued the statute authorizing independent counsels to investigate possible wrongdoing by government officials. "It is difficult to imagine a more compelling situation for appointing an independent counsel," Thompson quoted Freeh as arguing.

Thompson's revelation of the memorandum came at a Senate Judiciary Committee hearing at which Reno was testifying. She angrily defended her actions, saying she was determined to "call it like I see it, based on the evidence and the law."

A week later, Reno received a confidential report from another Justice Department official advocating appointment of an independent counsel to investigate Democratic fundraising in 1996. That report came from Charles La Bella, who had headed the department's campaign finance unit. La Bella sent his report to Reno just as he was leaving the department to become acting U.S. district attorney in San Diego.

Reno declined to follow La Bella's recommendation, but in late August and early September she reopened Justice Department investigations into two specific issues that had been subjects of inquiries in 1997: whether Gore had lied in testimony about telephone calls he had made soliciting donations for advertisements supporting Democrats, and whether Clinton and his aides had improperly evaded federal campaign laws by using state Democratic committees to pay for television ads on behalf of the Clinton-Gore campaign. Reno said she opened both probes in response to new information. In the Gore case, it was a new set of documents provided by Gore's office that raised questions about his earlier testimony. In the broader case of Democratic advertising, it was an audit by the Federal Election Committee challenging the propriety of how the party handled its spending.

Under the law authorizing appointment of independent counsels, Reno had ninety days to conduct preliminary investigations into each case before deciding whether to ask the U.S. District Court of Appeals in Washington to name a counsel. Reno used the full ninety days in both cases.

The specific issue in the Gore case was whether Gore had lied to Justice Department investigators in 1997 when he described telephone calls he had made in 1995 to raise money for advertisements supporting the Democratic Party. Gore had told the investigators that he had believed, at the time of the calls, that the advertisements were to be funded with soft money (raised from contributions to the Democratic Party) as opposed to hard money (raised from contributions directly to the Clinton-Gore campaign). Under the law, it would have been improper for Gore to have made calls from the White House soliciting hard money contributions. In July 1998 Gore's office turned over to the Justice Department notes taken by David Strauss, an aide to Gore, describing a November 1995 White House meeting on campaign fundraising; both Clinton and Gore attended that meeting. The notes appeared to show that the subject of hard money contributions for the advertisements was discussed at that meeting. That raised the question of whether Gore had misled investigators in 1997 when he said he had been unaware, at the time he made the calls, that hard money was involved in financing the advertisements.

Reno announced November 24 that she had determined that there were "no reasonable grounds" to believe that Gore had lied about the issue. Based on testimony from all fifteen people who attended the November 1995 White House meeting, Reno concluded that Gore did not lie to investigators.

Reno's decision came as a considerable relief to Gore, who was preparing to launch his presidential campaign for the 2000 election. An investigation by an independent counsel might have opened all of Gore's activities during the 1996 race to scrutiny and cast a cloud over his political future. Republicans expressed annoyance. Sen. Orrin G. Hatch, R-Utah, chairman of the Judiciary Committee, accused Reno of focusing on "narrow issues" while ignoring the "reckless fundraising practices" of President Clinton and other administration officials.

In the broader case involving Democratic advertisements, Reno said December 7 that she found no evidence of "criminal intent" on the part of the president or his aides to violate federal campaign spending laws. Reno noted that Clinton, Gore, and other officials had acted on the advice of lawyers when they raised money and approved the campaign advertisements. As a result, she said, there were "no reasonable grounds" to conclude that the officials had violated the law, and so further investigation by an independent counsel was unwarranted.

Once again, Reno's decision was welcomed by the White House and denounced by Republicans. "It's another banner day for the lawyers," Sen. Thompson said.

Reform Legislation Falters

Despite their objections to the Clinton administration's campaign finance tactics, Republican leaders in both chambers of Congress worked diligently in 1998 to block legislation reforming the campaign finance laws. Republicans complained that the legislation—intended to impose tough new limits on the use of soft money in federal campaigns—was unfair to their party because it did not restrict fundraising by labor unions, which historically favored Democratic candidates.

The Senate leadership succeeded, not once but twice, in blocking passage of the reform bill. The first vote came February 29 when fifty-one senators, a majority, voted to end a Republican filibuster against a reform bill (S 25) sponsored by John McCain, R-Ariz., and Russell D. Feingold, D-Wis. Sixty votes were needed to end a filibuster, however, and Majority Leader Trent Lott, of Mississippi, a staunch opponent of the bill, immediately pulled it from the Senate agenda.

In the meantime, House members of both parties pressed for a vote on a companion measure (HR 2183) sponsored by Rep. Christopher Shays, R-Conn., and Martin T. Meehan, D-Mass. House leaders used parliamentary tactics to block a vote on that bill in March, but supporters forced the issue to the floor in August. On the key vote, on August 3, the Shays-Meehan bill was carried 237–186 the House passed the measure, with amendments, three days later.

Buoyed by that success in the House, McCain and Feingold attempted again to bring the bill to a vote in the Senate. Once again, on September 10, they secured a majority (fifty-two votes) but not enough to end a Republican filibuster. Sponsors in both chambers vowed to press the campaign finance issue again in the 106th Congress.

Senate Committee Reports

Of all the investigations of 1996 campaign finance abuses, the most public—and the one that had the most potential to influence public opinion—was a probe by the Senate Governmental Affairs Committee. The committee held widely publicized hearings on the issue during 1997 and said it would issue a report in 1998. But Republicans and Democrats were unable to agree on a unified report, and so the two parties issued separate, sharply conflicting reports on March 5. The partisan bickering undermined any impact the committee's work might have had.

The majority report, signed by the panel's eight Republicans, contained harsh condemnations of the Clinton-Gore team's fundraising efforts, including use of the White House for overnight stays to reward contributors and the acceptance of illegal contributions from foreign donors— including several donations solicited by former Commerce Department official John Huang.

At the outset of the 1997 hearings, Thompson said he had evidence of a broad effort by the Chinese government to influence the presidential election and U.S. foreign policy through campaign donations. In their report, the Republicans acknowledged that they developed no proof of such a plot but insisted there was "strong circumstantial evidence" that China had intended to sway the 1996 elections.

The Republicans discussed only one campaign finance abuse attributed to members of their party: a $2.1 million loan guarantee by a Hong Kong businessman that was funneled to the Republican National Committee (RNC) through an intermediary. The Republicans said their investigation found nothing illegal in that deal, which Democrats had cited as one example of improper fundraising by the GOP.

The chief recommendation of the Republicans was a call for appointment of an independent counsel to "aggressively pursue illegal activity" described in the report. Republicans endorsed only narrow changes in federal campaign finance legislation.

The seven committee Democrats, led by John H. Glenn of Ohio, criticized fundraising efforts in 1996 by both parties, but rejected Republican suggestions that the Chinese government had any success in influencing U.S. elections or policy. Democrats said their own national committee had failed to supervise Huang's fundraising efforts, and they criticized the White House for allowing access to donors such as Roger Tamraz, a businessman who donated $300,000 to the Democratic Party in an unsuccessful effort to promote an oil pipeline route in the Middle East.

Democrats also challenged several Republican fundraising projects, including a $4.6 million donation by the RNC to a conservative group, Americans for Tax Reform, which used the money to counter anti-Republican advertisements during 1996. Democrats said that transaction allowed the party to evade specific campaign spending limits.

Following are excerpts from a report sent by Attorney General Janet Reno on November 24, 1998, to the Independent Counsel Division of the U.S. District Court of Appeals for the District of Columbia, in which she declined to recommend appointment of an independent counsel to investigate fundraising by Vice President Al Gore prior to the 1996 election:

Notification to the Court Pursuant to 28 U.S.C. § 592(b) of Results of Preliminary Investigation

On August 26, 1998, I notified this Court of the initiation of a preliminary investigation of Vice President of the United States Albert Gore, Jr. The preliminary investigation has now been concluded, and I have determined that there are no reasonable grounds to believe that further investigation is warranted of the matters that were under investigation. Therefore, appointment of an independent counsel is not being sought. In accordance with the requirements of 28 U.S.C. § 592(b), this notification will summarize the information received and the results of the preliminary investigation.

This preliminary investigation explored the question of whether there is sufficient evidence to warrant further investigation into whether the Vice President violated federal law, 18 U.S.C. § 1001, when he told attorneys and investigators last Fall that he did not know, at the time he made fundraising telephone calls from his West Wing Office, that the beneficiary of the solicitations, the media campaign run by the Democratic National Committee (DNC), was funded in part with federal money, and that he believed at the time of his telephone calls that federal money contributions to the DNC were limited to $2,000.

Information Received

a. The 1997 Investigation

In the Fall of 1997, the Department conducted a preliminary investigation into the question of whether the Vice President may have violated 18 U.S.C. § 607 when he made fundraising telephone calls from his White House office (hereinafter, 1997 Investigation). The 1997 Investigation led to my conclusion that there were no grounds to seek appointment of an independent counsel for two independent reasons: first, the overwhelming weight of the evidence supported the Vice President's statement that he was soliciting soft money contributions, outside the scope of section 607's ban on political fundraising from the federal workplace, when he made the telephone calls, and second, established Departmental policy precluded prosecutions under section 607 in the absence of aggravating circumstances, such as coercion, that were absent there.

In the course of the 1997 Investigation, we interviewed the Vice President. The Vice President explained that he believed he was soliciting soft money when he was making the telephone calls. The Vice President further explained that the telephone solicitations were intended to raise funds for the DNC's media fund, a series of so-called "issue advertisements" run during late 1995 and 1996. He further explained that he believed at the time he made the calls that the DNC media campaign was financed entirely with soft money, and that donors were limited to $2000 in hard money contributions. This belief was erroneous, but as a result, when he requested large contributions to the media fund, he believed that he could only have been requesting soft money contributions. The Vice President understood that there was a hard money component to the DNC's overall budget, and that some of its activities had to be financed with hard money, but believed that because the media fund involved so-called "issue ads," it could be financed entirely with soft money.

We explored this question further with the Vice President at the time, because we had obtained a number of memoranda addressed to the Vice President, among others, that mentioned the fact that the media campaign was funded with both hard and soft money, and we knew that a November 21, 1995 DNC budget meeting focused on the budget for the media fund. The agenda for the November 21 meeting suggested that the amount of funding for the media campaign and how to raise it was to have been a topic of discussion at the meeting, which we knew was attended by the Vice President.

The Vice President stated that he did not recall a discussion at this or any other meeting about the DNC's specific need for both hard and soft money in late 1995 to keep the advertisements on the air. The Vice President said that he believed that the fundraising phone calls probably were discussed during the meeting and that the general topic of the media fund budget being increased was raised and discussed. As for the memoranda that reflected a hard money component to the media fund, the Vice President said that as a rule he did not read memoranda on these topics, particularly from this author. This general practice was corroborated in the course of separate interviews with members of the Vice President's staff.

The Vice President's statements about his beliefs and intentions were a factor in my final conclusion in 1997 with respect to the alleged violations of 18 U.S.C. § 607, although a relatively minor one. Far more weighty was the substantial evidence derived from interviews of the donors themselves which substantiated my conclusion that they were in fact solicited for large soft money contributions to the DNC, to support the DNC's media campaign.

b. The New Information

On July 27, 1998, long after the conclusion of the 1997 Investigation, the Vice President's counsel provided the Department with a six-page set of newly discovered documents, responsive to document requests we had made during the 1997 Investigation. The documents were a copy of a set of documents already in our possession, which were distributed at the November 1995 meeting referenced above. The copies provided by the Vice President's counsel, however, included handwritten notes by a member of the Vice President's staff that strongly suggested that the hard money component to the media fund may have been expressly mentioned during the November 1995 meeting, which was attended by the Vice President.

Specifically, the notes—which set forth "65% soft/35% hard" opposite the term "media fund"—appear to reflect a phrase that may have been used at the meeting to describe the approximate proportions of hard and soft money used by the DNC to purchase television ads during this period. The notes also include what may be a statement of the hard money limit for gifts to the DNC.

Specifically, the note just below the "65%/35%" includes what appears to be an attempt to define soft money from the DNC's perspective as "corporate or anything over $20 k from an individual." In addition, while not clearly written, a second notation that appears to say "hard limit $20k" appears on page two of the set of documents.

These new documents, then, raised some new questions concerning the Vice President's statements about his understanding of the DNC's efforts to fund the media campaign. The notes suggested that during the November 1995 meeting, both the fact that the hard money limit on donations to the DNC was $20,000, and that the media campaign was funded by a mix of hard and soft money may have been discussed in the Vice President's presence. This could give rise to an inference that his subsequent statements that he believed at the time that hard money donations to the DNC were limited to $2,000 and that the media campaign was funded only by soft money may have been false.

I therefore initiated a preliminary investigation of this matter to fully explore the evidence concerning the Vice President's knowledge and intent.

Applicable Law

The false statement statute provides, in pertinent part:

> [w]hoever, in any matter within the jurisdiction of the executive, legislative, or judicial branch of the Government of the United States, knowingly and willfully ... makes any materially false, fictitious, or fraudulent statement or representation shall be [guilty of a felony].

18 U.S.C. § 1001. To obtain a conviction under section 1001, the government must prove (1) a statement, (2) falsity, (3) materiality, (4) specific intent, and (5) agency jurisdiction. *United States v. Herring*, 916 F. 2d 1543, 1546 (11th Cir. 1990), *cert. denied*, 500 U.S. 946 (1991). The elements in issue here are falsity and criminal intent; the other elements of the offense are not in dispute.

Scope of the Investigation

The handwritten notes alone are not sufficient to warrant a conclusion that the Vice President made a false statement. In an effort to determine whether the apparent disparity between what the Vice President told us he believed at the time he made the calls and what the notes indicate may have been said at a meeting he attended on these topics warrants further investigation, we interviewed the attendees of the meeting and others involved with these topics. These witnesses included the Vice President, current and former members of his staff, other current and former White House officials, officials of the Clinton/Gore '96 Committee (Clinton/Gore '96), and various officers and employees of the DNC. Documents were also obtained from the White House, the DNC, Clinton/Gore '96, and others, including an affidavit from the Vice President's counsel. We also reviewed depositions and testimony provided by various witnesses in the course of previous congressional and task force inquiries into various campaign fundraising matters. Finally, we reviewed all other documents and evidence that might support an inference that the Vice President's statements were false.

We were seeking to determine whether there was any evidence from which one might reasonably infer that the Vice President actually knew about the funding of the media campaign or the $20,000 contribution limit. Such an inference might be supported, for example, by information that these facts were discussed in sufficient detail and focus at the meeting that many other attendees specifically recall them, that the Vice President made comments or asked questions in the course of the discussion that would seem to reflect an active understanding of the details, that the participants recall any affirmative discussion of a need to raise hard money for the media fund, that the Vice President read memoranda that made these points, or that anyone spoke directly to the Vice President on any occasion about the need to raise hard money for the media campaign.

Results of the Investigation

As a threshold matter, the evidence we gathered during these interviews does support a conclusion that the Vice President attended a DNC budget meeting on November 21, 1995, and that at some point in the course of the meeting, the DNC media fund was discussed. The evidence also supports a conclusion that some reference was made in the course of the meeting to the fact that there was a hard money component to the financing of the media campaign.

Fifteen individuals, including the President and Vice President, attended the meeting. All fifteen were interviewed, with two exceptions: one who testified under oath in the course of a congressional investigation that he had no recollection of the meeting, and that if he attended at all, he likely would have left after just a few minutes; and the President, who provided us with a statement that he had no independent recollection of the meeting.

No attendees recall any particular questions or comments by the Vice President. No one who did not arrive at the meeting with a working knowledge of the DNC financing issues left with an accurate understanding of the fact that both hard and soft money were necessary to pay for the media campaign. Only two attendees of the meeting even recall the topic of a hard money component to the media fund being raised during the meeting.

While the author of the notes had no specific recollection of the meeting, he did confirm, based on his habit and practice, his belief that the words noted in his handwriting were things said during the meeting that he recorded as they were said. Reviewing his notes, this attendee could not recall who might have uttered the words "65% soft/35% hard"; "corporate or anything over $20k from an individual"; or "hard money limit $20k" during the meeting. He was also unable to provide an explanation about what each of the phrases might have meant within the context of the meeting. He did not recall the issue of "hard" and "soft" money being discussed by those attending but noted that these issues were often discussed at DNC budget meetings. He was also unable to say whether the words were used with regard to the media fund, the DNC's operating budget, or something else. Notably, this individual, who attended the meeting and was paying enough attention to what was being said to take verbatim notes of some points, also told us during his interview that he believed that the media campaign was financed entirely with soft money.

Two attendees specifically recall references to hard money in connection with the media fund being made at the meeting. The first, a White House official, recalls that the hard money component to the media fund was discussed. He also recalls a discussion of how much would have to be raised both in hard and in soft dollars for the media fund during the meeting. However, he has no specific recollection of any of the statements recorded in the notes.

The other, a DNC official, was the individual who made one of the quoted statements. He recalls answering a question about the "spending side" of the media campaign by noting that the expenses were generally averaging "65% soft/35% hard". The answer, according to this attendee, was one sentence without any elaboration. He does not remember who asked the question but volunteered that he did not think it was the Vice President since the Vice President did not often get into "that level of detail". He had no memory of anyone else mentioning hard or federal money during this preliminary discussion of the "spending side" of the media campaign. He does not recall a specific use of the terms hard, soft, federal or non-federal money during the discussion that centered around the "spending side" of the DNC.

He did remember some discussion about the fact that the DNC had sufficient funds available to borrow on their hard money line of credit but no borrowing capacity on the soft money side. There was a discussion about direct mail contributions to the DNC operating budget—all in hard money—that were available, if needed, for the media purchases. He recalled that both of these facts were mentioned as reasons why there was sufficient hard money on hand to keep the advertisements on the air through the end of the year, but that soft money would need to be raised. According to this witness, after these points were made at the meeting, the ensuing conversation about the funding of the media campaign and the money needed to be raised by the President and Vice President would have been focused on the need for soft money.

As noted above, in order to prove a violation of Section 1001 in this case, the government would have to prove beyond a reasonable doubt that, at the time he made the telephone calls that were at issue in the 1997 Investigation, the Vice President actually knew that the media campaign had a hard money component, or that the limit on hard money contributions was $20,000. In this case, there is no direct evidence of such knowledge. While the Vice President was present at the meeting, there is no evidence that he heard the statements or understood their implications, so as to suggest the falsity of his statement two years later that he believed the media fund was entirely soft money. Nor does anyone recall the Vice President asking any questions or making any comments at the meeting about the media fund, much less questions or comments indicating an understanding of the issue of the blend of hard and soft money needed for DNC media expenditures. Witnesses were also asked whether they recalled any other discussion with the Vice President about the hard money component of the media fund; none recalled any, nor did any recall the Vice President saying or doing anything at any other time that would indicate that indeed he knew, whether from the meeting or from some other source, that there was a hard money component to the media fund.

There is thus only weak circumstantial evidence of the Vice President's knowledge—his presence at a meeting where the subject was briefly discussed—that I do not believe provides reasonable grounds for proceeding further in this matter. Notably, others attending the meeting also left it with an inaccurate understanding of the funding of the media campaign. The range of impressions and vague misunderstandings among all the meeting attendees is striking, and undercuts any reasonable inference that mere attendance at the meeting should have served to communicate to the Vice President an accurate understanding of the facts.

In addition to the total lack of direct evidence suggesting that the Vice President was aware of the hard money component to the media fund, and the insubstantial nature of even the indirect evidence, I also find a lack of evidence to reasonably support a conclusion that he may have had a motive to falsely deny that he knew about the hard money component. The documentary evidence and the testimony from involved witnesses clearly establish that at the time, the DNC did not need to find ways of raising hard money in order to continue to run the advertisements. However, it was critically short of soft money, and had used up its soft money line of credit. Thus, when the Vice President was asked to help raise money by making telephone solicitations, the DNC's specific need was for soft money.

In other words, the Vice President did not need to deny knowledge of the fact that there was a hard money component to the fund in order to provide an innocent explanation for his telephone calls. His explanation would have been just as innocent if he had stated that while he knew there was a hard money component to the media campaign, soft money was what was needed at the time and therefore that was what he was raising. In fact, such an account, unlike the one he gave, would have been corroborated by the documentary evidence that was brought to the Vice President's attention.

It is also significant that there is evidence that this issue was specifically brought to the Vice President's attention before his interview with us during the 1997 Investigation. The Vice President's attorneys have provided us with their sworn statement that in the course of preparing him for his interview, the Vice President also told them that at the time he made the calls he believed that the media campaign was funded entirely with soft money. They explained to him that this belief was not accurate, and pointed out to him that there were documents, addressed to him, in conflict with his statement. Nevertheless, they averred, he stated that he would have to tell us that he believed the media fund was all soft money because it was the truth.

To summarize, it appears that at the time of his interview during the 1997 Investigation, the Vice President was expressly aware that he had little to gain and much to lose in admitting his misconception of the true facts. In fact, his explanation not only led to additional inquiries during the 1997 Investigation, because it was at odds with known documents, but led directly to this investigation as well. I can see no reasonable basis for concluding that he had a motive to tell this story if it were not true.

As mentioned above, the Vice President also told us in the course of the 1997 Investigation that he believed that the limit on hard money contributions was $2000, and some of the handwritten notes suggest that topic too may have been discussed at the November 1995 meeting. However, while some of the fifteen meeting attendees had a vague recollection of some of the topics of discussion, no one interviewed could remember the use of the note's terms "hard limit $20 k" and "corporate or anything over $20k from an individual" in this meeting. We thus have no evidence of what, if anything, was said, or in what context. Thus, with the exception of the notes themselves, the meaning of which is unclear, we are left with no evidence that the Vice President's statement that he believed the legal limit for hard money gifts to the DNC was the same as the limit for individual candidates—$2,000 per election cycle—is false. We found no independent evidence to suggest that the Vice President did not in fact believe that hard money contributions were so limited, and his belief is plausible in light of his previous experience with congressional campaigns. While it appears from the handwritten notes that some reference to the higher limit on hard money contributions to the DNC may have been made during the meeting, the fact that no one who attended the meeting recalled the statement—and a number of other attendees reported the same or similar mistaken belief about the limitation on the size of hard money contributions—leads me to the conclusion that I have insufficient evidence to warrant further investigation as to whether the Vice President made a false statement on this point.

As mentioned above, in the course of the 1997 Investigation, we obtained several memoranda addressed to the Vice President as one of several recipients, which contain brief internal references to the hard money component to the media fund. However, as we noted at the conclusion of the 1997 Investigation, the Vice President has stated, and several members of his staff have confirmed, that he did not read these types of memoranda that dealt with DNC budgetary issues. We discovered no new evidence during this investigation which contradicts this evidence or would lead me to revisit my previous conclusion that the mere existence of these memoranda, without any evidence that the Vice President actually read them, was not sufficient grounds to conclude that the Vice President might have been making a false statement about his knowledge of the hard money component to the media fund.

Finally, there were regular meetings held at the White House known as "Residence Meetings," because they were held in the White House. During the relevant period, the Residence Meetings were focused on political strategy and polling issues. Two Residence Meeting "agendas"—one dated September 7, 1995 and the other dated September 13, 1995—have one line each that indicates that the DNC issue ads under consideration were going to be paid for, in part, with hard money.

We were unable to establish whether the Vice President attended these particular meetings; indeed, we have been unable to establish that those two meetings were even held. They do not appear on either the President's or the Vice President's daily calendars, while other Residence Meetings do appear. Regular attendees of the Residence Meetings who were interviewed do not recall whether these particular meetings were held, or if they were held, whether the Vice President attended or whether these particular agenda items were actually discussed. Many of the attendees specifically stated that they do not recall the hard money component to the media fund ever being discussed at the Residence Meetings. Given this state of the evidence, I conclude that there is insufficient evidence to reasonably conclude that the Vice President was put on notice as to the hard money component to the media fund during or because of any discussion that may have been held on the topic in the course of the Residence Meetings.

I considered with care the reasonable implications that might be drawn from all of this evidence—the Vice President's attendance at the November 1995 meeting, the memoranda addressed to him, and the Residence meetings—along with all other evidence and information available to us concerning the Vice President's understanding of the media fund and how it was financed, including the affidavit of the Vice President's counsel. Taken altogether, I find the evidence fails to provide any reasonable support for a conclusion that the Vice President may have lied. As explained above, there are no reasonable grounds to conclude that the November 1995 meeting would have put the Vice President on notice of the hard money component of the media fund, there is no evidence that the Vice President actually read the memoranda in which the topic is mentioned (and considerable evidence that he did not), and there is insufficient evidence that the topic was addressed at the Residence Meetings or that the Vice President attended the meetings where the topic might have been raised. As a result, I conclude that there is no reasonable prospect that these facts could support a successful prosecution. Furthermore, I am unable to identify any additional investigation that might reasonably be expected to provide sufficient evidence to support a successful prosecution.

Conclusion

I conclude that the evidence supporting a conclusion that the Vice President may have provided false statements to investigators and attorneys during an interview in the 1997 Investigation is so insubstantial that there are no reasonable grounds for further investigation. Therefore, based on the results of the above-described investigation, I hereby notify this Court that no independent counsel should be appointed.

December

COMMISSION ON THE ROLE OF THE INDEPENDENT COUNSEL

December 7, 1998

One outcome of the impeachment of President Bill Clinton was likely to be an effort in Congress to abolish or severely limit the Office of the Independent Counsel (OIC). The office was established in 1978 in the aftermath of the Watergate scandal to help restore public confidence in the federal government by eliminating the inherent conflict of interest in having allegations of wrongdoing by top executive branch officials investigated by their subordinates. In an era when one political party controlled Congress and the other controlled the White House, some said the law was turning into a political tool rather than an objective mechanism for investigating and prosecuting abuses of power in the executive branch. Critics were particularly concerned that several investigations had gone well beyond their original scope, had lasted for years, and sometimes involved innocent people and trivial charges. The law was set to expire on June 30, 1999, unless Congress extended it.

The primary catalyst for the debate on renewing the law was Kenneth W. Starr, the independent counsel whose investigation of President Bill Clinton's affair with a White House intern led to the president's impeachment. Starr had spent more than four years and $50 million on the investigation, which had begun in 1994 with Clinton's involvement in the complex Whitewater land deal. The probe changed focus several times before Starr stumbled upon possible perjury and obstruction of justice in an unrelated sexual harassment suit against Clinton. Critics called Starr's pursuit of the president overzealous and out of control. But in many respects Starr's investigation of the president was similar to the investigations conducted by other independent counsels. (Clinton impeachment, p. 564, 695, 950; Starr report, p. 632)

One of the longest and costliest investigations on record was conducted by Lawrence E. Walsh. A retired federal judge, Walsh spent seven years and at least $47 million investigating the Reagan administration for alleged abuses of power in connection with the Iran-contra arms sales in the

1980s. *Walsh's investigation resulted in the convictions of several top White House officials, including a national security adviser, Admiral John M. Poindexter, and his aide, retired Marine lieutenant colonel Oliver L. North. Both men's convictions were dismissed on appeal.* (Walsh report, Historic Documents of 1994, p. 8)

More recently, Donald C. Smaltz spent four years and $17 million investigating and prosecuting Mike Espy on charges of corruption. Espy, who had been forced to resign as secretary of agriculture in 1994, was acquitted of all charges in 1998. (Espy resignation, Historic Documents of 1994, p. 403)

An exception to this pattern of lengthy, costly investigations was the inquiry by James C. McKay, who was appointed to look into alleged wrongdoing in connection with the personal finances of Attorney General Edwin Meese III, a close advisor to Ronald Reagan. Finishing his investigation in little more than a year, McKay did not bring an indictment against Meese but said the attorney general had "probably violated" the law. Two weeks before McKay's report was made public in July 1988, Meese had announced that he planned to resign the office. (Meese investigation, Historic Documents of 1988, p. 495)

Origin of the Office

Before 1978 investigations of top executive branch officials were conducted by Justice Department prosecutors. These "special prosecutors" had a fair amount of autonomy, but they were accountable to the attorney general and, ultimately, to the president. The inherent conflict of interest created by this situation was vividly demonstrated in 1973 when special prosecutor Archibald Cox was fired under orders from President Richard M. Nixon, the target of Cox's investigation into the Watergate scandal. Cox was fired by Solicitor General Robert H. Bork only after Attorney General Elliot Richardson and his deputy, William D. Ruckleshaus, resigned rather than carry out the order. This "Saturday night massacre," as it was quickly dubbed by the media, sparked the drive for Nixon's impeachment, which resulted in the president's resignation in August 1974.

The OIC was a direct outgrowth of this event. Under the law, which was first passed in 1978 and extended and amended three times since, about fifty top officials were potentially subject to this type of investigation. When the attorney general received "information sufficient to constitute grounds to investigate," he or she had thirty days to determine whether the allegations were specific and credible enough to trigger a preliminary investigation. If that investigation showed reasonable grounds for full investigation, the attorney general could recommend the appointment of an independent counsel.

Independent counsels were selected by the "special division," a panel of three federal appeals court judges chosen by the chief justice of the United States. An independent counsel could not be a government official and had to be "an individual who had appropriate experience and who will conduct the investigation and any prosecution in a prompt, responsible, and cost-

effective manner." The special division also set out the scope of the investigation; independent counsels had to apply to the attorney general or in some cases the special division for permission to expand the scope of their investigation.

Independent counsels had all the investigative and prosecutorial powers granted to the attorney general. Although they worked independently of the Justice Department, they were required to follow the department's legal policies. They were also required to file annual reports with Congress, file a final report with the special division, file expense reports, and submit to six-month audits by the General Accounting Office. The attorney general could remove an independent counsel "only for good cause, physical or mental disability . . . or any other condition that substantially" impaired the performance of the counsel's duties.

Since the law was enacted in 1978, at least twenty independent counsels had been appointed to investigate alleged wrongdoing by presidents, cabinet officials, and other top officials in the executive branch. Cumulative cost estimates range from $130 million to roughly $200 million. The law was upheld by the Supreme Court in 1988, in the case of Morrison v. Olson. (Constitutionality of the independent counsel, Historic Documents of 1988, p. 465)

Mounting Opposition to Extending the Law

The Clinton and Espy investigations illustrated two of the criticisms frequently heard about the independent counsel law—that it could be used to advance the cause of one political party at the expense of the other and that it led to witch hunts in which the target of the investigation was presumed guilty and the investigation was continued until a crime was found.

Clinton supporters, for example, charged that Starr was sympathetic to conservative Republicans who were intent on forcing the president out of office and that Starr searched for any evidence of wrongdoing that he could find. These critics, along with many prosecutors and defense attorneys, said that Starr's evidence that President Clinton had committed perjury and obstruction of justice would never have warranted an indictment in a regular criminal court. Similarly, Republicans charged that the Iran-contra investigation was a thinly disguised effort by the Democrats to weaken Reagan, if not oust him from office. "The 'ins' [the party in power] hate" the independent counsel law, said former independent counsel McKay, "and the 'outs' love it just for the purpose of bringing the 'ins' down."

Espy's supporters cited his case as the consummate example of an independent counsel who had lost his perspective. The former agriculture secretary was acquitted on December 2, 1998, of charges that he had accepted $34,000 worth of tickets to sporting events and other illegal gratuities from companies the department regulated. One juror told reporters after the trial that Smaltz's case against Espy "was the weakest, most bogus thing I ever saw. I can't believe Mr. Smaltz ever brought this to trial."

That opinion was shared by many attorneys and law professors who said that the case against Espy was overcharged and overprosecuted. Others suggested that Smaltz was acting as if his entire reputation depended on the outcome of his investigation. "The problem with this statute is that when a prosecutor is mandated to pursue one individual and is given unlimited resources and unlimited time, it is inevitable that it will become a witch hunt," said Ted Wells, Espy's attorney. "This decision is probably another nail in the coffin for the independent counsel statute, which was in a lot of trouble of begin with," said Irv Nathan, a former prosecutor in the Justice Department who studied the law for the American Bar Association. "It will be perceived as another example of excessive exuberance by an independent counsel and of poor judgment."

Legal experts differed over whether the law should be renewed, allowed to expire, or modified. Some argued that despite the law's shortcomings, it was a good mechanism for ensuring that wrongdoing was not covered up. "Today, there's no way that a sitting president can possibly prevent his own investigation by firing anybody because [the independent counsel law] will not permit it," said Joseph DeGenova, a former independent counsel. Others, like Stanford University law professor Kathleen Sullivan, argued that constitutional checks and balances were sufficient. "The greater the abuse and the closer it is to the executive," Sullivan said, "the more the pressure of impeachment does its job."

One organization that advocated an end to the law was the National Commission on the Separation of Powers, sponsored by the Miller Center of Public Affairs at the University of Virginia, a nonpartisan research institute that studied the American presidency. In a report released December 7, the commission said the independent counsel law was "seriously flawed" and should be allowed to die when it expired in 1999. The commission said there was no way to correct "the inherent absence of fairness from the procedure itself—chiefly the isolation of the putative defendant from the safeguards afforded to all other subjects of Federal criminal investigations." If Congress insisted on renewing the law, the commission said, it should be limited to criminal investigations involving the president, vice president, or attorney general.

Commission co-chairs were Griffin B. Bell, attorney general under President Jimmy Carter; and Howard H. Baker, a former Republican senator from Tennessee who became well-known during the Senate Watergate investigation. Baker was later chief of staff in the Reagan White House. Other members of the blue-ribbon commission included William P. Barr, attorney general in the Bush administration; Lawrence S. Eagleburger, secretary of state in the Bush administration; Lloyd N. Cutler, White House counsel for presidents Carter and Clinton; and William Webster, director of the FBI from 1978 to 1987 and director of the CIA from 1987 to 1991.

Following is an excerpt from the final report of the National Commission on the Separation of Powers, sponsored by the

Miller Center of Public Affairs at the University of Virginia, on the role of the independent counsel, released December 7, 1998:

Introduction

The separation of governmental powers is one of the hallmarks of the American Constitutional system. In Britain and in the many other countries that follow the Westminster model, the executive, legislative and judicial functions are all handled, wholly or in important measure, by the single entity known as parliament. In the United States, however, each of these functions is carried out by a separate branch of government, namely the Presidency, the Congress and the Judiciary.

The three are interrelated, not only in the way they derive their power but also in the way they exercise it. The President, senators and representatives are directly elected; judges and justices are appointed by the President with the consent of the Senate. Congress can remove a President from office by impeachment for "high crimes and misdemeanors." All three branches can be involved in the formulation of laws; Congress must pass them, the President must sign or veto them and the courts are frequently called upon to adjudge their constitutionality and meaning. This arrangement of separated and overlapping functions creates a system of checks and balances that is another hallmark of the American system.

Some of this is set out in the Constitution. Some is codified in the decisions of the Supreme Court, such as *Marbury v. Madison*, which established the right of the Court to rule on the constitutionality of acts of Congress. Many gray areas remain, however, where the delineation of powers is not so clear and where, in fact, the branches of government, usually the legislative and executive, grapple from time to time for dominance. Often these struggles take place deep within the bureaucracy, but sometimes, as in the extensive investigation of a sitting President by an independent counsel and the resulting consideration by Congress of his report, they become the stuff of national preoccupation.

One important struggle was recently decided by the Supreme Court when it declared unconstitutional the line-item veto statute passed by Congress after years of agitation for a Federal law giving Presidents the right, already enjoyed by many governors, to approve some parts and disapprove other parts of legislation. President Clinton signed the bill and used its powers on several occasions, but the Court subsequently found that it ceded to the President Congressional powers that Congress was not empowered to cede in the absence of a Constitutional amendment.

The Miller Center Commission on the Separation of Powers is the eighth such commission established by the Center to study aspects of the Federal government, in a series dating back to 1980. Like the others, it is independent of party and faction. Over the last two and one-half years, it has conducted a methodical and scholarly survey, examining a number of areas where the separation of powers is unclear and selecting five of them for detailed consideration. These are: The office of independent counsel, the uses of inspectors general throughout the government, the doctrine of executive privilege, the issuance of executive orders and the War Powers Resolution passed in 1973. All are related in some way to the contentious debates that arose out of the Vietnam War and the Watergate scandal. The Commission makes specifc recommendations on each.

Independent Counsel

Doubtless the most topical of these recommendations relates to the functioning of independent counsels, who operate under a law first passed in 1978 for a five-year period and renewed and amended several times since. This is a role born of the distrust in government created by Watergate. When the holders of specifed high offices, 49 in all, are alleged to have committed crimes, the authority of the Attorney General himself to investigate the matter is severely limited, and the Attorney General must consider requesting the judicial appointment of an independent counsel.

If such a counsel is deemed to be necessary, the duty to faithfully execute the laws, which is vested in the President by the Constitution, and normally exercised through the Department of Justice with respect to criminal law, is in effect transferred in cases where the President might have a conflict of interest. From November, 1979, to May, 1998, no fewer than 21 independent counsels have been named.

The Commission concludes that the law is seriously flawed. It finds that the Attorney General is unduly restricted in deciding the need for independent counsel. The Attorney General can remove the counsel, but only for cause, and that can be contested in the courts. In the practical world, no counsel is likely to be removed by an Attorney General. There are no realistic fiscal or time constraints on the counsel. In effect the law creates miniature departments of justice, independent of the Attorney General, to prosecute particular persons.

Driven by the fact that the independent counsel statute will expire next year unless Congress acts to revise or extend it, the Commission considered a number of ways in which the statute establishing the independent counsel could be reformed. It concludes that there is no way of correcting the inherent absence of fairness from the procedure itself—chiefly the isolation of the putative defendant from the safeguards afforded to all other subjects of Federal criminal investigations.

A paper discussing the law was prepared for the Commission by former Attorney General Griffin B. Bell, its co-chairman. The paper states, quoting from a 1988 brief that he wrote with two other former attorneys general: "The inherent checks and balances the system supplies heighten the occupational hazards of a prosecutor: taking too narrow a focus, a possible loss of perspective and a single-minded pursuit of alleged suspects seeking evidence of some misconduct. This search for a crime to fit the publicly identified suspect is generally unknown or should be unknown to our criminal justice system."

Judge Bell also criticized the provision of the statute requiring independent counsels to issue final reports. In some though not all cases, such as the Iran-contra investigation, he said, these can suggest guilt even though there is no indictment in the case.

Gerhard Casper, the president of Stanford University, who is a nationally recognized authority on the separation of powers, said recently that he doubted that the office of independent counsel could be eliminated because, he argued, once established, such institutions are hard to uproot.

The Commission urges that the independent counsel statute be permitted to expire next year under the five-year "sunset" provision. But the Commission recognizes that the possibility of conflicts of interest in investigations of high officials is far from imaginary. The difficulty lies in striking a balance between holding such officials accountable and protecting their inherent right to fair treatment. The Commission suggests that when the President, the Vice President or the Attorney General is involved in a criminal investigation, the Attorney General should be required under a new statute to recuse himself or herself from the case. The Attorney General, though recused, could appoint either outside counsel or a Justice Department offical who was not disqualified. The Attorney General would remain accountable as the responsible offical, entitled to dismiss the counsel or Justice Department official for cause.

SECRETARY OF STATE
ON NATO'S FUTURE
December 8, 1998

In preparation for the fiftieth anniversary of the Atlantic alliance in 1999, the Clinton administration during 1998 launched a drive for a broader role for the North Atlantic Treaty Organization (NATO). Administration officials said NATO needed to pay more attention to security and political threats of the post-cold war era, including terrorism and potential attacks by rogue states using chemical, biological, or nuclear weapons. The United States also pressed its European allies to modernize and streamline their military forces so they would be better equipped to confront those types of threats.

Most of Washington's allies agreed on the need to update NATO and its mission, but several resisted key aspects of the Clinton administration's approach. The French and German governments, in particular, expressed concerns that Washington was trying to convert NATO into a rapid-strike force to enforce U.S. foreign policy aims around the globe, perhaps without authorization from the United Nations. Alliance leaders were hoping to resolve these questions in time for a celebratory fiftieth anniversary NATO summit meeting in Washington in April 1999.

Many elements of the debate about NATO's future were present in deliberations during 1998 about how to handle the crisis in Kosovo—the province of Serbia where ethnic Albanians were fighting for independence. The Clinton administration was using the threat of NATO air strikes to try to force Serbian leaders to relax their grip on Kosovo. Several European governments were equally concerned about the possible spread of the Kosovo violence throughout the Balkans, but they were less willing than Washington to use NATO's vast military power to intervene in the conflict. (Kosovo conflict, p. 827)

NATO Background

The United States and its European allies (along with Canada) established NATO in 1949—four years after the end of World War II—in an attempt to prevent another world war and present a united Western front against the Soviet Union, which was then seen as a serious military and political threat. NATO proved to be one of the most successful and enduring strategic alliances in world history. Under Washington's acknowledged leadership, NATO blocked Soviet expansion westward and provided the security assurances that enabled the war-torn nations of Western Europe to recover and prosper as democracies.

The fall of the Berlin Wall in 1989 and the collapse of the Soviet Union at the end of 1991 raised questions about what NATO's future role should be. One of the first answers came in 1995 when the alliance decided to reach out to nations that had been part of the old "Warsaw Pact" alliance dominated by Moscow. The alliance began a Partnership for Peace program, which included seminars and planning sessions between representatives of NATO and East European nations.

In July 1997 NATO invited three former Soviet bloc nations to join as members (the Czech Republic, Hungary, and Poland), raising total NATO membership to nineteen nations. All three were coordinating their military operations with NATO so they would be ready for full membership prior to the 1999 Washington summit. To ease Russian concerns about NATO's eastward expansion, the alliance signed a "charter" establishing procedures for regular diplomatic and military consultations with Moscow. (NATO expansion, Historic Documents of 1997, p. 514)

U.S. Senate Debate on NATO

The admission of three new members to NATO technically required an amendment to the original 1949 Atlantic Alliance treaty—and the amendment had to be ratified by all current member nations. In the case of the United States, that meant approval by a two-thirds majority of the Senate, as well as the president's signature.

An unlikely coalition of conservative Republicans and liberal Democrats tried to block the treaty in the Senate. They expressed a variety of fears: extending NATO eastward would anger Russia and destabilize a fragile U.S. relationship with Moscow; a larger NATO would overextend U.S. military commitments by requiring Washington to help defend three more countries; the United States ultimately would end up having to pay a substantial part of the cost of modernizing NATO forces, including those of the three new members; and a NATO with members in Eastern Europe likely would be sucked into more regional conflicts, such as the wars in Croatia, Bosnia, and Kosovo.

The Clinton administration and supporters of NATO expansion argued that all those concerns were groundless or, at best, exaggerated. Most Senate leaders supported NATO expansion, and they worked to defeat nine amendments that would have delayed the expansion or imposed restrictions on how it was implemented. The Senate approved the expansion on bipartisan vote of 80–19. The fifteen other current NATO members also approved the alliance expansion by the end of 1998.

New NATO Roles

Even with the scheduled expansion of NATO, it was still unclear what role the alliance could or should play in such matters as sectarian conflict in the Balkans or the proliferation of nuclear arms and other weapons of mass destruction. NATO officials during 1998 turned their attention to these issues as they anticipated the landmark summit in 1999. The diplomatic discussions took place even as day-to-day events already were helping shape NATO's future. Nowhere was that more obvious than in the Balkans, where NATO since 1996 had provided armed troops to enforce the Dayton peace accords and where the threat of NATO air strikes was supposed to encourage a peaceful settlement in Kosovo. (Bosnia peace agreement, Historic Documents of 1995, p. 717)

The Clinton administration took the lead in articulating a general plan for NATO's future—what officials in Washington called a "strategic concept." The central tenant of the administration position was that NATO should be prepared to counter threats of an entirely different nature from the massive Soviet invasion that was feared for nearly a half-century. In the future, U.S. officials said, NATO member nations were more likely to face attacks by rogue nations, such as Iraq or Libya, that were capable of launching ballistic missiles carrying chemical or nuclear weapons. Such an attack, Secretary of State Madeleine K. Albright told her fellow NATO foreign ministers in Brussels on December 8, would be "every bit as much an Article V threat to our borders now as a Warsaw Pact tank was two decades ago." Under Article V of the NATO treaty, an attack on one NATO member was considered an attack on all members, requiring a collective response by the alliance.

Citing the experiences of Bosnia and Kosovo as examples, the Clinton administration said NATO also needed to be prepared to deal with regional crises—even those outside the borders of NATO nations—that could eventually threaten alliance members. "Common sense tells us that it is sometimes better to deal with instability when it is still at arm's length than to wait until it is at our doorstep," Albright said in Brussels.

To meet new challenges, the administration said, NATO's military forces, especially those of European nations, had to be more flexible than in the past. NATO's gigantic land, air, and sea forces that were intended to fend off a massive Soviet attack might not be the type of forces needed to counter the new threats of the twenty-first century, U.S. officials said. Defense Secretary William S. Cohen told his counterparts in November that the alliance needed to move from a "fixed, positional defense to a flexible, mobile defense"—meaning that troops, equipment, and supplies could be more quickly sent to hot spots.

In general, Washington's European allies agreed with the assessment that post-cold war threats likely would be different from those posed by the Soviet Union. And they agreed that battalions of infantry, backed by behemoth tanks, would not deter attacks of missiles carrying chemical weapons. But leaders of several European countries suggested that Washington seemed to be aiming for a "globalized" NATO, one capable of carrying out U.S. foreign policy interests, even in cases with little direct bearing on NATO member countries. The French government, historically the European power most resistant to U.S. leadership of NATO, took the lead in questioning the new approach. "We generally take the view that NATO should not be too elastic in interpreting its global interests," French foreign minister Hubert Vedrine said in a cautiously phrased response to Albright.

One of the most potentially troublesome issues between the United States and some of its allies involved what diplomats called "mandates"—how NATO military responses to regional disputes or unconventional attacks would be authorized under international law. The Clinton administration took the position that NATO should seek approval from the United Nations Security Council for its military actions whenever possible. But if Security Council approval was blocked by one of the five members holding a veto power (most likely China or Russia), U.S. officials said, NATO should be able to act anyway if its members felt compelled to do so. The alliance, Albright said, should "address this issue on a case-by-case basis."

Once again, the French government was the most vocal in expressing concerns about the U.S. position, saying NATO should act without UN Security Council approval only in extremely rare cases. Several European officials also said there was no need for NATO to duplicate the work of other international agencies—such as the International Atomic Energy Agency—that had the responsibility under UN treaties to monitor nuclear proliferation and similar security threats.

In their semi-annual meeting in Brussels on December 7-8, NATO foreign ministers discussed but did not resolve the issues posed by the U.S. initiatives to modernize the alliance. But they said they wanted agreement on a new "strategic concept" for the alliance in time for the April 1999 summit.

> *Following is an excerpt from a speech delivered in Brussels on December 8, 1998, by Secretary of State Madeleine K. Albright to the North Atlantic Council (the foreign minister's meeting of NATO):*

I would like now to take a few minutes to address the range of issues our Alliance confronts as we prepare for the Washington Summit in April.

This will be the largest diplomatic gathering at the Head of State level in that city's history. It will commemorate the vision and wisdom of our predecessors—and provide an historic test of our own.

For it is there and then that we will set the future course for our Alliance.

In Luxembourg, I spoke of President Clinton's desire to work together throughout 1999 to lay the foundation for a broad and comprehensive Euro-Atlantic Partnership for the twenty-first century. Our goal is to expand cooperation among partners on both sides of the Atlantic to advance our mutual security, prosperity, and democracy in Europe and beyond, as we continue to resolve our differences on specific issues.

I view NATO's future role in that broader partnership as the institution of choice when North America and Europe must act together militarily.

My vision of a new and better NATO can be summarized in one sentence: we want an Alliance strengthened by new members; capable of collective defense; committed to meeting a wide range of threats to our shared interests and values; and acting in partnership with others to ensure stability, freedom and peace in and for the entire trans-Atlantic area. This is the goal for our Summit, and one that I believe is within reach.

As we look to the Washington Summit, we may divide our work into seven essential tasks.

The first is to speak in clear and understandable terms to our public and parliaments about NATO's future role and purpose. At the Washington Summit, we should issue a concise, non-technical political declaration of our vision for a new and better NATO. That vision is of an Alliance fully equipped to deal with the security challenges of the future together with the other institutions and relationships that constitute the foundation of our broader Euro-Atlantic partnership.

Our second task is to develop, for unveiling at the Washington Summit, an updated Strategic Concept. This is our blueprint for the future. We need to get it right.

The NATO of the twenty-first century will confront a very different strategic environment than in the past. During the Cold War, we had no trouble identifying an Article V threat to our territory and security. It stared at us from across the Fulda Gap.

But the threats we face today and tomorrow could come from a number of different sources, including from areas beyond NATO's immediate borders. I often remind people that a ballistic missile attack using a weapon of mass destruction from a rogue state is every bit as much an Article V threat to our borders now as a Warsaw Pact tank was two decades ago.

But we should also recognize that NATO must be better equipped to respond to non-Article V crises as well. For if these threats are not addressed early and effectively, they could grow into Article V threats.

We must be prepared because we know that events beyond NATO's immediate borders can affect vital Alliance interests. This is why we acted in Bosnia. This is why we have come together to prevent renewed violence in Kosovo. Common sense tells us that it is sometimes better to deal with instability when it is still at arm's length than to wait until it is at our doorstep.

As President Clinton said in Berlin last May: "Yesterday's NATO guarded our borders against direct military invasion. Tomorrow's NATO must continue to defend enlarged borders and defend against threats to security from beyond them—the spread of weapons of mass destruction, ethnic violence and regional conflict."

The new Strategic Concept must find the right balance between affirming the centrality of Article V collective defense missions and ensuring that the fundamental tasks of the Alliance are intimately related to the broader defense of our common interests. Constructive engagement with Partners should also be explicitly recognized as a fundamental task for the Alliance.

I know that there are those who try to suggest that by assuming these new missions, or by talking about common Euro-Atlantic interests beyond collective defense, we are somehow tinkering with the original intent of the North Atlantic Treaty. I've said it before; I will repeat it again today: this is hogwash.

The founders of the Alliance were wise to allow us the flexibility to come together to meet common threats that could originate from beyond our immediate borders. Some 50 years ago my predecessor, Dean Acheson, pointed out that while the North Atlantic Treaty involves commitments to collective defense, it also allows us to come together to meet common threats that might originate from beyond the North Atlantic area.

We are neither altering the North Atlantic Treaty, nor attempting to create some kind of a new "global NATO." What we are doing is using the flexibility the Treaty always offered to adapt this Alliance to the realities of a new strategic environment and the challenges we must face together in the twenty-first century.

In this context, let me say a word about mandates. NATO will—in all cases—act in accordance with the principles of the UN Charter, while continuing to address this issue on a case-by-case basis.

The third task we face is to maintain our commitment to NATO enlargement. Our commitment to our Open Door strategy is central to our vision of a new and better NATO for the twenty-first century. Getting a robust and credible Open Door package is one of the key challenges we face for the Washington Summit.

We must underscore our commitment to the enlargement process by agreeing on a Madrid-plus package that will keep NATO's door open. Both what we say and do as an Alliance is critical.

We must agree on a robust Membership Action Plan to help aspiring partners, in practical and focused ways, to accelerate their efforts to become the strongest possible candidates. Without designating them in advance, we need to provide a road map that shows aspirants the way ahead. I welcome the discussions that Secretary-General Solana has begun on this issue and hope that we can soon reach consensus on how to proceed.

As an Alliance strengthened by new members, our fourth task must be to reach agreement on a long-term program to adapt NATO's defense capabilities to carry out the full spectrum of missions in the new Strategic Concept. We need military forces that are designed, equipped, and prepared for twenty-first century missions. We have all recognized the need to develop military forces that are mobile, effective, sustainable, and survivable. For this reason, my good friend Secretary of Defense Bill Cohen has been working closely with your Defense Ministers to develop a defense capabilities package and a common operational vision for the Washington Summit.

Our fifth task is related closely to the previous ones. The Summit should address the threat posed to our populations, territory and to our military forces by weapons of mass destruction, or WMD.

We have proposed a comprehensive WMD initiative that builds on the successful work we inaugurated at the 1994 summit. The initiative is designed to ensure that we can effectively address the threat posed by the proliferation of such weapons and their means of delivery. Our plan is to increase information and intelligence-sharing in the Alliance, accelerate the development of capabilities to deter and protect against potential WMD use, and underscore our shared commitment to prevent proliferation.

The Alliance needs to view the WMD issue not only in a defense context, but also as a political challenge that requires a more comprehensive response. We have no desire for NATO to duplicate or supplant other international efforts, but rather to complement and reinforce them. We should view NATO not as the, but rather an, institution of choice among the others addressing this challenge.

Our sixth task is working together to develop a European Security and Defense Identity, or ESDI, within the Alliance, which the United States has strongly endorsed. We enthusiastically support any such measures that enhance European capabilities. The United States welcomes a more capable European partner, with modern, flexible military forces capable of putting out fires in Europe's own back yard and working with us through the Alliance to defend our common interests.

The key to a successful initiative is to focus on practical military capabilities. Any initiative must avoid preempting Alliance decision-making by delinking ESDI from NATO, avoid duplicating existing efforts, and avoid discriminating against non-EU members. We all agree that we need to finish ESDI based on Berlin decisions by the April Summit.

Our seventh and final task is to further intensify and strengthen relations with our European partners. Indeed, in facing future security challenges, the Euro-Atlantic Partnership Council must also be seen as an instrument of choice. Specifically, the Alliance needs to define, in time for the Washington Summit, a framework for joint crisis response operations. We also welcome ideas on developing new mechanisms to improve Allied and Partner national and multinational forces' ability to act together.

With Russia, we must move ahead in the spirit of the Founding Act. We continue to work side by side with Russia in Bosnia, to consult closely on Kosovo, to discuss Summit preparations in the PJC and to develop common approaches on vital issues such as nonproliferation and the environment.

We need to continue to work with Russia on giving the PJC more substance. We are building the relationship, establishing patterns of cooperation and communication, and strengthening confidence between NATO and Russia. We—and they—are getting better at it. Our exchanges are becoming habit, a familiar practice. But we—and Russia—have to keep it up. We should base our engagement with Russia on mutual interests. We need to create an environment with a maximum degree of certainty, in which Russia can depend on us and we can depend on Russia, with "no surprises."

With Ukraine, we should continue to strengthen our distinctive partnership. Ukraine is a vital contributor to European security. It is in our interests to help it develop its capabilities to cooperate with NATO as a reliable partner and smooth its way fully into the mainstream of our community.

We must also move ahead with completion of CFE adaptation by the time of the OSCE Summit next year, a goal we all share. This issue relates directly to the character of NATO's partnerships and capabilities.

An adapted CFE Treaty must have enough flexibility built in to ensure that NATO can respond effectively to future crises without breaching it. It must be constructed so that it does not inhibit the political evolution of Europe or the Alliance. And it must not harm the military capabilities of our Alliance.

This is a complex negotiation. All thirty states involved have legitimate concerns. If NATO's interests are to be protected, we must be united. If we are to make progress in Vienna in the next months, we need to send a clear message tomorrow about both our commitment, and our redlines.

Some decades ago, in the depth of Cold War tensions, Walter Lippman wrote about the realities of his time in words that may serve as a warning to ours.

"With all the danger and worry it causes . . . the Soviet challenge may yet prove . . . a blessing. For . . . if our influence . . . were undisputed, we would, I feel sure, slowly deteriorate. Having . . . lost our daring because everything was . . . so comfortable. We would . . . enter into the decline which has marked . . . so many societies . . . when they have come to think there is no great work to be done. For then the night has come and they doze off and they begin to die."

Lippman s fear is being put to the test in this decade. Certainly, there are some in each of our countries who now believe "there is no great work to be done," and that all we have to do to ensure our prosperity, security and freedom is hold on and stay put.

Almost fifty years ago, a generation emerged from war with a fierce dedication to peace. That generation forged an Alliance to defend liberty that, throughout the Cold War, would mean as much to those denied their freedom as those already blessed by it.

Today the responsibility is ours to rise above the barrier of complacency of which Walter Lippman wrote, and to build a new framework for freedom. In so doing, we will rely not only on this Alliance, but on all the great institutions of this continent and of our Community. We will keep our door open to new allies and partners, to new ideas and approaches. We will derive inspiration from the enduring principles that brought our predecessors together at this century's midpoint. And we will prepare together with vigor and determination for the challenges of the next. . . .

UNICEF ON IMPROVING
EDUCATION WORLDWIDE
December 8, 1998

Most countries in the world were failing to fulfill one of their basic responsibilities—providing an adequate education for all their children—a United Nations agency reported in December. The UN International Emergency Children's Fund (UNICEF) said that at the close of the twentieth century nearly one billion people, about one-sixth of the world's population, could neither read nor write.

In its annual report on the state of the world's children, UNICEF said there were signs of progress around the world in making education universally available. But about 20 percent of the world's school-age children were not in school; many of them were required to work instead, and millions of them had no access to free schooling.

Providing expanded educational opportunities need not be expensive, the report said. UNICEF estimated that providing education for all the world's children would cost an additional $7 billion a year—roughly the amount that Americans spent each year on cosmetics.

The UNICEF Report

Each year UNICEF issued a report describing a specific issue concerning the world's children. In 1996 the report dealt with the impact on children of civil and ethnic strife. (Report background, Historic Documents of 1996, p. 777)

The agency's report for 1998 was a detailed examination of the state of education around the world. Although it concentrated on the developing world—as did most of UNICEF's work—the report contained information about industrialized countries, not all of it flattering. For example, the report noted that in Ireland, the United Kingdom, and the United States, more than 20 percent of adults were considered functionally illiterate because they could not fill out a job application or perform other basic tasks requiring the ability to read and write.

The main focus of the UNICEF report was on expanding access to education, particularly for girls. Citing statistics from various sources, the report said about 130 million (or about one-fifth) of the world's children of primary school age were not in school. Most of those children were in sub-Saharan Africa (40 million) and South Asia (50 million). Many of the unschooled children were working instead. According to the UN's International Labor Organization, 250 million children in the developing world worked full- or part-time.

Much of the report focused on inadequate educational opportunities for girls in the developing world. Especially in Africa, the Middle East, and South Asia, girls were less likely than boys to receive a full education, thus helping guarantee that women in those societies would be unable to advance as far as men. The lack of education for women had multiple impacts on society. Uneducated women, for example, rarely received adequate prenatal care, one of the chief determinants of the health of infants. Uneducated women were less able than educated women to provide adequate health care and educational opportunities for their children. Also, fertility rates were substantially higher for uneducated women than for educated women (in Brazil, for example, illiterate women bore an average of 6.5 children, while women with secondary educations had an average of 2.5 children). While the broad social benefits of educating girls "are almost universally acknowledged," the report said, many countries were still lagging behind in providing equal education for their girls.

Just getting children into school was not enough, the report said, noting that millions of schools around the world lacked even rudimentary teaching tools (such as blackboards and textbooks), trained teachers, or appropriate curricula. About one-half of all children in Latin America failed to attain basic literacy even after six years of schooling. Drop-out rates, another indicator of education success, were unacceptably high in much of the world; for example, more than 40 percent of all students dropped out of primary school in Haiti and Nicaragua. In many countries, schools were chronically underfinanced. The ideal of universal free education was more a dream than a reality; in many developing countries, families were charged for tuition and books, and often the fees were so high that only the wealthiest families could afford them.

Some of the most discouraging news in the report came from the former Soviet bloc countries, where many education standards had declined since the end of the cold war in the early 1990s. During the communist era, the report said, education was nearly universal, even though schools often were authoritarian, most learning was by rote, and critical thinking was discouraged. With the political, social, and economic turmoil since the collapse of the Soviet Union, many former east bloc countries had scaled back both the quantity and quality of their education systems. This was particularly true in Caucasus and Central Asia where, the report said, education was "spiralling down toward standards not seen in a generation."

The report cited numerous cases where education was working. Expanding educational opportunity in the developing world was not a hopeless task, it said. Among the creative ways for expanding educational opportunities were these examples: In the Philippines, corps of "ambulant"

921

teachers hiked through mountain regions, carrying books and lesson plans in their backpacks to reach remote villages that would otherwise have no access to schooling. Several Latin American countries had adapted the old one-room schoolhouse into "multigrade" schools in which children could graduate from one level to another at their own pace once they achieved specified objectives. Cambodia, with help from UNICEF and other international agencies, built "cluster" schools to serve several communities; some of the schools were floating houseboats that were moved on lakes and rivers as the rural population migrated with the changes of the seasons.

Nearly all the world's nations had signed and ratified a UN treaty in which they promised to provide adequate education for their children. The 1989 Convention on the Rights of the Child declared education to be a human right, similar to other civil and political rights guaranteed by the 1948 Universal Declaration of Human Rights. According to the report, the only two countries refusing to adopt the treaty were Somalia and the United States.

Investing in Education

Aiming its message at national leaders and the heads of international development agencies, the UNICEF report said providing adequate education was primarily a matter of "political will." Educators had developed new techniques to tailor schooling to local needs—whether for the high-technology requirements of industrialized nations such as the United States or basic education in impoverished nations in Africa. Putting those techniques into practice was simply a matter of paying for them, UNICEF said.

The primary responsibility for providing education rested with national governments, the report said. It noted that developing countries often plead poverty "as an excuse" for not putting resources into education. But evidence of the previous four decades showed that "even poor countries can work wonders if they only have the commitment." As examples, the report said Vietnam, with a per capita gross national product of $290, had achieved literacy rates of more than 90 percent, and Zimbabwe had increased its literacy rate from 50 percent at the time of independence in 1980 to 85 percent as of 1998.

International development agencies also had a responsibility, the report said. But the report suggested that even the World Bank, the agency with the biggest financial investment in education worldwide, still had an "inconsistent record" in funding education programs during the 1990s.

Citing figures from several of its sister UN agencies, UNICEF estimated that providing a primary school education for every child in the world would cost an additional $7 billion annually over a ten-year period (based on estimated total education spending worldwide of $80 billion as of 1998). Broken down by regions, the estimated additional costs would be: $1.9 billion in sub-Saharan Africa, $1.6 billion in the Middle East and North Africa, $1.6 billion in South Asia, $1.1 billion in Latin America and *the Caribbean, and $700 million in East Asia and the Pacific. Attempting to put the $7 billion figure in perspective, the report quoted figures showing that Americans spent that amount each year on cosmetics, while Europeans spent about $11 billion on ice cream.*

The UNICEF report argued that allocating more money for education was a matter of establishing priorities. It noted, for example, that the International Monetary Fund, the World Bank, the United States, and other lenders had acted quickly to pump more than $100 billion into Asian economies when their financial markets collapsed in 1997. "Imagine what a similar infusion of resources would do for education," the report said. (Asian financial crisis, p. 722)

> *Following is a summary, prepared by the United Nations International Children's Emergency Fund (UNICEF), of two sections from Chapter One of the agency's report,* The State of the World's Children 1999: Education, *released December 8, 1998:*

The Right to Education

An education revolution is absolutely essential. An estimated 855 million people (more than one sixth of humanity) will be functionally illiterate at the end of this century. At the same time, more than 130 million children of primary school age in the developing countries, including 73 million girls, are growing up without access to basic education. Millions of others languish in sub-standard learning situations where little learning takes place.

Without an education, people cannot work productively, care for their health, sustain and protect themselves and their families or live culturally enriched lives. Illiteracy makes it difficult for them to interact in society in a spirit of understanding, peace, tolerance and gender equality among all peoples and groups.

On a society-wide scale, the denial of education harms the cause of democracy and social progress—and, by extension, international peace and security.

The inclusion of the right to education in the Universal Declaration of Human Rights in 1948 was the beginning of a broad effort by the United Nations to promote social, economic and cultural rights in tandem with civil and political rights.

The indivisibility of these rights is guaranteed by the 1989 Convention on the Rights of the Child, which became binding international law on 2 September 1990 and has now been ratified by all but two nations (Somalia and the United States).

As a result, what were once seen as the needs of children have been elevated to something far harder to ignore: their rights.

Articles 28 and 29 of the Convention require countries to provide free, compulsory basic schooling that is aimed at developing each child's ability to the fullest. Access to school and high-quality education are vital to this. Articles 28 and 29 are buttressed by four other articles that assert overarching principles of law: article 2, on non-discrimination; article 3, on the best interests of the child; article 6, on the child's right to life, survival and development; and article 12, on the child's right to have opinions and express them freely.

The vision of education enshrined in the Convention and other human rights instruments recognizes the right to education as the underpinning for the practice of democratic citizenship. The Convention is thus a guide to the kind of education that is essential both to children's development and to social progress.

The 1990 World Conference on Education for All, held in Jomtien (Thailand), set out to accomplish for education what the International Conference on Primary Health Care (Alma Ata, 1978) had achieved for health. It called for universal quality education, with a particular focus on the world's poorest citizens.

Jomtien marked the emergence of an international consensus that education is the single most vital element in combating poverty, empowering women, protecting children from hazardous and exploitative labour and sexual exploitation, promoting human rights and democracy, protecting the environment and influencing population growth.

Previously, education had been assessed in terms of gross enrollment rates at primary, secondary and tertiary levels. At Jomtien, it became clear that as essential as access is, counting the number of children sitting on school benches is only part of the picture. Moving forward, education was to be assessed in terms of its quality and certain other key elements. The expanded vision of education embraced at Jomtien includes an emphasis on basic education, early childhood care and development, and learning through adolescence and adulthood. Essential elements also include: making girls' education a major priority; the recognition that learning begins at birth; and the acknowledgement that new partnerships among governments and groups at all levels are necessary to achieve Education For All.

Modelled on some of the principles that had driven the child survival revolution that UNICEF had sparked in the 1980s, the Jomtien conference established six key goals:

- expansion of early childhood care and development, especially for the poor;
- universal access to and completion of primary education by the year 2000;
- improvement in learning achievement based on an agreed-upon percentage of an age group (e.g., 80 per cent of 14-year-olds) attaining a defined level;
- reduction of the adult illiteracy rate to half its 1990 level by the year 2000, with special emphasis on female literacy;
- expansion of basic education and training for youth and adults;

- improved dissemination of the knowledge, skills and values required for better living and sustainable development.

Jomtien helped move education back to the centre of the international development agenda after the lost decade of the 1980s, when debt and structural adjustments had brought earlier progress in education to a halt. Each major United Nations summit and conference since Jomtien has recognized that education, particularly of girls and women, spans and links these areas of concern and is pivotal to progress in each.

Progress towards Education For All has, however, been much slower than those who attended the Jomtien conference had hoped, as a mid-decade review in Amman (Jordan) in June 1996 revealed. There was a sense that a central priority of Jomtien—girls' education—and the conference's integrated vision of basic education had been overshadowed by the drive to get all the world's children into primary school by the year 2000.

During the five years following the Jomtien conference, all evidence pointed to a girls' enrolment rate that was virtually static.

Overall primary enrolment was the brightest sign of progress by mid-decade, with some 50 million more children in developing countries enrolled in primary school than in 1990. Discouragingly, however, this figure only managed to keep pace with the numbers of children entering the 6- to 11-year-old age group over the period. Regionally, the rates of progress varied.

The poor quality of the education provided in most of the countries of the Latin America and Caribbean region—as well as the social and economic circumstances of many students—has led to both high rates of repetition and high drop-out rates.

Investing in Human Rights

In the years since Jomtien, significant possibilities have emerged to advance human welfare. At the same time, disparities between privileged and poor have widened and with them the threat of social instability and civil conflict, making the arguments for the education revolution as an investment to promote peace, prosperity and the advancement of human rights even stronger now than they were a decade ago.

However, without a major change in the approach to delivering schooling and ensuring learning, it will be impossible for most poor countries to deliver Education For All. The pioneering examples in the report clearly show the way forward. The world now has a much better understanding of how children learn, what kinds of schooling are most likely to promote this—and also how to deliver these more efficiently. Cost-effective successful models now abound, and many are simply waiting for the resources and commitment it would take to 'go to scale' with them—to apply the same principles countrywide.

In other words, the education revolution is under way, but if it is to embrace all schools, in rich and poor countries alike, it needs to be backed up by sufficient resources and the requisite political will, both nationally and internationally.

National and International Responsibility

The primary responsibility for basic education rests with national governments. Many have frankly failed to make it a sufficient priority. It is standard for developing countries to plead their own poverty as an excuse for not ploughing enough resources into the pursuit of Education For All, yet all the evidence from four decades of development suggests that even poor countries can work wonders if they only have the commitment.

UNICEF has made a detailed study of nine countries and the Indian state of Kerala that have achieved much better results in health and education than neighbouring countries with similar incomes. Regardless of their position on the ideological spectrum, all these countries have given strong state support for basic social services, refusing to rely on a trickle-down from economic growth or on the free play of market forces. In common, they have:

- consistently spent a higher proportion of their per capita income on primary education than their neighbours, while also maintaining relatively low unit costs;
- managed to improve quality by reducing pupil-teacher ratios while keeping repetition and drop-out rates low;
- kept primary schooling free of tuition fees;
- managed (except for one) to achieve universal primary enrolment including broadly equal participation by girls and boys—and the exception, Malaysia, is not far short.

The lesson is clear, says the report: National governments can and should do much more to fund the push towards Education For All. But international aid donors and lenders have, in general, also not significantly increased their funding of education since Jomtien. The proportion of bilateral aid committed to education in 1993–1994 was 10.1 per cent, compared with 10.2 per cent in 1989–1990 and with 11.0 per cent in 1987–1988.

Even the World Bank, one of the Jomtien conference convenors and now the greatest single provider of funds to the education sector, has an inconsistent record in funding education in the 1990s. Between 1989 and 1994 the proportion of Bank lending allocated to education went up from 4.5 per cent to 10.4 per cent. But by 1997, the proportion had fallen to 4.8 per cent. The trend seems to be changing again, and the Bank estimates that it will have allocated 8.6 per cent of its total lending to education in 1998.

More troubling, though, is the alarming fall-off in loans from its soft-loan subsidiary, the International Development Association (IDA), to countries in sub-Saharan Africa, unquestionably the region in direst need of help. IDA lent $417 million in 1993, but the figure has fallen precipitously each year since, arriving at a low point of $132 million in 1996—less than its average annual lending in the pre-Jomtien period of 1986–1990.

Education: The Best Investment

The World Bank's economic case for investing in primary education has had increasing influence as its research documents that the private rates of return—the amount earned by individuals in formal-sector employment in relation to that invested in their education—appears in all regions of the developing world to be higher for primary than for secondary and tertiary education.

In recent years, the Bank has lent its weight to the cause of girls' education. In a speech in 1992, Lawrence H. Summers, then Vice-President and Chief Economist of the World Bank, argued that "investment in the education of girls may well be the highest-return investment available in the developing world." Girls' schooling not only cuts child mortality and improves the nutrition and general health of children, it also reduces population growth, since educated women tend to marry later and choose to have fewer children.

The value of investing in basic education—and especially in the education of girls—is now almost universally accepted. Why, then, has the international community not rushed to embrace this most essential project, which comes closer than anything else to being the long-sought magic bullet that will deliver 'human development' worldwide?

The answer is disappointing but familiar, according to UNICEF: There has not been sufficient political will. When the international community decides that something is of urgent importance, it can move mountains.

The Shadow of Debt

A way to address the resource problem hamstringing education is to approach the developing world's indebtedness with the same sense of urgency and resolve as would accompany an economic collapse.

Developing countries in all regions except Latin America and the Caribbean are having to pay a higher percentage of their export earnings in debt repayments than they were in 1980. The most indebted countries of all must exist in the shadow of a debt many times the size of their national income—Nicaragua's debt, for example, was a chilling six times the size of its gross national product (GNP) in 1995. Tanzania, meanwhile, is not untypical in spending six times more to pay off its debt as it does on education.

The 1996 initiative of the International Monetary Fund (IMF) and the World Bank to relieve the most heavily indebted poor countries at first seemed highly promising but has now foundered badly. This inertia should embarrass an international community that responded so swiftly and munificently to the needs of much richer Asian countries in 1997-1998. When it comes to debt relief, according to a senior World Bank official with responsibility for African programmes: "This is clearly an area where we have failed these countries. The political will to do better just did not exist."

The Human Face of Capital

The stagnation on debt relief notwithstanding, the international economic agenda is perceptibly shifting. After almost two decades in which human development has taken a back seat to globalization and structural adjustment, we may be entering an era of investment in 'human and social capital' that will make the task of spreading the education revolution worldwide much easier, says *The State of the World's Children 1999*. A model is emerging among leading economists, including those at IMF and the World Bank, that privatization alone cannot assure long-term economic growth; equally essential are human capital (a nation's health, education and nutrition) and social capital (shared values, culture and a strong civil society).

The new economic thinking will add weight to the 20/20 Initiative advocated by UNICEF and other partners, which enjoins governments of donor and developing countries to allot 20 per cent of their official development assistance (ODA) and national budgets, respectively, to basic social services. This alone would, if implemented, certainly liberate sufficient resources to achieve Education For All within a decade, the cost of which UNICEF estimates to be an additional $7 billion a year, on average—less than is spent on cosmetics in the United States or on ice cream in Europe annually.

It is clear that the link between human rights and sustainable human development, envisioned 50 years ago in the Universal Declaration of Human Rights and articulated in the principles of the Convention on the Rights of the Child, foreshadowed the increasingly accepted argument for equitable Economic development.

And in this, education's role is especially vital and unique, as it increases human potential and development at the individual as well as the social level.

Conclusion

The UNICEF report concludes: "It may have taken almost 50 years for the education rights proclaimed in the Universal Declaration on Human Rights to be fully accepted. But those rights are no longer negotiable. It is the world's responsibility to fulfil them without further delay. We can move swiftly ahead knowing that Education For All—making the education revolution a global reality—is the soundest investment in a peaceful and prosperous future that we can make for our children."

NASA ON FIRST STAGE OF THE INTERNATIONAL SPACE STATION
December 11, 1998

One of the most complex and costly engineering projects in history got off the ground—literally—in late 1998: the building of a giant space station by the United States, Russia, and fourteen other nations. Construction of the International Space Station was expected to cost at least $60 billion, and operating it for its planned ten to fifteen year life cycle would bring the total price tag to about $110 billion, most of it paid by the United States.

Russia launched the first component of the space station into orbit on November 20. The crew of the U.S. shuttle Endeavor *worked from December 6 to 10 attaching a second component. On December 11 the National Aeronautics and Space Administration (NASA) declared that the space station was open "for business." U.S. and Russian crews were to attach three additional components during 1999, and a three-person crew was to begin living aboard the station in January 2000. If all went according to plans, the station would be completed in 2004.*

Scientists planned to use the station for long-term experiments and observations that could be conducted only in the weightless environment of space. The United States also planned to use the station as a platform to prepare for manned expeditions to the Moon and Mars during the twenty-first century.

The International Space Station was the latest—but by far the biggest and most expensive—project of its kind. The Soviet Union launched the first space station, called Salyut I, *in 1971. Two years later, the United States put its first and only space station, called* Skylab, *into orbit but used it for only nine months. For most of the next twenty years, the Soviets were more dedicated to the space station concept than were the Americans. They launched a series of* Salyut *stations and in 1986 put* Mir *into orbit. Consisting of seven modules and weighing more than one hundred tons,* Mir *was supposed to last only a decade, but it was still in service at the end of 1998, having outlasted the Soviet Union and hosted several dozen cosmonauts and American astronauts. Even as it was participating in work for the new space station, Russia, the successor state to the Soviet Union, was trying to figure out how to dismantle Mir so it would not fall to Earth when it was decommissioned.*

Launching of the space station components was the second high profile endeavor by NASA during 1998. John Glenn, the first American astronaut to orbit the Earth in 1962, returned to space aboard the shuttle Discovery in October, a nostalgic trip that reminded Americans of the early triumphs and uncertainties of the space program. (Glenn mission, p. 776)

Delays and Controversy

In 1984, as the Soviet Union was preparing to launch Mir, President Ronald Reagan proposed an international endeavor to build an orbiting laboratory in space. The European Space Agency and Japan agreed to cooperate in the project, and the first of a series of concepts for a space station was developed. As was typical of all construction projects, costs escalated; estimates of the U.S. share went from $8.5 billion in 1984 to more than $11 billion by the time President Bill Clinton took office in 1993.

The newly installed Clinton administration demanded a total revision of the project, and it was at that point that Russia came on board as a major partner. Administration officials argued that Russia had access to technology and know-how from its space program that would be difficult and costly to duplicate. Perhaps just as important, the Clinton administration wanted to make sure that Russian scientists were kept busy on peaceful projects, including the space program, so they would not be lured into building ballistic missiles and weapons for countries such as Iran and Iraq. By the mid-1990s, the total number of nations involved in the project had reached sixteen. Besides the United States and Russia, participants included Brazil, Canada, Japan, and the eleven member nations of the European Space Agency: Belgium, Denmark, France, Germany, Great Britain, Italy, the Netherlands, Norway, Spain, Sweden, and Switzerland.

The project was controversial among U.S. scientists. Many scientists in the space program argued for the space station as a unique opportunity for scientific research. But other scientists said the space station was draining dollars away from other high-priority projects, such as the superconducting super-collider, a giant atom-smasher that was never completed. Among the critics was the American Physical Society, the professional organization of physicists in the United States, which argued instead for increased funding of unmanned research missions. Some members of Congress also questioned the constantly escalating costs of the space station.

The project was hampered by numerous delays, most of them caused by the complexity of mounting a cooperative undertaking among so many nations. By 1997 the chief concern of space station planners in the United States was whether Russia would be able to produce the numerous components it had promised. The cash-strapped government in Moscow was unable to pay its scientists and contractors regularly, raising questions not only about whether the work would be done but whether it would meet the *rigorous specifications for service in space. By 1998 the United States was footing the bill for much of Russia's work: Washington paid the $240 million cost for the first Russian component launched in November, and the Clinton administration paid the Russian government another $60 million to subsidize further work. NASA told Congress in late 1998 that additional U.S. subsidies to Russia would total at least $660 million through 2004.*

Attending the October 29 launching of the space shuttle that carried Glenn into orbit, Clinton said the United States needed to continue funding the space station even if that meant paying for Russia's share. "I think we're doing the right thing with this space station and we need to stay with it," he said.

Space Station Plans

Putting together a space shuttle, with components from sixteen nations, would be a complex task even if done on Earth; when completed the shuttle would be larger than two football fields and would consist of millions of mechanical and electrical parts. Much of the final assembly of the space station was to take place not in laboratories on Earth but in space, about 230 miles above the Earth. Nearly one hundred major components were to be flown into space over a six-year period, then linked together by astronauts. NASA officials estimated that astronauts, in two-person teams, would spend about 960 hours on "spacewalks" to fit the components together. All together, U.S. and Russian crews would fly more than ninety missions to the space station by 2004—more flights than NASA's shuttles had flown in the previous eighteen years.

The first two launches of components for the space station went well. On November 20, a Russian Proton *rocket lifted off from the Baikonur Cosmodrome in Kazakstan, carrying the first component into orbit: the* Zarya *(Russian for "sunshine") control module. NASA described* Zarya *as an unmanned space "tugboat" that would provide propulsion, steering, and communications for the space station in its early months in orbit. In later years* Zarya *would be used primarily for its docking ports and fuel tanks.* Zarya *was built by Russian contractors but paid for with $240 million from NASA's budget.*

Two weeks later, on December 4, the shuttle Endeavor *took off from Kennedy Space Center in Florida carrying a $300 million connecting module for the space station named* Unity. *On December 6* Endeavor *astronaut Nancy J. Currie maneuvered a fifty-foot robot arm to snare* Zarya *from space and position it just above* Unity *so the two modules could be linked together. Astronauts spent the next three days wiring together cables and other components of the two modules. Three spacewalks were necessary, including one to dislodge two antennas on* Zarya *that had failed to deploy properly.*

The Endeavor *astronauts completed their construction work on December 10, and early the next day NASA announced that the space station was ready "for business."* Endeavor *returned to Earth on December 15, leaving the combined modules of the space station in unmanned orbit. "I've got to admit, we were all pretty tense at various phases of the mission," commander Robert Cabana said as the shuttle was preparing to land.*

The next step was to be a shuttle flight in May 1999 carrying supplies to the station. Plans called for Russia to launch the next major component of the space station in July 1999: a service module that would provide living quarters and propulsion and guidance systems in the early years of the station.

Following is the text of a statement released December 11, 1998, by the National Aeronautics and Space Administration (NASA) announcing the completion of a link-up between the first two components of the International Space Station:

Endeavour's astronauts opened the new International Space Station for business Thursday, entering the *Unity* and *Zarya* modules for the first time and establishing an S-band communications system that will enable U.S. flight controllers to monitor the outpost's systems.

Reflecting the international cooperation involved in building the largest space complex in history, Commander Bob Cabana and Russian Cosmonaut Sergei Krikalev opened the hatch to the U.S.-built *Unity* connecting module at 1:54 p.m. Central time Thursday and floated into the new station together.

The rest of the crew followed and began turning on lights and unstowing gear in the roomy hub to which other modules will be connected in the future. Each passageway within *Unity* was marked by a sign leading the way into tunnels to which new modules will be connected.

About an hour later, at 3:12 p.m., Cabana and Krikalev opened the hatch to the Russian-built *Zarya* control module, which will be the nerve center for the station in its embryonic stage. Joined by Pilot Rick Sturckow and Mission Specialists Jerry Ross, Jim Newman and Nancy Currie, Cabana and Krikalev hailed the historic entrance into the International Space Station and said the hatch opening signified the start of a new era in space exploration.

Ross and Newman went right to work in *Unity,* completing the assembly of an early S-band communications system that will allow flight controllers in Houston to send commands to *Unity*'s systems and to keep tabs on the health of the station with a more extensive communications capability than exists through Russian ground stations. The astronauts also conducted a successful test of the videoconferencing capability of the early communications system, which will be used by the first crew to permanently occupy the station in January 2000. Newman downlinked greetings to controllers in the station flight control room in Houston and to astronaut Bill Shepherd, who will command the first crew and live aboard the station with Krikalev and Cosmonaut Yuri Gidzenko.

Krikalev and Currie replaced a faulty unit in *Zarya* which controlled the discharging of stored energy from one of the module's six batteries. The battery had not been working properly in its automatic configuration, but the new unit was functioning normally shortly after it was installed.

The astronauts also unstowed hardware and logistical supplies stored behind panels in *Zarya*, relocating the items for use by the shuttle crew that will visit the station in May and Shepherd's expedition crew. Late this afternoon, the astronauts will complete their initial outfitting of the station.

The hatches to *Zarya* and *Unity* will be closed before *Endeavour* undocks from the new station Sunday, leaving the new complex to orbit the Earth unpiloted.

The astronauts begin an eight-hour sleep period at 2:36 a.m. Central time this morning and will be awakened at 10:36 a.m. to begin their ninth day in orbit.

Endeavour and the International Space Station are circling the globe every 90 minutes at an altitude of 247 statute miles with all systems operating in excellent shape.

CLINTON ON AIR STRIKES
AGAINST IRAQ
December 16 and 19, 1998

A series of confrontations during 1998 between Iraq and United Nations weapons inspectors ended late in the year with the collapse of an eight-year effort to locate and destroy Iraq's weapons of mass destruction. Frustrated by Iraqi president Saddam Hussein's repeated blocking of the weapons inspections, U.S. president Bill Clinton ordered a major bombing campaign against military targets in Iraq beginning December 16. That campaign continued for four days, but U.S. and British warplanes later resumed low-level attacks on Iraqi installations that lasted into 1999.

Clinton's decision to launch the biggest military attack on Iraq since the 1991 Persian Gulf War came at a tumultuous moment in American politics. The House of Representatives had been scheduled to begin debate on four articles of impeachment against Clinton on December 17. After the military engagement was underway, House Republican leaders reluctantly decided to delay the impeachment debate by one day. Several Republican leaders at first accused Clinton of using the military action to try to escape impeachment—but most of them later toned down their rhetoric on that issue. (Gulf War peace terms, Historic Documents of 1991, p. 191; impeachment debate, p. 958)

Pentagon officials said the bombing campaign caused significant damage to Iraqi military targets, perhaps setting back by a year any effort by Baghdad to revive its programs to develop nuclear, chemical, or biological weapons. But the bombing also spelled an end to UN weapons inspections. After the bombing, Iraq said it would never allow the UN inspectors back into the country. While the UN Security Council debated ways to gain Iraq's cooperation, the Clinton administration shifted the focus of its policy to trying to oust Saddam Hussein from power.

UN Inspections

Following the Gulf War, which expelled Iraq from its illegal occupation of neighboring Kuwait, the UN Security Council passed resolutions pro-

hibiting Iraq from developing or possessing ballistic missiles and chemical, biological, or nuclear weapons (so-called weapons of mass destruction). Inspectors—assigned to an agency called the United Nations Special Commission (UNSCOM)—had authority to search Iraq for those weapons and destroy any that they found.

Iraq pledged to cooperate with the inspections, but its cooperation was sporadic over the subsequent years. The Baghdad government posed numerous hurdles for the inspectors, including withholding or destroying important documents and restricting visits by the inspectors to key weapons installations. Each time Iraq resisted the work of the inspectors, the UN Security Council passed a resolution demanding its cooperation; in most cases, Iraq relented temporarily and allowed the inspections to continue, only to pose new hurdles a few weeks or months later. Despite this cat-and-mouse game throughout the 1990s, UN officials said they had been able to uncover and destroy most of Iraq's ballistic missiles and its laboratories that were developing nuclear weapons. (Previous confrontations, Historic Documents of 1997, p. 767)

By 1998 the UN inspectors were focusing on chemical and biological weapons that Iraq had develop prior to the Gulf War. Iraq acknowledged that it had acquired enormous quantities of weapons such as botulinum toxins and anthrax, both of which caused fatal diseases, and had loaded them into a small number of missile warheads and bombs. Inspectors said Iraq had developed enough of those weapons to destroy the entire population of the Earth many times over—if it had the capability of deploying the deadly agents. UNSCOM managed to locate and destroy some of those weapons, but Iraq withheld important information the inspectors needed to finish the job.

A confrontation between UNSCOM and Iraq late in 1997 ended with a deal, brokered by the Russians, enabling the inspectors to search for the prohibited weapons. But on January 13, 1998, Iraq barred inspectors from entering any of Saddam's eight presidential palaces. Iraq said the UN team included too many inspectors from the United States and Great Britain. After Clinton warned Iraq that the United States might launch a military attack, UN Secretary General Kofi Annan visited Baghdad in February and secured another agreement from the Iraqi leaders promising to cooperate with the inspections. Under that agreement, the inspectors were to be accompanied on their visits to the palaces by UN diplomats. Inspectors visited those sites in March and April, but UNSCOM reported to the Security Council in April that Iraq was still refusing to provide complete information about its biological weapons program.

During the late summer, Clinton administration policy on the inspections came under fire on Capitol Hill. William Scott Ritter Jr., an American who had worked for UNSCOM until he resigned in protest in August, alleged that the administration had repeatedly blocked the work of weapons inspectors. Ritter told the Senate Armed Services and Foreign Relations committees on September 3 that the United States had "undermined

UNSCOM's efforts through interference and manipulation." He accused Secretary of State Madeleine K. Albright of hindering UNSCOM inspections to avoid provoking a military confrontation with Iraq. Administration officials rejected Ritter's contentions, which touched off a heated partisan dispute between Democrats and Republicans in Congress. Republican leaders cited Ritter's testimony as evidence that Clinton administration policy toward Iraq had failed.

On August 5 Baghdad announced that it was halting all cooperation with the weapons inspectors until the Security Council restructured UNSCOM and completely lifted a UN embargo on Iraqi oil sales. That move set off another round of confrontations that ended—temporarily—on November 14 when Saddam's government sent the United Nations a letter promising to allow resumed inspections; the letter arrived at UN headquarters just minutes before the scheduled launching of U.S. air strikes against Iraq.

Inspectors resumed their work November 17, but four days later Iraq began a new series of challenges to the inspectors, ending December 9, when inspectors were prevented from entering offices of the ruling Ba'ath Party. On December 15, UNSCOM chairman Richard Butler sent Annan a report concluding that Saddam's government was not cooperating with the inspectors, as it had promised November 14. Butler concluded his report: "[I]n the absence of full cooperation by Iraq, it must regrettably be recorded again that the commission is not able to conduct the substantive disarmament work mandated to it by the Security Council and, thus, to give the Council the assurances it requires with respect to Iraq's prohibited weapons programs."

Butler ordered his inspectors to leave Iraq early the next day, and a few hours later U.S. and British ships and warplanes launched missiles and bombs against Iraqi military installations.

Clinton's Strike Against Iraq

In a televised speech from the White House in the early evening of December 16, Clinton announced the military strikes against Iraq. Clinton said targets included Iraq's nuclear, chemical, and biological weapons programs, as well as that country's "military capacity to threaten its neighbors." Clinton summarized the history of the confrontations with Baghdad over weapons inspections and recalled that U.S. forces had been prepared to attack Iraq just a month earlier when "Iraq backed down." Iraq had then refused to fulfill its latest promises of cooperation with UNSCOM, Clinton said, citing as examples the ban on inspections of a Ba'ath Party office in Baghdad and other sites. "Instead of the inspectors disarming Saddam, Saddam has disarmed the inspectors," Clinton said.

The president said he had ordered a "strong, sustained series of air strikes against Iraq" designed to "degrade Saddam's capacity to develop and deliver weapons of mass destruction and to degrade his ability to threaten his neighbors." Secretary of Defense William S. Cohen and other officials later said Clinton used the word **degrade** *because it was clear that air strikes could damage Iraqi military installations but not totally destroy them.*

Anticipating criticism that he had timed the air strikes to coincide with the House impeachment debate, Clinton said: "Saddam Hussein and the other enemies of peace may have thought that the serious debate currently before the House of Representatives would distract Americans or weaken our resolve to face him down. But once more the United States has proven that although we are never eager to use force, when we must act in America's vital interests, we will do so."

Clinton was correct in assuming that some would challenge his timing of the military action. Perhaps the strongest criticism came from Senate Majority Leader Trent Lott, R-Miss., who issued a statement saying, "I cannot support this military action in the Persian Gulf at this time. Both the timing and the policy are subject to question." Gerald B. H. Solomon, R-N.Y., chairman of the House Rules Committee, said: "It's obvious they're trying to do everything they can to postpone the vote in order to get as much leverage as they can." Robert L. Livingston, R-La., who had recently been designated by Republicans to take over as House Speaker in the 106th Congress, announced that the impeachment debate would be delayed, but he, too, raised questions about the timing of Clinton's action.

Lott and most other Republicans later modified their criticism when senior military officials briefed them on the reasons for the attack. Defense Secretary Cohen, a former Republican senator from Maine, was adamant in defending the president against criticism by his former colleagues: "I am prepared to place thirty years of public service on the line, to say the only factor that was important in this decision is what is in the American people's best interests."

The U.S. and British attacks lasted four days, and Clinton announced on December 19—the same day the House voted two articles of impeachment against him—that the military operation "is now complete." Clinton said the attacks had inflicted "significant damage on Saddam's weapons of mass destruction programs, on the command structures that direct and protect that capability, and on his military and security infrastructure." Over the long term, Clinton said, "the best way to end the threat that Saddam poses to his own people and the region is for Iraq to have a different government."

Looking for a New Policy

In the weeks after the military strikes, diplomats from the United States, Britain, France, Russia, and other countries represented on the Security Council debated how to salvage the failed policy of containing Iraq's military threat by diplomatic means. The French government on December 22 proposed replacing the UNSCOM monitors with a new weapons inspection system, but Paris offered few details. The Russian government, which had been considerably more sympathetic toward Iraq than most other Security Council members, demanded that Butler be replaced.

While the diplomats discussed what they called "modalities" for arms inspections, U.S. and British warplanes resumed what turned out to be a regular series of attacks on Iraqi military installations. On December 26 Iraq declared that it would fire on U.S. and British planes that were patrolling so-called no-fly zones in southern and northern Iraq; those zones were established after the Gulf War to prevent Iraqi planes from attacking Kurds in the northern part of the country and Islamic Shiites and other minority groups in the south. Iraqi planes began flying into the zones and Iraqi antiaircraft batteries fired on U.S. and British planes patrolling the zones. U.S. jets retaliated against an Iraqi antiaircraft missile battery on December 28, beginning a regular series of attacks and counterattacks that lasted into the early months of 1999.

Clinton administration officials said they were turning their attention to finding ways of removing Saddam Hussein from power. Among other steps, the administration resumed discussions with Iraqi opposition groups. Ousting Saddam had been the ultimate goal of U.S. policy for nearly a decade, and by late 1998 it was clear that Clinton was no more willing than his predecessor, George Bush, to launch the full-scale military invasion of Iraq that appeared to be the only guaranteed means of reaching that goal—short of waiting for Saddam to die.

Following is the text of a televised speech delivered by President Bill Clinton on December 16, 1998, in which he announced that U.S. and British air and naval forces were attacking military installations in Iraq, followed by a statement December 19, 1998, in which Clinton announced that the air attack had been concluded:

CLINTON ANNOUNCEMENT OF AIR STRIKES

Good evening. Earlier today, I ordered America's Armed Forces to strike military and security targets in Iraq. They are joined by British forces. Their mission is to attack Iraq's nuclear, chemical, and biological programs, and its military capacity to threaten its neighbors. Their purpose is to protect the national interest of the United States and, indeed, the interest of people throughout the Middle East and around the world. Saddam Hussein must not be allowed to threaten his neighbors or the world with nuclear arms, poison gas, or biological weapons.

I want to explain why I have decided, with the unanimous recommendation of my national security team, to use force in Iraq, why we have acted now and what we aim to accomplish.

Six weeks ago, Saddam Hussein announced that he would no longer cooperate with the United Nations weapons inspectors, called UNSCOM. They are highly professional experts from dozens of countries. Their job is to oversee the elimination of Iraq's capability to retain, create and use weapons of mass destruction, and to verify that Iraq does not attempt to rebuild that capability. The inspectors undertook this mission, first, seven and a half years ago, at the end of the Gulf War, when Iraq agreed to declare and destroy its arsenal as a condition of the cease-fire.

The international community had good reason to set this requirement. Other countries possess weapons of mass destruction and ballistic missiles. With Saddam, there's one big difference: he has used them, not once but repeatedly—unleashing chemical weapons against Iranian troops during a decade-long war, not only against soldiers, but against civilians; firing Scud missiles at the citizens of Israel, Saudi Arabia, Bahrain, and Iran—not only against a foreign enemy, but even against his own people, gassing Kurdish civilians in Northern Iraq.

The international community had little doubt then, and I have no doubt today, that left unchecked, Saddam Hussein will use these terrible weapons again.

The United States has patiently worked to preserve UNSCOM, as Iraq has sought to avoid its obligation to cooperate with the inspectors. On occasion, we've had to threaten military force, and Saddam has backed down. Faced with Saddam's latest act of defiance in late October, we built intensive diplomatic pressure on Iraq, backed by overwhelming military force in the region. The U.N. Security Council voted 15 to zero to condemn Saddam's actions and to demand that he immediately come into compliance. Eight Arab nations—Egypt, Syria, Saudi Arabia, Kuwait, Bahrain, Qatar, United Arab Emirates, and Oman—warned that Iraq alone would bear responsibility for the consequences of defying the U.N. When Saddam still failed to comply, we prepared to act militarily. It was only then, at the last possible moment, that Iraq backed down. It pledged to the U.N. that it had made—and I quote—"a clear and unconditional decision to resume cooperation with the weapons inspectors."

I decided then to call off the attack, with our airplanes already in the air, because Saddam had given in to our demands. I concluded then that the right thing to do was to use restraint and give Saddam one last chance to prove his willingness to cooperate.

I made it very clear at that time what "unconditional cooperation" meant, based on existing U.N. resolutions and Iraq's own commitments. And along with Prime Minister Blair of Great Britain, I made it equally clear that if Saddam failed to cooperate fully, we would be prepared to act without delay, diplomacy or warning.

Now, over the past three weeks, the U.N. weapons inspectors have carried out their plan for testing Iraq's cooperation. The testing period ended this weekend, and last night, UNSCOM's Chairman, Richard Butler, reported the results to U.N. Secretary General Annan. The conclusions are stark, sobering and profoundly disturbing.

In four out of the five categories set forth, Iraq has failed to cooperate. Indeed, it actually has placed new restrictions on the inspectors. Here are some of the particulars: Iraq repeatedly blocked UNSCOM from inspecting suspect sites. For example, it shut off access to the headquarters of its ruling party, and said it will deny access to the party's other offices, even though U.N. resolutions make no exception for them and UNSCOM has inspected them in the past.

Iraq repeatedly restricted UNSCOM's ability to obtain necessary evidence. For example, Iraq obstructed UNSCOM's effort to photograph bombs related to its chemical weapons program. It tried to stop an UNSCOM biological weapons team from videotaping a site and photocopying documents, and prevented Iraqi personnel from answering UNSCOM's questions.

Prior to the inspection of another site, Iraq actually emptied out the building, removing not just documents, but even the furniture and the equipment. Iraq has failed to turn over virtually all the documents requested by the inspectors; indeed, we know that Iraq ordered the destruction of weapons related documents in anticipation of an UNSCOM inspection.

So Iraq has abused its final chance. As the UNSCOM report concludes—and again I quote—"Iraq's conduct ensured that no progress was able to be made in the fields of disarmament. In light of this experience, and in the absence of full cooperation by Iraq, it must, regrettably, be recorded again that the Commission is not able to conduct the work mandated to it by the Security Council with respect to Iraq's prohibited weapons program." In short, the inspectors are saying that, even if they could stay in Iraq, their work would be a sham. Saddam's deception has defeated their effectiveness. Instead of the inspectors disarming Saddam, Saddam has disarmed the inspectors.

This situation presents a clear and present danger to the stability of the Persian Gulf and the safety of people everywhere. The international community gave Saddam one last chance to resume cooperation with the weapons inspectors. Saddam has failed to seize the chance.

And so we had to act, and act now. Let me explain why.

First, without a strong inspections system, Iraq would be free to retain and begin to rebuild its chemical, biological, and nuclear weapons programs in months, not years.

Second, if Saddam can cripple the weapons inspections system and get away with it, he would conclude that the international community, led by the United States, has simply lost its will. He will surmise that he has free rein to rebuild his arsenal of destruction. And some day, make no mistake, he will use it again, as he has in the past.

Third, in halting our air strikes in November, I gave Saddam a chance, not a license. If we turn our backs on his defiance, the credibility of U.S. power as a check against Saddam will be destroyed. We will not only have allowed Saddam to shatter the inspections system that controls his weapons of mass destruction program; we also will have fatally undercut the fear of force that stops Saddam from acting to gain domination in the region.

That is why, on the unanimous recommendation of my national security team, including the Vice President, Secretary of Defense, the Chairman of the Joint Chiefs of Staff, the Secretary of State, and the National Security Advisor, I have ordered a strong, sustained series of air strikes against Iraq. They are designed to degrade Saddam's capacity to develop and deliver weapons of mass destruction, and to degrade his ability to threaten his neighbors. At the same time, we are delivering a powerful message to Saddam: If you act recklessly, you will pay a heavy price.

We acted today because, in the judgment of my military advisors, a swift response would provide the most surprise and the least opportunity for Saddam to prepare. If we had delayed for even a matter of days from Chairman Butler's report, we would have given Saddam more time to disperse forces and protect his weapons.

Also, the Muslim holy month of Ramadan begins this weekend. For us to initiate military action during Ramadan would be profoundly offensive to the Muslim world, and therefore, would damage our relations with Arab countries and the progress we have made in the Middle East. That is something we wanted very much to avoid without giving Iraq a month's head start to prepare for potential action against it.

Finally, our allies, including Prime Minister Tony Blair of Great Britain, concurred that now is the time to strike. I hope Saddam will come into cooperation with the inspection system now and comply with the relevant U.N. Security Council resolutions. But we have to be prepared that he will not, and we must deal with the very real danger he poses. So we will pursue a long-term strategy to contain Iraq and its weapons of mass destruction, and work toward the day when Iraq has a government worthy of its people.

First, we must be prepared to use force again if Saddam takes threatening actions, such as trying to reconstitute his weapons of mass destruction or their delivery systems, threatening his neighbors, challenging allied aircraft over Iraq, or moving against his own Kurdish citizens. The credible threat to use force and, when necessary, the actual use of force, is the surest way to contain Saddam's weapons of mass destruction program, curtail his aggression and prevent another Gulf War.

Second, so long as Iraq remains out of compliance, we will work with the international community to maintain and enforce economic sanctions. Sanctions have caused Saddam more than $120 billion—resources that would have been used to rebuild his military. The sanctions system allows Iraq to sell oil for food, for medicine, for other humanitarian supplies for the Iraqi people. We have no quarrel with them. But without the sanctions, we would see the oil-for-food program become oil-for-tanks, resulting in a greater threat to Iraq's neighbors and less food for its people.

The hard fact is that so long as Saddam remains in power, he threatens the well-being of his people, the peace of his region, the security of the world. The best way to end that threat once and for all is with the new Iraqi government, a government ready to live in peace with its neighbors, a government that respects the rights of its people.

Bringing change in Baghdad will take time and effort. We will strengthen our engagement with the full range of Iraqi opposition forces and work with them effectively and prudently.

The decision to use force is never cost-free. Whenever American forces are placed in harm's way, we risk the loss of life. And while our strikes are focused on Iraq's military capabilities, there will be unintended Iraqi casualties. Indeed, in the past, Saddam has intentionally placed Iraqi civilians in harm's way in a cynical bid to sway international opinion. We must be prepared for these realities. At the same time, Saddam should have absolutely no doubt: If he lashes out at his neighbors, we will respond forcefully.

Heavy as they are, the costs of action must be weighed against the price of inaction. If Saddam defies the world and we fail to respond, we will face a far greater threat in the future. Saddam will strike again at his neighbors; he will make war on his own people. And mark my words, he will develop weapons of mass destruction. He will deploy them, and he will use them. Because we are acting today, it is less likely that we will face these dangers in the future.

Let me close by addressing one other issue. Saddam Hussein and the other enemies of peace may have thought that the serious debate currently before the House of Representatives would distract Americans or weaken our resolve to face him down. But once more, the United States has proven that, although we are never eager to use force, when we must act in America's vital interests, we will do so.

In the century we're leaving, America has often made the difference between chaos and community; fear and hope. Now, in a new century, we'll have a remarkable opportunity to shape a future more peaceful than the past—but only if we stand strong against the enemies of peace. Tonight, the United States is doing just that.

May God bless and protect the brave men and women who are carrying out this vital mission, and their families. And may God bless America.

CLINTON ON END OF AIR STRIKES

On Wednesday, I ordered our Armed Forces to strike military and strategic targets in Iraq. They were joined by British forces. That operation is now complete, in accordance with our 70-hour plan.

My national security team has just briefed me on the results. They are preliminary, but let me say just a few words about why we acted, what we have achieved, and where we want to go.

We began with this basic proposition: Saddam Hussein must not be allowed to develop nuclear arms, poison gas, biological weapons, or the means to deliver them. He has used such weapons before against soldiers and civilians, including his own people. We have no doubt that if left unchecked he would do so again.

Saddam must not be prepared to defy the will—be permitted—excuse me—to defy the will of the international community. Without a firm response he would have been emboldened to do that again and again.

For seven and a half years now, the United Nations weapons inspectors have done a truly remarkable job, in forcing Saddam to disclose and destroy weapons and missiles he insisted he did not have. But over the past year, Saddam has repeatedly sought to cripple the inspections system. Each time, through intensive diplomatic efforts backed by the threat of military action, Saddam has backed down. When he did so last month, I made it absolutely clear that if he did not give UNSCOM full cooperation this time, we would act swiftly and without further delay.

For three weeks, the inspectors tested Saddam's commitment to cooperate. They repeatedly ran into roadblocks and restrictions, some of them new. As their Chairman, Richard Butler, concluded in his report to the United Nations on Tuesday, the inspectors no longer were able to do their job. So far as I was concerned, Saddam's days of cheat and retreat were over.

Our objectives in this military action were clear: to degrade Saddam's weapons of mass destruction program and related delivery systems, as well as his capacity to attack his neighbors. It will take some time to make a detailed assessment of our operation, but based on the briefing I've just received, I am confident we have achieved our mission. We have inflicted significant damage on Saddam's weapons of mass destruction programs, on the command structures that direct and protect that capability, and on his military and security infrastructure. In a short while, Secretary Cohen and General Shelton will give you a more detailed analysis from the Pentagon.

So long as Saddam remains in power he will remain a threat to his people, his region and the world. With our allies, we must pursue a strategy to contain him and to constrain his weapons of mass destruction program, while working toward the day Iraq has a government willing to live at peace with its people and with its neighbors.

Let me describe the elements of that strategy going forward. First, we will maintain a strong military presence in the area, and we will remain ready to use it if Saddam tries to rebuild his weapons of mass destruction, strikes out at his neighbors, challenges allied aircraft, or moves against the Kurds. We also will continue to enforce no-fly zones in the North, and from the southern suburbs of Baghdad to the Kuwaiti border.

Second, we will sustain what have been among the most extensive sanctions in U.N. history. To date, they have cost Saddam more than $120 billion, resources that otherwise would have gone toward rebuilding his military. At the same time, we will support a continuation of the oil-for-food program, which generates more than $10 billion a year for food, medicine and other critical humanitarian supplies for the Iraqi people. We will insist that Iraq's oil be used for food, not tanks.

Third, we would welcome the return of UNSCOM and the International Atomic Energy Agency back into Iraq to pursue their mandate from the United Nations—provided that Iraq first takes concrete, affirmative and demonstrable actions to show that it will fully cooperate with the inspectors. But if UNSCOM is not allowed to resume its work on a regular basis, we will remain vigilant and prepared to use force if we see that Iraq is rebuilding its weapons programs.

Now, over the long-term the best way to end the threat that Saddam poses to his own people in the region is for Iraq to have a different government. We will intensify our engagement with the Iraqi opposition groups, prudently and effectively. We will work with Radio Free Iraq, to help news and information flow freely to the country. And we will stand ready to help a new leadership in Baghdad that abides by its international commitments and respects the rights of its own people. We hope it will return Iraq to its rightful place in the community of nations.

Let me say in closing again how terribly proud I am of our men and women in uniform. Once again, they have done a difficult job with skill, dedication and determination. I also want to say that I am very proud of our national security team. I want to thank Secretary Cohen and General Shelton; I want to thank Secretary Albright and Sandy Berger. The Vice President and I have relied on them very heavily—they have performed with extraordinary ability and restraint, as well as effectiveness. I am very, very grateful for the way this operation was planned and executed.

But again, foremost, I want to give my thanks to our men and women in uniform. We are waiting for the last planes to come home, and praying that we'll be able to tell you tomorrow that every last one of them has returned home safely.

Thank you very much.

METEOROLOGICAL ORGANIZATION ON RECORD HIGH TEMPERATURES
December 17, 1998

*A global warming trend throughout much of the twentieth century con-
tinued in 1998, which turned out to be the warmest year on record. Reports
issued by meteorologists showed that the decade of the 1990s set new
records for warmth, with seven of the ten warmest years on record.*

*The record temperatures helped bolster the conclusions of the scientific
community that mankind was contributing to the warming of the Earth's
environment. By the late 1990s the vast majority of scientists agreed that
the burning of fossil fuels—coal, petroleum products, wood, and natural
gas—was creating "greenhouse gases," principally carbon dioxide. Trapped
in the atmosphere, the greenhouse gases helped raise the Earth's surface
temperatures, according to this view. A minority of scientists, along with
representatives of industries that developed, marketed, and depended on
fossil fuels, disputed this theory and said any rise in global temperatures
was likely due to natural phenomena.*

*The dispute between these views was of more than scientific interest.
Embracing the general theory of global warming, 167 nations meeting in
Kyoto, Japan, in December 1997 adopted a United Nations treaty pledging
to take steps—such as reducing consumption of fossil fuels—to curb emissions of greenhouse gases. U.S. critics were able to block approval of the
treaty in Congress. They said adhering to the treaty would severely curtail
economic growth in the twenty-first century. The United States was by far
the biggest producer of greenhouse gases, and its adherence to the treaty
was generally considered essential to the success of the measure. (Kyoto
treaty, Historic Documents of 1997, p. 859)*

The Year's Records

*Many people around the world did not need sophisticated studies to tell
them that temperatures were rising and weather patterns seemed abnor-
mal. Among them were the residents of Texas, who suffered through the
hottest summer on record. The daily high temperature in much of Texas*

exceeded 100 degrees for sixty days, including twenty-nine days in a row. Record heat was at least partly responsible for widespread fires in Florida, Brazil, and Russia. Brazil, Chile, Russia, and parts of the South Pacific were among the areas that experienced severe droughts in 1998. China, by contrast, suffered from massive floods that displaced more than 50 million people.

Month by month during 1998 meteorologists compiled statistics showing that average temperatures were rising around the world. The record month was July, when temperatures globally averaged 61.7 degrees Fahrenheit, according to the U.S. National Oceanic and Atmospheric Administration (NOAA). That figure was about 1.26 degrees above the long-term average for July (as determined by records for the years 1961 through 1990), and about .5 degree above the previous record in July 1997.

Overall, NOAA reported that global surface temperatures for all of 1998 averaged 58.1 degrees Fahrenheit, which was 1.2 degrees above the long-term annual average. NOAA said 1998 was the twentieth consecutive year that average global temperatures were above the long-term average.

A similar report released December 17 by the World Meteorological Organization—a unit of the United Nations—noted that 1998 was the warmest year since 1860, generally considered the first year for accurate temperature records taken by thermometers. Further, the UN agency noted that the ten warmest years on record had all occurred since 1983. Seven of the ten warmest years were during the 1990s. All seven continents had above-average temperatures during the year, the UN agency said, except for the northern sections of Eurasia.

Despite the heat waves and record-high temperatures globally, some areas experienced periods of exceptionally cold weather, the UN agency said. January was unusually cold in Argentina and Uruguay, as was November in much of Europe.

Observing Long-Term Trends

Scientists said temperature variations were important even though they might appear, at first glance, to be slight—a matter of a degree or two. According to most estimates, global temperatures at the end of the twentieth century were only about 5 to 9 degrees higher than during the most recent Ice Age. In that perspective, the global increase of about 1.25 degrees during the twentieth century could have momentous consequences if the trend continued into the twenty-first century.

Two reports issued during 1998 attempted to show the 1998 record-high temperatures within a long-term perspective. The first, a study reported in April in the journal Nature, *traced weather patterns since 1400 using "proxy" evidence to substitute for thermometer readings that did not exist before the mid-1800s: growth rings in trees, cores from icebergs, marine fossils, lake sediments, and similar records. Michael E. Mann, a climatologist at the University of Massachusetts, and his colleagues found that natural phenomena—such as solar radiation, volcanic eruptions, and ocean currents—explained most of the annual variations in temperatures through the nineteenth century. But starting in the twentieth century, these scientists concluded, man-made greenhouse gases appeared to be the dominant factor in the steady rise in global temperatures.*

Similar findings were reported in December by Jonathan Overpeck, director of NOAA's Paleoclimatology Program in Boulder, Colorado. Overpeck said his research indicated that global temperatures at the end of the twentieth century were the highest in at least 1,200 years. Overpeck disputed a widely held view that global temperatures also were unusually higher between the ninth and fourteenth century, a "medieval warm period." Some scientists who were skeptical of the impact of man-made greenhouse gases had said that the twentieth century warming trend paralleled the centuries-long warming period during the Middle Ages. But Overpeck said his findings showed that the medieval warm period "did not exist" and that the high temperatures at the end of the twentieth century "are probably unprecedented in at least 1,200 years."

Kyoto Treaty

In endorsing the Kyoto global warming treaty, the United States and other industrialized nations agreed to curtail their emissions of greenhouse gases by 2012. The treaty called for U.S. emissions to drop below the 1990 levels by 7 percent. Organizations representing industry—especially in the energy sector—insisted that curbing emissions by that amount would require major cutbacks in U.S. consumption of fossil fuels, disrupt the economy, and force up to two million people out of work. Critics also expressed anger that the treaty exempted many developing countries, including China and India, from reducing their greenhouse gas emissions.

With Republican leaders in the Senate saying they would block ratification of the treaty, the Clinton administration adopted a stance of trying to negotiate changes that would make the measure politically acceptable in the United States. White House spokesman Joe Lockhart said the administration regarded the treaty as "a work in progress."

An international conference held in Buenos Aires, Argentina, in November was supposed to resolve some of the issues that threatened to hold up implementation of the treaty. But the conference succeeded only in highlighting the international differences over the treaty. The 160-plus nations that participated were able to agree only on an "action plan" for making decisions by 2000 on how to put the treaty into effect.

El Niño and La Niña

By the end of 1998 scientists and public officials were assessing the impact of one weather pattern that helped contribute to record temperatures—and they were preparing for a subsequent pattern that might help depress temperatures. The former was the "El Niño" of 1997–1998; the latter was a "La Niña" expected for 1998 and 1999.

947

An El Niño ("the little child" in Spanish) was a periodic weather pattern that formed in the equatorial Pacific Ocean and produced warm ocean currents, high levels of rainfall in some parts of the eastern Pacific but droughts in other areas, and other climate changes that extended over much of the Earth. At an international conference held in Ecuador in November, experts said the 1997–1998 El Niño caused floods and droughts that killed about 21,000 people and caused billions of dollars worth of damage, including setting back economic development in many poor countries.

La Niña ("the little girl") patterns tended to produce nearly opposite effects, stemming from unusually cold ocean temperatures in the eastern Pacific. Scientists said a La Niña was taking effect by mid-1998, immediately following the end of the El Niño. Among other effects, the 1998–1999 La Niña was expected to produce an unusually cold and wet winter in the north central United States but a milder and drier winter than usual in most southern areas.

Following is the text of a statement issued December 17, 1998, by the World Meteorological Organization summarizing global weather patterns during 1998:

The earth's global temperature in 1998 will be the highest since 1860, according to the World Meteorological Organization (WMO). The global mean surface temperature is estimated to be 0.58 degrees Celsius [1.04 degrees Fahrenheit] above the recent long-term average based on the period 1961–1990. As we approach the end of the century, global temperatures are almost 0.7 degrees Celsius [1.3 degrees Fahrenheit] above those at the end of the 19th century.

It will be the 20th consecutive year with an above normal global surface temperature. The ten warmest years have all occurred since 1983, with seven of them since 1990. As of October, new monthly temperature records have been set in each of the past 18 months. The previous warmest year, 1997, was 0.43 degrees Celsius [.77 degrees Fahrenheit] above average.

The regional temperature patterns (January through November) show all of the continents with above average temperatures, except for the northern sections of Eurasia. In the United States of America, spring and summer heat and drought caused massive wildfire outbreaks in Florida and damage to crops from the southern plains to the southeast. April-June was the driest period in 104 years of record in Florida, Texas, Louisiana, and New Mexico, and May-June was the warmest period on record.

February was the warmest in many regions of France and the UK for more than 100 years. A record-breaking heat wave during June in central Russia caused more than 100 deaths and started huge fires.

In New Zealand, at least five months of the year had unusually warm temperatures. Qatar experienced the hottest summer ever for four consecutive months from June to September, due principally to high minimum temperatures. A severe heat wave prevailed over many parts of India resulting in great loss of life in May 1998. There was widespread drought affecting large areas of Brazil inducing extensive wildfires. Rainfall deficits in some cities in Chile during July made it the driest in a century. Fiji and eastern New Zealand also experienced droughts.

Unusually low temperatures were recorded during January in Argentina and Uruguay, and during June in the USA. Also, during November, much of Europe experienced extremely cold conditions, which spread eastward through Siberia and into Korea and the northern sections of Japan by the end of the month.

Higher in the atmosphere, where regular measurements are made by instruments on weather balloons and satellites, record high temperatures also occurred. From the surface to 7 km altitude, record temperatures in 1998 were 0.47 degrees Celsius [.85 degrees Fahrenheit] higher than the average of the last 20 years, making 1998 by far the warmest year. In the lower stratosphere, 1998 was colder than usual, though not quite as cold as in 1995–1997 period.

Computer models of the atmosphere show that cold conditions in the lower stratosphere result from both increased carbon dioxide and depleted ozone. The ozone deficiency during the austral-spring season, September through November 1998, was the largest and strongest ever recorded. The area covered by the ozone-hole lasted for more than 100 continuous days, which was a new record. The area exceeded 25 million km2 for 20 days while in previous seasons the area exceeded 20–22 million km2 in area only for a few days. Poleward of 60 degrees South, the ozone deficiency was 25% more this season than the average of the previous seasons in the 1990s. Globally, carbon dioxide concentrations continued to increase at a rate of 1.5 parts per million per year.

Over the oceans, a slowly fading El Niño and the unprecedented warmth of the Indian Ocean contributed to this record warm year. The El Niño event which started in 1997, continued to influence the climate in 1998 including extremely dry conditions and fires in Indonesia, drought in Guyana and Papua New Guinea, and extensive flooding in Ecuador, Peru, and Kenya early in 1998. Devastating floods in China were linked to the final stages of the El Niño. Lingering El Niño conditions in the east Pacific were associated with extremely dry conditions in Mexico and southern USA.

The central equatorial Pacific warm El Niño waters gave way to colder than normal sea surface temperatures (La Niña condition) by mid-year. The switch to La Niña conditions was associated with extremely heavy rains in the West Pacific triggering landslides and floods in Indonesia.

El Niño contributed to the late start of the 1998 Atlantic Hurricane season which under the influence of La Niña, ended as one of the deadliest in history with 14 named storms. Hurricane Mitch triggered massive flooding and landslides in late October that killed over 9,000 people, displaced another 2.4 million, and damaged or destroyed over 130,000 homes in Central America.

In China, preliminary estimates show that 22 provinces suffered from severe flood disasters. With an affected area covering 8.5 million hectares, the death toll was more than 3,000 with a record number of rivers and lakes flooded.

Floods in India and Bangladesh took over 2,800 lives. In Bangladesh, three major floods occurred during July and August, leaving about 50% of the country under water, up to 3 meters deep, for periods of up to 67 days. Another 250 died in Nepal. There were also significant floods in the Republic of Korea and Vietnam, the Philippines, the Russian Federation, and Sudan. In January, eastern Canada suffered from the longest-duration ice storm in its history. More than 100 mm of freezing rain and drizzle fell for more than 80 hours.

The preliminary estimates for 1998 are based on observations up to mid-December from a network of ships, buoys and land-based weather stations. More extensive information will be made available in early January during the annual meeting of the American Meteorological Society in Dallas, Texas, USA.

Prof. G. O. P. Obasi, Secretary General of WMO, called upon the world community "to heed the anomalies and maximize their effort to implement the resolutions of the Fourth Conference of Parties of the UN Convention on Climate Change, particularly the resolution urging for the enhancement of the Global Climate Observing Systems." He added that "the Global estimates such as this are only possible thanks to the long-standing exchange of weather information facilitated by WMO through its Member countries and in particular the national Meteorological and Hydrological Services."

REP. LIVINGSTON ON HIS RESIGNATION FROM CONGRESS
December 19, 1998

Robert L. Livingston, the Louisiana Republican who was slated to take over the House Speaker's chair vacated by Newt Gingrich, enjoyed one of the shortest tenures of political power in modern American history. Just six weeks after helping push Gingrich from office, Livingston on December 19 announced that he, too, would resign from Congress. Livingston made his announcement after a Capitol Hill newspaper reported that he had repeatedly engaged in extramarital affairs.

Livingston's dramatic fall from power came as the House was preparing to vote on articles of impeachment against President Bill Clinton arising from the president's illicit affair with former White House intern Monica Lewinsky. Livingston said that by resigning he was setting an example "that I hope President Clinton will follow." Although the House proceeded to adopt two impeachment articles against Clinton, the president did not follow Livingston's example or advice. (Gingrich resignation, p. 799; Clinton impeachment, p. 950)

Livingston's Rise to the Top

Livingston was a widely respected conservative who gained national prominence after the 1994 elections when Republicans took control of Congress and Gingrich tapped him to chair the powerful House Appropriations Committee. Gingrich pushed Livingston ahead of two more senior Republicans, saying he had the energy and vision necessary for one of the most important posts in Congress.

During the next four years, Livingston was a central figure in the recurring budget battles between congressional Republicans and the Clinton administration. In December 1995, during a shutdown of much of the federal government resulting from the refusal by the Republicans to accept Clinton budget demands, Livingston stood on the House floor and said: "We will never, never, never give in [to Clinton on the budget]. We will stay here until doomsday . . . and Merry Christmas." A few months later, the

951

*Republicans did give into Clinton when it was clear they had no public
support for shutting down the government.*

*Despite his ties to Gingrich, Livingston was one of many House chair-
men who were dissatisfied with the tight rein Gingrich kept on the committees. While he had solid conservative credentials, Livingston occasionally took positions at odds with the most conservative elements of the
House Republican caucus; for example, he often blocked antiabortion
amendments on appropriations bills and he opposed term limits for members of Congress.*

*Livingston stepped into the full glare of national publicity at noontime
on November 6—four days after Republicans suffered embarrassing losses
in mid-term elections—when he announced that he would challenge
Gingrich for the Speakership in the 106th Congress. Livingston had alerted
Gingrich the day before that he was thinking of the challenge unless
Gingrich was willing to give him more leeway in running the
Appropriations Committee. A few hours after Livingston announced his
challenge, Gingrich made his own surprise announcement that he was
stepping down as Speaker and resigning from Congress.*

*Within a few days, Livingston had gathered majority support within the
Republican caucus, and on November 18 House Republicans formally
selected him as their candidate for Speaker. The Republicans retained the
next two most senior leaders, Majority Leader Dick Armey and Majority
Whip Tom DeLay, both of Texas, but J. C. Watts, the only black Republican
in Congress, scored an upset victory for the number four position, chairman of the Republican Conference.*

*In his acceptance speech, Livingston rejected suggestions by many
observers that the Republican Party no longer had the kind of compelling
agenda that helped it win control of Congress in 1994. "We didn't run out
of ideas, we simply neglected to run on our ideas," he said. He also said the
party need not be too discouraged about the November mid-term elections,
which were widely seen as a defeat: "Let's make sure we don't misinterpret
a warning for a whipping."*

A Sudden Fall

*With his endorsement from the party, Livingston became the effective
leader of House Republicans, even though Gingrich technically remained
as Speaker. It was in his position as Speaker-nominee that Livingston set
the agenda for House debate on the impeachment articles against Clinton,
scheduled to start in mid-December. Livingston also spoke for House
Republicans on December 16, after Clinton announced that U.S. and
British forces were attacking military sites in Iraq. Livingston said
Republicans would support American troops, but he was one of many in
his party who questioned whether Clinton had ordered the military action
to divert attention away from the impeachment. "We'll leave that [issue] to
the best judgment of the American people," Livingston told reporters.*

*One day later, on December 17, Roll Call, a Capitol Hill newspaper
devoted to coverage of Congress, posted an item on its Internet site alleging*

that Livingston had engaged in extramarital affairs. The newspaper made a vague reference to an investigation of the sex lives of Republicans being conducted by Larry Flynt, publisher of Hustler magazine. In September Flynt had taken an advertisement in the Washington Post offering to pay $1 million for information about the sexual misdeeds of leading Republicans.

Shortly after the Roll Call report became public, Livingston appeared before a closed-door meeting of his Republican colleagues and read a brief statement acknowledging that "I have on occasion strayed from my marriage." Livingston said he had sought marriage and spiritual counseling and had been forgiven by his wife of thirty-three years. He recalled that he had told a reporter a few weeks earlier that he was "running for Speaker, not sainthood." But Livingston also sought to distinguish between his behavior and the actions for which Clinton was facing impeachment. Unlike Clinton, Livingston said, he had not had an affair with an employee, and he had never committed perjury.

The news stunned Livingston's colleagues in both parties. Most Democrats chose to remain silent, and most Republicans immediately said they still supported Livingston. Several Republicans lashed out at the White House, voicing suspicion that the president's aides had somehow been involved in Flynt's muckraking campaign. In private sessions the following day, a handful of conservative Republicans raised concerns about whether Livingston could still be an effective leader, but few, if any, suggested that he should step aside.

On December 19, as the House was debating impeachment, Livingston strode to the lectern for his statement. He opened with an impassioned plea for members to "cool our raging tempers and return to an era when differences were confined to the debate and not of personal attack or assassination of character."

Livingston then launched into a brief analysis of Clinton's behavior in the Lewinsky scandal, concluding with a remark directed at the president: "You, sir, may resign your post." Those words brought boos and catcalls from several Democrats, who yelled that Livingston should be the one to resign. Livingston quelled the uproar with his very next statement, that he was "willing to heed my own words."

Begging the forgiveness of his wife, family, and colleagues, Livingston said he had determined that he could not "be the kind of leader that I would like to be under current circumstances, so I must set the example that I hope President Clinton will follow." Livingston said he would not stand for Speaker when the 106th Congress convened in January and would resign from Congress early in the new year.

Livingston's surprising announcement momentarily brought the House proceedings to a halt; it stunned members still trying to cope with the convergence of Clinton's military strikes against Iraq and the historic nature of the impeachment debate. Rep. Michael N. Castle, R-Del., reflected that mood: "There have been so many bombshells. We have bombshells in Baghdad and we have bombshells in the House of Representatives. You can't turn your back for ten seconds."

It was not long before the inbred partisanship of the House came to the surface. A handful of Republicans, led by DeLay, echoed Livingston's demand that Clinton resign immediately. Some Democrats, fearing a possible groundswell of support for that position, unsuccessfully pleaded with Livingston to change his mind about resignation. Several Democrats also suggested that Livingston had been a victim of the same type of "sexual McCarthyism" that they accused conservative Republicans of using against Clinton—referring to a variant of the extreme anticommunism of Sen. Joseph McCarthy and his followers during the 1950s.

Later on December 19, a majority of the House approved two articles of impeachment against Clinton and rejected two others. Even as the House was acting on impeachment, Gingrich and other Republicans were frantically working to salvage their leadership team. Gingrich, who still retained strong moral authority among Republicans, suggested Dennis Hastert, of Michigan, as a candidate for Speaker. Although he was a close associate of DeLay—one of the most fiercely partisan Republicans—Hastert was well liked by members of both parties. Gingrich and other leaders said Hastert might be just the man to improve relations between Democrats and Republicans. Hastert quickly won support from a majority of Republicans and was easily elected Speaker when the 106th Congress convened in January 1999.

In interviews in the days after his dramatic announcement, Livingston said he had decided to resign because it was clear he could not be an effective leader. Noting that Republicans had only a narrow margin in the House and that some Republicans were "disconcerted" about his past indiscretions, Livingston told the New York Times, *"I was facing an impossible situation."*

> *Following is the text of a speech delivered December 19, 1998, on the floor of the House of Representatives by Robert L. Livingston, R-La., in which he announced that he would not serve as Speaker in the 106th Congress and would resign his House seat in 1999:*

Mr. Speaker, I rise with the fondest hopes that the bitterness engendered in this debate will at its conclusion be put aside, and that all Members will return to their families for the holidays mindful of what has been done here by we as agents of principle. We have fulfilled our duty to our magnificent Constitution.

Yes, our young men and women in the uniformed Armed Services have in these last few days set about the task of ridding the earth of the threat of weapons of mass destruction in the hands of an enemy of civilization, Saddam Hussein, and they have performed their tasks with valor and fortitude, that we may freely engage in this most unpleasant aspect of self government as was envisioned by our forefathers.

I very much regret the enmity and hostility that has been bred in the Halls of Congress for the last months and years. I want so very much to pacify and cool our raging tempers and return to an era when differences were confined to the debate and not of personal attack or assassination of character.

I am proud to serve in this institution, and I respect every Member of this body. Each of us stands here because a majority of roughly 600,000 people had the confidence to vest us with this authority to act as their agents in a representative democracy.

When given the chance, we often find that aside from political and partisan differences we have much in common with one another. But we never discover what that common ground may be with the gulf between the sides of this narrow aisle.

The debate has done nothing to bring us together, and I greatly regret that it has become quite literally the opening gambit of the intended Livingston speakership. I most certainly would have written a different scenario, had I had the chance.

But we are all pawns on the chessboard, and we are playing our parts in a drama that is neither fiction nor unimportant. Indeed, it is of utmost significance in the course of American history, and my desire to create an environment for healing must take lesser precedence than must the search for responsibility, duty and justice within the format provided by the U.S. Constitution.

I believe we are in active pursuit of these goals, and I give great credit to the gentleman from Illinois [Mr. Hyde] and the gentleman from Michigan [Mr. Conyers], and Mr. Tom Mooney and all the members and staff, majority and minority, of the Committee on the Judiciary for their deliberate and conscientious effort on this most difficult task.

We are nearing completion, and however the vote turns out, no one may say that we did not own up to our constitutional responsibility as Members of Congress in a careful, respectful and insightful debate. Much credit is due our presiding officer, the gentleman from Illinois [Mr. LaHood], who has done an outstanding job.

Mr. Speaker, we differ on process. The minority believes that we acted too hastily in view of the troops in the field, and that we omitted an alternative from the options available for consideration. We in the majority believe we have properly begun the debate after setting aside a whole day to honor and praise our troops and the effort that they are extending on our behalf. General Schwarzkopf, the commander of the troops in Iraq several years ago, agreed with us on the *Brian Williams Show* on MSNBC just two nights ago. We believe, we believe that the Constitution envisioned that censure not be a part of the debate on whether or not to impeach the President, and we are supported there by comments by then majority leader Tip O'Neill during the Nixon impeachment proceedings.

So there are differences in process; what about substance? The minority has maintained that the President has not perjured himself and that even if he did, such perjury was not intended within the term "high crimes and misdemeanors" delineated in Article 2, Section 4 of our Constitution.

Surely no President has been impeached for perjury, but at least three Federal judges have been impeached and convicted under the perjury statutes, and so perjury, a felony punishable by up to 5 years in the penitentiary, is a crime for which the President may be held accountable, no matter the circumstances.

Perjury is a felony, as I have said, and fully 116 people are serving time in Federal prison as we speak for perjury today, and, yes, there have been several instances of people going to prison following convictions for perjury involving lies under oath under sexual circumstances.

The average citizen knows that he or she must not lie under oath. Ms. Christine Simms of Rockville, Maryland, wrote to the Committee on the Judiciary just 2 weeks ago and said, and I quote:

> I too was called upon to give answers under oath in interrogatories during a civil proceeding. Truthful answers to those questions would be embarrassing to me, and what I knew exposed me to criticism and had a potential to ruin my life, particularly as it related to my children whom I love very much. In short, I was scared to tell the truth. However, I did just that. I could not lie when I was sworn to tell the truth, no matter what the risks nor the degree of temptation to take the easy way out. Parts of my life have been difficult since that time because elements of that testimony have been used to scorn me. But I as a common citizen was compelled by my conscience to tell the truth.

Yes, our Nation is founded on law, not on the whim of man. We are not ruled by kings or emperors, and there is no divine right of Presidents. A President is an ordinary citizen, vested with the power to govern and sworn to preserve, protect and defend the Constitution of the United States. Inherent in that oath is the responsibility to live within its laws with no higher or lower expectations than the average citizen, just like Ms. Simms.

When the President appeared at the deposition of Ms. Jones and secondly before the Federal grand jury, he was sworn to a second oath, to tell the truth, the whole truth and nothing but the truth, so help you God. This, according to witnesses to the Committee on the Judiciary and before the Special Counsel, he did not do. For this I will vote to impeach the President of the United States and ask that his case be considered by the United States Senate, that other body of this great Congress, uphold their responsibility to render justice on these most serious charges.

But to the President I would say: "Sir, you have done great damage to this Nation over this past year, and while your defenders are contending that further impeachment proceedings would only protract and exacerbate the damage to this country, I say that you have the power to terminate that damage and heal the wounds that you have created. You, sir, may resign your post. And I can only challenge you in such fashion if I am willing to heed my own words."

To my colleagues, my friends and most especially my wife and family: I have hurt you all deeply, and I beg your forgiveness.

I was prepared to lead our narrow majority as Speaker, and I believe I had it in me to do a fine job. But I cannot do that job or be the kind of leader that I would like to be under current circumstances, so I must set the example that I hope President Clinton will follow.

Mr. Speaker, I will not stand for Speaker of the House on January 6, but rather I shall remain as a back bencher in this Congress that I so dearly love for approximately 6 months into the 106th Congress, whereupon I shall vacate my seat and ask my Governor to call a special election to take my place.

I thank my constituents for the opportunity to serve them; I hope they will not think badly of me for leaving. I thank Allen Martin, my chief of staff, and all of my staff for their tireless work on my behalf, and I thank my wife most especially for standing by me. I love her very much.

God bless America.

HOUSE VOTES TO IMPEACH PRESIDENT CLINTON
December 19, 1998

December 19 was perhaps one of the most tumultuous days in American political history. As U.S. planes bombed Iraq in retaliation for Iraqi president Saddam Hussein's refusal to cooperate with United Nations weapons inspectors, the House of Representatives voted to impeach President Bill Clinton on charges of perjury and obstruction of justice in his attempt to cover up an affair with former White House intern Monica Lewinsky. "This republic has never seen the convergence of perhaps the most important series of political decisions in its history together with an equally serious decision regarding our national security and that of our allies," said Sen. John W. Warner, R-Va.

As television networks preempted Saturday morning cartoons and switched between showing the debate on the House floor and bombs falling on Baghdad, the Republican-controlled, lame-duck House adopted two articles of impeachment against Clinton, largely along party lines. By a vote of 228–206, the House charged Clinton with committing perjury in his videotaped testimony to a federal grand jury on August 17. By a second vote of 221–212, the House charged Clinton with obstruction of justice for "using the powers of his high office" to "delay, impede, cover up and conceal" his involvement with Lewinsky. Two other articles of impeachment were defeated.

Although members spoke, almost reverently at times, of their constitutional duty and the solemnity of the occasion, political partisanship drove the proceedings, propelled by conservative Republicans who deeply disapproved of and mistrusted the president and seemed resolute on overturning the will of the electorate. President Clinton had won election to a second term in 1996 with 49 percent of the vote in a three-way race. Some members of the Republican leadership were so intent on impeaching Clinton that they refused to allow a vote on censure, a move favored by Democrats and some Republicans as a punishment more fitting the president's alleged misdeeds. These legislators argued that deceptions, while deplorable, were the understandable actions of a man trying to hide an illicit affair and did not rise to the level of "high crimes and misdemeanors" required by the Constitution for impeachment. Republicans, led by Judiciary Committee Chairman Henry J. Hyde, countered that the president had lied under oath and that impeachment was the only constitutional punishment to demonstrate that no one, not even the president of the United States, was above the law.

The impeachment debate was nearly upstaged by another political bombshell. Just hours before the scheduled votes on impeachment, Robert L. Livingston, the Republican chairman of the House Appropriations Committee who had been chosen less than a month earlier to succeed Newt Gingrich as Speaker when the 106th Congress convened in January 1999, announced that he was resigning from the House in response to his own sex scandal. Livingston called on the president to follow his example and resign. But at a South Lawn solidarity gathering with several dozen Democratic House members immediately following the impeachment votes, Clinton said that he had "accepted responsibility" for what he did and vowed to serve out his term.

Whether Clinton would be able to follow through on that pledge was up to the Senate, which was charged under the Constitution with trying impeachment cases. The Senate would not act until 1999, but most observers considered it unlikely that the president's opponents would be able to muster the two-thirds majority needed in the Senate for conviction and removal from office. With fifty-five Republican senators, the GOP would have to persuade at least twelve Democrats to abandon their party and their president.

It was only the second time that the full House voted to impeach a president. The first was in 1868, when the House, dominated by radical Republicans, voted to impeach President Andrew Johnson, a southern Democrat who had succeeded to the presidency when Abraham Lincoln was assassinated. Johnson's impeachment in the House and trial in the Senate—where he escaped being removed from office by a single vote—was also colored by partisanship. The radical Republicans made little secret of their desire to get rid of a president who continually opposed their efforts to punish the South by vetoing harsh Reconstruction legislation.

The impeachment of Johnson was not the only time Congress seriously sought to remove a president. In 1974 the House Judiciary Committee voted to impeach President Richard M. Nixon for his role in the Watergate scandal—the "third-rate burglary" of Democratic Party offices in a Washington office complex. Soon after this vote on August 9, 1974, Nixon became the first president to resign the office—escaping almost certain impeachment by the full House and conviction by the Senate for his involvement in the political sabotage and cover-up revealed by the Watergate investigation.

One direct outcome of the Watergate scandal was legislation establishing the Office of Independent Counsel (OIC). To ensure against conflicts of interest, that legislation gave independent counsels great leeway in conducting investigations of top executive branch officials and required little accountability. Thus, independent counsel Kenneth W. Starr, appointed in 1994 to investigate allegations against President Clinton in connection with a failed land deal while he was governor of Arkansas, was able to follow up on other allegations of wrongdoing in the president's personal life. If nothing else changed as a result of the year-long impeachment battle, it seemed a virtual certainty that the legislation authorizing the OIC would be significantly amended, if not discarded altogether, when it expired in June 1999. (Office of Independent Counsel, p. 905)

Road to Impeachment

The vote to impeach President Clinton represented a remarkable turnaround. Clinton's political fortunes hit a low point in late August and early September, first with his public admission on August 17 that he had misled the country by denying his affair with Lewinsky and then with the September 11 release of the independent counsel's report, which made its case for impeachment by setting out in graphic detail the president's encounters with Lewinsky. As the shock of public exposure of intimate details of the president's personal life subsided, Clinton began to gain back lost ground. Polls uniformly reported that Americans disapproved of the president's personal conduct but thought he was doing a good job as president. Roughly two-thirds did not want the president to be impeached. (Chronology of scandal, Clinton admission, p. 564; independent counsel report, p. 632)

On November 3 Democrats picked up a net of five House seats in the general elections, a great disappointment to Republicans who had predicted gains. The House Judiciary Committee, under the leadership of Hyde, seemed out of control and unfocused when it began its impeachment inquiry in the weeks immediately following the election. A month later, but by the time that committee voted along party lines to recommend four articles of impeachment to the full House, it seemed a virtual certainty that Clinton would lose his fight against impeachment. (House Judiciary Committee action, p. 695)

Two factors were seen as crucial in this turnaround. One was Clinton's response to a series of eighty-one questions posed by the Judiciary Committee. The president's responses, carefully phrased in the same legalistic manner that marked his grand jury testimony, disappointed legislators, including many moderates, who wanted the president to admit openly that he had lied under oath—regardless of how his political enemies might use such an admission or whether it would place him in greater jeopardy of criminal charges after he left the White House.

The second and probably more important factor was the decision by Republican leaders to deny a floor vote on a resolution censuring the president. Democrats and some Republicans argued that impeachment should be reserved for presidents who committed "high crimes and misde-

meanors" in the conduct of their official duties as president and not imposed in matters of a personal nature. Opponents of censure maintained that impeachment was the only permissible punishment under the Constitution for presidential misconduct of any type. Beyond that debate, Republicans favoring impeachment wanted to keep Republican ranks closed; they calculated that without the option of censure, most of the twenty or thirty Republicans who had expressed unease with impeachment would have no choice but to vote for it.

On December 12 Livingston notified the Democrats that a censure resolution would not be permitted on the floor. "Censure of the president would violate the careful balance of separation of powers and the scheme laid out by the Framers to address the issue of misconduct," he wrote. Shortly thereafter many of the Republicans who had been known to favor censure began to announce that they would vote to impeach.

Debate on the Articles of Impeachment

Clinton's decision to launch air strikes against Iraq starting on December 16, the night before the impeachment debate was scheduled to begin, drew harsh remarks in both the House and Senate, further poisoning the already acrid partisan atmosphere on Capitol Hill both before and after the debate. "Never underestimate a desperate president," warned House Rules Committee Chairman Gerald B. H. Solomon of New York. Senate Majority Leader Trent Lott said that both the "timing" of the strikes and the policy underlying them were "subject to question." House leaders nonetheless did not want to appear to be undercutting the military and so postponed the impeachment debate for one day. (Air strikes, p. 934)

Formal debate on the articles of impeachment began on the House floor at 9 a.m., December 18, with Ray LaHood, R-Ill., respected by members of both parties for his fairness, wielding the gavel. A Democratic motion to adjourn, offered to protest the Republican leadership's decision to proceed with the impeachment votes while air strikes against Iraq were underway, was easily turned aside. A nearly full House then sat quietly as the clerk read the four articles of impeachment. Judiciary Committee members began the debate with short statements summarizing the charges against the president. The speech by James E. Rogan, R-Calif., was typical. "The president was obliged, under his sacred oath, to faithfully execute our nation's laws," he said. "Yet he repeatedly perjured himself and obstructed justice."

The mood on the House floor darkened December 19, after Livingston announced that he would not serve as Speaker and would resign. Democrats and Republicans alike seemed stunned. Several Democrats asked Livingston to reconsider, saying that his decision to resign was as misguided as the impeachment effort. "It is a surrender to a developing sexual McCarthyism," said Jerrold Nadler, D-N.Y., a member of the Judiciary Committee. In an emotional speech that drew a standing ovation, Democratic Minority Leader Richard A. Gephardt of Missouri asked *for an end to the "fratricide" that "dominates our public debate. . . . America is held hostage with tactics of smear and fear. Let all of us here today say no to resignation, no to impeachment, no to hatred, no to intolerance of each other, and no to vicious self-righteousness."* (Livingston resignation, p. 951)

The voting then began. Republicans first won a procedural vote that prevented the Democrats from offering a censure resolution. The vote was 230–204. Democrats responded with a brief, staged walkout in protest. When they returned voting began on each of the four articles of impeachment contained in House Resolution 611.

By a vote of 228–206, with five Republicans and five Democrats crossing party lines, the House adopted the first article, which accused Clinton of having committed perjury in his August 17 grand jury testimony. This article had always been considered the most likely to succeed, legislators said, because Clinton's testimony was clearly material to Starr's investigation.

By a vote of 205–229, the House rejected the second article, which charged the president with committing perjury in his deposition in the sexual harassment suit brought by Paula Corbin Jones. (The presiding judge in that case had later dismissed the suit. Jones was in the process of appealing that dismissal when she and the president reached an out-of-court settlement in November 1998.) It was this deposition that was the basis for the president's later grand jury testimony, and many observers noted the irony of dismissing perjury charges connected to his deposition while pressing them in his grand jury testimony. On this article twenty-eight Republicans and five Democrats broke ranks with their party.

By a vote of 221–212, the House adopted the third article, which charged Clinton with obstruction of justice for his efforts to find Lewinsky a job, possibly in return for her silence, and his alleged witness tampering involving his personal secretary, Betty Currie. Five Democrats voted for this article, twelve Republicans voted against it.

By a vote of 148–285, the House rejected the fourth article, which accused the president of abuse of power. Among other things this article charged Clinton with "a pattern of deceit and obstruction" in providing misleading statements to the questions posed by the Judiciary Committee. Only one Democrat voted for this article, eighty-one Republicans voted against it.

After voting on the impeachment articles, the House authorized the appointment of thirteen Republican members of the Judiciary Committee to prosecute the case in the Senate. The "managers" as they were called then walked across the Capitol, where chairman Hyde presented a leather-bound book containing the two approved articles of impeachment to the secretary of the Senate.

At roughly the same time, several dozen loyal House Democrats arrived at the White House for a show of solidarity with President Clinton. Accompanied by his wife, and Vice President Al Gore, Clinton appeared somber but determined. "I will continue to do the work of the American people," the president vowed. "It's what I've tried to do for six years. It's what I intend to do for two more until the last hour of the last day of my term."

Effects of Impeachment

Whether or not the Senate convicted the president, there was already much speculation about the effect the second presidential impeachment in history would have on the president, the presidency, and American politics. Clearly, whether Clinton would be able to work effectively with House Republicans was an open question, but one likely to be tested early in 1999 as the president pushed forward his plans for ensuring a sound financial basis for Social Security, enacting a patient's bill of rights, and securing greater funding for education.

The effect on the presidency would not be apparent as quickly. Although Clinton's impeachment was cloaked in legal trappings and invoked in the name of upholding the law, many but not all constitutional scholars noted that impeachment was primarily a political tool, rather than a legal one. That was a fundamental point made by Clinton's attorneys, who argued that his political enemies in and out of Congress were bent on using almost any means to remove Clinton from office. Many constitutional experts warned that if politics remained so polarized, with the presidency controlled by one party and Congress by the other, impeachment could become more common. "My concern," explained Thomas Sargentich, a law professor at American University in Washington, D.C., "is that for the integrity of a government, for a workable system of checks and balances, impeachment should largely stay in the background. Otherwise we are changing our system of government and moving toward something that is more like a parliamentary system."

Others expressed concern that the men and women best qualified to serve their country would refuse government service to avoid the possibility that their most intimate secrets, however harmless, would be exposed to public view. Rep. Nadler summed up those concerns well during the impeachment debate: "We are losing sight of the distinction between sins, which ought to be between a person and his family and his God, and crimes, which are the concern of the state and of society as a whole."

Following is the text of House Resolution 611, the articles of impeachment against President William Jefferson Clinton that the House voted December 19, 1998, to refer to the Senate for trial; followed by excerpts of remarks by House Minority Leader Richard A. Gephardt, D-Mo., Vice President Al Gore, and Clinton on the South Lawn of the White House shortly after the impeachment vote:

ARTICLES OF IMPEACHMENT

Resolution, Impeaching William Jefferson Clinton, President of the United States, for high crimes and misdemeanors.

Resolved, that William Jefferson Clinton, President of the United States, is impeached for high crimes and misdemeanors, and that the following articles of impeachment be exhibited to the United States Senate:

Articles of impeachment exhibited by the House of Representatives of the United States of America in the name of itself and of the people of the United States of America, against William Jefferson Clinton, President of the United States of America, in maintenance and support of its impeachment against him for high crimes and misdemeanors.

Article I

In his conduct while President of the United States, William Jefferson Clinton, in violation of his constitutional oath faithfully to execute the office of the President of the United States, and to the best of his ability, preserve, protect, and defend the Constitution of the United States, and in violation of his constitutional duty to take care that the laws be faithfully executed, has willfully corrupted and manipulated the judicial process of the United States for his personal gain and exoneration, impeding the administration of justice, in that:

On August 17, 1998, William Jefferson Clinton swore to tell the truth, the whole truth and nothing but the truth before a Federal grand jury of the United States. Contrary to that oath, William Jefferson Clinton willfully provided perjurious, false and misleading testimony to the grand jury concerning one or more of the following: (1) the nature and details of his relationship with a subordinate government employee; (2) prior perjurious, false and misleading testimony he gave in a Federal civil rights action brought against him; (3) prior false and misleading statements he allowed his attorney to make to a Federal judge in that civil rights action; and (4) his corrupt efforts to influence the testimony of witnesses and to impede the discovery of evidence in that civil rights action.

In doing this, William Jefferson Clinton has undermined the integrity of his office, has brought disrepute on the Presidency, has betrayed his trust as President, and has acted in a manner subversive of the rule of law and justice, to the manifest injury of the people of the United States.

Wherefore, William Jefferson Clinton, by such conduct, warrants impeachment and trial, and removal from office and disqualification to hold and enjoy any office of honor, trust or profit under the United States.

Article II

In his conduct while President of the United States, William Jefferson Clinton, in violation of his constitutional oath faithfully to execute the office of President of the United States, and, to the best of his ability, preserve, protect, and defend the Constitution of the United States, and in violation of his constitutional duty to take care that the laws be faithfully executed, has willfully corrupted and manipulated the judicial process of the United States for his personal gain and exoneration, impeding the administration of justice, in that:

(1) On December 23, 1997, William Jefferson Clinton, in sworn answers to written questions asked as part of a Federal civil rights action brought against him, willfully provided perjurious, false and misleading testimony in response to questions deemed relevant by a Federal judge concerning conduct and proposed conduct with subordinate employees.

(2) On January 17, 1998, William Jefferson Clinton swore under oath to tell the truth, the whole truth, and nothing but the truth in a deposition given as part of a Federal civil rights action brought against him. Contrary to that oath, William Jefferson Clinton willfully provided perjurious, false and misleading testimony in response to questions deemed relevant by a Federal judge concerning the nature and details of his relationship with a subordinate government employee, his knowledge of that employee's involvement and participation in the civil rights action brought against him, and his corrupt efforts to influence the testimony of that employee.

In all of this, William Jefferson Clinton has undermined the integrity of his office, has brought disrepute on the Presidency, has betrayed his trust as president, and has acted in a manner subversive of the rule of law and justice, to the manifest injury of the people of the United States.

Wherefore William Jefferson Clinton, by such conduct, warrants impeachment and trial, and removal from office and disqualification to hold and enjoy any office of honor, trust or profit under the United States.

Article III

In his conduct, while President of the United States, William Jefferson Clinton, in violation of his constitutional oath faithfully to execute the office of President of the United States and, to the best of his ability, preserve, protect, and defend the Constitution of the United States, and in violation of his constitutional duty to take care that the laws be faithfully executed, has prevented, obstructed, and impeded the administration of justice, and has to that end engaged personally, and through his subordinates and agents, in a course of conduct or scheme designed to delay, impede, cover up, and conceal the existence of evidence and testimony related to a Federal civil rights action brought against him in a duly instituted judicial proceeding.

The means used to implement this course of conduct or scheme included one or more of the following acts:

(1) On or about December 17, 1997, William Jefferson Clinton corruptly encouraged a witness in a Federal civil rights action brought against him to execute a sworn affidavit in that proceeding that he knew to be perjurious, false and misleading.

(2) On or about December 17, 1997, William Jefferson Clinton corruptly encouraged a witness in a Federal civil rights action brought against him to

give perjurious, false and misleading testimony if and when called to testify personally in that proceeding.

(3) On or about December 28, 1997, William Jefferson Clinton corruptly engaged in, encouraged, or supported a scheme to conceal evidence that had been subpoenaed in a Federal civil rights action brought against him.

(4) Beginning on or about December 7, 1997, and continuing through and including January 14, 1998, William Jefferson Clinton intensified and succeeded in an effort to secure job assistance to a witness in a Federal civil rights action brought against him in order to corruptly prevent the truthful testimony of that witness in that proceeding at a time when the truthful testimony of that witness would have been harmful to him.

(5) On January 17, 1998, at his deposition in a Federal civil rights action brought against him, William Jefferson Clinton corruptly allowed his attorney to make false and misleading statements to a Federal judge characterizing an affidavit, in order to prevent questioning deemed relevant by the judge. Such false and misleading statements were subsequently acknowledged by his attorney in a communication to that judge.

(6) On or about January 18 and January 20-21, 1998, William Jefferson Clinton related a false and misleading account of events relevant to a Federal civil rights action brought against him to a potential witness in that proceeding, in order to corruptly influence the testimony of that witness.

(7) On or about January 21, 23, and 26, 1998, William Jefferson Clinton made false and misleading statements to potential witnesses in a Federal grand jury proceeding in order to corruptly influence the testimony of those witnesses. The false and misleading statements made by William Jefferson Clinton were repeated by witnesses to the grand jury, causing the grand jury to receive false and misleading information.

In all of this, William Jefferson Clinton has undermined the integrity of his office, has brought disrepute on the Presidency, has betrayed his trust as President, and has acted in a manner subversive to the rule of law and justice, to the manifest injury to the people of the United States.

Wherefore, William Jefferson Clinton, by such conduct, warrants impeachment and trial, and removal from office and disqualification to hold and enjoy any office of honor, trust or profit under the United States.

Article IV

Using the powers and influence of the office of the President of the United States, William Jefferson Clinton, in violation of his constitutional oath faithfully to execute the office of President of the United States and, to the best of his ability, preserve, protect, and defend the Constitution of the United States, and in disregard of his constitutional duty to take care that the laws be faithfully executed, has engaged in conduct that resulted in misuse and abuse of his high office, impaired the due and proper administration of justice and the conduct of lawful inquiries, and contravened the authority of the legislative branch and the truth-seeking purpose of a coordinate investigative proceeding, in that, as President, William Jefferson Clinton refused and failed to respond to certain written requests for admission and willfully made perjurious, false and misleading sworn statements in response to certain written requests for admission propounded to him as part of the impeachment inquiry authorized by the House of Representatives of the Congress of the United States.

William Jefferson Clinton, in refusing and failing to respond and in making perjurious, false and misleading statements, assumed to himself functions and judgments necessary to the exercise of the sole power of impeachment vested by the Constitution in the House of Representatives and exhibited contempt for the inquiry.

In doing this, William Jefferson Clinton has undermined the integrity of his office, has brought disrepute on the Presidency, has betrayed his trust as President, and has acted in a manner subversive of the rule of law and justice, to the manifest injury of the people of the United States.

Wherefore, William Jefferson Clinton, by such conduct, warrants impeachment and trial, and removal from office and disqualification to hold and enjoy any office of honor, trust or profit under the United States.

REMARKS AT THE WHITE HOUSE

Rep. Richard Gephardt, D-Mo.: Mr. President, Mr. Vice President, First Lady Hillary Clinton, we've just witnessed a partisan vote that was a disgrace to our country and our Constitution. [Judiciary Committee] Chairman Henry Hyde [R-Ill.] once called impeachment the ultimate weapon, and said that for it to succeed, ultimately, it has to be bipartisan. The fact that a vote as important as this occurred in such a partisan way violated the spirit of our democracy.

We must turn away now from the politics of personal destruction, and return to a politics of values. The American people deserve better than what they've received over these long five months. They want their Congress to bring this issue to a speedy compromise, closure. And they want their president, twice elected to his office, to continue his work fighting for their priorities.

The Democratic Caucus in the House will continue to stand alongside our president, and we will work to enact the agenda that we were sent here to pass.

We look forward to supporting his agenda in the upcoming session of Congress. The president has demonstrated his effectiveness as a national and world leader in the face of intense and unprecedented negative attacks by his opponents. I'm confident that he will continue to do so for the rest of his elected term of office.

Despite the worst efforts of the Republican leadership in the House, the Constitution will bear up under the strain, and our nation will survive. The constitutional process about to play out in the United States Senate will hopefully, finally, be fair, and allow us to put an end to this sad chapter of our history.

Ladies and gentlemen, it is now my honor to present our great vice president of these United States, Al Gore.

Vice President Al Gore: Thank you very much, Mr. Leader. To you and to David [E.] Bonior [D-Mich.] and to the entire Democratic Caucus leadership, thank you for what you have done for our country. I would also like to single out for special thanks and praise Congressman John Conyers [Jr., D-Mich.] and all of the members of the Judiciary Committee who are present here today.

And to you, Dick Gephardt, I would like to repeat a judgment that I made to the smaller group earlier. You and I came here on the same day 22 years ago, and in all that time, I don't believe I have heard a finer speech on the floor of the House of Representatives than the one that you delivered this morning.

But in all that time, I do believe this is the saddest day I have seen in our nation's capital, because today's vote in the House of Representatives disregarded the plain wishes and goodwill of the American people, and the plain meaning of our Constitution. Let me say simply, the president has acknowledged that what he did was wrong, but we must all acknowledge that invoking the solemn power of impeachment in the cause of partisan politics is wrong—wrong for our Constitution, wrong for the United States of America.

Republican leaders would not even allow the members of the House of Representatives to cast the vote they wanted to. They were not allowed to vote their conscience. What happened as a result does a great disservice to a man I believe will be regarded in the history books as one of our greatest presidents.

There is no doubt in my mind that the verdict of history will undo the unworthy judgment rendered a short while ago in the United States Capitol. But we do not have to wait for history. Instead, let us live up to the ideals of this season. Let us reach out to one another, and reach out for what is best in ourselves, our history, and our country. Let us heal this land, not tear it apart. Let us move forward, not toward bitter and angry division.

Our founders anticipated that there might be a day like this one, when excessive partisanship unlocked a form of vitriol and vehemence that hurts our nation. We all know that a process that wounds good people in both parties does no service to this country. What America needs is not resignations, but the renewal of civility, respect for one another, decency toward each other, and the certain belief that together we can serve this land and make a better life for all of our people.

That is what President Clinton has done. That is what he is doing, and that is what he will continue to do for the next two years. I feel extremely privileged to have been able to serve with him as his partner for the past six years. And I look forward to serving with him for the next two years. I have seen him close at hand, day after day, making the most important decisions about peace, prosperity, and our future, and making them always by asking what is right for the American people, what is right for all of the American people. I know him. I know his wonderful first lady. I know his heart, and his will, and I have seen his work.

Six years ago, he was left with the highest budget deficit in history, and he ended it. Six years ago, he was handed a failing economy. Today, because of his leadership, we are on the verge of the longest period of peacetime prosperity in all of American history. And I know nothing will stop him from doing the job that the American people sent him here to do.

I say to you today, President William Jefferson Clinton will continue and will complete his mission on behalf of the American people.

I'm proud to present to you my friend, America's great president, Bill Clinton.

President Bill Clinton: Thank you very much. Thank you. Good afternoon.

Let me begin by expressing my profound and heartfelt thanks to Congressman Gephardt and the leadership and all the members of the Democratic Caucus for what they did today. I thank the few brave Republicans who withstood enormous pressure to stand with them for the plain meaning of the Constitution, and for the proposition that we need to pull together to move beyond partisanship, to get on with the business of our country. I thank the millions upon millions of American citizens who have expressed their support and their friendship to Hillary, to me, to our family and to our administration during these last several weeks.

The words of the members here with me and others who were a part of their endeavor in defense of our Constitution were powerful and moving, and I will never forget them. The question is, what are we going to do now?

I have accepted responsibility for what I did wrong in my personal life, and I have invited members of Congress to work with us to find a reasonable, bipartisan, and proportionate response. That approach was rejected today by Republicans in the House. But I hope it will be embraced in the Senate. I hope there will be a constitutional and fair means of resolving this matter in a prompt manner.

Meanwhile, I will continue to do the work of the American people. We still, after all, have to save Social Security, and Medicare for the 21st century. We have to give all our children world-class schools. We have to pass a patient's bill of rights, we have to make sure the economic turbulence around the world does not curb our economic opportunity here at home. We have to keep America the world's strongest force for peace and freedom. In short, we have a lot to do before we enter the 21st century.

And we still have to keep working to build that elusive one America I have talked so much about. For six years now I have done everything I could to bring our country together across the lines that divide us, including bringing Washington together across party lines. Out in the country people are pulling together, but just as America is coming together, it must look from the country's point of view like Washington is coming apart.

I want to echo something Mr. Gephardt said. It is something I have felt strongly all my life. We must stop the politics of personal destruction. We must get rid of the poisonous venom of excessive partisanship, obsessive animosity, and uncontrolled anger. That is not what America deserves. That is not what America is about. We are doing well now. We are a good and decent country. But, we have significant challenges we have to face. In order to do it right, we have to have some atmosphere of decency and civility, some presumption of good faith, some sense of proportionality and balance in bringing judgment against those who are in different parties. We have important work to do.

We need a constructive debate that has all the different voices in this country heard in the halls of Congress. I want the American people to know today that I am still committed to working with people of good faith, and good will of both parties to do what's best for our country, to bring our nation together, to lift our people up, to move us all forward together. It's what I've tried to do for six years. It's what I intend to do for two more, until the last hour of the last day of my term.

So with profound gratitude for the defense of the Constitution and the best in America that was raised today by the members here and those who joined them, I ask the American people to move with me, to go on from here, to rise above the rancor, to overcome the pain and division, to be a repairer of the breach, all of us, to make this country as one America, what it can and must be for our children in the new century about to dawn.

Thank you very much.

STATE DEPARTMENT ON DEMISE
OF THE KHMER ROUGE
December 29, 1998

Nearly two decades after the murderous Khmer Rouge regime was ousted from power, Cambodia in late 1998 appeared to be on the verge of achieving two long elusive goals: peace and political stability. Pol Pot, the once-feared Khmer Rouge leader, died in April, and two of his chief lieutenants surrendered in late December, issuing a weak apology for the Khmer Rouge reign of terror from 1975 to 1979, when between one and two million Cambodians died.

Under international pressure, Cambodia held elections in July. Political bickering delayed formation of a new government until November, and it looked remarkably like the government that split apart in a violent coup in July 1997. Hun Sen—a former communist leader who ousted his coalition partner, Prince Norodom Ranariddh, in the coup—emerged as the prime minister with most of the country's political power. Ranariddh, who had fled Cambodia after the coup, fearing for his life, accepted a position as speaker of the National Assembly. Most observers said it appeared possible that Hun Sen and Ranariddh finally had reached an accommodation that would enable them to give Cambodia much-needed respite from war and political unrest. (Hun Sen coup, Historic Documents of 1997, p. 639)

Collapse of the Khmer Rouge

The previous three decades had seen almost an unending cycle of turmoil in Cambodia: first, spillover from the Vietnam War; then, four years of terror when the communist Khmer Rouge sought to forcibly transform Cambodia into their version of a nationalist, agrarian society; followed by a decade of occupation by Vietnam and civil war by Khmer Rouge guerrillas, ending in a peace agreement in 1991. An election in 1993 accomplished little more than set the stage for four years of political upheaval as Hun Sen and Ranariddh, leaders of the two major political factions in the country, tried to elbow each other out of power. (Peace accord, Historic Documents of 1991, p. 691)

The one positive factor during Cambodia's recent years was the gradual decline of the Khmer Rouge, whose fighters and leaders had taken refuge in the jungles of northern Cambodia and neighboring Thailand after they were ousted by the Vietnamese. In exile, the Khmer Rouge split into factions, several of which continued to wage war even after the 1991 peace treaty. The government in 1996 offered pardons to Khmer Rouge guerrillas, and in the following two years several thousand turned themselves into the government—often in exchange for control over large sections of the countryside.

In 1997 Pol Pot, who founded the Khmer Rouge and was its undisputed leader during the years in power, was deposed by Ta Mok, the group's former military commander (known as the "Butcher" because of his brutal methods of dealing with dissent). Ta Mok put Pol Pot under house arrest at a remote jungle camp near the northern border with Thailand, where he died April 15, impoverished and fearing for his life. Ta Mok insisted that Pol Pot died of a heart attack, but there were other reports that he either was poisoned or committed suicide because he feared being turned over to a United Nations war crimes tribunal. Whatever the cause, the truth of his death went up in flames when his remains were cremated three days later. A Khmer Rouge spokesman said: "There was no sadness or sorrow expressed at the cremation."

The last known sizable group of Khmer Rouge guerrillas laid down their arms on December 5. Cambodian officials said between 500 and 1,000 Khmer Rouge fighters were involved. An unknown number of their former colleagues remained at large in the jungles of Cambodia and Thailand, but observers said no large units of Khmer Rouge guerrillas remained.

On December 25 two of Pol Pot's chief aides surrendered to the Cambodian government. They were Khieu Samphan, a Khmer Rouge political leader who served as a front-man for Pol Pot during the years in power, and Nuon Chea, Pol Pot's second in command and the party's theorist. Chea reportedly designed the plan that in 1975 evacuated hundreds of thousands of Cambodians from the cities into forced labor, where many died from disease and starvation and others were executed.

Prime Minister Hun Sen, who had been a Khmer Rouge commander before breaking with the movement in 1977, stirred international outrage on December 28 when he said Cambodians should give "a bouquet of flowers for this pair, not a bullet or a pair of handcuffs." Hun Sen had previously called for an international tribunal to try Khmer Rouge leaders, but he reversed that position and said Cambodia needed to "bury the past." Hun Sen added: "In Cambodia, we know how to heal ourselves using our own medicines. If we try mixing in foreign medicine, it will not cure Cambodian disease."

At a news conference in Phnom Penh the following day, December 29, Khieu Samphan and Nuon Chea were questioned aggressively by reporters about whether they had any remorse for what the Khmer Rouge had done. Pressed repeatedly on the matter, Khieu Samphan reluctantly muttered in English that he was "sorry, very sorry" for the suffering of the Cambodian people. He repeated that phrase in the Khmer language at the urging of Cambodian journalists. He added: "We would like to apologize and ask our compatriots to forget the past so our nation can concentrate on the future."

Asked if he would offer an apology, Nuon Chea said: "Actually, we are very sorry not only for the lives of the people of Cambodia, but even for the lives of all animals that suffered because of the war." Observers noted that Nuon Chea referred to the civil war that raged in Cambodia for many years, not just the Khmer Rouge terror campaign from 1975 to 1979. His reference to animals appeared to reflect Buddhist philosophy equating the value of all creatures.

Both men also pleaded with journalists and their countrymen to leave the past to history. Speaking in English, Khieu Samphan said: "It is normal that those who have lost their families, that they, what to say, feel some resentment. But I feel that most of our compatriots understand that we have much more problems to resolve at the present and in the future and we have to forget the past."

Human rights groups and most foreign governments expressed outrage at the Khmer Rouge leaders' appeals and called for them to submit to justice. The U.S. State Department issued a statement saying that, "as leaders of the regime responsible for the deaths of up to two million people, they should be held accountable for their actions before an appropriate tribunal." A spokesman for Amnesty International said that Hun Sen's apparent willingness to forgive the Khmer Rouge leaders was "a black day for the Cambodian people and a black day for international justice." Thomas Hammarberg, the UN special representative for human rights in Cambodia, said the Khmer Rouge leaders should be tried by an international tribunal. "It would be extremely sad" if the Cambodian government blocked such a tribunal, Hammarberg said.

In the following days the question of how the Khmer Rouge leaders should be treated appeared to divide the Cambodian people and their rulers. King Norodom Sihanouk, who backed the Khmer Rouge in the early 1970s but lost at least a dozen family members during the years of Khmer Rouge rule, said December 30 that he would oppose a pardon and that he believed the majority of Cambodians held the same view. Sam Rainsy, a leading politician in opposition to the government, said the Khmer Rouge leaders should be tried for "crimes against humanity." Numerous survivors of the killings also rejected the Khmer Rouge leaders' apology and demanded that they be tried. "You know, millions of lives, including twenty of my relatives, were lost in their regime," Bun Sray, a Phnom Penh civil servant told Reuters news service. "OK, now I want to kill their wives and children and then say, 'I'm sorry.'" There were no mass protests, however, apparently reflecting the continuing fear among many Cambodians about anything having to do with the Khmer Rouge.

On December 31 the Cambodian government treated Khieu Samphan, Nuon Chea, and their wives to an oceanfront holiday at a resort hotel on the Gulf of Thailand—a move that provoked further outrage from human rights groups and foreign governments. Under continuing international pressure, Hun Sen appeared to be wavering on the question of whether the leaders should be put on trial.

New Elections, New–Old Government

After driving Prince Ranariddh from the coalition government in 1997 and killing dozens of his supporters, Hun Sen came under intense international pressure to hold new elections. In the wake of the coup, the United States and other donors had halted their aid for the troubled Cambodian economy until new elections were held and political stability was restored. The Clinton administration continued pressing for elections in 1998 even after several human rights groups and international election monitors argued for a postponement because of persistent instability in Cambodia.

In the elections, held July 26, Hun Sen's Cambodian People's Party won a plurality of the vote but was unable to capture the two-thirds majority necessary in the 122-seat National Assembly to form a government. Ranariddh's party, known as Funcinpec, finished second. The results led to more than three months of renewed bickering between Hun Sen and Ranariddh. During that period political violence escalated. On September 16 Hammarberg, the chief UN diplomat in Cambodia, issued a statement denouncing a government crackdown against the opposition and calling on all parties to resolve their differences "through dialogue."

Dialogue finally produced a political agreement on November 13, reportedly the result of pressure from King Sihanouk, the country's constitutional monarch and Ranariddh's father. Under the deal, Hun Sen became prime minister, Ranariddh became speaker of the National Assembly, and Hun Sen's party was given control of a new second chamber of parliament, a Senate with little more than advisory power. The new National Assembly took office November 25. Hun Sen and Ranariddh smiled and bowed to each other and promised to work together. Observers said that coalition might be more effective than the previous one because only one man—Hun Sen—held real power and Ranariddh was in a weaker position to pose a constant challenge to the stability of the government.

Following is the text of a statement issued December 29, 1998, by the U.S. State Department in response to the surrender of Cambodian Khmer Rouge leaders Khieu Samphan and Nuon Chea:

Former Khmer Rouge leaders Nuon Chea and Khieu Samphan are now in Phnom Penh. As leaders of the regime responsible for the deaths of up to two million people, they should be held accountable for their actions before an appropriate tribunal. While there have been a number of conflicting statements from Cambodian authorities, we note that Prime Minister Hun Sen has not ruled out the possibility of a trial.

The actions taken during the 1975–1979 period of Khmer Rouge rule were thoroughly documented by the Khmer Rouge themselves in a manner that leaves no doubt as to the way mass murder was planned and carried out. The records left by the Khmer Rouge makes it absolutely clear that the Khmer Rouge regime was among the most murderous in this century. The number of victims from the 1975-1979 period in Cambodia is up to four times as many as were killed in Rwanda in 1994 and up to ten times as many as were killed in Bosnia in 1992–1995.

We welcome the recent establishment of a coalition government in Cambodia, as well as Cambodia's return to the United Nations and its movement towards membership in the Association of Southeast Asian Nations (ASEAN). As Cambodia moves to fully regain its place in the community of nations, we hope that it will insist on accountability for the crimes of the 1975-1979 period. Its actions in this regard will shape its relations with the United States and the international community.

HOUSE ON CHINESE ACQUISITION
OF U.S. TECHNOLOGY
December 30, 1998

*A special committee of the House of Representatives completed a secret
report at the end of the year addressing what its chairman called "serious
problems" in the transfer of sensitive technology to China. The committee
reportedly identified cases in which the Chinese government stole information from the United States about nuclear weapons design. In its 1,100-
page report, the panel also detailed two cases during the mid-1990s in
which U.S. satellite manufacturers were said to have improperly given the
Chinese information on the design of ballistic missiles.*

*The committee's investigation capped the second straight year of contro-
versy in Washington about alleged efforts by the Chinese government to
gain political influence and obtain U.S. military secrets. Congressional
Republicans had charged in 1997 that Beijing had used intermediaries to
funnel illegal campaign contributions to President Bill Clinton's reelection
campaign in 1996. An investigation of that matter, and other campaign
finance issues, conducted by the Senate Governmental Affairs Committee
concluded in March 1998 with separate reports issued by the panel's
Republican and Democratic members. The Republican majority said it had
been unable to document a Chinese conspiracy to influence the U.S. elections.* (Campaign finance issues, p. 890)

*Aside from conducting investigations, Congress took only one major leg-
islative step on the China-technology issue during the year, reversing a
decision by President Clinton in 1996 to loosen U.S. government controls
over exports to China of satellite technology and supercomputers. Clinton
had shifted the job of reviewing high-technology exports to China from the
State Department (which, along with the Pentagon, emphasized foreign
policy and national security concerns) to the Commerce Department
(which tended to promote the commercial aspects of U.S. exports). The
Hughes Space and Communications Co., which wanted to expedite sales of
its satellites to China, had lobbied for the decision. Congress in 1998
passed legislation intended to force the president to give the export-review*

authority back to the State Department. The administration was expected to review this matter in 1999.

House Committee Investigation

Five Republicans and four Democrats served on the House Select Committee on U.S. National Security and Military/Commercial Concerns with the People's Republic of China. Christopher Cox, R-Calif., was the chairman, and Norman Dicks, D-Wash., was the co-chairman. The panel began its inquiry in June and held twenty-two closed hearings before approving its report by a unanimous vote on December 30. The committee staff included several current and former U.S. intelligence officials. Cox said the committee would work with the Clinton administration early in 1999 to prepare a declassified version of the report for public release.

House leaders formed the committee largely in response to stories by the New York Times *detailing allegedly improper dealings with China by two U.S. satellite manufacturers. Members said the inquiry quickly spread to broader issues involving Chinese efforts to obtain U.S. technology to bolster its military.*

The portion of the report that was certain to be the most controversial concerned allegations that the Chinese government had succeeded in obtaining information about the design of U.S. nuclear weapons. The New York Times *said the report had concluded that important aspects of weapons technology were "stolen" from U.S. laboratories, all of which were owned by the U.S. government or under exclusive government contracts. Other news organizations said the report focused on lax security at installations such as the Los Alamos nuclear laboratory in New Mexico, an Energy Department facility. The General Accounting Office had reported to Congress in 1997 that officials from China, Russia, and other countries were able to gain unauthorized access to sensitive information at those laboratories.*

Although some of the incidents cited in the report occurred on the Clinton administration's watch, the committee said the previous Reagan and Bush administrations also had failed to enforce security procedures or monitor technology exports to China. One topic of the committee report included allegations that China obtained information from U.S. weapons laboratories in the late 1980s that helped it develop a neutron bomb—an atomic weapon intended to kill people but cause little damage to buildings. Aspects of this matter had been reported by U.S. news outlets during the early 1990s.

The committee said it was making thirty-eight recommendations "to protect sensitive U.S. military technology" from China. Most of the recommendations reportedly dealt with tightening restrictions on technology transfers to China and enforcing tougher security rules at U.S. weapons facilities and technology installations. Some of the recommendations were for legislation; others were for actions by the executive branch. The only recommendation that was made public immediately was a reiteration of

the call by Congress for the State Department to have authority over tech-
nology transfers to China.

The Chinese government consistently denied that it had stolen U.S.
weapons secrets or done anything improper in its dealings with U.S. con-
tractors and government agencies. Responding to the House committee
report, Zhu Bangzao, a spokesman for the Chinese Foreign Ministry, said:
"The allegation is groundless and irresponsible, and we express our strong
resentment over this."

Hughes and Loral in China

The initial focus of the committee inquiry involved the alleged actions
by two major satellite manufacturers—Hughes Space and
Communications Co. and Loral Space and Communications Systems
Ltd.—in providing valuable technical information to the Chinese govern-
ment in the mid-1990s without the knowledge or approval of the U.S. gov-
ernment. The Defense Department notified Congress in December that an
air force investigation of the matter determined that Hughes had given
China a "defense service," the technical term for a technology transfer reg-
ulated by law and requiring advance approval of the U.S. government.

The Hughes incident reportedly occurred in 1995, when Chinese
Aerospace, the government corporation responsible for satellite launches,
requested help in determining why a Chinese rocket carrying a Hughes
satellite exploded when it was launched. Hughes technicians reportedly
helped the Chinese improve such matters as computer models for predict-
ing launch conditions and specifications for rockets. The New York Times
quoted the Pentagon report as saying that Hughes technicians provided the
Chinese with "specific insight into specific launch vehicle design and oper-
ational problems and corrective actions."

In a similar incident, one or more engineers from the Loral corporation
reportedly gave the Chinese information about the possible cause of
another rocket explosion in February 1996. That explosion destroyed a
Loral satellite. The allegations involving Loral were politically sensitive in
Washington because the company's chairman, Bernard L. Schwartz, was a
major financial contributor to the Democratic Party.

The House select committee said it had determined that the Hughes and
Loral incidents "damaged the national security." However, the committee
offered no details on the exact nature or extent of the damage. The New
York Times *quoted one Clinton administration official as saying that the*
techniques advised by Hughes and Loral could be helpful to the Chinese in
launching rockets carrying military warheads, as well as the communica-
tions satellites that had been on the failed launches.

However, the Washington Post *quoted Admiral Joseph W. Pueher, head of*
the U.S. Pacific Command, as saying that the information given the
Chinese helped their missile program "only incrementally, not [by] any
quantum leaps." Hughes Space and Communications Co. issued a state-
ment denying that any of its employees had provided information or tech-
nology that helped China with its missile technology; Hughes noted that the

978

company "makes satellites, not rockets." Loral also denied any wrongdoing or that its actions had damaged U.S. national security.

Both incidents were under investigation by a federal grand jury in Washington, D.C. No results of that inquiry had been reported as of the end of 1998.

Following are the text of a statement released December 30, 1998, by the House Select Committee on U.S. National Security and Military/Commercial Concerns with the People's Republic of China, and excerpts from a news conference held the same day by committee chairman Christopher Cox, R-Calif., and Norman Dicks, D-Wash.:

COMMITTEE STATEMENT

The Select Committee on U.S. National Security and Military/Commercial Concerns with the People's Republic of China [PRC] unanimously voted to approve a five-volume, 1,100-page report on the transfer of sensitive U.S. technology to the PRC. The report goes well beyond the two cases that spurred the investigation, involving Space Systems/Loral and Hughes, and addresses PRC targeting of not only so-called "dual-use" technologies, but also sensitive military technologies.

"These transfers are not limited to satellite and missile technology, but cover other militarily-significant technologies," said Committee Chairman Christopher Cox (R-Orange County). "Rather quickly, our investigation led to even more serious problems of PRC technology acquisition efforts targeted at the United States. The seriousness of these findings, and their enormous significance to our national security, led us to a unanimous report."

The Select Committee met for its 34th and final time December 30, capping a six-month effort launched by the near-unanimous vote of the House on June 18, 1998 to establish the Committee.

"Six months ago this Select Committee did not exist," Chairman Cox said. "It had no staff, no offices, no telephones. Within six months, the Select Committee assembled an extraordinarily professional staff, conducted a thorough, multi-faceted investigation, and prepared the report approved today."

The investigation was headed by professional investigators with significant national security experience. The staff included C. Dean McGrath, Jr., former Deputy Staff Director and Deputy Assistant to the President; Rick Cinquegrana, Deputy Inspector General of the CIA; Dan Silver, former General Counsel of the CIA and of NSA; Lewis Libby, former Deputy Under Secretary of Policy at the Department of Defense; Nicholas Rostow, former Legal Adviser to the National Security Council; Michael Sheehy, Minority Staff Director, House Permanent Select Committee on Intelligence; and Michael Davidson, former Counsel to the Senate.

The Committee held 22 hearings and heard more than 200 hours of testimony from more than 75 different witnesses. It conducted more than 700 hours of interviews and depositions of more than 150 individuals, issued 21 subpoenas, and conferred use immunity upon four witnesses with the concurrence of the Department of Justice.

Moreover, Chairman Cox added, "the investigation was completed on time and under budget."

"The investigation quickly turned to classified matters when it became clear that far more was involved in U.S. technology transfer to the PRC than just isolated cases," Chairman Cox said.

The report's entire 1,100 pages are temporarily classified "Top Secret." It was presented to the Speaker of the House and the Minority Leader on Saturday, January 2, 1999 and provided to the President and the House Permanent Select Committee on Intelligence for de-classification review.

In a statement in the Capitol announcing the unanimous vote, Chairman Cox said the Committee could not answer most questions relating to either classified or unclassified information until the report is reviewed by the Select Committee staff to carefully separate out the two.

"The classified and unclassified information is currently so intertwined that we would risk inadvertent disclosure of classified information if we did not first submit the report and our answers to your questions to staff review," he said.

The Committee did announce, based on unclassified information, that the transfer of sensitive U.S. technology to the People's Republic of China by both Hughes and Loral damaged the national security. These cases, which came to light after news reports that Loral received a waiver to launch a satellite in the PRC despite being the subject of a criminal investigation into prior technology transfers, were a significant reason that Congress created the Select Committee in late June 1998.

"The PRC's targeting of sensitive U.S. military technology is not limited to missiles and satellites, but covers other military technologies," Cox said. "Sensitive U.S. military technology has been the subject of serious PRC acquisition efforts over the last two decades, and continues today. A significant reason for the creation of the Select Committee was to determine whether Space Systems/Loral and Hughes were responsible for the transfer of technology that damaged the national security of the United States. Based on unclassified information, we have found that national security harm did occur. We have investigated these questions more thoroughly than any other part of the U.S. Government."

The Select Committee is making 38 recommendations to protect sensitive U.S. military technology from the PRC. These recommendations also recognize the need for continued American leadership in technology and continued U.S. international competitiveness.

A declassified version of the report will be made available to the public and press as soon as possible, Chairman Cox said.

NEWS CONFERENCE ON TECHNOLOGY TRANSFER

Rep. Christopher Cox, R-Calif.: The select committee has found that the transfer of sensitive U.S. technology to the People's Republic of China goes beyond the Hughes and Loral instances that were a significant part of the reason that the committee was formed. These transfers are not limited to missile-satellite technology, but cover militarily significant technologies.

United States' transfer of technology to the People's Republic of China has been the subject of serious and sustained PRC acquisition efforts over the last two decades, and continues today.

As I said, a significant reason for the creation of the select committee was to determine whether Space Systems Loral and Hughes were responsible for the transfer of technology that damaged the national security of the United States.

Based on unclassified information, I can tell you today that we have found that national security harm did occur.

We have investigated these questions more thoroughly than any other part of the United States government. The select committee's recommendations, along with its report, will be forwarded to the president of the United States as well as to relevant Cabinet departments and agencies and the select committee itself will brief both House and Senate committees at the earliest practicable date so that action can occur on our recommendations. I want, next and perhaps most importantly, to thank Norm Dicks, who is standing at my side, who has been not just the ranking Democrat on this select committee, but effectively, along with Porter Goss, the chairman of the Intelligence Committee, the co-chairman of this effort.

The members on both the Republican and Democratic sides are very expert in these matters and we have the speaker of the House and the minority leader to thank for these outstanding appointments of senior leaders in the Congress.

It's my pleasure now to yield to the ranking member of the select committee, Norm Dicks of Washington.

Rep. Norman Dicks, D-Wash.: I think the chairman said it quite well. Based on unclassified material, there was harm in some of the transfer of technology that occurred. It's also fair to say that this is not the only problem that we uncovered. And unfortunately, today we're stuck with the problem of classification, and these documents that we have assembled, the material we've assembled has to go through a process, as the chairman mentioned, of declassification. And we hope that when that is finished, that we'll be able to be more explicit about the problems that occurred.

But I will say this: These are serious problems that must be addressed by the administration and the Congress. We're going to not only—we have a series of recommendations and findings that clearly detail these problems. We are going to work diligently as members of Congress with the administration and the Congress to make certain that the problems that we've found will be corrected.

And some of it's going to require legislation. Some of it's going to require actions on the part of the executive branch. And I have been told by the White House that they are very willing to consider and to implement the recommendations of the select committee because they recognize that this is a bipartisan effort that has yielded a consensus product.

And that isn't easy to do in the climate that we were operating in, but it's a testament to the chairman's leadership and the bipartisan spirit that we were able to get this done. And I, too, want to congratulate the staff. The staff did an outstanding job. We had a joint investigative staff. We had a majority and minority staff, and we only had one press secretary. The chairman wanted to have a press secretary; we agreed to that. And we appreciate his fairness.

Again, he was very fair and was willing to work with everyone on the committee. We all had a chance to put in our recommendations and input. And I think this is a solid bipartisan product, and I'm proud to be associated with it.

CUMULATIVE INDEX, 1994–1998